B&B Guide
2012

AA Lifestyle Guides

42nd edition
© AA Media Limited 2011.
AA Media Limited retains the copyright in the current edition
© 2011 and in all subsequent editions, reprints and amendments to editions.
The information contained in this directory is sourced from the AA's establishment database.

Please contact:
The Editor, AA B&B Guide, Fanum House, Floor 13, Basing View, Basingstoke, Hampshire RG21 4EA
Advertising Sales Department: advertisingsales@theAA.com
Editorial Department: lifestyleguides@theAA.com
AA Hotel Scheme Enquiries: 01256 844455

AA Media Limited would like to thank the following photographers, companies and picture libraries for their assistance in the preparation of this book.

Abbreviations for the picture credits are as follows: (t) top; (b) bottom; (l) left; (r) right; (c) centre; (AA) AA World Travel Library.
Front cover: (t) L'Enclume; (bl) Ward/Alamy; (br) Little Span Farm.
Back cover: (l) Marmadukes Hotel; (c) Williams/Alamy; (r) The Horseshoe Inn.

Typeset by Servis Filmsetting Ltd, Manchester
Printed in Italy by Printer Trento SRL, Trento
Directory compiled by the AA Lifestyle Guides Department and managed in the Librios Information Management System and generated from the AA establishment database system.

Published by AA Publishing, which is a trading name of AA Media Limited whose registered office is: Fanum House, Basing View, Basingstoke, Hampshire RG21 4EA
Registered number 06112600

A CIP catalogue record for this book is available from the British Library.
ISBN: 978-0-7495-7069-9
A04613

Maps prepared by the
Mapping Services Department of
AA Publishing.

Maps © AA Media Limited 2011.

Contains Ordnance Survey data
© Crown copyright and database right 2011.
Licence number 100021153.

Land &
Property
Services. This is based upon Crown Copyright and is reproduced with the permission of Land & Property Services under delegated authority from the Controller of Her Majesty's Stationery Office. © Crown copyright and database rights 2011
Licence number 100,363.
Permit number 100175

Ordnance Survey
Ireland's National Mapping Agency
Republic of Ireland mapping based on © Ordnance Survey Ireland/ Government of Ireland Copyright Permit number MP000611

Information on National Parks in England provided by the Countryside Agency (Natural England).

Information on National Parks in Scotland provided by Scottish Natural Heritage.

Information on National Parks in Wales provided by The Countryside Council for Wales.

AA
★★★★★
Guest
Accommodation

Contents

How to Use the Guide

1 LOCATION, MAP REFERENCE & NAME

Each country is listed in alphabetical order by county then town/village. The Channel Islands and Isle of Man follow the England section and the Scottish islands follow the rest of Scotland. Establishments are listed alphabetically in descending order of Stars with any Yellow Stars first in each rating.

The map page number refers to the atlas at the back of the guide and is followed by the National Grid Reference. To find the town/ village, read the first figure across and the second figure vertically within the lettered square. You can find routes at theAA.com or www.AAbookings.ie. Farmhouse entries also have a six-figure National Grid Reference, which can be used with Ordnance Survey maps or **www.ordnancesurvey.co.uk**.

We also show the name of the proprietors, as often farms are known locally by their name.

2 CLASSIFICATION & DESIGNATOR

See pages 6 and 7.

Five Star establishments are highlighted as Premier Collection, and they are listed on page 20.

If the establishment's name is shown in *italics*, then details have not been confirmed by the proprietor for this edition.

⊛ **Rosettes** The AA's food award, see page 10.

🥚 **Egg cups and** 🥧 **pies** These symbols indicate that, in the experience of the inspector, either breakfast or dinner are really special, and have an emphasis on freshly prepared local ingredients.

3 E-MAIL ADDRESS & WEBSITE

E-mail and website addresses are included where they have been specified by the establishment. Such websites are not under the control of AA Media Limited, who cannot accept any responsibility or liability in respect of any and all matters whatsoever relating to such websites.

---

[1]

BERKSHIRE

[1] HUNGERFORD   Map 5 SU36 **[1]**

The Swan Inn
[2] ★★★★ 🥚 🥧 INN

[5]

Craven Rd, Inkpen RG17 9DX
[3] ☎ 01488 668326   📠 01488 668306
e-mail: enquiries@theswaninn-organics.co.uk
web: www.theswaninn-organics.co.uk
[4] dir: *3.5m SE of Hungerford. S on Hungerford High St past rail bridge, left to Hungerford Common, right signed Inkpen*

[6] This delightful village inn dates back to the 17th century has open fires and beams in the bar, and the bonus of a smart restaurant. Bedrooms are generally spacious and well equipped. Organic produce is available from the on-site farm shop, so the bar, restaurant and breakfast menus all feature local organic produce too.

[7] **Rooms** 10 en suite (2 fmly) S £60-£70; D £80-£95*
Facilities tea/coffee Dinner available Direct Dial Cen ht Wi-fi **Conf** Max 40 Thtr 40 Class 40 Board 12 **Parking** 50 **[8]**
Notes ⊗ Closed 25-26 Dec

[10]   **[9]**

4 DIRECTIONS & DISTANCES

Distances in **directions** are given in miles (m) and yards (yds), or kilometres (km) and metres (mtrs) in the Republic of Ireland.

5 PHOTOGRAPHS

Establishments may choose to include a photograph

6 DESCRIPTION

Written by the inspector at the time of his or her visit.

---

7 ROOMS

The number of letting bedrooms (rms), or rooms with a bath or shower en suite are shown. Bedrooms that have a private bathroom (pri facs) adjacent are indicated.

The number of bedrooms in an annexe of equivalent standard are also shown. Facilities may not be the same as in the main building.

Charges are per night:
S bed and breakfast per person
D bed and breakfast for two people sharing a room. If an asterisk (✳) follows the prices this indicates 2011 prices.
The euro is the currency of the Republic of Ireland.
Prices are indications only, so check before booking. Some places may offer free accommodation to children provided they share their parents' room.

8 FACILITIES

Most bedrooms will have TV. If this is important to you, please check when booking. If **TV4B** appears, this means that there are TVs in four bedrooms.
If **Dinner** is shown, you may have to order in advance. Please check when booking. For other abbreviations and symbols, see the table on the right.

9 PARKING

Parking is usually followed by the number of spaces. Motorists should be aware that some establishments may charge for parking. Please check when booking.

10 NOTES

Although many establishments allow dogs, they may be excluded from some areas of the accommodation and some breeds, particularly those requiring an exceptional license, may not be acceptable at all. Under the Disability Discrimination Act 1995 access should be allowed to guide dogs and assistance dogs. Please check

Key to Symbols and abbreviations

★	Classification (see page 6)
◎	AA Rosette award (see page 10)
Ⓐ	Associate entry (see page 7)
Ⓤ	Unclassified rating (see page 7)
☎	Phone number
🖹	Fax number
	A very special breakfast, with an emphasis on freshly prepared local ingredients
	A very special dinner, with an emphasis on freshly prepared local ingredients
S	Single room
D	Double room (2 people sharing)
pri fac	Private facilities
fmly	Family bedroom
GF	Ground floor bedroom
LB	Short/Leisure breaks
✳	2011 prices
Cen ht	Full central heating
ch fac	Special facilities for children
TVL	Lounge with television
TV4B	Television in four bedrooms
STV	Satellite television
FTV	Freeview television
Wi-fi	Wireless internet
⊗	Credit cards not accepted
tea/coffee	Tea and coffee facilities
Conf	Conference facilities
rms	Bedrooms in main building
Etr	Easter
fr	From
RS	Restricted service
⊗	No dogs
🏊	Indoor swimming pool
🏊	Heated indoor swimming pool
⌇	Outdoor swimming pool
⌇	Heated outdoor swimming pool
⚏	Croquet lawn
⚐	Tennis court
⚑	Putting green

the establishment's policy when making your booking.

No children - children cannot be accommodated, or a minimum age may be specified, e.g. No children 4yrs means no children under four years old.

Establishments with special facilities for children (**ch fac**) may include a babysitting service or baby-intercom system, playroom or playground, laundry facilities, drying and ironing facilities, cots, high chairs and special meals. If you have very young children, check before booking.

No coaches is published in good faith from details supplied by the establishment. Inns have well-defined legal obligations towards travellers; in the event of a query the customer should contact the proprietor or local licensing authority.

Additional facilities such as lifts or any leisure activities available are also listed.

LB indicates that Short or Leisure Breaks are available. Contact the establishment for details.

Establishments are open all year unless **Closed** days/dates/months are shown. Some places are open all year but offer a restricted service (**RS**) in low season. If the text does not say what the restricted services are you should check before booking.

Civ Wed 50 The establishment is licensed for civil weddings and can accommodate 50 guests for the ceremony.

⊗ shows that **credit/debit cards are not accepted**, but check when booking. Where credit cards are accepted there may be an extra charge.

Smoking Since July 1st 2007 smoking is banned in all public places in the United Kingdom and Ireland. The proprietor can designate one or more bedrooms with ventilation systems where the occupants can smoke, but communal areas must be smoke-free. Communal areas include the interior bars and restaurants in pubs and inns. We indicate number of smoking rooms (if any).

Conference facilities Conf indicates that facilities are available. Total number of delegates that can be accommodated is shown, plus maximum numbers in various settings.

AA Inspected Guest Accommodation

The AA inspects and classifies more than 2,800 guest houses, farmhouses and inns for its Guest Accommodation Scheme, under common quality standards agreed between the AA, VisitBritain, VisitScotland and VisitWales.
AA recognised establishments pay an annual fee according to the classification and the number of bedrooms. The classification is not transferable if an establishment changes hands.

The AA presents several awards within the Guest Accommodation scheme, including the **AA Friendliest Landlady of the Year**, which showcases the very finest hospitality in the country, **Guest Accommodation of the Year Awards**, presented to establishments in Scotland, Ireland, Wales and England, **AA London B&B of the Year**, and **AA Funkiest B&B of the Year**. See pages 12 and 14 for this year's winners.

Stars

AA Stars classify guest accommodation at five levels of quality, from one at the simplest, to five offering the highest quality. In order to achieve a one Star rating an establishment must meet certain minimum entry requirements, including:

- A cooked breakfast, or substantial continental option is provided.
- The proprietor and/or staff are available for your arrival, departure and at all meal times.
- Once registered, you have access to the establishment at all times unless previously notified.
- All areas of operation meet minimum quality requirements for cleanliness, maintenance and hospitality as well as facilities and the delivery of services.
- A dining room or similar eating area is available unless meals are only served in bedrooms.

Our research shows that quality is very important to visitors. To obtain a higher Star rating, an establishment must provide increased quality standards across all areas, with particular emphasis in four key areas:

- Cleanliness and housekeeping
- Hospitality and service
- Quality and condition of bedrooms, bathrooms and public rooms
- Food quality

There are also particular requirements in order for an establishment to achieve three, four or five Stars, for example:

Three stars and above

- access to both sides of all beds for double occupancy
- bathrooms/shower rooms cannot be used by the proprietor
- there is a washbasin in every guest bedroom (either in the bedrooms or the en suite/private facility)

Four stars

- half of bedrooms must be en suite or have private facilities

Five stars

- all bedrooms must be en suite or have private facilities

Establishments applying for AA recognition are visited by one of the AA's qualified accommodation inspectors as a mystery guest. Inspectors stay overnight to make a thorough test of the accommodation, food, and hospitality. After paying the bill the following morning they identify themselves and ask to be shown round the premises. The inspector completes a full report, resulting in a recommendation for the appropriate Star rating. After this first visit, the establishment will receive an annual visit to check that standards are maintained. If it changes hands, the new owners must re-apply for classification, as standards can change.

Guests can expect to find the following minimum standards at all levels:

- Pleasant and helpful welcome and service, and sound standards of housekeeping and maintenance
- Comfortable accommodation equipped to modern standards
- Bedding and towels changed for each new guest, and at least weekly if the room is taken for a long stay
- Adequate storage, heating, lighting and comfortable seating
- A sufficient hot water supply at reasonable times
- A full cooked breakfast. (If this is not provided, the fact must be advertised and a substantial continental breakfast must be offered)

When an AA inspector has visited a property, and evaluated all the aspects of the accommodation for comfort, facilities, attention to detail and presentation, you can be confident the Star rating will allow you to make the right choice for an enjoyable stay.

☆ Highly Commended

Yellow Stars indicate that an accommodation is in the top ten percent of its Star rating. Yellow Stars only apply to 3, 4 or 5 Star establishments.

Accommodation Designators

Along with the Star ratings, six designators have been introduced. The proprietors, in discussion with our inspectors, choose which designator best describes their establishment:

BED & BREAKFAST

A private house run by the owner with accommodation for no more than six paying guests.

GUEST HOUSE

Run on a more commercial basis than a B&B, the accommodation provides for more than six paying guests and there are usually more services; for example staff as well as the owner may provide dinner.

FARMHOUSE

The B&B or guest house accommodation is part of a working farm or smallholding.

INN

The accommodation is provided in a fully licensed establishment. The bar will be open to non-residents and can provide food in the evenings.

RESTAURANT WITH ROOMS

This is a destination restaurant offering overnight accommodation, with dining being the main business and open to non-residents. The restaurant should offer a high standard of food and restaurant service at least five nights a week. A liquor licence is necessary and there is a maximum of 12 bedrooms.

GUEST ACCOMMODATION

Any establishment that meets the minimum entry requirements is eligible for this general category.

Ⓤ Unclassified entries

A small number of establishments in this guide have this symbol because their Star classification was not confirmed at the time of going to press. This may be due to a change of ownership or because the establishment has only recently joined the AA rating scheme. For up-to-date information on these and other new establishments check **theAA.com.**

Ⓐ Associate entries

These establishments have been inspected and rated by VisitBritain, VisitScotland or VisitWales, and have joined the AA scheme on a marketing-only basis. A limited entry for these places appears in the guide, while descriptions for these establishments appear on **theAA.com.**

Why not spend less and relax more on UK breaks?

cottages4you
property ref GRL

Make AA Travel your first destination and you're on the way to a more relaxing short break or holiday.

AA Members and customers can get great deals on accommodation, from B&Bs to farmhouses, inns and hotels.

You can also save up to 10% at cottages4you, enjoy a 5% discount with Hoseasons, and up to 60% off the very best West End shows.

Thinking of going further afield?

Check out our attractive discounts on car hire, airport parking, ferry bookings, travel insurance and much more.

Then simply relax.

These are just some of our well-known partners:

Visit theAA.com/travel

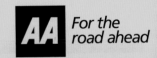

Useful Information

There may be restricted access to some establishments, particularly in the late morning and the afternoon, so do check when booking.

London prices tend to be higher than outside the capital, and normally only bed and breakfast is provided, although some establishments do provide a full meal service.

Farmhouses: Sometimes the land has been sold and only the house remains, but many are working farms and some farmers are happy to allow visitors to look around, or even to help feed the animals. However, you should always exercise care and never leave children unsupervised. Although the directory entry states the acreage and the type of farming, do check when booking to make sure that it matches your expectations. The farmhouses are listed under towns or villages, but do ask for directions when booking.

Inns: Traditional inns often have a cosy bar, convivial atmosphere, and good beer and pub food. Those listed in the guide will provide breakfast in a suitable room, and should also serve light meals during licensing hours. The character of the properties vary according to whether they are country inns or town establishments. Check before you book, including arrival times as these may be restricted to opening hours.

Booking

Book as early as possible, particularly for the peak holiday period (early June to the end of September) and for Easter and other public holidays. In some parts of Scotland the skiing season is also a peak holiday period. Some establishments only accept weekly bookings from Saturday, and some require a deposit on booking.

Prices

Minimum and maximum prices are shown for one (S) and two people (D) per night and include a full breakfast. If dinner is also included this is indicated in brackets (incl dinner). Where prices are for the room only, this is indicated.

Useful Information *continued*

Prices in the guide include VAT (and service where applicable), except the Channel Islands where VAT does not apply.

Where proprietors have been unable to provide us with their 2012 charges we publish the 2011 price as a rough guide (shown by an asterisk ✳). Where no prices are given, please make enquiries direct.

Cancellation

If you have to cancel a booking, let the proprietor know at once. If the room cannot be re-let you may be held legally responsible for partial payment; you could lose your deposit or be liable for compensation, so consider taking out cancellation insurance.

Food and drink

Some guest accommodation provides evening meals, ranging from a set meal to a full menu. Some even have their own restaurant. You may have to arrange dinner in advance, at breakfast, or on the previous day, so do ask when booking.

If you book on bed, breakfast and evening meal terms, you may find that the tariff includes only the set menu. If there is a carte you may be able to order from this and pay a supplement.

On Sundays, many establishments serve the main meal at midday, and provide only a cold supper in the evening. In some parts of Britain, particularly in Scotland, high tea (i.e. a savoury dish followed by bread and butter, scones and cakes) is sometimes served instead of, or as an alternative to, dinner.

Facilities for Disabled Guests

The Equality Act 2010 provides legal rights for disabled people including access to goods, services and facilities, and means that service providers may have to consider making adjustments to their premises. For more information about the Act see www.direct.gov.uk/en/DisabledPeople/ RightsAndObligations/DisabilityRights/ DG_4001068 or www.equalities.gov.uk. The establishments in this guide should be aware of their obligations under the Act. We recommend that you always telephone in advance to ensure that the establishment you have chosen has appropriate facilities

Please note: AA inspectors are not accredited to make inspections under the National Accessibility Scheme. We indicate in entries if an establishment has ground floor rooms; and if a B&B tells us they have disabled facilities this is included in the description.

AA Rosette Awards
The AA awards Rosettes to over 2,000 restaurants as the best in the UK.

Excellent local restaurants serving food prepared with care, understanding and skill, using good quality ingredients.

The best local restaurants, which aim for and achieve higher standards and better consistency, and where a greater precision is apparent in the cooking. There will be obvious attention to the selection of quality ingredients.

Outstanding restaurants that demand recognition well beyond their local area.

Among the very best restaurants in the British Isles, where the cooking demands national recognition.

The finest restaurants in the British Isles, where the cooking compares with the best in the world.

AA B&B Awards

Each year the AA likes to celebrate the cream of the Guest Accommodation scheme crop. Held this year at The Royal Horseguards Hotel, London, the event recognised and rewarded more than 30 very deserving finalists, for demonstrating all-round excellence and unfailing standards, and for providing outstanding service to their guests. All finalists were treated to a champagne reception followed by a formal four-course celebratory luncheon. They also received a personalised certificate and an engraved Villeroy & Boch decanter, as well as a goody bag to take home with them.

Above: Alistair Sandall, AA Key Account Manager (left) presenting Lisa with her award, accompanied by Nigel David, CEO of eviivo, sponsors of the AA Friendliest Landlady of the Year Award.

FRIENDLIEST LANDLADY OF THE YEAR

Sponsored by **eviivo**

Lisa Holloway,
COMPTON HOUSE ★★★★
Newark, Nottinghamshire Page 231

Lisa Holloway was chosen from a shortlist of just over 20 finalists nominated by the AA's hotel and guest accommodation inspectors. She welcomes guests to Compton House with the help of husband Mark, and has done since 2004. Her guest house is a renovated townhouse originally built for Alderman Cooper, Lord Mayor of Newark in 1849, and has a charming, welcoming atmosphere. Many guests return time and again, and have created what Lisa refers to as the 'Compton Community', a group that keep in touch with each other as well as with Lisa. Breakfasts run all the way from porridge with maple syrup to the Full English, all utilising the best local produce. Supper is a community event, and is ideal for meeting other guests and enjoying Lisa's hospitality. Lisa says, "You have to like people to run a B&B, and I love them and find them infinitely interesting." Read more about Lisa on page 16.

FUNKIEST B&B OF THE YEAR

THE WENSLEYDALE HEIFER
★★★★★ ◎◎

West Witton, North Yorkshire Page 356
In recent years, this 17th-century former coaching inn has been completely transformed. The rooms are a dazzling mix of top-quality furnishings and stylish and imaginative design. Rooms have themes which include whisky, chocolate, champagne, A Night at the Movies and James Herriot. Guests can "warm their cockles" in the Whisky Lounge, or enjoy an excellent meal in the Seafood Restaurant. David and Lewis Moss have done a great job of making this traditional pub into a destination restaurant and charming accommodation. They have also seen the Wensleydale Heifer enter the Guinness Book of Records, by cooking the world's largest portion of fish and chips in July 2011.

LONDON B&B OF THE YEAR

PARK GRAND PADDINGTON ★★★★
London WC2 Page 207
The Park Grand is very stylish operation at the heart of Paddington. Part of the Shaftesbury group, the property has been extensively refurbished throughout with impressive results. Modern and contemporary in style, bedrooms offer comfortable and spacious accommodation with modern facilities including plasma TVs and free internet connections. Service is both professional and attentive from an enthusiastic team. Meals are served in the vibrant Atlantic restaurant.

AA Guest Accommodation of the Year

Every year we ask our inspectors to nominate those establishments they feel come closest to the ideal of what a B&B should be. They consider location, food standards and quality of furniture and fittings, as well as charm and hospitality. From a shortlist of around 20, one is selected from each country in the guide.

ENGLAND

BLACKMORE FARM ★★★★
Bridgwater, Somerset page 258

Run as a dairy farm by the Dyer Family since 1952, Blackmore Farm is a superb example of farm diversification. It has a farm shop, produces its own ice cream, and offers self-catering and B&B accommodation. The Manor House is Grade I listed 15th-century, and has been continuously renovated over the years. Bedrooms are offered in the main house as well as a barn conversion. The former has lofty ceilings, a four-poster room and a tangible sense of history. The conversion is more contemporary, but equally comfortable. The Great Hall is the setting for a proper farmhouse breakfast, served on a huge, 20ft-long dining table, and highlighting local produce.

SCOTLAND

23 MAYFIELD ★★★★★
Edinburgh page 374

Ross Birnie has recently overseen a two-year refurbishment of 23 Mayfield, which has turned this Victorian detached house into a relaxing and atmospheric guest house, that combines dark wood panelling, stained glass, old paintings and four-poster beds with modern technology such as radio alarms, LCD TVs, Bose audio gear, and even an Xbox. Ross is an excellent host, and his customer care and hospitality are among the many reasons why people return to 23 Mayfield.

WALES

PLAS MAENAN COUNTRY HOUSE
★ ★ ★ ★ ★ ◉ ◉

Llanrwst, Conwy page 410

With stunning views over Conwy Valley, Plas Maenan is a beautiful house with high standards of quality and service. The team of professional, friendly staff are led from the front by hands-on owners James and Caroline Burt, who have lovingly refurbished this property. Mr Burt has worked at Buckingham Palace, and this has influenced the formal but friendly atmosphere. Bedrooms are individually furnished, combining traditional style with attention to detail. Guests can relax in a luxurious lounge or a library bar; both feature deeply comfortable sofas and quirky touches, such as 'fireside sheep' to keep guests company.

IRELAND

GORMAN'S CLIFFTOP HOUSE & RESTAURANT ★ ★ ★ ★ ★ ◉
Dingle, Co Kerry page 446

Gorman's is located perched on the cliffs overlooking Smerwick Harbour on the Dingle Peninsula. Síle and Vincent Gorman are devoted to their business, which they built about twenty years ago. Vincent is the Chef and Síle is front-of-house and bakery. She is very involved in Dingle Tourism, walking and music. Vincent was a fisherman who gave up the sea, attended Darina Allen's Cookery School in Ballymaloe and never looked back. He uses the best of local and quality ingredients, including many grown in their own garden.

A *natural*

Julia Hynard interviews Lisa Holloway, AA Landlady of the Year 2011-2012, from Compton House, Newark in Nottinghamshire

Lisa Holloway is a natural. It's obvious from the first time she picks up the phone – charming with her engaging personality, ready laugh and warm wit, and reassuring with her effortless professionalism. It is not surprising to learn that she has won the top award – Friendliest Landlady – from among the crème de la crème of the profession in the AA Landlady of the Year Awards 2011.

Lisa is thrilled: 'I've had so many lovely emails and messages of congratulation – I'm knocked out!' She says, 'It's great to have the recognition from the very organisation that has tested us so stringently all these years. After all the hard work, the early mornings and the late nights, it is a vindication of all I set out to achieve.'

As a great champion of the East Midlands, Lisa is also delighted to have brought a national award to the area, which she feels tends to get forgotten.

The Landlady of the Year presentation was held at The Royal Horseguards, a grand five-star hotel in Whitehall. This is not an area of London Lisa knows well,

but funnily enough on her last visit to the capital she saw the building and admired it. She recognised the building as she arrived, a surprise that enhanced the experience she describes as 'all so lovely!' remembering particularly the doorman in his bowler hat.

All 22 shortlisted finalists for the award are invited to the event, and being placed at the table furthest from the stage Lisa had no expectation of winning. She settled down to enjoy lunch and the company of the 'really interesting guests' at her table, including other friendly landladies, Nigel David from eviivo, the online booking service, and Henrietta Green, who is a culinary hero of Lisa's.

'Of course I was at Henrietta like an Exocet missile,' Lisa admitted, 'I am writing the Compton House Cookery Book, so I was discussing that with her and she has since sent me some helpful emails. Nigel, too, was very helpful as I want to set up an online booking system, and he gave me some great advice.'

As people were called forward

to receive their awards Lisa was thinking, 'It won't be me – I'll have another glass of wine', and then she was announced. She was presented with her winner's certificate and a beautifully engraved decanter. She says, 'It was really nice because all the finalists got one,' adding, wickedly, that she'd also rather hoped for a year's free membership of the AA!

**Above: Lisa & her Friendliest Landlady Award.
Right: Lisa at Compton House**

choice

Compton House - Some History

Lisa and her husband Mark opened the B&B at Compton House in 2004. Her two daughters had left home so it seemed like a good time to start her own business. Up till then she'd run a catering company for 12 years; established and managed a wedding venue in Leicestershire; followed by a stint at a small private hotel. Experience gained in those jobs dovetailed to provide the perfect skill set to starting her own B&B.

The Holloways initially planned to open a B&B in Yorkshire, where they had a cottage. But as 'the queen of procrastination' Lisa still hadn't found anywhere when her daughter urged her to take a look at a property for sale in Newark – a handsome Grade II listed town house. She went to view the house and instantly had a good feeling about it. A major plus was the separate apartment for the proprietors, as she didn't want to 'live in' any more. She had no business plan or anything, just a gut instinct, and she ran to the estate agent to make an offer.

Looking back on the conversion period, Lisa remembers how scary it was. It was the first time in 25 years that she didn't have a salary coming in and they lived for five months without floorboards. It was essential to get the business operating and some revenue in, so they were letting out the proprietors' apartment and sleeping in the drawing room. Lisa remembers cycling around Newark to drum up business. What really got things moving was the school for beauticians around the corner needing accommodation for its students and sending them to her.

Lisa acknowledges that Newark is not a holiday destination, but for her it was well placed in the country to get to and from the places people need to be. Newark also has a major antiques fair bringing in lots of visitors. Lisa was instrumental in setting up a forum for all the hotels and B&Bs in the town, so that they could work together to keep business in Newark.

The 'Compton Community'

Visitors from all over the world check in to Compton House and return again and again to what Lisa's calls the Compton Community. She says that when a Dutchman sits down to breakfast with a Chinese guest in her B&B, the next thing you know they're doing business in Beijing. Lisa's guests not only stay in touch with her, they stay in touch with each other. This sense of community really came to the fore during the 2011 Alabama earthquake and Japanese tsunami, when guests from all corners of the world were swapping enquiries and reports on the safety of regulars in those stricken areas.

Asking Lisa about the secret of her success, she says, 'You have to like people to run a B&B, and I love them

and find them infinitely interesting. You quickly get the drift of people, from their emails when they book, or within the first few minutes of meeting them. Some people want to tell you all their troubles, so you stay and listen and give them the attention they need. Others

– often the business guests – just want to be left in peace.'

In conclusion, she reflects: 'Anyone can open a B&B but you do need skills to make a success of it, and I've realised that friendliness is a skill in itself.'

❝ *You have to like people to run a B&B, and I love them and find them infinitely interesting* ❞

★★★★★ Premier Collection

ENGLAND

BERKSHIRE
HURLEY
Old Bell
WINDSOR
Magna Carta

BUCKINGHAMSHIRE
BEACONSFIELD
Crazy Bear Beaconsfield

CAMBRIDGESHIRE
ELTON
The Crown Inn

CHESHIRE
BURWARDSLEY
The Pheasant Inn
CHESTER
Dragonfly
Oddfellows
Stone Villa Chester
MALPAS
Tilston Lodge
WARMINGTON
The Bear's Paw

CORNWALL & ISLES OF SCILLY
BOSCASTLE
Trerosewill Farm
FALMOUTH
Dolvean House
LAUNCESTON
Primrose Cottage
LOOE
The Beach House
PADSTOW
The Seafood Restaurant
PENZANCE
Camilla House
The Summer House
PERRANUTHNOE
Ednovean Farm
POLPERRO
Trenderway Farm

ST AUSTELL
Anchorage House
Highland Court Lodge
Lower Barn
ST BLAZEY
Nanscawen Manor House
Penarwyn House
ST HILARY
Ennys
ST IVES
Beachcroft

CUMBRIA
AMBLESIDE
Drunken Duck
BORROWDALE
Hazel Bank Country House
BRAMPTON
Lanercost Bed & Breakfast
CARTMEL
L'enclume
CONISTON
Wheelgate Country Guest House
CROSTHWAITE
The Punchbowl Inn at Crosthwaite
GRASMERE
Moss Grove Organic
KESWICK
The Grange Country Guest House
KIRKBY LONSDALE
Hipping Hall
Plato's
The Sun Inn
LORTON
The Old Vicarage
Winder Hall Country House
NEAR SAWREY
Ees Wyke Country House
NEWBY BRIDGE
The Knoll Country House
PENRITH
Brooklands Guest House
TROUTBECK
Broadoaks Country House

WINDERMERE
Applegarth Villa & JR's Restaurant
Beaumont House
The Cranleigh
The Howbeck
Newstead
Oakbank House
Windermere Suites
The Woodlands

DERBYSHIRE
ASHBOURNE
Turlow Bank
BELPER
Chevin Green
Dannah Farm Country House
Shottle Hall
BRADWELL
The Samuel Fox Country Inn
BUXTON
Buxton's Victorian Guest House
HOPE
Underleigh House
MATLOCK
Holmefield
NEWHAVEN
The Smithy
WESTON UNDERWOOD
Park View Farm

DEVON
ASHWATER
Blagdon Manor
AXMINSTER
Kerrington House
CHAGFORD
Parford Well
CHILLATON
Tor Cottage
DARTMOUTH
Nonsuch House
HONITON
West Colwell Farm
HORNS CROSS
The Round House
LUSTLEIGH
Eastwrey Barton
Woodley House

LYDFORD
Moor View House
LYNMOUTH
The Heatherville
LYNTON
Highcliffe House
Victoria Lodge
ROUSDON
The Dower House
SIDMOUTH
The Salty Monk
STRETE
Strete Barton House
TEIGNMOUTH
Thomas Luny House
TORQUAY
The Cary Arms
Linden House
The Marstan

DORSET
BRIDPORT
The Roundham House
The Shave Cross Inn
CHRISTCHURCH
Druid House
The Lord Bute & Restaurant
DORCHESTER
Little Court
FARNHAM
Farnham Farm House
SHERBORNE
The Kings Arms
Munden House
WAREHAM
Kemps Country House
WIMBORNE MINSTER
Les Bouviers Restaurant with Rooms

ESSEX
CHIPPING ONGAR
Diggins Farm
WIX
Dairy House

GLOUCESTERSHIRE
BLOCKLEY
Lower Brook House
CHELTENHAM
Beaumont House
Cleeve Hill House
Georgian House
Lypiatt House
CHIPPING CAMPDEN
The Malt House
Staddlestones
Woodborough
NETHER WESTCOTE
The Feathered Nest Inn

HAMPSHIRE
BARTON-ON-SEA
Pebble Beach
BENTLEY
Bentley Green Farm
BROCKENHURST
The Cottage Lodge
CADNAM
The Log Cabin
LYMINGTON
The Olde Barn
MILFORD ON SEA
Ha'penny House
SOUTHAMPTON
Riverside Bed & Breakfast
White Star Tavern, Dining and Rooms
WINCHESTER
Giffard House
Orchard House
29 Christchurch Road

HEREFORDSHIRE
HEREFORD
Somerville House
LEOMINSTER
Hills Farm
The Old Rectory Pembridge
ROSS-ON-WYE
Orles Barn
Wilton Court Restaurant with Rooms

HERTFORDSHIRE
DATCHWORTH
Farmhouse B&B
HERTFORD HEATH
Brides Farm
Rushen

KENT
ASHFORD
The Wife of Bath
CANTERBURY
Magnolia House
Yorke Lodge
DEAL
Sutherland House
DODDINGTON
The Old Vicarage
DOVER
The Marquis at Alkham
FOLKESTONE
The Relish
HAWKHURST
Southgate-Little Fowlers
IVYCHURCH
Olde Moat House
MARDEN
Merzie Meadows
ROYAL TUNBRIDGE WELLS
Danehurst House

LANCASHIRE
WHITEWELL
The Inn at Whitewell

LEICESTERSHIRE
KEGWORTH
Kegworth House

LINCOLNSHIRE
HEMSWELL
Hemswell Court
HOUGH-ON-THE-HILL
The Brownlow Arms
LINCOLN
Bailhouse & Mews
Minster Lodge
MARKET RASEN
The Advocate Arms

★★★★★ Premier Collection *continued*

STAMFORD
Meadow View
Rock Lodge
WINTERINGHAM
Winteringham Fields

LONDON POSTAL DISTRICTS
NW1
York & Albany
SW3
San Domenico House

NORFOLK
BLAKENEY
Blakeney House
CLEY NEXT THE SEA
Old Town Hall House
GREAT YARMOUTH
Andover House
3 Norfolk Square
HINDRINGHAM
Field House
NORTH WALSHAM
White House Farm
NORWICH
Brasteds
SHERINGHAM
Ashbourne House
The Eiders Bed & Breakfast
The Eight Acres
THURSFORD
Holly Lodge

NORTHAMPTONSHIRE
AYNHO
Aynhoe Park

NORTHUMBERLAND
BELFORD
Market Cross
CHATTON
Chatton Park House
CORNHILL-ON-TWEED
Ivy Cottage
ROTHBURY
The Orchard House
WOOLER
The Old Manse

NOTTINGHAMSHIRE
ELTON
The Grange
HOLBECK
Browns
NOTTINGHAM
Restaurant Sat Bains with Rooms
SOUTHWELL
The Old Vicarage

OXFORDSHIRE
ABINGDON
B&B Rafters
BURFORD
Burford House
GORING
The Miller of Mansfield
HAMPTON POYLE
The Bell at Hampton Poyle
HENLEY-ON-THAMES
Crowsley House
OXFORD
Burlington House
STADHAMPTON
The Crazy Bear
WANTAGE
Brook Barn Country House

SHROPSHIRE
BRIDGNORTH
The Albynes
CHURCH STRETTON
Field House
Willowfield Guest House
IRONBRIDGE
The Library House
LUDLOW
The Clive Bar & Restaurant with Rooms
De Greys of Ludlow
MARKET DRAYTON
Ternhill Farm House &
The Cottage Restaurant
OSWESTRY
Greystones
SHREWSBURY
Drapers Hall
Mad Jack's Restaurant & Bar

SOMERSET
BATH
Apsley House
Ayrlington
Cheriton House
Chestnuts House
Dorian House
One Three Nine
Paradise House
Tasburgh House
DULVERTON
Tarr Farm Inn
FROME
Lullington House
TAUNTON
Elm Villa
WELLS
Beaconsfield Farm
WESTON-SUPER-MARE
Church House
9 The Park
WITHYPOOL
Kings Farm
YEOVIL
Little Barwick House

STAFFORDSHIRE
CHEDDLETON
Choir Cottage and Choir House
LICHFIELD
St Johns House
RUGELEY
Colton House
TAMWORTH
Oak Tree Farm

SUFFOLK
BURY ST EDMUNDS
Clarice House
HOLTON
Valley Farm
LAVENHAM
Lavenham Great House 'Restaurant With Rooms'
Lavenham Old Rectory
Lavenham Priory
SOUTHWOLD
Sutherland House

STOWMARKET
Bays Farm
YAXLEY
The Auberge

SURREY

CHIDDINGFOLD
The Crown Inn

EAST SUSSEX

DITCHLING
Tovey Lodge
EASTBOURNE
The Berkeley
The Gables
The Manse B & B
Ocklynge Manor
HALLAND
Tamberry Hall
HASTINGS & ST LEONARDS
Barn House Seaview B&B
The Cloudesley
The Laindons
Stream House
HERSTMONCEUX
Wartling Place
RYE
Jeake's House
Manor Farm Oast
White Vine House

WEST SUSSEX

CHICHESTER
Rooks Hill
The Royal Oak Inn
LINDFIELD
The Pilstyes
ROGATE
Mizzards
SIDLESHAM
The Crab & Lobster
WEST MARDEN
West Marden Farmhouse

TYNE & WEAR

GATESHEAD
The Stables Lodge
SUNNISIDE
Hedley Hall Country House

WARWICKSHIRE

ATHERSTONE
Chapel House Restaurant with Rooms
ETTINGTON
Fulready Manor
SHIPSTON ON STOUR
The Old Mill
STRATFORD-UPON-AVON
Cherry Trees

WEST MIDLANDS

BIRMINGHAM
Westbourne Lodge

ISLE OF WIGHT

GODSHILL
Godshill Park Farm House
NITON
Enchanted Manor
TOTLAND BAY
Sentry Mead
VENTNOR
The Hambrough
The Leconfield

WILTSHIRE

BRADFORD-ON-AVON
Bradford Old Windmill
BURTON
The Old House at Home
CORSHAM
The Methuen Arms
DEVIZES
Blounts Court Farm
SALISBURY
Quidhampton Mill

WORCESTERSHIRE

BEWDLEY
Number Thirty
BROADWAY
Abbots Grange

East House
Mill Hay House
Russell's

EAST RIDING OF YORKSHIRE

BEVERLEY
Burton Mount Country House
BRIDLINGTON
Marton Grange

NORTH YORKSHIRE

AMPLEFORTH
Shallowdale House
APPLETREEWICK
Knowles Lodge
BAINBRIDGE
Yorebridge House
BEDALE
Mill Close Farm
BOROUGHBRIDGE
The Crown Inn
GOLDSBOROUGH
Goldsborough Hall
GRASSINGTON
Ashfield House
Grassington House
HETTON
The Angel Inn
KIRKBY FLEETHAM
The Black Horse
KNARESBOROUGH
General Tarleton Inn
LEYBURN
Capple Bank Farm
Thorney Hall
OLDSTEAD
The Black Swan at Oldstead
PICKERING
17 Burgate
RIPON
Mallard Grange
THIRSK
Spital Hill
THORNTON WATLASS
Thornton Watlass Hall

★★★★★ Premier Collection *continued*

CHANNEL ISLANDS

JERSEY
ST AUBIN
The Panorama

ISLE OF MAN

PORT ST MARY
Aaron House

SCOTLAND

ARGYLL & BUTE
CONNEL
Ards House
HELENSBURGH
Lethamhill
OBAN
Blarcreen House

DUMFRIES & GALLOWAY
MOFFAT
Well View
THORNHILL
Gillbank House

CITY OF EDINBURGH
EDINBURGH
Elmview
Kew House
21212
23 Mayfield
The Witchery by the Castle

FIFE
PEAT INN
The Peat Inn
ST ANDREWS
The Paddock

HIGHLAND
AVIEMORE
The Old Minister's House
BRACLA
Loch Ness Lodge
DORNOCH
2 Quail
INVERNESS
Daviot Lodge
Trafford Bank
KINGUSSIE
The Cross at Kingussie
POOLEWE
Pool House

PERTH & KINROSS
ALYTH
Tigh Na Leigh Guesthouse

SCOTTISH BORDERS
MELROSE
Fauhope House

ISLE OF SKYE
STRUAN
Ullinish Country Lodge

SOUTH AYRSHIRE
AYR
The Crescent

STIRLING
STRATHYRE
Creagan House

WEST LOTHIAN
LINLITHGOW
Arden Country House
LIVINGSTONE
Ashcroft Farmhouse

WALES

ISLE OF ANGLESEY
BEAUMARIS
Ye Olde Bulls Head Inn

CARMARTHENSHIRE
ST CLEARS
Coedllys Country House

CEREDIGION
ABERAERON
Feathers Royal
The Harbourmaster
Ty Mawr Mansion
ABERYSTWYTH
Awel-Deg

CONWY
ABERGELE
The Kinmel Arms
BETWS-Y-COED
Penmachno Hall
Tan-y-Foel Country House
CONWY
Bryn Derwen
The Groes Inn
The Old Rectory Country House
LLANRWST
Plas Maenan Country House
RHOS-ON-SEA
Plas Rhos

DENBIGHSHIRE
DENBIGH
Castle House
LLANDRILLO
Tyddyn Llan Restaurant
LLANDYRNOG
Pentre Mawr Country House
RUTHIN
Firgrove Country House B&B
ST ASAPH
Tan-Yr-Onnen Guest House

GWYNEDD
CAERNARFON
Plas Dinas Country House
DOLGELLAU
Tyddynmawr Farmhouse

MONMOUTHSHIRE
SKENFRITH
The Bell at Skenfrith
WHITEBROOK
The Crown at Whitebrook

PEMBROKESHIRE
FISHGUARD
Erw-Lon
NARBETH
The Grove
ST DAVID'S
Ramsey House
SOLVA
Crug-Glas Country House
Lochmeyler Farm Guest House

POWYS
BRECON
Canal Bank
The Coach House
Peterstone Court
CAERSWS
The Talkhouse
CRICKHOWELL
Glangrwyney Court
LLANDRINDOD WELLS
Guidfa House
WELSHPOOL
Moors Farm B&B

SWANSEA
MUMBLES
Little Langland
PARKMILL
Maes-Yr-Haf Restaurant with Rooms
REYNOLDSTON
Fairyhill

NORTHERN IRELAND

ANTRIM
BUSHMILLS
Causewy Lodge
Whitepark House

DOWN
BANGOR
Hebron House

HOLYWOOD
Rayanne House

LONDONDERRY
COLERAINE
Greenhill House

TYRONE
DUNGANNON
Grange Lodge

REPUBLIC OF IRELAND

CLARE
LAHINCH
Moy House

CORK
BLARNEY
Ashlee Lodge
CLONAKILTY
An Garran Coir
KINSALE
Friar's Lodge
Old Bank House
Rivermount House
SHANAGARRY
Ballymaloe House
YOUGHAL
Ahernes

DUBLIN
DUBLIN
Butlers Town House
Glenogra Town House
Harrington Hall

KERRY
DINGLE
Emlagh House
Gormans Clifftop House & Restaurant
KILLARNEY
Foleys Town House
Fairview
Old Weir Lodge
KILLORGLIN
Carrig House Country House & Restaurant

KILDARE
ATHY
Coursetown Country House

MONAGHAN
GLASLOUGH
Tge Castle at Castle Leslie Estate

TIPPERARY
THURLES
The Castle
Inch House Country House & Restaurant

WATERFORD
BALLYMACARBRY
Hanoras Cottage
WATERFORD
Sion Hill House & Gardens

WEXFORD
CAMPILE
Kilmokea Country Manor & Gardens
GOREY
Woodlands Country House

England

Newton Wood, North York Moors National Park

BEDFORDSHIRE

DUNSTABLE — Map 11 TL02

The Highwayman

★★★ INN

London Rd LU6 3DX
☎ 01582 601122 📄 01582 603812
e-mail: 6466@greeneking.co.uk
web: www.oldenglish.co.uk
dir: *N'bound: M1 junct 9, A5, 6m on right. S'bound: M1 junct 11, A505, left on A5 towards London. Property on left*

This establishment continues to prove popular with business guests, partly due to its convenient location just south of the town, and for the ample parking space. The accommodation is comfortable, well equipped and cheerfully decorated. The public areas include a large public bar where meals are available.

Rooms 52 en suite (3 fmly) (24 GF) **Facilities** TVL tea/coffee Dinner available Direct Dial Cen ht **Parking** 76

MILTON ERNEST — Map 11 TL05

The Queens Head

★★★ INN

2 Rushden Rd MK44 1RU
☎ 01234 822412 📄 01234 822337
e-mail: 6495@greeneking.co.uk
dir: *From Bedford follow A6 towards Kettering, on left entering Milton Ernest*

This character inn provides good accommodation together with a wide range of dishes from the imaginative menu, and real ales from the cosy bar. Staff are friendly and polite. Ample parking is available.

Rooms 13 en suite (4 GF) **Facilities** tea/coffee Direct Dial Wi-fi **Parking**

WOBURN — Map 11 SP93

The Bell

★★★★ INN

21 Bedford St MK17 9QB
☎ 01525 290280 📄 01525 290017
e-mail: bell.woburn@oldenglishinns.co.uk
dir: *M1 junct 13/A507 to Woburn Sands. Take 1st left, then next left. At T-junct turn right*

The bar, restaurant and some of the bedrooms are housed in this charming inn, which has retained many original features. The rest of the bedrooms, together with a comfortable lounge, are located in a Georgian building directly opposite. Ample parking is provided behind both buildings.

Rooms 24 en suite (4 GF) **Facilities** tea/coffee Direct Dial **Parking** 50

BERKSHIRE

BEENHAM — Map 5 SU56

The Six Bells

★★★★ 🍽 INN

The Green RG7 5NX
☎ 0118 971 3368
e-mail: info@thesixbells.co.uk
web: www.thesixbells.co.uk
dir: *Off A4 between Reading/Newbury, follow signs for Beenham Village*

A traditional village pub with a good atmosphere, friendly service and comfortable, well-appointed bedrooms. The restaurant offers a good choice of well-prepared and tasty dishes. The establishment has good access to Thatcham and Newbury.

Rooms 4 en suite S £59.95; D £79.95* **Facilities** FTV tea/coffee Dinner available Cen ht **Conf** Max 40 Thtr 40 Class 40 Board 25 **Parking** 20 **Notes** ⊗ No Children 16yrs No coaches

BOXFORD — Map 5 SU47

High Street Farm Barn *(SU424714)*

★★★★ FARMHOUSE

RG20 8DD
☎ 01488 608783 & 07768 324707
Mr & Mrs Boden
e-mail: nboden@uk2.net
dir: *0.5m W of village centre. Off B4000 to Boxford, farm 1st on left opposite pub*

A converted barn situated on a small holding in the Berkshire village of Boxford. Bedrooms are smartly furnished and a comfortable lounge is available for guests use. Breakfast, which is served at one table, includes free-range eggs from the farm and home-made breads and marmalades.

Rooms 2 en suite (2 GF) S £55; D £70* **Facilities** FTV tea/coffee Cen ht **Parking** 4 **Notes** ⊗ 🐑 15 acres sheep

White Hart Cottage

★★★ BED AND BREAKFAST

Westbrook RG20 8DN
☎ 01488 608410
e-mail: gillian@jones-parry.orangehome.co.uk
dir: *0.3m NW of Boxford. Off B4000 to Boxford, left for Westbrook, premises on right*

Guests are ensured of a friendly welcome at this pretty cottage, peacefully located in the delightful village of Boxford. Newbury and the M4 are both just a short drive away. Bedrooms are attractively appointed and guests have access to a small TV lounge. A hearty breakfast is served at the large kitchen table.

Rooms 3 rms (1 en suite) (2 pri facs) S £35-£40; D £65-£70* **Facilities** TVL TV2B tea/coffee Cen ht **Parking** 6 **Notes** ⊗ No Children Closed 12 Dec-12 Jan 🐑

Bell@ Boxford

★★★ 🅰 INN

Lambourn Rd RG20 8DD
☎ 01488 608721 📄 01488 608502
e-mail: paul@bellatboxford.com
dir: *M4 junct 14 onto A338 towards Wantage. Turn right onto B4000 to x-rds, signed Boxford*

Rooms 10 en suite (4 GF) S £40-£75; D £50-£85* **Facilities** FTV tea/coffee Dinner available Direct Dial Cen ht Wi-fi Pool table **Conf** Max 12 Board 12 **Parking** 35

CHIEVELEY — Map 5 SU47

The Crab at Chieveley

★★★★ ⭐⭐ GUEST ACCOMMODATION

Wantage Rd RG20 8UE
☎ 01635 247550 📄 01635 247440
e-mail: info@crabatchieveley.com
dir: *1.5m W of Chieveley on B4494*

The individually themed bedrooms at this former pub have been appointed to a very high standard and include a full range of modern amenities. Ground-floor rooms have a small private patio area complete with a hot tub. The warm and cosy restaurant offers an extensive and award-winning range of fish and seafood dishes.

Rooms 8 en suite 5 annexe en suite (7 GF) **Facilities** FTV tea/coffee Dinner available Direct Dial Cen ht Licensed Wi-fi Hot Tub Japanese spa suite **Conf** Max 14 Thtr 14 Class 14 Board 14 **Parking** 80 **Notes** LB

COMPTON — Map 5 SU58

Compton Swan

★★★★ INN

High St RG20 6NJ
☎ 01635 579400 📄 01635 579199
e-mail: info@comptonswan.co.uk
dir: *M4 junct 13 N on A34 for 5m, follow signs for Compton*

Located in the peaceful Berkshire downland village of Compton, the Compton Swan offers a warm welcome,

Save on B&Bs and Hotels. Book at theAA.com/hotel

BERKSHIRE 29 ENGLAND

good food and smartly appointed bedrooms. Free Wi-fi and new flat-screen TVs with ample channel choice make the inn suitable for business and leisure guests alike. The bar and restaurant have varied and interesting menus.

Rooms 6 en suite (2 fmly) S £79.50-£95; D £89-£115* **Facilities** FTV tea/coffee Dinner available Cen ht Wi-fi **Conf** Max 45 Thtr 45 Class 24 Board 20 **Parking** 12 **Notes** RS Sun dinner residents only

EAST GARSTON   Map 5 SU37

Queens Arms

★★★★ INN

RG17 7ET
☎ 01488 648757
e-mail: info@queenshotel.co.uk
dir: *From A338 into Shefford, then follow signs to East Garston. On right as you enter village*

The perfect location for lovers of country pursuits, the Queens Arms is located in the beautiful Lambourn Valley. The individually themed bedrooms are well appointed and offer sumptuous beds, flat-screen TVs and Wi-fi. The bar is well stocked, and the restaurant serves great British food that is based on local produce.

Rooms 8 en suite (1 GF) **Facilities** FTV tea/coffee Dinner available Direct Dial Cen ht Wi-fi Golf 18 Fishing Riding **Parking** 30 **Notes** LB Closed 25 Dec

HUNGERFORD   Map 5 SU36

The Pheasant Inn

★★★★ INN

Ermin St, Shefford Woodlands RG17 7AA
☎ 01488 648284   01488 648971
e-mail: enquiries@thepheasant-inn.co.uk
web: www.thepheasant-inn.co.uk
dir: *M4 junct 14, 200yds N on A338 turn left onto B4000 towards Lambourn*

The Pheasant Inn is a friendly, traditional property conveniently located 400 yards from the M4 and close to the racing centre of Lambourn and Newbury racecourse. The horseracing theme runs throughout the traditional pub and restaurant where lunch and dinner are served daily. Bedrooms in contrast are contemporary in style providing guests with comfortable accommodation; all feature flat-screen TVs, free Wi-fi and in-room beverage making facilities.

Rooms 11 en suite (4 GF) **Facilities** FTV TVL tea/coffee Dinner available Cen ht Wi-fi Shooting & fishing by arrangement **Conf** Max 14 Board 14 **Parking** 100

Crown & Garter

★★★★ INN

Great Common, Inkpen RG17 9QR
☎ 01488 668325
e-mail: gill.hern@btopenworld.com
web: www.crownandgarter.com
dir: *4m SE of Hungerford. Off A4 into Kintbury, opp corner stores onto Inkpen Rd, straight for 2m*

Peacefully located in the attractive village of Inkpen, this charming 17th-century inn has a bar with large inglenook log fire where interesting well-prepared dishes are offered. The bedrooms surround a pretty garden, and are comprehensively equipped and attractively decorated in a country cottage style.

Rooms 9 annexe en suite (9 GF) S £79; D £99 **Facilities** FTV tea/coffee Dinner available Cen ht Wi-fi **Parking** 40 **Notes** LB ⊗ No Children 7yrs RS No lunch Mon/Tue or evening meal Sun No coaches

The Swan Inn

★★★★ INN

Craven Rd, Inkpen RG17 9DX
☎ 01488 668326   01488 668306
e-mail: enquiries@theswaninn-organics.co.uk
web: www.theswaninn-organics.co.uk
dir: *3.5m SE of Hungerford. S on Hungerford High St past rail bridge, left to Hungerford Common, right signed Inkpen*

This delightful village inn dates back to the 17th century has open fires and beams in the bar, and the bonus of a smart restaurant. Bedrooms are generally spacious and well equipped. Organic produce is available from the on-site farm shop, so the bar, restaurant and breakfast menus all feature local organic produce too.

Rooms 10 en suite (2 fmly) S £70-£80; D £85-£105* **Facilities** tea/coffee Dinner available Direct Dial Cen ht Wi-fi **Conf** Max 40 Thtr 40 Class 40 Board 12 **Parking** 50 **Notes** ⊗ Closed 25-26 Dec

HURLEY   Map 5 SU88

PREMIER COLLECTION

The Olde Bell Inn

★★★★★ ◎◎ INN

High St SL6 5LX
☎ 01628 825881   01628 825939
e-mail: oldebellreception@coachinginn.co.uk
dir: *M4 junct 8/9 follow signs for Henley. At rdbt take A4130 to Hurley, turn right to Hurley Village, 800yds on right*

Originally built in 1135, this charming coaching inn has lots of original features, and the cosy bar and lounge are warm and welcoming. There is a range of individually styled bedrooms, each with a modern well-equipped bathroom. The Olde Bell Inn has an award-winning restaurant and extensive landscaped gardens. The Tighe Barn and Malt House cater for functions and private parties, and there are a range of business facilities.

Rooms 11 en suite 37 annexe en suite (19 fmly) (21 GF) S £109-£225; D £109-£400* **Facilities** FTV tea/coffee Dinner available Direct Dial Cen ht Wi-fi ⊕ ⊕ **Conf** Max 130 Thtr 130 Class 50 Board 40 **Parking** 60 **Notes** Civ Wed 130

Black Boys Inn

★★★★ ◎◎ RESTAURANT WITH ROOMS

Henley Rd SL6 5NQ
☎ 01628 824212
e-mail: info@blackboysinn.co.uk
web: www.blackboysinn.co.uk
dir: *1m W of Hurley on A4130*

Just a short drive from Henley, the traditional exterior of this friendly establishment is a contrast to the smart modernity within. Popular with locals, the restaurant is the stage for Simon Bonwick's imaginative cuisine, and has a buzzing atmosphere. The well-appointed bedrooms are situated in converted barns close by.

Rooms 8 annexe en suite (5 GF) D £87.50-£140* **Facilities** FTV tea/coffee Dinner available Cen ht Wi-fi **Conf** Max 8 Board 8 **Parking** 40 **Notes** ⊗ No Children 12yrs No coaches

KNOWL HILL   Map 5 SU87

Bird in Hand Country Inn

★★★★ ⚐ INN

Bath Rd RG10 9UP
☎ 01628 826622 & 822781   01628 826748
e-mail: info@birdinhand.co.uk
dir: *M4 junct 8/9, take A404 towards Henley. At junct 9b onto A4 towards Reading, after 3m Knowl Hill on right after BP garage*

Rooms 3 en suite 12 annexe en suite (1 fmly) (6 GF) S £40-£80; D £60-£120 (room only)* **Facilities** FTV tea/coffee Dinner available Direct Dial Cen ht Wi-fi **Parking** 80 **Notes** LB

Pilgrims Guest House

★★★★ GUEST ACCOMMODATION

Oxford Rd RG14 1XB
☎ 01635 40694 📠 01635 44873
e-mail: office@pilgrimsgh.co.uk
web: www.pilgrimsnewbury.co.uk
dir: *Off Waitrose A4 rdbt onto B4494 towards Wantage, 0.5m on left*

Located close to the town centre, this smartly presented house has comfortable bedrooms with modern bathrooms; some rooms are located in a new annexe. Wi-fi is provided throughout the property and breakfast is served in the bright dining room. Parking is available.

Rooms 13 rms (9 en suite) 4 annexe en suite (1 fmly) (3 GF) S £43-£56.50; D £65* **Facilities** FTV tea/coffee Cen ht Wi-fi **Parking** 17 **Notes** ⊗ Closed 24 Dec-2 Jan

Rookwood Farm House

★★★★ GUEST ACCOMMODATION

Stockcross RG20 8JX
☎ 01488 608676 📠 01488 657961
e-mail: charlotte@rookwoodfarmhouse.co.uk
dir: *2m W of Newbury, at junct A4 & A34 onto B4000, 0.75m to Stockcross, 1st right signed Woodspeen, bear left, 1st on right*

This farmhouse enjoys wonderful views and is very much a family home. Bedrooms are attractively presented and feature fine pieces of furniture. Breakfast is served on one large table in the kitchen. The coach house has a kitchen and sitting room and, during the summer, visitors can enjoy the beautiful gardens and outdoor pool.

Rooms 2 rms (1 en suite) (1 pri facs) 2 annexe en suite (1 fmly) S fr £60; D fr £90 **Facilities** TVL tea/coffee Cen ht Wi-fi ⊰ 👪 **Conf** Max 16 Board 16 **Parking** 4 **Notes** ⊗

The Limes Guest House

★★★ GUEST HOUSE

368 London Rd RG14 2QH
☎ 01635 33082 📠 01635 580023
e-mail: s.j.sweeney@btinternet.com
web: www.limesguesthouse.co.uk
dir: *M4 junct 13, 3m S towards Newbury. Take A4 to towards Thatcham/Reading, 400yds past Newbury Business Park on left*

Built in 1910, this Edwardian house is convenient for Newbury and Thatcham, and Newbury Racecourse is only a mile away. The en suite bedrooms are individually decorated. Wi-fi internet access and ample parking are available. Dinner and breakfast are served in the light dining room overlooking the spacious gardens.

Rooms 17 en suite (2 fmly) (9 GF) S £62-£68; D £78-£98* **Facilities** FTV TVL tea/coffee Dinner available Direct Dial Cen ht Licensed Wi-fi **Parking** 20 **Notes** ⊗

Dolphin Inn

Ⓤ

113 Bartholomew St RG14 5DT
☎ 01635 232425 📠 01635 230356
e-mail: room@dolphin-inns.com
dir: *In town centre. Off A339 Sainsbury's rdbt into town centre, signs for council offices, inn opposite*

Currently the rating for this establishment is not confirmed. This may be due to a change of ownership or because it has only recently joined the AA rating scheme.

Rooms 8 en suite **Facilities** STV FTV TV4B tea/coffee Dinner available Direct Dial Cen ht Licensed **Conf** Max 50 Thtr 50 Class 50 Board 40 **Parking** 20 **Notes** ⊗ No Children 16yrs

Weir View House

★★★★ GUEST ACCOMMODATION

9 Shooters Hill RG8 7DZ
☎ 0118 984 2120 📠 0118 984 3777
e-mail: info@weirview.co.uk
web: www.weirview.co.uk
dir: *A329 N from Pangbourne, after mini rdbt under rail bridge, opp Swan pub*

A warm welcome is guaranteed at this delightful house, situated in the village of Pangbourne overlooking the River Thames. The spacious modern bedrooms have been

finished to a very high standard and the thoughtful extras include a well-stocked minibar. A continental breakfast is served in the bright and airy dining room, and freshly cooked meals can be delivered to your room from the pub across the road.

Wier View House

Rooms 9 en suite (6 fmly) (3 GF) S £90; D £90-£105* **Facilities** FTV TVL tea/coffee Direct Dial Cen ht Wi-fi **Parking** 10 **Notes** ⊗

Chestnuts Bed & Breakfast

★★★ BED AND BREAKFAST

Basingstoke Rd, Spencers Wood RG7 1AA
☎ 0118 988 6171 & 07903 956397
e-mail: chestnuts4bb@hotmail.com
dir: *M4 junct 11, A33 for Basingstoke, next rdbt onto B3349 Three Mile Cross, over white-spot rdbt, Chestnuts 1m on left between chemist & bakery*

This detached Georgian house is convenient for the business parks of Reading, just 1.5 miles from the M4 and with easy access to the M3. The house provides spacious bedrooms, warm hospitality, a good breakfast, and off-road parking.

Rooms 2 rms 2 annexe en suite S £35-£45; D £50-£60 **Facilities** FTV tea/coffee Cen ht Wi-fi **Parking** 4 **Notes** ⊗ No Children 16yrs 🍽

The Wee Waif

★★★ INN

Old Bath Rd, Charvil RG10 9RJ
☎ 0118 944 0066 📠 0118 969 1525

Located on the outskirts of Reading with easy access to popular transport networks. Bedrooms provide lodge style accommodation with guest comfort in mind. All day dining is available from the popular Hungry Horse restaurant and bar, where breakfast is also served. Ample parking is available.

Rooms 42 en suite **Parking**

La Baguette Reading

★★ GUEST ACCOMMODATION

7 Blagrave St RG1 1PJ
☎ 0118 956 0882 & 07966 263843 📠 0118 951 1447
e-mail: bookings@labaguettes.co.uk

Located a short walk from Reading town centre, and close to the main train station. Bedrooms vary in size and provide comfortable accommodation for the traveller. A varied choice of breakfast is served in the popular 'La Baguette' sandwich shop below.

Rooms 6 rms (6 pri facs) S £35-£45; D £55-£75*
Facilities STV FTV tea/coffee Cen ht Wi-fi **Notes** LB

SLOUGH	Map 6 SU97

Furnival Lodge

★★★★ 🅰 GUEST HOUSE

53-55 Furnival Av SL2 1DH
☎ 01753 570333 📠 01753 670038
e-mail: info@furnival-lodge.co.uk
web: www.furnival-lodge.co.uk
dir: Just off A355 (Farnham Rd) adjacent to BP garage
Rooms 10 en suite (1 fmly) (3 GF) **Facilities** TVL Cen ht Wi-fi **Parking** 7 **Notes** ⊗

WINDSOR	Map 6 SU97

PREMIER COLLECTION

Magna Carta

★★★★★ 🥄 GUEST ACCOMMODATION

Thames Side SL4 1QN
☎ 07836 551912
e-mail: dominic@magna-carta.co.uk
web: www.magna-carta.co.uk
dir: M4 junct 5 follow signs to Datchet, then Windsor. At Windsor & Eton riverside station turn right & down to river

A most exciting way to experience life-afloat, this superbly equipped barge offers bed and breakfast between charter cruising on the Thames. Accommodation is particularly comfortable and pleasantly spacious. The lounge and deck space is notable too, not only for the river views, but for the wealth of facilities, there is a hot-tub on deck, and an impressive range of books, DVD and music library, but also a well stocked bar, from where the large picture windows look on to the tranquil river. Breakfast cooked in the galley, is super, offering an excellent choice from local suppliers.

Rooms 4 en suite S £100-£130; D £130-£160*
Facilities tea/coffee Cen ht Licensed Wi-fi Hot tub
Conf Max 8 Board 8 **Notes** LB ⊗ RS pre-booked cruises

Park Farm

★★★★ GUEST ACCOMMODATION

St Leonards Rd SL4 3EA
☎ 01753 866823
e-mail: stay@parkfarm.com
dir: M4 junct 6, at end of dual-carriageway take 3rd exit. At T junct, turn right, Park Farm on left

Ideally situated between Windsor and Legoland, Park Farm offers a warm welcome and traditionally styled accommodation. Each bedroom has a range of useful facilities. Some rooms also have romantic wrought-iron beds. The owners aim to offer guests a friendly and personal service including advice and information on where to eat or what to do in the area. Bunk beds can be added for children.

Rooms 4 rms (3 en suite) (1 pri facs) (2 fmly) (2 GF) S £65-£85; D £85-£95* **Facilities** FTV tea/coffee Cen ht Wi-fi **Parking** 8 **Notes** ⊗ 📷

Clarence Guest House

★★★ GUEST HOUSE

9 Clarence Rd SL4 5AE
☎ 01753 864436 📠 01753 857060
e-mail: clarence.hotel@btconnect.com
web: www.clarence-hotel.co.uk
dir: M4 junct 6, dual carriageway to Windsor, left at 1st rdbt onto Clarence Rd

This Grade II listed Victorian house is in the heart of Windsor. Space in some rooms is limited, but all are well maintained and offer excellent value for money. Facilities include a lounge with a well-stocked bar, and a steam room. Breakfast is served in the dining room overlooking attractive gardens.

Rooms 20 en suite (6 fmly) (2 GF) (16 smoking) S £45-£77; D £55-£89* **Facilities** FTV TVL tea/coffee Cen ht Licensed Wi-fi Sauna Steam room **Parking** 4

The Windsor Trooper

★★★ INN

97 St Leonards Rd SL4 3BZ
☎ 01753 670123
e-mail: thewindsortrooper@live.co.uk
dir: M4 junct 6, at rdbt follow signs for Windsor, then straight over next 2 rdbts signed Staines, take 1st road on left

Located close to many local attractions and in walking distance of the town centre. This traditional inn provides comfortable annexed accommodation with some rooms suitable for families. Dinner is available in the bright and airy conservatory, where a range of daily specials are often available. A freshly prepared breakfast is served and limited secure car parking is available.

Rooms 4 en suite 5 annexe en suite (3 fmly) (5 GF) **Facilities** FTV tea/coffee Dinner available Cen ht Wi-fi **Parking** 9 **Notes** ⊗

WOKINGHAM	Map 5 SU86

Quarters

★★★★ GUEST ACCOMMODATION

14 Milton Rd RG40 1DB
☎ 0118 979 7071 📠 0118 977 0057
e-mail: elaineizod@hotmail.com
dir: From town centre on A321 towards Henley/Twyford. Left at 1st mini-rdbt onto Milton Rd

Located just a short walk from the town centre, a warm welcome is assured here. Stylishly decorated bedrooms are well equipped and spacious. A hearty breakfast is served around the communal dining table.

Rooms 3 en suite S £45-£50; D £65-£70* **Facilities** FTV tea/coffee Cen ht Wi-fi **Notes** ⊗ 📷

BRISTOL

BRISTOL   Map 4 ST57

Westfield House

★★★★ 🍽 BED AND BREAKFAST

37 Stoke Hill, Stoke Bishop BS9 1LQ
☎ 0117 962 6119 📠 0117 962 6119
e-mail: admin@westfieldhouse.net
web: www.westfieldhouse.net
dir: 1.8m NW of city centre in Stoke Bishop

A genuine welcome is assured at this friendly, family-run bed and breakfast in a quiet location on the edge of Durdham Downs. The very well-equipped bedrooms offer high levels of quality and comfort. Home-cooked dinners are available by arrangement, and in summer these can be enjoyed on the patio overlooking the large rear garden.

Rooms 3 en suite S £60-£93; D £75-£125 **Facilities** FTV TVL tea/coffee Dinner available Direct Dial Cen ht Wi-fi 🐾 **Conf** Max 10 Board 10 **Parking** 5 **Notes** LB ⊗ No Children 11yrs

Downlands House

★★★★ GUEST ACCOMMODATION

33 Henleaze Gardens, Henleaze BS9 4HH
☎ 0117 962 1639
e-mail: info@downlandshouse.co.uk
web: www.downlandshouse.com
dir: 2m NW of city centre off A4018. M5 junct 17, follow Westbury-on-Trym/City Centre signs, pass Badminton private girls' school. Henleaze Gdns on left

This elegant Victorian property is convenient for Durdham Downs, Clifton village and Bristol Zoo. The attractive bedrooms have lots of extra touches, there is a smart lounge, and breakfast is served in either the conservatory or the stylish dining room.

Rooms 10 rms (7 en suite) (3 pri facs) (1 fmly) (1 GF) S £45-£50; D £60-£77.50* **Facilities** FTV TVL tea/coffee Cen ht Wi-fi

Downs Edge

★★★★ GUEST HOUSE

Saville Rd, Stoke Bishop BS9 1JA
☎ 0117 968 3264 & 07885 866463 📠 0117 968 7063
e-mail: welcome@downsedge.com
dir: M5 junct 17, A4018, 4th rdbt right onto B4054 Parrys Ln, 1st left onto Saville Rd, 3rd right onto Hollybush Ln, left after 2nd speed ramp onto Downs Edge Drive

This attractive country house has a quiet countryside setting in the heart of the city, on the edge of Durdham Downs. It stands in glorious gardens and is furnished with period pieces and paintings. The pleasant, well-equipped bedrooms have en suite facilities and the added bonus of sweeping views across the Downs. A nice finishing touch to each room is a basket of life's little necessities. Breakfast is an impressive variety of hot and cold dishes. There is a drawing room with an open fire, and a library containing many books about Bristol.

Rooms 4 en suite 3 annexe en suite S £59-£65; D £79-£84* **Facilities** FTV tea/coffee Cen ht Wi-fi **Conf** Board 12 **Parking** 8 **Notes** ⊗ No Children 6yrs Closed Xmas & New Year

Greenlands (ST597636)

★★★★ FARMHOUSE

BS39 4ES
☎ 01275 333487 📠 01275 331211
Mrs J Cleverley

(For full entry see Stanton Drew (Somerset))

Valley Farm

★★★★ BED AND BREAKFAST

Sandy Ln BS39 4EL
☎ 01275 332723 & 07799 768161 📠 01275 332723
e-mail: valleyfarm2000@tiscali.co.uk

(For full entry see Stanton Drew (Somerset))

Westbury Park Guest House

★★★★ GUEST HOUSE

37 Westbury Rd, Westbury-on-Trym BS9 3AU
☎ 0117 962 0465
e-mail: westburypark@btconnect.com
dir: M5 junct 17, A4018, 3.5m opp gates of Badminton School

On the edge of Durdham Downs, this detached guest house is ideally located for many of Bristol's attractions.

Breakfast is served in the spacious dining room overlooking the front garden. Bedrooms and bathrooms come in a range of shapes and sizes, including one room on the ground floor.

Rooms 8 en suite (3 fmly) (1 GF) S fr £50; D fr £75* **Facilities** tea/coffee Cen ht Licensed Wi-fi **Parking** 3 **Notes** ⊗

Mayfair Lodge

★★★ GUEST HOUSE

5 Henleaze Rd, Westbury-on-Trym BS9 4EX
☎ 0117 962 2008 📠 0117 962 2008
e-mail: enquiries@mayfairlodge.co.uk
dir: M5 junct 17, A4018, after 3rd rdbt onto Henleaze Rd, Lodge 50yds on left

This charming Victorian house is in a residential area close to Durdham Downs and Bristol Zoo. Mayfair Lodge has well-equipped bedrooms of varying sizes and a relaxed, friendly atmosphere. Breakfast is served at separate tables in the bright dining room. Off-road parking is available behind the property.

Rooms 9 rms (6 en suite) S £38-£55; D £70-£75 **Facilities** FTV tea/coffee Cen ht Wi-fi **Parking** 6 **Notes** ⊗ No Children 10yrs Closed Xmas & New Year

The Washington

★★★ GUEST HOUSE

11-15 St Pauls Rd, Clifton BS8 1LX
☎ 0117 973 3980 📠 0117 973 4740
e-mail: washington@cliftonhotels.com
dir: A4018 into city, right at lights opp BBC, house 200yds on left

This large terraced house is within walking distance of the city centre and Clifton Village. The bedrooms, many refurbished, are well equipped for business guests. Public areas include a modern reception lounge and a bright basement breakfast room. The property has secure parking and a rear patio garden.

Rooms 46 rms (40 en suite) (4 fmly) (10 GF) S £40-£73; D £49-£89* **Facilities** FTV tea/coffee Direct Dial Cen ht Licensed Wi-fi Reduced rate pass for local health club **Parking** 16 **Notes** Closed 23 Dec-3 Jan

EASTON-IN-GORDANO   Map 4 ST57

The Tynings B & B

★★★ BED AND BREAKFAST

Martcombe Rd BS20 0QE
☎ 01275 372608 & 07794 898256
e-mail: enquiries@thetynings.com
dir: M5 junct 19, A369 towards Bristol (signed Clifton), 0.5m on right opp Rudgleigh Inn

The Tynings is just a ten-minute drive from central Bristol and has easy access to the M5. Bedrooms and bathrooms come in a range of sizes but all are well decorated and comfortably furnished. Breakfast is served in the small dining room, and guests may wish to opt for dinner in the pub just across the road. Off-street parking is available.

Rooms 6 rms (3 en suite) (3 pri facs) (4 fmly)
Facilities FTV TVL tea/coffee Cen ht Wi-fi **Parking** 8
Notes ⊗ Closed 25 & 26 Dec ⊜

BUCKINGHAMSHIRE

AMERSHAM   Map 6 SU99

Wildhatch

☆☆☆☆ BED AND BREAKFAST

Coles Hill Ln, Winchmore Hill HP7 0NT
☎ 01494 722611   🖨 01494 722611
e-mail: di.john.wildhatch@btinternet.com
dir: M40 junct 2 N on A355, after 1.5m left at Harte & Magpies public house. Fork left at Coleshill & continue to Winchmore Hill, house 2nd on left after 30mph sign

This beautifully presented modern house offers well-equipped bedrooms and comfortable public rooms. Hospitality is a major strength. Delicious, freshly cooked breakfasts are served in the dining room overlooking the gardens and surrounding countryside. Weather permitting breakfast may be taken on the terrace. Close to major motorway links.

Rooms 2 en suite (1 fmly) S £45-£50; D £60-£65*
Facilities TVL tea/coffee Dinner available Cen ht Wi-fi
Golf 18 cycle hire **Parking** 4 **Notes** ⊗ Closed 23 Dec-17 Jan ⊜

BEACONSFIELD   Map 6 SU99

PREMIER COLLECTION

Crazy Bear Beaconsfield

☆☆☆☆☆ ⊛ GUEST ACCOMMODATION

75 Wycombe End, Old Town HP9 1LX
☎ 01494 673086   🖨 01494 730183
e-mail: enquiries@crazybear-beaconsfield.co.uk
dir: M40 junct 2, 3rd exit from rdbt, next rdbt 1st exit. Over 2 mini-rdbts, on right

Located in the heart of the old town, this former inn dating from Tudor times has been completely restored to create an exciting and vibrant environment. Good food in both the Thai and the English restaurants, classic cocktails and an extensive wine list can be enjoyed. The rooms are individually appointed with unusual fabrics and dazzling colours. The Crazy Bear was a runner-up for the AA's Funkiest B&B of the Year award (2011-2012).

Rooms 6 en suite 4 annexe en suite (2 GF)
Facilities STV Dinner available Direct Dial Cen ht
Licensed Wi-fi ⚹ Jacuzzi **Conf** Max 40 Board 22
Parking 12 **Notes** ⊗

BRILL   Map 11 SP61

Poletrees Farm *(SP660160)*

★★★★ FARMHOUSE

Ludgershall Rd HP18 9TZ
☎ 01844 238276   🖨 01844 238276
Mrs A Cooper
e-mail: poletrees.farm@virgin.net
dir: S off A41 signed Ludgershall/Brill, after railway bridge 0.5m on left

Located between the villages of Ludgershall and Brill, this 16th-century farmhouse retains many original features including a wealth of exposed beams. The bedrooms are in converted outbuildings, and the cosy dining room is the setting for a wholesome breakfast.

Rooms 4 annexe en suite (4 GF) S fr £40; D £70-£80*
Facilities FTV TVL tea/coffee Cen ht **Parking** 6 **Notes** LB
⊗ No Children 10yrs 110 acres beef/sheep

CHALFONT ST GILES   Map 6 SU99

The White Hart

☆☆☆ INN

Three Households HP8 4LP
☎ 01494 872441   & 0845 608 6040
e-mail: 5630@greeneking.co.uk

At the heart of this beautiful village, is located this popular inn. The bedrooms are modern, well equipped and benefit from a recent refurbishment. Public areas feature a spacious lounge bar and a relaxed dining/conservatory area where a varied selection of dishes are available. Public parking is adjacent to the inn and there are also pleasant grounds.

Rooms 11 en suite (5 GF) S £50-£60; D £55-£75*
Facilities FTV tea/coffee Dinner available Cen ht Wi-fi
Conf Max 50 Thtr 50 Class 20 Board 20 **Parking** 34
Notes LB

DENHAM   Map 6 TQ08

The Falcon Inn

★★★★ INN

Village Rd UB9 5BE
☎ 01895 832125
e-mail: mail@falcondenham.com
web: www.falcondenham.com
dir: M40 junct 1 signed A40 Gerrards Cross. After approx 200yds, turn right onto Old Mill Rd, follow road, pub opp village green

The 18th-century inn stands in the heart of the picturesque village, opposite the green. The bedrooms, with smart shower rooms en suite, are well equipped and display original features. Carefully prepared dishes and a good selection of wines are available for lunch and dinner in the cosy restaurant.

Rooms 4 en suite S £78; D £90 (room only)*
Facilities FTV tea/coffee Dinner available Cen ht Wi-fi
Notes LB No Children 10yrs

FORD   Map 5 SP70

Dinton Hermit

☆☆☆ INN

Water Ln HP17 8XH
☎ 01296 747473   🖨 01296 748819
e-mail: relax@dintonhermit.co.uk
dir: 2m from A418

A restored 400-year-old, Grade II listed property that now provides a smart restaurant and atmospheric bedrooms in both the old inn and in the 200-year-old barn conversion. Bedrooms are well equipped and comfortable, and the restaurant is popular with locals and guests alike.

Rooms 7 rms (5 en suite) (2 pri facs) 6 annexe en suite
(8 GF) **Facilities** FTV tea/coffee Dinner available Cen ht
Wi-fi **Parking** 40 **Notes** LB

GREAT MISSENDEN · Map 6 SP80

Nags Head Inn & Restaurant

★★★★ ◉ INN

London Rd HP16 0DG
☎ 01494 862200 · 01494 862685
e-mail: goodfood@nagsheadbucks.com
web: www.nagsheadbucks.com
dir: N of Amersham on A413, turn left at Chiltern hospital onto London Rd signed Great Missenden

This delightful 15th-century inn located in the picturesque Chiltern Hills, has a popular reputation locally thanks to its extensive menu with local produce and carefully prepared dishes. Individually designed bedrooms are comfortable with a modern twist ensuring a home-from-home feel. Ample parking is available.

Rooms 5 en suite (1 fmly) S £80-£120; D £90-£130 **Facilities** FTV tea/coffee Dinner available Cen ht Wi-fi **Conf** Max 50 **Parking** 40

See advert on this page

HIGH WYCOMBE · Map 5 SU89

Clifton Lodge

★★★ GUEST HOUSE

210 West Wycombe Rd HP12 3AR
☎ 01494 440095 · 01494 536322
e-mail: mail@cliftonlodgehotel.com
web: www.cliftonlodgehotel.com
dir: A40 from town centre towards Aylesbury, on right after BP station & opp phone box

Located west of the town centre, this long-established, owner-managed establishment provides a range of bedrooms, popular with a regular commercial clientele. Public areas include an attractive conservatory-dining room and a cosy lounge. Ample parking behind the property.

Rooms 32 rms (20 en suite) (1 fmly) (7 GF) S £39-£75; D £55-£75* **Facilities** tea/coffee Dinner available Cen ht Licensed Wi-fi **Conf** Max 25 Thtr 25 Class 20 Board 15 **Parking** 28 **Notes** LB ⊗

IVINGHOE · Map 11 SP91

The Brownlow B&B

★★★★ GUEST ACCOMMODATION

LU7 9DY
☎ 01296 668787
e-mail: info@thebrownlow.com
dir: A41 to Tring onto B488 to Ivinghoe/Dunstable. Follow Leighton Buzzard sign on B488

The Brownlow at Ivinghoe was built in the early 1800s to serve the newly finished Grand Union Canal, it has remained in the same family ever since. The old stables have now been converted into well-appointed bedrooms, which offer plenty of modern amenities. Breakfast is served at the communal table overlooking the canal.

Rooms 5 en suite (5 GF) **Facilities** FTV TVL tea/coffee Cen ht Wi-fi **Parking** 6 **Notes** ⊗ No Children 6yrs

MILTON KEYNES · Map 11 SP83

The Cock

★★★ INN

72-74 High St, Stony Stratford MK11 1AH
☎ 01908 567733 · 01908 562109
e-mail: 6432@greeneking.co.uk
dir: In village centre

This historic 15th-century coaching inn is situated in the picturesque market town of Stony Stratford with the Silverstone Circuit nearby. The rooms are en suite and equipped with modern amenities, food is served all day whilst the function room is the perfect venue for all occasions. Parking is available.

Rooms 31 en suite (4 fmly) (7 GF) **Facilities** tea/coffee Dinner available Direct Dial Cen ht Wi-fi **Conf** Max 100 Thtr 100 Class 50 Board 45 **Parking** **Notes** ⊗ Civ Wed 100

NEWPORT PAGNELL Map 11 SP84

Mill Farm *(SP852454)*

★★★ FARMHOUSE

MK16 8LT
☎ 01908 611489 & 07714 719640
Mrs K Adams
e-mail: adamsmillfarm@aol.com
web: www.millfarmgayhurst.co.uk
dir: *B526 from Newport Pagnell, 2.5m left onto Haversham Rd, Mill Farm 1st on left*

Within easy reach of Newport Pagnell and the M1, this historic farmhouse has a peaceful setting with wonderful views over farmland. Bedrooms are decorated in a homely style and have a host of thoughtful extras. The sumptuous lounge-dining room is enhanced with fine antiques, and the extensive grounds include a tennis court.

Rooms 3 rms (2 en suite) 1 annexe en suite (1 fmly) (1 GF) S £25-£35; D £45-£65 **Facilities** FTV TVL tea/coffee Cen ht Wi-fi 🏊 Fishing rough shooting **Parking** 13 **Notes** 550 acres mixed

WADDESDON Map 11 SP71

The Five Arrows

★★★★ RESTAURANT WITH ROOMS

High St HP18 0JE
☎ 01296 651727 📠 01296 655716
e-mail: five.arrows@nationaltrust.org.uk

This Grade II listed building with elaborate Elizabethan chimney stacks, stands at the gates of Waddesdon Manor and was named after the Rothschild family emblem. Individually styled en suite bedrooms are comfortable and well appointed. Friendly staff are on hand to offer a warm welcome. Alfresco dining is possible in the warmer months.

Rooms 11 en suite (3 GF) S £60-£90; D £70-£230* **Facilities** FTV tea/coffee Dinner available Direct Dial Cen ht Wi-fi **Conf** Max 20 Thtr 20 Class 20 Board 20 **Parking** 40 **Notes** Civ Wed 60

CAMBRIDGESHIRE

BOXWORTH Map 12 TL36

The Golden Ball Inn

★★★★ INN

High St CB23 4LY
☎ 01954 267397 📠 01954 267497
e-mail: info@goldenballhotel.co.uk
dir: *In village centre*

The Golden Ball is a delightful 17th-century thatched inn with modern accommodation. The bedrooms are well appointed and each bathroom has a bath and power shower. The inn is very popular for its restaurant, pub meals and real ales, and service is helpful and friendly.

Rooms 11 en suite (1 fmly) (9 GF) S £80; D £90* **Facilities** FTV tea/coffee Dinner available Direct Dial Cen ht Wi-fi **Parking** 75

CAMBRIDGE Map 12 TL45

Benson House

★★★★ GUEST HOUSE

24 Huntingdon Rd CB3 0HH
☎ 01223 311594 📠 01223 311594
e-mail: bensonhouse@btconnect.com
dir: *0.5m NW of city centre on A604*

The popular guest house is well placed for the city centre and New Hall and Fitzwilliam colleges. Its pleasant bedrooms vary in size and style and are well equipped. Limited private parking behind the property.

Rooms 6 en suite (1 GF) S £65-£110; D £90-£110* **Facilities** FTV tea/coffee Cen ht Wi-fi **Parking** 5 **Notes** ⊗ No Children 12yrs Closed 31 Dec

Lynwood House

★★★★ GUEST HOUSE

217 Chesterton Rd CB4 1AN
☎ 01223 500776 & 07730 569630
e-mail: info@lynwood-house.co.uk
web: www.lynwood-house.co.uk
dir: *M11 N junct 13, A1303 towards city centre, left at mini-rdbt, house 1m on left*

Located close to the river and central attractions, this constantly improving guest house provides a range of thoughtfully equipped bedrooms, most of which have the benefit of modern en suite shower rooms. Organically sourced produce is a feature of the wholesome breakfasts which are taken in a stylish dining room. A warm welcome is assured.

Rooms 7 rms (5 en suite) (2 GF) **Facilities** FTV tea/coffee Cen ht Wi-fi **Parking** 3 **Notes** ⊗ No Children 12yrs

Rose Corner

★★★★ BED AND BREAKFAST

42 Woodcock Close, Impington CB24 9LD
☎ 01223 563136 & 07733 027581 📠 01223 233886
e-mail: wsalmon.rosecorner@virgin.net
web: www.rose-corner.co.uk
dir: *4m N of Cambridge. A14 junct 32, B1049 N into Impington, off Milton Rd*

The detached property is in a quiet cul-de-sac in the popular village of Impington, north of the city. Its spacious bedrooms are carefully furnished and thoughtfully equipped, and breakfast is served in the comfortable lounge/dining room overlooking the rear gardens.

Rooms 5 rms (3 en suite) S £30-£35; D £65-£70 **Facilities** FTV TVL tea/coffee Cen ht Wi-fi **Parking** 5 **Notes** ⊗ No Children 11yrs

Alpha Milton

★★★ GUEST ACCOMMODATION

61-63 Milton Rd CB4 1XA
☎ 01223 311625 📠 01223 565100
e-mail: info@alphamilton.com
dir: *0.5m NE of city centre*

The Alpha Milton is in a residential area just a short walk from the city centre. The attractive lounge-dining room overlooks the rear garden, and the pleasant bedrooms all have a good range of facilities.

Rooms 8 rms (7 en suite) (1 pri facs) (2 fmly) (2 GF) S £50-£70; D £70-£90 (room only)* **Facilities** TVL tea/coffee Cen ht Wi-fi **Parking** 8 **Notes** ⊗

CAMBRIDGE *continued*

Hamden

★★★ GUEST HOUSE

89 High St, Cherry Hinton CB1 9LU
☎ 01223 413263 🖷 01223 245960
e-mail: info@hamdenguesthouse.co.uk
web: www.hamdenguesthouse.co.uk
dir: *3m SE of city centre. Off A1134 to Cherry Hinton*

Expect a warm welcome at this small, family-run guest house, which is just a short drive from the city centre. The pleasant bedrooms are generally quite spacious and equipped with many thoughtful extras. Public rooms include a large kitchen-dining room where breakfast is served at individual tables.

Rooms 3 en suite (2 fmly) (1 GF) S £40; D £60
Facilities FTV tea/coffee Direct Dial Cen ht Wi-fi
Parking 6 **Notes** LB ⊗ No Children 5yrs

See advert on this page

Southampton Guest House

★★★ GUEST HOUSE

7 Elizabeth Way CB4 1DE
☎ 01223 357780 🖷 01223 314297
e-mail: southamptonhouse@btinternet.com
web: www.southamptonguesthouse.com
dir: *0.5m E of city centre*

The proprietors provide a friendly service at their terraced guest house, which is on the inner ring road, just a short walk from the Grafton Centre. The property has well-equipped bedrooms, and a comprehensive English breakfast is served.

Rooms 5 en suite (3 fmly) (1 GF) S £35-£45; D £55-£58*
Facilities tea/coffee Direct Dial Cen ht Wi-fi **Parking** 8
Notes ⊗ 🕸

ELTISLEY   Map 12 TL25

The Eltisley

★★ ◉ RESTAURANT WITH ROOMS

2 The Green PE19 6TG
☎ 01480 880308
e-mail: theeltisley@btconnect.com
dir: *Close to A428*

This popular restaurant with rooms is situated between St Neots and the historic City of Cambridge. The bedrooms are adjacent to the main building in a timber-framed block; each is pleasantly decorated and well equipped. The open-plan public rooms include a smart lounge bar, a restaurant and an alfresco dining area.

Rooms 7 en suite (6 GF) **Facilities** FTV TV6B tea/coffee Dinner available Cen ht Wi-fi 🍃 Giant chess & jenga **Parking** 15

ELTON Map 12 TL09

PREMIER COLLECTION

The Crown Inn

★★★★★ ⊛ INN

8 Duck St PE8 6RQ
☎ 01832 280232
e-mail: inncrown@googlemail.com
web: www.thecrowninn.org
dir: A1 junct 17 onto A605 W. In 3.5m right signed
Elton, 0.9m left signed Nassington. On village green

Expect a warm welcome at this delightful village pub,
situated opposite the village green. The property dates
back to the 16th century, and has recently undergone
major refurbishment yet retains many of its original
features, such as a large inglenook fireplace and oak-
beamed ceilings. The smartly decorated bedrooms are
tastefully appointed and thoughtfully equipped. Public
rooms include a large open-plan lounge bar, a small
relaxed dining area to the front, and a tastefully
appointed circular restaurant.

Rooms 3 en suite 2 annexe en suite (2 fmly) (2 GF)
Facilities tea/coffee Dinner available Cen ht Wi-fi
Conf Max 40 Thtr 25 Class 40 Board 25 **Parking** 15
Notes LB RS Sun eve & Mon (ex BH) Restaurant only
closed No coaches

See advert on this page

ELY Map 12 TL58

The Anchor Inn

★★★★ ⊛ RESTAURANT WITH ROOMS

Sutton Gault CB6 2BD
☎ 01353 778537 📠 01353 776180
e-mail: anchorinn@popmail.bta.com
dir: W of Ely. Sutton Gault signed off B1381 at S end of
Sutton

Located beside the New Bedford River with stunning
country views, this 17th-century inn has a wealth of
original features enhanced by period furniture. The
spacious bedrooms are tastefully appointed and equipped
with many thoughtful touches. The friendly team of staff
offer helpful and attentive service.

Rooms 4 en suite (2 fmly) **Facilities** FTV tea/coffee Dinner
available Direct Dial Cen ht Wi-fi **Parking** 16 **Notes** ⊗ No
coaches

The Nyton

★★★★ 🛏 GUEST ACCOMMODATION

7 Barton Rd CB7 4HZ
☎ 01353 662459 📠 01353 666217
e-mail: nytonhotel@yahoo.co.uk
dir: From S, A10 into Ely on Cambridge Rd, pass golf
course, 1st right

Set in two acres of mature gardens, this family-run
establishment offers comfortable bedrooms in a range of
sizes and styles. The pleasant public rooms include a
wood-panelled restaurant, a smart bar, and a
conservatory-lounge overlooking the gardens. Meals are
available in the dining room and informal light meals are
served in the lounge bar.

Rooms 9 en suite (3 fmly) (2 GF) **Facilities** FTV TVL tea/
coffee Dinner available Direct Dial Cen ht Licensed Wi-fi
Golf 18 **Conf** Max 40 Thtr 40 Class 20 Board 40
Parking 25 **Notes** ⊗ Civ Wed 100

The Three Pickerels

★★★★ INN

19 Bridge Rd, Mepal CB6 2AR
☎ 01353 777777 📠 01353 777891
e-mail: info@thethreepickerels.co.uk
web: www.thethreepickerels.co.uk

Situated in the tranquil village of Mepal on the outskirts
of Ely, this property sits on the banks of the New Bedford
River and has views of the surrounding grassland. Public
rooms include a smart bar, a dining room and a lovely
lounge overlooking the river. The smartly appointed
bedrooms are comfortable and well equipped.

Rooms 4 en suite (1 fmly) S fr £50; D fr £85*
Facilities FTV TVL tea/coffee Dinner available Cen ht Wi-fi
Fishing Pool table **Parking** 40 **Notes** LB ⊗

ELY *continued*

Castle Lodge

★★★ GUEST HOUSE

50 New Barns Rd CB7 4PW
☎ 01353 662276 📄 01353 666606
e-mail: castlelodgehotel@supanet.com
dir: *Off B1382 Prickwillow Rd, NE from town centre*

Located within easy walking distance of the cathedral, this extended Victorian house offers well-equipped bedrooms in a variety of sizes. Public areas include a traditionally furnished dining room and a comfortable air-conditioned bar lounge. Service is friendly and-helpful.

Rooms 11 rms (6 en suite) (3 fmly) **Facilities** TVL tea/coffee Dinner available Direct Dial Cen ht Licensed Wi-fi **Conf** Max 40 Board 40 **Parking** 6

HILTON   Map 12 TL26

Prince of Wales

★★★ INN

Potton Rd PE28 9NG
☎ 01480 830257 📄 01480 830257
dir: *A14 onto B1040 towards Biggleswade, 2m into village, Prince of Wales on left*

This popular village inn offers a choice of cosy traditional bars serving good food and real ales. The pleasantly decorated bedrooms are equipped with modern facilities. A hearty breakfast is served in the dining room at individual tables.

Rooms 4 en suite **Facilities** tea/coffee Dinner available Direct Dial Cen ht Pool table **Parking** 12 **Notes** No Children 5yrs

---

HINXTON   Map 12 TL44

The Red Lion Inn

★★★★ ⊛ INN

32 High St CB10 1QY
☎ 01799 530601 📄 01799 252601
e-mail: info@redlionhinxton.co.uk
dir: *Nbound only: M11 junct 9, towards A11, left onto A1301. Turn left to Hinxton. Or M11 junct 10, take A505 towards A11/Newmarket. At rdbt take 3rd exit onto A1301, right to Hinxton*

The Red Lion Inn is a 16th-century free house pub-restaurant, with high quality purpose-built accommodation, set in the pretty conservation village of Hinxton. In the winter guests can relax by the well-stoked fire, while in summer they can relax in the attractive walled garden, overlooked by a dovecote and the village church.

Rooms 8 annexe en suite (2 fmly) (8 GF) S £85; D £109-£130* **Facilities** FTV tea/coffee Dinner available Direct Dial Cen ht Wi-fi **Parking** 43 **Notes** LB

HOLYWELL   Map 12 TL37

The Old Ferryboat Inn

★★★ INN

Back Ln PE27 4TG
☎ 01480 463227 📄 01480 463245
e-mail: 8638@greeneking.co.uk

This delightful thatched inn sits in a tranquil setting beside the Great Ouse river, on the periphery of the village of Holywell. Said to be the oldest inn in England, with foundations dating back to 560AD, the inn retains much original character and charm. Bedrooms are soundly appointed, and the open-plan public rooms have a pleasing relaxed atmosphere: the extensive gardens, with views of the river, are a popular attraction in the summer months.

Rooms 7 en suite **Facilities** tea/coffee Dinner available Cen ht Wi-fi **Conf** Max 60 Thtr 60 Class 32 Board 24 **Parking** 70

HUNTINGDON   Map 12 TL27

Cheriton House

★★★★★ 🄰 BED AND BREAKFAST

Mill St, Houghton PE28 2AZ
☎ 01480 464004 📄 01480 496960
e-mail: sales@cheritonhousecambs.co.uk
dir: *In village of Houghton, through village square, signed to river & mill*

Rooms 2 en suite 3 annexe en suite (3 GF) S £70-£80; D £75-£90* **Facilities** FTV tea/coffee Cen ht Wi-fi 🛝 🛥 Golf 12 **Conf** Max 10 Thtr 10 Class 6 Board 8 **Parking** 7 **Notes** LB ⊗ No Children 14yrs

---

PETERBOROUGH   Map 12 TL19

Aaron Park

★★★★ GUEST ACCOMMODATION

109 Park Rd PE1 2TR
☎ 01733 564849 📄 01733 564855
e-mail: aaronparkhotel@yahoo.co.uk
dir: *A1 onto A1139 to junct 5, to city centre on Boongate, over rdbt onto Crawthorne Rd, over lights, next left*

Family service is both friendly and helpful at this Victorian house, which is situated in a tree-lined avenue just a short walk from the city centre and cathedral. Bedrooms come in a variety of styles and sizes; each room is nicely presented and has a good range of modern facilities. Freshly cooked breakfasts are carefully presented and provide a good start to the day.

Rooms 10 en suite (3 fmly) (2 GF) S £45; D £70* **Facilities** FTV tea/coffee Cen ht Wi-fi **Parking** 8 **Notes** ⊗ Closed Xmas

---

STETCHWORTH   Map 12 TL65

The Old Mill

★★★★ BED AND BREAKFAST

Mill Ln CB8 9TR
☎ 01638 507839 & 07831 179948
e-mail: gbell839@aol.com
dir: *In village centre off Tea Kettle Ln*

Situated in a delightful village, the accommodation comprises a thoughtfully equipped self-contained flat sleeping four, with a small kitchen, quality pine furniture and a DVD player. Access is via a private staircase leading to a sun terrace overlooking mature gardens. Breakfast is served at a large communal table in the main house.

Rooms 1 annexe en suite **Facilities** FTV TVL tea/coffee Cen ht Wi-fi 🛥 **Parking** 2 **Notes** LB ⊗

UFFORD   Map 12 TF00

The White Hart

★★★★ 🍽 INN

Main St PE9 3BH
☎ 01780 740250 📄 01780 740927
e-mail: info@whitehartufford.co.uk

This charming inn is home to Ufford Ales which are served in the bar. The property is built from local stone and retains many of its original features. The delightful bedrooms are split between the main house and a converted block; each one is tastefully furnished and thoughtfully equipped. Public rooms include a lounge bar, conservatory and restaurant.

Rooms 6 en suite (2 GF) **Facilities** tea/coffee Dinner available Cen ht Wi-fi ch fac **Conf** Max 30 Thtr 30 Class 20 Board 20 **Parking** 30 **Notes** Civ Wed 30

WILLINGHAM   Map 12 TL47

Willingham House

★★★★ 🍽 GUEST ACCOMMODATION

50 Church St CB4 5HT
☎ 01954 260606 📄 01954 260603
e-mail: willinghamhouse@hotmail.com
web: www.cambridgewillinghamhouse.com
dir: *A14 junct 29 onto B1050 to Willingham*

A former rectory, this elegant Victorian house has been sympathetically renovated and extended to provide high standards of comfort and facilities. Bedrooms are thoughtfully furnished, and imaginative dinners are served in an attractive dining room. Extensive conference facilities and pretty mature grounds are additional features.

Rooms 16 en suite 6 annexe en suite (7 GF) **Facilities** TVL tea/coffee Dinner available Cen ht Licensed Wi-fi Pool table **Conf** Max 40 Thtr 40 Class 23 Board 24 **Parking** 40 **Notes** ⊗ Closed 25-27 Dec

CHESHIRE

AUDLEM   Map 15 SJ64

Little Heath Farm *(SJ663455)*

★★★★ FARMHOUSE

CW3 0HE
☎ **01270 811324**
Mrs H M Bennion
e-mail: littleheath.farm@gmail.com
dir: *Off A525 in village onto A529 towards Nantwich for 0.3m. Farm opposite village green*

The 200-year-old brick farmhouse retains much original character, including low beamed ceilings. The traditionally furnished public areas include a cosy sitting room and a dining room where guests dine family style. The refurbished bedrooms are stylish, and the friendly proprietors create a relaxing atmosphere.

Rooms 3 en suite (1 fmly) S £30-£45; D £60-£70*
Facilities TVL tea/coffee Cen ht **Conf** Max 10 Board 10 **Parking** 6 **Notes** LB ⊛ 50 acres mixed

BURWARDSLEY   Map 15 SJ55

The Pheasant Inn

★★★★★ ⊜ INN

Higher Burwardsley CH3 9PF
☎ **01829 770434** 📠 **01829 771097**
e-mail: info@thepheasantinn.co.uk
web: www.thepheasantinn.co.uk
dir: *From A41, left to Tattenhall, right at 1st junct & left at 2nd Higher Burwardsley. At post office left, signed*

This delightful 300-year-old inn sits high on the Peckforton Hills and enjoys spectacular views over the Cheshire Plain. Well-equipped, comfortable bedrooms are housed in an adjacent converted barn. Creative dishes are served either in the stylish restaurant or in the traditional, beamed bar. Real fires are lit in the winter months.

Rooms 2 en suite 10 annexe en suite (2 fmly) (5 GF) S £75-£105; D £100-£155* **Facilities** FTV tea/coffee Dinner available Direct Dial Cen ht Wi-fi **Parking** 80

Cheshire Cheese Cottage

★★★★ BED AND BREAKFAST

Burwardsley Rd CH3 9NS
☎ **01829 770887** 📠 **01829 770887**
e-mail: r.rosney@yahoo.co.uk

A very warm welcome awaits at this delightful little cottage, which is set in its own extensive grounds and colourful gardens on the outskirts of the village. The accommodation consists of two modern bedrooms on ground floor level. There is also a conservatory which doubles as both lounge and breakfast room. Breakfasts are freshly cooked and hearty. Owner Rose Rosney is a qualified masseur and guests can book treatments if they wish.

Rooms 2 en suite (2 GF) D £75-£85 **Facilities** FTV TVL tea/coffee Direct Dial Cen ht Wi-fi Golf 18 Riding **Parking** 4 **Notes** ⊛ No Children ⊛

CHESTER   Map 15 SJ46

See also Malpas

Dragonfly

★★★★★ GUEST ACCOMMODATION

94 Watergate St CH1 2LF
☎ **01244 346740** 📠 **01244 346740**
e-mail: sleep@hoteldragonfly.com
dir: *M53 junct 12 follow A56 signed Chester. Take 2nd exit from rdbt - St Oswalds Way, next rdbt take 1st exit onto St Martin's*

Located a stone's throw from the Racecourse and within easy walking distance of city centre and attractions, this elegant Georgian terraced house has been sympathetically restored to provide high standards of comfort and facilities. Stylish and vibrant decor and furnishing schemes throughout the interior are matched by the many period features, and hospitality is natural and caring.

Rooms 5 en suite S £115-£150; D £115-£150 (room only) **Facilities** FTV tea/coffee Cen ht Wi-fi **Parking** 2 **Notes** ⊛ No Children 14yrs

Oddfellows

★★★★★ ⊛ RESTAURANT WITH ROOMS

20 Lower Bridge St CH1 1RS
☎ **01244 400001**
e-mail: reception@oddfellows.biz

Surrounded by designer shops and only a few minutes' walk from the Chester Rows, old meets new at this stylish Georgian mansion. The upper ground floor comprises a walled garden with ornamental moat, Arabic tents, a roofed patio, a cocktail bar with an excellent wine selection, a bustling brasserie and an Alice in Wonderland tea room. Fine dining, featuring local produce, is skilfully prepared in a second-floor formal restaurant and a sumptuous 'members' lounge is also available to diners and resident guests. Bedrooms have the wow factor with super beds and every conceivable guest extra.

Rooms 4 en suite **Facilities** FTV tea/coffee Dinner available Direct Dial Cen ht Wi-fi **Conf** Max 40 Thtr 40 **Parking** 4 **Notes** LB ⊛ No coaches Civ Wed 60

Stone Villa Chester

★★★★★ GUEST ACCOMMODATION

Stone Place, Hoole Rd CH2 3NR
☎ **01244 345014** 📠 **01244 345015**
e-mail: info@stonevillachester.co.uk
dir: *0.5m NE of city on A56 Hoole Rd*

A family run establishment tucked away in a quiet cul-de-sac, 50 yards from the main approach road into Chester. The guest bedrooms are well equipped and delightfully furnished. Hearty breakfasts are served in the pleasant rear dining room and special diets can be catered for. Private off-road parking is available.

Rooms 10 en suite (4 fmly) (3 GF) S £45-£55; D £75-£85 **Facilities** FTV tea/coffee Direct Dial Cen ht Wi-fi Golf 18 **Parking** 10 **Notes** LB ⊛

CHESTER *continued*

Mitchell's of Chester

★★★★★ 🅐 GUEST HOUSE

28 Hough Green CH4 8JQ
☎ 01244 679004 📄 01244 659567
e-mail: mitoches@dialstart.net
web: www.mitchellsofchester.com
dir: *1m SW of city centre. A483 onto A5104, 300yds on right in Hough Green*

Rooms 7 en suite (1 fmly) (1 GF) S £35-£51; D £65-£92*
Facilities FTV TVL tea/coffee Cen ht Licensed Wi-fi
Parking 5 **Notes** LB ⊗ No Children 8yrs Closed 21-29 Dec

Cheltenham Lodge

★★★★ GUEST ACCOMMODATION

58 Hoole Rd, Hoole CH2 3NL
☎ 01244 346767
e-mail: cheltenhamlodge@btinternet.com
web: www.cheltenhamlodge.co.uk
dir: *1m NE of city centre on A56*

This small, personally run guest accommodation lies midway between the city centre and M53. The attractive modern bedrooms, which include family rooms and some on the ground floor, are well equipped; a substantial breakfast is served in the smart dining room.

Rooms 5 en suite (2 fmly) (2 GF) **Facilities** FTV tea/coffee Cen ht **Parking** 5 **Notes** ⊗ Closed 23 Dec-7 Jan 🍴

Coach House Restaurant with Rooms

★★★★ RESTAURANT WITH ROOMS

29 Northgate St CH1 2HQ
☎ 01244 251900 📄 01244 351436
web: www.coachhousechester.co.uk

Ideally located in the centre of the city, this restaurant with rooms has been renovated to provide high standards of comfort and good facilities. Its sumptuous bedrooms have a wealth of thoughtful extras, and imaginative food is available in the bistro style restaurant or in the cosy bar area. A warm welcome is assured.

Rooms 9 en suite (3 fmly) **Facilities** FTV tea/coffee Dinner available Direct Dial Wi-fi **Notes** ⊗ Closed 25 Dec

Golborne Manor

★★★★ BED AND BREAKFAST

Platts Ln, Hatton Heath CH3 9AN
☎ 01829 770310 & 07774 695268 📄 01829 770370
e-mail: info@golbornemanor.co.uk
dir: *5m S off A14 (Whitchurch road). Right onto Platts Ln, 400yds on left*

The elegant Edwardian house stands in beautiful gardens with spectacular views across open countryside. Accommodation is in spacious bedrooms with either brass bedsteads or a richly carved antique Arabian bed. Breakfast is served around a large table in the dining room, and there is also a comfortable lounge.

Rooms 2 en suite (1 fmly) **Facilities** FTV tea/coffee Cen ht 🏓 table tennis **Conf** Max 10 **Parking** 6 **Notes** ⊗ RS wknds 🍴

Green Gables

★★★★ GUEST HOUSE

11 Eversley Park CH2 2AJ
☎ 01244 372243 📄 01244 376352
e-mail: perruzza_d@hotmail.com
dir: *Off A5116 Liverpool Rd signed Countess of Chester Hospital, right at 3rd pedestrian lights to Eversley Park*

The attractive Victorian house, set in pretty gardens, is in a quiet residential area close to the city centre. The well-equipped bedrooms include a family room, and there is a choice of sitting rooms. The bright breakfast room is strikingly decorated.

Rooms 2 en suite (1 fmly) S £44-£65; D £65-£70*
Facilities FTV TVL tea/coffee Cen ht Wi-fi **Parking** 8 **Notes** ⊗ 🍴

Lavender Lodge

★★★★ GUEST ACCOMMODATION

46 Hoole Rd CH2 3NL
☎ 01244 323204 📄 01244 329821
e-mail: bookings@lavenderlodgechester.co.uk
web: www.lavenderlodgechester.co.uk
dir: *1m NE of city centre on A56, opp All Saints church*

A warm welcome is assured at this smart late Victorian house located within easy walking distance of central attractions. The bedrooms are equipped with thoughtful extras and have modern bathrooms. Quality breakfasts are served in the attractive dining room.

Rooms 5 en suite (2 fmly) **Facilities** FTV tea/coffee Cen ht Wi-fi **Parking** 7 **Notes** ⊗ Closed 24 Dec-2 Jan

The Old Farmhouse B&B

★★★★ BED AND BREAKFAST

9 Eggbridge Ln, Waverton CH3 7PE
☎ 01244 332124 & 07949 820119
e-mail: jmitchellgreenwalls@hotmail.com
web: www.chestereggbridgefarm.co.uk
dir: *From A41 at Waverton turn left at Moor Ln, left onto Eggbridge Ln and over Canal Bridge, on the right*

A warm welcome is assured at this 18th-century former farmhouse, located in a village community three miles south of the city centre. Cosy bedrooms are equipped with a wealth of thoughtful extras and hearty breakfasts feature local or home-made produce.

Rooms 2 rms (1 en suite) (1 pri facs) S £35-£45; D £70-£75 **Facilities** FTV TVL tea/coffee Cen ht Wi-fi **Parking** 5 **Notes** LB ⊗ No Children 10yrs Closed 13-28 Feb

Summerhill Guest House

★★★★ GUEST HOUSE

4 Greenfield Ln, Hoole Village CH2 2PA
☎ 01244 400020 & 400334
e-mail: summerhill10@sky.com
dir: *1.5m NE of city centre. A56 onto A41, 1st right*

Summerhill is a converted Edwardian house with comfortable, well-equipped accommodation. All bedrooms include flat-screen televisions and complimentary Wi-fi is available throughout. The helpful owners provide a friendly atmosphere and hearty breakfasts in the attractive dining room overlooking the well maintained gardens

Rooms 4 en suite (1 fmly) S £30-£45; D £60-£80*
Facilities FTV TVL tea/coffee Cen ht Wi-fi **Parking** 4 **Notes** LB ⊗ No Children 8yrs

The Limes

★★★★ 🅐 GUEST ACCOMMODATION

12 Hoole Rd CH2 3NJ
☎ 01244 328239
e-mail: bookings@limes-chester.co.uk

Rooms 9 en suite (2 fmly) (2 GF) D £60-£70*
Facilities FTV tea/coffee Direct Dial Cen ht **Parking** 10 **Notes** LB ⊗ Closed Xmas-1 Jan

George & Dragon

★★★ INN

1 Liverpool Rd CH2 1AA
☎ 01244 380714 📠 01244 378461
e-mail: 7783@greeneking.co.uk

This former old coaching inn with its black and white Tudor façade is situated just 5 minutes from the city centre. Parking is available on-site. A traditional inn with sports viewing, cask ales, dining and weekly entertainment, with a late bar until midnight. Bedrooms have recently been refurbished and vary in size.

Rooms 14 en suite (2 fmly) **Facilities** FTV tea/coffee Dinner available Cen ht Wi-fi **Parking** 20 **Notes** ⊗ No coaches

Glen Garth

★★★ GUEST ACCOMMODATION

59 Hoole Rd CH2 3NJ
☎ 01244 310260 📠 01244 310260
e-mail: glengarthguesthouse@btconnect.com
dir: Exit M53 onto A56, 0.5m E of city

Situated within easy walking distance of the city, family-run Glen Garth provides well-equipped bedrooms, and hearty breakfasts served in the pleasant rear dining room. Friendly, attentive service is a strength here.

Rooms 5 rms (3 en suite) (2 pri facs) (3 fmly) **Facilities** FTV tea/coffee Cen ht Wi-fi **Parking** 5 **Notes** LB ⊗ 🐾

The Oaklands

★★ INN

93 Hoole Rd, Hoole CH2 3NB
☎ 01244 345528
e-mail: 7878@greeneking.co.uk

This busy and popular public house is conveniently located for access to both the city centre and the M56 motorway. A wide range of food is available in the stylish open plan bar and dining area. Bedrooms vary in size. Service is friendly and attentive.

Rooms 14 rms (13 en suite) (1 pri facs) (2 fmly) (4 GF) **Facilities** FTV TVL tea/coffee Dinner available Cen ht Wi-fi **Parking** 30 **Notes** ⊗

Edgar House

Ⓤ

22 City Walls CH1 1SB
☎ 01244 347007
e-mail: enquiries@edgarhouse.co.uk
web: www.edgarhouse.co.uk
dir: From city centre ring road (A5268) S down Lower Bridge St towards river. Last left onto Duke St

Currently the rating for this establishment is not confirmed. This may be due to a change of ownership or because it has only recently joined the AA rating scheme.

Rooms 8 en suite (3 GF) **Facilities** FTV TVL tea/coffee Cen ht Licensed Wi-fi **Parking** 8 **Notes** ⊗ No Children 14yrs

CONGLETON   Map 16 SJ86

The Plough At Eaton

★★★★ 🍴 INN

Macclesfield Rd, Eaton CW12 2NH
☎ 01260 280207 📠 01260 298458
e-mail: theploughinn@hotmail.co.uk
dir: On A536 (Congleton to Macclesfield road), 1.5m from Congleton town centre

A renovated traditional inn offering high quality meals and very comfortable bedrooms in an adjacent building. The rooms vary in style with some contemporary and others more traditionally furnished, all have very good en suite bathrooms. The spacious bar is appealing and there are also attractive outdoor seating areas.

Rooms 17 annexe en suite (2 fmly) (8 GF) **Facilities** tea/coffee Dinner available Direct Dial Cen ht Wi-fi **Parking** 78 **Notes** RS 25-26 Dec & 1 Jan Close at 6pm Civ Wed 60

Egerton Arms Country Inn

★★★★ INN

Astbury Village CW12 4RQ
☎ 01260 273946 📠 01260 277273
e-mail: egertonastbury@totalise.co.uk
dir: 1.5m SW of Congleton off A34, by St Mary's Church

This traditional country inn stands opposite the church in the pretty village of Astbury. The creative, good-value menus in the bars and restaurant attract a strong local following, and the bedrooms have been refurbished to provide high standards of comfort and facilities.

Rooms 6 en suite (1 fmly) S £50-£60; D £70-£80* **Facilities** FTV tea/coffee Dinner available Cen ht Wi-fi **Conf** Max 40 Thtr 40 Class 30 Board 20 **Parking** 100 **Notes** LB ⊗ No coaches

Sandhole Farm

★★★★ 🅐 GUEST ACCOMMODATION

Hulme Walfield CW12 2JH
☎ 01260 224419 📠 01260 224766
e-mail: veronica@sandholefarm.co.uk
dir: 2m N of Congleton. Off A34 down driveway

Rooms 16 annexe en suite (3 fmly) (7 GF) **Facilities** FTV TVL tea/coffee Direct Dial Cen ht Wi-fi **Conf** Thtr 80 Class 80 Board 50 **Parking** 50 **Notes** RS Xmas wk Self-catering only Civ Wed 150

FARNDON   Map 15 SJ45

The Farndon

Ⓤ

High St CH3 6PU
☎ 01829 270570 📠 01829 272060
e-mail: enquiries@thefarndon.co.uk
web: www.thefarndon.co.uk
dir: Just off A534 in village on main street

Currently the rating for this establishment is not confirmed. This may be due to a change of ownership or because it has only recently joined the AA rating scheme.

Rooms 5 en suite S £65-£75; D £85-£120* **Facilities** FTV TVL tea/coffee Dinner available Direct Dial Cen ht Licensed Wi-fi **Parking** 15 **Notes** LB ⊗

KNUTSFORD
Map 15 SJ77

The Hinton Guest House

★★★★ GUEST HOUSE

Town Ln, Mobberley WA16 7HH
☎ 01565 873484 📄 01565 873484
e-mail: the.hinton@virgin.net
dir: 1m NE on B5085 in Mobberley

This well-proportioned house offers a range of comfortable bedrooms with thoughtful extras. Comprehensive breakfasts, and dinners by arrangement, are served in the attractive dining room and a lounge is available.

Rooms 6 en suite (1 fmly) S £48; D £62* Facilities FTV tea/coffee Dinner available Cen ht Licensed Wi-fi Parking 8 Notes ⊗

The Cottage Restaurant & Lodge

★★★★ GUEST ACCOMMODATION

London Rd, Allostock WA16 9LU
☎ 01565 722470 📄 01565 722749
e-mail: reception@thecottageknutsford.co.uk
dir: M6 junct 18/19 onto A50, between Holmes Chapel & Knutsford

This well presented family-run establishment enjoys a peaceful location on the A50 between Knutsford and Holmes Chapel. Smart, spacious lodge-style bedrooms complement an attractive open-plan restaurant and bar lounge. Bedrooms are thoughtfully equipped and offer good levels of comfort. Conference and meeting facilities, as well as ample parking, are available.

Rooms 11 annexe en suite (4 fmly) (5 GF) S £50-£80; D £60-£95* Facilities FTV tea/coffee Dinner available Direct Dial Cen ht Licensed Wi-fi Conf Max 40 Thtr 40 Class 25 Board 25 Parking 40 Notes LB ⊗

The Dog Inn

★★★★ INN

Well Bank Ln, Over Peover WA16 8UP
☎ 01625 861421 📄 01625 864800
e-mail: thedoginnpeover@btconnect.com
web: www.doginn-overpeover.co.uk
dir: 4m SE of Knutsford. Off A50 at Whipping Stocks 2m to Peover Heath

Set in delightful Cheshire countryside, the front of this popular 18th-century inn is adorned with hanging baskets and tubs. The attractive bedrooms have many extras, while the lounge bar and restaurant offer a wide selection of ales and an extensive all-day menu using local produce.

Rooms 6 en suite Facilities FTV tea/coffee Dinner available Direct Dial Cen ht Wi-fi Pool table Parking 80

Rostherne Country House

★★★★ GUEST ACCOMMODATION

Rostherne Ln, Rostherne WA16 6RY
☎ 01565 832628
e-mail: info@rosthernehouse.co.uk

Set in its own spacious gardens in the village of Rostherne, this elegant Victorian house retains much original charm with spacious, well-equipped bedrooms and character lounges with open fires. It is a wonderful relaxing base for exploring the delights of Cheshire and dinner is available by arrangement. Other facilities include an honesty bar and a paddock for guests' horses. Courses in various subjects are also available.

Rooms 4 rms (3 en suite) (1 pri facs) (1 fmly) Facilities FTV TVL tea/coffee Dinner available Cen ht Wi-fi Guest arrangement for indoor swimming pool & spa Conf Max 20 Thtr 20 Parking 12

LOWER WITHINGTON
Map 15 SJ86

Holly Tree Farm (SJ802709)

★★★★ FARMHOUSE

Holmes Chapel Rd SK11 9DT
☎ 01477 571257 & 07979 910800 📄 01477 571257
Mrs Venables
e-mail: davidathollies@aol.com
web: www.hollytreefarm.org
dir: On A535 Holmes Chapel Rd in front of Jodrell Bank

Located close to Jodrell Bank, Holly Tree Farm offers a good base for the business person or for touring the local attractions. Rooms are located in the house adjacent to the farm and are attractive and well equipped. Hearty breakfasts are taken in the farmhouse, and the emphasis is on local produce from the farm's own shop.

Rooms 4 en suite (1 fmly) (1 GF) S £35; D £65-£70* Facilities FTV TVL tea/coffee Cen ht Wi-fi Parking 3 Notes ⊗ 100 acres beef/sheep/poultry

MALPAS
Map 15 SJ44

PREMIER COLLECTION

Tilston Lodge

★★★★★ GUEST ACCOMMODATION

Tilston SY14 7DR
☎ 01829 250223 📄 01829 250223
e-mail: kathie.ritchie@yahoo.co.uk
dir: A41 S from Chester for 10m, turn right for Tilston. Left at T-junct. Lodge 200yds on right

A former hunting lodge, this impressive Victorian house stands in 16 acres of rolling orchards and pasture, which are home to rare breeds of sheep and poultry. The spacious bedrooms are furnished with fine period pieces and a wealth of thoughtful extras. Ground-floor areas overlook immaculate gardens and a choice of lounges is available. The elegant dining room is the setting for memorable breakfasts.

Rooms 3 en suite (1 fmly) S £50-£56; D £80-£92 Facilities FTV TVL tea/coffee Cen ht Wi-fi 🐾 Hot tub Parking 8 Notes LB ⊗ 🐾

Hampton House Farm (SJ505496)

★★★★ FARMHOUSE

Stevensons Ln, Hampton SY14 8JS
☎ 01948 820588
Mrs E H Sarginson
e-mail: enquiries@hamptonhousefarm.co.uk
dir: 2m NE of Malpas. Off A41 onto Cholmondeley Rd, next left

Parts of this house are reputed to date from 1600, and quality furnishing styles highlight the many retained period features including a wealth of exposed beams. It is located on a quiet dairy farm and offers thoughtfully appointed accommodation and a warm welcome.

Rooms 3 en suite S £40-£45; D £60-£65* Facilities TVL tea/coffee Cen ht Wi-fi Parking 12 Notes ⊗ No Children 12yrs 🐾 180 acres mixed

The Paddock

★ ★ ★ ★ BED AND BREAKFAST

Malpas Rd, Tilston SY14 7DR
☎ 01829 250569 & 07754 857057
e-mail: info@thepaddocktilston.com
web: www.thepaddocktilston.com
dir: *Turn off A4, on entering Tilston, left at T-junct, 200mtrs on left, 1st drive after 40mph speed limit sign*

Set in the small village of Tilston, with easy access to Chester and Wrexham. A warm welcome can be expected at this family home which offers guests the choice of three comfortable, well-equipped bedrooms, with excellent bathroom facilities. There is a large summer house at the bottom of the garden where hosts Gail and Steve offer afternoon tea on warmer days for arriving guests. Well cooked breakfasts, made from locally sourced ingredients, are served in the cosy lounge. Wi-fi is available, and the property has its own parking.

Rooms 3 rms (2 en suite) (1 pri facs) (1 fmly) S £40-£60; D £80-£100 **Facilities** FTV tea/coffee Cen ht Wi-fi **Parking** 3 **Notes** ⊗ 🖼

NANTWICH   Map 15 SJ65

See also Wybunbury

Henhull Hall *(SJ641536)*

★ ★ ★ ★ FARMHOUSE

Welshmans Ln CW5 6AD
☎ 01270 624158 📠 01270 624158
Mr & Mrs Percival
e-mail: philippercival@hotmail.com
dir: *M6 junct 16 onto A500 towards Nantwich, then A51 past Reaseheath, turn left onto Welshmans Ln, 0.25m on left*

Expect a warm welcome at Henhull Hall, which has been in the Percival family since 1924. The Hall stands on the site of the Battle of Nantwich fought in 1644. The farmhouse is amidst acres of farmland with beautiful grounds and gardens surrounding the house. Bedrooms are spacious and individually decorated; breakfast is served in the attractive dining room and features fresh farm produce.

Rooms 2 rms (1 en suite) (1 pri facs) (1 fmly) S £35-£40; D £70-£80 **Facilities** TVL TV1B tea/coffee Cen ht Wi-fi 🐾 **Conf** Max 10 Thtr 10 Class 10 Board 10 **Parking** 4 **Notes** 🖼 345 acres dairy/arable

Oakland House

★ ★ ★ ★ GUEST ACCOMMODATION

252 Newcastle Rd, Blakelow, Shavington CW5 7ET
☎ 01270 567134
e-mail: enquiries@oaklandhouseonline.co.uk
dir: *2m E of Nantwich. Off A500 into Shavington, house 0.5m W of village*

Oakland House offers a friendly and relaxed atmosphere. Bedrooms, some of which are in a separate chalet, are attractively furnished and well equipped. There is a spacious sitting room, and a modern conservatory overlooks the pretty garden and the Cheshire countryside beyond. Substantial breakfasts are served either around one large table or at separate tables.

Rooms 3 en suite 6 annexe en suite (1 fmly) (6 GF) S £35-£40; D £50-£56* **Facilities** FTV TVL tea/coffee Cen ht Wi-fi **Parking** 13 **Notes** LB Closed 31 Dec

NORTHWICH   Map 15 SJ67

The Red Lion

★ ★ ★ INN

277 Chester Rd, Hartford CW8 1QL
☎ 01606 74597
e-mail: cathy.iglesias@tesco.net
web: www.redlionhartford.com
dir: *From A556 take Hartford exit. Red Lion at 1st junct on left next to church*

Located in the community of Hartford opposite the parish church, this popular inn provides a range of real ales and traditional pub food in the cosy public areas, or neat beer garden. Smart bedrooms feature many thoughtful extras in addition to efficient en suite shower rooms.

Rooms 3 en suite (1 fmly) S £44.95; D £60* **Facilities** FTV tea/coffee Dinner available Cen ht Wi-fi Pool table **Parking** 6 **Notes** ⊗ No coaches

PRESTBURY   Map 16 SJ87

Hilltop Country House

★ ★ ★ ★ GUEST ACCOMMODATION

Hill top, Flash Ln SK10 4ED
☎ 01625 829940
e-mail: enquiries@hilltopcountryhouse.co.uk
web: www.hilltopcountryhouse.co.uk
dir: *A523 from Macclesfield to Stockport. At 3rd rdbt turn right to Bollington. In 40mtrs turn left & follow signs*

Hilltop Country House is a hidden gem. Set in rural Cheshire, with easy access to motorway and rail links, this house offers a relaxing retreat. The four en suite bedrooms offer excellent quality, luxury and comfort. Breakfasts are served in the 17th-century dining room and guarantee a hearty start to the day.

Rooms 4 en suite (2 GF) S £60; D £84 **Facilities** FTV tea/coffee Dinner available Cen ht Wi-fi **Conf** Max 40 Thtr 40 Board 18 **Parking** 50 **Notes** LB ⊗ 🖼 Civ Wed 62

RAINOW   Map 16 SJ97

Common Barn Farm B&B *(SJ965764)*

★ ★ ★ ★ FARMHOUSE

Smith Ln SK10 5XJ
☎ 01625 574878 & 07779 816098
Mrs R Cooper
e-mail: g_greengrass@hotmail.com
web: www.cottages-with-a-view.co.uk
dir: *B5470 through Rainow towards Whaley Bridge, right onto Smith Ln, 0.5m on right down drive*

Located high in the Pennines and straddling the border of Cheshire and the Peak District, this new barn conversion provides a popular destination for walkers. Bedrooms are spacious and stylish, and all bathrooms offer modern power showers. A conservatory lounge is ideal for relaxation while enjoying stunning views. Hearty breakfasts are as memorable as the warmth of welcome. A coffee shop during the day provides light snacks and home-baked fare.

Rooms 5 annexe en suite (1 fmly) (3 GF) S £45-£55; D £65-£75 **Facilities** FTV TVL tea/coffee Cen ht Wi-fi Fishing **Conf** Max 25 **Parking** 40 **Notes** LB ⊗ 250 acres sheep

TARPORLEY   Map 15 SJ56

New Farm

★ ★ ★ ★ GUEST ACCOMMODATION

Long Ln, Wettenhall CW7 4DW
☎ 01270 528213
e-mail: Info@NewFarmCheshire.com
dir: *M6 junct 16 onto A51 (signed Nantwich/Chester), pass NWF feedmill over railway bridge. In Alphram turn right signed New Farm*

Set in the peaceful and picturesque Cheshire countryside, this recently converted milking parlour offers comfortable and modern facilities, all rooms are on the ground floor. At this family-run business you can expect a warm welcome and a hearty breakfast. Coarse fishing and caravan park are available on site.

Rooms 5 en suite (5 GF) **Facilities** FTV TVL tea/coffee Cen ht Wi-fi Golf 18 Fishing **Conf** Max 10 **Parking** 7 **Notes** LB ⊗

TARPORLEY *continued*

Alvanley Arms Inn

★★★★ ⇔ INN

Forest Rd, Cotebrook CW6 9DS
☎ 01829 760200
e-mail: info@alvanleyarms.co.uk
web: www.alvanleyarms.co.uk
dir: *2m NE of Tarporley on A49 in Cotebrook*

Records show that there has been a pub on this site since the 16th century, and renovations have uncovered original beams in some of the stylish, well-equipped bedrooms. Wide-ranging menus are available in the cosy bars, and the adjoining Shire Horse Centre and Countryside Park is popular with families. Delamere Forest Park and Oulton Park race circuit are nearby.

Rooms 7 en suite Facilities tea/coffee Dinner available Cen ht Wi-fi free entry for residents to Shire Horse Centre Parking 70 Notes No coaches

WARMINGHAM — Map 15 SJ76

PREMIER COLLECTION

The Bear's Paw

★★★★★ ⇔ INN

School Ln CW11 3QN
☎ 01270 526317
e-mail: info@thebearspaw.co.uk
web: www.thebearspaw.co.uk
dir: *M6 junct 17 onto A534/A533 signed Middlewich/Northwich. Continue on A533, left onto Mill Ln, left onto Warmingham Ln. Right onto Plant Ln, left onto Green Ln*

Located beside a small river within a rural Cheshire village, this 19th-century inn, totally refurbished in 2009, provides very comfortable and well equipped boutique bedrooms with a wealth of thoughtful and practical extras. A friendly team deliver imaginative food, utilising quality seasonal produce, in an attractive open-plan dining room, and a choice of sumptuous lounge areas is also available.

The Bear's Paw

Rooms 17 en suite (4 fmly) S £79-£120; D £99-£140* Facilities STV FTV tea/coffee Dinner available Direct Dial Cen ht Wi-fi Parking 75 Notes LB

WILMSLOW

See Manchester Airport (Greater Manchester)

WYBUNBURY — Map 15 SJ64

Lea Farm *(SJ717489)*

★★★ FARMHOUSE

Wrinehill Rd CW5 7NS
☎ 01270 841429
Mrs J E Callwood
e-mail: leafarm@hotmail.co.uk
dir: *1m E of Wybunbury church on unclassified road*

This working dairy farm is surrounded by delightful gardens and beautiful Cheshire countryside. The spacious bedrooms have modern facilities and there is a cosy lounge. Hearty breakfasts are served in the attractive dining room, which looks out over the garden with its resident peacocks.

Rooms 3 rms (2 en suite) (1 fmly) S £30-£35; D £50-£60* Facilities FTV TVL tea/coffee Cen ht Fishing Pool table Parking 24 Notes ⊕ 150 acres dairy/beef

CORNWALL & ISLES OF SCILLY

BODMIN — Map 2 SX06

Talamayne

★★★★ ⓘ BED AND BREAKFAST

Helland PL30 4PX
☎ 01208 264519 🖨 01208 264519
e-mail: martyn@talamayne.co.uk
dir: *From A30 follow signs for Helland, 2nd house on right on entering the village*

A professionally run bed and breakfast with an emphasis on high quality, comfortable accommodation in a home-from-home environment. Located within easy reach of many of the West Country's attractions in addition to the north and south coasts. On arrival guests are greeted with a warm welcome and freshly prepared Cornish cream tea. Award-winning breakfasts are Aga-cooked and feature local free range eggs and produce.

Rooms 3 en suite (1 GF) S £65; D £80-£85* Facilities FTV TVL tea/coffee Cen ht Parking 7 Notes ⊗ No Children ⊕

Castle Canyke Farm

★★★★ BED AND BREAKFAST

Priors Barn Rd PL31 1HG
☎ 01208 79109
e-mail: bookings@castlecanykefarm.co.uk
web: www.castlecanykefarm.co.uk
dir: *On A389/A38 Priory Rd between church & Carminow Cross rdbt*

A traditional bed and breakfast operation with very friendly hosts offering comfortable, well appointed rooms in a very handy location, with off-street parking. Hearty breakfasts are served in the conservatory, guests have their own lounge and are also welcome to use the pretty garden to the rear. Jane Dean was a finalist in this year's Friendliest Landlady of the Year award (2011-12).

Rooms 3 en suite (1 fmly) D £70-£80* Facilities FTV TVL tea/coffee Cen ht Wi-fi Parking 3 Notes LB ⊗ No Children 8yrs ⊕

Roscrea

★★★★ ⓘ BED AND BREAKFAST

18 Saint Nicholas' St PL31 1AD
☎ 01208 74400
e-mail: roscrea@btconnect.com
dir: *From Bodmin take B3268 to Lostwithiel. Roscrea 0.25m on left*

Dating back to 1805, this fascinating house was once the home of a celebrated local schoolmaster. Now sympathetically restored to its former glory, this is an excellent location for anyone wishing to explore all that Cornwall has to offer. Comfort and quality are evident throughout all areas, matched by the warmth of the welcome. Breakfast is a treat here, featuring local produce and eggs from the resident hens. Dinner is also available by prior arrangement.

Rooms 3 rms (2 en suite) (1 pri facs) S £45-£49; D £70-£78* Facilities FTV TVL tea/coffee Dinner available Cen ht Wi-fi Parking 2 Notes LB ⊗ ⊕

The Stables at Welltown

★★★★ ⓘ BED AND BREAKFAST

Cardinham PL30 4EG
☎ 01208 821316
e-mail: thestables@welltown.orangehome.co.uk

Enjoying a peaceful location away from hustle and bustle, this is a wonderful place to relax and enjoy the unspoilt delights of this rugged area. Guests are assured of a rewarding and pleasurable stay. Converted from stables, there is character and comfort in equal measure with an uncluttered contemporary feel. Breakfast from the Aga is a real treat with local produce in abundance. Additional facilities include a snug lounge and attractive garden.

Rooms 2 en suite Facilities FTV TVL tea/coffee Dinner available Cen ht Wi-fi Parking 2 Notes No Children 12yrs ⊕

Mount Pleasant Farm

★★★ GUEST ACCOMMODATION

Mount PL30 4EX
☎ 01208 821342
e-mail: info@mountpleasantcottages.co.uk
dir: *A30 from Bodmin towards Launceston for 4m, right signed Millpool, continue 3m*

Set in 10 acres, this is a wonderfully peaceful base from which to explore the delights of Cornwall. Originally a farmhouse dating back to the 17th century, there is something here for all the family with extensive facilities including a games barn and heated swimming pool. Cosy bedrooms are well furnished, while public areas include a spacious sun lounge and extensive gardens. Breakfast, served in the well-appointed dining room, features local produce and is a highlight of any stay; home-cooked evening meals are available by prior arrangement.

Rooms 6 en suite (3 fmly) S £32-£42; D £54-£74*
Facilities FTV TVL tea/coffee Dinner available Cen ht 🐕
Pool table Games barn **Parking** 8 **Notes** LB 🐾

BOSCASTLE Map 2 SX09

PREMIER COLLECTION

Trerosewill Farm *(SX095905)*

★★★★★ 🏠 FARMHOUSE

Paradise PL35 0BL
☎ 01840 250545 📠 01840 250727
Mr & Mrs Nicholls
e-mail: enquiries@trerosewill.co.uk
web: www.trerosewill.co.uk
dir: *Take B3266 at junct with B3263, towards Tintagel. After 0.2m, turn left by brown sign, 100yds along lane*

A genuine Cornish welcome, complete with tea and cake, is assured at the home of the Nicholls family. From this elevated position, the views over the village below to the sea beyond are truly spectacular. Bedrooms offer a host of thoughtful and generous extras from bathrobes to Wi-fi access. Breakfast is a showcase of locally sourced and home-made produce including eggs, sausages, breads and jams. Additional facilities include a hot tub.

Rooms 6 en suite 3 annexe en suite (2 fmly) (3 GF) D £72-£113* **Facilities** FTV TVL tea/coffee Cen ht Licensed Wi-fi Hot tub **Parking** 10 **Notes** LB 🐾 No Children 7yrs Closed Nov-Feb 50 acres beef/lamb

---

BUDE Map 2 SS20

Bangors Organic

★★★★ 🍴 GUEST HOUSE

Poundstock EX23 0DP
☎ 01288 361297
e-mail: info@bangorsorganic.co.uk
dir: *4m S of Bude. On A39 in Poundstock*

Situated a few miles south of Bude, this renovated Victorian establishment offers elegant accommodation with a good level of comfort. Bedrooms are furnished to a high standard and are located in the main house or the adjacent coach house; the latter being more contemporary in style. The bathrooms are a particular feature here, being impressively spacious and luxurious. Breakfast and dinner, featuring organic, local and home-made produce, are served in the pleasant dining room. The establishment is certified as being organic by the Soil Association.

Rooms 2 en suite 2 annexe en suite (1 GF) **Facilities** FTV TVL tea/coffee Dinner available Cen ht Licensed Wi-fi Badminton **Parking** 10 **Notes** 🐾 No Children 12yrs

Dylan's Guest House

★★★★ GUEST HOUSE

12 Downs View EX23 8RF
☎ 01288 354705
e-mail: dylansbude@tiscali.co.uk
dir: *From A39 onto A3073 at Stratton, at 2nd rdbt turn right to town centre, through town centre, signed to Downs View*

Refurbished to a high standard, this late Victorian house overlooks the golf course and is just a five-minute walk from the beach. There is a refreshing and appealing style here, derived from a combination of original features and a crisp, contemporary decor. The well-equipped bedrooms are light and airy with impressive levels of comfort. Plenty of choice is offered at breakfast, which is carefully prepared from quality produce and served in the attractive dining room.

Rooms 4 rms (3 en suite) (1 pri facs) (1 fmly) S £40-£50; D £55-£65* **Facilities** FTV TVL tea/coffee Cen ht **Notes** LB 🐾 Closed Dec-Jan 🐾

Fairway House

★★★★ GUEST HOUSE

8 Downs View EX23 8RF
☎ 01288 355059
e-mail: enquiries@fairwayguesthouse.co.uk
dir: *N through town to Flexbury, follow brown tourist signs to Downs View from golf course*

Genuine hospitality and attentive service await at this delightful Victorian terrace property, which overlooks the golf course and is close to the beach, the South West Coastal Footpath and the town centre. The comfortable bedrooms are of a high standard and have many thoughtful extra facilities. Breakfast uses local produce, including free range local farm eggs and extra thick back bacon, and is served at separate tables. Full English, omelettes, kippers or Continental options are available.

Rooms 7 rms (5 en suite) (2 pri facs) (1 fmly) S £32-£48; D £54-£66* **Facilities** FTV tea/coffee Cen ht Wi-fi **Notes** LB 🐾 Closed Dec-Jan 🐾

Atlantic House

★★★★ GUEST ACCOMMODATION

Summerleaze Crescent EX23 8HJ
☎ 01288 352451
e-mail: enq@atlantichousehotel.com
dir: *M5 junct 31 onto A30, then A386 to Bude*

This family-run establishment has much to offer and is situated high above Summerleaze Beach with lovely panoramic views across the town and the sea. Bedrooms provide ample comfort, and many have the added bonus of great views. Public areas include the stylish bar and impressive new restaurant where accomplished cuisine is not to be missed.

Rooms 15 en suite (2 fmly) S fr £40; D £80-£96* **Facilities** FTV TVL tea/coffee Dinner available Cen ht Licensed Wi-fi 🏊 Golf 18 ⛳ Squash Riding **Conf** Max 30 Thtr 30 Class 30 Board 30 **Parking** 7 **Notes** LB 🐾

Bude Haven

★★★★ GUEST ACCOMMODATION

Flexbury Av EX23 8NS
☎ 01288 352305 📠 01288 352662
e-mail: enquiries@budehavenhotel.com
dir: *0.5m N of Bude in Flexbury centre*

Quietly located within a short stroll of the town and beaches, this welcoming establishment is an ideal base from which to explore the spectacular North Cornish coast. Bedrooms provide good levels of space and comfort with all the expected little extras. Public areas include the bar/lounge and restaurant, where a selection of dishes is offered most nights of the week. Additional facilities include a hot tub for a relaxing soak at the end of the day.

Rooms 10 en suite (1 fmly) S £37-£42; D £74-£84* **Facilities** FTV tea/coffee Dinner available Cen ht Licensed Wi-fi Hot tub **Parking** 4 **Notes** LB 🐾

BUDE *continued*

The Cliff at Bude

★★★★ GUEST HOUSE

Maer Down, Crooklets Beach EX23 8NG
☎ 01288 353110 & 356833 📄 01288 353110
e-mail: cliff_hotel@btconnect.com
web: www.cliffhotel.co.uk
dir: *A39 through Bude, left at top of High St, pass
Sainsburys, 1st right between golf course, over x-rds,
premises at end on right*

Overlooking the sea from a clifftop location, this friendly
and efficient establishment provides spacious, well-
equipped bedrooms. The various public areas include a
bar and lounge and an impressive range of leisure
facilities. Delicious dinners and tasty breakfasts are
available in the attractive dining room.

Rooms 15 en suite (15 fmly) (8 GF) S £39.95-£44.95; D
£79.90-£89.90* **Facilities** FTV TVL tea/coffee Dinner
available Direct Dial Cen ht Licensed 🕙 ♨ ⌁ Gym Pool
table **Parking** 18 **Notes** LB Closed Nov-Mar

Pencarrol

★★★★ GUEST HOUSE

21 Downs View EX23 8RF
☎ 01288 352478
e-mail: pencarrolbude@aol.com
dir: *0.5m N of Bude. N from Bude into Flexbury village*

This cosy guest house is only a short walk from Bude
centre and Crooklets Beach, and has glorious views over
the golf course. Bedrooms are attractively furnished and
there is a first-floor lounge. Breakfast is served at
separate tables in the dining room.

Rooms 6 rms (3 en suite) (2 pri facs) (2 fmly) (1 GF) S
£31-£35; D £68-£76 **Facilities** FTV TVL tea/coffee Cen ht
Notes LB ⊗ Closed Nov-Feb ⊚

Surf Haven Guest House

★★★★ 🅐 GUEST HOUSE

31 Downs View EX23 8RG
☎ 01288 353923 & 07835 852205
e-mail: info@surfhaven.co.uk
web: www.surfhaven.co.uk
dir: *From A3072 follow signs to Bude town centre then
follow sign for Crooklets Beach*

Rooms 8 rms (7 en suite) (1 pri facs) (4 fmly) (1 GF) S
£25-£40; D £50-£66 **Facilities** FTV TVL tea/coffee Dinner
available Cen ht Wi-fi **Parking** 8 **Notes** LB

Sea Jade Guest House

★★★ GUEST ACCOMMODATION

15 Burn View EX23 8BZ
☎ 01288 353404 & 07737 541540
e-mail: seajadeguesthouse@yahoo.co.uk
dir: *A39 turn right follow signs for Bude & golf course*

A warm welcome awaits at this popular establishment
which is well located within a few minutes' walk of both
the town and beaches. Bedrooms are light and airy with a
simple, contemporary styling; some have views across the
golf course. Breakfast is a generous offering and
guaranteed to get the day off to a satisfying start.

Rooms 8 rms (7 en suite) (1 pri facs) (4 fmly) (2 GF) S
£30-£36; D £60-£68* **Facilities** FTV TVL tea/coffee Cen ht
Wi-fi Golf 18 **Notes** LB ⊗ ⊚

CALLINGTON   Map 3 SX36

Woodpeckers

★★★★ GUEST HOUSE

Rilla Mill PL17 7NT
☎ 01579 363717
e-mail: alisonmerchant@virgin.net
dir: *5m NW of Callington. Off B3254 at Upton Cross x-rds
for Rilla Mill*

Set in a conservation village, in a wooded valley, by a
tumbling stream, this modern, detached house offers
cosy, well equipped bedrooms with numerous thoughtful
extras. Home-cooked dinners, using the best of local
ingredients, are available by arrangement. The hot tub in
the garden is a welcome feature.

Rooms 3 en suite **Facilities** STV FTV tea/coffee Dinner
available Cen ht Gym Spa/Hot tub **Parking** 7 **Notes** LB ⊗
⊚

CAWSAND   Map 3 SX45

Wringford Down

★★★ GUEST ACCOMMODATION

Hat Ln PL10 1LE
☎ 01752 822287
e-mail: andrew@wringford.co.uk
dir: *A374 onto B3247, pass Millbrook, right towards
Cawsand & sharp right, 0.5m on right*

This family-run establishment has a peaceful location
near Rame Head and the South West Coast Path, and is
particularly welcoming to families. There is a nursery,
swimming pool, games room, and gardens with play
areas. A range of bedrooms, suites and self-catering
units is available. Breakfast is served in the spacious
dining room.

Rooms 5 en suite 2 annexe en suite (4 fmly) (5 GF) S
£46-£61; D £72-£102* **Facilities** FTV TVL tea/coffee
Cen ht Licensed Wi-fi ch fac 🕙 ♨ Golf 18 Pool table
Table tennis **Parking** 20 **Notes** LB Civ Wed 100

CRACKINGTON HAVEN   Map 2 SX19

Lower Tresmorn Farm *(SX164975)*

★★★★ 🍴 FARMHOUSE

EX23 0NU
☎ 01840 230667 & 07786 227437
Rachel Crocker
e-mail: rachel.crocker@talk21.com
web: www.lowertresmorn.co.uk
dir: *Take Tresmorn turn off coast road, 2m N of
Crackington Haven*

Set in the North Cornwall's heritage coast area, this
charming farmhouse dates, in part, back to medieval
times. The welcome is warm and genuine with a reviving
cup of tea and piece of cake always on offer. Bedrooms
are located in the main house and an adjacent converted
barn; all provide plenty of comfort. Breakfast and the
popular dinners (by prior arrangement) use local or farm
produce.

Rooms 3 rms (2 en suite) (1 pri facs) 3 annexe en suite
(2 fmly) (2 GF) S £35-£60; D £60-£80* **Facilities** FTV TVL
TV4B tea/coffee Dinner available Wi-fi **Parking** 6
Notes ⊗ No Children 8yrs RS 20 Dec-5 Jan B&B only 222
acres beef/sheep

Bears & Boxes Country Guest House

★★★★ 🛏 🍴 GUEST HOUSE

Penrose, Dizzard EX23 0NX
☎ 01840 230318
e-mail: rwfrh@btinternet.com
web: www.bearsandboxes.com
dir: *1.5m NE of St Gennys in Dizzard*

Dating in part from the mid 17th century, Bears & Boxes
is a small, family-run guest house situated 500 yards
from the coastal path. Guests are welcomed with a tray of
tea and home-made cake, and the caring owners are
always around to give advice on the local area. The cosy
bedrooms have numerous thoughtful extras, and evening
meals, using the very best of local ingredients and cooked
with flair, are served by arrangement.

Rooms 2 en suite S £35; D £63-£70* **Facilities** FTV TVL
tea/coffee Dinner available Cen ht Wi-fi **Parking** 6

CRAFTHOLE   Map 3 SX35

The Liscawn

★★★★ GUEST ACCOMMODATION

PL11 3BD
☎ 01503 230863
e-mail: enquiries@liscawn.co.uk
web: www.liscawn.co.uk
dir: *A374 onto B3247 to Crafthole, through village, left at rdbt, 0.3m on left*

A well established, friendly, family-run guest accommodation with comfortable rooms. Serving food every night of the week, The Liscawn sits in mature grounds and is a few minutes from the coastal path and Whitsand Bay.

Rooms 8 en suite 5 annexe en suite (3 fmly) (2 GF) S £45-£60; D £60-£90* **Facilities** FTV tea/coffee Dinner available Cen ht Licensed Children's play area **Conf** Max 60 Thtr 60 Class 40 Board 35 **Parking** 50 **Notes** Civ Wed 70

CRANTOCK   Map 2 SW76

Carrek Woth

★★★ GUEST ACCOMMODATION

West Pentire Rd TR8 5SA
☎ 01637 830530
web: www.carrekwoth.co.uk
dir: *W from Crantock towards West Pentire*

Many guests return to this friendly, family-run house where hospitality and service are noteworthy. Carrek Woth takes its name from the Cornish for Goose Rock, which can be seen in Crantock Bay. All the rooms are ground floor and neatly furnished, and some have good views. The lounge looks toward Newquay and the sea. Breakfast is served in the attractive dining room; Sunday lunch is also available.

Rooms 6 en suite (1 fmly) (6 GF) **Facilities** FTV TVL tea/coffee Cen ht **Parking** 6 **Notes** LB 🐾

FALMOUTH   Map 2 SW83

PREMIER COLLECTION

Dolvean House

★★★★★ GUEST ACCOMMODATION

50 Melvill Rd TR11 4DQ
☎ 01326 313658   📠 01326 313995
e-mail: reservations@dolvean.co.uk
web: www.dolvean.co.uk
dir: *On A39 near town centre & Maritime Museum*

A Victorian house with high standards throughout. Rooms are comfortable and well equipped and there is a guest lounge. Well located for the beach and town alike with ample off-street parking.

Rooms 10 en suite (2 GF) S £38.50-£44; D £77-£98* **Facilities** FTV TVL tea/coffee Cen ht Licensed Wi-fi **Parking** 11 **Notes** LB Closed Xmas

Bosanneth Guest House

★★★★ 🍴 GUEST HOUSE

Gyllyngvase Hill TR11 4DW
☎ 01326 314649   📠 01326 314649
e-mail: stay@bosanneth.co.uk
dir: *From Truro on A39 follow signs for beaches/docks, 3rd right mini-rdbt Melvil Rd, 3rd right onto Gyllyngvase Hill*

Well situated property with comfortable rooms and very friendly hosts. Some rooms have a sea view and dinner is served nightly. A full Cornish breakfast is served in the dining room.

Rooms 8 en suite S £40-£70; D £70-£125 **Facilities** FTV tea/coffee Dinner available Cen ht Licensed Wi-fi **Parking** 7 **Notes** LB 🐾 No Children 15yrs

Prospect House

★★★★ GUEST ACCOMMODATION

1 Church Rd, Penryn TR10 8DA
☎ 01326 373198   📠 01326 373198
e-mail: stay@prospecthouse-penryn.co.uk
web: www.prospecthouse-penryn.co.uk
dir: *Off A39 at Treluswell rdbt onto B3292, turn right at Penryn town centre sign. Left at junct to town hall, left onto Saint Gluivas St, at bottom on left*

Situated close to the waterside, Prospect House is an attractive building, built for a ship's captain around 1820. The original charm of the house has been carefully maintained and the attractive bedrooms are well equipped. A comfortable lounge is available, and freshly cooked breakfasts are served in the elegant dining room.

Rooms 3 en suite D £70-£75* **Facilities** FTV TVL tea/coffee Dinner available Cen ht Wi-fi **Conf** Max 6 **Parking** 4 **Notes** 🐾

The Rosemary

★★★★ GUEST ACCOMMODATION

22 Gyllyngvase Ter TR11 4DL
☎ 01326 314669
e-mail: stay@therosemary.co.uk
web: www.therosemary.co.uk
dir: *A39 Melvill Rd signed to beaches & seafront, right onto Gyllyngvase Rd, 1st left*

Centrally located with splendid views from many rooms over Falmouth Bay, this friendly establishment provides comfortable accommodation and hearty breakfasts. The attractive bedrooms are thoughtfully equipped, and guests can relax with a drink from the well stocked bar. A guest lounge and decked area in the rear garden are also available for guests.

Rooms 10 en suite (4 fmly) S £49-£61; D £75-£93* **Facilities** FTV tea/coffee Cen ht Licensed Wi-fi Golf 18 **Parking** 3 **Notes** LB Closed Dec-Jan

See advert on page 49

FALMOUTH *continued*

Anacapri

★★★★ GUEST ACCOMMODATION

Gyllyngvase Rd TR11 4DJ
☎ 01326 311454 📄 01326 311474
e-mail: anacapri@btconnect.com
web: www.hotelanacapri.co.uk
dir: *A39 (Truro to Falmouth), straight on at lights. Over next 2 rdbts onto Melvill Rd, down hill 2nd right onto Gyllyngvase Rd, Anacapri on right*

In an elevated position overlooking Gyllyngvase Beach with views of Falmouth Bay beyond, this family-run establishment extends a warm welcome to all. Bedrooms have similar standards of comfort and quality, and the majority have sea views. Public areas include a convivial bar, a lounge and the smart breakfast room with views out to sea.

Rooms 16 en suite **Facilities** FTV TVL tea/coffee Cen ht Licensed Wi-fi **Parking Notes** ⊗ No Children 10yrs Closed mid Dec–mid Jan

Cotswold House

★★★★ GUEST HOUSE

49 Melvill Rd TR11 4DF
☎ 01326 312077
e-mail: info@cotswoldhousehotel.com
dir: *On A39 near town centre & docks*

This smart Victorian house has splendid sea views, and is just a short walk from the town. The atmosphere is relaxed, the bar is popular, and the lounge provides a good level of comfort. A hearty breakfast is served in the dining room and dinner, featuring home-cooked dishes, is available by prior arrangement.

Cotswold House

Rooms 10 en suite (1 fmly) (1 GF) **Facilities** FTV TVL tea/coffee Dinner available Cen ht Licensed **Parking** 10 **Notes** ⊗ Closed Xmas

Esmond House

★★★★ GUEST HOUSE

5 Emslie Rd TR11 4BG
☎ 01326 313214
e-mail: esmondhouse@btopenworld.com
web: www.esmondhouse.com
dir: *Off A39 Melvill Rd right onto Emslie Rd*

The friendly and comfortable Edwardian house is just a short easy walk from the beach. Bedrooms vary in size and some have sea views; the rooms are on the first and second floors. A hearty, freshly cooked breakfast is served in the spacious, traditionally furnished front room, whose large bay windows create a light and airy environment.

Rooms 4 en suite D £60–£80* **Facilities** FTV tea/coffee Cen ht **Notes** LB ⊗ No Children 3yrs Closed Nov–Feb

Melvill House

★★★★ GUEST ACCOMMODATION

52 Melvill Rd TR11 4DQ
☎ 01326 316645 📄 01326 211608
e-mail: melvillhouse@btconnect.com
dir: *On A39 near town centre & docks*

Well situated for the beach, the town centre and the National Maritime Museum on the harbour, Melvill House is a family-run establishment with a relaxed atmosphere. Some bedrooms have four-poster beds, and breakfast is served in the smart dining room. Ample parking.

Rooms 7 en suite (2 fmly) (1 GF) S £30–£45; D £60–£80* **Facilities** FTV TVL tea/coffee Cen ht Wi-fi **Parking** 8 **Notes** LB ⊗

Park Grove

★★★★ GUEST HOUSE

Kimberley Park Rd TR11 2DD
☎ 01326 313276 📄 01326 211926
e-mail: reception@parkgrovehotel.com
web: www.parkgrovehotel.com
dir: *A39 from Truro to Falmouth, at lights left onto Kimberley Park Rd*

Within walking distance of the town centre, this friendly family-run establishment is situated in a pleasant residential area opposite Kimberley Park. Comfortable accommodation is provided and public areas include a relaxing and stylish lounge and a spacious dining room and bar. Bedrooms are also comfortable and well equipped.

Rooms 17 en suite (5 fmly) (2 GF) S £46–£94; D £69–£104* **Facilities** FTV TVL tea/coffee Direct Dial Cen ht Licensed Wi-fi Golf 18 **Parking** 16 **Notes** ⊗ Closed Dec–Feb

The Rathgowry

★★★★ GUEST HOUSE

Gyllyngvase Hill TR11 4DN
☎ 01326 313482
e-mail: enquiries@rathgowry.co.uk
web: www.rathgowry.co.uk
dir: *A39 from Truro bypass follow signs for docks & beaches until entering onto Melvill Rd. Gyllyngvase Hill is 3rd turning on right*

Located in a quieter residential area yet only a few minutes' stroll from the beach and 15 minutes from the town centre, this traditionally styled property offers a range of differently sized, well-equipped bedrooms and bathrooms. Extras include home-made biscuits and Wi-fi in all rooms. A varied menu is offered at breakfast including American pancakes with maple syrup and bacon, a full Continental and a complete English cooked option.

Rooms 9 rms (7 en suite) (2 pri facs) (5 fmly) S £35–£44; D £70–£88* **Facilities** FTV tea/coffee Cen ht Wi-fi Golf 18 **Parking** 7 **Notes** LB ⊗

Rosemullion

★★★★ GUEST ACCOMMODATION

Gyllyngvase Hill TR11 4DF
☎ 01326 314690 📄 01326 210098
e-mail: gail@rosemullionhotel.demon.co.uk

Recognisable by its mock-Tudor exterior, this friendly establishment is well situated for both the town centre and the beach. Some of the comfortable bedrooms are on the ground floor, while a few rooms on the top floor have views to Falmouth Bay. Hospitality and service are strengths. Breakfast, served in the panelled dining room, is freshly cooked and there is a well appointed lounge.

Rooms 13 rms (11 en suite) (2 pri facs) (3 GF) S £38-£45; D £68-£84* **Facilities** FTV tea/coffee Cen ht Wi-fi **Parking** 18 **Notes** LB ⊗ No Children Closed 23-31 Dec 🐕

The Westcott

★★★★ 🅰 GUEST ACCOMMODATION

Gyllyngvase Hill TR11 4DN
☎ 01326 311309 📄 01326 330222
e-mail: westcotthotel@btinternet.com
web: www.westcotthotelfalmouth.co.uk
dir: A39 from Truro to Falmouth. Gyllyngvase Hill on right 600yds before Princess Pavillion

Rooms 9 en suite S £35-£45; D £60-£80* **Facilities** FTV TVL tea/coffee Cen ht Wi-fi **Parking** 7 **Notes** LB ⊗ No Children 5yrs

Boswyn

★★★ BED AND BREAKFAST

1 Western Ter TR11 4QN
☎ 01326 314667
e-mail: eric.jermyn@sky.com

A traditional bed and breakfast with genuine hospitality and friendly service. The bedrooms are well equipped and well furnished, a guest lounge is available, and a separate dining room is the venue for breakfast. Conveniently located just a few minutes' walk from the seafront with on-street parking nearby.

Rooms 4 rms (3 en suite) (1 pri facs) (2 fmly) **Facilities** FTV TVL tea/coffee Cen ht Wi-fi **Notes** ⊗ 🐕

Broadmead

★★★ GUEST ACCOMMODATION

66/68 Kimberley Park Rd TR11 2DD
☎ 01326 315704 📄 01326 311048
e-mail: frontdesk@broadmead-hotel.co.uk
dir: A39 from Truro to Falmouth, at lights left onto Kimberley Park Rd, 200yds on left

Conveniently located, with views across the park and within easy walking distance of the beaches and town centre, this pleasant property is smart and comfortable. Bedrooms are well equipped and attractively decorated. A choice of lounges is available and, in the dining room, menus offer freshly prepared home-cooked dishes.

Rooms 12 en suite **Facilities** FTV tea/coffee Wi-fi

The Observatory

★★★ GUEST HOUSE

27 Western Ter TR11 4QL
☎ 01326 314509
e-mail: theobservatory@talktalk.net
dir: On A39, Dracaena Av onto Western Ter

This interesting house is in a pleasant location, close to the town and harbour. The proprietors are very friendly hosts. Bedrooms come in a range of sizes, and freshly cooked breakfasts, with vegetarian options, are served in the dining room. On-site parking is an added bonus.

Rooms 6 en suite (2 fmly) (3 GF) S £35-£55; D £55-£60* **Facilities** FTV tea/coffee Cen ht Wi-fi **Parking** 6 **Notes** LB ⊗ 🐕

Trevoil Guest House

★★★ GUEST HOUSE

25 Avenue Rd TR11 4AY
☎ 01326 314145 & 07966 409782 📄 01326 314145
e-mail: alan.jewel@btconnect.com
dir: Off A39 Melvill Rd left onto Avenue Rd, 150yds from Maritime Museum

Located within walking distance of the town centre, the friendly Trevoil is a comfortable and relaxed environment. Breakfast is enjoyed in the light, pleasant dining room.

Rooms 8 rms (4 en suite) (3 fmly) (1 GF) **Facilities** FTV tea/coffee Cen ht Wi-fi **Parking** 6

FALMOUTH *continued*

The Tudor Court

★★★ GUEST HOUSE

55 Melvill Rd TR11 4DF
☎ **01326 312807**
e-mail: enquiries@tudorcourthotel.com
dir: *A39 to Falmouth straight through Dracaena Av, onto Melvill Road. Tudor Court 300yds on right*

This mock Tudor establishment offers bright, well-equipped bedrooms, some having the benefit of distant sea views. A comfortable bar/lounge is available for guests and in the dining room, which overlooks the attractive garden, a freshly cooked, full English breakfast is served.

Rooms 10 rms (9 en suite) (1 pri facs) (1 fmly) S £30-£45; D £60-£80 **Facilities** FTV TVL tea/coffee Cen ht Licensed Wi-fi **Parking** 10 **Notes** LB

Eden Lodge

★★ GUEST HOUSE

54 Melvill Rd TR11 4DQ
☎ **01326 212989 & 07715 696218**
e-mail: edenlodge@hotmail.co.uk
dir: *On A39, on left 200yds past Fox Rosehill Gardens*

Very well located on Melvill Road with off-road parking, Eden Lodge boasts comfortable rooms and a swimming pool. The friendly hosts serve dinner by arrangement and do all they can to ensure a comfortable stay.

Rooms 5 rms (4 en suite) (2 fmly) (1 GF) **Facilities** FTV TVL tea/coffee Dinner available Cen ht Licensed Wi-fi 🐾 Gym Massage & aromatherapy by appointment **Parking** 9 **Notes** 🈲

FLUSHING   Map 2 SW83

Trefusis Barton Farmhouse B&B *(SW815341)*

★★★ FARMHOUSE

TR11 5TD
☎ **01326 374257 & 07866 045646** 📠 **01326 374257**
Mrs J Laity
e-mail: trefusisbarton@aol.com
dir: *Off A39 towards Carclew, follow signs to Mylor Bridge, left at mini-rdbt, after 0.5m straight across at x-rds*

This working farm is easily reached high above the village of Flushing. The friendly home is convenient for a relaxing break or for touring, and the comfortable bedrooms have many thoughtful extras. Breakfast is served at the farmhouse kitchen table, fresh from the Aga.

Rooms 3 en suite (1 GF) S £55-£68; D £65-£68* **Facilities** FTV tea/coffee Cen ht Wi-fi **Parking** 6 **Notes** 🈲 🈲 400 acres dairy/arable

FOWEY   Map 2 SX15

Trevanion

★★★★ GUEST ACCOMMODATION

70 Lostwithiel St PL23 1BQ
☎ **01726 832602**
e-mail: alisteve@trevanionguesthouse.co.uk
web: www.trevanionguesthouse.co.uk
dir: *A3082 into Fowey, down hill, left onto Lostwithiel St, Trevanion on left*

This 16th-century merchant's house provides friendly, comfortable accommodation within easy walking distance of the historic town of Fowey and is also convenient for visiting the Eden Project. A hearty farmhouse-style, cooked breakfast, using local produce, is served in the attractive dining room; other menu options are available.

Rooms 5 rms (4 en suite) (1 pri facs) (2 fmly) (1 GF) S £40-£45; D £60-£70* **Facilities** FTV tea/coffee Dinner available Cen ht Wi-fi **Parking** 6 **Notes** LB 🈲

GOLDSITHNEY   Map 2 SW53

Penleen

★★★ GUEST ACCOMMODATION

South Rd TR20 9LF
☎ **01736 710633**
e-mail: jimblain@penleen.com
web: www.penleen.com
dir: *A30 towards Penzance, left onto A394 at rdbt. Left into Goldsithney, 1st right onto South Rd*

Penleen is a quiet family home close to Penzance and Mount's Bay where the friendly proprietors ensure their guests have a comfortable stay. The lounge overlooks an attractive garden and freshly cooked breakfasts are served in the dining room. Bedrooms come with a good range of facilities.

Rooms 2 rms (1 en suite) (1 pri facs) D £60-£65* **Facilities** FTV tea/coffee Cen ht **Parking** 2 **Notes** 🈲 No Children 8yrs Closed 19 Dec-10 Jan 🈲

GORRAN   Map 2 SW94

Tregerrick Farm B&B *(SW992436)*

★★★★ FARMHOUSE

PL26 6NF
☎ **01726 843418** 📠 **01726 843418**
Mrs C Thomas
e-mail: fandc.thomas@btconnect.com
web: www.tregerrickfarm.co.uk
dir: *1m NW of Gorran. B3273 S from St Austell, right after Pentewan Sands campsite to The Lost Gardens of Heligan, continue 3m, farm on left*

Near many attractions, the family-run Victorian farmhouse offers a high standard of accommodation in peaceful countryside. Delicious breakfasts, featuring home-made breads and preserves, are served around the large dining table.

Rooms 2 en suite S £45; D £75-£80* **Facilities** FTV TVL tea/coffee Cen ht Wi-fi **Parking** 4 **Notes** LB 🈲 No Children 4yrs Closed Nov-Jan 🈲 280 acres arable/beef

GORRAN HAVEN   Map 2 SX04

The Mead

★★★★ BED AND BREAKFAST

PL26 6HU
☎ **01726 842981**
e-mail: maureengoff@tiscali.co.uk
dir: *A30 signed to St Austell continue towards Mevagissey. Signed for Gorran Haven, 1st right Wansford Meadows*

Guests are welcomed at this new, comfortable home, with a complimentary cream tea. Peacefully situated in Gorran Haven, within a ten-minute walk of the sandy beach, Heligan and the Eden Project are a short drive away. The bedrooms feature larger than average beds and numerous extra facilities. Hearty breakfasts are served in the ground-floor dining room and include free-range eggs from the owner's hens, whenever possible.

Rooms 2 en suite S £50; D £70 **Facilities** FTV tea/coffee Cen ht Wi-fi **Parking** 2 **Notes** 🈲 No Children Closed Xmas 🈲

HAYLE   Map 2 SW53

Calize Country House

★★★★ GUEST ACCOMMODATION

Prosper Hill, Gwithian TR27 5BW
☎ **01736 753268**
e-mail: jilly@calize.co.uk
dir: *2m NE of Hayle. B3301 in Gwithian at Red River Inn, house 350yds up hill on left*

The refurbished establishment has superb views of the sea and countryside, and is well located for the beaches and coves of West Penwith, walking, birdwatching, and the many gardens in the area. The attentive proprietors provide a most welcoming environment and invite you to share their comfortable lounge, which has a log-burning fire during colder months. Enjoyable breakfasts featuring delicious home-made fare are served around a communal table with sea views.

Rooms 4 en suite S £55-£65; D £80-£90* **Facilities** FTV TVL tea/coffee Cen ht Wi-fi **Parking** 6 **Notes** 🈲 No Children 12yrs 🈲

HELFORD   Map 2 SW72

Prince of Wales

★★★★ INN

Newtown, St Martin TR12 6DP
☎ 01326 231247

A newly refurbished traditional pub in a quiet village setting, privately owned and run with care and much pride. The bedrooms are bright, comfortable and well furnished and include such extras as iPod docking stations. Dinner is served every evening and breakfast features locally sourced, quality produce.

Rooms 3 en suite (2 fmly) S £60-£90; D £60-£90* **Facilities** FTV TVL tea/coffee Dinner available Direct Dial Cen ht Wi-fi Golf 18 **Parking** 70 **Notes** LB No coaches

HELSTON   Map 2 SW62

See also St Keverne

The Queens Arms

★★★ INN

Breage TR13 9PD
☎ 01326 573485
e-mail: chris-brazier@btconnect.com

A traditional inn in a quiet village location near to Helston, serving home-cooked food every night of the week. The bedrooms are bright, comfortable and well appointed, and the cosy bar is a great meeting place for locals and guests alike. Good food and good beer, coupled with commendable hospitality, make the Queens Arms a popular venue.

Rooms 2 en suite D £70-£80* **Facilities** FTV tea/coffee Dinner available Cen ht Wi-fi Pool table **Parking** 15 **Notes** LB No Children No coaches

LANLIVERY   Map 2 SX05

The Crown Inn

★★★ INN

PL30 5BT
☎ 01208 872707   📠 01208 871208
e-mail: thecrown@wagtailinns.com
web: www.wagtailinns.com
dir: Signed from A390, 2m W of Lostwithiel. Inn 0.5m down lane into village, opposite church

This character inn has a long history, reflected in its worn flagstone floors, aged beams, open fireplaces and ancient well. Dating in part from the 12th century, The Crown has undergone a faithful restoration. Dining is a feature and menus offer a wide choice of fresh fish, local produce and interesting dishes. The attractive bedrooms are more contemporary and are impressively appointed. The garden is a delight.

Rooms 2 en suite 7 annexe en suite (1 fmly) (7 GF) **Facilities** FTV tea/coffee Dinner available Cen ht Wi-fi **Parking** 50

LAUNCESTON   Map 3 SX38

PREMIER COLLECTION

Primrose Cottage

★★★★★ 🛏 🍽 BED AND BREAKFAST

Lawhitton PL15 9PE
☎ 01566 773645
e-mail: enquiry@primrosecottagesuites.co.uk
web: www.primrosecottagesuites.co.uk
dir: Exit A30 Tavistock, follow A388 through Launceston for Plymouth then B3362, Tavistock 2.5m

Originally a cottage, this impressive property has been imaginatively developed to provide stylish accommodation. From its elevated position, views across the lush countryside are wonderful. Two of the spacious suites have external entrances. All provide high levels of comfort with separate seating areas. Breakfast makes use of excellent local produce and a guest lounge is also available. Outside, guests can enjoy the garden, or perhaps take a stroll down to the River Tamar for a spot of fishing.

Rooms 2 en suite 1 annexe en suite (1 GF) S £70-£90; D £90-£130 **Facilities** FTV tea/coffee Dinner available Cen ht Wi-fi Fishing **Parking** 5 **Notes** ⊗ No Children 12yrs Closed 23-28 Dec

Hurdon *(SX333828)*

★★★★ 🍽 FARMHOUSE

PL15 9LS
☎ 01566 772955
Mrs M Smith
dir: A30 onto A388 to Launceston, at rdbt exit for hospital, 2nd right signed Trebullett, premises 1st on right

Genuine hospitality is assured at this delightful 18th-century granite farmhouse. The bedrooms are individually furnished and decorated, and equipped with numerous extras. The delicious dinners, by arrangement, use only the best local produce, and include home-made puddings and the farm's own clotted cream.

Rooms 6 en suite (1 fmly) (1 GF) S £32-£38; D £54-£70 **Facilities** FTV TVL tea/coffee Dinner available Cen ht **Parking** 10 **Notes** LB ⊗ Closed Nov-Apr ⊜ 400 acres mixed

Bradridge Farm *(SX328938)*

★★★★ FARMHOUSE

PL15 9RL
☎ 01409 271264
Mrs A Strout
e-mail: angela@bradridgefarm.co.uk
dir: 5.5m N of Launceston. Off B3254 at Ladycross sign for Boyton, Bradridge 2nd farm on right after Boyton school

The late Victorian farmhouse stands in glorious countryside on the border of Devon and Cornwall. The well-presented bedrooms have numerous thoughtful extras, and the Aga-cooked breakfasts feature farm-fresh eggs.

Rooms 4 rms (3 en suite) (1 fmly) **Facilities** FTV TVL tea/coffee Cen ht Fishing **Parking** 6 **Notes** Closed Nov-Feb ⊜ 250 acres arable/beef/sheep/hens

Tyne Wells House

★★★★ BED AND BREAKFAST

Pennygillam PL15 7EE
☎ 01566 775810
e-mail: btucker@talktalk.net
web: www.tynewells.co.uk
dir: 0.6m SW of town centre. Off A30 onto Pennygillam rdbt, house off rdbt

Situated on the outskirts of the town, Tyne Wells House has panoramic views over the countryside. A relaxed and friendly atmosphere prevails and the bedrooms are neatly furnished. A hearty breakfast is served in the dining room, which overlooks the garden.

Rooms 3 rms (2 en suite) (1 pri facs) (1 fmly) S £35-£40; D £56-£62* **Facilities** FTV tea/coffee Cen ht Wi-fi **Parking** 4 **Notes** LB ⊗ ⊜

B&B@ Rose Cottage

★★★ BED AND BREAKFAST

Rose Cottage, 5 Lower Cleaverfield PL15 8ED
☎ 01566 779292
e-mail: info@rosecottagecornwall.co.uk
dir: Exit A30 at Launceston onto A388. Lower Cleaverfield 200yds on left after 2nd mini rdbt

A warm and genuine welcome is extended to all guests at this charming cottage, parts of which date back several hundred years. A homely atmosphere ensures a relaxing and enjoyable stay with every effort made to help with any local information required. Bedrooms are very comfortable and breakfast is served in the attractive dining room with lovely views across the valley. Wi-fi access is also available.

Rooms 3 rms (2 en suite) (1 pri facs) S £29-£37; D £58-£78* **Facilities** FTV tea/coffee Cen ht Wi-fi **Parking** 4 **Notes** LB ⊗ No Children 9yrs

LISKEARD   Map 2 SX26

See also Callington

Redgate Smithy

★★★★ 🏠 BED AND BREAKFAST

Redgate, St Cleer PL14 6RU
☎ **01579 321578**
e-mail: enquiries@redgatesmithy.co.uk
web: www.redgatesmithy.co.uk
dir: *3m NW of Liskeard. Off A30 at Bolventor/Jamaica Inn onto St Cleer Rd for 7m, B&B just past x-rds*

This 200-year-old converted smithy is on the southern fringe of Bodmin Moor near Golitha Falls. The friendly accommodation offers smartly furnished, cottage-style bedrooms with many extra facilities. There are several dining options nearby, and the wide choice of freshly cooked breakfasts is served in the conservatory.

Rooms 3 rms (2 en suite) (1 pri facs) S £48; D £75*
Facilities FTV tea/coffee Cen ht Wi-fi **Parking** 3 **Notes** LB No Children 12yrs Closed Xmas & New Year

Trecarne House

★★★★ GUEST ACCOMMODATION

Penhale Grange, St Cleer PL14 5EB
☎ **01579 343543** 📠 **01579 343543**
e-mail: trish@trecarnehouse.co.uk
dir: *B3254 N from Liskeard to St Cleer. Right at Post Office, 3rd left after church, 2nd right, house on right*

A warm welcome awaits you at this large family home, peacefully located on the edge of the village. The stylish and spacious bedrooms, which have magnificent country views, feature pine floors and have many thoughtful extras. The buffet-style breakfast offers a wide choice, which can be enjoyed in the dining room or sun-filled conservatory overlooking rolling countryside.

Rooms 3 en suite (2 fmly) **Facilities** TVL tea/coffee Cen ht Table tennis Trampoline **Conf** Max 12 **Parking** 6 **Notes** ⊗

Elnor

★★★ GUEST HOUSE

1 Russell St PL14 4BP
☎ **01579 342472** 📠 **01579 345673**
e-mail: infoelnorguesthouse@talktalk.net
dir: *Off A38 from Plymouth into town centre, house on right opp florist on road to railway station, past British Legion and pub The Railway*

This well-established, friendly guest house is close to the town centre and railway station, and is just a short drive from Bodmin Moor and other places of interest. Bedrooms are neatly presented and well equipped, and some are on the ground floor. A cosy lounge and a small bar are available.

Rooms 6 rms (4 en suite) 3 annexe en suite (3 fmly) (4 GF) S £30-£35; D £55-£63* **Facilities** FTV TVL tea/coffee Direct Dial Cen ht Wi-fi **Parking** 7 **Notes** ⊗ ⊜

LOOE   Map 2 SX25

PREMIER COLLECTION

The Beach House

★★★★★ 🏠 GUEST ACCOMMODATION

Marine Dr, Hannafore PL13 2DH
☎ **01503 262598** 📠 **01503 262298**
e-mail: enquiries@thebeachhouselooe.co.uk
web: www.thebeachhouselooe.co.uk
dir: *From Looe W over bridge, left to Hannafore & Marine Dr, on right after Tom Sawyer Tavern*

This peaceful property has panoramic sea views and is just a short walk from the harbour, restaurants and town. Some rooms have been refurbished with stylish hand-made furniture, and the bedrooms are well equipped and have many extras. Hearty breakfasts are served in the first-floor dining room, a good start for the South West Coast Path that goes right by the house.

Rooms 5 en suite (4 GF) S £75; D £100-£140*
Facilities FTV tea/coffee Cen ht Wi-fi Beauty treatment room **Parking** 6 **Notes** LB ⊗ No Children 16yrs Closed Xmas

Barclay House

★★★★ ◉◉ GUEST ACCOMMODATION

St Martin's Rd PL13 1LP
☎ **01503 262929** 📠 **01503 262632**
e-mail: reception@barclayhouse.co.uk
web: www.barclayhouse.co.uk
dir: *1st house on left on entering Looe from A38*

This establishment stands in six acres of grounds overlooking Looe Harbour, and is within walking distance of the town. The thoughtfully furnished bedrooms have modern facilities, and there is a sitting room, a spacious bar, and a terrace where guests can enjoy an aperitif in the summer months. Enjoyable, freshly prepared dinners are served in the light and airy restaurant that proves popular with both locals and tourists alike. A heated swimming pool is available.

Rooms 11 en suite 1 annexe en suite (1 fmly) (1 GF) S £55-£117.50; D £110-£200 **Facilities** FTV tea/coffee Dinner available Direct Dial Cen ht Licensed Wi-fi ch fac ⟲ Sauna Gym Hair salon massage & beauty treatments **Conf** Max 40 Thtr 20 Class 10 Board 18 **Parking** 25 **Notes** LB ⊗ Civ Wed 70

See advert on opposite page

Bay View Farm *(SX282548)*

★★★★ 🚜 FARMHOUSE

St Martins PL13 1NZ
☎ **01503 265922** 📠 **01503 265922**
Mrs E Elford
e-mail: mike@looebaycaravans.co.uk
web: www.looedirectory.co.uk/bay-view-farm.htm
dir: *2m NE of Looe. Off B3253 for Monkey Sanctuary, farm signed*

The renovated and extended bungalow has a truly spectacular location with ever-changing views across

Looe Bay. The spacious bedrooms have many thoughtful extras. Add a genuine Cornish welcome, tranquillity and great food, and it's easy to see why guests are drawn back to this special place.

Bay View Farm

Rooms 3 en suite (3 GF) **Facilities** TVL tea/coffee Dinner available Cen ht **Parking** 3 **Notes** ⊗ No Children 5yrs ☺ 56 acres mixed/shire horses

Bucklawren Farm *(SX278540)*

★ ★ ★ ★ FARMHOUSE

St Martin-by-Looe PL13 1NZ
☎ 01503 240738 🖷 01503 240481 **Mrs J Henly**
e-mail: bucklawren@btopenworld.com
web: www.bucklawren.co.uk
dir: *2m NE of Looe. Off B3253 to Monkey Sanctuary, 0.5m right to Bucklawren, farmhouse 0.5m on left*

The spacious 19th-century farmhouse stands in 400 acres of farmland just a mile from the beach. The attractive bedrooms, including one on the ground floor, are well equipped, and the front-facing rooms have spectacular views across fields to the sea. Breakfast is served in the dining room, and tempting home-cooked evening meals are available at the Granary Restaurant, which is in a converted barn.

Rooms 6 en suite 1 annexe rms (1 pri facs) (3 fmly) (1 GF) S £35-£50; D £64-£80 **Facilities** TVL tea/coffee Cen ht Wi-fi ⚓ **Parking** 7 **Notes** LB ⊗ No Children 5yrs Closed Nov-Feb 400 acres arable/beef

Polgover Farm *(SX277586)*

★ ★ ★ ★ FARMHOUSE

Widegates PL13 1PY
☎ 01503 240248
Mrs L Wills
e-mail: enquiries@polgoverfarm.co.uk
dir: *4m NE of Looe. A38 S onto B3251 & B3252, 0.5m on right*

This attractive house stands in peaceful farmland with fine views. The welcoming proprietors ensure guests feel at home. Comfortable bedrooms are tastefully decorated with numerous thoughtful extras, and hearty breakfasts are served in the very pleasant lounge.

Rooms 3 rms (2 en suite) (1 pri facs) D £62-£74* **Facilities** FTV tea/coffee Cen ht Wi-fi **Parking** 9 **Notes** LB ⊗ No Children 12yrs Closed Nov-Feb 93 acres arable/sheep

LOOE *continued*

Polraen Country House

★★★★ 🛏 🍽 GUEST ACCOMMODATION

Sandplace PL13 1PJ
☎ 01503 263956
e-mail: enquiries@polraen.co.uk
web: www.polraen.co.uk
dir: *2m N of Looe at junct A387 & B3254*

This 18th-century stone house, formerly a coaching inn, sits in the peaceful Looe Valley. The charming hosts provide friendly service in a relaxed atmosphere, and the bedrooms and public areas are stylishly co-ordinated and well equipped. The licensed bar, lounge and dining room overlook the garden, and there are facilities for children. The excellent evening meals feature local produce.

Rooms 5 en suite (2 fmly) D £70-£105* **Facilities** FTV TVL tea/coffee Dinner available Cen ht Licensed Wi-fi ch fac Golf 18 **Conf** Max 20 Thtr 16 Class 16 Board 16 **Parking** 20 **Notes** LB ⊗ Closed 23-28 Dec RS Nov-Feb dinner by prior arrangement

Trehaven Manor

★★★★ 🛏 🍽 GUEST ACCOMMODATION

Station Rd PL13 1HN
☎ 01503 262028 📠 01503 265613
e-mail: enquiries@trehavenhotel.co.uk
web: www.trehavenhotel.co.uk
dir: *In East Looe between railway station & bridge. Trehaven's drive adjacent to The Globe PH*

Run by a charming family, the former rectory has a stunning location with magnificent views, and all are particularly well equipped. There is also a cosy lounge bar. Dinner, by arrangement, specialises in Oriental cuisine, and breakfast features traditional fare; the meals are memorable.

Rooms 7 en suite (1 fmly) (1 GF) **Facilities** TVL tea/coffee Dinner available Cen ht Licensed **Parking** 8 **Notes** ⊗

Tremaine Farm *(SX194558)*

★★★★ FARMHOUSE

Pelynt PL13 2LT
☎ 01503 220417 📠 01503 220417
Mrs R Philp
e-mail: tremainefarm@tiscali.co.uk
web: www.tremainefarm.co.uk
dir: *5m NW of Looe. B3359 N from Pelynt, left at x-rds*

Convenient for Fowey, Looe and Polperro, this pleasant working farm offers a comfortable stay. The proprietors provide friendly hospitality and attentive service, and the spacious bedrooms are well equipped with impressive bathrooms. A hearty breakfast is served in the dining room and there is a particularly pleasant guest lounge.

Rooms 2 rms (1 en suite) (1 pri facs) (1 fmly) **Facilities** FTV TVL tea/coffee Cen ht Wi-fi **Parking** 6 **Notes** LB ⊗ ⊛ 300 acres arable/sheep/potatoes

Coombe Farm

★★★★ GUEST ACCOMMODATION

Widegates PL13 1QN
☎ 01503 240223
e-mail: coombe_farm@hotmail.com
web: www.coombefarmhotel.co.uk
dir: *3.5m E of Looe on B3253 just S of Widegates*

Set in ten acres of grounds and gardens, Coombe Farm has a friendly atmosphere. The bedrooms are in a converted stone barn, and are comfortable and spacious. Each has a dining area, with breakfast delivered to your room.

Rooms 3 annexe en suite (1 fmly) (3 GF) **Facilities** STV FTV tea/coffee Direct Dial ⤳ Golf 18 **Parking** 20 **Notes** Closed 15 Dec-5 Jan

Down Ende Country House

★★★★ 🍽 GUEST ACCOMMODATION

Widegates PL13 1QN
☎ 01503 240213 📠 01503 240213
e-mail: teresa@downende.com
web: www.downende.com
dir: *A374 towards Looe, right A387 road becomes B3253 on left after Coombe Farm*

Set in its own grounds, guests are assured of a warm welcome at this young family's home. Bedrooms are comfortable and well equipped, the majority overlooking the gardens, to the front of the property. Home-cooked evening meals are a highlight and use the best of local produce, prepared with care and skill.

Rooms 7 en suite 1 annexe en suite (1 fmly) (2 GF) **Facilities** tea/coffee Dinner available Cen ht Licensed Wi-fi Golf 18 **Conf** Max 20 **Parking** 9 **Notes** ⊗

Shutta House

★★★★ GUEST ACCOMMODATION

Shutta PL13 1LS
☎ 01503 264233
e-mail: enquiries@shuttahouse.co.uk
web: www.shuttahouse.co.uk
dir: *From A58 Liskeard, follow A387 to Looe, opposite railway station*

This fine Victorian house was once the vicarage and has been sympathetically refurbished by the owners to create appealing and contemporary accommodation. All the bedrooms offer high standards of comfort with elegant styling and original character. Breakfasts, served in the light and airy dining room, utilise locally-sourced produce whenever possible. Guests are also welcome to use the garden which overlooks the East Looe River.

Rooms 3 en suite S £38-£65; D £56-£85* **Facilities** FTV tea/coffee Cen ht Wi-fi **Conf** Max 6 Thtr 6 Class 6 Board 6 **Parking** 1 **Notes** ⊗ No Children 11yrs

Woodlands

★★★★ GUEST HOUSE

St Martins Rd PL13 1LP
☎ 01503 264405
e-mail: lundyfishlock@googlemail.com
web: www.looedirectory.co.uk/woodlands.htm
dir: *On B3253, after Looe sign, St Martin's church on right. 1m further on left*

The charming Victorian country house looks over woodland and the Looe estuary, and is within walking distance of the harbour and beaches. The cosy bedrooms are well equipped, and public rooms include a lounge and the elegant dining room where breakfast is served.

Rooms 4 en suite (2 fmly) D £60-£80 **Facilities** FTV tea/coffee Dinner available Cen ht Licensed **Parking** 6 **Notes** LB ⊗ No Children 7yrs Closed Dec-Jan

Little Harbour

★★★ GUEST HOUSE

Church St PL13 2EX
☎ 01503 262474
e-mail: littleharbour@btinternet.com
web: www.looedirectory.co.uk
dir: *From harbour West Looe, right into Princess Sq, guest house on left*

Little Harbour is situated almost on Looe's harbourside in the historic old town; it has a pleasant and convenient location and parking is available. The proprietors are friendly and attentive and bedrooms are well appointed and attractively decorated. Breakfast is served freshly cooked in the dining room.

Rooms 5 en suite (1 fmly) **Facilities** FTV tea/coffee Cen ht Wi-fi **Parking** 3 **Notes** LB No Children 12yrs

The Old Malt House

★★★ BED AND BREAKFAST

West Looe Hill PL13 2HE
☎ 01503 264976
e-mail: stay@oldmalthouselooe.com
web: www.oldmalthouselooe.com
dir: *A387 to Looe, 1st left after bridge, right behind fire station, 100yds on left*

A short, level stroll from the harbour front, the Old Malt House dates back to 1650 and is very conveniently situated for all of Looe's amenities. The cosy bedrooms are well equipped and are approached via an external stone staircase, while a hearty breakfast using local produce is served in the ground floor dining room.

Rooms 3 en suite S £50; D £50-£60* **Facilities** FTV tea/coffee Cen ht Wi-fi **Parking** 3 **Notes** LB ⊗ No Children

St Johns Court

★★★ BED AND BREAKFAST

East Cliff PL13 1DE
☎ 01503 263792
e-mail: stay@stjohnscourtlooe.co.uk
dir: *300yds S of Looe bridge. Through Fore St, left at Ship Inn, 200yds on left*

With stunning views over Looe, the estuary and the beach, this late Victorian, stone-built property offers comfortable accommodation. Guests are assured of a very friendly, relaxed and informal atmosphere, along with a hearty breakfast each morning.

Rooms 3 en suite D £65-£80* **Facilities** FTV TVL tea/coffee Cen ht Wi-fi Golf 18 **Parking** 2 **Notes** LB ⊗ ☺

The Ship Inn

★★★ INN

Fore St PL13 1AD
☎ 01503 263124   ▤ 01503 263624
e-mail: reservations@smallandfriendly.co.uk
web: www.smallandfriendly.co.uk

This lively family pub is located in the very heart of bustling East Looe and has a local following. The bedrooms are comfortable and equipped with all the expected facilities. A wide range of popular dishes is served at lunch times and during the evenings, with light refreshments available throughout the day.

Rooms 8 en suite (1 fmly) **Facilities** FTV tea/coffee Dinner available Cen ht Wi-fi Pool table **Notes** LB

LOSTWITHIEL	Map 2 SX15

Penrose B&B

★★★★ GUEST ACCOMMODATION

1 The Terrace PL22 0DT
☎ 01208 871417   & 07766 900179   ▤ 01208 871101
e-mail: enquiries@penrosebb.co.uk
web: www.penrosebb.co.uk
dir: *A390 Edgcumbe Rd, Lostwithiel onto Scrations Ln, 1st right for parking*

Just a short walk from the town centre, this grand Victorian house offers comfortable accommodation and a genuine homely atmosphere. Many of the bedrooms have the original fireplaces and all are equipped with thoughtful extras. Breakfast is a generous offering and is served in the elegant dining room, with views over the garden. Wi-fi access is also available.

Rooms 7 en suite (3 fmly) (2 GF) D £40-£100 **Facilities** FTV TVL tea/coffee Cen ht Wi-fi **Parking** 8 **Notes** LB ☺

Hartswell Farm (SX119597)

★★★ FARMHOUSE

St Winnow PL22 0RB
☎ 01208 873419   ▤ 01208 873419
Mrs W Jordan
e-mail: hartswell@connexions.co.uk
web: www.connexions.co.uk/hartswell
dir: *1m E of Lostwithiel. S off A390 at Downend Garage, farm 0.25m up hill on left*

This 17th-century farmhouse has a wonderfully peaceful setting, and offers generous hospitality and a homely atmosphere. The cosy bedrooms look across rolling countryside, and breakfast includes tasty eggs fresh from the farm. A self-catering barn conversion is available, one with the Access Exceptional award. Hartswell Farm boasts a small herd of Red Poll cattle.

Rooms 2 rms (1 en suite) (1 pri facs) S £35-£45; D £56-£76* **Facilities** STV TVL TV1B tea/coffee Cen ht Wi-fi Sailing days for 5 night stays **Parking** 3 **Notes** LB ⊗ No Children 6yrs ☺ 52 acres rare breed cattle

MARAZION	Map 2 SW53

Godolphin Arms

★★★★ INN

TR17 0EN
☎ 01736 710202
e-mail: enquiries@godolphinarms.co.uk
dir: *From A30 follow Marazion signs for 1m to B&B. At end of causeway to St Michael's Mount*

A traditional inn overlooking St Michael's Mount and beyond, The Godolphin Arms is the heart of the community and caters for all ages. Bedrooms are stylish, modern, and appointed in pale colours. The staff are friendly. Food is served daily, and there are often special themed evenings. There's good reserved parking for guests.

Rooms 10 en suite (2 fmly) (2 GF) D £90-£180* **Facilities** STV tea/coffee Dinner available Direct Dial Cen ht Wi-fi Pool table **Parking** 10 **Notes** No coaches Civ Wed 60

MARAZION *continued*

Blue Horizon

★ ★ ★ GUEST ACCOMMODATION

Fore St TR17 0AW
☎ 01736 711199
e-mail: holidaybreaksmarazion@freeola.com
web: www.holidaybreaksmarazion.co.uk
dir: *E end of village centre*

Located in the heart of this market town, the rear of this establishment is almost at the water's edge and offers superb views of the sea from its garden, some of the bedrooms and the breakfast room. The atmosphere is laid back and relaxed. There are a number of additional facilities available (charged), including a laundry room, sauna cabin and barbeque facilities. Ample parking is also available.

Rooms 6 rms (5 en suite) (1 pri facs) (2 GF) S £38; D £65-£75* **Facilities** FTV TVL tea/coffee Wi-fi Sauna Hot tub, bike hire **Parking** 7 **Notes** LB ⊗ Closed Nov-mid Feb

Glenleigh

★ ★ ★ GUEST HOUSE

Higher Fore St TR17 0BQ
☎ 01736 710308
e-mail: info@marazionhotels.com
dir: *Off A394 to Penzance, opp Fire Engine Inn*

This proud granite house has an elevated position with wonderful views towards St Michael's Mount. The welcoming proprietors have owned this house for more than 30 years and many guests return. Dinners, by arrangement, are served in the comfortable dining room and feature fresh local produce where possible.

Rooms 9 en suite (1 fmly) (1 GF) S £36-£37; D £72-£74* **Facilities** FTV TVL tea/coffee Dinner available Cen ht Licensed Wi-fi **Parking** 9 **Notes** LB ⊗ No Children 3yrs Closed Nov-Mar ⊖

MEVAGISSEY	Map 2 SX04

Kerryanna Country House

★ ★ ★ ★ BED AND BREAKFAST

Treleaven Farm, Valley Rd PL26 6SA
☎ 01726 843558 📠 01726 843558
e-mail: enquiries@kerryanna.co.uk
dir: *B3273 St Austell to Mevagissey road, right at bottom of hill, next to playground*

Located on the peaceful outskirts of this fishing village, Kerryanna stands in two acres of gardens and looks across the countryside to the sea. The attractive bedrooms are comfortably furnished. There are three cosy lounges and a swimming pool.

Rooms 3 en suite D £72-£74* **Facilities** FTV tea/coffee Cen ht ⟋ **Parking** 6 **Notes** LB ⊗ No Children 15yrs Closed Oct-Apr ⊖

Headlands

★ ★ ★ GUEST ACCOMMODATION

Polkirt Hill PL26 6UX
☎ 01726 843453
e-mail: headlandshotel@talk21.com
dir: *One-way through village & ascend towards Port Mellon, Headlands on right*

Set on an elevated position with spectacular views over the bay, this family-run establishment offers friendly service and comfortable accommodation. The colourful bedrooms are well equipped, with many having sea views. Public rooms include a stylish lounge bar and dining room.

Rooms 14 rms (12 en suite) (1 fmly) (4 GF) **Facilities** FTV tea/coffee Cen ht Licensed **Parking** 10 **Notes** ⊗ Closed Dec-Jan

MITCHELL	Map 2 SW85

The Plume of Feathers

★ ★ ★ ★ INN

TR8 5AX
☎ 01872 510387 & 511122 📠 01872 511124
e-mail: enquiries@theplume.info
dir: *Just off A30 & A3076, follow signs*

A very popular inn with origins dating back to the 16th century, situated close to Newquay and the beaches. The restaurant offers a varied menu which relies heavily on local produce. The stylish bedrooms are decorated in neutral colours and have wrought-iron beds with quality linens. The garden makes an ideal place to enjoy a meal or a Cornish tea. The staff are very friendly.

Rooms 7 annexe en suite (1 fmly) (5 GF) S £60-£90; D £80-£120* **Facilities** FTV tea/coffee Dinner available Cen ht Wi-fi **Parking** 40 **Notes** LB No coaches

MORWENSTOW	Map 2 SS21

West Point B&B

★ ★ ★ ★ BED AND BREAKFAST

West Point, Crimp EX23 9PB
☎ 01288 331594
e-mail: bramhill@supanet.com
dir: *Take A361 to Barnstaple onto A39 towards Bude. 7m past Clovelly rdbt on right*

Ideally placed for exploring the beautiful countryside and coasts of north Cornwall and north Devon, this smartly

appointed establishment is surrounded by colourful gardens with far-reaching views to the rear. Guests are assured of a genuine welcome plus the freedom of all-day access. Both bedrooms are comfortable, light and airy; one has a four-poster bed and patio doors leading to the garden. Additional facilities include a guest lounge and dining room where local farm produce is on offer whenever possible.

Rooms 2 en suite (1 fmly) (2 GF) S £35; D £60 **Facilities** FTV TVL tea/coffee Cen ht **Parking** 4 **Notes** LB ⊗ Closed 22 Dec-2 Jan ⊖

MOUSEHOLE	Map 2 SW42

The Cornish Range Restaurant with Rooms

★ ★ ★ ★ ⊛ RESTAURANT WITH ROOMS

6 Chapel St TR19 6BD
☎ 01736 731488
e-mail: info@cornishrange.co.uk
dir: *From Penzance take B3315, through Newlyn to Mousehole. Along harbour, past Ship Inn, sharp right, left, establishment on right*

This is a memorable place to eat and stay. Stylish rooms, with delightful Cornish home-made furnishings, and attentive, friendly service create a relaxing environment. Interesting and accurate cuisine relies heavily on freshly-landed, local fish and shellfish, as well as local meat and poultry, and the freshest fruit and vegetables.

Rooms 3 en suite D £65-£110* **Facilities** FTV tea/coffee Dinner available Cen ht Wi-fi **Notes** ⊗ RS evenings only in winter months No coaches

MULLION	Map 2 SW61

Colvennor Farmhouse

★ ★ ★ ★ BED AND BREAKFAST

Cury TR12 7BJ
☎ 01326 241208 📠 01326 241208
e-mail: colvennor@btinternet.com
web: www.colvennorfarmhouse.com
dir: *A3083 (Helston-Lizard), over rdbt at end of airfield, next right to Cury/Poldhu Cove, farm 1.4m on right at top of hill*

Peacefully located, this Grade II listed former farmhouse is a wonderfully relaxing base from which to explore the picturesque delights of The Lizard. Parts of the house date back to the 17th century, but fortunately modern comforts are now in place with bedrooms and bathrooms offering high levels of quality and character. Breakfast utilises excellent local produce and is served in the attractive dining room. Guests also have a lovely lounge at their disposal that has a log burner to keep the chill off in cooler months; there is also a large garden.

Rooms 3 en suite (1 GF) S £45-£47; D £64-£70* **Facilities** FTV TVL tea/coffee Cen ht Wi-fi **Parking** 3 **Notes** ⊗ No Children 10yrs

NEWQUAY Map 2 SW86

Dewolf Guest House

★★★★ GUEST HOUSE

100 Henver Rd TR7 3BL
☎ 01637 874746
e-mail: holidays@dewolfguesthouse.com
dir: *A392 onto A3058 at Quintrell Downs rdbt, guest house on left just past mini-rdbts*

Making guests feel welcome and at home is the priority here. The bedrooms in the main house are bright and well equipped, and there are two more in a separate single storey building at the rear. The cosy lounge has pictures and items that reflect the host's interest in wildlife. The guest house is just a short walk from Porth Beach.

Rooms 4 en suite 2 annexe en suite (1 fmly) (3 GF) S £35-£45; D £60-£80* **Facilities** FTV tea/coffee Cen ht Licensed **Parking** 6 **Notes** LB

Fairview House

★★★★ GUEST HOUSE

2 Fairview Ter TR7 1RJ
☎ 01637 871179 & 07968 680957
e-mail: lindasheppsh@aol.com
dir: *From A30 exit at Newquay onto A392. Right onto Trevemper Rd. At rdbt turn left. At top of hill right at lights, left onto Fairview Terrace. Continue to bottom of road, house on left*

This very friendly guest house is conveniently located for access to the town centre, beaches and other amenities. It provides soundly maintained modern bedrooms and facilities include a lounge and bar.

Rooms 5 rms (3 en suite) (2 fmly) (1 GF) **Facilities** FTV tea/coffee Cen ht Licensed **Notes** ⊗ 🅴

Windward

★★★★ GUEST ACCOMMODATION

Alexandra Rd, Porth Bay TR7 3NB
☎ 01637 873185 📠 01637 851400
e-mail: enquiries@windwardhotel.co.uk
dir: *1.5m NE of town centre. A3508 towards Newquay, right onto B3276 Padstow road, 1m on right*

Windward is pleasantly located almost on Porth Beach and is convenient for the airport. It offers spectacular views, friendly hospitality, and a pleasant bar and terrace for relaxing. The spacious bedrooms, some with balcony, and many with sea views, are well equipped, and breakfast is served in the restaurant overlooking the beach.

Rooms 13 en suite (3 fmly) (3 GF) **Facilities** FTV TVL tea/coffee Dinner available Cen ht Licensed Wi-fi **Conf** Max 30 Thtr 30 Class 30 Board 30 **Parking** 15 **Notes** ⊗

Meadow View

★★★ GUEST ACCOMMODATION

135 Mount Wise TR7 1QR
☎ 01637 873132
e-mail: meadowview135@hotmail.com
web: www.meadowviewnewquay.co.uk
dir: *A392 into Newquay to Mountwise, Meadow View on left before rdbt to Pentire*

Expect a warm welcome at this detached property which is ideally located just a short walk from Newquay, and the famous Fistral Beach which is renowned for surfing. Waterworld, the Eden Project, and the Pentire Peninsular with its rolling green coastline are all just a short drive away. The bedrooms are comfortable and some have countryside views. A hearty breakfast is served in the pleasant dining room and there is a cosy sun lounge to relax in.

Rooms 7 en suite (2 fmly) D £60* **Facilities** tea/coffee Cen ht **Parking** 7 **Notes** LB ⊗ No Children 5yrs Closed 7 Nov-mid Feb 🅴

The Three Tees

★★★ GUEST ACCOMMODATION

21 Carminow Way TR7 3AY
☎ 01637 872055 📠 01637 872055
e-mail: greg@3tees.co.uk
web: www.3tees.co.uk
dir: *A30 onto A392 Newquay. Right at Quintrell Downs rdbt signed Porth, over x-rds & 3rd right*

Located in a quiet residential area just a short walk from the town and beach, this friendly family-run accommodation is comfortable and well equipped. There is a lounge, bar and a sun lounge for the use of guests. Breakfast is served in the dining room, where snacks are available throughout the day; the bar serves light snacks in the evenings.

Rooms 8 rms (7 en suite) (1 pri facs) 1 annexe en suite (4 fmly) (2 GF) D £60-£74* **Facilities** FTV TVL tea/coffee Cen ht Licensed Wi-fi **Parking** 11 **Notes** LB Closed Nov-Feb

Tregarthen Guest House

★★★ GUEST ACCOMMODATION

1 Arundel Way TR7 3BB
☎ 01637 873554 📠 01637 873554
e-mail: info@tregarthen.co.uk
web: www.tregarthen.co.uk
dir: *From A30 onto A392, at Quintrell onto A3058 Henver Rd, Arundel Way 4th right*

Located in a quiet residential area just a short walk from the beaches and town centre of Newquay. The owners of this delightful detached property provide warm hospitality along with comfortable accommodation which is smartly furnished and well-equipped. Evening meals can be provided by arrangement, and the hearty breakfast is served at individual tables in the spacious ground floor dining room. There is also a cosy lounge where guests can sit and relax. Parking is ample.

Rooms 5 en suite 2 annexe en suite (1 fmly) (6 GF) D £50-£75 **Facilities** FTV tea/coffee Dinner available Cen ht Wi-fi **Parking** 7 **Notes** LB ⊗ Closed Xmas RS Nov-Apr No evening meal

Wenden

★★★ GUEST HOUSE

11 Berry Rd TR7 1AU
☎ 01637 872604 📠 01637 872604
e-mail: wenden@newquay-holidays.co.uk
web: www.newquay-holidays.co.uk
dir: *In town centre off seafront Cliff Rd, near station*

The family-run guest house offers bright, modern accommodation near the beach and the town centre. Bedrooms have been carefully designed to make best use of space, and each is individually styled. Breakfast, served in the stylish dining room, is a filling start to the day.

Rooms 7 en suite D £55-£75* **Facilities** FTV tea/coffee Cen ht Wi-fi **Parking** 7 **Notes** LB ⊗ No Children 16yrs Closed 1wk Xmas RS Nov-Feb 2 nights stay minimum

Avalon

★★★ GUEST ACCOMMODATION

4 Edgcumbe Gardens TR7 2QD
☎ 01637 877522
e-mail: enquiries@avalonnewquay.co.uk
dir: *A30 at Quintrell Downs rdbt turn right onto A3058 signed St Columb Minor. After 1m turn left opposite Rocklands*

Conveniently situated within walking distance of the town centre and the beaches, Avalon provides comfortable accommodation. Located in a quiet, residential area, with the benefit of on-site parking, guests may enjoy the front-facing sun terrace during the summer months. Golfing holiday offers are available.

Rooms 6 rms (5 en suite) (1 pri facs) (1 fmly) S £25-£35; D £50-£70* **Facilities** FTV tea/coffee Wi-fi **Parking** 6 **Notes** LB

NEWQUAY *continued*

Copper Beech

★★★ GUEST HOUSE

70 Edgcumbe Av TR7 2NN
☎ **01637 873376**
e-mail: info@copperbeechnewquay.co.uk
web: www.copperbeechnewquay.co.uk
dir: *Exit A30 signed RAF St Mawgan, at rdbt take A3059 exit 6m. Right at T-junct, left at 1st mini-rdbt, straight over 2nd. 3rd on right opp tennis courts*

Set amidst pleasant gardens, Copper Beech is located in a peaceful area of the town opposite Trenance Gardens. Bedrooms are light and airy, with ground floor rooms available. Comprehensive breakfasts are served in an attractive dining room and a warm welcome is assured.

Rooms 13 en suite (2 fmly) (3 GF) S £33-£45; D £60-£70
Facilities FTV TVL tea/coffee Cen ht Licensed Wi-fi
Parking 13 **Notes** LB ⊗

The Croft

★★★ GUEST ACCOMMODATION

37 Mount Wise TR7 2BL
☎ **01637 871520** ▤ **01637 871520**
e-mail: info@the-crofthotel.co.uk
web: www.the-crofthotel.co.uk
dir: *In town centre nr Towan Beach, junct Mount Wise & Mayfield Rd*

Located just minutes away from the town centre and beach, this establishment is comfortable and the friendly hosts create a homely atmosphere. A full English breakfast is served in the informal bar-dining room.

Rooms 8 rms (6 en suite) (2 pri facs) (4 fmly)
Facilities FTV tea/coffee Cen ht Licensed **Parking** 7
Notes LB ⊗

Milber Guest House

★★★ GUEST HOUSE

11 Michell Av TR7 1BN
☎ **01637 872825**
e-mail: suemilber@aol.com
dir: *A392 Newquay straight ahead at Quintrell rdbt to Henver Rd/Berry Rd. Turn right onto Mount Wise, 2nd right to Michell Av*

This small and friendly guest house is situated in the centre of Newquay. Bedrooms are comfortable and offer lots of useful facilities. The bar is open most reasonable times, and guests get their own keys so they can come and go as they please.

Rooms 6 rms (4 en suite) (6 fmly) (1 GF) S £25-£35; D £40-£60* **Facilities** FTV tea/coffee Cen ht Licensed
Notes LB ⊗ 🐾

Pencrebar

★★★ GUEST ACCOMMODATION

4 Berry Rd TR7 1AT
☎ **01637 872037**
e-mail: enquiries@pencrebar.com
web: www.pencrebar.com
dir: *A30 onto A392, then right at boating lake on entering Newquay*

This friendly family-run house is a short walk from Newquay's popular beaches and the town centre. Bedrooms are all spacious and well planned. Delicious breakfasts are served in the attractive dining room. Secure car parking is available for guests.

Rooms 7 en suite (2 fmly) S £28-£35; D £48-£60*
Facilities FTV tea/coffee Cen ht Wi-fi Off site parking - charged all year **Notes** LB ⊗

Porth Lodge

★★★ GUEST ACCOMMODATION

Porth Bean Rd TR7 3LT
☎ **01637 874483**
e-mail: info@porthlodgehotel.co.uk

A popular venue with its own bowling alley. The property has recently been totally refurbished to provide bedrooms that are even more comfortable and well equipped. Food is served daily and the team are friendly and helpful.

Rooms 16 en suite (1 fmly) **Facilities** FTV tea/coffee Dinner available Cen ht Licensed Wi-fi Golf 18 Pool table Ten pin bowling alley **Conf** Thtr 40 Class 30 Board 20
Parking 20

Rolling Waves

★★★ GUEST HOUSE

Alexandra Rd, Porth TR7 3NB
☎ **01637 873236** ▤ **01637 873236**
e-mail: enquiries@rollingwaves.co.uk
dir: *A30 onto A392, A3058 towards Newquay, then B3276 to Porth, pass Mermaid public house*

A family owned and run guest house with great views across the bay. Rooms are comfortable, the hosts friendly and welcoming, and dinner is available on request.

Rooms 7 rms (6 en suite) (1 pri facs) (2 fmly) (3 GF) S £28-£36; D £56-£72* **Facilities** FTV TVL tea/coffee Dinner available Cen ht Licensed **Parking** 7 **Notes** LB ⊗

St Breca

★★★ GUEST HOUSE

22 Mount Wise TR7 2BG
☎ **01637 872745**
e-mail: enquiries@stbreca.co.uk
dir: *A30 onto A392. Follow signs to Newquay, then to Mount Wise*

This friendly guest house is conveniently located a few minutes walk from the town centre, beaches and other amenities. It provides soundly maintained, modern bedrooms and separate tables are provided in the attractive breakfast room.

Rooms 10 rms (8 en suite) (2 pri facs) (3 fmly) (2 GF)
Facilities tea/coffee Cen ht **Parking** 8 **Notes** ⊗

The Silver Jubilee

★★★ GUEST HOUSE

13 Berry Rd TR7 1AU
☎ **01637 874544** & **07779 518484**
e-mail: andrew.hatton@talktalk.net
dir: *Follow A3058 into Newquay. After railway station, left at lights, 3rd house on left*

Silver Jubilee is a small establishment situated on the level in the heart of Newquay. All amenities including shopping centre and beaches are about three minutes' walk away. Breakfast (and dinner Easter to September) are served in the dining room. There is also a bar/lounge for a pre-dinner drink or post-meal relaxation.

Rooms 7 en suite (3 fmly) S £35-£50; D £50-£80*
Facilities FTV tea/coffee Dinner available Cen ht Licensed Wi-fi **Parking** 4 **Notes** LB ⊗

Summer Breeze

★★★ GUEST HOUSE

20 Mount Wise TR7 2BG
☎ **01637 871518** & **07800 584681**
e-mail: summer-breeze@sky.com
web: www.summer-breeze.info
dir: *A30 onto A392 signed to Newquay, turn right at Pentire rdbt, 0.5m on left*

Guests are assured of a warm welcome at this centrally located guest house; just a couple of minutes from the town centre and not much further from the beaches. Bedrooms are neatly furnished and decorated, all equipped with modern facilities. Freshly cooked, hearty breakfasts are served each morning in the sunny breakfast room; prior notice is appreciated for the vegetarian option.

Rooms 6 en suite (3 fmly) (1 GF) D £50-£80*
Facilities FTV tea/coffee Cen ht Wi-fi **Parking** 4 **Notes** LB ⊗

Tir Chonaill

★★★ GUEST ACCOMMODATION

106 Mount Wise TR7 1QP
☎ 01637 876492
e-mail: tirchonailhotel@talk21.com
web: www.tirchonaill.co.uk
dir: A392 into Newquay, last rdbt right onto Mount Wise, signed

Expect a warm welcome at the long-established and family-owned Tir Chonaill, situated close to the beaches and the town centre. Some of the neat bedrooms have wonderful views across town to the sea, and the hearty breakfasts are sure to satisfy.

Rooms 9 en suite (9 fmly) (1 GF) S £35-£50; D £65-£95
Facilities FTV TVL tea/coffee Cen ht Wi-fi Golf 18
Parking 10 **Notes** LB

PADSTOW	Map 2 SW97

PREMIER COLLECTION

The Seafood Restaurant

★★★★★ ◉◉◉ RESTAURANT WITH ROOMS

Riverside PL28 8BY
☎ 01841 532700 📠 01841 532942
e-mail: reservations@rickstein.com
dir: Into town centre down hill, follow round sharp bend, restaurant on left

Food lovers continue to beat a well-trodden path to this legendary establishment. Situated on the edge of the harbour, just a stone's throw from the shops, the Seafood Restaurant offers stylish and comfortable bedrooms that boast numerous thoughtful extras; some have views of the estuary and a couple have stunning private balconies. Service is relaxed and friendly; booking is essential for both accommodation and a table in the restaurant.

Rooms 14 en suite 6 annexe en suite (6 fmly) (3 GF)
Facilities FTV tea/coffee Dinner available Direct Dial Cen ht Lift Wi-fi Cookery School **Parking** 12 **Notes** LB Closed 24-26 Dec RS 1 May restaurant closed No coaches

The Old Mill House

★★★★ 🏠 GUEST HOUSE

PL27 7QT
☎ 01841 540388 📠 01841 540406
e-mail: enquiries@theoldmillhouse.com
web: www.theoldmillhouse.com
dir: 2m S of Padstow. In centre of Little Petherick on A389

Situated in an Area of Outstanding Natural Beauty, the Old Mill House is a 16th-century corn mill with attractive secluded gardens beside a gentle stream. Guests enjoy an English breakfast in the room where the mill wheel still turns.

Rooms 7 en suite S £80-£120; D £80-£120*
Facilities FTV TVL tea/coffee Direct Dial Cen ht Licensed **Parking** 20 **Notes** ⊗ No Children 14yrs Closed Nov-Feb

Penjoly Guest House

★★★★ 🏠 GUEST HOUSE

Padstow Rd PL28 8LB
☎ 01841 533535 📠 01841 533535
e-mail: penjoly.padstow@btopenworld.com
dir: 1m S of Padstow. Off A389 near Padstow Holiday Park

A very professionally run establishment, where attention to detail and quality are noteworthy throughout. Bedrooms are delightfully decorated and complemented by an impressive range of extras. Breakfast is served in the attractive breakfast room or in the conservatory, and a guest lounge is also available. This is a perfect base for exploring the West Country's delights, and for seeking out the gastronomic restaurants of Cornwall. Guests have the convenience of off-road parking.

Rooms 3 en suite (3 GF) S £72.90-£81; D £81-£90*
Facilities STV FTV TVL tea/coffee Cen ht Wi-fi **Parking** 10 **Notes** ⊗ No Children 16yrs 🐾

Rick Stein's Café

★★★★ BED AND BREAKFAST

10 Middle St PL28 8AP
☎ 01841 532700 📠 01841 532942
e-mail: reservations@rickstein.com
dir: A389 into town, one way past church, 3rd right

Another Rick Stein success story, this lively café by day, restaurant by night, offers good food, quality accommodation, and is just a short walk from the harbour. Three bedrooms are available - each is quite different but have high standards of cosseting comfort. Friendly and personable staff complete the picture.

Rooms 3 en suite (1 fmly) D £97-£145* **Facilities** tea/coffee Dinner available Cen ht Licensed **Notes** LB Closed 1 May BH RS 24-26 Dec

Roselyn

★★★★ BED AND BREAKFAST

20 Grenville Rd PL28 8EX
☎ 01841 532756
e-mail: padstowbbroselyn@bushinternet.com
web: www.padstowbbroselyn.co.uk
dir: After blue 'Welcome to Padstow' sign, Grenville Rd 1st left

This charming small establishment is in a quiet residential area just a 10-minute walk from the centre of the delightful fishing port. Guests are assured of warm hospitality, and smartly furnished, well-equipped bedrooms. A good choice of breakfast options is available.

Rooms 3 en suite S £50-£70; D £70-£80* **Facilities** FTV tea/coffee Cen ht Wi-fi **Parking** 4 **Notes** LB ⊗ Closed Xmas & New Year

Treravel House

★★★★ BED AND BREAKFAST

PL28 8LB
☎ 01841 532931
e-mail: mandytreravel@tiscali.co.uk

Located just a few minutes outside Padstow, Treravel House provides rooms that are light and well furnished. Breakfast uses the house's own free-range eggs and is served in the bright breakfast room. Mandy Eddy provides a very warm welcome to all her guests and a pleasant stay is assured.

Rooms 3 en suite **Facilities** FTV tea/coffee Cen ht Wi-fi **Parking** 6 **Notes** ⊗ No Children 10yrs 🐾

Little Pentyre

★★ BED AND BREAKFAST

6 Moyle Rd PL28 8DG
☎ 01841 532246
e-mail: JujuLloyd@aol.com
dir: From A389, right onto Dennis Rd, bear right onto Moyle Rd

Within easy, level walking distance of the town centre, Little Pentyre is situated in a quiet residential area, adjacent to the Camel Estuary and Trail. The comfortable bedrooms are well equipped and guests enjoy a freshly cooked breakfast, featuring eggs from the hens in the rear garden.

Rooms 2 en suite (2 GF) S fr £30; D £55 **Facilities** FTV tea/coffee Cen ht **Parking** 2 **Notes** No Children 10yrs 🐾

PADSTOW *continued*

Wingfield House

★★ BED AND BREAKFAST

Dennis Ln PL28 8DP
☎ 01841 532617
e-mail: bedsidetheseaside@btinternet.com
dir: *Into Padstow on A389, 1st right onto Sarah's Ln. At bottom of hill, turn right onto Dennis Ln, 3rd entrance on right*

A very friendly, traditional bed and breakfast a few minutes' walk from Padstow town centre. The comfortable bedrooms are well appointed and have shared facilities. Hearty breakfasts are served at a large table in the dining room, and guests have the use of a TV lounge. There is off-road parking.

Rooms 3 rms (1 pri facs) (2 fmly) S £30-£37; D £60-£75*
Facilities FTV TVL tea/coffee Cen ht Wi-fi ch fac
Parking 5 **Notes** LB ⌖

| PAR | Map 2 SX05 |

Elmswood House

★★★★ GUEST ACCOMMODATION

73 Tehidy Rd, Tywardreath PL24 2QD
☎ 01726 814221
e-mail: enquiries@elmswoodhousehotel.co.uk
web: www.elmswoodhousehotel.co.uk
dir: *Right from Par station, then 1st left to top of hill, opp village church*

Elmswood is a fine Victorian house set in the middle of the village opposite the church, and many guests return for the warm welcome. Bedrooms have quality furnishings and many extra facilities, and the attractive dining room, lounge and bar overlook a beautiful garden.

Rooms 6 en suite (1 fmly) (1 GF) D £65-£80*
Facilities FTV TVL tea/coffee Cen ht Licensed Wi-fi
Parking 7 **Notes** ⌖ No Children 10yrs Closed Jan

The Royal Inn

★★★★ INN

66 Eastcliffe Rd, Tywardreath PL24 2AJ
☎ 01726 815601 ▤ 01726 816415
e-mail: info@royal-inn.co.uk
dir: *Adjacent to Par railway station*

Situated the local rail station, on the edge of Tywardreath, this free house provides high standards of comfort and quality. Only five minutes from Par Sands and four miles from the Eden Project, this is an ideal base for exploring Cornwall. The open-plan bar area has slate floors and a large open fire; the atmosphere is relaxed and diners can choose from the bar menu or can dine more formally in the restaurant or conservatory. All bedrooms have en suite facilities, along with TV, clock radio, direct-dial telephone, hairdryer and refreshment tray. All twin rooms have sofa beds (suitable for children under 14), and the family suite is suitable for families of 4 or 5.

Rooms 15 en suite (8 fmly) (4 GF) S fr £50; D fr £65*
Facilities STV FTV tea/coffee Dinner available Direct Dial Cen ht Wi-fi Golf Pool table **Conf** Max 20 Thtr 8 Class 8 Board 20 **Parking** 17 **Notes** LB Closed 23-26 Dec & 30 Dec-1 Jan

---

| PENZANCE | Map 2 SW43 |

Camilla House

★★★★★ GUEST HOUSE

12 Regent Ter TR18 4DW
☎ 01736 363771 ▤ 01736 363771
e-mail: enquiries@camillahouse.co.uk
web: www.camillahouse.co.uk
dir: *A30 to Penzance, at rail station follow road along harbour front onto Promenade Rd. Opp Jubilee Bathing Pool, Regent Ter 2nd right*

The friendly proprietors at this attractive Grade II listed terrace house do their utmost to ensure a comfortable stay. Wi-fi access is available throughout the house, and there is also access to computers in the lounge. Bedrooms and bathrooms are attractive, providing many added extras. Some bedrooms and the dining room provide delightful sea views.

Rooms 8 rms (7 en suite) (1 pri facs) (1 GF) S £35-£38.50; D £65-£89* **Facilities** FTV TVL tea/coffee Dinner available Cen ht Licensed Wi-fi **Parking** 6 **Notes** LB ⌖

Ennys

★★★★★ GUEST ACCOMMODATION

Trewhella Ln TR20 9BZ
☎ 01736 740262 ▤ 01736 740055
e-mail: ennys@ennys.co.uk
web: www.ennys.co.uk

(For full entry see St Hilary)

The Summer House

★★★★★ ⌖ ⌖ GUEST ACCOMMODATION

Cornwall Ter TR18 4HL
☎ 01736 363744 ▤ 01736 360959
e-mail: reception@summerhouse-cornwall.com
web: www.summerhouse-cornwall.com
dir: *A30 to Penzance, at rail station follow along harbour onto Promenade, pass Jubilee Pool, right after Queens Hotel. Summer House 30yds on left*

This house, in a delightful residential location close to the seafront and harbour, is decorated in a Mediterranean style. The walled garden also reflects the theme, with sub-tropical plantings and attractive blue tables and chairs; dinner and drinks are served here on summer evenings. Expect warm hospitality and attentive service in tastefully furnished surroundings.

Rooms 5 en suite S £105-£150; D £120-£150*
Facilities FTV TVL tea/coffee Dinner available Cen ht Licensed Wi-fi **Parking** 6 **Notes** LB ⌖ No Children 13yrs Closed Nov-Mar

Chy-an-Mor

★★★★ GUEST ACCOMMODATION

15 Regent Ter TR18 4DW
☎ 01736 363441
e-mail: reception@chyanmor.co.uk
dir: *A30 to Penzance, at rail station, follow along harbour front onto Promenade Rd. Pass Jubilee Pool, right at Stanley Guest House*

This elegant Grade II listed Georgian house has been appointed to provide high standards throughout. Bedrooms are individually designed and equipped with thoughtful extras, and many have spectacular views over Mount's Bay. The spacious lounge has similar views and tasty and satisfying breakfasts are served in the dining room. Ample off-street parking is available.

Rooms 9 en suite S £40-£44; D £70-£92 **Facilities** FTV tea/coffee Cen ht Wi-fi Beauty treatments available **Parking** 15 **Notes** ⊗ No Children 14yrs Closed 15 Nov-15 Mar

The Dunedin

★★★★ GUEST ACCOMMODATION

Alexandra Rd TR18 4LZ
☎ 01736 362652 ▤ 01736 360497
e-mail: info@dunedinhotel.co.uk
web: www.dunedinhotel.co.uk
dir: *A30 to Penzance, at rail station along harbour front onto Promenade Rd, right onto Alexandra Rd, Dunedin on right*

The house is in a tree-lined avenue just a stroll from the promenade and town centre. The friendly proprietors provide a relaxed atmosphere. Bedrooms are well equipped and smartly decorated to a high standard. There is a cosy lounge and hearty breakfasts are served in the dining room.

Rooms 8 rms (8 pri facs) (2 fmly) (2 GF) S £35-£50; D £60-£80* **Facilities** FTV TVL tea/coffee Cen ht Wi-fi **Notes** LB ⊗ No Children 5yrs Closed 12 Dec-2 Jan ⊛

The Old Vicarage

★★★★ BED AND BREAKFAST

Churchtown, St Hilary TR20 9DQ
☎ 01736 711508 & 07736 101230 ▤ 01736 711508
e-mail: johnbd524@aol.com
dir: *5m E of Penzance. Off B3280 in St Hilary*

Feel at home with a friendly welcome at this charming establishment. The spacious bedrooms are thoughtfully equipped, and there is a snooker room, a comfortable lounge and extensive gardens. Also available to guests, a trekking and riding school, run by the proprietors, who run a small stud farm as well.

Rooms 3 en suite (1 fmly) **Facilities** FTV TVL tea/coffee Cen ht Riding Snooker **Parking** 8

Mount Royal

★★★ GUEST ACCOMMODATION

Chyandour Cliff TR18 3LQ
☎ 01736 362233 ▤ 01736 362233
e-mail: mountroyal@btconnect.com
dir: *Off A30 onto coast road into town*

Part Georgian and part Victorian, the spacious Mount Royal has splendid views over Mount's Bay and is convenient for the town's attractions. The elegant dining room retains its original fireplace and ornate sideboard. Parking available to the rear of the property.

Rooms 7 en suite (3 fmly) (1 GF) S £60-£70; D £85-£95* **Facilities** tea/coffee Cen ht Wi-fi **Parking** 10 **Notes** LB ⊗ Closed Nov-Mar ⊛

The Carlton

★★★ GUEST HOUSE

Promenade TR18 4NW
☎ 01736 362081 ▤ 01736 362081
e-mail: carltonhotelpenzance@talk21.com
dir: *From A30 signs for harbour & Newlyn, on right after rdbt*

Situated on the pleasant promenade and having sea views from some of its rooms, the Carlton is an easy stroll from the town centre and amenities. Bedrooms are traditionally styled. There is a guest lounge and spacious dining room, both sea facing.

Rooms 12 rms (9 en suite) (3 smoking) S £25-£30; D £50-£60 **Facilities** FTV TVL tea/coffee **Notes** ⊗

The Coldstreamer Inn

★★★ ⊛ INN

Gulval TR18 3BB
☎ 01736 362072 ▤ 01736 322072
e-mail: info@coldstreamer-penzance.co.uk
dir: *1m NE of Penzance on B3311, right turn onto School Ln in Gulval, opp church*

Standing opposite the picturesque church in the pretty village of Gulval, this is very much the local hostelry with plenty of atmosphere and banter. Public areas have homely charm and the restaurant is the venue for impressive cuisine, prepared with skill, passion and excellent produce. After a relaxing evening, comfortable bedrooms await for a good night's sleep in preparation for a tasty, freshly cooked, breakfast.

Rooms 3 en suite S £60-£75; D £70-£85* **Facilities** FTV tea/coffee Dinner available Cen ht Wi-fi

The Dolphin Tavern

★★★ INN

Quay St TR18 4BD
☎ 01736 364106
e-mail: dolphintavern@tiscali.co.uk
dir: *Opp Penzance harbour*

A traditional inn just a few yards away from Penzance Harbour, usefully located for the Scillonian Ferry. Rooms are comfortable and well presented, staff are friendly and attentive, and food is available in the bar and restaurant daily from a wide menu with daily-changing specials.

Rooms 2 en suite S £70-£85; D £70-£85* **Facilities** FTV tea/coffee Dinner available Cen ht Wi-fi Pool table in winter only **Notes** ⊗ No coaches

PENZANCE *continued*

Mount View

★★★ INN

Longrock TR20 8JJ
☎ 01736 710416 📠 01736 710416
dir: *Off A30 at Marazion/Penzance rdbt, 3rd exit signed Longrock. On right after pelican crossing*

This Victorian inn, just a short walk from the beach and half a mile from the Isles of Scilly heliport, is a good base for exploring West Cornwall. Bedrooms are well equipped, including a hospitality tray, and the bar is popular with locals. Breakfast is served in the dining room and a dinner menu is available.

Rooms 5 rms (3 en suite) (2 fmly) (2 smoking) S £22-£34.50; D £44-£59 **Facilities** FTV tea/coffee Dinner available Wi-fi Pool table **Conf** Max 20 **Parking** 8 **Notes** RS Sun closed 4.30-7pm

Penmorvah

★★★ GUEST ACCOMMODATION

61 Alexandra Rd TR18 4LZ
☎ 01736 363711
e-mail: penmorvah_penzance@talktalk.net
dir: *A30 to Penzance, at railway station follow road along harbour front pass Jubilee pool. At mini-rdbt, right onto Alexandra Rd*

Well situated guest accommodation offering comfortable rooms, all of which are en suite. Penmorvah is just a few minutes walk from the seafront with convenient on-street parking nearby.

Rooms 8 en suite (2 fmly) (2 GF) S £30-£45; D £60-£70* **Facilities** FTV tea/coffee Cen ht **Notes** LB No Children 5yrs 📶

The Swordfish Inn

★★★ INN

The Strand, Newlyn TR18 5HN
☎ 01736 362830
e-mail: info@swordfishinn.co.uk
dir: *1m SW of Penzance*

Situated in the very heart of the fishing village of Newlyn, The Swordfish was totally renovated a couple of years ago. The spacious, comfortable bedrooms are well appointed, as are the en suite shower rooms. This establishment is a popular venue for locals and tourists alike.

Rooms 4 en suite (1 smoking) **Facilities** FTV tea/coffee Cen ht Wi-fi **Notes** ⊗ No coaches

PERRANARWORTHAL Map 2 SW73

Blankednick Farm

★★★★ BED AND BREAKFAST

Ponsanooth TR3 7JN
☎ 01872 863784 & 07799 054771
dir: *A39 Truro to Falmouth road, at Perranarworthal, 2nd right turn after Norway Inn. B&B signed*

This traditional bed and breakfast has very high standards throughout plus a very warm welcome from experienced hosts. Blankednick Farm is in a quiet yet accessible location and sits in 16 acres of grounds and gardens. The bedrooms are very well appointed, and hearty Aga-cooked breakfasts are served at a large table in the dining room.

Rooms 2 en suite D fr £80* **Facilities** FTV tea/coffee Cen ht Wi-fi ch fac **Parking** 10 **Notes** 📶

PERRANPORTH Map 2 SW75

St Georges Country House

★★★★ GUEST ACCOMMODATION

St Georges Hill TR6 0ED
☎ 01872 572184
e-mail: info@stgeorgescountryhouse.co.uk

Situated on an elevated position above Perranporth, St Georges is a very friendly and comfortable establishment. The owners and staff are attentive and very welcoming. Food is served most evenings and there is also a bar and large sitting room with comfy sofas and lots of books.

Rooms 7 en suite (2 fmly) **Facilities** FTV TVL tea/coffee Dinner available Cen ht Licensed Wi-fi **Conf** Max 20 Board 20 **Parking** 10 **Notes** LB Closed 23-30 Dec

PERRANUTHNOE Map 2 SW52

PREMIER COLLECTION

Ednovean Farm *(SW538295)*

★★★★★ 🏠 FARMHOUSE

TR20 9LZ
☎ 01736 711883
Mr & Mrs C Taylor
e-mail: info@ednoveanfarm.co.uk
web: www.ednoveanfarm.co.uk
dir: *Off A394 towards Perranuthnoe at Dynasty Restaurant, farm drive on left on bend by post box*

Tranquillity is guaranteed at this 17th-century farmhouse, which looks across the countryside towards St Michael's Mount. The bedrooms are individually styled and are most comfortable. The impressive Mediterranean style gardens are ideal to relax in. In addition to the sitting room, there is also a garden room and several patios. Breakfast is served family style at a magnificent oak table.

Rooms 3 en suite (3 GF) S £100-£115; D £100-£120 **Facilities** FTV tea/coffee Cen ht Wi-fi **Parking** 4 **Notes** LB ⊗ No Children 16yrs Closed 24-28 Dec 22 acres grassland/stud

The Victoria Inn

★★★ ⊛ INN

TR20 9NP
☎ 01736 710309
e-mail: enquiries@victoriainn-penzance.co.uk
dir: *Off A394 into village*

The attractive and friendly inn, popular with locals and visitors alike, reputedly originates from the Middle Ages. Daily specials in the cosy bar or the dining room include local fish, while the bedrooms are small but well equipped.

Rooms 2 en suite S £50-£75; D £75* **Facilities** FTV tea/coffee Dinner available Wi-fi **Parking** 10 **Notes** No Children 18yrs Closed 1wk Jan

POLPERRO   Map 2 SX25

PREMIER COLLECTION

Trenderway Farm *(SX214533)*

★★★★★ 🏠 FARMHOUSE

Pelynt PL13 2LY
☎ **01503 272214** 📠 **0870 705 9998**
Mr Yaron Peled & Jacq Harris
e-mail: stay@trenderwayfarm.com
web: www.trenderwayfarm.co.uk
dir: *Take A387 from Looe to Polperro, pass petrol station on left, right at farm sign & follow road across ford & up hill. Park on gravel yard*

Set in 200 acres on a working farm, warm hospitality is offered in this delightful 16th-century farmhouse. Stylish bedrooms, both in the farmhouse and in the adjacent barns, offer high levels of comfort and include Wi-fi access. Hearty breakfasts are served in the conservatory overlooking the lake, and free-range eggs from the farm, as well as high quality local produce, are served.

Rooms 2 en suite 5 annexe en suite (2 GF) D £95–£155* **Facilities** FTV tea/coffee Cen ht Wi-fi Lakes **Conf** Max 100 Thtr 100 Class 50 Board 15 **Parking** 8 **Notes** LB ⊗ No Children 200 acres beef/sheep/orchards

Trenake Manor Farm *(SX190555)*

★★★★ FARMHOUSE

Pelynt PL13 2LT
☎ **01503 220835** 📠 **01503 220835**
Mrs L Philp
e-mail: lorraine@cornishfarmhouse.co.uk
dir: *3.5m N of Polperro. A390 onto B3359 for Looe, 5m left at small x-rds*

The welcoming 15th-century farmhouse is surrounded by countryside and is a good base for touring Cornwall. Bedrooms have considerate finishing touches and there is a comfortable lounge. Breakfast, using local produce, is enjoyed in the cosy dining room (you may just spot the milking cows quietly passing the end of the garden).

Rooms 3 en suite (1 fmly) S £46; D £72–£76* **Facilities** FTV TVL tea/coffee Cen ht Wi-fi **Parking** 10 **Notes** LB 🅱 400 acres dairy/beef/arable

---

Penryn House

★★★★ GUEST ACCOMMODATION

The Coombes PL13 2RQ
☎ **01503 272157** 📠 **01503 273055**
e-mail: enquiries@penrynhouse.co.uk
web: www.penrynhouse.co.uk
dir: *A387 to Polperro, at mini-rdbt left down hill into village (ignore restricted access). 200yds on left*

Penryn House has a relaxed atmosphere and offers a warm welcome. Every effort is made to ensure a memorable stay. Bedrooms are neatly presented and reflect the character of the building. After a day exploring, enjoy a drink at the bar and relax in the comfortable lounge.

Rooms 12 en suite (3 fmly) S £41–£46; D £72–£102* **Facilities** FTV tea/coffee Licensed Wi-fi **Parking** 13 **Notes** LB

PORTHLEVEN   Map 2 SW62

Kota Restaurant with Rooms

★★★ ⚫ RESTAURANT WITH ROOMS

Harbour Head TR13 9JA
☎ **01326 562407** 📠 **01326 562407**
e-mail: kota@btconnect.com
dir: *B3304 from Helston into Porthleven. Kota on harbour opposite slipway*

Overlooking the water, this 300-year-old building is the home of Kota Restaurant (Kota is the Maori word for shellfish). The bedrooms are approached via a granite stairway at the side of the building. The family room is spacious and has the benefit of harbour views, while the smaller, double room is at the rear of the property. The enthusiastic young owners ensure that guests will enjoy their stay, and a meal in the restaurant should not be missed. Breakfast features the best local produce.

Rooms 2 annexe en suite (1 fmly) S £50–£70; D £60–£90* **Facilities** FTV tea/coffee Dinner available Wi-fi Golf 18 **Parking** 1 **Notes** ⊗ Closed Jan RS Nov-Mar Closed for lunch Mon-Thu & all day Sun No coaches

---

PORTLOE   Map 2 SW93

Carradale

★★★★ BED AND BREAKFAST

TR2 5RB
☎ **01872 501508**
e-mail: barbara495@btinternet.com
dir: *Off A3078 into Portloe, B&B 200yds from Ship Inn*

Carradale lies on the outskirts of this picturesque fishing village, a short walk from the South West Coast Path. It provides warm hospitality, a good level of comfort and well equipped bedrooms. There is an upper-floor lounge with a television. Breakfast is served around a communal table in the pleasant dining room.

Rooms 2 en suite (1 fmly) (1 GF) S £35–£40; D £60–£65 **Facilities** TVL tea/coffee Cen ht **Parking** 5 **Notes** ⊗ 🅱

REDRUTH   Map 2 SW64

Old Railway Yard

★★★★ BED AND BREAKFAST

Lanner Hill TR16 5SZ
☎ **01209 314514 & 07970 595598**
e-mail: g.s.collier@btinternet.com
dir: *A393 Redruth/Falmouth road, at brow of hill before Lanner village, turn right, 125mtrs*

The Old Railway Yard is a traditional bed and breakfast situated off Lanner Hill, with easy access to the A30. The hosts are friendly and attentive and make their guests really feel at home. The bedrooms are very well appointed; there is a small guest lounge and a conservatory, as well as the garden for guests to enjoy.

Rooms 2 rms (1 en suite) (1 pri facs) S £35–£60; D £70 **Facilities** FTV TVL tea/coffee Dinner available Cen ht Wi-fi **Parking** 8 **Notes** LB ⊗ No Children 6yrs

REDRUTH *continued*

Lanner Inn

★★ INN

The Square, Lanner TR16 6EH
☎ 01209 215611 📠 01209 214065
e-mail: info@lannerinn.co.uk
web: www.lannerinn.co.uk
dir: *2m SE of Redruth. In Lanner on A393*

Conveniently situated for access to Redruth and the A30, this traditional inn is situated in the centre of Lanner and has a good local following. At the time of inspection the property was undergoing refurbishment and there is now a new bar and dining room; the bedrooms are comfortable. This inn is owner-run and managed, and the team of staff are very friendly.

Rooms 5 en suite 1 annexe en suite (3 fmly) (1 GF)
Facilities FTV tea/coffee Dinner available Cen ht Wi-fi
Pool table **Parking** 16

RUAN MINOR Map 2 SW71

The Coach House

★★★★ GUEST ACCOMMODATION

Kuggar TR12 7LY
☎ 01326 291044
e-mail: mjanmakin@aol.com
dir: *1m N of Ruan Minor in Kuggar*

This 17th-century house is close to Kennack Sands and Goonhilly Downs nature reserve. The friendly proprietors provide a warm welcome for their guests, who can relax in the spacious lounge-dining room where a fire burns in colder months. Bedrooms, two of which are in a converted stable block, are attractively decorated.

Rooms 3 en suite S £40; D £70* **Facilities** FTV TVL tea/coffee Cen ht Wi-fi **Parking** 10 **Notes** LB ⊗ Closed Xmas 🍽

ST AGNES Map 2 SW75

The Aramay

★★★★ 🏠 GUEST ACCOMMODATION

Armay House, Quay Rd TR5 0RP
☎ 01872 553546
e-mail: amie@thearamay.com

Newly refurbished to very high standards, The Aramay offers stylish, contemporary surroundings with an intimate feel. Service is relaxed and informal, and an award-winning breakfast is served till late. Very well located with off-road parking. The Aramay was the Winner of last year's AA Funkiest B&B of the Year Award (2010-2011).

Rooms 5 en suite (1 GF) **Facilities** STV TVL tea/coffee Cen ht Licensed Wi-fi **Parking** 5 **Notes** ⊗ No Children 16yrs

Driftwood Spars

★★★★ 🚃 GUEST ACCOMMODATION

Trevaunance Cove TR5 0RT
☎ 01872 552428
e-mail: info@driftwoodspars.co.uk
dir: *A30 to Chiverton rdbt, right onto B3277, through village. Driftwood Spars 200yds before beach*

Partly built from shipwreck timbers, this 18th-century inn attracts locals and visitors alike. The attractive bedrooms, some in an annexe, are decorated in a bright, seaside style with many interesting features. Local produce, including delicious seafood, is served in the informal pub dining room and in the restaurant, together with a range from hand-pulled beers.

Rooms 9 en suite 6 annexe en suite (4 fmly) (5 GF) S £45-£66; D £86-£102* **Facilities** tea/coffee Dinner available Direct Dial Cen ht Licensed Wi-fi Pool table Table football **Conf** Max 50 Thtr 50 Class 25 Board 20 **Parking** 40 **Notes** LB RS 25 Dec no lunch/dinner, no bar in evening Civ Wed 80

Penkerris

★★ GUEST HOUSE

Penwinnick Rd TR5 0PA
☎ 01872 552262 📠 01872 552262
e-mail: info@penkerris.co.uk
web: www.penkerris.co.uk
dir: *A30 onto B3277 to village, on right after village sign*

Close to three surfing beaches and dramatic cliff walks, Penkerris is an elegant Edwardian house with a friendly atmosphere. An ideal place for families, the house has a large, lawned garden with plenty of toys and activities, and drinks can be served outside in warm weather. Bedrooms are comfortable and well appointed, and home-cooked meals are served by arrangement. A beach hut, complete with surf boards, is available for guests at nearby Trevaunance Cove.

Rooms 7 rms (4 en suite) (3 fmly) D £40-£70* **Facilities** FTV TVL tea/coffee Dinner available Licensed Wi-fi ch fac Badminton, volleyball **Parking** 9 **Notes** LB

ST AUSTELL Map 2 SX05

See also Gorran Haven & St Blazey

PREMIER COLLECTION

Anchorage House

★★★★★ 🏠 🚃 GUEST ACCOMMODATION

Nettles Corner, Tregrehan Mills PL25 3RH
☎ 01726 814071 📠 01726 814071
e-mail: info@anchoragehouse.co.uk
web: www.anchoragehouse.co.uk
dir: *2 m E of town centre off A390, opposite St Austell Garden Centre*

This Georgian style house is set in an acre of carefully landscaped gardens at the end of a private lane. Guests are met upon arrival with afternoon tea, often served on the patio, and dinner is served in the evening by arrangement. The luxurious bedrooms are equipped to the highest standard and include satellite TV, fresh fruit, magazines, bottled water and chocolates. Guests also have use of the pool, hot tub, gym and sauna. The house is a short distance from the Eden Project, the Lost Gardens of Heligan, Carlyon Bay and Charlestown Harbour.

Rooms 4 en suite 1 annexe en suite (1 GF) S £70-£115; D £90-£135* **Facilities** STV FTV tea/coffee Dinner available Cen ht Wi-fi 🏊 Sauna Gym Hot tub **Parking** 6 **Notes** ⊗ No Children 16yrs Closed Dec-Feb

PREMIER COLLECTION

Penarwyn House

★★★★★ 🏠 GUEST ACCOMMODATION

PL24 2DS
☎ 01726 814224 📠 01726 814224
e-mail: stay@penarwyn.co.uk
web: www.penarwyn.co.uk

(For full entry see St Blazey)

PREMIER COLLECTION

Highland Court Lodge

★★★★★ ≋ GUEST ACCOMMODATION

Biscovey Rd, Biscovey, Par PL24 2HW
☎ 01726 813320 🖺 01726 813320
e-mail: enquiries@highlandcourt.co.uk
web: www.highlandcourt.co.uk
dir: *2m E of St Austell. A390 E to St Blazey Gate, right onto Biscovey Rd, 300yds on right*

This is an extremely well presented and maintained contemporary building with stunning views over St Austell Bay, and is just over one mile from the Eden Project. Its impressive en suite bedrooms have luxurious fabrics and each room opens onto a private patio. There is a lounge with deep sofas, and the terrace shares the fine views. The local Cornish catch features strongly in the freshly prepared dinners, which, like breakfast are not to be missed. A spa and treatment room is now available.

Rooms 3 en suite (2 fmly) (3 GF) D £90-£190*
Facilities FTV tea/coffee Dinner available Cen ht Licensed Wi-fi Spa, 1 treatment room Conf Max 12 Class 12 Board 12 Parking 10 Notes LB ⊗

PREMIER COLLECTION

Lower Barn

★★★★★ ≋ GUEST ACCOMMODATION

Bosue, St Ewe PL26 6ET
☎ 01726 844881
e-mail: janie@bosue.co.uk
web: www.bosue.co.uk
dir: *3.5m SW of St Austell. Off B3273 at x-rds signed Lost Gardens of Heligan, Lower Barn signed 1m on right*

This converted barn, tucked away in countryside with easy access to local attractions, has huge appeal. Warm colours create a Mediterranean feel, complemented by informal and genuine hospitality. Bedrooms have a host of extras. Breakfast is served around a large table or on the patio deck overlooking the garden, which also has a hot tub.

Rooms 3 en suite (1 fmly) (1 GF) Facilities tea/coffee Dinner available Cen ht Sauna Hot tub Spa treatments Parking 7 Notes LB ⊗ Closed Jan

PREMIER COLLECTION

Nanscawen Manor House

★★★★★ GUEST ACCOMMODATION

Prideaux Rd, Luxulyan Valley PL24 2SR
☎ 01726 814488 & 07811 022423
e-mail: keith@nanscawen.com
web: www.nanscawen.com

(For full entry see St Blazey)

Hunter's Moon

★★★★ GUEST HOUSE

Chapel Hill, Polgooth PL26 7BU
☎ 01726 66445
e-mail: enquiries@huntersmooncornwall.co.uk
dir: *1.5m SW of town centre. Off B3273 into Polgooth, pass village shop on left, 1st right*

Hunter's Moon lies in a quiet village just a few miles from Heligan and within easy reach of the Eden Project. Service is friendly and attentive and the bedrooms are well equipped for business or leisure. There is a conservatory-lounge and a pretty garden to enjoy during warmer weather. Breakfast is served in the cosy dining room and the nearby village inn serves freshly prepared meals.

Rooms 4 en suite (2 fmly) S £55-£60; D £75-£80
Facilities FTV tea/coffee Cen ht Wi-fi Parking 5 Notes ⊗ No Children 14yrs 🖾

Sunnyvale Bed & Breakfast

★★★★ BED AND BREAKFAST

Hewas Water PL26 7JF
☎ 01726 882572
e-mail: jm.uden@hotmail.com
dir: *4m SW of St Austell. Off A390 in Hewas Water*

This house has pleasant gardens in a peaceful location, and the very friendly proprietor makes you feel most welcome. The bedrooms are both ground floor, one specifically designed for the disabled, and have an extensive range of facilities. Breakfast is either taken in the main house at separate tables, or for the less mobile, in the bedroom by prior arrangement.

Rooms 2 annexe en suite (2 GF) S £45; D £70
Facilities FTV tea/coffee Cen ht Wi-fi Parking 4 Notes ⊗ No Children 16yrs 🖾

The Elms

★★★★ BED AND BREAKFAST

14 Penwinnick Rd PL25 5DW
☎ 01726 74981 🖺 01726 74981
e-mail: pete@edenbb.co.uk
web: www.edenbb.co.uk
dir: *0.5m SW of town centre. On A390 junct Pondhu Rd*

Well located for the Eden Project or for touring Cornwall, this bed and breakfast offers a relaxed and friendly environment for leisure and business guests. Bedrooms, one with a four-poster bed, are well equipped and there is an inviting lounge. Breakfast is served in the conservatory dining room.

Rooms 3 en suite 1 annexe en suite (1 GF) S £35; D £70-£80* Facilities FTV TVL tea/coffee Cen ht Wi-fi Golf 18 Parking 3 Notes LB ⊗

Elmswood House

★★★★ GUEST ACCOMMODATION

73 Tehidy Rd, Tywardreath PL24 2QD
☎ 01726 814221
e-mail: enquiries@elmswoodhousehotel.co.uk
web: www.elmswoodhousehotel.co.uk

(For full entry see Par)

Polgreen Farm *(SX008503)*

★★★★ FARMHOUSE

London Apprentice PL26 7AP
☎ 01726 75151
Mr Berryman
e-mail: polgreen.farm@btinternet.com
web: www.polgreenfarm.co.uk
dir: *1.5m S of St Austell. Off B3273, turn left entering London Apprentice & signed*

Guests return regularly for the friendly welcome at this peaceful establishment located just south of St Austell. The spacious and well-equipped bedrooms are divided between the main house and an adjoining property, and each building has a comfortable lounge. Breakfast is served in a pleasant conservatory overlooking the garden.

Rooms 3 rms (2 en suite) (1 pri facs) 4 annexe en suite (1 fmly) (1 GF) S £30-£45; D £60-£70 Facilities FTV TVL tea/coffee Cen ht Parking 8 Notes LB ⊗ 64 acres livestock

ST AUSTELL *continued*

Sunnycroft

★★★★ GUEST ACCOMMODATION

28 Penwinnick Rd PL25 5DS
☎ 01726 73351 📠 01726 879409
e-mail: enquiries@sunnycroft.net
dir: *600yds SW of town centre on A390*

Just a short walk from the town centre, this 1930s house is conveniently situated for the Eden Project. The bright bedrooms offer good levels of comfort, and ground-floor rooms are available. Tasty and substantial breakfasts are served in the light and airy conservatory dining room. Ample off-road, secure parking is available too.

Rooms 5 en suite S £45-£75; D £65-£120 **Facilities** FTV tea/coffee Dinner available Cen ht Wi-fi Golf 18 **Parking** 10 **Notes** LB No Children 7yrs Closed 24-26 Dec

T'Gallants

★★★★ GUEST HOUSE

6 Charlestown Rd, Charlestown PL25 3NJ
☎ 01726 70203 📠 01726 70203
e-mail: enquiries@tgallants.co.uk
dir: *0.5m SE of town off A390 rdbt signed Charlestown*

The fine Georgian house partly dates from 1630. It overlooks the historic port of Charlestown, with its fleet of square-rigged sailing ships. Bedrooms are well presented and spacious, and one has a four-poster bed and views of the port. Breakfast is served in the attractive dining room with a choice of traditional or continental offered. A guest lounge is also available.

Rooms 7 en suite S fr £50; D £75-£100* **Facilities** FTV TVL tea/coffee Cen ht Wi-fi **Notes** ⊗

ST BLAZEY Map 2 SX05

PREMIER COLLECTION

Penarwyn House

★★★★★ 🏠 GUEST ACCOMMODATION

PL24 2DS
☎ 01726 814224 📠 01726 814224
e-mail: stay@penarwyn.co.uk
web: www.penarwyn.co.uk
dir: *A390 W through St Blazey, left before 2nd speed camera into Doubletrees School, Penarwyn straight ahead*

This large impressive Victorian house stands in tranquil surroundings close to main routes, with the Eden Project, The Lost Gardens of Heligan, Fowey, the coastal footpath and National Trust properties all close by. Painstakingly restored, the spacious house offers a host of facilities, and the bedrooms are particularly comfortable and delightfully appointed. On arrival, guests are welcomed with afternoon tea and cake, and breakfast is always a highlight. Jan and Mike offer very welcoming hospitality and place a great emphasis upon service.

Rooms 4 en suite (1 fmly) S £60-£75; D £80-£160 **Facilities** FTV tea/coffee Cen ht Wi-fi 3/4 size snooker table **Parking** 6 **Notes** LB ⊗ No Children 10yrs

PREMIER COLLECTION

Nanscawen Manor House

★★★★★ GUEST ACCOMMODATION

Prideaux Rd, Luxulyan Valley PL24 2SR
☎ 01726 814488 & 07811 022423
e-mail: keith@nanscawen.com
web: www.nanscawen.com
dir: *A390 W to St Blazey, right after railway, Nanscawen 0.75m on right*

This renovated manor house originates from the 14th century and provides a high standard of accommodation, with elegant bedrooms and bathrooms with spa baths. There are extra touches throughout to pamper you, a spacious lounge with a well-stocked honesty bar, and five acres of pleasant gardens with splendid woodland views. Breakfast, served in the conservatory, features fresh local produce.

Rooms 3 en suite S £40-£80; D £78-£120* **Facilities** STV FTV tea/coffee Direct Dial Cen ht Wi-fi 🔧 **Parking** 8 **Notes** ⊗ No Children 12yrs

---

ST BURYAN Map 2 SW42

Tregurnow Farm *(SW444242)*

★★★★ FARMHOUSE

TR19 6BL
☎ 01736 810255
Mr G Jeffery
e-mail: tregurnow@lamorna.biz

Tucked away near St Buryan, Tregurnow Farm offers traditional, quality farmhouse bed and breakfast and self-catering facilities. Peace and quiet, stunning views and hearty breakfasts are hallmarks of a stay here. Close to Mousehole, Minnack Theatre and Penzance, this is a good base for touring the far south-west of the county.

Rooms 3 en suite **Notes** Closed Oct-Apr

ST GENNYS Map 2 SX19

Rosecare Villa Farm

★★★★ GUEST ACCOMMODATION

EX23 0BG
☎ 01840 230474
e-mail: info@northcornwallholidays.com
dir: *9m S of Bude on A39, S of Wainhouse Corner*

This family-run establishment is close to the spectacular north Cornish coast, and dates back several hundred years. The house was once a slate captain's house and is now a smallholding complete with a small menagerie. Bedrooms are situated in the original stone barns surrounding the courtyard, and each has its own separate entrance. Breakfast features locally sourced produce, with eggs from the resident hens. Dinner is also available by prior arrangement.

Rooms 5 annexe en suite (5 GF) **Facilities** FTV tea/coffee Dinner available Cen ht **Parking** 8 **Notes** Closed 22-28 Dec

ST HILARY — Map 2 SW53

PREMIER COLLECTION

Ennys

★★★★★ ⌂ GUEST ACCOMMODATION

Trewhella Ln TR20 9BZ
☎ 01736 740262 📄 01736 740055
e-mail: ennys@ennys.co.uk
web: www.ennys.co.uk
dir: *1m N of B3280 Leedstown-Goldsithney road at end of Trewhella Ln*

Set off the beaten track, this 17th-century manor house is a perfect place to unwind. A friendly welcome awaits you, and a complimentary afternoon tea is laid out in the kitchen. Ennys retains much original character and the rooms are impressively furnished. A delightful Cornish breakfast is served in the dining room, using a wealth of fresh local ingredients and home-produced fresh eggs. Three self-catering cottages available.

Rooms 3 en suite 2 annexe en suite (1 GF) S £90-£130; D £105-£150* **Facilities** FTV tea/coffee Cen ht Wi-fi ⚡ 🏊 Yoga studio & classes **Parking** 8 **Notes** ⊗ No Children 16yrs Closed Nov-28 Mar

ST IVES — Map 2 SW54

PREMIER COLLECTION

Beachcroft

★★★★★ GUEST ACCOMMODATION

Valley Rd, Carbis Bay TR26 2QS
☎ 01736 794442
e-mail: enquiries@beachcroftstives.co.uk
web: www.beachcroftstives.co.uk
dir: *From A30/A3074 rdbt, follow signs to St Ives, through Carbis Bay, turn right onto Valley Rd*

After a total refurbishment and transformation Beachcroft now offers a tranquil haven of peace and calm in truly top class surroundings. The hosts offer genuine warmth and hospitality and their focus is guest relaxation and enjoyment. Egyptian cotton, flat screen televisions, Villeroy & Boch bathrooms and Molton Brown toiletries are only a few examples of the quality to be expected here.

Rooms 5 en suite **Facilities** FTV TVL tea/coffee Cen ht Licensed Wi-fi **Parking** 5 **Notes** ⊗ No Children 12yrs Closed 30 Nov-Feb RS New Year & 14 Feb wknd open for guests

Lamorna Lodge

★★★★ GUEST ACCOMMODATION

Boskerris Rd, Carbis Bay TR26 2NG
☎ 01736 795967
e-mail: lamorna@tr26.wanadoo.co.uk
dir: *A30 onto A3074, right after playground in Carbis Bay, establishment 200yds on right*

A truly genuine welcome is assured at this quietly situated establishment which is just a short walk from Carbis Bay beach. Wonderful views over St Ives Bay to Godrevy Lighthouse can be enjoyed from the spacious lounge, a view also shared by some of the stylish bedrooms. Breakfast and dinner are served in the elegant surroundings of the dining room where home-cooked food is prepared from local produce.

Rooms 9 en suite (2 fmly) (2 GF) **Facilities** FTV tea/coffee Dinner available Cen ht Wi-fi **Conf** Max 18 Thtr 18 Class 18 Board 18 **Parking** 9 **Notes** ⊗ Closed 5 Nov-10 Mar

The Nook

★★★★ GUEST ACCOMMODATION

Ayr TR26 1EQ
☎ 01736 795913
e-mail: info@nookstives.co.uk
web: www.nookstives.co.uk
dir: *A30 to St Ives left at NatWest, right at rdbt & left at top of hill*

Having undergone an extensive refurbishment, The Nook is an ideal base for exploring Cornwall's spectacular coastline, gardens and countryside. The comfortable bedrooms are furnished in a contemporary style and are equipped with numerous facilities. There is a wide variety on offer at breakfast, from full English or continental, to scrambled eggs with smoked salmon.

Rooms 11 en suite (1 fmly) (1 GF) S £39-£50; D £72-£102* **Facilities** FTV TVL tea/coffee Cen ht Wi-fi **Parking** 10 **Notes** LB ⊗

Treliska

★★★★ ⌂ GUEST ACCOMMODATION

3 Bedford Rd TR26 1SP
☎ 01736 797678 📄 01736 797678
e-mail: info@treliska.com
web: www.treliska.com
dir: *A3074 to St Ives, fork at Porthminster Hotel into town, at T-junct facing Barclays Bank left onto Bedford Rd, house on right*

This stylish, friendly and relaxed home is close to the seafront, restaurants and galleries. There is a refreshing approach here with a contemporary feel throughout. Impressive bathrooms have invigorating showers, while the attractive bedrooms are configured to maximise comfort. Enjoyable, freshly cooked Cornish breakfasts are

served in the lounge-dining room with a choice of coffee available at all times to guests. Additional facilities include internet and Wi-fi connections.

Rooms 5 en suite **Facilities** FTV tea/coffee Cen ht Wi-fi **Notes** ⊗ No Children 10yrs 🎁

Wheal-e-Mine Bed & Breakfast

★★★★ ⌂ BED AND BREAKFAST

9 Belmont Ter TR26 1DZ
☎ 01736 795051 & 07523 332018 📄 01736 795051
e-mail: whealemine@btinternet.com
web: www.stivesbedandbreakfast.com
dir: *A3074 into town, left at x-rds onto B3306, right at rdbt, left at top of hill*

Guests are assured of a warm, friendly welcome at this Victorian terraced property, which over the last few years has been fully upgraded with style and flair. Bedrooms are well appointed and each boasts distant sea views. A hearty breakfast is served each morning in the attractive dining room. On-site parking at the rear of the property is an added bonus.

Rooms 3 en suite D £74-£92* **Facilities** FTV tea/coffee Cen ht Free membership to local gym **Parking** 3 **Notes** LB ⊗ No Children 18yrs Closed Oct-Mar 🎁

Borthalan

★★★★ GUEST ACCOMMODATION

Off Boskerris Rd, Carbis Bay TR26 2NQ
☎ 01736 795946 📄 01736 795946
e-mail: borthalanhotel@btconnect.com
dir: *A3074 into Carbis Bay, right onto Boskerris Rd, 1st left onto cul-de-sac*

Quietly situated, this welcoming establishment is just a short walk from Carbis Bay station, from where you can take the 3-minute journey to St Ives without the hassle of car parking. The friendly proprietors provide a relaxing environment, with every effort made to ensure an enjoyable stay. Bedrooms are all well equipped and smartly presented, some with lovely sea views. There is a cosy lounge and an attractive garden, and breakfast is served in the bright dining room.

Rooms 7 en suite **Facilities** TVL tea/coffee Cen ht Licensed **Parking** 7 **Notes** ⊗ No Children 12yrs Closed Xmas

ST IVES *continued*

Chy Conyn

★★★★ BED AND BREAKFAST

8 Ayr Ter TR26 1ED
☎ 01736 798068
e-mail: mail@chyconyn.co.uk

Located in a pleasant residential area, just above the town, this comfortable bed and breakfast offers refurbished accommodation in a range of sizes; all rooms have plenty of useful extras. Breakfast is served in the relaxing and well-presented dining room. Wi-fi is available. There is a car park is to the rear of the property.

Rooms 3 en suite (1 fmly) S £60-£75; D £65-£80*
Facilities FTV tea/coffee Cen ht Wi-fi **Parking** 2 **Notes** ⊗

Coombe Farmhouse

★★★★ BED AND BREAKFAST

TR27 6NW
☎ 01736 740843
e-mail: coombefarmhouse@aol.com
web: www.coombefarmhouse.com
dir: *1.5m W of Lelant. Off A3074 to Lelant Downs*

Built of sturdy granite, this early 19th-century farmhouse is in a delightful location tucked away at the southern foot of Trencrom Hill, yet convenient for St Ives. The comfortable bedrooms are attractively decorated. There is a cosy lounge, and substantial breakfasts, featuring farm-fresh eggs, are served in the dining room overlooking the garden.

Rooms 3 rms (2 en suite) (1 pri facs) S £45; D £76-£82*
Facilities TVL tea/coffee Cen ht **Parking** 3 **Notes** ⊗ No Children 12yrs Closed Dec ⊜

Edgar's

★★★★ 🏠 GUEST ACCOMMODATION

Chy-an-Creet, Higher Stennack TR26 2HA
☎ 01736 796559 📠 01736 796559
e-mail: stay@edgarshotel.co.uk
web: www.edgarshotel.co.uk
dir: *0.5m W of town centre on B3306, opp Leach Pottery*

High standards of comfort are provided at this friendly, family-run property. Public areas are spacious and include a comfortable guest lounge, and bedrooms, some on the ground floor, are well equipped. Breakfast, served in the dining room, includes home-made preserves and makes good use of local produce. Good off-road parking available.

Rooms 7 en suite (2 fmly) (3 GF) S £55-£85; D £72-£98
Facilities FTV TVL tea/coffee Cen ht Wi-fi **Parking** 7
Notes LB Closed Nov-Feb

Glanmor

★★★★ GUEST ACCOMMODATION

The Belyars TR26 2BX
☎ 01736 795613
e-mail: margaret@glanmor.net
dir: *A3074 to St Ives, left at Porthminster Hotel & up Talland Rd*

The relaxed and friendly atmosphere at the Glanmor draws guests back time after time. It is just a short walk from the town centre and beaches, and offers attractive, well-equipped bedrooms. There is a comfortable lounge and conservatory, and the pretty landscaped gardens have seating on warm sunny days. Carefully prepared breakfasts are served in the light and airy dining room.

Rooms 6 en suite (3 fmly) (1 GF) **Facilities** TVL tea/coffee Cen ht Wi-fi **Parking** 6 **Notes** ⊗ No Children 3yrs ⊜

Little Leaf Guest House

★★★★ GUEST ACCOMMODATION

16 Park Av TR26 2DN
☎ 01736 795427 & 07855 490831
e-mail: hello@littleleafguesthouse.co.uk
dir: *A3074 through Lelant into St Ives, turn right at Porthminster Hotel. Left onto Gabriel St, Park Av on left*

There's an engaging, fresh and contemporary style at Little Leaf, which boasts stunning views over the roof tops of St Ives to the harbour and sea beyond. Bedrooms are light, bright and individually designed with plenty of comfort; one has a sea-facing balcony. The tasty breakfasts, featuring daily specials, are served in the attractive dining room which incorporates a small guest lounge area.

Rooms 5 en suite (1 fmly) S £50-£90; D £60-£95*
Facilities FTV tea/coffee Cen ht Wi-fi Easel hire for painters **Notes** LB ⊗ No Children 7yrs Closed 5-31 Jan

The Mustard Tree

★★★★ GUEST HOUSE

Sea View Meadows, St Ives Rd, Carbis Bay TR26 2JX
☎ 01736 795677 & 07840 072323
e-mail: enquiries@mustard-tree.co.uk
dir: *A3074 to Carbis Bay, The Mustard Tree on right opp Methodist church*

Set in delightful gardens and with sea views, this attractive house is just a short drive from the centre of St Ives, and the coastal path leads from Carbis Bay to St Ives. The pleasant bedrooms are very comfortable and have many extra facilities. A splendid choice is offered at breakfast, with vegetarian and continental options; a range of 'lite bites' is available in the early evening.

Rooms 9 rms (8 en suite) (1 pri facs) (2 fmly) (4 GF) S £33-£42; D £66-£130* **Facilities** FTV TVL tea/coffee Dinner available Cen ht Wi-fi **Conf** Max 20 **Parking** 9 **Notes** ⊗

The Old Count House

★★★★ GUEST HOUSE

1 Trenwith Square TR26 1DQ
☎ 01736 795369 📠 01736 799109
e-mail: counthouse@btconnect.com
web: www.theoldcounthouse-stives.co.uk
dir: *Follow signs to St Ives, house between leisure centre & school*

Situated in a quiet residential area with on-site parking, the Old Count House is a granite stone house, where Victorian mine workers collected their wages. Guests are assured of a warm welcome and an extensive choice at breakfast. Bedrooms vary in size, with all rooms being well equipped. The town centre and all its restaurants is only a five-minute walk away.

Rooms 10 rms (9 en suite) (1 pri facs) (2 GF) S £40-£44; D £80-£90* **Facilities** FTV TVL tea/coffee Cen ht Wi-fi Sauna **Parking** 9 **Notes** ⊗ No Children Closed 20-29 Dec

Old Vicarage

★★★★ 🏠 GUEST HOUSE

Parc-an-Creet TR26 2ES
☎ 01736 796124
e-mail: stay@oldvicarage.com
web: www.oldvicarage.com
dir: *From A3074 in town centre take B3306, 0.5m right into Parc-an-Creet*

This former Victorian rectory stands in secluded gardens in a quiet part of St Ives and is convenient for the seaside, town and Tate St Ives. The bedrooms are enhanced by modern facilities. A good choice of local produce is offered at breakfast, plus home-made yoghurt and preserves.

Rooms 6 en suite (4 fmly) S £63-£67; D £84-£94*
Facilities FTV TVL tea/coffee Cen ht Licensed Wi-fi ♿
Parking 12 **Notes** LB Closed Dec-Jan Civ Wed 40

The Regent

★★★★ GUEST ACCOMMODATION

Fernlea Ter TR26 2BH
☎ 01736 796195 📠 01736 794641
e-mail: keith@regenthotel.com
web: www.regenthotel.com
dir: *In town centre, near bus & railway station*

This popular and attractive property stands on an elevated position convenient for the town centre and seafront. The Regent has well-equipped bedrooms, some with spectacular sea vistas, and the comfortable lounge also has great views. The breakfast choices, including vegetarian, are excellent.

Rooms 10 rms (8 en suite) (1 fmly) S £38-£80; D £80-£110* **Facilities** TVL tea/coffee Cen ht Wi-fi **Parking** 12 **Notes** LB ⊗ No Children 16yrs

Rivendell Guest House

★★★★ GUEST HOUSE

7 Porthminster Ter TR26 2DQ
☎ 01736 794923 & 07837 468875
e-mail: rivendellstives@aol.com
web: www.rivendell-stives.co.uk
dir: *A3074 to St Ives, left at junct, left again & up hill, over road, 50yds on right*

Just a short walk from the town centre and harbour, this friendly and welcoming establishment has much to offer those visiting this lovely area. Bedrooms are all well appointed with contemporary comforts; some also have the benefit of sea views. Breakfast is served in the attractive dining room, which leads through to the guest lounge.

Rooms 7 rms (6 en suite) (1 pri facs) S £32-£35; D £66-£86* **Facilities** FTV TVL tea/coffee Cen ht Wi-fi **Parking** 5 **Notes** LB ⊗ Closed 23-27 Dec

The Rookery

★★★★ GUEST ACCOMMODATION

8 The Terrace TR26 2BL
☎ 01736 799401
e-mail: therookerystives@hotmail.com
dir: *A3074 through Carbis Bay, right fork at Porthminster Hotel, The Rookery 500yds on left*

This friendly establishment stands on an elevated position overlooking the town and sandy beach. The attractive bedrooms include one on the ground floor and a luxurious suite, all of which are well equipped and offer a good level of comfort. Breakfast is served in the first-floor dining room at separate tables.

Rooms 7 en suite (1 GF) **Facilities** FTV tea/coffee Cen ht Wi-fi **Parking** 7 **Notes** ⊗ No Children 7yrs

St Dennis

★★★★ 🏠 BED AND BREAKFAST

6 Albany Ter TR26 2BS
☎ 01736 795027
e-mail: info@staystives.co.uk
dir: *A3074 to St Ives, pass St Ives Motor Co on right, continue down hill, Albany Ter 1st left, signed Edward Hain Hospital*

St Dennis is a friendly and comfortable place to stay and is within walking distance of the town and beaches. Breakfast is a real treat with an emphasis on excellent local organic produce; the comprehensive menu includes choices for vegetarians and lighter, healthier options. The bedrooms are attractively decorated and have many thoughtful touches. Ample parking is available.

Rooms 3 en suite D £72-£91* **Facilities** FTV tea/coffee Cen ht **Parking** 5 **Notes** ⊗ No Children 12yrs Closed Oct-Mar

Thurlestone Guest House

★★★★ GUEST ACCOMMODATION

St Ives Rd, Carbis Bay TR26 2RT
☎ 01736 796369
e-mail: thurlestoneguesthouse@yahoo.co.uk
dir: *A3074 to Carbis Bay, pass convenience store on left, 0.25m on left next to newsagent*

The granite chapel, built in 1843, now offers stylish, comfortable accommodation. The welcoming proprietors provide a relaxed environment, and many guests return regularly. Now totally upgraded, the property offers a cosy lounge bar and well-equipped bedrooms, some with sea views.

Rooms 7 en suite (1 fmly) (1 GF) S £37-£42; D £64-£84* **Facilities** FTV TVL tea/coffee Cen ht Licensed Wi-fi **Parking** 5 **Notes** ⊗ Closed Nov-Mar

The Woodside

★★★★ GUEST ACCOMMODATION

The Belyars TR26 2DA
☎ 01736 795681
e-mail: woodsidehotel@btconnect.com
dir: *A3074 to St Ives, left at Porthminster Hotel onto Talland Rd, 1st left onto Belyars Ln, Woodside 4th on right*

This attractive house is in a peaceful location overlooking St Ives Bay. The friendly proprietors provide a welcoming and relaxing environment, and the bedrooms, some with sea views, come in a range of sizes. Hearty breakfasts are served in the dining room, and there is a comfortable lounge and a well-stocked bar.

Rooms 10 en suite (3 fmly) S £40-£55; D £80-£120* **Facilities** FTV TVL tea/coffee Cen ht Licensed Pool table **Parking** 12 **Notes** LB ⊗ No Children 5yrs Closed Xmas

Penlee International Guest House

★★★ GUEST ACCOMMODATION

St Ives Rd, Carbis Bay TR26 2SX
☎ 01736 795497
e-mail: enquiries@penleeinternational.co.uk
dir: *A30 onto A3074, 75yds after Carbis Bay sign left onto Polmennor Dr, 1st left into car park*

Situated in Carbis Bay, with distant coastal views, Penlee International is a small friendly establishment. In the comfortable bedrooms, the best possible use has been made of the available space. Guests can relax and spend enjoyable evenings in the cosy bar.

Rooms 8 en suite (3 fmly) **Facilities** FTV TVL tea/coffee Cen ht Licensed **Parking** 6 **Notes** LB ⊗ No Children

Portarlington

★★★ GUEST ACCOMMODATION

11 Parc Bean TR26 1EA
☎ 01736 797278 📠 01736 797278
e-mail: info@portarlington.co.uk
web: www.portarlington.co.uk

This pleasant home is convenient for the town, beaches and Tate St Ives. The friendly proprietors have long welcomed guests to their home and many return regularly. Bedrooms are well furnished and some have sea views. There is a comfortable lounge, and enjoyable breakfasts are served in the attractive dining room.

Rooms 4 en suite (3 fmly) **Facilities** FTV TVL tea/coffee Cen ht **Parking** 4 **Notes** ⊗ No Children 3yrs Closed Nov-Jan 🐾

St Margaret's Guest House

★★★ GUEST HOUSE

3 Park Av TR26 2DN
☎ 01736 795785
e-mail: btrevena@aol.com
web: www.stmargaretsguesthouse.co.uk
dir: *A3074 to town centre, left onto Gabriel St & The Stennack, left onto Park Av*

Guests feel comfortable at St Margaret's, with its panoramic views of the town and bay, and just a short walk from the sandy beaches. Breakfast is served in a pleasant dining room and dinner is available by arrangement.

Rooms 6 rms (4 en suite) (2 pri facs) (1 fmly) S £37.50; D £70-£75* **Facilities** FTV tea/coffee Dinner available Wi-fi **Parking** 2 **Notes** LB ⊗ Closed Nov-Mar

ST IVES *continued*

The Sloop Inn

★★★ INN

The Wharf TR26 1LP
☎ 01736 796584 📠 01736 793322
e-mail: sloopinn@btinternet.com
web: www.sloop-inn.co.uk
dir: *On St Ives harbour by middle slipway*

This attractive, historic inn has an imposing position on the harbour. Each of the guest rooms has a nautical name, many with pleasant views, and all have impressive modern facilities. A good choice of dishes is offered at lunch and dinner in the atmospheric restaurant-bar.

Rooms 18 en suite (6 fmly) (3 GF) (3 smoking)
Facilities FTV tea/coffee Dinner available Cen ht Wi-fi
Parking 6 **Notes** LB No coaches

ST JUST (NEAR LAND'S END) Map 2 SW33

The Wellington

★★ INN

Market Square TR19 7HD
☎ 01736 787319 📠 01736 787906
e-mail: wellingtonhotel@msn.com
dir: *6m W of Penzance*

This friendly inn, situated in busy Market Square, offers comfortable accommodation and is popular with locals and visitors alike. Bedrooms are spacious and well equipped. Home-cooked food and local ales from the well-stocked bar make for a pleasant stay.

Rooms 5 en suite 6 annexe en suite (4 fmly) (3 GF) S £45-£50; D £75-£80* **Facilities** tea/coffee Dinner available Direct Dial Cen ht Wi-fi Golf 18 Pool table **Conf** Max 20 **Notes** LB

ST KEVERNE Map 2 SW72

Gallen-Treath Guest House

★★★ GUEST HOUSE

Porthallow TR12 6PL
☎ 01326 280400 📠 01326 280400
e-mail: gallentreath@btclick.com
dir: *1.5m SE of St Keverne in Porthallow*

Gallen-Treath has super views over the countryside and sea from its elevated position above Porthallow. Bedrooms are individually decorated and feature many personal touches. Guests can relax in the large, comfortable lounge complete with balcony. Hearty breakfasts and dinners (by arrangement) are served in the bright dining room.

Rooms 5 rms (4 en suite) (1 pri facs) (1 fmly) (1 GF) S £27-£34; D £54-£68* **Facilities** FTV TVL tea/coffee Dinner available Cen ht Licensed **Parking** 6

ST MAWGAN Map 2 SW86

The Falcon Inn

★★★★ INN

TR8 4EP
☎ 01637 860225 📠 01637 860884
e-mail: info@thefalconinn-stmawgan.co.uk
dir: *A30 towards Newquay airport, follow signs for St Mawgan. Turn right, signed, Falcon Inn at bottom of hill*

Traditional village pub serving good food and drink along with two well presented and comfortable en suite bedrooms. Pleasant atmosphere, friendly owners and staff and a quiet location with plenty of off-street parking make this a popular venue. The pub is closed between 3-6pm but access for accommodation can be arranged outside of these times.

Rooms 2 en suite **Facilities** STV FTV tea/coffee Dinner available Direct Dial Cen ht Wi-fi Pool table **Parking** 20 **Notes** Closed 25 Dec RS 24 Dec No B&B available No coaches

---

SALTASH Map 3 SX45

Smeaton Farm *(SX387634)*

★★★★ 🏠 🚜 FARMHOUSE

PL12 6RZ
☎ 01579 351833 📠 01579 351833
Mr & Mrs Jones
e-mail: info@smeatonfarm.co.uk
web: www.smeatonfarm.co.uk
dir: *1m N of Hatt & 1m S of St Mellion just off A388*

This elegant Georgian farmhouse is surrounded by 450 acres of rolling Cornish farmland, providing a wonderfully peaceful place to stay. Home to the Jones family, the atmosphere is relaxed and hospitable, with every effort made to ensure a comfortable and rewarding break. Bedrooms are spacious, light and airy. Enjoyable dinners often feature home-reared meats and the sausages at breakfast come highly recommended.

Rooms 3 en suite (1 fmly) S £50-£60; D £75-£85* **Facilities** FTV TVL tea/coffee Dinner available Cen ht Licensed Wi-fi Golf Riding Cornish maze guided farm tours **Conf** Board 10 **Parking** 8 **Notes** LB ⊗ 450 acres arable/beef/sheep/organic

Crooked Inn

★★★★ INN

Stoketon Cross, Trematon PL12 4RZ
☎ 01752 848177 📠 01752 843203
e-mail: info@crooked-inn.co.uk
dir: *1.5m NW of Saltash. A38 W from Saltash, 2nd left to Trematon, sharp right*

The friendly animals that freely roam the courtyard add to the relaxed country style of this delightful property. The spacious bedrooms are well equipped, and freshly cooked dinners are available in the bar and conservatory. Breakfast is served in the cottage-style dining room.

Rooms 18 annexe rms 15 annexe en suite (5 fmly) (7 GF) **Facilities** tea/coffee Dinner available Cen ht ⚲ **Conf** Max 60 **Parking** 45 **Notes** Closed 25 Dec

The Holland Inn

★★★ INN

Callington Rd, Hatt PL12 6PJ
☎ 01752 844044 📠 01752 849701
e-mail: hollandinn@myopal.net
web: www.hollandinn.co.uk
dir: *2m NW of Saltash on A388*

This popular country inn provides spacious and comfortable accommodation in countryside near the A38. The wide choice for lunch and dinner includes a carvery, and a good selection of ales and wines is available at the bar.

Rooms 30 en suite (5 fmly) (30 GF) **Facilities** FTV tea/coffee Dinner available Direct Dial Cen ht Wi-fi Pool table 9 hole crazy golf **Conf** Max 50 Thtr 50 Class 50 **Parking** 30 **Notes** ⊗ Civ Wed 50

SCILLY, ISLES OF

ST MARY'S Map 2 SV91

Crebinick House

★★★★ GUEST HOUSE

Church St TR21 0JT
☎ 01720 422968
e-mail: aa@crebinick.co.uk
web: www.crebinick.co.uk
dir: *House 500yds from quay through Hugh Town; (airport bus to house)*

Many guests return time and again to this friendly, family-run house close to the town centre and the seafront. The granite-built property dates from 1760 and has smart, well equipped bedrooms; two are on the ground floor. There is a quiet lounge for relaxing.

Rooms 6 en suite (2 GF) D £76-£94* **Facilities** FTV TVL tea/coffee Cen ht Wi-fi **Notes** ⊗ No Children 10yrs Closed Nov-Mar 🈺

TRESCO   Map 2 SV81

New Inn

★★★★ ⊛ INN

TR24 0QQ
☎ 01720 422844 & 423006 📄 01720 423200
e-mail: newinn@tresco.co.uk
web: www.tresco.co.uk
dir: By New Grimsby Quay

This friendly, popular inn is located at the island's centre point and offers bright, attractive and well-equipped bedrooms, many with splendid sea views. Guests have an extensive choice from the menu at both lunch and dinner and can also choose where they take their meals - either in the airy bistro-style Pavilion, the popular bar which serves real ales, or the elegant restaurant. A heated outdoor pool is also available.

Rooms 16 en suite (2 GF) S £75-£150; D £150-£220*
Facilities Dinner available Wi-fi ↖ 🏊 Fishing Pool table
Notes LB ⊗ No coaches

SENNEN   Map 2 SW32

Mayon Farmhouse

★★★★ BED AND BREAKFAST

TR19 7AD
☎ 01736 871757
e-mail: mayonfarmhouse@hotmail.co.uk
web: www.mayonfarmhouse.co.uk
dir: A30 into Sennen, driveway opp Post Office

Guests receive a genuine welcome and a cream tea at this 19th-century, granite former farmhouse. About one mile from Land's End, and conveniently situated for visiting the Minack Theatre, it has country and distant coastal views. The attractive bedrooms are comfortable and well equipped, and an imaginative choice is offered at breakfast.

Rooms 4 rms (3 en suite) (1 pri facs) (1 fmly) S £60; D £85 **Facilities** FTV TVL tea/coffee Cen ht Wi-fi **Parking** 30 **Notes** LB ⊗ No Children 14yrs

TINTAGEL   Map 2 SX08

Pendrin House

★★★★ GUEST HOUSE

Atlantic Rd PL34 0DE
☎ 01840 770560
e-mail: info@pendrintintagel.co.uk
dir: Through village, pass entrance to Tintagel Castle, last house on right before Headlands Caravan Park

Located close to coastal walks, castle and the town centre, this Victorian house provides comfortable accommodation with most rooms having sea or country views. There is a cosy lounge.

Rooms 9 rms (5 en suite) (4 pri facs) S £30-£35; D £60-£70 **Facilities** FTV TVL tea/coffee Cen ht **Parking** 6 **Notes** ⊗ No Children 12yrs

Reevescott

★★★ BED AND BREAKFAST

Trethevy PL34 0BG
☎ 01840 770533 & 07814 503034
e-mail: fenann@live.co.uk

Situated twixt Boscastle and Tintagel, this is a great location for exploring the stunning coast and countryside of North Cornwall. The welcome here is warm and genuine with a relaxed and homely approach, the perfect place to de-stress. Bedrooms offer all the expected comforts with one located on the ground floor. Breakfast is a treat for the taste buds and the eyes, with breathtaking views from the dining room, across the fields to Bossiney Cove.

Rooms 2 en suite (1 GF) D £55-£65* **Facilities** TVL tea/coffee Cen ht Wi-fi **Parking** 2 **Notes** LB ⊗ Closed Oct-Etr 🐾

TRURO   Map 2 SW84

Bissick Old Mill

★★★★ GUEST HOUSE

Ladock TR2 4PG
☎ 01726 882557
e-mail: enquiries@bissickoldmill.plus.com
dir: 6m NE of Truro. Off B3275 in Ladock village centre by Falmouth Arms pub

This charming family-run mill, dates back some 300 years. Low ceilings, beams, stone walls and an impressive fireplace all contribute to its character. Equally inviting is the hospitality extended to guests, who are instantly made welcome. The breakfast menu offers a range of hot dishes, is freshly prepared and is a memorable aspect of any stay.

Rooms 3 en suite 1 annexe en suite (1 fmly) (1 GF) S £50-£60; D £77.50-£87.50 **Facilities** FTV TVL tea/coffee Direct Dial Cen ht Wi-fi **Parking** 6 **Notes** LB

Bodrean Manor Farm (SW851480)

★★★★ FARMHOUSE

Trispen TR4 9AG
☎ 07970 955857
Mrs M Marsh
e-mail: bodrean@hotmail.co.uk
web: www.bodreanmanorfarm.co.uk
dir: 3m NE of Truro. A30 onto A39 towards Truro, left after Trispen signed Frogmore & Trehane, farm drive 100yds

This friendly farmhouse is located in peaceful countryside, convenient for Truro or as a touring base. It has all the charm of an historic house but is styled and fitted with modern facilities. Bedrooms are thoughtfully and extensively equipped, and the bathrooms are well provisioned with soft towels and a host of toiletries. The home-cooked breakfast served in the smartly appointed dining room, around a large communal table, is a feature. Storage for motorbikes and cycles is available.

Rooms 3 rms (2 en suite) (1 pri facs) (1 fmly) **Facilities** FTV TVL tea/coffee Cen ht Wi-fi **Parking** 6 **Notes** ⊗ 🐾 220 acres mixed

The Haven

★★★★ BED AND BREAKFAST

Truro Vean Ter TR1 1HA
☎ 01872 264197
e-mail: thehaven7@btinternet.com
dir: Entering Truro from A39 or A390, right at 1st rdbt, through 2 sets of lights, next right then immediately left. On left (no through road)

A recently refurbished and extended property within a few minutes' walk of the city centre with off-street parking and views of the cathedral. The owners are very friendly. The rooms are bright and well furnished, the beds are very comfortable and bathrooms well equipped. Freshly cooked hearty breakfasts are served at a large table in the separate breakfast room.

Rooms 3 rms (2 en suite) (1 pri facs) (3 GF) S £55-£65; D £65-£75* **Facilities** FTV tea/coffee Cen ht Wi-fi **Parking** 3 **Notes** ⊗ No Children 7yrs Closed Nov-Jan 🐾

Manor Cottage

★★★★ GUEST ACCOMMODATION

Tresillian TR2 4BN
☎ 01872 520212
e-mail: manorcottage@live.co.uk
dir: 3m E of Truro on A390, on left opp river

Located just a few minutes drive of Truro this well-run establishment is friendly and comfortable. Breakfast is served in the conservatory and dinner is available with prior notice.

Rooms 3 rms (2 en suite) (1 pri facs) (1 fmly) S £38-£65; D £65-£78 **Facilities** tea/coffee Dinner available Wi-fi **Parking** 8 **Notes** LB ⊗

TRURO *continued*

Oxturn House

★★★★ BED AND BREAKFAST

Ladock TR2 4NQ
☎ 01726 884348
e-mail: oxturnhouse@hotmail.com
web: www.oxturnhouse.co.uk
dir: *6m NE of Truro. B3275 into Ladock, onto lane opp Falmouth Arms, up hill 200yds, 1st right after end 30mph sign, Oxturn on right*

A friendly welcome is assured at this large family house, set slightly above the village and close to a pub and several dining venues. Bedrooms are spacious and a pleasant lounge is available. In summer you can enjoy the country views from the patio. Hearty breakfasts are served in the dining room.

Rooms 2 rms (1 en suite) (1 pri facs) D £64-£76*
Facilities TVL tea/coffee Cen ht Wi-fi **Parking** 4 **Notes** ⊗ No Children 12yrs Closed Dec-Jan ⊛

The Whitehouse Inn & Luxury Lodge

★★★★ INN

Penhallow TR4 9LQ
☎ 01872 573306 ▤ 01872 572062
e-mail: whitehouseinn@btconnect.com
web: www.whitehousecornwall.co.uk
dir: *A3075 between Newquay & Redruth*

This popular inn now offers recently constructed, very well appointed bedrooms. Conveniently located mid-way between Truro and Newquay, the Whitehouse Inn has a busy bar and restaurant, appealing to all palates and pockets. In addition to the local and international artists performing at weekends, widescreen TVs, pool tables and both indoor and outdoor children's play areas are provided. A wide range of meals is available, including the carvery which offers great value for money.

Rooms 12 en suite (3 fmly) (6 GF) **Facilities** FTV tea/coffee Dinner available Direct Dial Cen ht Lift Wi-fi Golf 9 Pool table Go-Karts Crazy golf **Parking** 200 **Notes** ⊗

Spires

★★★ BED AND BREAKFAST

45 Treyew Rd TR1 2BY
☎ 01872 277621
dir: *0.5m W of town centre on A39, opp Truro City Football Club*

This comfortable establishment enjoys a homely atmosphere and friendly host. The city centre is just a short drive away, or a walk for the more energetic (downhill there, uphill back). Bedrooms are light and airy; one room is spacious and has a splendid view of the city and cathedral. Breakfast is served in the cosy dining room. The nearby pub-restaurant offers an extensive choice of meals.

Rooms 2 rms (1 en suite) (1 pri facs) (1 fmly) S £45; D £60* **Facilities** FTV tea/coffee Cen ht Wi-fi **Parking** 2 **Notes** ⊗ ⊛

Cliftons

★★★ GUEST ACCOMMODATION

46 Tregolls Rd TR1 1LA
☎ 01872 274116 ▤ 01872 274116
e-mail: cliftonsbandb@hotmail.com
dir: *0.5m NE of city centre on A390*

This lovely Victorian property has character, provides a relaxed atmosphere and is within walking distance of the city centre. Bedrooms, including one on the ground floor, have considerate extras. There is a lounge for guest use, which exhibits a large tropical fish tank. The breakfast menu offers a good choice of dishes in the bright dining room.

Rooms 6 en suite (1 fmly) (1 GF) S £43-£45; D £63-£65*
Facilities FTV tea/coffee Cen ht Wi-fi **Parking** 6 **Notes** ⊗

Coronation Guest House

★★★ BED AND BREAKFAST

2 Coronation Ter TR1 3HJ
☎ 01872 274514
e-mail: email@coronationguesthouse.com
dir: *Opp railway station*

Located just a short distance from the city centre and close to the railway station, this Victorian accommodation is attentively cared for. Bedrooms, although not spacious, are clean and bright. A freshly prepared traditional English breakfast is taken in the pleasant dining room at the rear of the house.

Rooms 3 rms (2 pri facs) S £30-£35; D £60-£65*
Facilities FTV tea/coffee Cen ht **Notes** ⊗ No Children 8yrs ⊛

Donnington Guest House

★★★ GUEST ACCOMMODATION

43 Treyew Rd TR1 2BY
☎ 01872 222552 & 07787 555475
e-mail: info@donnington-guesthouse.co.uk

A well located property within 12 minutes walk of the city centre, Donnington Guest House is actually two houses operating as one with breakfast being taken in the breakfast room of one of them. Well-appointed rooms, a friendly host and good off-road parking make this a very popular venue.

Rooms 14 rms (12 en suite) (2 pri facs) (5 fmly) (3 GF) **Facilities** FTV tea/coffee Cen ht Lift Wi-fi ch fac Golf 18 **Parking** 11 **Notes** ⊛

The Laurels

★★★ BED AND BREAKFAST

Penwethers TR3 6EA
☎ 07794 472171
e-mail: annie.toms@hotmail.com
dir: *From A39 right onto A390 Tregolls Rd, through 3 rdbts. Take exit towards Redruth, Treyew Rd, next left to Penwethers*

A traditional bed and breakfast operation offering comfortable accommodation in a home-from-home environment. It is ideally located in a quiet location, yet is just minutes from the cathedral city of Truro. Off-road parking is available.

Rooms 3 rms (1 en suite) (1 pri facs) (2 fmly)
Facilities FTV TV2B tea/coffee Wi-fi **Parking** 3 **Notes** ⊗ ⊛

Polsue Manor Farm (SW858462)

★★★ FARMHOUSE

Tresillian TR2 4BP
☎ 01872 520234
Mrs G Holliday
e-mail: geraldineholliday@hotmail.com
dir: *2m NE of Truro. Farm entrance on A390 at S end of Tresillian*

The 190-acre sheep farm is in peaceful countryside a short drive from Truro. The farmhouse provides a relaxing break from the city, with hearty breakfasts and warm hospitality. The spacious dining room has pleasant views and three large communal tables. Bedrooms do not offer televisions but there is a homely lounge equipped with a television and video recorder with a selection of videos for viewing.

Rooms 5 rms (2 en suite) (3 fmly) (1 GF) **Facilities** TVL tea/coffee **Parking** 5 **Notes** Closed 21 Dec-2 Jan 190 acres mixed/sheep/horses

Resparveth Farm (SW914499)

★★★ FARMHOUSE

Grampound Rd TR2 4EF
☎ 01726 882382 ▤ 01726 882382
Ms Lisa Willey
e-mail: lisawilley83@hotmail.com

The new, young owners of this traditional farmhouse bed and breakfast do all they can to make a stay as comfortable as possible. Handy location for St Austell, the Eden Project and Truro, offering comfortable rooms and freshly cooked breakfasts at one large table in the breakfast room featuring an original Cornish Range.

Rooms 3 en suite **Facilities** FTV TVL tea/coffee Cen ht Wi-fi **Parking** 4 **Notes** 65 acres dairy

The Bay Tree

★★ GUEST ACCOMMODATION

28 Ferris Town TR1 3JH
☎ 01872 240274

A well established friendly property within a few minutes walk of the railway station and the city centre. Rooms are comfortable and have shared facilities, and breakfast is served at large tables in the dining room.

Rooms 4 rms (1 fmly) S £35-£40; D £55-£60* **Facilities** tea/coffee Cen ht Wi-fi **Notes** 🐾

VERYAN   Map 2 SW93

Elerkey Guest House

★★★★ GUEST HOUSE

Elerkey House TR2 5QA
☎ 01872 501261 & 501160
e-mail: enquiries@elerkey.co.uk
web: www.elerkey.co.uk
dir: In village, 1st left after church & water gardens

This peaceful home is surrounded by attractive gardens in a tranquil village. The proprietors and their family provide exemplary hospitality and many guests return time and again. The pleasantly appointed bedrooms have many considerate extras.

Rooms 4 en suite (1 fmly) S £45-£80; D £60-£80 **Facilities** FTV tea/coffee Direct Dial Cen ht Wi-fi Art gallery & gift shop art tuition **Parking** 4 **Notes** LB 🐾 Closed Dec-Feb

---

ZENNOR   Map 2 SW43

The Gurnard's Head

★★★ ◉ INN

Treen TR26 3DE
☎ 01736 796928
e-mail: enquiries@gurnardshead.co.uk
dir: 5m from St Ives on B3306, 4.5m from Penzance via New Mill

This inn is ideally located for enjoying the beautiful coastline, and is very popular with walkers keen to rest their weary legs. The style is relaxed with a log fire in the bar providing a warm welcome on colder days, and outside seating ideal for enjoying the sun. Lunch and dinner are available either in the bar or the adjoining restaurant area. The dinner menu is not extensive but there are interesting choices and everything is home-made, including the bread. Breakfast is also a treat with newspapers on the bar to peruse whilst easing into the day.

Rooms 7 en suite S £65-£125; D £95-£165* **Facilities** tea/coffee Dinner available Wi-fi **Parking** 40 **Notes** Closed 25 Dec & 4 days mid Jan No coaches

---

CUMBRIA

ALSTON   Map 18 NY74

See also Cowshill (Co Durham)

Alston House

★★★★ 🍴 RESTAURANT WITH ROOMS

Townfoot CA9 3RN
☎ 01434 382200 📠 01434 382493
e-mail: alstonhouse@fsmail.net
web: www.alstonhouse.co.uk
dir: On A686 opposite Spar garage

Located at the foot of the town, this family-owned restaurant with rooms provides well-equipped, stylish and comfortable accommodation. The kitchen serves both modern and traditional dishes with flair and creativity. Alston House runs a café during the day serving light meals and afternoon teas.

Rooms 7 en suite (3 fmly) S £40-£55; D £80-£100 **Facilities** tea/coffee Dinner available Cen ht Wi-fi ch fac Golf 9 Fishing **Conf** Max 70 Thtr 70 Class 30 Board 30 **Parking** 20 **Notes** Civ Wed

---

Lowbyer Manor Country House

★★★★ 🏠 GUEST HOUSE

Hexham Rd CA9 3JX
☎ 01434 381230 📠 01434 381425
e-mail: stay@lowbyer.com
web: www.lowbyer.com
dir: 250yds N of village centre on A686. Pass South Tynedale Railway on left, turn right

Located on the edge of the village, this Grade II listed Georgian building retains many original features, which are highlighted by the furnishings and decor. Cosy bedrooms are filled with a wealth of thoughtful extras and day rooms include an elegant dining room, a comfortable lounge and bar equipped with lots of historical artefacts.

Rooms 9 en suite (1 fmly) S £36-£60; D £72-£86* **Facilities** tea/coffee Cen ht Licensed **Parking** 9 **Notes** LB

AMBLESIDE   Map 18 NY30

PREMIER COLLECTION

Drunken Duck

★★★★★ ◉◉ 🏠 INN

Barngates LA22 0NG
☎ 015394 36347 📠 015394 36781
e-mail: info@drunkenduckinn.co.uk
web: www.drunkenduckinn.co.uk
dir: B5286, S from Ambleside towards Hawkshead, 2.5m signed right, 0.5m up hill

This 400-year-old, traditional coaching inn has been stylishly modernised to offer a high standard of accommodation. Superior rooms are in a courtyard house looking out over private gardens and a tarn. The bar retains its original character and is the hub of the inn. Fresh, local produce features on the imaginative menus served there and in the cosy restaurant. The on-site brewery ensures a fine selection of award-winning ales.

Rooms 8 en suite 9 annexe en suite (5 GF) S £71.25-£172.50; D £95-£295* **Facilities** FTV Dinner available Direct Dial Cen ht Wi-fi Fishing **Parking** 40 **Notes** Closed 25 Dec No coaches

AMBLESIDE continued

Riverside

★★★★ 🏠 GUEST HOUSE

Under Loughrigg LA22 9LJ
☎ 015394 32395 📠 015394 32440
e-mail: info@riverside-at-ambleside.co.uk
web: www.riverside-at-ambleside.co.uk
dir: *A593 from Ambleside to Coniston, over stone bridge, right onto Under Loughrigg Ln, Riverside 150yds left*

A friendly atmosphere prevails at this refurbished Victorian house, situated on a quiet lane by the River Rothay, below Loughrigg Fell. Bedrooms, all with lovely views, are very comfortable, stylishly furnished and feature homely extras; some have spa baths. A log-burning stove warms the lounge in winter. Guests can use the garden, which has seating for morning and evening sun.

Rooms 6 en suite (1 fmly) **Facilities** TVL tea/coffee Cen ht Licensed Fishing Jacuzzi **Parking** 15 **Notes** ⊗ No Children 5yrs Closed Xmas & New Year

Wateredge Inn

★★★★ INN

Waterhead Bay LA22 0EP
☎ 015394 32332 📠 015394 31878
e-mail: rec@wateredgeinn.co.uk
web: www.wateredgeinn.co.uk
dir: *On A59, at Waterhead, 1m S of Ambleside. Inn at end of promenade by lake*

This modern inn has an idyllic location on the shore of Windermere at Waterhead Bay. The pretty bedrooms are particularly smart and generally spacious, and all offer a high standard of quality and comfort. The airy bar-restaurant opens onto attractive gardens, which have magnificent lake views. There is also a comfortable lounge, bar and dining area.

Rooms 15 en suite 7 annexe en suite (4 fmly) (3 GF) S £40-£60; D £75-£170* **Facilities** tea/coffee Dinner available Cen ht Wi-fi Complimentary membership of nearby leisure club **Parking** 40 **Notes** LB Closed 25-26 Dec

Ambleside Lodge

★★★★ GUEST HOUSE

Rothay Rd LA22 0EJ
☎ 015394 31681 📠 015394 34547
e-mail: enquiries@ambleside-lodge.com
web: www.ambleside-lodge.com

Located close to the centre of this historic market town, this Grade II listed 18th-century residence has a peaceful atmosphere. The stylishly decorated, elegant accommodation includes attractive bedrooms with antique and contemporary pieces, including four-poster beds. Attentive, personal service is provided.

Rooms 18 en suite (2 fmly) (1 GF) S £35-£45; D £80-£150 **Facilities** FTV tea/coffee Cen ht Wi-fi **Parking** 20 **Notes** LB

Broadview Guest House

★★★★ 🏠 GUEST HOUSE

Lake Rd LA22 0DN
☎ 015394 32431
e-mail: enquiries@broadviewguesthouse.co.uk
web: www.broadviewguesthouse.co.uk
dir: *On A591 S side of Ambleside, on Lake Rd opposite Garden Centre*

Just a short walk from the centre of Ambleside a warm welcome is assured at this popular guest house, where regular improvements enhance the guest experience. Bedrooms are thoughtfully furnished and comprehensive breakfasts provide an excellent start to the day.

Rooms 6 rms (3 en suite) (1 pri facs) S £40-£100; D £50-£100* **Facilities** FTV tea/coffee Cen ht Wi-fi Access to nearby leisure club **Notes** LB ⊗

Cherry Garth

★★★★ GUEST HOUSE

Old Lake Rd LA22 0DH
☎ 015394 33128 📠 015394 33885
e-mail: reception@cherrygarth.com
dir: *M6 junct 36, follow signs for Windermere, A591 N into Ambleside, over lights, 800yds on right*

Set on the southern approach to the town, this detached house sits in well-landscaped gardens giving views of Loughrigg Fell and Wetherlam. Bedrooms offer a range of styles, are spacious and have modern fittings with all of the expected facilities. Traditional Lakeland breakfasts are served in the lounge-breakfast room overlooking the

front garden. Amy and Vivienne Eccles were runners-up in this year's AA Friendliest Landlady of the Year Award (2011-12).

Rooms 11 en suite (2 fmly) (3 GF) S £40-£75; D £80-£150 **Facilities** STV tea/coffee Cen ht Licensed Wi-fi **Parking** 14 **Notes** LB

Haven Cottage Guest House

★★★★ GUEST HOUSE

Rydal Rd LA22 9AY
☎ 015394 33270
e-mail: enquiries@amblesidehavencottage.co.uk
web: www.amblesidehavencottage.co.uk
dir: *250yds N of town centre on A591*

At Haven Cottage a warm welcome awaits along with home baking and refreshments served on arrival. Lindsey and Tim create a definite home-away-from-home, making their guests feel very welcome, with plenty of extras provided. Haven Cottage is located on the edge of Ambleside and benefits from off-road parking. Very good breakfast; see how many puzzles you can work out.

Rooms 7 en suite (2 fmly) S £45-£55; D £80-£150* **Facilities** FTV tea/coffee Cen ht Licensed Wi-fi **Parking** 6 **Notes** LB ⊗ No Children 8yrs

Kent House

★★★★ GUEST HOUSE

Lake Rd LA22 0AD
☎ 015394 33279
e-mail: mail@kent-house.com
web: www.kent-house.com
dir: *From town centre, pass Post Office on one-way system 300mtrs on left on terrace above main road*

From an elevated location overlooking the town, this traditional Lakeland house offers comfortable, well-equipped accommodation with attractive bedrooms. Traditional breakfasts featuring the best of local produce are served at individual tables in the elegant dining room.

Rooms 5 rms (4 en suite) (1 pri facs) (2 fmly) **Facilities** FTV tea/coffee Cen ht Wi-fi **Parking** 2

Lake House

★★★★ GUEST ACCOMMODATION

Waterhead Bay LA22 0HD
☎ 015394 32360 📠 015394 31474
e-mail: info@lakehousehotel.co.uk
dir: *From S: M6 junct 36, A590, then A591 towards Kendal & Windermere. House 3m N of Windermere. From N: M6 junct 40, A66 to Keswick, then A591 to Ambleside. House just S of town*

Set on a hillside with lake views, this delightful house has very stylish accommodation and a homely atmosphere. The bedrooms are all individual in style and include many homely extras. Dinner is available at the nearby sister property with complimentary transport, and leisure facilities are available there too. Breakfast is an interesting and substantial cold buffet.

Rooms 12 en suite 7 annexe en suite (3 fmly) (4 GF) S £65-£95; D £89-£149* **Facilities** FTV TVL tea/coffee Cen ht Licensed Wi-fi Use of pool at Regent Hotel **Parking** 19 **Notes** LB ⊗ No Children 14yrs

The Log House

★★★★ ֎ RESTAURANT WITH ROOMS

Lake Rd LA22 0DN
☎ 015394 31077
e-mail: info@loghouse.co.uk
web: www.loghouse.co.uk
dir: *From Windermere into Ambleside on A591. On left after Hayes Garden Centre*

This charming and historic Norwegian building is located midway between the town centre and the shore of Lake Windermere, just five minutes' walk to each. Guests can enjoy delicious meals in the attractive restaurant, which also has a bar area. There are three comfortable bedrooms, each equipped with thoughtful accessories such as DVD/VCR players and hairdryers. Wi-fi is also available.

Rooms 3 en suite D £60-£92.25* **Facilities** FTV tea/coffee Dinner available Cen ht Wi-fi **Parking** 3 **Notes** LB ⊗ Closed 3 Jan-1 Feb No coaches

Rysdale Guesthouse

★★★★ GUEST ACCOMMODATION

Rothay Rd LA22 0EE
☎ 015394 32140 ▤ 015394 33999
e-mail: info@rysdalehotel.co.uk
dir: *A591 into Ambleside, one-way system to A593, Rysdale on right facing church*

This Edwardian house is only a stroll from the village centre and overlooks the church and the park. The friendly proprietors offer attractive, well-equipped bedrooms, carefully decorated throughout with co-ordinated soft fabrics. Some have period furniture, and most enjoy superb mountain views, as does the smart dining room. There is also a cosy lounge with an inglenook fire place.

Rooms 9 rms (7 en suite) (2 pri facs) (1 fmly) S £32-£50; D £64-£100 **Facilities** tea/coffee Cen ht Complimentary pass to Lanedale Country Club **Parking** 2 **Notes** ⊗ No Children 4yrs Closed 23-26 Dec RS Jan wknds only ֎

Wanslea Guest House

★★★★ GUEST HOUSE

Low Fold, Lake Rd LA22 0DN
☎ 015394 33884 ▤ 015394 33884
e-mail: information@wanslea.co.uk
dir: *On S side of town, opp garden centre*

Located between town centre and lakeside pier, this Victorian house provides a range of thoughtfully furnished bedrooms, some of which are individually themed and equipped with spa baths. Comprehensive breakfasts are served in the spacious dining room and a cosy lounge is available.

Rooms 8 en suite (1 fmly) S £35-£50; D £60-£90* **Facilities** FTV tea/coffee Cen ht Wi-fi **Notes** LB ⊗ No Children 6yrs Closed 23-26 Dec

The Old Vicarage

★★★★ Ⓐ GUEST ACCOMMODATION

Vicarage Rd LA22 9DH
☎ 015394 33364 ▤ 015394 34734
e-mail: info@oldvicarageambleside.co.uk
web: www.oldvicarageambleside.co.uk
dir: *In town centre. Off Compston Rd onto Vicarage Rd*
Rooms 15 en suite (4 fmly) (2 GF) D £99-£144* **Facilities** FTV tea/coffee Cen ht Wi-fi ⓣ ♨ Riding Sauna Pool table Hot tub **Parking** 17 **Notes** LB Closed 23-28 Dec

The Rothay Garth

★★★★ Ⓐ GUEST ACCOMMODATION

Rothay Rd LA22 0EE
☎ 015394 32217 ▤ 015394 34400
e-mail: book@rothay-garth.co.uk
dir: *M6 junct 36, A591 to Ambleside. 1st lights straight over, then left onto Wansfell Rd. At T-junct turn right, located on right*

Rooms 14 en suite 1 annexe en suite (3 fmly) (4 GF) S £54-£60; D £88-£120* **Facilities** FTV TVL tea/coffee Direct Dial Cen ht Licensed Wi-fi **Parking** 18 **Notes** LB

APPLEBY-IN-WESTMORLAND   **Map 18 NY62**

Hall Croft

★★★★ ֎ BED AND BREAKFAST

Dufton CA16 6DB
☎ 017683 52902
e-mail: hallcroft@phonecoop.coop
dir: *3m N of Appleby. In Dufton by village green*

Standing at the end of a lime-tree avenue, Hall Croft, built in 1882, has been restored to its original glory. Bedrooms are comfortably proportioned, traditionally furnished and well equipped. Breakfasts, served in the lounge-dining room, are substantial and include a range of home-made produce. Guests can enjoy the lovely garden, which has views of the Pennines.

Rooms 3 rms (2 en suite) (1 pri facs) **Facilities** FTV tea/coffee Cen ht Wi-fi **Parking** 3 **Notes** Closed 24-26 Dec ֎

ARMATHWAITE   **Map 18 NY54**

The Dukes Head Inn

★★★ INN

Front St CA4 9PB
☎ 016974 72226
e-mail: info@dukeshead-hotel.co.uk
web: www.dukeshead-hotel.co.uk
dir: *In village centre opp post office*

Located in the peaceful village of Armathwaite close to the River Eden, the Dukes Head offers comfortable accommodation in a warm friendly atmosphere. There is a relaxing lounge bar with open fires, and a wide choice of meals are available either here or in the restaurant.

Rooms 5 rms (3 en suite) (2 pri facs) **Facilities** FTV TV4B tea/coffee Dinner available Cen ht Wi-fi **Parking** 20 **Notes** Closed 25 Dec

BOOT   **Map 18 NY10**

Brook House Inn

★★★★ ☞ INN

CA19 1TG
☎ 01946 723288 ▤ 01946 723160
e-mail: stay@brookhouseinn.co.uk
web: www.brookhouseinn.co.uk
dir: *In village centre. 0.5m NE of Dalegarth station*

Located in the heart of Eskdale, this impressive inn dates from the early 18th century and has been renovated to offer comfortable accommodation with smart, modern bathrooms for weary walkers and travellers. Wholesome meals using local produce are served in the traditionally furnished dining room or attractive bar, the latter featuring real ales and country memorabilia.

Rooms 8 en suite (2 fmly) S £52.50-£62.50; D £80-£95* **Facilities** FTV tea/coffee Dinner available Cen ht Wi-fi **Conf** Max 35 **Parking** 24 **Notes** LB Closed 25 Dec

BORROWDALE — Map 18 NY21

PREMIER COLLECTION

Hazel Bank Country House

★★★★★ GUEST ACCOMMODATION

Rosthwaite CA12 5XB
☎ 017687 77248 📄 017687 77373
e-mail: info@hazelbankhotel.co.uk
dir: From Keswick, follow B5289 towards Borrowdale, turn left after sign for Rosthwaite

Arrival at this grand Victorian house is impressive, reached via a picturesque hump back bridge and winding drive. Set on an elevated position surrounded by four acres of gardens and woodland, Hazel Bank enjoys magnificent views of Borrowdale. Carefully cooked dishes are served in the elegant dining room; the daily-changing, four-course dinner menu features fresh, local ingredients. There is a friendly atmosphere here and the proprietors are very welcoming.

Rooms 8 en suite (2 GF) S £90-£96; D £180-£178* (incl.dinner) **Facilities** FTV tea/coffee Dinner available Cen ht Licensed Wi-fi 💪 **Parking** 8 **Notes** ⊗ No Children 10yrs

BOWNESS-ON-WINDERMERE

See Windermere

BRAITHWAITE — Map 18 NY22

The Cottage in the Wood

★★★★ ⚫⚫ 🍴 RESTAURANT WITH ROOMS

Whinlatter Pass CA12 5TW
☎ 017687 78409
e-mail: relax@thecottageinthewood.co.uk
dir: M6 junct 40, A66 W. After Keswick exit for Braithwaite via Whinlatter Pass (B5292), establishment at top of pass

This charming property sits on wooded hills with striking views of Skiddaw, and it is in a conveniently placed for Keswick. The professional owners provide excellent hospitality in a relaxed manner. The award-winning food, freshly prepared and locally sourced, is served in the bright and welcoming conservatory restaurant that has stunning views. The comfortable bedrooms are well appointed and have many useful extras.

Rooms 9 en suite (1 GF) S fr £90; D £110-£180* **Facilities** FTV tea/coffee Dinner available Direct Dial Cen ht Wi-fi **Parking** 15 **Notes** LB ⊗ No Children 10yrs Closed Jan RS Mon closed No coaches

The Royal Oak

★★★ INN

CA12 5SY
☎ 017687 78533 📄 017687 78533
e-mail: info@royaloak-braithwaite.co.uk
web: www.royaloak-braithwaite.co.uk
dir: In village centre

The Royal Oak, in the pretty village of Braithwaite, has delightful views of Skiddaw and Barrow, and is a good base for tourists and walkers. Some of the well-equipped bedrooms are furnished with four-poster beds. Hearty meals and traditional Cumbrian breakfasts are served in the restaurant, and there is an atmospheric, well-stocked bar.

Rooms 10 en suite (1 fmly) S £43-£46; D £78-£92* **Facilities** STV FTV tea/coffee Dinner available Cen ht Wi-fi 👤 **Parking** 20 **Notes** LB

BRAMPTON — Map 21 NY56

PREMIER COLLECTION

Lanercost Bed & Breakfast

★★★★★ 🏠 GUEST ACCOMMODATION

Lanercost CA8 2HQ
☎ 016977 42589 & 07976 977204
e-mail: info@lanercostbedandbreakfast.co.uk
web: www.lanercostbedandbreakfast.co.uk
dir: Follow signs to Lanercost Priory

Built in 1840 in the grounds of Lanercost Priory close to Hadrian's Wall. Individually designed bedrooms of a good size with quality fixtures and fittings. Public areas are warm and welcoming enhanced with artwork and objet d'art. Hearty award-winning breakfasts use local produce offering a wonderful start to the day. Gardens are pleasing to the eye looking onto the priory.

Rooms 4 en suite **Facilities** FTV tea/coffee Dinner available Cen ht Wi-fi Golf 18 Fishing Riding **Conf** Max 10 Thtr 10 Class 10 Board 10 **Parking** 6 **Notes** LB ⊗

The Blacksmiths Arms

★★★★ INN

Talkin Village CA8 1LE
☎ 016977 3452 & 42111 📄 016977 3396
e-mail: blacksmithsarmstalkin@yahoo.co.uk
web: www.blacksmithstalkin.co.uk
dir: B6413 from Brampton to Castle Carrock, after level crossing 2nd left signed Talkin

Dating from the early 19th century and used as a smithy until the 1950s, this friendly village inn offers good home-cooked fare and real ales, with two Cumbrian cask beers always available. Bedrooms are well equipped, and three are particularly smart. An extensive menu and daily specials are offered in the cosy bar lounges or the smart, panelled Old Forge Restaurant.

Rooms 5 en suite 3 annexe en suite (2 fmly) (3 GF) S £50-£55; D £70-£80* **Facilities** FTV tea/coffee Dinner available Direct Dial Cen ht Wi-fi Golf **Parking** 20 **Notes** ⊗ No coaches

Hullerbank

★★★★ GUEST ACCOMMODATION

Talkin CA8 1LB
☎ 016977 46668 📄 016977 46668
e-mail: info@hullerbank.co.uk
web: www.hullerbank.co.uk
dir: B6413 from Brampton for 2m, over railway & after golf club left to Talkin, onto Hallbankgate Rd & signs to Hullerbank

Dating from 1635, Hullerbank is a delightful farmhouse set in well-tended gardens, convenient for Hadrian's Wall, the Lake District and the Borders. Bedrooms are comfortably proportioned, attractively decorated and well equipped. There is a cosy ground-floor lounge with an inglenook fireplace, and traditional hearty breakfasts are served in the dining room.

Rooms 3 rms (2 en suite) (1 pri facs) D £74 **Facilities** FTV TVL tea/coffee Cen ht **Parking** 6 **Notes** ⊗ No Children 12yrs Closed Nov-Etr

Save on B&Bs and Hotels. Book at **theAA.com/hotel**

CUMBRIA 77 **ENGLAND**

CALDBECK — Map 18 NY34

Swaledale Watch Farm

★★★★ GUEST ACCOMMODATION

Whelpo CA7 8HQ
☎ 016974 78409 📠 016974 78409
e-mail: nan.savage@talk21.com
web: www.swaledale-watch.co.uk
dir: 1m SW of Caldbeck on B5299

This attractive farmhouse, set in its own nature reserve, is in a peaceful location with a backdrop of picturesque fells. The en suite bedrooms are spacious and well equipped. Two rooms are in an adjacent converted farm building and share a comfortable sitting room. Traditional hearty breakfasts are served in the attractive dining room overlooking the garden, with views of the fells.

Rooms 2 en suite 2 annexe en suite (2 fmly) (4 GF) S £30-£33; D £50-£60* **Facilities** FTV TVL tea/coffee Cen ht Wi-fi 100 acre Nature Reserve, badger watching evenings **Parking** 8 **Notes** Closed 24-26 Dec

CARLISLE — Map 18 NY35

See also Brampton

Cambro House

★★★★ GUEST ACCOMMODATION

173 Warwick Rd CA1 1LP
☎ 01228 543094
e-mail: davidcambro@aol.com
dir: M6 junct 43, onto Warwick Rd, 1m on right before St Aidan's Church

This smart Victorian house is close to the town centre and motorway. The beautifully refurbished and spacious bedrooms are brightly decorated, smartly appointed and thoughtfully equipped. A hearty Cumbrian breakfast is served in the cosy morning room.

Rooms 3 en suite (1 GF) S £35-£40; D £55-£60* **Facilities** FTV tea/coffee Cen ht Wi-fi **Parking** 2 **Notes** LB ⊗ No Children 5yrs

No1 Guest House

★★★★ BED AND BREAKFAST

1 Etterby St CA3 9JB
☎ 01228 547285 & 07899 948711
e-mail: sheila@carlislebandb.co.uk
dir: M6 junct 44 onto A7, right at 7th lights onto Etterby St, house 1st on left

This small friendly house is on the north side of the city within walking distance of the centre. The attractive, well-equipped en suite bedrooms consist of a double, a twin and a single room. Hearty traditional breakfasts featuring the best of local produce, are served in the ground-floor dining room.

Rooms 3 en suite S £35; D £60* **Facilities** FTV tea/coffee Dinner available Cen ht Wi-fi **Parking** 1 **Notes** LB ⊗

Angus House & Almonds Restaurant

★★★ ⌂ GUEST ACCOMMODATION

14-16 Scotland Rd CA3 9DG
☎ 01228 523546 📠 01228 531895
e-mail: hotel@angus-hotel.co.uk
web: www.angus-hotel.co.uk
dir: 0.5m N of city centre on A7

Situated just north of the city, this family-run establishment is ideal for business and leisure. A warm welcome is assured and the accommodation is well equipped. Almonds Restaurant provides enjoyable food and home baking, and there is also a lounge and a large meeting room.

Rooms 10 en suite (2 fmly) **Facilities** FTV tea/coffee Dinner available Direct Dial Cen ht Licensed Wi-fi **Conf** Max 25 Thtr 25 Class 16 Board 16 **Notes** LB

Marlborough House

★★★ GUEST ACCOMMODATION

2 Marlbourgh Gardens, Stanwix CA3 9NW
☎ 01228 512174 & 07714 091538
e-mail: ian_mc_brown@hotmail.com
dir: M6 junct 44, 2m to Carlisle, left at Crown Inn

A warm welcome awaits you at Marlborough House, situated within easy walking distance of the city centre. This friendly guest accommodation offers individually decorated, pleasantly furnished, and thoughtfully equipped bedrooms. There is a comfortable conservatory room where hearty breakfasts are served at individual tables. Parking is available.

Rooms 4 en suite (1 fmly) (1 GF) **Facilities** TVL tea/coffee Dinner available Cen ht Wi-fi Golf 18 **Parking** 8 **Notes** ⊗

CARTMEL — Map 18 SD37

PREMIER COLLECTION

L'enclume

★★★★★ ⌂⌂⌂⌂⌂ RESTAURANT WITH ROOMS

Cavendish St LA11 6PZ
☎ 015395 36362
e-mail: info@lenclume.co.uk
dir: From A590 turn left for Cartmel before Newby Bridge

A delightful 13th-century property in the heart of this lovely village offering 21st-century cooking that is more than worth travelling some distance for. Simon Rogan cooks imaginative and adventurous food in this stylish restaurant. Individually designed, modern, en suite rooms vary in size and style, and are either in the main property or dotted about the village only a few moments' walk from the restaurant.

Rooms 7 en suite 5 annexe en suite (3 fmly) (3 GF) **Facilities** STV tea/coffee Dinner available Direct Dial Cen ht **Parking** 11 **Notes** No coaches

CONISTON — Map 18 SD39

PREMIER COLLECTION

Wheelgate Country Guest House

★★★★★ ⌂ GUEST HOUSE

Little Arrow LA21 8AU
☎ 015394 41418 📠 015394 41114
e-mail: enquiry@wheelgate.co.uk
dir: 1.5m S of Coniston, on W side of road

Dating from the 17th century, this charming farmhouse has original oak beams, panelling and low ceilings. An intimate bar, laundry facilities and a comfortable lounge with open fire are provided. There are impressive views over the well-tended gardens and the beautiful Lakeland countryside. A warm welcome can be expected.

Rooms 4 en suite 1 annexe en suite (1 GF) S £40-£45; D £70-£90* **Facilities** FTV tea/coffee Cen ht Licensed **Parking** 5 **Notes** LB ⊗ No Children 8yrs Closed Nov-Apr

CROSTHWAITE — Map 18 SD49

PREMIER COLLECTION

The Punchbowl Inn at Crosthwaite

★★★★★ ◉◉ INN

Lyth Valley LA8 8HR
☎ 015395 68237 ▪ 015397 68875
e-mail: info@the-punchbowl.co.uk
dir: *M6 junct 36 signed Barrow, on A5074 towards Windermere, turn right for Crosthwaite. At E end of village beside church*

Located in the stunning Lyth Valley alongside the village church, this historic inn has been renovated to provide excellent standards of comfort and facilities. Its sumptuous bedrooms have a wealth of thoughtful extras, and imaginative food is available in the elegant restaurant or in the rustic-style bar with open fires. A warm welcome and professional service is assured.

Rooms 9 en suite S £95–£221.25; D £120–£295*
Facilities FTV Dinner available Direct Dial Cen ht Wi-fi
Parking 25 **Notes** No coaches Civ Wed 50

Crosthwaite House

★★★★ GUEST HOUSE

LA8 8BP
☎ 015395 68264 ▪ 015395 68264
e-mail: bookings@crosthwaitehouse.co.uk
web: www.crosthwaitehouse.co.uk
dir: *A590 onto A5074, 4m right to Crosthwaite, 0.5m turn left*

Enjoying stunning views across the Lyth Valley, this friendly Georgian house is a haven of tranquillity. Bedrooms are spacious and offer a host of thoughtful extras. The reception rooms include a comfortable lounge and a pleasant dining room with polished floorboards and individual tables.

Rooms 6 en suite **Facilities** FTV TVL tea/coffee Cen ht Wi-fi **Parking** 10 **Notes** Closed mid Nov-Mar RS early Nov & Feb-Mar

FAUGH — Map 18 NY55

The String of Horses Inn

★★★★ Ⓐ INN

CA8 9EG
☎ 01228 670297
e-mail: info@stringofhorses.com
web: www.stringofhorses.com
dir: *A69 turn towards Heads Nook at Corby Hill lights. 1m through Heads Nook, turn left*

Rooms 11 en suite (1 fmly) **Facilities** FTV TVL tea/coffee Dinner available Direct Dial Cen ht Wi-fi **Conf** Max 60 Thtr 60 Class 30 Board 30 **Parking** 30 **Notes** LB ⊗

GRANGE-OVER-SANDS — Map 18 SD47

Corner Beech House

★★★★ GUEST ACCOMMODATION

Methven Ter, Kents Bank Rd LA11 7DP
☎ 015395 33088
e-mail: info@cornerbeech.co.uk
web: www.cornerbeech.co.uk
dir: *M6 junct 36 onto A590, then off B5277, Kents Bank Rd*

Overlooking Morecambe Bay, this Edwardian house is well maintained and offers a friendly atmosphere. Hearty breakfasts featuring home-made and local produce are served in the attractive dining room. All bedrooms are en suite and well equipped with sitting area, widescreen digital televisions and DVD players.

Rooms 3 en suite S £49; D £68-£80 **Facilities** FTV tea/coffee Cen ht Wi-fi **Parking** 5 **Notes** ⊗ No Children 14yrs

Greenacres Country Guest House

★★★★ Ⓐ GUEST HOUSE

Lindale LA11 6LP
☎ 015395 34578 & 07776 211616 ▪ 015395 34578
e-mail: greenacres-lindale@gmail.com
dir: *M6 junct 36 take 1st exit onto A590 to Kendal/Barrow. After 3m 1st exit at rdbt continue on A590, then 1st exit at rdbt onto B5277, on right before mini rdbt*

Rooms 4 en suite 1 annexe en suite D £78-£82*
Facilities FTV TVL TV4B tea/coffee Cen ht **Parking** 5 **Notes** LB ⊗

GRASMERE — Map 18 NY30

PREMIER COLLECTION

Moss Grove Organic

★★★★★ GUEST ACCOMMODATION

LA22 9SW
☎ 015394 35251 ▪ 015394 35306
e-mail: enquiries@mossgrove.com
web: www.mossgrove.com
dir: *From S, M6 junct 36 onto A591 signed Keswick, from N M6 junct 40 onto A591 signed Windermere*

Located in the centre of Grasmere, this impressive Victorian house has been refurbished using as many natural products as possible with ongoing dedication to causing minimal environmental impact. The stylish bedrooms are decorated with beautiful wallpaper and natural clay paints, featuring handmade beds and furnishings. Bose home entertainment systems, flat screen TVs and luxury bathrooms add further comfort. Extensive continental breakfasts are served in the spacious kitchen, where guests can help themselves and dine at the large wooden dining table in the guest lounge.

Rooms 11 en suite (2 GF) S £95-£154; D £110-£250*
Facilities STV tea/coffee Cen ht Licensed Wi-fi
Parking 11 **Notes** LB No Children 14yrs Closed 24-25 Dec

Silver Lea Guest House

★★★★ GUEST HOUSE

Easedale Rd LA22 9QE
☎ 015394 35657 & 07818 678109 ▪ 015394 35657
e-mail: info@silverlea.com
dir: *Easedale Rd opp village green, Silver Lea 300yds on right*

A friendly welcome is assured at this ivy-clad Lakeland-stone house, just a short walk from the village. Delicious, freshly cooked breakfasts are served in the cosy cottage dining room. Bedrooms, some having their own sitting area, are fresh in appearance and very comfortable. Silver Lea is an ideal base for walking and exploring the Lake District.

Rooms 4 en suite D £80-£98* **Facilities** FTV tea/coffee Cen ht Wi-fi **Parking** 4 **Notes** LB ⊗ No Children 11yrs

White Moss House

★★★★ GUEST HOUSE

Rydal Water LA22 9SE
☎ 015394 35295 ▪ 015394 35516
e-mail: sue@whitemoss.com
web: www.whitemoss.com
dir: *On A591 1m S of Grasmere, 2m N of Ambleside*

This traditional Lakeland house was once bought by Wordsworth for his son. It benefits from a central location and has a loyal following. The individually styled bedrooms are comfortable and thoughtfully equipped.

There is also a two-room suite in a cottage on the hillside above the house. Afternoon tea is served in the inviting lounge. It is possible to book all five rooms for a private 'house party', dinner is then available by arrangement.

Rooms 5 en suite S £72-£92; D £94-£118* **Facilities** FTV tea/coffee Direct Dial Cen ht Licensed Wi-fi Fishing Free use of local leisure club & fishing permits **Parking** 10 **Notes** LB ⊗ Closed Dec-Jan

---

GRIZEDALE   Map 18 SD39

Grizedale Lodge
★★★★ GUEST ACCOMMODATION

LA22 0QL
☎ 015394 36532 ▤ 015394 36572
e-mail: enquiries@grizedale-lodge.com
dir: From Hawkshead follow signs S to Grizedale. Lodge 2m on right

Set in the heart of the tranquil Grizedale Forest Park, this charming establishment provides particularly comfortable bedrooms, some with four-poster beds and splendid views. Hearty breakfasts are served in the attractive dining room, which leads to a balcony for relaxing on in summer.

Rooms 8 en suite (1 fmly) (2 GF) **Facilities** STV TVL tea/coffee Dinner available Cen ht Licensed Wi-fi **Conf** Max 10 **Parking** 20

HAWKSHEAD   Map 18 SD39

See also Near Sawrey

PREMIER COLLECTION

Ees Wyke Country House
★★★★★ ⊛ ≜ GUEST HOUSE

LA22 0JZ
☎ 015394 36393
e-mail: mail@eeswyke.co.uk
web: www.eeswyke.co.uk

(For full entry see Near Sawrey)

The Queen's Head
★★★★ ⊛ INN

Main St LA22 0NS
☎ 015394 36271 ▤ 015394 36722
e-mail: enquiries@queensheadhotel.co.uk
web: www.queensheadhotel.co.uk
dir: M6 junct 36, then A590 to Newby Bridge. Over rdbt, 1st right into Hawkshead

This 16th-century inn features a wood-panelled bar with low, oak-beamed ceilings and an open log fire. Substantial, carefully prepared meals are served in the cosy bar and in the traditional style dining room. The bedrooms, some of which are in an adjacent cottage, are attractively furnished and include some four-poster rooms.

Rooms 10 en suite 3 annexe rms 2 annexe en suite (1 pri facs) (3 fmly) (2 GF) S £45-£60; D £75-£130* **Facilities** FTV tea/coffee Dinner available Cen ht Wi-fi Golf 18 **Notes** LB ⊗

Sawrey Ground
★★★★ ≜ GUEST ACCOMMODATION

Hawkshead Hill LA22 0PP
☎ 015394 36683
e-mail: mail@sawreyground.com
dir: B5285 from Hawkshead, 1m to Hawkshead Hill, sharp right after Baptist chapel, signs to Tarn Hows for 0.25m. Sawrey Ground on right

Set in the heart of the Lake District, this charming 17th-century farmhouse has a superb setting on the doorstep of Tarn Hows. The flagstone entrance hall leads to a sitting room with a beamed ceiling, where an open fire burns on winter nights. Hearty breakfasts featuring fresh fruit and home-baked bread are served in the dining room. The traditional bedrooms are furnished in pine and oak.

Rooms 2 en suite D £78-£90* **Facilities** FTV tea/coffee Cen ht Wi-fi **Parking** 6 **Notes** ⊗ No Children 8yrs Closed mid Nov-beg Mar ⊛

See advert on this page

HAWKSHEAD *continued*

The Sun Inn

★★★★ INN

Main St LA22 0NT
☎ 015394 36236 📄 015394 36747
e-mail: rooms@suninn.co.uk
web: www.suninn.co.uk

Situated in the popular village of Hawkshead, The Sun Inn is full of character. The 16th-century inn features a wood-panelled bar with low, oak-beamed ceilings. Substantial, carefully prepared meals are served in the bar and dining room. The bedrooms are modern in style, attractively furnished and include a four-poster room.

Rooms 8 en suite (1 fmly) S £50-£80; D £59-£99*
Facilities FTV tea/coffee Dinner available Cen ht Wi-fi Fishing Pool table **Conf** Max 20 Thtr 20 Class 20 Board 12 **Notes** LB

Kings Arms

★★★ INN

LA22 0NZ
☎ 015394 36372 📄 015394 36006
e-mail: info@kingsarmshawkshead.co.uk
web: www.kingsarmshawkshead.co.uk
dir: *M6 junct 36 onto A591, left onto A593 at Waterhead. After 1m onto B5286 to Hawkshead, in main square*

A traditional Lakeland inn in the heart of a conservation area. The cosy, thoughtfully equipped bedrooms retain much character and are traditionally furnished. A good choice of freshly prepared food is available in the lounge bar and the neatly presented dining room.

Rooms 8 en suite (3 fmly) S £52-£65; D £74-£96
Facilities FTV tea/coffee Dinner available Direct Dial Cen ht Wi-fi 🏊 Golf 18 Fishing Riding Bowling green **Notes** LB Closed 25 Dec

HOLMROOK   Map 18 SD09

The Lutwidge Arms

★★★ INN

CA19 1UH
☎ 019467 24230 📄 019467 24100
e-mail: mail@lutwidgearms.co.uk
dir: *M6 junct 36 onto A590 towards Barrow. Follow A595 towards Whitehaven/Workington, in centre of Holmrook*

This Victorian roadside inn is family-run and offers a welcoming atmosphere. The name comes from the Lutwidge family of Holmrook Hall, who included Charles Lutwidge Dodgson, better known as Lewis Caroll. The bar and restaurant offer a wide range of meals during the evening. Bedrooms are comfortably equipped.

Rooms 11 en suite 5 annexe en suite (5 fmly) (5 GF)
Facilities FTV TVL tea/coffee Dinner available Direct Dial Cen ht Wi-fi Pool table **Parking** 30 **Notes** ⊗

IREBY   Map 18 NY23

Woodlands Country House

★★★★ 🍴 GUEST HOUSE

CA7 1EX
☎ 016973 71791 📄 016973 71482
e-mail: stay@woodlandsatireby.co.uk
web: www.woodlandsatireby.co.uk
dir: *M6 junct 40 onto A66, pass Keswick at rdbt turn right onto A591. At Castle Inn turn right signed Ireby, then 2nd left signed Ireby. Pass church on left, last house in village*

Previously a vicarage, this lovely Victorian home is set in well tended gardens that attract lots of wildlife. Guests are given a warm welcome by the friendly owners and delicious home-cooked evening meals are available by prior arrangement. A peaceful lounge and cosy bar with snug are also available. Bedrooms are attractively furnished and thoughtfully equipped.

Rooms 4 en suite 3 annexe en suite (3 fmly) (3 GF) S £45-£60; D £75-£105 **Facilities** FTV TVL tea/coffee Dinner available Cen ht Licensed Wi-fi **Parking** 11 **Notes** LB

KESWICK   Map 18 NY22

See also Lorton

PREMIER COLLECTION

The Grange Country Guest House

★★★★★ GUEST HOUSE

Manor Brow, Ambleside Rd CA12 4BA
☎ 017687 72500 📄 0707 500 4885
e-mail: info@grangekeswick.com
web: www.grangekeswick.com
dir: *M6 junct 40, A66 15m. A591 for 1m, turn right onto Manor Brow*

This stylish Victorian residence stands in beautiful gardens just a stroll from the town centre and offers a relaxed atmosphere and professional service. The spacious bedrooms are well equipped and some have beams and mountain views. Spacious lounges and ample parking are available. The proprietors are keen to give advice on walks and local activities.

Rooms 10 en suite (1 GF) S £78-£86; D £100-£120
Facilities FTV tea/coffee Direct Dial Cen ht Licensed Wi-fi **Parking** 10 **Notes** LB ⊗ No Children 10yrs Closed Jan

Badgers Wood

★★★★ GUEST HOUSE

30 Stanger St CA12 5JU
☎ 017687 72621 📄 017687 72621
e-mail: enquiries@badgers-wood.co.uk
web: www.badgers-wood.co.uk
dir: *In town centre off A5271(main street)*

A warm welcome awaits guests at this delightful Victorian terrace house, located in a quiet area close to the town centre. The smart bedrooms are furnished to a high standard and are well equipped; the attractive breakfast room at the front of the house overlooks the fells. Off-road parking is an added benefit.

Rooms 6 en suite S £38; D £72-£76 **Facilities** FTV tea/coffee Cen ht Wi-fi **Parking** 4 **Notes** ⊗ No Children 12yrs Closed Nov-Jan 🍴

Dalegarth House

★★★★ 🛏 🍴 GUEST ACCOMMODATION

Portinscale CA12 5RQ
☎ 017687 72817 & 07769 794912
e-mail: allerdalechef@aol.com
dir: *Off A66 to Portinscale, pass Farmers Arms, 100yds on left*

The friendly family-run establishment stands on an elevated position in the village of Portinscale, and has fine views from the well-tended garden. The attractive bedrooms are well equipped, and there is a peaceful lounge, a well-stocked bar, and a spacious dining room where the resident owner-chef produces hearty breakfasts and delicious evening meals.

Rooms 8 en suite 2 annexe en suite (2 GF) S £40-£45; D £80-£95* **Facilities** FTV tea/coffee Dinner available Cen ht Licensed **Parking** 14 **Notes** LB ⊗ No Children 12yrs Closed Dec-1 Mar

Save on B&Bs and Hotels. Book at **theAA.com/hotel**

CUMBRIA 81 ENGLAND

The Edwardene

★★★★ 🏠 GUEST ACCOMMODATION

26 Southey St CA12 4EF
☎ 017687 73586
e-mail: info@edwardenehotel.com
dir: *M6 junct 40 onto A66 follow 1st sign to Keswick, turn right onto Penrith Rd. Sharp left by war memorial onto Southey St, 150mtrs on right*

Located close to the heart of the town centre. This Victorian Lakeland stone building retains many of its original features. Bedrooms are well equipped with many thoughtful extras provided throughout this three storey building. A comfortable lounge is available, and the generous Cumbrian breakfast is served in the stylish dining room.

Rooms 11 en suite (1 fmly) S fr £45; D £84-£92*
Facilities FTV TVL tea/coffee Cen ht Licensed Wi-fi
Parking 2 **Notes** LB ⊗

Rooms 36

★★★★ GUEST ACCOMMODATION

36 Lake Rd CA12 5DQ
☎ 017687 72764 & 74416
e-mail: andy@rooms36.co.uk
web: www.rooms36.co.uk
dir: *M6 junct 40 onto A66 to Keswick then signs for Borrowdale and the lake. Right onto The Heads, left to end*

Recently refurbished to a high standard and renamed, Rooms 36 overlooks Hope Park at the end of Lake Road. Modern bedrooms feature iPod docking stations, Tassimo coffee machines, comfortable beds and Herdwick wool carpets as standard. En suites are well appointed and public area decor is enhanced with wonderful artwork by local artist Tessa Kennedy.

Rooms 6 en suite (4 fmly) S £60-£90; D £90-£110*
Facilities STV FTV TVL tea/coffee Cen ht Wi-fi **Parking** 2

Sunnyside Guest House

★★★★ GUEST HOUSE

25 Southey St CA12 4EF
☎ 017687 72446
e-mail: enquiries@sunnysideguesthouse.com
web: www.sunnysideguesthouse.com
dir: *200yds E of town centre. Off A5271 Penrith Rd onto Southey St, Sunnyside on left*

This stylish guest house is in a quiet area close to the town centre. Bedrooms have been refurbished to a high standard and are comfortably furnished and well equipped. There is a spacious and comfortable lounge with plenty of books and magazines. Breakfast is served at individual tables in the airy and attractive dining room, and private parking is available.

Rooms 7 en suite S £46-£48; D £74-£80* **Facilities** FTV
tea/coffee Cen ht Wi-fi **Parking** 8 **Notes** LB ⊗ No
Children 12yrs Closed 3 Jan-10 Feb

Amble House

★★★★ GUEST HOUSE

23 Eskin St CA12 4DQ
☎ 017687 73288
e-mail: info@amblehouse.co.uk
web: www.amblehouse.co.uk
dir: *400yds SE of town centre. Off A5271 Penrith Rd onto Greta St & Eskin St*

An enthusiastic welcome awaits you at this Victorian mid-terrace house, close to the town centre. The thoughtfully equipped bedrooms have co-ordinated decor and are furnished in pine. Healthy breakfasts are served in the attractive dining room.

Rooms 5 en suite S £40-£50; D £66-£76* **Facilities** tea/
coffee Cen ht Wi-fi **Notes** LB ⊗ No Children 16yrs Closed
24-26 Dec

Claremont House

★★★★ GUEST ACCOMMODATION

Chestnut Hill CA12 4LT
☎ 017687 72089
e-mail: claremonthouse@btinternet.com
web: www.claremonthousekeswick.co.uk
dir: *A591 N onto Chestnut Hill, Keswick. Pass Manor Brow on left, Claremont House 100yds on right*

This attractive and well-maintained family home stands in mature grounds overlooking the town. Bedrooms are pine furnished and thoughtfully equipped, while the welcoming dining room has good views towards the fells.

Rooms 6 en suite S £45-£75; D £65-£75* **Facilities** FTV
tea/coffee Cen ht **Parking** 6 **Notes** LB ⊗ No Children
10yrs Closed 23-26 Dec ⊛

Craglands Guest House

★★★★ GUEST ACCOMMODATION

Penrith Rd CA12 4LJ
☎ 017687 74406
e-mail: craglands@msn.com
dir: *0.5m E of Keswick centre on A5271 (Penrith Rd) at junct A591*

This Victorian house occupies an elevated position within walking distance of the town centre. The good value accommodation provides attractive, well equipped bedrooms. Pauline and Mark offer a warm welcome and serve delicious breakfasts with local produce and home-made breads.

Rooms 7 rms (5 en suite) S £32-£50; D £64-£100*
Facilities FTV tea/coffee Dinner available Cen ht Wi-fi
Parking 6 **Notes** LB ⊗ No Children 8yrs

Cragside

★★★★ GUEST ACCOMMODATION

39 Blencathra St CA12 4HX
☎ 017687 73344 📠 017687 73344
e-mail: cragside-keswick@hotmail.com
dir: *A591 Penrith Rd into Keswick, under rail bridge, 2nd left*

Expect warm hospitality at this establishment, located within easy walking distance of the town centre. The attractive bedrooms are well equipped, and many have fine views of the fells. Hearty Cumbrian breakfasts are served in the breakfast room, which overlooks the small front garden. Visually or hearing impaired guests are catered for, with Braille information, televisions with teletext, and a loop system installed in the dining room.

Rooms 4 en suite (1 fmly) S £40-£60; D £50-£70
Facilities FTV tea/coffee Cen ht Wi-fi **Notes** No Children
4yrs

Dorchester House

★★★★ GUEST ACCOMMODATION

17 Southey St CA12 4EG
☎ 017687 73256
e-mail: dennis@dorchesterhouse.co.uk
dir: *200yds E of town centre. Off A5271 Penrith Rd onto Southey St, 150yds on left*

A warm welcome awaits you at this property, just a stroll from the town centre and its amenities. The comfortably proportioned, well-maintained bedrooms offer pleasing co-ordinated decor. Hearty breakfasts are served in the attractive ground-floor dining room.

Rooms 8 rms (7 en suite) (1 pri facs) (2 fmly) S £32-£42;
D £68-£76* **Facilities** FTV tea/coffee Cen ht Wi-fi
Notes LB ⊗ No Children 6yrs

Eden Green Guest House

★★★★ GUEST HOUSE

20 Blencathra St CA12 4HP
☎ 017687 72077 📠 017687 80870
e-mail: enquiries@edengreenguesthouse.com
web: www.edengreenguesthouse.com
dir: *A591 Penrith Rd into Keswick, under railway bridge, 2nd left, house 500yds on left*

This mid-terrace house, faced with local stone, offers well-decorated and furnished bedrooms, some suitable for families and some with fine views of Skiddaw. Traditional English and vegetarian breakfasts are served in the neat breakfast room, and packed lunches can be provided on request.

Rooms 5 en suite (1 fmly) (1 GF) **Facilities** tea/coffee
Cen ht Wi-fi **Notes** ⊗ No Children 8yrs

KESWICK *continued*

Elm Tree Lodge

★★★★ GUEST ACCOMMODATION

16 Leonard St CA12 4EL
☎ 017687 71050 & 07980 521079
e-mail: info@elmtreelodge-keswick.co.uk
dir: *Off A66, pass ambulance depot, left before pedestrian crossing, then left again onto Southey St. 3rd left onto Helvellyn St, 1st right onto Leonard St, property 3rd on right*

Close to the town centre, this tastefully decorated Victorian house offers a variety of room sizes, bedrooms feature stripped pine, period furniture, crisp white linen and modern en suites or private shower room. Hearty breakfasts are served in the charming dining room and feature local produce. A friendly welcome is guaranteed. Tim Mosedale was a finalist in this year's Friendliest Landlady of the Year award (2011-12).

Rooms 4 rms (3 en suite) (1 pri facs) D £60-£75*
Facilities FTV tea/coffee Cen ht Wi-fi **Parking** 2 **Notes** LB
⊗ No Children 8yrs

Hazelmere

★★★★ GUEST ACCOMMODATION

Crosthwaite Rd CA12 5PG
☎ 017687 72445
e-mail: info@hazelmerekeswick.co.uk
web: www.hazelmerekeswick.co.uk
dir: *Exit A66 at Crosthwaite rdbt (A591 junct) for Keswick, Hazelmere 400yds on right*

Peacefully located overlooking the River Greta and perfect for walking in the surrounding fells or to the shores of Derwentwater. The market place is only a short stroll away. The house has benefited from complete refurbishment by the friendly owners who can offer advice on local walks and cycle routes. All bedrooms feature stunning views and are well equipped. Guests can also enjoy watching the birds and other wildlife visiting the garden.

Rooms 6 en suite (1 fmly) S £37; D £74-£80*
Facilities FTV tea/coffee Cen ht Wi-fi **Parking** 7 **Notes** No Children 8yrs

Hedgehog Hill Guest House

★★★★ GUEST HOUSE

18 Blencathra St CA12 4HP
☎ 017687 80654
e-mail: keith@hedgehoghill.co.uk
dir: *M6 junct 40, take A66 to Keswick. Left onto Blencathra St*

Expect warm hospitality at this Victorian terrace house. Hedgehog Hill is convenient for the town centre, local attractions and many walks. Bedrooms are comfortably equipped and offer thoughtful extras. Hearty breakfasts are served in the light and airy dining room with vegetarians well catered for.

Rooms 6 rms (4 en suite) S £30-£33; D £64-£80*
Facilities FTV tea/coffee Cen ht Wi-fi **Notes** ⊗ No Children 12yrs Closed 23-26 Dec

The Hollies

★★★★ GUEST HOUSE

Threlkeld CA12 4RX
☎ 017687 79216
e-mail: info@theholliesinlakeland.co.uk
dir: *M6 junct 40 W on A66 towards Keswick. Turn right into Threlkeld, on main village road opp village hall*

The Hollies is located in the picturesque village of Threlkeld with commanding views up to Blencathra and across to the Helvellyn range. A warm and genuine welcome awaits, along with refreshments and home baking. Bedrooms are well appointed and comfortable with thoughtful extras provided as standard. Quality breakfasts are served on individual tables.

Rooms 4 en suite S £43-£58; D £66-£86* **Facilities** FTV tea/coffee Cen ht Wi-fi **Parking** 6 **Notes** Closed 25 Dec

Honister House

★★★★ 🏠 BED AND BREAKFAST

1 Borrowdale Rd CA12 5DD
☎ 017687 73181
e-mail: honisterhouse@btconnect.com
web: www.honisterhouse.co.uk
dir: *100yds S of town centre, off Market Sq onto Borrowdale Rd*

This charming family home is one of the oldest properties in Keswick, dating from the 18th century, and has attractive and well-equipped bedrooms. John and Susie Stakes are the friendly proprietors, who offer a warm welcome and serve hearty breakfasts utilising high quality local, organic and Fair Trade produce wherever possible.

Rooms 3 en suite D £75-£77 **Facilities** FTV tea/coffee Cen ht Wi-fi **Notes** LB ⊗

Keswick Lodge

★★★★ INN

Main St CA12 5HZ
☎ 017687 74584
e-mail: relax@keswicklodge.co.uk

Located on the corner of the vibrant market square this large, friendly 18th-century coaching inn offers a wide range of meals throughout the day and evening. There is a fully stocked bar complete with well-kept cask ales. Bedrooms vary in size but all are contemporary, smartly presented and feature quality accessories such as LCD TVs. There is also a drying room.

Rooms 19 en suite (2 fmly) S £75-£99; D £99-£120*
Facilities FTV tea/coffee Dinner available Cen ht **Notes** LB

Keswick Park

★★★★ GUEST ACCOMMODATION

33 Station Rd CA12 4NA
☎ 017687 72072 🖷 017687 74816
e-mail: reservations@keswickparkhotel.com
web: www.keswickparkhotel.com
dir: *200yds NE of town centre. Off A5271 Penrith Rd onto Station Rd*

A friendly welcome awaits at this comfortable Victorian house, situated within a short walking distance of the town centre. Bedrooms are mostly of a good size, and have homely extras. The breakfast room is divided into two sections and there is also a cosy bar. Guests might like to sit on the front garden patio while enjoying refreshments.

Rooms 16 en suite (2 fmly) **Facilities** FTV TVL tea/coffee Direct Dial Cen ht Licensed Wi-fi **Parking** 8 **Notes** ⊗

Low Nest Farm B&B

★★★★ GUEST ACCOMMODATION

Castlerigg CA12 4TF
☎ 017687 72378
e-mail: info@lownestfarm.co.uk
dir: *2m S of Keswick, off A591 (Windermere road)*

Low Nest Farm is a small, family-run farm set in some typically breath-taking Cumbrian scenery. Bedrooms are very comfortable with smart en suites and lovely views. Dog owners are especially well catered for. There are of course, any number of walks available in the area, and Keswick is just two miles away.

Rooms 6 en suite (4 GF) **Facilities** FTV TVL tea/coffee Cen ht Wi-fi **Parking** 8 **Notes** LB No Children 14yrs Closed mid Dec-mid Feb 🐾

Avondale Guest House

★★★★ 🄰 GUEST ACCOMMODATION

20 Southey St CA12 4EF
☎ 01768 772735
e-mail: enquiries@avondaleguesthouse.com
dir: *A66 to Keswick. A591 towards town centre, left at war memorial onto Station St. Sharp left onto Southey St, 100yds on right*

Rooms 6 en suite S £34-£42; D £68-£84* **Facilities** FTV tea/coffee Cen ht Wi-fi **Notes** ⊗ No Children 12yrs

Sandon Guesthouse

★★★★ 🄰 GUEST HOUSE

13 Southey St CA12 4EG
☎ 017687 73648
e-mail: enquiries@sandonguesthouse.com
dir: *200yds E of town centre. Off A5271 Penrith Rd onto Southey St*

Rooms 6 rms (5 en suite) (1 pri facs) S £30-£38; D £60-£76 **Facilities** FTV tea/coffee Cen ht **Notes** ⊗ No Children 4yrs Closed 24 Dec (day), 25-26 Dec

Watendlath

★★★★ Ⓐ GUEST HOUSE

15 Acorn St CA12 4EA
☎ **017687 74165** ▤ **017687 74165**
e-mail: info@watendlathguesthouse.co.uk
dir: *350yds SE of town centre. Off A5271 Penrith Rd onto Southey St, left onto Acorn St*

Rooms 4 en suite (2 fmly) **Facilities** tea/coffee Cen ht **Notes** ⊗ Closed Xmas 🐾

Brierholme

★★★ GUEST ACCOMMODATION

21 Bank St CA12 5JZ
☎ **017687 72938**
e-mail: enquiries@brierholme.co.uk
dir: *On A591, 100yds from Post Office*

Benefiting from a great location just a few minutes walk from the town centre. Limited off-road parking is available along with a lock-up facility for bikes and motorcycles. A rolling programme of refurbishment in the bedrooms is showing good results. Bedrooms on the higher floors offer some wonderful views and the hearty Lakeland breakfast will provide a great start to the day.

Rooms 6 en suite D £70–£80 **Facilities** FTV tea/coffee Cen ht Wi-fi **Parking** 6 **Notes** LB ⊗ No Children 5yrs

The George

★★★ 🍴 INN

Saint Johns St CA12 5AZ
☎ **017687 72076** ▤ **017687 75968**
e-mail: rooms@thegeorgekeswick.co.uk
dir: *M6 junct 40 onto A66, take left filter road signed Keswick, pass pub on left. At x-rds turn left onto Station St, 150yds on left*

Located in the centre of town this property is Keswick's oldest coaching inn. There is an abundance of character with wooden beamed bar, cosy seating areas and an atmospheric, candle-lit dining room. Food is a highlight with a wide choice of freshly prepared dishes. Bedrooms are simply presented and comfortable. Parking permits and storage for cycles are available.

Rooms 12 en suite (2 fmly) D £100 **Facilities** FTV tea/coffee Dinner available Cen ht **Parking Notes** No coaches

---

PREMIER COLLECTION

Hipping Hall

★★★★★ ◉◉ 🍽 RESTAURANT WITH ROOMS

Cowan Bridge LA6 2JJ
☎ **015242 71187** ▤ **015242 72452**
e-mail: info@hippinghall.com
dir: *M6 junct 36 take A65 through Kirkby Lonsdale towards Skipton. On right after Cowan Bridge*

Close to the market town of Kirkby Lonsdale, Hipping Hall offers spacious, feature bedrooms, designed in soft shades with sumptuous textures and fabrics; the bathrooms use natural stone, slate and limestone to great effect. There are also three spacious cottage suites that create a real hideaway experience. The sitting room, with large, comfortable sofas has a traditional feel. The restaurant is a 15th-century hall with tapestries and a minstrels' gallery that is as impressive as it is intimate.

Rooms 6 en suite 3 annexe en suite (1 GF) **Facilities** Dinner available Direct Dial Cen ht 🌱 **Parking** 30 **Notes** No Children 12yrs Closed 3-8 Jan No coaches Civ Wed 42

PREMIER COLLECTION

Plato's

★★★★★ 🍴 RESTAURANT WITH ROOMS

2 Mill Brow LA6 2AT
☎ **01524 274180**
e-mail: sally@platoskirkby.co.uk
dir: *M6 junct 36, A65 Kirkby Lonsdale, after 5m at rdbt take 1st exit, onto one-way system*

Tucked away in the heart of the popular market town, Plato's is steeped in history. Sumptuous bedrooms have a wealth of thoughtful extras, and imaginative food is available in the elegant restaurant with its open-plan kitchen. The lounge bar is more rustic in style with fires to relax by. A warm welcome and professional service is assured. The Pop Shop offers Plato's cuisine to take away.

Rooms 8 en suite **Facilities** FTV TVL tea/coffee Dinner available Cen ht Wi-fi ch fac 🌱 Golf 18 **Notes** No coaches

---

PREMIER COLLECTION

The Sun Inn

★★★★★ ◉ INN

6 Market St LA6 2AU
☎ **015242 71965** ▤ **015242 72485**
e-mail: email@sun-inn.info
web: www.sun-inn.info
dir: *From A65 follow signs to town centre. Inn on main street*

A 17th-century inn situated in a historic market town, overlooking St Mary's Church. The atmospheric bar features stone walls, wooden beams and log fires with real ales available. Delicious meals are served in the bar and more formal, modern restaurant. Traditional and modern styles are blended together in the beautifully appointed rooms with excellent en suites.

Rooms 11 en suite (1 fmly) S £72–£134; D £102–£154* **Facilities** FTV tea/coffee Cen ht Wi-fi 🌱 Golf 18 **Notes** LB No coaches

The Copper Kettle

★★★ Ⓐ GUEST ACCOMMODATION

3-5 Market St LA6 2AU
☎ **015242 71714** ▤ **015242 71714**
e-mail: gamble_p@btconnect.com
dir: *In town centre, down lane by Post Office*

Rooms 5 en suite (2 fmly) S £31; D £45–£55* **Facilities** FTV tea/coffee Dinner available Licensed **Parking** 3 **Notes** LB

Brownber Hall Country House

★★★★ GUEST ACCOMMODATION

Newbiggin-on-Lune CA17 4NX
☎ **015396 23208**
e-mail: enquiries@brownberhall.co.uk
web: www.brownberhall.co.uk
dir: *5m from M6 junct 38 along A685 towards Kirkby Stephen*

Having an elevated position with superb views of the surrounding countryside, Brownber Hall, built in 1860, has been restored to its original glory. The en suite bedrooms are comfortably proportioned, attractively decorated and well equipped. The ground floor has two lovely reception rooms, which retain many original features, and a charming dining room where traditional breakfasts are served.

Rooms 10 rms (8 en suite) (2 pri facs) (1 fmly) (1 GF) S £40–£50; D £70–£90* **Facilities** FTV TVL tea/coffee Cen ht Lift Licensed Wi-fi Golf 18 **Parking** 8 **Notes** LB Closed 22-28 Dec

LITTLE LANGDALE — Map 18 NY30

Three Shires Inn

★★★★ INN

LA22 9NZ
☎ 015394 37215 📄 015394 37127
e-mail: enquiry@threeshiresinn.co.uk
dir: Turn off A593, 3m from Ambleside at 2nd junct signed for Langdales. 1st left after 0.5m, 1m along lane

Enjoying an outstanding rural location, this family-run inn was built in 1872. The brightly decorated bedrooms are individual in style and many offer panoramic views. The attractive lounge features a roaring fire in the cooler months and there is a traditional style bar with a great selection of local ales. Meals can be taken in either the bar or cosy restaurant.

Rooms 10 en suite (1 fmly) D £86-£124 **Facilities** FTV TVL tea/coffee Dinner available Cen ht Wi-fi Use of local country club **Parking** 15 **Notes** LB Closed 25 Dec RS Dec & Jan wknds & New Year only No coaches

LORTON — Map 18 NY12

PREMIER COLLECTION

The Old Vicarage

★★★★★ 🏠 🍽 GUEST HOUSE

Church Ln CA13 9UN
☎ 01900 85656
e-mail: info@oldvicarage.co.uk
web: www.oldvicarage.co.uk
dir: B5292 onto B5289 N of Lorton. 1st left signed Church, house 1st on right

This delightful Victorian house offers spacious accommodation in the peaceful Lorton Vale, at the heart of the Lake District National Park. A converted coach-house offers two rooms with exposed stone walls, and is ideal for families with older children. Bedrooms in the main house are well equipped and have excellent views of the distant mountains. Delicious home cooking is served in the bright dining room.

Rooms 6 en suite 2 annexe en suite (1 GF) S £80-£90; D £115-£135* **Facilities** FTV tea/coffee Dinner available Cen ht Licensed Wi-fi **Parking** 10 **Notes** ⊗ No Children 8yrs

PREMIER COLLECTION

Winder Hall Country House

★★★★★ 🏠 🍽 GUEST ACCOMMODATION

CA13 9UP
☎ 01900 85107 📄 01900 85479
e-mail: stay@winderhall.co.uk
web: www.winderhall.co.uk
dir: A66 W from Keswick, at Braithwaite onto B5292 to Lorton, left at T-junct signed Buttermere, Winder Hall 0.5m on right

Impressive Winder Hall dates from the 14th century. The lounge is luxuriously furnished and the elegant, spacious dining room is the venue for skilfully prepared meals using local produce. The smart, individually styled bedrooms are thoughtfully equipped, and all are furnished with fine antiques or pine. Two rooms have beautiful four-poster beds.

Rooms 7 en suite 3 annexe rms (3 pri facs) (4 fmly) **Facilities** FTV TV7B tea/coffee Dinner available Direct Dial Cen ht Licensed Wi-fi Fishing Sauna Hot tub **Conf** Max 25 Class 25 Board 25 **Parking** 10 **Notes** ⊗ Closed 2-31 Jan Civ Wed 65

LOWESWATER — Map 18 NY12

Kirkstile Inn

★★★★ 🍽 INN

CA13 0RU
☎ 01900 85219
e-mail: info@kirkstile.com
web: www.kirkstile.com
dir: A66 onto B5292 into Lorton, left signed Buttermere. Signs to Loweswater, left signed Kirkstile Inn

This historic 16th-century inn lies in a valley surrounded by mountains. Serving great food and ale, its rustic bar and adjoining rooms are a mecca for walkers. There is also a cosy restaurant offering a quieter ambiance. Bedrooms retain their original character. There is a spacious family suite in an annexe, with two bedrooms, a lounge and a bathroom.

Rooms 7 en suite 3 annexe en suite (1 fmly) (2 GF) S £62.50-£90; D £90-£107* **Facilities** TVL TV3B tea/coffee Dinner available Cen ht **Parking** 30 **Notes** LB Closed 25 Dec No coaches

MILNTHORPE — Map 18 SD48

The Cross Keys

★★★★ INN

1 Park Rd LA7 7AB
☎ 015395 62115 📄 015395 62446
e-mail: stay@thecrosskeyshotel.co.uk
dir: In Milnthorpe at A6 x-rds

This is a family-run inn that has undergone a major modernisation programme. It is within walking distance of Milnthorpe's new Millennium Square, Dallam Towers, and the Kent estuary with its wealth of wildlife. The well-appointed bedrooms are en suite, and some have sitting areas. The public areas include a limed-oak panelled bar and a superb new snooker room. Food is served every day in the dining room or in the relaxed bar. The inn is a Robinson's house with real ales on draught and is holder of several Best Kept Cellar awards.

Rooms 8 en suite (2 fmly) S fr £47.50; D £65-£70* **Facilities** STV FTV tea/coffee Dinner available Direct Dial Cen ht Wi-fi Snooker **Conf** Max 60 Thtr 60 Class 60 Board 30 **Parking** 40 **Notes** LB

NEAR SAWREY — Map 18 SD39

PREMIER COLLECTION

Ees Wyke Country House

★★★★★ ◉ 🏠 GUEST HOUSE

LA22 0JZ
☎ 015394 36393
e-mail: mail@eeswyke.co.uk
web: www.eeswyke.co.uk
dir: On B5285 on W side of village

A warm welcome awaits you at this elegant Georgian country house with views over Esthwaite Water and the surrounding countryside. The thoughtfully equipped bedrooms have been decorated and furnished with care. There is a charming lounge with an open fire, and a splendid dining room where a carefully prepared five-course dinner is served. Breakfasts have a fine reputation due to the skilful use of local produce.

Rooms 8 en suite (1 GF) S £56-£86; D £112-£138* **Facilities** FTV tea/coffee Dinner available Cen ht Licensed **Parking** 12 **Notes** LB ⊗ No Children 12yrs

NEWBY BRIDGE	Map 18 SD38

PREMIER COLLECTION

The Knoll Country House

★★★★★ 🏠 🍽 GUEST ACCOMMODATION

Lakeside LA12 8AU
☎ 015395 31347   📠 015395 30850
e-mail: info@theknoll-lakeside.co.uk
dir: *A590 W to Newby Bridge, over rdbt, signed right for Lake Steamers, house 0.5m on left*

This delightful Edwardian villa stands in a leafy dell on the western side of Windermere. Public areas have many original features, including an open fire in the cosy lounge and dining room. The attractive bedrooms vary in style and outlook, but are all very stylish. Jenny and her enthusiastic team extend a very caring and natural welcome. Jenny also prepares a very good range of excellent dishes at breakfast and dinner.

Rooms 8 en suite 1 annexe rms (1 pri facs) S £75-£95; D £90-£250 **Facilities** STV FTV TVL tea/coffee Dinner available Direct Dial Cen ht Licensed Wi-fi Use of nearby hotel leisure spa **Conf** Max 40 Thtr 40 Class 20 Board 12 **Parking** 9 **Notes** LB ⊗ No Children 16yrs Closed 24-26 Dec Civ Wed 40

Hill Crest Country Guest House

★★★★ 🏠 BED AND BREAKFAST

Brow Edge LA12 8QP
☎ 015395 31766
e-mail: enquiries@hill-crestguesthouse.co.uk
dir: *1m SW of Newby Bridge. Off A590 onto Brow Edge Rd, house 0.75m on right*

Set in picturesque surroundings with stunning views offering a high standard of en suite accommodation at this well kept Lakeland home. All rooms are individual and well maintained. The lounge doubles as a breakfast room and opens out on to a large patio to the rear. The breakfast menu makes good use of fresh local produce. Warm and genuine hospitality is guaranteed.

Rooms 3 en suite (2 fmly) (1 GF) **Facilities** TVL tea/coffee Cen ht use of local leisure club if staying 5 nights **Parking** 4 **Notes** ⊗ Closed 22-26 Dec

Lyndhurst Country House

★★★★ 🏠 GUEST HOUSE

LA12 8ND
☎ 015395 31245
e-mail: chris@lyndhurstcountryhouse.co.uk
dir: *On junct of A590 & A592 at Newby Bridge rdbt*

This 1920s house is situated close to the southern tip of Lake Windermere. Accommodation consists of three comfortable, tastefully decorated bedrooms, each with en suite shower room. Hearty breakfasts feature local produce and are served in the pleasant dining room, which also has a lounge area opening onto the garden.

Rooms 3 en suite D £70-£80* **Facilities** FTV tea/coffee Cen ht Wi-fi **Parking** 3 **Notes** ⊗ No Children 8yrs Closed 23-28 Dec

The Coach House

★★★★ BED AND BREAKFAST

Hollow Oak LA12 8AD
☎ 015395 31622
e-mail: coachho@talk21.com
web: www.coachho.com
dir: *2.5m SW of Newby Bridge. Off A590 onto B5278 signed Cark & 1st left into rear of white house*

This converted coach house stands in delightful gardens south of Lake Windermere. The hosts offer a warm welcome and are a good source of local knowledge. The modern bedrooms are light and airy, and there is a cosy lounge. Breakfast is served in a converted stable.

Rooms 3 rms (2 en suite) (1 pri facs) S £33-£38; D £51-£60* **Facilities** FTV TVL tea/coffee Cen ht **Parking** 3 **Notes** LB ⊗ No Children 10yrs 🐾

Lakes End

★★★★ GUEST HOUSE

LA12 8ND
☎ 015395 31260   📠 015395 31260
e-mail: info@lakes-end.co.uk
web: www.lakes-end.co.uk
dir: *On A590 in Newby Bridge, 100yds from rdbt*

In a sheltered, wooded setting away from the road, Lakes End is convenient for the coast and the lakes. The bedrooms have been thoughtfully furnished and equipped. Traditional English breakfasts are served, and delicious home-cooked evening meals can be provided by arrangement.

Rooms 4 en suite (1 fmly) (1 GF) **Facilities** STV FTV tea/coffee Dinner available Cen ht Licensed **Parking** 6 **Notes** ⊗

PENRITH	Map 18 NY53

PREMIER COLLECTION

Brooklands Guest House

★★★★★ 🏠 GUEST HOUSE

2 Portland Place CA11 7QN
☎ 01768 863395   📠 01768 863395
e-mail: enquiries@brooklandsguesthouse.com
web: www.brooklandsguesthouse.com
dir: *From town hall onto Portland Place, 50yds on left*

In the bustling market town of Penrith this beautifully refurbished house offers individually furnished bedrooms with high quality accessories and some luxury touches. Nothing seems to be too much trouble for the friendly owners, and from romantic breaks to excellent storage for cyclists, all guests are very well looked after. Delicious breakfasts featuring Cumbrian produce are served in the attractive dining room.

Rooms 6 en suite (1 fmly) **Facilities** FTV tea/coffee Cen ht Wi-fi **Parking** 2 **Notes** ⊗ Closed 24 Dec-4 Jan

Roundthorn Country House

★★★★★ 🅰 GUEST ACCOMMODATION

Beacon Edge CA11 8SJ
☎ 01768 863952   📠 01768 864100
e-mail: info@roundthorn.co.uk
dir: *1.2m NE of town centre. Off A686 signed Roundthorn*

Rooms 10 en suite (3 fmly) S £69-£89; D £99-£125* **Facilities** tea/coffee Dinner available Direct Dial Cen ht Licensed Wi-fi ch fac Golf 18 **Conf** Max 200 Thtr 200 Class 200 Board 50 **Parking** 60 **Notes** LB ⊗ Civ Wed 100

Brandelhow

★★★★ 🏠 GUEST HOUSE

1 Portland Place CA11 7QN
☎ 01768 864470
e-mail: enquiries@brandelhowguesthouse.co.uk
web: www.brandelhowguesthouse.co.uk
dir: *In town centre on one-way system, left at town hall*

Situated within easy walking distance of central amenities, this friendly guest house is also convenient for the Lakes and M6. The bedrooms are thoughtfully furnished and some are suitable for families. Breakfasts, utilising quality local produce, are served in a Cumbria-themed dining room overlooking the pretty courtyard garden. Afternoon and high teas are available by arrangement.

Rooms 5 rms (4 en suite) (1 pri facs) (2 fmly) **Facilities** FTV tea/coffee Cen ht Wi-fi **Notes** ⊗ Closed 31 Dec & 1 Jan

PENRITH *continued*

Acorn Guest House

★★★★ GUEST HOUSE

Scotland Rd CA11 9HL
☎ 01768 868696
e-mail: acornguesthouse@fsmail.net
web: www.acorn-guesthouse.co.uk

This house, newly refurbished, is on the edge of the town and is popular with walkers and cyclists. Bedrooms are generally spacious and a substantial, freshly cooked breakfast made with local produce is served. Drying facilities and safe storage for bikes are available. High teas can be provided by arrangement.

Rooms 8 en suite (2 fmly) **Facilities** FTV tea/coffee Cen ht Wi-fi **Parking** 8 **Notes** ⊗

Albany House

★★★★ GUEST HOUSE

5 Portland Place CA11 7QN
☎ 01768 863072
e-mail: info@albany-house.org.uk
dir: *Left at town hall onto Portland Place. 30yds on left*

A well maintained Victorian house located close to Penrith town centre. Bedrooms are spacious, comfortable and thoughtfully equipped. Wholesome breakfasts utilising local ingredients are served in the attractive breakfast room.

Rooms 5 rms (3 en suite) (2 pri facs) (2 fmly) D £60-£75 **Facilities** FTV tea/coffee Cen ht Wi-fi **Notes** LB ⊗

Glendale

★★★★ GUEST HOUSE

4 Portland Place CA11 7QN
☎ 01768 210061
e-mail: glendaleguesthouse@yahoo.co.uk
web: www.glendaleguesthouse.com
dir: *M6 junct 40, follow town centre signs. Pass castle, turn left before town hall*

This friendly family-run guest house is part of a Victorian terrace only a stroll from the town centre and convenient for the lakes and Eden Valley. Drying facilities are available. Bedrooms vary in size, but all are attractive, and well equipped and presented. Hearty breakfasts are served at individual tables in the charming ground-floor dining room.

Rooms 7 en suite (3 fmly) **Facilities** FTV tea/coffee Cen ht Wi-fi

Tymparon Hall *(NY467300)*

★★★★ 🅰 FARMHOUSE

Newbiggin, Stainton CA11 0HS
☎ 017684 83236
Mrs M R Taylor
e-mail: margaret@tymparon.co.uk
web: www.tymparon.co.uk
dir: *M6 junct 40, A66 towards Keswick for 1.75m, right turn for Newbiggin, Tymparon Hall on right*

Rooms 3 rms (2 en suite) (1 pri facs) (2 fmly) S £40-£45; D £70-£80* **Facilities** TVL tea/coffee Cen ht **Parking** 4 **Notes** LB ⊗ No Children 3yrs RS Nov-Mar ⊛ 130 acres sheep

RAVENSTONEDALE   Map 18 NY70

The Black Swan

★★★★ 🍴 🍽 INN

CA17 4NG
☎ 015396 23204   📠 015396 23204
e-mail: enquiries@blackswanhotel.com
dir: *M6 junct 38. Black Swan on A685, W of Kirkby Stephen*

Set in the heart of this quiet village, the inn is popular with visitors and locals and offers a very friendly welcome. Bedrooms are individually styled and comfortably equipped. There is an informal atmosphere in the bar areas and home-made meals can be taken in the bar or the stylish dining room. Relax by the fire in the cooler months and enjoy the riverside garden in the summer.

Rooms 10 rms (9 en suite) (1 pri facs) 4 annexe en suite (3 fmly) (4 GF) S £50; D £75-£125* **Facilities** FTV tea/coffee Dinner available Cen ht Wi-fi ch fac 🏌 Golf 9 Fishing Snooker **Conf** Max 14 Thtr 14 Class 14 Board 14 **Parking** 20 **Notes** LB

RYDAL

See Ambleside

SEASCALE   Map 18 NY00

Cumbrian Lodge

★★★★ 🏅 RESTAURANT WITH ROOMS

Gosforth Rd CA20 1JG
☎ 019467 27309   📠 019467 27158
e-mail: cumbrianlodge@btconnect.com
web: www.cumbrianlodge.com
dir: *Off A595 at Gosforth onto B5344 signed Seascale, 2m on left*

A relaxed and friendly atmosphere prevails at this well-run restaurant with rooms, where tasty, well-prepared dinners prove popular locally. The decor and fixtures are modern throughout, and the bedrooms are well-equipped for both business and leisure guests. The thatched garden buildings provide a delightful opportunity for eating alfresco under canvas panels, for up to 12 diners.

Rooms 6 en suite (1 fmly) **Facilities** STV tea/coffee Dinner available Direct Dial Cen ht Wi-fi 🏖 **Parking** 15 **Notes** ⊗

SHAP   Map 18 NY51

Brookfield

★★★★ GUEST HOUSE

CA10 3PZ
☎ 01931 716397   📠 01931 716397
e-mail: info@brookfieldshap.co.uk
dir: *M6 junct 39, A6 towards Shap, 1st accommodation off motorway, on right*

Having a quiet rural location within easy reach of the M6, this inviting house stands in well-tended gardens. Bedrooms are thoughtfully appointed and well maintained. There is a comfortable lounge, and a small bar area next to the traditional dining room where substantial, home-cooked breakfasts are served at individual tables.

Rooms 4 rms (3 en suite) (1 pri facs) S £40-£50; D £70-£80 **Facilities** FTV TVL tea/coffee Cen ht Licensed Wi-fi **Conf** Max 20 **Parking** 20 **Notes** ⊗ No Children 12yrs Closed Dec-Feb ⊛

TEMPLE SOWERBY   Map 18 NY62

Skygarth Farm *(NY612261)*

★★★ FARMHOUSE

CA10 1SS
☎ 01768 361300   📠 01768 361300
Mrs Robinson
e-mail: enquire@skygarth.co.uk
dir: *Off A66 at Temple Sowerby for Morland, Skygarth 500yds on right, follow signs*

Skygarth is just south of the village, half a mile from the busy main road. The house stands in a cobbled courtyard surrounded by cowsheds and with gardens to the rear, where red squirrels feed. There are two well-proportioned bedrooms and an attractive lounge where tasty breakfasts are served.

Rooms 2 rms (2 fmly) **Facilities** FTV TVL tea/coffee Cen ht **Parking** 4 **Notes** ⊗ Closed Dec-Jan ⊛ 200 acres mixed

The Queens Head Inn

– Luxury in the Lakes –

The UK has some of the most stunning landscape in the world, boasting superb scenery, rolling hills, and views to remember. No more so is this true than in the Lake District, so we've found the ideal base from which you can experience all this and more – The Queen's Head Inn.

Tucked away in the Troutbeck Valley near Windermere (only three miles away), this warm and welcoming accommodation awaits your arrival, where you'll experience first hand the luxurious rooms on offer, as well as an array of tantalising dishes. Plus, you'll have no trouble discovering all the area has to offer, with a maze of footpaths linking ancient hamlets, as well as luring you into some beautiful gardens.

Take a break from the stresses and strains of everyday life and savour the moment within comfortable and attractive surroundings. You can expect a choice of double and fabulous four-poster beds, as well as being enticed by the textures and themes that complement each room. From the original coaching inn to the beautifully transformed ancient barn, your room will just be the tip of the iceberg when it comes to comfort.

During your stay you'll also no doubt want to sample the extensive menu on offer, with locally sourced produce, including poached local duck eggs, prime cut fillet steak, slowly braised ham hock parcel, locally reared lamb shank, as well as the old favourite of real ale battered fish and chips! With so much choice, it seems that the most stressful part of your break will be what to choose from the menu and there's even a selection of real ales to wash everything down!

So, take advantage of The Queen's Head Inn NOW and book your next Lakeland adventure.

**The Queen's Head Inn, Townhead, Troutbeck,
Near Windermere, Cumbria, LA23 1PW**

Tel 015394 32174

www.queensheadtroutbeck.co.uk

TROUTBECK (NEAR WINDERMERE) Map 18 NY40

PREMIER COLLECTION

Broadoaks Country House

★★★★★ GUEST ACCOMMODATION

Bridge Ln LA23 1LA
☎ 015394 45566 📠 015394 88766
e-mail: enquiries@broadoakscountryhouse.co.uk
web: www.broadoakscountryhouse.co.uk
dir: Exit A591 junct 36 pass Windermere. Filing station on left, 1st right 0.5m

This impressive Lakeland stone house has been restored to its original Victorian grandeur and is set in seven acres of landscaped grounds with stunning views of the Troutbeck Valley. Individually furnished bedrooms are well appointed and en suite bathrooms feature either whirlpool or Victorian roll top baths. Spacious day rooms include the music room, featuring a Bechstein piano. Meals are served by friendly and attentive staff in the elegant dining room.

Rooms 11 en suite 4 annexe en suite (5 fmly) (4 GF) S £75-£260; D £110-£270* **Facilities** FTV tea/coffee Dinner available Direct Dial Cen ht Licensed Wi-fi 🦢 🛴 Fishing Arrangement with local leisure facility
Conf Max 62 Thtr 40 Class 45 Board 45 **Parking** 40
Notes LB Civ Wed 62

The Queen's Head

★★★★ INN

Townhead LA23 1PW
☎ 015394 32174 📠 015394 31938
e-mail: reservations@queensheadtroutbeck.co.uk
web: www.queensheadtroutbeck.co.uk
dir: M6 junct 36 onto A591, past Windermere towards Ambleside. At mini-rdbt, right onto A592 for Ullswater, 3m on left

This 17th-century coaching inn has stunning views of the Troutbeck valley. The delightful bedrooms, several with four-poster beds, are traditionally furnished and equipped with modern facilities. Beams, flagstone floors, and a bar that was once an Elizabethan four-poster, provide a wonderful setting in which to enjoy imaginative food, real ales and fine wines.

Rooms 10 en suite 5 annexe en suite (1 fmly) (2 GF) S £75-£90; D £120-£150* **Facilities** FTV tea/coffee Dinner available Cen ht Wi-fi **Parking** 65 **Notes** LB RS 25 Dec pre-booked lunch only & 31 Dec pre-booked dinner only No coaches

See advert on page 87

ULVERSTON Map 18 SD27

Church Walk House

★★★★ BED AND BREAKFAST

Church Walk LA12 7EW
☎ 01229 582211 & 07774 368331
e-mail: martinchadd@btinternet.com
dir: In town centre opposite Stables furniture shop on corner of Fountain St & Church Walk

This Grade II listed 18th-century residence stands in the heart of the historic market town. Stylishly decorated, the accommodation includes attractive bedrooms with a mix of antiques and contemporary pieces. Service is attentive and there is a small herbal garden and patio.

Rooms 3 rms (2 en suite) (1 pri facs) S £30-£40; D £65-£75* **Facilities** TVL tea/coffee Cen ht **Notes** LB

WASDALE HEAD Map 18 NY10

Wasdale Head Inn

★★★ INN

CA20 1EX
☎ 019467 26229 📠 019647 26334
e-mail: reception@wasdale.com
dir: Leave A595 at Santon Bridge or Gosforth if travelling S. Follow signs for Wasdale

Wasdale Head is known as the "Birthplace of British Climbing" for good reason. The setting is breath-taking, surrounded by the Fells with the brooding Wast Water close by. Inside, the decor is enhanced with objet d'art and photos of climbing and mountains. Bedrooms and public areas are being refurbished and are comfortable. Service is relaxed and informal. Real ales and good food are served in the rustic bar while a separate restaurant is available for residents.

Rooms 10 en suite (4 fmly) (4 GF) S £62.50-£72.50; D £130-£145* **Facilities** Dinner available Direct Dial Cen ht Wi-fi **Parking** 30 **Notes** LB No coaches

WATERMILLOCK Map 18 NY42

Brackenrigg

★★★ INN

CA11 0LP
☎ 017684 86206 📠 017684 86945
e-mail: enquiries@brackenrigginn.co.uk
web: www.brackenrigginn.co.uk
dir: M6 junct 40, A66 towards Keswick. In 0.5m take A592 at Rheged Services rdbt towards Ullswater. In 5m right at T-junct at lake. 1m to Watermillock sign. Inn 300yds on right. (NB car park entrance before inn)

An 18th-century coaching inn with superb views of Ullswater and the surrounding countryside. Freshly prepared dishes and daily specials are served by friendly staff in the traditional bar and restaurant. The bedrooms include six attractive rooms in the stable cottages.

Rooms 11 en suite 6 annexe en suite (8 fmly) (3 GF) **Facilities** tea/coffee Dinner available Cen ht Wi-fi **Conf** Max 48 Thtr 36 Class 12 Board 16 **Parking** 40 **Notes** LB

WHITEHAVEN Map 18 NX91

Glenfield Guest House

★★★★ GUEST HOUSE

Back Corkickle CA28 7TS
☎ 01946 691911 & 07810 632890 📠 01946 694060
e-mail: glenfieldgh@gmail.com
web: www.glenfield-whitehaven.co.uk
dir: 0.5m SE of town centre on A5094

The imposing, family-run Victorian house is in a conservation area close to the historic town centre and harbour. Margaret and Andrew provide a relaxed environment with friendly but unobtrusive service, and this is a good start point for the Sea to Sea (C2C) cycle ride.

Rooms 6 en suite (2 fmly) S £40; D £65* **Facilities** FTV TVL tea/coffee Dinner available Cen ht Licensed Wi-fi **Notes** ⊗

WINDERMERE
Map 18 SD49

PREMIER COLLECTION

The Cranleigh
★★★★★ GUEST HOUSE

Kendal Rd, Bowness LA23 3EW
☎ 015394 43293 📄 015394 47283
e-mail: enquiries@thecranleigh.com
web: www.thecranleigh.com
dir: Lake Rd onto Kendal Rd, 150yds on right

Just a short walk from Lake Windermere this smartly appointed period property has been transformed to provide stylish accommodation. Bedrooms are divided between the main house and adjacent building. Luxury and superior rooms are impressive, featuring spa baths, illuminated showers and an excellent range of accessories. The new Sanctuary Suite comes with its own hot tub. Guests have complimentary use of leisure facilities at a nearby hotel.

Rooms 11 en suite 6 annexe en suite (3 GF)
Facilities FTV tea/coffee Direct Dial Cen ht Licensed Wi-fi 🌀 Squash Snooker Sauna Solarium Gym Complimentary use of off-site leisure facilities
Parking 13 **Notes** ⊗ No Children 15yrs

PREMIER COLLECTION

The Howbeck
★★★★★ 📖 GUEST HOUSE

New Rd LA23 2LA
☎ 015394 44739
e-mail: relax@howbeck.co.uk
dir: A591 through Windermere town centre, left towards Bowness

Howbeck is a delightful Victorian villa, convenient for the village and the lake. Bedrooms are well appointed and feature lovely soft furnishings, along with luxurious spa baths in some cases. There is a bright lounge with internet access and an attractive dining room where home-prepared hearty Cumbrian breakfasts are served at individual tables.

Rooms 10 en suite 1 annexe en suite (3 GF)
Facilities STV FTV TVL tea/coffee Cen ht Licensed Wi-fi Free membership to spa & leisure club 0.5m
Parking 12 **Notes** ⊗ Closed 24-25 Dec

PREMIER COLLECTION

Windermere Suites
★★★★★ 📖 BED AND BREAKFAST

New Rd LA23 2LA
☎ 015394 44739
e-mail: pureluxury@windermeresuites.co.uk
dir: Through village on one-way system towards Bowness-on-Windermere. 0.25m on left after The Howbeck

Close to Windermere and Bowness, Windermere Suites is a very special boutique town house which offers eight individual suites, all combining contemporary designer furniture with cutting edge entertainment technology and sheer elegance. Each suite has its own lounge area, and the bathrooms have large spa baths complete with TV, mood lighting and power showers. Rooms also have mini-bars and room service up to 10 at night. An unusual feature is the 'living showroom' element, if you like an item of furniture or decoration you can order it at a discount.

Rooms 8 en suite (3 GF) **Facilities** STV FTV TVL tea/coffee Dinner available Cen ht Licensed Wi-fi Free use of spa & leisure club 0.5m **Parking** 9 **Notes** ⊗

PREMIER COLLECTION

Applegarth Villa & JR's Restaurant
★★★★★ GUEST ACCOMMODATION

College Rd LA23 1BU
☎ 015394 43206 📄 015394 46636
e-mail: info@lakesapplegarth.co.uk
web: www.lakesapplegarth.co.uk
dir: M6 junct 36 onto A591 towards Windermere. On entering the town turn left after NatWest Bank onto Elleray Rd then 1st right onto College Rd, Applegarth on right

This period building set in the centre of Windermere, offers elegant and comfortable accommodation with high quality furnishings. The attractive and elegant conservatory dining room offers stunning views of the mountains. Private off-road parking is a bonus.

Rooms 15 en suite S £62-£67; D £120-£206*
Facilities FTV tea/coffee Dinner available Direct Dial Cen ht Licensed Wi-fi Complimentary leisure facilities at nearby hotel **Parking** 16 **Notes** LB ⊗ No Children 18yrs

PREMIER COLLECTION

Beaumont House
★★★★★ GUEST HOUSE

Holly Rd LA23 2AF
☎ 015394 47075 📄 015394 88311
e-mail: enquiries@lakesbeaumont.co.uk
web: www.lakesbeaumont.co.uk
dir: M6 junct 36 onto A591 then A590 & left into Windermere, through one-way system left onto Ellerthwaite Rd, then 1st left onto Holly Rd

A warm welcome awaits you at this smart, traditional house, in a peaceful location just a stroll from the town centre. Bedrooms, some with four-poster beds, are individually furnished to a high standard, as are the modern bathrooms. The spacious lounge has an honesty bar, and hearty breakfasts are served in the smartly appointed dining room.

Rooms 10 en suite (4 GF) **Facilities** FTV TVL tea/coffee Cen ht Licensed Wi-fi **Parking** 10 **Notes** ⊗ No Children 16yrs

PREMIER COLLECTION

Newstead
★★★★★ GUEST HOUSE

New Rd LA23 2EE
☎ 015394 44485 📄 015394 88904
e-mail: info@newstead-guesthouse.co.uk
dir: 0.5m from A591 between Windermere & Bowness

A family home set in landscaped gardens, this spacious Victorian house offers very comfortable well-equipped accommodation. The attractive bedrooms are very individual and retain original features such as fireplaces and include many thoughtful extra touches. There is an elegant lounge and a smart dining room where freshly cooked breakfasts are served at individual tables.

Rooms 9 en suite (1 fmly) **Facilities** FTV TV7B tea/coffee Cen ht Wi-fi Free use of Parklands Leisure Club **Parking** 10 **Notes** ⊗ No Children 7yrs 📧

WINDERMERE *continued*

PREMIER COLLECTION

Oakbank House

★★★★★ 🏠 GUEST HOUSE

Helm Rd LA23 3BU
☎ 015394 43386 📠 015394 47965
e-mail: enquiries@oakbankhousehotel.co.uk
web: www.oakbankhousehotel.co.uk
dir: *Off A591 through town centre into Bowness, Helm Rd 100yds on left after cinema*

Oakbank House is just off the main street in Bowness village, overlooking Windermere and the fells beyond. Bedrooms are individually styled, attractive and very well equipped; most have stunning lake views. There is an elegant lounge with a perpetual coffee pot, and delicious breakfasts are served at individual tables in the dining room.

Rooms 12 rms (11 en suite) (1 pri facs) (3 GF) D £60-£120* **Facilities** FTV tea/coffee Cen ht Wi-fi Free membership of local country club **Parking** 14 **Notes** LB ⊗ RS 20-26 Dec

PREMIER COLLECTION

The Woodlands

★★★★★ GUEST HOUSE

New Rd LA23 2EE
☎ 015394 43915 📠 015394 43915
e-mail: enquiries@woodlands-windermere.co.uk
web: www.woodlands-windermere.co.uk
dir: *One-way system through town down New Rd towards lake, premises by war memorial clock*

Just a short walk from Lake Windermere, guests can expect stylish accommodation and friendly, attentive service. Bedrooms (including two contemporary 4-poster rooms) have been individually decorated and feature quality furnishings and accessories, such as flat screen televisions. Guests are welcome to relax in the comfortable lounge where there is also a well stocked bar offering beers, wine, champagnes and rich Italian coffees. A wide choice is offered at breakfast which is served in the spacious dining room.

Rooms 14 en suite (2 fmly) (3 GF) **Facilities** tea/coffee Dinner available Cen ht Licensed Free facilities at local leisure/sports club **Parking** 17

Dene House

★★★★ GUEST ACCOMMODATION

Kendal Rd LA23 3EW
☎ 015394 48236 📠 015394 48236
e-mail: denehouse@ignetics.co.uk
dir: *0.2m S of Bowness centre on A5074, next to Burnside Hotel*

A friendly welcome awaits you at this smart Victorian house, in a peaceful location just a short walk from the centre of Bowness. The elegant bedrooms are generally spacious, individually decorated and are particularly well equipped. Afternoon tea is served on the patio, which overlooks a well-tended garden. A car park is available.

Rooms 7 rms (6 en suite) (1 pri facs) (1 fmly) (1 GF) S £39-£45; D £72-£90* **Facilities** FTV tea/coffee Cen ht Wi-fi Adjacent leisure centre facilities available **Parking** 7 **Notes** LB ⊗ No Children 10yrs

Fairfield House and Gardens

★★★★ 🏠 GUEST HOUSE

Brantfell Rd, Bowness-on-Windermere LA23 3AE
☎ 015394 46565 📠 015394 46564
e-mail: tonyandliz@the-fairfield.co.uk
web: www.the-fairfield.co.uk
dir: *Into Bowness town centre, turn opp St Martin's Church & sharp left by Spinnery restaurant, house 200yds on right*

Situated just above Bowness and Lake Windermere this Lakeland country house is tucked away in a half acre of secluded, peaceful gardens. The house has been beautifully refurbished to combine Georgian and Victorian features with stylish, contemporary design. Guests are shown warm hospitality and can relax in the delightful lounge. Bedrooms are well furnished, varying in size and style with some featuring luxurious bathrooms. Delicious breakfasts are served in the attractive dining room or on the terrace in warmer weather.

Rooms 10 en suite (2 fmly) (3 GF) **Facilities** TVL tea/coffee Dinner available Cen ht Licensed Wi-fi 🏊 **Conf** Max 20 Thtr 20 Class 10 Board 12 **Parking** 10 **Notes** No Children 10yrs

See advert on opposite page

The Hideaway at Windermere

★★★★ ⚛⚛ RESTAURANT WITH ROOMS

Phoenix Way LA23 1DB
☎ 015394 43070
e-mail: eatandstay@thehideawayatwindermere.co.uk
web: www.thehideawayatwindermere.co.uk
dir: *Exit A591 at Ravensworth B&B, onto Phoenix Way, The Hideaway 100mtrs on right*

Tucked away quietly this beautiful Victorian Lakeland house is personally run by owners Richard and Lisa. Delicious food, individually designed bedrooms and warm hospitality ensure an enjoyable stay. There is a beautifully appointed lounge looking out to the garden and the restaurant is split between two light and airy rooms; here guests will find the emphasis is on fresh, local ingredients and attentive, yet friendly service. Bedrooms vary in size and style - the larger rooms feature luxury bathrooms.

Rooms 10 en suite 1 annexe en suite S £52-£152; D £65-£190* **Facilities** FTV tea/coffee Dinner available Direct Dial Cen ht Wi-fi **Parking** 15 **Notes** LB ⊗ No Children 12yrs Closed Jan-mid Feb RS Mon & Tue Restaurant closed for dinner (ex New Year) No coaches

The Wild Boar

★★★★ INN

Crook LA23 3NF
☎ 015394 45225 📠 015394 42498
e-mail: thewildboar@englishlakes.co.uk
dir: *2.5m S of Windermere on B5284. From Crook 3.5m, on right*

Steeped in history this former coaching inn enjoys a peaceful rural location close to Windermere. Public areas include a welcoming lounge and a cosy bar where an extensive choice of wines, ales and whiskies are served. The Grill and recent addition of a Smokehouse feature quality local and seasonal ingredients. Bedrooms, some with four-poster beds, vary in style and size. Leisure facilities are available close by.

Rooms 33 en suite (2 fmly) (9 GF) S £70-£110; D £80-£160* **Facilities** FTV tea/coffee Dinner available Direct Dial Cen ht **Conf** Thtr 40 Class 10 Board 20 **Parking** 60 **Notes** LB

Save on B&Bs and Hotels. Book at **theAA.com/hotel**

CUMBRIA 91 ENGLAND

Blenheim Lodge

★★★★ GUEST ACCOMMODATION

Brantfell Rd, Bowness-on-Windermere LA23 3AE
☎ 015394 43440
e-mail: enquiries@blenheim-lodge.com
dir: From Windermere to Bowness village, left at mini
rdbt, up to top of Brantfell Rd & turn right

From a peaceful position above the town of Bowness,
Blenheim Lodge has some stunning panoramic views of
Lake Windermere. Bedrooms are well equipped featuring
antique furnishings and pocket-sprung mattresses. Most
beds are antiques themselves and include two William IV
four-posters and three Louis XV beds. There is a
comfortable lounge and a beautifully decorated dining
room.

Rooms 11 rms (10 en suite) (1 pri facs) (2 fmly) (2 GF) S
£61.50-£64; D £88-£150 **Facilities** FTV TVL tea/coffee
Licensed 2 free fishing permits/free c-club membership
Parking 11 **Notes** LB ⊗ Closed 25 Dec RS 20-27 Dec
may open, phone for details

The Coach House

★★★★ GUEST ACCOMMODATION

Lake Rd LA23 2EQ
☎ 015394 44494
e-mail: enquiries@lakedistrictbandb.com
web: www.lakedistrictbandb.com
dir: A591 to Windermere house 0.5m on right opp St
Herbert's Church

Expect a relaxed and welcoming atmosphere at this
stylish house, which has a minimalist interior with bright
decor and cosmopolitan furnishings. The attractive
bedrooms are well equipped. There is a reception lounge,
and a breakfast room where freshly prepared breakfasts
feature the best of local produce.

Rooms 5 en suite (1 fmly) D £60-£85* **Facilities** FTV tea/
coffee Cen ht Wi-fi Use of local health & leisure club
Parking 5 **Notes** LB ⊗ No Children 5yrs Closed 24-26 Dec

The Coppice

★★★★ 🏠 🍽 GUEST HOUSE

Brook Rd LA23 2ED
☎ 015394 88501 📠 015394 42148
e-mail: chris@thecoppice.co.uk
web: www.thecoppice.co.uk
dir: 0.25m S of village centre on A5074

This attractive detached house lies between Windermere
and Bowness. There are colourful public rooms and
bedrooms, and a restaurant serving freshly prepared
local produce. The bedrooms vary in size and style and
have good facilities.

Rooms 9 en suite (2 fmly) (1 GF) **Facilities** tea/coffee
Dinner available Cen ht Licensed Wi-fi Private leisure
club membership **Parking** 10

The Cottage

★★★★ 🏠 GUEST ACCOMMODATION

Elleray Rd LA23 1AG
☎ 015394 44796
e-mail: enquiries@thecottageguesthouse.com
dir: A591, past Windermere Hotel, in 150yds turn left onto
Elleray Rd. The Cottage 150yds on left

Built in 1847, this attractive house has been extensively
refurbished to offer a blend of modern and traditional
styles. The tastefully furnished bedrooms are well
equipped and comfortable. A wide choice of freshly
cooked breakfasts are served in the spacious dining room
at individual tables.

Rooms 8 en suite (2 GF) S £32-£45; D £60-£95
Facilities FTV tea/coffee Cen ht **Parking** 8 **Notes** ⊗ No
Children 11yrs Closed Nov-Jan

Fir Trees

★★★★ GUEST HOUSE

Lake Rd LA23 2EQ
☎ 015394 42272 📠 015394 42512
e-mail: enquiries@fir-trees.co.uk
web: www.fir-trees.co.uk
dir: Off A591 through town, Lake Rd in 0.5m, Fir Trees on
left after clock tower

Located halfway between Windermere town and the lake,
this spacious Victorian house offers attractive and well
equipped accommodation. Bedrooms are generously
proportioned and have many thoughtful extra touches.
Breakfasts, featuring the best of local produce, are
served at individual tables in the smart dining room.

Rooms 9 en suite (2 fmly) (3 GF) **Facilities** tea/coffee
Dinner available Cen ht Wi-fi Fishing **Parking** 9 **Notes** LB
⊗

Fairfield House and Gardens

The Fairfield is a charming Georgian house set in quiet
secluded grounds with its own car park. Located in a
quiet cul-de-sac, yet just a few steps from the waterfront,
shops, pubs, clubs and restaurants of Bowness.

A spacious terrace and a large lounge are available. We are
licensed for alcohol, and free Internet access and Wi-fi are
available. We have four-poster rooms, deluxe rooms with
spa bath's and a roofspace penthouse.

Brantfell Road, Bowness Bay, Windermere, Cumbria LA23 3AE
Tel: 015394 46565   Fax: 015394 46564
Website: www.the-fairfield.co.uk

WINDERMERE *continued*

Glencree

★★★★ GUEST HOUSE

Lake Rd LA23 2EQ
☎ 015394 45822 & 07974 697114 ▤ 05603 420040
e-mail: h.butterworth@btinternet.com
web: www.glencreelakes.co.uk
dir: *From town centre signs for Bowness & The Lake, Glencree on right after large wooded area on right*

Colourful hanging baskets and floral displays adorn the car park and entrance to Glencree, which lies between Windermere and Bowness. Bedrooms are brightly decorated and individually furnished. The attractive lounge, with an honesty bar, is next to the dining room, where breakfasts are served at individual tables.

Rooms 6 en suite (1 fmly) (1 GF) S £45-£60; D £70-£90* **Facilities** FTV TVL tea/coffee Dinner available Cen ht Licensed Wi-fi **Parking** 6 **Notes** LB ⊗

Glenville House

★★★★ GUEST HOUSE

Lake Rd LA23 2EQ
☎ 015394 43371 ▤ 015394 48457
e-mail: mail@glenvillehouse.co.uk
dir: *Off A591 into Windermere, B5074 to Bowness, Glenville 0.5m on right next to St John's Church*

This traditional Lakeland stone house has a relaxing and friendly atmosphere, and is just a short walk from the town centre and Lake Windermere. Breakfast, including a wide choice of cooked dishes, is served in the pleasant dining room. Bedrooms are attractively decorated and furnished with good quality en suite bathrooms.

Rooms 7 en suite (1 GF) S £65-£85; D £75-£105* **Facilities** STV tea/coffee Cen ht Wi-fi **Parking** 7 **Notes** LB ⊗ No Children

The Haven

★★★★ BED AND BREAKFAST

10 Birch St LA23 1EG
☎ 015394 44017
e-mail: thehaven.windermere@btopenworld.com
dir: *On A5074 enter one-way system, 3rd left onto Birch St*

Built from Lakeland slate and stone, this Victorian house is just a stroll from the town centre and shops. The bright, spacious bedrooms offer en suite or private facilities, and one has a Victorian brass bed. A hearty Cumbrian breakfast is served in the well-appointed dining room that doubles as a lounge.

Rooms 3 en suite (1 fmly) D £50-£72* **Facilities** FTV tea/coffee Cen ht Wi-fi **Parking** 3 **Notes** LB ⊗ No Children 7yrs

Holly-Wood Guest House

★★★★ GUEST HOUSE

Holly Rd LA23 2AF
☎ 015394 42219
e-mail: info@hollywoodguesthouse.co.uk
web: www.hollywoodguesthouse.co.uk
dir: *A591 towards Windermere, left into town, left again onto Ellerthwaite Rd, next left onto Holly Rd*

This attractive Victorian end terrace is located in a quiet residential area just a few minutes' walk from the town centre. Guests are offered a friendly welcome, comfortable, well equipped bedrooms and a freshly prepared breakfast. Limited off-street parking is also available.

Rooms 6 en suite (1 fmly) S £37.50-£42.50; D £65-£85 **Facilities** FTV tea/coffee Cen ht Wi-fi **Parking** 3 **Notes** ⊗ No Children 10yrs Closed 23-27 Dec

Invergarry Guest House

★★★★ GUEST HOUSE

3 Thornbarrow Rd LA23 2EW
☎ 015394 44561 ▤ 015394 43960
e-mail: invergarryguesthouse@btinternet.com
dir: *From Kendal, follow signs to Windermere, take 1st left in town. Around one-way system onto New Rd, then Lake Rd towards lake, 1st left after zebra crossing*

Invergarry is a small traditional Lakeland Guest House. The rooms are comfortable with modern look and feel fabrics and flat screen TVs, as well as some traditional pieces of furniture. All rooms are en suite with comfortably sized shower rooms. Garden rooms are spacious and welcome well behaved dogs. The location of the house is ideal for touring the Lakes or visiting local attractions such as the Beatrix Potter attraction. Wi-fi also available.

Rooms 4 en suite 1 annexe en suite (1 GF) D £78-£99* **Facilities** tea/coffee Cen ht Wi-fi **Parking** 1 **Notes** LB No Children Closed Nov-Mar

Jerichos

★★★★ ◉◉ RESTAURANT WITH ROOMS

College Rd LA23 1BX
☎ 015394 42522 ▤ 015394 88899
e-mail: info@jerichos.co.uk
dir: *A591 to Windermere, 2nd left onto Elleray Rd then 1st right onto College Rd*

Dating back to around 1870, this centrally located property has been lovingly restored by its current owners over the years. All the elegantly furnished bedrooms are en suite and the top floor rooms have views of the fells. Breakfast is served in the Restaurant Room, and the comfortable lounge has a real fire to relax by on chillier days. The chef/proprietor has established a strong reputation for his creative menus that use the best local and seasonal produce. The restaurant is always busy so booking is essential. Wi-fi is available.

Rooms 10 en suite S £40-£55; D £70-£125* **Facilities** FTV tea/coffee Dinner available Cen ht Wi-fi **Parking** 12 **Notes** LB ⊗ No Children 12yrs Closed 20 Nov-10 Dec & 3wks from 8 Jan No coaches

The Old Court House

★★★★ GUEST HOUSE

Lake Rd LA23 3AP
☎ 015394 45096
e-mail: alison@theoch.co.uk
dir: *On Windermere-Bowness road at junct Longlands Rd*

Guests are given a warm welcome at this attractive former Victorian police station and courthouse, located in the centre of Bowness. Comfortable, pine-furnished bedrooms offer a good range of extra facilities. Freshly prepared breakfasts are served in the bright ground-floor dining room.

Rooms 6 en suite (2 GF) **Facilities** tea/coffee Cen ht Wi-fi **Parking** 6 **Notes** ⊗ No Children 10yrs

Save on B&Bs and Hotels. Book at **theAA.com/hotel**

CUMBRIA 93 ENGLAND

The Willowsmere

★★★★ 🛏 GUEST HOUSE

Ambleside Rd LA23 1ES
☎ 015394 43575 📠 015394 44962
e-mail: info@thewillowsmere.com
web: www.thewillowsmere.com
dir: On A591, 500yds on left after Windermere station, towards Ambleside

The Willowsmere is a friendly, family-run establishment within easy walking distance of the town centre. It stands in a colourful, well-tended garden, with a patio and water feature to the rear. The attractive bedrooms are spacious, and there is a choice of inviting lounges and a well-stocked bar. Delicious breakfasts are served at individual tables in the stylish dining room.

Rooms 12 en suite (1 GF) S £40-£45; D £68-£90*
Facilities TVL tea/coffee Cen ht Licensed Wi-fi Free use of pool, sauna and gym at local hotel **Parking** 15 **Notes** LB ⊗ No Children 12yrs

Broadlands

★★★ GUEST HOUSE

19 Broad St LA23 2AB
☎ 015394 46532
e-mail: enquiries@broadlandsbandb.co.uk
dir: From A591 follow one-way system, left onto Broad St after pedestrian crossing

Warm and genuine hospitality is offered at this attractive house opposite the park and library, convenient for central amenities. Bedrooms are pleasantly co-ordinated and comfortably furnished. Freshly prepared breakfasts featuring local and home-made produce are served in the attractive ground floor dining room.

Rooms 4 en suite S £50; D £60-£75* **Facilities** FTV tea/coffee Cen ht Wi-fi Golf 36 **Notes** LB ⊗ No Children Closed Dec-Feb

St Johns Lodge

★★★ 🛏 GUEST ACCOMMODATION

Lake Rd LA23 2EQ
☎ 015394 43078 📠 015394 88054
e-mail: mail@st-johns-lodge.co.uk
web: www.st-johns-lodge.co.uk
dir: On A5074 between Windermere & lake

Located between Windermere and Bowness, this large property offers a refreshingly friendly welcome. Bedrooms vary in size and style but all are neatly furnished and decorated. Freshly prepared traditional breakfasts, including vegetarian, vegan, gluten and dairy-free options, are served in the well-appointed basement dining room. Facilities include free internet access.

Rooms 9 en suite (1 fmly) **Facilities** tea/coffee Cen ht Wi-fi Free access to local leisure club **Parking** 3 **Notes** LB ⊗ No Children 12yrs Closed Xmas

Adam Place Guest House

★★★ GUEST HOUSE

1 Park Av LA23 2AR
☎ 015394 44600 & 07879 640757 📠 015394 44600
e-mail: adamplacewindermere@yahoo.co.uk
web: www.adam-place.co.uk
dir: Off A591 into Windermere, through town centre, left onto Ellerthwaite Rd & Park Av

Located in a mainly residential area within easy walking distance of lake and town centre, this stone Victorian house has been renovated to provide comfortable and homely bedrooms. Comprehensive breakfasts are served in the cosy dining room and there is a pretty patio garden.

Rooms 5 en suite (2 fmly) S £39-£44; D £68-£78
Facilities FTV tea/coffee Cen ht **Notes** LB ⊗ No Children 6yrs

Brook House

★★★ GUEST HOUSE

30 Ellerthwaite Rd LA23 2AH
☎ 015394 44932
e-mail: stay@brookhouselakes.co.uk
dir: M6 junct 36 onto A591, through one-way system. Ellerthwaite Rd 2nd left, 200yds on right

Brook House is a Lakeland stone Victorian guest house located in a quiet part of Windermere and offers a very relaxed friendly atmosphere. Accessible with or without a car and close to all amenities is a perfect base for exploring the Lake District. Private parking and a guest lounge are also available. Whisky warmer weekends are run through winter.

Rooms 5 en suite (1 fmly) **Facilities** FTV tea/coffee Cen ht **Parking** 5 **Notes** ⊗ ♿

Green Gables Guest House

★★★ GUEST HOUSE

37 Broad St LA23 2AB
☎ 015394 43886
e-mail: info@greengablesguesthouse.co.uk
dir: Off A591 into Windermere, 1st left after pelican crossing, opp car park

Aptly named, Green Gables is a friendly guest house looking onto Elleray Gardens. Just a short walk from the centre, the house is attractively furnished and offers bright, fresh and well appointed bedrooms. There is a comfortable bar-lounge, and substantial breakfasts are served in the spacious dining room.

Rooms 7 rms (4 en suite) (3 pri facs) (3 fmly) (1 GF)
Facilities TVL tea/coffee Cen ht Licensed **Notes** ⊗ Closed 23-27 Dec

WORKINGTON Map 18 NY02

The Sleepwell Inn

★★★ GUEST ACCOMMODATION

Washington St CA14 3AY
☎ 01900 65772 📠 01900 68770
e-mail: kawildwchotel@aol.com
dir: M6 junct 40, W on A66. At bottom of Ramsay Brow turn left onto Washington St, 300yds on left

Comfortable, well appointed accommodation situated just 100 meters from the sister property the Washington Central Hotel. Guests have full use of these facilities and this is where breakfast is served. Limited off-road car parking is available to the rear. Rooms differ in size and styles with some inter-connecting rooms available.

Rooms 24 en suite (4 fmly) (12 GF) S £38.95-£50; D £70 (room only)* **Facilities** FTV TVL tea/coffee Dinner available Direct Dial Cen ht Licensed Wi-fi Facilities available at Washington Central Hotel **Parking** 32 **Notes** LB ⊗

DERBYSHIRE

ASHBOURNE | Map 10 SK14

PREMIER COLLECTION

Turlow Bank

★★★★★ 🏠 BED AND BREAKFAST

Hognaston DE6 1PW
☎ 01335 370299 📄 01335 370299
e-mail: turlowbank@w3z.co.uk
web: www.turlowbank.co.uk
dir: Off B5035 to Hognaston (signed Hognaston only), through village towards Hulland Ward, Turlow Bank 0.5m, look for clock tower

Set in delightful gardens on a superb elevated position close to Carsington Water, this extended 19th-century farmhouse provides high levels of comfort with excellent facilities. Bedrooms are equipped with many thoughtful extras and feature quality modern bathrooms. Comprehensive breakfasts, which include free-range chicken or duck eggs, are served at a family table in the cosy dining room. A spacious lounge is available. Hospitality is memorable.

Rooms 2 en suite S £45-£55; D £76-£90*
Facilities TVL tea/coffee Cen ht Wi-fi 🏌 **Parking** 6
Notes ⊗ No Children 12yrs Closed 25-27 Dec 🐾

Compton House

★★★★ GUEST ACCOMMODATION

27-31 Compton DE6 1BX
☎ 01335 343100
e-mail: jane@comptonhouse.co.uk
web: www.comptonhouse.co.uk
dir: A52 from Derby into Ashbourne, over lights at bottom of hill, house 100yds on left opp garage

Within easy walking distance of the central attractions, this conversion of three cottages has resulted in a house with good standards of comfort and facilities. Bedrooms are filled with homely extras and comprehensive breakfasts are served in the cottage-style dining room.

Rooms 5 en suite (2 fmly) (1 GF) **Facilities** TVL tea/coffee Cen ht Wi-fi **Parking** 6

Mercaston Hall (SK279419)

★★★★ FARMHOUSE

Mercaston DE6 3BL
☎ 01335 360263 & 07836 648102
Mr & Mrs A Haddon
e-mail: mercastonhall@btinternet.com
dir: Off A52 in Brailsford onto Luke Ln, 1m turn right at 1st x-rds, house 1m on right

Located in a pretty hamlet, this medieval building retains many original features. Bedrooms are homely, and additional facilities include an all-weather tennis court and a livery service. This is a good base for visiting local stately homes, the Derwent Valley mills and Dovedale.

Rooms 3 en suite S £50-£55; D £70-£75* **Facilities** FTV tea/coffee Cen ht Wi-fi 🐴 **Parking** 3 **Notes** No Children 8yrs Closed Xmas 🐾 60 acres mixed

The Wheel House

★★★★ 🏠 BED AND BREAKFAST

Belper Rd, Hulland Ward DE6 3EE
☎ 01335 372837 📄 01335 372837
e-mail: thewheelhouse@btinternet.com
dir: Between Ashbourne & Belper on A517

This comfortably furnished house is set in open countryside on the main road between Ashbourne and Belper. The bedrooms are well furnished and a cosy lounge is also available. Breakfasts are hearty, and guests can expect friendly and attentive service.

Rooms 3 en suite S £45-£50; D £60-£70 **Facilities** FTV TVL tea/coffee Cen ht Wi-fi **Parking** 5 **Notes** LB ⊗

Homesclose House

★★★ BED AND BREAKFAST

DE6 2DA
☎ 01335 324475
e-mail: gilltomlinson@tiscali.co.uk
dir: Off A52 into village centre

Stunning views of the surrounding countryside and manicured gardens are a feature of this beautifully maintained dormer bungalow. Bedrooms are filled with homely extras, and an attractive dining room with one family table is the setting for breakfast.

Rooms 3 rms (2 en suite) (1 fmly) (1 GF) S £27.50-£35; D £48-£50* **Facilities** FTV tea/coffee Cen ht Wi-fi **Parking** 4 **Notes** LB Closed Dec-Jan 🐾

Thistle Bank Guest House

★★★ GUEST ACCOMMODATION

24A Derby Rd DE6 1BE
☎ 01335 300451 📄 01335 342814
e-mail: cindy.swann@hotmail.co.uk
dir: M1 junct 25, A52 to Derby, A52 to Ashbourne, located at bottom of hill on right

Set on the outskirts of Ashbourne, Thistle Bank offers four spacious, well equipped, modern en suite bedrooms. Breakfasts are hearty, and guests can expect friendly and attentive service. An ideal location to explore the Peak District National Park.

Rooms 4 en suite (3 fmly) S £30-£40; D £60-£70* **Facilities** TVL tea/coffee Cen ht Wi-fi **Parking** 5 **Notes** 🐾

Air Cottage Farm (SK142523)

★★ FARMHOUSE

Ilam DE6 2BD
☎ 01335 350475
Mrs J Wain
e-mail: aircottagedovedale@btinternet.com
dir: A515 from Ashbourne, left signed Thorpe/Dovedale/Ilam, in Ilam right at memorial stone to Alstonfield, right at 1st cattle grid gate on right leaving village, 2nd farm on drive

This 18th-century farmhouse has a magnificent elevated position with stunning views over the countryside and Dovedale. It provides traditional standards of accommodation and is very popular with serious walkers, climbers and artists visiting this beautiful part of the Peak District.

Rooms 3 rms (3 GF) S £30-£35; D £60-£70* **Facilities** TVL tea/coffee Cen ht **Parking** 4 **Notes** ⊗ Closed Nov-Feb 🐾 70 acres beef/cattle/sheep

BAKEWELL | Map 16 SK26

Avenue House

★★★★ GUEST ACCOMMODATION

The Avenue DE45 1EQ
☎ 01629 812467
dir: Off A6 onto The Avenue, 1st house on right

Located a short walk from the town centre, this impressive Victorian house has original features complemented by the decor and furnishings. Bedrooms have many thoughtful extras and the modern bathrooms contain power showers. Hearty English breakfasts are served in the traditionally furnished dining room.

Rooms 3 en suite S £40-£45; D £55-£65* **Facilities** FTV tea/coffee Cen ht **Parking** 3 **Notes** ⊗ 🐾

Bourne House

★★★★ GUEST HOUSE

The Park, Haddon Rd DE45 1ET
☎ 01629 813274
dir: 300yds S of town centre on A6, on left before park

This impressive former manse stands in mature gardens and is located overlooking the park a few minutes' walk from the town centre. Bedrooms are spacious and lots of thoughtful extras enhance guest comfort. Breakfast is taken in an attractive period-furnished dining room and a warm welcome is assured.

Rooms 3 en suite S £35-£40; D £56-£70 **Facilities** tea/coffee Cen ht Golf 9 **Parking** 5 **Notes** ⊗ No Children 7yrs Closed Dec-Feb ⊜

Croft Cottages

★★★★ GUEST ACCOMMODATION

Coombs Rd DE45 1AQ
☎ 01629 814101
e-mail: croftco@btinternet.com
dir: A619 E from town centre over bridge, right onto Station Rd & Coombs Rd

A warm welcome is assured at this Grade II listed stone building close to the River Wye and town centre. Thoughtfully equipped bedrooms are available in the main house or in an adjoining converted barn suite. Breakfast is served in a spacious lounge dining room.

Rooms 3 rms (2 en suite) (1 pri facs) 1 annexe en suite (1 fmly) D £60-£85 **Facilities** tea/coffee Cen ht **Parking** 2 **Notes** ⊜

Wyedale

★★★★ BED AND BREAKFAST

Wyedale House, 25 Holywell DE45 1BA
☎ 01629 812845
dir: 500yds SE of town centre, off A6 (Haddon Rd)

Wyedale is close to the town centre and is ideal for relaxing or touring. Bedrooms, one of which is on the ground floor, are spacious and freshly decorated. Breakfast is served in the attractive dining room, which overlooks the rear patio.

Rooms 4 en suite (1 fmly) (1 GF) **Facilities** tea/coffee Cen ht **Parking** 5 **Notes** ⊗ Closed 31 Dec RS 24 Dec

Everton

★★★ GUEST HOUSE

Haddon Rd DE45 1AW
☎ 01629 815028
e-mail: trish@evertonbandb.co.uk
dir: S of Bakewell on A6

Ideally located opposite a public park and a few minutes walk from central attractions, this large semi-detached house provides comfortable homely bedrooms. Delicious cooked breakfasts are served in an attractive pine-furnished dining room.

Rooms 3 rms (2 en suite) (1 pri facs) (1 fmly) **Facilities** tea/coffee Cen ht **Parking** 6 **Notes** LB ⊗ Closed 24-26 Dec RS 30-31 Dec ⊜

Wyeclose

★★★ BED AND BREAKFAST

5 Granby Croft DE45 1ET
☎ 01629 813702
e-mail: h.wilson@talk21.com
dir: Off A6 Matlock St onto Granby Rd & Granby Croft

Located in a quiet cul-de-sac in the town centre, this Edwardian house provides thoughtfully furnished bedroom accommodation with smart modern bathrooms and an attractive dining room, the setting for comprehensive breakfasts. Original family art is a feature in the ground-floor areas.

Rooms 2 rms (1 en suite) (1 pri facs) D £60-£70 **Facilities** STV FTV tea/coffee Cen ht **Parking** 3 **Notes** ⊗ No Children 8yrs Closed Xmas & New Year ⊜

BAMFORD   Map 16 SK28

Yorkshire Bridge Inn

★★★★ INN

Ashopton Rd S33 0AZ
☎ 01433 651361   📠 01433 651361
e-mail: info@yorkshire-bridge.co.uk
web: www.yorkshire-bridge.co.uk
dir: From A57 between Sheffield & Glossop take A6013 to Bamford. Or from Sheffield take A625, then A6187, through Hathersage, right onto A6013 to Bamford

A well-established country inn, ideally located beside the Ladybower Reservoir and within reach of the Peak District's many beauty spots, the Yorkshire Bridge Inn offers a wide range of excellent dishes in both the bar and dining area, along with a good selection of real ales. Bedrooms are attractively furnished, comfortable and well-equipped.

Rooms 14 en suite (3 fmly) (4 GF) S £60-£65; D £76-£120* **Facilities** tea/coffee Dinner available Direct Dial Cen ht Wi-fi **Conf** Max 20 **Parking** 50 **Notes** LB

Thornhill View

★★★ GUEST ACCOMMODATION

Hope Rd, Bamford, Hope Valley S33 0AL
☎ 01433 651823   & 07792 782565
e-mail: thornhill4bb@aol.com
dir: 0.5m SW of Bamford. On A6187 pass Thornhill Ln junct

Comfortable accommodation in a secluded location, set back from the main road running through the Hope Valley near to the Rising Sun Inn. Compact bedrooms are well equipped, and Jo Fairbairn is a caring hostess.

Rooms 3 rms (2 en suite) (1 pri facs) (2 GF) S £35; D £60* **Facilities** tea/coffee Cen ht **Parking** 3 **Notes** LB ⊜

BEELEY   Map 16 SK26

The Devonshire Arms at Beeley

★★★★ ⊛⊛ INN

Devonshire Square DE4 2NR
☎ 01629 733259   📠 01629 734542
e-mail: enquiries@devonshirebeeley.co.uk
web: www.devonshirebeeley.co.uk
dir: B6012 towards Matlock, pass Chatsworth House. After 1.5m turn left, 2nd entrance to Beeley

The Devonshire Arms is a picturesque country inn at the heart of village life. It offers all the charm and character of an historic inn with a warm and comfortable interior full of oak beams and stone crannies, but venture inside a little further and you will find the startlingly different decor of the brasserie with its contemporary bar, glass fronted wine store and colourful furnishings. For the ultimate escape, there are four stylish cottage bedrooms.

Rooms 4 en suite 4 annexe en suite (1 fmly) (2 GF) S fr £114; D £134-£197* **Facilities** STV tea/coffee Dinner available Direct Dial Cen ht Wi-fi **Parking** 40 **Notes** No coaches

BELPER
Map 11 SK34

PREMIER COLLECTION

Dannah Farm Country House

★★★★★ 🏠 GUEST ACCOMMODATION

Bowmans Ln, Shottle DE56 2DR
☎ 01773 550273 & 550630 📠 01773 550590
e-mail: slack@dannah.co.uk
web: www.dannah.co.uk
dir: *A517 from Belper towards Ashbourne, 1.5m right into Shottle after Hanging Gate pub on right, over x-rds & right*

Part of the Chatsworth Estates at Shottle, on an elevated position with stunning views, this impressive Georgian house and outbuildings have been renovated to provide high standards of comfort and facilities. Many original features have been retained, and are enhanced by quality decor and furnishings. The bedrooms are filled with a wealth of thoughtful extras. One room has an outdoor hot tub. The Mixing Place restaurant is the setting for memorable breakfasts, which make use of the finest local produce.

Rooms 8 en suite (1 fmly) (2 GF) S £79-£95; D £150-£275* **Facilities** FTV tea/coffee Direct Dial Cen ht Licensed Wi-fi Sauna Leisure cabin, hot tub **Conf** Max 10 Thtr 10 Class 10 Board 10 **Parking** 20 **Notes** LB ⊗ Closed 24-26 Dec

PREMIER COLLECTION

Chevin Green Farm

★★★★★ GUEST ACCOMMODATION

Chevin Rd DE56 2UN
☎ 01773 822328 📠 01773 822328
e-mail: davidrmarley@btinternet.com
dir: *Off A6 opp Strutt Arms at Milford onto Chevin Rd, 1.5m on left*

Mr and Mrs Marley welcome guests to this beautiful stone building refurbished to a high standard with original beams, lovely finishing touches and stunning views of the Derwent Valley and beyond. Bedrooms are individually styled, featuring high quality furnishings and excellent bathrooms. Breakfast focuses on home-made and local ingredients. The lounge and wonderful gardens also provide additional space for guests to relax.

Rooms 5 en suite (1 fmly) (1 GF) S £45-£70; D £70-£90* **Facilities** FTV TVL tea/coffee Cen ht **Parking** 5 **Notes** LB ⊗ No Children 16yrs Closed Xmas & New Year

PREMIER COLLECTION

Shottle Hall

★★★★★ GUEST ACCOMMODATION

White Ln, Shottle DE56 2EB
☎ 01773 550577 📠 01332 440260
e-mail: Joanne.nicol@shottlehall.co.uk
dir: *M1 junct 25, A52 to Derby follow signs for Matlock. A6 at Duffield take B5023 signed Wirksworth & Hazelwood; from N - M1 junct 28, A6 to Belper onto A517 signed Shottle Hall*

Shottle Hall is set on the edge of the Peak District National Park and is part of the Chatsworth House Estate. Standing in beautiful grounds and gardens, the hall is a country house that offers spacious public areas, a feature dining room and individually designed bedrooms. All bedrooms have modern bathrooms, some with roll-top baths. The property is ideal for corporate functions, weddings and business meetings.

Rooms 8 en suite (4 fmly) S £78-£98; D £115-£128* **Facilities** FTV tea/coffee Direct Dial Cen ht Licensed Wi-fi Golf 18 **Conf** Max 200 Thtr 200 Class 100 Board 20 **Parking** 50 **Notes** Closed 25-28 Dec Civ Wed 200

BONSALL
Map 16 SK25

Pig of Lead

★★★★ GUEST ACCOMMODATION

Via Gellia Rd DE4 2AJ
☎ 01629 820040 📠 01629 820040
e-mail: pigoflead@aol.com
dir: *0.5m SE of Bonsall on A5012*

This delightful property dating back over two hundred years was once an inn named after a measurement of lead, which used to be mined locally. Only five minutes from Matlock Bath, this is a good base for exploring the area. Individually styled bedrooms are comfortable and well appointed. A warm welcome and hearty breakfasts featuring local produce can be assured here.

Rooms 3 en suite S £45-£65; D £65-£90* **Facilities** tea/coffee Cen ht Wi-fi **Parking** 3 **Notes** ⊗ No Children 14yrs 🐾

BRADWELL
Map 16 SK18

PREMIER COLLECTION

The Samuel Fox Country Inn

★★★★★ @@ INN

Stretfield Rd S33 9JT
☎ 01433 621562 📠 01433 623770
e-mail: thesamuelfox@hotmail.co.uk
dir: *M1 junct 29, A617 towards Chesterfield, A619 signed Baslow & Buxton, 2nd rdbt A623 for 7m, take B6049 to Bradwell, through village on left*

Recently renamed after Bradwell's most famous son, industrial magnate Samuel Fox, who built the steelworks at Stocksbridge, The Samuel Fox has undergone a full refurbishment and is modern and stylish while retaining its rustic charm. Bedrooms are both immaculately presented and extensively equipped. Service is highly attentive. Modern British cuisine is served in the restaurant with breathtaking views over Bradwell.

Rooms 4 en suite S £85; D £125* **Facilities** tea/coffee Dinner available Direct Dial Cen ht Wi-fi **Parking** 15 **Notes** LB ⊗

BUXTON   Map 16 SK07

PREMIER COLLECTION

Buxton's Victorian Guest House

★★★★★ GUEST HOUSE

3A Broad Walk SK17 6JE
☎ 01298 78759   📠 01298 74732
e-mail: buxtonvictorian@btconnect.com
web: www.buxtonvictorian.co.uk
dir: *Signs to Opera House, proceed to Old Hall Hotel,
right onto Hartington Rd, car park 100yds on right*

Standing in a prime position overlooking the Pavilion
Gardens, this delightfully furnished house has an
interesting Victorian style. Bedrooms are individually
themed and have many thoughtful extras. A
comfortable lounge is available. Excellent breakfasts
are served in the Oriental breakfast room and
hospitality is first class.

Rooms 7 en suite (2 fmly) (1 GF) S £50-£70; D
£78-£100* **Facilities** FTV tea/coffee Cen ht Wi-fi Riding
Parking 9 **Notes** LB ⊗ No Children 4yrs Closed 22
Dec-12 Jan

Oldfield

★★★★ ⌂ GUEST HOUSE

8 Macclesfield Rd SK17 9AH
☎ 01298 78264
e-mail: avril@oldfieldhousebuxton.co.uk
web: www.oldfieldhousebuxton.co.uk
dir: *On B5059 0.5m SW of town centre*

Located within easy walking distance of the centre, this
impressive Victorian house provides spacious bedrooms
with modern en suites. Comprehensive breakfasts are
served in the bright dining room, and a cosy lounge is
available.

Rooms 5 en suite (1 GF) D £75-£85* **Facilities** FTV TVL
tea/coffee Cen ht Golf 18 **Parking** 7 **Notes** LB ⊗ No
Children 7yrs Closed Xmas

Grosvenor House

★★★★ ⌂ GUEST HOUSE

1 Broad Walk SK17 6JE
☎ 01298 72439
e-mail: grosvenor.buxton@btopenworld.com
dir: *In town centre*

This Victorian house is centrally located overlooking the
Pavilion Gardens and Opera House. Bedrooms are
carefully furnished and have many thoughtful extras.
There is a comfortable period-style sitting room, and
freshly prepared imaginative breakfasts are served in the
cosy dining room.

Rooms 8 en suite (1 fmly) S £50; D £65-£85
Facilities FTV tea/coffee Cen ht Wi-fi **Parking** 2 **Notes** ⊗
Closed Xmas-New Year

Roseleigh

★★★★ GUEST HOUSE

19 Broad Walk SK17 6JR
☎ 01298 24904   📠 01298 24904
e-mail: enquiries@roseleighhotel.co.uk
web: www.roseleighhotel.co.uk
dir: *A6 to Morrisons rdbt, onto Dale Rd, right at lights,
100yds left by Swan pub, down hill & right onto
Hartington Rd*

This elegant property has a prime location overlooking
Pavilion Gardens, and quality furnishings and decor
highlight the many original features. Thoughtfully
furnished bedrooms have smart modern shower rooms
and a comfortable lounge is also available.

Rooms 14 rms (12 en suite) (2 pri facs) (1 GF) S
£39-£90; D £76-£90* **Facilities** tea/coffee Cen ht Wi-fi
Parking 9 **Notes** ⊗ No Children 6yrs Closed 16 Dec-16
Jan

Nat's Kitchen

★★★ ⊛ RESTAURANT WITH ROOMS

9-11 Market St SK17 6JY
☎ 01298 214642
e-mail: natskitchen@btconnect.com
dir: *On Market St, just off Buxton's market place*

Set in one of the Peak District's most well known
destinations, Nat's Kitchen offers an intimate restaurant
with a warm welcome. Accessed via a separate entrance,
the accommodation is situated above the dining room
and comes in a range of bedrooms with en suite facilities.

Rooms 5 en suite **Facilities** FTV tea/coffee Dinner
available Cen ht Wi-fi **Notes** ⊗ Closed 27 Dec-7 Jan No
coaches

CHINLEY   Map 16 SK08

The Old Hall Inn

★★★★ Ⓐ INN

Whitehough SK23 6EJ
☎ 01663 750529
e-mail: info@old-hall-inn.co.uk
Rooms 4 en suite S £49-£69; D £59-£89* **Facilities** FTV
tea/coffee Dinner available Cen ht Wi-fi **Parking** 20
Notes LB

CROMFORD   Map 16 SK25

Alison House

★★★★ GUEST ACCOMMODATION

Intake Ln DE4 3RH
☎ 01629 822211   📠 01629 822316
e-mail: info@alison-house-hotel.co.uk

This very well furnished and spacious 18th-century house
stands in seven acres of grounds just a short walk from
the village. Public rooms are comfortable and bedrooms
are mostly very spacious.

Rooms 16 en suite (1 fmly) (4 GF) S fr £55; D fr £85*
Facilities tea/coffee Dinner available Direct Dial Cen ht
Licensed Wi-fi 🍴 **Conf** Max 40 Thtr 40 Class 40 Board 40
Parking 30 **Notes** LB Civ Wed 50

DERBY   Map 11 SK33

See also Belper & Melbourne

The Derby Conference Centre

★★★★ GUEST ACCOMMODATION

London Rd DE24 8UX
☎ 0845 880 8101   0870 890 0030
e-mail: reservations@thederbyconferencecentre.com
web: www.thederbyconferencecentre.com
dir: *M1 junct 25, A52 towards Derby. Filter left onto A5111 signed Ring Road. At Raynesway Park rdbt take 3rd exit signed Ring Road/Alvaston. At next rdbt take A6 towards Derby centre. Pass Wickes, turn left into entrance*

Formerly a railway training centre, this Grade II-listed art deco building has undergone a major refurbishment to modernise the public areas, meeting rooms and accommodation, yet it still retains original features such as the wall paintings by Norman Wilkinson. Day rooms offer good flexibility and comforts, while updated conference facilities can cater for small to very large gatherings. The studio bedroom accommodation is soundly appointed and equipped.

Rooms 50 en suite (10 GF) S £35-£53; D £45-£63*
Facilities FTV TVL tea/coffee Dinner available Cen ht
Licensed Wi-fi Pool table **Conf** Max 1000 Thtr 400 Class
80 Board 50 **Parking** 250 **Notes** ⊗ Closed 24 Dec-4 Jan
Civ Wed 400

Chambers House

★★★ GUEST ACCOMMODATION

110 Green Ln DE1 1RY
☎ 01332 746412
web: www.chambershouse.co.uk
dir: *In city centre on Green Lane. Approach car park via Wilson St*

Located a short walk from the centre, this impressive Victorian house retains many original features. The attractive bedrooms are generally spacious; some are en suite whilst others have shared facilities. A car park is available.

Rooms 8 rms (4 en suite) (2 fmly) (1 GF) **Facilities** tea/coffee Cen ht **Parking** 6 **Notes** ⊗ ⊜

FENNY BENTLEY   Map 16 SK14

Bentley Brook Inn

★★★ INN

DE6 1LF
☎ 01335 350278   01335 350422
e-mail: all@bentleybrookinn.co.uk
dir: *2m N of Ashbourne at junct of A515 & B5056*

This popular inn is located in the Peak District National Park, just north of Ashbourne. It is a charming building with an attractive terrace, sweeping lawns, and nursery gardens. A well-appointed family restaurant dominates the ground floor, where a wide range of dishes is available all day. The character bar serves beer from its own micro-brewery. Bedrooms are well appointed and thoughtfully equipped.

Rooms 11 en suite (1 fmly) (2 GF) **Facilities** TVL tea/coffee Dinner available Direct Dial Cen ht Wi-fi **Conf** Max 11 Thtr 11 Class 11 Board 11 **Parking** 100 **Notes** Civ Wed 40

FOOLOW   Map 16 SK17

The Bulls Head Inn

★★★★ INN

S32 5QR
☎ 01433 630873   01433 631738
e-mail: wilbnd@aol.com
dir: *Off A623 into Foolow*

Located in the village centre, this popular inn retains many original features and offers comfortable, well-equipped bedrooms. Extensive and imaginative bar meals are served in the traditionally furnished dining room or in the cosy bar areas. The inn welcomes well-behaved dogs in the bar (and even muddy boots on the flagstone areas).

Rooms 3 en suite (1 fmly) **Facilities** tea/coffee Dinner available Cen ht Golf 18 **Parking** 20

FROGGATT   Map 16 SK27

The Chequers Inn

★★★★ ◉ INN

S32 3ZJ
☎ 01433 630231   01433 631072
e-mail: info@chequers-froggatt.com
dir: *On A625 between Sheffield & Bakewell, 0.75m from Calver*

A very popular 16th-century inn offering an extensive range of well-cooked food. The bedrooms are comprehensively equipped with all modern comforts and the hospitality is professional and sincere. A good location for touring Derbyshire, the Peak Park, and visiting Chatsworth.

Rooms 5 en suite D £77-£102* **Facilities** tea/coffee Dinner available Direct Dial Cen ht Wi-fi **Parking** 45 **Notes** LB ⊗ Closed 25 Dec No coaches

GLOSSOP   Map 16 SK09

Allmans Heath Cottage Bed & Breakfast

★★★★ BED AND BREAKFAST

Woodhead Rd SK13 7QE
☎ 01457 857867 & 07783 842900
e-mail: julie@allmansheathcottage.co.uk
dir: *From Glossop town centre lights, proceed up Norfolk St towards Woodhead for 1m. Continue through tunnel of trees, on left turning in at farm gate*

Just one mile from Glossop, this converted farm cottage has beamed ceilings, open fires and many original features. All the rooms command spectacular views over open countryside, and hospitality is warm and friendly.

Rooms 2 rms (1 en suite) (1 pri facs) S £45; D £70 **Facilities** FTV TVL tea/coffee Cen ht Wi-fi **Parking** 6 **Notes** ⊗ ⊜

Woodlands

★★★★ BED AND BREAKFAST

Woodseats Ln, Charlesworth SK13 5DP
☎ 01457 866568
e-mail: brian.mairs@sky.com
dir: *3m SW of Glossop. Off A626, 0.5m from Charlesworth towards Marple*

This delightful Victorian house stands in well-tended grounds and offers very well-equipped and delightfully furnished bedrooms. There is a comfy lounge and a conservatory serving very good breakfasts, lunches and cream teas.

Rooms 3 rms (2 en suite) (1 pri facs) S £40-£45; D £55-£75* **Facilities** FTV TVL tea/coffee Cen ht Licensed Wi-fi **Parking** 6 **Notes** LB ⊗ No Children 12yrs

Rock Farm *(SK027907)*

★★★★ FARMHOUSE

Monks Rd SK13 6JZ
☎ 01457 861086 & 07780 670568 📄 01457 861086
Mrs Dennett
e-mail: rockfarmbandb@btinternet.com
dir: *Off A624 onto Monks Rd, signed Charlesworth. After 1m, Rock Farm on left, follow farm track past Higher Plainsteads Farm*

Located down a winding track, with spectacular views over Kinder Scout and the surrounding hills from all rooms, Rock Farm is a restored family home. Walkers, horses, and riders, as well as young families, are offered a particularly warm welcome. Fresh eggs are used at breakfast.

Rooms 2 rms Facilities FTV TVL tea/coffee Dinner available Cen ht Wi-fi Stabling & grazing available for guests horses Parking 4 Notes ⊗ Closed Nov-Feb ☺ 6 acres non-working

---

GREAT HUCKLOW   Map 16 SK17

The Queen Anne

★★★ ➣ INN

SK17 8RF
☎ 01298 871246 📄 01298 873504
e-mail: angelaryan100@aol.com
web: www.queenanneinn.co.uk
dir: *Off A623 onto B6049 to Great Hucklow*

Set in the heart of this pretty village, the Queen Anne has been a licensed inn for over 300 years and the public areas retain many original features. The bedrooms are in a separate building with direct access, and have modern shower rooms en suite.

Rooms 2 annexe en suite (2 GF) Facilities TVL tea/coffee Dinner available Cen ht Parking 20 Notes LB ⊗ No Children 10yrs Closed Xmas & New Year

---

HARTINGTON   Map 16 SK16

Bank House

★★★★ GUEST ACCOMMODATION

Market Place SK17 0AL
☎ 01298 84465
dir: *B5054 into village centre*

Bank House is a very well-maintained Grade II listed Georgian building that stands in the main square of this delightful village. Bedrooms are neat and fresh in appearance, and there is a comfortable television lounge. A hearty breakfast is served in the ground-floor cottage-style dining room.

Rooms 5 rms (3 en suite) (3 fmly) S £32-£37; D £58-£62 Facilities TVL tea/coffee Cen ht Parking 2 Notes LB ⊗ Closed Xmas RS 22-28 Dec ☺

Charles Cotton

★★★★ ➣ INN

SK17 0AL
☎ 01298 84229 📄 01298 84301
e-mail: info@charlescotton.co.uk
dir: *M1 junct 23A/A50 to Sudbury, follow A515 to Ashbourne then follow signs for Buxton. On B5054 1m S of A515 half way between Buxton & Ashbourne*

A 17th-century inn in the centre of a pretty village in the Peak District. The cosy traditional bar, which features real ales and an open fire, blends with stylish design in the restaurant and attractive bedrooms. Complimentary Wi-fi is available. Food is a highlight and menus feature local ingredients.

Rooms 11 en suite 6 annexe en suite (3 fmly) (3 GF) S £55-£75; D £65-£105* Facilities TVL tea/coffee Dinner available Cen ht Wi-fi Fishing Conf Max 50 Thtr 50 Class 35 Board 45 Parking 25 Notes LB

HARTSHORNE   Map 10 SK32

The Mill Wheel

★★★★ ➣ INN

Ticknall Rd DE11 7AS
☎ 01283 550335 📄 01283 552833
e-mail: info@themillwheel.co.uk
web: www.themillwheel.co.uk
dir: *M42 junct 2 follow signs for A511 to Woodville, left onto A514 towards Derby to Hartshorne*

This popular inn and restaurant provides a wide range of well-prepared food and has a large mill wheel in the bar. Bedrooms are modern and well-equipped while friendly and attentive service is provided.

Rooms 4 en suite (2 GF) D fr £50.95* Facilities FTV tea/coffee Dinner available Cen ht Wi-fi Parking 55 Notes ⊗

HATHERSAGE   Map 16 SK28

The Millstone Inn

★★★★ INN

Sheffield Rd S32 1DA
☎ 01433 650258 📄 01433 651664
e-mail: jerry@millstoneinn.co.uk
web: www.millstoneinn.co.uk
dir: *0.5m SE of village on A6187*

This timber and stone inn stands on an elevated position overlooking the Hope Valley. It offers modern, well-equipped bedrooms, and real ales and exciting food are served in the friendly bar. The smart Terrace fish restaurant offers fine dining with great views over the valley. Wi-fi and free use of the local gym are benefits.

Rooms 8 en suite (3 fmly) Facilities tea/coffee Dinner available Direct Dial Cen ht Wi-fi Gym membership free to guests Conf Max 40 Thtr 40 Class 40 Board 40 Parking 80

The Plough Inn

★★★★ ⊛ INN

Leadmill Bridge S32 1BA
☎ 01433 650319 📄 01433 651049
e-mail: sales@theploughinn-hathersage.co.uk
web: www.theploughinn-hathersage.co.uk
dir: *1m SE of Hathersage on B6001. Over bridge, 150yds beyond at Leadmill*

This delightful 16th-century inn with beer garden has an idyllic location by the River Derwent. A selection of real ales and imaginative food is served in the spacious public areas, and original fireplaces and exposed beams have been preserved. The attractive, well equipped bedrooms include several recently refurbished luxury rooms and Wi-fi access is available throughout.

Rooms 3 en suite 2 annexe en suite (1 GF) Facilities tea/coffee Dinner available Direct Dial Cen ht Parking 50 Notes ⊗ Closed 25 Dec No coaches

HATHERSAGE *continued*

The Scotsman's Pack Inn

★★★★ INN

School Ln S32 1BZ
☎ 01433 650253 📠 01433 650712
e-mail: scotsmans.pack@btinternet.com
dir: *A625 into Hathersage, turn right onto School Ln towards the church, Scotsman's Pack 100yds on right*

This comfortable inn on the edge of the village provides a wide range of well-prepared food. The bedrooms are compact, well-furnished and thoughtfully equipped, while the bar, which contains 'Little John's chair', is a great place to meet the locals. Hearty breakfasts are served in the separate dining room, and the staff are very friendly.

Rooms 5 en suite **Facilities** tea/coffee Dinner available Cen ht **Conf** Max 20 **Parking** 17 **Notes** LB ⊗ RS 25 Dec eve no food served

HOPE	Map 16 SK18

PREMIER COLLECTION

Underleigh House

★★★★★ 🏠 GUEST ACCOMMODATION

Lose Hill Lane S33 6AF
☎ 01433 621372 📠 01433 621324
e-mail: info@underleighhouse.co.uk
web: www.underleighhouse.co.uk
dir: *From village church on A6187 onto Edale Rd, 1m left onto Losehill Ln*

Situated at the end of a private lane, surrounded by glorious scenery, Underleigh House was converted from a barn and cottage that dates from 1873, and now offers carefully furnished and attractively decorated bedrooms with modern facilities. One room has a private lounge and others have access to the gardens. There is a very spacious lounge with comfortable chairs and a welcoming log fire. Memorable breakfasts are served at one large table in the dining room.

Rooms 5 en suite (2 GF) S £65-£85; D £85-£105*
Facilities TVL tea/coffee Direct Dial Cen ht Licensed Wi-fi **Parking** 6 **Notes** LB No Children 12yrs Closed Xmas, New Year & 23 Jan-23 Feb

Stoney Ridge

★★★★ 🏠 GUEST ACCOMMODATION

Granby Rd, Bradwell S33 9HU
☎ 01433 620538
e-mail: info@stoneyridge.org.uk
web: www.stoneyridge.org.uk
dir: *From N end of Bradwell, Gore Ln uphill past Bowling Green Inn, turn left onto Granby Rd*

This large, split-level bungalow stands in attractive mature gardens at the highest part of the village and has extensive views. Hens roam freely in the landscaped garden, and their fresh eggs add to the hearty breakfasts. Bedrooms are attractively furnished and thoughtfully equipped, and there is a spacious comfortable lounge and a superb indoor swimming pool.

Rooms 4 rms (3 en suite) (1 pri facs) S £47-£55; D £74*
Facilities STV FTV TVL tea/coffee Cen ht Wi-fi 🖲
Parking 3 **Notes** LB No Children 10yrs RS Winter Pool may be closed for maintenance

Poachers Arms

★★★★ 🅰 INN

95 Castleton Rd S33 6SB
☎ 01433 620380
e-mail: btissington95@aol.com
web: www.poachersarms.co.uk
dir: *On A625/A6187 between Hope & Castleton*

Rooms 4 en suite **Facilities** tea/coffee Dinner available Cen ht Wi-fi **Parking** 30 **Notes** ⊗ No coaches

Round Meadow Barn

★★★ BED AND BREAKFAST

Parsons Ln S33 6RB
☎ 01433 621347 & 07836 689422 📠 01433 621347
e-mail: rmbarn@bigfoot.com
dir: *Off A625 (Hope Rd) N onto Parsons Ln, over rail bridge, in 200yds right into hay barnyard, through gates, across 3 fields, house on left*

This converted barn, with original stone walls and exposed timbers, stands in open fields in the picturesque Hope Valley. The bedrooms are large enough for families and there are two modern bathrooms. Breakfast is served at one large table adjoining the family kitchen.

Rooms 3 rms (1 en suite) (2 pri facs) (1 fmly) S £35-£45; D £60-£66* **Facilities** tea/coffee Cen ht Golf 18 Riding **Parking** 8 **Notes** LB 🖲

MATLOCK	Map 16 SK35

PREMIER COLLECTION

Holmefield

★★★★★ 🍴 GUEST HOUSE

Dale Road North, Darley Dale DE4 2HY
☎ 01629 735347
e-mail: holmefieldguesthouse@btinternet.com
web: www.holmefieldguesthouse.co.uk
dir: *Between Bakewell & Matlock on A6. 1m from Rowsley & Chatsworth Estate, 0.5m from Peak Rail*

Standing in mature grounds between Matlock and Bakewell, this elegant Victorian house has been furnished with flair to offer good levels of comfort and facilities. Imaginative dinners feature seasonal local produce, including some from the Chatsworth Estate. Warm hospitality and attentive service are assured.

Rooms 4 en suite 3 annexe en suite (1 fmly) (2 GF)
Facilities tea/coffee Dinner available Direct Dial Cen ht Wi-fi Pool table **Parking** 10 **Notes** ⊗

Hearthstone Farm (SK308583)

★★★★ FARMHOUSE

Hearthstone Ln, Riber DE4 5JW
☎ 01629 534304
Mrs Gilman
e-mail: enquiries@hearthstonefarm.co.uk
web: www.hearthstonefarm.co.uk
dir: *A615 at Tansley 2m E of Matlock, turn opp Royal Oak towards Riber, at gates to Riber Hall left onto Riber Rd and 1st left onto Hearthstone Ln, farmhouse on left*

Situated on a stunning elevated location, this traditional stone farmhouse retains many original features and is stylishly decorated throughout. Bedrooms are equipped with a wealth of homely extras and comprehensive breakfasts feature the farm's organic produce. There is a very comfortable lounge, and the farm animals in the grounds are an attraction.

Rooms 3 en suite S £50-£55; D £70-£75* **Facilities** FTV TVL tea/coffee Cen ht **Parking** 6 **Notes** LB Closed Xmas & New Year 🖲 150 acres beef/lamb

Save on B&Bs and Hotels. Book at **theAA.com/hotel**

DERBYSHIRE 101 | ENGLAND

Hodgkinsons

★★★★ ☞ GUEST ACCOMMODATION

150 South Pde, Matlock Bath DE4 3NR
☎ 01629 582170 📠 01629 584891
e-mail: enquiries@hodgkinsons-hotel.co.uk
dir: *On A6 in village centre, corner of Waterloo Rd & South Parade*

This fine Georgian building was renovated in the Victorian era and has many interesting and unusual features. Bedrooms are equipped with fine antique furniture and a wealth of thoughtful extras. The elegant dining room is the setting for imaginative dinners and a comfortable lounge is also available.

Rooms 8 en suite (1 fmly) S £42-£85; D £93-£145*
Facilities tea/coffee Dinner available Direct Dial Cen ht Licensed Wi-fi garden **Conf** Max 12 Thtr 12 Class 12 Board 12 **Parking** 5 **Notes** LB Closed 24-26 Dec

The Pines

★★★★ 🗕 BED AND BREAKFAST

12 Eversleigh Rd, Darley Bridge DE4 2JW
☎ 01629 732646
e-mail: info@thepinesbandb.co.uk
dir: *From Bakewell or Matlock take A6 to Darley Dale. Turn at Whitworth Hotel onto B5057, pass Square & Compass pub & The 3 Stags Heads, The Pines on right*

Dating from the 1820s this home as been authentically restored. Standing in a secluded and pretty garden, The Pines makes an ideal location for visiting the Peak District. Three spacious en suite bedrooms are stylishly furnished using rich fabrics. Comprehensive breakfasts, utilising quality local produce, offer a hearty start to the day.

Rooms 3 en suite S £40-£60; D £70-£80* **Facilities** tea/coffee Dinner available Cen ht Wi-fi **Parking** 5 **Notes** LB 🐾

Yew Tree Cottage

★★★★ 🗕 BED AND BREAKFAST

The Knoll, Tansley DE4 5FP
☎ 01629 583862 & 07799 541903
e-mail: enquiries@ytcbb.co.uk
dir: *1.2m E of Matlock. Off A615 into Tansley centre*

This 18th-century cottage has been renovated to provide high standards of comfort while retaining original character. Memorable breakfasts are served in the elegant dining room, and a cosy lounge is available. A warm welcome and attentive service are assured.

Rooms 3 en suite S £65-£75; D £75-£90* **Facilities** FTV TVL tea/coffee Cen ht Wi-fi Sauna **Parking** 3 **Notes** LB No Children 12yrs

Glendon

★★★★ GUEST HOUSE

Knowleston Place DE4 3BU
☎ 01629 584732
e-mail: sylvia.elliott@tesco.net
dir: *250yds SE of town centre. Off A615, car park before Glendon sign*

Glendon is set beside a park just a short walk from the town centre. The spacious bedrooms are pleasantly decorated and well equipped, and one is suitable for families. The comfortable third-floor lounge has lovely views over Bentley Brook and the local church.

Rooms 3 en suite (1 fmly) S fr £40; D fr £68
Facilities TVL tea/coffee Cen ht **Parking** 4 **Notes** 🚫 No Children 3yrs Closed Dec 🐾

Old Sunday School

★★★★ BED AND BREAKFAST

New St DE4 3FH
☎ 01629 583347 📠 01629 583347
e-mail: davhpatrick@hotmail.com
dir: *In town centre. Off A6 rdbt to Crown Sq, turn left onto Bank Rd, New St 4th on right*

A warm welcome is assured at this converted Victorian chapel, built of mellow sandstone and just a short walk from central attractions. The homely bedroom is complemented by a modern shower room, and the spacious living area includes a period dining table, the setting for comprehensive breakfasts.

Rooms 1 en suite (1 fmly) S £30; D £55* **Facilities** STV TVL tea/coffee Cen ht Wi-fi **Notes** LB 🚫 Closed 23 Dec-4 Jan 🐾

Woodside

★★★★ BED AND BREAKFAST

Stanton Lees DE4 2LQ
☎ 01629 734320 📠 01629 734320
e-mail: kmptr21@googlemail.com
web: www.woodsidestantonlees.co.uk
dir: *4m NW of Matlock. A6 onto B5057 into Darley Bridge, opp pub turn right to Stanton Lees & right fork in village*

Located on an elevated position with stunning views of the surrounding countryside, this mellow stone house has been renovated to provide high standards of comfort and facilities. Carefully decorated bedrooms come with a wealth of thoughtful extras, and ground floor areas include a comfortable lounge and conservatory overlooking the garden, which is home to a variety of wild birds.

Rooms 3 en suite S £40-£42; D £62-£70 **Facilities** FTV TVL tea/coffee Cen ht **Parking** 3 **Notes** 🚫 No Children 3yrs 🐾

The Red Lion

★★★ INN

Matlock Green DE4 3BT
☎ 01629 584888
dir: *500yds SE of town centre on A632*

This comfortable free house is a good base for exploring Matlock and the surrounding Derbyshire countryside. Each bedroom is comfortably furnished, and one comes complete with a four-poster. Public areas include a lounge and games area with open fires, and a restaurant where a wide selection of meals is on offer. Private parking is a bonus.

Rooms 6 en suite **Facilities** tea/coffee Dinner available Cen ht Pool table **Parking** 20 **Notes** 🚫

Farley *(SK294622)*

★★★ FARMHOUSE

Farley DE4 5LR
☎ 01629 582533 & 07801 756409 📠 01629 584856
Mrs Brailsford
e-mail: eric.brailsford@btconnect.com
dir: *1m N of Matlock. From A6 rdbt towards Bakewell, 1st right, right at top of hill, left up Farley Hill, 2nd farm on left*

You can expect a warm welcome at this traditional stone farmhouse. In addition to farming, the proprietors also breed dogs and horses. The bedrooms are pleasantly decorated and equipped with many useful extras. A hearty farmhouse breakfast offers a good start to any day.

Rooms 2 en suite (3 fmly) S £35-£40; D £60-£64
Facilities TVL tea/coffee Dinner available Cen ht Riding **Parking** 8 **Notes** LB 🐾 165 acres arable/beef/dairy

MATLOCK *continued*

Red House Carriage Museum

★★★ GUEST ACCOMMODATION

Old Rd, Darley Dale DE4 2ER
☎ 01629 733583 📠 01629 733583
e-mail: redhousestables@hotmail.co.uk
dir: *2m N of Matlock, left off A6, 200yds on left*

Located in a famous working carriage-driving school and museum, this detached house provides homely and thoughtfully equipped bedrooms, one on the ground floor and one in a former stable. Comprehensive breakfasts are served at a family table in an attractive dining room, and the comfortable lounge area overlooks the spacious gardens.

Rooms 2 rms (1 en suite) 2 annexe en suite (1 fmly) (1 GF) **Facilities** tea/coffee Cen ht Horse & carriage trips **Parking** 5 **Notes** ⊗ RS Nov-Mar Mon-Sat 10-4 & Sun 10-2 🐾

MELBOURNE	Map 11 SK32

The Coach House

★★★★ GUEST HOUSE

69 Derby Rd DE73 8FE
☎ 01332 862338 📠 01332 695281
e-mail: enquiries@coachhouse-hotel.co.uk
web: www.coachhouse-hotel.co.uk
dir: *Off B587 in village centre*

Located in the heart of a conservation area and close to Donington Park and East Midlands Airport, this traditional cottage has been restored to provide good standards of comfort and facilities. Bedrooms are thoughtfully furnished, and two are in converted stables. A lounge and secure parking are available.

Rooms 6 en suite (1 fmly) (3 GF) S £36-£41; D £52-£66* **Facilities** FTV TVL tea/coffee Cen ht Wi-fi **Parking** 6 **Notes** LB ⊗

The Melbourne Arms

★★★ INN

92 Ashby Rd DE73 8ES
☎ 01332 864949 📠 01332 865525
e-mail: info@melbournearms.co.uk
web: www.melbournearms.co.uk
dir: *3m from East Midlands Airport*

Well located for the airport and Donington Park, this Grade-II listed inn provides modern, thoughtfully equipped bedrooms, one of which is in a converted outbuilding. Ground floor areas include two bars, a coffee shop and an elegant Indian restaurant.

Rooms 9 en suite (1 fmly) (2 GF) S £30-£45; D £50-£70 **Facilities** FTV TVL tea/coffee Dinner available Cen ht Wi-fi Fishing Riding Bouncy Castle for children (weather permitting) **Conf** Max 25 Thtr 15 Class 15 Board 15 **Parking** 52 **Notes** Closed 26 Dec

NEWHAVEN	Map 16 SK16

PREMIER COLLECTION

The Smithy

★★★★★ 🏠 GUEST ACCOMMODATION

SK17 0DT
☎ 01298 84548
e-mail: lynnandgary@thesmithybedandbreakfast.co.uk
web: www.thesmithybedandbreakfast.co.uk
dir: *0.5m S of Newhaven on A515. Next to Biggin Ln, private driveway opp Ivy House*

Set in a peaceful location close to the Tissington and High Peak trails, the 17th-century drovers' inn and blacksmith's workshop have been carefully renovated. Bedrooms, which are in a former barn, are well equipped. Enjoyable breakfasts, which include free-range eggs and home-made preserves, are served in the forge, which features the original bellows on the vast open hearth. Lynn and Gary Jinks were finalists in this year's Friendliest Landlady of the Year award (2011-12).

Rooms 4 en suite (2 GF) S £40-£50; D £70-£90* **Facilities** TVL tea/coffee Cen ht Wi-fi **Conf** Max 20 Thtr 15 Board 10 **Parking** 8 **Notes** LB ⊗ No Children 🐾

NEW MILLS	Map 16 SK08

Pack Horse Inn

★★★★ 🅰 INN

Mellor Rd SK22 4QQ
☎ 01663 742365 📠 01663 741674
e-mail: info@packhorseinn.co.uk
dir: *A6 onto A6015, left at lights. Right at rdbt, after 0.5m left, onto Mellor Rd*

Rooms 7 en suite 5 annexe en suite (1 fmly) (2 GF) S £57.50-£77.50; D £77.50-£97.50* **Facilities** tea/coffee Dinner available Cen ht Wi-fi **Parking** 50 **Notes** ⊗ No coaches

PILSLEY	Map 16 SK27

Holly Cottage

★★★★ BED AND BREAKFAST

DE45 1UH
☎ 01246 582245
e-mail: hollycottagebandb@btinternet.com
dir: *Follow brown tourist signs for Chatsworth & Pilsley. Holly Cottage next to post office in Pilsley village*

A warm welcome is assured at this mellow stone cottage, part of a combined Post Office and shop in the conservation area of Pilsley, which is owned by the adjacent Chatsworth Estate. The cosy bedrooms feature a wealth of thoughtful extras, and comprehensive breakfasts, utilising quality local produce, are taken in an attractive pine-furnished dining room.

Rooms 3 en suite D £65-£75* **Facilities** tea/coffee Cen ht Wi-fi **Notes** LB ⊗ No Children 10yrs

Devonshire Arms Pilsley

★★★ INN

The High St DE45 1UL
☎ 01246 583258
e-mail: res@devonshirehotels.co.uk
dir: *From A619, in Baslow, at rdbt take 1st exit onto B6012. Follow signs to Chatsworth, 2nd right to Pilsley*

The newest addition to the Devonshire Hotels and Restaurant group, The Devonshire Arms at Pilsley is just two miles from Chatsworth House, and also a minute's walk from the Chatsworth farm shop which provides much of the food served. All rooms are en suite, quite individual in design and offer very impressive quality and comfort.

Rooms 7 en suite (1 fmly) S £89-£114; D £89-£114* **Facilities** tea/coffee Dinner available Cen ht **Parking** 10 **Notes** ⊗ No coaches

ROWSLEY — Map 16 SK26

The Grouse and Claret
★★★★ INN

Station Rd DE4 2EB
☎ 01629 733233   ▤ 01629 735194
e-mail: grouseandclaret.matlock@marstons.co.uk
dir: M1 junct 28, A6 5m from Matlock, 3m from Bakewell

A busy inn with a wide range of dishes available in the spacious bars. Bedrooms are pleasantly furnished and staff are friendly and attentive.

Rooms 8 en suite (2 fmly) **Facilities** STV tea/coffee Dinner available Cen ht Wi-fi **Parking** 78 **Notes** ⊗ No coaches

SWADLINCOTE — Map 10 SK21

Overseale House
★★★ BED AND BREAKFAST

Acresford Rd, Overseal DE12 6HX
☎ 01283 763741
e-mail: oversealehouse@hotmail.com
web: www.oversealehouse.co.uk
dir: On A444 between Burton upon Trent & M42 junct 11

Located in the village, this well-proportioned Georgian mansion, built for a renowned industrialist, retains many original features including a magnificent dining room decorated with ornate mouldings. The period-furnished ground floor areas include a cosy sitting room, and bedrooms contain many thoughtful extras.

Rooms 4 en suite 1 annexe en suite (3 fmly) (2 GF) S £30; D £70 **Facilities** tea/coffee Cen ht Wi-fi **Conf** Max 14 Board 14 **Parking** 6 **Notes** ⊛

TIDESWELL — Map 16 SK17

Poppies
★★★ GUEST ACCOMMODATION

Bank Square SK17 8LA
☎ 01298 871083
e-mail: poptidza@dialstart.net
dir: On B6049 in village centre opp NatWest bank

A friendly welcome is assured at this non-smoking house, located in the heart of a former lead-mining and textile community, a short walk from the 14th-century parish church. The two bedrooms are homely and practical. There is a third room presented as a comfortable lounge, which is also available as an additional bedroom if needed.

Rooms 3 rms (1 en suite) (1 fmly) **Facilities** tea/coffee Cen ht **Notes** ⊛

WESTON UNDERWOOD — Map 10 SK24

PREMIER COLLECTION

Park View Farm (SK293425)
★★★★★ FARMHOUSE

DE6 4PA
☎ 01335 360352   & 07771 573057
▤ 01335 360352
Mrs Adams
e-mail: enquiries@parkviewfarm.co.uk
web: www.parkviewfarm.co.uk
dir: From A52/A38 rdbt W of Derby, take A38 N, 1st left to Kedleston Hall. Continue for 1.5m past the Hall, farm on left as you enter the village

This impressive, vine-covered, Victorian farmhouse is surrounded by beautiful gardens, and forms part of a working organic sheep farm. Each bedroom has an antique four-poster bed, attractive decor, period furniture and pleasant touches such as flowers and books. Breakfasts come straight from the Aga and include home-made bread, fresh fruit compotes, and fresh eggs from the farm's own chickens. Guests have use of a drawing room. There are also two self-catering cottages on the farm.

Rooms 3 en suite S £60; D £85-£90* **Facilities** FTV TVL tea/coffee Cen ht Wi-fi **Parking** 10 **Notes** LB ⊗ No Children 8yrs Closed Xmas ⊛ 370 acres organic arable/sheep

WINSTER — Map 16 SK26

Brae Cottage
★★★★ ⚑ GUEST ACCOMMODATION

East Bank DE4 2DT
☎ 01629 650375
dir: A6 onto B5057, driveway on right past pub
Rooms 2 annexe en suite (1 fmly) (2 GF) S £40-£60; D £60-£70* **Facilities** tea/coffee Cen ht **Parking** 2 **Notes** ⊗ No Children 11yrs ⊛

YOULGREAVE — Map 16 SK26

The George
★★★ INN

Church St DE45 1UW
☎ 01629 636292   ▤ 01632 636292
dir: 3m S of Bakewell in Youlgreave, opp church

The public bars of the 17th-century George are popular with locals and tourists. Bedroom styles vary, and all have shower rooms en suite. Breakfast is served in the lounge bar, and a range of bar meals and snacks is available.

Rooms 3 en suite (1 fmly) **Facilities** tea/coffee Dinner available Cen ht Fishing **Parking** 12 **Notes** ⊛

DEVON

APPLEDORE — Map 3 SS43

Appledore House
★★★★ GUEST ACCOMMODATION

Meeting St EX39 1RJ
☎ 01237 421471   & 07825 141459
e-mail: info@appledore-house.co.uk
web: www.appledore-house.co.uk
dir: A361 N Devon Link Road, follow signs to Bideford, then Appledore

An imposing house set on the hill overlooking the town and across the water towards Instow with a number of rooms having impressive views. A house with high standards and proprietors with a genuine concern for their guests' comfort and wellbeing.

Rooms 5 en suite (1 fmly) S £55-£75; D £75-£110* **Facilities** FTV tea/coffee Cen ht Wi-fi **Parking** 2 **Notes** LB ⊗

ASHBURTON — Map 3 SX77

Greencott
★★★★ GUEST HOUSE

Landscove TQ13 7LZ
☎ 01803 762649
dir: 3m SE of Ashburton. Off A38 at Peartree junct, Landscove signed on slip road, village green 2m on right, opp village hall

Greencott has a peaceful village location and superb country views. Your hosts extend a very warm welcome and there is a relaxed home-from-home atmosphere. Service is attentive and caring and many guests return time and again. Bedrooms are attractive, comfortable and very well equipped. Delicious country cooking is served around an oak dining table.

Rooms 2 en suite S £25; D £50* **Facilities** TVL tea/coffee Dinner available Cen ht **Parking** 3 **Notes** LB ⊗ Closed 25-26 Dec ⊛

ASHBURTON *continued*

Gages Mill Country Guest House

★★★★ GUEST ACCOMMODATION

Buckfastleigh Rd TQ13 7JW
☎ 01364 652391
e-mail: katestone@gagesmill.co.uk
dir: *Off A38 at Peartree junct, turn right then left at fuel station, Gages Mill 500yds on left*

Conveniently situated within easy access of the A38, this Grade II listed building was formerly a woollen mill. Very much a family home, there is a relaxed and welcoming style here with every effort made to ensure a rewarding and memorable stay. The bedrooms provide good standards of comfort and many have lovely views across the surrounding fields. Breakfast provides a substantial and enjoyable start to the day with plenty of choice for all appetites.

Rooms 7 en suite (1 fmly) (1 GF) S £55; D £70-£80*
Facilities TVL tea/coffee Cen ht Licensed Wi-fi **Parking** 7
Notes ⊗ Closed 23 Oct-1 Mar ⊛

The Rising Sun

★★★★ ⇔ INN

Woodland TQ13 7JT
☎ 01364 652544
e-mail: admin@therisingsunwoodland.co.uk
dir: *A38, exit signed Woodland/Denbury, continue straight on for 1.5m, Rising Sun on left*

Peacefully situated in scenic south Devon countryside, this inn is just a short drive from the A38. A friendly welcome is extended to all guests; business, leisure and families alike. Bedrooms are comfortable and well equipped. Dinner and breakfast feature much local and organic produce. A good selection of home-made puddings, West Country cheeses, local wines and quality real ales are available.

Rooms 5 en suite (2 fmly) (2 GF) S £45; D £55-£65
Facilities FTV tea/coffee Dinner available Cen ht Wi-fi
Parking 30 **Notes** Closed 25 Dec No coaches

Sladesdown Farm *(SX765684)*

★★★★ FARMHOUSE

Landscove TQ13 7ND
☎ 01364 653973   📠 01364 653973
Mr & Mrs Mason
e-mail: sue@sladesdown.co.uk
dir: *2m S of Ashburton. Off A38 at Peartree junct, Landscove signed on slip road, left at 2nd x-rds, farm 100yds right*

Surrounded by lush green fields, woodland and rolling hills, Sladesdown is a picturesque choice for anyone looking for a peaceful, rural hideaway, with easy access to the A38. This modern farmhouse offers spacious, attractive and homely accommodation with a natural and genuine welcome assured. Bedrooms provide impressive levels of comfort with lovely views being an added bonus. A hearty breakfast, featuring delicious local and home-made produce, is the perfect start to the day.

Rooms 4 rms (2 en suite) (2 pri facs) (1 fmly) S £35-£45;
D £60-£65* **Facilities** tea/coffee Cen ht **Parking** 8
Notes ⊗ ⊛ 40 acres beef/turkeys/chickens

ASHWATER	Map 3 SX39

PREMIER COLLECTION

Blagdon Manor

★★★★★ ⊛⊛ 🍴 RESTAURANT WITH ROOMS

EX21 5DF
☎ 01409 211224   📠 01409 211634
e-mail: stay@blagdon.com
web: www.blagdon.com
dir: *A388 towards Launceston/Holsworthy. Approx 2m N of Chapman's Well take 2nd right for Ashwater. Next right beside Blagdon Lodge, 0.25m to manor*

Located on the borders of Devon and Cornwall within easy reach of the coast, and set in its own beautifully kept natural gardens, this small and friendly restaurant with rooms offers a charming home-from-home atmosphere. The tranquillity of the secluded setting, the character and charm of the house and its unhurried pace ensure calm and relaxation. High levels of service, personal touches and thoughtful extras are all part of a stay here. Steve Morey cooks with passion and his commitment to using only the finest local ingredients speaks volumes.

Rooms 7 en suite S £85-£110; D £135-£195*
Facilities FTV tea/coffee Dinner available Direct Dial
Cen ht Wi-fi ⚲ Giant chess **Parking** 13 **Notes** No Children
12yrs Closed Jan RS Mon & Tue closed No coaches

ATHERINGTON	Map 3 SS52

West Down *(SS582228)*

★★★★ ⇔ FARMHOUSE

Little Eastacombe EX37 9HP
☎ 01769 560551   📠 01769 560551
Mr & Mrs Savery
e-mail: info@westdown.co.uk
web: www.westdown.co.uk
dir: *0.5m from Atherington on B3227 to Torrington, turn right, 100yds on left*

Set within 25 acres of lush Devon countryside, this establishment makes a good base for exploring the area. A peaceful atmosphere, together with caring hospitality are assured. Bedrooms are equipped with a host of thoughtful extras, and every effort is made to ensure an enjoyable stay. A choice of homely lounges is available; breakfast and scrumptious dinners are served in the sun lounge.

Rooms 2 en suite 2 annexe en suite (2 GF) S £43-£45; D £68-£76* **Facilities** TVL tea/coffee Dinner available Cen ht Wi-fi **Parking** 8 **Notes** LB ⊗ ⊛ 25 acres sheep/chickens

AXMINSTER	Map 4 SY29

PREMIER COLLECTION

Kerrington House

★★★★★ 🏅 ⇔ GUEST ACCOMMODATION

Musbury Rd EX13 5JR
☎ 01297 35333   📠 01297 35345
e-mail: info@kerringtonhouse.com
dir: *0.5m from Axminster on A358 towards Seaton, house on left*

This former Victorian gentleman's residence has been decorated and furnished to very high standards to provide guests with much comfort throughout their visit. Bedrooms and bathrooms include a range of welcome extras. Afternoon tea may be enjoyed in the comfortably furnished lounge, or in the warmer months, outside overlooking the landscaped gardens. Locally sourced produce is used both at breakfast, and at dinner which is available by prior arrangement.

Rooms 5 en suite (1 fmly) **Facilities** FTV tea/coffee Dinner available Cen ht Licensed Wi-fi **Conf** Max 12 Board 12 **Parking** 6 **Notes** LB ⊗

BAMPTON	Map 3 SS92

The Bark House

★★★★ ⇔ GUEST ACCOMMODATION

Oakfordbridge EX16 9HZ
☎ 01398 351236
dir: *A361 to rdbt at Tiverton onto A396 for Dulverton, then onto Oakfordbridge. House on right*

Located in the stunning Exe Valley and surrounded by wonderful unspoilt countryside, this is a perfect place to

Save on B&Bs and Hotels. Book at **theAA.com/hotel**

DEVON 105 **ENGLAND**

relax and unwind. Hospitality is the hallmark here and a cup of tea by the fireside is always on offer. Both breakfast and dinner make use of the excellent local produce, and are served in the attractive dining room, overlooking fields and the river. Bedrooms have a homely, cottage-style feel with comfy beds to ensure a peaceful night's sleep.

Rooms 6 rms (5 en suite) (1 pri facs) (1 fmly) **Facilities** tea/coffee Dinner available Cen ht Licensed **Parking** 6

Newhouse Farm *(SS892228)*

★★★★ 🐄 FARMHOUSE

EX16 9JE
☎ **01398 351347**
Mrs A Boldry
e-mail: anne.boldry@btconnect.com
web: www.newhouse-farm-holidays.co.uk
dir: *5m W of Bampton on B3227*

Set in 42 acres of rolling farmland, this delightful farmhouse provides a friendly and informal atmosphere. The smart, rustic-style bedrooms are well equipped with modern facilities, and imaginative and delicious home-cooked dinners, using the best local produce, are available by arrangement. Home-made bread and preserves feature at breakfast which can be enjoyed outside on the patio in the summer months.

Rooms 3 en suite (1 GF) S £40-£45; D £65-£75
Facilities FTV tea/coffee Dinner available Cen ht Fishing **Parking** 3 **Notes** LB ⊗ No Children 10yrs Closed Xmas & New Year 42 acres beef/sheep

The Quarrymans Rest

★★★★ 🏵 INN

Briton St EX16 9LN
☎ **01398 331480**
e-mail: paul@thequarrymans.co.uk
dir: *M5 junct 27 towards Tiverton on A361, at rdbt right signed Bampton. At next rdbt take 2nd exit signed Bampton, on right*

This popular and atmospheric inn is located in the bustling town of Bampton, a perfect location for exploring the beautiful scenery of the Exmoor National Park. There's always plenty of good natured banter around the bar which features a range of local ales. Bedrooms are varied in size, but all have a number of thoughtful extras, as do the bathrooms with fluffy towels and quality toiletries. Local produce is very much to the fore in well executed dishes ranging from pub classics to more creative offerings.

Rooms 3 en suite **Facilities** STV tea/coffee Dinner available Cen ht Wi-fi Golf 18 Pool table **Parking** 6 **Notes** No coaches

---

Cresta Guest House

★★★ GUEST HOUSE

26 Sticklepath Hill EX31 2BU
☎ **01271 374022**
e-mail: peter.davis170@virgin.net
dir: *On A3215, 0.6m W of town centre, top of hill on right*

A warm welcome is assured at this family-run establishment, situated on the western outskirts of Barnstaple. The well-equipped, individually styled bedrooms are smartly appointed and include ground-floor rooms. A hearty breakfast is served in the modern and comfortable dining room.

Rooms 6 rms (4 en suite) (2 pri facs) 2 annexe en suite (2 fmly) (2 GF) S £25; D £50* **Facilities** FTV tea/coffee Cen ht Wi-fi **Parking** 6 **Notes** ⊗ Closed 2wks Xmas

Cedars Lodge

★★★ INN

Bickington Rd EX31 2HP
☎ **01271 371784** 🖨 **01271 325733**
e-mail: cedars.barnstaple@oldenglishinns.co.uk

Once a private country house, this popular establishment stands in three-acre gardens, situated just outside Barnstaple and within easy reach of the M5 and major roads. Bedrooms are located in the adjacent lodge which is set around a courtyard facing the main house; all rooms offer generous levels of comfort and modern facilities. The popular conservatory restaurant serves a wide choice of dishes.

Rooms 2 en suite 32 annexe en suite (7 fmly)
Facilities FTV TVL tea/coffee Dinner available Direct Dial Cen ht Wi-fi Golf 18 **Conf** Max 250 Thtr 250 Class 100 Board 100 **Parking** 200 **Notes** Civ Wed

---

Anchor Inn

★★★★ INN

Fore St EX12 3ET
☎ **01297 20386** 🖨 **01297 24474**
e-mail: 6403@greeneking.co.uk
dir: *A3052 at Hangmans Stone onto B3174 into Beer, located on slipway*

Overlooking the sea in the idyllic village of Beer, this perennially popular inn has a well deserved reputation for the warmth of its welcome and convivial atmosphere. A number of the well appointed bedrooms have the added bonus of sea views. The menu makes plentiful use of the excellent local fish, much of which is landed just yards away. The cliff-top beer garden is a wonderful spot in summer months to soak up some sun whilst enjoying freshly barbecued food.

Rooms 6 rms (5 en suite) (1 pri facs) D £75-£95*
Facilities STV FTV tea/coffee Dinner available Cen ht Wi-fi **Notes** LB

The Cricket Inn

★★★★ 🏵 INN

TQ7 2EN
☎ **01548 580215**
e-mail: enquiries@thecricketinn.com
dir: *From Kingsbridge follow A379 towards Dartmouth, at Stokenham mini-rdbt turn right for Beesands*

Dating back to 1867 this charming seaside inn is situated almost on the beach at Start Bay. The well-appointed bedrooms have fantastic views, comfortable beds and flat-screen TVs. The daily-changing fish menu includes locally-caught crabs, lobster and perhaps hand-dived scallops.

Rooms 8 en suite (1 fmly) **Facilities** FTV tea/coffee Dinner available Cen ht Wi-fi **Parking** 30 **Notes** No coaches

See advert on page 107

BERRYNARBOR — Map 3 SS54

Berry Mill House

★★★★ GUEST ACCOMMODATION

Mill Ln EX34 9SH
☎ **01271 882990**
e-mail: enquiries@berrymillhouse.co.uk
web: www.berrymillhouse.co.uk
dir: *500yds NW of village centre. A399 W through Combe Martin, 2nd left at bottom of the hill, house on left*

In a wooded valley on the edge of the village, this former grain mill is a 5-minute walk on the coastal path. Guests are assured of a warm reception from the owners, who enjoy welcoming guests to their home. The freshly cooked breakfast provides a substantial start to the day while home-cooked evening meals are available by arrangement.

Rooms 3 en suite S £50-£60; D £70-£80 **Facilities** FTV TVL tea/coffee Dinner available Cen ht Licensed Wi-fi **Parking** 6 **Notes** LB ⊗ No Children 12yrs Closed Nov-1 Mar 🌐

BIDEFORD — Map 3 SS42

The Mount

★★★★ GUEST HOUSE

Northdown Rd EX39 3LP
☎ **01237 473748** 📠 **01271 373813**
e-mail: andrew@themountbideford.co.uk
web: www.themountbideford.co.uk
dir: *Bideford turning off A39, right after Rydon garage, premises on right after 600yds at mini-rdbt*

A genuinely warm welcome is assured at this delightful, centrally located Georgian property. Bedrooms are comfortably furnished and well equipped; there is a ground-floor bedroom that offers easier access. A hearty breakfast is served in the elegant dining room, and there is a cosy sitting room.

Rooms 8 en suite (3 fmly) (1 GF) S £32.50-£40; D £65-£80* **Facilities** FTV tea/coffee Cen ht Licensed Wi-fi **Parking** 6 **Notes** LB ⊗ Closed Xmas

Pines at Eastleigh

★★★★ GUEST ACCOMMODATION

The Pines, Eastleigh EX39 4PA
☎ **01271 860561** 📠 **01271 861689**
e-mail: pirrie@thepinesateastleigh.co.uk
dir: *A39 onto A386 signed East-the-Water. 1st left signed Eastleigh, 500yds next left, 1.5m to village, house on right*

Friendly hospitality is assured at this Georgian house, set in seven acres of hilltop. Two of the comfortable bedrooms are located in the main house, the remainder in converted barns around a charming courtyard that has a pretty pond and well. A delicious breakfast, featuring local and home-made produce, is served in the dining room, and a lounge and honesty bar are also available.

Rooms 6 en suite (1 fmly) (4 GF) S £55-£69; D £79-£89 **Facilities** FTV tea/coffee Direct Dial Cen ht Licensed Wi-fi 🌐 Table Tennis, Archery, Table Football **Conf** Max 25 Thtr 20 Board 20 **Parking** 20 **Notes** LB No Children 9yrs

BOVEY TRACEY — Map 3 SX87

The Cromwell Arms

★★★★ INN

Fore St TQ13 9AE
☎ **01626 833473** 📠 **01626 836873**
e-mail: info@thecromwellarms.co.uk
dir: *From A38 from Exeter towards Plymouth take A382 at Drumbridges rdbt & follow Bovey Tracey signs. At mini rdbt take 2nd exit, follow town centre signs. At next rdbt take 3rd exit into Station Rd (B3344) & up hill*

A traditional country inn situated in the heart of Bovey Tracey, on the southern edge of Dartmoor and approximately three miles from Newton Abbot, The Cromwell dates back from the 1600s, is full of original charm and has been enhanced with 21st-century facilities. This is an atmospheric, friendly pub with lots of character, which is suitable for all ages and is open all day every day.

Rooms 12 en suite (2 fmly) S £50-£60; D £70-£80* **Facilities** FTV tea/coffee Dinner available Direct Dial Cen ht Wi-fi **Conf** Max 40 Thtr 40 Class 25 Board 25 **Parking** 25

BRIXHAM — Map 3 SX95

Harbour View Brixham

★★★ GUEST ACCOMMODATION

65 King St TQ5 9TH
☎ **01803 853052**
e-mail: hello@harbourviewbrixhambandb.co.uk
dir: *A3022 to town centre/harbour, left at lights, right at T-junct, premises on right of inner harbour*

Aptly named, with lovely views across the harbour and out to sea, this refurbished establishment is an excellent base for exploring the locale. Bedrooms all provide good levels of quality, character and comfort with many having the bonus of the wonderful outlook. Breakfast proudly boasts a local provenance and is served in the engaging lounge/dining room.

Rooms 8 rms (7 en suite) (1 pri facs) (1 fmly) S £45-£65; D £60-£75* **Facilities** FTV Cen ht Wi-fi **Parking** 7 **Notes** LB ⊗ No Children 5yrs

Anchorage Guest House

[U]

170 New Rd TQ5 8DA
☎ **01803 852960** & 07950 536362
e-mail: enquiries@brixham-anchorage.co.uk
dir: *A3022, enter Brixham, left at lights at junct with Monksbridge Rd. Pass Toll House immediately on right*

Currently the rating for this establishment is not confirmed. This may be due to a change of ownership or because it has only recently joined the AA rating scheme.

Rooms 7 rms (6 en suite) (1 pri facs) (1 fmly) (4 GF) S £28-£39; D £52-£71* **Facilities** FTV tea/coffee Cen ht Wi-fi **Parking** 6 **Notes** ⊗

BUCKFAST — Map 3 SX76

Furzeleigh Mill

★★★ GUEST ACCOMMODATION

Old Ashburton Rd TQ11 0JP
☎ **01364 643476**
e-mail: enquiries@furzeleigh.co.uk
web: www.furzeleigh.co.uk
dir: *Off A38 at Dartbridge junct, right at end slip road, right opp Little Chef signed Ashburton/Prince Town (do not cross River Dart bridge), 200yds right*

This Grade II listed, 16th-century converted corn mill stands in its own grounds and is a good base for touring Dartmoor. Spacious family rooms are available as well as a lounge and a bar. All meals are served in the dining room and use local produce.

Rooms 14 en suite (2 fmly) **Facilities** FTV TVL tea/coffee Dinner available Cen ht Licensed Wi-fi **Conf** Max 20 Thtr 20 **Parking** 32 **Notes** No Children 8yrs Closed 23 Dec-2 Jan

"THE INN ON THE SHORE"

The Cricket Inn opened its doors in 1867 to serve the thirsty fishermen of this sleepy beachside South Hams village, although there are only a few working fishermen left, the village still retains its charm, and the Cricket serves both locals and tourist alike.

A refurbishment in the spring of 2010 consisted of a new restaurant and 4 extra rooms, making 8 rooms in total, 5 with glorious sea views of Start Bay, including twins and family rooms. All rooms are en-suite with 4ft x 3ft walk-in showers, flat screen TVs (some with DVD players), and all the doubles are king size.

The Restaurant specialises in fresh seafood brought straight out the bay in front of the Inn, including diver caught scallops, lobster and crab plus locally reared beef for those steak lovers. There is something for everyone, including the kids.

The Cricket Inn, Beesands, Kingsbridge, South Devon, TQ7 2EN

01548 580215

enquiries@thecricketinn.com   www.thecricketinn.com

LAT. 50 15.0573N   LONG. 003 39.3197W

BUCKFASTLEIGH — Map 3 SX76

Kilbury Manor

★★★★ 🏠 GUEST ACCOMMODATION

Colston Rd TQ11 0LN
☎ 01364 644079
e-mail: info@kilburymanor.co.uk
web: www.kilburymanor.co.uk
dir: *Off A38 onto B3380 to Buckfastleigh, left onto Old Totnes Rd, at bottom turn right, Kilbury Manor on left*

Dating back to the 17th century, this charming Devon longhouse is situated in the tranquil surroundings of the Dart Valley with access to the river across the meadow. Bedrooms have an abundance of character and are located in the main house and in adjacent converted barns; all provide high levels of comfort. The stylish bathrooms are also appointed to impressive standards. Breakfast is served in the elegant dining room with local produce very much in evidence. Julia Blundell was a finalist in this year's Friendliest Landlady of the Year award (2011-12).

Rooms 4 rms (3 en suite) (1 pri facs) (1 GF) S £60-£75; D £75-£95 Facilities FTV tea/coffee Cen ht Wi-fi Parking 5 Notes No Children 7yrs ⊛

Dartbridge Inn

★★★ 🅰 INN

Totnes Rd TQ11 0JR
☎ 01364 642214 📠 01364 643839
e-mail: dartbridgeinn@oldenglishinns.co.uk
web: www.oldenglishinns.co.uk
dir: *0.5m NE of town centre. A38 onto A384, 250yds on left*

Rooms 10 en suite (1 fmly) Facilities tea/coffee Direct Dial Conf Max 150 Thtr 150 Class 75 Board 40 Parking 100

BUDLEIGH SALTERTON — Map 3 SY08

Hansard House

★★★★ GUEST ACCOMMODATION

3 Northview Rd EX9 6BY
☎ 01395 442773 📠 01395 442475
e-mail: enquiries@hansardhousehotel.co.uk
web: www.hansardhousehotel.co.uk
dir: *500yds W of town centre*

Hansard House is quietly situated a short walk from the town centre. Many of the well-presented bedrooms have commanding views across the town to the countryside and estuary beyond. Several are located on the ground floor and have easier access. Guests enjoy a varied selection at breakfast including a range of healthy options. The dining room and lounge are both comfortably furnished.

Rooms 12 en suite (1 fmly) (3 GF) S £52-£57; D £89-£98* Facilities STV TVL tea/coffee Direct Dial Cen ht Lift Licensed Wi-fi Parking 11 Notes LB

CHAGFORD — Map 3 SX78

PREMIER COLLECTION

Parford Well

★★★★★ BED AND BREAKFAST

Sandy Park TQ13 8JW
☎ 01647 433353
e-mail: tim@parfordwell.co.uk
web: www.parfordwell.co.uk
dir: *A30 onto A382, after 3m left at Sandy Park left towards Drewsteignton, house 50yds on left*

Set in delightful grounds on the edge of Dartmoor, this attractive house is a restful and friendly home. Quality and style combine in the comfortable bedrooms; the lounge overlooks the well-tended gardens and breakfast is served at tables laid with crisp linen and silverware in one of two dining rooms. Carefully cooked, top local ingredients are hallmarks of a breakfast that makes the perfect start to a day exploring the moors.

Rooms 3 rms (2 en suite) (1 pri facs) S £50-£95; D £80-£95 Facilities TVL tea/coffee Cen ht Wi-fi Parking 4 Notes ⊗ No Children 8yrs ⊛

Easton Court

★★★★ GUEST ACCOMMODATION

Easton Cross TQ13 8JL
☎ 01647 433469
e-mail: stay@easton.co.uk
web: www.easton.co.uk
dir: *1m E of Chagford at junct A382 & B3206*

Set in Dartmoor National Park, the age of this picturesque house is evident in the oak beams and thick granite walls. Guests can come and go via a separate entrance. Relaxation is obligatory, either in the lovely garden or in the snug surroundings of the lounge. The delightful bedrooms all have country views.

Rooms 5 en suite (2 GF) S £50-£70; D £65-£85* Facilities STV FTV tea/coffee Cen ht Wi-fi Golf 18 Parking 5 Notes No Children 10yrs

CHILLATON — Map 3 SX48

PREMIER COLLECTION

Tor Cottage

★★★★★ 🏠 GUEST ACCOMMODATION

PL16 0JE
☎ 01822 860248 📠 01822 860126
e-mail: info@torcottage.co.uk
web: www.torcottage.co.uk
dir: *A30 Lewdown exit through Chillaton towards Tavistock, 300yds after Post Office right signed 'Bridlepath No Public Vehicular Access' to end*

Tor Cottage, located in its own valley with 18 acres of grounds, is a welcome antidote to the fast pace of everyday life. Rooms are spacious and elegant; the cottage-wing bedroom has a separate sitting room, and the garden rooms have their own wood burners. The gardens are delightful, with a stream and heated outdoor pool. An exceptional range of dishes is offered at breakfast, which can be enjoyed either in the conservatory dining room or on the terrace.

Rooms 1 en suite 3 annexe en suite (3 GF) S £98; D £140-£150 Facilities FTV TVL tea/coffee Cen ht Wi-fi ⚡ Parking 8 Notes LB ⊗ No Children 14yrs Closed mid Dec-beg Feb

Save on B&Bs and Hotels. Book at **theAA.com/hotel**

DEVON 109 ENGLAND

CHULMLEIGH — Map 3 SS61

Old Bakehouse

★★★★ GUEST HOUSE

South Molton St EX18 7BW
☎ 01769 580074 & 580137 ▤ 01769 580074
e-mail: oldbakehouse@colinandholly.co.uk
web: www.colinandholly.co.uk
dir: A377 onto B3096 into village centre, left into South
Molton St, 100yds on left

This 16th-century, thatched house is situated in the
centre of Chulmleigh, a hilltop town which stands above
a beautiful river valley. The charming bedrooms are
equipped with many extras such as DVD players (library
available) and are located across a pretty, secluded
courtyard garden in the former village bakery. A wealth of
beams, thick cob walls and wood-burning stove all
contribute to the character and comfort. A generous
choice is offered at breakfast with an emphasis on
excellent local produce.

Rooms 3 en suite (1 GF) S £50-£75; D £75* **Facilities** FTV
tea/coffee Cen ht Golf 18 **Notes** LB ⊗ No Children 11yrs

CLOVELLY — Map 3 SS32

East Dyke Farmhouse (SS312235)

★★★★ ▣ FARMHOUSE

East Dyke Farm, Higher Clovelly EX39 5RU
☎ 01237 431216
Mrs H Goaman
e-mail: steve.goaman@virgin.net
web: www.bedbreakfastclovelly.co.uk
dir: A39 onto B3237 at Clovelly Cross rdbt, farm 500yds
on left

Adjoining an Iron Age hill fort, this working farm has
glorious views across of Bideford Bay in the distance. The
farmhouse has a friendly atmosphere and offers
attractively co-ordinated bedrooms. A key feature here are
the breakfasts - local produce and delicious home-made
preserves are served around one large table.

Rooms 3 rms (2 en suite) (1 pri facs) (1 fmly) S £35-£45;
D £60-£70 **Facilities** FTV TVL tea/coffee Cen ht Wi-fi
Parking 6 **Notes** ⊗ Closed 24-26 Dec ☺ 350 acres beef/
arable

COLEFORD — Map 3 SS70

The New Inn

★★★★ INN

EX17 5BZ
☎ 01363 84242 ▤ 01363 85044
e-mail: enquiries@thenewinncoleford.co.uk
dir: Off A377 into Coleford, inn after 1.5m

Originally dating back to the 13th century, this charming
thatched village inn has much to offer, and provides a
relaxing base from which to explore this beautiful corner
of Devon. Bedrooms are spacious, comfortable and well
appointed with lovely snuggly beds and lots of period
features retained. Roaring fires, flagged floors and
Captain, the resident parrot, all combine to create an
engaging atmosphere. A choice of carefully prepared
dishes is on offer in the bar and lounges, with local
produce strongly featured.

Rooms 6 en suite (1 fmly) (1 GF) **Facilities** tea/coffee
Dinner available Direct Dial Cen ht Wi-fi Golf 18
Parking 50 **Notes** LB Closed 25-26 Dec No coaches

CROYDE — Map 3 SS43

The Whiteleaf

★★★★★ ▣ ▢ GUEST HOUSE

Croyde Rd EX33 1PN
☎ 01271 890266
dir: On B3231 entering Croyde, on left at 'Road Narrows'
sign

A warm, family welcome awaits guests at this attractive
house within easy walking distance of the pretty village
and the sandy beach. Each of the well-equipped
bedrooms has its own charm, and three rooms have
decked balconies. Ambitious and imaginative dinners,
using fresh seasonal produce, are served in elegant
restaurant.

Rooms 5 en suite (2 fmly) S £62-£68; D £80-£100
Facilities FTV tea/coffee Dinner available Direct Dial
Cen ht Licensed **Parking** 10 **Notes** LB ⊗ Closed 24-26
Dec

Denham House

★★★★ ▲ BED AND BREAKFAST

North Buckland EX33 1HY
☎ 01271 890297 ▤ 01271 890106
e-mail: info@denhamhouse.co.uk
web: www.denhamhouse.co.uk
dir: From Barnstaple A361, 2nd left after Knowle, follow
lane into North Buckland, house on right

Rooms 6 en suite (2 fmly) D £60-£70 **Facilities** FTV TVL
tea/coffee Cen ht Licensed Snooker Pool table Table
tennis Skittle Alley Games Room **Parking** 7 **Notes** LB ⊗

CULLOMPTON — Map 3 ST00

Lower Ford Farm (SS978095)

★★★★ ▢ FARMHOUSE

EX15 1LX
☎ 01884 252354 **Ms Diane Pring**
e-mail: lowerfordfarm@hotmail.com
dir: M5 junct 28 Cullompton, take road by HSBC bank. At
Whitedown x-rds turn left then 1st left

A peacefully located 15th-century farmhouse offering
naturally welcoming hospitality with a real home-from-
home atmosphere. Surrounded by delightful countryside,
this working farm provides a peaceful retreat. Bedrooms
are comfortably furnished and equipped with some
welcome extras to add to guest comfort. A spacious
lounge is also available. In addition to the large,
farmhouse breakfast, the wonderful home-cooked dinners
(available by prior arrangement) should not be missed.

Rooms 3 en suite (1 fmly) **Facilities** FTV TVL tea/coffee
Dinner available Wi-fi **Parking** 6 **Notes** ⊗ Closed Nov-Jan
☺ 350 acres beef/sheep/arable

Weir Mill Farm (ST040108)

★★★★ FARMHOUSE

Jaycroft, Willand EX15 2RE
☎ 01884 820803 **Mrs R Parish**
e-mail: rita@weirmill-devon.co.uk
dir: 2m N of Cullompton. M5 junct 27, B3181 to Willand,
left at rdbt onto B3340 signed Uffculme, 50yds right onto
Willand Moor Rd, after Lupin Way left onto lane

Set in extensive farmland, this charming 19th-century
farmhouse offers comfortable accommodation with a
relaxed and homely atmosphere. The spacious bedrooms
are attractively decorated and equipped with an
impressive range of thoughtful extras. A good choice is
offered at breakfast in the well-appointed dining room.

Rooms 3 en suite (1 fmly) S £35; D £60 **Facilities** FTV TVL
tea/coffee Cen ht Wi-fi **Parking** 5 **Notes** ⊗ 100 acres
arable/beef

Wishay Farm (SS994056)

★★★ FARMHOUSE

Trinity EX15 1PE
☎ 01884 33223 ▤ 01884 33223
Mrs Baker
e-mail: wishayfarm@btopenworld.com
dir: 2m SW of Cullompton. From town centre onto Colbrook
Ln, 1.5m to junct, continue over, farm 200yds on left

This is a 280-acre, working arable and beef farm with a
modernised Grade II listed farmhouse. The house has a
peaceful location with pleasant country views. The two
bedrooms are spacious and comfortably furnished. A
traditional farmhouse breakfast is served in the dining
room, and a separate guest lounge is also available.

Rooms 2 rms (1 en suite) (1 pri facs) (2 fmly) S £35; D
£58-£60* **Facilities** FTV TVL tea/coffee Cen ht Wi-fi
Parking 3 **Notes** LB ⊗ 280 acres arable/beef

DARTMEET   Map 3 SX67

Brimpts Farm

★★★ GUEST ACCOMMODATION

PL20 6SG
☎ 01364 631450   📠 01364 631179
e-mail: info@brimptsfarm.co.uk
web: www.brimptsfarm.co.uk
dir: *Dartmeet at E end of B3357, establishment signed on right at top of hill*

A popular venue for walkers and lovers of the great outdoors, Brimpts is peacefully situated in the heart of Dartmoor and has been a Duchy of Cornwall farm since 1307. Bedrooms are simply furnished and many have wonderful views across Dartmoor. Dinner is served by arrangement. Additional facilities include a sauna and spa, and a children's play area. Brimpts is also home to the Dartmoor Pony Heritage Trust.

Rooms 10 en suite (2 fmly) (7 GF) S £35; D £60
Facilities TVL TV1B tea/coffee Dinner available Cen ht Licensed Wi-fi Sauna Pool table Farm walks & trails, Hot tub **Conf** Max 60 Thtr 60 Class 40 Board 25 **Parking** 50 **Notes** LB

DARTMOUTH   Map 3 SX85

PREMIER COLLECTION

Nonsuch House

★★★★★ 🛏 🍴 GUEST ACCOMMODATION

Church Hill, Kingswear TQ6 0BX
☎ 01803 752829   📠 01803 752357
e-mail: enquiries@nonsuch-house.co.uk
web: www.nonsuch-house.co.uk
dir: *A3022 onto A379 2m before Brixham. Fork left onto B3205. Left up Higher Contour Rd, down Ridley Hill, house on bend on left at top of Church Hill*

This delightful Edwardian property has fabulous views across the Dart estuary. The marvellous hosts combine friendliness with unobtrusive service. Bedrooms are spacious and superbly appointed, each with a spectacular panorama of the harbour. Fresh, local ingredients are served at dinner, including top-quality meat, fish, and farmhouse cheeses. Breakfast, on the patio in good weather, features freshly squeezed juice, local sausages and home-baked bread.

Rooms 4 en suite (2 GF) S £85-£125; D £110-£170*
Facilities FTV tea/coffee Dinner available Cen ht Wi-fi Membership of local spa **Parking** 4 **Notes** LB ⊗ No Children 12yrs RS Sat & Tue-Wed no dinner available

PREMIER COLLECTION

Strete Barton House

★★★★★ GUEST HOUSE

Totnes Rd TQ6 0RU
☎ 01803 770364   📠 01803 771182
e-mail: info@stretebarton.co.uk
web: www.stretebarton.co.uk

(For full entry see Strete)

Angélique Rooms

★★★★ RESTAURANT WITH ROOMS

51 Victoria Rd TQ6 9RT
☎ 01803 839425   📠 01803 839505
e-mail: info@angeliquedartmouth.co.uk
dir: *In Dartmouth take one-way system, 1st left at NatWest Bank*

This terrace property offers very comfortable, contemporary accommodation, equipped with numerous extra facilities including a complimentary half bottle of champagne. Breakfast is a feature, and includes freshly squeezed orange juice; specials such as eggs Benedict and scrambled eggs with smoked salmon should not be missed.

Rooms 6 en suite (2 fmly) S £85-£105; D £95-£125*
Facilities FTV tea/coffee Dinner available Cen ht Wi-fi Golf 18 **Notes** LB ⊗ Closed Jan No coaches

Strete Barton House - South Hams Luxury Coastal Guest House

16th Century Manor House set in the picturesque village of Strete, near Dartmouth. Panoramic sea views. Only one mile from award winning beaches of Blackpool Sands and Slapton Sands. The South West Coast Path a mere 50 metres away. Contemporary interior; Egyptian cotton sheets; fluffy white towels; feather-down pillows; luxury toiletries; beverage tray; flat screen TV and DVD/CD player.

T: 01803 770364   **F:** 01803 771182   **E:** info@stretebarton.co.uk   **W:** www.stretebarton.co.uk

AA
★★★★★
Guest House

Save on B&Bs and Hotels. Book at **theAA.com/hotel**

DEVON 111 ENGLAND

Captain's House

★★★★ GUEST ACCOMMODATION

18 Clarence St TQ6 9NW
☎ **01803 832133**
e-mail: thecaptainshouse@aol.com
web: www.captainshouse.co.uk
dir: B3122 into Dartmouth, Clarence St parallel with river

Dating from 1730, this charming house retains many original features and is only a short walk from the quayside and town centre. The attractive bedrooms are comfortable and well equipped. Enjoyable breakfasts are served in the dining room and include local produce and a large selection of quality preserves.

Rooms 5 en suite **Facilities** FTV tea/coffee Cen ht Wi-fi Golf **Notes** ⊗ No Children 5yrs

Cherub's Nest

★★★★ GUEST ACCOMMODATION

15 Higher St TQ6 9RB
☎ **01803 832482**
e-mail: cherubsnest4bb@aol.com
web: www.cherubsnest.co.uk
dir: From Lower Dartmouth ferry along Lower St, left onto Smith St, left onto Higher St, Cherub's Nest 50yds on left

Dating from 1710, this former merchant's house, bedecked with flowers during the summer, is located in the very heart of historic Dartmouth. Full of character, the individually decorated bedrooms vary in size, but all are attractive and well equipped. A choice of breakfasts is served in the cosy dining room.

Rooms 3 en suite S £50-£85; D £70-£90* **Facilities** FTV tea/coffee Cen ht Wi-fi **Notes** LB ⊗ No Children 10yrs

DODDISCOMBSLEIGH
Map 3 SX88

The Nobody Inn

★★★★ ⊜ INN

EX6 7PS
☎ **01647 252394** 🖷 **01647 252978**
e-mail: info@nobodyinn.co.uk
web: www.nobodyinn.co.uk
dir: From A38 turn off at top of Haldon Hill, follow signs to Doddiscombsleigh

Dating back to the 16th century, this fascinating inn is something of a mecca for lovers of wine, whisky and local ale - the choices are extensive. Of course, that's not forgetting the impressive food, much of which is sourced locally including an extensive cheese selection. Bedrooms and bathrooms have been totally refurbished to provide high levels of quality, comfort and individuality. Reassuringly, the bars and lounges remain unchanged with charmingly mis-matched furniture, age-darkened beams and an inglenook fireplace.

Rooms 5 rms (4 en suite) (1 pri facs) (1 fmly) S £40-£65; D £60-£95* **Facilities** FTV tea/coffee Dinner available Direct Dial Wi-fi **Conf** Max 24 **Parking** 50 **Notes** No Children 5yrs Closed 25-26 Dec & 31 Dec pm-1 Jan No coaches

EXETER
Map 3 SX99

See also Rockbeare

Chi Restaurant & Bar with Accommodation

★★★★ ⊜ RESTAURANT WITH ROOMS

Fore St, Kenton EX6 8LD
☎ **01626 890213** 🖷 **01626 891678**
e-mail: enquiries@chi-restaurant.co.uk
web: www.chi-restaurant.co.uk
dir: 5m S of Exeter. M5 junct 30, A379 towards Dawlish, in village centre

This former pub has been spectacularly transformed into a chic and contemporary bar, allied with a stylish Chinese restaurant. Dishes are beautifully presented with an emphasis on quality produce and authenticity, resulting in a memorable dining experience. Bedrooms are well equipped and all provide good levels of space and comfort, along with modern bathrooms.

Rooms 5 en suite (2 fmly) **Facilities** FTV TVL tea/coffee Dinner available Direct Dial Cen ht Wi-fi **Parking** 26 **Notes** ⊗ No coaches

Holbrook Farm

★★★★ GUEST ACCOMMODATION

Clyst Honiton EX5 2HR
☎ **01392 367000** 🖷 **01392 367000**
e-mail: heatherglanvill@holbrookfarm.co.uk
web: www.holbrookfarm.co.uk
dir: M5, A3052 for Sidmouth, pass Westpoint (county showground) & Cat and Fiddle pub, 500yds left at Cat Adoption Centre, signed for 1m

This friendly, modern farmhouse stands in lush rolling countryside and has spectacular views. All bedrooms are located on the ground floor, have their own entrance and offer bright, attractive and spacious accommodation. Breakfast features the best fresh local produce. Holbrook Farm is convenient for Exeter, the coast and moor, and there are several popular inns and restaurants nearby.

Rooms 3 en suite (1 fmly) (3 GF) S £40-£55; D £60-£65* **Facilities** FTV tea/coffee Cen ht Wi-fi **Parking** 4 **Notes** LB ⊗ ⊜

Mill Farm *(SX959839)*

★★★★ FARMHOUSE

Kenton EX6 8JR
☎ **01392 832471**
Mrs D Lambert
e-mail: info@millfarmstay.co.uk
dir: A379 from Exeter towards Dawlish, over mini-rdbt by Swans Nest, farm 1.75m on right

Located just a short drive from the Powderham Estate, this imposing farmhouse is surrounded by pasture. Each of the spacious bedrooms (single, twin, double and family) is stylishly co-ordinated and comfortably furnished; all rooms have countryside views. Breakfast (including vegetarian options) is served in the sunny dining room and a lounge is also provided. A packed breakfast can be prepared if a very early start is required.

Rooms 5 en suite (3 fmly) S £40-£45; D £65 **Facilities** FTV TVL tea/coffee Cen ht Wi-fi **Parking** 12 **Notes** LB ⊗ No Children 6yrs Closed Xmas 30 acres horses

EXMOUTH
Map 3 SY08

Barn

★★★★ GUEST ACCOMMODATION

Foxholes Hill, Marine Dr EX8 2DF
☎ **01395 224411** 🖷 **01395 225445**
e-mail: exmouthbarn@googlemail.com
web: www.barnhotel.co.uk
dir: From M5 junct 30 take A376 to Exmouth, then follow signs to seafront. At rdbt last exit into Foxholes Hill. Located on right

This Grade II listed establishment has a prime location, close to miles of sandy beaches. Equally pleasant is the immaculate rear garden, which is sea-facing and features a terrace and swimming pool for use during the summer. Service is attentive and friendly, and spectacular sea views are enjoyed from most of the well-equipped bedrooms and public rooms. Breakfast is served in the elegant surroundings of the dining room.

Rooms 11 en suite (4 fmly) S £35-£50; D £65-£105* **Facilities** FTV tea/coffee Direct Dial Cen ht Licensed Wi-fi ⚲ **Parking** 30 **Notes** LB Closed 23 Dec-10 Jan

EXMOUTH *continued*

The Devoncourt

★★★★ GUEST ACCOMMODATION

16 Douglas Av EX8 2EX
☎ 01395 272277 📠 01395 269315
e-mail: enquiries@devoncourt.com
web: www.devoncourthotel.com
dir: *M5/A376 to Exmouth, follow seafront to Maer Rd, right at T-junct*

The Devoncourt stands in four acres of mature, subtropical gardens, sloping gently towards the sea and overlooking two miles of sandy beaches. It offers extensive leisure facilities, and the smartly furnished bedrooms are exceptionally well equipped. The spacious public areas are available to timeshare owners as well as guests. For meals there is a choice between the informal bar and the restaurant.

Rooms 52 en suite 2 annexe en suite (35 fmly) (8 GF) (49 smoking) **Facilities** FTV TVL tea/coffee Dinner available Direct Dial Cen ht Lift Licensed Wi-fi 🕙 ≷ ᠍ 🎿 ﻼ Snooker Sauna Solarium Gym Pool table Sun shower, Jacuzzi **Parking** 50 **Notes** ⊗ Civ Wed

---

| GALMPTON | Map 3 SX64 |

Burton Farmhouse *(SX693404)*

★★★★ 🍴 FARMHOUSE

TQ7 3EY
☎ 01548 561210
Ms A Rossiter
e-mail: anne@burtonfarm.co.uk
web: www.burtonfarm.co.uk
dir: *Off A381 at Malborough towards Galmpton & Hope Cove, 1m on left onto lane, signed*

Situated in the beautiful South Hams, close to the picturesque fishing village of Hope Cove, this 15th-century farmhouse is a perfect place for rest and relaxation. The welcome is always genuine and guests can sample a delicious cream tea for a real taste of Devon. Bedrooms are traditional and homely with lovely countryside views. Dinner and breakfast, served in the attractive garden room restaurant, are real treats with local produce always featured.

Rooms 13 en suite (6 fmly) (3 GF) S £70-£85; D £85-£107.50* **Facilities** FTV tea/coffee Dinner available Cen ht Licensed Wi-fi ch fac Pool table **Parking** 60 **Notes** LB ⊗ Closed 23 Dec-4 Jan Civ Wed 75 325 acres sheep/arable

---

| HOLSWORTHY | Map 3 SS30 |

The Bickford Arms

★★★★ INN

Brandis Corner EX22 7XY
☎ 01409 221318
e-mail: info@bickfordarms.com

This roadside inn has been providing rest and sustenance for weary travellers for many years, a tradition which continues today with a genuine welcome and relaxed atmosphere. A crackling fire warms the spacious bar in cooler months and there are always a few locals ready for a natter over a pint of local ale. The bar menu is supplemented with daily specials with ample space to find a quiet table at which to enjoy a relaxing meal. The attractive bedrooms provide high levels of comfort, likewise the impressive and well-appointed bathrooms.

Rooms 5 en suite S £55; D £90 **Facilities** FTV tea/coffee Dinner available Cen ht Wi-fi **Conf** Max 100 **Parking** 80 **Notes** LB

Clawford Vineyard

★★★★ GUEST HOUSE

Clawton EX22 6PN
☎ 01409 254177 📠 01409 254177
e-mail: john.ray@clawford.co.uk
dir: *A388 (Holsworth to Launceston road), left at Clawton x-rds, 1.5m to T-junct, left, 0.5m left again*

Situated in the peaceful Claw Valley and with splendid views over fishing lakes and woodland, this working cider orchard and vineyard property offers spacious and comfortable bedrooms. There is a large lounge, a well-stocked bar, a conservatory and a restaurant. Freshly cooked dishes are well prepared and attractively presented at dinner and breakfast. Self-catering apartments, overlooking the lakes, are also available.

Rooms 11 en suite (7 fmly) **Facilities** TVL tea/coffee Dinner available Cen ht Licensed Fishing Pool table Coarse & game fishing **Parking** 60 **Notes** ⊗ No Children 6yrs

The Hollies Farm Guest House *(SS371001)*

★★★★ FARMHOUSE

Clawton EX22 6PN
☎ 01409 253770 & 07929 318033
Mr & Mrs G Colwill
e-mail: theholliesfarm@hotmail.com
web: www.theholliesfarm.co.uk
dir: *Off A388 at Clawton village signed vineyard, after 2m turn left, The Hollies in lane on left after T-junct, signed. At end of farm lane, fork right*

This sheep and beef farm offers comfortable, modern accommodation with a family atmosphere. There are pleasant views across the countryside from most bedrooms; all are well appointed. Breakfast is served in the conservatory, and dinner is available by arrangement. There is also a barbecue area with a gazebo.

Rooms 3 en suite (3 fmly) S £27-£35; D £52-£58* **Facilities** TVL tea/coffee Dinner available Cen ht Outdoor hot tub **Parking** 6 **Notes** LB ⊗ Closed 24-25 Dec ⊛ 25 acres beef/sheep

---

| HONITON | Map 4 ST10 |

PREMIER COLLECTION

West Colwell Farm

★★★★★ 🛏 BED AND BREAKFAST

Offwell EX14 9SL
☎ 01404 831130
e-mail: stay@westcolwell.co.uk
dir: *Off A35 to village, at church downhill, farm 0.5m on right*

Peacefully situated down a country lane, in an Area of Outstanding Natural Beauty, this establishment offers stylish bedrooms in a converted dairy. The two rooms on the ground floor have direct access to their own terraces. Breakfast is served in the split-level dining room overlooking the wooded valley and fields, where there is a roaring log-burning stove in cooler months.

Rooms 3 en suite (2 GF) S £60; D £80-£90* **Facilities** FTV tea/coffee Cen ht **Parking** 3 **Notes** LB ⊗ No Children 12yrs Closed Dec & Jan

Monkton Court

★★★★ 🍴 RESTAURANT WITH ROOMS

Monkton EX14 9QH
☎ 01404 42309
e-mail: enquiries@monktoncourthotel.co.uk
dir: *2m E A30 from Honiton*

Located on the A30 near Honiton and on the edge of the ancient Blackdown Hills, Monkton Court is a former vicarage steeped in history. There is a range of well-equipped and comfortably furnished bedrooms and bathrooms in addition to a relaxing lounge and spacious restaurant. Both dinner and breakfast utilise a range of local produce, and offer an enjoyable selection of dishes.

Rooms 7 en suite (1 fmly) (1 GF) S £72.50-£99; D £99-£125* **Facilities** FTV tea/coffee Dinner available Direct Dial Cen ht Wi-fi **Conf** Max 75 Thtr 50 Class 30 Board 50 **Parking** 19 **Notes** ⊗

Save on B&Bs and Hotels. Book at **theAA.com/hotel**

DEVON 113 **ENGLAND**

Ridgeway Farm

★★★★ GUEST ACCOMMODATION

Awliscombe EX14 3PY
☎ 01404 841331 📠 01404 841119
e-mail: jessica@ridgewayfarm.co.uk
dir: 3m NW of Honiton. A30 onto A373, through
Awliscombe to near end of 40mph area, right opp Godford
Farm, farm 500mtrs up narrow lane, sign on entrance

This 18th-century farmhouse has a peaceful location on
the slopes of Hembury Hill, and is a good base for
exploring nearby Honiton and the east Devon coast.
Renovations have brought the cosy accommodation to a
high standard and the atmosphere is relaxed and homely.
The proprietors and their family pets assure a warm
welcome.

Rooms 2 en suite S £34-£38; D £60-£66 Facilities FTV
TVL tea/coffee Dinner available Cen ht Wi-fi Parking 4
Notes LB ⊛

Threshays

★★★ BED AND BREAKFAST

Awliscombe EX14 3QB
☎ 01404 43551 & 07811 675800 📠 01404 43551
e-mail: threshays@btinternet.com
dir: 2.5m NW of Honiton on A373

A converted threshing barn, situated on a non-working
farm, Threshays has wonderful views over open
countryside. With tea and cake offered on arrival, this
family-run establishment provides comfortable
accommodation in a friendly atmosphere. The lounge-
dining room is a light and airy setting for the enjoying the
good breakfasts. Ample parking is a bonus.

Rooms 2 rms (1 fmly) S £30; D £54 Facilities TVL tea/
coffee Cen ht Wi-fi Parking 4 Notes ⊛ ⊛

HOPE COVE　　　　　　　Map 3 SX64

Cottage

★★★ GUEST ACCOMMODATION

TQ7 3HJ
☎ 01548 561555 📠 01548 561455
e-mail: info@hopecove.com
dir: From Kingsbridge on A381 to Salcombe. 2nd right at
Marlborough, left for Inner Hope

Glorious sunsets can be seen over the attractive bay from
this popular accommodation. Friendly and attentive
service from the staff and management mean many
guests return here. Bedrooms, many with sea views and
some with balconies, are well equipped. The restaurant
offers an enjoyable dining experience.

Rooms 34 rms (31 en suite) (3 pri facs) (5 fmly) (7 GF) S
£50.30-£75; D £100.60-£190* (incl.dinner) Facilities FTV
TVL TV32B tea/coffee Dinner available Direct Dial
Licensed Wi-fi ch fac Golf 18 Table tennis Conf Max 70
Thtr 60 Class 60 Board 30 Parking 50 Notes LB Closed
early Jan-early Feb

HORNS CROSS　　　　　　Map 3 SS32

PREMIER COLLECTION

The Round House

★★★★★ GUEST HOUSE

EX39 5DN
☎ 01237 451687
e-mail: michael.m.clifford@btinternet.com
web: www.the-round-house.co.uk
dir: 1m W of Horns Cross on A39, 0.5m past Hoops Inn
towards Bude

This charming converted barn stands in landscaped
gardens within easy reach of Clovelly. Guests receive a
warm welcome and a complimentary cream tea on
arrival, which may be served in the lounge with its
exposed beams and inglenook fireplace. Bedrooms are
comfortable with numerous thoughtful extra facilities.
A varied choice is offered at breakfast.

Rooms 3 en suite (1 fmly) (1 GF) S £40; D £65*
Facilities FTV TVL tea/coffee Cen ht Wi-fi Parking 8
Notes ⊛ No Children 12yrs

ILFRACOMBE　　　　　　Map 3 SS54

Strathmore

★★★★ GUEST ACCOMMODATION

57 St Brannock's Rd EX34 8EQ
☎ 01271 862248 📠 01271 862248
e-mail: info@the-strathmore.co.uk
web: www.the-strathmore.co.uk
dir: A361 from Barnstaple to Ilfracombe, Strathmore
1.5m from Mullacot Cross entering Ilfracombe

Situated within walking distance of the town centre and
beach, this charming Victorian property offers a very
warm welcome. The attractive bedrooms are comfortably
furnished, while public areas include a well-stocked bar,

---

an attractive terraced garden, and an elegant breakfast
room.

Rooms 8 en suite (3 fmly) S £35-£40; D £65-£76*
Facilities FTV tea/coffee Cen ht Licensed Wi-fi Parking 7
Notes LB

Collingdale Guest House

★★★★ GUEST HOUSE

13 Larkstone Ter EX34 9NU
☎ 01271 863770
e-mail: stay@thecollingdale.co.uk
web: www.thecollingdale.co.uk
dir: Take A399 E through Ilfracombe, on left past B3230
turning

Overlooking the harbour, this Victorian guest house is
within easy walking distance of the town centre and
seafront. The well-presented bedrooms, many with
sweeping sea views, are furnished to a high standard
with many thoughtful extras. The comfortable lounge and
elegant dining room share the magnificent views. A cosy
bar is also available for a tipple before bedtime.

Rooms 9 rms (8 en suite) (1 pri facs) (3 fmly) S £42-£50;
D £64-£80* Facilities FTV TVL tea/coffee Licensed Wi-fi
Golf 18 Notes LB ⊛ No Children 8yrs Closed Nov-Feb

Marine Court

★★★★ GUEST HOUSE

Hillsborough Rd EX34 9QQ
☎ 01271 862920
e-mail: marinecourthotel@btconnect.com
dir: M5 junct 27, A361 to Barnstaple, continue to
Ilfracombe

This friendly and welcoming establishment, opposite the
Old Thatched Inn, offers comfortable and homely
accommodation. The light and airy bedrooms have
benefited from refurbishment and provide good levels of
comfort with thoughtful extras. Breakfast is served in the
spacious dining room which is next to the bar. On-site
and adjacent parking is a bonus.

Rooms 8 en suite (2 fmly) S £40-£45; D £64-£78
Facilities FTV tea/coffee Cen ht Licensed Parking 3
Notes LB ⊛ No Children 8yrs Closed Nov-Jan

ILFRACOMBE *continued*

Norbury House

★★★★ GUEST HOUSE

Torrs Park EX34 8AZ
☎ 01271 863888
e-mail: info@norburyhouse.co.uk
dir: *From A399 to end of High St/Church St. At mini-rdbt after lights take 1st exit onto Church Rd. Bear left onto Osbourne Rd. At T-junct left onto Torrs Park. House at top of hill on right*

This detached Victorian residence has a refreshingly different, contemporary style, and the genuinely warm welcome is allied with a helpful and attentive approach. A variety of bedrooms styles is offered but all provide impressive levels of comfort and quality. An elegant lounge leads through to a conservatory which has an honesty bar. Outside, the peaceful terraced gardens have lovely views. Cuisine is taken seriously here, with breakfast featuring quality, local produce.

Rooms 6 en suite (2 fmly) D £85-£115* **Facilities** FTV tea/coffee Cen ht Licensed Wi-fi **Conf** Max 18 Thtr 14 Class 14 Board 12 **Parking** 6 **Notes** LB ⊗

The Graystoke

★★★★ 🅰 GUEST HOUSE

58 St Brannocks Rd EX34 8EQ
☎ 01271 862328
e-mail: info@thegraystoke.co.uk
web: www.thegraystoke.co.uk
dir: *1.5m from rdbt at Mullacott Cross*

Rooms 7 en suite S £35-£40; D £60-£75* **Facilities** FTV TVL tea/coffee Cen ht Licensed Wi-fi **Parking** 6 **Notes** LB ⊗ No Children 15yrs Closed Nov-Mar

Avalon

★★★ GUEST HOUSE

6 Capstone Crescent EX34 9BT
☎ 01271 863325 📄 01271 866543
e-mail: avalon_ilfracombe@yahoo.co.uk
web: www.avalon-hotel.co.uk
dir: *A361 to Ilfracombe, left at 1st lights, straight on 2nd lights, left at end of one-way system & left again*

Conveniently located near the centre of Ilfracombe, this well-established guest house has magnificent sea views

from the bedrooms and dining room. Avalon offers well-equipped bedrooms, one of which is located on the ground floor. Breakfast is served at separate tables in the well-appointed dining room and parking is available free of charge nearby.

Rooms 9 en suite (3 fmly) (1 GF) S £32-£64; D £54-£64* **Facilities** FTV tea/coffee Dinner available **Parking** 7 **Notes** LB ⊗ No Children 6yrs Closed Xmas & New Year

KENTISBEARE Map 3 ST00

Orway Crescent Farm Bed & Breakfast

★★★★ BED AND BREAKFAST

Orway Crescent Farm, Orway EX15 2EX
☎ 01884 266876 & 0845 658 8472 📄 01884 266876
e-mail: orway.crescentfarm@btinternet.com
dir: *M5 junct 28 onto A373 towards Honiton. After 5m Keepers Cottage pub on right, take next left for Sheldon - Broad Rd. 3rd on left to Orway, farm at bottom of hill*

Located in a sleepy rural hamlet, this welcoming home has now been refurbished to an impressive standard and is just five miles from the M5. Bedrooms combine comfort and quality in equal measure with numerous useful extras which typify the caring and helpful approach here. The stylish modern bathrooms are simply superb, either for an invigorating shower or relaxing soak in the bath. The dining room is the venue for substantial breakfasts with lovely views across the fields to woodland beyond.

Rooms 3 en suite (1 fmly) (1 GF) **Facilities** STV FTV tea/coffee Cen ht Wi-fi **Parking** 3 **Notes** ⊗

KENTISBURY Map 3 SS64

Night In Gails

★★★★ 🏠 GUEST ACCOMMODATION

Kentisbury Mill EX31 4NF
☎ 01271 883545
e-mail: info@kentisburymill.co.uk
dir: *M5 junct 27 onto A361 towards Barnstaple, then A399 to Blackmoor Gate. Turn left at Blackmoor Gate onto A39, then right onto B3229 at Kentisbury Ford, 1m on right*

Originally consisting of an 18th-century cottage and mill, this relaxing hideaway has been sympathetically renovated to provide impressive levels of comfort, allied with caring hospitality. Bedrooms offer an appealing blend of old and new, with views over the extensive gardens. A guest lounge is also provided with plenty of local information for those wanting to explore the dramatic coast and countryside. Breakfast is Aga-cooked and includes superb eggs laid by the resident hens, together with other wonderful local produce - a perfect start to the day.

Rooms 4 en suite **Facilities** FTV tea/coffee Cen ht Wi-fi **Parking** 6 **Notes** ⊗ Closed Xmas

LEWDOWN Map 3 SX48

Lobhill Accommodation

★★★★ BED AND BREAKFAST

Lewdown EX20 4DT
☎ 01566 783542 & 07817 244687
e-mail: jane.colwill@btopenworld.com
web: www.lobhilldevon.com
dir: *Leave A30 at Sourton Cross, follow signs for Lewdown onto old A30. Lobhill 1m before Lewdown*

Ideally situated for easy access to moorland and the Devon and Cornwall coasts, this stone farmhouse dates back some 130 years. Peacefully located, its renovation has resulted in impressive levels of quality, whilst retaining a reassuringly traditional and homely feel. The bedrooms (including one on the ground floor with separate access) have views of the countryside. Tasty and satisfying breakfasts are cooked on the Aga and served, either in the dining room, or at the kitchen table. Guests are welcome to make use of the lovely gardens and summerhouse, or explore the woodland walks.

Rooms 3 en suite (1 fmly) (1 GF) S £45-£50; D £70-£90* **Facilities** FTV tea/coffee Cen ht Wi-fi **Parking** 8 **Notes** LB

LIFTON Map 3 SX38

The Old Coach House

★★★★ BED AND BREAKFAST

The Thatched Cottage, Sprytown PL16 0AY
☎ 01566 784224 📄 01566 784334
e-mail: tochsprytown@aol.com
web: www.theoldcoach-house.co.uk
dir: *Off A30 through Lifton, 0.75m E to Sprytown x-rds, right to Thatched Cottage in 100yds*

Set in a colourful cottage garden near the Cornwall border, the Old Coach House offers a warm welcome. The comfortable bedrooms have numerous extras including a welcome basket. Hearty breakfasts, served in the beamed dining room in the adjacent thatched cottage, feature good, local produce including vegetarian options.

Rooms 4 annexe en suite (3 fmly) (2 GF) **Facilities** tea/coffee Direct Dial **Parking** 6 **Notes** ⊗

Tinhay Mill Guest House and Restaurant

★★★★ ◉ RESTAURANT WITH ROOMS

Tinhay PL16 0AJ
☎ 01566 784201 🖷 01566 784201
e-mail: tinhay.mill@talk21.com
web: www.tinhaymillrestaurant.co.uk
dir: *A30/A388 approach Lifton, establishment at bottom of village on right*

These former mill cottages are now a delightful restaurant with charming rooms. Beams and open fireplaces set the scene, with everything geared to ensure a relaxed and comfortable stay. Bedrooms are spacious and well equipped, with many thoughtful extras. Cuisine is taken seriously here, and uses the best local produce.

Rooms 6 en suite (1 GF) S £55-£70; D £75-£90 **Facilities** FTV TVL Dinner available Cen ht Wi-fi **Parking** 13 **Notes** LB ⊗ No Children 14yrs Closed Dec-Jan No coaches

---

LUSTLEIGH   Map 3 SX78

PREMIER COLLECTION

Eastwrey Barton

🖘 GUEST ACCOMMODATION

Moretonhampstead Rd TQ13 9SN
☎ 01647 277338 🖷 01647 277133
e-mail: info@eastwreybarton.co.uk
web: www.eastwreybarton.co.uk
dir: *On A382 between Bovey Tracey & Moretonhampstead, 6m from A38 (Drumbridges junct)*

Warm hospitality and a genuine welcome are hallmarks at this family-run establishment, situated inside the Dartmoor National Park. Built in the 18th century, the house retains many original features and has views across the Wray Valley. Bedrooms are spacious and well equipped, while public areas include a snug lounge warmed by a crackling log fire. Breakfast and dinner showcase local produce with an impressive wine list to accompany the latter.

Rooms 5 en suite (1 fmly) D £100-£120* **Facilities** FTV tea/coffee Dinner available Cen ht Licensed Wi-fi **Parking** 18 **Notes** ⊗ No Children 10yrs

---

PREMIER COLLECTION

Woodley House

★★★★★ 🖼 GUEST ACCOMMODATION

Caseley Hill TQ13 9TN
☎ 01647 277214 🖷 01647 277126
dir: *Off A382 into village, at T-junct right to Caseley, house 2nd on left*

Set just a stroll from the village pub, church and tea room, Woodley House is a peaceful and tranquil retreat, with super views over the rolling countryside. A hearty breakfast, featuring as many as 12 home-made preserves, home-baked bread and a vast range of cooked breakfast options, can be enjoyed in the charming dining room. A good base for walkers, and dogs are welcome too.

Rooms 1 en suite D £70-£72* **Facilities** FTV TVL tea/coffee Cen ht **Parking** 3 **Notes** No Children 10yrs ⊛

LYDFORD   Map 3 SX58

PREMIER COLLECTION

Moor View House

🖘 GUEST ACCOMMODATION

Vale Down EX20 4BB
☎ 01822 820220 🖷 01822 820220
dir: *4m from Sourton A30/A386, signed Tavistock, NE of Lydford*

Built around 1870, this charming house once changed hands over a game of cards. The elegant bedrooms are furnished with interesting pieces and retain many original features. Breakfast, and dinner by arrangement, are served house-party style at a large oak table. The two acres of moorland gardens give access to Dartmoor.

Rooms 4 en suite S £45-£50; D £70-£85 **Facilities** FTV TVL tea/coffee Dinner available Cen ht Licensed 🍴 **Parking** 15 **Notes** LB ⊗ No Children 12yrs Closed 23 Dec-2 Jan ⊛

LYNMOUTH   Map 3 SS74

PREMIER COLLECTION

The Heatherville

★★★★★ 🖼 🖘 GUEST ACCOMMODATION

Tors Park EX35 6NB
☎ 01598 752327 🖷 01598 753893
e-mail: theheatherville@aol.com
dir: *Off A39 onto Tors Rd, 1st left fork into Tors Park*

This wonderful Victorian establishment stands high above Lynmouth, from where the views across the wooded valley are quite superb. There is an abundance of charm and quality here with each bedroom being individually styled and providing impressive levels of comfort and character. Public rooms are also inviting with an elegant lounge and snug bar, whilst the dining room is the attractive venue for skilfully prepared dinners and substantial breakfasts.

Rooms 6 en suite D £80-£106* **Facilities** FTV TVL tea/coffee Dinner available Cen ht Licensed Wi-fi **Parking** 6 **Notes** LB No Children 16yrs Closed Nov-Mar

---

Rock House

★★★★ GUEST ACCOMMODATION

Manor Grounds EX35 6EN
☎ 01598 753508 🖷 0800 7566964
e-mail: enquiries@rock-house.co.uk
dir: *On A39, at foot of Countisbury Hill right onto drive, pass Manor green/play area to Rock House*

Located next to the river with wonderful views of the harbour and out to sea, this enchanting establishment dates back to the 18th century and has much to offer. Bedrooms are well appointed, and many have the benefit of wonderful views of the rolling waves. A choice of menus is offered, either in the spacious lounge/bar or in the smart dining room. The garden is a popular venue for cream teas in the summer.

Rooms 8 en suite (1 GF) **Facilities** TVL tea/coffee Dinner available Cen ht Licensed Wi-fi ⅃ **Parking** 8 **Notes** Closed 24-25 Dec

LYNMOUTH *continued*

River Lyn View

★★★ GUEST ACCOMMODATION

26 Watersmeet Rd EX35 6EP
☎ 01598 753501
e-mail: riverlynview@aol.com
dir: *On A39, 200yds past St John's church on right*

A warm welcome awaits at River Lyn View, just a stroll from the picturesque harbour at Lynmouth. Exmoor National Park is a short drive away or guests can enjoy a walk along the East Lyn River's tranquil tree-lined banks. Much of the accommodation overlooks the river; all bedrooms are comfortable and offer a good range of extras. There is a choice of lounges, and a hearty breakfast is served at individual tables in the open-plan dining area.

Rooms 4 en suite (2 fmly) S £35-£40; D £54-£60
Facilities FTV TVL tea/coffee Cen ht Wi-fi **Parking** 2

LYNTON	Map 3 SS74

PREMIER COLLECTION

Victoria Lodge

★★★★★ GUEST ACCOMMODATION

30-31 Lee Rd EX35 6BS
☎ 01598 753203
e-mail: info@victorialodge.co.uk
web: www.victorialodge.co.uk
dir: *Off A39 in village centre opp Post Office*

A warm welcome awaits at this elegant villa, built in the 1880s and located in the heart of Lynton. Named after Queen Victoria's children and grandchildren, and reflecting the style of the period, bedrooms are decorated in rich colours and feature coronets, half-tester and four-poster beds.

Rooms 8 en suite S £60-£119; D £70-£140*
Facilities FTV tea/coffee Cen ht Wi-fi **Parking** 6
Notes ⊗ No Children 11yrs Closed Nov-23 Mar

PREMIER COLLECTION

Highcliffe House

★★★★★ ⊞ GUEST ACCOMMODATION

Sinai Hill EX35 6AR
☎ 01598 752235
e-mail: info@highcliffehouse.co.uk
web: www.highcliffehouse.co.uk
dir: *Off A39 into Lynton, signs for Old Village, at Crown pub up steep hill, house 150yds on left*

Highcliffe House has stunning views of Exmoor and the coast, and across to South Wales. Built in the 1880s as a summer residence, this wonderful house is a good base for exploring the area. Bedrooms are spacious and elegant, likewise the lounges and conservatory dining room where wonderful breakfasts are accompanied by a spectacular outlook.

Rooms 7 en suite S £75-£112.50; D £96-£150*
Facilities FTV tea/coffee Cen ht Licensed Wi-fi
Parking 7 **Notes** LB ⊗ No Children 16yrs Closed Nov-Mar

St Vincent House

★★★★ GUEST ACCOMMODATION

Castle Hill EX35 6JA
☎ 01598 752244
e-mail: welcome@st-vincent-hotel.co.uk
web: www.st-vincent-hotel.co.uk
dir: *Off Lynmouth Hill onto Castle Hill, take left fork after NCP car park. 50mtrs on right, next to Exmoor museum*

A warm welcome is assured at this engaging Grade II listed house, which is handily placed for exploring the quaint delights of Lynton. The individually furnished bedrooms are well equipped, and an open fire burns in the charming drawing room during cooler months. The garden is available to guests in the summer months where you can enjoy classic Belgian beers.

Rooms 6 en suite D £75-£80* **Facilities** STV FTV tea/coffee Cen ht Licensed Wi-fi **Parking** 2 **Notes** LB ⊗ No Children 14yrs Closed Nov-Etr

Sinai House

★★★★ GUEST ACCOMMODATION

Lynway EX35 6AY
☎ 01598 753227 🖃 01598 752663
e-mail: enquiries@sinaihouse.co.uk
dir: *A39 onto B3234 through town, pass church, house on right overlooking main car park*

This Victorian residence has spectacular views over Lynton, Lynmouth and across the Bristol Channel. Guests are assured of a friendly welcome from the owners. Bedrooms are well furnished and the comfortable public rooms include a spacious, well-appointed lounge, a cosy bar and smartly presented dining room.

Rooms 8 rms (6 en suite) (2 pri facs) **Facilities** TVL tea/coffee Cen ht Licensed **Parking** 8 **Notes** ⊗ No Children 12yrs Closed 15 Nov-28 Dec & 3 Jan-15 Feb

MORETONHAMPSTEAD	Map 3 SX78

Moorcote Country Guest House

★★★★ GUEST HOUSE

Chagford Cross TQ13 8LS
☎ 01647 440966
e-mail: enquiries@moorcotehouse.co.uk
dir: *500yds NW of village centre on A382, past hospital on right*

Perched on a hill overlooking the town and surrounded by attractive mature country gardens, this Victorian house is a good base for exploring Dartmoor and only a short walk from the town centre. Friendly owners Pat and Paul Lambert extend a warm welcome to their guests, many of whom return on a regular basis.

Rooms 3 en suite (1 fmly) **Facilities** FTV tea/coffee Cen ht **Parking** 6 **Notes** LB ⊗ No Children 5yrs Closed Dec ⊜

Great Sloncombe *(SX737864)*

★★★★ Ⓐ FARMHOUSE

TQ13 8QF
☎ 01647 440595 🖃 01647 440595
Mrs T Merchant
e-mail: hmerchant@sloncombe.freeserve.co.uk
dir: *A382 from Moretonhampstead towards Chagford, 1.5m left at sharp double bend & farm 0.5m up lane*

Rooms 3 en suite S £45-£50; D £70-£80* **Facilities** FTV tea/coffee Cen ht Wi-fi **Parking** 3 **Notes** 170 acres beef/horses

Cookshayes Country Guest House

★★★ ⬛ GUEST HOUSE

33 Court St TQ13 8LG
☎ 01647 440374 ▤ 01647 440453
e-mail: cookshayes@aol.com
web: www.cookshayes.co.uk
dir: A38 onto A382 to Moretonhampstead. Take B3212 towards Princetown. Cookshayes 400yds on left

A genuine welcome awaits at this secluded Victorian house, a perfect base for exploring the delights of Dartmoor. Bedrooms are comfortably furnished and well appointed, and one has a four-poster bed. The smart dining room is the venue for scrumptious breakfasts and excellent dinners, where local produce is cooked with skill and enthusiasm. Additional facilities include a cosy lounge which overlooks the attractive garden.

Rooms 7 rms (5 en suite) (2 pri facs) (1 fmly) (1 GF)
Facilities TVL tea/coffee Dinner available Cen ht Licensed **Conf** Max 16 Class 10 Board 10 **Parking** 10 **Notes** No Children 5yrs

NEWTON ABBOT   Map 3 SX87

See also Widecombe in the Moor

Bulleigh Park *(SX860660)*

★★★★ ▦ FARMHOUSE

Ipplepen TQ12 5UA
☎ 01803 872254 ▤ 01803 872254
Mrs A Dallyn
e-mail: bulleigh@lineone.net
dir: 3.5m S of Newton Abbot. Off A381 at Parkhill Cross by petrol station for Compton, continue 1m, signed

Bulleigh Park is a working farm, producing award-winning Aberdeen Angus beef. The owners have also won an award for green tourism by reducing the impact of the business on the environment. Expect a friendly welcome at this family home set in glorious countryside, where breakfasts are notable for the wealth of fresh, local and home-made produce, and the porridge is cooked using a secret recipe.

Rooms 2 en suite 1 annexe en suite (1 fmly) S £42-£45; D £72-£80* **Facilities** FTV TVL tea/coffee Cen ht Wi-fi ch fac **Parking** 6 **Notes** LB Closed Dec-1 Feb 60 acres beef/sheep/hens

Lyndale Bed and Breakfast

★★★★ BED AND BREAKFAST

Lyndale Leygreen, Teigngrace TQ12 6QW
☎ 01626 332491
e-mail: sue.haddy@btinternet.com
dir: Going S from Exeter on A38, pass Chudleigh exit, after 1.5m exit for Teigngrace. 1m on right

Peacefully located in the quiet village of Teigngrace, Lyndale is a modern detached bungalow surrounded by pleasant countryside views. The two well decorated and comfortably furnished bedrooms and bathrooms provide guests with plenty of space. Breakfast is taken in the bright conservatory overlooking the gardens, and outdoor seating is available for sunnier days.

Rooms 2 en suite (2 GF) S £40-£42; D £60-£70*
Facilities tea/coffee Cen ht **Parking** 4 **Notes** ⊗ No Children 16yrs ⬤

NEWTON POPPLEFORD   Map 3 SY08

Moores' Restaurant & Rooms

★★★ ◉◉ RESTAURANT WITH ROOMS

6 Greenbank, High St EX10 0EB
☎ 01395 568100
e-mail: info.moores@btconnect.com
dir: On A3052 in village centre, 3m from Sidmouth

Centrally located in the village, this small restaurant offers very comfortable, practically furnished bedrooms. Guests are assured of a friendly welcome and relaxed, efficient service. Good quality, locally sourced ingredients are used to produce imaginative dishes full of natural flavours.

Rooms 3 rms (1 en suite) (2 fmly) S £40; D £50-£60
Facilities FTV tea/coffee Dinner available Cen ht ch fac **Conf** Max 12 Board 12 **Notes** LB ⊗ Closed 1st 2wks Jan No coaches

OKEHAMPTON   Map 3 SX59

See also Holsworthy

Week Farm Country Holidays *(SX519913)*

★★★★ FARMHOUSE

Bridestowe EX20 4HZ
☎ 01837 861221 ▤ 01837 861221
Mrs Margaret Hockridge
e-mail: margaret@weekfarmonline.com
web: www.weekfarmonline.com
dir: Leave A30 at Sourton Cross & cross A386, fork right, left at x-rds towards Bridestowe. After 2m, take centre lane at lights (turning right) through x-rds, pass Week Cottage to Week Farm

A delicious complimentary cream tea awaits at this 17th-century farmhouse. Surrounded by undulating

countryside, the farm also has three coarse fishing lakes, set in a conservation area. Traditional farmhouse breakfasts can be enjoyed in the dining room. The comfortable bedrooms are furnished in traditional style, and one ground-floor room has easier access.

Rooms 5 en suite (2 fmly) (1 GF) **Facilities** FTV TVL tea/coffee Cen ht Wi-fi ⬛ Fishing 3 Coarse fishing lakes **Conf** Max 12 **Parking** 10 **Notes** Closed 25 Dec 180 acres sheep/cattle

OTTERY ST MARY   Map 3 SY19

Fluxton Farm

★★ BED AND BREAKFAST

Fluxton EX11 1RJ
☎ 01404 812818 ▤ 01404 814843
web: www.fluxtonfarm.co.uk
dir: 2m SW of Ottery St Mary. B3174, W from Ottery over river, left, next left to Fluxton

A haven for cat lovers, Fluxton Farm offers comfortable accommodation with a choice of lounges and a large garden, complete with pond and ducks. Set in peaceful farmland four miles from the coast, this 16th-century longhouse has a wealth of beams and open fireplaces.

Rooms 7 en suite S £27.50-£30; D £55-£60*
Facilities FTV TVL tea/coffee Cen ht **Parking** 15 **Notes** LB No Children 8yrs RS Nov-Apr pre-booked & wknds only ⬤

PAIGNTON   Map 3 SX86

Merritt House B&B

★★★★ ▦ GUEST ACCOMMODATION

7 Queens Rd TQ4 6AT
☎ 01803 528959
e-mail: bookings@merritthouse.co.uk
dir: From Paignton seafront, turn right onto Torbay Rd, then 1st left onto Queens Rd, house on right

Just a five-minute stroll from the seafront and town centre, this elegant Victorian property is ideally situated to make the most of this traditional resort. The owners take understandable pride in their establishment and will assist in any way possible to ensure a relaxed and rewarding stay. Bedrooms and bathrooms are thoughtfully furnished and generously equipped to ensure a cosseting and comfortable stay. Breakfast is a real treat with plenty of choice, and an emphasis on local and home-made produce.

Rooms 7 en suite (3 GF) S £27-£34; D £54-£72*
Facilities FTV tea/coffee Cen ht Wi-fi **Parking** 4 **Notes** No Children 14yrs Closed 20 Dec-7 Jan

PAIGNTON *continued*

The Wentworth Guest House

★★★★ GUEST HOUSE

18 Youngs Park Rd, Goodrington TQ4 6BU
☎ 01803 557843
e-mail: enquiries@wentworthguesthouse.co.uk
dir: *Through Paignton on A378, 1m left at rdbt, sharp right onto Roundham Rd, right & right again onto Youngs Park Rd*

Quietly located opposite a pretty park, this is an ideal location for exploring the many and varied attractions of the English Riviera. Goodrington's lovely beaches are just a short stroll away and the town centre is a 10-15 minute walk away. The caring owners make every effort to ensure guests enjoy a relaxing break, and are always on hand to assist with local information. Bedrooms offer good levels of comfort and include both dog-friendly and family rooms. Breakfast is served in the informal dining room with a cosy guest lounge also provided.

Rooms 10 en suite (2 fmly) (1 GF) S £26-£30; D £52-£70* **Facilities** FTV TVL tea/coffee Cen ht Licensed Wi-fi **Parking** 5 **Notes** LB Closed 16 Dec-2 Jan

Bay Cottage

★★★ GUEST ACCOMMODATION

4 Beach Rd TQ4 6AY
☎ 01803 525729
web: www.baycottagepaignton.co.uk
dir: *Along B3201 Esplanade Rd past Paignton Pier, Beach Rd 2nd right*

Quietly located in a level terrace, the seafront, park, harbour and shops are all just a short stroll away. Run in a friendly and relaxed manner, Bay Cottage offers a range of bedrooms of various shapes and sizes, with a guest lounge also made available. Dinner is offered by prior arrangement and includes enjoyable home cooking in hearty portions.

Rooms 8 en suite (3 fmly) S £22-£25; D £44-£50* **Facilities** FTV TVL tea/coffee Dinner available Cen ht Wi-fi **Notes** LB ⊗

The Park

★★★ GUEST ACCOMMODATION

Esplanade Rd TQ4 6BQ
☎ 01803 557856   📠 01803 555626
e-mail: stay@parkhotel.me.uk
web: www.theparkhotel.net
dir: *On Paignton seafront, nearly opp pier*

This large establishment has a prominent position on the seafront with excellent views of Torbay. The pleasant bedrooms are all spacious and available in a number of options, and several have sea views. Entertainment is provided on some evenings in the lounge. Dinner and breakfast are served in the spacious dining room, which overlooks the attractive front garden.

Rooms 47 en suite (5 fmly) (3 GF) **Facilities** tea/coffee Dinner available Cen ht Lift Licensed Wi-fi Pool table Games room with 3/4 snooker table & table tennis **Conf** Max 120 Board 12 **Parking** 38

The Clydesdale

[U]

5 Polsham Park TQ3 2AD
☎ 01803 558402   📠 01803 558402
e-mail: theclydesdale@hotmail.co.uk
dir: *Off A3022 Torquay Rd onto Lower Polsham Rd, 2nd right into Polsham Park*

Currently the rating for this establishment is not confirmed. This may be due to a change of ownership or because it has only recently joined the AA rating scheme.

Rooms 7 en suite (1 fmly) (2 GF) S £26-£30; D £52-£60 **Facilities** FTV TVL tea/coffee Dinner available Cen ht Wi-fi **Parking** 6 **Notes** LB Closed Xmas & New Year

Berkeley's of St James

★★★★ GUEST ACCOMMODATION

4 St James Place East, The Hoe PL1 3AS
☎ 01752 221654   📠 01752 221654
e-mail: enquiry@onthehoe.co.uk
dir: *Off A38 towards city centre, left at sign The Hoe, over 7 sets of lights, left onto Athenaeum St, right to Crescent Av, 1st left*

Located in a quiet square close to The Hoe and just a short walk from the city centre, this is a good choice for business and leisure. Bedrooms are comfortable, attractive and equipped with a number of thoughtful extras. An enjoyable breakfast using organic and local produce, whenever possible, is served in the dining room.

Rooms 5 en suite (1 fmly) (1 GF) S £45-£50; D £65-£70 **Facilities** FTV tea/coffee Cen ht Wi-fi **Parking** 3 **Notes** LB ⊗ Closed 23 Dec-1 Jan

Brittany Guest House

★★★★ GUEST ACCOMMODATION

28 Athenaeum St, The Hoe PL1 2RQ
☎ 01752 262247
e-mail: thebrittanyguesthouse@btconnect.com
dir: *A38/City Centre follow signs for Pavillions, bear left at mini-rdbt, turn left at lights onto Athenaeum St*

Situated in a pleasant street, within walking distance of Plymouth's many attractions, this well presented house offers comfortable and well-equipped accommodation. The proprietors provide friendly hospitality, and many guests return frequently. Freshly cooked breakfast is served in the attractive dining room. Parking available.

Rooms 10 en suite (3 fmly) (1 GF) S £35-£39; D £49-£55* **Facilities** FTV tea/coffee Cen ht Wi-fi **Parking** 6 **Notes** ⊗ No Children 5yrs Closed 20 Dec-2 Jan

Jewell's

★★★★ GUEST ACCOMMODATION

220 Citadel Rd, The Hoe PL1 3BB
☎ 01752 254760 ≣ 01752 254760
e-mail: jewellsguest@btconnect.com
dir: *A38 towards city centre, follow sign for Barbican, then The Hoe. Left at lights, right at top of road onto Citadel Rd. Jewell's 0.25m*

This smart, comfortable, family-run establishment is only a short walk from The Hoe and is convenient for the city centre and The Barbican. Bedrooms come with a wide range of extra facilities, and breakfast is served in the pleasant dining room. Some secure parking is available.

Rooms 10 rms (7 en suite) (5 fmly) **Facilities** FTV tea/coffee Cen ht Wi-fi **Parking** 3 **Notes** ⊗

Ashgrove House

★★★ GUEST ACCOMMODATION

218 Citadel Rd, The Hoe PL1 3BB
☎ 01752 664046 ≣ 01752 252112
e-mail: ashgroveho@aol.com
dir: *Follow signs for The Hoe*

Conveniently situated within walking distance of all the city's attractions, this personally-run establishment offers well-presented accommodation; ideal for commercial visitors and also welcoming to children. Freshly-cooked breakfasts are provided and a comfortable lounge is available for guests.

Rooms 10 en suite (5 fmly) **Facilities** FTV TVL tea/coffee Cen ht Wi-fi **Notes** ⊗

The Cranbourne

★★★ GUEST ACCOMMODATION

278-282 Citadel Rd, The Hoe PL1 2PZ
☎ 01752 263858 & 224646 & 661400
≣ 01752 263858
e-mail: info@cranbournehotel.co.uk
web: www.cranbournehotel.co.uk
dir: *Behind the Promenade, Plymouth Hoe*

This attractive Georgian terrace house is located just a short walk from The Hoe, The Barbican and the city centre. Bedrooms are practically furnished and well equipped. Hearty breakfasts are served in the elegant dining room and there is also a cosy bar.

Rooms 40 rms (28 en suite) (5 fmly) (2 GF) S £27-£40; D £48-£60* **Facilities** FTV TVL tea/coffee Cen ht Licensed Wi-fi **Parking** 14

Devonshire

★★★ GUEST ACCOMMODATION

22 Lockyer Rd, Mannamead PL3 4RL
☎ 01752 220726 ≣ 01752 220766
e-mail: devonshiregh@blueyonder.co.uk
dir: *At Hyde Park pub on traffic island turn left onto Wilderness Rd. After 60yds turn left onto Lockyer Rd*

This comfortable Victorian house is located in a residential area close to Mutley Plain high street, from where there is a regular bus service to the city centre. The well-proportioned bedrooms are bright and attractive, and guests can use the comfy lounge. Parking is available.

Rooms 10 rms (5 en suite) (4 fmly) (3 GF) S £26-£45; D £48-£56 **Facilities** FTV TVL tea/coffee Cen ht Licensed Wi-fi **Parking** 6 **Notes** LB ⊗

The Firs Guest Accommodation

★★★ GUEST ACCOMMODATION

13 Pier St, West Hoe PL1 3BS
☎ 01752 262870 & 300010
e-mail: thefirsguesthouse@hotmail.co.uk

A well-located and-well established house on the West Hoe with convenient on-street parking. Friendly owners and comfortable rooms make it a popular destination.

Rooms 7 rms (2 en suite) (2 fmly) S £25-£35; D £45-£65* **Facilities** FTV tea/coffee Dinner available Cen ht Wi-fi **Notes** LB

The Lamplighter

★★★ GUEST ACCOMMODATION

103 Citadel Rd, The Hoe PL1 2RN
☎ 01752 663855 & 07793 360815
e-mail: stay@lamplighterplymouth.co.uk
web: www.lamplighterplymouth.co.uk
dir: *Near war memorial*

With easy access to The Hoe, The Barbican and the city centre, this comfortable house provides a good base for leisure or business. Bedrooms, including family rooms, are light and airy and furnished to a consistent standard. Breakfast is served in the dining room, which has an adjoining lounge area.

Rooms 9 rms (7 en suite) (2 pri facs) (2 fmly) S £30-£40; D £50-£60 **Facilities** FTV TVL tea/coffee Cen ht Wi-fi **Parking** 4

Rainbow Lodge Guest House

★★★ GUEST HOUSE

29 Athenaeum St, The Hoe PL1 2RQ
☎ 01752 229699
e-mail: info@rainbowlodgeplymouth.co.uk
web: www.rainbowlodgeplymouth.co.uk
dir: *A38 onto A374. Follow City Centre signs for 3m, onto Exeter St. Bear left onto Breton Side at lights, follow road, left onto Athenaeum St at Walrus pub*

Just a short stroll from The Hoe, this small and friendly establishment is well placed for exploring the city. Bedrooms are varied in size and style, some of which are suitable for family use. Substantial breakfasts are served in the homely dining room.

Rooms 11 rms (7 en suite) (1 pri facs) (2 fmly) (1 GF) S £32-£48; D £48-£65* **Facilities** FTV tea/coffee Cen ht Wi-fi **Parking** 6 **Notes** LB ⊗ No Children 5yrs Closed 22 Dec-5 Jan

Riviera

★★★ GUEST HOUSE

8 Elliott St, The Hoe PL1 2PP
☎ 01752 667379 ≣ 01752 623318
e-mail: riviera-hoe@btconnect.com
dir: *Follow signs to city centre, then The Hoe, located off Citadel Rd*

This late Victorian building retains many of the features typical of the period, and is only a short walk from Plymouth Hoe where Sir Francis Drake finished playing his game of bowls prior to defeating the approaching Spanish armada in 1588. Linda and Lester Wrench are committed to providing a highly personalised guest experience. Guests have use of a lounge and bar, and breakfast is served in the breakfast room.

Rooms 11 rms (8 en suite) (1 fmly) S £36-£41; D £58-£59* **Facilities** FTV TVL tea/coffee Cen ht Wi-fi **Notes** ⊗ Closed mid Dec-early Jan

ROCKBEARE Map 3 SY09

3 Cherry Tree Close

★★★ BED AND BREAKFAST

EX5 2HF
☎ 01404 822047
dir: *In village centre between bridge & church. 3.5m from M5 off old A30*

Guests are assured of a warm welcome and a homely atmosphere at this spacious bungalow set in its own garden in the village of Rockbeare. The property is convenient for the M5, Exeter International Airport and Westpoint Arena, and is only a short drive from Dartmoor. One of the two bedrooms overlooks fields, and both come complete with tea- and coffee-making facilities. A TV lounge is available for guests, and breakfast is served in the dining room.

Rooms 2 rms (2 GF) **Facilities** TVL tea/coffee Cen ht **Parking** 3 **Notes** LB No Children Closed 23 Dec-4 Jan ☻

ROUSDON — Map 4 SY29

PREMIER COLLECTION

The Dower House

★★★★★ 🍴 🚭 GUEST ACCOMMODATION

DT7 3RB
☎ 01297 21047 📄 01428 661387
e-mail: info@dhhotel.com
dir: Off A3052, 3m W of Lyme Regis

Handily placed, a short drive from Lyme Regis and the coast, this fine old Victorian building has an interesting and varied history. The atmosphere is warm and welcoming with all bedrooms offering lots of comfort and character. The friendly bar lounge has doors opening onto a decked area with wonderful views across the rolling countryside. Local produce, including excellent fish, features on the daily-changing menu, and is served in the elegant dining room. There is a heated outdoor swimming pool.

Rooms 10 en suite (2 fmly) (1 GF) **Facilities** FTV tea/coffee Dinner available Direct Dial Cen ht Licensed Wi-fi **Conf** Max 45 Thtr 45 Class 20 Board 20 **Parking** 25 **Notes** Closed 2-31 Jan Civ Wed 140

SEATON — Map 4 SY29

Mariners

★★★★ 🚭 🍴 GUEST ACCOMMODATION

East Walk Esplanade EX12 2NP
☎ 01297 20560
web: www.marinershotelseaton.co.uk
dir: Off A3052 signed Seaton, Mariners on seafront

Located just yards from the beach and cliff paths, this comfortable establishment has a friendly and relaxed atmosphere. Bedrooms, some with sea views, are well equipped, and public rooms are light and airy. The dining room is the venue for enjoyable breakfasts that utilise quality local produce; afternoon teas are also available on the seafront terrace.

Rooms 10 en suite (1 fmly) (2 GF) **Facilities** tea/coffee Dinner available Cen ht Licensed **Parking** 10 **Notes** ⊗ No Children 5yrs RS Nov-Jan Closed at certain times

Holmleigh House Bed and Breakfast

★★★★ 🅰 GUEST ACCOMMODATION

Sea Hill EX12 2QT
☎ 01297 625671
e-mail: contact@holmleighhouse.com
Rooms 3 en suite S £48-£55; D £70-£80 **Facilities** TVL tea/coffee Cen ht Wi-fi **Notes** LB ⊗ Closed 23-28 Dec 🐾

SHALDON

See Teignmouth

SIDMOUTH — Map 3 SY18

See also Ottery St Mary

PREMIER COLLECTION

The Salty Monk

★★★★★ 🍴🍴 🚭 RESTAURANT WITH ROOMS

Church St, Sidford EX10 9QP
☎ 01395 513174
e-mail: saltymonk@btconnect.com
web: www.saltymonk.co.uk
dir: On A3052 opposite church

Set in the village of Sidford, this attractive property dates from the 16th century. There's oodles of style and appeal here and each bedroom has a unique identity. Bathrooms are equally special with multi-jet showers, spa baths and cosseting robes and towels. The output from the kitchen is impressive with excellent local produce very much in evidence, served in the elegant surroundings of the restaurant. A mini spa facility is available.

Rooms 5 en suite 1 annexe en suite (3 GF) S £70-£150* **Facilities** FTV tea/coffee Dinner available Cen ht Wi-fi Golf 18 Sauna Hot tub **Conf** Max 14 Board 14 **Parking** 20 **Notes** LB Closed 2wks Nov & 3wks Jan No coaches

Blue Ball Inn

★★★★ INN

Stevens Cross, Sidford EX10 9QL
☎ 01395 514062 📄 01395 519584
e-mail: rogernewton@blueballinn.net
dir: On A3052, at Sidford straight over lights. Inn 600yds

Ideally placed for exploring the many delights of east Devon, this long established inn has been overseen by five generations of the Newton family since 1912, and can trace its history back to 1385. After a devastating fire in 2006, the inn has been lovingly rebuilt and now provides impressive levels of comfort and quality. The bedrooms and stylish bathrooms provide an appealing blend of old and new. The extensive bars have cosy nooks in which to enjoy the food and drink on offer, with an attractive garden also available.

Rooms 9 en suite (2 fmly) (1 GF) **Facilities** FTV tea/coffee Dinner available Cen ht Wi-fi Golf 18 **Conf** Max 65 **Parking** 80 **Notes** LB ⊗

The Groveside

★★★★ GUEST HOUSE

Vicarage Rd EX10 8UQ
☎ 01395 513406
e-mail: info@thegroveside.co.uk
web: www.thegroveside.co.uk
dir: 0.5m N of seafront on A375

Conveniently situated a short, level walking distance from the town centre, the Groveside offers 'boutique-style' accommodation. A number of influences, such as Art Deco, have been used to impressive effect in the bedrooms, while bathrooms also show individuality and flair. Guests are assured of attentive service and a relaxed and friendly atmosphere, with every effort made to produce an enjoyable stay. Home-cooked evening meals are served by prior arrangement. On-site parking is an added bonus.

Rooms 9 rms (8 en suite) (1 pri facs) S £35-£40; D £70-£80 **Facilities** FTV TVL tea/coffee Dinner available Cen ht Wi-fi Pamper wknds in Nov **Conf** Max 14 Class 14 Board 14 **Parking** 9 **Notes** LB ⊗ No Children 12yrs 🐾

The Old Farmhouse

★★★★ GUEST ACCOMMODATION

Hillside Rd EX10 8JG
☎ 01395 512284
dir: A3052 from Exeter to Sidmouth, right at Bowd x-rds, 2m left at rdbt, left at mini-rdbt, next right, over hump-back bridge, bear right on the corner

This beautiful 16th-century thatched farmhouse, in a quiet residential area just a stroll from the Esplanade and shops, has been lovingly restored. Bedrooms are attractively decorated and the charming public rooms feature beams and an inglenook fireplace. The welcoming proprietors provide memorable dinners using traditional recipes and fresh local ingredients.

Rooms 3 en suite 3 annexe en suite (1 fmly) (1 GF) D £64-£80 **Facilities** TVL TV3B tea/coffee Dinner available Cen ht Licensed **Parking** 4 **Notes** LB No Children 12yrs Closed Nov-Feb 🐾

Dukes

★★★★ 🛏 INN

The Esplanade EX10 8AR
☎ 01395 513320 📄 01395 519318
e-mail: dukes@hotels-sidmouth.co.uk
web: www.hotels-sidmouth.co.uk
dir: *A3052, take 1st exit to Sidmouth on right, left onto Esplanade*

Situated in the heart of Sidmouth, this stylish inn offers a relaxed and convivial atmosphere created by a great team of attentive staff. Bedrooms provide good levels of comfort and a number have the benefit of sea views. The menu utilises the seasonal produce that this area has to offer. A choice of dining areas is available including the patio garden - perfect for soaking up the sun.

Rooms 13 en suite (5 fmly) **Facilities** FTV tea/coffee Dinner available Direct Dial Cen ht Wi-fi **Parking** 9 **Notes** RS 25 Dec Bar & rest for residents only

Glendevon

★★★★ GUEST HOUSE

Cotmaton Rd EX10 8QX
☎ 01395 514028
e-mail: enquiries@glendevon-hotel.co.uk
web: www.glendevon-hotel.co.uk
dir: *A3052 onto B3176 to mini-rdbt. Right, house 100yds on right*

Located in a quiet residential area just a short walk from the town centre and beaches, this stylish Victorian house offers neat, comfortable bedrooms. Guests are assured of a warm welcome from the resident owners, who provide attentive service and wholesome home-cooked evening meals by arrangement. A lounge is also available.

Rooms 8 en suite S £34-£38; D £68-£76* **Facilities** FTV tea/coffee Dinner available Cen ht Licensed **Notes** LB 🚭 No Children 🐾

Bramley Lodge Guest House

★★★ GUEST HOUSE

Vicarage Rd EX10 8UQ
☎ 01395 515710
e-mail: bramleyowner@btinternet.com
dir: *0.5m N of seafront on A375*

Guests are assured of a warm and friendly welcome at this family-run, small guest house, located about a half mile from the sea. The neatly furnished bedrooms vary in size, and all are equipped to a good standard. Home-cooked evening meals are available, by prior arrangement, with special diets on request.

Rooms 6 rms (5 en suite) (1 fmly) S £32-£36; D £64-£72 **Facilities** FTV tea/coffee Dinner available Cen ht **Parking** 6 **Notes** Closed mid Nov-mid Feb RS 1st wk Aug week long bookings only 🐾

Enstone House B&B

★★ BED AND BREAKFAST

Lennox Av EX10 8TX
☎ 01395 514444
e-mail: enstonehouse@hotmail.com
dir: *A375 Vicarage Rd into Sidmouth, left onto Lennox Av*

Situated in colourful gardens at the end of a quiet cul-de-sac, this family-run B&B is just 200 yards from the town centre, and a short walk from the seafront. Bedrooms are neatly furnished with the best use made of the available space.

Rooms 3 rms (2 en suite) (1 fmly) (1 GF) S £30-£35; D £50-£60* **Facilities** FTV TVL tea/coffee Cen ht **Parking** 4 **Notes** LB 🚭 No Children 2yrs Closed Oct-Mar 🐾

SOURTON   Map 3 SX59

Bearslake Inn

★★★★ 🛏 INN

Lake EX20 4HQ
☎ 01837 861334 📄 01837 861108
e-mail: enquiries@bearslakeinn.com
dir: *A30 from Exeter onto A386 signed Sourton/Tavistock, 2m on left from junct*

Situated on the edge of the Dartmoor National Park, this thatched inn is believed to date back to the 13th century and was originally part of a working farm. There is character in abundance here with beams, flagstone floors and low ceilings, all of which contribute to an engaging atmosphere. Bedrooms have great individuality and provide period features combined with contemporary comforts. Local produce is very much in evidence on the menu with dinner served in the attractive Stable Restaurant. The beer garden is bordered by a moorland stream with wonderful views across open countryside.

Rooms 6 en suite (3 fmly) (1 GF) S £65-£75; D £90-£100* **Facilities** FTV tea/coffee Dinner available Cen ht Wi-fi **Parking** 35 **Notes** LB No coaches

SOUTH MOLTON   Map 3 SS72

The Coaching Inn

★★★ INN

Queen St EX36 3BJ
☎ 01769 572526
dir: *In town centre*

This long established, former coaching inn, has been providing a warm welcome for weary travellers for many years. Situated in the heart of this bustling town, guests are assured of a relaxing stay with a genuine, family-run atmosphere. Bedrooms provide good levels of comfort with a number benefiting from refurbished bathrooms. An extensive menu is provided with an emphasis on quality and value for money.

Rooms 10 en suite (2 fmly) **Facilities** tea/coffee Dinner available Cen ht Wi-fi Pool table **Conf** Max 100 Thtr 40 Class 40 Board 40 **Parking** 40 **Notes** 🚭

SOUTH ZEAL — Map 3 SX69

The Oxenham Arms

★★★★ INN

EX20 2JT
☎ 01837 840244 & 840577 📠 01837 840791
e-mail: relax@theoxenhamarms.com
web: www.theoxenhamarms.co.uk

Dating back to the 12th century, this fascinating inn, still very much the village local, was first licensed in 1477. Extensive refurbishment has blended contemporary styling with the historic features. Bedrooms have lots of character and no two are alike. The stylish restaurant offers varied cuisine, often utilising produce from the owner's rare breeds farm. In summer, meals can be taken in the extensive garden with stunning views of Dartmoor.

Rooms 7 en suite S £70-£110; D £90-£170*
Facilities STV FTV TVL tea/coffee Dinner available Direct Dial Cen ht Wi-fi **Conf** Max 30 Thtr 30 Class 27 Board 24 **Parking** 8

STOWFORD — Map 3 SX48

Townleigh Farm (SX425876)

★★★★ FARMHOUSE

EX20 4DE
☎ 01566 783186
Mr Stubbs
e-mail: mail@townleigh.com
dir: M5 junct 31, take A30 southbound Roadford, turn off left, left again, follow lane for approx 2m

This 19th-century farmhouse, in 350 acres of picturesque countryside, has something to offer just about everyone. The Victorian architecture, complemented by all the expected modern luxuries, creates an understated grandeur. Bedrooms have much charm, comfort and character together with lovely views, and public areas are equally special with a sumptuous drawing room and elegant dining room. The estate also has a number of self-catering cottages, fishing lakes, an equestrian centre and, in season, pheasant shoots.

Rooms 3 rms (2 en suite) (1 pri facs) **Facilities** TVL tea/coffee Dinner available Cen ht Wi-fi 🦢 Fishing **Parking** 8 **Notes** 250 acres country sports/horses

STRETE — Map 3 SX84

PREMIER COLLECTION

Strete Barton House

★★★★★ GUEST HOUSE

Totnes Rd TQ6 0RU
☎ 01803 770364 📠 01803 771182
e-mail: info@stretebarton.co.uk
web: www.stretebarton.co.uk
dir: Off A379 coastal road into village, just below church

This delightful 16th-century farmhouse has been refurbished to blend stylish accommodation with its original character. Bedrooms are very comfortably furnished and well equipped with useful extras. Breakfast utilises quality local produce and is served in the spacious dining room. Guests are also welcome to use the very comfortable lounge, complete with log burning stove for the cooler months. The village lies between Dartmouth and Kingsbridge and has easy access to the natural beauty of the South Hams as well as local pubs and restaurants.

Rooms 5 rms (4 en suite) (1 pri facs) 1 annexe en suite D £100-£150* **Facilities** FTV tea/coffee Cen ht Wi-fi **Parking** 4 **Notes** LB No Children 8yrs

See advert on page 110

TAVISTOCK — Map 3 SX47

PREMIER COLLECTION

Tor Cottage

★★★★★ 🏠 GUEST ACCOMMODATION

PL16 0JE
☎ 01822 860248 📠 01822 860126
e-mail: info@torcottage.co.uk
web: www.torcottage.co.uk

(For full entry see Chillaton)

The Coach House

★★★ GUEST ACCOMMODATION

PL19 8NS
☎ 01822 617515 📠 01822 617515
e-mail: estevens255@aol.com
web: www.thecoachousehotel.co.uk
dir: 2.5m NW of Tavistock. A390 from Tavistock to Gulworthy Cross, at rdbt take 3rd exit towards Chipshop Inn turn right to Ottery, 1st building in village

Dating from 1857, this building was constructed for the Duke of Bedford and converted by the current owners. Some bedrooms are on the ground floor and in an adjacent barn conversion. Dinner is available in the cosy dining room or the restaurant, which leads onto the south-facing garden.

Rooms 6 en suite 3 annexe en suite (1 fmly) (4 GF) **Facilities** FTV tea/coffee Dinner available Direct Dial Cen ht Licensed Wi-fi **Parking** 24 **Notes** No Children 5yrs

Sampford Manor

★★★ BED AND BREAKFAST

Sampford Spiney PL20 6LH
☎ 01822 853442
e-mail: manor@sampford-spiney.fsnet.co.uk
web: www.sampford-spiney.fsnet.co.uk
dir: B3357 towards Princetown, right at 1st x-rds. Next x-rds Warren Cross left for Sampford Spiney. 2nd right, house below church

Once owned by Sir Francis Drake, this manor house is tucked away in a tranquil corner of Dartmoor National Park. The family home is full of character, with exposed beams and slate floors, while outside, a herd of award-winning alpacas graze in the fields. Genuine hospitality is assured together with scrumptious breakfasts featuring home-produced eggs. Children, horses (stabling available) and dogs are all equally welcome.

Rooms 3 rms (2 pri facs) (1 fmly) S £27-£35; D £50-£70* **Facilities** FTV tea/coffee Cen ht **Parking** 3 **Notes** Closed Xmas 🐾

Save on B&Bs and Hotels. Book at **theAA.com/hotel**

DEVON 123 **ENGLAND**

TEIGNMOUTH
Map 3 SX97

PREMIER COLLECTION

Thomas Luny House

★★★★★ 🏠 GUEST ACCOMMODATION

Teign St TQ14 8EG
☎ 01626 772976
e-mail: alisonandjohn@thomas-luny-house.co.uk
dir: *A381 to Teignmouth, at 3rd lights turn right to quay, 50yds turn left onto Teign St, after 60yds turn right through white archway*

Built in the late 18th century by marine artist Thomas Luny, this charming house offers unique and comfortable accommodation in the old quarter of Teignmouth. Bedrooms are individually decorated and furnished, and all are well equipped with a good range of extras. An elegant drawing room with French windows leads into a walled garden with a terraced sitting area. A superb breakfast, featuring local produce, is served in the attractive dining room.

Rooms 4 en suite S £64-£75; D £80-£102*
Facilities FTV tea/coffee Direct Dial Cen ht Licensed Wi-fi **Parking** 8 **Notes** LB ⊗ No Children 12yrs Closed early Jan-mid Feb

The Minadab Cottage

★★★★ BED AND BREAKFAST

60 Teignmouth Rd TQ14 8UT
☎ 01626 772044
e-mail: enquiries@minadab.co.uk
dir: *M5 onto A380, 2nd left onto B3192, left at T-lights onto A379, cottage approx 1m*

Minadab Cottage is a unique thatched, Grade II listed property built for a Royal Navy commander who fought in the Battle of Trafalgar. This is an engagingly different place with real character. The individually styled bedrooms, named after ships in Nelson's fleet, are stylish with flat-screen TVs and DVD players. Just a short distance from the sea, the property has lovely views and pretty gardens. Breakfast, served in the attractive dining area, makes use of quality local produce.

Rooms 3 rms (2 en suite) (1 pri facs) (1 GF) S £65; D £79* **Facilities** FTV tea/coffee Dinner available Cen ht Wi-fi DVD's & games available for use **Parking** 4 **Notes** ⊗ No Children 16yrs Closed 18 Nov-18 Mar

Potters Mooring

★★★★ GUEST ACCOMMODATION

30 The Green, Shaldon TQ14 0DN
☎ 01626 873225 🖷 01626 872909
e-mail: mail@pottersmooring.co.uk
web: www.pottersmooring.co.uk
dir: *A38 onto A380 signed Torquay, B3192 to Teignmouth & Shaldon, over river signs to Potters Mooring*

A former sea captain's residence dating from 1625, Potters Mooring has been refurbished to provide charming accommodation of a very high standard, including a four-poster room. The friendly proprietors make every effort to ensure an enjoyable stay and the Captain Potter's breakfast features tasty local produce.

Rooms 5 rms (4 en suite) (1 pri facs) (1 fmly)
Facilities FTV tea/coffee Cen ht Wi-fi **Parking** 8

TIVERTON
Map 3 SS91

Hornhill Farmhouse *(SS965117)*

★★★★ 🏠 FARMHOUSE

Exeter Hill EX16 4PL
☎ 01884 253352
Mrs B Pugsley
e-mail: hornhill@tinyworld.co.uk
web: www.hornhill-farmhouse.co.uk
dir: *Signs to Grand Western Canal, right fork up Exeter Hill. Farmhouse on left at top of hill*

Hornhill has a peaceful hilltop setting with panoramic views of the town and the Exe Valley. Elegant decor and furnishings enhance the character of the farmhouse, which in part dates from the 18th century. Bedrooms are beautifully equipped with modern facilities and there is a lovely sitting room with a log fire. Breakfast is served at one large table in the spacious dining room.

Rooms 3 rms (1 en suite) (2 pri facs) (1 GF) S £37-£45; D £60-£70 **Facilities** FTV tea/coffee Wi-fi 🐾 **Parking** 5 **Notes** ⊗ No Children 12yrs 🐄 75 acres beef/sheep

Quoit-At-Cross *(ST923188)*

★★★ FARMHOUSE

Stoodleigh EX16 9PJ
☎ 01398 351280
Mrs L Hill
e-mail: quoit-at-cross@hotmail.co.uk
dir: *M5 junct 27 for Tiverton. A396 N for Bampton, after 3.5m turn left over bridge for Stoodleigh, farmhouse on 1st junct in village centre*

This delightful, stone-built farmhouse commands lovely views over rolling Devonshire countryside and is a great place from which to explore this picturesque area. A warm and genuine welcome is assured with a homely and relaxed atmosphere. The comfortable, attractive bedrooms are well furnished and have many extra facilities. A crackling fire keeps the lounge snug and warm during colder nights, whilst in the summer, the pretty garden is available to guests.

Rooms 4 en suite (2 fmly) S £30-£35; D £60-£70*
Facilities FTV TVL tea/coffee Dinner available Cen ht Fishing Riding Pool table Wildlife garden & trail **Parking** 4 **Notes** LB ⊗ 🐄 160 acres organic/mixed

TORBAY

See Brixham, Paignton and Torquay

TORQUAY
Map 3 SX96

PREMIER COLLECTION

The Cary Arms

★★★★★ INN

Babbacombe Beach TQ1 3LX
☎ 01803 327110 🖷 01803 323221
e-mail: enquiries@caryarms.co.uk
web: www.caryarms.co.uk
dir: *A380 at Ashcombe Cross onto B3192 to Teignmouth. Right at lights to Torquay on A379, bear left at lights continue to Babbacombe. Left onto Babbacombe Downs Rd, left onto Beach Rd*

Located on the water's edge at Babbacombe, this seaside retreat has been refurbished to the highest of standards; the rooms have sea views and nearly all have terraces or balconies. A dedicated team of hosts who will assist in planning your day, or simply impart local knowledge. Bedrooms and bathrooms are fitted to a high standard with many thoughtful extras and unique touches to make a stay memorable. This is a popular dining venue whether eating inside, or on the terraces that lead down to the water's edge; in summer there's a BBQ and wood-fired oven.

Rooms 8 en suite (1 fmly) (3 GF) S £105-£210; D £155-£260* **Facilities** FTV tea/coffee Dinner available Cen ht Wi-fi ch fac Golf 18 Pool table Spa treatment room, sea fishing **Parking** 15 **Notes** LB No coaches Civ Wed 40

TORQUAY *continued*

Linden House

★★★★ GUEST ACCOMMODATION

31 Bampfylde Rd TQ2 5AY
☎ **01803 212281**
e-mail: lindenhouse.torquay@virgin.net
web: www.lindenhousetorquay.co.uk
dir: *Onto A3022, 1st left opposite playing fields*

This elegant Victorian building has been refurbished in a classic style with soft neutral colours providing charm and elegance. An especially warm welcome is provided by the enthusiastic proprietors. Bedrooms and bathrooms provide a range of welcome extras and include a garden room with its own patio. Gluten-free breakfasts can be provided.

Rooms 7 en suite (1 GF) S £55-£65; D £75-£90
Facilities FTV TVL tea/coffee Cen ht Wi-fi **Parking** 7
Notes LB ⊗ No Children 16yrs Closed 24 Dec-2 Jan

The Marstan

★★★★★ GUEST HOUSE

Meadfoot Sea Rd TQ1 2LQ
☎ **01803 292837** 🖨 **01803 299202**
e-mail: enquiries@marstanhotel.co.uk
dir: *A3022 to seafront, left onto A379 Torbay Rd & Babbacombe Rd, right onto Meadfoot Rd, Marstan on right*

This elegant mid 19th-century villa provides high levels of comfort and quality throughout. The hospitality and service are excellent, and every effort is made to create a relaxed and enjoyable atmosphere. Public areas include an impressive dining room, a bar and a comfortable lounge. Outdoors, guests can enjoy a heated swimming pool and hot tub in the secluded garden.

Rooms 9 en suite (1 fmly) (2 GF) S £55-£67; D £80-£150* **Facilities** FTV tea/coffee Direct Dial Cen ht Licensed Wi-fi ⌇ Hot tub **Parking** 8 **Notes** LB ⊗

The Berburry

★★★★★ ⚡ GUEST ACCOMMODATION

64 Bampfylde Rd TQ2 5AY
☎ **01803 297494**
e-mail: stay@berburryhotel.co.uk
web: www.berburryhotel.co.uk
dir: *At Torre railway station lights bear right onto Avenue Rd signposted Seafront. 50yds before 2nd lights, 300yds from seafront*

Rooms 9 en suite (2 GF) S £62-£82; D £80-£108
Facilities FTV TVL tea/coffee Dinner available Cen ht Licensed Wi-fi **Parking** 9 **Notes** LB ⊗ No Children 18yrs Closed 16 Oct-20 Mar

Meadfoot Bay Guest House

★★★★ GUEST ACCOMMODATION

Meadfoot Sea Rd TQ1 2LQ
☎ **01803 294722** 🖨 **01803 214473**
e-mail: stay@meadfoot.com
dir: *A3022 to seafront, onto A379 & right onto Meadfoot Rd, 0.5m on right*

This detached Victorian villa dates from 1850 and was originally a gentleman's residence; it is just a short stroll from Meadfoot Beach, the town and the harbour. A number of the smart bedrooms have private balconies or patios and ground-floor rooms are also available. Public areas offer high levels of comfort and quality with a choice of lounges. Outside, there are four decked areas for relaxing with a drink.

Rooms 19 en suite (3 GF) **Facilities** FTV TVL tea/coffee Cen ht Licensed Wi-fi Golf 18 Access to nearby health club **Parking** 16 **Notes** ⊗ No Children 14yrs

Ashfield Guest House

★★★★ GUEST ACCOMMODATION

9 Scarborough Rd TQ2 5UJ
☎ **01803 293537**
e-mail: enquiries@ashfieldguesthouse.co.uk
dir: *Torquay Seafront onto Belgrave Rd, 300mtrs turn right onto Scarborough Rd, 100mtrs on left*

On a quiet side street, and just a short walk from the bustling town centre, this fine mid-terrace property offers comfortable bedrooms. The house has been sympathetically restored in recent years and guests have the sole use of the large lounge. Breakfasts are served at individual tables in the bright airy dining room.

Rooms 6 en suite (2 fmly) (2 GF) S £30-£35; D £55-£65* **Facilities** FTV TVL tea/coffee Cen ht Wi-fi **Parking** 3 **Notes** LB ⊗ Closed Dec-Mar

Aveland House

★★★★ GUEST ACCOMMODATION

Aveland Rd, Babbacombe TQ1 3PT
☎ **01803 326622** & 328940
e-mail: avelandhouse@aol.com
web: www.avelandhouse.co.uk
dir: *A3022 to Torquay, left onto B3199 Hele Rd onto Westhill Rd. Then Warbro Rd, 2nd left onto Aveland Rd*

Set in well-tended gardens in a peaceful area of Babbacombe, close to the South West Coastal Path, beaches, shops and attractions, Aveland House is within easy walking distance of Torquay harbour and town. This family-run house offers warm and attentive service. The attractive bedrooms are well equipped, with free Wi-fi throughout. A pleasant bar and two comfortable TV lounges are available. Hearing-impaired visitors are especially welcome, as both the proprietors are OCSL signers. Evening meals and bar snacks are available by arrangement. Coeliacs and special diets can be catered for.

Rooms 10 en suite (2 fmly) S £38-£40; D £76-£80
Facilities TVL tea/coffee Dinner available Cen ht Licensed Wi-fi Licensed bar **Parking** 10 **Notes** LB ⊗ No Children 2yrs RS Sun no evening meals

Barclay Court

★★★★ GUEST ACCOMMODATION

29 Castle Rd TQ1 3BB
☎ **01803 292791**
e-mail: enquiries@barclaycourthotel.co.uk
dir: *M5 onto A38 then A380 to Torquay. A3022 Newton Rd left onto Upton Rd, right towards Lymington Rd. Right to Castle Circus, Castle Rd on left*

The delightful, personally-run Barclay Court is within easy walking distance of Torquay's attractions and offers a friendly, relaxed atmosphere. Individually decorated rooms vary in size, but all are en suite and well equipped. There is a games room on the lower-ground floor and the garden is a quiet retreat especially in the summer months.

Save on B&Bs and Hotels. Book at **theAA.com/hotel**

DEVON 125 ENGLAND

Rooms 4 en suite 6 annexe en suite (1 fmly) (1 GF)
Facilities FTV TVL tea/coffee Games room **Parking** 7
Notes ⊗ Closed 25 Dec & New Year RS Nov-Mar Limited
rooms available 🐾

Berkeley House

★★★★ GUEST HOUSE

39 Babbacombe Downs Rd, Babbacombe TQ1 3LN
☎ 01803 322429
e-mail: reception@berkeleyhousetorquay.co.uk
dir: *A380 to Babbacombe, off Babbacombe Rd onto
Princes St to seafront*

Warm and friendly hospitality awaits you at this very
pleasant guest house, which is situated on the
Babbacombe seafront. The bedrooms vary in size and
style, but all are thoughtfully equipped. Three rooms have
sea views. Separate tables are provided in the dining
room, where breakfast is served.

Rooms 4 en suite S £45-£55; D £50-£75* **Facilities** FTV
tea/coffee Cen ht Licensed Wi-fi **Parking** 4 **Notes** LB ⊗
No Children 5yrs

Blue Conifer

★★★★ GUEST ACCOMMODATION

Higher Downs Rd, The Seafront, Babbacombe TQ1 3LD
☎ 01803 327637
dir: *Signs for Babbacombe & seafront, premises 500yds
from model village, opp cliff railway*

Surrounded by neat gardens with splendid views across
beaches to the bay, this attractive property provides a
relaxed and friendly atmosphere. Bedrooms, many with
sea views, are well equipped and one is on the ground
floor. A relaxing lounge and spacious car park are
welcome additions.

Rooms 7 en suite (3 fmly) (1 GF) S £37-£43; D £58-£74*
Facilities FTV tea/coffee Cen ht **Parking** 9 **Notes** LB
Closed Nov-Feb 🐾

Brooklands

★★★★ GUEST HOUSE

5 Scarborough Rd TQ2 5UJ
☎ 01803 296696 🖷 01803 296696
e-mail: enquiries@brooklandsguesthousetorquay.com
dir: *From seafront onto Belgrave Rd, Scarborough Rd
300mtrs on right*

This Victorian terraced property is in a convenient
location for both the seafront and town centre; an ideal
base for visiting the attractions of the English Riviera.
This is a personally-run guest house that offers friendly
hospitality. Bedrooms have good facilities with a
thoughtful range of extras. The attractive breakfast room,
has separate tables, and there is also a separate lounge.
Dinner is available during the summer season. On-street
parking is available, or at the rear on request.

Rooms 5 en suite (1 fmly) S £30-£40; D £50-£60
Facilities FTV TVL tea/coffee Dinner available Cen ht Wi-fi
Use of nearby health and fitness centre **Parking** 1
Notes LB ⊗ No Children 2yrs

Court Prior

★★★★ GUEST HOUSE

St Lukes Road South TQ2 5NZ
☎ 01803 292766
e-mail: courtprior@btconnect.com
dir: *A380 to Torquay, at Halfords right at lights onto
Avenue Rd to seafront, left at next lights up Sheddon Hill,
2nd right onto St Lukes Rd*

Located in a quiet residential area within walking
distance of the seafront and town centre, this charming
house, built in 1860, offers comfortable accommodation.
The bedrooms are spacious, well decorated and
pleasantly furnished throughout. There is also a large
comfortable lounge.

Rooms 9 en suite (3 fmly) (1 GF) S £29-£31; D £58-£62*
Facilities FTV TVL tea/coffee Cen ht Wi-fi **Parking** 9
Notes LB ⊗ No Children 12yrs

The Downs, Babbacombe

★★★★ GUEST ACCOMMODATION

41-43 Babbacombe Downs Rd, Babbacombe TQ1 3LN
☎ 01803 328543
e-mail: manager@downshotel.co.uk

Originally built in the 1850s, this elegant building forms
part of a seafront terrace with direct access to the
promenade and Babbacombe Downs. The warmth of
welcome is matched by attentive service, with every effort
made to ensure a rewarding and relaxing stay. Bedrooms
offer impressive levels of comfort and most have
spectacular views across Lyme Bay with balconies being
an added bonus. For guests with limited mobility,
assisted access is available to the first floor. Additional
facilities include the convivial lounge/bar and spacious
restaurant where enjoyable dinners and breakfasts are
offered.

Rooms 12 en suite (4 fmly) S £50-£64; D £65-£79*
Facilities FTV TVL tea/coffee Dinner available Direct Dial
Cen ht Licensed Wi-fi **Parking** 8 **Notes** LB

The Elmington

★★★★ GUEST ACCOMMODATION

St Anges Ln, Chelston TQ2 6QE
☎ 01803 605192 🖷 01803 690489
e-mail: mail@elmimgton.co.uk
web: www.elmington.co.uk
dir: *At rear of rail station*

Set in sub-tropical gardens with views over the bay, this
splendid Victorian villa has been lovingly restored. The
comfortable bedrooms are brightly decorated and vary in
size and style. There is a spacious lounge, bar and dining
room. Additional facilities include an outdoor pool and
terrace.

Rooms 19 en suite S £40-£45; D £68-£90* **Facilities** FTV
TVL tea/coffee Dinner available Cen ht Licensed Wi-fi ☇
⛳ Golf Pool table **Parking** 24 **Notes** ⊗ Closed Nov-Mar

Glenorleigh

★★★★ GUEST ACCOMMODATION

26 Cleveland Rd TQ2 5BE
☎ 01803 292135 🖷 01803 213717
e-mail: glenorleighhotel@btinternet.com
web: www.glenorleigh.co.uk
dir: *A380 from Newton Abbot onto A3022, at Torre station
lights right onto Avenue Rd & 1st left, across 1st junct,
200yds on right*

Located in a residential area, the Glenorleigh provides a
range of smart bedrooms with some on ground floor level.
Offering guests a solarium, a heated outdoor pool with
terrace and a convivial bar, this family-run establishment
is ideal for both leisure or business guests. Breakfast
provides a hearty start to the day, and dinner is available
with prior notice.

Rooms 15 rms (14 en suite) (6 fmly) (7 GF) S £30-£40; D
£60-£80 **Facilities** FTV TVL tea/coffee Dinner available
Cen ht Licensed Wi-fi ☇ Solarium Pool table **Parking** 10
Notes LB ⊗

Headland View

★★★★ GUEST HOUSE

37 Babbacombe Downs, Babbacombe TQ1 3LN
☎ 01803 312612 & 07762 960230
e-mail: reception@headlandview.com
dir: *A379 S to Babbacombe, off Babbacombe Rd left onto
Portland Rd & Babbacombe Downs Rd & seafront*

Positioned on Babbacombe Downs, this elegant Victorian
house boasts superb views of the coast of Lyme Bay, a
World Heritage Site. Bedrooms are individually styled with
most having French doors leading onto balconies
overlooking the spectacular bay. Many period features
have been retained which add to the character and
appeal of the building. A spacious guest lounge is also
available, whilst the excellent breakfasts are served in
the pretty dining room.

Rooms 6 rms (4 en suite) (2 pri facs) (1 fmly) S £45-£50;
D £60-£68* **Facilities** FTV TVL tea/coffee Cen ht Wi-fi
Parking 4 **Notes** LB ⊗ No Children 5yrs 🐾

TORQUAY *continued*

Iona

★★★★ GUEST ACCOMMODATION

5 Cleveland Rd TQ2 5BD
☎ 01803 294918 ▤ 01803 294918
e-mail: stay@hoteliona.co.uk
dir: *A380 to Riviera rdbt, 1st exit onto A3022 towards
seafront. Take left onto Vine Rd, right onto Cleveland Rd*

Dating back to the 1860s, this grand Victorian villa is
situated in a quiet location just a short stroll from the
town centre, harbour and many attractions. A variety of
bedroom sizes is offered; all provide good levels of
comfort and the expected necessities. Public areas are
elegant with a number of period features retained. Dinner
and breakfast are served in the light and airy
conservatory, and a bar is also provided.

Rooms 9 en suite (2 fmly) **Facilities** FTV TVL tea/coffee
Dinner available Cen ht Licensed Wi-fi **Parking** 8

Kelvin House

★★★★ GUEST ACCOMMODATION

46 Bampfylde Rd TQ2 5AY
☎ 01803 209093 ▤ 01803 209093
e-mail: kelvinhousehotel@hotmail.com
dir: *M5 take A3032 (Newton Rd) into Torquay. At lights
at Torre Station turn right onto Avenue Rd. Bampfylde
Rd on left*

This attractive Victorian house was built in the 1880s
and sits on a lovely tree-lined road. All rooms are en suite
and have been refurbished to a high standard with many
extras. A large elegant sitting room is available for guests
and hearty breakfasts are served in the dining room or on
the patio in good weather. This is a family-run property
with a relaxed, friendly home-from-home atmosphere.
Close to transport links, it makes an ideal base for
touring the Torquay Riviera.

Rooms 8 en suite (1 fmly) (2 GF) S £50-£60; D £55-£70*
Facilities FTV TVL tea/coffee Cen ht Licensed **Parking** 6
Notes LB ⊗

Kingsholm

★★★★ GUEST ACCOMMODATION

539 Babbacombe Rd TQ1 1HQ
☎ 01803 297794 ▤ 01803 897121
e-mail: thekingsholm@sky.com
dir: *A3022 left onto Torquay seafront, left at clock tower
rdbt, Kingsholm 400mtrs on left*

An elegant, personally run establishment situated in a
conservation area, only 350 metres from the bustling
harbour. This fine Edwardian house offers excellent
accommodation appointed to a high standard, and many
rooms overlook Torwood Gardens. All bedrooms have
Freeview TV, free Wi-fi, hairdryers and hospitality trays.
There is also a guest lounge, a spacious dining room with
separate tables and a licensed bar. Parking is free. The
owners, June and Carl offer a friendly welcome.

Rooms 9 en suite S £28-£33; D £55-£65 **Facilities** FTV
TVL tea/coffee Cen ht Licensed Wi-fi **Parking** 9 **Notes** No
Children 10yrs

Mariners Guest House

★★★★ GUEST ACCOMMODATION

35 Belgrave Rd TQ2 5HX
☎ 01803 291604
e-mail: marinersguesthouse@btinternet.com
dir: *A380 onto A3022 to seafront, left onto Belgrave Rd,
left at lights onto Lucius St, then 1st left*

This personally run guest accommodation provides
friendly hospitality and willing service. It is within easy
reach of the town centre, and the modern bedrooms are
being refurbished to a good standard. Separate tables
are provided in the attractive breakfast room.

Rooms 7 en suite (2 fmly) (2 GF) S £30-£55; D £45-£60*
Facilities FTV tea/coffee Cen ht Wi-fi **Parking** 4 **Notes** LB
⊗

Millbrook House

★★★★ GUEST ACCOMMODATION

1 Old Mill Rd, Chelston TQ2 6AP
☎ 01803 297394
e-mail: marksj@sky.com

The delightful, personally run Millbrook House is within
easy walking distance of Torquay's attractions and has a
friendly and relaxed atmosphere. The well-maintained
bedrooms provide many useful facilities; a room with a
king-size bed and another with a four-poster are
available. There is a bar on the lower-ground floor with
pool and darts, and the garden has a summer house for
guests to relax in on hotter days.

Rooms 10 en suite (1 fmly) (2 GF) **Facilities** FTV TVL tea/
coffee Cen ht Licensed Pool table **Parking** 8 **Notes** ⊗
Closed Nov-Feb

Newton House

★★★★ GUEST ACCOMMODATION

31 Newton Rd TQ2 5DB
☎ 01803 297520 ▤ 01803 297520
e-mail: newtonhouse_torquay@yahoo.com
web: www.newtonhouse-tq.co.uk
dir: *From Torre station bear left at lights, Newton House
40yds on left*

You are assured of a warm welcome at Newton House,
which is close to the town centre and attractions. The
comfortable bedrooms, some at ground level, have
thoughtful extras, and a lounge is available. Breakfast is
enjoyed in the pleasant dining room.

Rooms 9 en suite (3 fmly) (5 GF) **Facilities** FTV tea/coffee
Cen ht Wi-fi Drying room for hikers **Parking** 15 **Notes** ⊗

Robin Hill

★★★★ GUEST ACCOMMODATION

74 Braddons Hill Road East TQ1 1HF
☎ 01803 214518 ▤ 01803 291410
e-mail: stay@robinhillhotel.co.uk
dir: *From A38 to seafront then left to Babbacombe. Pass
theatre to Clock Tower rdbt, take 1st exit & through 2 sets
of lights, Braddons Hill Road East on left*

Dating back to 1896, this fascinating building has
character in abundance and is located a short stroll from
the harbour and shops. Every effort is made to ensure a
stay is enjoyable; assistance is readily available at all
times. Bedrooms, in varying styles, provide all the
expected necessities; a number have now been
impressively refurbished. Public areas include the
inviting lounge and light and airy dining room where
breakfast can be enjoyed.

Rooms 10 en suite (2 fmly) (1 GF) S £35-£40; D
£65-£78* **Facilities** FTV TVL tea/coffee Cen ht Licensed
Wi-fi ⌣ Golf 18 **Parking** 10 **Notes** LB Closed Nov-Mar

Stover Lodge

★★★★ GUEST ACCOMMODATION

29 Newton Rd TQ2 5DB
☎ 01803 297287 ▤ 01803 297287
e-mail: enquiries@stoverlodge.co.uk
web: www.stoverlodge.co.uk
dir: *Follow signs to Torquay town centre, at station/
Halfords left lane. Lodge on left after lights*

Located close to the town centre, the family-run Stover
Lodge is relaxed and friendly. Children and babies are
welcome, and a cot and high chair can be provided on
request. Hearty breakfasts, with a vegetarian option, are
served in the dining room. There is a garden to enjoy in
summer.

Rooms 9 rms (8 en suite) (1 pri facs) (3 fmly) (2 GF) S
£28-£46; D £52-£60* **Facilities** FTV tea/coffee Cen ht
Wi-fi **Parking** 10 **Notes** LB ⊗

Summerlands

★★★★ GUEST ACCOMMODATION

19 Belgrave Rd TQ2 5HU
☎ 01803 299844
e-mail: summerlands@fsmail.net
web: www.summerlandsguesthousetorquay.com
dir: *A3022 onto Newton Rd, towards seafront & town centre, onto Belgrave Rd. Summerlands on left just past lights*

Located just five minutes walk from the seafront, Summerlands offers a friendly and relaxed environment. There are six well equipped, modern and comfortable bedrooms, all of which are en suite. Breakfasts are served on the lower-ground floor and provide a satisfying start to the day.

Rooms 6 en suite (2 fmly) (1 GF) **Facilities** FTV tea/coffee Cen ht Wi-fi **Parking** 4 **Notes** ✖ No Children 5yrs

Torcroft

★★★★ GUEST ACCOMMODATION

28-30 Croft Rd TQ2 5UE
☎ 01803 298292 ▤ 01803 291799
e-mail: info@torcrofthotel.co.uk
dir: *A390 onto A3022 to Avenue Rd, follow seafront signs, turn left. Cross lights, up Shedden Hill,1st left onto Croft Rd*

Located a short stroll away from the seafront, within a quiet residential area, this elegant establishment is well situated for exploring this area. Bedrooms have good levels of comfort and some have the added bonus of balconies with sea views. Public areas include a spacious dining room and stylish bar/lounge where drinks can be enjoyed. A lovely, secluded garden is available with ample space to sit and enjoy some summer sunshine.

Rooms 15 en suite (1 fmly) S £40-£45; D £71-£81* **Facilities** FTV TVL tea/coffee Cen ht Licensed Wi-fi ch fac Golf 18 **Parking** 10 **Notes** LB ✖ Closed Jan-Feb

Crown Lodge

★★★★ ⓐ GUEST ACCOMMODATION

83 Avenue Rd TQ2 5LH
☎ 01803 298772 ▤ 01803 291155
e-mail: john@crownlodgehotel.co.uk
web: www.crownlodgehotel.co.uk
dir: *A380 through Kingskerswell, over rbt & 6 lights, right at Torre station, 200yds on left*

Rooms 6 en suite (2 GF) D £59-£85* **Facilities** FTV tea/coffee Dinner available Cen ht Wi-fi **Parking** 7 **Notes** LB ✖ No Children 9yrs

Grosvenor House

★★★★ ⓐ GUEST HOUSE

Falkland Rd TQ2 5JP
☎ 01803 294110
e-mail: aa@grosvenorhousehotel.co.uk
dir: *From Newton Abbot to Torquay, at Torre station right by Halfords, left at 2nd lights onto Falkland Rd*

Rooms 10 en suite (4 fmly) (3 GF) **Facilities** FTV TVL tea/coffee Dinner available Cen ht Licensed Wi-fi **Parking** 7 **Notes** ✖ Closed Oct-Etr

The Norwood

★★★★ ⓐ GUEST ACCOMMODATION

60 Belgrave Rd TQ2 5HY
☎ 01803 294236 & 07792 186806 ▤ 01803 294224
e-mail: enquiries@norwoodhoteltorquay.co.uk
dir: *From Princess Theatre towards Paignton, 1st lights right onto Belgrave Rd, over x-rds, 3rd building on left*

Rooms 10 en suite (5 fmly) (1 GF) S £30-£40; D £48-£60* **Facilities** FTV tea/coffee Dinner available Cen ht Licensed Wi-fi **Parking** 3 **Notes** LB

The Sandpiper Guest House

★★★★ ⓐ GUEST HOUSE

Rowdens Rd TQ2 5AZ
☎ 01803 292779 ▤ 01803 292806
e-mail: enquiries@sandpiperguesthouse.co.uk
dir: *From A380 onto A3022 (Riviera Way) follow signs for seafront along Avenue Rd. Left onto Bampfylde Rd, right onto Rowdens Rd*

Rooms 11 rms (9 en suite) (2 pri facs) (1 fmly) (2 GF) S £28-£32; D £50-£60 **Facilities** FTV TVL tea/coffee Dinner available Cen ht Licensed Wi-fi **Parking** 8 **Notes** LB

Walnut Lodge

★★★★ ⓐ GUEST ACCOMMODATION

48 Bampfylde Rd TQ2 5AY
☎ 01803 200471 ▤ 01803 200471
e-mail: stay@walnutlodgetorquay.co.uk
dir: *M5 onto A3032 into Torquay, through lights at Torre Station, turn right signed sea front. After 1st of lights next left onto Bampfylde Rd*

Rooms 6 en suite (1 fmly) (2 GF) **Facilities** FTV TVL tea/coffee Cen ht Wi-fi **Parking** 5 **Notes** ✖

The Westgate

★★★★ ⓐ GUEST ACCOMMODATION

Falkland Rd TQ2 5JP
☎ 01803 295350 ▤ 01803 213710
e-mail: stay@westgatehotel.co.uk
dir: *A380 to Torquay, at A3022 junct sharp left onto Falkland Rd, 300yds on left*

Rooms 10 en suite (2 fmly) (1 GF) **Facilities** FTV TVL tea/coffee Dinner available Cen ht Licensed Wi-fi **Parking** 10 **Notes** ✖ No Children 5yrs

Mulberry House

★★★ GUEST ACCOMMODATION

1 Scarborough Rd TQ2 5UJ
☎ 01803 213639
e-mail: mulberryguesthouse@yahoo.co.uk
web: www.mulberryguesthousetorquay.co.uk
dir: *From Torquay seafront onto Belgrave Rd (B3199), Scarborough Rd 1st right, house on opp end of road*

Tucked away in a quiet residential area, but only a short stroll from the seafront, this is an ideal base from which to explore the local area. The elegant building has much period charm, combined with more contemporary influences, all of which contribute to a relaxed and comfortable stay. Breakfast is served in the attractive dining room which opens into the guest lounge.

Rooms 3 en suite **Facilities** tea/coffee Cen ht Wi-fi **Notes** ✖ No Children

Wayfarer Guest House

★★★ GUEST ACCOMMODATION

37 Belgrave Rd TQ2 5HX
☎ 01803 299138 ▤ 01803 299138
e-mail: wayfarertorquay@hotmail.com
web: www.wayfarertorquay.co.uk
dir: *A380 onto A3022 to seafront, left, onto Belgrave Rd, left at lights onto Lucious St, 1st left to car park*

The Wayfarer offers friendly accommodation, which is convenient for the town centre and the many seaside attractions. Bedrooms are smartly presented, well equipped and comfortable. Freshly prepared breakfasts and dinners are served at individual tables in the stylish dining room.

Rooms 6 en suite (2 fmly) (1 GF) **Facilities** FTV tea/coffee Cen ht Wi-fi **Parking** 3 **Notes** LB ✖

Atlantis

★★★ GUEST ACCOMMODATION

68 Belgrave Rd TQ2 5HY
☎ 01803 292917 ▤ 01803 292917
e-mail: info@atlantis-torquay.co.uk
dir: *Signs to Torquay seafront, turn left, left at lights onto Belgrave Rd, over next lights, premises on left*

Convenient for the beach, theatre and conference centre, the Atlantis is a thoughtfully equipped home-from-home. There is a genuine welcome here with each bedroom offering good levels of comfort. There is a guest lounge leading through to the dining room, where tasty breakfasts provide a satisfying start to the day.

Rooms 10 rms (9 en suite) (1 pri facs) (7 fmly) S £25-£40; D £45-£60* **Facilities** FTV TVL tea/coffee Cen ht Wi-fi **Parking** 3 **Notes** LB ✖

TORQUAY *continued*

Silverlands B&B

★★★ GUEST ACCOMMODATION

27 Newton Rd TQ2 5DB
☎ 01803 292013 & 07878 376714
e-mail: enquiries@silverlandsguesthouse.co.uk
web: www.silverlandsguesthouse.co.uk
dir: *A380 onto A3022 for Torquay, premises on left after Torre station lights*

Convenient for the town centre and the beaches, this friendly establishment has a homely atmosphere. Some of the well-presented bedrooms are on the ground floor, and a hearty, freshly cooked breakfast is served in the dining room.

Rooms 9 rms (7 en suite) (2 pri facs) (2 fmly) (4 GF) S £25-£35; D £50-£58* Facilities FTV tea/coffee Cen ht Wi-fi Parking 10 Notes LB ⊗

Tyndale

★★★ GUEST ACCOMMODATION

68 Avenue Rd TQ2 5LF
☎ 01803 380888
dir: *A380 onto A3022, pass Torre station onto Avenue Rd, 1st lights right onto Old Mill Rd & right into car park*

Close to the seaside attractions and the town centre, this neatly presented house is only a short level walk from the railway station. Bedrooms are brightly decorated in a range of sizes. A comfortable lounge is provided and a freshly cooked, traditional British breakfast is served in the dining room.

Rooms 3 en suite (1 GF) S £20; D £40 Facilities FTV TVL tea/coffee Cen ht Parking 5 Notes LB ⊗ ⊗ ⊜

TOTNES   Map 3 SX86

The Old Forge at Totnes

★★★★ GUEST HOUSE

Seymour Place TQ9 5AY
☎ 01803 862174
e-mail: enq@oldforgetotnes.com
dir: *From Totnes town centre cross river bridge & 2nd right*

Over 600 years old, this delightful property is close to the town centre and Steamer Quay. A range of bedroom styles is offered from spacious suites to cosy cottage-style. All are thoughtfully equipped with numerous extras. Public areas include a conservatory complete with hot tub, which overlooks the garden. Breakfast is a leisurely and enjoyable affair, served in the pleasantly appointed dining room.

Rooms 9 rms (8 en suite) (1 pri facs) (2 fmly) (2 GF) S £50-£75; D £69-£98 Facilities FTV tea/coffee Cen ht Licensed Wi-fi Parking 7 Notes LB ⊗

Steam Packet Inn

★★★★ ⊜ INN

St Peter's Quay TQ9 5EW
☎ 01803 863880 📠 01803 862754
e-mail: steampacket@buccaneer.co.uk
web: www.steampacketinn.co.uk
dir: *Off A38 at Totnes to Dartington & Totnes. Over 1st lights, pass railway station, signs for town centre at next rdbt. Over mini-rdbt, River Dart on left, inn 100yds on left*

This friendly and popular riverside inn offers a warm welcome to visitors and locals alike. Complete with its own quay, the property has a long history. Bedrooms are well equipped and comfortable; some have river views. Public areas have open fires and a choice of dining options including the heated waterside patio area, ideal for relaxing on a warm day. Interesting and well-cooked dishes are offered at lunch and dinner, while breakfast provides a satisfying start to the day.

Rooms 4 en suite (1 fmly) S £59.50; D £79.50* Facilities tea/coffee Dinner available Cen ht Wi-fi 4 private moorings Parking 15 Notes LB

WIDECOMBE IN THE MOOR   Map 3 SX77

Manor Cottage

★★★ BED AND BREAKFAST

TQ13 7TB
☎ 01364 621218
e-mail: di.richard@btinternet.com
dir: *A382 to Bovey Tracey, left onto B3387 to Widecombe, cottage on right after old inn*

Located in the centre of the historic village, this attractive cottage, standing in a large and pleasant garden, has a lot of character. It offers friendly hospitality and spacious, comfortable bedrooms. Breakfast is served in the cosy dining room and features good home cooking that uses fresh, local produce.

Rooms 3 rms (1 en suite) D £50-£60* Facilities FTV TV2B tea/coffee Cen ht Wi-fi 🐎 Riding Parking 3 Notes ⊗ No Children 15yrs Closed Xmas ⊜

WOOLACOMBE   Map 3 SS44

The Castle

★★★★ GUEST ACCOMMODATION

The Esplanade EX34 7DJ
☎ 01271 870788 📠 01271 870812
e-mail: the.castlehotel@amserve.net
dir: *A361 from Barnstaple to Ilfracombe, turn right at Woolacombe sign*

Built in 1898 in the style of a castle, this Victorian stone folly has stunning views over the bay. The attractively decorated bedrooms are comfortable and well equipped. The lounge has a carved-wood ceiling and interesting panelling. There is also a lounge-bar, and breakfast is served in the elegant dining room.

Rooms 8 en suite (2 fmly) (5 GF) Facilities TVL tea/coffee Cen ht Licensed Parking 8 Notes ⊗ No Children 5yrs Closed Oct-Mar

YELVERTON   Map 3 SX56

Harrabeer Country House

★★★★ GUEST ACCOMMODATION

Harrowbeer Ln PL20 6EA
☎ 01822 853302
e-mail: reception@harrabeer.co.uk
web: www.harrabeer.co.uk
dir: *In village. Off A386 Tavistock Rd onto Grange Rd, right onto Harrowbeer Ln*

A warm welcome awaits at this historic Devon longhouse situated on the edge of Dartmoor. It provides an excellent base for exploring this beautiful area; the accommodation has all the expected modern comforts with a lounge, bar and dining room overlooking the garden. Dinners are available by arrangement with special diets catered for. There are also two self-catering units.

Rooms 6 rms (5 en suite) (1 pri facs) (2 fmly) (1 GF) S £61-£71; D £71-£81 Facilities tea/coffee Dinner available Dial Cen ht Licensed Wi-fi Golf 18 Conf Max 20 Board 20 Parking 10 Notes Closed 3rd wk Dec, 2nd wk Jan

Overcombe House

★★★★ 🅰 GUEST HOUSE

Old Station Rd, Horrabridge PL20 7RA
☎ 01822 853501
e-mail: enquiries@overcombehotel.co.uk
web: www.overcombehotel.co.uk
dir: *Signed 100yds off A386 at Horrabridge*

Rooms 8 en suite (2 GF) S £49.50-£69.50; D £75-£95 Facilities FTV tea/coffee Cen ht Licensed Wi-fi Parking 7 Notes ⊗ No Children 12yrs Closed 25 Dec

DORSET

ABBOTSBURY   Map 4 SY58

East Farm House (SY578853)

★★★ FARMHOUSE

2 Rosemary Ln DT3 4JN
☎ 01305 871363 📠 01305 871363
Mrs W M Wood
e-mail: eastfarmhouse@uwclub.net
web: www.eastfarmhouse.co.uk
dir: *B3157 W into Abbotsbury, Swan Inn on left, farmhouse 1st right onto Rosemary Ln*

This unspoiled and charming farmhouse is in the centre of the village and has been in the owner's family since 1729. The house has a homely atmosphere, traditionally furnished with much character, and filled with memorabilia. Hearty breakfasts are served in the lounge-dining room, where a log fire burns in winter.

Rooms 3 en suite **Facilities** tea/coffee Dinner available Cen ht **Parking** 3 **Notes** No Children 14yrs 20 acres horse stud/rare breed pigs

ASKERSWELL   Map 4 SY59

The Spyway Inn

★★★★ INN

DT2 9EP
☎ 01308 485250 📠 01308 485250
e-mail: spywayinn@sky.com
dir: *From A35 follow Askerswell sign, then follow Spyway Inn sign*

Peacefully located in the rolling Dorset countryside, this family-run inn offers a warm and genuine welcome to all. Bedrooms are spacious and well appointed with a number of extras provided, including bath robes. Real ales are on tap in the bar, where locals congregate to put the world to rights. Menus feature home-cooked food with many dishes utilising local produce both at dinner and breakfast. The extensive beer garden, with wonderful views, is popular in summer.

Rooms 3 en suite (1 fmly) S £35-£45; D £50-£70* **Facilities** FTV tea/coffee Dinner available Cen ht Wi-fi **Parking** 40 **Notes** LB ⊗

BEAMINSTER   Map 4 ST40

Watermeadow House (ST535001)

★★★★★ Ⓐ FARMHOUSE

Bridge Farm, Hooke DT8 3PD
☎ 01308 862619 📠 01308 862619
Mrs P M Wallbridge
e-mail: enquiries@watermeadowhouse.co.uk
web: www.watermeadowhouse.co.uk
dir: *3m E of Beaminster, in Hooke*

Rooms 2 rms (1 en suite) (1 pri facs) (1 fmly) S £35-£45; D £60-£70* **Facilities** tea/coffee Cen ht Wi-fi **Parking** 6 **Notes** LB ⊗ Closed Nov-Mar 280 acres dairy/beef

BLANDFORD FORUM   Map 4 ST80

Portman Lodge

★★★★ BED AND BREAKFAST

Whitecliff Mill St DT11 7BP
☎ 01258 453727 📠 01258 453727
e-mail: enquiries@portmanlodge.co.uk
web: www.portmanlodge.co.uk
dir: *On NW end of Blandford's one-way system, to access follow signs from town centre to Shaftesbury & hospital*

Built in the Victorian period and once used as a music school, this substantial detached house now provides elegant accommodation and a warm welcome. All bedrooms and bathrooms are well decorated and comfortably furnished. Breakfast utilises good quality ingredients and is served at a communal table.

Rooms 3 en suite D £70* **Facilities** STV TVL tea/coffee Cen ht Wi-fi **Parking** 8 **Notes** ⊗ No Children Closed 24-31 Dec 🐾

The Anvil Inn

★★★★ INN

Salisbury Rd, Pimperne DT11 8UQ
☎ 01258 453431 📠 01258 480182
e-mail: theanvil.inn@btconnect.com
dir: *2m NE of Blandford on A354 in Pimperne*

Located in a village near Blandford, this 16th-century thatched inn provides a traditional country welcome. Bedrooms have been appointed to high standards. Dinner is a varied selection of home-made dishes, plus there is a tempting variety of hand-pulled ales and wines by the glass.

Rooms 12 en suite **Facilities** STV tea/coffee Dinner available Direct Dial Cen ht **Parking** 18 **Notes** LB No coaches

St Martin's House

★★★★ BED AND BREAKFAST

White Cliff Mill St DT11 7BP
☎ 01258 451245 & 07818 814381
e-mail: info@stmartinshouse.co.uk
dir: *Off Market Pl onto Salisbury St & left onto White Cliff Mill St, on right before traffic island*

Dating from 1866, this restored property was once part of the choristers' house for a local church. The bedrooms are comfortable, homely and well equipped. The hosts offer warm hospitality and attentive service. Breakfast, which features local and home-made items, is enjoyed around a communal table.

Rooms 2 rms (2 pri facs) (1 fmly) S £45-£50; D £65-£70* **Facilities** tea/coffee Cen ht Wi-fi **Parking** 3 **Notes** LB ⊗ 🐾

The Old Bakery

★★★ BED AND BREAKFAST

Church Rd, Pimperne DT11 8UB
☎ 01258 455173 & 07799 853784
e-mail: jjtanners@hotmail.com
web: www.theoldbakerydorset.co.uk
dir: *2m NE of Blandford. Off A354 into Pimperne*

Dating from 1890 and once, as the name suggests, the village bakery, this family home offers comfortable accommodation in a convenient location. Popular with business travellers, families can also be accommodated, with cots available. Substantial breakfasts featuring home-made bread and marmalade are served in the dining room.

Rooms 3 en suite (1 GF) S £30-£32.50; D £60* **Facilities** TVL tea/coffee Dinner available Cen ht Wi-fi **Parking** 2 **Notes** LB ⊗ 🐾

Pennhills Farmhouse (ST819101)

★★★ FARMHOUSE

Sandy Ln, Shillingstone DT11 0TF
☎ 01258 860491
Mrs Watts
dir: *6.5m NW of Blandford. Off A357 at Shillingstone Post Office onto Gunn Ln, bear right to T-junct, left onto Lanchard Ln, signed*

Located in a quiet location with views over the countryside, this delightful, family-run farmhouse provides spacious rooms. The substantial English breakfast consists of home-produced items, served house-party style around one large table in the lounge dining room, where an open fire burns during the winter.

Rooms 2 en suite (1 fmly) (1 GF) **Facilities** FTV TVL tea/coffee Cen ht **Parking** 4 **Notes** ⊗ Closed 22 Dec-3 Jan 🐾 120 acres mixed

BOURNEMOUTH

Map 5 SZ09

Fenn Lodge

★★★★ GUEST ACCOMMODATION

11 Rosemount Rd, Alum Chine BH4 8HB
☎ 01202 761273 📠 01202 761273
e-mail: fennlodge@btconnect.com
web: www.fennlodge.co.uk
dir: *A338 into Poole, at rdbt onto B3065 signed Alum Chine & Sandbanks. Left at lights, right at rdbt onto Alumhurst Rd, 3rd left onto Rosemount Rd*

Located within walking distance of Alum Chine and the beach, this stylish accommodation is friendly and relaxed. The hosts ensure their guests are well cared for and provide many thoughtful extras. Bournemouth and Poole are just a short drive away. Guests have use of an elegant comfortable lounge.

Rooms 11 rms (10 en suite) (1 pri facs) (1 fmly) (1 GF) S £29-£35.50; D £53-£67* **Facilities** TVL tea/coffee Cen ht Wi-fi **Parking** 6 **Notes** LB ⊗ Closed Nov-Apr

The Maples

★★★★ BED AND BREAKFAST

1 Library Rd, Winton BH9 2QH
☎ 01202 529820
e-mail: jeffreyhurrell@yahoo.co.uk
dir: *1.5m N of town centre. Off A3060 Castle Ln West onto Wimborne Rd, The Maples 1m on right after police station*

A warm welcome awaits you at The Maples, which is just off Winton High Street. The atmosphere is friendly and bedrooms are quiet, comfortable and equipped with considerate extras. Breakfast is enjoyed in the pleasant dining room around a communal table.

Rooms 2 en suite (1 fmly) S £25-£30; D £50-£60* **Facilities** FTV tea/coffee Cen ht Wi-fi **Parking** 2 **Notes** ⊗ No Children 7yrs 🐾

Newlands

★★★★ GUEST ACCOMMODATION

14 Rosemount Rd, Alum Chine BH4 8HB
☎ 01202 761922 📠 01202 769872
e-mail: newlandshotel@totalise.co.uk
web: www.newlandsguesthouse.com
dir: *A338/A35 to Liverpool Victoria rdb, exit for Alum Chine, left at lights, right at small rdbt onto Alumhurst Rd, 3rd left*

A warm welcome is guaranteed at this attractive Edwardian house which is in a quiet area near Alum Chine beach and within easy driving distance of Bournemouth and Poole centres. Offering comfortable accommodation with Wi-fi and a guest lounge.

Rooms 8 en suite (3 fmly) S £26-£35; D £54-£70 **Facilities** TVL tea/coffee Cen ht Wi-fi **Parking** 8 **Notes** LB ⊗ Closed Dec, Jan & Feb

Rosscourt Guest House

★★★★ GUEST ACCOMMODATION

6 St Johns Rd, Boscombe Spa BH5 1EL
☎ 01202 397537
e-mail: enquiries@rosscourthotel.co.uk

Located just a moment's walk from Boscombe town centre, this accommodation is suitable for both business and leisure travellers looking to relax in child-free surroundings. Bedrooms are designed with comfort in mind; en suite shower rooms are well furnished. Guests have access to complimentary Wi-fi and use of the guest lounge. A genuine warm and friendly welcome is assured here, whilst a hearty breakfast sets you up for the day ahead. Off-road parking is an additional plus.

Rooms 8 en suite (1 GF) S £40-£65; D £55-£100 (room only)* **Facilities** FTV TVL tea/coffee Cen ht Wi-fi **Parking** 9 **Notes** LB ⊗ No Children Closed 21-30 Dec RS Jan

Thanet House

★★★★ GUEST ACCOMMODATION

2 Drury Rd, Alum Chine BH4 8HA
☎ 01202 761135
e-mail: stay@thanethouse.co.uk
dir: *Signs for Alum Chine Beach. On corner of Alumhurst Rd & Drury Rd*

A delightful and friendly Edwardian house, ideally located for the Jurassic Coast, the New Forest and within walking distance of Westbourne and Alum Chine beaches. The bedrooms are filled with many homely extras and the whole house can be hired for a party or special event.

Rooms 7 rms (6 en suite) (1 pri facs) (1 fmly) S £30-£37.50; D £60-£75* **Facilities** FTV TVL tea/coffee Cen ht Licensed Wi-fi **Parking** 5 **Notes** LB ⊗

Wood Lodge

★★★★ GUEST ACCOMMODATION

10 Manor Rd, East Cliff BH1 3EY
☎ 01202 290891 📠 01202 290892
e-mail: enquiries@woodlodgehotel.co.uk
web: www.woodlodgehotel.co.uk
dir: *A338 to St Pauls rdbt, 1st exit left. Straight over next 2 rdbts, immediate left*

Expect a warm welcome from this family-run guest accommodation. Set in beautiful gardens minutes from the seafront and a 10 minute walk from the town centre. Bedrooms, which vary in size, are well presented. Home-cooked evening meals and hearty breakfasts are served in the smart dining room.

Rooms 15 rms (14 en suite) (1 pri facs) (1 fmly) (4 GF) S £35-£50; D £70-£100* **Facilities** TVL tea/coffee Dinner available Cen ht Licensed Wi-fi 🎱 🏓 Pool table **Conf** Max 30 Thtr 30 Class 30 Board 30 **Parking** 12 **Notes** LB

The Woodside

★★★★ GUEST HOUSE

29 Southern Rd, Southbourne BH6 3SR
☎ 01202 427213 & 07772 450403
e-mail: enquiries@the-woodside.co.uk
dir: *Follow A35 from Bournemouth. Take B3059 at Pokesdown Station. Right at Boots. Straight on to Southern Rd*

Well located with some off-street parking The Woodside offers comfortable rooms and is run by friendly hosts. Dinner is available by prior arrangement and is served in a light and airy dining room.

Rooms 7 rms (6 en suite) (1 pri facs) D £65-£70 **Facilities** FTV TVL tea/coffee Dinner available Cen ht Wi-fi **Parking** 4 **Notes** LB ⊗ No Children 16yrs

Blue Palms

★★★★ ⒶBED AND BREAKFAST

26 Tregonwell Rd, West Cliff BH2 5NS
☎ 01202 554968 📠 01202 294197
e-mail: bluepalmshotel@btopenworld.com
web: www.bluepalmshotel.com
dir: *Off A338 at Bournemouth West rdbt signed town centre, Triangle, next rdbt onto Durley Chine Rd, at rdbt onto West Hill Rd, Tregonwell Rd 3rd left*

Rooms 9 en suite (1 fmly) (2 GF) S £40-£50; D £65-£90*
Facilities FTV TVL tea/coffee Cen ht Licensed Wi-fi
Parking 8 **Notes** LB ⊗ No Children 5yrs Closed Dec-5 Jan

Carlton Lodge

★★★ GUEST ACCOMMODATION

12 Westby Rd, Boscombe BH5 1HD
☎ 01202 303650 📠 01202 303650
e-mail: enquiries@thecarltonlodge.com
dir: *A338 Wessex Way turn left signed to football ground, right at rdbt, left onto Ashley Rd/Christchurch Rd. 1st right onto Crabton Close Rd, 2nd right onto Westby Rd*

This relaxing home-from-home, family-run guest accommodation is only a five minute stroll from the beach and shopping centre at Boscombe. The en suite bedrooms are spacious and individually decorated. Hearty breakfasts feature home-made preserves and excellent locally sourced bacon and sausages. Bournemouth is a short drive away with Poole, Swanage and Christchurch on the doorstep.

Rooms 5 en suite (2 fmly) (2 GF) S £40-£70; D £60-£80
Facilities FTV tea/coffee Cen ht **Parking** 6 **Notes** LB

Commodore

★★★ INN

Overcliff Dr, Southbourne BH6 3TD
☎ 01202 423150 📠 01202 423519
e-mail: 7688@greeneking.co.uk
web: www.thecommodore.co.uk
dir: *1m E of town centre on seafront*

Situated on the cliff top at Southbourne, the Commodore is adjacent to Fisherman's Walk. Popular with locals, the

bar boasts spectacular views across Poole Bay and serves an extensive range of dishes.

Rooms 12 en suite (1 fmly) **Facilities** tea/coffee Dinner available Cen ht Lift Golf 18 **Conf** Max 30 Thtr 30 Class 18 Board 20 **Parking** 12 **Notes** LB ⊗

Denewood

★★★ GUEST ACCOMMODATION

1 Percy Rd, Boscombe BH5 1JE
☎ 01202 394493 & 309913 📠 01202 391155
e-mail: info@denewood.co.uk
dir: *500yds NE of Boscombe Pier, signed*

Located within walking distance of the beach and Boscombe shopping centre, and close to Bournemouth centre, the Denewood offers individually decorated bedrooms. A full English breakfast is served at individual tables in the delightful dining room, and the beauty salon is perfect for a little indulgence.

Rooms 10 en suite (3 fmly) S £25-£40; D £50-£80*
Facilities FTV TVL tea/coffee Cen ht Wi-fi Golf 18 health & beauty salon **Conf** Thtr 35 Class 30 Board 20 **Parking** 14 **Notes** LB

The Hop Inn

★★★ INN

6 Westcliff Rd BH2 5EY
☎ 01202 244626
e-mail: thehopinn@btinternet.com
dir: *A31 Bournemouth Wessex Way, left at Bournemouth West rdbt, follow signs for BIC, Hop Inn on left*

Centrally located on the West Cliff, The Hop Inn offers light, airy modern en suite accommodation in a contemporary style. The busy bar with big screens shows all major sporting events; there is a lively atmosphere and meals are available in the evening. Groups are welcome by arrangement.

Rooms 12 en suite **Facilities** STV tea/coffee Dinner available Cen ht Wi-fi Golf 18 Pool table **Parking** 3 **Notes** No coaches

Pinedale

★★★ GUEST ACCOMMODATION

40 Tregonwell Rd, West Cliff BH2 5NT
☎ 01202 553733 & 292702 📠 01202 553733
e-mail: thepinedalehotel@btconnect.com
dir: *A338 at Bournemouth West rdbt, signs to West Cliff, Tregonwell Rd 3rd left after passing Wessex Hotel*

This friendly guest accommodation is enthusiastically run by two generations of the same family, and offers comfortable accommodation within a short walk of the seafront and local attractions. The fresh-looking bedrooms are equipped with useful extras. There is also an attractive licensed bar and an airy dining room where you can enjoy wholesome home-cooked meals.

Rooms 15 rms (10 en suite) (1 fmly) S £20-£40; D £40-£80* **Facilities** TVL tea/coffee Dinner available Direct Dial Licensed Wi-fi **Parking** 15 **Notes** ⊗

Trouville Lodge

★★★ GUEST ACCOMMODATION

9 Priory Rd BH2 5DF
☎ 01202 552262 📠 01202 293324
e-mail: reception@trouvillehotel.com

Professionally run, this well managed establishment offers an impressive standard of accommodation and facilities. Bedrooms are situated in an annexe to the Trouville Hotel next door. All rooms are stylishly appointed and comfortably furnished. Facilities are in the hotel. The Deauville restaurant offers a very good menu choice, and the well-stocked Le Café Bar provides an informal and pleasant environment. There is also a large pool and sauna as well as a resident beautician.

Rooms 19 en suite (4 fmly) (4 GF) S £40.95-£50.95; D £81.90-£101.90 (room only) **Facilities** FTV tea/coffee Cen ht Wi-fi **Parking** 14 **Notes** LB

BRIDPORT	Map 4 SY49

See also Chideock

PREMIER COLLECTION

The Shave Cross Inn

★★★★★ 🍴 INN

Marshwood Vale DT6 6HW
☎ 01308 868358 📠 01308 867064
e-mail: roy.warburton@virgin.net
web: www.theshavecrossinn.co.uk
dir: *From B3165 turn at Birdsmoorgate and follow brown signs.*

This historic inn has been providing refreshment to weary travellers for centuries and continues to offer a warm and genuine welcome. The snug bar is dominated by a wonderful fireplace with crackling logs creating just the right atmosphere. Bedrooms are located in a separate Dorset flint and stone building. Quality is impressive throughout with wonderful stone floors and oak beams, combined with feature beds and luxurious bathrooms. Food, using excellent local produce, has a distinct Caribbean and international slant, including a number of authentic dishes.

Rooms 7 en suite (1 fmly) (3 GF) **Facilities** STV FTV tea/coffee Dinner available Direct Dial Cen ht Wi-fi Pool table **Parking** 29 **Notes** No Children RS Mon (ex BH) Closed for lunch & dinner No coaches

BRIDPORT *continued*

The Roundham House

★★★★★ GUEST ACCOMMODATION

Roundham Gardens, West Bay Rd DT6 4BD
☎ 01308 422753 📄 01308 421500
e-mail: cyprencom@compuserve.com
dir: *A35 into Bridport, at Crown Inn rdbt take exit signed West Bay. House 400yds on left*

The hosts here are always on hand to welcome guests to their lovely home, which has well-tended gardens and views to the coast. Bedrooms come in a variety of sizes and are filled with useful extras. Public areas include a comfortable lounge and well-appointed dining room.

Rooms 8 rms (7 en suite) (1 fmly) S £52-£58; D £92-£98* **Facilities** FTV tea/coffee Cen ht Licensed Wi-fi **Parking** 10 **Notes** No Children 6yrs Closed Dec-Feb

Willowhayne Farm

★★★★ BED AND BREAKFAST

DT6 6HY
☎ 01297 489042
e-mail: wickes@willowhayne.co.uk
dir: *A35 E of Chideock, turn S towards sea (by speed camera), last house on left (with flag pole)*

This lovely farmhouse has now been updated to provide an engaging blend of traditional and contemporary. Situated just a 15-minute walk from the Jurassic Coast, its setting is stunning with views across the rolling countryside. Bedrooms have a wonderful outlook and provide equal measures of comfort and quality, allied with stunning modern bathrooms. The atmosphere here is relaxed and homely, typified by the convivial breakfasts (using local produce) served around the dining room table.

Rooms 2 en suite D £70-£80* **Facilities** FTV TVL tea/coffee Cen ht Wi-fi Golf 18 Fishing **Parking** 6 **Notes** LB No Children 16yrs 🐾

Britmead House

★★★★ GUEST ACCOMMODATION

West Bay Rd DT6 4EG
☎ 01308 422941 & 07973 725243
e-mail: britmead@talk21.com
web: www.britmeadhouse.co.uk
dir: *1m S of town centre, off A35 onto West Bay Rd*

Britmead House is located south of Bridport, within easy reach of the town centre and West Bay harbour. Family-run, the atmosphere is friendly and the accommodation well-appointed and comfortable. Suitable for business and leisure, many guests return regularly. A choice of breakfast is served in the light and airy dining room.

Rooms 8 en suite (2 fmly) (2 GF) S £40-£58; D £64-£80 **Facilities** FTV TVL tea/coffee Cen ht Wi-fi **Parking** 12 **Notes** LB Closed 24-27 Dec

Oxbridge Farm (SY475977)

★★★★ FARMHOUSE

DT6 3UA
☎ 01308 488368 & 07766 086543
Mrs C Marshall
e-mail: jojokillin@hotmail.com
web: www.oxbridgefarm.co.uk
dir: *From A3066 Bridport to Beaminster. Take 1st right signed Oxbridge 1m*

Oxbridge Farm sits in the rolling hills of West Dorset in an Area of Outstanding Natural Beauty. The bedrooms are well equipped and offer a very good degree of comfort. A hearty breakfast is served in the attractive dining room overlooking the wonderful views.

Rooms 3 rms (2 en suite) (1 pri facs) (2 fmly) **Facilities** FTV TVL tea/coffee Dinner available Cen ht Wi-fi Golf 18 **Parking** 6 **Notes** LB 🐾 🐾 40 acres sheep

Rose Cottage

★★★★ BED AND BREAKFAST

Main St DT6 6JQ
☎ 01297 489994 & 07980 400904
e-mail: enquiries@rosecottage-chideock.co.uk
web: www.rosecottage-chideock.co.uk
dir: *On A35 in village centre, on left in W direction*

Located in the centre of a charming village, this 300-year-old cottage provides very well-appointed, attractive accommodation and a friendly welcome is assured. A delicious breakfast can be enjoyed in the renovated dining room which has many interesting features, and in finer weather guests can relax in the pretty garden.

Rooms 2 en suite S £55; D £70* **Facilities** FTV tea/coffee Cen ht Wi-fi **Parking** 2 **Notes** LB 🐾 No Children 12yrs Closed 31 Dec

Warren House

★★★★ GUEST ACCOMMODATION

DT6 6JW
☎ 01297 489996
e-mail: kathy@warren-house.com
dir: *Off A35 in village centre signed North Chideock, parking signed 60yds*

Expect a friendly welcome on arriving at this thatched long house, built in the early 17th century, and situated in this picturesque Dorset village. Bedrooms, which are all named after local hills, are spacious and comfortable. Enjoy afternoon tea in the secluded garden. Private parking is available.

Rooms 4 en suite (2 fmly) **Facilities** FTV tea/coffee Cen ht Wi-fi **Parking** 5 **Notes** Closed Xmas 🐾

Druid House

★★★★★ 🏆 GUEST ACCOMMODATION

26 Sopers Ln BH23 1JE
☎ 01202 485615 📄 01202 473484
e-mail: reservations@druid-house.co.uk
web: www.druid-house.co.uk
dir: *A35 exit Christchurch main rdbt onto Sopers Ln, establishment on left*

Overlooking the park, this delightful family-run establishment is just a stroll from the high street, the priory and the quay. Bedrooms, some with balconies, are very comfortably furnished, and have many welcome extras including CD players. There is a pleasant rear garden, patio and relaxing lounge and bar areas.

Rooms 8 en suite (3 fmly) (4 GF) S £35-£60; D £70-£96* **Facilities** STV tea/coffee Direct Dial Cen ht Licensed **Parking** 8 **Notes** LB 🐾

The Lord Bute & Restaurant

★★★★★ ⚜ GUEST ACCOMMODATION

179-181 Lymington Rd, Highcliffe on Sea BH23 4JS
☎ 01425 278884 📄 01425 279258
e-mail: mail@lordbute.co.uk
web: www.lordbute.co.uk
dir: *A337 towards Highcliffe*

The elegant Lord Bute stands directly behind the original entrance lodges of Highcliffe Castle close to the beach and historic town of Christchurch. Bedrooms have been finished to a very high standard with many thoughtful extras including spa baths. Excellent food is available in the smart restaurant, and conferences and weddings are catered for.

Rooms 9 en suite 4 annexe en suite (1 fmly) (6 GF) **Facilities** FTV tea/coffee Dinner available Direct Dial Cen ht Licensed **Conf** Max 25 Thtr 25 Class 15 Board 18 **Parking** 40 **Notes** LB RS Mon Restaurant closed (open bkfst)

Save on B&Bs and Hotels. Book at **theAA.com/hotel**

DORSET 133 **ENGLAND**

The Manor

★★★★★ 🅰 GUEST ACCOMMODATION

15-17 Salisbury Rd, Burton BH23 7JG
☎ 01202 477189 📄 0872 110 8939
e-mail: info@themanorchristchurch.co.uk
dir: *Off A35 Christchurch Bypass onto Salisbury Rd*

Rooms 10 en suite (1 fmly) S £55-£65; D £80-£95*
Facilities FTV TVL tea/coffee Dinner available Cen ht
Licensed Wi-fi **Conf** Max 20 Thtr 20 Class 20 Board 20
Parking 100 **Notes** LB

Windy Willums

★★★★ BED AND BREAKFAST

38 Island View Av BH23 4DS
☎ 01425 277046 & 07973 235082
e-mail: enquiries@windywillums.co.uk
dir: *A35 Somerford rdbt take A337 for Highcliffe, mini-rdbt last exit 2nd left after Sandpiper pub*

Just a two minute walk from Mudeford beach, this
establishment is an ideal base for windsurfing, sailing or
for exploring the New Forest. The proprietor is passionate
about gardening and has created a truly beautiful and
peaceful outdoor space for guests to relax in.

Rooms 3 rms (2 en suite) (1 pri facs) (3 fmly) S £35-£60;
D £60-£80* **Facilities** FTV tea/coffee Cen ht Wi-fi
Parking 3 **Notes** LB ⊗ No Children 8yrs 🐾

Ashbourne

★★★★ GUEST ACCOMMODATION

47 Stour Rd BH23 1LN
☎ 01202 475574 📄 01202 482905
e-mail: ashcroftb@hotmail.com
dir: *A35 (Christchurch to Bournemouth), left at lights
onto Stour Rd, over lights, 4th house on right*

Convenient for the historic market town of Christchurch,
the scenic River Stour, the New Forest and nearby
beaches, this delightful guest house provides a relaxed
and friendly environment. Bedrooms and bathrooms are
all neatly furnished and equipped with many extra
facilities. Large cooked breakfasts are served in the
bright dining room.

Rooms 7 rms (5 en suite) (2 pri facs) (1 fmly) S £45-£50;
D £60-£70 **Facilities** STV tea/coffee Cen ht Wi-fi
Parking 6 **Notes** ⊗ Closed Xmas & New Year 🐾

Beautiful South

★★★★ BED AND BREAKFAST

87 Barrack Rd BH23 2AJ
☎ 01202 568183 & 07958 597686
e-mail: kevin.lovett1@ntlworld.com
web: www.christchurchbandb.co.uk
dir: *0.25m from Christchurch town centre on A35, opp
Pizza Hut at Bailey Bridge*

A convenient location near to the main road on the
outskirts of Christchurch makes this friendly bed and

breakfast a good choice for leisure and business. Totally
refurbished throughout by the proprietor, public areas
and bedrooms are bright and inviting, and hearty dinners,
by arrangement, can be enjoyed in the pleasantly
appointed dining room.

Rooms 3 en suite (1 fmly) **Facilities** FTV tea/coffee Dinner
available Cen ht Wi-fi **Parking** 4 **Notes** ⊗ 🐾

Bure Farmhouse

★★★★ BED AND BREAKFAST

107 Bure Ln, Friars Cliff BH23 4DN
☎ 01425 275498
e-mail: info@burefarmhouse.co.uk
dir: *A35 & A337 E from Christchurch towards Highcliffe,
1st rdbt right onto The Runway. Bure Lane 3rd turn sharp
right onto service road, farmhouse on left*

A friendly welcome is assured at this family home.
Individually decorated bedrooms offer comfort and
provide useful extras. Hearty breakfasts are served
farmhouse style in the dining room overlooking the
attractive gardens.

Rooms 3 rms (2 en suite) (1 pri facs) (1 fmly) **Facilities**
tea/coffee Cen ht **Parking** 3 **Notes** LB ⊗ No Children 4yrs
🐾

Grosvenor Lodge

★★★★ GUEST HOUSE

53 Stour Rd BH23 1LN
☎ 01202 499008 📄 01202 486041
e-mail: bookings@grosvenorlodge.co.uk
dir: *A35 from Christchurch to Bournemouth, at 1st lights
left onto Stour Rd, Lodge on right*

A friendly and popular guest house near the centre of this
historic town. The bedrooms are brightly and individually
decorated and have lots of useful extras. Hearty
breakfasts are served in the cheerful dining room and
there is an extensive selection of local restaurants for
lunch and dinner.

Rooms 7 en suite (4 fmly) (1 GF) **Facilities** FTV tea/coffee
Cen ht Wi-fi **Parking** 10 **Notes** ⊗

Riversmead

★★★★ GUEST ACCOMMODATION

61 Stour Rd BH23 1LN
☎ 01202 487195
e-mail: riversmead.dorset@googlemail.com
dir: *A338 to Christchurch. Left turn to town centre, turn
right over railway bridge*

Ideally located close to the town centre, beaches and the
New Forest with excellent access to all local transport,
Riversmead is the perfect base for a short break or longer
stay. This comfortable house offers a range of facilities
including enclosed off-road parking, fridges in rooms and
an excellent breakfast.

Rooms 3 en suite (1 fmly) S £45; D £50-£70*
Facilities FTV tea/coffee Cen ht Wi-fi **Parking** 9 **Notes** LB
⊗ 🐾

The Rothesay

★★★★ GUEST ACCOMMODATION

175, Lymington Rd, Highcliffe BH23 4JS
☎ 01425 274172
e-mail: reservations@therothesayhotel.com
web: www.therothesayhotel.com
dir: *A337 to Highcliffe towards The Castle, 1m on left*

Set on the edge of Highcliffe village, the Rothesay is a
great base for exploring the Dorset-Hampshire coast.
Highcliffe Castle is just a 5 minute walk away, and there
are clifftop walks and views to the Isle of Wight. The
indoor pool is a real benefit, as are the pretty gardens
and large car park.

Rooms 12 en suite 3 annexe en suite (1 fmly) (7 GF)
Facilities FTV TVL tea/coffee Cen ht Licensed Wi-fi 🕓
Sauna Pool table **Conf** Max 30 Thtr 30 Class 30 Board 30
Parking 21 **Notes** ⊗ No Children 8yrs

The White House

★★★★ GUEST ACCOMMODATION

428 Lymington Rd, Highcliffe On Sea BH23 5HF
☎ 01425 271279 📄 01425 276900
e-mail: enquiries@thewhitehouse-christchurch.co.uk
dir: *Off A35, signs to Highcliffe. After rdbt The White
House 200yds on right*

This charming Victorian house is just a short drive from
Highcliffe beach, the New Forest and the historic town of
Christchurch. Comfortable, well-appointed
accommodation is provided, and a generous, freshly-
cooked breakfast is served in the cosy dining room.

Rooms 6 en suite **Facilities** tea/coffee Cen ht Wi-fi
Parking 6 **Notes** LB ⊗

CHRISTCHURCH *continued*

Brantwood Guest House

★★★ GUEST ACCOMMODATION

55 Stour Rd BH23 1LN
☎ 01202 473446 📠 01202 473446
e-mail: brantwoodbookings@gmail.com
dir: *A338 Bournemouth, 1st exit to Christchurch, right after railway bridge, cross lights, 200yds on right*

Relaxed and friendly guest accommodation where the proprietors create a home-from-home atmosphere. Bedrooms and bathrooms are all well decorated and comfortably furnished. The town centre is just a stroll away and off-road parking is available.

Rooms 5 rms (4 en suite) (1 pri facs) (2 fmly) (1 GF) S £25-£35; D £45-£60* **Facilities** tea/coffee Cen ht Wi-fi **Parking** 5 **Notes** ⊗ Ⓔ

Southern Comfort Guest House

★★★ GUEST ACCOMMODATION

51 Stour Rd BH23 1LN
☎ 01202 471373
e-mail: scomfortgh@aol.com
dir: *A338 onto B3073 towards Christchurch, 2m onto B3059 (Stour Rd)*

Convenient for Bournemouth, Christchurch and Southbourne, this practical and friendly guest accommodation offers spacious bedrooms. Breakfast, served in the bright lounge-dining room, is a relaxed affair with a good choice of hot items.

Rooms 3 en suite (3 fmly) S £25-£30; D £50-£70* **Facilities** TVL tea/coffee Cen ht Wi-fi **Parking** 4 **Notes** LB ⊗

Three Gables

★★★ BED AND BREAKFAST

11 Wickfield Av BH23 1JB
☎ 01202 481166
e-mail: enquiries@3gables-christchurch.co.uk
web: www.3gables-christchurch.co.uk
dir: *A35 to Christchurch, at Fountain rdbt exit onto Sopers Ln. 1st left onto Wickfield Av*

Located in a residential area and only five minutes walk from the town centre, this family-run establishment offers comfortable bedrooms and bathrooms which have been recently redecorated. Wi-fi is available throughout the house. Breakfast is served at the communal table in the dining room and there is off-road parking.

Rooms 3 en suite (2 fmly) S £50; D £70* **Facilities** tea/coffee Cen ht Wi-fi **Parking** 5 **Notes** LB ⊗ Ⓔ

CORFE MULLEN Map 4 SY99

Kenways

★★★ BED AND BREAKFAST

90a Wareham Rd BH21 3LQ
☎ 01202 694655
e-mail: eileen@kenways.com
web: www.kenways.com
dir: *2m SW of Wimborne. Off A31 to Corfe Mullen. Over B3074 rdbt, B&B 0.3m on right*

Expect to be welcomed as one of the family at this homely bed and breakfast between Wimborne Minster and Poole. The spacious bedrooms are well provisioned with thoughtful extras, and breakfast is served in the pleasant conservatory overlooking the attractive gardens.

Rooms 3 rms (3 pri facs) (2 GF) **Facilities** FTV TVL tea/coffee Cen ht Wi-fi Table tennis Snooker table **Parking** 4 **Notes** Ⓔ

DORCHESTER Map 4 SY69

PREMIER COLLECTION

Little Court

★★★★★ 🏠 GUEST ACCOMMODATION

5 Westleaze, Charminster DT2 9PZ
☎ 01305 261576 📠 01305 261359
e-mail: info@littlecourt.net
dir: *A37 from Dorchester, 0.25m right at Loders Garage, Little Court 0.5m on right*

Built in 1909 in the style of Lutyens, Little Court sits in over four acres of attractive grounds and gardens. The property has been appointed to a very high standard and the friendly proprietors are on hand to ensure a pleasant stay. A delicious breakfast, including home-grown produce, can be enjoyed in the stylish dining room.

Rooms 8 en suite (1 fmly) **Facilities** FTV tea/coffee Cen ht Licensed Wi-fi ⚲ ⛳ Golf **Parking** 10 **Notes** LB ⊗ Closed Xmas & New Year

---

Baytree House Dorchester

★★★★ BED AND BREAKFAST

4 Athelstan Rd DT1 1NR
☎ 01305 263696
e-mail: info@baytreedorchester.com
dir: *0.5m SE of town centre*

Friendly, family-run bed and breakfast situated in the heart of Dorchester, not far from the village of Higher Bockham - the birthplace of Thomas Hardy. Bedrooms are furnished in an appealing contemporary style and provide high levels of comfort. Breakfast is farmhouse style in the open-plan kitchen/dining area. Parking is available.

Rooms 3 en suite **Facilities** FTV TVL tea/coffee Cen ht **Parking** 3 **Notes** LB ⊗ ⊗ Ⓔ

Beggars Knap

★★★★ GUEST ACCOMMODATION

2 Weymouth Av DT1 1QS
☎ 01305 268191 & 07768 690691
e-mail: beggarsknap@hotmail.co.uk

Conveniently situated in the heart of the town, this renovated, detached Victorian property has connections with the local brewery and Thomas Hardy. Guests are greeted with warmth and in an efficient manner. The bedrooms are spacious and furnished in a variety of styles. The freshly-cooked breakfast, using the best of locally sourced ingredients, are served at one large table. Off-street parking is available.

Rooms 3 en suite (2 fmly) **Facilities** TVL tea/coffee Cen ht **Parking** 3 **Notes** RS Xmas & New Year open by reservation only Ⓔ

Westwood House

★★★★ GUEST ACCOMMODATION

29 High West St DT1 1UP
☎ 01305 268018
e-mail: reservations@westwoodhouse.co.uk
web: www.westwoodhouse.co.uk
dir: *On B2150 in town centre*

Originally built in 1815, Westwood House is centrally located in the historic town of Dorchester and is ideal for leisure visitors as well as business travellers. This attractive property, run by a husband and wife team, offers well-appointed rooms with modern facilities presented in an informal, stylish environment.

Rooms 7 rms (5 en suite) (2 pri facs) (2 fmly) **Facilities** FTV tea/coffee Cen ht Wi-fi **Notes** ⊗

Bramlies

★★★ BED AND BREAKFAST

107 Bridport Rd DT1 2NH
☎ **01305 265778**
e-mail: bramlies@btinternet.com
web: www.bramlies.co.uk
dir: On B3150 on W side of Dorchester

A traditional bed and breakfast on the outskirts of the town and within easy walking distance of the centre, and close to the hospital. The hospitality is excellent and the proprietors do all they can to make guests feel at home.

Rooms 1 en suite 2 annexe en suite (1 fmly) (2 GF) S £38-£50; D £68-£85* **Facilities** FTV tea/coffee Cen ht Wi-fi **Parking** 5 **Notes** LB ⊗ ⊕

EVERSHOT   Map 4 ST50

The Acorn Inn

★★★★ ⊕ INN

DT2 0JW
☎ **01935 83228** 🖷 **01935 83707**
e-mail: stay@acorn-inn.co.uk
web: www.acorn-inn.co.uk
dir: 0.5m off A37 between Yeovil & Dorchester, signed Evershot & Holywell

This delightful 16th-century coaching inn is located in the heart of the village. Several of the bedrooms feature interesting four-poster beds, and all the rooms have been individually decorated and furnished. The public rooms retain many original features including oak panelling, open fires and stone-flagged floors. Fresh local produce is included on the varied menu.

Rooms 10 en suite (2 fmly) S £79-£89; D £99-£149 **Facilities** FTV TVL tea/coffee Dinner available Direct Dial Cen ht Wi-fi Pool table Use of spa opposite - charged **Conf** Max 30 Thtr 30 Board 30 **Parking** 40 **Notes** LB

FARNHAM   Map 4 ST91

PREMIER COLLECTION

Farnham Farm House

★★★★★ GUEST ACCOMMODATION

DT11 8DG
☎ **01725 516254** 🖷 **01725 516306**
e-mail: info@farnhamfarmhouse.co.uk
dir: Off A354 Thickthorn x-rds into Farnham, continue NW from village centre T-junct, 1m bear right at sign

A country house on 350 acres of arable farmland, offering a high level of quality, comfort and service. The atmosphere is friendly and the accommodation charming and spacious. In winter, a log fire burns in the attractive dining room, where a delicious breakfast, featuring local produce, is served; from here views across the rolling countryside can be enjoyed. Added features include an outdoor pool and the Sarpenela Natural Therapies Centre in the converted stable.

Rooms 3 en suite (1 fmly) S £60-£70; D £75-£90* **Facilities** FTV tea/coffee ↘ ⤇ Holistic Therapies Centre **Parking** 7 **Notes** ⊗ Closed 25-26 Dec

---

The Museum Inn

★★★★ ⊕⊕ INN

DT11 8DE
☎ **01725 516261** 🖷 **01725 516988**
e-mail: enquiries@museuminn.co.uk
dir: Village signed off A354 Blandford to Salisbury road

Located in a peaceful Dorset village, this traditional style inn offers cosy log fires, flagstone floors and a welcoming bar combined with efficient service and a friendly welcome. Bedrooms include larger, stylish rooms in the main building or a selection of cosy rooms in an adjacent building. Food here, whether dinner or breakfast, utilises the finest quality produce and should not be missed.

Rooms 4 en suite 4 annexe en suite (4 GF) S fr £110; D £140-£170* **Facilities** FTV tea/coffee Dinner available Direct Dial Cen ht Wi-fi Golf 18 **Conf** Max 40 Thtr 40 Class 40 Board 40 **Parking** 14 **Notes** No coaches

---

FERNDOWN   Map 5 SU00

City Lodge

★★★★ GUEST ACCOMMODATION

Ringwood Rd BH22 9AN
☎ **01202 578828** 🖷 **01202 572620**
e-mail: bournemouth@citylodge.co.uk

Close to Bournemouth and the airport, City Lodge provides an ideal base for exploring the Dorset coastline. Situated on the edge of the River Stour, many of the rooms have the benefit of beautiful riverside views. Recently refurbished, offering modern facilities such as en suite bathrooms, LCD TVs and free Wi-fi. A large bar and restaurant serve meals and snacks while parking is gated and secure.

Rooms 45 en suite (4 fmly) (11 GF) S £29.95-£89.95; D £29.95-£89.95 (room only) **Facilities** FTV tea/coffee Dinner available Cen ht Licensed Wi-fi Fishing **Conf** Max 120 Thtr 80 Class 60 Board 40 **Parking** 300 **Notes** LB ⊗ Civ Wed 120

HIGHCLIFFE

For accommodation details see Christchurch

LOWER ANSTY   Map 4 ST70

The Fox Inn

★★★★ INN

DT2 7PN
☎ **01258 880328** 🖷 **01258 881440**
e-mail: fox@anstyfoxinn.co.uk
web: www.anstyfoxinn.co.uk
dir: Off A354 at Millbourne St Andrew, follow brown signs to Ansty

This popular inn has a long and interesting history including strong links to the Hall & Woodhouse Brewery. Surrounded by beautiful Dorset countryside, this is a great base for exploring the area. Bedrooms are smartly appointed and offer high levels of comfort. The interesting menu focuses on excellent local produce, with a choice of dining options including the oak-panelled dining room. An extensive garden and patio area are also available.

Rooms 11 en suite (7 fmly) S £50-£75; D £60-£125 **Facilities** FTV TVL tea/coffee Dinner available Direct Dial Cen ht Wi-fi **Conf** Max 60 Thtr 60 Class 40 Board 45 **Parking** 30 **Notes** LB

See also Axminster (Devon)

Old Lyme Guest House

★ ★ ★ ★ GUEST ACCOMMODATION

29 Coombe St DT7 3PP
☎ **01297 442929**
e-mail: oldlyme.guesthouse@virgin.net
web: www.oldlymeguesthouse.co.uk
dir: *In town centre onto Coombe St at lights*

Comfort is a high priority at this delightful 18th-century former post office, which is just a short walk from the seafront. Bedrooms, which vary in size, are all well equipped and include many thoughtful extras. A wide choice is offered at breakfast, served in the cheerful dining room.

Rooms 5 rms (4 en suite) (1 pri facs) (1 fmly) D £76-£85* **Facilities** FTV TVL tea/coffee Cen ht Wi-fi **Notes** LB ⊗ No Children 5yrs ⊜

St Cuthberts

★ ★ ★ ★ BED AND BREAKFAST

Charmouth Rd DT7 3HG
☎ **01297 445901**
e-mail: info@stcuthbertsoflyme.co.uk
web: www.stcuthbertsoflyme.co.uk
dir: *A35 from Dorchester, at Charmouth rdbt onto B3052 for 2m. Next to Timbervale Caravan Park on right*

Located just a ten minute walk above the main town and harbour, this detached home is set within mature gardens and has its own parking. Bedrooms and bathrooms offer plenty of quality and comfort as well as many extras to add to guest enjoyment. A lounge with log burner is available in addition to a decked terrace. Breakfast, served around one large table, offers a varied choice including delicious pancakes with bacon and maple syrup.

Rooms 3 en suite (1 GF) S fr £60; D £80-£85* **Facilities** FTV TVL tea/coffee Cen ht Golf 18 **Parking** 3 **Notes** ⊗ No Children 7yrs ⊜

Albany

★ ★ ★ ★ GUEST ACCOMMODATION

Charmouth Rd DT7 3DP
☎ **01297 443066**
e-mail: albany@lymeregis.com
dir: *300yds NE of town centre on A3052*

Situated on the outskirts of this popular town and within easy walking distance of the seafront, this attractive house provides comfortable accommodation and a home-from-home atmosphere. Bedrooms are comfortably furnished, the public rooms are inviting and guests are welcome to use the garden. Breakfast, featuring local ingredients, is served in the homely dining room.

Rooms 6 en suite (1 fmly) (1 GF) S £39-£42; D £68-£80* **Facilities** FTV TVL tea/coffee Cen ht Wi-fi **Parking** 6 **Notes** ⊗ No Children 5yrs ⊜

Cleveland

★ ★ ★ ★ BED AND BREAKFAST

Pound St DT7 3JA
☎ **01297 442012**
e-mail: clevelandlyme@aol.com
dir: *A3052 Lyme Regis/Sidmouth road, 250yds up hill from Lyme Regis High St*

Delightfully positioned just a short stroll from the main high street and a five-minute walk to the sea, this relaxing bed and breakfast offers a range of welcome extras including the benefit of off-street parking. The stylish bedrooms and bathrooms have now been completed to modern standards, as has the comfortable breakfast room where a range of carefully chosen produce is available.

Rooms 2 en suite (2 GF) S £70-£84; D £80-£89 **Facilities** FTV tea/coffee Cen ht Wi-fi **Parking** 3 **Notes** ⊗ No Children 18yrs ⊜

The Mariners

★ ★ ★ ★ ⊛ INN

Silver St DT7 3HS
☎ **01297 442753** 📠 **01297 442431**
e-mail: enquiry@hotellymeregis.co.uk
dir: *From A35 onto A3052 to Lyme Regis. In town bear right onto Silver St. 350mtrs to The Mariners*

Now refurbished throughout, this delightful building combines traditional character and ambience with a modern and stylish upgrade. Bedrooms and bathrooms vary in space, but include a range of welcome extras;q many have views over the bay. Public areas include a relaxing lounge, comfortable bar and modern restaurant. Guests can choose a full dinner, utilising local fish and seafood, or a varied range of lighter options from the bar menu. Outdoor seating is available.

Rooms 14 en suite (2 fmly) S fr £65; D fr £100* **Facilities** FTV tea/coffee Dinner available Direct Dial Cen ht Wi-fi **Conf** Max 30 Thtr 24 Class 16 Board 30 **Parking** 16 **Notes** LB ⊗

Fishmore Hill Farm *(ST799013)*

★ ★ ★ FARMHOUSE

DT11 0DL
☎ **01258 881122** & **07708 003561** 📠 **01258 881122**
Mr & Mrs N Clarke
e-mail: sarah@fishmorehillfarm.com
dir: *Off A354 signed Milton Abbas, 3m left on sharp bend, up steep hill, 1st left*

This working sheep farm and family home is surrounded by beautiful Dorset countryside, close to historic Milton Abbas and only a short drive from the coast. Bedrooms,

which vary in size, are comfortable and have useful extras. The atmosphere is friendly and relaxed. Breakfast is served in the smart dining room around a communal table.

Rooms 3 en suite S £35; D £70* **Facilities** TVL tea/coffee Cen ht **Parking** 4 **Notes** Closed Xmas & New Year ⊜ 50 acres sheep/horses

The Coppleridge Inn

★ ★ ★ INN

SP7 9HW
☎ **01747 851980** 📠 **01747 851858**
e-mail: thecoppleridgeinn@btinternet.com
web: www.coppleridge.com
dir: *Off A350 to Motcombe, under railway bridge, 400yds right to Mere, inn 300yds on left*

This village inn set within its own 15 acres of land offers ten en suite bedrooms located in a pretty courtyard. All have been refurbished to a very high standard providing a very comfortable stay. Staff offer a warm welcome, and the inn serves good food with many daily specials. There are tennis courts and Boules, plus a children's play area. Clay pigeon shooting can also be arranged.

Rooms 10 en suite (2 fmly) (10 GF) S £50; D £90* **Facilities** FTV TVL tea/coffee Dinner available Direct Dial Cen ht Wi-fi ch fac ⚲ Pool table boules pitch **Conf** Max 60 Thtr 60 Class 60 Board 30 **Parking** 100 **Notes** LB Civ Wed 80

Longpuddle

★ ★ ★ ★ BED AND BREAKFAST

4 High St DT2 7TD
☎ **01300 348532**
e-mail: ann@longpuddle.co.uk
dir: *From Dorchester (A35) take B3143, after entering village 1st thatched house on left after village cross*

This purpose-built annexed accommodation is perfectly located for exploring the delightful Dorset countryside and coast. Bedrooms are spacious, very well furnished and equipped with thoughtful extras such as mini fridges. Breakfast is served in the dining room of the main house, where a guest lounge is also located overlooking the lovely gardens.

Rooms 2 annexe en suite (2 fmly) S £50-£60; D £80-£90* **Facilities** FTV TVL tea/coffee Cen ht Wi-fi **Parking** 3 **Notes** RS Dec-Jan Prior bookings only ⊜

Save on B&Bs and Hotels. Book at **theAA.com/hotel**

DORSET 137 **ENGLAND**

PIDDLETRENTHIDE — Map 4 SY79

The Piddle Inn

★★★★ INN

DT2 7QF
☎ 01300 348468 ☐ 01300 348102
e-mail: piddleinn@aol.com
web: www.piddleinn.co.uk
dir: *7m N of Dorchester on B3143 in middle of Piddletrenthide*

This inn is situated deep in the heart of the Dorset countryside in the Piddle Valley. Fresh flowers are put in each bedroom and most have lovely views. Dinner is served in the friendly bar downstairs, and the menu includes the fresh fish of the day. The gardens are perfect for alfresco dining.

Rooms 3 en suite (1 fmly) **Facilities** tea/coffee Dinner available Direct Dial Cen ht Wi-fi Golf 18 Pool table **Parking** 15 **Notes** No coaches

PLUSH — Map 4 ST70

The Brace of Pheasants

★★★★ INN

DT2 7RQ
☎ 01300 348357
e-mail: info@braceofpheasants.co.uk
web: www.braceofpheasants.co.uk
dir: *A35 onto B3142, right to Plush 1.5m*

Situated in the heart of Dorset, this picturesque thatched pub offers a warm and genuine welcome to both visitors and locals alike. Very much a real pub, the atmosphere is convivial, with plenty of good-natured banter. Bedrooms are split between the main building and the former skittle alley - all offer exceptional standards of comfort and individual style with wonderful bathrooms. The food here should not be missed, with excellent local produce used throughout the appealing menu.

Rooms 4 en suite 4 annexe en suite (4 GF) S £89; D £99* **Facilities** FTV tea/coffee Dinner available Direct Dial Cen ht Wi-fi **Parking** 15 **Notes** Closed 25 Dec

POOLE — Map 4 SZ09

Bona Vista Bed & Breakfast

★★★★ BED AND BREAKFAST

36 Sea View Rd, Upton BH16 5NG
☎ 01202 622675
e-mail: leonora.godfrey@tiscali.co.uk
web: www.bonavista.org.uk
dir: *From A31 onto A350 Sbound signed Upton, at rdbt (A35/A350) take 2nd exit. 0.5m 2nd exit at mini-rdbt onto Dorchester Rd, 3rd left onto Sea View Rd. Bona Vista at end of road on left*

A warm welcome and an attentive service are offered at this family-run bed and breakfast located in a residential area. The one bedroom is of a generous size and offers all modern amenities. Guests have the choice of having breakfast in their room or the patio during warm months.

Rooms 1 en suite (1 GF) **Facilities** STV FTV tea/coffee Cen ht Wi-fi **Parking Notes** ☺

Acorns

★★★★ GUEST ACCOMMODATION

264 Wimborne Rd, Oakdale BH15 3EF
☎ 01202 672901 ☐ 01202 672901
e-mail: enquiries@acornsguesthouse.co.uk
web: www.acornsguesthouse.co.uk
dir: *On A35, approx 1m from town centre, opp Esso station*

A warm welcome is assured at Acorns, located with easy access to the town, ferry terminal, business parks and attractions. The bedrooms are furnished to a high standard, and an English breakfast is served in the charming dining room. There is also a quiet cosy lounge.

Rooms 4 en suite (1 GF) D £65-£72 **Facilities** FTV TVL tea/coffee Cen ht Wi-fi **Parking** 6 **Notes** LB ☒ No Children 14yrs Closed 23 Dec-1 Jan ☺

Milsoms Poole

★★★★ RESTAURANT WITH ROOMS

47 Haven Rd, Canford Cliffs BH13 7LH
☎ 01202 609000
e-mail: poole@milsomshotel.co.uk

Milsoms Poole is located in the Canford Cliffs area, moments from some of the country's best beaches and the picturesque Purbeck Hills. Stylish en suite accommodation is situated above the popular seafood Loch Fyne Restaurant. The friendly and helpful team provide a warm welcome. Limited on-site parking is available.

Rooms 8 en suite (1 fmly) (1 GF) S £70-£85; D £70-£85* **Facilities** FTV tea/coffee Dinner available Cen ht Wi-fi **Parking** 12 **Notes** ☒ No coaches

Towngate

★★★ GUEST HOUSE

58 Wimborne Rd BH15 2BY
☎ 01202 668552
e-mail: ayoun19@ntlworld.com
dir: *B3093 from town centre, guest house on right*

Guests are assured of a warm welcome at this centrally located house, within walking distance of the town centre and harbour, and just a short drive from the ferry terminal. The well-equipped bedrooms are comfortable and nicely furnished.

Rooms 3 en suite **Facilities** tea/coffee Cen ht **Parking** 4 **Notes** ☒ No Children 10yrs Closed mid Dec-mid Jan ☺

Antelope Inn

★★★ INN

8 High St BH15 1BP
☎ 01202 672029 ☐ 01202 678286
e-mail: 6603@greeneking.co.uk

Close to Poole Quay, which is one of the town's main attractions, this famous old coaching inn is the oldest licensed premises in Poole, and has long been a popular meeting point. All rooms are furnished to a good standard with modern facilities, and include some feature rooms. Public areas include a busy bar and a restaurant.

Rooms 23 en suite

The Burleigh

★★★ GUEST ACCOMMODATION

76 Wimborne Rd BH15 2BZ
☎ 01202 673889 ☐ 01202 685283
dir: *Off A35 onto A349*

Suited to business and leisure, this well-kept guest accommodation is close to the town centre and ferry terminal. The individually furnished and decorated bedrooms are of a good standard. Breakfast is served at separate tables and there is a small, attractive lounge.

Rooms 8 rms (4 en suite) (1 fmly) **Facilities** TVL tea/coffee Cen ht Wi-fi **Parking** 5

Centraltown

★★★ GUEST HOUSE

101 Wimborne Rd BH15 2BP
☎ 01202 674080 ☐ 01202 674080
dir: *From town centre onto A3093, Barclays International building on left, guest house 500yds*

This friendly and well-maintained guest house is within easy access of the town centre, ferry terminals, speedway and many other attractions. Bedrooms are attractive and equipped with many useful extra facilities. A full English breakfast is served in the bright, cosy dining room.

Rooms 3 en suite S £40; D £55* **Facilities** tea/coffee Cen ht Wi-fi **Parking** 6 **Notes** ☒ No Children ☺

POOLE continued

Seacourt

★★★ GUEST ACCOMMODATION

249 Blandford Rd, Hamworthy BH15 4AZ
☎ **01202 674995**
dir: Off A3049/A35 signed to Hamworthy

Within a short distance of the ferry port and town centre, this friendly establishment is well maintained and efficiently run. The comfortable bedrooms, some located on the ground floor, are all nicely decorated and equipped with useful extra facilities. Breakfast is served in the pleasant dining room at separate tables.

Rooms 5 en suite (1 fmly) (3 GF) (5 smoking) **Facilities** tea/coffee Cen ht Wi-fi **Parking** 5 **Notes** ⊗ No Children 5yrs ⊛

Shah of Persia

★★★ INN

173 Longfleet Rd BH15 2HS
☎ **01202 676587** 🖹 **01202 679327**
e-mail: shahofpersia.poole@marstons.co.uk
dir: On A35, 0.5m from Poole General Hospital

The Shah of Persia is located just a short distance from the town centre of Poole and is popular with visitors and locals alike. The accommodation consists of well equipped en suite rooms, some located in an adjacent annexe. The carvery restaurant has a friendly atmosphere and offers a wide range of freshly prepared dishes, and a large drinks selection including beers and wines which is available all day.

Rooms 11 en suite 4 annexe en suite (3 fmly) (4 GF) **Facilities** tea/coffee Dinner available Direct Dial Cen ht Wi-fi **Parking** 40 **Notes** No coaches

PORTLAND Map 4 SY67

Queen Anne House

★★★★ GUEST ACCOMMODATION

2/4 Fortuneswell DT5 1LP
☎ **01305 820028**
e-mail: margaretdunlop@tiscali.co.uk
dir: A354 to Portland then Fortuneswell. House on left 200mtrs past Royal Portland Arms

This delightful Grade II listed building is a charming and comfortable place to stay; particularly delightful are the Italianate gardens to the rear. Ideal for business and for leisure, Queen Anne House is close to the famous Chesil Beach, Portland Bill and Weymouth. Bedrooms are particularly attractive and pleasantly furnished. At breakfast, where guests are seated at one large table, there is a wide choice of options.

Rooms 3 en suite S £48-£50; D £75-£190 **Facilities** FTV TVL tea/coffee Cen ht Wi-fi **Parking** 4 **Notes** ⊗ ⊛

Beach House

★★★ GUEST HOUSE

51 Chiswell DT5 1AW
☎ **01305 821155**
e-mail: pete@beach-house-bandb.co.uk
dir: A354, after causeway take right lane to Victoria Square & into Chiswell. 150mtrs on right

Dating back to the early 19th century, this grand building was formerly a public house, but more recently has been providing relaxed and welcoming accommodation. Situated at the side of the stunning sweep of Chesil Beach, this establishment is also handy for the sailing academy. Bedrooms provide good levels of comfort and quality, many having stripped wooden floors and simple, stylish decor. A lounge and bar are also available, together with a light and airy breakfast room.

Rooms 7 rms (5 en suite) (2 pri facs) (2 fmly) S £40-£50; D £78-£90* **Facilities** FTV TVL tea/coffee Cen ht Licensed Wi-fi **Parking** 8 **Notes** LB ⊗

Portland Lodge

★★★ GUEST ACCOMMODATION

Easton Ln DT5 1BW
☎ **01305 820265** 🖹 **01305 860359**
e-mail: info@portlandlodge.com
dir: Signs to Easton/Portland Bill, rdbt at Portland Heights Hotel 1st right. Portland Lodge 200yds

Situated on the fascinating island of Portland, this modern, lodge style establishment provides comfortable accommodation including a number of ground-floor bedrooms. Breakfast is served in the spacious dining room with a friendly team of staff on hand. This is an ideal location for those wishing to explore the World Heritage coastline.

Rooms 30 annexe en suite (15 fmly) (7 GF) S £35-£48; D £48-£64 (room only)* **Facilities** FTV tea/coffee Cen ht Wi-fi **Parking** 50 **Notes** LB ⊗

PUNCKNOWLE Map 4 SY58

Offley Bed & Breakfast

★★★★ GUEST ACCOMMODATION

Looke Ln DT2 9BD
☎ **01308 897044** & **07792 624977**
dir: Off B3157 into village centre, left after Crown Inn onto Looke Ln, 2nd house on right

With magnificent views over the Bride Valley, this village house provides comfortable, quality accommodation. Guests are assured of a warm, friendly welcome; an ideal venue to enjoy the numerous local attractions. There are several local inns, one in the village which is just a gentle stroll away.

Rooms 3 rms (2 en suite) (1 pri facs) **Facilities** FTV TVL tea/coffee Cen ht **Parking** 3 **Notes** LB ⊛

ST LEONARDS Map 5 SU10

St Leonards

★★★ INN

Ringwood Rd BH24 2NP
☎ **01425 471220** 🖹 **01425 480274**
e-mail: 9230@greeneking.co.uk
web: www.oldenglish.co.uk
dir: At end of M27 continue to 1st rdbt. Take slip road on left

Close to Ringwood and Bournemouth, this inn has an attractive bar and restaurant offering an extensive menu of popular dishes and a children's menu. The spacious bedrooms are furnished to a high standard with modern facilities.

Rooms 35 en suite (5 fmly) (15 GF) **Facilities** tea/coffee Direct Dial Lift **Parking** 500 **Notes** Civ Wed 60

SHAFTESBURY Map 4 ST82

La Fleur de Lys Restaurant with Rooms

★★★★★ ⊛⊛ RESTAURANT WITH ROOMS

Bleke St SP7 8AW
☎ **01747 853717** 🖹 **01747 853130**
e-mail: info@lafleurdelys.co.uk
web: www.lafleurdelys.co.uk
dir: From junct of A30 & A350, 0.25m towards town centre

Located just a few minutes' walk from the famous Gold Hill, this light and airy restaurant with rooms combines efficient service in a relaxed and friendly atmosphere. Bedrooms, which are suitable for both business and leisure guests, vary in size but all are well equipped, comfortable and tastefully furnished. A relaxing guest lounge and courtyard are available for afternoon tea or pre-dinner drinks.

Rooms 7 en suite (2 fmly) (1 GF) S £75-£95; D £100-£175* **Facilities** FTV TVL tea/coffee Dinner available Direct Dial Cen ht Wi-fi **Conf** Max 12 Board 10 **Parking** 10 **Notes** LB ⊗ Closed 3rd wk Jan No coaches

SHERBORNE   Map 4 ST61

PREMIER COLLECTION

The Kings Arms

★★★★★ ⇔ INN

Charlton Horethorne DT9 4NL
☎ 01963 220281 📠 01963 220496
e-mail: admin@thekingsarms.co.uk
web: www.thekingsarms.co.uk
dir: *From A303 follow signs for Templecombe &
Sherborne onto B3145 to Charlton Horethorne*

Situated in the heart of this engaging village, The
Kings Arms offers impressive standards throughout.
The experienced owners have created something for
everyone with a convivial bar, snug and choice of
dining environments, including the garden terrace with
lovely countryside views. Bedrooms have individuality,
quality and style with marble bathrooms, robes and
wonderful showers. Food is taken seriously here with
assured cooking from a menu showcasing the best of
local produce.

Rooms 10 en suite (1 fmly) D £110-£125 **Facilities** FTV
tea/coffee Dinner available Direct Dial Cen ht Lift Wi-fi
⛳ Golf 18 **Conf** Thtr 80 Class 45 Board 50 **Parking** 30
Notes No coaches

PREMIER COLLECTION

Munden House

★★★★★ ⇔ GUEST ACCOMMODATION

Munden Ln, Alweston DT9 5HU
☎ 01963 23150
e-mail: stay@mundenhouse.co.uk
dir: *A352 from Sherborne, left onto A3030 to Alweston,
pass village shop on right, 250yds on left at Oxfords
Bakery sign*

Delightful property set in a quiet lane away from the
main road with pleasant views over the surrounding
countryside. Bedrooms and bathrooms come in a
variety of shapes and styles but all are very well
decorated and furnished; the beds are especially
comfortable. Guests are welcome to use to lounge and
garden, and delicious home-cooked dinners
(accompanied by an Italian wine list) are available by
prior arrangement. Breakfast includes a selection of
high quality hot and cold dishes, all carefully prepared
to order.

Rooms 4 en suite 3 annexe en suite (3 fmly) (4 GF) S
£70-£95; D £80-£130* **Facilities** FTV tea/coffee Dinner
available Cen ht Licensed Wi-fi ⛳ **Parking** 14
Notes LB

Avalon Townhouse

★★★★ BED AND BREAKFAST

South St DT9 3LZ
☎ 01935 814748
e-mail: enquiries@avalontownhouse.co.uk
web: www.avalontownhouse.co.uk
dir: *A30 from Shaftesbury, towards Sherborne town
centre, left onto South St*

Avalon is a spacious and comfortable Edwardian
townhouse in the heart of historic Sherborne. The building
is appointed to a high standard, and each stylish
bedroom has Freeview, flat-screen TV, free Wi-fi, tea and
coffee making facilities and luxury toiletries. The husband
and wife team extend a warm welcome and offer fine,
freshly prepared food that utilises local produce.

Rooms 3 en suite **Facilities** FTV TVL tea/coffee Cen ht
Wi-fi **Notes** ⊗ No Children 18yrs

Thorn Bank

★★★★ BED AND BREAKFAST

Long St DT9 3BS
☎ 01935 813795
e-mail: savileplatt@hotmail.com
dir: *A30 onto North Rd, then St Swithin's Rd. Right onto
Long St, 75yds on right*

Located just a short walk from the centre of town and the
abbey, this elegantly appointed Grade II listed, Georgian
townhouse is a perfect base from which to explore this
delightful area. The attentive service is noteworthy here
with every effort made to ensure an enjoyable and
relaxing stay. The spacious bedrooms, with lovely views
over the garden, are appointed to an impressive
standard. Breakfast makes use of local Dorset produce,
and in summer months guests are welcome to eat
alfresco on the lovely patio.

Rooms 1 en suite 1 annexe en suite S £70-£75; D
£90-£95* **Facilities** FTV tea/coffee Cen ht Wi-fi **Parking** 2
Notes LB ⊗ No Children 18yrs

The Alders

★★★★ BED AND BREAKFAST

Sandford Orcas DT9 4SB
☎ 01963 220666 📠 01963 220666
e-mail: jonsue@btinternet.com
web: www.thealdersbb.com
dir: *3m N of Sherborne. Off B3148 signed Sandford Orcas,
near Manor House in village*

Located in the charming conservation area of Sandford
Orcas and set in a lovely walled garden, this delightful
property offers attractive, well-equipped bedrooms.
Guests have their own entrance leading from the garden.
A large inglenook fireplace with a wood-burning stove can
be found in the comfortable sitting room, which also
features the owner's watercolours. Massage therapies are
available.

Rooms 3 en suite (1 fmly) D £60-£75 **Facilities** FTV TVL
tea/coffee Cen ht Wi-fi **Parking** 4 **Notes** ⊗ ⓐ

Venn *(ST684183)*

★★★ FARMHOUSE

Milborne Port DT9 5RA
☎ 01963 250598 📠 01963 250598
Mrs Pauline Tizzard
e-mail: info@colintizzard.co.uk
dir: *3m E of Sherborne on A30 on edge of Milborne Port*

Expect a friendly welcome at this farmhouse, set in a
good location for exploring west Dorset, which specialises
in training National Hunt race horses. The individually
furnished bedrooms are comfortable, and bathrooms are
fitted with power showers. Downstairs, a farmhouse
breakfast is served in the lounge-dining room.

Rooms 3 en suite S £40-£60; D £56-£60* **Facilities** FTV
TVL tea/coffee Cen ht Fishing **Parking** 6 **Notes** No
Children 5yrs Closed Xmas ⓐ 375 acres dairy/mixed/race
horses

STURMINSTER NEWTON   Map 4 ST71

The Old Post Office

Ⓤ

Marnhull Rd, Hinton St Mary DT10 1NG
☎ 01258 475590 📠 01258 475590
e-mail: info@northdorsetbandb.co.uk
web: www.northdorsetbandb.co.uk
dir: *A30 onto B3092 signed Sturminster Newton, on right
after 5m*

Currently the rating for this establishment is not
confirmed. This may be due to a change of ownership or
because it has only recently joined the AA rating scheme.

Rooms 2 rms (1 en suite) (1 pri facs) S £45; D £60*
Facilities TVL tea/coffee Cen ht Wi-fi **Parking** 2 **Notes** ⊗
No Children 14yrs ⓐ

A Great Escape Guest House

★★★★ GUEST ACCOMMODATION

6 Argyle Rd BH19 1HZ
☎ 01929 475853 & 07867 508724
e-mail: stay@agreatescapeguesthouse.co.uk

This newly renovated guest accommodation is located in a quiet part of Swanage within easy reach of the town centre and the beach. The top floor rooms offer beautiful views of the surrounding areas and beyond. Rooms are tastefully decorated and equipped with an ample choice of amenities.

Rooms 5 rms (4 en suite) (1 pri facs) (1 fmly) (1 GF)
Facilities FTV tea/coffee Cen ht Wi-fi **Notes** ⊗

Rivendell

★★★★ GUEST HOUSE

58 Kings Rd BH19 1HR
☎ 01929 421383
e-mail: kevin@rivendellguesthouse.co.uk

This beautiful period house, located within easy reach of the beach and town centre, has been lovingly restored to retain many of the original features. The bedrooms have been upgraded to a very good standard and can accommodate a diverse clientele. An award-winning breakfast is served in the cosy dining room.

Rooms 9 en suite (1 fmly) **Facilities** FTV TVL tea/coffee Cen ht Wi-fi **Notes** ⊗

Swanage Haven

★★★★ GUEST HOUSE

3 Victoria Rd BH19 1LY
☎ 01929 423088 🖶 01929 421912
e-mail: info@swanagehaven.com
web: www.swanagehaven.com

A boutique style guest house close to Swanage Beach and coastal path. Exclusively for adults, the accommodation is modern and contemporary with many extras such as fluffy robes, slippers, Wi-fi and a hot tub. Hands-on owners provide excellent hospitality with relaxed and friendly service. Breakfasts are superb; top quality organic and local produce from an extensive menu.

Rooms 7 en suite D £70-£100* **Facilities** FTV TVL tea/coffee Cen ht Licensed Wi-fi ⦙ Golf Hot tub, Holistic treatment room **Parking** 7 **Notes** LB ⊗ No Children

The Limes

★★★★ GUEST HOUSE

48 Park Rd BH19 2AE
☎ 01929 422664
e-mail: info@limeshotel.net
dir: Follow one-way system, signed to Durlston Country Park. Pass restaurant on left, turn right onto Park Rd, 200mtrs on right

Ideally located for both the town centre and the seafront being just a few minutes' stroll from either, this comfortable establishment offers a variety of different bedroom shapes and sizes. In addition to the pleasant dining room, guests are able to use a small bar area and a popular games room.

Rooms 12 rms (10 en suite) (7 fmly) **Facilities** FTV tea/coffee Cen ht Licensed Wi-fi Pool table **Parking** 8

Ocean Lodge

★★★ GUEST ACCOMMODATION

3 Park Rd BH19 2AA
☎ 01929 422805 🖶 01929 425225
e-mail: oceanlodgeswanage@gmail.com

This Victorian townhouse is centrally located in the picturesque coastal town of Swanage, within walking distance of the Blue Flag beach, restaurants, pubs and the shops. Bedrooms are comfortable with modern decor and furnishings. A continental or hearty cooked breakfast can be enjoyed in the dining room.

Rooms 5 en suite (2 fmly) S £35-£55; D £50-£68* **Facilities** FTV tea/coffee Cen ht Wi-fi **Notes** ⊗ No Children 3yrs

Railway Cottage

★★★ BED AND BREAKFAST

26 Victoria Av BH19 1AP
☎ 01929 425542
e-mail: foxysh@btinternet.com

Ideally located and only a short stroll from both the town centre and the seafront, this is a relaxed and welcoming family-run establishment with bedrooms of varying sizes. Breakfast is served in the pleasant dining room; parking is available either to the rear of the property or in the main car park opposite.

Rooms 6 en suite (1 fmly) (1 GF) S £30-£60; D £60-£90* **Facilities** tea/coffee Cen ht Wi-fi **Parking** 5 **Notes** LB ⊜

The Langton Arms

★★★★ INN

DT11 8RX
☎ 01258 830225 🖶 01258 830053
e-mail: info@thelangtonarms.co.uk
dir: Off A354 in Tarrant Hinton to Tarrant Monkton, through ford, Langton Arms opp

Tucked away in this sleepy Dorset village, the Langton Arms offers stylish, light and airy accommodation and is a good base for touring this attractive area. Bedrooms, all on the ground-floor level in the modern annexe, are very well equipped and comfortable. There is a choice of dining options - the relaxed bar-restaurant or the more formal Stables Restaurant, offering innovative and appetising dishes. Breakfast is served in the conservatory dining room just a few steps through the pretty courtyard.

Rooms 6 annexe en suite (6 fmly) (6 GF) S £70; D £90* **Facilities** tea/coffee Dinner available Direct Dial Cen ht Wi-fi **Conf** Max 70 Thtr 70 Class 70 Board 70 **Parking** 100 **Notes** Civ Wed 60

Kemps Country House

★★★★★ ⦿ GUEST ACCOMMODATION

East Stoke BH20 6AL
☎ 0845 8620315 🖶 0845 8620316
e-mail: info@kempscountryhouse.co.uk
web: www.kempshotel.com
dir: Follow A352 W from Wareham, 3m on right in village of East Stoke

Located within easy reach of the Dorset coastline, this former rectory provides a calming, friendly atmosphere and is the perfect base for touring the area. The refurbished bedrooms are spacious and well appointed, and benefit from plenty of modern extras; super king-size beds, flatscreen TV and power showers. Breakfast and dinner are served in the elegant dining room and offer an imaginative choice of modern British cuisine.

Rooms 4 en suite 12 annexe en suite (2 fmly) (6 GF) **Facilities** FTV tea/coffee Dinner available Direct Dial Cen ht Licensed Wi-fi **Parking** 24 **Notes** ⊗

Purbeck Vineyard

★★★★ 🏠 🍴 GUEST ACCOMMODATION

Valley Rd, Harmans Cross BH20 5HU
☎ **01929 481525 & 07780 614050**
e-mail: info@vineyard.uk.com
dir: *From Corfe on A351 in Harmans Cross, on right*

This unique establishment situated on a working vineyard benefits from several bedrooms which overlook the stunning countryside and is only a few minutes' drive from the equally scenic south coast. Accommodation is comfortable and furnished to a very high standard; bathrooms have powerful showers with generously sized fluffy towels. Enjoy a freshly prepared dinner made using a number of locally sourced ingredients and try a glass of the delicious house wine from the vineyard. Breakfast is heartily substantial, creating a fabulous start to the day.

Rooms 9 en suite (3 fmly) (1 GF) S £85; D £110*
Facilities FTV tea/coffee Dinner available Direct Dial Cen ht Licensed Wi-fi ch fac **Conf** Max 24 Thtr 12 Class 12 Board 12 **Parking** 10 **Notes** LB ⊗

Hyde Cottage Bed & Breakfast

★★★★ BED AND BREAKFAST

Furzebrook Rd, Stoborough BH20 5AX
☎ **01929 553344**
e-mail: hydecottbb@yahoo.co.uk
dir: *2m S of Wareham. Off A351 rdbt for Furzebrook/Blue Pool, premises on right*

Easy to find, on the Corfe Castle side of Wareham, this friendly bed and breakfast has a great location. Bedrooms are all large with lounge seating and some are suitable for families. All are well equipped with extras such as fridges. Meals are served en famille in the dining area downstairs.

Rooms 3 en suite (2 fmly) (1 GF) S £35-£40; D £66-£80
Facilities FTV tea/coffee Dinner available Cen ht Wi-fi **Parking** 4 **Notes** LB ⊗ Closed 24-27 Dec 🐾

Luckford Wood House *(SY872864)*

★★★★ FARMHOUSE

East Stoke BH20 6AW
☎ **01929 463098 & 07888 719002**
Mr & Mrs Barnes
e-mail: luckfordleisure@hotmail.co.uk
web: www.luckfordleisure.co.uk
dir: *3m W of Wareham. Off A352, take B3070 to Lulworth, turn right onto Holme Ln, signed East Stoke. 1m right onto Church Ln*

Rurally situated about three miles west of Wareham, this family home offers comfortable accommodation. Situated on the edge of woodland, there is abundant wildlife to see. Guests can be assured of a friendly welcome and an extensive choice at breakfast.

Rooms 6 rms (5 en suite) (1 pri facs) (3 fmly) (1 GF) S £40-£65; D £70-£85 **Facilities** FTV TVL tea/coffee Cen ht Wi-fi Golf 27 **Parking** 6 **Notes** LB 122 acres sheep

The Old Granary *(SY886858)*

★★★★ FARMHOUSE

West Holme Farm BH20 6AQ
☎ **01929 552972**
Mrs Venn Goldsack
e-mail: theoldgranarybandb@googlemail.com
web: www.theoldgranarybandb.co.uk
dir: *A352 from Wareham onto B3090, turn into Holme for Gardens, house on right*

A friendly, well run farmhouse with an experienced host, this is a former granary to the working farm, architect-designed with high ceilings and lots of light. Rooms are comfortable and well maintained and the hearty breakfast is a great start to the day.

Rooms 2 en suite (1 GF) **Facilities** STV FTV tea/coffee Cen ht Wi-fi **Parking** 2 **Notes** ⊗ No Children 16yrs Closed 19 Dec-3 Jan 50 acres horticultural

Worgret Manor

★★★★ GUEST ACCOMMODATION

Worgret Rd BH20 6AB
☎ **01929 552957** 📠 **01929 554804**
e-mail: admin@worgretmanorhotel.co.uk
dir: *0.5m from town centre towards Dorchester*

On the edge of Wareham, with easy access to major routes, this privately owned Georgian manor house has a friendly, cheerful atmosphere. The bedrooms come in a variety of sizes. Public rooms are well presented and comprise a popular bar and a quiet lounge.

Rooms 13 en suite (1 fmly) (4 GF) S fr £65; D fr £90* **Facilities** FTV TVL tea/coffee Direct Dial Cen ht Licensed Wi-fi Golf 18 **Conf** Max 65 Thtr 65 Class 65 Board 65 **Parking** 25 **Notes** ⊗ Closed 23 Dec-3 Jan

WEST LULWORTH　　　　**Map 4 SY88**

Lulworth Cove Inn

★★★ INN

Main Rd BH20 5RQ
☎ **01929 400333** 📠 **01929 400534**
e-mail: inn@lulworth-cove.com

Located within a moments walk of the picturesque Lulworth Cove (a World Heritage Site) this long-established coaching inn provides comfortable en suite accommodation in traditional surroundings. Rooms are well presented with some offering sizable balconies and views to the sea beyond. A range of bar snacks and meals are available in the popular bar and restaurant.

Rooms 13 en suite (2 fmly) **Facilities** STV tea/coffee Dinner available Direct Dial Cen ht Wi-fi Pool table **Notes** ⊗

WEYMOUTH　　　　**Map 4 SY67**

See also Portland

Channel View

★★★★ GUEST HOUSE

10 Brunswick Ter, The Esplanade DT4 7RW
☎ **01305 782527** 📠 **01305 782527**
e-mail: channelviewweymouth@hotmail.co.uk
dir: *Off A353 The Esplanade onto Dorchester Rd, right onto Westerall Rd, 1st left at lights to Brunswick Ter*

Just off The Esplanade, this guest house is in a superb spot close to the beach and within walking distance of the attractions. Bedrooms are on three floors and vary in size. Some have lovely views over the bay and all offer good levels of comfort and decor. Guests receive a warm welcome and breakfast is served in the well-appointed dining room.

Rooms 7 rms (6 en suite) (1 pri facs) (1 fmly) S £30-£40; D £60-£80* **Facilities** FTV TVL tea/coffee Cen ht Wi-fi **Notes** ⊗

The Esplanade

★★★★ GUEST ACCOMMODATION

141 The Esplanade DT4 7NJ
☎ **01305 783129 & 07515 657116** 📠 **01305 783129**
e-mail: stay@theesplanadehotel.co.uk
web: www.theesplanadehotel.co.uk
dir: *On seafront, between Jubilee Clock & pier bandstand*

Dating from 1835, this attractive property is located on the seafront and offers wonderful views from the elegant dining room and stylish first-floor lounge. There's a genuine enthusiasm here, with a warm welcome assured and every effort provided to ensure a relaxing and rewarding stay. The comfortable bedrooms are thoughtfully equipped including Egyptian cotton sheets and towels; many rooms have sea views. Breakfast is a showcase of local produce with an extensive menu from which to choose. Rob Cole was a finalist in this year's Friendliest Landlady of the Year award (2011-12).

Rooms 11 en suite (3 fmly) (2 GF) S £50-£60; D £80-£120 **Facilities** FTV TVL tea/coffee Cen ht Licensed Wi-fi **Parking** 9 **Notes** LB ⊗ Closed Nov-Feb

WEYMOUTH *continued*

The Heritage Restaurant with Rooms

★★★★ 🍽 RESTAURANT WITH ROOMS

8 East St, Chickerell DT3 4DS
☎ 01305 783093 📠 01305 786668
e-mail: mail@the-heritage.co.uk
dir: *In village centre*

Located just three miles from Weymouth and less than a mile from the spectacular Chesil Beach, this building dates back to 1769. Attentive service and a friendly, caring approach are hallmarks here, with every effort made to ensure a relaxing stay. Excellent Dorset produce is featured on the menus that are offered in the elegant restaurant. After dinner, the comfortable bedrooms await, each individually styled and well appointed.

Rooms 6 en suite (1 fmly) **Facilities** tea/coffee Dinner available Direct Dial Cen ht Wi-fi **Conf** Max 14 Board 14 **Parking** 10 **Notes** No coaches

Kingswood

★★★★ GUEST ACCOMMODATION

55 Rodwell Rd DT4 8QX
☎ 01305 784926 📠 01305 788016
e-mail: robbie.f@btinternet.com
dir: *On A354 up hill towards Portland from inner harbour, on left after lights*

Handily located for both Weymouth and Portland, this welcoming establishment provides spacious guest accommodation. The building has a long and interesting history and was even commandeered during World War II for American officers. The bedrooms are well appointed and comfortable, as are the public areas with breakfast being served in the attractive dining room. Just a stroll away is Brewers Quay, a lovely area in which to while away an hour or two.

Rooms 10 rms (9 en suite) (1 pri facs) (2 fmly) (2 GF) **Facilities** FTV tea/coffee Cen ht Wi-fi **Parking** 20 **Notes** ⊗

St John's Guest House

★★★★ GUEST ACCOMMODATION

7 Dorchester Rd DT4 7JR
☎ 01305 775523
e-mail: stjohnsguesthouse@googlemail.com
dir: *Opp St John's Church*

Located just 70 yards from the beach, this elegant Victorian property was built around 1880. Hospitality here is warm and genuine. The property has an appealing, uncluttered style, and standards are high throughout. Bedrooms are all well equipped with such extras as DVD players, Wi-fi access and comfy beds. Breakfast is served in the light and airy dining room with a lounge area also available for guests.

Rooms 7 en suite (2 fmly) (3 GF) S £32-£35; D £64-£70* **Facilities** FTV tea/coffee Cen ht Wi-fi **Parking** 10 **Notes** LB ⊗ No Children 4yrs

Wenlock House

★★★★ GUEST ACCOMMODATION

107 The Esplanade DT4 7EE
☎ 01305 786674 & 0800 781 3949
e-mail: stay@wenlockweymouth.co.uk
dir: *On A353 (The Esplanade) King St junct*

Wenlock House offers a good standard of accommodation and a friendly atmosphere. The attractive bedrooms are well equipped and many have excellent views. The hosts are very attentive and always happy to help. The house is situated on the seafront, just a short walk from the station and town centre.

Rooms 10 rms (8 en suite) (3 fmly) **Facilities** FTV tea/coffee Cen ht Wi-fi **Parking** 10 **Notes** LB ⊗ No Children 5yrs Closed 30 Nov-Dec

The Alendale Guest House

★★★ GUEST HOUSE

4 Waterloo Place DT4 7NX
☎ 01305 788817
e-mail: bowie538@aol.com
dir: *Turn left at clock tower, through 2nd set of lights, Alendale 20mtrs on left*

This friendly property is located just 50 yards from the beach, and provides a warm, homely environment with easy access to the town centre and ferry terminals. Bedrooms are light and airy with an uncluttered contemporary style and come equipped with useful extras.

The attractive dining room is the venue for excellent local Dorset produce which is utilised in the imaginative and extensive breakfast menu, including both full English and Scottish options. Ample off-road parking is also a bonus here.

Rooms 5 en suite (2 fmly) S £34-£44; D £60-£68* **Facilities** FTV TVL tea/coffee Cen ht Wi-fi **Parking** 6 **Notes** LB ⊗

Kimberley Guest House

★★★ GUEST HOUSE

16 Kirtleton Av DT4 7PT
☎ 01305 783333 📠 01305 839603
e-mail: kenneth.jones@btconnect.com
dir: *Off A384 Weymouth road right onto Carlton Rd North, opp Rembrandt Hotel, Kirtleton Av on left*

This friendly guest house is in a quiet residential area near the seafront. Bedrooms are well presented, and in addition to a hearty breakfast, traditional home-cooked meals using fresh local and seasonal produce are served by arrangement.

Rooms 11 rms (9 en suite) (1 pri facs) (2 fmly) (1 GF) S £23-£25; D £50-£54* **Facilities** FTV tea/coffee Dinner available Cen ht **Parking** 8 **Notes** LB ⊗ Closed 1-29 Dec 🚫

The Cavendale

★★★ BED AND BREAKFAST

10 The Esplanade DT4 8EB
☎ 01305 786960
e-mail: laraine.holder@virgin.net

Conveniently located right on the seafront with splendid views from some of the bedrooms, this cosy bed and breakfast offers a range of differing sized bedrooms, some with shared bathrooms. Guests are welcome to use the lounge, where in addition to a large range of videos, they can join in with the current on-the-go jigsaw. Helpfully, parking permits for nearby car parks are available.

Rooms 9 rms (6 en suite) (3 pri facs) (5 fmly) (1 smoking) S £25-£28; D £60-£68* **Facilities** FTV TVL tea/coffee **Notes** LB ⊗ Closed 24 Dec-2 Jan

Molyneux Guest House

★★★ GUEST HOUSE

9 Waterloo Place, The Esplanade DT4 7PD
☎ 01305 774623 & 07947 883235
e-mail: stay@molyneuxguesthouse.co.uk
web: www.molyneuxguesthouse.co.uk
dir: *A354 to Weymouth seafront, onto The Esplanade, Molyneux on right*

Located close to the seafront and beautiful beaches of Weymouth, this guest house offers a genuine warm welcome. Bedrooms are brightly decorated and comfortable and there is also a lounge. Breakfast is enjoyed in the smart dining room. Off-road parking to the rear is a bonus.

Rooms 6 rms (5 en suite) (1 pri facs) (2 fmly) (1 GF) S £25-£40; D £50-£70* **Facilities** FTV TVL tea/coffee Cen ht Licensed Wi-fi **Parking** 6 **Notes** LB ⊗

Philbeach Guest House

★★★ GUEST ACCOMMODATION

11 Waterloo Place DT4 7PD
☎ 01305 785344
e-mail: stay@philbeachguesthouse.co.uk

Just across the road from the wonderful beach at Weymouth, this is an ideal property from which to explore the town and attractions. A warm welcome is always on offer together with helpful advice about the area. The bedrooms are thoughtfully equipped and include a family room and ground-floor options. Breakfast is served in the attractive dining room with a generous offering of hot and cold items to enjoy.

Rooms 5 en suite (1 fmly) (1 GF) S £40-£50; D £55-£85* **Facilities** FTV tea/coffee Wi-fi **Notes** ⊗

Tara

★★★ GUEST HOUSE

10 Market St DT4 8DD
☎ 01305 766235
dir: From Alexandra Gardens on The Esplanade right onto Belle Vue, right & left onto Market St

Neatly presented, this welcoming establishment is set just back from the seafront at the harbour end of town. Strictly non-smoking, the guest house provides a relaxed and friendly atmosphere. Bedrooms offer good levels of comfort. Home-cooked evening meals are served every day except Sundays.

Rooms 6 en suite (1 fmly) S £27-£32; D £54-£64 **Facilities** tea/coffee Dinner available Cen ht **Notes** LB ⊗ No Children 14yrs 🐾

The Trelawney

★★★ GUEST ACCOMMODATION

1 Old Castle Rd DT4 8QB
☎ 01305 783188 📠 01305 783181
e-mail: info@trelawneyhotel.com
dir: From Harbourside follow Portland signs, Trelawney 700yds on left

This charming Victorian house stands amid attractive gardens in a quiet residential area a short walk from the town centre and beach. The friendly proprietors provide a comfortable environment, and many guests return regularly. Generous English breakfasts are offered in the light and airy dining room, and a comfortable lounge is available.

Rooms 8 en suite (3 fmly) **Facilities** FTV TVL tea/coffee Cen ht Licensed Wi-fi ♿ **Parking** 12 **Notes** LB ⊗ No Children 5yrs Closed Nov-1 Apr

Wadham Guesthouse

★★★ GUEST HOUSE

22 East St DT4 8BN
☎ 01305 779640
e-mail: p.middleton22@aol.com
dir: Off S end of A353 The Esplanade

This pleasant, town centre property offers a range of rooms, and is a good base for touring and for a short stay. The comfortable bedrooms are attractively decorated, and home-cooked breakfasts are served in the ground-floor dining room. Parking permits are available.

Rooms 9 en suite (3 fmly) (1 GF) S £30-£35; D £60-£70 **Facilities** FTV TVL tea/coffee Cen ht **Notes** LB ⊗ No Children 4yrs Closed Xmas 🐾

Fieldbarn House

★★ GUEST ACCOMMODATION

44 Fieldbarn Dr, Southill DT4 0EE
☎ 01305 779140
dir: 1m NW of town centre. Off A354 Weymouth Way rdbt onto Fieldbarn Dr (Southill), 300yds on right

Located on a residential estate on the outskirts of the town, yet only a short drive from sandy beaches and the town centre, this modern home is family run and provides guests with comfortable accommodation. A full English breakfast is served at a communal table overlooking the well-tended rear garden.

Rooms 3 rms (1 fmly) S £22-£26; D £44-£52* **Facilities** FTV tea/coffee Cen ht **Parking** 4 **Notes** LB ⊗ No Children 3yrs Closed 15-31 Dec 🐾

WIMBORNE MINSTER Map 5 SZ09

PREMIER COLLECTION

Les Bouviers Restaurant with Rooms

★★★★★ ⊛⊛ 🍴 RESTAURANT WITH ROOMS

Arrowsmith Rd, Canford Magna BH21 3BD
☎ 01202 889555 📠 01202 639428
e-mail: info@lesbouviers.co.uk
web: www.lesbouviers.co.uk
dir: A31 onto A349. In 0.6m turn left. In approx 1m right onto Arrowsmith Rd. Establishment approx 100yds on right

An excellent restaurant with rooms in a great location, set in five and a half acres of grounds. Food is a highlight of any stay here as is the friendly, attentive service. Chef/patron James Coward's team turn out impressive cooking which has reached AA 2 Rosette status. Cream tea can be taken on the terrace. Bedrooms are extremely well equipped and beds are supremely comfortable.

Rooms 6 en suite (4 fmly) S £88-£183; D £94-£215* **Facilities** FTV tea/coffee Dinner available Direct Dial Cen ht Wi-fi All bathrooms have steam showers or air baths **Conf** Max 120 Thtr 100 Class 100 Board 100 **Parking** 50 **Notes** LB RS Sun eve restricted opening & restaurant closed Civ Wed 120

Ashton Lodge

★★★★ GUEST ACCOMMODATION

10 Oakley Hill BH21 1QH
☎ 01202 883423 📠 01202 883423
e-mail: ashtonlodge@tiscali.co.uk
web: www.ashton-lodge.co.uk
dir: Off A31 S of Wimborne onto A349 for Poole, left next rdbt signed Wimborne/Canford Magna, house 200yds on right

A warm welcome is assured at this delightful modern home, which provides comfortable bedrooms, stylishly furnished with attractively coordinated decor and fabrics. All rooms are well equipped, with many extra facilities provided. Hearty breakfasts are served in the spacious dining room, which overlooks the well-maintained garden.

Rooms 5 rms (2 en suite) (1 pri facs) (2 fmly) S £38; D £70-£79* **Facilities** FTV TVL tea/coffee Cen ht Wi-fi ch fac **Parking** 4 **Notes** LB ⊗ 🐾

WIMBOURNE MINSTER *continued*

The Kings Head

★★★ INN

The Square BH21 1JG
☎ 01202 880101 📄 01202 881667
e-mail: 6474@greeneking.co.uk
dir: *From A31 Dorchester take B3073 into Wimborne. Follow signs to town centre, in square on left*

Situated in the town square this establishment offers accommodation that includes one room with a four poster and also a family room. The restaurant specialises in seafood and there is also Laing's Bar that serves bar food and real ales. There are facilities for small meetings and wedding receptions.

Rooms 27 en suite (1 fmly) **Facilities** tea/coffee Direct Dial Lift

---

WINTERBOURNE ABBAS Map 4 SY69

The Coach & Horses

★★★ INN

DT2 9LU
☎ 01305 889340 📄 01305 889766
e-mail: info@thecoachandhorsesdorset.co.uk
dir: *On A35 between Dorchester & Bridport*

This former coaching inn dates back to the 1800s and provides an ideal base for exploring the wonderful Dorset countryside or perhaps as a stopover on the journey further into the West Country. The welcome is warm and genuine with caring staff making every effort to ensure guests have a relaxing and memorable stay. An extensive menu is offered, along with a popular carvery plus a choice of local beers. Bedrooms offer good levels of space and comfort.

Rooms 5 en suite **Facilities** tea/coffee Dinner available Cen ht **Parking** 45 **Notes** ⊗ Closed 24 Dec-1 Jan

---

CO DURHAM

AYCLIFFE Map 19 NZ22

The County Restaurant with Rooms

★★★★ 🍽 RESTAURANT WITH ROOMS

12 The Green DL5 6LX
☎ 01325 312273 📄 01325 317131
e-mail: info@thecountyaycliffevillage.com
dir: *A1(M) junct 59, A167 towards Newton Aycliffe. In Aycliffe turn onto village green*

Located overlooking the pretty village green yet convenient for the A1, the focus here is on fresh, home-cooked meals, real ales and friendly service. There is a relaxed atmosphere in the bar area, and the restaurant where attractive artwork is displayed. The bedrooms in the smart townhouse next door are all furnished to a high standard.

Rooms 7 en suite (3 GF) S £49; D £70-£110*
Facilities FTV TVL tea/coffee Dinner available Cen ht Wi-fi **Parking** 25 **Notes** LB ⊗ Closed 25 Dec & 1 Jan No coaches

---

BARNARD CASTLE Map 19 NZ01

Homelands Guest House

★★★★ 🏠 🍽 GUEST HOUSE

85 Galgate DL12 8ES
☎ 01833 638757
e-mail: carol@homelandsguesthouse.co.uk
dir: *From A1 onto A67, on left on Galgate*

This beautiful Victorian town house is conveniently located for the Yorkshire Dales and is only 20 minutes from the A1(M). The friendly proprietors provide a warm welcome; there is a comfortable lounge and delicious home-cooked suppers are available by prior arrangement. The attractively presented bedrooms are thoughtfully equipped and include a garden room.

Rooms 4 rms (3 en suite) (1 pri facs) 1 annexe en suite (1 GF) S £43-£53; D £73-£78* **Facilities** STV FTV tea/coffee Dinner available Cen ht Licensed Wi-fi Golf **Notes** Closed 15 Dec-15 Jan

---

COWSHILL Map 18 NY84

Low Cornriggs Farm *(NY845413)*

★★★★ 🏠 🍽 FARMHOUSE

Cowshill-in-Weardale DL13 1AQ
☎ 01388 537600 & 07760 766794
Mrs J Elliott
e-mail: cornriggsfarm@btconnect.com
web: www.cornriggsfarm.co.uk
dir: *0.6m NW of Cowshill on A689*

Situated in the heart of Weardale yet also close to Cumbria, this delightful farmhouse has stunning views. Original stone and stripped pine are combined to provide a house with real character. Excellent home-cooked dinners are offered along with charming hospitality. Bedrooms are attractive and thoughtfully equipped with many homely extras.

Rooms 3 en suite 4 annexe en suite (1 fmly) (3 GF) S £40-£44; D £60-£64* **Facilities** TVL tea/coffee Dinner available Cen ht Wi-fi Golf 9 **Parking** 6 **Notes** LB ⊗ 42 acres beef

---

DARLINGTON Map 19 NZ21

See also Aldbrough St John (Yorkshire, North)

Raby Hunt Inn and Restaurant with Rooms

★★★★ RESTAURANT WITH ROOMS

Summerhouse DL2 3UD
☎ 01325 374237
e-mail: enquiries@rabyhuntrestaurant.co.uk
web: www.rabyhuntrestaurant.co.uk
dir: *A1(M) junct 58 onto A68 N, then B6275 & B6279*

This Grade II listed building, situated in the quiet village of Summerhouse, is a family-owned restaurant with rooms providing well-equipped, stylish and comfortable accommodation. Both bedrooms are en suite and have many thoughtful extras. The comfortable and contemporary restaurant serves modern British and European dishes with flair and creativity.

Rooms 2 en suite S £65-£105; D £105* **Facilities** STV FTV tea/coffee Dinner available Cen ht Wi-fi **Parking** 8 **Notes** ⊗ No Children 13yrs No coaches

Save on B&Bs and Hotels. Book at **theAA.com/hotel**

CO DURHAM – ESSEX 145 ENGLAND

DURHAM	Map 19 NZ24

The Old Mill

★★★★ INN

Thinford Rd, Metal Bridge DH6 5NX
☎ 01740 652928 ▤ 01740 657230
e-mail: office@theoldmill.uk.com
web: www.theoldmill.uk.com
dir: *5m S of Durham. A1(M) junct 61, onto A688 S for 1.5m, left at rdbt & sharp right*

This traditional, family-owned inn offers a friendly welcome. The stylish bedrooms are very well equipped, and the bar offers a comprehensive list of wines and beer, and a very good selection of meals.

Rooms 8 en suite **Facilities** STV tea/coffee Dinner available Direct Dial Cen ht Jacuzzi/Spa **Conf** Max 40 Thtr 40 Class 40 Board 25 **Parking** 40 **Notes** ⊗ Closed 26 Dec RS 25 Dec

---

HASWELL PLOUGH	Map 19 NZ34

The Gables

★★★ 🅰 GUEST ACCOMMODATION

Front St DH6 2EW
☎ 0191 526 2982 ▤ 0191 526 2982
e-mail: jmgables@aol.com
web: www.thegables.co.uk
dir: *On B1283 in village centre*
Rooms 5 en suite (1 fmly) **Facilities** STV FTV TVL tea/coffee Dinner available Cen ht Licensed Wi-fi **Parking** 30

SEAHAM	Map 19 NZ44

The Seaton Lane Inn

★★★★ INN

Seaton Ln, Seaton Village SR7 0LP
☎ 0191 581 2036
e-mail: info@seatonlaneinn.com
dir: *A19 S of Sunderland on B1404 between Seaham & Houghton*

Set on the edge of the quiet village of Seaton, yet close to Seaham and the A19, the inn is popular with visitors and locals. Recently refurbished offering a blend of modern and traditional. The emphasis is on food here with interesting home-made dishes offered in the restaurant and bar areas. Bedrooms are modern, spacious and smartly furnished and are located in the adjoining building.

Rooms 18 en suite (1 GF) S £69.95-£90; D £79.95-£120* **Facilities** FTV TVL tea/coffee Dinner available Direct Dial Cen ht Wi-fi Golf 18 Fishing **Parking** 36 **Notes** ⊗

STOCKTON-ON-TEES	Map 19 NZ41

The Parkwood Inn

★★★ INN

64-66 Darlington Rd, Hartburn TS18 5ER
☎ 01642 587933
e-mail: theparkwoodhotel@aol.com
web: www.theparkwoodhotel.com
dir: *1.5m SW of town centre. A66 onto A137 signed Yarm & Stockton West, left at lights onto A1027, left onto Darlington Rd*

Expect a very friendly welcome at this family-run establishment. The well-equipped en suite bedrooms come with many homely extras, and a range of professionally prepared meals are served in the cosy bar lounge, conservatory, or the attractive dining room.

Rooms 6 en suite **Facilities** tea/coffee Dinner available Cen ht **Parking** 36 **Notes** No coaches

---

ESSEX

CHIPPING ONGAR	Map 6 TL50

PREMIER COLLECTION

Diggins Farm *(TL582082)*

★★★★★ FARMHOUSE

Fyfield CM5 0PP
☎ 01277 899303 ▤ 01277 899015
Mrs M Frost
dir: *B184 N from Fyfield, right after Black Bull pub, farm 0.75m on left*

This delightful Grade II listed 16th-century farmhouse is set amid open farmland in the Roding Valley, and is only a short drive from Stansted Airport. The spacious bedrooms are attractively decorated, carefully furnished and well equipped.

Rooms 2 rms (1 en suite) (1 pri facs) **Facilities** tea/coffee Cen ht **Parking** 20 **Notes** ⊗ No Children 12yrs Closed 15 Dec-3 Jan ☺ 440 acres arable

---

CLACTON-ON-SEA	Map 7 TM11

The Chudleigh

★★★★ GUEST ACCOMMODATION

13 Agate Rd, Marine Parade West CO15 1RA
☎ 01255 425407 ▤ 01255 470280
e-mail: chudleighhotel@btconnect.com
dir: *With sea on left, cross lights at pier, turn onto Agate Rd*

Conveniently situated for the seafront and shops, this immaculate property has been run by the friendly owners Peter and Carol Oleggini for more than 30 years. Bedrooms are most attractive with co-ordinating decor and well chosen fabrics. Breakfast is served in the smart dining room and there is a cosy lounge with plush sofas.

Rooms 10 en suite (2 fmly) (2 GF) S £50-£55; D £80-£85 **Facilities** FTV TVL tea/coffee Direct Dial Cen ht Licensed Wi-fi **Parking** 7 **Notes** No Children 1yr Closed Oct

---

COLCHESTER	Map 13 TL92

Fridaywood Farm *(TL985213)*

★★★★ FARMHOUSE

Bounstead Rd CO2 0DF
☎ 01206 573595 ▤ 01206 547011
Mrs J Lochore
e-mail: lochorem8@aol.com
dir: *3m S of Colchester, from A12 follow signs for zoo to Mersea, cross B1026. At Maypole pub, right for Bounstead Rd*

Fridaywood Farm is a traditional farmhouse surrounded by wooded countryside. Bedrooms are generally quite spacious, and each one is carefully decorated, furnished with well-chosen pieces, and equipped with many thoughtful touches. Public rooms include an elegant dining room where breakfast is served at a large communal table, and a cosy sitting room.

Rooms 2 en suite D £65-£80* **Facilities** tea/coffee Cen ht Wi-fi 🐾 🏇 **Parking** 6 **Notes** ⊗ No Children 12yrs ☺ 500 acres sheep/arable

---

The Old Manse

★★★★ BED AND BREAKFAST

15 Roman Rd CO1 1UR
☎ 01206 545154 & 07773 948082 ▤ 01206 545153
e-mail: wendyanderson15@hotmail.com
web: www.theoldmanse.uk.com
dir: *In town centre, 250yds E of castle. Off High St-East Hill onto Roman Rd*

Expect a warm welcome from the caring host at this Victorian house, situated just a short walk from the castle and High Street. Bedrooms are carefully decorated with co-ordinated soft furnishings and equipped with many thoughtful touches. Breakfast is served seated at a large communal table in the attractive dining room and there is a comfortable lounge.

Rooms 3 rms (2 en suite) (1 pri facs) S £48-£65; D £70-£80 **Facilities** tea/coffee Cen ht Wi-fi **Parking** 1 **Notes** ⊗ No Children 8yrs Closed 23-31 Dec ☺

DEDHAM — Map 13 TM03

The Sun Inn

★★★★★ ⚬ 🛏 INN

High St CO7 6DF
☎ 01206 323351 📠 01206 323964
e-mail: office@thesuninndedham.com
dir: In village centre opp church

A charming 15th-century coaching inn situated in the centre of Dedham opposite the church. The carefully decorated bedrooms include four-poster and half tester beds, along with many thoughtful touches. The open-plan public rooms have a wealth of character with inglenook fires, oak beams and fine oak panelling.

Rooms 5 en suite **Facilities** tea/coffee Dinner available Cen ht **Parking** 15 **Notes** LB Closed 25-28 Dec Civ Wed 100

Marlborough Head Inn

★★★ INN

Mill Ln CO7 6DH
☎ 01206 323250
e-mail: jen.pearmain@tiscali.co.uk

A period building with many original features, The Marlborough Head is ideally located to explore "Constable Country". The three en suite bedrooms are traditionally appointed and offer modern amenities. There are two bars, two restaurants and a comfortable lounge. Parking is provided and there is a well maintained garden.

Rooms 3 en suite **Facilities** FTV tea/coffee Dinner available Cen ht Wi-fi **Parking Notes** No Children

FRINTON-ON-SEA — Map 7 TM22

Uplands

★★★ GUEST ACCOMMODATION

41 Hadleigh Rd CO13 9HQ
☎ 01255 674889 & 07921 640772 📠 01255 674889
e-mail: info@uplandsguesthouse.co.uk
web: www.uplandsguesthouse.com
dir: B1033 into Frinton, over level crossing, Hadleigh Rd 3rd left, Uplands 250yds on left

This large Edwardian house stands in a peaceful side road just a short walk from the shops and seafront. Bedrooms are pleasantly decorated and thoughtfully equipped with a good range of useful extras. Public rooms include a large lounge-dining room where breakfast is served at individual tables.

Rooms 5 rms (4 en suite) (1 fmly) S £30-£35; D £60-£65* **Facilities** TVL tea/coffee Dinner available Cen ht Wi-fi **Parking** 4 **Notes** LB ⊗

GREAT DUNMOW — Map 6 TL62

Homelye Farm

★★★★ GUEST ACCOMMODATION

Homelye Chase, Braintree Rd CM6 3AW
☎ 01371 872127 📠 01371 876428
e-mail: info@homelye.co.uk
web: www.homelye.co.uk
dir: 1.5m E of Great Dunmow. Off B1256 at water tower

Expect a warm welcome at this working farm situated in a peaceful rural location just a short drive from the town centre. The spacious bedrooms are in converted outbuildings; each one features exposed beams, co-ordinated fabrics and attractive pine furnishings. Breakfast is taken at individual tables in the original farmhouse.

Rooms 13 annexe en suite (1 fmly) (13 GF) S £47-£55; D £57-£85* **Facilities** FTV TVL tea/coffee Cen ht Licensed Wi-fi **Parking** 16 **Notes** ⊗ Closed 24-27 Dec

Blatches Farm (TL669225)

★★★ FARMHOUSE

Braintree Rd, Stebbing CM6 3AL
☎ 01371 856770 📠 01371 856770
David & Liz Walsh
e-mail: walsh57@btinternet.com

Blatches Farm has a lot to offer; newly built and well-appointed cottage style accommodation, a parking area, the sound of nature and the tranquillity one would expect from a rural location. In addition, Stansted Airport is only seven miles away. The husband and wife team is welcoming, attentive and hospitable.

Rooms 8 en suite **Parking**

GREAT TOTHAM — Map 7 TL81

The Bull at Great Totham

★★★★★ ⚬⚬ RESTAURANT WITH ROOMS

2 Maldon Rd CM9 8NH
☎ 01621 893385 & 894020 📠 01621 894029
e-mail: reservations@thebullatgreattotham.co.uk
web: www.thebullatgreattotham.co.uk
dir: Exit A12 at Witham junct to Great Totham

Located in the village of Great Totham, this stylish restaurant with rooms has been tastefully restored following a complete refurbishment. A 16th-century coaching inn, The Bull now offers comfortable en suite bedrooms with stylish decor and furnishings and satellite TVs with Freeview; Wi-fi is available throughout. Guests can enjoy dinner in the gastropub or in the AA 2 Rosette, fine dining restaurant, The Willow Room.

Rooms 4 en suite (2 GF) S £59-£79; D £69-£85* **Facilities** STV FTV tea/coffee Dinner available Cen ht Wi-fi Golf 18 **Conf** Max 60 Thtr 40 Class 40 Board 16 **Parking** 80 **Notes** LB ⊗

GREAT YELDHAM — Map 13 TL73

The White Hart

★★★★★ ⚬⚬ RESTAURANT WITH ROOMS

Poole St CO9 4HJ
☎ 01787 237250 📠 01787 238044
e-mail: mjwmason@yahoo.co.uk
dir: On A1017 in village

A large timber-framed character building houses the main restaurant and bar areas whilst the bedrooms are located in the converted coach house; all are smartly appointed and well equipped with many thoughtful extras. A comfortable lounge-bar area and beautifully landscaped gardens provide areas for relaxation. Locally sourced produce is used in the main house restaurant, popular with local residents and guests alike.

Rooms 11 en suite (2 fmly) (6 GF) S £55; D £75-£120* **Facilities** FTV TVL tea/coffee Dinner available Direct Dial Cen ht Wi-fi **Conf** Max 200 Thtr 200 Class 200 Board 50 **Parking** 80 **Notes** LB Civ Wed 130

HALSTEAD — Map 13 TL83

The Bull

★★★ INN

Bridge St CO9 1HU
☎ 01787 472144 📠 01787 472496
e-mail: bull.halstead@oldenglishinns.co.uk
dir: Off A131 at bottom of hill on High St

A charming inn situated in the heart of this bustling town that is between Sudbury and Braintree. Public areas include a large lounge bar, cosy restaurant and meeting rooms. Bedrooms are full of original character; each one is pleasantly decorated and equipped with modern facilities.

Rooms 10 en suite 6 annexe en suite **Facilities** tea/coffee Direct Dial **Parking** 25 **Notes** Civ Wed 50

HATFIELD HEATH — Map 6 TL51

Lancasters Farm (TL544149)

★★★★ FARMHOUSE

Chelmsford Rd CM22 7BB
☎ 01279 730220 📠 01279 730220
Mrs M Hunt
dir: A1060 from Hatfield Heath for Chelmsford, 1m left on sharp right bend, through white gates

Guests are made to feel at home at this delightfully spacious house, which is the heart of this large working arable farm close to Stansted Airport. Bedrooms vary in size and style but all are smartly decorated and thoughtfully equipped. Garaging can be arranged, as can transport to and from the airport.

Rooms 4 rms (2 en suite) (2 pri facs) S £40; D £80* **Facilities** FTV tea/coffee Cen ht **Parking** 6 **Notes** ⊗ No Children 12yrs Closed 14 Dec-4 Jan ⊜ 260 acres arable

MANNINGTREE   Map 13 TM13

PREMIER COLLECTION

Dairy House *(TM148293)*

★★★★★ FARMHOUSE

Bradfield Rd CO11 2SR
☎ 01255 870322
Mrs B Whitworth
e-mail: bridgetwhitworth@btinternet.com
web: www.dairyhousefarm.info

(For full entry see Wix)

SAFFRON WALDEN   Map 12 TL53

Warner's Farm

★★★★ BED AND BREAKFAST

Top Rd, Wimbish Green CB10 2XJ
☎ 01799 599525
e-mail: info@warnersfarm.co.uk
web: www.warnersfarm.co.uk
dir: *4m SE of Saffron Walden. Off B184 to Wimbish Green*

Expect a warm welcome at this delightful property set in five acres of grounds and surrounded by open countryside. The comfortable bedrooms have a wealth of character; each one has cordinated fabrics and many thoughtful touches. Breakfast is taken in the smart dining room and guests have the use of a lounge with an open fireplace.

Rooms 4 en suite (2 fmly) **Facilities** FTV TVL tea/coffee Cen ht Wi-fi ⚲ **Parking** 15 **Notes** ⊗ No Children 1-10yrs Closed 22 Dec-4 Jan ⊛

SOUTHEND-ON-SEA   Map 7 TQ88

Ilfracombe House

★★★★ GUEST ACCOMMODATION

9-13 Wilson Rd SS1 1HG
☎ 01702 351000   🖷 01702 393989
e-mail: info@ilfracombehotel.co.uk
web: www.ilfracombehotel.co.uk
dir: *500yds W of town centre. Off A13 at Cricketers pub onto Milton Rd, 3rd left onto Cambridge Rd, 4th right, car park in Alexandra Rd*

Ilfracombe House lies in Southend's conservation area, just a short walk from the cliffs, gardens and the beach. The public rooms include a dining room, lounge and a cosy bar, and the well-equipped bedrooms include deluxe options and two four-poster rooms.

Rooms 20 en suite (3 fmly) (2 GF) **Facilities** STV FTV TVL tea/coffee Dinner available Direct Dial Cen ht Licensed **Parking** 9 ⊗

Terrace Guest House

★★★ GUEST ACCOMMODATION

8 Royal Ter SS1 1DY
☎ 01702 348143   🖷 01702 348143
e-mail: info@terraceguesthouse.co.uk
dir: *From pier up Pier Hill onto Royal Terrace*

Set on a terrace above the Western Esplanade, this comfortable guest house has an informal atmosphere. There is a cosy bar, and an elegant sitting room and breakfast room. The spacious, well-planned bedrooms include four en suite front and rear-facing rooms, and several front-facing rooms that share two bathrooms.

Rooms 9 rms (6 en suite) (2 fmly) S £39-£45; D £59-£65* **Facilities** FTV TVL tea/coffee Cen ht Wi-fi **Notes** LB Closed 21 Dec-4 Jan

STANSTED AIRPORT   Map 6 TL52

See also Bishop's Stortford (Hertfordshire)

The White House

★★★★ GUEST ACCOMMODATION

Smiths Green CM22 6NR
☎ 01279 870257   🖷 01279 870423
e-mail: enquiries@whitehousestansted.co.uk
web: www.whitehousestansted.co.uk
dir: *M11 junct 8, B1256 towards Takeley. Through lights at Four Ashes x-rds. 400yds, corner of B1256 & Smiths Green*

The White House is a delightful 16th-century property situated close to Stansted Airport (but not on the flight path). The stylish bedrooms feature superb beds, luxurious bathrooms and many thoughtful touches. Traditional breakfasts are served in the farmhouse-style kitchen, using local ingredients. Evening meals are available at the Lion and Lamb, a nearby pub/restaurant owned by the proprietors, who can usually provide transport.

Rooms 3 rms (2 en suite) (1 pri facs) (3 fmly) S £65; D £75* **Facilities** FTV tea/coffee Dinner available Cen ht Wi-fi **Conf** Max 25 **Parking** 6 **Notes** ⊗ Closed 24-25, 31 Dec & 1 Jan

THAXTED   Map 12 TL63

The Farmhouse Inn

★★★ INN

Monk Street CM6 2NR
☎ 01371 830864   🖷 01371 831196
e-mail: info@farmhouseinn.org
dir: *M11 to A120 to B184, 1m from Thaxted, between Thaxted & Great Dunmow*

This 16th-century inn overlooks the Chelmer Valley, and is surrounded by open countryside. The property is ideally situated in the quiet hamlet of Monk Street about two miles from the historic town of Thaxted. Bedrooms are pleasantly decorated and equipped with modern facilities. Public rooms include a cosy lounge bar and a large smartly appointed restaurant.

Rooms 11 annexe en suite **Facilities** FTV tea/coffee Dinner available Cen ht Wi-fi **Conf** Max 80 Thtr 80 Class 60 Board 50 **Parking** 35

The Swan

★★★ INN

Bullring, Watling St CM6 2PL
☎ 01371 830321   🖷 01371 831186
e-mail: swan.thaxted@greeneking.co.uk
web: www.oldenglish.co.uk
dir: *M11 junct 8, A120 to Great Dunmow, then B164 to Thaxted. At N end of high street, opposite church*

This popular village inn is situated in the town centre opposite the parish church. Public areas feature a large open-plan beamed bar/restaurant serving real ales and appealing dishes. Bedrooms are located in the main building or the more peaceful rear annexe; each one is pleasantly decorated and well equipped.

Rooms 13 en suite 6 annexe en suite (2 fmly) (3 GF) **Facilities** tea/coffee **Parking** 15

THORPE BAY

See Southend-on-Sea

TOPPESFIELD
Map 12 TL73

Ollivers Farm
★★★ BED AND BREAKFAST

CO9 4LS
☎ 01787 237642 ▤ 01787 237602
e-mail: bandbolliversfarm@tesco.net
web: www.essex-bed-breakfast.co.uk
dir: 500yds SE of village centre. Off A1017 in Great Yeldham to Toppesfield, farm 1m on left before T-junct to village

Impressive 16th-century farmhouse full of charm and character set amid pretty landscaped gardens in a peaceful rural location. Bedrooms are pleasantly decorated and thoughtfully equipped. Public rooms have a wealth of original features including exposed beams and a huge open fireplace in the reception hall.

Rooms 3 rms (1 en suite) (1 pri facs) S £50; D £70-£80 Facilities tea/coffee Wi-fi Shed for bikes Parking 4 Notes ⊗ No Children 10yrs Closed 23 Dec-1 Jan ⊛

WESTCLIFF-ON-SEA
Map 7 TQ88

See also Southend-on-Sea

The Trinity
★★★ GUEST ACCOMMODATION

3 Trinity Av SS0 7PU
☎ 01702 342282
e-mail: enquiries@thetrinityhotel.co.uk
dir: A13 to Milton Rd, at lights turn right towards Cliffs pavilion, left onto Cambridge Rd and right onto Trinity Av

New life has been injected in this property, a contemporary establishment with en suite accommodation within a short distance of the Westcliff sea front. All rooms are beautifully appointed and comfortably equipped. A freshly prepared breakfast is taken at the communal table in the attractive breakfast room.

Rooms 7 en suite (1 fmly) Facilities FTV tea/coffee Cen ht Notes ⊗

WIX
Map 13 TM12

PREMIER COLLECTION

Dairy House (TM148293)
★★★★★ FARMHOUSE

Bradfield Rd CO11 2SR
☎ 01255 870322
Mrs B Whitworth
e-mail: bridgetwhitworth@btinternet.com
web: www.dairyhousefarm.info
dir: Off A120 into Wix, turn at x-rds to Bradfield, farm 1m on left

This Georgian house stands amid 700 acres of arable land, with stunning views of the surrounding countryside. Extensively renovated in the Victorian style, it still retains original decorative tiled floors, moulded cornices and marble fireplaces. The spacious bedrooms are carefully furnished and equipped with many thoughtful touches. Breakfast is served in the elegant antique-furnished dining room and there is a cosy lounge.

Rooms 3 en suite S fr £44; D fr £64* Facilities FTV TVL tea/coffee Cen ht Wi-fi 🎣 Farm reservoir fishing Parking 8 Notes ⊗ No Children 12yrs ⊛ 700 acres arable

GLOUCESTERSHIRE

ALDERTON
Map 10 SP03

Tally Ho Bed & Breakfast
★★★★ BED AND BREAKFAST

20 Beckford Rd GL20 8NL
☎ 01242 621482 & 07966 593169
e-mail: tallyhobb@aol.com
dir: M5 junct 9, A46 signed Evesham, through Ashchurch. Take B4077 signed Stow-on-the-Wold & Alderton. Left in 1.5m opp garage signed Alderton

Convenient for the M5, this friendly establishment stands in a delightful quiet village. Bedrooms, including two on the ground floor, offer modern comforts and attractive co-ordinated furnishings. Breakfast is served in the stylish dining room, and for dinner, the village pub is just a stroll away.

Rooms 3 en suite (1 fmly) (2 GF) S £35-£45; D £65-£70* Facilities FTV tea/coffee Cen ht Wi-fi Parking 3 Notes LB

See advert on opposite page

ARLINGHAM
Map 4 SO71

The Old Passage Inn
★★★★ ⍟⍟ 🍴 RESTAURANT WITH ROOMS

Passage Rd GL2 7JR
☎ 01452 740547 ▤ 01452 741871
e-mail: oldpassage@ukonline.co.uk
dir: A38 onto B4071 through Arlingham. Through village to river

Delightfully located on the very edge of the River Severn, this relaxing restaurant with rooms combines high quality food with an air of tranquillity. Bedrooms and bathrooms are decorated in a modern style and include a range of welcome extras such as air conditioning and a well-stocked mini-bar. The menu offers a wide range of seafood and shellfish dishes including crab, oysters and lobsters from Cornwall (kept alive in seawater tanks). An outdoor terrace is available in warmer months.

Rooms 3 en suite Facilities FTV tea/coffee Dinner available Cen ht Wi-fi Parking 30 Notes Closed 25 & 26 Dec No coaches

BERKELEY
Map 4 ST69

The Malt House
★★★ INN

22 Marybrook St GL13 9BA
☎ 01453 511177 ▤ 01453 810257
e-mail: the-malthouse@btconnect.com
web: www.themalthouse.uk.com
dir: A38 into Berkeley, at town hall follow road to right, premises on right past hospital & opposite school

Well located for business and leisure, this family-run inn has a convivial atmosphere. Bedrooms are soundly appointed while public areas include a choice of bars, a skittle alley and an attractive restaurant area. Local attractions include Berkeley Castle, and the Wildfowl & Wetlands Trust at Slimbridge.

Rooms 10 rms (9 en suite) (2 fmly) Facilities FTV tea/coffee Dinner available Cen ht Wi-fi Pool table Skittle Alley Parking 30 Notes ⊗

BIBURY   Map 5 SP10

The Catherine Wheel

★★★★ ➾ INN

Arlington GL7 5ND
☎ 01285 740250
e-mail: rooms@catherinewheel-bibury.co.uk
dir: *On B4425 between Burford & Cirencester*

Located in the middle of this pleasant village, this
family-run inn provides a pleasant welcome and
traditional country inn ambience. A range of seating is
available from the cosy bar or more formal dining room
where a selection of carefully prepared dishes is offered
throughout the day and evening. Bedrooms are in an
adjacent building and include smaller standard rooms or
larger superior rooms - all comfortably furnished and
with some welcome extras.

Rooms 4 annexe en suite (4 GF) **Facilities** FTV TVL tea/
coffee Dinner available Cen ht Wi-fi **Parking** 23

Cotteswold House

★★★★ BED AND BREAKFAST

Arlington GL7 5ND
☎ 01285 740609   📠 01285 740609
e-mail: enquiries@cotteswoldhouse.net
web: www.cotteswoldhouse.net
dir: *On B4425, 500yds W of village centre*

Convenient for exploring the Cotswolds, Cotteswold House
offers a warm welcome together with high levels of
comfort. The spacious bedrooms are equipped with
thoughtful extras, and there is a cosy lounge which offers
useful local information for guests.

Rooms 3 en suite S £50-£55; D £70-£75* **Facilities** FTV
tea/coffee Cen ht Wi-fi **Parking** 3 **Notes** LB ⊗

BLOCKLEY   Map 10 SP13

PREMIER COLLECTION

Lower Brook House

★★★★★ 🏠 ➾ GUEST ACCOMMODATION

Lower St GL56 9DS
☎ 01386 700286   📠 01386 701400
e-mail: info@lowerbrookhouse.com
web: www.lowerbrookhouse.com
dir: *In village centre*

Dating from the 17th century, this enchanting house is
the perfect place to relax. Genuine hospitality and
attentive service are hallmarks here, and bedrooms
come in all shapes and sizes. There's a lot of character
in the public areas, with beams, flagstone floors, huge
fireplace and deep stone walls. Enjoy a delicious
breakfast and an aperitif in the garden, but leave room
for the skilfully prepared dinner.

Rooms 6 en suite S £80-£190; D £80-£190*
Facilities FTV tea/coffee Dinner available Cen ht
Licensed Wi-fi **Parking** 8 **Notes** ⊗ No Children 10yrs
Closed Xmas

BOURTON-ON-THE-WATER   Map 10 SP12

Larks Rise

★★★★ BED AND BREAKFAST

Old Gloucester Rd GL54 3BH
☎ 01451 822613   & 07884 438498
e-mail: larks.rise@virgin.net
web: www.larksrisehouse.co.uk
dir: *0.5m W of village. A249 onto A436, 1st driveway
on left*

A relaxed and welcoming establishment that sits in an
acre of gardens on the edge of the village. Comfort and
style are of paramount importance at this delightful
property where the proprietors offer a very warm welcome.
The bedrooms are really comfortable with cotton sheets
on pocket sprung mattresses and high quality en suite
facilities. Breakfasts feature locally sourced produce, and
there is ample parking.

Rooms 3 rms (2 en suite) (1 pri facs) (1 GF) D £70-£95
Facilities FTV tea/coffee Cen ht Wi-fi **Parking** 6 **Notes** ⊗
No Children 12yrs

Old Manse

★★★ INN

Victoria St GL54 2BX
☎ 01451 820082   📠 01451 810381
e-mail: 6488@greeneking.co.uk
web: www.oldenglish.co.uk
dir: *A429 Bourton turn off, property at far end of village
high street next to Cotswold Motor Museum*

Formerly a residence for Baptist ministers back in 1748,
this establishment has lots of traditional Cotswold
charm, and is located just a few feet from the River
Windrush. There is an extensive bar menu and a very
good restaurant menu. Bedrooms are modern and well
equipped with comfortable beds. In the winter guests can
relax by a roaring log fire and in the summer enjoy the
beer garden overlooking the river.

Rooms 12 en suite 3 annexe en suite S £65-£120; D
£65-£120 **Facilities** FTV tea/coffee Dinner available
Direct Dial Cen ht Wi-fi **Conf** Max 40 Thtr 40 Class 20
Board 16 **Parking** 12

BOURTON-ON-THE-WATER *continued*

The Cotswold House

★★★ BED AND BREAKFAST

Lansdowne GL54 2AR
☎ 01451 822373
e-mail: meadowscotswoldhouse@btinternet.com
dir: *Off A429 into Lansdowne, continue 0.5m to Cotswold House on right opp Mousetrap Inn*

A warm welcome is assured at this well maintained, mellow-stone house. Just a short walk from the church and the many attractions of this popular village, this is a great base for touring the Cotswolds. Bedrooms are comfortably furnished, and one is a self-contained conversion of the former village telephone exchange, set within immaculate gardens.

Rooms 3 en suite 1 annexe en suite (2 fmly) (1 GF) S £35-£60; D £55-£70* **Facilities** TVL tea/coffee Cen ht Wi-fi **Parking** 5 **Notes** LB ⊗ Closed Xmas 🅴

The Mousetrap Inn

★★★ INN

Lansdowne GL54 2AR
☎ 01451 820579
e-mail: thebatesies@gmail.com

A traditional and informal Cotswold inn located on the edge of this idyllic village yet just a few minutes' stroll from the centre. A selection of real ales and also home-cooked dinners (except Sundays and Mondays) are offered in the relaxed bar. Bedrooms and bathrooms vary for size and include three at ground floor level that have easy access. Breakfast includes home-made sausages and free range eggs.

Rooms 10 en suite (3 GF) S £40-£73; D £50-£73* **Facilities** tea/coffee Dinner available Cen ht Wi-fi **Parking** 10 **Notes** ⊗ No Children 10yrs

Strathspey

★★★ BED AND BREAKFAST

Lansdowne GL54 2AR
☎ 01451 810321 & 07889 491993
e-mail: information@strathspey.org.uk
web: www.strathspey.org.uk
dir: *Off A429 into Lansdowne, 200yds on right*

This friendly Edwardian-style cottage is just a short riverside walk from the charming village centre, the perfume factory and the famous model village. Bedrooms, including one at ground floor level with its own front door, are well presented with many useful extras. Substantial breakfasts are part of the caring hospitality.

Rooms 2 en suite 1 annexe en suite (1 fmly) (1 GF) **Facilities** TVL tea/coffee Cen ht **Parking** 4 **Notes** 🅴

CHELTENHAM Map 10 SO92

PREMIER COLLECTION

Beaumont House

★★★★★ GUEST ACCOMMODATION

56 Shurdington Rd GL53 0JE
☎ 01242 223311 🖷 01242 520044
e-mail: reservations@bhhotel.co.uk
web: www.bhhotel.co.uk
dir: *S side of town on A46 to Stroud*

Built as a private residence, this popular establishment exudes genteel charm. Public areas include a large lounge and an elegant dining room which overlooks the garden. Many improvements have taken place recently and include new studio bedrooms on the top floor. These complement the already completed 'Out of Asia' and 'Out of Africa' bedrooms, which are luxuriously furnished and very well equipped. Bedrooms situated to the rear of the building have views over Leckhampton Hill and there are also bedrooms on the lower ground floor.

Rooms 16 en suite (3 fmly) S £69-£79; D £89-£190* **Facilities** STV FTV tea/coffee Dinner available Direct Dial Cen ht Licensed Wi-fi **Parking** 16 **Notes** LB ⊗ Closed 24-26 Dec

PREMIER COLLECTION

Cleeve Hill House

★★★★★ GUEST ACCOMMODATION

Cleeve Hill GL52 3PR
☎ 01242 672052 🖷 01242 679969
e-mail: info@cleevehill-hotel.co.uk
dir: *3m N of Cheltenham on B4632*

Many of the bedrooms and the lounge at this Edwardian property have spectacular views across to the Malvern Hills. Room shapes and sizes vary but all are comfortably furnished with many welcome extras; some have four-poster beds. In addition to the relaxing guest lounge, an honesty bar is in place. Breakfast, served in the pleasant conservatory, offers a good selection of carefully presented hot and cold items.

Rooms 10 en suite (1 GF) **Facilities** STV FTV tea/coffee Direct Dial Cen ht Licensed Wi-fi **Parking** 11 **Notes** ⊗ No Children 8yrs

---

PREMIER COLLECTION

Georgian House

★★★★★ BED AND BREAKFAST

77 Montpellier Ter GL50 1XA
☎ 01242 515577 🖷 01242 545929
e-mail: penny@georgianhouse.net
web: www.georgianhouse.net
dir: *M5 junct 11, A40 into town centre & onto Montpellier Ter, Georgian House on right after park*

Dating from 1807, this elegant Georgian house is located in the fashionable area of Montpellier. Renovation has resulted in delightful accommodation with quality and comfort throughout. Bedrooms are individually styled, with contemporary comforts cleverly interwoven with period furnishings to great effect. Warm hospitality and attentive service ensure a memorable stay.

Rooms 3 en suite S £65-£75; D £85-£105* **Facilities** FTV tea/coffee Cen ht Wi-fi **Parking** 2 **Notes** ⊗ No Children 16yrs Closed Xmas & New Year

PREMIER COLLECTION

Lypiatt House

★★★★★ GUEST ACCOMMODATION

Lypiatt Rd GL50 2QW
☎ 01242 224994 🖷 01242 224996
e-mail: stay@lypiatt.co.uk
web: www.lypiatt.co.uk
dir: *M5 junct 11 to town centre. At Texaco petrol station mini-rdbt take exit signed Stroud. Fork right, pass shops, turn sharp left onto Lypiatt Rd*

Close to the fashionable area of Montpellier, set in its own grounds with ample parking, Lypiatt House is built in a typical Victorian style. Contemporary decor enhances the traditional features of the building. Bedrooms and bathrooms come in a range of shapes and sizes but all rooms are decorated and maintained to high standards, and include a range of welcome extras. Guests may use the elegant drawing room and the conservatory, which has an honesty bar.

Rooms 10 en suite (2 GF) S £78-£95; D £95-£130* **Facilities** FTV tea/coffee Direct Dial Cen ht Licensed Wi-fi **Conf** Max 10 Board 10 **Parking** 10 **Notes** LB ⊗ No Children 10yrs

The Wyastone

★★★★★ Ⓐ GUEST ACCOMMODATION

Parabola Rd GL50 3BG
☎ 01242 245549
e-mail: reservations@wyastonehotel.co.uk
Rooms 13 en suite (4 fmly) S £69-£89; D £99-£145*
Facilities FTV TVL tea/coffee Direct Dial Cen ht Licensed
Wi-fi Use of swimming pool & gym nearby **Parking** 6
Notes LB ⊗ Closed 23 Dec-3 Jan

Clarence Court

★★★★ 🛏 GUEST ACCOMMODATION

Clarence Square GL50 4JR
☎ 01242 580411   🖷 01242 224609
e-mail: enquiries@clarencecourthotel.co.uk
web: www.clarencecourthotel.com

Situated in an attractive, tree-lined Georgian square, this
property was once owned by the Duke of Wellington.
Sensitive refurbishment is returning the building to its
former glory with elegant public rooms reflecting the
grace of a bygone age. Spacious bedrooms offer ample
comfort and quality, with many original features retained.
The convenience of the peaceful location is a great asset,
only a 5-minute stroll from the town centre. A varied
range of carefully prepared dishes is offered in the
relaxing café restaurant from noon to 9pm.

Rooms 20 en suite (3 fmly) (7 GF) S £55-£70; D
£70-£120* **Facilities** FTV TVL tea/coffee Dinner available
Direct Dial Cen ht Licensed Wi-fi **Parking** 21

Badger Towers

★★★★ GUEST ACCOMMODATION

133 Hales Rd GL52 6ST
☎ 01242 522583   🖷 01242 574800
e-mail: mrbadger@badgertowers.co.uk
web: www.badgertowers.co.uk
dir: Off A40 (London Rd) onto Hales Rd, 0.5m on right
towards Prestbury & race course

Located in the residential area of Battledown, close to the
racecourse, town centre and GCHQ, this elegant Victorian
house offers thoughtfully furnished bedrooms, a light and
airy breakfast room, and a spacious lounge complete with
piano. The well-cooked breakfasts, with an emphasis on
local produce, are a satisfying start to the day.

Rooms 6 en suite (2 GF) S £60-£75; D £75-£125
Facilities FTV tea/coffee Cen ht Wi-fi **Parking** 6 **Notes** LB
Closed Xmas & New Year

The Battledown

★★★★ GUEST HOUSE

125 Hales Rd GL52 6ST
☎ 01242 233881
e-mail: battledown125@hotmail.com
dir: 0.5m E of town centre. A40 onto B4075, 0.5m on right

This elegant and well-proportioned Grade II listed house
offers comfortable accommodation close to the town
centre and racecourse. The refurbished bedrooms and
bathrooms provide plenty of quality and comfort with
some welcome extras, while the smart dining room is an
attractive setting for breakfast.

Rooms 7 en suite (2 fmly) S £49-£55; D fr £69* **Facilities**
tea/coffee Cen ht Wi-fi **Parking** 7 **Notes** LB ⊗ Closed
Xmas

Cotswold Grange

★★★★ 🛏 GUEST ACCOMMODATION

Pittville Circus Rd GL52 2QH
☎ 01242 515119   🖷 01242 241537
e-mail: info@cotsworldgrange.co.uk
dir: From town centre, follow Prestbury signs. Right at 1st
rdbt, next rdbt straight over, 100yds on left

A delightful building located in a quieter, mainly
residential area of Cheltenham, near Pitville Park and
just a short walk to the town centre. The Grange offers a
relaxed and welcoming atmosphere; there are many
useful extras such as Wi-fi in the bedrooms. A range of
carefully cooked and presented dishes is served in the
comfortable restaurant.

Rooms 24 en suite (3 fmly) S £60-£75; D £75-£95*
Facilities FTV TVL tea/coffee Dinner available Direct
Dial Cen ht Licensed Wi-fi Golf 18 Complimentary access to
nearby gym **Parking** 21 **Notes** LB Closed 25-31 Dec

Hope Orchard

★★★★ GUEST ACCOMMODATION

Gloucester Rd, Staverton GL51 0TF
☎ 01452 855556   🖷 01452 530037
e-mail: info@hopeorchard.com
web: www.hopeorchard.com
dir: A40 onto B4063 at Arlecourt rdbt, Hope Orchard
1.25m on right

Situated midway between Gloucester and Cheltenham,
Hope Orchard is a good base for exploring the area. The
comfortable bedrooms are next to the main house, and all
are on the ground floor and have their own separate
entrances. There is a large garden, and ample off-road
parking is available.

Rooms 8 en suite (8 GF) **Facilities** FTV tea/coffee Direct
Dial Cen ht Wi-fi **Parking** 10

33 Montpellier

★★★★ GUEST ACCOMMODATION

33 Montpellier Ter GL50 1UX
☎ 01242 526009
e-mail: montpellierhotel@btopenworld.com
dir: M5 junct 11, A40 to rdbt at Montpellier, over rdbt &
100yds on right

The friendly and welcoming Montpellier forms part of an
elegant Georgian terrace overlooking the municipal
gardens in a fashionable area of town convenient for
shops, restaurants and amenities. Bedrooms are light,
airy and well equipped with a range of practical extras
and thoughtful touches. Breakfast is served in the lower
ground floor dining room.

Rooms 7 en suite (5 fmly) **Facilities** FTV TVL tea/coffee
Cen ht Licensed Wi-fi **Notes** ⊗

White Lodge

★★★★ GUEST ACCOMMODATION

Hatherley Ln GL51 6SH
☎ 01242 242347   🖷 01242 242347
e-mail: pamela@whitelodgebandb.co.uk
dir: M5 junct 11, A40 to Cheltenham, 1st rdbt 4th exit
Hatherley Ln, White Lodge 1st on right

Built around 1900, this well cared for, smart and friendly
establishment is very convenient for access to the M5.
Bedrooms, of varying sizes, offer quality and many extra
facilities, including fridges and Wi-fi. The very
comfortable dining room, where breakfast is served
around a grand table, looks out across the pleasant and
extensive gardens.

Rooms 4 en suite (1 GF) S £42-£45; D £60-£65
Facilities FTV tea/coffee Cen ht Wi-fi **Parking** 6 **Notes** 🐾

CHELTENHAM *continued*

Wishmoor House

★★★★ GUEST ACCOMMODATION

147 Hales Rd GL52 6TD
☎ **01242 238504** 📠 **01242 226090**
e-mail: wishmoor@hotmail.co.uk
dir: *A40 onto B4075 Hales Rd signed Prestbury, racecourse, crematorium, 0.5m on right*

Wishmoor House is an elegantly modernised spacious Victorian residence, situated between the town centre and racecourse with easy access from all major roads and ample parking. Inside you can expect charming period features, wonderful views and a warm welcome. Free Wi-fi is available.

Rooms 10 rms (9 en suite) (1 pri facs) (2 fmly)
Facilities FTV tea/coffee Cen ht Wi-fi **Conf** Max 10 Thtr 10 Class 10 Board 10 **Parking** 9 **Notes** ⊗

The Beaufort Arms

★★★ GUEST ACCOMMODATION

184 London Rd GL52 6HJ
☎ **01242 526038** 📠 **01242 526038**
e-mail: beaufort.arms@blueyonder.co.uk
dir: *On A40*

Located on the main road, just outside of the town centre, this traditional inn offers a friendly welcome and a relaxed style of service and hospitality. Bedrooms, some with en suite and some sharing bathrooms, have been refurbished to provide sound standards throughout. A selection of real ales is available.

Rooms 5 rms (2 en suite) (1 fmly) S £27.50-£35; D £50-£60* **Facilities** FTV TVL tea/coffee Cen ht Licensed Wi-fi Pool table **Parking** 5 **Notes** ⊗

Cheltenham Guest House

★★★ GUEST HOUSE

145 Hewlett Rd GL52 6TS
☎ **01242 521726**
e-mail: info@cheltenhamguesthouse.biz
dir: *A40 London Rd into town, 3rd set of lights after church; From M5 pass Kwik Fit on left continue straight onto Hewlett Road*

This quietly located guest house is just outside the main town, yet within easy walking distance of it. Bedrooms and bathrooms come in a variety of shapes and sizes; all are well equipped. The bright and comfortable breakfast room provides an ideal setting for carefully prepared breakfasts including some extra options such as omelettes.

Rooms 9 rms (7 en suite) (1 fmly) S £40-£50; D £55-£70* **Facilities** FTV tea/coffee Cen ht Wi-fi **Parking** 6 **Notes** ⊗ Closed 23-27 Dec

---

See also Blockley

PREMIER COLLECTION

The Malt House

★★★★★ 🏠 GUEST HOUSE

Broad Campden GL55 6UU
☎ **01386 840295** 📠 **01386 841334**
e-mail: info@malt-house.co.uk
web: www.malt-house.co.uk
dir: *0.8m SE of Chipping Campden in Broad Campden, by church*

Formed from the village malt house and adjacent cottages, this beguiling house dates from the 16th century. Original features are mixed with contemporary comforts, and bedrooms have quality soft fabrics and period furniture. There is a choice of lounges, an elegant breakfast room, and a wonderful garden with croquet lawn and relaxing seating.

Rooms 4 en suite 3 annexe en suite (3 fmly) (1 GF) S £95; D £140-£150 **Facilities** FTV TVL tea/coffee Cen ht Licensed Wi-fi 🚲 **Conf** Max 8 Board 8 **Parking** 10 **Notes** ⊗ Closed 22-28 Dec

PREMIER COLLECTION

Staddlestones

★★★★★ BED AND BREAKFAST

7 Aston Rd GL55 6HR
☎ **01386 849288**
e-mail: info@staddle-stones.com
web: www.staddle-stones.com
dir: *From Chipping Campden take B4081 signed Mickleton, 200mtrs. House on right opposite gravel lane*

A warm welcome can be expected from host Pauline Kirton at this delightful property, situated just a short walk from the Cotswold village of Chipping Campden; this makes an ideal base for walking, cycling, golf or just relaxing. There are three bedrooms offering quality and comfort plus some thoughtful extras. A hearty breakfast is served in the dining room around the communal table, and there's a good choice of mostly organic produce sourced from local farms.

Rooms 2 en suite 1 annexe en suite (1 fmly) D £65-£85* **Facilities** FTV tea/coffee Cen ht Wi-fi **Parking** 6 **Notes** No Children 12yrs 📧

PREMIER COLLECTION

Woodborough

★★★★★ BED AND BREAKFAST

Aston Rd GL55 6HR
☎ **01386 841585**
e-mail: enquiries@chippingcampdenbandb.co.uk

Individual attention is assured at this very comfortable bed and breakfast located just a short stroll from the main High Street of Chipping Campden. The one spacious bedroom has a separate lounge area providing plenty of quality and comfort throughout. Breakfast is served in the well furnished dining room and includes a selection of carefully prepared, high quality produce.

Rooms 1 en suite (1 fmly) S £85; D £85 **Facilities** TVL Cen ht Wi-fi Golf 18 **Parking** 3 **Notes** LB ⊗ No Children 10yrs 📧

Bramley House

★★★★ BED AND BREAKFAST

6 Aston Rd GL55 6HR
☎ **01386 840066** & **07855 760113**
e-mail: povey@bramleyhouse.co.uk
dir: *Off High St onto B4081 towards Mickleton, house 0.5m opp cul-de-sac Grevel Ln & post box*

A warm welcome and refreshments on arrival await at Bramley House. With ample off-road parking and situated just a stroll from the centre of the popular market town, this friendly, family home offers attractively co-ordinated accommodation, with many thoughtful extras. The tranquil rear room offers superb field views. A delicious breakfast, featuring organic produce whenever possible, is served in the smart dining room around a large communal table.

Rooms 2 en suite 1 annexe en suite S fr £58; D £68-£90* **Facilities** tea/coffee Cen ht Wi-fi **Parking** 3 **Notes** ⊗ No Children 12yrs Closed 6-14 Feb 📧

The Chance

★★★★ 🏠 BED AND BREAKFAST

1 Aston Rd GL55 6HR
☎ **01386 849079**
e-mail: enquiries@the-chance.co.uk
web: www.the-chance.co.uk
dir: *B4081 towards Mickleton from Chipping Campden, signed on right hand side*

Located just a short stroll from the pleasant town of Chipping Campden, The Chance offers three well decorated and well maintained bedrooms where a range of extras are helpfully provided for guests. A friendly welcome from the resident proprietor may well include the offer of tea and home-made cakes. Breakfast is a real treat with a varied menu utilising fresh local produce with something to suit all tastes.

Save on B&Bs and Hotels. Book at **theAA.com/hotel**

GLOUCESTERSHIRE 153 **ENGLAND**

Rooms 3 en suite S £65-£75; D £65-£75* **Facilities** FTV tea/coffee Cen ht Wi-fi **Parking** 6 **Notes** LB ⊗ No Children 12yrs Closed Xmas & New Year RS mid Dec-mid Jan ⊛

The Kings

★★★★ ⊛ RESTAURANT WITH ROOMS

The Square GL55 6AW
☎ 01386 840256 & 841056 📠 01386 841598
e-mail: info@kingscampden.co.uk
dir: *In centre of town square*

Located in the centre of this delightful Cotswold town, The Kings effortlessly blends a relaxed and friendly welcome with efficient service. Bedrooms and bathrooms come in a range of shapes and sizes but all are appointed to high levels of quality and comfort. Dining options, whether in the main restaurant or the comfortable bar area, include a tempting menu to suit all tastes, from light salads and pasta to meat and fish dishes.

Rooms 14 en suite 5 annexe en suite (3 fmly) (3 GF) **Facilities** FTV TV14B tea/coffee Dinner available Direct Dial Cen ht Wi-fi **Conf** Thtr 30 Class 20 Board 20 **Parking** 8 **Notes** Civ Wed 60

Seagrave Arms

★★★★ ⊛ INN

Friday St, Weston-sub-Edge GL55 6QH
☎ 01386 840192
e-mail: info@seagravearms.co.uk
web: www.seagravearms.co.uk
dir: *From Moreton-in-Marsh take A44 towards Evesham. In approx 7m right onto B4081 signed Chipping Campden. Road becomes Sheep St. At junct with High Street left, into Dyers Ln. 0.5m over Dovers Hill, into Weston-sub-Edge, road becomes Church St. Pub on left*

Ideally located for exploring many of the popular Cotswold villages, The Seagrave Arms is a Grade II listed building with parts dating back to the 16th century. Now

refurbished throughout, the inn now offers a delightful combination of contemporary-styled bedrooms and bathrooms together with plenty of character retained in the bar and restaurant areas. The food at breakfast and dinner is a highlight, and carefully sourced, high quality produce is used.

Rooms 5 en suite 1 annexe en suite (1 GF) D £95-£115* **Facilities** STV tea/coffee Dinner available Cen ht Wi-fi **Parking** 15 **Notes** No coaches

Catbrook House

★★★★ BED AND BREAKFAST

Catbrook GL55 6DE
☎ 01386 841499
e-mail: m.klein@virgin.net
dir: *B4081 into Chipping Campden, signs for Broad Campden until Catbrook House on right*

Along with stunning rural views and close proximity to the town centre, this mellow-stone house provides comfortable, homely bedrooms. The attentive hosts extend a friendly welcome. A traditional English breakfast is served in the comfortably furnished dining room.

Rooms 3 rms (1 en suite) (2 pri facs) S fr £45; D fr £56* **Facilities** TV2B tea/coffee Cen ht **Parking** 3 **Notes** ⊗ No Children 9yrs Closed Xmas ⊛

Holly House

★★★★ BED AND BREAKFAST

Ebrington GL55 6NL
☎ 01386 593213
e-mail: info.hollyhouse@btinternet.com
web: www.hollyhousebandb.co.uk
dir: *B4035 from Chipping Campden towards Shipston on Stour, 0.5m left to Ebrington & signed*

Set in the heart of the pretty Cotswold village of Ebrington, this late Victorian house offers thoughtfully equipped accommodation. Bedrooms are housed in buildings that were formerly used by the local wheelwright, and offer level access, seclusion and privacy. Quality English breakfasts are served in the light and airy dining room. For other meals, the village pub is just a short walk away.

Rooms 2 en suite 1 annexe en suite (2 fmly) (3 GF) S £50-£65; D £65-£75 **Facilities** tea/coffee Cen ht **Parking** 5 **Notes** ⊗ Closed Xmas ⊛

Lygon Arms

★★★★ 🛏 🍺 INN

High St GL55 6HB
☎ 01386 840318 & 840089 📠 01386 841088
e-mail: sandra@lygonarms.co.uk
dir: *In town centre near church*

This charming and welcoming inn sits on the high street of this delightful village - a tranquil location with lots of tempting antique shops and restaurants. Well managed by a friendly team, the inn has a cosy bar with open log fires and oak beams. Spacious and very well appointed accommodation is provided in the main building and in mews houses. Dinner and breakfast are hearty and not to be missed.

Rooms 10 en suite (3 fmly) (1 GF) **Facilities** FTV tea/coffee Dinner available Direct Dial Wi-fi **Parking** 12 **Notes** No coaches

Manor Farm *(SP124412)*

★★★★ FARMHOUSE

Weston-sub-Edge GL55 6QH
☎ 01386 840390 & 07889 108812 📠 0870 1640638
Mrs L King
e-mail: lucy@manorfarmbnb.demon.co.uk
web: www.manorfarmbnb.demon.co.uk
dir: *2m NW of Chipping Campden. On B4632 in Weston-sub-Edge*

A genuine welcome is extended at this 17th-century mellow Cotswold-stone farmhouse. Bedrooms are comfortable and homely with thoughtful extras. Facilities include a lounge with a wood-burning stove, and an elegant dining room where mouth-watering breakfasts are served.

Rooms 3 en suite S £55-£70; D £65-£70* **Facilities** STV FTV TVL tea/coffee Cen ht Wi-fi Golf 18 **Parking** 8 **Notes** LB ⊗ 800 acres arable/cattle/horses/sheep

Stonecroft Bed & Breakfast

★★★★ BED AND BREAKFAST

Stonecroft, George Ln GL55 6DA
☎ 01386 840486
e-mail: info@stonecroft-chippingcampden.co.uk

Quietly located in a residential area just a stroll from the High Street, this well-maintained property offers relaxing accommodation. Guests have the key to their own entrance and can come and go as they please. Breakfast is served around one large table in the compact but well-furnished dining room.

Rooms 2 en suite (1 fmly) S £60; D £73* **Facilities** FTV tea/coffee Cen ht Wi-fi **Parking** 2 **Notes** ⊗ No Children 12yrs ⊛

The Moda House

★★★★ GUEST ACCOMMODATION

1 High St BS37 6BA
☎ 01454 312135   📠 01454 850090
e-mail: enquiries@modahouse.co.uk
web: www.modahouse.co.uk
dir: *In town centre*

This popular Grade II listed Georgian house has an imposing position at the top of the High Street. It has been appointed to provide modern bedrooms of varying shapes and sizes and comfortable public areas, while retaining many original features. Room facilities include satellite TV and phones.

Rooms 8 en suite 3 annexe en suite (3 GF) S £62-£67; D £82-£95* Facilities STV TVL tea/coffee Direct Dial Cen ht Licensed Wi-fi Conf Max 20 Thtr 10 Board 10

Hare & Hounds

★★★★ 🍴 INN

Fosse-Cross, Chedworth GL54 4NN
☎ 01285 720288
e-mail: stay@hareandhoundsinn.com
dir: *4.5m NE of Cirencester. On A429 by speed camera*

This traditional country inn built of Cotswold stone, near the Fosse Way, offers delicious home-cooked food in one of the elegant dining rooms and in the garden in fine weather. The smart and comfortable en suite bedrooms are set round a peaceful courtyard. Ample parking is available to the rear of the inn.

Rooms 10 en suite (2 fmly) (8 GF) Facilities tea/coffee Dinner available Direct Dial Cen ht Wi-fi Parking 40 Notes LB ⊗

The Old Bungalow Guest House

★★★★ 🅰 GUEST ACCOMMODATION

93 Victoria Rd GL7 1ES
☎ 01285 654179
e-mail: info@bandbcirencester.co.uk
dir: *Follow signs to town centre from A419 or A417, at 1st set of lights left onto Victoria Rd, 300yds on left*

Rooms 6 en suite (3 fmly) (2 GF) S fr £53; D fr £68 Facilities FTV TVL tea/coffee Cen ht Licensed Wi-fi Parking 9 Notes ⊗ No Children 10yrs

The Fleece

🅄

Market Place GL7 2NZ
☎ 01285 658507   📠 01285 651017
e-mail: relax@fleecehotel.co.uk

Currently the rating for this establishment is not confirmed. This may be due to a change of ownership or because it has only recently joined the AA rating scheme.

Rooms 28 en suite

Rising Sun

★ ★ ★ INN

GL52 3PX
☎ 01242 676281   📠 01242 673069
e-mail: 9210@greeneking.co.uk
dir: *On B4632, 4m N of Cheltenham*

This popular establishment is situated on Cleeve Hill and offers commanding views across the Severn Vale to the Malvern Hills and beyond. There is a pleasant range of public rooms which include a large bar-bistro and a reception lounge. Bedrooms are well equipped and smartly presented, and many have glorious views. A large garden is also available for summer drinking and dining.

Rooms 24 en suite (3 fmly) (6 GF) S £45-£80; D £65-£140 Facilities tea/coffee Dinner available Direct Dial Cen ht Wi-fi Parking 70 Notes LB

Dryslade Farm *(SO581147)*

★ ★ ★ ★ FARMHOUSE

English Bicknor GL16 7PA
☎ 01594 860259   📠 01594 860259
Mrs D Gwilliam
e-mail: daphne@drysladefarm.co.uk
web: www.drysladefarm.co.uk
dir: *3m N of Coleford. Off A4136 onto B4432, right towards English Bicknor, farm 1m*

Visitors are warmly welcomed at this 184-acre working farm, which dates from 1780 and has been in the same family for almost 100 years. The en suite bedrooms are attractively furnished in natural pine and are well equipped. The lounge leads onto a conservatory where hearty breakfasts are served.

Rooms 3 en suite (1 GF) D £66-£72 Facilities FTV TVL tea/coffee Cen ht Wi-fi Parking 6 Notes LB 🐾 184 acres beef

The Rock B&B

★★★★ GUEST ACCOMMODATION

GL16 7NY
☎ 01594 837893
e-mail: chris@stayattherock.com
web: www.stayattherock.com
dir: *A40 at Monmouth onto A4136, after 5m turn left at Five Acres onto Park Rd. At Christchurch turn right & immediately left towards Symonds Yat Rock, 0.75m S of Symonds Yat Rock*

The Rock offers stylish modern accommodation and is located on the outskirts of Coleford, near the famous Symonds Yat Rock. Bedrooms are attractively presented and very comfortable, with the new garden rooms making the most of the spectacular views over the Wye Valley. Very popular with walkers, the Rock also caters well for business guests. Breakfasts are served in the spacious dining room overlooking the garden.

Rooms 7 annexe en suite (5 GF) S £40-£45; D £50-£95* Facilities FTV tea/coffee Cen ht Lift Wi-fi Hot tub Parking 20 Notes LB No Children 12yrs

The Green Dragon

★★★★ 🍴 INN

Cockleford GL53 9NW
☎ 01242 870271
e-mail: green-dragon@buccaneer.co.uk

This establishment offers all the charm and character of an English country pub combined with a relaxed atmosphere and carefully prepared food made from local produce. Bedrooms, some at ground floor level, are individually furnished and vary in size. There is a terrace to the front where guests may enjoy a drink on warm sunny days.

Rooms 9 en suite (4 GF) Facilities tea/coffee Dinner available Direct Dial Cen ht Wi-fi Conf Max 65 Thtr 65 Class 65 Board 65 Parking 11

Save on B&Bs and Hotels. Book at theAA.com/hotel

GLOUCESTERSHIRE 155 ENGLAND

EBRINGTON
Map 10 SP14

The Ebrington Arms
★★★★ @ INN

GL55 6NH
☎ 01386 593223
e-mail: info@theebringtonarms.co.uk
web: www.theebringtonarms.co.uk
dir: From Chipping Campden take B4035 towards
Shipston-on-Stour, left to Ebrington

Located in the quiet, unspoilt village of Ebrington, just a
couple of miles from Chipping Campden, this 17th-
century inn provides an excellent selection of real ales,
fine wines and really enjoyable home-made dishes
utilising the finest of produce. Food is served in the
traditional ambience of the bar or the cosy dining room
with roaring open fire. Bedrooms are full of character and
include some welcome extras. A large beer garden and
car park are also available.

Rooms 3 en suite Facilities FTV tea/coffee Dinner
available Cen ht Conf Max 32 Thtr 32 Class 32 Board 25
Parking 10

FORD
Map 10 SP02

The Plough Inn
★★★★ ⊜ INN

GL54 5RU
☎ 01386 584215 📠 01386 584042
e-mail: info@theploughinnatford.co.uk
web: www.theploughinnatford.co.uk
dir: On B4077 in village

Popular with locals and the racing fraternity, this
charming 16th-century inn retains many original features
such as Cotswold stone walls, open fires and beamed
ceilings. Cheltenham, Tewkesbury and many popular
Cotswold towns and villages are in close proximity.
Home-cooked food featuring local produce is a highlight.
Bedrooms are situated in a restored stable block across a
courtyard, adjacent to the delightful beer garden.

Rooms 3 annexe en suite (2 fmly) Facilities FTV tea/
coffee Dinner available Cen ht Parking 50 Notes LB ⊗

FOSSEBRIDGE
Map 5 SP01

The Inn at Fossebridge
★★★★ ⊜ INN

GL54 3JS
☎ 01285 720721
e-mail: info@fossebridgeinn.co.uk
dir: On A429, 3m S of A40 & 6m N of Cirencester

Located not too far from Stratford-upon-Avon,
Cheltenham and Cirencester this inn is around 300 years
old, and was once a coaching inn on the old Fosse Way.
Today it is a beautiful Cotswold retreat with wonderful
accommodation and grounds. Fine food is served in the
character bar and dining areas, and a warm welcome
awaits all visitors.

Rooms 9 en suite (1 fmly) D £110-£165 Facilities FTV
TVL tea/coffee Dinner available Cen ht Wi-fi ch fac
Fishing Conf Max 70 Thtr 50 Class 40 Board 14
Parking 40 Notes LB Civ Wed 70

FRAMPTON MANSELL
Map 4 SO90

The Crown Inn
★★★★ INN

GL6 8JG
☎ 01285 760601
e-mail: enquiries@thecrowninn-cotswolds.co.uk
dir: Off A419 signed Frampton Mansell, 0.75m at village
centre

This establishment was a cider house in the 17th century,
and guests today will find that roaring log fires, locally
brewed ales and traditional, home-cooked food are all on
offer. The comfortable, well-equipped bedrooms are in an
annexe, and ample parking is available.

Rooms 12 en suite (1 fmly) (4 GF) S £67.50-£87.50; D
£87.50-£101.50* Facilities tea/coffee Dinner available
Cen ht Wi-fi Conf Max 40 Parking 35 Notes LB

GLOUCESTER
Map 10 SO81

The Wharf House
★★★★ @ RESTAURANT WITH ROOMS

Over GL2 8DB
☎ 01452 332900 📠 01452 332901
e-mail: thewharfhouse@yahoo.co.uk
dir: Off A40 between Gloucester & Highnam at Over

The Wharf House was built to replace the old lock cottage
and, as the name suggests, it is located at the very edge
of the river; it has pleasant views and an outdoor terrace.
The bedrooms and bathrooms have been decorated and
appointed to high levels of quality and comfort, and there
are plenty of guest extras. Seasonal, local produce can be
enjoyed both at breakfast and dinner in the delightfully
relaxing restaurant.

Rooms 7 en suite (1 fmly) (1 GF) D £85-£135*
Facilities STV FTV TVL tea/coffee Dinner available Direct
Dial Cen ht Wi-fi Fishing Parking 37 Notes Closed 24
Dec-4 Jan No coaches

The New Inn
★★★ INN

16 Northgate St GL1 1SF
☎ 01452 522177 📠 01452 301054
e-mail: newinn@relaxinnz.co.uk

This establishment is located in the centre of Gloucester
and has been described as one of the finest examples of
a medieval galleried inn in Britain. As expected the
building, dating back to 1430, has plenty of character.
The bedrooms come in a range of shapes and sizes on
several floors around the inner courtyard. The restaurant
has a traditional carvery, and there is also a separate bar
and coffee shop.

Rooms 33 en suite (2 fmly) S £39-£54; D £49-£71
Facilities FTV TVL tea/coffee Dinner available Cen ht Wi-fi
Conf Max 80 Thtr 80 Class 80 Board 30 Notes LB ⊗

GUITING POWER
Map 10 SP02

Guiting Guest House
★★★★ GUEST HOUSE

Post Office Ln GL54 5TZ
☎ 01451 850470
e-mail: info@guitingguesthouse.com
web: www.guitingguesthouse.com
dir: In village centre

In keeping with all the surrounding houses, this engaging
family home is built of mellow Cotswold stone. Charming
and comfortable bedrooms offer both individuality and
character, as do the public rooms, which include the
stylish dining room and snug lounge. Breakfast (and
dinner by arrangement) uses excellent local produce
whenever possible. Barbara Millar was a finalist in this
year's Friendliest Landlady of the Year award (2011-12).

Rooms 3 rms (2 en suite) (1 pri facs) 2 annexe en suite
(2 GF) D £78-£88* Facilities tea/coffee Dinner available
Cen ht Wi-fi Parking 3 Notes LB

LECHLADE ON THAMES
Map 5 SU29

Cambrai Lodge
★★★★ GUEST ACCOMMODATION

Oak St GL7 3AY
☎ 01367 253173 & 07860 150467
e-mail: info@cambrailodgeguesthouse.co.uk
web: www.cambrailodgeguesthouse.co.uk
dir: In town centre, off High St onto A361 Oak St

This delightful house is just a stroll from the centre of the
historic market town with its many pubs that serve
meals. The individually styled bedrooms offer plenty of
quality and comfort, and include a four-poster room and
two ground-floor rooms. Breakfast is served in the
pleasant conservatory overlooking the gardens.

Rooms 3 en suite (2 GF) S £45-£55; D £60-£75*
Facilities FTV tea/coffee Cen ht Parking 12 Notes ⊛

New House Farm B&B *(SO685229)*

★★★★ FARMHOUSE

Barrel Ln, Aston Ingham GL17 0LS
☎ **01452 830484** & 07768 354922 ☐ 01452 830484
Ms R Smith
e-mail: scaldbrain@btinternet.com
dir: *A40 onto B4222, Barrel Ln on right before Aston Ingham or M50 junct 3 towards Newent, turn right at Kilcot to Aston Ingham*

Located in tranquil wooded countryside, this working farm is a good touring base on the Gloucestershire-Herefordshire border. Set in 65 acres, the welcoming farmhouse will certainly appeal to nature lovers, and there is a comfortable lounge and bar. Breakfast consists of a good selection of carefully prepared local produce.

Rooms 3 en suite (1 fmly) **Facilities** FTV TVL tea/coffee Dinner available Cen ht Wi-fi ⚓ **Conf** Max 15 **Parking** 10 **Notes** ⊗ No Children 10yrs Closed Xmas & New Year 65 acres sheep/cattle/woodland

Lord Nelson Inn

★★★ INN

SN14 8LP
☎ **01225 891820**
e-mail: thelordnelsoninn@btinternet.com
web: www.thelordnelsoninn.info
dir: *M4 junct 18 onto A46 towards Bath. Left at Cold Ashton rdbt towards Marshfield*

Located at one end of the pleasant village of Marshfield, the Lord Nelson is a traditional coaching inn with a pleasant ambience. The spacious bar provides a good opportunity to mix with the locals, while the candlelit restaurant offers a quieter environment in which to enjoy the excellent selection of carefully prepared home-made dishes. Bedrooms and bathrooms are all well decorated and furnished.

Rooms 3 en suite S £35-£47.50; D £65-£77.50*
Facilities FTV tea/coffee Dinner available Cen ht
Conf Max 80 Thtr 40 Class 30 Board 30 **Notes** LB

Red Lion Inn

★★★ ⌐ INN

Little Compton GL56 0RT
☎ **01608 674397**
e-mail: info@theredlionlittlecompton.co.uk
dir: *On A44 between Chipping Norton & Moreton-in-Marsh*

Built in 1748 as a coaching inn the Red Lion retains much of the charm and character of a friendly country pub. It has been sympathetically restored and the inglenook fireplaces, stone walls and oak beams remain a real feature. The comfortable bedrooms are stylishly presented and overlook the neat gardens with the beautiful Cotswold countryside beyond. Comprehensive breakfast choices are available, and evening meals should not to be missed.

Rooms 2 en suite **Facilities** FTV tea/coffee Dinner available Cen ht Wi-fi Pool table **Parking** 15 **Notes** LB

Wild Garlic Restaurant and Rooms

★★★★ ◉◉ RESTAURANT WITH ROOMS

3 Cossack Square GL6 0DB
☎ **01453 832615**
e-mail: info@wild-garlic.co.uk
dir: *M4 junct 18. A46 towards Stroud. Enter Nailsworth, left at rdbt, immediate left. Establishment opposite Britannia Pub*

Situated in a quiet corner of this charming Cotswold town, this restaurant with rooms offers a delightful combination of welcoming, relaxed hospitality and high quality cuisine. The spacious and well equipped bedrooms are situated above the restaurant. The small and friendly team of staff ensure guests are very well looked after throughout their stay.

Rooms 3 rms (2 en suite) (1 pri facs) (2 fmly) S £59.50-£75; D £65-£85* **Facilities** STV FTV tea/coffee Dinner available Cen ht Wi-fi Golf 18 **Notes** ⊗ No coaches

Mill View

★★★★ GUEST HOUSE

2 Mill View GL54 3AF
☎ **01451 850586**
e-mail: patricia@millview.myzen.co.uk
web: www.millviewguesthousecotswolds.com
dir: *Off B4068 to E end of village*

Lying opposite a historic watermill, this former family home has been extended and modernised to provide every comfort. A warm welcome and attentive care is assured in this non-smoking house, which has one bedroom equipped for easier access. The accommodation provides a good base for walkers or for touring Gloucestershire.

Rooms 3 en suite (1 GF) S £45-£55; D £65-£80*
Facilities TVL tea/coffee Dinner available Cen ht **Parking** 4 **Notes** LB ⊗ ⊜

The Feathered Nest Inn

◉◉ 🍴 INN

OX7 6SD
☎ **01993 833030** ☐ 01993 833031
e-mail: info@thefeatherednestinn.co.uk
web: www.thefeatherednestinn.co.uk
dir: *A424 between Burford & Stow-on-the-Wold, follow signs*

Located in the picturesque Cotswold village of Nether Westcote with rolling views over the Evenlode Valley, this charming village inn has been restored with care offering a cosy base in which to explore the idyllic Cotswolds. There are four luxurious en suite bedrooms all individually designed combining quality antiques and modern extras which will ensure a memorable stay. Service is attentive and helpful whilst the food is a delight, offering a selection of carefully crafted dishes using the best of quality, seasonal produce.

Rooms 4 en suite (1 fmly) **Facilities** STV FTV TVL tea/coffee Dinner available Direct Dial Cen ht Wi-fi **Parking** 45 **Notes** ⊗ Closed 25 Dec No coaches Civ Wed 200

Three Choirs Vineyards

★★★★ ◉◉ RESTAURANT WITH ROOMS

GL18 1LS
☎ **01531 890223** ☐ 01531 890877
e-mail: info@threechoirs.com
web: www.threechoirs.com
dir: *On B4215 N of Newent, follow brown tourist signs*

This thriving vineyard continues to go from strength to strength and provides a wonderfully different place to stay. The restaurant, which overlooks the 100-acre estate, enjoys a popular following thanks to well-executed dishes that make good use of local produce. Spacious, high quality bedrooms are equipped with many extras, and each opens onto a private patio area which has wonderful views.

Rooms 11 annexe en suite (1 fmly) (11 GF) S £115-£145; D £125-£155* **Facilities** FTV tea/coffee Dinner available Direct Dial Cen ht Wine tasting Vineyard Tours **Conf** Max 20 Thtr 20 Class 15 Board 20 **Parking** 11 **Notes** LB Closed 24-27 Dec No coaches

OLD SODBURY   Map 4 ST78

The Sodbury House

★★★★ GUEST HOUSE

Badminton Rd BS37 6LU
☎ **01454 312847**   📠 **01454 273105**
e-mail: info@sodburyhouse.co.uk
web: www.sodburyhouse.co.uk
dir: *M4 junct 18, A46 N, 2m left onto A432 to Chipping Sodbury, house 1m on left*

This comfortably furnished 19th-century farmhouse stands in six acres of grounds. The bedrooms, many located on the ground floor and in buildings adjacent to the main house, have many extra facilities. Breakfast offers a varied choice and is served in the spacious breakfast room.

Rooms 6 en suite 9 annexe en suite (2 fmly) (7 GF)
Facilities FTV TVL tea/coffee Direct Dial Cen ht Wi-fi ♨
Conf Thtr 40 Class 25 Board 20 **Parking** 30 **Notes** ⊗
Closed 24 Dec-3 Jan

The Cross Hands

★★★ INN

BS37 6RJ
☎ **01454 313000**   📠 **01454 324409**
e-mail: 6435@greeneking.co.uk
dir: *M4 junct 18 signed to Cirencester/Stroud on A46. After 1.5m, on right at 1st lights*

The Cross Hands is a former posting house dating back to the 14th century that is just off the main road, and within easy reach of both Bath and Bristol. The bedrooms are well equipped and some are at ground-floor level. The public areas include a bar, comfortable seating area and a spacious split-level restaurant which offers a selection of home-cooked dishes. Alternatively, guests may choose to eat from the extensive menu in the bar area.

Rooms 21 en suite (1 fmly) (9 GF) **Facilities** tea/coffee Dinner available Direct Dial Cen ht Wi-fi **Conf** Max 80 Thtr 80 Class 24 Board 16 **Parking** 120 **Notes** Civ Wed 80

PAINSWICK   Map 4 SO80

St Michaels

★★★★ ◉ 🍴 RESTAURANT WITH ROOMS

Victoria St GL6 6QA
☎ **01452 814555**   📠 **01452 814606**
e-mail: info@stmickshouse.co.uk

This 17th-century Grade II listed building has a wealth of character and overlooks the famous Church of St Michaels with its 99 Yew trees. Each stylish bedroom has its own theme and is equipped with a host of thoughtful extras. The award-winning restaurant has an imaginative menu based on the best local produce. A warm welcome is guaranteed and the delicious breakfasts should not be missed. Situated in the heart of the very pretty Cotswold village of Painswick this establishment makes an ideal base for exploring the beautiful Cotswolds.

Rooms 3 en suite **Facilities** Dinner available Cen ht Wi-fi Golf 18 **Notes** Closed 21 Dec-1 Feb & 6-15 Jun No coaches

Hambutts Mynd Guest House

★★★ GUEST ACCOMMODATION

Edge Rd GL6 6UP
☎ **01452 812352**
e-mail: ewarland@supanet.com

Built in the 1700s as a corn mill, this property has an interesting history. In 1801 it was converted into a school, and much later it commenced its role of offering guest accommodation. Homely and welcoming hospitality is delivered and the bedrooms benefit from delightful views over the valley and the hills. A number of pleasant Cotswold walks are available directly from the house and Painswick itself is a just a five-minute stroll away.

Rooms 3 en suite **Facilities** STV FTV TVL tea/coffee Cen ht **Parking** 3 **Notes** No Children 10yrs Closed Jan RS Mar 🍴

PAXFORD   Map 10 SP13

Churchill Arms

★★★★ ◉◉ 🍴 INN

GL55 6XH
☎ **01386 594000**
e-mail: info@thechurchillarms.com
dir: *A429 onto A44 to Bourton-on-the-Hill, through village then turn right. Through Blockley to Paxford, pub on right*

Set in the peaceful village of Paxford, this delightful Cotswold inn combines the atmosphere of a traditional village hostelry (real ale, log fires, wooden beams etc) with modern comforts in the well-appointed bedrooms and bathrooms. All food here, from the bar menu's light options to the carefully-prepared dishes at dinner and at breakfast, is of the highest quality.

Rooms 4 en suite (2 fmly) **Facilities** tea/coffee Dinner available Direct Dial Cen ht Wi-fi **Notes** No coaches

ST BRIAVELS   Map 4 SO50

The Florence

★★★★ GUEST ACCOMMODATION

Bigsweir GL15 6QQ
☎ **01594 530830**   📠 **01594 530830**
e-mail: enquiries@florencehotel.co.uk
dir: *On A466 between Monmouth & Chepstow*

Located on the Wye Valley road, The Florence has delightful views across the river and stands in over five acres of gardens with woodland walks. Bedrooms, some in the main house and the others in an adjacent cottage, come in a range of sizes and styles. Guests can enjoy cream teas in the garden, a drink in the snug, and choose from a wide selection of carefully prepared dishes at both lunch and dinner.

Rooms 4 en suite 4 annexe en suite (1 fmly) (2 GF) S £35-£50; D £70-£100* (incl.dinner) **Facilities** FTV tea/coffee Dinner available Cen ht Licensed Wi-fi Fishing **Parking** 30 **Notes** LB ⊗ No Children 10yrs Closed Nov-Jan

STOW-ON-THE-WOLD   Map 10 SP12

Woodlands Guest House

★★★★ GUEST ACCOMMODATION

Upper Swell GL54 1EW
☎ **01451 832346**
e-mail: amandak247@talktalk.net
dir: *Upper Swell 1m from Stow-on-the-Wold, take B4077 (Tewkesbury Road)*

Situated in the small hamlet of Upper Swell, Woodlands provides an ideal base for exploring many charming nearby villages. This establishment enjoys delightful rural views and has comfortably appointed bedrooms with a good range of extra accessories. Breakfast is served in the welcoming dining room around the communal dining table. Off-road parking is available.

Rooms 5 en suite (2 GF) S £40-£50; D £65-£80* **Facilities** FTV tea/coffee Cen ht Wi-fi **Parking** 8 **Notes** LB ⊗ 🍴

STOW-ON-THE-WOLD *continued*

Aston House

★★★★ BED AND BREAKFAST

Broadwell GL56 0TJ
☎ 01451 830475
e-mail: fja@astonhouse.net
dir: *A429 from Stow-on-the-Wold towards Moreton-in-Marsh, 1m right at x-rds to Broadwell, Aston House 0.5m on left*

Peacefully located on the edge of the village of Broadwell, this is an ideal base from which to explore the charming delights of the Cotswolds. A warm and genuine welcome is guaranteed and every effort is made to ensure a relaxed and enjoyable stay. Great care and attention are hallmarks here, and bedrooms come equipped with many thoughtful extras such as electric blankets.

Rooms 3 rms (2 en suite) (1 pri facs) (1 GF) D £75-£85
Facilities FTV tea/coffee Cen ht Wi-fi stairlift **Parking** 3
Notes ⊗ No Children 10yrs Closed Nov-Feb ⊜

The Kings Head Inn

★★★★ @ INN

The Green, Bledington OX7 6XQ
☎ 01608 658365 ▤ 01608 658902
e-mail: info@kingsheadinn.net
web: www.kingsheadinn.net
dir: *4m SE off B4450*

Located on the delightful village green near the river, this 16th-century inn has spacious public areas with open fires, wobbly floors, beams and wood furnishings. The comfortable restaurant offers excellent dining and the bedrooms have been creatively decorated and well furnished; some rooms are in a converted annexe.

Rooms 6 en suite 6 annexe en suite (3 GF) **Facilities** FTV TVL tea/coffee Dinner available Direct Dial Cen ht Wi-fi **Parking** 24 **Notes** ⊗ Closed 25-26 Dec RS wkdays Closed every afternoon 3-6 low season No coaches

Corsham Field Farmhouse *(SP217249)*

★★★ FARMHOUSE

Bledington Rd GL54 1JH
☎ 01451 831750 ▤ 01451 832247
Mr R Smith
e-mail: farmhouse@corshamfield.co.uk
dir: *2m SE of Stow on B4450*

This establishment, which has views of the surrounding countryside from its elevated position, is a popular choice with walking groups and families. The modern bedrooms are practically equipped and located in two separate houses. Enjoyable breakfasts are taken in the spacious dining room, which also provides a lounge. The local pub is just a short walk away and has a reputation for good food.

Rooms 7 rms (5 en suite) (2 pri facs) (3 fmly) (2 GF) S £35-£50; D £50-£70* **Facilities** FTV tea/coffee Cen ht Wi-fi **Parking** 10 **Notes** LB ⊗ ⊜ 100 acres arable

---

1 Woodchester Lodge

★★★★ ⊜ BED AND BREAKFAST

Southfield Rd, North Woodchester GL5 5PA
☎ 01453 872586
e-mail: anne@woodchesterlodge.co.uk
dir: *A46 onto Selsley Rd, take 2nd left, 200yds on left*

Close to the newly re-routed Cotswold Way, this late Victorian former timber merchant's house is set in the peaceful village of North Woodchester and is just a short drive from Stroud. In its own landscaped gardens, this large house has spacious, sympathetically restored bedrooms and a comfortable lounge. Evening meals and freshly prepared breakfasts are not to be missed.

Rooms 3 rms (1 en suite) (2 pri facs) (1 fmly) S £45-£48; D £65-£70* **Facilities** FTV TVL tea/coffee Dinner available Cen ht Wi-fi **Parking** 4 **Notes** ⊗ Closed Xmas & Etr

Hyde Crest

★★★★ BED AND BREAKFAST

Cirencester Rd GL6 8PE
☎ 01453 731631
e-mail: stay@hydecrest.co.uk
dir: *Off A419, 5m E of Stroud, signed Minchinhampton & Aston Down, house 3rd right opp Ragged Cot pub*

Hyde Crest lies on the edge of the picturesque Cotswold village of Minchinhampton. Bedrooms are located at ground floor level, each with a private patio where welcome refreshments are enjoyed upon arrival (weather permitting). Guests are attentively cared for and scrumptious breakfasts are served in the small lounge-dining room around a communal table.

Rooms 3 en suite (3 GF) S fr £45; D fr £70* **Facilities** FTV TVL tea/coffee Cen ht Wi-fi **Parking** 6 **Notes** No Children 10yrs RS Xmas & New Year no meals available ⊜

The Withyholt Guest House

★★★★ GUEST HOUSE

Paul Mead, Edge GL6 6PG
☎ 01452 813618 ▤ 01452 812375
e-mail: info@thewithyholtbedandbreakfast.com

A peacefully located property in a quiet residential area very close to Painswick; delightful walks in the Cotswolds are available right from the doorstep. The bedrooms and bathrooms are comfortably appointed, and the spacious public areas include a lounge and snooker room. Breakfast offers a good selection of well cooked and well presented hot and cold dishes.

Rooms 4 rms (2 en suite) (1 pri facs) 1 annexe en suite (1 GF) S fr £35; D £65-£70 **Facilities** STV FTV TVL tea/coffee Dinner available Cen ht ch fac Snooker Sauna **Parking** 4 **Notes** ⊜

The Great Tythe Barn Accommodation

★★★ GUEST ACCOMMODATION

Folly Farm, Long Newton GL8 8XA
☎ 01666 502475 ▤ 01666 502358
e-mail: info@gtb.co.uk
web: www.gtb.co.uk
dir: *M4 junct 17, B4014 signed Tetbury, on right after Welcome to Tetbury sign*

Folly Farm is located amidst rolling countryside just a 10-minute walk from Tetbury. The well-equipped bedrooms are adjacent to a huge tithe barn, that together with the pleasant grounds surrounding it, makes this a popular wedding venue. Breakfast is taken in the comfortable and relaxing Orangery that offers a well presented continental selection.

Rooms 12 en suite (2 fmly) (6 GF) **Facilities** FTV tea/coffee Cen ht Licensed Wi-fi ⤸ **Conf** Max 180 Thtr 100 Class 64 Board 65 **Parking** 100 **Notes** LB ⊗ Civ Wed 180

Hunters Hall

★★★ INN

Kingscote GL8 8XZ
☎ 01453 860393 ▤ 01453 860707
e-mail: huntershall.kingscote@greeneking.co.uk
dir: *M4 junct 18, take A46 towards Stroud. Turn left signed Kingscote, to T-junct left, 0.5m on left*

Situated close to Tetbury, this 16th-century inn has a wealth of charm and character, enhanced by beamed ceilings and open fires. There are three bars and a restaurant offering freshly prepared home-cooked, traditional food from an extensive menu. The bedrooms, situated in the converted stable block, are comfortable with a good range of extras. One ground-floor room has facilities for disabled guests. There is a large garden and play area.

Rooms 12 annexe en suite (1 fmly) (8 GF) **Facilities** tea/coffee Direct Dial Pool table **Parking** 100

TEWKESBURY   Map 10 SO83

The Bell

★★★★ INN
----

52 Church St GL20 5SA
☎ **01684 293293** 📠 **01684 295938**
e-mail: 6408@greeneking.co.uk
dir: *M5 junct 9, follow brown tourist signs for Tewkesbury Abbey, directly opposite Abbey*

This 14th-century former coaching house is situated on the edge of the town, opposite the Norman abbey. The bar and lounge are the focal point of this atmospheric and friendly establishment, with a large open fire providing warmth. Bedrooms offer good levels of comfort and quality with some welcome extra facilities provided.

Rooms 24 en suite (1 fmly) (4 GF) **Facilities** tea/coffee Direct Dial Wi-fi **Parking** 20

Willow Cottages

★★★ GUEST ACCOMMODATION

Shuthonger Common GL20 6ED
☎ **01684 298599** 📠 **01684 298599**
e-mail: RobBrd1@aol.com
dir: *1m N of Tewkesbury, on A38, house on right; or 1m S of M50 junct 1, on A38 house on left*

Located to the north of Tewkesbury in pretty rural surroundings, this welcoming house offers comfortable homely bedrooms with efficient modern bathrooms and a cosy, pine furnished breakfast room. This establishment makes an excellent base for those visiting this picturesque area whether for work or pleasure.

Rooms 3 en suite (1 fmly) S £20-£32; D £46-£56 **Facilities** tea/coffee Dinner available Cen ht **Parking** 6 **Notes** LB ⊗

THORNBURY   Map 4 ST69

Thornbury Golf Lodge

★★★★ GUEST ACCOMMODATION

Bristol Rd BS35 3XL
☎ **01454 281144**
e-mail: info@thornburygc.co.uk
web: www.thornburygc.co.uk
dir: *M5 junct 16, A38 towards Thornbury. At lights (Berkeley Vale Motors) turn left, 1m on left*

With good access to both the M4 and M5 this golfing lodge offers a popular retreat for both business and

leisure guests. Surrounded by pleasant scenery including the golf course, dinner and breakfast can be enjoyed in the clubhouse-style dining area where a good choice is offered. The spacious and comfortable bedrooms are located in a lodge adjacent to the main clubhouse. An excellent golf driving range is also available.

Rooms 11 en suite **Facilities** tea/coffee **Notes** Closed 25 Dec

---

WICK   Map 4 ST77

Southwood House B&B

★★★ BED AND BREAKFAST
----

2 Bath Rd BS30 5RL
☎ **0117 937 2649** & **07792 980087** 📠 **0117 937 3361**
e-mail: mail@southwoodhouse.com

Conveniently located with easy access to both Bristol and Bath, this welcoming, family-run bed and breakfast offers a peaceful ambience and comfortable rooms. Two rooms are located in the main house, and one larger room in an adjacent building. Breakfasts utilise fresh, local produce including eggs from the hens in the back garden, and also home-made jams. There's a good choice of pubs nearby including a couple within easy walking distance.

Rooms 2 en suite 1 annexe en suite (1 GF) S £45-£50; D £65-£70* **Facilities** FTV tea/coffee Cen ht Wi-fi **Parking** 3 **Notes** LB ⊗ 🐾

WINCHCOMBE   Map 10 SP02

Manor Farm *(SP025300)*

★★★★ FARMHOUSE

Greet GL54 5BJ
☎ **01242 602423** & **07748 077717** 📠 **01242 602423**
Mr & Mrs Richard Day
e-mail: janet@dickandjanet.fsnet.co.uk
dir: *M5 junct 9 onto A46 then B4077 towards Stow-on-the-Wold, right onto B4078. In 2m turn left to Greet*

Peacefully located in the quiet village of Greet, this impressive building is full of character and charm. Bedrooms and bathrooms come in a range of shapes and sizes but all are comfortable and well equipped. Breakfast is taken in traditional farmhouse style at one large table in the well furnished dining room. The views from this working farm over the surrounding hills are delightful whatever the time of year.

Rooms 3 en suite S £50; D £75* **Facilities** FTV TVL tea/coffee Cen ht 🐾 **Parking** 50 **Notes** ⊗ Closed 22-28 Dec 🐾 500 acres arable/beef

---

Sudeley Hill Farm *(SP038276)*

★★★★ FARMHOUSE

GL54 5JB
☎ **01242 602344** 📠 **01242 602344**
Mrs B Scudamore
e-mail: scudamore4@aol.com
dir: *Off B4632 in Winchcombe onto Castle St, White Hart Inn on corner, farm 0.75m on left*

Located on an 800-acre mixed arable and sheep farm, this 15th-century mellow stone farmhouse is full of original features including fires and exposed beams. Genuine hospitality is always on offer here with a relaxed and welcoming atmosphere. The comfortable bedrooms are filled with thoughtful extras, and memorable breakfasts are served in the elegant dining room overlooking immaculate gardens.

Rooms 3 en suite (1 fmly) S £40-£50; D £70-£80* **Facilities** TVL tea/coffee Cen ht **Parking** 10 **Notes** ⊗ Closed Xmas 🐾 800 acres sheep/arable

---

Wesley House

★★★★ ⊛⊛ 🍴 RESTAURANT WITH ROOMS

High St GL54 5LJ
☎ **01242 602366** 📠 **01242 609046**
e-mail: enquiries@wesleyhouse.co.uk
web: www.wesleyhouse.co.uk
dir: *In town centre*

This 15th-century, half-timbered property is named after John Wesley, founder of the Methodist Church, who stayed here while preaching in the town. Bedrooms are small but full of character. In the rear dining room, a unique lighting system changes colour to suit the mood required, and also highlights the various floral creations by a world-renowned flower arranger. A glass atrium covers the outside terrace.

Rooms 5 en suite **Facilities** tea/coffee Dinner available Cen ht Wi-fi **Conf** Thtr 30 Class 40 **Notes** ⊗ RS Sun eve Restaurant closed Civ Wed 60

GREATER MANCHESTER

ALTRINCHAM — Map 15 SJ78

Ash Farm Country House

★★★★ GUEST ACCOMMODATION

Park Ln, Little Bollington WA14 4TJ
☎ 0161 929 9290
e-mail: ashfarm@googlemail.com
dir: Turn off A56 at Home pub onto Park Ln, at bottom of lane on right

A warm welcome is guaranteed at this charming 18th century National Trust farmhouse, which enjoys a peaceful rural location along a quiet country lane. The bedrooms are attractively presented and public areas include a book-filled lounge with its crackling log fire and cosy sofas. Free Wi-fi is available and the house is equally popular with business and leisure guests. The Dunham Massey Hall and Deerpark is a short stroll from the house and Manchester Airport is a 15 minute drive away.

Rooms 3 en suite 1 annexe en suite (1 GF) S £49-£61; D £77-£86* **Facilities** FTV tea/coffee Cen ht Licensed Wi-fi **Conf** Max 10 Class 10 **Parking** 12 **Notes** LB ⊗ No Children 12yrs

Rostherne Country House

★★★★ GUEST ACCOMMODATION

Rostherne Ln, Rostherne WA16 6RY
☎ 01565 832628
e-mail: info@rosthernehouse.co.uk

(For full entry see Knutsford (Cheshire))

BOLTON — Map 15 SD70

Broomfield House

★★★ GUEST HOUSE

33-35 Wigan Rd, Deane BL3 5PX
☎ 01204 61570 📄 01204 650932
e-mail: contact@broomfieldhotel.co.uk
dir: M61 junct 5, A58 to 1st lights, straight onto A676, premises on right

A friendly relaxed atmosphere prevails at Broomfield House, close to the motorway and west of the town centre. There is a comfy lounge and separate bar area. Hearty breakfasts are served in the dining room.

Rooms 20 en suite (2 fmly) (2 GF) (6 smoking) S £33-£43; D £48-£58 **Facilities** FTV TVL tea/coffee Cen ht Licensed Wi-fi **Parking** 12

CHEADLE — Map 16 SJ88

The Governors House

★★★ INN

43 Ravenoak Rd, Cheadle Hulme SK8 7EQ
☎ 0161 488 4222
e-mail: 4718@greeneking.co.uk
web: www.gkpubs.co.uk/cheadle-hulme/governors-house

Located close to Manchester and Stockport, this establishment is an ideal base for exploring the Cheshire countryside. Bedrooms are tastefully decorated and furnished, with a good range of accessories. The bar and restaurant are popular with residents and locals, and alfresco dining can be enjoyed in the summer months. Children are welcome. Park and Fly Manchester is available.

Rooms 9 en suite (1 fmly) S fr £45.50; D £55* **Facilities** FTV tea/coffee Dinner available Direct Dial Cen ht Wi-fi **Conf** Thtr 20 Class 14 Board 14 **Parking** 87 **Notes** LB ⊗ No coaches

DELPH — Map 16 SD90

Wellcroft House

★★★★ GUEST ACCOMMODATION

Bleak Hey Nook OL3 5LY
☎ 01457 875017
e-mail: wellcrofthouse@hotmail.co.uk
web: www.wellcrofthouse.co.uk
dir: Off A62 on Standedge Foot Rd near A670 junct

Commanding superb views down the valley below, this former weaver's cottage offers warm traditional hospitality to walkers on the Pennine Way and those touring the Pennine towns and villages. Modern comforts in all bedrooms and transport from local railway or walks is routinely provided by the friendly proprietors.

Rooms 3 rms (2 en suite) (1 GF) S £30-£65; D £50-£65* **Facilities** FTV TVL tea/coffee Dinner available Cen ht Wi-fi Pool table **Parking** 1 **Notes** LB ⊕

LITTLEBOROUGH — Map 16 SD91

Hollingworth Lake Bed & Breakfast

★★★★★ Ⓐ GUEST ACCOMMODATION

164 Smithy Bridge Rd OL15 0DB
☎ 01706 376583 📄 01706 374054
dir: M62 junct 21, take A640 N follow brown signs to Hollingworth Lake Country Park, at T-junct onto small rdbt, right onto Smithy Bridge Rd, 50yds on right

Rooms 3 en suite 2 annexe en suite (1 fmly) (2 GF) S £37.50; D £50* **Facilities** STV FTV tea/coffee Cen ht Wi-fi **Conf** Max 10 **Parking** 8 **Notes** RS 25-26 Dec & 1 Jan No breakfast

MANCHESTER — Map 15 SJ89

The Ascott

★★★★ GUEST ACCOMMODATION

6 Half Edge Ln, Ellesmere Park, Eccles M30 9GJ
☎ 0161 950 2453 📄 0161 661 7063
e-mail: ascotthotelmanchester@yahoo.co.uk
web: www.ascotthotelmanchester.co.uk
dir: M602 junct 2, left onto Wellington Rd, 0.25m right onto Abbey Grove & left onto Half Edge Ln

Set in a mainly residential area close to major routes, this early Victorian house, once the home of the mayor of Eccles, has been renovated to provide thoughtfully furnished bedrooms with smart modern bathrooms. A choice of breakfast rooms is available and there is an elegant lounge.

Rooms 14 en suite (1 fmly) (4 GF) S £45-£85; D £65-£105 (room only) **Facilities** FTV TVL tea/coffee Direct Dial Cen ht Wi-fi **Parking** 12 **Notes** ⊗ Closed 22 Dec-2 Jan RS Sun & Fri Closed 1-5pm

Thistlewood

★★★ GUEST HOUSE

203 Urmston Ln, Stretford M32 9EF
☎ 0161 865 3611 📄 0161 866 8133
e-mail: iain.campbell30@ntlworld.com
dir: M60 junct 7, A56 towards Stretford, left onto A5181 & Sandy Ln, left onto A5213

This grand Victorian house is set in attractive grounds in a residential area close to the M60, and within easy reach are Old Trafford and the airport. The bedrooms are well equipped, and the public rooms, including a lounge, are spacious and comfortable.

Rooms 9 en suite **Facilities** FTV TVL tea/coffee Cen ht Licensed Wi-fi **Parking** 12 **Notes** ⊗

MANCHESTER AIRPORT — Map 15 SJ88

Rylands Farm Guest House

★★★ GUEST ACCOMMODATION

Altrincham Rd SK9 4LT
☎ 01625 535646 & 548041 📄 01625 255256
e-mail: info@rylandsfarm.com
web: www.rylandsfarm.com
dir: M56 junct 6, A538 towards Wilmslow, house 1.5m on left after Wilmslow Moat House

Next to the main road, very convenient for Manchester Airport and yet situated in attractive gardens. There is a range of well furnished bedrooms. Most are located in the converted farm buildings adjacent to the main house. Breakfast is served in a conservatory dining room and there is outside seating for guests to enjoy the garden in warmer weather.

Rooms 3 en suite 6 annexe en suite (3 fmly) (3 GF) **Facilities** TVL tea/coffee Dinner available Cen ht Licensed **Conf** Max 30 Class 30 **Parking** 15 **Notes** Closed 24-25 Dec & 31 Dec-1 Jan

MELLOR Map 16 SJ98

The Moorfield Arms
★★★★ INN

Shiloh Rd SK6 5NE
☎ 0161 427 1580 📄 0161 427 1582
e-mail: info@moorfieldarms.co.uk
dir: *1m NE of Mellor. Off A6015 towards Mellor, right onto Shiloh Rd, 0.3m on left*

Located in an elevated position with stunning views of the surrounding countryside including Kinder Scout, this 400-year-old property has been renovated and extended to provide spacious, comfortable public areas and tastefully furnished modern bedrooms in a sympathetic barn conversion.

Rooms 4 annexe en suite (1 fmly) (3 GF) **Facilities** FTV tea/coffee Dinner available Cen ht **Conf** Max 90 Class 40 Board 25 **Parking** 100 **Notes** LB ⊗ Closed Mon (ex BHs)

SALE Map 15 SJ79

The Belmore
★★★★ GUEST ACCOMMODATION

143 Brooklands Rd M33 3QN
☎ 0161 973 2538 📄 0161 973 2665
e-mail: belmore@jwlees.co.uk
dir: *M56 junct 3a or junct 2 (from Manchester) onto A560 towards Altrincham, at large rdbt turn right onto Brooklands Rd, on corner of Norris Rd*

This grand building, built in 1875, is located within easy reach of the motorway, and stands in attractive well tended grounds. The bedrooms are spacious and comfortable and have all of the expected facilities. Fresh, tasty food is available in the adjoining pub restaurant.

Rooms 20 en suite (4 fmly) **Facilities** FTV TVL tea/coffee Dinner available Cen ht Licensed Wi-fi ch fac **Conf** Max 64 Thtr 64 Class 20 Board 28 **Parking** 20 **Notes** ⊗

WIGAN Map 15 SD50

The Beeches
★★★ RESTAURANT WITH ROOMS

School Ln, Standish WN6 0TD
☎ 01257 426432 & 421316 📄 01257 427503
e-mail: mail@beecheshotel.co.uk
dir: *M6 junct 27, A5209 into Standish on School Ln*

Located a short drive from M6, this elegant Victorian house has been appointed to provide high standards of comfort. Bedrooms are equipped with practical and homely extras, and public areas include spacious lounges, a popular brasserie, and a self-contained function suite.

Rooms 10 en suite (4 fmly) **Facilities** FTV tea/coffee Dinner available Cen ht **Conf** Max 120 Thtr 100 Board 40 **Parking** 120 **Notes** ⊗ Civ Wed 60

HAMPSHIRE

ALRESFORD

See New Alresford

ALTON Map 5 SU73

The Anchor Inn
★★★★ ◉◉ INN

Lower Froyle GU34 4NA
☎ 01420 23261
e-mail: info@anchorinnatlowerfroyle.co.uk
dir: *On A31, exit towards Bentley*

The Anchor Inn is located in the tranquil Hampshire village of Lower Froyle. Luxury rooms are designed to reflect the traditional English inn style with charming decor, pictures and a selection of books. The restaurant welcomes residents and the local population with classic pub cooking, and impressive surroundings, with wooden floors and period furnishings.

Rooms 5 en suite S £110-£140; D £110-£140* **Facilities** STV FTV tea/coffee Dinner available Direct Dial Cen ht Wi-fi Golf **Parking** 30 **Notes** Closed 25 Dec Civ Wed 60

Beech Barns Guest House
★★★★ GUEST ACCOMMODATION

61 Wellhouse Rd, Beech GU34 4AQ
☎ 01420 85575 & 07759 723112 📄 01420 85575
e-mail: timsiggs@yahoo.com
dir: *1.5m W of Alton. Off A339 towards Beech, 2nd right onto Wellhouse Rd, 0.5m on left*

This well-appointed property has easy access to the motorway system. Set on the outskirts of Alton in its own grounds at the end of a quiet lane, there is no shortage of walking and cycling around this picturesque village. The proprietors are welcoming and friendly, and bedrooms are smartly appointed in contemporary style to provide a good range of facilities. A separate lounge is available for guest use, and dinner can be offered on request.

Rooms 9 en suite (2 fmly) (6 GF) **Facilities** TVL tea/coffee Dinner available Cen ht ⬥ **Conf** Max 18 Class 18 **Parking** 12

The Swan
★★★ INN

High St GU34 1AT
☎ 01420 83777 📄 01420 87975
e-mail: 6518@greeneking.co.uk
dir: *B3004 into Alton, follow signs for town centre*

Located in the centre of the town, The Swan is a traditional coaching inn where guests have been welcomed over many hundreds of years. Bedrooms and bathrooms vary in size but are generally comfortably furnished and include some welcome extras. A varied choice of enjoyable meals is available from the all-day menu, and a good selection of well-prepared dishes is offered at breakfast.

Rooms 37 en suite (1 fmly) S £59-£65; D £69-£95* **Facilities** STV FTV TVL tea/coffee Dinner available Direct Dial Cen ht Wi-fi Golf 9 **Conf** Max 120 Thtr 120 Class 80 Board 80 **Parking** 50 **Notes** LB Civ Wed 120

ANDOVER Map 5 SU34

The Barn House B&B
★★★★★ ⚠ BED AND BREAKFAST

Forton SP11 6NU
☎ 01264 720544
e-mail: hello@thebarnhousebandb.co.uk
web: www.thebarnhousebandb.co.uk
dir: *M3 junct 8 onto A303, onto B3048 to Longparish. Right to Forton, 2nd drive on left*

Rooms 2 en suite S £60-£75; D £80-£95* **Facilities** FTV tea/coffee Cen ht Wi-fi **Parking** 4 **Notes** ⊗

May Cottage
★★★★ ⚠ BED AND BREAKFAST

SP11 8LZ
☎ 01264 771241 & 07768 242166 📄 01264 771770
e-mail: info@maycottage-thruxton.co.uk
web: www.maycottage-thruxton.co.uk
dir: *3.5m W of Andover. Off A303 signed Thruxton (Village Only), opp George Inn*

Rooms 3 en suite (1 GF) S £45-£65; D £70-£90 **Facilities** STV TVL tea/coffee Cen ht Wi-fi **Parking** 5 **Notes** LB ⊗ ⊜

ASHURST — Map 5 SU31

The Willows

★★★ BED AND BREAKFAST

72 Lyndhurst Rd SO40 7BE
☎ 023 8029 2745 & 07980 937862
e-mail: thewillowsashurst@hotmail.co.uk
dir: *M27 junct 3 onto M271. After 1.5m at rdbt A35 signed Lyndhurst, continue straight for Ashurst. The Willows on right before bus stop*

Located in Ashurst, 'the gateway into the New Forest', The Willows offers bedrooms that are traditional in style with modern fixtures and furnishings. Free Wi-fi is available. Bathrooms have floor-to-ceiling tiles and high quality fixtures following a complete refurbishment. Guests can enjoy a cooked or continental breakfast in the dining room.

Rooms 3 en suite (1 fmly) S £30-£40; D £65-£70* **Facilities** tea/coffee Cen ht Wi-fi **Parking** 4 **Notes** Closed 2wks Xmas & New Year

Forest Gate Lodge

★★★ 🅰 GUEST HOUSE

161 Lyndhurst Rd SO40 7AW
☎ 023 8029 3026 📄 023 8029 3026
e-mail: forestgatelodge@hotmail.co.uk
dir: *On A35 in village*

Rooms 4 en suite (1 fmly) D £60-£70* **Facilities** FTV tea/coffee Cen ht Golf **Parking** 6 **Notes** LB ⊗ No Children 5yrs 🌐

Kingswood Cottage

🆄

10 Woodlands Rd SO40 7AD
☎ 023 8029 2582 & 07866 455322
e-mail: kingswoodcottage@yahoo.co.uk
dir: *Off A35 Lyndhurst to Ashurst, in village turn right over bridge signed Woodlands. Gates on right after 1st turning*

Currently the rating for this establishment is not confirmed. This may be due to a change of ownership or because it has only recently joined the AA rating scheme.

Rooms 3 en suite S £30-£45; D £60-£75 **Facilities** FTV TVL tea/coffee Cen ht Wi-fi **Parking** 3 **Notes** LB ⊗ No Children 5yrs Closed 12 Dec-2 Jan 🌐

BARTON-ON-SEA — Map 5 SZ29

Pebble Beach

★★★★★ 🍽 RESTAURANT WITH ROOMS

Marine Dr BH25 7DZ
☎ 01425 627777 📄 01425 610689
e-mail: mail@pebblebeach.uk.com
dir: *A35 from Southampton onto A337 to New Milton, left onto Barton Court Av to clifftop*

Situated on the cliff top the restaurant at this establishment boasts stunning views towards The Needles. Bedrooms and bathrooms, situated above the restaurant, are well equipped and provide a range of accessories to enhance guest comfort. A freshly cooked breakfast is served in the main restaurant.

Rooms 4 rms (3 en suite) (1 pri facs) S £69.95; D £89.95-£99.95* **Facilities** FTV tea/coffee Dinner available Cen ht Wi-fi **Conf** Max 8 **Parking** 20 **Notes** ⊗ RS 25 Dec & 1 Jan dinner not available No coaches

BENTLEY — Map 5 SU74

Bentley Green Farm

★★★★★ BED AND BREAKFAST

The Drift GU10 5JX
☎ 01420 23246 & 07711 981614 📄 01252 737916
e-mail: enquiries@bentleygreenfarm.co.uk
web: www.bentleygreenfarm.co.uk
dir: *500yds S of village. Off A31 Farnham-Alton signed Bentley, left at T-junct & 1st right*

Situated off the A31, a short drive from the village centre, this Grade II listed farm offers outstanding luxury. The first-floor smaller double in the main house boasts a private bathroom and wet room shower. A separate ground floor private lounge with fireplace is the ideal place to sample owners Glenda and Chris Powell's excellent hospitality. The annexe suite of rooms includes lounge, dining and kitchen area overlooking the gardens and swimming pool. Breakfast is served in the dining room around a big oak table. 39 acres surrounds the house which includes a tennis court, spa pool and private fishing.

Rooms 1 rms (1 pri facs) 1 annexe en suite (1 fmly) (1 GF) S £85-£95; D £95-£105 **Facilities** STV FTV TVL tea/coffee Cen ht Wi-fi 🎣 ⛳ Golf 18 Fishing Trampolines, tree house, hot tub **Parking** 13 **Notes** LB ⊗ 🌐

BRANSGORE — Map 5 SZ19

Tothill House

★★★★ BED AND BREAKFAST

Black Ln, off Forest Rd BH23 8EA
☎ 01425 674414
dir: *M27 onto A31 or A35, house is 0.75m NE of Bransgore centre*

Built for an admiral in 1908, Tothill House is located in the southern part of the New Forest. The garden backs on to the forest, where deer, ponies and other wildlife are frequent visitors. The spacious bedrooms are furnished to a high standard, reflecting the character of the house. There is an elegant library, and a generous breakfast is served in the dining room.

Rooms 3 rms (2 en suite) (1 pri facs) D £70* **Facilities** FTV tea/coffee Cen ht **Parking** 6 **Notes** ⊗ No Children 16yrs Closed Nov-Feb 🌐

BROCKENHURST — Map 5 SU30

The Cottage Lodge

★★★★★ 🏡 GUEST ACCOMMODATION

Sway Rd SO42 7SH
☎ 01590 622296 📄 01590 623014
e-mail: enquiries@cottagelodge.co.uk
web: www.cottagelodge.co.uk
dir: *Off A337 opp Careys Manor Hotel onto Grigg Ln, 0.25km over x-rds, cottage next to war memorial*

This 17th-century forester's cottage in the town centre is a good base for exploring the New Forest. The comfortable bedrooms are individually furnished and thoughtfully equipped. There is a cosy bar lounge with a fire, where tea can be served and a small selection of drinks is available.

Rooms 11 en suite 4 annexe en suite (7 GF) S £50-£120; D £60-£160* **Facilities** tea/coffee Cen ht Licensed Wi-fi **Parking** 15 **Notes** LB No Children 10yrs Closed Xmas

Save on B&Bs and Hotels. Book at **theAA.com/hotel**

HAMPSHIRE 163 ENGLAND

CADNAM — Map 5 SU31

PREMIER COLLECTION

The Log Cabin

★★★★★ GUEST ACCOMMODATION

Rangoon, Southampton Rd SO40 2NG
☎ 0845 230 6106 & 07788 873460
📠 023 8081 3423
e-mail: thelogcabin2009@live.co.uk
dir: M27 junct 1 onto A336

Located on the edge of the New Forest in Cadnam, this unique log cabin is built in the garden of the owner's house. Stylishly decorated throughout, it has a spacious interior with a separate lounge and an outside decking area. An extensive cooked or continental breakfast can be enjoyed in the main house or on the cabin's deck in the summer months.

Rooms 1 annexe en suite (1 GF) Facilities FTV TVL tea/coffee Dinner available Cen ht Wi-fi Parking 1 Notes ⊗

COLDEN COMMON — Map 5 SU42

The Dell

★★★★ BED AND BREAKFAST

27 Main Rd SO21 1RP
☎ 01962 714710 & 07554 882131
e-mail: thedellguesthouse@googlemail.co.uk
dir: M3 junct 11, B3335 to Twyford/Fair Oak through Twyford to Colden Common. On left on entering village opp restaurant

This beautiful 15th-century house oozes charm and boasts colourful gardens which lead to a stunning small wooded clearing; hence the name 'The Dell'. Winchester is only a few miles away and this establishment is located within walking distance of a number of dining options; the bus stop is just a stroll away. Original features have been retained in the smart and comfortable bedrooms and bathrooms and guests can enjoy a delicious home-cooked breakfast in the characterful dining room.

Rooms 2 en suite (1 fmly) (1 GF) S £60; D £80–£90 Facilities STV tea/coffee Cen ht Wi-fi Parking 6 Notes ⊗

DUMMER — Map 5 SU54

Tower Hill House

★★★ BED AND BREAKFAST

Tower Hill, Winchester Rd RG25 2AL
☎ 01256 398340 📠 01256 398340
e-mail: martin.hyndman@virgin.net
web: www.accommodationinbasingstoke.co.uk
dir: In village. M3 junct 7, onto A30 towards Winchester, 2nd left, opp sign for North Waltham

Ideally situated for access to the M3 and A30, while overlooking fields and countryside, this family-run bed and breakfast is in the pretty village of Dummer, just 10 minutes away from the centre of Basingstoke. Bedrooms are simply, but comfortably furnished and a well-prepared breakfast is served in the cheerful dining room.

Rooms 4 rms (2 en suite) (1 pri facs) Facilities tea/coffee Cen ht Wi-fi Parking 6

EAST TYTHERLEY — Map 5 SU22

The Star Inn

★★★★ ⊛ INN

SO51 0LW
☎ 01794 340225
e-mail: info@starinn.co.uk
dir: 1m S of East Tytherley

This charming coaching inn offers bedrooms in a purpose-built annexe, separate from the main pub. The spacious rooms have high levels of quality and comfort, and an outdoor children's play area is available. The inn has a loyal following of locals and visitors, drawn especially by the excellent food.

Rooms 3 annexe en suite (3 GF) Facilities FTV tea/coffee Dinner available Wi-fi Conf Max 30 Thtr 24 Class 24 Board 30 Parking 50 Notes RS Sun eve & Mon

EMSWORTH — Map 5 SU70

Hollybank House

★★★★ BED AND BREAKFAST

Hollybank Ln PO10 7UN
☎ 01243 375502 📠 01243 378118
e-mail: anna@hollybankhouse.com
web: www.hollybankhouse.com
dir: 1m N of town centre. A259 onto B2148, 1m right onto Southleigh Rd, 3rd left onto Hollybank Ln, house at top

The Georgian country house stands in a 10-acre woodland garden with a tennis court on the outskirts of Emsworth, and looks out to Chichester Harbour. Emsworth has a variety of restaurants, pubs and harbour walks.

Rooms 4 rms (3 en suite) (1 pri facs) (1 fmly) Facilities tea/coffee Cen ht Wi-fi ⊱ Parking 85

Jingles

★★★★ GUEST ACCOMMODATION

77 Horndean Rd PO10 7PU
☎ 01243 373755 📠 01243 431377
e-mail: info@thejingles.co.uk
dir: A3 (M) junct 2, follow signs for Emsworth, 4m, 1st building in Emsworth

Jingles is a family-run business, located in the charming maritime village of Emsworth. Situated adjacent to open farmland, it's a great location for discovering both Portsmouth and Chichester. All bedrooms are en suite and decorated to a high standard. The dining room is the setting for a cooked English breakfast, and a drawing room is available for relaxing in. Wi-fi is available if required.

Rooms 28 en suite (2 fmly) (7 GF) Facilities FTV tea/coffee Cen ht Wi-fi Parking 35 Notes ⊗

36 on the Quay

★★★★ ⊛⊛⊛ RESTAURANT WITH ROOMS

47 South St PO10 7EG
☎ 01243 375592 & 372257

Occupying a prime position with far reaching views over the estuary, this 16th-century house is the scene for some accomplished and exciting cuisine. The elegant restaurant occupies centre stage with peaceful pastel shades, local art and crisp napery together with glimpses of the bustling harbour outside. The contemporary bedrooms offer style, comfort and thoughtful extras.

Rooms 5 en suite Facilities tea/coffee Dinner available Cen ht Parking 6 Notes Closed 3wks Jan, 1wk late May & 1wk late Oct

The Crown

★★★ INN

High St PO10 7AW
☎ 01243 307461 📠 01243 370082
e-mail: thecrownemsworth@aol.co.uk

An historic property conveniently located in the centre of town with ample parking at the back. Long winding stairs and uneven corridors lead to well-appointed bedrooms which offer a range of amenities such as flat-screen TVs and Wi-fi. Freshly prepared food is served in the well-stocked bar and the restaurant.

Rooms 9 rms (7 en suite) (2 pri facs) (2 fmly) Facilities FTV tea/coffee Dinner available Cen ht Wi-fi Conf Max 24 Board 24 Parking 16

FAREHAM
Map 5 SU50

Wisteria House

★★★★ BED AND BREAKFAST

14 Mays Ln, Stubbington PO14 2EP
☎ 01329 511940 & 07742 400242
e-mail: info@wisteria-house.co.uk
dir: M27 junct 9, take A27 to Fareham. Right onto B3334, at rdbt left onto Mays Ln

Wisteria House is located on the edge of the village of Stubbington, just a short walk from local amenities, and only one mile from the beach at Lee-on-the-Solent. The charming and comfortable bedrooms have en suite bathrooms, are located on the ground floor, and also now have Wi-fi. Off-road parking is available.

Rooms 2 en suite (2 GF) S £50; D £65 **Facilities** FTV tea/coffee Cen ht Wi-fi **Parking** 2 **Notes** ⊗ No Children 8yrs

Bembridge House

★★★★ GUEST ACCOMMODATION

32 Osborn Rd PO16 7DS
☎ 01329 317050
e-mail: bembridgehouse@live.co.uk
web: www.bembridge-house.co.uk
dir: M27 junct 11 follow signs to Fareham town centre, then signs to Ferneham Hall, Bembridge House opp

Bembridge House is a haven of tranquillity yet it is located within walking distance of the town centre with its varied choice of restaurants and shops. The house has been sympathetically restored and offers well appointed accommodation. Breakfast is served in the attractive dining room, which overlooks the front garden.

Rooms 4 en suite (4 fmly) S £60-£70; D £100-£120 **Facilities** FTV tea/coffee Cen ht Wi-fi **Conf** Max 30 Thtr 30 Board 18 **Parking** 9 **Notes** ☺

Catisfield Cottage

★★ 🅰 BED AND BREAKFAST

1 Catisfield Ln PO15 5NW
☎ 01329 843301
dir: Off A27 at Highlands Rd lights, Catisfield Ln 2nd left
Rooms 6 rms (3 en suite) (1 fmly) S £30-£40; D £58.50-£72* **Facilities** FTV TVL tea/coffee Cen ht **Parking** 6 **Notes** Closed 24 Dec-5 Jan

FARNBOROUGH
Map 5 SU85

Tudorwood Guest House

★★★★ GUEST HOUSE

164 Farnborough Rd GU14 7JJ
☎ 01252 541123
e-mail: info@tudorwood.net
dir: Off A325 (Farnborough Rd) left onto Sycamore Rd, left onto Salisbury Rd, left onto Cedar Rd & right onto Farnborough Rd

A delightful Tudor-style house located just a few minutes from the town centre. Individually decorated bedrooms are well appointed with a range of useful facilities. Public areas include a pleasant conservatory lounge and intimate dining room where home-cooked dinners are available. Ample parking is provided to the front of the property.

Rooms 2 en suite 4 annexe en suite (1 fmly) (4 GF) **Facilities** TVL tea/coffee Dinner available Cen ht Wi-fi DVD & CD library **Conf** Max 20 Thtr 20 Class 16 Board 16 **Parking** 7 **Notes** ⊗ Closed 24-29 Dec

HAVANT
Map 5 SU70

The Bear

★★★ INN

15-17 East St PO9 1AA
☎ 023 9248 6501 ▤ 023 9247 0551
e-mail: 9110@greeneking.co.uk

This listed, former coaching inn is located in the heart of the town and has informal public rooms, which include a small cocktail bar and the Elizabethan public bar. The fully equipped bedrooms are well laid out and equally suited to both the business and leisure guest.

Rooms 42 en suite (3 fmly) S £29-£59; D £59-£79 **Facilities** TVL tea/coffee Dinner available Direct Dial Cen ht Wi-fi ch fac Pool table **Conf** Max 100 Thtr 100 Class 40 Board 40 **Parking** 80

HAWKLEY
Map 5 SU72

The Hawkley Inn

★★★ INN

Pococks Ln GU33 6NE
☎ 01730 827205 ▤ 01730 827954
e-mail: info@hawkleyinn.co.uk
dir: A3 Liss rdbt towards Liss B3006. Right at Spread Eagle 2.5m turn left at Pococks Ln

This inn is conveniently situated just off the A3 and is a perfect base for ramblers, and leisure and business guests alike. The rustic bar areas are in contrast to the style of the contemporary, thoughtfully-equipped bedrooms; the bathrooms have powerful showers. Delicious home-made 'comfort food' is on offer at lunchtime and in the evenings, and breakfast provides a great start to the day.

Rooms 5 en suite (1 fmly) (1 GF) S £65-£100; D £65-£100* **Facilities** FTV tea/coffee Dinner available Cen ht Wi-fi **Parking** 2 **Notes** ⊗ No coaches

HAYLING ISLAND
Map 5 SU70

Ravensdale

★★★★ BED AND BREAKFAST

19 St Catherines Rd PO11 0HF
☎ 023 9246 3203 & 07802 188259
e-mail: phil.taylor@tayloredprint.co.uk
web: www.ravensdale-hayling.co.uk
dir: From A27 onto A3023 at Langstone, cross Hayling Bridge, 3m to mini rdbt, right onto Manor Rd 1m. Right by Barley Mow onto Station Rd, 3rd left onto St Catherines Rd

A warm welcome awaits you to this comfortable home, quietly situated near the beach and golf course. Bedrooms are attractive, very comfortable and enhanced with numerous thoughtful extras. Home cooking can be enjoyed at breakfast (and dinner by arrangement) in the dining room, and there is also a lounge area.

Rooms 3 rms (2 en suite) (1 pri facs) **Facilities** TVL tea/coffee Dinner available Cen ht Wi-fi **Parking** 4 **Notes** ⊗ No Children 8yrs Closed last 2wks Dec ☺

Redwalls

★★ BED AND BREAKFAST

66 Staunton Av PO11 0EW
☎ 023 9246 6109
e-mail: daphne@redwalls.co.uk
dir: A3023 to South Hayling seafront, right along seafront & 4th right

Built around the turn of the 20th century, the characterful home of Daphne and Noel Grover offers a peaceful retreat close to the seafront and local attractions. The bedrooms and public areas enjoy a homely ambience and there is a garden and conservatory lounge for guests to use.

Rooms 3 en suite S £35; D £50* **Facilities** TVL tea/coffee Cen ht **Parking** 4 **Notes** ⊗ No Children Closed Xmas & New Year ☺

HOOK   Map 5 SU75

Oaklea Guest House

★★★★ GUEST HOUSE

London Rd RG27 9LA
☎ 01256 762673
e-mail: reception@oakleaguesthouse.co.uk
dir: From village centre, 500yds on right on A30 towards Basingstoke

You can be sure of a warm welcome at this Victorian house located just a short drive from the M3. Bedrooms are well appointed with modern facilities. There is a comfortable lounge, and the large dining room has a bar.

Rooms 15 en suite (2 fmly) (1 GF) S £50-£58; D £65* **Facilities** TVL tea/coffee Cen ht Licensed Wi-fi **Parking** 15

Cherry Lodge Guest House

★★★ GUEST ACCOMMODATION

Reading Rd RG27 9DB
☎ 01256 762532   🖶 01256 766068
e-mail: cherrylodge@btinternet.com
dir: On B3349 (Reading Rd), next to Hook garden centre

This pleasant bungalow is peacefully set back from the Reading Road, and is convenient for the M3. Cherry Lodge provides extremely friendly hospitality and is popular with business guests. Breakfast is served from 6.30am. A spacious lounge is provided and bedrooms are well equipped.

Rooms 10 en suite (1 fmly) (10 GF) **Facilities** STV TVL tea/coffee Direct Dial Cen ht Wi-fi **Parking** 20 **Notes** ⊗ Closed Xmas-New Year

HURSLEY   Map 5 SU42

Kings Head

★★★★ INN

SO21 2JW
☎ 01962 775208   🖶 01962 775954
e-mail: info@kingsheadhursley.co.uk
dir: M3 junct 11 onto A3090. Pass through Standon, Kings Head on left in centre of Hursley opposite church

A traditional coaching inn recently refurbished to its former glory with modern amenities and stylish interior decor sympathetic to its historical past. Bedrooms are deeply comfortable, individually designed and named after previous incumbents of the Hursley Estate. The cosy bar features changing guest ales and a very good wine list. Dining takes inspiration from local suppliers with a varied and interesting menu; popular with both residents and locals alike.

Rooms 7 en suite 1 annexe en suite (1 fmly) S £55-£65; D £85-£115* **Facilities** FTV tea/coffee Dinner available Cen ht Wi-fi Skittle alley, games room **Conf** Thtr 30 Class 40 Board 24 **Parking** 30 **Notes** RS 24-25 Dec No accommodation available No coaches

HYTHE   Map 5 SU40

Four Seasons B&B

★★★★ GUEST ACCOMMODATION

Hamilton Rd SO45 3PD
☎ 023 8084 5151   🖶 023 8084 6285
e-mail: the-four-seasons@btconnect.com
dir: M27 junct 2 onto A326. At 4th rdbt take exit signed Hythe, on left after 500mtrs

The Four Seasons B&B is located in Hythe with easy access to both Southampton and the New Forest. Bedrooms are tastefully decorated with modern decor and furnishings. All rooms are equipped with Freeview TV and there is free Wi-fi throughout. The dining room and guest lounge is open plan with a small preparation kitchen area. There's also a TV, a DVD library and a computer with broadband. Cooked and continental breakfasts are available, and for the early riser is served from 6:30am on weekdays.

Rooms 12 rms (7 en suite) (2 fmly) (2 GF) S £29-£32; D £72* **Facilities** FTV TVL tea/coffee Cen ht Wi-fi **Parking** 11 **Notes** LB ⊗

ISLE OF WIGHT

See Wight, Isle of

LEE-ON-THE-SOLENT   Map 5 SU50

West Wind Guest House

★★★★ GUEST ACCOMMODATION

197 Portsmouth Rd PO13 9AA
☎ 023 9255 2550
e-mail: info@west-wind.co.uk
dir: M27 junct 11 follow signs for Gosport & Fareham, B3385 for Lee-on-the-Solent. At seafront left along Marine Pde, 600mtrs left onto Portsmouth Rd, West Wind on right

This family-run guest accommodation is found in a quiet, residential location and within walking distance of the beach and town centre. The bedrooms are comfortable and nicely appointed, some with flat screen TV and all with free Wi-fi. There is an attractive breakfast room and off-street parking.

Rooms 6 en suite (1 GF) S £50-£55; D £65-£70 **Facilities** FTV tea/coffee Cen ht Wi-fi **Parking** 6 **Notes** ⊗ No Children 8yrs

Apple Tree Cottage B&B

★★★ BED AND BREAKFAST

159 Portsmouth Rd PO13 9AD
☎ 023 9255 1176   🖶 023 9235 2492
e-mail: appletreecottage@ntlworld.com
web: www.leeonthesolentbedandbreakfast.com
dir: From Marine Pde pass Old Ship public house onto Portsmouth Rd. Pass Inn by the Sea on right, 4th house along

Situated just 50 yards from the seafront and Sailing Club, Apple Tree Cottage is a small, family-run establishment offering a warm welcome, individual attention, and high standards of comfort. Both rooms have a maritime theme and enjoy a wide range of useful facilities including DVD players and Wi-fi, along with high quality linen and towels. The Lighthouse Room has a 4-poster with drapes, and the Solent can be seen from the bedrooms. Breakfast is served in the pretty dining room.

Rooms 3 en suite (1 fmly) S £42-£47; D £52-£56 **Facilities** FTV TV2B tea/coffee Cen ht Wi-fi **Parking** 3 **Notes** ⊗ No Children 6yrs ☺

LYMINGTON   Map 5 SZ39

See also Milford-on-Sea & Sway

PREMIER COLLECTION

The Olde Barn

★★★★★ BED AND BREAKFAST

Christchurch Rd, Downton SO41 0LA
☎ 01590 644939 & 07813 679757
📠 01590 644939
e-mail: julie@theoldebarn.co.uk
dir: *On A337 3m W of Lymington, in Downton*

A 17th-century barn and associated buildings have been restored to provide stylish accommodation. Bedrooms are smartly decorated and furnished, and the spacious bathrooms have power showers. There is a comfortable lounge, and a traditional English breakfast is served around a farmhouse table in the attractive dining room.

Rooms 3 annexe en suite (3 GF) S £50-£70; D £65-£80* **Facilities** FTV TVL tea/coffee Cen ht Golf 27 **Parking** 6 **Notes** ⊗ No Children 10yrs

Gorse Meadow Guest House

★★★★ GUEST HOUSE

Sway Rd SO41 8LR
☎ 01590 673354 📠 01590 673336
e-mail: gorsemeadow@btconnect.com
web: www.gorsemeadowguesthouse.co.uk
dir: *Off A337 from Brockenhurst, right onto Sway Rd before Toll House pub, Gorse Meadow 1.5m on right*

This imposing Edwardian house is situated in 14 acres of grounds, and most of the bedrooms enjoy views across the gardens and paddocks. Situated just one mile from Lymington, this is an excellent base for enjoying the many leisure pursuits that the New Forest has to offer. Meals are also available here, and Mrs Tee often uses the local wild mushrooms in her dishes.

Rooms 5 en suite (2 fmly) (2 GF) S £35-£50; D £70-£120* **Facilities** tea/coffee Dinner available Cen ht Licensed Wi-fi Health Club Membership **Conf** Max 12 Board 12 **Parking** 20

Harts Lodge

★★★★ BED AND BREAKFAST

242 Everton Rd, Everton SO41 0HE
☎ 01590 645902
dir: *From Lymington 2.5m W to Everton, off A337 onto Everton Rd, 0.5m on left*

This attractive bungalow is situated in three acres of peaceful gardens and paddocks. The bedrooms are furnished to a high standard and feature many thoughtful touches; one room has outside access. Public areas include a lounge and a pleasant breakfast room, with views of the garden and a small pond.

Rooms 3 en suite (1 fmly) (3 GF) S £40-£60; D £65-£75* **Facilities** FTV tea/coffee Cen ht **Parking** 6 **Notes** LB ⊗ No Children 8yrs 🐾

Rosewood B&B

★★★ BED AND BREAKFAST

45 Ramley Rd SO41 8GZ
☎ 01590 677970
e-mail: diwillford@gmail.com
dir: *M27 to Lyndhurst then A337 to Lymington. Continue towards Christchurch, right before shops at Pennington onto South St, past church onto Ramley Rd. Rosewood 0.5m on right*

Expect a warm welcome with an African theme at this family-run establishment. Located opposite Pennington Common on the edge of Lymington, this is an ideal area for exploring the area around the New Forest. Breakfast is served in the dining room which leads into a large conservatory.

Rooms 2 rms (1 en suite) (1 pri facs) S £30-£40; D £60-£70 **Facilities** tea/coffee Cen ht **Parking** 2 **Notes** LB Closed Xmas 🐾

LYNDHURST   Map 5 SU30

Temple Lodge

★★★★ GUEST ACCOMMODATION

2 Queens Rd SO43 7BR
☎ 023 8028 2392 📠 023 8028 4910
e-mail: templelodge@btinternet.com
web: www.templelodge-guesthouse.com
dir: *M27 junct 2/3 onto A35 to Ashurst/Lyndhurst, Temple Lodge on 2nd corner on right, opposite forest*

Temple Lodge is a well appointed Victorian house with very friendly hosts. Guests will enjoy easy access to the New Forest and Lyndhurst town centre, with good off-road parking. The bedrooms feature lots of thoughtful extras including mini bars. The breakfasts should not be missed.

Rooms 6 en suite (2 fmly) D £60-£120 **Facilities** FTV TVL tea/coffee Cen ht Wi-fi **Parking** 6 **Notes** LB ⊗ No Children 12yrs

Whitemoor House

★★★★ GUEST ACCOMMODATION

Southampton Rd SO43 7BU
☎ 023 8028 3043
e-mail: whitemoorhouse@tiscali.co.uk
dir: *0.5m NE of town centre on A35*

A warm welcome is assured at this well-run establishment in the New Forest. The comfortable bedrooms are brightly decorated and well equipped. A full English breakfast is served with home-made preserves in the tastefully appointed breakfast room. John and Stephanie Drew were finalists in this year's Friendliest Landlady of the Year award (2011-12).

Rooms 6 en suite (1 fmly) S £40-£50; D £70-£90 **Facilities** FTV TVL tea/coffee Cen ht Licensed Wi-fi Golf 9 **Parking** 6 **Notes** ⊗ No Children 10yrs Closed 16 Dec-25 Jan 🐾

Clayhill House

★★★★ BED AND BREAKFAST

SO43 7DE
☎ 023 8028 2304 📠 023 8028 2093
e-mail: clayhillhouse@tinyworld.co.uk
web: www.clayhillhouse.co.uk
dir: *Exit M27 junct 2. A35 to Lyndhurst then A337 signed Brockenhurst, 0.75m from village*

Set at the edge of this attractive town, and convenient for visiting the New Forest and coastal attractions nearby, Clayhill House is a well-appointed property, which offers friendly service and comfortable accommodation. The bedrooms are particularly well equipped with thoughtful extras. Freshly-cooked breakfasts are served in the dining room.

Rooms 3 en suite (1 fmly) S £35-£50; D £70-£80* **Facilities** FTV tea/coffee Cen ht Wi-fi **Parking** 6 **Notes** LB ⊗ No Children 7yrs Closed 22 Dec-4 Jan

Save on B&Bs and Hotels. Book at **theAA.com/hotel**

HAMPSHIRE 167 ENGLAND

Little Hayes

★★★★ GUEST ACCOMMODATION

43 Romsey Rd SO43 7AR
☎ 023 8028 3816
e-mail: wendy@littlehayes.co.uk
dir: *M27 junct 1 onto A337. On entering Lyndhurst, 200yds on right*

A friendly, well-run guest accommodation located a few moments walk from the town centre, pubs and restaurants. Breakfast featuring local produce is served in the cosy dining room. Little Hayes provides an ideal base for touring the New Forest National Park, and benefits from off-road parking.

Rooms 6 rms (5 en suite) (1 pri facs) S £45-£50; D £70-£82* **Facilities** FTV tea/coffee Cen ht Wi-fi **Parking** 6 **Notes** ✖ No Children Closed Dec-Jan

The Rufus House

★★★★ GUEST ACCOMMODATION

Southampton Rd SO43 7BQ
☎ 023 8028 2930
e-mail: stay@rufushouse.co.uk
dir: *From Lyndhurst centre onto A35 (Southampton Rd), 300yds on left*

Located on the edge of town, this delightful family-run Victorian property is well situated for exploring the New Forest. The brightly decorated bedrooms are appointed to a high standard, while the turret lounge and the garden terrace are great spots for relaxing.

Rooms 10 en suite (1 fmly) (2 GF) **Facilities** tea/coffee Cen ht Wi-fi Golf 18 **Parking** 12 **Notes** ✖ No Children 5yrs

Burwood Lodge

★★★★ 🅰 GUEST ACCOMMODATION

27 Romsey Rd SO43 7AA
☎ 023 8028 2445 & 07717 767997 📠 023 8028 2057
e-mail: burwoodlodge@yahoo.co.uk
Rooms 7 en suite (2 fmly) (1 GF) **Facilities** FTV TVL tea/coffee Cen ht Wi-fi **Parking** 10 **Notes** ✖ No Children 6yrs ♿

Heather House

★★★ GUEST ACCOMMODATION

Southampton Rd SO43 7BQ
☎ 023 8028 4409 📠 023 8028 4431
e-mail: enquiries@heatherhouse.co.uk
web: www.heatherhouse.co.uk
dir: *M27 junct 1, A337 to Lyndhurst. At lights in centre turn left, establishment 800yds on left*

This impressive double-fronted Edwardian house stands in attractive gardens on the edge of town with views of the New Forest. Bedrooms are comfortably appointed with some suitable for families. Breakfast is served in the pleasant dining room.

Rooms 10 en suite (1 fmly) (1 GF) S £25-£48; D £60-£90* **Facilities** FTV TVL tea/coffee Cen ht Licensed Wi-fi **Parking** 12 **Notes** LB ✖ No Children 7yrs Closed 23 Dec-2 Jan

---

MICHELDEVER   Map 5 SU53

The Dove Inn

★★★★ INN

Andover Rd SO21 3AU
☎ 01962 774288 📠 01962 774952
e-mail: info@the-dove-inn.co.uk
web: www.the-dove-inn.co.uk
dir: *M3 junct 8 merge onto A303, take exit signed Micheldever Station, follow station signs onto Andover Rd, on left*

Set in the Hampshire countryside close to Micheldever railway station, this traditional inn serves guest ales and has a popular dining room with both blackboard specials and à la carte options. Bedrooms have been refurbished and feature a range of comfortable accessories to enhance guest comfort. The en suite bathrooms are well appointed with good quality toiletries. Complimentary Wi-fi throughout the building is a positive enhancement for business travellers. Ample parking is available.

Rooms 5 en suite (1 fmly) S £65; D £85* **Facilities** STV FTV tea/coffee Dinner available Cen ht Wi-fi Pool table **Conf** Max 50 Thtr 50 Class 20 Board 30 **Parking** 20 **Notes** LB

MILFORD ON SEA   Map 5 SZ29

PREMIER COLLECTION

Ha'penny House

★★★★★ GUEST ACCOMMODATION

16 Whitby Rd SO41 0ND
☎ 01590 641210
e-mail: info@hapennyhouse.co.uk
web: www.hapennyhouse.co.uk
dir: *A337 at Everton onto B3058, through village onto Cliff Rd, right onto Cornwallis Rd, right at T-junct onto Whitby Rd, house 50yds on left*

This delightful house is in a peaceful residential area close to the clifftop with its stunning views towards the Isle of Wight. Individually styled bedrooms are beautifully appointed and equipped with a host of thoughtful extras. There is a stylish lounge, and an elegant dining room where superb breakfasts are served.

Rooms 4 en suite S £50-£55; D £78-£85* **Facilities** FTV TVL tea/coffee Cen ht Wi-fi **Parking** 7 **Notes** LB ✖ No Children 12yrs

MILFORD ON SEA *continued*

Alma Mater

★★★★ BED AND BREAKFAST

4 Knowland Dr SO41 0RH
☎ 01590 642811
web: www.almamaternewforest.co.uk
dir: *A337 at Everton onto B3058 to Milford on Sea. Pass South Lawn Hotel, right onto Manor Rd, 1st left onto Knowland Dr, 3rd bungalow on right*

Alma Mater is in a quiet residential area within walking distance of the village centre and beaches. The comfortable bedrooms are all well appointed with many thoughtful touches including digital TV and toiletries. One room is on the ground floor and has twin beds, and the elegant dining room also has a conservatory where a wide choice of breakfasts can be enjoyed.

Rooms 3 en suite (3 fmly) (1 GF) S £40-£50; D £68-£70* **Facilities** TVL tea/coffee Cen ht **Parking** 4 **Notes** LB ⊗ No Children 15yrs ⊜

Pilgrims Rest

★★★★ GUEST ACCOMMODATION

Westover Rd SO41 0PW
☎ 01590 641167
e-mail: pilgrimsrestbandb@yahoo.co.uk
dir: *From Lymington follow New Milton signs, in 2m left onto B3058 through village, 2nd left*

A traditional establishment with friendly hosts, very well appointed rooms and a breakfast that is a great start to the day. Pilgrims Rest lies within walking distance of the beach and the town of Milford on Sea. All rooms are en suite.

Rooms 4 en suite **Facilities** FTV tea/coffee Cen ht Wi-fi **Parking** 6 **Notes** ⊗ ⊜

NEW ALRESFORD   **Map 5 SU53**

Haygarth

★★★ 🅰 BED AND BREAKFAST

82 Jack Lyns Ln SO24 9LJ
☎ 01962 732715 & 07986 372895
dir: *B3046 from New Alresford centre for Cheriton, Haygarth 0.5m on right*
Rooms 3 rms (2 en suite) (1 pri facs) (3 GF) **Facilities** TVL tea/coffee Cen ht **Parking** 7 **Notes** LB ⊗ ⊜

NORTHINGTON   **Map 5 SU53**

The Woolpack Inn

★★★★ ◉◉ INN

Totford SO24 9TJ
☎ 01962 734184 & 0845 293 8066   📠 0845 293 8055
e-mail: info@thewoolpackinn.co.uk
web: www.thewoolpackinn.co.uk
dir: *M3 junct 6 take A339 towards Alton, turn right onto B3046. In Totford on left*

Situated in the small village of Totford, a tranquil and picturesque location that is within easy reach of main transport routes. This traditional establishment has benefited from extensive refurbishment resulting in a fine balance of contemporary styling and traditional features. The bedrooms (named after game birds) and the bathrooms are well appointed with many thoughtful extras making guest comfort a top priority. The award-winning dining room showcases local produce with regularly changing specials enhancing the carte options.

Rooms 7 en suite (1 fmly) (4 GF) S £85-£105; D £85-£105* **Facilities** FTV tea/coffee Dinner available Direct Dial Cen ht Wi-fi Pool table Cycling, fishing trips, hiking, clay pigeon shoots **Conf** Max 15 Thtr 15 Class 12 Board 12 **Parking** 20 **Notes** Closed 25 Dec eve

---

PORTSMOUTH & SOUTHSEA   **Map 5 SU60**

St Margaret's Lodge

★★★★ GUEST HOUSE

3 Craneswater Gate PO4 0NZ
☎ 023 9282 0097   📠 023 9282 0097
e-mail: enquiries@stmargarets-southsea.co.uk
web: www.stmargarets-southsea.co.uk
dir: *From South Parade Pier E along A288 St Helens Parade, 2nd left*

This establishment is in a quiet residential area close to the seafront and town centre. The attractive bedrooms have co-ordinated soft furnishings and many thoughtful extras. Breakfast is served in the smart dining room and there are two lounges and a cosy bar.

Rooms 14 en suite (1 fmly) S fr £38; D fr £60* **Facilities** FTV TVL tea/coffee Cen ht Wi-fi **Parking** 5 **Notes** ⊗ Closed 21 Dec-2 Jan

Upper Mount House

★★★★ GUEST ACCOMMODATION

The Vale, Southsea PO5 2EQ
☎ 023 9282 0456   📠 023 9282 0456
e-mail: uppermountportsmouth@btconnect.com
dir: *Off M275 for D-Day Museum onto road opposite Museum, over x-rds, right at T-junct, right again*

This impressive Victorian villa retains many original features and is peacefully located in a residential cul-de-sac. Public areas include a comfortable lounge and an attractive dining room where a fine collection of Venetian glassware is displayed. The bedrooms are spacious and well equipped, and come in a variety of styles.

Rooms 15 en suite (3 fmly) (7 GF) **Facilities** FTV TVL tea/coffee Direct Dial Cen ht Wi-fi **Parking** 17 **Notes** ⊗ Closed 2wks Xmas

The Festing Grove

★★★ GUEST ACCOMMODATION

8 Festing Grove, Southsea PO4 9QA
☎ 023 9273 5239
e-mail: thefestinggrove@ntlworld.com
dir: *E along seafront to South Parade Pier, after pier sharp left, around lake, 3rd left & 2nd right*

A well-presented property situated within easy walking distance of the seafront and pier. A continual programme of upgrading ensures that the rooms enjoy a high standard of decor and comfort. Breakfast is served in the homely dining room, and there is a well-appointed lounge.

Rooms 6 rms (1 en suite) (1 pri facs) (2 fmly) **Facilities** FTV TVL tea/coffee Cen ht Wi-fi **Notes** ⊗

Amberley Court

★★★ GUEST ACCOMMODATION

97 Waverley Rd, Southsea PO5 2PL
☎ 023 9273 7473   📠 023 9275 2343
e-mail: mail@amberleycourt.co.uk
dir: *Off A288 South Parade near pier onto B2155 Clarendon Rd & Waverley Rd*

Amberley Court has a convenient location less than half a mile from the seafront and attractions. The comfortable bedrooms have bright modern co-ordinated fabrics, and come with good facilities. Some rooms and a smart conservatory-dining room are in a second house nearby.

Rooms 9 en suite (4 fmly) **Facilities** TVL tea/coffee Cen ht Wi-fi **Parking** 4 **Notes** ⊗

Save on B&Bs and Hotels. Book at **theAA.com/hotel**

HAMPSHIRE 169 **ENGLAND**

RINGWOOD
Map 5 SU10

Moortown Lodge

★★★★ GUEST ACCOMMODATION

244 Christchurch Rd BH24 3AS
☎ 01425 471404 📄 01425 476527
e-mail: enquiries@moortownlodge.co.uk
dir: 1m S of Ringwood. Off A31 at Ringwood onto B3347, signs to Sopley, Lodge next to David Lloyds Leisure Club

The light and airy accommodation is finished to a very high standard, with digital TV and broadband in each room. Two of the well-equipped bedrooms are at ground-floor level, and one features a four-poster bed. Breakfast is served at separate tables in the smart lounge-dining room.

Rooms 7 en suite (3 fmly) (2 GF) D £86-£96*
Facilities FTV tea/coffee Direct Dial Cen ht Wi-fi Access to facilities of adjoining leisure club **Parking** 9 **Notes** LB

Amberwood

★★★★ GUEST ACCOMMODATION

3/5 Top Ln BH24 1LF
☎ 01425 476615 📄 01425 476615
e-mail: maynsing1@sky.com
dir: A31 onto B3347, over rdbt, left onto School Ln, left onto Top Ln

This delightful Victorian home is situated in a quiet residential area within easy walking distance of the town centre. Bedrooms are attractively furnished and decorated, with many thoughtful extras. A substantial breakfast is served around one large table in the conservatory, which overlooks the well-tended garden. A lounge is also available.

Rooms 2 en suite (1 fmly) S £35-£40; D £60
Facilities FTV TVL tea/coffee Direct Dial Cen ht Wi-fi
Parking 2 **Notes** LB ⊗ No Children 12yrs Closed Xmas & New Year 🍴

Little Forest Lodge

★★★★ GUEST HOUSE

Poulner Hill BH24 3HS
☎ 01425 478848 📄 01425 473564
dir: 1.5m E of Ringwood on A31

A warm welcome is given to you, and your pet, at this charming Edwardian house set in two acres of woodland. Bedrooms are pleasantly decorated and equipped with thoughtful extras. Both the attractive wood-panelled dining room and the delightful lounge, with bar and wood-burning fire, overlook the gardens.

Rooms 6 en suite (3 fmly) (1 GF) **Facilities** tea/coffee Cen ht Licensed 🦮 **Parking** 10

Candlesticks Inn

★★★ GUEST HOUSE

136 Christchurch Rd BH24 3AP
☎ 01425 472587 📄 01425 471600
e-mail: info@hotelnewforest.co.uk
web: www.hotelnewforest.co.uk
dir: 0.5m SE of town centre on B3347

This 15th-century thatched property offers accommodation with a restaurant on the edge of town, and is convenient for Bournemouth and the New Forest National Park. Ample parking.

Rooms 8 annexe en suite (1 fmly) (4 GF) S £30-£50; D £50-£75* **Facilities** FTV tea/coffee Dinner available Direct Dial Cen ht Licensed Wi-fi Sauna Sauna also available for wheelchair users **Parking** 30 **Notes** LB ⊗ Closed 23 Dec-10 Jan

SOUTHAMPTON
Map 5 SU41

PREMIER COLLECTION

Riverside Bed & Breakfast

★★★★★ BED AND BREAKFAST

4 Tides Reach, 53 Whitworth Rd SO18 1GE
☎ 023 8063 0315 📄 023 8063 0315
e-mail: gordon-funnelle@supanet.com
dir: 2m NE of city centre. M27 junct 5, A335 onto Thomas Lewis Way, left onto A3035 over river, sharp right onto Whitworth Crescent & Whitworth Rd

Located in a quieter part of Southampton, just five minutes walk away from public transport links and a ten-minute drive from the airport, this small and homely house has wonderful river views. Bedrooms have many thoughtful touches and guests have their own comfortable lounge. A wonderful continental breakfast is served in the dining room or on the balcony in warmer weather.

Rooms 2 rms (2 pri facs) S £35-£60; D £60-£80* **Facilities** FTV tea/coffee Cen ht **Parking** 1 **Notes** ⊗ No Children 14yrs 🍴

PREMIER COLLECTION

White Star Tavern, Dining and Rooms

★★★★★ ⊛⊛ INN

28 Oxford St SO14 3DJ
☎ 023 8082 1990 📄 023 8090 4982
e-mail: reservations@whitestartavern.co.uk
web: www.whitestartavern.co.uk
dir: M3 junct 14 onto A33, towards Ocean Village

This stylish tavern is conveniently located in the popular Oxford Street area, a moment's walk to the city centre. Bedrooms take their name from the ships of the White Star Line, and are smartly appointed and well equipped with many thoughtful extras. The main bar and restaurant areas provide comfortable seating in well styled surroundings. Award-winning cuisine is served in the White Star restaurant whilst in the morning an à la carte breakfast is served in the bar area. Private meeting space is also available.

Rooms 13 en suite **Facilities** FTV TVL tea/coffee Dinner available Direct Dial Cen ht Wi-fi **Conf** Max 12 Board 12 **Notes** ⊗

Heather Gables

★★★★ GUEST ACCOMMODATION

Dodwell Ln, Bursledon SO31 1DJ
☎ 023 8040 4925
e-mail: heather.gables@talktalk.net
web: www.heathergables.co.uk
dir: M27 junct 8, 600yds N on Hedge End Rd

Suitable for both business and leisure travellers, Heather Gables offers comfortable en suite accommodation. Both bedrooms feature balconies overlooking the well manicured garden and countryside. Friendly proprietors are on hand to assist with local dining recommendations. Award-winning breakfasts are served at the communal dining table or on the terrace in the warmer summer months. Off-road parking is an additional plus.

Rooms 2 en suite S £49; D £69 **Facilities** FTV tea/coffee Cen ht Wi-fi **Parking** 2 **Notes** ⊗ 🍴

SOUTHAMPTON *continued*

Alcantara Guest House

★★★★ GUEST ACCOMMODATION

20 Howard Rd, Shirley SO15 5BN
☎ 023 8033 2966   📠 023 8049 6163
e-mail: alcantaraguesthouse@sky.com
dir: *0.5m NW of city centre. Off A3057 onto Howard Rd*

A warm welcome is assured at this Victorian property,
named after the ocean liner to reflect the establishment's
shipping connections and location close to the city centre.
Bedrooms are comfortable and well decorated and have
many thoughtful extras. An appetising breakfast can be
served in the bright and airy dining room. Secure off-road
parking is available.

Rooms 9 rms (6 en suite) (3 fmly) (2 GF) **Facilities** FTV
tea/coffee Cen ht Wi-fi **Parking** 7 **Notes** ⊗ No Children
12yrs RS 2wks Xmas

Eversley Guest House

★★★★ GUEST ACCOMMODATION

Eversley, Kanes Hill, West End SO19 6AJ
☎ 023 8046 4546
e-mail: info@eversleyguesthouse.org.uk
web: www.eversleyguesthouse.org.uk
dir: *M27 junct 7, take A334 towards Southampton. At
rdbt, 2nd exit onto A27, 0.5m on right*

Within easy driving distance of Southampton city centre,
Eversley offers a quiet retreat where a friendly welcome
awaits you. Bedrooms are comfortable, thoughtfully
equipped and are complemented by smart en suite
facilities. Memorable breakfasts are served in an
attractive dining room, and Wi-fi is a bonus.

Rooms 5 en suite (1 fmly) **Facilities** FTV tea/coffee Cen ht
Wi-fi **Parking** 5 **Notes** ⊗

Hunters Lodge

★★★★ GUEST ACCOMMODATION

25 Landguard Rd, Shirley SO15 5DL
☎ 023 8022 7919
e-mail: hunterslodge.hotel@virgin.net
web: www.hunterslodgehotel.net
dir: *500yds NW of Southampton Central station. Off
A3057 Shirley Rd onto Languard Rd*

Located in a leafy residential area close to the city centre
and convenient for the docks, ferry terminal, university
and hospital, this double-fronted Victorian house
provides business and leisure guests with comfortable,
well-equipped bedrooms. Full English breakfast is served
at shared tables in the elegant dining room. There is also
a television lounge and a well-stocked bar.

Rooms 14 en suite (1 fmly) (1 GF) S £40-£48; D
£70-£77* **Facilities** FTV TVL tea/coffee Direct Dial Cen ht
Licensed Wi-fi **Parking** 16 **Notes** ⊗

Landguard Lodge

★★★ GUEST HOUSE

21 Landguard Rd SO15 5DL
☎ 023 8063 6904   📠 023 8063 2258
e-mail: info@landguardlodge.co.uk
web: www.landguardlodge.co.uk
dir: *500yds NW of Southampton Central station. Off
A3057 Shirley Rd onto Landguard Rd*

This Victorian house is in a quiet residential area a short
walk from the railway station. The bedrooms are bright,
comfortable and well equipped with many thoughtful
extras.

Rooms 11 en suite (1 fmly) (2 GF) S £42; D £65*
Facilities FTV tea/coffee Cen ht Wi-fi **Parking** 3 **Notes** ⊗
No Children 5yrs

The Brimar

★★ GUEST ACCOMMODATION

10-14 High St, Totton SO40 9HN
☎ 023 8086 2950   📠 023 8086 1301
e-mail: info@brimar-guesthouse.co.uk
dir: *3m W of city centre, off A35 in Totton High St*

This property offers practical, comfortable
accommodation at reasonable prices. Not all rooms are
en suite but bathrooms are well situated. Breakfast is
served in the dining room or as a take-away option. The
Brimar is well placed for the M27 and Southampton
docks, and off-road parking is available.

Rooms 21 rms (8 en suite) (13 pri facs) (2 fmly) (8 GF) (3
smoking) **Facilities** Cen ht Wi-fi **Parking** 20 **Notes** ⊗

Mayview Guest House

★★ 🅰 GUEST HOUSE

30 The Polygon SO15 2BN
☎ 023 8022 0907   & 07973 874194   📠 07977 017921
e-mail: info@mayview.co.uk
Rooms 9 rms (1 en suite) (1 fmly) (1 GF) S £25-£30; D
£45-£60* **Facilities** FTV tea/coffee Cen ht Wi-fi **Notes** ⊗
Closed 25 Dec

SOUTHSEA

See Portsmouth & Southsea

STOCKBRIDGE   Map 5 SU33

York Lodge

★★★★ BED AND BREAKFAST

Five Bells Ln, Nether Wallop SO20 8HE
☎ 01264 781313
e-mail: bradley@york-lodge.co.uk
web: www.york-lodge.co.uk
dir: *Turn off A30 or A343 onto B3084, turn onto Hosketts
Ln, fork left onto Five Bells Ln, 1st house on right*

Located in the picturesque village used as one of the sets
for the *Miss Marple* TV series, this charming house has

comfortable accommodation in a self-contained wing.
Bedrooms are stylishly presented with many thoughtful
extra facilities. The dining room overlooks peaceful
gardens.

Rooms 2 en suite (2 GF) **Facilities** FTV tea/coffee Cen ht
Wi-fi **Parking** 4 **Notes** No Children 8yrs ⊛

The Three Cups Inn

★★★ INN

High St SO20 6HB
☎ 01264 810527
e-mail: manager@the3cups.co.uk

A former coaching inn on the high street in a popular
town, with its own parking. Rooms are comfortable and
well equipped, and food is available every evening.

Rooms 8 en suite (3 fmly) **Facilities** tea/coffee Dinner
available Cen ht Wi-fi Fishing **Parking** 15

The Grosvenor

★★★ INN

23 High St SO20 6EU
☎ 01264 810606   📠 01264 810747
e-mail: 9180@greeneking.co.uk

Located between the historic cathedral cities of
Winchester and Salisbury and a stones throw from the
River Test, The Grosvenor provides en suite
accommodation within the traditional setting of this
Georgian building. Bedrooms have recently been
refurbished and have been designed with guest comfort
in mind. The 'Tom Cannon' restaurant is popular with
both residents and locals alike and provides a good range
of locally sourced produce and game (when in season).

Rooms 14 en suite 12 annexe en suite (6 GF) S £59; D
£79-£89* **Facilities** tea/coffee Dinner available Direct
Dial Cen ht Wi-fi Fishing **Conf** Max 105 Thtr 105 Class 85
Board 40 **Parking** 16 **Notes** Civ Wed 85

SWAY   Map 5 SZ29

The Nurse's Cottage Restaurant
with Rooms

★★★★ 🍴 🛏 GUEST ACCOMMODATION

Station Rd SO41 6BA
☎ 01590 683402
e-mail: stay@nursescottage.co.uk
web: www.nursescottage.co.uk
dir: *Off B3055 in village centre, close to shops*

Enjoying a prominent position in the New Forest village of
Sway, the Nurse's Cottage is the recipient of numerous
hospitality awards. Quality is paramount in each of the
individually styled bedrooms and each room offers a host
of thoughtful extras including flat-screen TVs, DVDs,
complimentary soft drinks, Wi-fi and delicious hand-
made chocolates. The conservatory restaurant overlooks
the neat garden and the seasonally changing dinner
menu features the best in local produce. A wide ranging

choice of hot and cold dishes at breakfast guarantees a good start to the day.

Rooms 5 en suite (5 GF) **Facilities** FTV tea/coffee Dinner available Direct Dial Cen ht Licensed Wi-fi **Parking** 5

Acorn Shetland Pony Stud

★★★★ BED AND BREAKFAST

Meadows Cottage, Arnewood Bridge Rd SO41 6DA
☎ **01590 682000 & 07506 079373**
e-mail: meadows.cottage@virgin.net
dir: *M27 junct 1, A337 to Brockenhurst, B3055 to Sway, pass Birchy Hill Nursing Home, over x-rds, 2nd entrance left*

Located on the outskirts of Sway, this comfortable establishment is set in over six acres of pony paddocks and a water garden. The ground-floor bedrooms are well furnished and have direct access onto patios. The enjoyable, freshly cooked breakfasts use a range of fine produce including delicious home-made bread.

Rooms 3 en suite (1 fmly) (3 GF) **Facilities** tea/coffee Cen ht Wi-fi Carriage driving with Shetland ponies, clock golf **Parking** 30 **Notes** 🐾

WARNFORD	Map 5 SU62

George & Falcon

★★★★ INN

Warnford Rd SO32 3LB
☎ **01730 829623** 📄 **01730 352222**
e-mail: reservations@georgeandfalcon.com
web: www.georgeandfalcon.com
dir: *Adjacent to A32 in village*

Set within the picturesque village of Warnford located close to major transport links to Winchester, Portsmouth and Southampton. Rooms are tastefully appointed following a recent refurbishment, featuring modern appointments yet keeping the charm and character of this traditional coaching inn. Traditional fayre is served in the popular restaurant and bar, whilst the large decking area is a welcome addition for summer months.

Rooms 6 en suite (1 fmly) S £59-£99; D £59-£109
Facilities FTV tea/coffee Dinner available Cen ht Wi-fi Golf 18 Fishing Riding **Conf** Max 30 Thtr 30 Class 15 Board 15 **Parking** 47 **Notes** LB Closed Xmas & 1 Jan

---

WINCHESTER	Map 5 SU42

PREMIER COLLECTION

Giffard House

★★★★★ GUEST HOUSE

50 Christchurch Rd SO23 9SU
☎ **01962 852628** 📄 **01962 856722**
e-mail: giffardhotel@aol.com
dir: *M3 junct 11, at rdbt 3rd exit onto A333 St Cross road for 1m. Pass BP garage on right, take next left then 2nd right. 150mtrs on left*

A warm welcome awaits at this stunning 19th-century Victorian house. The accommodation is luxurious, comfortable and well equipped for both the business and leisure traveller. There is also a fully licensed bar set in the elegant conservatory.

Rooms 13 en suite (1 fmly) (4 GF) **Facilities** STV FTV tea/coffee Direct Dial Cen ht Licensed Wi-fi **Conf** Max 15 Thtr 15 Class 15 Board 13 **Parking** 13 **Notes** 🐾 Closed 24 Dec-2 Jan

---

PREMIER COLLECTION

Orchard House

★★★★★ BED AND BREAKFAST

3 Christchurch Gardens, St Cross SO23 9TH
☎ **01962 861544** 📄 **01962 861988**
e-mail: h.hope@hotmail.co.uk
dir: *B3335 to Winchester & St Cross, after 2nd lights left onto Barnes Close, right onto Christchurch Rd, right again onto Christchurch Gdns, last house on right*

This friendly, family-run B&B is in a peaceful cul-de-sac, close to Winchester and the famous college, yet within easy reach of the M3. It offers a relaxed atmosphere, professional service and warm hospitality. The bedroom is spacious, comfortable and very well equipped for either the business or leisure guest alike. Gardens are well tended, and the balcony overlooking the rear garden can be used for breakfast on warmer summer mornings. There is also ample parking.

Rooms 1 en suite S £55-£60; D £80-£90*
Facilities STV FTV TVL tea/coffee Cen ht Wi-fi
Parking 2 **Notes** 🐾 No Children 6yrs 🐾

PREMIER COLLECTION

29 Christchurch Road

★★★★★ BED AND BREAKFAST

29 Christchurch Rd SO23 9SU
☎ **01962 868661** 📄 **01962 868661**
e-mail: dilke@waitrose.com
dir: *M3 junct 11 follow signs for Winchester & St Cross B3335, through 2 sets of lights, pass BP garage, left onto Ranelagh Rd. Take 2nd right onto Christchurch Rd, house at junct of Grafton Rd*

Located a short distance from the historic city of Winchester, this quality accommodation is tastefully appointed and offers comfortable bedrooms and bathrooms. The guest terrace is the ideal place to relax on a summer's afternoon within the well kept garden. A wide selection of breakfast items are served in the dining room around the communal table. Ample on-street parking is available.

Rooms 3 rms (2 en suite) (1 pri facs) **Facilities** FTV tea/coffee Cen ht Wi-fi **Notes** 🐾 No Children 5yrs 🐾

The Old Vine

★★★★ INN

8 Great Minster St SO23 9HA
☎ **01962 854616**
e-mail: reservations@oldvinewinchester.com
web: www.oldvinewinchester.com
dir: *M3 junct 11 towards St Cross, turn right at Green Man Pub, left onto Symonds St, left onto Little Minster St*

Overlooking the cathedral, this historic inn has been extensively and sympathetically restored and updated. Rooms are named and themed after various designers, there is permit parking, and food is served in the restaurant and bar downstairs.

Rooms 5 en suite (1 fmly) S £90-£165; D £100-£195*
Facilities FTV tea/coffee Dinner available Cen ht Wi-fi
Notes No coaches

WINCHESTER *continued*

Running Horse Inn

★★★★ ⊛ INN

88 Main Rd, Littleton SO22 6QS
☎ **01962 880218** 📠 **01962 886596**
e-mail: runninghorseinn@btconnect.com
dir: *B3049 out of Winchester 1.5m, turn right into Littleton after 1m, Running Horse on right*

Situated in a pretty rural location, yet with easy access to the M3, this is a great location for business and leisure travellers visiting Hampshire. Offering quality accommodation, the Running Horse is minimalist in its design, and provides comfortable beds and a small workstation area. Highlights of a stay here are a meal in the smart restaurant or a drink in the bar.

Rooms 9 annexe en suite (1 fmly) (9 GF) S £65; D £90*
Facilities tea/coffee Dinner available Cen ht Wi-fi
Parking 70 **Notes** No coaches

---

24 Clifton Road

★★★ BED AND BREAKFAST

SO22 5BU
☎ **01962 851620**
e-mail: a.williams1997@btinternet.com
dir: *500yds NW of city centre. B3090 Romsey Rd W from city centre, Clifton Rd 2nd right*

This delightful house is in a quiet residential area close to the railway station and High Street. It combines town-house elegance with a homely cottage charm, and is handy for local walks. The bedroom is comfortably furnished and the bathroom has a deep claw-foot bath. There is a lounge and a dining room.

Rooms 1 rms (1 pri facs) S £35; D £55 **Facilities** TVL tea/coffee Cen ht **Parking** 2 **Notes** ⊗ No Children 6yrs ⊜

The Westgate Inn

★★★ INN

2 Romsey Rd SO23 8TP
☎ **01962 820222** 📠 **01962 820222**
e-mail: wghguy@yahoo.co.uk
dir: *M3 junct 9 follow signs to city centre, on corner of Romsey Rd & Upper High St*

The Westgate Inn is well placed at the west end of the city near the castle. A popular restaurant serves good, home-prepared Indian meals and snacks. The traditional

bar is always busy. The attractive and good-sized bedrooms on two floors are well equipped.

Rooms 8 rms (6 en suite) (8 smoking) D £70-£85*
Facilities FTV tea/coffee Dinner available Direct Dial Cen ht Wi-fi **Conf** Max 12 Board 12 **Notes** No Children 10yrs No coaches

---

HEREFORDSHIRE

ADFORTON — Map 9 SO47

Brick House Farm

★★★★ 🏠 ⊜ BED AND BREAKFAST

SY7 0NF
☎ **01568 770870**
e-mail: info@adforton.com
dir: *On A4110 in Adforton opposite St Andrew's Church*

Very much at the heart of the village community, this 16th-century longhouse has been sympathetically renovated to provide high standards of comfort. Superb beds are just one feature of the thoughtfully furnished accommodation, and smart modern private bathrooms are an additional benefit. Comprehensive breakfasts and imaginative set dinners featuring locally-sourced produce including home-grown items are served in a cosy combined sitting/dining room. A warm welcome is assured.

Rooms 2 rms (2 pri facs) D fr £75* **Facilities** STV FTV tea/coffee Dinner available Cen ht Wi-fi **Parking** 2 **Notes** LB No Children 12yrs

---

BODENHAM — Map 10 SO55

The Coach House at England Gate's Inn

★★★★ ⊜ INN

HR1 3HU
☎ **07500 833498**
e-mail: englandsgate@btconnect.com

This fine black and white 16th-century inn is run by the McNeil family, who pride themselves on quality service. The inn is set in attractive gardens which are ideal for alfresco dining on warmer days. The detached coach house has comfortable bedrooms with modern en suite facilities; the views are spectacular from the upstairs rooms. Continental breakfast is served in the coach house dining area on weekdays, and a full cooked breakfast is available at weekends.

Rooms 7 en suite (2 fmly) (4 GF) S £68-£123; D £68-£123* **Facilities** FTV tea/coffee Dinner available Direct Dial Cen ht Wi-fi **Conf** Max 12 Board 12 **Parking** 30

BROCKHAMPTON — Map 10 SO53

Ladyridge Farm

★★★★ ⊜ GUEST HOUSE

HR1 4SE
☎ **01989 740220** 📠 **01989 740220**
e-mail: carolgrant@ladyridgefarm.fsworld.co.uk
dir: *Off B4224 signed Brockhampton Church between How Caple & Fownhope. 400yds on right after thatched church*

This working farm, set in delightful countryside, provides a peaceful haven and is also home to rare breed ducks, poultry and sheep. The traditionally styled bedrooms are spacious and thoughtfully equipped. Meals, served family-style in the attractive dining room, use local, fresh ingredients and home-produced free-range eggs.

Rooms 3 rms (2 pri facs) (1 fmly) **Facilities** tea/coffee Dinner available Cen ht **Parking** 6 **Notes** ⊗ ⊜

BROMYARD — Map 10 SO65

Linton Brook Farm *(SO676538)*

★★★★ FARMHOUSE

Malvern Rd, Bringsty WR6 5TR
☎ **01885 488875**
Mrs S Steeds
e-mail: stay@lintonbrookfarm.com
dir: *Off A44 1.5m E of Bromyard onto B4220 signed Malvern. Farm 0.5m on left*

Dating back some 400 years, this large house has a wealth of character and has been renovated to provide modern comforts. Accommodation is spacious and there is a comfortable sitting room with a welcoming wood-burning stove. The breakfast room has exposed beams, antique furniture and an inglenook fireplace.

Rooms 3 rms (2 en suite) (1 pri facs) S £45-£60; D £75-£85* **Facilities** STV FTV TVL tea/coffee Dinner available Cen ht Wi-fi **Parking** 12 **Notes** LB ⊗ Closed Xmas & New Year RS Nov-Feb No single person single night bookings ⊜ 68 acres grassland

Save on B&Bs and Hotels. Book at **theAA.com/hotel**

HEREFORDSHIRE 173 **ENGLAND**

Little Hegdon Farm House

★★★★ BED AND BREAKFAST

Hegdon Hill, Pencombe HR7 4SL
☎ 01885 400263 & 07779 595445
e-mail: howardcolegrave@hotmail.com
web: www.littlehegdonfarmhouse.co.uk
dir: *4m SW of Bromyard. From Bromyard to Pencombe, 1.5m towards Risbury, at top of Hegdon Hill down farm lane for 500yds*

Located in a pretty hamlet, this traditional house has been renovated to provide high standards of comfort. Original features include exposed beams and open fires, and the bedrooms, with stunning countryside views, are equipped with lots of thoughtful extras.

Rooms 2 en suite (1 GF) S £35–£40; D £60 **Facilities** TVL tea/coffee Cen ht ⚓ Riding Pool table **Parking** 4 **Notes** ⊛

GOODRICH   Map 10 S051

Granton House B&B

★★★★ BED AND BREAKFAST

Church Pitch HR9 6JE
☎ 01600 890277
e-mail: granton@stayonwye.com
web: www.stayonwye.com
dir: *A40 S from Ross-on-Wye, 2nd Goodrich exit into village, pass Cross Keys continue straight for approx 0.5m*

A genuinely warm and friendly welcome awaits at Granton House, parts of which date back to the late 18th century. It is situated in extensive grounds and gardens, in a picturesque rural area on the edge of Goodrich. The house, which was once the home of Victorian artist Joshua Cristall, has been extensively and tastefully renovated to provide high quality, thoughtfully equipped accommodation.

Rooms 3 en suite (1 fmly) D £80–£95* **Facilities** FTV tea/coffee Cen ht Wi-fi Golf 18 **Parking** 4 **Notes** LB ⊛ No Children 12yrs Closed 18 Dec-2 Jan

HEREFORD   Map 10 S053

See also Little Dewchurch

PREMIER COLLECTION

Somerville House

★★★★★ GUEST ACCOMMODATION

12 Bodenham Rd HR1 2TS
☎ 01432 273991 📠 01432 268719
e-mail: enquiries@somervillehouse.net
web: www.somervillehouse.net
dir: *A465, at Aylestone Hill rdbt towards city centre, left at Southbank Rd, leading to Bodenham Rd*

A detached late-Victorian villa situated in a quiet tree-lined residential road, that is a boutique-style experience. Expect a warm and friendly welcome from Rosie and Bill who offer quality accommodation with high standards of luxury and comfort. All bedrooms are spacious and provide a good range of quality extras. Breakfast is served in the light and contemporary dining room at individual tables. There is a terraced garden to the rear where guests can sit and relax, or indoors, they can make use of the comfortable lounge. There is ample parking.

Rooms 12 en suite (2 fmly) (1 GF) S £60; D £77–£112* **Facilities** FTV tea/coffee Cen ht Licensed Wi-fi Arrangement with health spa **Conf** Max 10 Thtr 10 Class 10 Board 10 **Parking** 10 **Notes** LB ⊛

Holly House Farm *(S0456367)*

★★★★ FARMHOUSE

Allensmore HR2 9BH
☎ 01432 277294 & 07889 830223
Mrs D Sinclair
e-mail: hollyhousefarm@aol.com
web: www.hollyhousefarm.org.uk
dir: *A465 S to Allensmore, right signed Cobhall Common, at small x-rds right into lane, house on right*

Surrounded by open countryside, this spacious farmhouse is a relaxing base for those visiting this beautiful area. The homely and comfortable bedrooms offer lovely views over the fields. Breakfast makes use of local produce together with home-made jams and marmalade. Pets are very welcome here and the proprietor is happy to look after them during the day if required.

Rooms 2 rms (1 en suite) (1 pri facs) D £50–£70* **Facilities** FTV tea/coffee Cen ht **Parking** 32 **Notes** Closed 25-26, 31 Dec & 1 Jan ⊛ 11 acres horses

Norfolk House

★★★★ GUEST ACCOMMODATION

23 Saint Martin St HR2 7RD
☎ 01432 340900
e-mail: info@norfolkhousehereford.co.uk
web: www.norfolkhousehereford.co.uk

Norfolk House is a large mid-terraced Georgian property situated south of the River Wye in Hereford, only 100 metres from the city's old bridge and the Left Bank Village. An ideal location for exploring the nearby towns of Leominster, Ludlow, Ledbury, Kington, Ross-on-Wye and Worcester. There are five comfortable en suite bedrooms including doubles (with king-sized beds) and twin rooms. In the welcoming dining room a hearty breakfast, made from fresh local produce, is provided. Wi-fi is available.

Rooms 5 en suite (1 fmly) **Facilities** FTV tea/coffee Cen ht Wi-fi **Parking** 3 **Notes** ⊛ No Children 5yrs

Sink Green *(S0542377)*

★★★★ FARMHOUSE

Rotherwas HR2 6LE
☎ 01432 870223 📠 01432 870223
Mr D E Jones
e-mail: enquiries@sinkgreenfarm.co.uk
web: www.sinkgreenfarm.co.uk
dir: *3m SE of city centre. Off A49 onto B4399 for 2m*

This charming 16th-century farmhouse stands in attractive countryside and has many original features, including flagstone floors, exposed beams and open fireplaces. Bedrooms are traditionally furnished and one has a four-poster bed. The pleasant garden has a comfortable summer house, hot tub and barbecue.

Rooms 3 en suite S £35–£40; D £70–£80* **Facilities** FTV TVL tea/coffee Cen ht Wi-fi Fishing Hot Tub **Parking** 10 **Notes** LB ⊛ 180 acres beef

Heron House

★★★ ⚿ BED AND BREAKFAST

Canon Pyon Rd, Portway HR4 8NG
☎ 01432 761111 📠 01432 760603
e-mail: info@theheronhouse.com
web: www.theheronhouse.com
dir: *A4103 onto A4110 until Portway x-rds, Heron House 200yds on left*

Rooms 2 rms (1 en suite) **Facilities** tea/coffee Cen ht **Parking** 5 **Notes** ⊛ No Children 10yrs ⊛

HEREFORD *continued*

No 21

Ⓤ

21 Aylestone Hill HR1 1HR
☎ 01432 279897 & 07967 525403
dir: *On A4103 from Worcester to rdbt at approach to Hereford. Take 1st exit to town centre (A465)*

Currently the rating for this establishment is not confirmed. This may be due to a change of ownership or because it has only recently joined the AA rating scheme.

Rooms 4 en suite (1 GF) S £35-£45; D £60-£80*
Facilities FTV tea/coffee Cen ht Wi-fi **Parking** 8 **Notes** ⊖

| **LEDBURY** | **Map 10 SO73** |

Church Farm *(SO718426)*

★★★★ FARMHOUSE

Coddington HR8 1JJ
☎ 01531 640271 & 07861 358549
Mrs West
web: www.dexta.co.uk

A warm welcome awaits at Church Farm, a Grade II listed, 16th-century farmhouse, located in a peaceful location in the depths of rural Herefordshire. Aga-cooked breakfasts including home-made preserves, are served around the shared kitchen table or in the separate dining room. Church Farm is a working farm with a beautiful garden and rural views. There is much to explore in the area, and numerous activities including golf, canoeing, cycling and various walks. The Malvern Hills are only five miles away.

Rooms 3 rms (2 en suite) (1 pri facs) S fr £37; D fr £74*
Facilities TVL tea/coffee Cen ht **Parking** 6 **Notes** Closed 17 Dec-17 Jan ⊖ 150 acres arable

Moor Court Farm *(SO639447)*

★★★★ FARMHOUSE

Stretton, Grandison HR8 2TP
☎ 01531 670408 📠 01531 670408
Mrs E Godsall
dir: *1.5m E of A417 at Upper Eggleton*

This 15th-century house is situated on a mixed farm with working oast houses where hops are dried. Bedrooms are thoughtfully equipped and furnished, and one has a four-poster. Public areas include a comfortable lounge with an impressive stone fireplace and a dining room, where breakfast includes local produce and eggs from the farm.

Rooms 3 en suite **Facilities** tea/coffee Dinner available Cen ht Licensed Fishing **Parking** 5 **Notes** ⊗ No Children 8yrs ⊖ 200 acres mixed/livestock/hops

The Seven Stars

★★★★ ⇔ INN

11 The Homend HR8 1BN
☎ 01531 635800
e-mail: paulford@sevenstars.co.uk
web: www.sevenstarsledbury.co.uk
dir: *4m from M50*

This 16th-century high street inn is reputedly the oldest in this picturesque market town. Owners Paul and Sharon are welcoming and friendly. The interior of the inn is modern and contemporary with a stylish dining area to the rear. The bedrooms have very comfortable beds and good space with some thoughtful extras. Breakfast is freshly prepared and hearty. Parking is available at the nearby public car park.

Rooms 3 en suite (2 fmly) **Facilities** STV tea/coffee Dinner available Cen ht Wi-fi **Notes** ⊗ No coaches

Wall Hills House

★★★★ ⇔ GUEST ACCOMMODATION

Hereford Rd HR8 2PR
☎ 01531 632833
e-mail: wallhills@btinternet.com
dir: *Leave Ledbury on A438, entrance to drive within 200yds on left after rdbt*

Expect a friendly welcome at Wall Hills House, which is set amongst fields and woodland half a mile from the main road and close to the old market town of Ledbury. The area is ideal for walkers, with the wonderful scenery of the nearby Malvern Hills. Bedrooms are spacious, reflecting the Georgian era in which the house was built, and the front-facing rooms command views over rural Herefordshire. Dinner is freshly prepared using fresh, local ingredients including vegetables from the garden, and served in the cosy dining room at individual tables.

Rooms 3 rms (2 en suite) (1 pri facs) D £84-£90
Facilities tea/coffee Dinner available Cen ht Licensed Wi-fi **Parking** 6 **Notes** LB ⊗ Closed Xmas & New Year

| **LEOMINSTER** | **Map 10 SO45** |

PREMIER COLLECTION

The Old Rectory Pembridge

★★★★★ BED AND BREAKFAST

Bridge St, Pembridge HR6 9EU
☎ 01544 387968
e-mail: lynnpickard@hotmail.co.uk
web: www.theoldrectorypembridge.co.uk
dir: *A44 into Pembridge onto Bridge St towards river, house on right before bridge*

Set in a peaceful location close to the River Arrow on the Black & White Village Trail, this 1852 Gothic building has been lovingly refurbished to provide luxurious accommodation by the present owners who extend a warm welcome to all their guests. The bedrooms have antique furniture and quality soft furnishings along with a range of thoughtful extras; the spacious en suite bathrooms add to the luxury experience. Public areas include a large lounge with a log fire, and an elegant dining room where excellent breakfasts are served around a communal table. Lynn and Philip Pickard were finalists in this year's Friendliest Landlady of the Year award (2011-12).

Rooms 3 en suite D £90-£110 **Facilities** FTV TVL tea/coffee Cen ht Wi-fi **Parking** 6 **Notes** ⊗ No Children

Save on B&Bs and Hotels. Book at **theAA.com/hotel**

HEREFORDSHIRE 175 **ENGLAND**

PREMIER COLLECTION

Hills Farm (SO564638)

★★★★★ 🏠 FARMHOUSE

Leysters HR6 0HP
☎ 01568 750205
Mrs J Conolly
e-mail: info@thehillsfarm.co.uk
web: www.thehillsfarm.co.uk
dir: Off A4112 (Leominster to Tenbury Wells), on
outskirts of Leysters

Set in a peaceful location with views over the
countryside, this property dates in part from the 16th
century. The friendly, attentive proprietors provide a
relaxing and homely atmosphere. The attractive
bedrooms, in the converted barns, are spacious and
comfortable. Breakfasts, served in the dining room and
conservatory, feature fresh local produce.

Rooms 3 annexe en suite (1 GF) S £52-£55; D £84-£90
Facilities FTV tea/coffee Cen ht **Parking** 8 **Notes** ⊗ No
Children 12yrs Closed Dec & Jan 120 acres arable

LITTLE DEWCHURCH   Map 10 SO53

Cwm Craig (SO535322)

★★★★ FARMHOUSE

HR2 6PS
☎ 01432 840250   📠 01432 840250
Mrs G Lee
e-mail: leead@btconnect.com
dir: Off A49 into Little Dewchurch, turn right in village,
Cwm Craig 1st farm on left

This Georgian farmhouse is situated on the outskirts of
the village in glorious countryside and offers spacious
accommodation. Bedrooms are carefully furnished and
public areas consist of a comfortable lounge, games
room and dining rooms; one is offered for the use of
families. Hearty breakfasts include eggs from the farm's
hens.

Rooms 3 en suite (1 fmly) S £35-£40; D £60-£70
Facilities FTV TVL tea/coffee Cen ht Pool table **Parking** 6
Notes ⊗ ⊜ 190 acres organic arable

ROSS-ON-WYE   Map 10 SO52

See also Goodrich

PREMIER COLLECTION

Wilton Court Restaurant with Rooms

★★★★★ ◉◉ 🍴 RESTAURANT WITH ROOMS

Wilton Ln HR9 6AQ
☎ 01989 562569   📠 01989 768460
e-mail: info@wiltoncourthotel.com
dir: M50 junct 4, A40 towards Monmouth at 3rd rdbt
left signed Ross-on-Wye, 1st right, on right

Dating back to the 16th century, this establishment
has great charm and a wealth of character. Standing
on the banks of the River Wye and just a short walk
from the town centre, there is a genuinely relaxed,
friendly and unhurried atmosphere created by hosts
Roger and Helen Wynn and their reliable team.
Bedrooms are tastefully furnished and well equipped,
while public areas include a comfortable lounge,
traditional bar and pleasant restaurant with a
conservatory extension overlooking the garden. High
standards of food, using fresh, locally sourced
ingredients, are offered.

Rooms 10 en suite (1 fmly) S £100-£155; D
£125-£175* **Facilities** FTV TVL tea/coffee Dinner
available Direct Dial Cen ht Wi-fi 🏌 Golf 18 Fishing
Conf Thtr 50 Class 20 Board 20 **Parking** 20 **Notes** LB
Closed 3-15 Jan Civ Wed 50

PREMIER COLLECTION

Orles Barn

★★★★★ ◉◉ 🍴 RESTAURANT WITH ROOMS

Wilton HR9 6AE
☎ 01989 562155   📠 01989 768470
e-mail: reservations@orles-barn.co.uk
web: www.orles-barn.co.uk
dir: A49/A40 rdbt outside Ross-on-Wye, take slip road
between petrol station & A40 to Monmouth. 100yds
on left

The proprietors of this character property offer a warm
welcome to all their guests. Older sections of the
property date back to the 14th and 17th centuries when
it was a farmhouse with a barn. The property offers
comfortable bedrooms, a smart cosy lounge with a bar
and a spacious restaurant. Dinner and Sunday lunch
are offered on a balanced menu of fresh local and
seasonal ingredients. Breakfast also utilises quality
local produce and makes a good start to the day.

Rooms 5 en suite (1 fmly) (1 GF) S £95-£135; D
£135-£175* **Facilities** FTV tea/coffee Dinner available
Cen ht Wi-fi **Conf** Max 100 Thtr 100 Class 50 Board 40
Parking 20 **Notes** LB Civ Wed 100

Brookfield House

★★★★ GUEST ACCOMMODATION

Over Ross St HR9 7AT
☎ 01989 562188
e-mail: info@brookfield-house.co.uk
dir: 500yds N of town centre. Off B4234 Over Ross St onto
Brookmead & up driveway

Dating from the 18th century, this large detached house
lies just north of the town centre with easy access to the
M50 then the M5. The new owners Robin and Kaye extend
a warm welcome to all their guests. Bedrooms are very
spacious, comfortably appointed and well equipped with
many thoughtful extras. Breakfast is served in the light
and airy dining room at separate tables. A relaxing lounge
is available for guest use, as are the attractive gardens.
Parking is available to the rear of the property.

Rooms 3 en suite (1 fmly) **Facilities** tea/coffee Cen ht
Parking 12 **Notes** ⊗

ROSS-ON-WYE *continued*

Lumleys

★★★★ BED AND BREAKFAST

Kern Bridge, Bishopswood HR9 5QT
☎ 01600 890040 ▨ 0870 706 2378
e-mail: helen@lumleys.force9.co.uk
web: www.thelumleys.co.uk
dir: *Off A40 onto B4229 at Goodrich, over Kern Bridge, right at Inn On The Wye, 400yds opp picnic ground*

This pleasant and friendly bed and breakfast overlooks the River Wye, and has been a hostelry since Victorian times. It offers the character of a bygone era combined with modern comforts and facilities. Bedrooms are individually and carefully furnished and one has a four-poster bed and its own patio. Comfortable public areas include a choice of sitting rooms. Helen Mattis and Judith Mills-Haworth were finalists in this year's Friendliest Landlady of the Year award (2011-12).

Rooms 3 en suite D £70-£75* **Facilities** STV FTV TVL tea/coffee Direct Dial Cen ht Wi-fi ⚲ **Parking** 15 **Notes** Closed Nov-end Mar ⊕

Benhall Farm

★★★★ ⬜ BED AND BREAKFAST

Wilton HR9 6AG
☎ 01989 563900 & 07900 26412 ▨ 01989 563900
e-mail: info@benhallfarm.co.uk
web: www.benhallfarm.co.uk
dir: *From Wilton rdbt (junct A40/A49), take exit in direction M50. On dual-carriageway turn immediately left onto No Through Road, Benhall Farm at end of lane*

A warm welcome can be expected at Benhall Farm which is a working dairy/arable farm of 335 acres and has been part of the Duchy of Cornwall Estate since 2000. The location is on the outskirts of Ross-on-Wye on the banks of the River Wye and has easy access to the M50, Hereford, Abergavenny, Monmouth, and the Forest of Dean. Bedrooms are comfortable, spacious and many guest extras are provided, including Wi-fi. A lounge is available for guests use and the dining room is also part of the comfortable lounge where hearty breakfasts are provided at the communal table. Parking is available to the front of the property.

Rooms 3 en suite D £70-£80 **Facilities** FTV TVL tea/coffee Cen ht Wi-fi Fishing **Parking** 6 **Notes** LB Closed 20 Dec-10 Jan

Lea House

★★★★ ⬜ ⬚ GUEST ACCOMMODATION

Lea HR9 7JZ
☎ 01989 750652 ▨ 01989 750652
e-mail: enquiries@leahouse.co.uk
web: www.leahouse.co.uk
dir: *4m SE of Ross on A40 towards Gloucester in Lea*

This former coaching inn, near Ross-on-Wye, makes a good base for exploring the Forest of Dean and the Wye Valley, and the atmosphere is relaxed and comfortable. The individually furnished bedrooms are thoughtfully equipped and very homely. Breakfast in the oak-beamed dining room offers home-made breads, freshly squeezed juice, fresh fruit platters, local sausages and fish choices. Home-cooked dinners are available by prior arrangement.

Rooms 3 rms (2 en suite) (1 pri facs) (1 fmly) S £40-£55; D £65-£75* **Facilities** FTV TVL tea/coffee Dinner available Cen ht Wi-fi **Parking** 4 **Notes** LB

Nature's Choice

★★★★ GUEST HOUSE

Raglan House, 17 Broad St HR9 7EA
☎ 01989 763454 ▨ 01989 763064
e-mail: deanclarke@surfree.co.uk
dir: *Market Place onto Broad St, 100yds on left*

Anna and Dean Clarke extend a friendly welcome at this Grade II listed Queen Anne property, located in the town centre, close to all amenities. As the name suggests, the emphasis here is on healthy food with vegetarian and gluten-free options in the café area where food is available all day; Anna's speciality is Russian style cooking. Discounted meals are available to guests.

Rooms 4 en suite (1 fmly) S £25-£39.50; D £55-£59.50* **Facilities** FTV tea/coffee Dinner available Cen ht Licensed Wi-fi **Notes** ⊗

Thatch Close

★★★★ GUEST ACCOMMODATION

Llangrove HR9 6EL
☎ 01989 770300
e-mail: info@thatchclose.co.uk
web: www.thatchclose.co.uk
dir: *Off A40 at Symonds Yat West/Whitchurch junct to Llangrove, right at x-rds after Post Office & before school. Thatch Close 0.6m on left*

Standing in 13 acres, this sturdy 18th-century farmhouse is full of character. Expect a wonderfully warm atmosphere with a genuine welcome from your hosts. The homely bedrooms are equipped for comfort with many thoughtful extras. Breakfast is served in the elegant dining room, and a lounge is available. The extensive patios and gardens are popular in summer, providing plenty of space to find a quiet corner and relax with a good book.

Rooms 3 en suite S £45-£55; D £70-£80* **Facilities** TVL tea/coffee Cen ht Wi-fi **Parking** 8 **Notes** LB ⊕

The Whitehouse Guest House

★★★ GUEST HOUSE

Wye St HR9 7BX
☎ 01989 763572
e-mail: whitehouseross@aol.com
dir: *Exit A40 dual-carriageway at Wilton, pass over bridge, take 1st left White House on right*

A warm welcome awaits at this 18th-century guest house which is located adjacent to the River Wye and just a short walk to the town centre. The bedrooms are tastefully appointed and provide a thoughtful range of extras including Wi-fi access. There are four-poster rooms and single rooms. A hearty breakfast is provided at individual tables in the dining room; evening meals are available with prior notice. Parking is on the road to the front.

Rooms 7 en suite (2 fmly) **Facilities** tea/coffee Dinner available Cen ht Licensed Wi-fi **Notes** No Children 12yrs Closed 24-25 Dec

SHOBDON	Map 9 SO46

The Bateman Arms

★★★★ INN

HR6 9LX
☎ 01568 708374 ▨ 08701 236418
e-mail: diana@batemanarms.co.uk
web: www.batemanarms.co.uk
dir: *On B4362 in Shobdon*

Located in the village, parts of this inn date back over 400 years; Bill and Diana Mahood offer a warm welcome to all their guests. The accommodation comprises six modern bedrooms located in a separate building, all are comfortable and well appointed. There are plenty of oak beams and a large log fire adds to the warm ambience of the public areas. In addition to the friendly welcome, the food, using carefully prepared local produce, is a key feature.

Rooms 6 annexe en suite (2 fmly) (3 GF) S £55-£60; D £85-£95* **Facilities** FTV tea/coffee Dinner available Cen ht Wi-fi Pool table Games room **Parking** 40 **Notes** LB

STAPLOW	Map 10 SO64

The Oak Inn

★★★★ INN

HR8 1NP
☎ 01531 640954
e-mail: oakinn@wyenet.co.uk
dir: *2m N of Ledbury on B4214*

A privately owned, delightful country inn surrounded by a cider apple orchard. Situated north of the market town of Ledbury, yet within easy access of the Malvern Hills, this 17th-century building has been totally renovated. The bedrooms are modern, spacious and well appointed with under-floor heating and beds that have quality pocket-sprung mattresses. The public areas feature log-burning fires, flagstone floors and wooden beams. Dining is available seven days a week, and the open-plan kitchen allows diners to see their meals being prepared. Wi-fi is accessible throughout.

Rooms 4 en suite (1 fmly) **Facilities** FTV tea/coffee Dinner available Cen ht Wi-fi **Parking Notes** No coaches

SYMONDS YAT (EAST)   Map 10 SO51

See also Coleford (Gloucestershire)

The Royal Lodge

★★★★ ≜ GUEST ACCOMMODATION

HR9 6JL
☎ 01600 890238 ▤ 01600 891425
e-mail: info@royalhotel-symondsyat.com
web: www.royallodgesymondsyat.co.uk
dir: *Midway between Ross and Monmouth exit A40 at signs for Goodrich & B4229 to Symonds Yat East*

The Royal Lodge stands at the top end of the village overlooking the River Wye and parking is available. The bedrooms are spacious and comfortable, and have flat-screen TVs and many guest extras; the bathrooms offer modern facilities. There is a cosy lounge with an open fireplace and two bars are available. The welcoming restaurant provides carefully prepared meals using fresh and local ingredients. The staff are pleasant and friendly.

Rooms 20 en suite (5 fmly) S £39-£55; D £49-£99
Facilities TVL tea/coffee Dinner available Direct Dial Cen ht Licensed Wi-fi **Conf** Max 70 Thtr 70 Class 20 Board 30 **Parking** 150 **Notes** LB Civ Wed 80

Saracens Head Inn

★★★★ ⊜ INN

HR9 6JL
☎ 01600 890435
e-mail: contact@saracensheadinn.co.uk
web: www.saracensheadinn.co.uk
dir: *Off A40 at Little Chef, signed Symonds Yat East, 2m*

Dating from the 16th century, the friendly, family-run Saracens Head faces the River Wye and has wonderful views. The well-equipped bedrooms are decorated in a cottage style, and there is a cosy lounge, an attractive dining room, and a popular public bar with a riverside patio. All meals are offered from a comprehensive menu changed regularly, and include locally-sourced produce.

Rooms 8 en suite 2 annexe en suite (1 GF) S £59-£70; D £94-£138* **Facilities** FTV TVL tea/coffee Dinner available Direct Dial Cen ht Wi-fi Fishing Pool table **Conf** Max 25 Thtr 25 Class 25 Board 25 **Parking** 35 **Notes** LB No Children 7yrs No coaches

VOWCHURCH   Map 9 SO33

Yew Tree House

★★★★ ⚑ BED AND BREAKFAST

Bacho Hill HR2 9PF
☎ 01981 251195 ▤ 01981 251195
e-mail: enquiries@yewtreehouse-hereford.co.uk
web: www.yewtreehouse-hereford.co.uk
dir: *On B4348 between Kingstone & Vowchurch*

Rooms 3 en suite (2 fmly) D £70-£85 **Facilities** FTV TVL tea/coffee Dinner available Cen ht Wi-fi **Parking** 4 **Notes** LB ⊛

WHITCHURCH   Map 10 SO51

Portland House Guest House

★★★★ ≜ GUEST ACCOMMODATION

HR9 6DB
☎ 01600 890757
e-mail: info@portlandguesthouse.co.uk
web: www.portlandguesthouse.co.uk
dir: *Off A40 between Monmouth & Ross on Wye. Take turn for Whitchurch/Symonds Yat West*

Portland House is an impressive dwelling, dating in part to the 17th century, and situated in the picturesque Wye Valley. Comfortable bedrooms include a large family room, an accessible bedroom on the ground floor, and a four-poster suite. All have a thoughtful range of extras. Walkers can use the Boot Room and guests have use of the laundry, the terrace garden area, and the attractive lounge. Breakfast, with home-made bread and up to eight kinds of home-made preserve, is served around the shared dining table, or at a separate table in the dining room. With prior arrangement, evening meals can be provided.

Rooms 6 en suite (2 fmly) (1 GF) S £55-£70; D £70-£95 **Facilities** FTV TVL tea/coffee Dinner available Cen ht Licensed Wi-fi ⤙ **Parking** 6 **Notes** LB Closed 25-26 Dec

YARKHILL   Map 10 SO64

Garford Farm *(SO600435)*

★★★★ FARMHOUSE

HR1 3ST
☎ 01432 890226 ▤ 01432 890707
Mrs H Parker
e-mail: garfordfarm@btconnect.com
dir: *Off A417 at Newtown x-rds onto A4103 for Hereford, farm 1.5m on left*

This black and white timber-framed farmhouse, set on a large arable holding, dates from the 17th century. Its character is enhanced by period furnishings, and fires burn in the comfortable lounge during colder weather. The traditionally furnished bedrooms, including a family room, have modern facilities.

Rooms 2 en suite (1 fmly) S fr £35; D fr £60* **Facilities** tea/coffee Cen ht ⤙ Fishing **Parking** 6 **Notes** No Children 2yrs Closed 25-26 Dec ⊛ 700 acres arable

HERTFORDSHIRE

ASHWELL   Map 12 TL23

The Three Tuns

★★★ ⚑ INN

6 High St SG7 5NL
☎ 01462 742107 ▤ 01462 743662
e-mail: info@threetunshotel.co.uk
dir: *A1M junct 10, after 1m signs for Ashwell*

Rooms 6 en suite (2 fmly) S £39-£53; D £53-£69*
Facilities FTV tea/coffee Dinner available Cen ht Wi-fi **Conf** Max 36 Thtr 24 Class 36 Board 18 **Parking** 24 **Notes** Civ Wed 150

BISHOP'S STORTFORD   Map 6 TL42

Broadleaf Guest House

★★★ BED AND BREAKFAST

38 Broadleaf Av CM23 4JY
☎ 01279 835467
e-mail: b-pcannon@sky.com
dir: *1m SW of town centre. Off B1383 onto Whittinton Way & Friedburge Av, Broadleaf Av 6th left*

A delightful detached house situated in a peaceful residential area close to the town centre, and within easy striking distance of the M11 and Stansted Airport. The pleasantly decorated bedrooms are carefully furnished and equipped with many thoughtful touches. Breakfast is served in the smart dining room, which overlooks the pretty garden.

Rooms 2 rms (1 fmly) **Facilities** FTV tea/coffee Cen ht **Parking** 2 **Notes** ⊛

BUNTINGFORD   Map 12 TL32

Sword Inn Hand

★★★★ INN

Westmill SG9 9LQ
☎ 01763 271356
e-mail: welcome@theswordinnhand.co.uk
web: www.theswordinnhand.co.uk
dir: *In Westmill, off A10 S of Buntingford*

Set within the peaceful village of Westmill amid rolling countryside, this charming 14th-century inn offers excellent accommodation and a friendly and relaxed atmosphere. The purpose-built, ground-floor bedrooms are located just off the rear gardens; they are very well-equipped and carefully appointed rooms that have their own access. Character public rooms offer a choice of restaurant and bar dining options, along with a choice of draught ales.

Rooms 4 en suite (4 GF) **Facilities** STV FTV TVL tea/coffee Dinner available Cen ht Wi-fi **Parking** 25 **Notes** ⊗

CODICOTE — Map 6 TL21

The Rustic Pub Company

★★★ INN

65 High St SG4 8XD
☎ 01438 821600 📠 01438 821700
e-mail: info@thebellcodicote.co.uk
dir: A1(M) onto B656 to Codicote, on High St

This well presented country inn offers cottage-style en
suite accommodation, ample parking space and an
attractive restaurant with an appealing menu for both
lunch and dinner. The pub has a warm atmosphere and a
well-stocked bar. The accommodation is comfortable and
has a good range of amenities.

Rooms 25 en suite (4 fmly) (25 GF) Facilities tea/coffee
Dinner available Direct Dial Cen ht Wi-fi Conf Max 40 Thtr
20 Class 40 Board 20 Parking 30

DATCHWORTH — Map 6 TL21

PREMIER COLLECTION

Farmhouse B&B

★★★★★ BED AND BREAKFAST

Hawkins Grange Farm, Hawkins Hall Ln SG3 6TF
☎ 01438 813369
e-mail: mail@hawkinsgrangefarm.com
web: www.hawkinsgrangefarm.com
dir: A1(M) junct 7 onto A602 (Hertford). From Bragbury
End right onto Bragbury Ln, 1m, then 50yds on left
after phone box

This detached property is set in several acres of
grassland on the edge of the pretty village of
Datchworth. A warm and professional welcome is
provided by your host Jane. Bedrooms are comfortably
furnished with an abundance of accessories. Full
English or continental breakfast is served, including
organic, local produce and home-made items.

Rooms 3 rms (2 en suite) (1 pri facs) Facilities FTV
tea/coffee Cen ht Wi-fi Parking 8 Notes ✖

HARPENDEN — Map 6 TL11

The Silver Cup

★★★★ INN

5 St Albans Rd AL5 2JF
☎ 01582 713095 📠 01582 469713
e-mail: info@silvercup.co.uk
web: www.silvercup.co.uk
dir: 200yds SW of Harpenden station on A1081 St Albans
Rd

Located south of Harpenden High Street opposite the
common, this small family-owned inn offers comfortable,
well equipped rooms with many additional extras such as
an honesty bar and home-made biscuits. Public areas are
stylish and well presented and the attractive restaurant

serves a superior quality menu, complemented by real
ales and a good wine list. Service is friendly and helpful.

Rooms 6 en suite (1 fmly) Facilities TVL tea/coffee Dinner
available Cen ht Wi-fi Parking 7 Notes ✖ No coaches

HERTFORD HEATH — Map 6 TL31

PREMIER COLLECTION

Brides Farm

★★★★★ BED AND BREAKFAST

The Roundings SG13 7PY
☎ 01992 463315 📠 01992 478776
e-mail: rjbartington@btinternet.com
dir: Take B1197 to Hertford Heath. Right at College
Arms into The Roundings. Left to Brides Farm

This is an elegant country house in a parkland setting
with quiet gardens for guests to enjoy. The
accommodation is very comfortable and well equipped.
There is a large sitting room overlooking the gardens
and a formal dining room where continental and
English breakfasts are served. Ample parking is
available.

Rooms 3 en suite 1 annexe en suite S £40; D £70*
Facilities FTV tea/coffee Cen ht Wi-fi Parking 10
Notes LB

PREMIER COLLECTION

Rushen

★★★★★ BED AND BREAKFAST

Mount Pleasant SG13 7QY
☎ 01992 581254 📠 01992 534737
e-mail: wilsonamwell@btinternet.com
dir: From A10 exit at Hertford slip road, 1st left onto
B1502. 1st right at top of lane, bear left at village
green. Rushen on left at end of green

Guests will receive a warm welcome at Rushen, which
is situated at the end of the village green in Hertford
Heath. Bedrooms are comfortable and well appointed.
Breakfast offers a good choice and local and organic
produce is used whenever possible.

Rooms 3 rms (2 en suite) (1 pri facs) S £40; D £80*
Facilities FTV tea/coffee Cen ht Wi-fi Parking 3
Notes ✖ Closed 22 Dec-3 Jan

HITCHIN — Map 12 TL12

The Sun

★★★ INN

Sun St SG5 1AF
☎ 01462 432092 & 438411 📠 01462 431488
e-mail: sun.hitchin@greeneking.co.uk
web: www.sunhotel-hitchin.com
dir: A1(M) junct 8 onto A602 to Hitchin. At 1st rdbt take
4th exit & at mini-rdbt straight over. 2nd left onto Biggin
Ln & follow road to car park

This attractive 16th-century coaching inn is situated in
the centre of town. Bedrooms are equipped with modern
facilities and some retain their original character with
exposed beams. Public areas offer an informal restaurant
and a comfortably appointed bar.

Rooms 26 en suite 6 annexe en suite (6 GF) (6 smoking)
Facilities tea/coffee Dinner available Direct Dial Cen ht
Conf Max 100 Thtr 100 Class 60 Board 30 Parking 20
Notes Civ Wed 100

MUCH HADHAM — Map 6 TL41

High Hedges Bed & Breakfast

★★★★ BED AND BREAKFAST

High Hedges, Green Tye SG10 6JP
☎ 01279 842505
e-mail: info@high-hedges.co.uk
dir: From B1004 turn off to Green Tye at Prince of Wales
pub, turn into private road, 1st on right

Expect a warm welcome at High Hedges. Bedrooms are
well presented and comfortable, and come with many
thoughtful extra touches. A substantial breakfast is
served in the comfortable dining room. Half Moon Holistic
Therapies is part of the B&B, and offers a range of
massages and other treatments.

Rooms 3 rms (2 en suite) (1 pri facs) (1 GF)
Facilities FTV tea/coffee Cen ht Wi-fi Holistic therapies
Parking 3 Notes ✖ Closed 25-26 Dec & 31 Dec-1 Jan 🈯

NUTHAMPSTEAD — Map 12 TL43

The Woodman Inn

★★★ INN

SG8 8NB
☎ 01763 848328 📠 01763 848328
e-mail: woodman.inn@virgin.net
dir: *A505 to Royston, take right onto B1368 to Barkway, 1st left past Tally Ho, in 2m turn right. Inn on left*

This 17th-century inn has many fine features, and is close to the Duxford Imperial War Museum. The practical bedrooms are decorated in a traditional style. The kitchen offers a good range of British meals, plus a generous breakfast.

Rooms 4 rms (3 en suite) (1 pri facs) (2 GF) **Facilities** TVL TV2B tea/coffee Dinner available Cen ht Wi-fi Golf 18 Pool table Shooting range by arrangement **Parking** 30 **Notes** ⊗ RS Sun eve & Mon lunch, bar & restaurant closed

ST ALBANS — Map 6 TL10

Fern Cottage

★★★★ 🅰 BED AND BREAKFAST

116 Old London Rd AL1 1PU
☎ 01727 834200
e-mail: bookinginfo@ferncottage.uk.net
dir: *M25 junct 22, A1081 to St Albans, 3rd exit off London Colney rdbt for 1m, under railway bridge, over mini-rdbt & 2nd left onto Old London Rd. Fern Cottage 400yds on left*

Rooms 3 en suite (1 GF) **Facilities** tea/coffee Cen ht Wi-fi **Parking** 3 **Notes** ⊛

STAPLEFORD — Map 6 TL31

Papillon Woodhall Arms

★★★ INN

17 High Rd SG14 3NW
☎ 01992 535123 📠 01992 587030
e-mail: papillonwoodhall@aol.com
web: www.papillon-woodhallarms.com
dir: *2.5m from Hertford town (A414)*

Located in the village centre, this Victorian house has been sympathetically renovated and extended to provide good standards of comfort and facilities. Bedrooms are equipped with both practical and thoughtful extras and public areas include a spacious restaurant offering a wide range of international dishes.

Rooms 10 en suite (1 fmly) S £29.50-£35; D £46-£55 (room only)* **Facilities** TVL tea/coffee Dinner available Cen ht Wi-fi **Conf** Max 50 Thtr 50 Class 30 Board 20 **Parking** 33 **Notes** ⊗

WARE — Map 6 TL31

Feathers Inn

★★★ INN

Wadesmill SG12 0TN
☎ 01920 462606 📠 01920 469994
e-mail: feathers.wadesmill@newbridgeinns.co.uk

This coaching inn is situated beside the A10 on the Cambridge side of Ware. An adjacent modern annexe provides cottage-style rooms and a good array of modern facilities. Meals are taken in the inn where there is a choice of a carvery and informal restaurant operations; the bar remains open all day.

Rooms 31 en suite

WATFORD — Map 6 TQ19

Travel Stop Inn

★★★ GUEST ACCOMMODATION

26-28 Upton Rd WD18 0JF
☎ 01923 224298 📠 01923 253553
e-mail: info@travelstopinn.com
web: www.travelstopinn.com
dir: *M1 junct 5, A4008 to Watford centre. On ring road stay in centre lane, past T-lights at Market St, bus stop on left. Take next left Upton Rd*

Located within easy walking distance of the town centre, this renovation of two Edwardian houses provides a range of bedrooms equipped with lots of homely extras. There is a cocktail bar and restaurant in the White House Hotel opposite, which is under the same ownership; it is here that guests check in and take breakfast.

Rooms 26 annexe en suite (1 fmly) (7 GF) **Facilities** STV TVL tea/coffee Dinner available Direct Dial Cen ht Licensed Complimentay use of local gym **Conf** Max 200 Thtr 200 Class 80 Board 60 **Parking** 35 **Notes** ⊗ RS Xmas/New Year Reduced restaurant service Civ Wed 120

WELWYN GARDEN CITY — Map 6 TL21

The Brocket Arms

★★★★ INN

Ayot St Lawrence AL6 9BT
☎ 01438 820250
e-mail: bookings@brocketarms.com
dir: *A1(M) junct 4 follow signs to Wheathampstead, then Shaw's Corner. Pub past Shaw's Corner on right*

This delightful 14th-century hostelry retains many traditional features of a country pub and offers fully refurbished accommodation which is comfortable and tastefully appointed. The bars and restaurant, with their low ceilings and oak beams, offer a variety of real ales, a range of wines and a seasonally changing menu.

Rooms 3 rms (2 en suite) (1 pri facs) 3 annexe en suite (2 fmly) (3 GF) **Facilities** FTV tea/coffee Dinner available Cen ht Wi-fi Fishing **Parking** 6 **Notes** LB

The Fairway Tavern

★★★ GUEST ACCOMMODATION

Old Herns Ln AL7 2ED
☎ 01707 336007 & 339349 📠 01707 376154
e-mail: info@fairwaytavern.co.uk
web: www.fairwaytavern.co.uk
dir: *Exit A1 junct 6 to B1000 through Digswell for 2m, follow signs for golf complex*

Enjoying a picturesque location, this property is located on Panshanger Golf Complex, with lodge style bedrooms opening out onto views of the golf course and rolling countryside. Bedrooms are smartly presented and are well equipped for business and leisure guests. Breakfast and meals up to 5pm are served by the friendly staff in the adjacent pub. A large peaceful garden and a function room for private hire are available.

Rooms 7 en suite (2 fmly) (7 GF) S £40-£55; D £50-£65 (room only)* **Facilities** tea/coffee Dinner available Direct Dial Cen ht Lift Licensed Wi-fi Golf 18 ⅃ Squash **Conf** Thtr 120 Class 80 Board 25 **Parking** 200 **Notes** ⊗ Civ Wed 100

KENT

ASHFORD — Map 7 TR04

PREMIER COLLECTION

The Wife of Bath

★★★★★ ⊛⊛ 🍴 RESTAURANT WITH ROOMS

4 Upper Bridge St, Wye TN25 5AF
☎ 01233 812232 📠 01233 813630
e-mail: relax@thewifeofbath.com
dir: *4m NE of Ashford. M20 junct 9, A28 for Canterbury, 3m right to Wye*

The Wife of Bath is set in the medieval village of Wye which is close to Dover, Canterbury and Ashford. Bedrooms are tastefully decorated and provide guests with comfortable accommodation; each is equipped with LCD TVs and DVD players (a range of DVDs is available). The stylish restaurant, with a small separate bar area, is open for lunch and dinner daily; a cooked or continental breakfast is served here in the morning. Free Wi-fi is available throughout.

Rooms 3 en suite 2 annexe en suite (2 GF) S £75; D £95-£115* **Facilities** FTV tea/coffee Dinner available Cen ht Wi-fi **Parking** 12 **Notes** No coaches

ASHFORD *continued*

The Croft

★★★ GUEST ACCOMMODATION

Canterbury Rd, Kennington TN25 4DU
☎ 01233 622140 📄 01233 635271
e-mail: info@thecroft.biz
dir: *M20 junct 10, 2m on A28 signed Canterbury*

An attractive red-brick house situated in two acres of landscaped grounds just a short drive from Ashford railway station. The generously proportioned bedrooms are in the main house and in pretty cottages; all are pleasantly decorated and thoughtfully equipped. Public rooms include a smart Italian restaurant, a bar, and a cosy lounge.

Rooms 14 en suite (4 GF) **Facilities** tea/coffee Dinner available Direct Dial Cen ht Licensed Wi-fi **Conf** Max 40 Thtr 40 Class 20 Board 22 **Parking** 30 **Notes** Civ Wed 40

AYLESFORD Map 6 TQ75

Wickham Lodge

★★★★★ 🅰 GUEST ACCOMMODATION

The Quay, 73 High St ME20 7AY
☎ 01622 717267 📄 01622 792855
e-mail: wickhamlodge@aol.com
web: www.wickhamlodge.co.uk
dir: *M20 junct 5, signs to Aylesford. The Quay on small road beside Chequers pub*

Rooms 3 rms (2 en suite) (1 pri facs) (1 fmly) (1 GF) S £45; D £90* **Facilities** FTV tea/coffee Cen ht Wi-fi **Parking** 4

BENENDEN Map 7 TQ83

Apple Trees B&B

★★★★ BED AND BREAKFAST

Goddards Green TN17 4AR
☎ 01580 240622
e-mail: garryblanch@aol.com
web: www.appletreesbandb.co.uk
dir: *3m E of Cranbrook. Off A262 at Sissinghurst S onto Chaple Ln, over x-rds, 2m left to Goddards Green, 1m on right*

This spacious rural cottage is situated in the heart of the Kentish countryside, and is convenient for those visiting Sissinghurst Castle and Great Dixter. Bedrooms are attractively presented and include plenty of thoughtful extras. TV can be watched in the comfortable lounge, and breakfast is served in the rustic dining room with picturesque views of the garden.

Rooms 3 rms (1 en suite) (2 pri facs) (3 GF) S £50-£65; D £60-£75* **Facilities** TVL TV1B tea/coffee Cen ht Wi-fi ch fac Golf 18 **Parking** 6 **Notes** ⊗ 🐾

BIDDENDEN Map 7 TQ83

Heron Cottage

★★★★ GUEST ACCOMMODATION

TN27 8HH
☎ 01580 291358 📄 01580 291358
e-mail: susantwort@hotmail.com
web: www.heroncottage.info
dir: *1m NW of Biddenden. A262 W from Biddenden, 1st right, 0.25m across sharp left bend through stone pillars, left onto unmade road*

Expect a warm welcome at this picturesque extended cottage, set in immaculate, mature gardens in peaceful Kent countryside. The bedrooms are thoughtfully equipped and have co-ordinated soft furnishings. Breakfast is served in the smart dining room, and the cosy sitting room has an open fireplace.

Rooms 7 rms (6 en suite) (2 fmly) (1 GF) S £50-£65; D £60-£75 **Facilities** TVL tea/coffee Dinner available Cen ht Wi-fi 🎣 Fishing **Parking** 8 **Notes** Closed Dec-Feb 🐾

BROADSTAIRS Map 7 TR36

Bay Tree Broadstairs

★★★★ GUEST ACCOMMODATION

12 Eastern Esplanade CT10 1DR
☎ 01843 862502 📄 01843 860589
dir: *A255 onto Rectory Rd & Eastern Esplanade*

Expect a warm welcome at this family-run establishment, situated on an elevated position overlooking East Cliff. The attractive bedrooms are well equipped and some have a balcony with a sea view. There is a comfortable lounge bar, and a good breakfast menu is offered in the dining room.

Rooms 10 en suite (1 GF) S £44-£69; D £88-£98* **Facilities** TVL tea/coffee Cen ht Licensed **Parking** 11 **Notes** LB ⊗ No Children 10yrs Closed Xmas & New Year

---

BROOKLAND Map 7 TQ92

Dean Court

★★★★ BED AND BREAKFAST

TN29 9TD
☎ 01797 344244 📄 01797 344102
e-mail: anne_furnival@hotmail.com
dir: *M20 junct 10, A2070 towards Hastings (follow Brenzett signs). At Brenzett take A259 signed Hastings & Rye. Through Brookland, sharp left. In 0.5m to house*

A very warm welcome is assured at this Victorian farmhouse located on a working farm in the middle of Romney Marsh. The bedrooms are well appointed and suitable for both the leisure and business guest. There is a spacious seating room and a well-kept garden for the warmer months.

Rooms 3 rms (2 en suite) (1 pri facs) (1 fmly) S £40-£50; D £75-£85* **Facilities** FTV TVL tea/coffee Cen ht Wi-fi **Parking** 5 **Notes** Closed 20 Dec-4 Jan 🐾

CANTERBURY Map 7 TR15

Magnolia House

★★★★★ GUEST ACCOMMODATION

36 St Dunstan's Ter CT2 8AX
☎ 01227 765121 & 07776 236459
📄 01227 765121
e-mail: info@magnoliahousecanterbury.co.uk
web: www.magnoliahousecanterbury.co.uk
dir: *A2 E onto A2050 for city centre, 1st rdbt left signed University of Kent. St Dunstan's Ter 3rd right*

This charming property combines a warm welcome with superbly appointed bedrooms, equipped with lots of extra amenities including internet access. Evening meals (by arrangement from November to February) are delightful, served in the dining room overlooking the attractive walled garden. A wide range of items are offered at breakfast.

Rooms 7 en suite (1 GF) S £55; D £95-£125 **Facilities** FTV tea/coffee Dinner available Cen ht Wi-fi **Parking** 5 **Notes** ⊗ No Children 12yrs

PREMIER COLLECTION

Yorke Lodge

★★★★★ GUEST ACCOMMODATION

50 London Rd CT2 8LF
☎ 01227 451243 ▤ 01227 462006
e-mail: info@yorkelodge.com
web: www.yorkelodge.com
dir: *From London M2/A2, 1st exit signed Canterbury. At 1st rdbt left onto London Rd*

The charming Victorian property stands in a tree-lined road just ten minutes walk from the town centre and railway station. The spacious bedrooms are thoughtfully equipped and carefully decorated; some rooms have four-poster beds. The stylish dining room leads to a conservatory-lounge, which opens onto a superb terrace.

Rooms 8 en suite (1 fmly) S £58-£70; D £90-£130
Facilities FTV tea/coffee Cen ht Wi-fi **Parking** 5
Notes LB No Children 5yrs

Castle House

★★★★ GUEST ACCOMMODATION

28 Castle St CT1 2PT
☎ 01227 761897
e-mail: enquiries@castlehousehotel.co.uk
web: www.castlehousehotel.co.uk
dir: *Opposite Canterbury Castle ruins, off A28 ring road*

Conveniently located in the city centre opposite the imposing ruins of the ancient Norman castle; part of the building dates back to 1730s. Bedrooms are spacious, all with en suite facilities and many little extras such as Wi-fi. There is a walled garden in which to relax during the warm months.

Rooms 7 en suite 5 annexe en suite (4 fmly) (2 GF)
Facilities TVL tea/coffee Dinner available Cen ht Wi-fi
Conf Max 35 **Parking** 12 **Notes** ⊗

Chislet Court Farm *(TR224644)*

★★★★ FARMHOUSE

Chislet CT3 4DU
☎ 01227 860309 & 07980 841890 ▤ 01227 860444
Mr & Mrs M Wilkinson
e-mail: kathy@chisletcourtfarm.com
web: www.chisletcourtfarm.com
dir: *Off A28 in Upstreet, farm on right 100yds past church*

This delightful 18th-century house is situated in a pretty village close to Canterbury. The house is smartly maintained and set in delightful grounds. The en suite bedrooms are extremely spacious, well appointed, and have smart modern bathrooms. A hearty Aga-cooked breakfast is served in the charming conservatory overlooking the garden.

Rooms 2 en suite S £50; D £80* **Facilities** FTV tea/coffee
Cen ht Wi-fi **Parking** 4 **Notes** ⊗ No Children 12yrs Closed
Xmas ⊛ 800 acres arable

House of Agnes

★★★★ GUEST ACCOMMODATION

71 Saint Dunstans St CT2 8BN
☎ 01227 472185 ▤ 01227 470478
e-mail: info@houseofagnes.co.uk
dir: *On A290 between London Rd & Orchard St, 300mtrs from West Gate*

This historic 14th-century property has been refurbished as a luxury guest accommodation and offers individually themed rooms, ranging from the traditional to the more exotic. All rooms have a nice range of amenities such as flat-screen TVs and Wi-fi. This establishment is also licensed for weddings.

Rooms 8 en suite 8 annexe en suite (2 fmly) (8 GF) S
£60-£130; D £70-£130 **Facilities** FTV tea/coffee Cen ht
Licensed Wi-fi ᨓ Boules **Conf** Thtr 30 Class 12 Board 20
Parking 13 **Notes** LB ⊗ No Children 5yrs Closed 24-26
Dec Civ Wed 46

The White House

★★★★ GUEST ACCOMMODATION

6 St Peters Ln CT1 2BP
☎ 01227 761836
e-mail: info@whitehousecanterbury.co.uk
dir: *A2 into Canterbury at London Rd rdbt take 2nd exit (A2050), at next rdbt 1st exit onto St Peters Pl. At Westgate Tower rdbt turn right, before next rdbt turn right. Left at end & St Peters Ln on right*

This listed Regency establishment is ideally located in the heart of Canterbury, within a two-minute walk of the famous cathedral. All bedrooms are modern with a bright, airy decor and have LCD TVs and Wi-fi. Breakfast can be enjoyed in the ground-floor dining room and there's additional space for guests to relax during their stay.

Rooms 7 en suite S £65-£85; D £90-£140* **Facilities** FTV
tea/coffee Cen ht Wi-fi **Notes** ⊗ No Children 16yrs

Peregrine House

★★★★ GUEST ACCOMMODATION

18 Hawks Ln CT1 2NU
☎ 01227 761897
e-mail: enquiries@castlehousehotel.co.uk

Peregrine House is centrally located right in the heart of historic Canterbury. This is a sister property to Castle House, guests register at Castle House and then take a short walk to Peregrine House, alternatively a courtesy car is available to help transport guests and their luggage. Following a complete renovation, bedrooms and bathrooms offer clean, modern comfortable accommodation. Within seconds, guests are on the main high street close to Canterbury Cathedral, shops and restaurants.

Rooms 13 rms (11 en suite) (2 pri facs) (5 fmly) (3 GF)
Facilities TVL tea/coffee Dinner available Cen ht Licensed
Wi-fi **Parking** 14 **Notes** ⊗

Canterbury Cathedral Lodge

★★★★ A GUEST ACCOMMODATION

The Precincts CT1 2EH
☎ 01227 865350 ▤ 01227 865388
e-mail: stay@canterbury-cathedral.org
Rooms 29 en suite 6 annexe en suite (1 fmly) (13 GF) S
£75-£109; D £85-£119 **Facilities** FTV TVL tea/coffee
Direct Dial Cen ht Lift Licensed Wi-fi **Conf** Max 250 Thtr
250 **Parking** 15 **Notes** LB ⊗

CANTERBURY *continued*

Duke William

★★★ ⬮ INN

Ickham CT3 1QP
☎ 01227 721308 & 721244
e-mail: goodfood@dukewilliam.biz
dir: *A257(Canterbury to Sandwich) into Littlebourne, turn left opp The Anchor onto Nargate St. After 0.5m turn right onto Drill Ln & right onto The Street*

Located in the quiet village of Ickham and just five miles from Canterbury, this family-run pub has a spacious bar and restaurant boasting original features and a large open fireplace, there is also a rear garden with seating for guests to enjoy lunch with great views of the East Kent countryside. Bedrooms are well appointed with modern, comfortable decor and free Wi-fi throughout. Lunch and dinner are available daily and a cooked or continental breakfast is served in the restaurant.

Rooms 4 en suite S £65; D £65* **Facilities** STV tea/coffee Dinner available Cen ht Wi-fi Golf 18 **Conf** Class 30 Board 30

Canterbury Pilgrims

★★★ INN

18 The Friars CT1 2AS
☎ 01227 464531 📠 01227 762514
e-mail: pilgrimshotel@aol.com
web: www.pilgrimshotel.com
dir: *Signs for Marlowe Theatre, establishment opp*

Situated in the centre of historic Canterbury opposite the Marlowe Theatre, parts of the Pilgrims date back some 350 years. Bedrooms are comfortably appointed and well equipped. The public rooms include a spacious bar, a smart meeting room and a contemporary style restaurant, where a good selection of dishes is available.

Rooms 15 en suite (1 fmly) **Facilities** tea/coffee Dinner available Direct Dial Cen ht **Conf** Max 30 Thtr 25 Class 25 Board 20 **Parking** 10 **Notes** ⊗

Cathedral Gate

★★★ GUEST ACCOMMODATION

36 Burgate CT1 2HA
☎ 01227 464381 📠 01227 462800
e-mail: cgate@cgate.demon.co.uk
dir: *In city centre. Next to main gateway into cathedral precincts*

Dating from 1438, this house has an enviable central location next to the cathedral. Old beams and winding corridors are part of the character of the property. Bedrooms are traditionally furnished, equipped to modern standards and many have cathedral views. Luggage can be unloaded at reception before parking in a nearby car park.

Rooms 13 rms (2 en suite) 12 annexe rms 10 annexe en suite (5 fmly) **Facilities** tea/coffee Dinner available Direct Dial Cen ht Licensed Wi-fi

Ersham Lodge

★★★ GUEST ACCOMMODATION

12 New Dover Rd CT1 3AP
☎ 01227 463174
e-mail: info@ersham-lodge.co.uk
dir: *From Cantebury ring road take A2050 (signs for Dover, A2) premises on right 40mtrs after lights opp road entrance to Cantebury College*

This attractive twin-gabled Victorian house is just a short walk from the college, cathedral and the city's attractions. Bedrooms are smartly decorated and comfortable, and there is a cosy lounge and a spacious breakfast room which looks out onto the well-kept patio and garden. Free guest parking is available.

Rooms 10 en suite (1 fmly) (5 GF) S fr £45; D fr £80* **Facilities** tea/coffee Cen ht Wi-fi **Conf** Max 30 Class 30 Board 20 **Parking** 10 **Notes** LB ⊗

St Stephens Guest House

★★★ GUEST ACCOMMODATION

100 St Stephens Rd CT2 7JL
☎ 01227 767644
e-mail: info@ststephensguesthouse.co.uk
dir: *A290 from city Westgate & sharp right onto North Ln, 2nd rdbt left onto St Stephens Rd, right onto Market Way, car park on right*

St Stephens Guest House offers comfortable yet basic accommodation. All rooms are well equipped with beverage making facilities and free Wi-fi throughout. Located just 10 minutes' walk from Canterbury town centre and conveniently located near the University of Kent and Christchurch College. The dining room is traditionally decorated and has views of the garden; guests can enjoy a cooked and continental breakfast.

Rooms 2 en suite 8 annexe en suite (1 fmly) (3 GF) **Facilities** tea/coffee Cen ht Wi-fi **Parking** 11 **Notes** ⊗ Closed 18 Dec-mid Jan

Rising Sun

★★★ INN

Fawkham Green DA3 8NL
☎ 01474 872291 📠 01474 872779
dir: *M25 junct 3, A20 Brands Hatch. Turn onto Scratchers Ln until sign for Fawkham. Left onto Brandshatch Rd, inn on left*

This popular inn overlooks the village green just a short drive from Brands Hatch. All the en suite bedrooms are spacious, pleasantly decorated and comfortable. There is a busy character bar, restaurant, and a patio for alfresco dining in warmer weather.

Rooms 5 en suite (1 fmly) (2 GF) S £50-£55; D £75* **Facilities** FTV tea/coffee Dinner available Cen ht Wi-fi **Parking** 20 **Notes** ⊗ No coaches

PREMIER COLLECTION

Sutherland House

★★★★★ GUEST ACCOMMODATION

186 London Rd CT14 9PT
☎ 01304 362853 📠 01304 381146
e-mail: info@sutherlandhouse.fsnet.co.uk
dir: *0.5m W of town centre/seafront on A258*

This stylish accommodation demonstrates impeccable taste with its charming, well-equipped bedrooms and a comfortable lounge. A fully stocked bar, books, free Wi-fi, Freeview TV and radio are some of the many amenities offered. The elegant dining room is the venue for a hearty breakfast and dinner is available by prior arrangement.

Rooms 4 en suite (1 GF) S £60-£75; D £70-£85* **Facilities** FTV tea/coffee Dinner available Direct Dial Cen ht Licensed Wi-fi **Conf** Max 12 Thtr 12 Class 12 Board 12 **Parking** 7 **Notes** LB No Children 5yrs

Sondes Lodge

★★★ GUEST ACCOMMODATION

14 Sondes Rd CT14 7BW
☎ 01304 368741 & 07817 178186
e-mail: sondes.lodge@tiscali.co.uk
web: www.sondeslodge.co.uk
dir: *From Dover take A258 to Deal, pass Deal Castle, towards town centre. 4th right onto Sondes Rd. Lodge on right hand side*

Expect a warm welcome at this smart guest accommodation situated in a side road just off the seafront and a short walk from the town centre. The pleasant bedrooms have co-ordinated fabrics and many thoughtful touches. Breakfast is served at individual tables in the lower ground-floor dining room.

Rooms 3 en suite (1 fmly) (1 GF) S £40-£60; D fr £60*
Facilities FTV TVL tea/coffee Cen ht Wi-fi

DODDINGTON   Map 7 TQ95

PREMIER COLLECTION

The Old Vicarage

★★★★★ GUEST ACCOMMODATION

Church Hill ME9 0BD
☎ 01795 886136 📠 01795 886136
e-mail: claire@oldvicaragedoddington.co.uk
dir: *From A2 take Faversham Rd signed Doddington for 4.4m. Turn right towards church*

The Old Vicarage is a stunning Grade II listed property situated at the edge of the village beside the old church. Spacious rooms come with flat-screen TVs, and special touches such as binoculars and bird reference books. Guests can relax in the elegant lounge, and a bountiful breakfast is served in the stylish dining room overlooking endless trees and green fields.

Rooms 3 en suite (2 fmly) S £55-£65; D £79-£85*
Facilities FTV tea/coffee Cen ht Wi-fi **Parking** 6
Notes ⊗ No Children 3yrs Closed 25 Dec-2 Jan

DOVER   Map 7 TR34

PREMIER COLLECTION

The Marquis at Alkham

★★★★★ ◎◎ 🍴 RESTAURANT WITH ROOMS

Alkham Valley Rd, Alkham CT15 7DF
☎ 01304 873410 📠 01304 873418
e-mail: info@themarquisatalkham.co.uk
web: www.themarquisatalkham.co.uk
dir: *From Dover take A256, at rdbt 1st exit onto London Rd, left onto Alkham Rd, Alkham Valley Rd. Establishment 1.5m after sharp bend*

Located between Dover and Folkestone, this modern, contemporary restaurant with rooms offers luxury accommodation with modern features - flat-screen TVs, Wi-fi, power showers and bathrobes to name but a few. All the stylish bedrooms are individually designed and have fantastic views of the Kent Downs. The award-winning restaurant, open for lunch and dinner, serves modern British cuisine. Continental and a choice of cooked breakfasts are offered.

Rooms 5 en suite (1 fmly) S £75-£145; D £115-£235*
Facilities FTV TVL Dinner available Cen ht Wi-fi
Conf Max 20 Thtr 20 Class 20 Board 16 **Parking** 22
Notes LB ⊗ Civ Wed 45

Hubert House Guesthouse & Bistro

★★★★ GUEST HOUSE

9 Castle Hill Rd CT16 1QW
☎ 01304 202253 📠 01304 210142
e-mail: stay@huberthouse.co.uk
web: www.huberthouse.co.uk
dir: *On A258 by Dover Castle*

This charming Georgian house is within walking distance of the ferry port and the town centre. Bedrooms are sumptuously decorated and furnished with an abundance of practical extras. Breakfast, including full English and healthy options, is served in the smart coffee house, which is open all day. Families are especially welcome.

Rooms 6 en suite (4 fmly) S fr £45; D fr £60*
Facilities FTV tea/coffee Dinner available Cen ht Licensed Wi-fi **Parking** 6 **Notes** LB

Beulah House

★★★★ GUEST ACCOMMODATION

94 Crabble Hill, London Rd CT17 0SA
☎ 01304 824615 📠 01304 828850
e-mail: owen@beulahhouse94.freeserve.co.uk
web: www.beulahguesthouse.co.uk
dir: *On A256*

An impressive Victorian house located just a stroll from the town centre and close to the ferry port. The spacious bedrooms are pleasantly decorated and thoughtfully equipped. Public rooms include two conservatories and a comfortable lounge. The impressive garden has an interesting display of topiary and a small menagerie.

Rooms 8 en suite **Facilities** TVL tea/coffee Cen ht Wi-fi
Parking 8 **Notes** ⊗ No Children 12yrs

Bleriot's

★★★ GUEST ACCOMMODATION

Belper House, 47 Park Av CT16 1HE
☎ 01304 211394
e-mail: info@bleriots.net
dir: *A20 to Dover, left onto York St, right at lights into Ladywell. Left at next lights onto Park Av*

This large, family-run Victorian property is convenient for the ferry port and town centre. Guests receive a warm welcome and can enjoy a range of comfortable, spacious en suite bedrooms. The attractive dining room is the venue for a wholesome breakfast to start the day.

Rooms 8 en suite (2 fmly) S £32-£48; D £50-£58 (room only) **Facilities** FTV tea/coffee Cen ht **Parking** 8 **Notes** LB ⊗

Ardmore Guest House

★★★ GUEST ACCOMMODATION

18 Castle Hill Rd CT16 1QW
☎ 01304 205895 📠 01304 208229
e-mail: res@ardmoreph.co.uk
web: www.ardmoreph.co.uk
dir: *On A258 by Dover Castle*

Dating from 1796, this delightful house is adjacent to Dover Castle. Convenient for the town centre and ferry port, the Ardmore offers comfortable accommodation and friendly hospitality. The non-smoking bedrooms are spacious and airy. Public rooms include a comfortable lounge and a well-appointed breakfast room.

Rooms 4 en suite (1 fmly) D £50-£68* **Facilities** tea/coffee Cen ht **Notes** ⊗ Closed Xmas

DOVER *continued*

Kernow

★★★ GUEST ACCOMMODATION

189 Folkestone Rd CT17 9SJ
☎ 01304 207797
dir: *B2011 W from town centre onto Folkestone Rd*

This welcoming guest accommodation is convenient for the ferries and railway station. The neat accommodation is well maintained, and two bathrooms are available. There is adequate parking at the front of the property, and breakfast can be arranged to suit your travel arrangements.

Rooms 3 rms Facilities TVL tea/coffee Cen ht Parking 4 Notes ⊗

St Martins

★★★ GUEST ACCOMMODATION

17 Castle Hill Rd CT16 1QW
☎ 01304 205938 📄 01304 208229
e-mail: res@stmartinsgh.co.uk
web: www.stmartinsgh.co.uk
dir: *On A258 by Dover Castle*

Located close to the castle, ferry port and town centre, this smart guest accommodation offers a friendly welcome. The thoughtfully equipped en suite bedrooms are attractively decorated, and most rooms enjoy a sunny aspect. Breakfast is served in the pine-furnished dining room, and there is also a comfortable lounge.

Rooms 6 en suite (3 fmly) D £50-£55* Facilities tea/coffee Cen ht Notes ⊗ Closed Xmas

The Swingate Inn

★★★ INN

Deal Rd CT15 5DP
☎ 01304 204043 📄 01304 204043
e-mail: info@swingate.co.uk
dir: *Dover Eastern Docks. Turn right at rdbt up Jubilee Way for 1m, at rdbt turn right onto A258 to Deal*

Situated in a convenient location on the outskirts of Dover and very convenient for the ferries. Bedrooms are traditionally decorated and offer comfortable accommodation. The bar is spacious and offers an informal, friendly atmosphere. There is an outside bar and garden and plenty of parking spaces. Cooked or continental breakfasts are available.

Rooms 10 en suite (2 fmly) Facilities tea/coffee Dinner available Cen ht Wi-fi Conf Max 30 Thtr 30 Class 30 Board 20 Parking 60 Notes ⊗ Civ Wed 120

DYMCHURCH   Map 7 TR12

Waterside

★★★★ GUEST ACCOMMODATION

15 Hythe Rd TN29 0LN
☎ 01303 872253 📄 01303 872253
e-mail: info@watersideguesthouse.co.uk
dir: *M20 junct 11 onto A259 follow signs for Hythe then Dymchurch, 0.5m past village sign*

Waterside is located overlooking a picturesque stream, and sandy beaches are a few minutes away. Bedrooms are comfortably appointed and have sparkling en suite bathrooms. Breakfast is served in the cosy dining room and a small bar and lounge is provided for added guest comfort. Parking is available.

Rooms 5 en suite (1 fmly) S £45-£70; D £65-£70* Facilities tea/coffee Dinner available Cen ht Licensed Wi-fi Conf Max 16 Thtr 16 Class 16 Board 12 Parking 6 Notes LB ⊗

FAVERSHAM   Map 7 TR06

Court Lodge B&B

★★★★ GUEST ACCOMMODATION

Court Lodge, Church Rd, Oare ME13 0QB
☎ 01795 591543 📄 01795 591543
e-mail: d.wheeldon@btconnect.com
dir: *A2 onto B2045, left onto The Street, right onto Church Rd, 0.25m on left*

Surrounded by arable land, and commanding fabulous views, this charming farmhouse has been restored to a very high standard. Inside is a mini museum of antique furniture and Victorian fittings include caringly restored bathtubs, sinks and kitchen appliances. Modern additions such as free Wi-fi are provided. Home-made cakes and jams and the warm hospitality of owners Dennise and John guarantee a memorable stay.

Rooms 2 rms (1 en suite) (1 pri facs) S fr £50; D fr £70* Facilities tea/coffee Cen ht Wi-fi Parking 10 Notes ⊗ ⊗

FOLKESTONE   Map 7 TR23

The Relish

★★★★★ GUEST ACCOMMODATION

4 Augusta Gardens CT20 2RR
☎ 01303 850952 📄 01303 850958
e-mail: reservations@hotelrelish.co.uk
web: www.hotelrelish.co.uk
dir: *Off A2033 (Sandgate Rd)*

Expect a warm welcome at this impressive Victorian terrace property, which overlooks Augusta Gardens in the fashionable West End of town. The bedrooms feature beautiful contemporary natural-wood furniture, lovely co-ordinated fabrics and many thoughtful extras like DVD players and free broadband access. Public rooms include a modern lounge-dining room, and a sun terrace where breakfast is served in the summer.

Rooms 10 en suite (2 fmly) S fr £69; D £95-£145* Facilities FTV tea/coffee Direct Dial Cen ht Wi-fi Conf Max 20 Thtr 20 Class 10 Board 20 Notes ⊗ Closed 23 Dec-2 Jan

Chandos Guest House

★★★ GUEST ACCOMMODATION

77 Cheriton Rd CT20 1DG
☎ 01303 851202 & 07799 886297
e-mail: don@chandosguesthouse.com
web: www.chandosguesthouse.co.uk
dir: *M20 junct 13. Right towards Folkestone. At 2nd set of lights, take middle lane. Continue for 1m, straight over rdbt, premises 0.25m on right*

Close to the town centre and only a five minute drive from the Eurotunnel, this pleasant guest accommodation is ideal for continental travellers. Bedrooms and bathrooms are well equipped, bright and comfortable. Free Wi-fi is available. A hearty breakfast is served in the spacious ground-floor dining room. Early morning departures are catered for.

Rooms 10 rms (6 en suite) (4 pri facs) (4 fmly) S £25-£35; D £50-£70 (room only)* Facilities FTV tea/coffee Cen ht Wi-fi Parking 6 Notes LB ⊗

Langhorne Garden

★★★ GUEST ACCOMMODATION

10-12 Langhorne Gardens CT20 2EA
☎ 01303 257233 　 01303 242760
e-mail: info@langhorne.co.uk
web: www.langhorne.co.uk
dir: *Exit M20 junct 13, follow signs for The Leas, 2m*

Once a Victorian villa, Langhorne Garden is close to the seafront, shops and restaurants. Bright spacious bedrooms are traditionally decorated with plenty of original charm. Public rooms include a choice of comfortable lounges and a bar, a spacious dining room and a popular local bar in the basement with billiards, darts and table football.

Rooms 29 en suite (8 fmly) S fr £37; D fr £60*
Facilities STV FTV tea/coffee Dinner available Direct Dial Cen ht Lift Licensed Wi-fi Pool table **Notes** LB Closed Xmas RS Jan-Etr no evening meal

---

| GOUDHURST | Map 6 TQ73 |

The Star & Eagle

★★★★ ⇔ INN

High St TN17 1AL
☎ 01580 211512 　 01580 212444
e-mail: starandeagle@btconnect.com
web: www.starandeagle.co.uk
dir: *Off A21 to Hastings rd, take A262, inn at top of village next to church*

A warm welcome is assured at this 15th-century inn located in the heart of a delightful village. Within easy reach of Royal Tunbridge Wells and the Weald this is a great base for walkers. Both bedrooms and public areas boast original features and much character. A wide range of delicious home-made dishes is available in the restaurant and bar.

Rooms 10 rms (8 en suite) (2 pri facs) D £80-£140*
Facilities FTV Dinner available Direct Dial Cen ht Wi-fi **Conf** Max 30 Thtr 30 Class 15 Board 12 **Parking** 20 **Notes** ⊗ RS 25-26 Dec eve closed Civ Wed 50

| HAWKHURST | Map 7 TQ73 |

PREMIER COLLECTION

Southgate-Little Fowlers

★★★★★ 　 GUEST ACCOMMODATION

Rye Rd TN18 5DA
☎ 01580 752526 　 01580 752526
e-mail: susan.woodard@southgate.uk.net
dir: *0.25m E of Hawkhurst on A268*

A warm welcome is assured at this wonderful 300-year-old former dower house. Set in immaculate mature gardens, the renovated property provides attractive accommodation throughout. Spacious bedrooms are carefully decorated and equipped with many thoughtful extras. A hearty breakfast is served at individual tables in the delightful Victorian conservatory.

Rooms 2 en suite (1 fmly) **Facilities** TVL tea/coffee Cen ht Wi-fi **Parking** 5 **Notes** ⊗ No Children 8yrs Closed Nov-Feb 　

| HYTHE | Map 7 TR13 |

Seabrook House

★★★★ GUEST ACCOMMODATION

81 Seabrook Rd CT21 5QW
☎ 01303 269282 　 01303 237822
e-mail: seabrookhouse@hotmail.co.uk
web: www.seabrook-house.co.uk
dir: *0.9m E of Hythe on A259*

A stunning Victorian house situated just a few miles from the M20 and Eurotunnel. The property is set in pretty gardens and within easy walking distance of the beach. The attractive bedrooms are carefully furnished and thoughtfully equipped. Public rooms include an elegant lounge, where tea and coffee are served in the evening, a sunny conservatory and large dining room.

Rooms 13 en suite (4 fmly) (4 GF) **Facilities** TVL tea/coffee Cen ht **Parking** 13 **Notes** ⊗

| IVYCHURCH | Map 7 TR02 |

PREMIER COLLECTION

Olde Moat House

★★★★★ 　 GUEST ACCOMMODATION

TN29 0AZ
☎ 01797 344700 　 01797 343919
e-mail: oldemoathouse@hotmail.com
web: www.oldemoathouse.co.uk
dir: *Off junct A2070 & A259 into Ivychurch, left & 0.75m on left*

Situated eight miles north-east of Rye this charming character property sits peacefully amongst carefully tended gardens. Spacious bedrooms are elegantly furnished and an abundance of accessories are provided for guest comfort. The elegant dining room overlooks the gardens, and a cosy lounge with oak beams and open fireplace is furnished with comfortable sofas.

Rooms 3 en suite S £50-£60; D £80-£110
Facilities TVL tea/coffee Dinner available Cen ht **Parking** 10 **Notes** LB ⊗ No Children 16yrs

---

| MAIDSTONE | Map 7 TQ75 |

See also Marden

The Black Horse Inn

★★★★ ⇔ INN

Pilgrims Way, Thurnham ME14 3LD
☎ 01622 737185 & 630830 　 01622 739170
e-mail: info@wellieboot.net
web: www.wellieboot.net/home_blackhorse.htm
dir: *M20 junct 7, N onto A249. Right into Detling, opp pub onto Pilgrims Way for 1m*

This charming inn dates from the 17th century, and the public areas have a wealth of oak beams, exposed brickwork and open fireplaces. The stylish bedrooms are in a series of cosy cabins behind the premises; each one is attractively furnished and thoughtfully equipped.

Rooms 30 annexe en suite (8 fmly) (30 GF) **Facilities** FTV tea/coffee Dinner available Cen ht Wi-fi **Parking** 40 **Notes** LB No coaches Civ Wed 40

MAIDSTONE *continued*

Aylesbury House

★★★★ GUEST ACCOMMODATION

56-58 London Rd ME16 8QL
☎ 01622 762100 📄 01622 664673
e-mail: mail@aylesburyhouse.co.uk
dir: *M20 junct 5, A20 to Maidstone. Aylesbury House on left before town centre*

Located just a short walk from the town centre, this smartly maintained establishment offers a genuine welcome. The carefully decorated bedrooms have co-ordinated soft fabrics and many thoughtful touches. Breakfast is served in the smart dining room overlooking a walled garden.

Rooms 8 en suite S £58-£65; D £69-£80 Facilities FTV tea/coffee Cen ht Wi-fi Parking 8

Rock House Bed & Breakfast

★★★ GUEST ACCOMMODATION

102 Tonbridge Rd ME16 8SL
☎ 01622 751616 📄 01622 756119
e-mail: rock.house@btconnect.com
dir: *On A26, 0.5m from town centre*

This friendly, family-run property is just a short walk from the town centre. Breakfast is served in the conservatory dining room that overlooks the attractive walled garden. Bedrooms are brightly decorated and equipped with modern facilities.

Rooms 14 rms (8 en suite) (4 fmly) (3 GF) Facilities FTV TVL tea/coffee Cen ht Wi-fi Parking 7 Notes ⊗

Maidstone Lodge

★★★ 🅰 GUEST ACCOMMODATION

22/24 London Rd ME16 8QL
☎ 01622 758778 📄 01622 609984
e-mail: maidstonelodge@btinternet.com
dir: *400yds W of town centre on A20*
Rooms 10 rms (1 GF) (3 smoking) S £40-£45; D £80*
Facilities FTV TVL tea/coffee Cen ht Licensed Parking 10
Notes ⊗ Closed 24 Dec-1 Jan

| MARDEN | Map 6 TQ74 |

Merzie Meadows

★★★★★ BED AND BREAKFAST

Hunton Rd TN12 9SL
☎ 01622 820500 & 07762 713077
📄 01622 820500
e-mail: pamela@merziemeadows.co.uk
dir: *A229 onto B2079 for Marden, 1st right onto Underlyn Ln, 2.5m large Chainhurst sign, right onto drive*

A detached property set in 20 acres of mature gardens in the Kent countryside. The generously proportioned bedrooms are housed in two wings, which overlook a terrace; each room is carefully decorated, thoughtfully equipped and furnished with well-chosen pieces. The attractive breakfast room has an Italian tiled floor and superb views of the garden.

Rooms 2 en suite (1 fmly) (2 GF) D £95-£100*
Facilities STV FTV TVL tea/coffee Cen ht Wi-fi
Parking 4 Notes ⊗ No Children 15yrs Closed mid Dec-mid Feb ⊛

Tanner House

★★★★ BED AND BREAKFAST

Tanner Farm, Goudhurst Rd TN12 9ND
☎ 01622 831214 📄 01622 832472
e-mail: lesley@tannerhouse.wanadoo.co.uk
dir: *From A21 or A229 onto B2709, between Marden & Goudhurst*

This traditional style Tudor farmhouse is located just outside the village of Marden. Part of a 150-acre family run farm with caravan and camping park on site, this bed and breakfast is completely separate and boasts views of the spacious gardens and period outbuildings. Bedrooms are traditional in style and provide comfortable accommodations with modern amenities including free Wi-fi and Freeview TVs. There is a guest lounge which provides additional space for guests to relax, and breakfast can be enjoyed in the dining room which boasts a large inglenook fireplace.

Rooms 3 en suite S £45-£75; D £65-£75 Facilities FTV TVL tea/coffee Cen ht Wi-fi Fishing Parking 3 Notes ⊗ No Children 12yrs Closed 25-26 Dec

---

| NEW ROMNEY | Map 7 TR02 |

Honeychild Manor Farmhouse *(TR062276)*

★★★★ 🏠 FARMHOUSE

St Mary In The Marsh TN29 0DB
☎ 01797 366180 & 07951 237821 📄 01797 366925
Mrs V Furnival
e-mail: honeychild@farming.co.uk
dir: *2m N of New Romney off A259. S of village centre*

This imposing Georgian farmhouse is part of a working dairy farm on Romney Marsh. Walkers and dreamers alike will enjoy the stunning views and can relax in the beautifully landscaped gardens or play tennis on the full-sized court. A hearty breakfast is served in the elegant dining room and features quality local produce. Bedrooms are pleasantly decorated, well furnished and thoughtfully equipped. This establishment is pet friendly.

Rooms 3 rms (1 en suite) (2 pri facs) (1 fmly) S £40; D fr £85* Facilities tea/coffee Dinner available Cen ht Wi-fi ⌁ Parking 10 Notes LB ⊛ 1500 acres arable/dairy

---

| SANDGATE | Map 7 TR23 |

The Suite at Tsunami

★★★★ GUEST ACCOMMODATION

Helena Corniche CT20 3TD
☎ 01303 268535
e-mail: thesuite@btinternet.com
dir: *M20 junct 12, A20 (Cheriton exit). 1st right, left at lights, 2nd left onto Horn St. Right onto Church Rd, right onto Pond Hill Rd, right onto North Rd. Down Hospital Hill, Helena Corniche on left*

Located in the quiet area of Sandgate, this establishment benefits from views of the English Channel and is in close proximity to both Folkestone and Dover. There is one main suite, which includes a private patio, a spacious bedroom with modern decor and furnishings, and an en suite bathroom. There is a comfortable lounge where breakfast is also served.

Rooms 1 rms (1 pri facs) D £70-£130* Facilities FTV TVL tea/coffee Cen ht Wi-fi Parking 2 Notes LB ⊗ No Children 1yr

SANDWICH　　　Map 7 TR35

The New Inn
★★★ INN

2 Harnet St CT13 9ES
☎ 01304 612335　📠 01304 619133
e-mail: new.inn@thorleytaverns.com
dir: Off A256, one-way system into town centre, inn on right

A popular inn situated in the heart of this busy historic town. The large open-plan lounge bar offers an extensive range of beers and an interesting choice of home-made dishes. Bedrooms are furnished in pine and have many useful extras.

Rooms 5 en suite (3 fmly) (2 smoking) S £55-£75; D £79-£95* **Facilities** STV tea/coffee Dinner available Direct Dial Cen ht **Parking** 17 **Notes** ⊗ No coaches

SEVENOAKS　　　Map 6 TQ55

Yew Tree Barn
★★★★ GUEST ACCOMMODATION

Long Mill Ln, Crouch, Borough Green TN15 8QB
☎ 01732 780461
e-mail: bartonje@hotmail.com
web: www.yewtreebarn.com
dir: A25 (Maidstone Road) turn left after Esso garage. Crouch Lane 1m, right to Crouch. Yew Tree Barn on left

Situated in the picturesque village of Crouch this attractively converted barn is in an ideal position from which to explore the beautiful Kent countryside. Brands Hatch racing circuit and The London Golf Club are just a short drive away as well as Leeds and Lullingstone Castles. Welcoming hosts Tricia and James offer spaciously comfortable bedrooms with free Wi-fi. The charming dining room and guest lounge overlook the well-tended gardens.

Rooms 2 en suite (2 fmly) (1 GF) S £40-£50; D £65-£75* **Facilities** TVL tea/coffee Cen ht Wi-fi **Parking** 5 **Notes** LB ⊗ ☺

SITTINGBOURNE　　　Map 7 TQ96

The Beaumont
★★★★ ≜ GUEST ACCOMMODATION

74 London Rd ME10 1NS
☎ 01795 472536　📠 01795 425921
e-mail: info@thebeaumont.co.uk
web: www.thebeaumont.co.uk
dir: From M2 or M20 take A249 N. Exit at A2, 1m on left towards Sittingbourne

This Georgian farmhouse is a charming family-run property that offers the best hospitality and service. Comfortable bedrooms and bathrooms are well equipped for business and leisure guests. Breakfast in the bright, spacious conservatory makes good use of local produce and home-made preserves. Off-road parking is available.

Rooms 9 rms (6 en suite) (3 pri facs) (3 GF) S £44-£70; D £66-£84* **Facilities** STV TVL tea/coffee Cen ht Wi-fi **Conf** Max 12 Thtr 12 Class 12 Board 12 **Parking** 9 **Notes** Closed 24 Dec-1 Jan

Sandhurst Farm Forge
★★★ BED AND BREAKFAST

Seed Rd, Newnham ME9 0NE
☎ 01795 886854
e-mail: rooms.forge@btinternet.com
dir: Off A2 into Newnham, onto Seed Rd by church, establishment 1m on right

A warm welcome is assured at this peaceful location, which also features a working forge. The spacious bedrooms are in a converted stable block and provide smartly furnished accommodation. Breakfast is served in the dining room adjoining the bedrooms. The owner has won an award for green tourism by reducing the impact of the business on the environment.

Rooms 2 annexe en suite (2 GF) S £40-£45; D £75 **Facilities** STV FTV tea/coffee Cen ht Wi-fi **Parking** 6 **Notes** No Children 12yrs Closed 23 Dec-1 Jan

STELLING MINNIS　　　Map 7 TR14

Heathwood Lodge B&B
★★★★ ≜ BED AND BREAKFAST

Wheelbarrow Town CT4 6AH
☎ 01227 709315　& 07831 347395　📠 01227 709475
e-mail: enquiries@heathwoodlodge.co.uk
dir: B2068 from Canterbury, left into Stelling Minnis. Right at T-junct, pass village hall, after 0.5m round right-hand corner, last yellow house on left

Heathwood Lodge is located in a quiet village area of Stelling Minnis, boasting scenic views, spacious gardens for guests to enjoy during summer months and easily accessible from both Canterbury and Dover. Bedrooms are tastefully appointed, comfortable and all have en suite facilities. The guest lounge provides additional space for guests to relax and features an open fire place. Traditionally styled dining room serves both a cooked and

continental breakfast with all high quality ingredients sourced from the surrounding area.

Rooms 3 en suite S £50-£85; D £60-£100* **Facilities** FTV TVL tea/coffee Cen ht Wi-fi **Parking** 8 **Notes** LB ☺

TUNBRIDGE WELLS (ROYAL)　　　Map 6 TQ53

PREMIER COLLECTION

Danehurst House
★★★★★ ≜ BED AND BREAKFAST

41 Lower Green Rd, Rusthall TN4 8TW
☎ 01892 527739　📠 01892 514804
e-mail: info@danehurst.net
web: www.danehurst.net
dir: 1.5m W of Tunbridge Wells in Rusthall. Off A264 onto Coach Rd & Lower Green Rd

Situated in pretty gardens in a quiet residential area, this Victorian gabled house is located to the west of the historic spa town. The house retains many original features and is attractively decorated throughout. Public areas include a comfortable lounge with a small bar. The homely bedrooms come with a wealth of thoughtful extras, and excellent breakfasts are served in the conservatory.

Rooms 4 en suite (1 fmly) **Facilities** TVL tea/coffee Cen ht Licensed **Parking** 6 **Notes** ⊗ No Children 8yrs Closed Xmas

The Beacon
★★★★ ⊜ INN

Tea Garden Ln, Rusthall TN3 9JH
☎ 01892 524252　📠 01892 534288
e-mail: beaconhotel@btopenworld.com
web: www.the-beacon.co.uk
dir: 1.5m W of Tunbridge Wells. Signed off A264 onto Tea Garden Ln

This charming 18th-century inn is situated on an elevated position amid 16 acres of land and surrounded by open countryside. The open-plan public areas are full of character and include ornate fireplaces and stained glass windows. The spacious bedrooms are attractively decorated, comfortably furnished and have many thoughtful touches.

Rooms 3 en suite S £80; D £115* **Facilities** TV2B tea/coffee Dinner available Direct Dial Cen ht Wi-fi Fishing **Conf** Thtr 50 Class 40 Board 30 **Parking** 42 **Notes** No coaches Civ Wed 100

WESTERHAM — Map 6 TQ45

Corner Cottage

★★★★ GUEST ACCOMMODATION

Toys Hill TN16 1PY
☎ 01732 750362 📠 01732 750754
e-mail: cornercottagebandb@jshmanco.com
dir: *A25 to Brasted, onto Chart Ln signed Fox & Hounds. Turn right onto Puddledock Ln, 1st house on left*

Set in a charming village, this spacious, well-equipped annexe is comfortably furnished and includes many thoughtful touches. In the main cottage a hearty Aga-cooked breakfast is served in the rustic dining room with stunning views of the countryside.

Rooms 1 annexe en suite (1 fmly) S fr £60; D fr £80*
Facilities tea/coffee Dinner available Cen ht Wi-fi
Parking 2 **Notes** ⓦ

Kings Arms

★★★ INN

Market Square TN16 1AN
☎ 01959 562990 📠 01959 561240
e-mail: kingsarms.westerham@oldenglishinns.co.uk
dir: *Exit M25 junct 6 & follow A25 to Westerham*

The Kings Arms is located in the centre of Westerham and is in close proximity to Sevenoaks, Tunbridge Wells and Maidstone. The bedrooms are spacious and feature original oak beams; some have four-poster beds. The bar and restaurant are modern, and breakfast can be enjoyed in the conservatory. Free Wi-fi is available throughout.

Rooms 17 en suite (1 fmly) **Facilities** tea/coffee Dinner available Direct Dial Cen ht Wi-fi **Conf** Max 50 **Parking** 33
Notes Civ Wed 50

WROTHAM — Map 6 TQ65

The Bull

★★★ ⓖ INN

Bull Ln TN15 7RF
☎ 01732 789800 📠 01732 886288
e-mail: info@thebullhotel.com
dir: *In centre of village*

Dating back to 1385 and first licensed in 1495, this property offers modern facilities yet retains many traditional features including original exposed beams. High quality meals can be enjoyed at breakfast, lunch and dinner; the inn sources local produce from nearby farms, south coast landed fish and real ales from Dark Star microbrewery. The bedrooms, including one four-poster room, are decorated with modern furnishings. The Buttery function room was originally the village bakery.

Rooms 11 en suite (3 fmly) S £61-£69; D £72-£79*
Facilities FTV tea/coffee Dinner available Cen ht Wi-fi
Conf Max 40 Thtr 40 Class 40 Board 30 **Parking** 18

WROTHAM HEATH — Map 6 TQ65

Pretty Maid House B&B

★★★★ GUEST ACCOMMODATION

London Rd TN15 7RU
☎ 01732 886445 📠 01732 886439
e-mail: stay@prettymaid.co.uk
dir: *M26 junct 2A towards Maidstone on A20, through lights, 300mtrs on left*

Situated close to Brands Hatch, and within easy reach of the Bluewater shopping centre and Lullingstone Castle, this family home has been carefully designed to offer spacious, comfortable accommodation. Well-appointed bedrooms vary in size and provide many thoughtful extras including free Wi-fi. Breakfast is served in the large, bright dining room or can be offered as room service. Seasonal rates are available.

Rooms 7 en suite (2 fmly) (2 GF) S £52-£58; D £65-£71*
Facilities FTV tea/coffee Cen ht Wi-fi **Parking** 8
Notes Closed 24 Dec-4 Jan

LANCASHIRE

ACCRINGTON — Map 18 SD72

The Maple Lodge

★★★★ GUEST ACCOMMODATION

70 Blackburn Rd, Clayton-le-Moors BB5 5JH
☎ 01254 301284 📠 0560 112 5380
e-mail: info@stayatmaplelodge.co.uk
dir: *M65 junct 7, signs for Clitheroe, right at T-junct onto Blackburn Rd*

This welcoming house is convenient for the M65, and provides comfortable, well-equipped bedrooms, as well as an inviting lounge with well-stocked bar. Freshly cooked dinners (by arrangement) and hearty breakfasts are served in the attractive dining room.

Rooms 4 en suite 4 annexe en suite (1 fmly) (4 GF) S £40-£44; D £58-£62* **Facilities** FTV TVL tea/coffee Dinner available Direct Dial Cen ht Licensed Wi-fi **Parking** 6
Notes LB

Pilkington's Guest House

★★★ GUEST HOUSE

135 Blackburn Rd BB5 0AA
☎ 01254 237032 📠 01254 237032
e-mail: pilkybuses@hotmail.com

Located close to the railway station, this family-run property has two comfortable bedrooms in the main house and four further bedrooms in the carefully refurbished terrace a short way along the street. Home-cooked breakfasts are served in the main house.

Rooms 2 rms (2 pri facs) 4 annexe rms (2 fmly) (2 GF)
Facilities FTV tea/coffee Cen ht Snooker Pool table
Conf Max 100 Thtr 100 Class 100 Board 100 **Parking** 6
Notes ⊗ ⓦ

BLACKBURN — Map 18 SD62

Fernhurst

★★★★ INN

466 Bolton Rd BB2 4JP
☎ 01254 693541
e-mail: info@thefernhurst.co.uk
dir: *M65 junct 4, A666 towards Blackburn. Fernhurst on left in approx 0.5m*

Situated close to Blackburn town centre and positioned opposite Ewood Park, home of Blackburn Rovers, Fernhurst is the official away-supporters' pub on match days. Guests can enjoy the big match atmosphere and watch Sky sports in the pub on large screens. Bedrooms are situated adjacent to the main building and all are contemporary in style and comfortable.

Rooms 30 annexe en suite (4 fmly) (15 GF) S £53-£80; D £60-£100* **Facilities** FTV tea/coffee Dinner available Cen ht Wi-fi **Parking** 50 **Notes** LB ⓦ

BLACKPOOL — Map 18 SD33

Bona Vista

★★★★ GUEST ACCOMMODATION

104-106 Queens Promenade FY2 9NX
☎ 01253 351396 📠 01253 594985
e-mail: enquires@bonavistahotel.com
dir: *0.25m N of Uncle Toms Cabin & Castle Casino*

The Bona Vista has a peaceful seafront location on North Shore within reach of the town's amenities. Its attractive bedrooms are well equipped and some have sea views. There is a spacious dining room and a comfortable bar and lounges. Sixteen parking spaces are available, a boon in busy Blackpool.

Rooms 19 rms (17 en suite) (4 fmly) S £25-£34; D £50-£68* **Facilities** FTV TVL tea/coffee Dinner available Cen ht Licensed Wi-fi Pool table **Conf** Max 50 Thtr 50 Class 50 Board 50 **Parking** 16 **Notes** LB

Save on B&Bs and Hotels. Book at theAA.com/hotel

LANCASHIRE 189 ENGLAND

The Craigmore

★★★★ GUEST HOUSE

8 Willshaw Rd, Gynn Square FY2 9SH
☎ 01253 355098
e-mail: enquiries@thecraigmore.com
dir: *1m N of Tower. A584 N over Gynn rdbt, 1st right onto Willshaw Rd. The Craigmore 3rd on left*

This well-maintained property is in an attractive location overlooking Gynn Square gardens, with the Promenade and tram stops just yards away. Several of the smart modern bedrooms are suitable for families. There is a comfortable lounge, a sun lounge and patio, and the pretty dining room has a small bar.

Rooms 7 en suite (4 fmly) S £30-£40; D £50-£70*
Facilities FTV TVL tea/coffee Dinner available Cen ht Licensed Wi-fi **Notes** LB ⊗ Closed Dec-Feb RS Feb-Mar open wknds & BHs

The Ramsay

★★★★ GUEST ACCOMMODATION

90-92 Queen Promenade FY2 9NS
☎ 01253 352777 ▤ 01253 351207
e-mail: enquiries@theramsayhotel.co.uk
dir: *M55 exit towards Blackpool, left onto Central Drive then 1st left towards promenade. At lights turn right, at Gynn rdbt straight over, just past Uncle Toms Cabin*

This family-run guest accommodation occupies a prime location on the North Shore promenade. The bedrooms are restful and those at the front enjoy panoramic sea views. The public rooms are spacious, and include a cosy lounge with comfortable seating providing an ideal area to relax and have a drink from the bar. Dinner is available on request.

Rooms 22 en suite (2 fmly) **Facilities** FTV TVL tea/coffee Dinner available Cen ht Lift Licensed Wi-fi Golf **Parking** 8 **Notes** LB ⊗

The Baron

★★★★ A GUEST ACCOMMODATION

296 North Promenade FY1 2EY
☎ 01253 622729 ▤ 0161 297 0464
e-mail: baronhotel@f2s.com
web: www.baronhotel.co.uk
Rooms 21 en suite (1 fmly) (3 GF) (2 smoking)
Facilities FTV tea/coffee Dinner available Cen ht Lift Licensed Wi-fi **Conf** Max 20 Thtr 20 Class 20 Board 20 **Parking** 16 **Notes** ⊗ No Children 12yrs

Homecliffe

★★★★ A GUEST ACCOMMODATION

5 - 6 Wilton Pde FY1 2HE
☎ 01253 625147 ▤ 01253 292667
e-mail: enquiry@homecliffehotel.com
dir: *From the Promenade at North Pier, turn right onto Wilton Parade after Imperial Hotel, half way along on left*
Rooms 22 en suite (1 fmly) S £25-£40; D £50-£120*
Facilities FTV TVL tea/coffee Direct Dial Cen ht Licensed Wi-fi Golf 18 Pool table **Parking** 10 **Notes** LB ⊗

The Old Coach House

★★★★ A GUEST ACCOMMODATION

50 Dean St FY4 1BP
☎ 01253 347657
e-mail: info@theoldcoachhouse.co.uk
Rooms 11 en suite (2 GF) S fr £50; D £77-£97
Facilities FTV TVL tea/coffee Cen ht Licensed Wi-fi
Conf Max 25 **Parking** 11 **Notes** ⊗ No Children Closed Nov-Feb

The Valentine

★★★★ A GUEST ACCOMMODATION

35 Dickson Rd FY1 2AT
☎ 01253 622775
e-mail: anthony@anthonypalmer.orangehome.co.uk
Rooms 12 en suite (1 fmly) D £48-£70* **Facilities** FTV TVL tea/coffee Dinner available Cen ht Licensed Wi-fi **Notes** LB ⊗ Closed Nov-Mar

Hartshead

★★★ GUEST ACCOMMODATION

17 King Edward Av, North Shore FY2 9TA
☎ 01253 353133 & 357111
e-mail: info@hartshead-hotel.co.uk
dir: *M55 junct 4, A583 & A584 to North Shore, off Queens Promenade onto King Edward Av*

Popular for its location near the seafront, this enthusiastically run establishment has modern bedrooms of various sizes, equipped with a good range of practical extras. A veranda-sitting room is available, in addition to a comfortable lounge bar, and breakfast and pre-theatre dinners are served in the attractive dining room.

Rooms 9 en suite (3 fmly) S £21-£36; D £40-£62*
Facilities FTV TVL tea/coffee Dinner available Cen ht Licensed Wi-fi **Parking** 6 **Notes** LB ⊗

Sunny Cliff

★★★ GUEST ACCOMMODATION

98 Queens Promenade, North Shore FY2 9NS
☎ 01253 351155
dir: *On A584, 1.5m N of Blackpool Tower, just past Sheraton Hotel*

Under the same ownership for four decades, this friendly guest accommodation overlooking the seafront offers a genuine home-from-home atmosphere. The pretty bedrooms, some with sea views, are neatly furnished. There is a cosy bar, a sun lounge, a comfortable lounge, and a smart dining room where good home cooking features.

Rooms 9 en suite (3 fmly) (2 smoking) S £26-£27; D £52-£54* **Facilities** FTV TVL tea/coffee Dinner available Cen ht Licensed **Parking** 6 **Notes** LB ⊗ Closed 9 Nov-Etr ⊗

Denely

★★★ GUEST HOUSE

15 King Edward Av, North Shore FY2 9TA
☎ 01253 352757
e-mail: denely-hotel@btconnect.com
dir: *1m N of Blackpool Tower*

Just a stroll from the Promenade and Gynn Square Gardens, this welcoming guest house offers a spacious lounge and a bright dining room along with simply furnished bedrooms. The friendly resident owners provide attentive service, and evening meals are available by arrangement.

Rooms 9 en suite (3 fmly) **Facilities** FTV TVL tea/coffee Dinner available Cen ht **Parking** 6 **Notes** LB ⊗ Closed Dec-Jan

Derby Lodge & Bistro

★★★ GUEST HOUSE

8 Derby Rd FY1 2JF
☎ 01253 753444 ▤ 01253 753444
e-mail: derbylodgehotel@btconnect.com
web: www.derbylodgehotelandrestaurant.com
dir: *From M55 follow signs for Promenade, north (with sea on left), right onto Derby Rd, located on right*

Located close to the seafront and the town centre, Derby Lodge offers spacious well-equipped accommodation in a friendly atmosphere. Dinner is available in the attractive restaurant and there is a small bar.

Rooms 7 en suite (3 fmly) **Facilities** FTV tea/coffee Dinner available Licensed Wi-fi **Conf** Max 24 Thtr 24 Class 24 Board 20 **Parking** 4 **Notes** ⊗

BLACKPOOL *continued*

Funky Towers

★★★ GUEST ACCOMMODATION

297 The Promenade FY1 6AL
☎ 01253 400123
e-mail: stay@funkytowers.com
web: www.funkytowers.com
dir: *On seafront promenade halfway between The Tower & Pleasure Beach*

The friendly, family-run property has a prime location facing the sea, between the Pleasure Beach and Central Pier. There is a spacious bar and a modern café with direct access to the seafront. The bedrooms are equipped with lots of extras; some feature four-posters and others have great sea views. Rebecca and Adam Lancaster were runners-up in this year's AA Friendliest Landlady of the Year Award (2011-12).

Rooms 14 en suite (5 fmly) (1 GF) S £35-£45; D £60-£99 **Facilities** FTV TVL tea/coffee Cen ht Licensed Wi-fi Pool table **Parking** 3 **Notes** ⊗

The Sandalwood

★★★ GUEST HOUSE

3 Gynn Av FY1 2LD
☎ 01253 351795   📄 01253 351795
e-mail: peter.gerald@btconnect.com
web: www.sandalwoodhotel.co.uk
dir: *North of tower along promenade. 1st right, then 1st left after Hilton Hotel*

Situated on Blackpool's North Shore, The Sandalwood offers a friendly atmosphere and attractive, well-equipped accommodation. There is a comfortable lounge, and dinner or lighter snacks are available by arrangement.

Rooms 9 rms (7 en suite) (2 fmly) **Facilities** TVL tea/coffee Dinner available Cen ht Licensed **Parking** 2 **Notes** ⊗ Closed 20-30 Dec

Wilmar

★★★ GUEST HOUSE

42 Osborne Rd FY4 1HQ
☎ 01253 346229 & 07931 668305   📄 01253 200343
e-mail: info@thehotelwilmar.co.uk
dir: *Exit M55 junct 4, straight on at rdbt. Straight on at next rdbt (Total Garage on left). Right at next rdbt (at Aldi). Left at lights onto Waterloo Rd, left at next rdbt onto Lytham Rd. Right just before rail bridge onto Osborne Rd*

This friendly, family-run guest house has a convenient location close to the Pleasure Beach, Sandcastles and all the resort's major South Promenade attractions. Bedrooms are brightly appointed, smartly maintained and include a family suite. A cosy lounge and bar are available and dinner is served by arrangement.

Rooms 7 rms (6 en suite) (1 pri facs) (1 fmly) S £28-£30; D £55-£60* **Facilities** FTV TVL tea/coffee Dinner available Cen ht Licensed Wi-fi **Notes** LB ⊗

Carn-Brae

★★★ 🅰 GUEST ACCOMMODATION

657-659 New South Promenade FY4 1RN
☎ 01253 345938   📄 01253 341790
e-mail: mail@the carnbrae.co.uk
web: www.thecarnbrae.co.uk
dir: *M6 junct 32 onto M55, exit onto A5230. Pass Blackpool Airport to seafront right at lights Carn Brae on right*

Rooms 30 en suite (6 fmly) S £30-£40; D £50-£70 **Facilities** FTV tea/coffee Dinner available Cen ht Lift Licensed Wi-fi Pool table **Notes** LB ⊗ Closed Jan-Mar

The Montclair

★★★ 🅰 GUEST HOUSE

95 Albert Rd FY1 4PW
☎ 01253 625860
e-mail: chrissbowen@aol.com
Rooms 15 en suite (4 fmly) **Facilities** FTV TVL Dinner available Cen ht Licensed **Parking** 7 **Notes** ⊗

Briny View

★★ 🅰 GUEST ACCOMMODATION

2 Woodfield Rd FY1 6AX
☎ 01253 346584
e-mail: brinyviewhotel@aol.com
dir: *Off A584 Promenade between Central Pier & South Pier, opposite St Chads headland*

Rooms 9 rms (7 en suite) (1 pri facs) (5 fmly) S £20-£30; D £40-£50* **Facilities** FTV TVL tea/coffee Cen ht Licensed **Notes** LB ⊗ Closed Dec RS Winter months wknds only

BOLTON-BY-BOWLAND   Map 18 SD74

Middle Flass Lodge

★★★★ 🍽 GUEST HOUSE

Settle Rd BB7 4NY
☎ 01200 447259   📄 01200 447300
e-mail: middleflasslodge@btconnect.com
web: www.middleflasslodge.co.uk
dir: *2m N of Bolton by Bowland. Off A59 for Sawley, N to Forest Becks, over bridge, 1m on right*

Set in peaceful countryside in the Forest of Bowland, this smart house provides a warm welcome. Stylishly converted from farm outbuildings, exposed timbers feature throughout, including the attractive restaurant and cosy lounge. The modern bedrooms include a family room. Thanks to the accomplished chef, the restaurant is also popular with non-residents.

Rooms 5 en suite 2 annexe en suite (1 fmly) S £46-£52; D £68-£75* **Facilities** FTV TVL tea/coffee Dinner available Cen ht Licensed Wi-fi **Parking** 14 **Notes** LB ⊗

CHORLEY

See Eccleston

ECCLESTON   Map 15 SD51

Parr Hall Farm

★★★★ GUEST ACCOMMODATION

8 Parr Ln PR7 5SL
☎ 01257 451917   📄 01257 453749
e-mail: enquiries@parrhallfarm.com
dir: *M6 junct 27 onto B5250 N for 5m to Parr Ln on right hand side. 1st property on left*

This attractive, well-maintained farmhouse, located in a quiet corner of the village, yet close to the M6, dates back to the 18th century. The majority of bedrooms are located in a sympathetic barn conversion and include luxury en suite bathrooms and lots of thoughtful extras. A comprehensive continental breakfast is included in the room price.

Rooms 10 annexe en suite (1 fmly) (5 GF) S £40-£45; D £70-£80 **Facilities** FTV tea/coffee Cen ht Wi-fi Golf 9 Guided Walks **Parking** 20 **Notes** ⊗

LANCASTER
Map 18 SD46

Lancaster Town House

★★★ A GUEST ACCOMMODATION

11/12 Newton Ter, Caton Rd LA1 3PB
☎ 01524 65527   📠 01524 383148
e-mail: hedge-holmes@talk21.com
dir: *M6 junct 34, 1m towards Lancaster, house on right*
Rooms 7 en suite (1 fmly) S fr £35; D fr £60*
Facilities FTV TVL tea/coffee Cen ht Wi-fi **Notes** ⊗

LYTHAM ST ANNES
Map 18 SD32

Strathmore

★★★ GUEST ACCOMMODATION

305 Clifton Drive South FY8 1HN
☎ 01253 725478
dir: *In centre of St Annes opp Post Office*

This friendly, family-run property has a central location close to the promenade. The long-established Strathmore offers smartly furnished and well-equipped bedrooms. There is an elegant lounge where you can enjoy a relaxing drink, and a smart dining room.

Rooms 8 rms (5 en suite) S £24-£31; D £48-£62
Facilities tea/coffee Cen ht Wi-fi **Parking** 8 **Notes** LB ⊗ No Children 9yrs ☻

MORECAMBE
Map 18 SD46

Yacht Bay View

★★★★ GUEST HOUSE

359 Marine Road East LA4 5AQ
☎ 01524 414481
e-mail: yachtbayview@hotmail.com
dir: *0.5m NE of town centre on seafront promenade*

Overlooking Morecambe Bay, this family-run property offers comfortable bedrooms, some with impressive views, and all with en suite shower rooms. Guests are given a warm welcome and breakfast is served in the dining room, which also has a lounge area.

Rooms 7 en suite (1 fmly) S £30-£35; D £60-£70*
Facilities FTV TVL tea/coffee Wi-fi **Notes** LB ⊗

Broadwater Guest House

★★★ GUEST HOUSE

356 Marine Road East LA4 5AQ
☎ 01524 41333
e-mail: enquiries@thebroadwaterhotel.co.uk
web: www.thebroadwaterhotel.co.uk
dir: *M6 junct 34 follow signs for Morecambe, then signs for E Promenade*

Located on Morecambe's sea front this guest house offers a refreshingly friendly welcome. Bedrooms vary in size, but all are en suite, and well equipped with thoughtful extras including free Wi-fi. Substantial breakfasts are served in the pleasant dining room with sea views.

Rooms 8 en suite S fr £29; D £58-£66* **Facilities** FTV tea/coffee Wi-fi **Notes** ⊗

Beach Mount

★★★ GUEST ACCOMMODATION

395 Marine Road East LA4 5AN
☎ 01524 420753
e-mail: beachmounthotel@aol.com
dir: *M6 junct 34/35, follow signs to Morecambe. Beach Mount 0.5m from town centre on E Promenade*

This spacious property overlooks the bay and features a range of room styles that includes a family room and a junior suite. Guests have use of a comfortable lounge with fully licensed bar, and breakfasts are served in a pleasant separate dining room.

Rooms 10 en suite (1 GF) (10 smoking) S £25.50-£28.75; D £52.50-£59.50* **Facilities** FTV tea/coffee Cen ht Licensed **Notes** LB Closed Nov-Mar

Belle Vue

★★★ GUEST ACCOMMODATION

330 Marine Rd LA4 5AA
☎ 01524 411375   📠 01524 411375
dir: *On seafront between lifeboat house & bingo hall*

With fine views over the promenade and Morecambe Bay, the Belle Vue provides a range of bedrooms styles on

three floors; most are accessible by lift. There are comfortable lounges, and a spacious lounge bar where entertainment is provided at peak times. A choice of dishes is available in the large dining room.

Rooms 41 rms (34 en suite) (3 fmly) S £25-£30; D £40-£50 (room only) **Facilities** TVL tea/coffee Dinner available Cen ht Lift Licensed **Parking** 3 **Notes** LB ⊗ No Children 14yrs Closed Jan-Mar

PRESTON
Map 18 SD52

See also Blackburn

Birch Croft Bed & Breakfast

★★★ BED AND BREAKFAST

Gill Ln, Longton PR4 4SS
☎ 01772 613174 & 07761 817187
e-mail: johnsuts@btinternet.com
web: www.birchcroftbandb.co.uk
dir: *From A59 right at rdbt to Midge Hall. Premises 4th on left*

Located only 10 minutes away from major motorway links (M6, M65, M61) this establishment is on the doorstep of many attractions and close to Southport, Preston and Blackpool. This is a friendly, family-run business which offers comfortable accommodation in a very peaceful location.

Rooms 3 en suite (1 fmly) **Facilities** FTV TVL tea/coffee Cen ht Wi-fi **Parking** 11 **Notes** LB ⊗ ☻

Ashton Lodge Guest House

★★ GUEST ACCOMMODATION

37 Victoria Pde, Ashton PR2 1DT
☎ 01772 728414   📠 01772 720580
e-mail: greathospitality@btconnect.com
dir: *M6 junct 31, A59 onto A5085, 3.3m onto A5072 Tulketh Rd, 0.3m onto Victoria Pde*

This detached Victorian guest house offers good value accommodation. Bedrooms vary in size; some are located on the ground floor. The dining room is the setting for hearty traditional breakfasts served at individual tables.

Rooms 8 rms (3 en suite) (5 fmly) (3 GF) S £28-£35; D £40-£48* **Facilities** FTV TVL tea/coffee Cen ht Wi-fi **Parking** 7 **Notes** ⊗

WHITEWELL · Map 18 SD64

PREMIER COLLECTION

The Inn at Whitewell

★★★★★ ⍟ INN

Forest of Bowland, Clitheroe BB7 3AT
☎ 01200 448222 ▤ 01200 448298
e-mail: reception@innatwhitewell.com
dir: *M6 junct 31a, B6243 to Longridge. Left at mini-rdbt. After 3 rdbts leave Longridge. Approx 3m, sharp left bend (with white railings), then right. Approx 1m left, right at T-junct. Next left, 3m to Whitewell*

This long-established culinary destination is hidden away in quintessential Lancashire countryside just 20 minutes from the M6. The fine dining restaurant is complemented by two historic and cosy bars with roaring fires, real ales and polished service. Bedrooms are richly furnished with antiques and eye-catching bijouterie, while many of the bathrooms have Victorian brass showers.

Rooms 19 en suite 4 annexe en suite (1 fmly) (2 GF) S £88-£187; D £120-£231* **Facilities** STV FTV tea/coffee Dinner available Direct Dial Cen ht Wi-fi Golf 18 Fishing Horse stabling can be arranged **Conf** Max 45 Thtr 45 Board 35 **Parking** 60 **Notes** No coaches Civ Wed 80

LEICESTERSHIRE

BARROW UPON SOAR · Map 11 SK51

The Hunting Lodge

★★★★ INN

38 South St LE12 8LZ
☎ 01509 412337 ▤ 01509 410838
web: www.thehuntinglodgebarrowonsoar.co.uk
dir: *M1 junct 23 onto A6, 1st exit to Barrow upon Soar. At rdbt onto South St, 200yds on right*

The themed bedrooms at this modern inn include a Fagin room, a Chopin room and a Dali room; all are well equipped and have good facilities. There is a popular bar and a good range of interesting food is served in the brasserie.

Rooms 6 en suite (2 fmly) **Facilities** FTV tea/coffee Dinner available Cen ht Wi-fi **Conf** Max 50 Thtr 50 Class 50 Board 30 **Parking** 60

BELTON · Map 11 SK42

The Queen's Head

★★★★ ⍟⍟ ▤ RESTAURANT WITH ROOMS

2 Long St LE12 9TP
☎ 01530 222359 ▤ 01530 224680
e-mail: enquiries@thequeenshead.org
web: www.thequeenshead.org
dir: *From Loughborough left onto B5324, 3m to Belton*

This well furnished establishment is found in the village centre and has public rooms with a modern feel. The individually designed bedrooms feature crisp white linen, fluffy duvets and pillows, 19-inch LCD TVs with Freeview and DVD players. The restaurant has earned a well deserved reputation for its AA 2 Rosette-worthy cuisine; the menus are based on the freshest, locally sourced produce.

Rooms 6 en suite (2 fmly) **Facilities** FTV TVL tea/coffee Dinner available Cen ht Wi-fi **Conf** Max 40 Thtr 40 Class 18 Board 30 **Parking** 20 **Notes** Civ Wed 50

CASTLE DONINGTON

See East Midlands Airport

EAST LANGTON · Map 11 SP79

The Bell Inn

★★★ INN

Main St LE16 7TW
☎ 01858 545278
e-mail: nickatthebell@btconnect.com
web: www.thebellinn-eastlangton.co.uk

Set in the pretty village of East Langton, The Bell Inn is a traditional English pub with two comfortable en suite bedrooms, both of which come with TV and Wi-fi. Staff are on hand to offer a warm and friendly welcome. A wide range of food and ales is available, and is served seven days a week in the spacious restaurant. In the summer months, guests can enjoy alfresco dining in the attractive garden.

Rooms 2 en suite (1 fmly) **Facilities** FTV TVL tea/coffee Dinner available Cen ht Wi-fi **Parking** 20 **Notes** No coaches

EAST MIDLANDS AIRPORT · Map 11 SK42

PREMIER COLLECTION

Kegworth House

★★★★★ GUEST HOUSE

42 High St DE74 2DA
☎ 01509 672575 ▤ 01509 670645
e-mail: info@kegworthhouse.co.uk
web: www.kegworthhouse.co.uk
dir: *M1 junct 24, A6 to Loughborough. 0.5m 1st right onto Packington Hill. Left at junct, Kegworth House 50yds on left*

Convenient for major roads and East Midlands Airport, this impressive Georgian house with an immaculate walled garden has been lovingly restored. The individually styled bedrooms are luxuriously appointed and equipped with a wealth of thoughtful extras. The elegant dining room is the setting for memorable dinners by arrangement for six or more, and wholesome breakfasts featuring local produce are served in the kitchen.

Rooms 11 en suite (2 fmly) (2 GF) S £55-£90; D £67-£140* **Facilities** FTV TVL tea/coffee Direct Dial Cen ht Licensed Wi-fi Free access to health club & swimming pool **Conf** Max 12 Board 12 **Parking** 25 **Notes** LB ⊗ No Children 8yrs

HUSBANDS BOSWORTH · Map 11 SP68

Croft Farm B&B (SP634860)

★★★★ FARMHOUSE

Leicester Rd LE17 6NW
☎ 01858 880679
Mrs Smith
e-mail: janesmith06@aol.com
web: www.croftfarm.org.uk
dir: *Take A5199 from Husbands Bosworth towards Leicester, Croft Farm 0.25m on left*

This very spacious and delightfully furnished house stands on the edge of the village in very well cared for grounds. Bedrooms are thoughtfully equipped and there is a very comfortable guests' lounge. Expect a substantial breakfast together with friendly and attentive service.

Rooms 4 en suite (2 fmly) **Facilities** TVL tea/coffee Cen ht Wi-fi **Parking** 15 **Notes** ⊗ ⊜ 350 acres sheep/arable/beef/mixed

KEGWORTH

See East Midlands Airport

Save on B&Bs and Hotels. Book at **theAA.com/hotel**

LEICESTERSHIRE 193 **ENGLAND**

KNIPTON   Map 11 SK83

The Manners Arms

★★★★ ⊛ RESTAURANT WITH ROOMS

Croxton Rd NG32 1RH
☎ 01476 879222   📄 01476 879228
e-mail: info@mannersarms.com
web: www.mannersarms.com
dir: *Off A607 into Knipton*

Part of the Rutland Estate and built as a hunting lodge for the 6th Duke, the Manners Arms offers thoughtfully furnished bedrooms designed by the present Duchess. Public areas include the intimate Beater's Bar and attractive Red Coats Restaurant, popular for its imaginative menus.

Rooms 10 en suite (1 fmly) **Facilities** TVL tea/coffee Dinner available Direct Dial Cen ht Wi-fi **Conf** Max 50 Thtr 50 Class 25 Board 20 **Parking** 60 **Notes** No coaches Civ Wed 50

LEICESTER   Map 11 SK50

Stoney Croft

★★★ GUEST ACCOMMODATION

5-7 Elmfield Av, Off London Rd LE2 1RB
☎ 0116 270 7605   📄 0116 270 6067
e-mail: reception@stoneycrofthotel.co.uk
web: www.stoneycrofthotel.co.uk
dir: *Near city centre on A6 to Market Harborough*

Stoney Croft provides comfortable accommodation and helpful service. Public rooms include a foyer-lounge area, breakfast room and conference facilities. The modern bedrooms come with desks. There is also a large restaurant-bar where a good selection of freshly cooked dishes is available.

Rooms 41 en suite (4 fmly) (6 GF) S £29.50-£49; D £59-£69* **Facilities** FTV TVL tea/coffee Dinner available Direct Dial Cen ht Licensed Wi-fi Pool table **Conf** Max 150 Thtr 150 Class 20 Board 30 **Parking** 30 **Notes** LB Civ Wed 120

LONG WHATTON   Map 11 SK42

The Royal Oak

★★★★★ ⊛ 🛏 INN

26 The Green LE12 5DB
☎ 01509 843694
e-mail: enquiries@theroyaloaklongwhatton.co.uk

Following a substantial renovation project The Royal Oak has been transformed into a popular gastropub with rooms and located in a small village just 4 miles from East Midlands airport. The young team offer a warm welcome and service is attentive. The seven spacious en suite bedrooms are set externally to the rear of the property and have been designed with comfort and style in mind. There is plenty of parking available and a small garden for the warmer months.

Rooms 7 en suite (1 fmly) (7 GF) S £79-£95; D £79-£95* **Facilities** FTV tea/coffee Dinner available Cen ht Wi-fi **Parking** 28 **Notes** ⊗

The Falcon Inn

★★★ INN

64 Main St LE12 5DG
☎ 01509 842416   📄 01509 646802
e-mail: enquiries@thefalconinnlongwhatton.com
dir: *M1 junct 23 N or junct 24 S, follow signs to Airport. After lights 1st left to Diseworth, left at T-junct, left towards Long Whatton, on right*

This late 18th-century traditional country pub sits in the quiet village of Long Whatton. Inside, the relaxed and friendly atmosphere is complemented by a good choice of freshly made meals, real ales and efficient service. Smartly appointed bedrooms are housed in a converted former school house and stable block at the rear of the main inn. Ample private parking is provided.

Rooms 11 annexe en suite (5 GF) **Facilities** FTV tea/coffee Dinner available Cen ht Wi-fi petanque pitch **Conf** Max 30 Thtr 20 Class 20 Board 20 **Parking** 46 **Notes** ⊗

MARKET BOSWORTH   Map 11 SK40

Softleys

★★★ GUEST ACCOMMODATION

2 Market Place CV13 0LE
☎ 01455 290464
e-mail: softleysrestaurant@tiscali.co.uk
dir: *On B585 in Market Place*

Softleys is a Grade II listed building dating back to 1794. The bedrooms are en suite and set on the third floor offering picturesque views over Market Bosworth. Quality food is served using locally sourced ingredients.

Rooms 3 en suite (1 fmly) S £69; D £85* **Facilities** FTV tea/coffee Dinner available Direct Dial Cen ht Licensed Wi-fi **Conf** Max 26 Thtr 26 Class 26 Board 26 **Notes** RS Sun eve & Mon no food available

MEDBOURNE   Map 11 SP89

Medbourne Grange *(SP815945)*

★★★★ FARMHOUSE

LE16 8EF
☎ 01858 565249   & 07730 956116
📄 01858 565257   Mrs S Beaty
e-mail: sally.beaty@googlemail.com
dir: *2m NE of Medbourne. Between Market Harborough & Uppingham off B664*

This 150-year-old working farm has unrivalled views of the Welland Valley and is well situated for Rutland Water, Uppingham or Market Harborough. Mrs Beaty is a natural host, ensuring that guests receive a warm welcome and friendly service. Individually furnished bedrooms are complemented by comfortable day rooms, and freshly prepared breakfasts are served in the smart dining room.

Rooms 3 en suite S £36-£40; D £60-£66* **Facilities** FTV TVL tea/coffee Cen ht Wi-fi 🎣 **Parking** 6 **Notes** ⊗ 🚭 500 acres arable

MELTON MOWBRAY   Map 11 SK71

Bryn Barn

★★★★ GUEST ACCOMMODATION

38 High St, Waltham-on-the-Wolds LE14 4AH
☎ 01664 464783   & 07914 222407
e-mail: glenarowlands@onetel.com
web: www.brynbarn.co.uk
dir: *4.5m NE of Melton. Off A607, in Waltham-on-the-Wolds centre*

A warm welcome awaits at this attractive, peacefully located cottage within easy reach of Melton Mowbray, Grantham, Rutland Water and Belvoir Castle. Bedrooms are smartly appointed and comfortably furnished, while public rooms include an inviting lounge overlooking a wonderful courtyard garden. Meals are available at one of the nearby village pubs.

Rooms 4 rms (3 en suite) (1 pri facs) (2 fmly) (1 GF) S £35-£50; D £60-£70 **Facilities** FTV TVL tea/coffee Cen ht Wi-fi **Parking** 4 **Notes** LB Closed 21 Dec-4 Jan

MOUNTSORREL   Map 11 SK51

The Swan Inn

★★★★ INN

10 Loughborough Rd LE12 7AT
☎ 0116 230 2340   0116 237 6115
e-mail: office@swaninn.eu
web: www.the-swan-inn.eu
dir: In village centre

This traditional 17th-century inn is in the centre of the village and offers well produced meals in the bar, together with a wide range of real ales. The accommodation consists of a luxury suite which includes a double bedroom, a lounge, a large bathroom and an office. Continental breakfast is available in the suite.

Rooms 1 en suite S £70-£98; D £80-£108* Facilities FTV TVL tea/coffee Dinner available Direct Dial Cen ht Wi-fi Parking 12 Notes No coaches

NARBOROUGH   Map 11 SP59

Fossebrook B&B

★★★★ GUEST ACCOMMODATION

Coventry Rd, Croft LE9 3GP
☎ 01455 283517   01455 283517
dir: 0.6m SE of village centre on B4114

This friendly guest accommodation stands in a quiet rural location with good access to major roads. Bedrooms are spacious, very comfortable and offer an excellent range of facilities including a range of videos in all rooms. Breakfast is served in the bright dining room, which overlooks pleasant gardens and grounds.

Rooms 4 en suite (4 GF) S £40; D £40* Facilities tea/coffee Cen ht Wi-fi Parking 16 Notes ⊗ Closed 24 Dec-2 Jan

RAVENSTONE   Map 11 SK41

Ravenstone Guesthouse

★★★★ GUEST HOUSE

Church Lane Farm House LE67 2AE
☎ 01530 810536
e-mail: annthorne@ravenstone-guesthouse.co.uk
web: www.ravenstone-guesthouse.co.uk
dir: 1.5m W of Coalville. Off A447 onto Church Ln for Ravenstone, 2nd house on left

Situated in the heart of Ravenstone village, this early 18th-century house is full of character. The bedrooms are individually decorated and feature period furniture, and local produce is used for dinner and in the extensive breakfast menu. The beamed dining room has an honesty bar and there is also a cosy lounge.

Rooms 4 en suite Facilities FTV TVL tea/coffee Dinner available Cen ht Licensed Wi-fi Painting tuition Parking 6 Notes Closed 23-30 Dec & 1 Jan RS 31 Dec-1 Jan No breakfast on 1 Jan

REDMILE   Map 11 SK73

The Peacock Inn

★★★★ INN

Main St NG13 0GA
☎ 01949 842554
e-mail: reservations@thepeacockinnredmile.co.uk
dir: Off A52 between Bingham & Bottesford, follow signs for Belvoir Castle, then Redmile

Between Nottingham and Grantham in a peaceful village, this period inn provides well-equipped bedrooms, which are named after wild animals, and all have efficient bathrooms. Public areas retain many fine original features and in addition to a wide range of bar meals, an à la carte menu is available in a formal restaurant on two weekend evenings.

Rooms 10 en suite (1 fmly) S £62.50; D £84.95* Facilities tea/coffee Dinner available Direct Dial Cen ht Wi-fi Conf Max 50 Thtr 40 Class 50 Board 40 Parking 40 Notes LB

SIBSON   Map 11 SK30

The Millers

★★★ INN

Twycross Rd CV13 6LB
☎ 01827 880223   01827 880990
e-mail: millerssibsonreservations@greeneking.co.uk
dir: A5 onto A444 towards Burton. Property 3m on right

This inn was once a bakery and water mill and several original features have been retained - the water wheel is a feature of the public bar along with the log-burning fireplace. The well-equipped bedrooms have modern facilities. The bar and restaurant are popular with the locals, and there is a conference suite in a separate building which is ideal for small groups.

Rooms 39 en suite (2 fmly) (15 GF) Facilities tea/coffee Dinner available Direct Dial Cen ht Wi-fi Conf Max 60 Thtr 60 Class 30 Board 40 Parking 60 Notes ⊗ Civ Wed 60

SUTTON IN THE ELMS   Map 11 SP59

The Mill on the Soar

★★★ INN

Coventry Rd LE9 6QA
☎ 01455 282419   01455 285937
e-mail: 1968@greeneking.co.uk
web: www.oldenglish.co.uk
dir: M1 junct 21, follow signs for Narborough, 3m, inn on left

This is a popular inn, set in grounds with two rivers and a lake, that caters especially well for family dining. The open-plan bar offers meals and snacks throughout the day, and is divided into family and adults-only areas; for the summer months, there is also an attractive patio. Practical bedrooms are housed in a lodge-style annexe in the grounds.

Rooms 20 en suite 5 annexe en suite (19 fmly) (13 GF) Facilities FTV tea/coffee Direct Dial Children's outdoor play area Pool room Parking 80 Notes ⊗

WIGSTON   Map 11 SP69

Plough Inn

★★★★ INN

44 Bushloe Rd LE18 2BA
☎ 0116 281 0078   0116 210 0674
e-mail: theploughwigston@ntlworld.com
dir: Just off A599 (old A50), next to All Saints church

Located within easy travelling distance from Leicester, this half timbered and red brick inn provides a range of thoughtfully furnished bedrooms located in a separate accommodation wing, ensuring a peaceful night's sleep. A wide range of food and ales is available in the spacious public areas and hospitality is natural and thoughtful.

Rooms 7 annexe en suite (1 fmly) (7 GF) Facilities tea/coffee Dinner available Cen ht Parking 32 Notes ⊗ No coaches

WOODHOUSE EAVES   Map 11 SK51

The Wheatsheaf Inn

★★★★ INN

90 Brand Hill LE12 8SS
☎ 01509 890320
e-mail: richard@wheatsheafinn.net
web: www.wheatsheafinn.net

Originally built around 1800 by the local miners of Swithland slate mines, this charming inn offers a friendly service, good food and modern accommodation in the adjacent self-contained cottage. The first-floor restaurant proves very popular with locals, offering specials and bistro menus that include traditional English dishes, and fresh fish appears on the blackboard specials.

Rooms 2 annexe en suite S £60; D £80* Facilities FTV TVL tea/coffee Dinner available Cen ht Wi-fi Conf Thtr 18 Class 12 Board 14 Parking 70 Notes No coaches

Save on B&Bs and Hotels. Book at **theAA.com/hotel**

LINCOLNSHIRE 195 **ENGLAND**

LINCOLNSHIRE

CLEETHORPES — Map 17 TA30

Adelaide

★★★★ GUEST ACCOMMODATION

41 Isaac's Hill DN35 8JT
☎ 01472 693594 📠 01472 329717
e-mail: adelaide.hotel@ntlworld.com
dir: *500yds W of seafront. Junct A180 & A46 onto A1098 Isaac's Hill, on right at bottom of hill*

This beautifully presented house offers well-equipped bedrooms and comfortable public rooms, and hospitality is a major strength. Good home cooking is provided and there is a small lounge with a bar. Secure parking is available.

Rooms 5 rms (3 en suite) (1 fmly) **Facilities** STV TVL tea/coffee Dinner available Cen ht Licensed **Notes** ⊗ No Children 4yrs

Aristocrat Guest House

★★★★ GUEST HOUSE

15 Clee Rd DN35 8AD
☎ 01472 234027 & 07957 388475 📠 01472 318086
e-mail: aristocrat@ntlworld.com
web: www.aristocrat-guesthouse.co.uk
dir: *A180 follow signs for Cleethorpes, over fly over through 3 sets of lights. At rdbt turn right onto Clee Rd, 30yds on left*

Located just a few minutes' walk from the seafront, restaurants, bars and main attractions, this lovely, carefully refurbished house is family run. The attractively decorated bedrooms are well equipped with thoughtful accessories such as fridges and DVD players, and Wi-fi is available.

Rooms 4 rms (2 en suite) (2 pri facs) (1 fmly) S £30-£35; D £60-£65 **Facilities** FTV tea/coffee Cen ht Wi-fi **Parking** 2 **Notes** LB ⊗

The Comat

★★★★ GUEST ACCOMMODATION

26 Yarra Rd DN35 8LS
☎ 01472 694791 📠 01472 238113
e-mail: comat-hotel@ntlworld.com
web: www.comat-hotel.co.uk
dir: *Off A1098 (Alexandra Rd), on left of library*

A short walk from the shops and seafront, the welcoming Comat offers cosy, well-equipped bedrooms, one with a four-poster bed. Tasty English breakfasts are served in the bright dining room, and a quiet sitting room and bar overlook the colourful flower terrace.

Rooms 6 en suite (2 fmly) (2 GF) D £65-£73* **Facilities** FTV TVL tea/coffee Cen ht Licensed Wi-fi **Notes** LB ⊗ No Children 3yrs

Alpine House

★★★ GUEST ACCOMMODATION

55 Clee Rd DN35 8AD
☎ 01472 690804
e-mail: nw.sanderson@ntlworld.com
dir: *On A46 before junct A180 & A1098 Isaac's Hill rdbt*

Carefully run by the resident owners, and convenient for the town centre and attractions, this friendly guest accommodation offers compact, well-equipped bedrooms and a comfortable lounge.

Rooms 5 rms (2 fmly) S £20-£24; D £36-£48* **Facilities** FTV TVL tea/coffee Cen ht Wi-fi **Parking** 3 **Notes** LB ⊗ No Children 2yrs 🐾

Brier Park Guest House

★★★ GUEST ACCOMMODATION

27 Clee Rd DN35 8AD
☎ 01472 605591 & 07849 639923
e-mail: graham.sherwood2@ntlworld.com
dir: *Left at bottom of Isaac's Hill, 150yds on left*

A private house personally managed by the owner offering a friendly atmosphere and comfortable compact bedrooms that are brightly decorated. Breakfast is freshly cooked to order, and convenient parking in front is a bonus.

Rooms 6 rms (3 en suite) (3 pri facs) (1 fmly) (2 GF) **Facilities** FTV TVL tea/coffee Cen ht Wi-fi **Parking** 2 **Notes** LB ⊗ No Children 5yrs 🐾

Holmhirst

★★★ GUEST ACCOMMODATION

3 Alexandra Rd DN35 8LQ
☎ 01472 692656 📠 01472 692656
e-mail: holmhirst@aol.com

Overlooking the sea and the pier, this Victorian terrace house offers comfortable well-equipped bedrooms, many with showers en suite. Tasty English breakfasts and a range of lunchtime and evening meals are available. There is a well-stocked bar, and the resident owners are fluent in several languages.

Rooms 8 rms (5 en suite) **Facilities** TVL TV7B tea/coffee Dinner available Cen ht Licensed **Notes** ⊗

Ginnies

★★★ 🅰 GUEST HOUSE

27 Queens Pde DN35 0DF
☎ 01472 694997 📠 01472 593153
e-mail: enquiries@ginnies.co.uk
dir: *On A1098 Queens Parade, off seafront Kingsway*

Rooms 7 rms (5 en suite) (2 pri facs) (3 fmly) (1 GF) D £45-£60 **Facilities** FTV TVL tea/coffee Cen ht Wi-fi **Parking** 4 **Notes** LB ⊗ RS 24 Dec-2 Jan 24-25 & 31 Dec room only

EPWORTH — Map 17 SE70

Wesley Guest House

★★★★ GUEST ACCOMMODATION

16 Queen St DN9 1HG
☎ 01427 874512 & 07738 867801 📠 01427 874592
e-mail: enquiries@wesleyguesthouse.com
web: www.wesleyguesthouse.com
dir: *In town centre, 200yds off Market Place*

Situated near the Market Cross and close to The Old Rectory, this detached guest accommodation offers a friendly welcome, modern, non-smoking en suite rooms, and secure off-road parking. Finningley Airport is close by.

Rooms 4 en suite 2 annexe en suite (1 fmly) (1 GF) **Facilities** FTV tea/coffee Cen ht Wi-fi Golf 18 Infra red sauna & therapy room **Parking** 7 **Notes** ⊗

GAINSBOROUGH — Map 17 SK88

See also Marton

Eastbourne House

★★★★ GUEST HOUSE

81 Trinity St DN21 1JF
☎ 01427 679511
e-mail: info@eastbournehouse.co.uk
dir: *In town centre. Off A631 onto A159 Trinity St*

Located in a residential area west of the town centre, this impressive Victorian house has been restored to provide high standards of comfort and facilities. Bedrooms are thoughtfully furnished and the comprehensive breakfast uses quality local produce.

Rooms 5 rms (3 en suite) (2 pri facs) (1 fmly) S £40; D £60-£75 **Facilities** FTV tea/coffee Cen ht Wi-fi **Parking** 1 **Notes** ⊗

GRANTHAM — Map 11 SK93

The Welby Arms

★★★★ INN

The Green, Allington NG32 2EA
☎ 01400 281361 📄 01400 281361
dir: 4m NW of Grantham. Off A52 into Allington village

Set in the pleasant village of Allington, The Welby Arms is just off the busy A1, handy for Grantham but deep in the countryside. There are three purpose built en suites in a former byre behind a popular village inn that serves a wide range of real ales and an extensive menu that is very popular with locals.

Rooms 3 annexe en suite **Facilities** FTV Dinner available Cen ht **Parking** 30 **Notes** ⊗

Beaver House

★★★ BED AND BREAKFAST

School Ln, Old Somerby NG33 4AH
☎ 01476 565011
e-mail: cuttlers@btinternet.com
web: www.beaverhouse.co.uk
dir: From Grantham A52 E for 2m. At rdbt take exit signed Old Somerby, then 1st left, 1st house on right 1m from rdbt

Located on a mainly residential avenue in the quiet village of Old Somerby, just five minutes' drive from Grantham, a warm welcome awaits you at Beaver House. The accommodation has been thoughtfully designed, and is well equipped and very comfortable. Breakfasts are served in the dining room overlooking the manicured garden, and there is a restaurant within walking distance. For those with children, a highchair and travel cot can be provided.

Rooms 3 rms (1 en suite) (1 pri facs) S £30-£40; D £40-£50 **Facilities** TVL tea/coffee Cen ht **Parking** 3 **Notes** ⊗ 🐾

The Kingston Guest House

[U]

25 Avenue Rd NG31 6TH
☎ 01476 591395 & 07414 202846
e-mail: thekingstonguesthouse@yahoo.com
web: www.thekingston.co.uk
dir: In town centre, council offices on right, turn right onto Avenue Rd, 200mtrs on right

Currently the rating for this establishment is not confirmed. This may be due to a change of ownership or because it has only recently joined the AA rating scheme.

Rooms 5 rms (4 en suite) (1 pri facs) (1 fmly) S fr £30; D fr £55* **Facilities** FTV TVL tea/coffee Cen ht Wi-fi **Parking** 4 **Notes** LB ⊗

HEMSWELL — Map 17 SK99

Hemswell Court

★★★★★ ⌂ GUEST ACCOMMODATION

Lancaster Green, Hemswell Cliff DN21 5TQ
☎ 01427 668508 📄 01427 667335
e-mail: function@hemswellcourt.com
dir: 1.5m SE of Hemswell on A631 in Hemswell Cliff

Originally an officers' mess, Hemswell Court is now a venue for conferences, weddings or private gatherings. The modern bedrooms and many suites are ideal for families or groups of friends, and all rooms are well equipped. The lounges and dining rooms are enhanced by many antique pieces.

Rooms 23 en suite (2 fmly) (4 GF) **Facilities** TVL tea/coffee Dinner available Cen ht Licensed Wi-fi 🛜 🐾 **Conf** Max 200 Thtr 200 Class 150 Board 150 **Parking** 150 **Notes** ⊗ Closed Xmas & New Year Civ Wed 200

HORNCASTLE — Map 17 TF26

Greenfield Farm (TF175745)

★★★★ FARMHOUSE

Mill Ln/Cow Ln, Minting LN9 5PJ
☎ 01507 578457 & 07768 368829 📄 01507 578457
Mrs J Bankes Price
e-mail: info@greenfieldfarm.net
web: www.greenfieldfarm.net
dir: A158 NW from Horncastle. 5m left at The New Midge pub, farm 1m on right

A beautifully appointed, spacious farmhouse located just one mile from the A158 and within easy reach of many attractions. The stunning grounds, wildlife pond and surrounding countryside ensure a peaceful stay. A warm welcome is certain along with comfortable, fully equipped bedrooms (two doubles and a twin room available) and a hearty Lincolnshire breakfast. There is also a lovely sitting room and complimentary Wi-fi access.

Rooms 3 en suite S £42; D £60-£67* **Facilities** FTV TVL tea/coffee Cen ht Wi-fi **Parking** 12 **Notes** LB ⊗ No Children 10yrs Closed Xmas & New Year 🌾 387 acres arable

HOUGH-ON-THE-HILL — Map 11 SK94

The Brownlow Arms

★★★★★ ⊛ INN

High Rd NG32 2AZ
☎ 01400 250234 📄 01400 271193
e-mail: armsinn@yahoo.co.uk
web: www.thebrownlowarms.com

This beautiful 16th-century property enjoys a peaceful location in the picturesque village, located between Newark and Grantham. Tastefully appointed and spacious public areas have many original features, and include a choice of luxurious lounges and an elegant restaurant offering imaginative cuisine. The bedrooms are stylish, comfortable and particularly well equipped.

Rooms 4 en suite 1 annexe en suite (1 GF) S £65-£70; D £98-£110 **Facilities** FTV tea/coffee Dinner available Direct Dial Wi-fi **Parking** 20 **Notes** ⊗ No Children 12yrs Closed 25-27 Dec & 31 Dec-1 Jan No coaches

LACEBY — Map 17 TA20

Oaklands Hall

[U]

Barton St DN37 7LF
☎ 01472 753101 & 872248 📄 01472 878143
e-mail: info@oaklandshallhotel.co.uk
dir: Signed from Laceby rdbt, junct of A46 & A18

Currently the rating for this establishment is not confirmed. This may be due to a change of ownership or because it has only recently joined the AA rating scheme.

Rooms 45 en suite (10 fmly) (10 GF) S £49-£149; D £59-£169 **Facilities** STV FTV TVL tea/coffee Dinner available Direct Dial Cen ht Licensed Wi-fi Golf 18 **Conf** Max 280 Thtr 200 Class 200 Board 80 **Parking** 150 **Notes** LB Civ Wed 80

LINCOLN   Map 17 SK97

See also Horncastle, Marton & Swinderby

PREMIER COLLECTION

Bailhouse & Mews

★★★★★ GUEST ACCOMMODATION

34 Bailgate LN1 3AP
☎ **01522 541000 & 07966 152329**
📠 **01522 521829**
e-mail: info@bailhouse.co.uk
dir: *100yds W of cathedral*

This renovated 18th-century building in the cathedral quarter offers high levels of modern comfort. One room has an exposed cruck beam of a surviving 14th-century hall. Breakfast is served in the adjacent tea room. A private car park surrounds an old chapel. Customer care is of the highest standard.

Rooms 10 rms (8 en suite) (2 pri facs) (1 fmly) (3 GF) S £59-£175; D £79-£175 (room only)* **Facilities** TVL tea/coffee Direct Dial Cen ht Licensed Wi-fi 🌂 **Parking** 15 **Notes** LB ⊗

PREMIER COLLECTION

Minster Lodge

★★★★★ GUEST ACCOMMODATION

3 Church Ln LN2 1QJ
☎ **01522 513220** 📠 **01522 513220**
e-mail: info@minsterlodge.co.uk
dir: *400yds N of cathedral*

A charming house in a convenient location close to the cathedral and castle. Spacious bedrooms are enhanced by newly refurbished bathrooms and are full of thoughtful extras. A large comfortable sitting room with deep sofas, and an attractive dining room where Aga-cooked breakfasts can be enjoyed, ensure guests have a memorable stay.

Rooms 6 en suite (3 fmly) **Facilities** FTV TVL tea/coffee Direct Dial Cen ht Wi-fi **Parking** 11

See advert on this page

Carholme Guest House

★★★★ GUEST HOUSE

175 Carholme Rd LN1 1RU
☎ **01522 531059 & 07795 964706**
e-mail: root@carholmeguesthouse.com
dir: *From A1 take A57. From A46 take A57, 0.5m on left after racecourse*

Situated a short walk from Lincoln Marina and the University, this small family-run guest house provides well appointed accommodation that is attractively decorated and well maintained, equipped with many useful extras; a ground floor bedroom is available. A freshly cooked breakfast is served in a pleasant dining area and guests have use of a comfortable ground floor lounge.

Rooms 5 rms (4 en suite) (1 pri facs) (1 fmly) (1 GF) S £32-£45; D £55-£85* **Facilities** FTV tea/coffee Cen ht **Parking** 3 **Notes** ⊗ Closed 23 Dec-2 Jan

Carline

★★★★ GUEST HOUSE

1-3 Carline Rd LN1 1HL
☎ **01522 530422** 📠 **01522 530422**
e-mail: sales@carlineguesthouse.co.uk
dir: *Left off A1102, A15 N. Premises 1m from A46 bypass & A57 into city*

This smart double-fronted Edwardian house is within easy walking distance of the castle and the cathedral. Bedrooms are particularly smartly appointed and have a host of useful extras. Breakfast is served at individual tables in the spacious dining room.

Rooms 9 en suite (1 fmly) (3 GF) S £40; D £60 **Facilities** tea/coffee Cen ht Wi-fi **Parking** 6 **Notes** LB ⊗ No Children 3yrs Closed Xmas & New Year 🍽

LINCOLN *continued*

Eagles Guest House

★★★★ GUEST ACCOMMODATION

552A Newark Rd, North Hykeham LN6 9NG
☎ 01522 686346
e-mail: eaglesguesthouse@yahoo.co.uk
dir: *A46 onto A1434, signed Lincoln south, North Hykeham, South Hykeham, 0.5m on right opp Cornflower Way*

This large, modern detached house is situated within easy access of the A46 and the historic city of Lincoln. The smartly appointed, thoughtfully equipped bedrooms are bright and fresh in appearance. A substantial breakfast is served in the pleasant dining room and free Wi-fi is available throughout the property.

Rooms 5 en suite (1 fmly) (1 GF) S £37-£42; D £50-£65* **Facilities** FTV tea/coffee Cen ht Wi-fi **Parking** 6 **Notes** ⊗ No Children 9yrs

The Loudor

★★★★ GUEST ACCOMMODATION

37 Newark Rd, North Hykeham LN6 8RB
☎ 01522 680333 📠 01522 802770
e-mail: info@loudorhotel.co.uk
dir: *3m from city centre. A46 onto A1434 for 2m, on left opp shopping centre*

Opposite the Forum shopping centre and a short walk from the sports centre, this friendly house offers well-equipped bedrooms. Breakfast is served at individual tables in the spacious dining room. There is ample parking.

Rooms 9 en suite 2 annexe rms (1 fmly) (2 GF) S £38; D £55* **Facilities** tea/coffee Cen ht Wi-fi **Parking** 8 **Notes** ⊗

The Old Bakery

★★★★ ⍟⍟ RESTAURANT WITH ROOMS

26/28 Burton Rd LN1 3LB
☎ 01522 576057
e-mail: enquiries@theold-bakery.co.uk
dir: *Exit A46 at Lincoln North follow signs for cathedral. 3rd exit at 1st rdbt, 1st exit at next rdbt*

Situated close to the castle at the top of the town, this converted bakery offers well-equipped bedrooms and a delightful dining operation. The cooking is international

and uses much local produce. Expect good friendly service from the dedicated staff.

Rooms 4 rms (2 en suite) (2 pri facs) (1 fmly) S fr £50; D £55-£65 (room only) **Facilities** FTV tea/coffee Dinner available Cen ht Wi-fi **Notes** ⊗

St Clements Lodge

★★★★ GUEST ACCOMMODATION

21 Langworth Gate LN2 4AD
☎ 01522 521532 & 07906 184266 📠 01522 521532
e-mail: enquiries@stclementslodge.co.uk
dir: *350yds E of cathedral, down Eastgate onto Langworth Gate*

A warm welcome awaits at St Clements Lodge, which is just a short walk from Lincoln Cathedral and Castle. This constantly improving accommodation offers three very comfortable bedrooms, two of which are en suite. Off-road parking is available.

Rooms 3 rms (2 en suite) (1 pri facs) (1 fmly) S fr £50; D fr £68* **Facilities** FTV tea/coffee Cen ht Wi-fi **Parking** 3 **Notes** ⊗ 🐾

South Park Guest House

★★★★ GUEST HOUSE

11 South Park LN5 8EN
☎ 01522 887136 📠 01522 887136
e-mail: enquiry@southparkguesthouse.co.uk
dir: *1m S of city centre on A15*

A Victorian house situated on the inner ring road facing South Park. The staff are friendly and attentive, and bedrooms, though compact, are well equipped. Breakfast is served in a modern dining room overlooking the park.

Rooms 6 en suite 1 annexe en suite (2 fmly) (1 GF) S £30-£40; D fr £50* **Facilities** FTV tea/coffee Dinner available Cen ht Wi-fi **Parking** 7 **Notes** LB ⊗

Stables B&B

★★★★ BED AND BREAKFAST

32 Saxon St LN1 3HQ
☎ 01522 851750
e-mail: info@stableslincoln.co.uk
dir: *A46/A15 to Cathedral, right onto Rasen Ln, 2nd right on Saxon St, then Saint Nicholas St*

A converted Victorian stable in a quiet location with courtyard parking. Near the Cathedral Quarter and restaurants, it makes an ideal choice for relaxing breaks and business visits to Lincoln. Stables offers modern comfortable bedrooms with Wi-fi. Breakfasts, using local produce, are freshly prepared to order.

Rooms 3 en suite (1 GF) S £45-£110; D £65-£110* **Facilities** FTV tea/coffee Cen ht Wi-fi **Parking** 3 **Notes** ⊗ No Children 12yrs

The Tennyson

★★★★ GUEST HOUSE

7 South Park LN5 8EN
☎ 01522 521624
e-mail: enquiries@thetennyson.com
web: www.thetennyson.com
dir: *S of city centre on A15, near South Park Common*

This smart house is just one mile from the city centre, situated on the ring road overlooking South Park. Bedrooms are attractively appointed and have a host of thoughtful extras. There is a modern lounge and a smart dining room where impressive breakfasts are served.

Rooms 8 en suite (2 GF) S £45-£50; D £60 **Facilities** FTV tea/coffee Cen ht Wi-fi **Parking** 8 **Notes** LB ⊗ Closed 24-31 Dec

Newport Guest House

★★★ GUEST HOUSE

26-28 Newport Rd LN1 3DF
☎ 01522 528590 📠 01522 542868
e-mail: info@newportguesthouse.com
web: www.newportguesthouse.com
dir: *600mtrs N of cathedral*

Situated in the quieter upper part of the city and just a few minutes' walk from the cathedral, this double-fronted terrace house offers well-equipped and comfortable bedrooms with broadband access. The pleasing public areas include a very comfortable sitting room and a bright and attractive breakfast room.

Rooms 9 en suite (2 GF) **Facilities** FTV TVL tea/coffee Cen ht Wi-fi **Parking** 4

Save on B&Bs and Hotels. Book at theAA.com/hotel

LINCOLNSHIRE 199 ENGLAND

LOUTH	Map 17 TF38

The Manse B&B

★★★ BED AND BREAKFAST

Middlesykes Ln, Grimoldby LN11 8TE
☎ 01507 327495
e-mail: knowles578@btinternet.com
dir: *Grimoldby 4m from Louth on B1200 onto Tinkle St, turn right onto Middlesykes Ln*

Located in a quiet country lane, this pleasantly appointed house offers comfortable accommodation and a warm welcome. Proprietors are enthusiastic and helpful, making every effort to make guests feel welcomed to their home; freshly cooked evening meals are available by prior arrangement. An ideal location for exploring the delights of the Wolds.

Rooms 4 rms (3 en suite) (1 pri facs) (1 fmly) (1 GF) S £45; D £55-£65* **Facilities** TVL tea/coffee Dinner available Cen ht Wi-fi **Parking** 5 **Notes** LB ⊗ No Children 5yrs Closed 25 Dec ⊜

MABLETHORPE	Map 17 TF58

Park View Guest House

★★★ GUEST HOUSE

48 Gibraltar Rd LN12 2AT
☎ 01507 477267 & 07906 847841 ▤ 01507 477267
e-mail: malcolm@pvgh.freeserve.co.uk
dir: *Take A1104, at beach turn right onto Gibraltar Rd*

This well-established guest house is ideally situated just beside Mablethorpe's golden beach and the Queens Park, and also within easy walking distance of the main town centre amenities. Service is both helpful and friendly, provided by the resident proprietors, Debbie and Malcolm. The accommodation is soundly presented and of varying sizes, the ground-floor bedrooms proving particularly popular.

Rooms 5 rms (2 en suite) (1 fmly) (3 GF) S £25-£27.50; D £50-£55* **Facilities** FTV TVL tea/coffee Dinner available Cen ht Licensed Wi-fi **Parking** 6 **Notes** LB ⊜

MARKET RASEN	Map 17 TF18

PREMIER COLLECTION

The Advocate Arms

★★★★★ ⊜ RESTAURANT WITH ROOMS

2 Queen St LN8 3EH
☎ 01673 842364
e-mail: info@advocatearms.co.uk
dir: *In town centre*

Appointed to a high standard this 18th-century property is located in the heart of Market Rasen and combines historic character and contemporary design. The operation centres around the stylish restaurant where service is friendly yet professional and the food is a highlight. The attractive bedrooms are very well equipped and feature luxury bathrooms.

Rooms 10 en suite (2 fmly) D £50-£90 (room only)* **Facilities** FTV tea/coffee Dinner available Cen ht Wi-fi Golf 18 **Conf** Max 22 Thtr 18 Class 22 Board 18 **Parking** 6 **Notes** ⊗

Wold View House B&B

★★★ ⊜ BED AND BREAKFAST

Bully Hill Top, Tealby LN8 6JA
☎ 01673 838226 & 07976 563473
e-mail: enquiries@woldviewhouse.co.uk
dir: *A46 onto B1225 towards Horncastle, after 7m Wold View House at x-rds*

Situated at the top of Bully Hill with expansive views across The Wold, this smart teashop with bed and breakfast offers modern bedrooms and warm hospitality. Ideal for walking, riding, or touring the charming nearby villages and coastline, the house is also only a short drive from Lincoln.

Rooms 3 rms (2 en suite) (1 pri facs) (1 fmly) S £35-£40; D £60-£65* **Facilities** TVL tea/coffee Cen ht Licensed Wi-fi **Parking** 15 **Notes** LB ⊜

MARTON (VILLAGE)	Map 17 SK88

Black Swan Guest House

★★★★ GUEST ACCOMMODATION

21 High St DN21 5AH
☎ 01427 718878
e-mail: info@blackswanguesthouse.co.uk
web: www.blackswanguesthouse.co.uk
dir: *On A156 in village centre at junct A1500*

Centrally located in the village, this 18th-century former coaching inn retains many original features, and offers good hospitality and homely bedrooms with modern facilities. Tasty breakfasts are served in the cosy dining room and a comfortable lounge with Wi-fi access is available. Transport to nearby pubs and restaurants can be provided.

Rooms 6 en suite 4 annexe en suite (3 fmly) (4 GF) S £45-£50; D £68* **Facilities** FTV TVL tea/coffee Cen ht Licensed Wi-fi **Parking** 10 **Notes** LB

SKEGNESS	Map 17 TF56

Sunnyside B&B

★★★ GUEST ACCOMMODATION

34 Scarborough Av PE25 2TA
☎ 01754 765119 & 07990 534757
e-mail: form@skegness-accommodation.co.uk
dir: *From A52 or A158 follow signs for seafront. Scarborough Av opposite pier, Sunnyside on left before church*

Sunnyside B&B is ideally situated in a quiet avenue, close to Skegness Pier and the northern promenade. The bedrooms are pleasantly decorated and have a good range of useful facilities such as fridges, Freeview TV and DVD players. Breakfast is served at individual tables in the breakfast room and guests also have the use of a conservatory.

Rooms 8 en suite (2 fmly) (1 GF) D £50-£55* **Facilities** FTV TVL tea/coffee Cen ht Wi-fi **Parking** 4 **Notes** LB ⊗ Closed 20-28 Dec

SKILLINGTON — Map 11 SK82

The Cross Swords Inn

★★★ INN

The Square NG33 5HB
☎ 01476 861132
e-mail: harold@thecross-swordsinn.co.uk
dir: Between Grantham & Stamford, W off A1 at
Colsterworth junct

Located at the crossroads at the centre of the award-
winning village of Skillington, and very popular with the
local community, this traditional inn offers three modern,
well-equipped bedrooms that are housed in an attractive
cottage at the top of the courtyard, and named in keeping
with the history of the village. All are very comfortable
and coupled with smart modern bathrooms. The inn
provides imaginative food and a range of real ales in a
rustic period atmosphere.

Rooms 3 annexe en suite (3 GF) **Facilities** FTV tea/coffee
Dinner available Cen ht Gliding club **Parking** 12 **Notes** ⊗
No Children 10yrs RS Sun eve & Mon lunch bar and
restaurant closed

STAMFORD — Map 11 TF00

PREMIER COLLECTION

Meadow View

★★★★★ BED AND BREAKFAST

Wothorpe Rd PE9 2JR
☎ 01780 762133 & 07833 972577
dir: Off A1 signed Stamford, follow road past entrance
to Burley House, bottom of hill, left at lights. Follow
road round, 1st house on left

A stylish property situated just a short walk from the
town centre and Burghley House. The tastefully
appointed bedrooms are contemporary in style with
lovely co-ordinated soft furnishings and many
thoughtful touches. Breakfast is served at a large
communal table in the open-plan kitchen/dining room,
and guests have the use of a smartly appointed lounge.

Rooms 3 en suite S £45-£55; D £65-£80*
Facilities FTV TVL tea/coffee Cen ht **Parking** 2
Notes LB ⊗ ⊗

PREMIER COLLECTION

Rock Lodge

★★★★★ GUEST ACCOMMODATION

1 Empingham Rd PE9 2RH
☎ 01780 481758 📠 01780 481757
e-mail: rocklodge@innpro.co.uk
dir: Off A1 at A606 signed Oakham, into Stamford,
Rock Lodge 1.25m on left

Philip and Jane Sagar have considerable experience in
managing luxury hotels and offer a warm welcome to
their imposing 1900 house near the town centre. The
attractive bedrooms are individually furnished and
have a good range of facilities. Character public rooms
include the oak-panelled drawing room with mullion
windows. Breakfast is served in a sunny room
overlooking the gardens.

Rooms 6 en suite (1 fmly) (2 GF) S £82-£85; D
£92-£115* **Facilities** STV FTV TVL tea/coffee Cen ht
Wi-fi **Parking** 7 **Notes** ⊗

The Bull & Swan at Burghley

★★★★ ⊛ INN

St Martins PE9 2LJ
☎ 01780 766412 📠 01780 767061
e-mail: enquiries@thebullandswan.co.uk
dir: A1 onto Old Great North Rd, left onto B1081, follow
signs for Stamford

This delightful inn dates back to the 16th century when it
is said to have been a gentleman's drinking club. The
public rooms include a large bar with full height tables
and a range of ales; there is a separate restaurant. The
stylish bedrooms are extremely well appointed with lovely
co-ordinated soft furnishings and a range of thoughtful
touches.

Rooms 7 en suite (2 fmly) S £80-£90; D £90-£100*
Facilities FTV tea/coffee Dinner available Direct Dial
Cen ht Wi-fi **Parking** 7 **Notes** LB No coaches

Candlesticks

★★★ RESTAURANT WITH ROOMS

1 Church Ln PE9 2JU
☎ 01780 764033 📠 01780 756071
e-mail: info@candlestickshotel.co.uk
dir: On B1081 High Street St Martins. Church Ln opposite
St Martin Church

A 17th-century property situated in a quiet lane in the
oldest part of Stamford, Candlesticks is just a short walk
from the centre of town. The bedrooms are pleasantly
decorated and equipped with a good range of useful
extras. Public rooms feature Candlesticks restaurant, a
small lounge and a cosy bar.

Rooms 8 en suite **Facilities** STV FTV tea/coffee Dinner
available Direct Dial Cen ht **Parking** 8 **Notes** LB ⊗ RS
Mon No restaurant or bar service No coaches

SUTTON ON SEA — Map 17 TF58

Athelstone Lodge

★★★ GUEST ACCOMMODATION

25 Trusthorpe Rd LN12 2LR
☎ 01507 441521
e-mail: athelstone@googlemail.com
dir: On A52, N of village

Situated between Mablethorpe and Skegness and close to
the promenade, Athelstone Lodge has pleasant, soundly
maintained bedrooms equipped with many useful extras.
Breakfast is served in the dining room and a bar and a
lounge are also available. A variety of enjoyable home-
cooked dinners is served.

Rooms 6 rms (5 en suite) (1 fmly) S £30-£32; D
£60-£64* **Facilities** FTV TVL tea/coffee Dinner available
Cen ht Licensed **Parking** 6 **Notes** LB Closed Nov-Feb

SWINDERBY — Map 17 SK86

Halfway Farm Motel

★★★ GUEST ACCOMMODATION

Newark Road (A46) LN6 9HN
☎ 01522 868749 📠 01522 868082
e-mail: halfwayfarmmotel@hotmail.com
web: www.halfway-farm-motel.co.uk
dir: On A46 opp Swinderby rbt

This 300-year-old farmhouse is set back from the A46,
midway between Lincoln and Newark. Spacious bedrooms
are traditional in the main house, while motel-style rooms
are located around a courtyard to the rear. There is a
bright, airy dining room and comfortable lounge. A good
base for touring or antique hunting.

Rooms 6 rms (5 en suite) 10 annexe en suite (1 fmly) (13
GF) **Facilities** tea/coffee Direct Dial Cen ht **Conf** Max 30
Parking 25 **Notes** ⊗

TIMBERLAND — Map 17 TF15

The Penny Farthing

★★★★ ⊜ INN

Station Rd LN4 3SA
☎ 01526 378359 📠 01526 378915
e-mail: pennyfarthing@talktalkbusiness.net
dir: Junct of B1191 & B1189, signed 1m to Timberland

A warm welcome awaits at this charming inn situated in
the heart of a delightful Lincolnshire village. Public areas
include a large open plan lounge/bar/dining area as well
as an additional restaurant to the front of the property.
The bedrooms are tastefully decorated and thoughtfully
equipped with a good range of useful facilities.

Rooms 7 en suite (1 fmly) **Facilities** FTV tea/coffee Dinner
available Cen ht Wi-fi **Parking** 12

WHAPLODE   Map 12 TF32

Westgate House & Barn

★★★★ BED AND BREAKFAST

Little Ln PE12 6RU
☎ 01406 370546
e-mail: enquiries@westgatehousebandb.co.uk
web: www.westgatehousebandb.co.uk
dir: *Follow brown signs in Whaplode (on A151)*

Set in a peaceful rural location, in well-established
cottage gardens and grounds, Westgate House offers
comfortably appointed accommodation in a delightful
barn conversion. Breakfast is taken in the main house, in
a charming room with wood-burning stove and garden
views. The freshly cooked breakfast includes good locally
sourced ingredients and home-made preserves.

Rooms 2 annexe en suite **Facilities** tea/coffee Cen ht
Parking 2 **Notes** LB ⊗ No Children 6yrs 🐾

WINTERINGHAM   Map 17 SE92

PREMIER COLLECTION

Winteringham Fields

★★★★★ ⊚⊚ ☗ RESTAURANT WITH ROOMS

DN15 9ND
☎ 01724 733096 📄 01724 733898
e-mail: reception@winteringhamfields.co.uk
dir: *In village centre at x-rds*

This highly regarded restaurant with rooms, located
deep in the countryside in Winteringham village, is six
miles west of the Humber Bridge. Public rooms and
bedrooms, some of which are housed in renovated
barns and cottages, are delightfully cosseting. AA 2
Rosette award-winning food is served in the
restaurant.

Rooms 4 en suite 7 annexe en suite (2 fmly) (3 GF) S
£140-£180; D £165-£220* **Facilities** tea/coffee Dinner
available Direct Dial Cen ht **Conf** Max 50 Thtr 50 Class
50 Board 50 **Parking** 14 **Notes** LB Closed 25 Dec for 2
wks, last wk Oct, 2 wks Aug No coaches Civ Wed 60

WOODHALL SPA   Map 17 TF16

The Claremont Guest House

★★★ GUEST HOUSE

9/11 Witham Rd LN10 6RW
☎ 01526 352000
e-mail: claremontgh@live.co.uk
web: www.theclaremontguesthouse.co.uk
dir: *In town centre on B1191 near mini-rdbt*

A Victorian townhouse with a lovely dining room, guest
lounge and Wi-fi access. Having benefited from recent
refurbishment by the friendly new owners, bedrooms are
well equipped and vary in size from cosy singles to family
rooms. The house is pet friendly, with lock up facilities for
cyclists and golfers also available.

Rooms 11 rms (6 en suite) (5 pri facs) (3 fmly) (2 GF)
Facilities FTV TVL tea/coffee Cen ht Wi-fi **Parking** 4

LONDON

N8

White Lodge   PLAN 2 F5

★★★ GUEST ACCOMMODATION

1 Church Ln, Hornsey N8 7BU
☎ 020 8348 9765 📄 020 8340 7851
e-mail: info@whitelodgehornsey.co.uk
web: www.whitelodgehornsey.co.uk
dir: *A406 to Bounds Green, Hornsey High Rd & Church Ln*

This well-maintained, friendly guest accommodation is in
a convenient location close to shops and restaurants.
Bedrooms are traditionally appointed and airy public
areas include an attractive lounge and spacious dining
room where continental breakfast is served.

Rooms 16 rms (8 en suite) (5 fmly) (1 GF) S £46-£52; D
£58-£75* **Facilities** FTV TVL tea/coffee Cen ht Wi-fi
Notes ⊗

N12   Map 6 TQ29

Glenlyn Guest House

★★★ GUEST ACCOMMODATION

6 Woodside Park Rd N12 8RP
☎ 020 8445 0440 📄 020 8446 2902
e-mail: contactus@glenlynhotel.com
web: www.glenlynhotel.com
dir: *M25 junct 23 towards High Barnet, A1000 into North
Finchley on right after Sainsburys*

Located in the heart of Finchley and set in four large
Victorian terraced houses, the Glenlyn offers a choice of
rooms spanning from cosy loft rooms to interconnecting
family rooms. Guests can relax in the private bar or
unwind in the garden. Breakfast is served in the airy
conservatory.

Rooms 27 en suite (4 fmly) (3 GF) S £65; D £75*
Facilities FTV TVL tea/coffee Direct Dial Cen ht Licensed
Wi-fi **Parking** 14 **Notes** ⊗

NW1

PREMIER COLLECTION

York & Albany PLAN 2 E4

★★★★★ ⊛⊛⊛ 🏛 RESTAURANT WITH ROOMS

127-129 Parkway NW1 7PS
☎ **020 7387 5700** 📠 **020 7255 9250**
e-mail: yandareception@gordonramsay.com
dir: *Overlooking Regent's Park*

Overlooking Regent's Park, the York & Albany has been stylishly appointed to retain many original features and with guest comfort in mind. The property showcases a restaurant, bar, Nonna's delicatessen and meeting space in addition to the very well appointed bedrooms and suites. AA 3 Rosette award-winning cuisine is served in the restaurant and uses ingredients from some of the best suppliers. Picnics for alfresco eating in the park can be ordered from Nonna's.

Rooms 10 en suite D £155-£575 (room only)*
Facilities STV FTV Dinner available Direct Dial Cen ht Lift Wi-fi **Conf** Max 40 Thtr 40 Board 30 **Notes** ⊗ No coaches Civ Wed 40

Superior Guest Accommodation PLAN 1 C5

★★★★ 🍽 GUEST ACCOMMODATION

81-103 Euston St NW1 2EZ
☎ **020 7380 0001** 📠 **020 7387 5300**
e-mail: sales@micentre.com
web: www.micentre.com
dir: *Euston Rd left at lights onto Melton St, 1st left onto Euston St, 100yds on left*

Located within walking distance of Euston station, this smart property is convenient for central London. Stylish air-conditioned bedrooms are thoughtfully equipped for business and leisure. The airy Atrium Bar and Restaurant offers drinks, light snacks and an evening menu. Extensive conference and meeting facilities are available.

Rooms 28 en suite (2 fmly) S £139; D £149*
Facilities STV TVL tea/coffee Dinner available Direct Dial Cen ht Lift Licensed Wi-fi **Conf** Max 150 Thtr 150 Class 50 Board 45 **Parking** 2 **Notes** LB ⊗ Civ Wed

---

Euston Square PLAN 1 C5

★★★ GUEST ACCOMMODATION

152-156 North Gower St NW1 2LU
☎ **020 7388 0099** 📠 **020 7788 9699**
e-mail: reservations@euston-square-hotel.com
web: www.euston-square-hotel.com
dir: *On junct Euston Rd, next to Euston Sq tube station*

Over the tube station, this property is ideal for both the business and leisure markets. The smart compact bedrooms and en suite bathrooms are well designed. Small conference facilities and a modern reception area are available. Breakfast and light meals are served in the bar lounge area, FAB.

Rooms 75 en suite (4 GF) **Facilities** STV TVL tea/coffee Dinner available Direct Dial Cen ht Lift Licensed Wi-fi **Conf** Thtr 120 Class 50 Board 50 **Notes** ⊗

NW3

The Langorf PLAN 2 E4

★★★★ GUEST ACCOMMODATION

20 Frognal, Hampstead NW3 6AG
☎ **020 7794 4483** 📠 **020 7435 9055**
e-mail: info@langorfhotel.com
web: www.langorfhotel.com
dir: *Off A41 (Finchley Rd), near Finchley Rd tube station*

Located on a leafy and mainly residential avenue within easy walking distance of shops and restaurants, this elegant Edwardian property has been appointed to provide high standards of comfort and facilities. Bedrooms are furnished with flair and a warm welcome is assured.

Rooms 31 en suite (4 fmly) (3 GF) **Facilities** STV TVL tea/coffee Direct Dial Cen ht Lift Licensed Wi-fi **Conf** Max 30 Thtr 30 Class 20 Board 15 **Parking Notes** ⊗

La Gaffe PLAN 2 E4

★★★ GUEST ACCOMMODATION

107-111 Heath St NW3 6SS
☎ **020 7435 8965 & 7435 4941** 📠 **020 7794 7592**
e-mail: info@lagaffe.co.uk
dir: *On A502, 250yds N of Hampstead tube station*

This family owned and run guest accommodation, just north of Hampstead High Street, offers charm and warm hospitality. The Italian restaurant, which is open most lunchtimes and for dinner, is popular with locals. Bedrooms are compact, but all are en suite.

Rooms 11 en suite 7 annexe en suite (2 fmly) (2 GF) S £75-£105; D £99-£129* **Facilities** FTV tea/coffee Dinner available Direct Dial Cen ht Licensed Wi-fi **Conf** Max 10 Board 10 **Notes** ⊗ RS 26 Dec Restaurant closed

NW8

The New Inn PLAN 2 E4

★★★ INN

2 Allitsen Rd, St Johns Wood NW8 6LA
☎ **020 7722 0726** 📠 **020 7722 0653**
e-mail: thenewinn@gmail.com
web: www.newinnlondon.co.uk
dir: *Off A41 by St Johns Wood tube station onto Acacia Rd, last right, to end on corner*

Built in 1810, this popular inn is in a leafy suburb only a stroll from Regent's Park. Bedrooms are appointed to a high standard, while Thai cuisine and traditional fare are offered in the atmospheric bar lounge.

Rooms 5 en suite S £85; D £85 (room only)*
Facilities FTV tea/coffee Dinner available Cen ht Wi-fi **Notes** ⊗ No coaches

NW9

Kingsland PLAN 2 C5

★★★ GUEST ACCOMMODATION

Kingsbury Circle, Kingsbury NW9 9RR
☎ **020 8206 0666** 📠 **020 8206 0555**
e-mail: stay@kingslandhotel.co.uk
web: www.kingslandhotel.co.uk
dir: *Kingsbury Circle junct A4006 & A4140*

Located at the roundabout near Kingsbury Station, shops, restaurants and Wembley complex, the Kingsland provides modern bedrooms with smart bathrooms en suite. A continental breakfast is supplied, and a passenger lift and car park are available.

Rooms 28 en suite (5 fmly) (6 GF) S £50–£60; D £65–£75* **Facilities** STV tea/coffee Direct Dial Cen ht Lift Wi-fi **Parking** 30 **Notes** ⊗

SW1

Best Western Corona
PLAN 1 C1

★★★★ GUEST ACCOMMODATION

87–89 Belgrave Rd SW1V 2BQ
☎ 020 7828 9279   📄 020 7931 8576
e-mail: info@coronahotel.co.uk
dir: *From Pimlico St take exit 2 onto Tachbrook St. Make 1st left, 1st right onto Belgrave Rd*

Centrally located, this elegant Victorian property is appointed to a high standard. The smart, well-equipped bedrooms offer comfortable, modern accommodation. A continental breakfast is served in the basement dining room, and room service is also available.

Rooms 51 en suite (8 fmly) (7 GF) **Facilities** STV tea/coffee Direct Dial Lift Wi-fi **Notes** ⊗

Sidney London-Victoria
PLAN 1 C1

★★★★ GUEST ACCOMMODATION

68–76 Belgrave Rd SW1V 2BP
☎ 020 7834 2738   📄 020 7630 0973
e-mail: reservations@sidneyhotel.com
web: www.sidneyhotel.com
dir: *A202 (Vauxhall Bridge Rd) onto Charlwood St & junct with Belgrave Rd*

This smart property near Pimlico offers brightly decorated bedrooms that are well equipped for business use, while several rooms are suitable for families. Public areas include a bar lounge and an airy breakfast room.

Rooms 82 en suite (13 fmly) (9 GF) **Facilities** STV TVL tea/coffee Direct Dial Cen ht Lift Licensed Wi-fi **Conf** Thtr 30 Class 15 Board 14 **Notes** ⊗

See advert on this page

The Windermere
PLAN 1 C1

★★★★ GUEST ACCOMMODATION

142/144 Warwick Way, Victoria SW1V 4JE
☎ 020 7834 5163   📄 020 7630 8831
e-mail: reservations@windermere-hotel.co.uk
web: www.windermere-hotel.co.uk
dir: *On B324 off Buckingham Palace Rd, at junct with Alderney St*

The Windermere is a relaxed, informal and family-run establishment within easy reach of Victoria Station and many of the capital's attractions. Bedrooms, although varying in size, are stylish, comfortable and well equipped. The Pimlico restaurant serves delicious evening meals and hearty cooked breakfasts.

Rooms 19 en suite (3 fmly) (3 GF) S fr £115; D fr £145 **Facilities** FTV TVL tea/coffee Dinner available Direct Dial Cen ht Lift Licensed Wi-fi **Notes** ⊗

SW1 *continued*

Best Western Victoria Palace PLAN 1 C1

★★★ GUEST ACCOMMODATION

60-64 Warwick Way SW1V 1SA
☎ 020 7821 7113 ▤ 020 7630 0806
e-mail: info@bestwesternvictoriapalace.co.uk
web: www.bestwesternvictoriapalace.co.uk

An elegant, 19th-century building located in the heart of
London, near to Belgravia and a five minute walk from
Victoria rail, underground and coach stations. The
bedrooms have en suite shower rooms. A buffet-style
breakfast is served in the basement dining room.

Rooms 50 en suite (4 fmly) (4 GF) **Facilities** STV TVL tea/
coffee Direct Dial Cen ht Lift **Notes** ⊗

Central House PLAN 1 C1

★★★ GUEST ACCOMMODATION

39 Belgrave Rd SW1V 2BB
☎ 020 7834 8036 ▤ 020 7834 1854
e-mail: info@centralhousehotel.co.uk
dir: *Near Victoria station*

Located a short walk from Victoria station, the Central
House offers sound accommodation. Bedroom sizes vary,
and each room is suitably appointed, with en suite
compact modular shower rooms. A self-service
continental breakfast is offered in the lower ground-floor
dining room.

Rooms 54 en suite (4 fmly) **Facilities** TVL tea/coffee
Direct Dial Cen ht Lift

Comfort Inn PLAN 1 C1

★★★ GUEST ACCOMMODATION

8-12 St Georges Dr SW1V 4BJ
☎ 020 7834 2988 ▤ 020 7821 5814
e-mail: info@comfortinnbuckinghampalacerd.co.uk
dir: *Off Buckingham Palace Rd onto Elizabeth Bridge &
St Georges Dr*

Located just a short walk south from Victoria station, this
establishment is a good base for visiting the capital's
attractions. All bedrooms and public areas are smartly
appointed and offer very good levels of comfort. An
extensive continental breakfast is served.

Rooms 51 en suite (4 fmly) (7 GF) **Facilities** STV TVL tea/
coffee Direct Dial Cen ht Lift **Conf** Max 20 Thtr 20 Class
20 Board 20 **Notes** ⊗

Comfort Inn Victoria PLAN 1 C1

★★★ GUEST ACCOMMODATION

18-24 Belgrave Rd, Victoria SW1V 1QF
☎ 020 7233 6636 ▤ 020 7932 0538
e-mail: stay@comfortinnvictoria.co.uk

Having a prime location close to Victoria station, this
property offers brightly appointed en suite
accommodation that is thoughtfully equipped for

business and leisure guests. A continental breakfast is
offered in the basement dining room.

Rooms 48 en suite (16 fmly) (9 GF) **Facilities** STV FTV TVL
tea/coffee Direct Dial Cen ht Lift Wi-fi **Notes** ⊗

Victoria Inn PLAN 1 C1

★★★ GUEST HOUSE

65-67 Belgrave Rd, Victoria SW1V 2BG
☎ 020 7834 6721 & 7834 0182 ▤ 020 7931 0201
e-mail: welcome@victoriainn.co.uk
web: www.victoriainn.co.uk
dir: *On A3213, 0.4m SE of Victoria station, near Pimlico
tube station*

A short walk from Victoria station, this Victorian property
offers modern, well-equipped accommodation for
business and leisure guests. There is a comfortable
reception lounge, and a limited self-service buffet
breakfast is available in the basement breakfast room.

Rooms 43 en suite (7 fmly) **Facilities** STV tea/coffee
Direct Dial Cen ht Lift Wi-fi **Notes** ⊗

Winchester PLAN 1 C1

★★★ GUEST ACCOMMODATION

17 Belgrave Rd SW1V 1RB
☎ 020 7828 2972 ▤ 020 7828 5191
e-mail: info@winchester-hotel.net
web: www.winchester-hotel.net
dir: *On A3213, 300yds SE of Victoria station*

Conveniently located close to Victoria this welcoming,
well maintained house provides an ideal base for tourists.
Bedrooms vary in size and style but all are well equipped,
decorated in bright colours and boast comfortable
modern beds. Freshly cooked breakfasts are served in the
traditionally styled dining room. Staff are friendly and
keen to please.

Rooms 19 en suite (2 fmly) (2 GF) **Facilities** STV tea/
coffee Direct Dial Cen ht **Notes** ⊗ No Children 5yrs

Stanley House PLAN 1 C1

★★ Ⓐ BED AND BREAKFAST

19-21 Belgrave Rd, Victoria SW1V 1RB
☎ 020 7834 5042 & 7834 7292 ▤ 020 7834 8439
e-mail: cmahotel@aol.com
web: www.londonbudgethotels.co.uk
dir: *Near Victoria station*

Rooms 44 rms (41 en suite) (7 fmly) (8 GF) **Facilities** FTV
TVL Direct Dial Cen ht Wi-fi **Notes** LB ⊗ No Children 5yrs

PREMIER COLLECTION

San Domenico House PLAN 1 B1

★★★★★ GUEST ACCOMMODATION

29-31 Draycott Place SW3 2SH
☎ 020 7581 5757 ▤ 020 7584 1348
e-mail: info@sandomenicohouse.com

This stunning property in the heart of Chelsea offers
beautiful, individually styled bedrooms, all with
antique and period pieces, and well appointed en
suites complete with Italian Spa toiletries. A
sumptuous drawing room with wonderful works of art is
available for guests to relax in or maybe to enjoy
afternoon tea. Breakfast is served either in guests'
bedrooms or in the lower ground floor elegant dining
room. Staff are friendly and attentive.

Rooms 13 en suite (9 smoking) **Facilities** STV Direct
Dial Cen ht Lift Licensed **Notes** ⊗

Best Western The Boltons PLAN 2 E3

★★★★ GUEST ACCOMMODATION

19-21 Penywern Rd, Earls Court SW5 9TT
☎ 020 7373 8900 ▤ 020 7244 6835
e-mail: reservations@theboltonshotel.co.uk
dir: *A3220 from Cromwell Rd, follow road past Earls Court
station, 1st right into Penywern Rd. Located on left*

This smart, newly renovated property boasts an excellent
location, just seconds walk from Earls Court tube station
and exhibition centre, and with easy reach of museums
and major shopping areas. Both public areas and
bedrooms have an airy contemporary feel with stylish
furnishings and fittings. En suite bedrooms have comfy
beds, flat-screen satellite TV and Wi-fi. 24-hour room
service and buffet breakfast are available.

Rooms 57 en suite (4 fmly) (4 GF) S £80-£100; D
£130-£150 (room only) **Facilities** STV FTV TVL tea/coffee
Direct Dial Cen ht Lift Wi-fi **Notes** ⊗

Best Western
Shaftesbury Kensington PLAN 2 E3

★★★★ GUEST ACCOMMODATION

33-37 Hogarth Rd, Kensington SW5 0QQ
☎ 020 7370 6831 ▤ 020 7373 6179

Well appointed to a high standard, this property has a
smart modern feel and is conveniently located for the
exhibition centre, the West End and local transport links.
Bedrooms are furnished and decorated to a very high
standard, offering guests a comprehensive range of
modern facilities and amenities.

Rooms 133 en suite (7 GF) **Facilities** STV tea/coffee
Dinner available Direct Dial Cen ht Lift Licensed Wi-fi
Gym Fitness centre **Conf** Max 15 Board 15 **Notes** ⊗

The Mayflower
PLAN 2 E3

★★★★ GUEST ACCOMMODATION

26-28 Trebovir Rd SW5 9NJ
☎ 020 7370 0991 📄 020 7370 0994
e-mail: info@mayflower-group.co.uk
web: www.mayflowerhotel.co.uk
dir: *Left from Earls Court tube station & 1st left into Trebovir Rd, premises on left in 50yds*

This smart guest accommodation is a short walk from Earls Court, and close to Olympia and West London's museums and attractions. Stylish, individually designed bedrooms vary in size but all are extremely well equipped and have smart, modern en suites. There is a comfortable, stylish lounge and an airy dining room where breakfast is served.

Rooms 47 en suite (4 fmly) (5 GF) S £95-£120; D £120-£199* **Facilities** FTV tea/coffee Direct Dial Cen ht Lift Wi-fi **Conf** Max 25 Thtr 25 Class 25 Board 25 **Notes** LB ⊗

See advert on this page

Quality Crown Kensington
PLAN 2 E3

★★★★ GUEST ACCOMMODATION

162 Cromwell Rd, Kensington SW5 0TT
☎ 020 7244 2400 📄 020 7244 2500
e-mail: stay@qualitycrown.com

This delightful property enjoys a prime location adjacent to the famous Cromwell Road Hospital, within easy reach of the V&A Museum and the chic shops of Knightsbridge and South Kensington. Bedrooms are extremely well equipped and along with the comfortable public areas have a stylish, contemporary feel. The popular smart bar is a feature.

Rooms 82 en suite **Facilities** STV TVL tea/coffee Dinner available Direct Dial Cen ht Lift Licensed **Parking** 8 **Notes** ⊗

My Place
PLAN 2 E3

★★★ GUEST ACCOMMODATION

1-3 Trebovir Rd SW5 9LS
☎ 020 7373 0833 📄 020 7373 9998
e-mail: info@myplacehotel.co.uk
dir: *A4 West Cromwell Rd onto Earls Court Rd, 3rd right*

This Victorian house is in a quiet residential street close to Earls Court station with easy access to the West End. The smart bedrooms vary in size and have an extremely good range of modern facilities. Breakfast is served in the dining room overlooking a spacious garden. Free entry to the on-site nightclub is included.

Rooms 49 en suite (6 fmly) S £75-£100; D £95-£135 **Facilities** FTV TVL Direct Dial Cen ht Lift Licensed Wi-fi Night Club **Conf** Max 100 Thtr 100 Class 100 Board 20 **Notes** LB ⊗

SW7

Ashburn
PLAN 1 A2

★★★★ GUEST ACCOMMODATION

111 Cromwell Rd SW7 4DP
☎ 020 7244 1999 📄 020 7244 1998
e-mail: reservations@ashburn-hotel.co.uk
dir: *On Cromwell Rd, close to junct with Gloucester Rd*

This stunning establishment benefits from a great location in a peaceful Kensington side street which is less than a five minute walk from Gloucester Road tube station. All areas including the guest lounge, bar, dining room and accommodation have been stylishly renovated to a very high standard with guest comfort a priority. Light hot and cold snacks are available during the day and evening. A continental or full English breakfast is served in the attractive dining room located on the lower ground floor.

Rooms 38 en suite (3 GF) (3 smoking) S £149-£209; D £159-£215* **Facilities** STV FTV TVL tea/coffee Dinner available Direct Dial Cen ht Lift Wi-fi **Notes** ⊗

Best Western The Cromwell
PLAN 1 A2

★★★★ GUEST ACCOMMODATION

110-112 Cromwell Rd, Kensington SW7 4ES
☎ 020 7244 1720 📄 020 7373 3706
e-mail: reception@thecromwell.com
dir: *M4/A4 towards London, pass Cromwell Hospital, 0.5m*

Just minutes away from the tube station and within easy access of all main tourist attractions, this property offers comfortable, modern accommodation. Fully air-conditioned and with free Wi-fi, this is an ideal location for both leisure and business guests. Amenities include an on-site meeting room, and secure parking is available nearby.

Rooms 85 en suite (4 fmly) (11 GF) **Facilities** STV tea/coffee Direct Dial Lift Wi-fi Fitness room **Notes** ⊗

SW7 continued

The Gainsborough
PLAN 1 A2

★★★★ GUEST ACCOMMODATION

7-11 Queensberry Place, South Kensington SW7 2DL
☎ 020 7957 0000 📄 020 7970 1805
e-mail: reservations@eeh.co.uk
web: www.eeh.co.uk
dir: Off A4 Cromwell Rd opp Natural History Museum, near South Kensington tube station

This smart Georgian house is in a quiet street near South Kensington's museums. Bedrooms are individually designed with fine fabrics, quality furnishings and co-ordinated colours. A choice of breakfasts is offered in the attractive dining room. There is also a delightful lobby lounge, and 24-hour room service is available.

Rooms 48 en suite (5 fmly) Facilities STV tea/coffee Dinner available Direct Dial Cen ht Lift Licensed Wi-fi Conf Max 40 Class 40 Board 30 Notes ⊗

The Gallery
PLAN 1 A2

★★★★ GUEST ACCOMMODATION

8-10 Queensberry Place, South Kensington SW7 2EA
☎ 020 7915 0000 📄 020 7970 1805
e-mail: reservations@eeh.co.uk
web: www.eeh.co.uk
dir: Off A4 Cromwell Rd opp Natural History Museum, near South Kensington tube station

This stylish property, close to Kensington and Knightsbridge, offers friendly hospitality, attentive service and sumptuously furnished bedrooms, some with a private terrace. Public areas include a choice of lounges (one with internet access) and an elegant bar. There is an option of English or continental breakfast, and 24-hour room service is available.

Rooms 36 en suite Facilities STV tea/coffee Dinner available Direct Dial Cen ht Lift Licensed Wi-fi Conf Max 40 Thtr 40 Board 30 Notes ⊗

W1

The Sumner
PLAN 1 B4

★★★★ GUEST ACCOMMODATION

54 Upper Berkeley St, Marble Arch W1H 7QR
☎ 020 7723 2244 📄 020 7705 8767
e-mail: hotel@thesumner.com

Centrally located just five minutes' walk from Marble Arch, The Sumner is part of a Georgian terrace. Refurbished throughout to a very high standard, this delightful property combines much of the original character of the building with modern comfort. Air-conditioned rooms have all been designer decorated and feature widescreen LCD TVs, free broadband, as well as a range of traditional amenities. The breakfast buffet is included in the rate and there is also an elegant lounge for guests to relax in.

Rooms 20 en suite Facilities FTV Direct Dial Cen ht Lift Licensed Wi-fi Notes ⊗ No Children 5yrs

Best Western Premier Shaftesbury
PLAN 1 D3

★★★★ GUEST ACCOMMODATION

65-73 Shaftesbury Av W1D 6EX
☎ 020 7871 6000
e-mail: reservations@shaftesburyhotel.co.uk
dir: From Piccadilly Circus 300yds up Shaftesbury Av, at junct with Dean St

In the centre of the West End, this boutique property offers plenty of warm, traditional hospitality. The Shaftesbury is next to two major underground stations, with comfortably sized public areas, a refreshment lounge, the Premier Bar, restaurants, conference facilities, and a fitness room.

Rooms 67 en suite (2 fmly) Facilities STV tea/coffee Direct Dial Lift Licensed Gym Conf Max 12 Board 12 Notes ⊗

Hart House
PLAN 1 B4

★★★★ GUEST ACCOMMODATION

51 Gloucester Place, Portman Sq W1U 8JF
☎ 020 7935 2288 📄 020 7935 8516
e-mail: reservations@harthouse.co.uk
web: www.harthouse.co.uk
dir: Off Oxford St behind Selfridges, near Baker St & Marble Arch tube stations

This elegant Georgian house is only a short walk from Oxford Street, Selfridges and Madame Tussaud's. Bedrooms and public areas are smartly furnished, stylishly decorated and have been carefully restored to retain much of the house's original character. English breakfast is served in the stylish dining room.

Rooms 15 en suite (4 fmly) (4 GF) S £95-£110; D £135-£165 Facilities FTV tea/coffee Direct Dial Cen ht Wi-fi Notes ⊗

See advert on this page

The St George
PLAN 1 B4

★★★★ GUEST ACCOMMODATION

49 Gloucester Place W1U 8JE
☎ 020 7486 8586   📠 020 7486 6567
e-mail: reservations@stgeorge-hotel.net
dir: Off Marylebone Rd, between Marble Arch & Baker St tube stations

This attractive, Grade II listed house is in the heart of the West End near Oxford Street. Bedrooms are furnished to a high standard and offer many facilities such as modem points, safes, hairdryers and mini-fridges. There is a smart breakfast room and the friendly staff offer a very warm welcome.

Rooms 19 en suite (3 fmly) (3 GF) **Facilities** STV FTV TVL tea/coffee Direct Dial Cen ht Wi-fi **Conf** Max 20 Thtr 15 Class 20 Board 20 **Notes** ⊗

The Regency
PLAN 1 B4

★★★ GUEST ACCOMMODATION

19 Nottingham Place W1U 5LQ
☎ 020 7486 5347   📠 020 7224 6057
e-mail: enquiries@regencyhotelwestend.co.uk
web: www.regencyhotelwestend.co.uk
dir: A501 Marylebone Rd S onto Baker St, left onto Paddington St, left onto Nottingham Place

The Regency, a converted mansion, is close to Baker Street tube station, Madame Tussaud's, the West End shops and Harley Street. Bedrooms are well equipped and some rooms are suitable for families. Breakfast is served in the brightly appointed basement breakfast room. Free Wi-fi is available.

Rooms 20 en suite (2 fmly) (5 smoking) **Facilities** STV TVL tea/coffee Dinner available Direct Dial Cen ht Lift Wi-fi **Notes** LB ⊗

W2

AA GUEST ACCOMMODATION OF THE YEAR, LONDON

Park Grand Paddington
PLAN 1 A4

★★★★ GUEST ACCOMMODATION

1-2 Queens Gardens, Paddington W2 3BA
☎ 020 7298 9800   📠 020 7262 5414
e-mail: info@parkgrandlondon.co.uk
dir: Exit Paddington station via Praed St, turn right. After 3 sets of lights right onto Devonshire Terrace, 100mtrs to Park Grand

Enjoying a central location moments walk from Paddington Station and Hyde Park not to mention the main shopping districts and attractions. Rooms vary in size and are completed to a very high standard. A number of stylish suites are also available. The Atlantic bar serves a range of light snacks throughout the day and evening. Additional facilities include state of the art technology with free internet access, satellite TV and fridges. Park Grand Paddington is the AA Guest Accommodation of the Year for London (2011-2012).

Rooms 157 en suite (11 fmly) (23 GF) **Facilities** FTV TVL tea/coffee Dinner available Direct Dial Cen ht Lift Licensed Wi-fi Fitness room **Notes** ⊗

Best Western Mornington
PLAN 1 A3

★★★★ GUEST ACCOMMODATION

12 Lancaster Gate W2 3LG
☎ 020 7262 7361   📠 020 7706 1028
e-mail: london@mornington.co.uk
dir: N of Hyde Park, off A402 Bayswater Rd

This fine Victorian building is located in a quiet road, close to Lancaster Gate station for easy access to the West End. The bedrooms have been appointed to provide comfortable, stylish accommodation. There is a lounge/bar and an attractive dining room where an extensive Scandinavian-style breakfast is served.

Rooms 66 en suite (9 fmly) (2 GF) (20 smoking) **Facilities** STV tea/coffee Direct Dial Cen ht Lift Licensed Wi-fi **Conf** Max 14 Thtr 14 Class 14 Board 14

Best Western Shaftesbury Paddington Court London
PLAN 1 A4

★★★★ GUEST ACCOMMODATION

27 Devonshire Ter W2 3DP
☎ 020 7745 1200   📠 020 7745 1221
e-mail: info@paddingtoncourt.com
web: www.paddingtoncourt.com
dir: From A40 take exit before Paddington flyover, follow Paddington Station signs. Devonshire Ter is off Craven Rd

This establishment benefits from its convenient location close to Paddington mainline train station including links to the underground and the Heathrow Express terminal. Situated next to Hyde Park and Kensington Palace Gardens, this establishment offers smart and comfortable guest accommodation and a guaranteed substantial breakfast. Club Rooms are also available with additional extras including the exclusive use of the Club Lounge. A room is available for small meetings by prior arrangement.

Rooms 165 en suite 35 annexe en suite (43 fmly) **Facilities** STV TVL tea/coffee Direct Dial Lift Licensed

Commodore
PLAN 1 A3

★★★★ GUEST ACCOMMODATION

50 Lancaster Gate, Hyde Park W2 3NA
☎ 020 7402 5291   📠 020 7262 1088
e-mail: reservations@commodore-hotel.com

Located in a quiet area of Bayswater, close to Hyde Park and the buzzy shopping area of Oxford Street, is the recently redecorated Commodore. This attractive establishment was originally three townhouses, and facilities include a stylish dining area where evening meals and substantial breakfasts are served daily. 24-hour room service and day-time refreshments are available in the ornate, high ceilinged lounge area.

Rooms 83 en suite (1 fmly) (8 GF) (8 smoking) S £110-£155; D £130-£250 **Facilities** STV tea/coffee Dinner available Direct Dial Cen ht Lift Licensed Wi-fi Gym **Notes** ⊗

W2 *continued*

Grand Royale London Hyde Park
PLAN 2 E3

★★★★ GUEST ACCOMMODATION

1 Inverness Ter W2 3JP
☎ 020 7313 7900 ▤ 020 7221 1169
e-mail: info@shaftesburyhotels.com
dir: *On A40 Bayswater Rd*

Located adjacent to Hyde Park, fashionable Notting Hill and within easy reach of the West End, the Grand Royale combines its rich heritage with the needs of the modern traveller. The accommodation is contemporary in style and very well equipped. Breakfast is served in the staterooms.

Rooms 188 en suite (2 GF) S £159-£350; D £179-£395 (room only)* **Facilities** tea/coffee Direct Dial Cen ht Lift Licensed Wi-fi **Conf** Max 20 Thtr 20 Class 20 Board 20 **Notes** ✛

Hyde Park Radnor
PLAN 1 A4

★★★★ GUEST ACCOMMODATION

7-9 Sussex Place, Hyde Park W2 2SX
☎ 020 7723 5969 ▤ 020 7262 8955
e-mail: hydeparkradnor@btconnect.com
web: www.hydeparkradnor.com
dir: *Off A402 Bayswater Rd onto Lancaster Ter & Sussex Gardens, right onto Sussex Place*

This smart property is within walking distance of Paddington station and close to all London's central attractions. The smart bedrooms are brightly appointed, well equipped and have modern en suites. English breakfast is served in the lower ground-floor dining room.

Rooms 36 en suite (10 fmly) (5 GF) **Facilities** STV TVL tea/coffee Direct Dial Cen ht Lift **Parking** 2 **Notes** ✛

The New Linden
PLAN 2 E3

★★★★ GUEST ACCOMMODATION

59 Leinster Square, Notting Hill W2 4PS
☎ 020 7221 4321 ▤ 020 7727 3156
e-mail: newlindenhotel@mayflower-group.co.uk
dir: *Off A402, Bayswater Rd*

The friendly New Linden has a good location north of Kensington Gardens. Its stylish en suite bedrooms are richly furnished and thoughtfully equipped with CD players and safes. A good continental breakfast is served in the basement dining room.

Rooms 50 en suite S £89-£120; D £120-£250* **Facilities** STV FTV TVL tea/coffee Direct Dial Cen ht Lift Wi-fi **Notes** ✛

See advert on this page

Quality Crown Hyde Park
PLAN 1 A4

★★★★ GUEST ACCOMMODATION

8-14 Talbot Square W2 1TS
☎ 020 7262 6699 ▤ 020 7723 3233
e-mail: res.hydepark@lth-hotels.com
dir: *SE of Paddington station off Sussex Gardens*

This well-presented property is convenient for Hyde Park, Paddington and Marble Arch. The modern bedrooms are furnished to a good standard and the executive rooms are particularly impressive. Public areas include a compact but stylish bar and lounge, and a basement restaurant where hearty breakfasts are served.

Rooms 75 en suite (8 fmly) (8 GF) **Facilities** FTV TVL tea/coffee Direct Dial Cen ht Lift Licensed Wi-fi **Notes** ✛

Quality Crown Paddington
PLAN 1 A4

★★★★ GUEST ACCOMMODATION

144 Praed St, Paddington W2 1HU
☎ 020 7706 8888 ▤ 020 7706 8800
e-mail: stay@qualitycrown.com

This contemporary, stylish property enjoys a central location, adjacent to Paddington Station. Bedrooms and en suites vary in size but all are extremely smartly appointed and boast a host of extra facilities including CD players, flat-screen TVs, room safes and internet access. A small gym, stylish lounge and meeting rooms are also available.

Rooms 83 en suite **Facilities** STV TVL tea/coffee Dinner available Direct Dial Cen ht Lift Licensed **Conf** Max 22 Board 22 **Notes** ✛

Shaftesbury Hyde Park International　　PLAN 2 E3

★★★★ GUEST ACCOMMODATION

52-55 Inverness Ter W2 3LB
☎ **020 7985 8300** 🖷 **020 7792 0157**
e-mail: info@shaftesburyhotels.com
dir: On A40 Bayswater road

This smart, modern establishment is located near to Bayswater, Queensway and Paddington underground stations and it is within walking distance of a myriad of dining options. Bedrooms and bathrooms are decorated to a very high standard with a good range of in-room facilities including flat screen televisions, irons and ironing boards and complimentary internet or Wi-fi access. Continental and cooked buffet breakfasts are served daily. There is a limited number of off-road parking spaces.

Rooms 70 en suite (2 GF) S £159-£350; D £179-£395 (room only)* **Facilities** STV TVL tea/coffee Direct Dial Cen ht Lift Licensed Wi-fi Gym **Parking** 3 **Notes** ⊗

Shaftesbury Metropolis London Hyde Park　　PLAN 1 A4

★★★★ GUEST ACCOMMODATION

78-84 Sussex Gardens, Hyde Park W2 1UH
☎ **020 7723 7723** 🖷 **020 7402 6318**

This establishment is in an ideal location close to Paddington station with express links to Heathrow Airport. Smartly decorated bedrooms with highly comfortable beds are available in a range of bedroom sizes, all with stylish en suite provision. On-site facilities include complimentary internet or Wi-fi, and continental and full English breakfasts are served every day. Reception is staffed 24 hours a day.

Rooms 90 en suite (14 GF) **Facilities** STV FTV TVL tea/coffee Direct Dial Cen ht Lift Licensed Wi-fi small fitness centre **Notes** ⊗

The Shaftesbury Premier London Hyde Park　　PLAN 1 A4

★★★★ GUEST ACCOMMODATION

78-82 Westbourne Ter, Paddington W2 6QA
☎ **020 7262 4521** 🖷 **020 7262 7610**
e-mail: reservations@londonpremierhotels.co.uk
dir: Off A40 onto Lancaster Ter, at crossing left onto slip road

This attractive property enjoys a central location within easy reach of central London shops and attractions. The en suite bedrooms and public areas have a smart contemporary feel. Although rooms vary in size, all boast many useful facilities such as free internet access, mini-fridges and irons.

Rooms 119 en suite (2 GF) S £118.80-£350; D £154.80-£395 (room only)* **Facilities** STV tea/coffee Direct Dial Lift Licensed Wi-fi **Parking** 12 **Notes** ⊗

Shaftesbury Premier London Notting Hill　　PLAN 2 E3

★★★★ GUEST ACCOMMODATION

5-7 Princes Square, Bayswater W2 4NP
☎ **020 7792 1414** 🖷 **020 7792 0099**

This smart establishment offers friendly, professional service and comfortable rooms. Situated conveniently for many attractions yet peacefully located in a quiet, leafy square, the property has stylish public rooms and offers free Wi-fi as well as hard-wire connectivity in the extremely well equipped bedrooms. Breakfast is served in the dining room and offers a good choice of freshly cooked traditional breakfast and continental items.

Rooms 68 en suite (2 GF) **Facilities** STV TVL tea/coffee Direct Dial Cen ht Lift Wi-fi Gym

Shaftesbury Premier Paddington　　PLAN 1 A4

★★★★ GUEST ACCOMMODATION

55-61 Westbourne Ter W2 6QA
☎ **020 7723 3434** 🖷 **020 7402 0433**
dir: Off A40 onto Lancaster Ter

This smart property enjoys a convenient location within walking distance of Hyde Park and of many of London's major shops and attractions. Bedrooms are smartly appointed and boast modern technology. A hearty breakfast is served in the airy dining room. Limited off-street parking (chargeable) is a bonus. The staff are friendly and attentive.

Rooms 118 en suite (2 GF) S £118.80-£350; D £154.80-£395* **Facilities** STV tea/coffee Dinner available Direct Dial Cen ht Lift Licensed Wi-fi **Notes** ⊗

Admiral　　PLAN 1 A4

★★★ GUEST ACCOMMODATION

143 Sussex Gardens, Hyde Park W2 2RY
☎ **020 7723 7309** 🖷 **020 7723 8731**
e-mail: enquiries@admiral-hotel.com

The Admiral is a short walk from Paddington station and is convenient for Hyde Park and the West End. The smart bedrooms are enhanced with attractive artworks, and a full English breakfast is provided.

Rooms 21 en suite (12 fmly) (1 GF) **Facilities** STV FTV TVL tea/coffee Dinner available Direct Dial Cen ht Licensed Wi-fi **Conf** Max 30 Class 25 Board 25 **Parking** 3 **Notes** ⊗

Comfort Inn　　PLAN 1 A3

★★★ GUEST ACCOMMODATION

73 Queensborough Ter, Bayswater W2 3SU
☎ **020 7229 6424** 🖷 **020 7221 4772**
e-mail: info@comforthydepark.com
dir: Off Bayswater Rd near Queensway tube station

A short walk from Kensington Gardens and fashionable Queensway, this property has been converted to provide practically equipped bedrooms, with bright and well appointed bathrooms. Breakfast is served in the basement dining room.

Rooms 29 en suite (1 fmly) (3 GF) **Facilities** STV FTV tea/coffee Direct Dial Cen ht Lift **Notes** ⊗

Kingsway Park Guest Accommodation　　PLAN 1 A4

★★★ GUEST ACCOMMODATION

139 Sussex Gardens W2 2RX
☎ **020 7723 5677** & 7724 9346 🖷 **020 7402 4352**
e-mail: info@kingswaypark-hotel.com
web: www.kingswaypark-hotel.com

This Victorian property has a central location within walking distance of Marble Arch, Hyde Park and Paddington. Bedrooms offer well-equipped value accommodation. Public areas include a reception lounge and a basement breakfast room adorned with interesting artwork. A limited number of parking spaces is available.

Rooms 22 en suite (5 fmly) (2 GF) **Facilities** STV FTV TVL tea/coffee Direct Dial Cen ht Licensed **Conf** Max 30 **Parking** 3 **Notes** ⊗

Parkwood at Marble Arch　　PLAN 1 B4

★★★ GUEST ACCOMMODATION

4 Stanhope Place, Marble Arch W2 2HB
☎ **020 7402 2241** 🖷 **020 7402 1574**
e-mail: reception@parkwoodhotel.com
web: www.parkwoodhotel.com
dir: Near Marble Arch tube station

Located in a quiet residential street next to Marble Arch and Oxford Street, the friendly Parkwood provides a central base for budget-conscious shoppers and tourists. Family rooms are available, and a freshly cooked breakfast is served in the attractive basement dining room.

Rooms 16 rms (12 en suite) (1 fmly) (2 GF) **Facilities** STV FTV TVL tea/coffee Direct Dial Cen ht Wi-fi **Notes** ⊗

W2 continued

Princes Square
PLAN 2 E3

★★★ GUEST ACCOMMODATION

23-25 Princes Square, off Ilchester Gardens, Bayswater
W2 4NJ
☎ 020 7229 9876 📠 020 7229 4664
e-mail: info@princessquarehotel.co.uk
dir: From Bayswater 1st left onto Moscow Rd, then 3rd
right into Ilchester Gardens

This fine building is in a quiet road close to tube stations
for easy access to the West End. The comfortable
bedrooms provide stylish accommodation, and there is a
small bar and an attractive dining room where a
continental breakfast is served.

Rooms 50 en suite (3 fmly) (6 GF) **Facilities** STV tea/
coffee Direct Dial Cen ht Lift Wi-fi **Notes** ⊗

Soroptimist Residential Club
PLAN 1 A3

★★★ GUEST ACCOMMODATION

63 Bayswater Rd W2 3PH
☎ 020 7723 8575 📠 020 7723 1061
e-mail: info@soropclub63.org.uk

This friendly establishment offers a surprisingly tranquil
environment located less than one minute's walk from
Lancaster Gate Underground and situated directly
opposite Hyde Park. All bedrooms are comfortable with en
suite facilities and comprise of a range of singles and
twins; there is also a room which can accommodate three
guests. Hot snacks are available throughout the
afternoon and evening by prior arrangement and a good
continental breakfast is served in the mornings. A room is
available for meetings and private functions. Parking
arrangements can be made.

Rooms 16 en suite (1 fmly) S fr £69; D fr £115*
Facilities TVL tea/coffee Dinner available Cen ht Lift
Licensed Wi-fi **Conf** Max 40 Class 40 Board 20 **Notes** ⊗
Closed 21-31 Dec

Barry House
PLAN 1 A4

★★★ 🅰 BED AND BREAKFAST

12 Sussex Place, Hyde Park W2 2TP
☎ 020 7723 7340 📠 020 7723 9775
e-mail: hotel@barryhouse.co.uk
web: www.barryhouse.co.uk
dir: 300yds SE of Paddington station
Rooms 18 rms (16 en suite) (5 fmly) (2 GF) S £45-£75; D
£75-£120 **Facilities** FTV tea/coffee Direct Dial Cen ht
Wi-fi **Notes** ⊗

W7

Hanwell Bed and Breakfast
PLAN 2 B4

★★ BED AND BREAKFAST

110A Grove Av, Hanwell W7 3ES
☎ 020 8567 5015 & 020 8840 8555
e-mail: tassanimation@aol.com
web:
www.ealing-hanwell-bed-and-breakfast.co.uk/new/about.html
dir: 1.5m from Greenford Rd

Hanwell occupies a convenient and peaceful location
close to regular bus routes, Ealing Hospital and Ealing
golf course. An array of restaurants offering menus to
suit all palates is available within minutes. The
accommodation is comfortable and the top floor en suite
bedroom is available for longer term stays (minimum
seven nights). Breakfast provides an excellent start to the
day.

Rooms 2 rms (1 en suite) (1 pri facs) (1 fmly) **Facilities**
tea/coffee Dinner available Cen ht Wi-fi **Parking** 2
Notes LB ⊗ Closed 25 Dec 🍽

W8

Seraphine
PLAN 2 E3

★★★★ GUEST ACCOMMODATION

7-11 Kensington High St W8 5NP
☎ 020 7368 2222 & 7938 5911 📠 020 7368 2221
e-mail: info@seraphinehotel.co.uk
dir: B325 Gloucester Road, continue for 0.5m, left at
A315 Kensington Road

This smart property enjoys a prime location opposite
Kensington Palace and is ideally positioned for Hyde Park,
The Royal Albert Hall, shops and museums. Bedrooms
vary in size but all are well equipped with interactive flat-
screen TV, iPod docking, laptop safes and free Wi-fi. En
suites are modern with powerful showers. An extensive
continental breakfast is included.

Rooms 22 en suite S £90-£399; D £120-£499*
Facilities STV FTV TVL tea/coffee Direct Dial Cen ht Lift
Licensed Wi-fi **Notes** ⊗

Seraphine Kensington Olympia
PLAN 2 E3

★★★★ GUEST ACCOMMODATION

225 Kensington High St W8 6SA
☎ 020 7938 5911 📠 020 7938 5912
e-mail: olympia@seraphinehotel.co.uk

This chic and intimate property enjoys a prime location in
the heart of High Street Kensington, and is ideally
positioned for Holland Park, local attractions, shops and
museums. Bedrooms vary in size but all are well equipped
with interactive flat-screen TV, iPod docking, laptop safes
and free Wi-fi. En suites are modern with powerful
showers. An extensive continental breakfast is included
and full cooked breakfasts upon request.

Rooms 17 en suite S £90-£499; D £120-£699
Facilities FTV TVL tea/coffee Direct Dial Cen ht Lift
Licensed Wi-fi **Notes** ⊗

W14

Avonmore
PLAN 2 D3

★★★ GUEST ACCOMMODATION

66 Avonmore Rd W14 8RS
☎ 020 7603 4296 & 7603 3121 ▤ 056 0153 5230
e-mail: reservations@avonmorehotel.co.uk
web: www.avonmorehotel.co.uk
dir: Off Hammersmith Rd opp Olympia Exhibition Centre

Avonmore occupies a convenient location only a few
minutes' walk from Kensington Olympia and is one stop
on the District Line underground from Earls Court. The
accommodation provided is comfortable and bedrooms
are equipped with mini bars and fans; Wi-fi is available
throughout the establishment. The team at Avonmore are
friendly and guest focused.

Rooms 9 rms (7 en suite) (2 pri facs) (3 fmly) (2 GF)
Facilities TVL tea/coffee Direct Dial Cen ht Licensed Wi-fi
Notes ⊗

WC1

Euro
PLAN 1 D5

★★★ GUEST ACCOMMODATION

51-53 Cartwright Gardens, Russell Square WC1H 9EL
☎ 020 7387 4321 ▤ 020 7383 5044
e-mail: reception@eurohotel.co.uk
dir: Off Euston Rd onto Judd St, right onto Leigh St &
Cartwright Gardens. Near Euston tube station

This friendly guest accommodation is in a leafy Georgian
crescent only a short walk from Russell Square tube
station with its direct link to Heathrow, as well as Euston.
Bedrooms are well equipped and most have en suite
bathrooms. Breakfast is served at individual tables in the
attractive dining room.

Rooms 31 rms (25 en suite) (6 pri facs) (9 fmly) (4 GF)
Facilities STV FTV tea/coffee Direct Dial Cen ht Wi-fi ⌣
Notes ⊗

The George
PLAN 1 D5

★★★ GUEST ACCOMMODATION

58-60 Cartwright Gardens WC1H 9EL
☎ 020 7387 8777 ▤ 020 7387 8666
e-mail: ghotel@aol.com
web: www.georgehotel.com
dir: From St Pancras 2nd left onto Marchmont St & 1st
left onto Cartwright Gardens

The George is within walking distance of Russell Square
and the tube, and convenient for London's central
attractions. The brightly appointed bedrooms vary in size,
many have en suites, and some rooms are suitable for
families. A substantial breakfast is served in the
attractive ground-floor dining room.

Rooms 40 rms (14 en suite) (14 fmly) (4 GF)
Facilities STV TVL tea/coffee Direct Dial Cen ht Wi-fi ⌣
Free Internet access Notes ⊗

The Jesmond Dene
PLAN 1 D5

★★★ GUEST ACCOMMODATION

27 Argyle St, Kings Cross WC1H 8EP
☎ 020 7837 4654 ▤ 020 7833 1633
e-mail: info@jesmonddenehotel.co.uk
web: www.jesmonddenehotel.co.uk

Less than five minutes' walk from the main line and
underground station of Kings Cross is The Jesmond Dene.
Accommodation comprises comfortable bedrooms, some
of which benefit from their own en suite facilities; some
bathroom facilities are shared. Warm service and
hospitality is provided along with a well cooked breakfast
served in the bright dining room.

Rooms 22 rms (11 en suite) (4 fmly) (5 GF) Facilities STV
FTV tea/coffee Cen ht Wi-fi Parking 6 Notes ⊗

GREATER LONDON

BARNET
Map 6 TQ29

Savoro Restaurant with Rooms

★★★ ◉ RESTAURANT WITH ROOMS

206 High St EN5 5SZ
☎ 020 8449 9888 ▤ 020 8449 7444
e-mail: savoro@savoro.co.uk
web: www.savoro.co.uk
dir: M25 junct 23, A1000. In crescent behind Hadley
Green Jaguar Garage

Set back from the main high street, the traditional
frontage of this establishment belies the stylishly modern
bedrooms and well designed bathrooms within. The
award-winning restaurant is an additional bonus.

Rooms 11 rms (9 en suite) (2 pri facs) (2 fmly) (3 GF) S
£45-£85; D £75-£125* Facilities FTV tea/coffee Dinner
available Cen ht Wi-fi Parking 9 Notes LB ⊗ No coaches

CRANFORD

See London Plan 2 A3 For accommodation details see
Heathrow Airport

CROYDON
Map 6 TQ36

Kirkdale

★★★ GUEST ACCOMMODATION

22 St Peters Rd CR0 1HD
☎ 020 8688 5898 ▤ 020 8680 6001
e-mail: reservations@kirkdalehotel.co.uk
dir: A23 onto A232 W & A212 Lower Coombe St, 500yds
right

Close to the town centre, this Victorian property retains
many original features. Public areas include a small
lounge bar and an attractive breakfast room, and the
bedrooms have good facilities. There is a sheltered patio
for the summer.

Rooms 16 en suite (5 GF) Facilities TVL tea/coffee Direct
Dial Cen ht Licensed Wi-fi Parking 12 Notes ⊗

FELTHAM

See London Plan 2 A2 For accommodation details see
Heathrow Airport

HARROW ON THE HILL

See London Plan 2 B5

Old Etonian

★★★ GUEST ACCOMMODATION

36-38 High St HA1 3LL
☎ 020 8423 3854 & 8422 8482 ▤ 020 8423 1225
e-mail: info@oldetonian.com
web: www.oldetonian.com
dir: In town centre. On B458 opp Harrow School

In the heart of this historic part of London and opposite
the prestigious school, this friendly guest accommodation
is a delight. Recently redecorated bedrooms are
attractive, well appointed and comfortable. A continental
breakfast is served in the dining room, which in the
evening is home to a lively restaurant. On-road parking
available.

Rooms 9 en suite (1 GF) S £69.50-£82; D £77.50-£87.50*
Facilities FTV TVL tea/coffee Dinner available Direct Dial
Cen ht Licensed **Conf** Max 30 Thtr 20 Class 20 Board 20
Parking 3 Notes ⊗

HEATHROW AIRPORT

See London plan 2 A2

The Cottage

★★★★ GUEST ACCOMMODATION

150-152 High St TW5 9WB
☎ 020 8897 1815
e-mail: info@the-cottage.eu
dir: *M4 junct 3, A312 towards Feltham, left at lights, left after 1st pub on left*

This beautiful property is a peacefully situated oasis, family run within five minutes of Heathrow Airport. It offers comfortable and spacious accommodation, decorated tastefully in the main house and six new bedrooms located at the rear of the garden, connected to the main building by a covered walkway overlooking the stunning courtyard.

Rooms 14 en suite 6 annexe en suite (4 fmly) (12 GF) **Facilities** tea/coffee Cen ht Wi-fi **Parking** 20 **Notes** ⊗ Closed 24-26 Dec & 31 Dec-1 Jan

Crompton Guest House

★★★★ GUEST HOUSE

49 Lampton Rd TW3 1JG
☎ 020 8570 7090 🖨 020 8577 1975
e-mail: cromptonguesthouse@btinternet.com
dir: *M4 junct 3, follow signs for Hounslow. Turn onto Bath Rd (A3005), left at Yates pub. 200yds on right just before bridge*

Located just a moment's walk away from Hounslow underground station this accommodation is popular with both business and leisure travellers. Bedrooms and bathrooms are comfortable and well equipped with good facilities. Breakfast is served in the intimate dining room where a freshly prepared breakfast is served. Ample off-street parking is an additional plus.

Rooms 11 en suite (5 fmly) (2 GF) **Facilities** STV FTV tea/coffee Dinner available Direct Dial Cen ht Wi-fi **Parking** 12 **Notes** LB ⊗

HOUNSLOW

See London Plan 2 B2 For accommodation details see under Heathrow Airport

ILFORD

See London Plan 2 H5

Best Western Ilford

★★★★ GUEST ACCOMMODATION

3-5 Argyle Rd IG1 3BH
☎ 020 8911 6083 🖨 020 8554 4726
e-mail: manager@expresslodging.co.uk

This newly refurbished establishment is conveniently located for easy access to the Olympic Village and central London. The accommodation is very comfortable and offers a range of amenities such as free internet and a new, state-of-the-art Media Hub. 24-hour room service and parking is also provided.

Rooms 34 en suite (15 GF) **Facilities** FTV tea/coffee Direct Dial Wi-fi **Parking** 12 **Notes** ⊗

KINGSTON UPON THAMES

See London Plan 2 C1

Chase Lodge House

★★★ GUEST ACCOMMODATION

10 Park Rd, Hampton Wick KT1 4AS
☎ 020 8943 1862 🖨 020 8943 9363
e-mail: info@chaselodgehotel.com
web: www.chaselodgehotel.com
dir: *A308 onto A310 signed Twickenham, 1st left onto Park Rd*

This independent establishment is set in a quiet residential area, a short walk from Kingston town centre, Bushey Park and the River Thames. The individually decorated rooms vary in size and are all well-appointed and feature a range of useful extras. An attractive lounge-bar-restaurant is provided where breakfast, snacks and dinner by pre-arrangement are served. Children and dogs are most welcome, and on-road parking is available.

Rooms 13 en suite (2 smoking) **Facilities** FTV Direct Dial Wi-fi ch fac **Conf** Max 65 Thtr 50 Class 65 Board 30 **Notes** LB

NEW MALDEN

See London Plan 2 D1

J J Lodge

★★ GUEST ACCOMMODATION

22-24 Somerset Close KT3 5RF
☎ 020 8336 0082
e-mail: jjlodge99@googlemail.com

Situated close to the A3/Malden Way, JJ Lodge caters mainly to Korean guests. The owner is Korean, so fluent Korean can be expected.

Rooms 12 en suite

RICHMOND (UPON THAMES)

See London Plan 2 C2

Hobart Hall

★★★ GUEST ACCOMMODATION

43-47 Petersham Rd TW10 6UL
☎ 020 8940 0435   📠 020 8332 2996
e-mail: hobarthall@aol.com
dir: 200yds S of Richmond Bridge on A307

Built around 1690, this impressive yet friendly establishment stands beside the River Thames close to Richmond Bridge. Many of the spacious bedrooms have river views and a good range of modern facilities. There is a comfortable lounge, an attractive breakfast room, and a meeting room that overlooks the river.

Rooms 33 rms (18 en suite) (5 fmly) (3 GF) S £50-£75; D £90-£105* Facilities TVL tea/coffee Direct Dial Cen ht Wi-fi Parking 14 Notes ⊗ RS 25-26 Dec & 1 Jan

MERSEYSIDE

BROMBOROUGH   Map 15 SJ38

The Dibbinsdale

★★★★ INN

Dibbinsdale Rd CH63 0HQ
☎ 0151 334 9818
e-mail: info@thedibbinsdale.co.uk
dir: M53 junct 4 towards Bebbington. Right at 1st lights, after 1.8m on this road

Located in a peaceful residential area, a few minutes' walk from shops and transport links, this popular inn has been sympathetically renovated to offer high standards of comfort and facilities. Bedrooms are equipped for both business and leisure guests and spacious public areas are a perfect setting for freshly prepared food, a wide selection of real ales and live entertainment is provided on a regular basis.

Rooms 11 en suite (1 fmly) S £55-£90; D £65-£120* Facilities FTV tea/coffee Dinner available Cen ht Wi-fi Parking 20 Notes LB

LIVERPOOL   Map 15 SJ39

Roscoe House

★★★★ GUEST ACCOMMODATION

27 Rodney St L1 9EH
☎ 0151 708 0532   📠 0151 203 3076
e-mail: stay@a2zrooms.com
dir: On corner of Rodney St & Hardman St in city centre

This fine Georgian house was once the home of the writer William Roscoe and enjoys a very convenient location close to Liverpool city centre and all the major attractions. Roscoe House has been sympathetically restored and offers stylish modern accommodation, while still retaining lots of period features. A delicious continental breakfast is served to guests in their rooms and free Wi-fi is available to residents.

Rooms 15 en suite (5 fmly) (4 GF) Facilities FTV tea/coffee Cen ht Wi-fi Golf 18 Conf Max 20 Thtr 20 Class 15 Board 15 Notes Closed 24-26 Dec

SOUTHPORT   Map 15 SD31

Bay Tree House B&B

★★★★ 🏠 GUEST ACCOMMODATION

No1 Irving St, Marine Gate PR9 0HD
☎ 01704 510555   📠 0870 753 6318
e-mail: baytreehouseuk@aol.com
web: www.baytreehousesouthport.co.uk
dir: Off Leicester St

A warm welcome is assured at this immaculately maintained house, located a short walk from the promenade and central attractions. Bedrooms are equipped with a wealth of thoughtful extras, and delicious imaginative breakfasts are served in an attractive dining room overlooking the pretty front patio garden.

Rooms 6 en suite Facilities FTV tea/coffee Dinner available Direct Dial Cen ht Licensed Wi-fi Parking 2 Notes Closed 14 Dec-1 Feb

The Baytrees

★★★★ GUEST ACCOMMODATION

4 Queens Rd PR9 9HN
☎ 01704 536513   📠 01704 536513
e-mail: baytreeshotel@hotmail.co.uk
web: www.baytreeshotel.co.uk
dir: From B565 (Lord St) towards fire station, right at rdbt onto Manchester Rd, left at lights, 200yds on right

Located a short walk from Lord Street, this elegant late Victorian house has been well appointed to provide thoughtfully furnished bedrooms with smart modern en suite bathrooms. Breakfast is served in the attractive dining room overlooking the pretty rear garden, and a lounge is also available.

Rooms 12 en suite (5 fmly) (2 GF) S £29.50-£35; D £39.50-£72* Facilities FTV TVL tea/coffee Cen ht Parking 11 Notes ⊗ Closed Xmas

Bowden Lodge

★★★★ GUEST ACCOMMODATION

18 Albert Rd PR9 0LE
☎ 01704 543531   📠 01704 539112
e-mail: stay@bowdenlodge.co.uk
web: www.bowdenlodge.co.uk
dir: A565 N from town centre, over rdbt, 150yds on right

This stylish house is in a quiet residential area just a stroll from Lord Street and the town's attractions. Bedrooms, many suitable for families, are smartly furnished and well equipped. Day rooms include a lounge with deep sofas, and a bright dining room where hearty cooked breakfasts are served. Value for money and a friendly welcome are assured. Ideal venue for walkers and cyclists.

Rooms 10 en suite (3 fmly) S £35-£60; D £65-£100* Facilities FTV TVL tea/coffee Dinner available Cen ht Licensed Wi-fi Parking 10 Notes LB ⊗

Rosedale

★★★★ GUEST ACCOMMODATION

11 Talbot St PR8 1HP
☎ 01704 530604   📠 01704 530604
e-mail: info@rosedale-hotel.co.uk
dir: A570 into Southport, left onto Talbot St

The smart and friendly Rosedale stands in a quiet street only a short walk from the town's attractions. The bright bedrooms are thoughtfully equipped, and there is a comfortable lounge, a cosy bar and a lovely garden.

Rooms 9 rms (8 en suite) (1 pri facs) (2 fmly) Facilities TVL tea/coffee Dinner available Cen ht Licensed Parking 6 Notes ⊗ Closed 21 Dec-3 Jan

Lyndhurst

★★ GUEST HOUSE

101 King St PR8 1LQ
☎ 01704 537520   & 07759 526864   📠 01704 537520
dir: Off A570 Eastbank St at McDonalds onto King St

This well maintained friendly guest house is situated just a short walk from Lord Street and the town's main attractions. It offers brightly decorated, comfortable accommodation. Public areas include a cosy lounge that leads onto the breakfast room.

Rooms 6 rms S £22; D £44* Facilities FTV TVL tea/coffee Cen ht Parking 2 Notes LB No Children 12yrs Closed Xmas & New Year 🐾

NORFOLK

ALBURGH
Map 13 TM28

The Dove Restaurant with Rooms

★★★★ ◎◎ ☖ RESTAURANT WITH ROOMS

Holbrook Hill IP20 0EP
☎ 01986 788315 🖹 01986 788315
e-mail: thedovenorfolk@freeola.com
dir: Between Harleston & Bungay at junct A143 & B1062

A warm welcome awaits at this restaurant with rooms.
Bedrooms are pleasantly decorated, furnished with pine
pieces and have modern facilities. Public rooms include a
lounge area with a small bar, and a smart restaurant
with well-spaced tables.

Rooms 2 rms (1 en suite) (1 pri facs) (1 fmly) S fr £40; D
fr £60* Facilities tea/coffee Dinner available Cen ht
Wi-fi Parking 20 Notes ⊗ No coaches

ATTLEBOROUGH
Map 13 TM09

Rylstone B&B

★★★★ BED AND BREAKFAST

Bell Rd, Rockland St Peter NR17 1UL
☎ 01953 488199 🖹 0844 7744562
e-mail: margaret@hneale.f9.co.uk
dir: 4m W of Attleborough. B1077 to Rockland St Peter, at
x-rds onto Chapel St & Bell Rd

A delightful detached property situated in a peaceful
rural location on the edge of the village. The pleasantly
decorated bedrooms have co-ordinated fabrics and many
thoughtful touches. Public rooms include a large lounge
with a log burner, and a conservatory with views of the
surrounding countryside.

Rooms 3 rms (2 en suite) (1 pri facs) D fr £70*
Facilities FTV tea/coffee Cen ht Wi-fi Parking 3 Notes LB
⊗ 🐾

BARNEY
Map 13 TF93

The Old Brick Kilns

★★★★ BED AND BREAKFAST

Little Barney Ln NR21 0NL
☎ 01328 878305 🖹 01328 878948
e-mail: enquiries@old-brick-kilns.co.uk
web: www.old-brick-kilns.co.uk
dir: Off B1354 to Barney, 0.3m left onto Little Barney Ln,
B&B 0.75m at end

This delightful country house, originally three separate
cottages, provides attractive accommodation in peaceful
grounds. Breakfasts are served at a communal table in
the lounge-dining room. Due to the narrow access road
guests should arrive after 1pm.

Rooms 3 en suite Facilities FTV TVL tea/coffee Cen ht
Licensed Wi-fi Fishing Pool table Parking 20 Notes ⊗ No
Children 16yrs

BLAKENEY
Map 13 TG04

PREMIER COLLECTION

Blakeney House

★★★★★ GUEST HOUSE

High St NR25 7NX
☎ 01263 740561 🖹 01263 741750
e-mail: admin@blakeneyhouse.com
web: www.blakeneyhouse.com
dir: In village centre

A stunning Victorian manor house set amid two acres
of attractive landscaped grounds just a short walk
from the quay and town centre. The stylish, individually
decorated bedrooms have co-ordinated fabrics and
many thoughtful touches. Breakfast is served at
individual tables in the smart dining room, which
overlooks the well-stocked front garden.

Rooms 8 rms (7 en suite) (1 pri facs) (1 fmly)
Facilities tea/coffee Cen ht Wi-fi Golf 18 Parking 8
Notes ⊗ No Children 12yrs

BRISLEY
Map 13 TF92

The Brisley Bell Inn & Restaurant

★★★ INN

The Green NR20 5DW
☎ 01362 668686
e-mail: info@brisleybell-inn.co.uk
web: www.brisleybell-inn.co.uk
dir: Between Fakenham & East Dereham on B1145

Delightful village inn situated in a peaceful location just
a short drive from the town centre. The bedrooms are
generally quite spacious, and each one is smartly
appointed with modern furniture and co-ordinated soft
furnishings. Public rooms include a beamed bar and a
cosy restaurant serving an interesting choice of dishes.

Rooms 3 rms (1 en suite) (1 fmly) S £45-£54; D
£50-£68* Facilities FTV tea/coffee Dinner available
Cen ht Wi-fi Conf Max 40 Thtr 40 Class 36 Board 20
Parking 30 Notes LB ⊗

BROOKE
Map 13 TM29

Old Vicarage

★★★★ BED AND BREAKFAST

48 The Street NR15 1JU
☎ 01508 558329
dir: Off B1332 in village centre near church

Set in mature gardens in a peaceful village, this
charming house is within easy driving distance of
Norwich. The individually decorated bedrooms are
thoughtfully furnished and equipped, and one room has a
lovely four-poster bed. There is an elegant dining room
and a cosy lounge, and dinner is available by
arrangement. Service is genuinely helpful, provided in a
relaxed and friendly manner.

Rooms 2 en suite S £40; D £60* Facilities TVL tea/coffee
Dinner available Cen ht Parking 4 Notes LB ⊗ No
Children 15yrs 🐾

CASTLE ACRE   Map 13 TF81

Ostrich Inn

★★★★ ⇔ INN

Stocks Green PE32 2AE
☎ 01760 755398
e-mail: info@ostrichcastleacre.com
web: www.ostrichcastleacre.com
dir: *0.3m on right of Castle Acre Priory*

This 15th-century inn is situated adjacent to the village green in the centre of Castle Acre. The warm and inviting public areas have a wealth of original features such as exposed brickwork, oak beams and open fires. The spacious bedrooms are in an adjacent building; each room has been sympathetically renovated and has modern facilities.

Rooms 6 en suite (1 fmly) (1 GF) **Facilities** FTV tea/coffee Dinner available Direct Dial Cen ht Wi-fi **Conf** Max 25 Thtr 25 Class 25 Board 25 **Parking** 30 **Notes** LB

CLEY NEXT THE SEA   Map 13 TG04

PREMIER COLLECTION

Old Town Hall House

★★★★★ 🖫 BED AND BREAKFAST

Coast Rd NR25 7RB
☎ 01263 740284
e-mail: louise@oldtownhallhouse.co.uk
web: www.oldtownhallhouse.co.uk
dir: *On A149 in centre of Cley. Opposite old red phone box*

Expect a warm welcome from the caring hosts at this delightful detached property situated in the heart of a bustling North Norfolk village, which has been designated as an Area of Outstanding Natural Beauty, and has a superb bird watching reserve on its outskirts. The tastefully appointed bedrooms have lovely co-ordinated soft fabrics and many thoughtful touches. Breakfast, using locally sourced produce, is served at individual tables in the stylish dining room.

Rooms 3 en suite **Facilities** tea/coffee Cen ht Wi-fi **Notes** ⊗ No Children Closed Xmas & Jan

COLTISHALL   Map 13 TG21

The Hedges

★★★★ GUEST ACCOMMODATION

Tunstead Rd NR12 7AL
☎ 01603 738361   📠 01603 738983
e-mail: info@hedgesbandb.co.uk
web: www.hedgesbandb.co.uk
dir: *Off B1354 onto White Lion Rd & right fork*

A delightful family-run guest accommodation situated close to the Norfolk Broads. The spacious bedrooms have co-ordinated fabrics and many thoughtful touches; most rooms have lovely views of the surrounding countryside. Breakfast is served in the dining room and guests have the use of a smart conservatory which overlooks the garden.

Rooms 5 en suite (2 fmly) (2 GF) **Facilities** TVL tea/coffee Cen ht **Parking** 5 **Notes** ⊗ Closed 23-28 Dec

COLTON   Map 13 TG10

The Ugly Bug Inn

★★★★ INN

High House Farm Ln NR9 5DG
☎ 01603 880794
e-mail: info@uglybuginn.co.uk

This popular inn is located in a peaceful rural location on the edge of the village, close to the A47 that has links to Norwich and the Norfolk coast. Public rooms include a large lounge bar and a smart restaurant. The bedrooms are smartly appointed with modern facilities, and most rooms have views of the countryside.

Rooms 4 en suite (1 GF) S £40-£55; D £60-£75* **Facilities** FTV tea/coffee Dinner available Cen ht Wi-fi Golf 18 **Parking** 40 **Notes** No Children 16yrs

CROMER   Map 13 TG24

See also Sheringham

Shrublands Farm *(TG246393)*

★★★★ FARMHOUSE

Church St, Northrepps NR27 0AA
☎ 01263 579297   📠 01263 579297
Mrs A Youngman
e-mail: youngman@farming.co.uk
web: www.shrublandsfarm.com
dir: *Off A149 to Northrepps, through village, past Foundry Arms, cream house 50yds on left*

Expect a warm welcome from the caring host at this delightful 18th-century farmhouse, set in landscaped grounds and surrounded by 300 acres of arable farmland. Public areas include a cosy lounge with a wood-burning stove, and breakfast is served at a communal table in the elegant dining room.

Rooms 2 rms (1 en suite) (1 pri facs) S £44-£47.50; D £68-£75* **Facilities** FTV TVL tea/coffee Cen ht **Parking** 5 **Notes** LB ⊗ No Children 12yrs 300 acres arable

The White Horse Overstrand

★★★★ ֎֎ INN

34 High St, Overstrand NR27 0AB
☎ 01263 579237
e-mail: reservations@whitehorseoverstrand.co.uk
dir: *From A140, before Cromer, turn right onto Mill Rd. At bottom turn right onto Station Rd. After 2m, bear left onto High St, White Horse on left*

A smartly appointed inn ideally situated in the heart of this popular village on the north Norfolk coastline. The modern bedrooms are tastefully appointed and equipped with a good range of useful extras. Public rooms include a large open-plan lounge bar with comfortable seating and a relaxed dining area.

Rooms 7 en suite (1 fmly) **Facilities** TVL tea/coffee Dinner available Cen ht Wi-fi Pool table **Parking** 6

CROMER *continued*

Beachcomber Guest House

★★★★ GUEST HOUSE

17 Macdonald Rd NR27 9AP
☎ **01263 513398**
e-mail: info@beachcomber-guesthouse.co.uk
dir: *Off A149 Runton Rd, 500yds W of pier*

A smartly maintained Edwardian house situated in a
peaceful side road close to the seafront and town centre.
The pleasant bedrooms are carefully furnished and
equipped with many thoughtful touches. Breakfast is
served in the smart dining room and there is a
comfortable lounge with sofas.

Rooms 5 en suite (1 fmly) S £45-£50; D £60-£64*
Facilities TVL tea/coffee Cen ht Wi-fi **Notes** LB ⊗ No
Children 8yrs ⊛

Bon Vista

★★★★ GUEST ACCOMMODATION

12 Alfred Rd NR27 9AN
☎ **01263 511818**
e-mail: jim@bonvista-cromer.co.uk
web: www.bonvista-cromer.co.uk
dir: *From pier onto A148 (coast road), in 400yds left onto
Alfred Rd*

This delightful Victorian terraced house, situated in a
peaceful side road adjacent to the seafront, just a short
walk from the town centre, promises a warm welcome.
The individually decorated bedrooms have co-ordinated
soft fabrics, and the public rooms include an attractive
dining room and a spacious first-floor lounge.

Rooms 5 en suite (2 fmly) S £45-£62; D £64-£85*
Facilities TVL tea/coffee Cen ht Wi-fi **Parking** 2 **Notes** LB
⊗ ⊛

Corner House

★★★★ BED AND BREAKFAST

2 Station Rd NR27 9QD
☎ **01263 838540** & **07769 800831** 🖷 **01263 838540**
e-mail: linjimhoward@btinternet.com
web: www.cornerhousenorfolk.com

(For full entry see West Runton)

Homefield Guest House

★★★★ GUEST HOUSE

48 Cromer Rd, West Runton NR27 9AD
☎ **01263 837337**
e-mail: homefield@hotmail.co.uk
web: www.homefieldguesthouse.co.uk
dir: *On A149 (coast road) between Sheringham & Cromer*

This large Victorian house was previously owned by the
Canon of Cromer and is situated in the peaceful village of
West Runton between Cromer and Sheringham. The
pleasantly co-ordinated bedrooms have many useful
extras. Breakfast, which includes locally sourced produce,
is served at individual tables in the smart dining room.

Rooms 6 en suite **Facilities** STV TVL tea/coffee Cen ht
Wi-fi **Parking** 8 **Notes** ⊗ No Children 14yrs

The Red Lion Food and Rooms

★★★★ 🍽 INN

Brook St NR27 9HD
☎ **01263 514964** 🖷 **01263 512834**
e-mail: info@redlion-cromer.co.uk

A charming Victorian inn situated in an elevated position
in the heart of the town centre overlooking the beach and
the sea. The open-plan public areas include a billiard
room, lounge bar, a popular restaurant, a sunny
conservatory and a first-floor residents' lounge with
superb sea views. The spacious bedrooms are tastefully
decorated with co-ordinated soft furnishings and include
many thoughtful touches.

Rooms 12 en suite S £60-£70; D £100-£150*
Facilities FTV tea/coffee Dinner available Direct Dial
Cen ht Wi-fi Golf Snooker **Parking** 20 **Notes** LB

Williams Restaurant

★★★★ ⊛ RESTAURANT WITH ROOMS

2 Brook St NR27 9EY
☎ **01263 519619**
e-mail: eat@williams-restaurant.co.uk

A lovely restored Victorian property situated just a stone's
throw from the beach and pier. The guest bedroom is
situated above the restaurant; it has been appointed with
stylish fixtures and fittings, and provides high levels of
quality and comfort. Breakfast and dinner are served in
the contemporary restaurant.

Rooms 1 en suite

Glendale

★★★ GUEST HOUSE

33 Macdonald Rd NR27 9AP
☎ **01263 513278**
e-mail: glendalecromer@btconnect.com
dir: *A149 (coast road) from Cromer centre, 4th left*

Victorian property situated in a peaceful side road
adjacent to the seafront, just a short walk from the town
centre. Bedrooms are pleasantly decorated, well
maintained and equipped with a good range of useful
extras. Breakfast is served at individual tables in the
smart dining room.

Rooms 5 rms (1 en suite) S £25-£40; D £50-£80
Facilities FTV tea/coffee **Parking** 2 **Notes** LB Closed 20
Oct-6 Apr

The Sandcliff

★★★ GUEST HOUSE

Runton Rd NR27 9AS
☎ **01263 512888** 🖷 **01263 512785**
e-mail: admin@sandcliffhotel.com
dir: *500yds W of town centre on A149*

Ideally situated on the seafront just a short walk from the
town centre, this guest house offers a large lounge bar
with comfortable seating and a spacious dining room
where breakfast and dinner are served. The bedrooms are
pleasantly decorated, thoughtfully equipped and some
have superb sea views.

Rooms 23 rms (17 en suite) (10 fmly) (3 GF) S
£47.50-£65; D £65-£105* **Facilities** FTV TVL tea/coffee
Dinner available Licensed Wi-fi Golf 18 **Parking** 10
Notes LB

Westgate Lodge B&B

★★★ BED AND BREAKFAST

10 MacDonald Rd NR27 9AP
☎ **01263 512840**
e-mail: info@westgatelodge.co.uk
dir: *Along seafront & left after the Cliftonville Hotel,
Westgate Lodge 50yds on right*

Situated in a peaceful side road next to the seafront and
just a short walk from the centre of town. Bedrooms vary
in size and style; each one is pleasantly decorated and
has many thoughtful touches. Breakfast is served in the
smart dining room and there is a cosy lounge.

Rooms 3 en suite D £52-£64* **Facilities** tea/coffee
Cen ht **Parking** 5 **Notes** LB ⊗ No Children 3yrs Closed
Xmas & New Year ⊛

Save on B&Bs and Hotels. Book at **theAA.com/hotel**

NORFOLK 217 **ENGLAND**

DEREHAM — Map 13 TF91

Orchard Cottage

★★★★ BED AND BREAKFAST

The Drift, Gressenhall NR20 4EH
☎ 01362 860265
e-mail: ann@walkers-norfolk.co.uk
dir: *2m NE of Dereham. Off B1146 in Beetley to Gressenhall, right at x-crds onto Bittering St, right at x-crds, 2nd right*

Orchard Cottage is an attractive newly-built Norfolk flint building situated in the historic rural village of Gressenhall near Dereham. The comfortable country style bedrooms are smartly decorated and situated on the ground floor; one of the rooms has a superb wet room. Public rooms include a lounge, a dining room and a study. Dinner is available by arrangement.

Rooms 2 en suite (2 GF) S £48-£54; D £64-£70
Facilities FTV TVL tea/coffee Dinner available Cen ht Wi-fi
Parking 2 **Notes** LB ⊗

DOCKING — Map 13 TF73

Jubilee Lodge

★★★★ GUEST ACCOMMODATION

Station Rd PE31 8LS
☎ 01485 518473 📠 01485 518473
e-mail: eghoward62@hotmail.com
web: www.jubilee-lodge.co.uk
dir: *400yds N of village centre on B1153*

Ideally placed for touring the North Norfolk coast, with Sandringham, Hunstanton, Burnham Market and Fakenham within easy striking distance. Bedrooms are pleasantly decorated, thoughtfully equipped and come with en suite facilities. Public rooms include a cosy guest lounge, and breakfast is served at individual tables in the smart dining room.

Rooms 3 en suite S £30; D £50* **Facilities** FTV TVL tea/coffee Cen ht 🎣 Fishing **Parking** 3 **Notes** LB ⊗ No Children 16yrs ⊠

DOWNHAM MARKET — Map 12 TF60

Crosskeys Riverside House

★★★ BED AND BREAKFAST

Bridge St, Hilgay PE38 0LD
☎ 01366 387777 📠 01366 387777
e-mail: crosskeyshouse@aol.com
web: www.crosskeys.info
dir: *2m S of Downham Market. Off A10 into Hilgay, Crosskeys on bridge*

Situated in the small village of Hilgay on the banks of the River Wissey, this former coaching inn offers comfortable accommodation that includes a number of four-poster bedrooms; many rooms have river views. Public rooms include a dining room with oak beams and inglenook fireplace, plus a small, rustic residents' bar.

Rooms 4 en suite (1 fmly) (2 GF) S £30-£55; D £55-£60*
Facilities FTV tea/coffee Cen ht Wi-fi Fishing Rowing boat for guests use **Parking** 10

FAKENHAM — Map 13 TF92

See also Barney

Abbott Farm *(TF975390)*

★★★ FARMHOUSE

Walsingham Rd, Binham NR21 0AW
☎ 01328 830519 📠 01328 830519
Mrs E Brown
e-mail: abbot.farm@btinternet.com
web: www.abbottfarm.co.uk
dir: *NE of Fakenham. From Binham SW onto Walsingham Rd, farm 0.6m on left*

A detached red-brick farmhouse set amidst 190 acres of arable farmland and surrounded by open countryside. The spacious bedrooms are pleasantly decorated and thoughtfully equipped; they include a ground-floor room with a large en suite shower. Breakfast is served in the attractive conservatory, which has superb views of the countryside.

Rooms 3 en suite (2 GF) S £30; D £60 **Facilities** TVL tea/coffee Cen ht **Parking** 20 **Notes** Closed 24-26 Dec ⊠ 190 acres arable

Fieldview Guest House

Ⓤ

West Barsham Rd, East Barsham NR21 0AR
☎ 01328 820083
e-mail: info@fieldview.net

Currently the rating for this establishment is not confirmed. This may be due to a change of ownership or because it has only recently joined the AA rating scheme.

Rooms 4 en suite S £35-£45; D £58*

GORLESTON ON SEA — Map 13 TG50

Avalon

★★★★ GUEST ACCOMMODATION

54 Clarence Rd NR31 6DR
☎ 01493 662114 📠 01493 668528
e-mail: info@avalon-gorleston.co.uk
web: www.avalon-gorleston.co.uk
dir: *A12 past James Paget Hospital. Take 2nd exit at rdbt towards Gorleston. Next rdbt 2nd exit, 1st right*

This Edwardian terraced house is just a short walk from the promenade and beach. Breakfast and evening meals are served in the smart dining room and there is a cosy lounge bar; service is both helpful and friendly. Bedrooms are pleasantly appointed, each thoughtfully equipped and well furnished.

Rooms 10 en suite (6 fmly) (1 GF) S £35; D £55-£65*
Facilities TVL tea/coffee Dinner available Cen ht Licensed Wi-fi **Notes** ⊗

Jennis Lodge

★★★★ GUEST HOUSE

63 Avondale Rd NR31 6DJ
☎ 01493 662840
e-mail: bookings@jennis-lodge.co.uk
dir: *A12, past James Paget Hospital, rdbt 2nd exit, next rdbt 2nd exit, left & 2nd right*

Jennis Lodge is a friendly, family-run guest house situated close to the seafront, marine gardens and town centre. The smartly decorated bedrooms have pine furniture and many thoughtful touches that include TV, DVD or video plus broadband connection. Breakfast and dinner are served in the smart dining room and guests have the use of a cosy lounge with comfy sofas.

Rooms 8 en suite (2 fmly) S £30; D £55* **Facilities** FTV TVL tea/coffee Dinner available Cen ht ch fac **Notes** LB

GREAT ELLINGHAM — Map 13 TM09

Aldercarr Hall

★★★★ GUEST ACCOMMODATION

Attleborough Rd NR17 1LQ
☎ 01953 455766 & 07710 752213 📠 01953 457993
e-mail: bedandbreakfast@aldercarr-limited.com
dir: *On B1077 500yds SE of village*

Aldercarr Hall is set in extensive grounds and surrounded by open countryside on the edge of Great Ellingham. Public rooms include a comfortably appointed conservatory and a delightful dining room where breakfast is served around a large table. The excellent facilities include a health, beauty and hairdressing studio, an indoor swimming pool, a Jacuzzi and a large function suite.

Rooms 3 annexe en suite (1 fmly) (3 GF) **Facilities** TVL tea/coffee Cen ht Wi-fi 🕾 Golf Fishing Riding Snooker Sauna Pool table **Conf** Max 125 Board 9 **Parking** 200 **Notes** ⊗

PREMIER COLLECTION

Andover House

★★★★★ ◉◉ RESTAURANT WITH ROOMS

28-30 Camperdown NR30 3JB
☎ 01493 843490   📄 01493 852546
e-mail: info@andoverhouse.co.uk
web: www.andoverhouse.co.uk
dir: *Opposite Wellington Pier turn into Shadingfield Close, right into Kimberley Terrace, follow into Camperdown. Property on left*

A lovely three-storey Victorian town house which was totally transformed by the current owners a few years ago. The property features a series of contemporary spaces that include a large open-plan lounge bar, a brasserie-style restaurant serving modern British cuisine, a cosy lounge and a smart sun terrace. Bedrooms are tastefully appointed with co-ordinated soft furnishings and have many thoughtful touches.

Rooms 20 en suite S £67-£69; D £77-£97*
Facilities STV FTV TVL tea/coffee Dinner available Direct Dial Cen ht Wi-fi **Conf** Max 40 Thtr 40 Class 40 Board 15 **Notes** ⊗ No Children 16yrs No coaches

PREMIER COLLECTION

3 Norfolk Square

★★★★★ GUEST HOUSE

3 Norfolk Square NR30 1EE
☎ 01493 843042   & 07734 735001
📄 01493 857276
e-mail: info@3norfolksquare.co.uk
web: www.3norfolksquare.co.uk
dir: *From Britannia Pier, 200yds N along seafront, left onto Albemarle Rd*

Delightful refurbished property situated in a peaceful side road just a short walk from the seafront and town centre. The bedrooms are smartly decorated, with co-ordinated soft furnishings and many thoughtful touches. Breakfast is served in the lower ground floor dining room/bar, and guests also have the use of a large lounge.

Rooms 8 en suite (2 GF) D £55-£100* **Facilities** FTV TVL tea/coffee Cen ht Licensed Wi-fi **Conf** Max 20 Class 20 Board 20 **Parking** 3 **Notes** LB ⊗ No Children 18yrs

Barnard House

★★★★ BED AND BREAKFAST

2 Barnard Crescent NR30 4DR
☎ 01493 855139
e-mail: enquiries@barnardhouse.com
dir: *0.5m N of town centre. Off A149 onto Barnard Crescent*

A friendly, family-run bed and breakfast, set in mature landscaped gardens in a residential area. The smartly decorated bedrooms are thoughtfully equipped. Breakfast is served in the stylish dining room and there is an elegant lounge with comfy sofas. A warm welcome is assured.

Rooms 3 rms (2 en suite) (1 pri facs) S £45-£50; D £65-£75 **Facilities** FTV TVL tea/coffee Cen ht Wi-fi **Parking** 3 **Notes** LB Closed Xmas & New Year

The Classic Lodge

★★★★ BED AND BREAKFAST

13 Euston Rd NR30 1DY
☎ 01493 852851   📄 01493 852851
web: www.classiclodge.com
dir: *A12 to A47, follow signs for seafront. Turn left Sainsbury's, ahead at lights 200mtrs on right, 100mtrs from seafront*

The Classic Lodge is an impressive Victorian villa situated just a short stroll from the seafront and town centre. Breakfast is served at individual tables in the large lounge-dining room, and the spacious bedrooms are carefully furnished and equipped with a very good range of facilities. Secure parking is provided at the rear of the property.

Rooms 3 en suite **Facilities** FTV TVL tea/coffee Cen ht Wi-fi **Parking** 7 **Notes** LB ⊗ No Children 18yrs Closed Nov-Apr ◉

All Seasons Guest House

★★★★ GUEST HOUSE

10 Nelson Road South NR30 3JL
☎ 01493 852713   & 07810 560079
e-mail: m.kenmore@sky.com
dir: *From seafront (with sea on left) turn onto Kings Rd, Nelson Rd South, 150yds on right*

A well maintained terrace property situated just a short walk from the beach and town centre. Bedrooms are pleasantly decorated with co-ordinated fabrics and have a good range of useful facilities. Breakfast is served at individual tables in the dining room and guests have the use of a comfy lounge.

Rooms 8 en suite (3 fmly) (1 GF) S £22.50-£35; D £45-£70* **Facilities** STV FTV TVL tea/coffee Dinner available Cen ht Wi-fi Golf 18 **Conf** Max 16 Thtr 16 Class 16 Board 16 **Notes** LB ⊗

The Chequers

★★★★ GUEST HOUSE

27 Nelson Road South NR30 3JA
☎ 01493 853091
e-mail: mitchellsatchequers@hotmail.co.uk
dir: *Off A47 signed Seafront, right onto Marine Parade & Kings Rd, 1st right*

Guests will receive a warm welcome from the caring hosts at this privately-run establishment situated just a short walk from Wellington pier and the beach. Public rooms include a cosy bar, residents' lounge and a smart dining room. Bedrooms are cheerfully decorated and have many thoughtful touches.

Rooms 8 rms (7 en suite) (1 pri facs) (2 fmly) S £22-£33; D £44-£64 **Facilities** FTV TVL tea/coffee Dinner available Cen ht Licensed Wi-fi **Notes** LB ⊗

The Hamilton

★★★★ GUEST HOUSE

23-24 North Dr NR30 4EW
☎ 01493 844662   📄 01493 745772
e-mail: enquiries@hamilton-hotel.co.uk

Overlooking the beach with fantastic views of the sea, this property is ideally situated for the theatre, tourist attractions, town centre and Yarmouth Racecourse. Public rooms include a smart lounge bar with leather seating, a breakfast room and a residents' lounge with comfy sofas. Bedrooms are bright and airy with many thoughtful touches; most rooms have lovely sea views.

Rooms 21 en suite (1 fmly) (1 GF) **Facilities** TVL tea/coffee Dinner available Cen ht Licensed Wi-fi **Conf** Max 40 Thtr 40 Class 26 Board 26 **Parking** 20 **Notes** ⊗

Knights Court

★★★★ GUEST ACCOMMODATION

22 North Dr NR30 4EW
☎ 01493 843089   📄 01493 850780
e-mail: enquiries@knights-court.co.uk
dir: *600yds N of Britannia Pier, opp Waterways & Gardens*

Knights Court stands on the seafront overlooking the Venetian waterways and the beach. The spacious bedrooms are carefully decorated and equipped with many thoughtful touches, and most rooms have lovely sea views. Breakfast and dinner are served in the smart dining room and there is a cosy lounge bar.

Rooms 14 en suite 6 annexe en suite (5 fmly) (6 GF) S £35-£47; D £62-£76* **Facilities** FTV tea/coffee Dinner available Direct Dial Cen ht Licensed Wi-fi **Parking** 21 **Notes** LB ⊗ Closed 30 Oct-20 Mar

Marine Lodge

★★★★ GUEST ACCOMMODATION

19-20 Euston Rd NR30 1DY
☎ 01493 331120
e-mail: res@marinelodge.co.uk
dir: *Follow signs for seafront, 300mtrs N of Britannia Pier*

This establishment's enviable seafront position has panoramic views of the bowling greens and beach, and is within easy walking distance of Britannia Pier. Bright modern bedrooms are complemented by smart public areas that include a bar area where light snacks are available during the evening. Guests also have complimentary use of the indoor swimming pool at the sister Palm Court Hotel.

Rooms 40 en suite (5 fmly) (5 GF) **Facilities** FTV TVL tea/coffee Cen ht Lift Licensed Wi-fi **Conf** Thtr 50 Class 35 Board 25 **Parking** 38 **Notes** ⊗

Swiss Cottage B&B Exclusively for Non Smokers

★★★★ GUEST ACCOMMODATION

31 North Dr NR30 4EW
☎ 01493 855742 & 07986 399857 📄 01493 843547
e-mail: info@swiss-cottage.info
dir: *0.5m N of town centre. Off A47 or A12 to to seafront, 750yds N of pier. Turn left at Britannia Pier. Swiss Cottage on left opposite Water Gardens*

A charming detached property situated in the peaceful part of town overlooking the Venetian waterways and the sea beyond. The comfortable bedrooms are pleasantly decorated with co-ordinated fabrics and have many useful extras. Breakfast is served in the smart dining room and guests have use of an open-plan lounge area.

Rooms 8 en suite 1 annexe en suite (2 GF) S £33-£42; D £55-£83* **Facilities** FTV tea/coffee Cen ht Wi-fi **Parking** 9 **Notes** LB No Children 11yrs Closed Nov-Feb

The Winchester

★★★★ GUEST ACCOMMODATION

12 Euston Rd NR30 1DY
☎ 01493 843950
e-mail: enquiries@winchesterprivatehotel.com
dir: *A12 onto A47, signs for seafront, left at Sainsbury's over lights, premises 400yds on right*

Just off the sea front, the friendly hosts at The Winchester give a warm welcome. The pleasant bedrooms vary in size and style and are thoughtfully equipped. Public rooms include a large lower ground-floor dining room, a small conservatory and a foyer with sofas.

Rooms 14 en suite (2 fmly) (5 GF) S £25-£35; D £50-£70* **Facilities** TVL tea/coffee Dinner available Cen ht Wi-fi **Parking** 10 **Notes** LB ⊗ No Children 12yrs Closed Dec-Jan RS Oct-Etr No evening meals 🍽

Haydee

★★★ GUEST HOUSE

27 Princes Rd NR30 2DG
☎ 01493 844580 📄 01493 844580
e-mail: info@haydee.co.uk
web: www.haydee.co.uk
dir: *Off A47 to seafront, Princes Rd opp Britannia Pier*

The Haydee is in a side road just a stroll from the seafront, pier and town centre. The pleasant bedrooms vary in size and style, but all are well equipped. Breakfast is served in the smart dining room and there is a cosy lounge bar.

Rooms 8 en suite (2 fmly) (2 smoking) S £22-£27; D £44-£54* **Facilities** TVL tea/coffee Cen ht Licensed **Notes** LB ⊗

Senglea Lodge

★★★ GUEST ACCOMMODATION

7 Euston Rd NR30 1DX
☎ 01493 859632 & 07775 698819
e-mail: senglealodge@fsmail.net
dir: *From A4 straight over 1st 2 rdbts. At lights left towards seafront. Through next lights, Lodge on right*

Delightful terrace property situated just off the seafront and very close to the town centre. Bedrooms are pleasantly decorated, have co-ordinated soft furnishings, and a good range of useful extras. Breakfast is served at individual tables in the smart open-plan lounge/dining room.

Rooms 6 rms (4 en suite) (2 fmly) (2 smoking) S £20-£25; D £40-£45* **Facilities** FTV TVL tea/coffee Cen ht Wi-fi **Notes** LB ⊗ Closed 23 Dec-2 Jan

Shemara Guest House

★★★ GUEST HOUSE

11 Wellesley Rd NR30 2AR
☎ 01493 844054 & 07771 882054
e-mail: info@shemaraguesthouse.co.uk
dir: *A47 to Great Yarmouth, follow signs for seafront, take 4th right, Shemara on right*

Shemara is ideally situated in the heart of this busy resort, as it is just a short walk from the town centre and seafront. Bedrooms come in a variety of sizes and styles, each one is pleasantly decorated and well equipped. Breakfast is served at individual tables in the open-plan lounge/dining room.

Rooms 7 en suite (2 fmly) S £20-£30; D £40-£60 **Facilities** FTV TVL tea/coffee Dinner available Cen ht **Notes** LB ⊗ 🍽

Victoria

★★★ GUEST ACCOMMODATION

2 Kings Rd NR30 3JW
☎ 01493 843872 & 842132 📄 01493 843872
e-mail: booking@hotelvictoria.org.uk
web: www.hotelvictoria.org.uk
dir: *Off seafront, opposite model village*

Large detached property situated just off the seafront close to Wellington Pier and the town centre. Bedrooms come in a variety of sizes and styles; each one is pleasantly decorated and thoughtfully equipped. Dinner and breakfast are served in the open plan lounge/dining room. The Victoria also has a smart outdoor swimming pool.

Rooms 36 en suite (12 fmly) (2 GF) S £25-£35; D £45-£70* **Facilities** FTV TVL tea/coffee Dinner available Cen ht Lift Licensed Wi-fi 🎱 Pool table **Conf** Max 50 Thtr 50 Class 50 Board 30 **Parking** 20 **Notes** LB ⊗

Rhonadean

★★ GUEST HOUSE

110-111 Wellesley Rd NR30 2AR
☎ 01493 842004
e-mail: barbara@6wheeler0.wanadoo.co.uk
dir: *500yds N of town centre. Off A47 onto B1141 Fuller's Hill towards seafront, onto St Nicholas Rd & 3rd right*

Rhonadean is situated in a side road adjacent to the seafront and just a short walk from the town centre. Public rooms include a small lounge bar and a dining room where breakfast and dinner are served at individual tables. Bedrooms vary in size and style; each one is pleasantly decorated and well equipped.

Rooms 18 rms (17 en suite) (1 pri facs) (7 fmly) (8 GF) S £16-£26; D £32-£52* **Facilities** TVL tea/coffee Dinner available Cen ht Licensed Pool table **Notes** ⊗ Closed 24-26 Dec

GREAT YARMOUTH *continued*

The Harbour

[U]

20 Pavilion Rd, Gorleston on Sea NR31 6BY
☎ 01493 661031 & 07816 891900
e-mail: sales@theharbourhotel.co.uk
web: www.theharbourhotel.co.uk
dir: *A47 signs for Gorleston on Sea, pier & Quay Rd,
premises near lighthouse*

Currently the rating for this establishment is not
confirmed. This may be due to a change of ownership or
because it has only recently joined the AA rating scheme.

Rooms 10 rms (4 en suite) (5 fmly) S £28-£40; D
£36-£60 **Facilities** tea/coffee Licensed Wi-fi **Notes** LB ⊗

HARLESTON — Map 13 TM28

Heath Farmhouse

★★★★ BED AND BREAKFAST

Homersfield IP20 0EX
☎ 01986 788417
e-mail: julia.john.hunt@googlemail.com
dir: *A143 onto B1062 towards Flixton, over bridge past
Suffolk sign & 2nd farm entrance on left at AA sign*

A charming 16th-century farmhouse set amid attractive
landscaped grounds that include a croquet lawn. The
property retains much of its original character with
exposed beams, open fireplaces and wood-burning
stoves. The pleasant bedrooms are carefully furnished
and have many thoughtful touches. Breakfast and dinner
are served in the smart dining room overlooking the
garden.

Rooms 2 rms (1 fmly) **Facilities** TVL tea/coffee Dinner
available Cen ht ⬤ Table tennis **Parking** 8 **Notes** ⊗ ⊛

HINDRINGHAM — Map 13 TF93

PREMIER COLLECTION

Field House

★★★★★ ⬛ BED AND BREAKFAST

Moorgate Rd NR21 0PT
☎ 01328 878726
e-mail: stay@fieldhousehindringham.co.uk
web: www.fieldhousehindringham.co.uk
dir: *Off A148 to Hindringham, onto Moorgate Rd at
Lower Green, Field House on left*

A warm friendly welcome and genuine hospitality are
offered by the caring hosts at this delightful property.
Field House is situated in a peaceful rural location
amid pretty landscaped gardens. The individually
decorated bedrooms are tastefully furnished and have
co-ordinated soft fabrics as well as many thoughtful
touches. Breakfast is served in the lounge-dining room
and features quality, locally sourced produce.

Rooms 2 en suite 1 annexe en suite S £70-£75; D
£90-£110 **Facilities** FTV tea/coffee Cen ht Wi-fi ⬤
Parking 3 **Notes** LB ⊗ No Children 10yrs Closed 25-26
Dec ⊛

HOLT — Map 13 TG03

See also Thurning

Kadina

★★★★ BED AND BREAKFAST

Warren Close, High Kelling NR25 6QX
☎ 01263 710116 & 07900 928729 📠 01263 710116
e-mail: enquiries@kadinanorfolk.co.uk
dir: *Turn off A148 onto Bridge Rd, turn right onto Warren
Rd. Right again onto Warren Close, Kadina fourth on left*

Modern detached chalet bungalow situated close to the
Georgian town of Holt, in the peaceful village of High
Kelling. The smartly appointed bedrooms have pine
furniture, co-ordinated soft furnishings and many
thoughtful touches. Breakfast is served at a large pine
table in the kitchen/dining room, and dinner is available
by prior arrangement.

Rooms 2 en suite (1 GF) S £50-£55; D £70-£75*
Facilities tea/coffee Dinner available Cen ht Wi-fi
Parking 5 **Notes** LB ⊗ No Children ⊛

The Lawns Wine Bar

★★★★ ⬤ RESTAURANT WITH ROOMS

26 Station Rd NR25 6BS
☎ 01263 713390
e-mail: mail@lawnsatholt.co.uk
dir: *A148 (Cromer road). 0.25m from Holt rdbt, turn left,
400yds along Station Rd*

A superb Georgian house situated in the centre of this
delightful north Norfolk market town. The open-plan
public areas include a large wine bar, a conservatory and
a smart restaurant. The spacious bedrooms are tastefully
appointed with co-ordinated soft furnishings and have
many thoughtful touches.

Rooms 8 en suite S £75-£95; D £85-£125* **Facilities** FTV
TVL tea/coffee Dinner available Cen ht Wi-fi Petanque
Conf Max 20 Thtr 20 Class 12 **Parking** 14

The Old Telephone Exchange Bed & Breakfast

★★★★ BED AND BREAKFAST

37 New St NR25 6JH
☎ 01263 712992
e-mail: christopher.manders@btinternet.com
dir: *Off High St onto New St, establishment 200yds on left*

Expect a warm welcome at this small, family-run bed and
breakfast situated in a quiet side road close to the town
centre. The immaculate bedrooms are tastefully
appointed and equipped with many thoughtful touches.
Public rooms feature a comfortable lounge-dining area
with a wide-screen television, sofas, books and games.

Rooms 3 rms (2 en suite) (1 pri facs) (3 GF) S £55-£65; D
£57-£75* **Facilities** FTV TVL tea/coffee Cen ht **Parking** 2
Notes LB ⊗ No Children 10yrs ⊛

White Cottage B&B

★★★★ GUEST ACCOMMODATION

Norwich Rd NR25 6SW
☎ 01263 713353
e-mail: enquiries@whitecottageholt.co.uk
dir: *From A148 from Holt take B1149, 0.5m on left after
police station*

A delightful detached cottage situated just a short walk
from this busy town centre. Breakfast is served at
individual tables in the smart dining room and guests
have the use of a cosy lounge. The bedrooms are
pleasantly decorated and equipped with a good range of
useful extras.

Rooms 2 en suite **Facilities** tea/coffee Cen ht **Notes** ⊗
No Children 10yrs Closed 21 Dec-7 Jan RS Jan-Feb
Telephone to confirm ⊛

Save on B&Bs and Hotels. Book at **theAA.com/hotel**

NORFOLK 221 ENGLAND

Claremont

★★★★ GUEST HOUSE

35 Greevegate PE36 6AF
☎ **01485 533171**
e-mail: claremontgh@tiscali.co.uk
dir: Off A149 onto Greevegate, house before St Edmund's Church

This Victorian guest house, close to the shops, beach and gardens, has individually decorated bedrooms with a good range of useful extras. There are also a ground-floor room and two feature rooms, one with a four-poster, and another with a canopied bed.

Rooms 7 en suite (1 fmly) (1 GF) **Facilities** TVL tea/coffee Cen ht **Parking** 4 **Notes** LB No Children 5yrs Closed 15 Nov-15 Mar ❸

The Neptune Restaurant with Rooms

★★★★ ❸❸❸ RESTAURANT WITH ROOMS

85 Old Hunstanton Rd, Old Hunstanton PE36 6HZ
☎ **01485 532122**
e-mail: reservations@theneptune.co.uk
web: www.theneptune.co.uk
dir: On A149, past Hunstanton, 200mtrs on left after post office

This charming 18th-century coaching inn, now a restaurant with rooms, is ideally situated for touring the Norfolk coastline. The smartly appointed bedrooms are brightly finished with co-ordinated fabrics and hand-made New England furniture. Public rooms feature white clapboard walls, polished dark wood floors, fresh flowers and Lloyd Loom furniture. The food is very much a draw here with the carefully prepared, award-winning cuisine utilising excellent local produce, from oysters and mussels from Thornham to quinces grown on a neighbouring farm.

Rooms 6 en suite S £75-£120; D £110-£120* **Facilities** FTV tea/coffee Dinner available Direct Dial Cen ht Wi-fi **Parking** 6 **Notes** ⊗ No Children 10yrs Closed 2wks Nov & 3wks Jan RS Oct-Apr Closed Mon No coaches

Gemini Lodge Guest House

★★★★ GUEST HOUSE

5 Alexandra Rd PE36 5BT
☎ **01485 533902**

This guest house is situated in an elevated position close to the centre of town and seafront. The bedrooms are smartly decorated in neutral colours with lovely co-ordinated soft furnishings and fabrics; some rooms have lovely views of the sea. Public rooms include a smart lounge with plush sofas, and breakfast is served at a large communal table in the contemporary dining room.

Rooms 3 en suite D £50-£60* **Facilities** FTV TVL tea/coffee Cen ht **Parking** 3 **Notes** LB No Children ❸

The King William IV Country Inn & Restaurant

★★★★ ⚑ INN

Heacham Rd, Sedgeford PE36 5LU
☎ **01485 571765** 📠 **01485 571743**
e-mail: info@thekingwilliamsedgeford.co.uk
web: www.thekingwilliamsedgeford.co.uk
dir: A149 to Hunstanton, right at Norfolk Lavender in Heacham onto B1454, signed Docking. 2m to Sedgeford

Rooms 9 en suite (4 fmly) S £60-£70; D £90-£105* **Facilities** tea/coffee Dinner available Cen ht Wi-fi Golf 18 Leisure/Tennis centre 0.5m by arrangement **Parking** 60 **Notes** LB No coaches

Rosamaly

★★★★ ⚑ GUEST ACCOMMODATION

14 Glebe Av PE36 6BS
☎ **01485 534187** & **07775 724484**
e-mail: vacancies@rosamaly.co.uk
dir: A149 to Hunstanton. At rdbt take 3rd exit staying on A149 towards Cromer. In 1m church on left, Glebe Av 2nd left, Rosamaly 50yds on left

Rooms 6 en suite (2 fmly) (1 GF) S £30-£70; D £60-£70* **Facilities** FTV TVL tea/coffee Dinner available Cen ht **Notes** LB Closed 24 Dec-1 Jan ❸

The White Cottage

★★★ GUEST ACCOMMODATION

19 Wodehouse Rd PE36 6JW
☎ **01485 532380**

A charming cottage situated in a quiet side road in Old Hunstanton, The White Cottage has been owned and run by Mrs Burton for over 25 years. The spacious bedrooms are attractively decorated, and some have lovely sea views. Dinner is served in the smart dining room and there is a cosy sitting room with a television.

Rooms 3 rms (1 en suite) **Facilities** TVL TV1B Dinner available Cen ht **Parking** 4 **Notes** LB No Children 10yrs ❸

Richmond House Bed & Breakfast

★★★ GUEST HOUSE

6-8 Westgate PE36 5AL
☎ **01485 532601**
e-mail: richmondhousehotel@xln.co.uk
dir: Off A149 onto Westgate

This well-maintained guest house is well situated for the seafront and town centre. Its pleasant bedrooms vary in size and style, but all are well equipped and some rooms have superb sea views. Public rooms feature a smart restaurant and a cosy lounge bar.

Rooms 14 rms (10 en suite) (5 GF) **Facilities** tea/coffee Dinner available Cen ht Lift Licensed **Notes** ⊗ No Children 18yrs Closed Nov-Etr ❸

KELLING — Map 13 TG04

Sandpipers

★★★★ BED AND BREAKFAST

The Street NR25 7EL
☎ 01263 588604
e-mail: inastew@hotmail.co.uk
dir: *From A149 into Kelling, 200mtrs on right next to phone box*

Located in this peaceful village on the North Norfolk Coast. The tastefully appointed self-contained accommodation has a double bedroom, en suite bathroom, a separate lounge with plush sofas and a well equipped kitchenette. Breakfast is served in the main house conservatory, which overlooks the garden.

Rooms 1 annexe en suite (1 GF) D £71-£80 **Facilities** STV TVL tea/coffee Cen ht **Parking** 2 **Notes** ⊗ No Children ☻

KING'S LYNN — Map 12 TF62

Guanock

★★★ GUEST ACCOMMODATION

10-11 Guanock Place PE30 5QJ
☎ 01553 772959 ᐧ 01553 772959
dir: *Signs to town centre, premises on right of South Gates*

Located within easy walking distance of the town centre, this friendly, family-run guest accommodation offers comfortable, practical rooms. Public areas include a lounge bar, pool room, and a bright dining room where breakfast is served at individual tables. There is also a delightful little roof garden.

Rooms 17 rms (5 fmly) (1 GF) S £30-£33; D £54* **Facilities** STV tea/coffee Cen ht Licensed Pool table **Parking** 8 **Notes** ⊗ Closed 24 Dec-3 Jan

LITCHAM — Map 13 TF81

Bramley

★★★★ BED AND BREAKFAST

Weasenham Rd PE32 2QT
☎ 01328 701592 ᐧ 01328 701592
e-mail: bramleybandb@hotmail.co.uk
web: www.bramley-litcham.co.uk
dir: *A1065 onto B1145. Left at x-rds, left at school, 4th house on left*

A warm welcome awaits at this delightful detached house, set in a peaceful location on the village fringe, with ample safe parking in generous grounds. The mostly spacious bedrooms are thoughtfully furnished to ensure guest comfort and have smartly appointed en suite shower rooms. A hearty, freshly-cooked breakfast is served at individual tables in the separate elegant dining room.

Rooms 4 en suite (1 fmly) **Facilities** TV3B tea/coffee Cen ht Wi-fi **Parking** 4 **Notes** LB ⊗ ☻

LITTLE WALSINGHAM — Map 13 TF93

The Old Bakehouse Tea Room & Guest House

★★★★ GUEST HOUSE

33 High St NR22 6BZ
☎ 01328 820454 ᐧ 01328 820454
e-mail: theoldbakehouseguesthouse@yahoo.co.uk
dir: *Exit A148 (Fakenham Bypass) to Wells & Walsingham (B1105). Do not turn left at x-rds, continue straight ahead into Walsingham. Next to post office*

Ideally situated in the heart of the historical shrine village of Little Walsingham, The Old Bakehouse offers spacious bedrooms with pine furniture, co-ordinated soft furnishings and many thoughtful touches. Breakfast is served in the large dining room, which is now a traditional tea room during the day.

Rooms 3 en suite S £50; D £80* **Facilities** tea/coffee Dinner available Cen ht Wi-fi **Notes** ⊗

NORTH WALSHAM — Map 13 TG23

White House Farm

★★★★★ GUEST ACCOMMODATION

Knapton NR28 0RX
☎ 01263 721344 & 07879 475220
e-mail: info@whitehousefarmnorfolk.co.uk

The caring hosts at this delightful Grade II listed 18th-century flint cottage are particularly welcoming. The property is surrounded by open farmland and has been restored to retain many of its original features. Bedrooms are attractively decorated, tastefully furnished and equipped with many thoughtful touches. Breakfast is served in the smart dining room and guests have the use of a cosy lounge.

Rooms 3 en suite (1 fmly) **Facilities** FTV TVL tea/coffee Cen ht Wi-fi **Parking** 8 **Notes** ⊗ No Children 12yrs

Chimneys

★★★★ ☻ BED AND BREAKFAST

51 Cromer Rd NR28 0HB
☎ 01692 406172 & 07952 117701
e-mail: jenny.harmer8@virgin.net
dir: *0.5m NW of town centre on A149*

A delightful Edwardian-style town house set amidst mature secluded grounds close to the town centre. Bedrooms are tastefully furnished and thoughtfully equipped, the superior room has a Jacuzzi bath. Breakfast is served in the smart dining room and guests are welcome to sit on the balcony, which overlooks the garden. Dinner is available by prior arrangement.

Rooms 3 en suite (1 fmly) S £40-£55; D £60-£75* **Facilities** FTV tea/coffee Dinner available Cen ht Wi-fi **Parking** 6

The Scarborough Hill Country Inn

★★★★ INN

Old Yarmouth Rd NR28 9NA
☎ 01692 402151 ᐧ 01692 406686
e-mail: scarboroughhill@nascr.net
web: www.arlingtonhotel.co.uk
dir: *From Norwich B1150, straight through lights, across mini-rdbt, right at next rdbt, 1m on right*

A delightful inn with a country house feel situated on the outskirts of town, in a peaceful location amidst landscaped grounds. Public rooms include a smart lounge bar with plush sofas, an intimate dining room and a large conservatory. Bedrooms are generally quite spacious; each one is pleasantly furnished and thoughtfully equipped.

Rooms 8 en suite 1 annexe en suite (1 fmly) (1 GF) **Facilities** FTV TVL tea/coffee Dinner available Direct Dial Cen ht Wi-fi **Parking** 80 **Notes** ⊗ Civ Wed

Save on B&Bs and Hotels. Book at **theAA.com/hotel**

NORFOLK 223 ENGLAND

NORWICH
Map 13 TG20

PREMIER COLLECTION

Brasteds

★★★★★ ◎◎ ⌂ RESTAURANT WITH ROOMS

Manor Farm Barns, Framingham Pigot NR14 7PZ
☎ 01508 491112 ▤ 01508 491113
e-mail: enquiries@brasteds.co.uk
web: www.brasteds.co.uk
dir: *A11 onto A47 towards Great Yarmouth, then A146. After 0.5m turn right into Fox Rd, 0.5m on left*

Brasteds is a lovely detached property set in 20 acres of mature, landscaped parkland on the outskirts of Norwich. The tastefully appointed bedrooms have beautiful soft furnishings and fabrics along with comfortable seating and many thoughtful touches. Public rooms include a cosy snug with plush sofas, and a smart dining room where breakfast is served. Dinner is available in Brasteds Restaurant, which can be found in an adjacent building.

Rooms 6 en suite (1 fmly) (3 GF) S £80-£100; D £130-£175 **Facilities** FTV TVL tea/coffee Dinner available Direct Dial Cen ht Wi-fi **Conf** Max 120 Thtr 120 Class 100 Board 40 **Parking** 50 **Notes** LB No coaches Civ Wed 160

Catton Old Hall

★★★★★ ⬛ GUEST ACCOMMODATION

Lodge Ln, Old Catton NR6 7HG
☎ 01603 419379 ▤ 01603 400379
e-mail: enquiries@catton-hall.co.uk
dir: *A11 outer ring road (A140/A1042) to rdbt signed North Walsham on B1150. At lights turn left onto George Hill then right onto Spixworth Rd. At lights left onto Lodge Ln, on right*

Rooms 7 en suite D £70-£150* **Facilities** FTV TVL tea/coffee Direct Dial Cen ht Licensed Wi-fi **Parking** 9 **Notes** LB No Children 12yrs

Gothic House Bed & Breakfast

★★★★ GUEST ACCOMMODATION

King's Head Yard, Magdalen St NR3 1JE
☎ 01603 631879
e-mail: charvey649@aol.com
dir: *Follow signs for A147, turn off at rdbt past flyover into Whitefriars. Right again onto Fishergate, at end, right onto Magdalen St*

Gothic House is an elegant Grade II listed Regency townhouse set in a quiet courtyard in the heart of Norwich. The property has been lovingly restored and retains much of its original character. The spacious bedrooms are individually decorated and have many thoughtful touches. Breakfast, which includes locally sourced produce, is served in the elegant dining room.

Rooms 2 rms (2 pri facs) S £65; D £95 **Facilities** STV FTV tea/coffee Cen ht Wi-fi **Parking** 2 **Notes** ⊗ No Children 18yrs Closed Feb ⊛

Old Thorn Barn

★★★★ GUEST ACCOMMODATION

Corporation Farm, Wymondham Rd, Hethel NR14 8EU
☎ 01953 607785 & 07894 203208 ▤ 01953 601909
e-mail: enquires@oldthornbarn.co.uk
dir: *6m SW of Norwich. Follow signs for Lotus Cars from A11or B1113, on Wymondham Rd*

A delightful Grade II listed barn situated in a peaceful rural location just a short drive from the city centre. The property has stylish, thoughtfully equipped bedrooms with polished wood floors and antique pine furniture. Breakfast is served in the open-plan barn, which also has a wood-burning stove and a cosy lounge area.

Rooms 5 en suite 2 annexe en suite (7 GF) S £36-£40; D £64-£68 **Facilities** FTV TVL tea/coffee Cen ht Wi-fi **Parking** 14 **Notes** ⊗

Church Farm

★★★★ GUEST ACCOMMODATION

Church St, Horsford NR10 3DB
☎ 01603 898020 ▤ 01603 891649
e-mail: churchfarmgh@aol.com
dir: *5m NW of city centre. A140 onto B1149, right at x-rds*

Set in a peaceful rural location just a short drive from Norwich airport and the city centre. The spacious bedrooms are smartly decorated, pleasantly furnished and have many thoughtful touches. Breakfast is served at individual tables in the conservatory-style lounge-dining room, which overlooks the garden and sun terrace.

Rooms 10 en suite (1 fmly) (3 GF) **Facilities** FTV TVL tea/coffee Cen ht Wi-fi **Parking** 20 **Notes** ⊗

Cringleford Guest House

★★★★ GUEST HOUSE

1 Gurney Ln, Cringleford NR4 7SB
☎ 01603 451349 & 07775 725933
e-mail: robandkate@cringlefordguesthouse.co.uk
web: www.cringlefordguesthouse.co.uk
dir: *From A11/A47 Thickthorn rdbt signs to Norwich, 0.25m slip road to Cringleford, left at junct onto Colney Ln, Gurney Ln 5th on right*

A delightful property, situated just a short drive from the hospital, University of East Anglia and major roads. The pleasant, well-equipped bedrooms have co-ordinated fabrics and pine furniture. Breakfast is served at individual tables in the smart dining room.

Rooms 6 en suite 1 annexe en suite (3 fmly) (2 GF) S £45-£55; D £70-£75* **Facilities** TVL tea/coffee Cen ht Wi-fi **Conf** Max 10 Thtr 10 Class 10 Board 10 **Parking** 7 **Notes** LB ⊗

Wensum Guest House

★★★★ GUEST HOUSE

225 Dereham Rd NR2 3TF
☎ 01603 621069 ▤ 01603 618445
e-mail: info@wensumguesthouse.co.uk
dir: *From A47 1st exit into Norwich A1074 Dereham Rd*

Expect a warm welcome at this modern refurbished guest house situated just a short walk from the city centre. Public rooms include a smart open-plan dining room and a cosy lounge with flat screen TV and leather sofas. The contemporary style bedrooms are pleasantly decorated and thoughtfully equipped.

Rooms 9 rms (5 en suite) (4 pri facs) 9 annexe rms 7 annexe en suite (2 pri facs) (4 fmly) (8 GF) S £45-£55; D £65-£90* **Facilities** FTV tea/coffee Cen ht Wi-fi **Parking** 16 **Notes** LB ⊗ Closed 24 Dec-3 Jan

NORWICH *continued*

Edmar Lodge

★ ★ ★ GUEST ACCOMMODATION

64 Earlham Rd NR2 3DF
☎ 01603 615599   📠 01603 495599
e-mail: mail@edmarlodge.co.uk
web: www.edmarlodge.co.uk
dir: *Off A47 S bypass onto B1108 Earlham Rd, follow university and hospital signs*

Located just a ten minute walk from the city centre, this friendly family-run guest accommodation offers a convenient location and ample private parking. Individually decorated bedrooms are smartly appointed and well equipped. Freshly prepared breakfasts are served in the cosy dining room; a microwave and a refrigerator are also available.

Rooms 5 en suite (1 fmly) S £38-£45; D £48-£55
Facilities FTV tea/coffee Cen ht Wi-fi **Parking** 6

RINGSTEAD
Map 12 TF74

The Gin Trap Inn

★★★★ 🌐 INN

6 High St PE36 5JU
☎ 01485 525264
e-mail: thegintrap@hotmail.co.uk
dir: *A149 from King's Lynn towards Hunstanton. In 15m turn right at Heacham for Ringstead into village centre*

This delightful 17th-century inn is in a quiet village just a short drive from the coast. The public rooms include a large open-plan bar and a cosy restaurant. The accommodation is luxurious. Each individually appointed bedroom has been carefully decorated and thoughtfully equipped.

Rooms 3 en suite **Facilities** tea/coffee Dinner available Cen ht Wi-fi **Parking** 20 **Notes** No Children No coaches

---

SHERINGHAM
Map 13 TG14

See also Cromer

PREMIER COLLECTION

The Eight Acres

★ ★ ★ ★ ★ 🏠 BED AND BREAKFAST

Glebe Farm, Holt Rd, Aylmerton NR11 8QA
☎ 01263 838094 & 07891 717713
📠 01263 838094
dir: *On A148 3m from Cromer, 6m from Holt*

A warm welcome is assured at this modern detached farmhouse, which is set amid open countryside just off the A148. Bedrooms are smartly decorated with co-ordinated soft furnishings, lovely pine furniture and many extras such as flat-screen digital TVs with built-in DVD. Public rooms feature a large open-plan lounge/dining room.

Rooms 2 en suite S £50-£70; D £65* **Facilities** FTV tea/coffee Cen ht Wi-fi DVD players available in rooms **Parking** 2 **Notes** ⊗ No Children 16yrs Closed Nov-Feb 🍴

PREMIER COLLECTION

Ashbourne House

★ ★ ★ ★ ★ 🏠 BED AND BREAKFAST

1 Nelson Rd NR26 8BT
☎ 01263 821555 & 07807 629868
e-mail: nailligill@yahoo.co.uk
dir: *Take A149 Cromer road towards Cromer, turn left over Beeston Common. Under bridge, at top of Curtis Ln turn left, situated on right*

This superb detached property has been tastefully refurbished to a very high standard by the current owners. The smartly appointed bedrooms have lovely soft furnishings and are full of thoughtful touches. Public rooms include a large entrance hall and a guest lounge. Breakfast is served in the stylish panelled dining room, which overlooks the smart landscaped gardens that slope upwards to the cliff top.

Rooms 3 en suite S £45-£50; D £65-£75 **Facilities** TVL tea/coffee Cen ht Wi-fi **Parking** 3 **Notes** ⊗ No Children 12yrs 🍴

PREMIER COLLECTION

The Eiders Bed & Breakfast

★ ★ ★ ★ ★ BED AND BREAKFAST

Holt Rd, Aylmerton NR11 8QA
☎ 01263 837280
e-mail: enquiries@eiders.co.uk
web: www.eiders.co.uk
dir: *From Cromer on A148, enter Aylmerton, pass garage on left. After x-rds, 2nd entrance on right*

The Eiders is situated just a short drive from the centre of town and is ideally placed for touring the north Norfolk coast. The tastefully appointed bedrooms have lovely co-ordinated fabrics and many thoughtful touches. Breakfast is served at individual tables in the conservatory which overlooks the gardens and duck pond. Guests have the use of a heated swimming pool which is open from May to September.

Rooms 6 en suite (2 fmly) (6 GF) S £70-£90; D £80-£125* **Facilities** FTV TVL tea/coffee Cen ht Wi-fi 🎿 **Parking** 7 **Notes** LB ⊗ 🍴

At Knollside

★ ★ ★ ★ BED AND BREAKFAST

43 Cliff Rd NR26 8BJ
☎ 01263 823320 & 07771 631980
e-mail: avril@at-knollside.co.uk
web: www.at-knollside.co.uk
dir: *250yds E of town centre. A1082 to High St, onto Wyndham St & Cliff Rd*

Expect a warm welcome from the caring hosts at this delightful Victorian house overlooking the beach and sea. Bedrooms are tastefully furnished, have co-ordinated fabrics and enjoy many thoughtful touches. Breakfast is served in the elegant dining room and features local produce. Guests also have the use of a comfortable lounge.

Rooms 3 en suite D £70-£80* **Facilities** tea/coffee Cen ht Golf 36 ⛳ **Parking** 3 **Notes** LB ⊗ No Children 3yrs 🍴

Bay Leaf Guest House

★ ★ ★ ★ BED AND BREAKFAST

10 St Peters Rd NR26 8QY
☎ 01263 823779
e-mail: bayleafgh@aol.com
dir: *A149 (Weybourne Rd) onto Church St, 2nd right*

This lovely Victorian property is situated just a short walk from the golf course, steam railway and town centre. There is a smart lounge bar, and breakfast is served in the conservatory-dining room which overlooks the patio.

Rooms 7 en suite (2 fmly) (2 GF) S £35-£50; D £64-£80 **Facilities** tea/coffee Cen ht Licensed **Parking** 5 **Notes** LB ⊗ No Children 8yrs 🍴

Brambles Bed & Breakfast

★★★★ GUEST ACCOMMODATION

5 Nelson Rd NR26 8BT
☎ 01263 825567 & 07791 429093 📠 01263 825567
e-mail: enquiries@stayatbrambles.co.uk
dir: Leave A148 into Sheringham across rdbt, right at Lobster pub. Left onto Cliff Rd, right onto Nelson Rd

A warm welcome is offered by the caring hosts at this delightful detached property situated just a short walk from the seafront and town centre. The well-equipped bedrooms are pleasantly decorated. Breakfast is served in the smart dining room.

Rooms 3 en suite (2 fmly) (1 GF) S £45-£55; D £60-£75* **Facilities** FTV tea/coffee Cen ht Wi-fi **Parking** 6 **Notes** LB ⊗ 🐾

Highfield

★★★★ GUEST HOUSE

5 Montague Rd NR26 8LN
☎ 01263 825524 & 07769 628817
e-mail: gmcaldwell@aol.com
dir: Off A148, left at mini rdbt, 1st right. Left at church, left onto South St & Montague Rd

This delightful guest house is situated in a peaceful side road within easy walking distance of the shops and beach. It offers smart, thoughtfully equipped bedrooms, and breakfast is served at individual tables in the attractive dining room.

Rooms 6 rms (5 en suite) (1 pri facs) (2 fmly) **Facilities** TVL tea/coffee Cen ht **Conf** Max 20 Board 20 **Parking** 2 **Notes** ⊗ No Children 8yrs Closed 22 Dec-1 Feb 🐾

The Old Barn

★★★★ 🅰 BED AND BREAKFAST

Cromer Rd, West Runton NR27 9QT
☎ 01263 838285
e-mail: mkelliott2@aol.com
dir: A149 from Cromer to West Runton, 2m opp church
Rooms 3 rms (2 en suite) (1 pri facs) (1 GF) D £68-£80 **Facilities** TVL tea/coffee Cen ht Wi-fi **Parking** 6 **Notes** ⊗ No Children 18yrs 🐾

The Bell

★★★ INN

King St IP24 2AZ
☎ 01842 754455 📠 01842 755552
e-mail: bell.thetford@oldenglishinns.co.uk
dir: From S exit A11, 2m to 1st set of lights, turn right onto A134. 100yds turn left onto Bridge St, 150yds & over bridge

A 15th-century coaching inn situated in the heart of the old part of town. The historic charm and character permeates through much of the building. The accommodation is split between the main building and the more modern bedroom wings. Public areas include a bar, a lounge, and restaurant as well as conference facilities.

Rooms 46 en suite (1 fmly) **Facilities** tea/coffee Direct Dial **Parking** 55

The Chequers Inn

★★★★ 🅰 INN

Griston Rd IP24 1PX
☎ 01953 483360 📠 01953 488092
e-mail: richard@thompsonchequers.co.uk
dir: NE of Thetford. Off A1075 to Thompson village x-rds
Rooms 3 annexe en suite (1 fmly) (3 GF) S £45; D £65* **Facilities** FTV tea/coffee Dinner available Direct Dial Cen ht Wi-fi Fishing **Parking** 35

PREMIER COLLECTION

Holly Lodge

★★★★★ 🍴 BED AND BREAKFAST

The Street NR21 0AS
☎ 01328 878465 📠 01328 878465
e-mail: info@hollylodgeguesthouse.co.uk
dir: Off A148 into Thursford, village green on left. 2nd driveway on left past green

Holly Lodge is an award-winning 18th-century property situated in a picturesque location surrounded by open farmland. The stylish cottage bedrooms are in a converted stable block, each room individually decorated, beautifully furnished and equipped with many useful extras. The attractive public rooms have a wealth of character, with flagstone floors, oak beams and open fireplaces. There are also superb landscaped grounds to enjoy.

Rooms 3 en suite (3 GF) S £70-£100; D £90-£120 **Facilities** TVL tea/coffee Dinner available Cen ht Wi-fi **Parking** 6 **Notes** LB ⊗ No Children 14yrs

The Old Forge Seafood Restaurant

★★★★ 🍴 RESTAURANT WITH ROOMS

Seafood Restaurant, Fakenham Rd NR21 0BD
☎ 01328 878345
e-mail: sarah.goldspink@btconnect.com
dir: On A148 (Fakenham to Holt road)

Expect a warm welcome at this delightful relaxed restaurant with rooms. The open-plan public areas include a lounge bar area with comfy sofas, and an intimate restaurant with pine tables. Bedrooms are pleasantly decorated and equipped with a good range of useful facilities.

Rooms 3 en suite S £35-£55; D £65* **Facilities** STV FTV tea/coffee Dinner available Cen ht Wi-fi Riding **Conf** Max 28 Class 28 **Parking** 14 **Notes** No Children 5yrs No coaches

Red House Farm Bed & Breakfast

★★★★ BED AND BREAKFAST

Station Rd NR15 2DJ
☎ 01379 676566
e-mail: office@redhousefarm.info
dir: 500mtrs from A140

A warm welcome is assured at this delightful 17th-century barn conversion, situated on a small working farm in a peaceful rural location. The tastefully appointed bedrooms have modern furniture and lovely countryside views. Breakfast, which includes home-grown produce, is served at a large communal table in the smart kitchen.

Rooms 2 en suite **Facilities** TVL tea/coffee Cen ht Wi-fi **Parking** 4 **Notes** 🐾

Kilcoroon

★★★ BED AND BREAKFAST

Chancery Ln NR23 1ER
☎ 01328 710270 & 07733 112108
e-mail: terry@kilcoroon.co.uk
dir: Exit B1105 onto Mill Rd. 3rd right onto Buttlands. Left of Crown Hotel

Delightful detached period property situated by the green, just off the Buttlands and a short walk from the town centre. The spacious bedrooms are pleasantly decorated with co-ordinated fabrics and equipped with modern facilities. Breakfast is served at a large communal table in the elegant dining room.

Rooms 2 en suite S £60; D £70-£75* **Facilities** tea/coffee Cen ht Wi-fi **Notes** ⊗ No Children 10yrs Closed 23-31 Dec 🐾

WEST RUNTON
Map 13 TG14

Corner House

★★★★ BED AND BREAKFAST

2 Station Rd NR27 9QD
☎ 01263 838540 & 07769 800831 ▤ 01263 838540
e-mail: linjimhoward@btinternet.com
web: www.cornerhousenorfolk.com
dir: Station Rd, N off A149, in village centre, B&B 1st on right

A warm welcome is to be expected from the caring hosts at this delightful property situated just off the main coast road on the outskirts of Sheringham. Bedrooms are cheerfully decorated, have co-ordinated fabrics, and benefit from many thoughtful touches. Public areas include a large breakfast room and a cosy TV lounge.

Rooms 3 rms (1 en suite) (2 pri facs) S £43-£45; D £66-£70 **Facilities** TVL tea/coffee Cen ht **Notes** ⊗ No Children 8yrs ⊜

WORSTEAD
Map 13 TG32

The Ollands

★★★★ ▨ ⊜ GUEST HOUSE

Swanns Yard NR28 9RP
☎ 01692 535150 ▤ 01692 535150
e-mail: theollands@btinternet.com
dir: Off A149 to village x-rds, off Back St

This charming detached property is set in the heart of the picturesque village of Worstead. The well-equipped bedrooms are pleasantly decorated and carefully furnished, and breakfasts served in the elegant dining room feature local produce.

Rooms 3 en suite (1 GF) S £40-£42.50; D £66-£70* **Facilities** TVL tea/coffee Dinner available Cen ht Wi-fi **Parking** 8 **Notes** LB

NORTHAMPTONSHIRE

AYNHO
Map 11 SP53

PREMIER COLLECTION

Aynhoe Park

★★★★★ GUEST ACCOMMODATION

OX17 3BG
☎ 01869 810636 ▤ 01869 811059
e-mail: thebutler@aynhoepark.co.uk
web: www.aynhoepark.co.uk

Located in the quaint village of Aynhoe and within a short distance of both Silverstone and the M40, Aynhoe Park is a Grade I listed 17th-century house located on the border between Oxfordshire and Northamptonshire. For the first time it is now open for private hire and individual bookings. Bedrooms and bathrooms have been refurbished to offer luxury accommodation, and the public areas are spacious with contemporary decor. The large dining room can host private dinners and this is also where guests can enjoy a cooked or continental breakfast. Features include a large chandelier and a menagerie of animals. The grounds benefit from uninterrupted views of the Oxfordshire countryside and feature a large collection of sculptures.

Rooms 12 en suite D £175-£300*

CASTLE ASHBY
Map 11 SP85

The Falcon

★★★ INN

NN7 1LF
☎ 01604 696200 ▤ 01604 696673
e-mail: 6446@greeneking.co.uk
dir: Off A428

Set in the heart of a peaceful village, the inn consists of a main house and a neighbouring cottage. Bedrooms are all individually decorated and provide a wealth of thoughtful extras. Character public rooms, in the main house, include a cellar bar, a choice of lounges and a pretty restaurant serving good quality cuisine.

Rooms 5 en suite 10 annexe en suite (1 fmly) **Facilities** TVL tea/coffee Dinner available Cen ht Wi-fi **Conf** Max 100 Thtr 100 Class 60 Board 30 **Parking** 75 **Notes** LB Civ Wed 60

EASTON-ON-THE-HILL
Map 11 TF00

The Exeter Arms

★★★★★ ◉ INN

21 Stamford Rd PE9 3NS
☎ 01780 756321 ▤ 01780 753171
e-mail: reservations@theexeterarms.net
dir: A1 Nbound take exit signed Easton-on-the-Hill; A1 Sbound take exit signed A47/A43 Corby/Kettering, on left entering village

This lovely village inn is situated in north-eastern Northamptonshire just a short drive from Stamford. The public rooms have many original features such as stone walls and open fireplaces; they include a lounge bar and the Orangery Restaurant which opens out onto the terrace for alfresco dining. The modern, well-equipped bedrooms are very stylish.

Rooms 5 en suite 1 annexe en suite (2 fmly) S £60-£150; D £65-£150 **Facilities** FTV tea/coffee Dinner available Direct Dial Cen ht Wi-fi Golf 18 **Parking** 40 **Notes** No coaches

ECTON
Map 11 SP86

The World's End

★★★★ INN

Main St NN6 0QN
☎ 01604 414521 ▤ 01604 400334
e-mail: info@theworldsend.org
dir: On A4500 on outskirts of Ecton. A45 for Cogenhoe/ Great Billing, follow Ecton signs

The World's End is a modern inn with striking interior, wooden floors, leather sofas, mirrors and downlighters. Smart, well appointed, bedrooms have flat-screen TVs, broadband and power showers along with all the expected amenities. The restaurant offers plenty of choice to suit all appetites. There is an outdoor decking area for alfresco dining.

Rooms 20 en suite (9 GF) **Facilities** tea/coffee Dinner available Direct Dial Cen ht Lift Wi-fi **Conf** Max 35 Thtr 35 Class 16 Board 16 **Parking** 50 **Notes** ⊗

NASSINGTON — Map 12 TL09

The Queens Head Inn

★★★★ ◉ INN

54 Station Rd PE8 6QB
☎ 01780 784006 🖹 01780 781539
e-mail: info@queensheadnassington.co.uk
web: www.queensheadnassington.co.uk
dir: A1 Nbound exit junct 17, follow signs for Yarwell, then Nassington. Queens Head on left on entering the village

A friendly atmosphere and a warm welcome are to be expected at this delightful Inn situated on the banks of the River Nene in the picturesque village of Nassington. The adjacent bedrooms are constructed from local stone; each one is smartly appointed and well equipped. Public rooms include a smart lounge bar, a restaurant and a smart conservatory dining room.

Rooms 9 en suite (2 fmly) (9 GF) S £50-£120; D £50-£120* **Facilities** FTV tea/coffee Dinner available Direct Dial Cen ht Wi-fi Fishing **Conf** Max 50 Thtr 50 Class 20 Board 20 **Parking** 45 **Notes** LB ⊗

TOWCESTER — Map 11 SP64

The Saracens Head

★★★ INN

219 Watling St NN12 7BX
☎ 01327 350414 & 0800 917 3085 🖹 01327 359879
e-mail: saracenshead.towcester@greeneking.co.uk
dir: M1 junct 15A onto A43, at rdbt take 1st exit onto A5 (Towcester), on right

This historic coaching inn is rumoured to be the inspiration for Dickens' *Pickwick Papers*. There are smart bedrooms and a convivial bar and restaurant. Staff are young and friendly and the Saracens Head provides an excellent base for horse racing enthusiasts visiting the Towcester course and for motor racing fans heading for Silverstone.

Rooms 21 en suite (5 fmly) **Facilities** FTV tea/coffee Direct Dial Cen ht Wi-fi **Conf** Max 100 Thtr 100 Class 60 Board 50 **Parking** 32 **Notes** ⊗ No coaches Civ Wed 90

NORTHUMBERLAND

ALNWICK — Map 21 NU11

Bondgate House

★★★★ 🏠 GUEST HOUSE

20 Bondgate Without NE66 1PN
☎ 01665 602025
e-mail: enquiries@bondgatehouse.co.uk
web: www.bondgatehouse.co.uk
dir: A1 onto B6346 into town centre, 200yds past war memorial on right

Originally a doctor's house, this Georgian building stands close to the historic gateway into the town centre. Friendly service complements an attractive breakfast room, memorable breakfasts and the cosy lounge. Bedrooms are all well equipped and thoughtfully furnished and include three rooms in converted stables set in a secluded garden behind the house.

Rooms 3 en suite 3 annexe en suite (1 fmly) (1 GF) D £80-£100* **Facilities** FTV TVL tea/coffee Cen ht Wi-fi **Parking** 8 **Notes** ⊗ No Children 5yrs Closed Xmas ◉

BARDON MILL — Map 21 NY76

Gibbs Hill Farm B&B *(NY749693)*

★★★★ 🅰 FARMHOUSE

NE47 7AP
☎ 01434 344030 🖹 01434 344030
Mrs V Gibson
e-mail: val@gibbshillfarm.co.uk
dir: Off A69 at Bardon Mill, signs to Oncebrewed, over B6318, up hill, 1m right at sign to Gibbs Hill

Rooms 3 en suite (1 fmly) S £45-£60; D £70-£75* **Facilities** FTV TVL tea/coffee Dinner available Cen ht Fishing Riding **Parking** 10 **Notes** LB ⊗ No Children 10yrs Closed Nov-Apr 750 acres mixed

BELFORD — Map 21 NU13

PREMIER COLLECTION

Market Cross

★★★★★ 🏠 GUEST ACCOMMODATION

1 Church St NE70 7LS
☎ 01668 213013
e-mail: info@marketcross.net
web: www.marketcross.net
dir: Off A1 into village, opp church

Lying in the heart of the village, this Grade II listed building offers delightful, individually styled and thoughtfully equipped bedrooms. A friendly welcome awaits you, and breakfast is also a real treat, an extensive and impressive range of delicious cooked dishes using local produce.

Rooms 4 en suite S £60-£90; D £80-£120 **Facilities** FTV TVL tea/coffee Cen ht Wi-fi Golf 18 **Parking** 4 **Notes** LB

BERWICK-UPON-TWEED — Map 21 NT95

Lindisfarne Inn

★★★ INN

Beal TD15 2PD
☎ 01289 381223 🖹 01289 381223
e-mail: enquiries@lindisfarneinn.co.uk
dir: On A1, turn off for Holy Island

The Lindisfarne Inn stands on the site of the old Plough Hotel at Beal, on the road leading to Holy Island. Now totally refurbished and re-opened with a traditional bar, rustic style restaurant and comfortably equipped courtyard bedrooms in the adjacent wing. Food is available all day.

Rooms 21 annexe en suite (20 fmly) (10 GF) S £60; D £80* **Facilities** FTV TVL tea/coffee Dinner available Cen ht Wi-fi **Parking** 25

CHATTON — Map 21 NU02

PREMIER COLLECTION

Chatton Park House

★★★★★ 🏠 BED AND BREAKFAST

NE66 5RA
☎ 01668 215507 🖹 01668 215446
e-mail: enquiries@chattonpark.com
web: www.chattonpark.com
dir: A1 N or S onto B6348 for 4m, on right

This charming Georgian house is nestled in four acres of gardens, with views out to the Northumberland countryside and Cheviots hills. Once home to the current Duke of Northumberland, whose family seat is Alnwick Castle. Spacious bedrooms are very elegantly furnished, one is a suite. The dining room and drawing room overlook the gardens and both have open fires. A warm welcome is guaranteed.

Rooms 4 en suite S £100-£130; D £130-£160* **Facilities** FTV tea/coffee Cen ht Wi-fi ♨ **Parking** 4 **Notes** ⊗ No Children 18yrs Closed Jan

CORNHILL-ON-TWEED — Map 21 NT83

PREMIER COLLECTION

Ivy Cottage

★★★★★ 🏠 GUEST ACCOMMODATION

1 Croft Gardens, Crookham TD12 4ST
☎ 01890 820667 📠 01890 820667
e-mail: stay@ivycottagecrookham.co.uk
web: www.ivycottagecrookham.co.uk
dir: *4m E of Cornhill. Off A697 onto B6353 into Crookham*

Hospitality is second to none at this pristine modern house set in delightful gardens in a quiet village. Three rooms are available and all thoughtfully furnished with either a super private bathroom or full en suite. Delicious Aga-cooked breakfasts are served either in the farmhouse-style kitchen or the cosy dining room, and dinners are available by arrangement. Guests can enjoy tea in the spacious lounge or cosy summerhouse.

Rooms 3 rms (1 en suite) (2 pri facs) (1 GF) S £47-£55; D £70-£88* **Facilities** FTV TVL tea/coffee Dinner available Cen ht Wi-fi **Parking** 2 **Notes** LB ⊗ No Children 8yrs 🐾

FALSTONE — Map 21 NY78

The Blackcock Country Inn and Restaurant

★★★★ INN

NE48 1AA
☎ 01434 240200
e-mail: thebcinn@yahoo.co.uk
dir: *From Hexham take A6079 to Bellingham, then left at church. In village centre, towards Kielder Water*

This traditional family-run village inn lies close to Kielder Water. A cosy pub, it has a very homely atmosphere, with welcoming fires in the colder weather. The bedrooms are very comfortable and well equipped. Evening meals are served here or in the restaurant. The inn is closed during the day on Wednesday throughout winter.

Rooms 6 rms (4 en suite) (2 pri facs) (1 fmly) S £45-£62; D £85* **Facilities** STV tea/coffee Dinner available Cen ht Wi-fi Fishing Riding Pool table Children's play area clay pigeon shooting **Parking** 15 **Notes** LB RS Wed Closed during low season

Pheasant Inn

★★★★ 🍽 INN

Stannersburn NE48 1DD
☎ 01434 240382 📠 01434 240382
e-mail: stay@thepheasantinn.com
web: www.thepheasantinn.com
dir: *1m S of Falstone. Off B6320 to Kielder Water, via Bellingham or via Hexham A69 onto B6320 via Wall-Wark-Bellingham*

This charming establishment epitomises the traditional country inn; it has character, good food and warm hospitality. Bright modern bedrooms, some with their own entrances, are all contained in stone buildings adjoining the inn. Delicious home-cooked meals are served in the bar with its low-beamed ceilings and exposed stone walls, or in the attractive dining room.

Rooms 8 annexe en suite (1 fmly) (5 GF) S £50-£60; D £90-£95* **Facilities** tea/coffee Dinner available Cen ht ch fac Golf 18 **Parking** 40 **Notes** LB ⊗ Closed 4 days Xmas RS Nov-Mar closed Mon & Tue No coaches

HALTWHISTLE — Map 21 NY76

See also Brampton (Cumbria)

Vallum Lodge

★★★★ GUEST HOUSE

Military Rd, Twice Brewed NE47 7AN
☎ 01434 344248
e-mail: stay@vallum-lodge.co.uk
web: www.vallum-lodge.co.uk
dir: *On B6318, 400yds W of Once Brewed National Park visitors' centre*

Set in the Northumberland National Park, a real home-from-home atmosphere is found at this well-equipped roadside guest house, which provides easy access to Hadrian's Wall. The en suite bedrooms feature homely extras. Breakfast is served in the smart dining room and there is a cosy lounge. The Lodge is licensed and all accommodation is on the ground floor.

Rooms 6 en suite (1 fmly) (6 GF) D £75-£85* **Facilities** FTV TVL tea/coffee Cen ht Licensed Wi-fi **Parking** 15 **Notes** ⊗

HEXHAM — Map 21 NY96

Peth Head Cottage

★★★★ 🏠 BED AND BREAKFAST

Juniper NE47 0LA
☎ 01434 673286 📠 01434 673038
e-mail: peth_head@btopenworld.com
web: www.peth-head-cottage.co.uk
dir: *B6306 S from Hexham, 200yds fork right, next left. Continue 3.5m, house 400yds on right after Juniper sign*

Warm and caring hospitality is assured at this lovely sandstone cottage located in the peaceful hamlet of Juniper. Guests can enjoy home-made biscuits on arrival and home-baked bread and preserves at breakfast. The attractive bedrooms are equipped with lots of thoughtful extras and day rooms feature a cosy lounge-breakfast room. Self-catering is also available.

Rooms 2 en suite S £30; D £60* **Facilities** FTV TVL tea/coffee Cen ht **Parking** 2 **Notes** LB ⊗

MORPETH — Map 21 NZ18

Eshott Hall

[U]

Eshott NE65 9EN
☎ 01670 787454 & 07966 226283 📠 01670 786011
e-mail: info@eshotthall.co.uk
dir: *Eshott signed off A1. N of Morpeth*

Currently the rating for this establishment is not confirmed. This may be due to a change of ownership or because it has only recently joined the AA rating scheme.

Rooms 11 en suite (3 fmly) S £120-£210; D £120-£280* (incl.dinner) **Facilities** FTV tea/coffee Dinner available Cen ht Licensed Wi-fi 🎣 ⛳ Golf 18 Fishing **Conf** Max 100 Thtr 100 Class 50 Board 20 **Parking** 50 **Notes** LB Closed 24-27 Dec Civ Wed 100

NEWTON-ON-THE-MOOR · Map 21 NU10

The Cook and Barker Inn

★★★★ ⊜ INN

NE65 9JY
☎ 01665 575234 ▤ 01665 575234
e-mail: info@cookandbarkerinn.co.uk
dir: *North on A1, pass Morpeth. A1 becomes single carriageway for 8m, then dual carriageway. Up slight incline 3m, follow signs on left to Newton-on-the-Moor*

Set in the heart of a quiet village this inn is popular with visitors and locals. The emphasis is on food here with interesting home-made dishes offered in the restaurant and bar areas. Bedrooms are smartly furnished and well equipped and are split between the main house and the adjacent annexe.

Rooms 4 en suite 14 annexe en suite (2 fmly) (7 GF) S fr £65; D fr £85* **Facilities** tea/coffee Dinner available Direct Dial Cen ht Wi-fi **Conf** Max 50 Thtr 50 Class 50 Board 25 **Parking** 64 **Notes** LB ⊗

ROTHBURY · Map 21 NU00

PREMIER COLLECTION

The Orchard House

★★★★★ ≜ GUEST ACCOMMODATION

High St NE65 7TL
☎ 01669 620684
e-mail: graham@orchardhouserothbury.com
web: www.orchardhouserothbury.com
dir: *In village centre*

This delightful accommodation is located in an attractive Georgian period house within easy walking distance of the village amenities. Full of character, the restful atmosphere is enhanced by genuinely friendly service and hospitality. Individually styled bedrooms are all finished to a high standard and are very well equipped. The elegant lounge is richly styled and very comfortable, the elegant dining room has an honesty bar and interesting breakfasts featuring the best of local and organic produce are served here.

Rooms 5 en suite (1 fmly) **Facilities** tea/coffee Cen ht Licensed Golf 18 **Notes** ⊗ Closed Xmas & New Year

SEAHOUSES · Map 21 NU23

The Olde Ship Inn

★★★★ INN

NE68 7RD
☎ 01665 720200 ▤ 01665 721383
e-mail: theoldeship@seahouses.co.uk
dir: *Lower end of main street above harbour*

Under the same ownership since 1910, this friendly inn overlooks the harbour and is full of character. Lovingly maintained, its sense of history is evident by the amount of nautical memorabilia on display. Public areas include a character bar, cosy snug, restaurant and guests' lounge. The individual bedrooms are smartly presented. Two separate buildings contain executive apartments, all with sea views.

Rooms 12 en suite 6 annexe en suite S £51-£59; D £102-£130* **Facilities** FTV TVL tea/coffee Dinner available Direct Dial Cen ht Wi-fi Pool table **Parking** 18 **Notes** LB ⊗ No Children 10yrs Closed Dec-Jan No coaches

Bamburgh Castle Inn

★★★ INN

NE68 7SQ
☎ 01665 720283 ▤ 01665 720284
e-mail: enquiries@bamburghcastleinn.co.uk
web: www.bamburghcastleinn.co.uk
dir: *A1 onto B1341 to Bamburgh, B1340 to Seahouses, follow signs to harbour*

Situated in a prime location on the quayside in the popular coastal resort of Seahouses, this establishment has arguably the best viewpoint along the coast. Dating back to the 18th century, the inn has been transformed in recent years and has superb dining and bar areas, with outside seating available in warmer weather. There are smart, comfortable bedrooms, many with views of the Farne Islands and the inn's famous namesake Bamburgh Castle.

Rooms 27 en suite 2 annexe en suite (6 fmly) (8 GF) **Facilities** FTV TVL tea/coffee Dinner available Cen ht Sauna Solarium Gym Access to Ocean Club Spa **Conf** Max 50 **Parking** 35 **Notes** LB

WOOLER · Map 21 NT92

PREMIER COLLECTION

The Old Manse

★★★★★ ≜ GUEST ACCOMMODATION

New Rd, Chatton NE66 5PU
☎ 01668 215343 & 07811 411808
e-mail: chattonbb@aol.com
web: www.oldmansechatton.co.uk
dir: *4m E of Wooler. On B6348 in Chatton*

Built in 1875, this elegant former manse is located on the edge of the village convenient for St Cuthbert's Way. There is a four-poster and double room upstairs, and a ground-floor room with its own entrance, sitting room and patio; all are thoughtfully equipped with a wealth of thoughtful extras including fridge with fruit, CD player, juices and biscuits. Sumptuous day rooms include wood-burning stoves. Impressive breakfasts are served in a conservatory overlooking the pretty gardens and a warm welcome is assured.

Rooms 3 en suite (1 GF) S £50-£65; D £86-£100* **Facilities** TVL tea/coffee Cen ht Wi-fi **Parking** 4 **Notes** ⊗ No Children 14yrs Closed Nov-Feb ⊛

NOTTINGHAMSHIRE

BINGHAM · Map 11 SK73

Yeung Sing

★★★ GUEST ACCOMMODATION

15 Market St NG13 8AB
☎ 01949 831831 & 831222 ▤ 01949 838833
e-mail: manager@yeung-sing.co.uk
dir: *Off junct A52 & A46*

This family-run guest accommodation is in the centre of the market town. The smart ground-floor public rooms include a bar and the highly successful Yeung Sing restaurant, which serves a fine selection of Cantonese and regional Chinese dishes. The bedrooms are well equipped and have modern en suites.

Rooms 15 en suite (2 fmly) S £49-£52; D £69-£75* **Facilities** FTV TVL tea/coffee Dinner available Direct Dial Cen ht Lift Licensed **Conf** Max 100 Thtr 100 Class 30 Board 30 **Parking** 30 **Notes** LB ⊗ Closed 25-26 Dec

COTGRAVE   Map 11 SK63

Jerico Farm *(SK654307)*

★★★★ 🏠 FARMHOUSE

Fosse Way NG12 3HG
☎ 01949 81733
Mrs S Herrick
e-mail: info@jericofarm.co.uk
web: www.jericofarm.co.uk
dir: *Farm driveway off A46, 1m N of junct A46 & A606*

A friendly relaxed atmosphere is offered at this attractive farmhouse, which stands in peaceful extensive grounds just off the A46, close to Nottingham, Melton Mowbray and the Vale of Belvoir. Day rooms include a comfortable lounge and a separate dining room overlooking the gardens, in which substantial tasty breakfasts are served. Spacious bedrooms are beautifully appointed and thoughtfully equipped.

Rooms 3 en suite S £45-£50; D £65-£80* **Facilities** FTV TVL tea/coffee Cen ht Wi-fi Fishing **Conf** Max 6 **Parking** 4 **Notes** ⊗ No Children 10yrs Closed 24 Dec-2 Jan 150 acres mixed

EASTWOOD   Map 11 SK44

The Sun Inn

★★★ INN

6 Derby Rd NG16 3NT
☎ 01773 712940 📠 01773 531563

Built in 1705, this Grade II listed building is located right in the centre of Eastwood with easy access to the Derbyshire Dales for walkers and Nottingham for shoppers. The well-equipped bedrooms are all en suite and offer modern facilities.

Rooms 15 en suite (1 fmly) **Facilities** FTV tea/coffee Dinner available Cen ht Wi-fi Pool table **Conf** Max 15 Thtr 15 Class 8 Board 15 **Parking** 8 **Notes** ⊗

EDWINSTOWE   Map 16 SK66

The Forest Lodge

★★★★ INN

Church St NG21 9QA
☎ 01623 824443 📠 01623 824686
e-mail: reception@forestlodgehotel.co.uk
dir: *A614 into Edwinstowe. On B6034, opp St Mary's church*

Situated in the heart of Sherwood Forest, The Forest Lodge is a 17th-century coaching inn, lovingly restored and refurbished to provide the visitor with a warm and homely base from which to explore the unique attractions of this fascinating and historic area. The rooms have been tastefully modernised and the bar provides home comforts and good company. Food is served in the bar or in the restaurant.

Rooms 8 en suite 5 annexe en suite (2 fmly) (5 GF) S £67-£75; D £85-£90* **Facilities** FTV tea/coffee Dinner

---

available Cen ht Wi-fi **Conf** Max 75 Thtr 75 Class 45 Board 50 **Parking** 35

The Dukeries Lodge

[U]

Main St NG21 9HS
☎ 01623 822553
e-mail: mark.gallagher@pubpeople.com

Currently the rating for this establishment is not confirmed. This may be due to a change of ownership or because it has only recently joined the AA rating scheme.

Rooms 17 en suite S £45; D £75*

ELTON   Map 11 SK73

PREMIER COLLECTION

The Grange

★★★★★ BED AND BREAKFAST

Sutton Ln NG13 9LA
☎ 07887 952181
web: www.thegrangebedandbreakfastnotts.co.uk
dir: *From Grantham A1 onto A52 to Elton x-rds, left 200yds, B&B on right*

Parts of this lovely house date back to the early 17th century and the rooms command fine views across the gardens and rolling open countryside. Bedrooms contain many thoughtful extras and fine hospitality is assured from the proprietors.

Rooms 3 en suite S £45-£55; D £70-£75 **Facilities** FTV TVL tea/coffee Cen ht Wi-fi **Parking** 8 **Notes** ⊗ ⊛

HOLBECK   Map 16 SK57

PREMIER COLLECTION

Browns

★★★★★ 🏠 BED AND BREAKFAST

The Old Orchard Cottage, Holbeck Ln S80 3NF
☎ 01909 720659 📠 01909 720659
e-mail: browns.holbeck@btconnect.com
dir: *0.5m off A616 Sheffield-Newark road, turn for Holbeck at x-rds*

Set amid beautifully tended gardens with lily-ponds and extensive lawns, this mid 18th-century cottage is a tranquil rural hideaway. Breakfasts are served in the Regency-style dining room, and the elegant bedrooms have four-poster beds and many extras. The friendly owners provide attentive service, including courtesy transport to nearby restaurants if required.

Rooms 3 annexe en suite (3 GF) S £59-£67; D £77-£87 **Facilities** FTV tea/coffee Cen ht **Parking** 3 **Notes** ⊗ No Children 15yrs Closed Xmas wk ⊛

HOLME PIERREPONT   Map 11 SK63

Holme Grange Cottage

★★★ GUEST ACCOMMODATION

Adbolton Ln NG12 2LU
☎ 0115 981 0413
e-mail: jean.colinwightman@talk21.com
dir: *Off A52 SE of Nottingham, opp National Water Sports Centre main entrance*

A stone's throw from the National Water Sports Centre, this establishment with its own all-weather tennis court is ideal for the active guest. Indeed, when not providing warm hospitality and freshly cooked breakfasts, the proprietor is usually on the golf course.

Rooms 3 rms (1 en suite) (1 fmly) S £32-£36; D £52-£58 **Facilities** TVL tea/coffee Cen ht Wi-fi 🎾 **Parking** 6 **Notes** LB Closed Xmas ⊛

MANSFIELD   Map 16 SK56

Bridleways Holiday Homes & Guest House

★★★★ GUEST HOUSE

Newlands Rd, Forest Town NG19 0HU
☎ 01623 635725 📠 01623 635725
e-mail: bridleways@webnet2000.net
web: www.stayatbridleways.co.uk
dir: *Off B6030*

Beside a quiet bridleway that leads to Vicar Water Country Park and Sherwood Pines Forest Park this friendly guest house is a good touring base for walkers, cyclists or sightseeing. The new double, twin and family bedrooms are particularly spacious and all are en suite. Lovely breakfasts are served in a cottage style dining room.

Rooms 9 en suite (1 fmly) (2 GF) S £37; D £70* **Facilities** FTV tea/coffee Wi-fi **Parking** 14 **Notes** ⊗

NEWARK-ON-TRENT
Map 17 SK75

Compton House

★★★★ 🛏 🍽 GUEST HOUSE

117 Baldertongate NG24 1RY
☎ **01636 708670**
e-mail: info@comptonhousenewark.com
web: www.comptonhousenewark.com
dir: *500yds SE of town centre. Off B6326 onto Sherwood Av, 1st right onto Baldertongate*

Located a short walk from the central attractions, this elegant period house has been renovated to provide high standards of comfort. Individually themed bedrooms come with a wealth of thoughtful extras and smart modern bathrooms. Comprehensive breakfasts, and wholesome dinners by arrangement, are served in the attractive dining room and a lounge is available. Lisa Holloway is the winner of this year's AA Friendliest Landlady of the Year Award (2011-12).

Rooms 7 rms (6 en suite) (1 pri facs) (1 fmly) (1 GF) S £45-£75; D £90-£115* **Facilities** FTV tea/coffee Dinner available Cen ht Wi-fi **Conf** Max 10 Thtr 10 Class 10 Board 10 **Parking** 2 **Notes** ⊗ Closed Xmas

Acers Services Apartments

★★★★ GUEST ACCOMMODATION

150 London Rd NG24 3BN
☎ **01636 610357**
e-mail: macdougallmeg@gmail.com

Situated on the London Road with easy assess to Newark. Bedrooms are situated in an annexe at the rear of the property. They are comfortably furnished, well equipped and offer a small kitchenette. A continental-style breakfast is provided in your room.

Rooms 4 en suite (4 GF) S fr £40; D fr £55 **Facilities** FTV tea/coffee Cen ht Wi-fi **Parking** 4 **Notes** ⊗ 🍽

NOTTINGHAM
Map 11 SK53

See also Cotgrave

PREMIER COLLECTION

Restaurant Sat Bains with Rooms

★★★★★ 🏵🏵🏵🏵🏵 🛏
RESTAURANT WITH ROOMS

Trentside, Lenton Ln NG7 2SA
☎ **0115 986 6566** 📠 **0115 986 0343**
e-mail: info@restaurantsatbains.net
dir: *M1 junct 24 take A453 Nottingham S. Over River Trent in central lane to rdbt. Left then left again towards river. Establishment on left after bend*

This charming restaurant with rooms, a stylish conversion of Victorian farm buildings, is situated on the river and close to the industrial area of Nottingham. The bedrooms create a warm atmosphere by using quality soft furnishings together with antique and period furniture; suites and four-poster rooms are available. Public areas are chic and cosy, and the delightful restaurant complements the truly outstanding cuisine.

Rooms 4 en suite 4 annexe en suite (6 GF) **Facilities** STV Dinner available Direct Dial Cen ht **Parking** 22 **Notes** ⊗ Closed 1st wk Jan & 2wks mid Aug RS Sun & Mon rooms & restaurant closed

Cockliffe Country House

★★★★ 🏵 RESTAURANT WITH ROOMS

Burntstump Country Park, Burntstump Hill, Arnold NG5 8PQ
☎ **0115 968 0179** 📠 **0115 968 0623**
e-mail: enquiries@cockliffehouse.co.uk

Expect a warm welcome at this delightful property situated in a peaceful rural location amidst neat landscaped grounds, close to Sherwood Forest. Public areas include a smart breakfast room, a tastefully appointed restaurant and a cosy lounge bar. The individually decorated bedrooms have co-ordinated soft furnishings and many thoughtful touches.

Rooms 7 en suite 4 annexe en suite (5 GF) S £79-£89; D £109-£155* **Facilities** FTV tea/coffee Dinner available Direct Dial Cen ht Wi-fi 🍽 **Conf** Max 30 Thtr 30 Class 25 Board 30 **Parking** 60 **Notes** No coaches Civ Wed 60

Beech Lodge

★★★★ GUEST ACCOMMODATION

222 Porchester Rd NG3 6HG
☎ **0115 952 3314 & 07961 075939**
e-mail: paulinegoodwin222@hotmail.com
web: www.beechlodgeguesthouse.com
dir: *Off A684 onto Porchester Rd, 8th left, Punchbowl pub on right corner, Beech Lodge on left corner*

A friendly welcome is assured at Beech Lodge and the modern accommodation is well presented and suitably equipped. The ground-floor lounge is particularly comfortable, and there is a small conservatory. Breakfast is a good choice of freshly cooked and carefully presented fare served in the dining area next to the lounge.

Rooms 4 en suite (1 fmly) S £35; D £65* **Facilities** FTV TVL tea/coffee Cen ht Wi-fi **Parking** 4 **Notes** LB ⊗

The Yellow House

★★★★ BED AND BREAKFAST

7 Littlegreen Rd, Woodthorpe NG5 4LE
☎ **0115 926 2280**
e-mail: suzanne.prewsmith1@btinternet.com
web: www.bandb-nottingham.co.uk
dir: *Off A60 Mansfield Rd N from city centre onto Thackery's Ln, over rdbt, right onto Whernside Rd to x-rds, left onto Littlegreen Rd, house on left*

This semi-detached private house is in a quiet residential suburb to the north-east of the city, with easy access. A warm welcome is assured; the one purpose-built bedroom contains many thoughtful extras, and the family's pet dog is also very friendly.

Rooms 1 en suite S fr £45; D fr £65 **Facilities** FTV tea/coffee Cen ht **Parking** 1 **Notes** ⊗ No Children Closed Xmas & New Year 🍽

Hall Farm House

★★★ GUEST ACCOMMODATION

Gonalston NG14 7JA
☎ **0115 966 3112**
web: www.hallfarmhousebandb.com
dir: *NE of Nottingham. Off A612 x-rds into Gonalston, 1st right after post box*

This charming 17th-century former farmhouse is tucked away behind trees in the pretty village of Gonalston. Bedrooms are comfortable, and the beamed living rooms are full of character. There are extensive grounds, and a good choice of pubs for evening meals nearby.

Rooms 4 rms (2 en suite) (1 fmly) **Facilities** TVL TV3B tea/coffee Cen ht 🐾 🍽 Table tennis **Parking** 5 **Notes** LB ⊗ Closed 20 Dec-2 Jan 🍽

NOTTINGHAM *continued*

Old Rectory Farm B&B

★★★ 🛏 BED AND BREAKFAST

Main St, Strelley Village NG8 6PE
☎ 0115 929 8838
e-mail: enq@oldrectoryfarm.com
dir: *M1 junct 26 onto A6002, after 1m turn right to Strelley village, 0.5m opp church*

Located in the pretty village of Strelley opposite the notable All Saints parish church, this period property has been sympathetically restored to provide modern comfort in a home-from-home atmosphere. Bedrooms are equipped with lots of thoughtful extras, and memorable breakfasts feature eggs from the farm's own chickens, along with home-made preserves.

Rooms 4 rms (2 en suite) (1 fmly) (1 GF) **Facilities** TVL tea/coffee Cen ht Wi-fi **Parking** 6 **Notes** LB 🐾

Fairhaven

★★ GUEST ACCOMMODATION

19 Meadow Rd, Beeston NG9 1JP
☎ 0115 922 7509 📠 0115 922 5344
e-mail: info@fairhavennottingham.com
web: www.fairhavennottingham.com
dir: *A52 onto B6005 for Beeston station, 200yds after bridge*

This well-established guest accommodation is in the quiet residential suburb of Beeston on the outskirts of Nottingham. The public rooms offer a stylish reception lounge, and breakfast is served in the cosy dining room. The bedrooms vary in style and size.

Rooms 14 rms (10 en suite) (1 fmly) (1 GF) S £30-£42; D £52* **Facilities** tea/coffee Cen ht Licensed Wi-fi **Parking** 13

SOUTHWELL	**Map 17 SK65**

PREMIER COLLECTION

The Old Vicarage

★★★★★ 🍴 RESTAURANT WITH ROOMS

Westhrope NG25 0NB
☎ 01636 815989 📱 07787 534635
📠 0872 352 1940
e-mail: reservations@vicarageboutiquehotel.co.uk

The Old Vicarage provides high standards of accommodation and service. Bedrooms and bathrooms are individually designed and retain many original features. The public areas have a real contemporary look and feel, including wooden floors and highly polished tables. The dining room, overlooking the lovely gardens, is spacious with lots of natural light. Outside there is a hot tub and seating area. The establishment is owner-managed ensuring first-class service and attention to detail.

Rooms 8 en suite (2 fmly) (1 GF) S £85-£95; D £95-£188 **Facilities** STV FTV TVL tea/coffee Dinner

available Direct Dial Cen ht Lift Wi-fi **Conf** Max 15 Thtr 15 Class 10 Board 12 **Parking** 25 **Notes** 🐾 Civ Wed 60

The Old Forge

★★★ GUEST HOUSE

Burgage Ln NG25 0ER
☎ 01636 812809 📠 01636 816302
e-mail: theoldforgesouthwell@yahoo.co.uk
dir: *Off A612 past Minster, Church St, left onto Newark Rd, 2nd left onto Burgage Ln*

An interesting house packed with pictures and antique furniture, the Old Forge is central and handy for the Minster, while its own parking also makes this a good touring base. Bedrooms are comfortable, and a secluded conservatory-lounge and spacious breakfast room are available.

Rooms 3 en suite 1 annexe en suite (1 GF) **Facilities** tea/coffee Direct Dial Cen ht **Parking** 4

WELLOW	**Map 17 SK66**

Scotts Farm B&B

★★★ BED AND BREAKFAST

Wellow Park Stables, Rufford Ln NG22 0EQ
☎ 01623 861040 📱 07860 869378 📠 01623 835292
e-mail: wellowpark@btconnect.com
web: www.wellowpark.co.uk
dir: *A616 SE from New Ollerton, 1m right onto Rufford Ln*

Scotts Farm is a part of Wellow Park Stables, a family equestrian centre located on the quiet outskirts of Wellow in Sherwood Forest. Breakfast is served in the kitchen. Stabling, dressage instruction, showjumping and cross-country rides are available by arrangement.

Rooms 3 rms (1 en suite) (3 fmly) **Facilities** tea/coffee Cen ht Riding **Parking** 6 **Notes** LB 🐾

WORKSOP	**Map 16 SK57**

Acorn Lodge

★★★★ GUEST ACCOMMODATION

85 Potter St S80 2HL
☎ 01909 478383 📠 01909 478383
e-mail: info@acornlodgeworksop.co.uk
dir: *A1 onto A57. Take B6040 (town centre) through Manton, Lodge on right, 100mtrs past Priory*

Originally part of the community house of the Priory Church, this property has been modernised to offer comfortable, well-appointed accommodation. Good breakfasts are served in the pleasant breakfast room and ample private parking is available at the rear.

Rooms 7 en suite (2 fmly) **Facilities** FTV tea/coffee Cen ht Wi-fi **Parking** 15 **Notes** 🐾

OXFORDSHIRE

ABINGDON	**Map 5 SU49**

PREMIER COLLECTION

B&B Rafters

★★★★★ 🛏 BED AND BREAKFAST

Abingdon Rd OX13 6NU
☎ 01865 391298 📠 01865 391173
e-mail: enquiries@bnb-rafters.co.uk
web: www.bnb-rafters.co.uk
dir: *A34 onto A415 towards Witney, Rafters on A415 in Marcham next to pedestrian crossing, on the right*

Set amid immaculate gardens, this modern house is built in a half-timbered style and offers spacious accommodation together with a warm welcome. Bedrooms are stylishly furnished and equipped with a range of homely extras. Comprehensive breakfasts feature local and organic produce when possible.

Rooms 4 en suite S £52-£89; D £95-£120* **Facilities** FTV tea/coffee Cen ht Wi-fi **Parking** 4 **Notes** 🐾

The Dog House

★★★ INN

Faringdon Rd, Frilford Heath OX13 6QJ
☎ 01865 390830 📠 01865 390860
e-mail: doghouse.frilfordheath@oldenglishinns.co.uk

As its name suggests, The Dog House was once the kennels (and the stables) for a local manor house. Situated in the heart of the Oxfordshire countryside, this is a popular inn with a spacious bar and restaurant that offer a wide variety of meals and lighter options, with carvery available on Sundays. Conference facilities and weddings are also catered for.

Rooms 20 en suite (2 fmly) (4 GF) **Facilities** tea/coffee Dinner available Direct Dial Cen ht Wi-fi **Conf** Thtr 30 Class 10 Board 18 **Parking** 40

ADDERBURY   Map 11 SP43

Red Lion
★★★ INN

The Green, Oxford Rd OX17 3LU
☎ 01295 810269 📠 01295 811906
e-mail: 6496@greeneking.co.uk
web: www.oldenglish.co.uk
dir: *M40 junct 11 into Banbury, take A4260 towards Bodicote into Adderbury, on left*

This charming former coaching inn was once an important stop-over on the old Banbury to Oxford road. The atmosphere typifies an English inn, and dedicated staff provide a warm welcome. The comfortable and spacious bedrooms are attractively decorated - some are split-level and one has a four-poster. Honest, fresh food is served in the restaurant and the bar.

Rooms 12 en suite (1 GF) **Facilities** FTV tea/coffee Direct Dial Wi-fi **Notes** ⊗

ARDINGTON   Map 5 SU48

The Boar's Head
★★★★ ⊚⊚ INN

Church St OX12 8QA
☎ 01235 833254 📠 01235 833254
e-mail: info@boarsheadardington.co.uk
dir: *In village next to church*

This characterful inn has been serving the local community for over 150 years and is set in a beautiful and seemingly timeless village. Great care has gone into creating a stylish ambience in the comfortable bedrooms, and the welcoming bar and restaurant where Bruce Buchan's accomplished cuisine can be enjoyed.

Rooms 3 en suite (1 fmly) **Facilities** tea/coffee Dinner available Direct Dial Cen ht Wi-fi **Parking** 20 **Notes** No coaches

ASTON ROWANT   Map 5 SU79

Lambert Arms
★★★★★ ⊚ 🔒 INN

London Rd OX49 5SB
☎ 0845 4593736 📠 01844 351893
e-mail: info@lambertarms.com
web: www.lambertarms.com
dir: *M40 junct 6, follow signs to Chinnor (B4009) then left to Thame (A40)*

Completely transformed inside, yet retaining original, historical features, this lovely coaching inn has been caringly restored to its former glory, with a modern twist. You'll find a comfortable and friendly bar with open log fires, real ales and a mouth-watering array of food, including favourite pub classics using fresh, seasonal locally sourced produce.

Rooms 9 rms (8 en suite) (1 pri facs) 35 annexe en suite (13 fmly) (16 GF) **Facilities** STV FTV tea/coffee Dinner available Direct Dial Cen ht Lift Wi-fi Golf Gym Ella Bache Treatment rooms **Conf** Max 140 Thtr 120 Class 62 Board 38 **Parking** 75 **Notes** Civ Wed 120

BAMPTON   Map 5 SP30

Upham House Bed & Breakfast
★★★★ BED AND BREAKFAST

The Lanes OX18 2JG
☎ 01993 852703 & 07946 625563 📠 01993 852703
e-mail: pat@uphamhouse.co.uk
web: www.uphamhouse.co.uk
dir: *A4095 between Faringdon & Brize Norton*

A delightful stone-built house in a traditional country style, Upham House provides well-appointed and tastefully decorated accommodation, with a welcoming atmosphere; quality linens and towels, comfortable beds, fresh flowers and local produce used wherever possible. Situated in part of the Conservation Area of Bampton, with no passing traffic, yet only five minutes' walk from the village centre, it is just a short drive from the River Thames and Kelmscott Manor - home of William Morris. Bampton is just eight miles from Burford, 'the gateway to the Cotswolds.'

Rooms 2 rms (1 en suite) (1 pri facs) S fr £35; D £60-£70 **Facilities** FTV TVL tea/coffee Cen ht Wi-fi **Parking** 3 **Notes** ⊗ No Children 2yrs Closed 10 Dec-5 Jan 🐾

BANBURY   Map 11 SP44

The Cromwell Lodge
★★★★ INN

9-11 North Bar OX16 0TB
☎ 01295 259781 📠 01295 276619
e-mail: 6434@greeneking.co.uk
dir: *M40 junct 11 towards Banbury, through 3 sets of lights, property on left just before Banbury Cross*

Enjoying a central location, this 17th-century property is full of character and has been sympathetically refurbished. Diners can choose between the lounge, the delightful walled garden and patio, or the smart restaurant. The comfortable bedrooms are furnished and equipped to a good standard. Parking is available at the rear of the building.

Rooms 23 en suite (1 fmly) (3 GF) **Facilities** Direct Dial **Parking** 20

The Blinking Owl
★★★ INN

Main St, North Newington OX15 6AE
☎ 01295 730650
e-mail: theblinkingowl@btinternet.com
dir: *B4035 from Banbury, 2m sharp bend, right to North Newington, inn opp green*

An important part of the community in the pretty village of North Newington, this former 17th-century inn retains many original features including impressive open fires. Straight forward food and a range of real ales are served in the beamed bar-lounges. The converted barn houses the three bedrooms and the restaurant, which is open at weekends.

Rooms 3 en suite **Facilities** tea/coffee Dinner available Cen ht **Parking** 14 **Notes** ⊗ 🐾

Fairlawns
★★★ GUEST ACCOMMODATION

60 Oxford Rd OX16 9AN
☎ 01295 262461 & 07831 330220 📠 01295 261296
e-mail: fairlawnsgh@aol.com
dir: *0.5m S of Banbury Cross on A4260 opp Horton Hospital*

This extended Edwardian house retains many original features and has a convenient location. Bedrooms are mixed in size, and all are neatly furnished, some with direct access to the car park. A comprehensive breakfast is served in the traditional dining room and a selection of soft drinks and snacks is also available.

Rooms 11 rms (10 en suite) 6 annexe en suite (5 fmly) (9 GF) S £54; D £64* **Facilities** FTV tea/coffee Direct Dial Cen ht Wi-fi **Parking** 17

BICESTER   Map 11 SP52

Manor Farm B&B

★★★★ BED AND BREAKFAST

Hethe OX27 8ES
☎ **01869 277602**
e-mail: chrmanor@aol.com
web: www.freewebs.com/manorfarm
dir: *Off B4100 signed Hardwick, 2m to Hethe. In village 1st house after church (entrance through thatched arch)*

Guests are warmly welcomed at this delightful stone farmhouse in the peaceful village of Hethe, close to the M40 and Bicester, and a short drive from Oxford. The property retains many original features such as Georgian beams and open fireplaces, and offers comfortable spacious accommodation with beautiful stylish bathrooms. A hearty breakfast with home-made preserves is included.

Rooms 2 rms (1 en suite) (1 pri facs) S £45-£75; D £75-£85 **Facilities** FTV tea/coffee Cen ht Wi-fi **Parking** 2 **Notes** LB ⊗ ⊛

BURFORD   Map 5 SP21

PREMIER COLLECTION

Burford House

★★★★★ GUEST ACCOMMODATION

99 High St OX18 4QA
☎ **01993 823151** 📄 **01993 823240**
e-mail: stay@burfordhouse.co.uk
dir: *Off A40 onto A361, on right half way down hill*

This charming house provides superb quality with a professional and friendly welcome. The bedrooms offer very good quality, space and comfort. Wonderful lunches and afternoon teas are served daily, while dinners are available by prior arrangement.

Rooms 8 en suite (1 fmly) (1 GF) **Facilities** STV tea/coffee Dinner available Direct Dial Cen ht Licensed Wi-fi **Notes** ⊗

The Bull at Burford

★★★★ ⊛⊛ 🍴 RESTAURANT WITH ROOMS

105 High St OX18 4RG
☎ **01993 822220** 📄 **01993 824055**
e-mail: info@bullatburford.co.uk
dir: *In town centre*

Situated in the heart of a pretty Cotswold town, The Bull has undergone major refurbishment. Originally built in 1475 as a rest house for the local priory, it now has stylish, attractively presented bedrooms that still reflect charm and character. Dinner should not be missed and the award-winning restaurant has an imaginative menu along with an excellent choice of wines. Lunch is served daily and afternoon tea is popular. There is a residents' lounge, and free Wi-fi is available.

Rooms 12 en suite (1 fmly) S £60-£105; D £70-£140 **Facilities** FTV tea/coffee Dinner available Cen ht Wi-fi **Conf** Thtr 24 Class 12 Board 12 **Parking** 6 **Notes** LB

Potters Hill Farm *(SP300148)*

★★★★ FARMHOUSE

Leafield OX29 9QB
☎ **01993 878018** 📄 **01993 878018**
Mrs K Stanley
e-mail: potterabout@freenet.co.uk
dir: *4.5m NE of Burford. A361 onto B4437, 1st right, 1st left, 1.5m on left*

Located on a working farm in peaceful parkland with diverse wildlife, this converted coach house stands next to the farmhouse. It has been refurbished to offer comfortable bedrooms with many original features. Breakfast served in the main farmhouse features local produce.

Rooms 3 annexe en suite (1 fmly) (2 GF) S £30-£50; D £65-£70* **Facilities** tea/coffee Dinner available Cen ht Wi-fi **Parking** 5 **Notes** ⊗ ⊛ 770 acres mixed/sheep

---

The Golden Pheasant

★★★ INN

91 High St OX18 4QA
☎ **01993 823223** 📄 **01993 822621**
e-mail: andrew@goldenpheasant-burford.co.uk
web: www.goldenpheasant-burford.co.uk

Ideally located in the heart of Burford, this privately owned, 18th-century property offers comfortable accommodation for the leisure and business traveller. It is also the ideal base for exploring the surrounding Cotswold area. Meals are served in the attractive restaurant with its period fireplace.

Rooms 10 rms (9 en suite) (1 pri facs) **Facilities** tea/coffee Dinner available Direct Dial Cen ht Wi-fi **Parking** 8

The Inn For All Seasons

★★★ RESTAURANT WITH ROOMS

The Barringtons OX18 4TN
☎ **01451 844324** 📄 **01451 844375**
e-mail: sharp@innforallseasons.com
web: www.innforallseasons.com
dir: *3m W of Burford on A40 towards Cheltenham*

This charming 16th-century coaching inn is close to the pretty village of Burford. The individually styled bedrooms are comfortable, and include a four-poster room, as well as a family room that sleeps four. The public areas include a cosy bar with oak beams and real fires. There is a good choice on the bar menu, and evening meals feature the best of local Cotswold produce. The inn is a dog-friendly establishment and two of the ground-floor bedrooms have direct access to the garden and an exercise area.

Rooms 10 en suite (1 fmly) **Facilities** Dinner available

CHIPPING NORTON — Map 10 SP32

PREMIER COLLECTION

The Feathered Nest Inn

★ ★ ★ ★ ★ ◉◉ 🍴 INN

OX7 6SD
☎ 01993 833030 📄 01993 833031
e-mail: info@thefeatherednestinn.co.uk
web: www.thefeatherednestinn.co.uk

(For full entry see Nether Westcote (Gloucestershire))

Wild Thyme Restaurant with Rooms

U

10 New St OX7 5LJ
☎ 01608 645060
e-mail: enquiries@wildthymerestaurant.co.uk
dir: On A44 in town centre off Market Sq

Currently the rating for this establishment is not confirmed. This may be due to a change of ownership or because it has only recently joined the AA rating scheme.

Rooms 3 en suite S £55-£75; D £65-£85* **Facilities** tea/coffee Dinner available Cen ht Licensed Wi-fi **Notes** ✖ Closed 2wks Jan & 1 wk in Spring

CHISELHAMPTON — Map 5 SU59

Coach & Horses

★ ★ ★ 🍴 INN

Watlington Rd OX44 7UX
☎ 01865 890255 📄 01865 891995
e-mail: enquiries@coachhorsesinn.co.uk
dir: On B480

Located six miles south-east of Oxford, this 16th-century inn retains original exposed beams and open fires, while furniture styles enhance the character of the building. A wide range of imaginative food is served, and the practically equipped chalet-style bedrooms have lovely rural views.

Rooms 9 annexe en suite **Facilities** tea/coffee Dinner available Direct Dial Cen ht **Conf** Max 12 **Parking** 30

EAST HENDRED — Map 5 SU48

Mather House

★ ★ ★ ★ GUEST ACCOMMODATION

White Rd OX12 8JG
☎ 01235 833338 📄 01235 821632
e-mail: greensands@btconnect.com

Located within easy reach of transport networks, this newly refurbished accommodation benefits from a peaceful rural setting. Bedrooms and bathrooms are spacious and comfortably appointed with a number of thoughtful accessories. A hearty breakfast is served in the bright breakfast room. The property provides ample parking.

Rooms 4 en suite **Facilities** FTV tea/coffee Cen ht Wi-fi **Parking** 10 **Notes** ✖

FARINGDON — Map 5 SU29

Chowle Farmhouse Bed & Breakfast (SU272925)

★ ★ ★ ★ FARMHOUSE

SN7 7SR
☎ 01367 241688
Mr & Mrs Muir
e-mail: info@chowlefarmhouse.co.uk
web: www.chowlefarmhouse.co.uk
dir: From Faringdon rdbt on A420, 2m W on right. From Watchfield rdbt 1.5m E on left

Chowle is a delightful modern farmhouse in a quiet setting, just off the A420 and ideally placed for visiting Oxford and Swindon. Bedrooms are very well equipped, and there is a charming and airy downstairs breakfast room. An outdoor pool and hot tub are available to guests. There is ample parking space.

Rooms 4 en suite (1 GF) **Facilities** FTV tea/coffee Cen ht Wi-fi ⚲ Golf 9 Fishing Riding Sauna Gym Clay pigeon shooting, Indoor spa **Parking** 10 **Notes** LB 10 acres pedigree beef cattle

The Trout at Tadpole Bridge

★ ★ ★ ★ ◉ INN

Buckland Marsh SN7 8RF
☎ 01367 870382 📄 01367 870912
e-mail: info@troutinn.co.uk
web: www.troutinn.co.uk
dir: A420 Swindon to Oxford road, turn signed Bampton. Inn 2m on right

The Trout is located 'where the River Thames meets the Cotswolds'. The peaceful location offers riverside walks from the door and berthing for up to six boats. Bedrooms and bathrooms are located adjacent to the inn and all rooms are very comfortable and well equipped with welcome extras. The main bar and restaurant offer an excellent selection of carefully prepared local produce at both lunch and dinner, together with cask ales and a varied choice of wines by the glass.

Rooms 3 en suite 3 annexe en suite (1 fmly) (4 GF) **Facilities** FTV tea/coffee Dinner available Cen ht Wi-fi Fishing **Conf** Max 20 Thtr 20 Class 20 Board 20 **Parking** 40 **Notes** LB Closed 25-26 Dec No coaches

The Eagle

U

Little Coxwell SN7 7LW
☎ 01367 241879
e-mail: eaglelittlecoxwell@gmail.com
dir: M4 junct 15, 3rd exit onto A419 then A420 signed Oxford, turn right into village

Currently the rating for this establishment is not confirmed. This may be due to a change of ownership or because it has only recently joined the AA rating scheme.

Rooms 6 en suite S £60-£70; D £65-£75 **Facilities** FTV Dinner available Cen ht Licensed Wi-fi **Notes** LB

GORING · Map 5 SU68

PREMIER COLLECTION

The Miller of Mansfield

⊛ RESTAURANT WITH ROOMS

High St RG8 9AW
☎ 01491 872829 📠 01491 873100
e-mail: reservations@millerofmansfield.com
web: www.millerofmansfield.com
dir: *M40 junct 7, S on A329 towards Benson, A4074 towards Reading, B4009 towards Goring. Or M4 junct 12, S on A4 towards Newbury. 3rd rdbt onto A340 to Pangbourne. A329 to Streatley, right at lights onto B4009 into Goring*

The frontage of this former coaching inn hides sumptuous rooms with a distinctive and individual style, an award-winning restaurant that serves appealing dishes using locally sourced ingredients, and a comfortable bar, which serves real ales, fine wines, afternoon tea and a bar menu for a quick bite to eat.

Rooms 13 en suite (2 fmly) **Facilities** FTV tea/coffee Dinner available Direct Dial Cen ht Wi-fi **Conf** Max 14 Thtr 14 Class 14 Board 14 **Parking** 2 **Notes** LB

See advert on opposite page

HAILEY · Map 11 SP31

Bird in Hand Inn

★★★★ INN

Whiteoak Green OX29 9XP
☎ 01993 868321 📠 01993 868702
e-mail: welcome@birdinhandinn.co.uk
web: www.birdinhandinn.co.uk

Situated on the edge of the Cotswolds, The Bird in Hand is ideally located to discover the natural beauty of the area plus the culture heritage of nearby Oxford. The attractive en suite bedrooms combine style and comfort, while the restaurant offers an imaginative seasonal menu using the finest, local produce and the bar serves traditional local ales.

Rooms 16 annexe en suite (2 fmly) (9 GF) **Facilities** FTV tea/coffee Dinner available Direct Dial Cen ht Wi-fi **Conf** Max 40 Thtr 40 Class 40 Board 40 **Parking** 100

HAMPTON POYLE · Map 11 SP51

PREMIER COLLECTION

The Bell at Hampton Poyle

★★★★★ INN

11 Oxford Rd OX5 2QD
☎ 01865 376242
e-mail: contactus@thebelloxford.co.uk
dir: *From N, turn off A34 signed Kidlington, 0.25m; From S, N from Kidlington Sainsburys rdbt, with Sainsburys on left, on left 0.25m*

This property with its attractive period features has been fully renovated and is ideally located for exploring Oxford and the surrounding countryside. The accommodation is contemporary in style and well appointed, while the restaurant offers an appealing menu including stone-baked pizza and shellfish dishes.

Rooms 9 en suite (3 GF) **Facilities** FTV tea/coffee Dinner available Cen ht Wi-fi Golf 18 Fishing Riding **Conf** Max 30 **Parking** 31 **Notes** No Children 5yrs No coaches

HENLEY-ON-THAMES · Map 5 SU78

PREMIER COLLECTION

Crowsley House

★★★★★ 🏠 BED AND BREAKFAST

Crowsley Rd, Lower Shiplake RG9 3JT
☎ 0118 940 6708
e-mail: info@crowsleyhouse.co.uk
dir: *A4155 onto Station Rd in Shiplake. Right onto Crowsley Rd, 2nd house on right*

Situated close to the popular village of Henley-on-Thames and a moment's walk from Shiplake railway station. Bedrooms are smartly appointed and very well equipped with many thoughtful extras. A comfortable lounge area and beautifully landscaped gardens provide areas in which to relax. Breakfast is served around the dining table in the well styled dual aspect dining room. A two or three course dinner option is available on request.

Rooms 3 rms (2 en suite) (1 pri facs) **Facilities** FTV Dinner available Cen ht Wi-fi **Parking** 6 **Notes** ⊛ No Children 14yrs

The Baskerville

★★★★ INN

Station Rd, Lower Shiplake RG9 3NY
☎ 0118 940 3332
e-mail: enquiries@thebaskerville.com
web: www.thebaskerville.com
dir: *2m S of Henley in Lower Shiplake. Off A4155 onto Station Rd, inn signed*

Located close to Shiplake station and just a short drive from Henley, this smart accommodation is perfect for a business or leisure break. It is a good base for exploring the Oxfordshire countryside, and the enjoyable hearty meals served in the cosy restaurant use good local produce.

Rooms 4 en suite (1 fmly) S £77.50; D £87.50*
Facilities STV tea/coffee Dinner available Cen ht Wi-fi **Conf** Max 15 Thtr 15 Class 15 Board 15 **Parking** 15 **Notes** No coaches

Save on B&Bs and Hotels. Book at **theAA.com/hotel**

OXFORDSHIRE 237 ENGLAND

Leander Club

★★★★ ⌂ GUEST ACCOMMODATION

Leander Way RG9 2LP
☎ 01491 575782 ▤ 01491 410291
e-mail: events@leander.co.uk
web: www.leander.co.uk
dir: *M4 junct 8/9 follow signs for Henley (A404M & A4130). Turn right immediately before Henley Bridge to Club & car park*

This historic rowing club has opened its doors and made its delightful facilities available to guests. The location is breathtaking, particularly in the morning, when the rowers can be seen setting out on the river. The rooms are each named after various colleges and universities, and each is packed with interesting photos and memorabilia linking them with the Leander Club. Public areas also feature lots of trophies, pictures and artefacts, and it all makes for a most interesting place to stay.

Rooms 11 en suite (1 fmly) S £120; D £120-£145* **Facilities** STV FTV TVL tea/coffee Dinner available Direct Dial Cen ht Lift Licensed Wi-fi **Conf** Max 120 Thtr 120 Class 40 Board 20 **Parking** 60 **Notes** ⊗ No Children 10yrs Closed Xmas-New Year RS 1st wk Jul Henley Royal Regatta Civ Wed 120

Milsoms Henley-on-Thames

★★★★ RESTAURANT WITH ROOMS

20 Market Place RG9 2AH
☎ 01491 845780 & 845789 ▤ 01491 845781
e-mail: henley@milsomshotel.co.uk
dir: *In centre of town, close to town hall*

The seven en suite bedrooms are located in a listed building above the Loch Fyne Restaurant in Henley's Market Place. Each bedroom is individually appointed and equipped to meet the needs of the modern traveller; particular care has been taken to incorporate original features into the contemporary design. The restaurant has a commitment to offer ethically sourced seafood.

Rooms 7 en suite (2 fmly) (1 GF) D £50-£95* **Facilities** tea/coffee Dinner available Cen ht Wi-fi **Parking** 7 **Notes** ⊗ No coaches

Phyllis Court Club

★★★★ GUEST ACCOMMODATION

Marlow Rd RG9 2HT
☎ 01491 570500 ▤ 01491 570528
e-mail: enquiries@phylliscourt.co.uk
dir: *A404 onto A4130 into town centre. Follow A4155, 150mtrs on right*

Phyllis Court was founded in 1906 as a private members' club and has welcomed many distinguished visitors over the years. Set in 18 acres, with lawns sweeping down to the River Thames, it offers a unique blend of traditional elegance and modern comforts. The club takes centre stage during Henley Royal Regatta week, being positioned opposite the race finishing line. The individually styled bedrooms are well appointed and very comfortable. There is restricted meal service two days before and after the regattas in June and July. An excellent range of function venues is available, and the Grade II listed Grandstand Pavilion is perfect for weddings.

Rooms 17 en suite **Facilities** FTV TVL tea/coffee Dinner available Direct Dial Cen ht Lift Licensed Wi-fi ⌂ **Conf** Max 250 Thtr 250 Class 100 Board 30 **Parking** 200 **Notes** RS 26-28 Dec, 2-3 Jan, regattas Jun-Jul Civ Wed 250

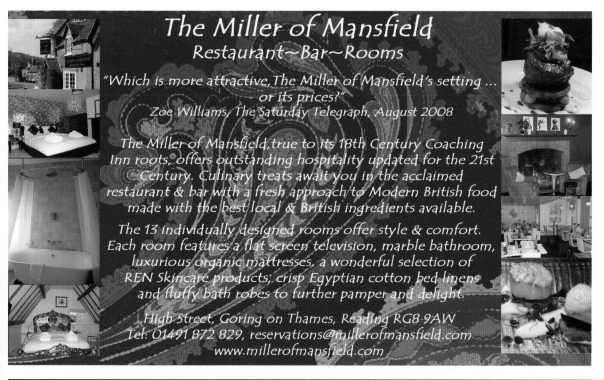

HENLEY-ON-THAMES *continued*

Slater's Farm

★★★ Ⓐ BED AND BREAKFAST

Peppard Common RG9 5JL
☎ 01491 628675
e-mail: stay@slatersfarm.co.uk
dir: *3m W of Henley. A4130 onto B481 to Rotherfield Peppard, pass Ruchetta Restaurant left to primary school, house 200yds on right*

Rooms 3 rms (1 pri facs) S £45; D £65* **Facilities** FTV tea/coffee Dinner available Cen ht Wi-fi ⌁ Golf 18 **Parking** 7 **Notes** ⊗ Closed Xmas ⊛

IDBURY   Map 10 SP21

Bould Farm *(SP244209)*

★★★★ FARMHOUSE

OX7 6RT
☎ 01608 658850   ▤ 01608 658850
Mrs L Meyrick
e-mail: meyrick@bouldfarm.co.uk
web: www.bouldfarm.co.uk
dir: *Off A424 signed Idbury, through village, down hill, round two bends, on right*

This delightful 17th-century farmhouse stands amid pretty gardens between Stow-on-the-Wold and Burford. The spacious bedrooms are carefully furnished and thoughtfully equipped, and some have stunning views of the surrounding countryside. Breakfast is served in the cosy dining room which features a cast-iron stove and stone-flagged floors.

Rooms 3 rms (2 en suite) (1 pri facs) (1 fmly) S fr £50; D £65-£70* **Facilities** TVL tea/coffee Cen ht **Parking** 6 **Notes** ⊗ Closed Dec-Jan ⊛ 400 acres arable/sheep/beef cows

---

KINGHAM   Map 10 SP22

The Kingham Plough

★★★★★ ⊛⊛ ⓘ INN

The Green OX7 6YD
☎ 01608 658327
e-mail: book@thekinghamplough.co.uk
dir: *On the green in Kingham Village*

The Kingham Plough is a quintessential Cotswold inn, sympathetically refurbished and set in the pretty village of Kingham, just minutes away from the well known Daylesford Organic estate. The seven en suite bedrooms have Cotswold character and offer impressive quality and comfort. Dining is memorable both for evening meals and at breakfast; the team here deliver excellence using locally sourced produce.

Rooms 7 en suite (2 fmly) S £75-£105; D £90-£130* **Facilities** FTV tea/coffee Dinner available Cen ht Wi-fi **Parking** 25 **Notes** Closed 25 Dec

---

Moat End

★★★★ ⓘ BED AND BREAKFAST

The Moat OX7 6XZ
☎ 01608 658090 & 07765 278399
e-mail: moatend@gmail.com
web: www.moatend.co.uk
dir: *Off B4450/A436 into village centre*

This converted barn lies in a peaceful Cotswold village and has splendid country views. Its well-appointed bedrooms either have a jacuzzi or large shower cubicles, one with hydro-massage jets. The attractive dining room leads to a comfortable beamed sitting room with a stone fireplace. Quality local ingredients are used in the wholesome breakfasts. The owner has won an award for green tourism by reducing the impact of the business on the environment.

Rooms 3 en suite (1 fmly) S £55-£60; D £70-£80* **Facilities** TVL tea/coffee Cen ht Wi-fi **Parking** 4 **Notes** LB Closed Xmas & New Year ⊛

The Tollgate Inn & Restaurant

★★★★ ⇌ INN

Church St OX7 6YA
☎ 01608 658389
e-mail: info@thetollgate.com

Situated in the idyllic Cotswold village of Kingham, this Grade II listed Georgian building has been lovingly restored to provide a complete home-from-home among some of the most beautiful countryside in Britain. The Tollgate provides comfortable, well-equipped accommodation in pleasant surroundings. A good choice of menu for lunch and dinner is available with fine use made of fresh and local produce. You can also be sure of a hearty breakfast provided in the modern, well-equipped dining room.

Rooms 5 en suite 4 annexe en suite (1 fmly) (4 GF) **Facilities** tea/coffee Dinner available Cen ht Wi-fi **Conf** Max 15 **Parking** 12

MILTON COMMON   Map 5 SP60

Byways

★★★★ ⓘ BED AND BREAKFAST

Old London Rd OX9 2JR
☎ 01844 279386   ▤ 01844 279386
e-mail: byways.mott@tiscali.co.uk
web: www.bywaysbedandbreakfast.co.uk
dir: *Between M40 juncts 7 & 8A*

A friendly welcome awaits you at Byways, situated a few minutes from the M40. Bedrooms are comfortable and tastefully decorated, and the emphasis is on a peaceful and relaxing stay away from it all. Breakfast is home produced, organic and obtained locally where possible. There is a large garden for guests to enjoy. Please note that Byways is a TV-free establishment.

Rooms 3 rms (2 en suite) (1 pri facs) (3 GF) S £40-£45; D £70 **Facilities** tea/coffee Cen ht **Parking** 3 **Notes** ⊗ No Children 7yrs ⊛

OXFORD   Map 5 SP50

PREMIER COLLECTION

Burlington House

★★★★★ ⓘ GUEST ACCOMMODATION

374 Banbury Rd, Summertown OX2 7PP
☎ 01865 513513   ▤ 01865 311785
e-mail: stay@burlington-house.co.uk
dir: *Opposite Oxford Conference Centre on A4165 on corner of Hernes Rd & Banbury Rd*

Guests are assured of a warm welcome and attentive service at this smart, beautifully maintained Victorian house, within walking distance of Summertown's fashionable restaurants. Elegant, contemporary bedrooms are filled with a wealth of thoughtful extras, and some open onto a pretty patio garden. Memorable breakfasts, served in the delightful dining room, include home-made preserves, fruit breads, granola and excellent coffee.

Rooms 10 en suite 2 annexe en suite **Facilities** FTV tea/coffee Direct Dial Cen ht Wi-fi **Parking** 5 **Notes** ⊗ No Children 12yrs Closed 24 Dec-2 Jan

Claddagh Guest House

★★★★ GUEST HOUSE

112 The Slade, Headington OX3 7DX
☎ 01865 751641
e-mail: info@claddaghguesthouse.co.uk
dir: *At Headington rdbt take 1st exit onto A420 signed city centre. At traffic signals left onto Windmill Rd (B4495) signed Nuffield Orthopaedic Centre. 0.6m on left onto The Slade*

A family-run guest house, where guests can relax and unwind. Three rooms are en suite whilst the single room has a private bathroom. All have TVs and courtesy trays as well as thoughtful extras including Wi-fi. Breakfast is served at the communal table in the attractive breakfast room overlooking the garden.

Rooms 4 rms (3 en suite) (1 pri facs) S £45-£55; D £70-£75* **Facilities** STV FTV tea/coffee Cen ht Wi-fi **Parking** 8 **Notes** ⊗ ⊛

Conifers Guest House

★★★★ GUEST ACCOMMODATION

116 The Slade, Headington OX3 7DX
☎ 01865 763055 🖹 01865 742232
e-mail: stay@conifersguesthouse.co.uk
web: www.conifersguesthouse.co.uk
dir: *Off ring road onto A420 towards city centre. Left onto B4495 (Windmill Rd), straight over at lights, house on left past Nuffield Orthopaedic Centre*

Located in a residential area close to the hospitals, this impressive Edwardian house has been renovated to provide attractive, pine-furnished bedrooms. Breakfast is served in a smart, front-facing dining room. Private car park.

Rooms 11 en suite (4 fmly) **Facilities** FTV TV9B tea/coffee Cen ht Wi-fi **Parking** 8 **Notes** ⊗

Cotswold House

★★★★ GUEST ACCOMMODATION

363 Banbury Rd OX2 7PL
☎ 01865 310558 🖹 01865 310558
e-mail: d.r.walker@talk21.com
web: www.cotswoldhouse.co.uk
dir: *A40 onto A423 into Oxford city centre, following signs to Summertown, 0.5m on right*

Situated in a leafy avenue close to the northern ring road and Summertown, this well-maintained house offers comfortable, well-equipped bedrooms and a relaxed atmosphere. Enjoy a traditional, hearty breakfast with vegetarian choice, including home-made muesli and fresh fruit, served in the bright attractive dining room.

Rooms 8 en suite (2 fmly) (2 GF) S £58-£65; D £95-£120 **Facilities** FTV tea/coffee Cen ht Wi-fi **Parking** 6 **Notes** ⊗ No Children 5yrs

Galaxie

★★★★ GUEST ACCOMMODATION

180 Banbury Rd OX2 7BT
☎ 01865 515688 🖹 01865 556824
e-mail: info@galaxie.co.uk
web: www.galaxie.co.uk
dir: *1m N of Oxford centre, on right before shops in Summertown*

Situated in the popular Summertown area of the city, the Galaxie has a welcoming atmosphere and very good quality accommodation. The well-equipped bedrooms are all very comfortable and have a good range of extra facilities. The attractive conservatory-dining room looks over the Oriental garden.

Rooms 32 rms (28 en suite) (3 fmly) **Facilities** TVL TV31B tea/coffee Direct Dial Cen ht Lift **Parking** 30 **Notes** ⊗

Marlborough House

★★★★ GUEST ACCOMMODATION

321 Woodstock Rd OX2 7NY
☎ 01865 311321 🖹 01865 515329
e-mail: enquiries@marlbhouse.co.uk
web: www.marlbhouse.co.uk
dir: *1.5m N of city centre. Off junct A34 & A44 for city centre, onto A4144 (Woodstock Rd), premises on right by lights*

Marlborough House is just 1.5 miles north of Oxford's historic city centre, and is within easy reach of the M40 and the A34 ring road. Custom built in 1990 to a traditional design, the house sits comfortably alongside its Victorian neighbours in a predominantly residential area. All 17 bedrooms have en suite facilities, kitchenettes and mini-bars so guests aren't tied to any routine. Wi-fi covers the lounge and many of the rooms.

Rooms 13 en suite 4 annexe en suite (3 fmly) (4 GF) **Facilities** FTV tea/coffee Direct Dial Cen ht Licensed Wi-fi **Parking** 6 **Notes** ⊗

Pickwicks

★★★★ GUEST HOUSE

15-17 London Rd, Headington OX3 7SP
☎ 01865 750487 🖹 01865 742208
e-mail: pickwicks@tiscali.co.uk
web: www.pickwicksguesthouse.co.uk
dir: *Off ring road onto A420 towards city centre, Pickwicks 0.9m on right at junct with Sandfield Rd*

Just a short walk from the bustling community of Headington, this double-fronted Edwardian house has been renovated to provide good standards of overall comfort. Bedrooms offer a useful range of facilities, and an attractive breakfast room overlooks the pretty gardens.

Rooms 15 rms (13 en suite) (2 pri facs) (4 fmly) (4 GF) S £30-£55; D £65-£90* **Facilities** FTV TVL tea/coffee Direct Dial Cen ht Licensed Wi-fi **Parking** 12 **Notes** Closed 23 Dec-2 Jan

OXFORD *continued*

Red Mullions Guest House

★★★★ GUEST HOUSE

23 London Rd, Headington OX3 7RE
☎ 01865 742741 📠 01865 769944
e-mail: stay@redmullions.co.uk
dir: *M40 junct 8 onto A40. At Headington rdbt, 2nd exit signed Headington onto London Rd*

Red Mullions takes its name from the brick columns between the windows of the building. Modern bedrooms provide comfortable accommodation set within easy reach of motorway networks and Oxford city centre. Hearty breakfasts provide a good start to any day.

Rooms 13 rms (12 en suite) (1 pri facs) (3 fmly) (4 GF) S £70-£85; D £80-£110* **Facilities** FTV tea/coffee Cen ht Wi-fi **Parking** 9 **Notes** ⊗

Acorn Guest House

★★★ GUEST ACCOMMODATION

260-262 Iffley Rd OX4 1SE
☎ 01865 247998
e-mail: kate@oxford-acorn.co.uk
dir: *Off ring road onto A4158 towards city centre, 1m on left after VW garage*

This double-fronted Victorian house is located between the ring road and the city centre, and offers good value accommodation. The lounge leads out to a quiet enclosed rear garden.

Rooms 15 rms (7 en suite) (1 pri facs) (1 fmly) S £35-£60; D £72-£75* **Facilities** tea/coffee Cen ht Lift Wi-fi **Parking** 6

All Seasons

★★★ GUEST ACCOMMODATION

63 Windmill Rd, Headington OX3 7BP
☎ 01865 742215 📠 01865 429667
e-mail: info@allseasonshouse.com
web: www.allseasonshouse.com
dir: *Off ring road onto A420 towards city centre. 1m left at lights onto Windmill Rd, house 300yds on left*

Within easy walking distance of the suburb of Headington, this double-fronted Victorian house provides comfortable homely bedrooms equipped with practical and thoughtful extras. The elegant dining room features an original fireplace, and secure parking is available behind the property.

Rooms 6 rms (4 en suite) (2 pri facs) (1 fmly) **Facilities** FTV TVL tea/coffee Cen ht Wi-fi **Parking** 6 **Notes** ⊗

Athena Guest House

★★★ GUEST ACCOMMODATION

255 Cowley Rd, Cowley OX4 1XQ
☎ 01865 425700 & 07748 837144 📠 01865 240566
e-mail: info@athenaguesthouse.com
web: www.athenaguesthouse.com
dir: *1.5m SE of city centre on B480*

Located close to the shops and amenities in Cowley, this Victorian brick house offers smart modern bedrooms on three floors with many useful extras. Breakfast is served in the bright and relaxing dining room, and limited parking is available.

Rooms 6 en suite (2 fmly) (2 GF) **Facilities** STV TVL tea/coffee Cen ht Wi-fi **Conf** Max 15 **Parking** 4 **Notes** ⊗

Green Gables

★★★ GUEST ACCOMMODATION

326 Abingdon Rd OX1 4TE
☎ 01865 725870 📠 01865 723115
e-mail: green.gables@virgin.net
web: www.greengables.uk.com
dir: *Off ring road onto B4144 towards city centre, Green Gables 0.5m on left*

A warm welcome is assured at this Edwardian house, located within easy walking distance of the city centre. Bedrooms are equipped with a range of practical and homely extras, and a comprehensive breakfast is served in the cosy dining room. Guests have free access to the internet in the smart conservatory-lounge, and private parking is available.

Rooms 11 en suite (2 fmly) (4 GF) S £48-£52; D £70-£80 **Facilities** FTV TVL tea/coffee Direct Dial Cen ht Wi-fi **Parking** 9 **Notes** ⊗ Closed 23-31 Dec

Heather House

★★★ GUEST ACCOMMODATION

192 Iffley Rd OX4 1SD
☎ 01865 249757 📠 01865 249757
e-mail: stay@heatherhouseoxford.com
web: www.heatherhouseoxford.com
dir: *Off A40 at Headington rdbt, S onto A4142 to Littlemore rdbt onto A4158 Iffley Rd then house 1.25m. On left after pedestrian crossing near Chester St*

A short walk from the colleges, city centre and Oxford Brookes campus, this detached Edwardian house stands in a residential area and has its own parking. The en suite bedrooms are bright and comfortable, and come complete with useful facilities including TV and CD/DVD players. There is Wi-fi, a computer station (with Skype) and a relaxing lounge with lots of tourist information. A choice of breakfasts is available.

Rooms 6 rms (5 en suite) (1 pri facs) (2 fmly) (1 GF) **Facilities** FTV TVL tea/coffee Direct Dial Cen ht Wi-fi **Parking** 6 **Notes** ⊗

Highfield

★★★ GUEST ACCOMMODATION

91 Rose Hill OX4 4HT
☎ 01865 774083
e-mail: highfield.house@tesco.net
dir: *Off A4142 Eastern Bypass Rd onto A4158, continue 250yds*

This attractive detached house stands in immaculate gardens close to Cowley and provides homely bedrooms equipped with quality pine furniture. The attractive front dining room is the setting for comprehensive breakfasts and there is also a spacious lounge.

Rooms 7 rms (5 en suite) (2 pri facs) (1 fmly) S £30-£38; D £65-£70* **Facilities** FTV TVL tea/coffee Cen ht Wi-fi **Parking** 6 **Notes** ⊗ Closed Xmas

Lina Guest House

★★★ GUEST HOUSE

308 Banbury Rd OX2 7ED
☎ 01865 511070 📠 01865 510060
e-mail: info@linaguesthouse.com

This beautifully refurbished Victorian townhouse offers well appointed accommodation with all modern facilities to provide a base for leisure and business guests alike. Breakfast is served in the front room whilst the rear garden can be enjoyed in the warmer months. Parking is available on a first-come first-served basis.

Rooms 7 en suite (1 fmly) (1 GF) S £45-£60; D £75-£90* **Facilities** FTV TVL Cen ht Wi-fi **Parking** 5 **Notes** ⊗

Save on B&Bs and Hotels. Book at **theAA.com/hotel**

OXFORDSHIRE 241 ENGLAND

Sports View Guest House

★★★ GUEST ACCOMMODATION

106-110 Abingdon Rd OX1 4PX
☎ 01865 244268 📠 01865 249270
e-mail: stay@sportsviewguesthouse.co.uk
web: www.sportsviewguesthouse.co.uk
dir: *Exit Oxford S at Kennington rdbt towards city centre, 1.25m on left*

This family-run Victorian property, overlooks the Queens College sports ground. Situated south of the city it is within walking distance of the centre. Rooms are comfortable, and the property benefits from off-road parking.

Rooms 20 rms (19 en suite) (1 pri facs) (4 fmly) (5 GF) S £42-£56; D £72-£84* **Facilities** FTV tea/coffee Direct Dial Cen ht Wi-fi **Parking** 10 **Notes** ⊗ No Children 3yrs Closed 25-26 Dec & 1 Jan

Tower House

★★★ GUEST ACCOMMODATION

15 Ship St OX1 3DA
☎ 01865 246828 📠 01865 247508
e-mail: generalmanager.towerhousehotel@ohiml.com
dir: *Follow signs to city centre, turn left onto Turl St, then right onto Ship St*

Tower House is a charming 17th-century house set on a quiet street in the heart of Oxford city centre. Bedrooms are all individually decorated in keeping with the age of the property. A light Continental breakfast is served in the quaint breakfast room on the ground floor.

Rooms 7 rms (4 en suite) (1 fmly) **Facilities** FTV tea/coffee Cen ht Wi-fi **Notes** ⊗

Newton House

★★★ 🅰 BED AND BREAKFAST

82-84 Abingdon Rd OX1 4PL
☎ 01865 240561 📠 01865 244647
e-mail: newton.house@btinternet.com
dir: *On A4144 (Abingdon Rd)*
Rooms 13 rms (2 en suite) (11 pri facs) (4 fmly) (4 GF) **Facilities** FTV tea/coffee Direct Dial Cen ht Wi-fi **Parking** 8 **Notes** ⊗

SOUTH STOKE   Map 5 SU58

Perch & Pike

★★★ INN

The Street RG8 0JS
☎ 01491 872415 📠 01491 871001
e-mail: info@perchandpike.co.uk
dir: *From A4074 take B4009 S to South Stoke*

Set in the quiet village of South Stoke, minutes from the River Thames, this cosy inn offers a very warm welcome. The four en suite bedrooms are comfortable and well equipped. Public areas are spacious and include a separate dining room. Enjoy local asparagus, when in season, or trout caught that day by the proprietor.

Rooms 4 en suite (1 fmly) **Facilities** FTV tea/coffee Dinner available Cen ht **Parking** 25 **Notes** ⊗ No coaches

---

STADHAMPTON   Map 5 SU69

PREMIER COLLECTION

The Crazy Bear

★★★★★ ◉◉ GUEST ACCOMMODATION

Bear Ln OX44 7UR
☎ 01865 890714 📠 01865 400481
e-mail: enquiries@crazybear-stadhampton.co.uk
web: www.crazybeargroup.co.uk
dir: *M40 junct 7, A329. In 4m left after petrol station, left onto Bear Lane*

This popular and attractive guest accommodation, successfully combines modern chic with old world character. Cuisine is extensive and varied, with award-winning Thai and English restaurants under the same roof (both with AA Rosettes). Those choosing to make a night of it can enjoy the concept bedrooms, all presented to a very high standard and styled with exciting themes; the 'infinity suites' have state-of-the-art facilities.

Rooms 5 en suite 12 annexe en suite (3 fmly) (4 GF) **Facilities** STV FTV Dinner available Direct Dial Cen ht Licensed Wi-fi **Conf** Max 40 Thtr 30 Class 30 Board 30 **Parking** 100 **Notes** ⊗ Civ Wed 200

SWINBROOK   Map 5 SP21

The Swan Inn

★★★★★ ◉◉ INN

OX18 4DY
☎ 01993 823339
e-mail: swaninnswinbrook@btconnect.com
web: www.theswanswinbrook.co.uk
dir: *1m from A40, 2m E of Burford*

The idyllic location and award-winning food are only two of the reasons why this is the perfect place for a comfortable business visit or a relaxed weekend. The bar offers real ales, local lagers and an appealing wine list. The accommodation is sumptuous and combines modern facilities with traditional comfort.

Rooms 6 en suite (1 fmly) (4 GF) **Facilities** FTV tea/coffee Dinner available Cen ht Wi-fi Golf 18 Riding **Parking** 20 **Notes** Closed 25 Dec No coaches

---

WANTAGE   Map 5 SU38

PREMIER COLLECTION

Brook Barn Country House

★★★★★ 🏠 ➡ GUEST ACCOMMODATION

Brook Barn, Letcombe Regis OX12 9JD
☎ 01235 766502 📠 01235 766873
e-mail: info@brookbarn.com
web: www.brookbarn.com
dir: *M4 junct 14 onto A338 to Wantage. Left onto B4507 signed Ashbury, after 1m take left signed Letcombe Regis. House 0.75m on left*

A bijou country house hideaway with luxurious bedrooms. Brook Barn is set in over an acre of gardens which include an orchard, and a beautiful chalk stream allowing guests to enjoy the tranquillity of the Oxfordshire countryside. This house is equipped to the highest standards, and is a perfect respite for business travellers or holiday-makers alike.

Rooms 5 rms (4 en suite) (1 pri facs) (4 GF) S £80-£170; D £120-£250* **Facilities** STV FTV tea/coffee Dinner available Direct Dial Cen ht Licensed Wi-fi ➳ Outdoor hot tub **Parking** 6 **Notes** LB ⊗ No Children 16yrs

See advert on page 242

WANTAGE *continued*

La Fontana Restaurant with Accommodation

★★★★ 🍴 RESTAURANT WITH ROOMS

Oxford Rd, East Hanney OX12 0HP
☎ 01235 868287 📠 01235 868019
e-mail: anna@la-fontana.co.uk

Guests are guaranteed a warm welcome at this family-run Italian restaurant which is located on the outskirts of the busy town of Wantage. The stylish bedrooms are individually designed, well equipped and very comfortable. Dinner should not to be missed - the menu features a wide range of regional Italian specialities.

Rooms 8 en suite 7 annexe en suite (2 fmly) (3 GF) S £65-£70; D £85-£90* **Facilities** FTV TVL tea/coffee Dinner available Direct Dial Cen ht Wi-fi **Parking** 30 **Notes** LB ⊗

Greensands Guest House

★★★ GUEST HOUSE

Reading Rd OX12 8JE
☎ 01235 833338 📠 01235 821632
e-mail: info@greensandsguesthouse.co.uk.
web: www.greensandsguesthouse.co.uk
dir: *A4185 to Rowstock rdbt, take A417, 1m on right*

This guest house in a peaceful rural setting has good access to local towns, attractions and transport networks. Bedrooms vary in size and are comfortably appointed. Hearty breakfasts are served overlooking the attractive gardens. Ample parking available.

Rooms 7 rms (6 en suite) (1 pri facs) (2 fmly) (3 GF) **Facilities** tea/coffee Cen ht Wi-fi **Parking** 9

Hill Barn *(SU337852)*

★★★ FARMHOUSE

Sparholt Firs OX12 9XB
☎ 01235 751236 & 07885 368918
Mrs Joanna Whittington
e-mail: jmw@hillbarn.plus.com
dir: *W of B4001 on The Ridgeway, 4m N of Wantage*

This working farm offers en suite bedrooms with beautiful distant views over the countryside. The atmosphere is friendly, and guests are able to relax either in the sitting room or in the garden. Breakfast is a highlight with home-made jams and produce from the farm, when available.

Rooms 2 en suite **Facilities** TVL tea/coffee Dinner available Cen ht **Parking** 3 **Notes** LB ⊛ 100 acres horses

Down Barn Farm *(SU332852)*

★★ FARMHOUSE

Sparsholt Down OX12 9XD
☎ 01367 820272
Mrs P A Reid
e-mail: pendomeffect@aol.com
dir: *4m SW of Wantage. Off B4507 S onto Kingston Lisle-Seven Barrows road*

Popular with walkers and horse riders (stabling is available), this working farm has glorious views over the Downs and is near to the famous Ridgeway. Bedrooms and public areas have a homely and comfortable aspect while home-produced veal, beef and pork can be anticipated for dinner.

Rooms 3 rms (1 en suite) (1 pri facs) (3 GF) **Facilities** TVL Dinner available Cen ht Riding **Parking** 4 **Notes** Closed Xmas ⊛ 100 acres organic beef/pigs

Corn Croft Guest House

★★★★ GUEST ACCOMMODATION

69-71 Corn St OX28 6AS
☎ 01993 773298 📠 01993 773298
e-mail: richardturner4@btconnect.com
web: www.corncroft.co.uk
dir: *A40 to town centre, from Market Square onto Corn Street, 400mtrs on left*

Located in the quieter end of town, yet close to the centre, Corn Croft offers comfortable well equipped accommodation in a friendly atmosphere. Substantial breakfasts featuring local produce are served in the attractive dining room.

Rooms 11 en suite (1 fmly) (2 GF) **Facilities** FTV tea/coffee Cen ht Wi-fi **Notes** Closed 24-26 Dec

Save on B&Bs and Hotels. Book at **theAA.com/hotel**

OXFORDSHIRE – RUTLAND 243 **ENGLAND**

The Fleece

★★★ ➔ INN

1 Church Green OX28 4AZ
☎ 01993 892270 🖹 0871 8130458
e-mail: fleece@peachpubs.com
dir: A40 to Witney town centre, on Church Green

Set in the centre of Witney overlooking the church green, The Fleece offers ten well equipped en suite modern bedrooms. The popular destination pub offers food all day including breakfast, and a great selection of wines and real ales.

Rooms 7 en suite 3 annexe en suite (1 fmly) (1 GF)
Facilities tea/coffee Dinner available Direct Dial Cen ht Wi-fi **Conf** Max 30 Thtr 25 Class 16 Board 22 **Parking** 12 **Notes** Closed 25 Dec

WOODSTOCK   Map 11 SP41

Duke of Marlborough Country Inn

★★★★ INN

Woodleys OX20 1HT
☎ 01993 811460 🖹 01993 810165
e-mail: sales@dukeofmarlborough.co.uk
dir: 1m N of Woodstock on A44 x-rds

The Duke of Marlborough is just outside the popular town of Woodstock, convenient for local attractions including Blenheim Palace. Bedrooms and bathrooms are in an adjacent lodge-style building and offer high standards of quality and comfort. Dinner includes many tempting home-cooked dishes, complemented by a good selection of ales and wines.

Rooms 13 annexe en suite (2 fmly) (7 GF) **Facilities** tea/coffee Dinner available Direct Dial Cen ht Wi-fi **Conf** Max 20 Thtr 20 Class 16 Board 12 **Parking** 42 **Notes** ⊗

Kings Head House

★★★★ GUEST ACCOMMODATION

Chapel Hill, Wootton OX20 1DX
☎ 01993 811340
e-mail: t.fay@kings-head.co.uk
web: www.kings-head.co.uk
dir: 2m N of Woodstock. Off A44 to Wootton, close to village church

Set in the pretty village of Wootton, this mellow stone house has undergone a major refurbishment while still retaining many of the original features, including exposed oak beams and open fires. The light-filled dining room has lovely views over the private garden, and the new individually styled bedrooms are attractively presented and very comfortable.

Rooms 2 en suite 1 annexe en suite (1 fmly) (1 GF)
Facilities tea/coffee Cen ht Wi-fi **Parking** 2 **Notes** ⊗ No Children 12yrs Closed Xmas

The Blenheim Guest House & Tea Rooms

★★★★ 🅰 GUEST ACCOMMODATION

17 Park St OX20 1SJ
☎ 01993 813814 🖹 01993 813810
e-mail: theblenheim@aol.com
web: www.theblenheim.com
dir: Off A44 in Woodstock to County Museum, after museum on left

Rooms 6 rms (5 en suite) (1 pri facs) (2 fmly) S fr £55; D £67.50-£85* **Facilities** tea/coffee Cen ht Licensed Wi-fi

RUTLAND

CLIPSHAM   Map 11 SK91

Beech House

★★★★★ ◉◉ 🛏 INN

Main St LE15 7SH
☎ 01780 410355 🖹 01780 410000
e-mail: rooms@theolivebranchpub.com
dir: From A1 take B668 signed Stretton & Clipsham

Beech House stands over the road from the Olive Branch restaurant. It offers very well furnished bedrooms which include DVD players. Breakfasts are served in the Olive Branch. Excellent lunches and dinners are also available.

Rooms 5 en suite 1 annexe en suite (2 fmly) (3 GF) S £97.50-£180; D £115-£195* **Facilities** FTV tea/coffee Dinner available Direct Dial Cen ht Wi-fi **Conf** Max 20 Thtr 20 Class 16 Board 16 **Parking** 10 **Notes** LB No coaches

EMPINGHAM   Map 11 SK90

The White Horse Inn

★★★ INN

Main St LE15 8PS
☎ 01780 460221 🖹 01780 460521
e-mail: info@whitehorserutland.co.uk
web: www.whitehorserutland.co.uk
dir: On A606 (Oakham to Stamford road)

This attractive stone-built inn, offering bright, comfortable accommodation, is conveniently located just minutes from the A1. Bedrooms in the main building are spacious and include a number of family rooms. Public areas include a well-stocked bar, a bistro and restaurant where a wide range of meals is served.

Rooms 4 en suite 9 annexe en suite (4 fmly) (5 GF) S £53-£63; D £70* **Facilities** TVL tea/coffee Dinner available Direct Dial **Conf** Max 25 Thtr 25 Class 20 Board 20 **Parking** 60 **Notes** Closed 25 Dec

LYDDINGTON   Map 11 SP89

The Marquess of Exeter

★★★★ ➔ INN

52 Main St LE15 9LT
☎ 01572 822477 🖹 08082 801159
e-mail: info@marquessexeter.co.uk
dir: M1 junct 19 onto A14 to Kettering, then A6003 to Caldecott. Turn right onto Lyddington Rd, 2m to village

Situated in the picturesque Rutland countryside, the inn has been refurbished with a contemporary touch whilst retaining many original features such as timber beam ceilings, open log fires and flagstone floors. The stylish bedrooms, situated across a courtyard, are individually decorated and comfortable. The food is imaginative with the chef's 'sharing dishes' being particularly noteworthy.

Rooms 18 en suite (2 fmly) (10 GF) **Facilities** FTV tea/coffee Dinner available Direct Dial Cen ht Wi-fi **Conf** Max 50 Thtr 50 Class 40 Board 40 **Parking** 60 **Notes** No coaches

Old White Hart

★★★★ INN

51 Main St LE15 9LR
☎ 01572 821703 🖹 01572 821978
e-mail: mail@oldwhitehart.co.uk
dir: 1m S of Uppingham on main street, opp village green

Set opposite the village green in the heart of Lyddington, The Old White Hart offers a personal, attentive welcome. The accommodation is set in converted cottages situated alongside the public house. All have been thoughtfully renovated. Each is individually designed, but all offer very good quality and comfort. Enjoy home prepared food either in one of the cosy restaurants, the bar, or alfresco dining in the garden during the summer months.

Rooms 2 en suite 8 annexe en suite (1 fmly) (2 GF) S £60-£70; D £85-£95* **Facilities** FTV tea/coffee Dinner available Direct Dial Cen ht Wi-fi Petanque **Conf** Max 20 Thtr 15 Class 15 Board 18 **Parking** 50 **Notes** LB ⊗ Closed 25 Dec

OAKHAM   Map 11 SK80

The Finch's Arms

★★★★ INN

Oakham Rd, Hambleton LE15 8TL
☎ 01572 756575 🖹 01572 771142
e-mail: enquiries@finchsarms.co.uk

Set in the heart of Hambleton village with priceless views over Rutland water, this inn offers contemporary modern accommodation equipped with many thoughtful extras. Public areas include an open-plan dining room and two snug areas of cosy seating with open fires in the winter months.

Rooms 4 en suite 6 annexe en suite S £75-£95; D £115-£125* **Facilities** FTV tea/coffee Dinner available Cen ht Wi-fi **Conf** Max 20 Thtr 20 Class 10 Board 20 **Parking** 35 **Notes** LB ⊗

OAKHAM *continued*

Kirkee House

★★★★ BED AND BREAKFAST

35 Welland Way LE15 6SL
☎ 01572 757401
e-mail: carolbeech@kirkeehouse.demon.co.uk
dir: *S of town centre. Off A606 High St onto Mill St, over level crossing, 400yds on left*

Located on a leafy avenue a short walk from the town centre, this immaculately maintained modern house provides comfortable bedrooms filled with homely extras. Comprehensive breakfasts, including local sausages and home-made jams, are served in the elegant conservatory-dining room, which overlooks the pretty garden.

Rooms 2 en suite S £40-£45; D £65-£70* **Facilities** FTV tea/coffee Cen ht Wi-fi **Parking** 2 **Notes** ⊗ No Children 7yrs ⊛

UPPINGHAM   Map 11 SP89

The Lake Isle

★★★★ ⊛⊛ 🛏 RESTAURANT WITH ROOMS

16 High Street East LE15 9PZ
☎ 01572 822951   📠 01572 824400
e-mail: info@lakeisle.co.uk
web: www.lakeisle.co.uk
dir: *From A47, turn left at 2nd lights, 100yds on right*

This attractive townhouse centres round a delightful restaurant and small elegant bar. There is also an inviting first-floor guest lounge, and the bedrooms are extremely well appointed and thoughtfully equipped; spacious split-level cottage suites situated in a quiet courtyard are also available. The imaginative cooking and an extremely impressive wine list are highlights.

Rooms 9 en suite 3 annexe rms (3 pri facs) (1 fmly) (1 GF) S £57.50-£67.50; D £80-£110* **Facilities** FTV tea/coffee Dinner available Direct Dial Cen ht Wi-fi **Conf** Max 16 Board 16 **Parking** 7 **Notes** ⊗ RS Sun eve & Mon lunch closed No coaches

WING   Map 11 SK80

Kings Arms Inn & Restaurant

★★★★ ⊛⊛ 🛏 INN

13 Top St LE15 8SE
☎ 01572 737634   📠 01572 737255
e-mail: info@thekingsarms-wing.co.uk
dir: *1.5m off A6003 in village centre*

This traditional village inn, with its open fires, flagstone floors and low beams, dates from the 17th century. The refurbished restaurant is more contemporary and offers a wide range of interesting freshly produced dishes. Service is attentive and friendly. The spacious, well-equipped bedrooms are in The Old Bake House and Granny's Cottage, in the nearby courtyard.

Rooms 8 en suite (2 fmly) (4 GF) S £50; D £60-£80 (room only)* **Facilities** FTV tea/coffee Dinner available Cen ht Wi-fi **Conf** Max 20 Thtr 16 Class 16 Board 16 **Parking** 30 **Notes** ⊗ RS Nov-Apr closed Mon, Tue lunch & Sun eve (ex BHs)

SHROPSHIRE

BISHOP'S CASTLE   Map 15 SO38

The Sun at Norbury

★★★★ 🛏 ⊜ INN

Norbury SY9 5DX
☎ 01588 650680
web: www.sunatnorbury.co.uk
dir: *3m NE of Bishop's Castle. Off A488/A489 into Norbury*

This delightful stone inn stands in the quiet village of Norbury. Exposed beams and log-burning stoves are enhanced by period furnishings, and the attractive, traditionally appointed bedrooms have modern facilities. Wholesome home-cooked food is available in the elegant dining room or in the popular bar.

Rooms 3 rms (2 en suite) (1 pri facs) 3 annexe en suite (1 GF) S £75-£90; D £90-£120* **Facilities** FTV tea/coffee Dinner available Cen ht **Parking** 20 **Notes** LB ⊗ No Children 12yrs No coaches

Shuttocks Wood

★★★★ BED AND BREAKFAST

Norbury SY9 5EA
☎ 01588 650433   & 07712 443283   📠 01588 650433
e-mail: info@shuttocks.co.uk
dir: *From A489, turn left signed Norbury 3m, on the left past Norbury school*

Peacefully located in rural Norbury, this modern detached house stands on pretty mature gardens and provides good standards of comfort and facilities. Bedrooms are equipped with thoughtful extras; there is a separate annexe, and breakfasts feature local fresh produce. Kennels are available for dogs.

Rooms 3 en suite 1 annexe en suite (1 fmly) (1 GF) S £45-£55; D £70-£90* **Facilities** TV3B tea/coffee Dinner available Cen ht Wi-fi **Parking** 10 **Notes** LB No Children 10yrs

BRIDGNORTH   Map 10 SO79

PREMIER COLLECTION

The Albynes

★★★★★ BED AND BREAKFAST

Nordley WV16 4SX
☎ 01746 762261
e-mail: thealbynes@hotmail.com
dir: *In Nordley on B4373, 500yds past Nordley sign*

This imposing farmhouse features grand staircases, high ceilings and idyllic views. Melissa Woolley is a charming hostess, while husband Hayden looks after the crops and sheep. Bedrooms are comfortable, spacious, and offer many thoughtful extras. Day rooms retain many original features and guests can enjoy traditional breakfasts, home-cooked on the Aga.

Rooms 3 en suite S £45-£50; D £60-£70 **Facilities** FTV TVL tea/coffee Cen ht **Parking** 6 **Notes** ⊗ No Children 12yrs Closed Xmas-New Year ⊛

Save on B&Bs and Hotels. Book at **theAA.com/hotel**

SHROPSHIRE 245 ENGLAND

The Laurels

☆☆☆☆ GUEST HOUSE

Broadoak, Six Ashes WV15 6EQ
☎ 01384 221546 & 07813 925319
e-mail: george.broadoak75@btinternet.com
web: www.thelaurelsbandb.co.uk
dir: *On right 5m from Bridgnorth towards Stourbridge on A458*

Located on pretty gardens in a hamlet between Bridgnorth and Stourbridge, this immaculately maintained property provides a range of homely bedrooms, some of which are in converted stables. Breakfast is served in an attractive conservatory-dining room, and a lounge and indoor swimming pool are additional attractions.

Rooms 2 en suite 5 annexe en suite (1 fmly) (5 GF) S £25-£30; D £55* **Facilities** FTV TVL tea/coffee Dinner available Cen ht Wi-fi ⓢ **Parking** 9 **Notes** ⊗ ⊛

Bearwood Lodge Guest House

★★★★ GUEST ACCOMMODATION

10 Kidderminster Rd WV15 6BW
☎ 01746 762159
e-mail: dawnjones604@yahoo.co.uk
dir: *On A442, 50yds S of Bridgnorth bypass island*

This friendly guest accommodation is situated on the outskirts of Bridgnorth. It provides soundly maintained modern bedrooms, including one on the ground floor. The bright and pleasant breakfast room has an adjacent conservatory, which opens onto the attractive and colourful garden. There is also a comfortable lounge.

Rooms 4 en suite (1 GF) S £45; D £65* **Facilities** FTV TVL tea/coffee Cen ht Wi-fi **Parking** 8 **Notes** LB ⊛

The Halfway House Inn

★★★ INN

Cleobury Mortimer Rd WV16 5LS
☎ 01746 762670 🖷 01746 768063
e-mail: info@halfwayhouseinn.co.uk
web: www.halfwayhouseinn.co.uk
dir: *1m from town centre on B4363 to Cleobury Mortimer*

Located in a rural area, this 16th-century inn has been renovated to provide good standards of comfort, while retaining its original character. The bedrooms, most of which are in converted stables and cottages, are especially suitable for families and groups.

Rooms 10 en suite (10 fmly) (6 GF) S £50-£75; D £60-£95* **Facilities** FTV TVL tea/coffee Dinner available Cen ht Wi-fi Golf 18 Fishing Pool table **Conf** Max 30 Thtr 30 Class 24 Board 20 **Parking** 30 **Notes** LB Closed 25-26 Dec RS Sun eve (ex BHs)

Wyndene

★★ BED AND BREAKFAST

57 Innage Ln WV16 4HS
☎ 01746 764369 & 07977 943074
e-mail: wyndene@bridgnorth2000.freeserve.co.uk
dir: *500yds NW of town centre. Off B4373 onto Innage Ln*

Situated within walking distance of the centre of Bridgnorth, this small property is a home from home. Bedrooms are carefully decorated and one has a four-poster bed. Home-cooked breakfasts are served in an attractive dining room and parking space is available.

Rooms 3 rms (1 en suite) S £35; D £50-£55* **Facilities** FTV TVL tea/coffee Cen ht **Parking** 3 **Notes** ⊗ ⊛

BURLTON Map 15 SJ42

Burlton Inn

★★★★ ⬭ INN

SY4 5TB
☎ 01939 270284
e-mail: enquiries@burltoninn.com
dir: *A528 Ellesmere to Shrewsbury road*

This 18th-century building, in its own grounds, is situated between Shrewsbury and Ellesmere. Hosts, Lindsay and Paul, and their staff offer a warm welcome to all guests. The en suite bedrooms are furnished in a modern style and located in a separate building at the rear. Classic cuisine, using fresh, locally sourced ingredients, is offered. There is a terrace area for guests to enjoy on warmer days.

Rooms 6 en suite (3 GF) S £67.50-£105; D £67.50-£105* **Facilities** FTV tea/coffee Dinner available Cen ht Wi-fi **Parking** 30 **Notes** ⊗ Closed 24-26 Dec RS Sun eve closed No coaches

---

CHURCH STRETTON Map 15 SO49

PREMIER COLLECTION

Field House

★★★★★ GUEST HOUSE

Cardington Moor, Cardington SY6 7LL
☎ 01694 771485
e-mail: pjsecrett@talktalk.net
dir: *A49 onto B4371 at lights in Church Stretton. After 3.5m turn left signed Cardington, after 1m turn left, 0.5m on right*

This delightful old cottage is set by nine acres of grounds and gardens quietly located in a picturesque valley. It has been considerably renovated and extended to provide tastefully appointed, modern accommodation including a bedroom on the ground-floor. Evening meals are available and separate tables are provided in the pleasant dining room. There is also a conservatory lounge.

Rooms 3 en suite (1 GF) D £67-£71 **Facilities** FTV tea/coffee Dinner available Direct Dial Cen ht Licensed Pool table Table tennis **Parking** 3 **Notes** ⊗ Closed Nov-Feb ⊛

PREMIER COLLECTION

Willowfield Guest House

★★★★★ GUEST HOUSE

Lower Wood SY6 6LF
☎ 01694 751471
e-mail: willowfieldlowerwood@tiscali.co.uk
dir: *A5 onto A49 to Leebotwood, follow sign for Lower Wood, 0.5m on left*

Set in spacious and immaculate gardens, this Edwardian house, parts of which are much older, provides high standards of comfort. The bedrooms are well equipped and have many thoughtful extras as well as stunning views, while stylish decor and period furnishings add to the charm. A comfortable lounge is available, plus two elegant dining rooms where hearty breakfasts are served.

Rooms 4 en suite (1 GF) S £40-£45; D £60-£70* **Facilities** tea/coffee Cen ht **Parking** 6 **Notes** LB ⊗ ⊛

CHURCH STRETTON *continued*

Belvedere

★★★★ GUEST HOUSE

Burway Rd SY6 6DP
☎ 01694 722232 📠 01694 722232
e-mail: info@belvedereguesthouse.co.uk
dir: *Off A49 into town centre, over x-rds onto Burway Rd*

Popular with walkers and cyclists and located on the lower slopes of the Long Mynd, this impressive, well-proportioned Edwardian house has a range of homely bedrooms, equipped with practical extras and complemented by modern bathrooms. Ground-floor areas include a cottage-style dining room overlooking the pretty garden and a choice of lounges.

Rooms 7 rms (6 en suite) (2 fmly) S £33-£40; D £58-£68
Facilities TVL tea/coffee Cen ht Wi-fi **Parking** 9 **Notes** LB

Brereton's Farm *(SO424871)*

★★★★ FARMHOUSE

Woolston SY6 6QD
☎ 01694 781201 📠 01694 781201
Mrs J Brereton
e-mail: info@breretonsfarm.co.uk
web: www.breretonsfarm.co.uk
dir: *A49 N from Craven Arms, at Jewsons turn left A489. Under bridge turn right, Wistonstow. At top of village, left, signed Woolston 1.75m. Farm on right*

Located among undulating hills in the pretty hamlet of Woolston, this impressive early-Victorian red-brick house provides thoughtfully equipped bedrooms with stunning country views. Comprehensive breakfasts are served in an elegant dining room, and the lounge has a wood-burning fire.

Rooms 2 en suite S £35; D £60* **Facilities** TVL tea/coffee Cen ht **Parking** 6 **Notes** ⊗ Closed 30 Nov-Mar ➔ 350 acres mixed

The Bucks Head

★★★★ INN

42 High St SY6 6BX
☎ 01694 722898 & 07811 364416
e-mail: lloyd.nutting@btconnect.com
web: www.the-bucks-head.co.uk
dir: *A49 N or S, turn into Church Stretton. At top of town turn left, Bucks Head on right*

Located in the heart of an historic market town, this period hostelry has become a vibrant modern inn after a total renovation. There are high levels of comfort and up-to-date facilities together with original charm and character. The comfortable bedrooms are complemented by smart en suite bathrooms, and the attractive open-plan public areas are the perfect setting for enjoying food and drinks. The hospitality is warm and genuine.

Rooms 4 en suite **Facilities** tea/coffee Dinner available Cen ht **Notes** ⊗ No Children 5yrs No coaches

Court Farm *(SO514951)*

★★★★ FARMHOUSE

Gretton SY6 7HU
☎ 01694 771219 📠 01694 771219
e-mail: alison@courtfarm.eu
dir: *Turn off B4371at Longville, left at x-rds, 1st on left*

Located in the pretty village of Gretton, this 17th-century impressive stone-built Tudor house has been sympathetically renovated to provide high standards of comfort and facilities. The bedrooms overlook the pretty gardens and are equipped with a wealth of thoughtful extras. Comprehensive breakfasts are taken in an elegant dining room and a comfortable guest lounge is also available.

Rooms 2 en suite S £40; D £60-£70* **Facilities** FTV TVL tea/coffee Cen ht **Parking** 4 **Notes** ⊗ No Children 12yrs ➔ 330 acres mixed

North Hill Farm

★★★★ BED AND BREAKFAST

Cardington SY6 7LL
☎ 01694 771532
e-mail: cbrandon@btinternet.com
dir: *From Cardington village S onto Church Stretton road, right signed Cardington Moor, farm at top of hill on left*

This delightful house has been modernised to provide comfortable accommodation. It is located on a fairly remote 20-acre sheep-rearing holding amid the Shropshire hills. The lounge, with exposed beams, has log fires in colder weather. Guests share one large table in the breakfast room. There are two bedrooms in the main house and two in different buildings, one newly built to provide high quality spacious accommodation.

Rooms 2 rms (2 pri facs) 2 annexe en suite (2 GF) S £35; D £56-£80* **Facilities** FTV tea/coffee Cen ht Wi-fi **Parking** 6 **Notes** LB Closed Xmas ➔

CRAVEN ARMS — Map 9 SO48

Castle View

★★★★ BED AND BREAKFAST

Stokesay SY7 9AL
☎ 01588 673712
e-mail: castleviewb_b@btinternet.com
dir: *On A49 S of Craven Arms opp turning to Stokesay Castle*

This Victorian cottage, extended about 20 years ago, stands in delightful gardens on the southern outskirts of Craven Arms, close to Stokesay Castle. Bedrooms are thoughtfully furnished, and breakfasts, featuring local produce, are served in the cosy, traditionally furnished dining room.

Rooms 3 rms (1 en suite) (2 pri facs) S £35-£40; D £60-£68* **Facilities** tea/coffee Cen ht **Parking** 4 **Notes** LB No Children 3yrs ➔

Strefford Hall Farm *(SO444856)*

★★★★ FARMHOUSE

Strefford SY7 8DE
☎ 01588 672383 📠 0870 132 3818
Mrs C Morgan
e-mail: strefford@btconnect.com
dir: *A49 from Church Stretton, S for 5.5m to Strefford, 0.25m past Travellers Rest Inn signed left. Strefford Hall 0.25m on right*

This well-proportioned Victorian house stands at the foot of Wenlock Edge. The spacious bedrooms, filled with homely extras, have stunning views of the surrounding countryside. Breakfast is served in the elegant dining room and a comfortable lounge is also available.

Rooms 3 en suite (1 fmly) (3 smoking) **Facilities** TVL tea/coffee Cen ht **Parking** 3 **Notes** ⊗ RS end Feb-end Oct ➔ 350 acres arable/beef/sheep/pigs

DORRINGTON — Map 15 SJ40

Caro's Bed & Breakfast

★★★ BED AND BREAKFAST

1 Higher Netley SY5 7JY
☎ 01743 718790 & 07739 285263
e-mail: info@carosbandb.co.uk
dir: *1m SW of Dorrington. Off A49 in Dorrington signed Picklescott, 1m left onto driveway by stone bridge, signed Higher Netley*

Self-contained accommodation is provided in this converted barn, south-west of Dorrington. Bedrooms, with smart modern bathrooms, are equipped with thoughtful extras and the open-plan ground-floor contains a dining area and a comfortable lounge with a wood-burning stove.

Rooms 2 en suite (1 fmly) S £35-£55; D £35-£55* **Facilities** FTV tea/coffee Cen ht Wi-fi **Parking** 4 **Notes** LB ⊗ Closed 21-28 Dec

GRINSHILL — Map 15 SJ52

The Inn at Grinshill

★★★★ ⊛ INN

The High St SY4 3BL
☎ 01939 220410 📠 01939 220397
e-mail: info@theinnatgrinshill.co.uk
dir: *N of Shrewsbury on A49, after 7m turn left, Inn 500yds on left*

This inn is part Grade II listed and many areas have been restored to highlight the original features. It is located under the lee of Grinshill in a delightful village with beautiful countryside close by; the Welsh border is within easy driving distance as are Shrewsbury, Telford and Welshpool. The accommodation is comfortable, and real ales and award-winning food are available in the spacious restaurant. Guests are very welcome to make use of the grounds.

Rooms 6 en suite S fr £60; D £120 **Facilities** FTV Dinner available Cen ht Wi-fi ⛳ Golf 36 **Parking** 30 **Notes** LB No coaches

Save on B&Bs and Hotels. Book at **theAA.com/hotel**

SHROPSHIRE 247 ENGLAND

HADNALL Map 15 SJ52

Hall Farm House

★★★★ BED AND BREAKFAST

Shrewsbury Rd SY4 4AG
☎ 01939 210269
e-mail: hallfarmhouse@tiscali.co.uk
web: www.hallfarmhouse.co.uk
dir: On A49 in centre of Hadnall

Parts of this elegant former farmhouse, situated in pretty, mature gardens in the village, date from the 16th century. Accommodation is offered in two thoughtfully equipped bedrooms and comprehensive breakfasts are taken in a spacious, traditionally furnished dining room.

Rooms 2 en suite (1 fmly) S £35-£45; D £60-£70
Facilities tea/coffee Cen ht Wi-fi Parking 6 Notes LB ⊗ No Children 1yr ⊛

Saracens at Hadnall

★★★★ ⊛⊛ RESTAURANT WITH ROOMS

Shrewsbury Rd SY4 4AG
☎ 01939 210877 📠 01939 210877
e-mail: reception@saracensathadnall.co.uk
web: www.saracensathadnall.co.uk
dir: M54 onto A5, at junct of A5/A49 take A49 towards Whitchurch. Follow A49 to Hadnall, diagonally opposite church

This Georgian Grade II listed former farmhouse and village pub has been tastefully converted into a very smart restaurant with rooms, without any loss of original charm and character. The bedrooms are thoughtfully equipped and include a family room. Skilfully prepared meals are served in either the elegant dining room or the adjacent conservatory where there is a glass-topped well.

Rooms 5 en suite (1 fmly) Facilities tea/coffee Dinner available Cen ht Parking 20 Notes LB ⊗ RS Sun eve-Mon Closed No coaches

IRONBRIDGE Map 10 SJ60

PREMIER COLLECTION

The Library House

★★★★★ ⬛ GUEST ACCOMMODATION

11 Severn Bank TF8 7AN
☎ 01952 432299
e-mail: info@libraryhouse.com
web: www.libraryhouse.com
dir: 50yds from Iron Bridge

A warm welcome is assured at this renovated Georgian house, once the local library. Bedrooms, named after writers of note, have a wealth of thoughtful extras and the immaculate gardens and hanging baskets are stunning during spring and summer. Memorable breakfasts are served in the pine- and copper-furnished dining room, and a comfortable guest lounge is also available.

Rooms 4 en suite S £65-£75; D £80-£90*
Facilities FTV TVL tea/coffee Cen ht Licensed Wi-fi
Notes LB ⊗ No Children

Broseley House

★★★★ GUEST HOUSE

1 The Square, Broseley TF12 5EW
☎ 01952 882043 & 07790 732723
e-mail: info@broseleyhouse.co.uk
web: www.broseleyhouse.co.uk
dir: 1m S of Ironbridge in Broseley town centre

A warm welcome is assured at this impressive Georgian house in the centre of Broseley. Quality individual decor and soft furnishings highlight the many original features, and thoughtfully furnished bedrooms are equipped with a wealth of homely extras. Comprehensive breakfasts are taken in an elegant dining room and a stylish apartment is also available.

Rooms 7 en suite (2 fmly) (1 GF) S £50-£60; D £70-£90*
Facilities FTV TV6B tea/coffee Cen ht Wi-fi Notes LB No Children 5yrs

LUDLOW Map 10 SO57

PREMIER COLLECTION

The Clive Bar & Restaurant with Rooms

★★★★★ ⊛⊛ RESTAURANT WITH ROOMS

Bromfield SY8 2JR
☎ 01584 856565 & 856665 📠 01584 856661
e-mail: info@theclive.co.uk
web: www.theclive.co.uk
dir: 2m N of Ludlow on A49 in Bromfield

The Clive is just two miles from the busy town of Ludlow and is a convenient base for visiting the local attractions or for business. The bedrooms, located outside the main restaurant area, are spacious and very well equipped; some are suitable for families and many are on the ground-floor level. Meals are available in the well-known Clive Restaurant or in the bar areas. The property also has a small meeting room.

Rooms 15 annexe en suite (9 fmly) (11 GF) S £65-£90; D £90-£115* Facilities FTV tea/coffee Dinner available Direct Dial Cen ht Wi-fi Conf Max 40 Thtr 40 Class 40 Board 24 Parking 100 Notes LB ⊗ Closed 25-26 Dec

PREMIER COLLECTION

De Greys of Ludlow

★★★★★ GUEST HOUSE

5-6 Broad St SY8 1NG
☎ 01584 872764 📠 01584 879764
e-mail: degreys@btopenworld.com
web: www.degreys.co.uk
dir: Off A49, in town centre, 50yds beyond clock tower

This 16th-century timber-framed property is situated in the town centre. It has recently been extensively refurbished to provide high quality accommodation with modern facilities, including two suites and one bedroom on ground floor level, all with the added confidence of an electronic security system. Careful renovation of the original beams combined with lush fabrics and beautiful wooden furniture has created a real fusion of the past and present. Breakfast is taken in the adjacent tearoom/restaurant and bakery shop.

Rooms 9 en suite (1 GF) Facilities tea/coffee Cen ht Licensed Notes ⊗ Closed 26 Dec & 1 Jan

Number Twenty Eight

★★★★ ⬛ BED AND BREAKFAST

28 Lower Broad St SY8 1PQ
☎ 01584 875466
e-mail: enquiries@no28ludlow.co.uk
dir: In town centre. Over Ludford Bridge onto Lower Broad St, 3rd house on right

A warm welcome is assured at this 200-year-old property just a stroll from the centre. There are two double bedrooms, each well-equipped, and containing thoughtful extras and welcoming touches. Day rooms include an antique furnished combined lounge and sitting room, and a small roof terrace that overlooks the pretty rear garden.

Rooms 2 en suite D £80-£90* Facilities FTV tea/coffee Cen ht Wi-fi Notes ⊗ No Children 16yrs Closed Nov-May

LUDLOW *continued*

Angel House

★★★★ BED AND BREAKFAST

Angel Bank, Bitterley SY8 3HT
☎ 01584 891377 ▤ 08723 520921
e-mail: angelhousebandb@googlemail.com
dir: *On A4117, 4m E of Ludlow on Clee Hill*

Located in an elevated position five miles from Ludlow, this sympathetically renovated 17th-century former pub provides high standards of comfort and facilities. Thoughtfully furnished bedrooms have stunning rural views, and comprehensive breakfasts are served in an attractive dining room. A guest lounge is also available and a warm welcome is assured.

Rooms 2 en suite (1 fmly) S fr £68; D fr £78*
Facilities FTV tea/coffee Dinner available Cen ht Wi-fi
Parking 7 **Notes** No Children 7yrs

The Charlton Arms

★★★★ ⇌ INN

Ludford Bridge SY8 1PJ
☎ 01584 872813
dir: *From town centre onto Broad St, over Ludford Bridge, Charlton Arms on right*

The accommodation at this riverside inn reflects the character of the historic building whilst offering all the comforts of modern living. The restaurant provides fresh locally-sourced ingredients, and as a free house also offers a fine selection of local beers. There is one bedroom which has a private terrace and a hot tub, and there are decking areas to enjoy drinks or a meal on warmer days.

Rooms 10 en suite (2 fmly) **Facilities** tea/coffee Dinner available Cen ht Wi-fi Fishing **Conf** Max 100 Thtr 100 Class 80 Board 70 **Parking** 25 **Notes** Civ Wed 80

Church Inn

★★★★ INN

The Buttercross SY8 1AW
☎ 01584 872174 ▤ 01584 877146
web: www.thechurchinn.com
dir: *In town centre at top of Broad St, behind Buttercross*

Set right in the heart of the historic town, this Grade II listed inn has been renovated to provide quality accommodation with smart modern bathrooms, some with spa baths. Other areas include a small lounge, a well-equipped meeting room, and cosy bar areas where imaginative food and real ales are served.

Rooms 8 en suite (3 fmly) **Facilities** TVL tea/coffee Dinner available Direct Dial Cen ht **Conf** Max 38 **Notes** No coaches

Haynall Villa (SO543674)

★★★★ FARMHOUSE

Little Hereford SY8 4BG
☎ 01584 711589 ▤ 01584 711589
Mrs R Edwards
e-mail: rachelmedwards@hotmail.com
web: www.haynallvilla.co.uk
dir: *A49 onto A456, at Little Hereford right signed Leysters & Middleton on the Hill. Villa 1m on right*

Located in immaculate gardens in the pretty hamlet of Little Hereford, this Victorian house retains many original features, which are enhanced by the furnishings and decor. Bedrooms are filled with lots of homely extras and the lounge has an open fire.

Rooms 3 rms (2 en suite) (1 pri facs) (1 fmly)
Facilities FTV TVL tea/coffee Dinner available Cen ht Wi-fi Fishing **Parking** 3 **Notes** No Children 6yrs Closed mid Dec-mid Jan ⊛ 72 acres arable

Moor Hall

★★★★ GUEST HOUSE

Cleedownton SY8 3EG
☎ 01584 823209
e-mail: enquiries@moorhall.co.uk
dir: *A4117 Ludlow to Kidderminster, left to Bridgnorth. B4364, follow for 3.2m, Moor Hall on right*

This impressive Georgian house, once the home of Lord Boyne, is surrounded by extensive gardens and farmland. Bedrooms are richly decorated, well equipped, and one room has a sitting area. Public areas are spacious and comfortably furnished. There is a choice of sitting rooms and a library bar. Guests dine family-style in an elegant dining room.

Rooms 3 en suite S £40-£45; D £60-£70* **Facilities** tea/coffee Dinner available Cen ht Licensed **Conf** Max 14 Thtr 14 Class 14 Board 14 **Parking** 7 **Notes** LB Closed 25-26 Dec ⊛

130 Corve Street

★★★★ BED AND BREAKFAST

130 Corve St SY8 2PG
☎ 01584 875548 ▤ 08723 523397
e-mail: info@130corvestreet.co.uk
dir: *N side of town on B4361, adjacent to Tesco supermarket*

Expect a warm welcome at this Grade II listed building, situated within easy access of the town's many interesting attractions and restaurants. The attractive bedrooms, situated on the ground floor at the rear, are comfortable and have their own independent entrances. Hearty breakfasts are served in the first-floor dining room. There is off-road parking close by.

Rooms 3 en suite (3 GF) **Facilities** FTV tea/coffee Cen ht Wi-fi **Parking** 3 **Notes** LB ⊗ No Children 12yrs

Tean House

★★★★ BED AND BREAKFAST

8 Ledwyche Close, Middleton SY8 3EP
☎ 01584 875891
dir: *A4117 onto B4364, 0.7m on right*

Located in a small rural hamlet a few minutes' drive from the town centre, this impressive modern, detached house offers comfortable bedrooms that are equipped with a range of homely extras. The comprehensive breakfasts provide a good start to the day and a warm welcome is assured.

Rooms 3 rms (1 en suite) (1 pri facs) S £38; D £60*
Facilities FTV TVL tea/coffee Cen ht Wi-fi **Parking** 3
Notes ⊗ No Children 5yrs ⊛

37 Gravel Hill

★★★★ BED AND BREAKFAST

SY8 1QR
☎ 01584 877524
e-mail: angelastraker@btinternet.com
dir: *Close to town centre*

This charming old house is within walking distance of the town centre. It provides good quality, thoughtfully equipped accommodation, and there is also a comfortable sitting room. Guests share one large table in the elegant breakfast room.

Rooms 2 rms (1 en suite) (1 pri facs) **Facilities** TVL tea/coffee Cen ht **Notes** ⊛

PREMIER COLLECTION

Ternhill Farm House & The Cottage Restaurant

★★★★★ ◎◎ 🍴 RESTAURANT WITH ROOMS

Ternhill TF9 3PX
☎ 01630 638984
e-mail: info@ternhillfarm.co.uk
web: www.ternhillfarm.co.uk
dir: On junct A53 & A41, archway off A53 to back of property

This elegant Grade II listed Georgian farmhouse stands in a large pleasant garden and has been modernised to provide quality accommodation. There is a choice of comfortable lounges, and the Cottage Restaurant features imaginative dishes using local produce. Secure parking is an additional benefit.

Rooms 5 en suite (2 fmly) S £45-£60; D £65-£90*
Facilities FTV tea/coffee Dinner available Cen ht Wi-fi
Parking 18 **Notes** LB ⊗

The Four Alls Inn

★★★ INN

Woodseaves TF9 2AG
☎ 01630 652995 📠 01630 653930
e-mail: inn@thefouralls.com
web: www.thefouralls.com
dir: On A529 1m S of Market Drayton

This country inn provides spacious open-plan public areas and has a strong local following for its food and real ales. Bedrooms, which are in a purpose-built chalet block, offer a good balance between practicality and homeliness. Superb beer gardens adorned with attractive floral displays are a feature during the summer.

Rooms 9 annexe en suite (4 fmly) (9 GF) S £47; D £65*
Facilities FTV tea/coffee Dinner available Direct Dial Cen ht Wi-fi **Conf** Max 100 Thtr 100 Class 100 Board 30 **Parking** 60 **Notes** LB ⊗ Closed 24-26 Dec

The Tudor House

★★★ INN

1 Cheshire St TF9 1PD
☎ 01630 657523 & 01257 248012 📠 01630 657806
e-mail: tudor@alfatravel.co.uk
dir: From A53 onto A529 Adderley Rd, at next rdbt 2nd exit onto Cheshire St

This beautiful property and former coaching inn is located in the heart of the town and has a characterful public bar. The fully equipped bedrooms are well laid out and equally suited to both the business and leisure guest.

Rooms 10 en suite (3 fmly) S £40-£55; D £60-£90*
Facilities FTV TVL tea/coffee Dinner available Cen ht Wi-fi **Conf** Thtr 40 Class 6 Board 12 **Notes** ⊗ No coaches

The Lowfied Inn

★★★★ INN

SY21 9JX
☎ 01743 891313
e-mail: lowfieldinn@tiscali.co.uk
dir: From A5 (Shrewsbury ring road) onto B4386 signed Montgomery

Rooms 4 en suite (1 fmly) S £50; D £70 **Facilities** FTV tea/coffee Dinner available Cen ht Wi-fi Pool table **Parking** 30

Pool Cottage

★★★★ BED AND BREAKFAST

Gravels SY5 0JD
☎ 01743 891621
e-mail: reservations@poolcottage.com
dir: Off A488, signed Pool Cottage

This small, pleasant and friendly bed and breakfast is quietly located being set well back from the A488 amid open country, five miles south of Minsterley. It provides well-maintained, modern accommodation, as well as a cosy breakfast room where guests are seated around one table.

Rooms 3 en suite (1 fmly) (1 GF) S fr £40; D fr £70*
Facilities FTV tea/coffee Cen ht Wi-fi Stabling available **Parking** 7 **Notes** ⊗ Closed Xmas

Yew Tree (SO543958)

★★★★ FARMHOUSE

Longville In The Dale TF13 6EB
☎ 01694 771866
Mr & Mrs Hilbery
e-mail: enquiries@yewtreefarmshropshire.co.uk
dir: 5m SW of Much Wenlock. N off B4371 at Longville, left at pub, right at x-rds, farm 1.2m on right

Yew Tree is peacefully located between Much Wenlock and Church Stretton in ten acres of unspoiled countryside, where pigs, sheep and chickens are reared, and own produce is a feature on the comprehensive breakfast menu. Bedrooms are equipped with thoughtful extras and a warm welcome is assured.

Rooms 2 rms (1 en suite) (1 pri facs) S £35-£45; D £50-£70* **Facilities** FTV TVL tea/coffee Cen ht Wi-fi **Parking** 4 **Notes** LB Closed 24-30 Dec 🌐 10 acres smallholding/sheep/pigs

Talbot Inn

★★★ 🅰 INN

High St TF13 6AA
☎ 01952 727077 📠 01952 728436
e-mail: the_talbot_inn@hotmail.com
web: www.the-talbot-inn.com
dir: In village centre on A458

Rooms 6 annexe en suite (1 GF) **Facilities** TVL tea/coffee Dinner available Cen ht **Parking** 6 **Notes** ⊗ Closed 25 Dec

Crown Country Inn

★★★★ ◎◎ 🍴 INN

SY7 9ET
☎ 01584 841205
e-mail: info@crowncountryinn.co.uk
dir: Off B4368 into village

Located between Much Wenlock and Craven Arms, this impressive pastel-coloured and half-timbered Tudor inn is full of character and charm with stone floors, exposed beams and blazing log fires during winter. The smart pine-furnished bedrooms are in a converted stable block, and the spacious public areas include two dining rooms.

Rooms 3 en suite (1 fmly) (1 GF) S £60-£90; D £90*
Facilities tea/coffee Dinner available Cen ht Wi-fi **Conf** Max 30 Thtr 30 Class 30 Board 20 **Parking** 20 **Notes** LB ⊗ Closed 25 Dec RS Closed Sun eve Closed Mon lunch/eve for food

Moreton Hall Farm B&B

★★★★ GUEST HOUSE

Moreton TF10 9DY
☎ 01952 691544 & 07816 755045 📠 01952 691544
e-mail: sarabloor@moretonhallfarm.com
web: www.moretonhallfarm.com
dir: Exit M54 junct 3, A41 Chester. Turn right Stockton, Moreton, Church Eaton 1.5m, turn left to farm

Peacefully located close to major road links, a warm welcome is assured at this 18th-century farmhouse, which stands in pretty mature gardens and benefits from a swimming pool. Bedrooms are equipped with lots of homely extras, and locally-sourced produce is featured in the breakfast selection.

Rooms 3 rms (2 en suite) (1 pri facs) (1 fmly) S £40-£60; D £65-£100* **Facilities** FTV tea/coffee Cen ht Wi-fi ch fac ⚓ **Parking** 6 **Notes** ⊗ 🌐

OSWESTRY Map 15 SJ22

PREMIER COLLECTION

Greystones

★★★★★ 🏛 ⬟ BED AND BREAKFAST

Crickheath SY10 8BW
☎ 07976 740141
e-mail: enquiry@stayatgreystones.co.uk
web: www.stayatgreystones.co.uk
dir: *From A483 follow B4396, turn right through village take No Through Road, Greystones on right*

A warm welcome is assured at this impressive detached house, located on pretty mature gardens in the hamlet of Crickheath. Bedrooms are equipped with a wealth of thoughtful extras and smart modern bathrooms. Comprehensive breakfasts and imaginative dinners, featuring the best of seasonal produce, are available in the elegant dining room. A comfortable guest lounge is also available.

Rooms 3 en suite (2 fmly) S £69; D £90-£99*
Facilities FTV TVL tea/coffee Dinner available Cen ht Licensed Wi-fi ⬟ Fishing **Conf** Board 10 **Parking** 20 **Notes** LB ⊗ No Children 14yrs

The Pentre

★★★★ ⬟ GUEST HOUSE

Trefonen SY10 9EE
☎ 01691 653952
e-mail: helen@thepentre.com
web: www.thepentre.com
dir: *4m SW of Oswestry. Off Oswestry-Treflach road onto New Well Ln & signed The Pentre*

This 500-year-old stone farmhouse retains many original features, including a wealth of exposed beams and a superb inglenook fireplace with blazing wood burner during colder months. Bedrooms are equipped with a range of thoughtful extras, and breakfast and dinner are memorable, with quality produce cooked with flair on an Aga.

Rooms 3 en suite (1 fmly) (1 GF) S £40-£50; D £68-£76*
Facilities TVL tea/coffee Dinner available Cen ht **Parking** 10 **Notes** LB ⊗ ⬟

The Bradford Arms

★★★★ INN

Llanymynech SY22 6EJ
☎ 01691 830582 📠 01691 839009
e-mail: catelou@tesco.net
dir: *5.5m S of Oswestry on A483 in Llanymynech*

Once a coaching inn on the Earl of Bradford's estate, the Bradford Arms provides a range of carefully furnished bedrooms with a wealth of thoughtful extras. The elegant ground-floor areas include lounges, bars, and a choice of formal or conservatory restaurants, the settings for imaginative food and fine wines.

Rooms 5 en suite (2 fmly) (2 GF) S £40; D £60*
Facilities FTV tea/coffee Dinner available Direct Dial Cen ht Wi-fi Golf 18 Fishing Riding Pool table **Parking** 20

Riseholme

★★★★ BED AND BREAKFAST

4 Hampton Rd SY11 1SJ
☎ 01691 656508
e-mail: ssparnell1234@googlemail.com

Located in a residential area within easy walking distance of the town centre, via the attractive memorial gardens, comfortable bedrooms are complemented by smart modern bathrooms at this attractive home. Comprehensive breakfasts are taken in a cosy dining room and a spacious guest lounge is also available.

Rooms 3 en suite (1 fmly) **Facilities** TVL tea/coffee Cen ht Wi-fi **Parking** 5 **Notes** No Children 12yrs ⬟

Carreg-Y-big Farm

★★★ BED AND BREAKFAST

Carreg-y-big, Selattyn SY10 7HX
☎ 01691 654754
e-mail: info@carreg-y-bigfarm.co.uk
dir: *Off B4580 at Old Racecourse, signed Selattyn. 1m on right on Offa's Dyke*

Incorporated within The Oswestry Equestrian Centre on the edge of Selattyn, this former farmhouse provides a range of simply appointed bedrooms, ideal for walkers on nearby Offas's Dyke. Comprehensive breakfasts, and dinners by arrangement, are served at one table in an attractive beamed dining room; a small guest lounge is also available.

Rooms 4 rms (1 pri facs) (1 GF) **Facilities** TVL Dinner available Cen ht Riding **Parking** 10 **Notes** ⬟

RUYTON-XI-TOWNS Map 15 SJ32

Brownhill House

★★★ BED AND BREAKFAST

SY4 1LR
☎ 01939 261121 📠 01939 260626
e-mail: brownhill@eleventowns.co.uk
web: www.eleventowns.co.uk
dir: *A5 onto B4397, 2m to Ruyton-XI-Towns. Through village. Brownhill House on left of right-hand bend*

A warm welcome is assured at this charming house, parts of which date from the 18th century. The large terraced garden has been painstakingly created on the side of a steep hill above the River Perry, and guests are welcome to explore. All bedrooms have modern facilities and guests share one large table in a cosy kitchen-dining room.

Rooms 3 en suite (1 GF) S £29-£35.50; D £50-£60*
Facilities TVL tea/coffee Cen ht Wi-fi ⬟ Fishing **Parking** 5 **Notes** LB ⊗ RS Xmas

SHIFNAL Map 10 SJ70

The Anvil Lodge

★★★★ GUEST ACCOMMODATION

22 Aston Rd TF11 8DU
☎ 01952 460125 📠 01952 460125
e-mail: michaeldavies234@btinternet.com

A friendly welcome is assured at Anvil Lodge, just a short stroll from the market town of Shifnal. Delicious, freshly cooked breakfasts are served around the dining room table. Bedrooms are spacious, are fresh in appearance and very comfortable with modern bathrooms complete with bath and separate shower. Off-road secure parking is available.

Rooms 4 annexe en suite (2 fmly) (2 GF) **Facilities** FTV Cen ht **Parking** 8 **Notes** ⊗

SHREWSBURY   Map 15 SJ41

See also Criggion (Powys), Ruyton-XI-Towns, Wem & Westbury

PREMIER COLLECTION

Drapers Hall

★★★★★ ◉◉ RESTAURANT WITH ROOMS

10 Saint Mary's Place SY1 1DZ
☎ 01743 344679
e-mail: goodfood@drapershallrestaurant.co.uk

This 16th-century timber-framed property is situated in the heart of the market town of Shrewsbury. It provides high quality accommodation, including two suites, with modern facilities. Careful renovation of the original beams and wood panels together with beautiful wooden furniture has created a harmony of the past and present. Accomplished dining, headed up by Nigel Huxley, can be enjoyed in the main restaurant, Huxleys at Drapers Hall.

Rooms 4 en suite (2 fmly) **Facilities** FTV TVL tea/coffee Dinner available Cen ht Wi-fi **Conf** Max 20 Thtr 20 Class 20 Board 20 **Notes** ⊗

PREMIER COLLECTION

Mad Jack's Restaurant & Bar

★★★★★ ◉ RESTAURANT WITH ROOMS

15 Saint Mary's St SY1 1EQ
☎ 01743 358870 & 761220 🖷 01743 344422
e-mail: info@madjacks.uk.com
dir: *Follow one-way system around town, opposite St Mary's church*

This fine property is located in the heart of the town. Its name comes from a eccentric squire in the 18th century who squandered a fortune and then landed in jail for his drunken and riotous behaviour. The four individually designed bedrooms, including a suite, are very comfortable and have spacious and contemporary bathrooms. Downstairs the award-winning, vibrant bar and restaurant specialises in British food with a classic twist. Breakfast offers a quality range of dishes. Secure parking is available in a nearby public car park.

Rooms 4 en suite (1 fmly) S £70-£120; D £80-£145* **Facilities** tea/coffee Dinner available Cen ht Wi-fi **Notes** LB ⊗ Closed 25 Dec No coaches

Fieldside

★★★★ GUEST HOUSE

38 London Rd SY2 6NX
☎ 01743 353143
e-mail: robrookes@btinternet.com
dir: *A5 onto A5064, premises 1m on left*

Located in manicured grounds within easy walking distance of the town centre, this well maintained, early Victorian house provides a range of tastefully furnished bedrooms equipped with a wealth of thoughtful extras. Breakfast is taken in an elegant spacious dining room and a warm welcome is assured.

Rooms 8 rms (5 en suite) (3 pri facs) **Facilities** FTV tea/coffee Cen ht Wi-fi **Parking** 8 **Notes** No Children 10yrs ⊛

Tudor House

★★★★ 🗎 GUEST HOUSE

2 Fish St SY1 1UR
☎ 01743 351735 & 07870 653040
e-mail: enquiry@tudorhouseshrewsbury.co.uk
web: www.tudorhouseshrewsbury.co.uk
dir: *Enter town over English Bridge, ascend Wyle Cop, in 50yds take 1st right*

Located in the beautiful medieval town centre, this fine 15th-century house has original beams and fireplaces, enhanced by the stylish decor and furnishings. The bedrooms are filled with thoughtful extras, and breakfast features local organic produce.

Rooms 3 rms (2 en suite) (1 pri facs) **Facilities** tea/coffee Cen ht **Notes** ⊗ No Children 11yrs ⊛

Abbey Court

★★★★ GUEST HOUSE

134 Abbey Foregate SY2 6AU
☎ 01743 364416
e-mail: info@abbeycourt.biz
web: www.abbeycourt.biz
dir: *N of river off A5112*

Located within easy reach of the town centre, this Grade II listed house offers a range of homely bedrooms, some of which are in an attractive extension. Comprehensive breakfasts are served in a cosy dining room and a warm welcome is assured.

Rooms 6 en suite 4 annexe en suite (1 fmly) (4 GF) S £40-£45; D £65-£70 **Facilities** FTV tea/coffee Direct Dial Cen ht **Parking** 10 **Notes** LB ⊗ RS 23-27 Dec room only

TELFORD   Map 10 SJ60

Church Farm Guest House

★★★★ ◉ 🗎 GUEST ACCOMMODATION

Wrockwardine Village, Wellington TF6 5DG
☎ 01952 251927 & 07976 897528 🖷 01952 427511
e-mail: info@churchfarm-shropshire.co.uk
dir: *M54 junct 7 towards Wellington, 1st left, 1st right, then right at end of road. 0.5m on left opp St Peters church*

Located in the pretty rural village of Wrockwardine, this impressive period former farmhouse provides high standards of comfort and good facilities. Attractive bedrooms, furnished in minimalist style, offer a wealth of thoughtful extras including complimentary Wi-fi. The spacious day rooms include a comfortable lounge and an elegant dining room, the setting for imaginative cooking.

Rooms 4 rms (3 en suite) (1 pri facs) (1 fmly) S £55-£65; D £70-£80 **Facilities** FTV tea/coffee Dinner available Cen ht Wi-fi Golf 18 ♨ Sauna Solarium Gym **Conf** Max 20 Thtr 20 Class 20 Board 14 **Parking** 12

WELLINGTON   Map 10 SJ61

The Old Orleton Inn

★★★★★ 🅰 INN

Holyhead Rd TF1 2HA
☎ 01952 255011 & 07515 352538
e-mail: info@theoldorleton.com
dir: *M54 junct 7, 400yds on left on corner of Haygate Rd & Holyhead Rd*

Rooms 10 en suite S £65-£88; D £65-£118* **Facilities** FTV tea/coffee Dinner available Direct Dial Cen ht Wi-fi Golf 18 Discounted access to local gym/spa **Conf** Max 15 Thtr 15 Class 15 Board 15 **Parking** 25 **Notes** LB ⊗ No Children 5yrs Closed 1st 2wks Jan

WEM
Map 15 SJ52

Soulton Hall

★★★★ GUEST ACCOMMODATION

Soulton SY4 5RS
☎ 01939 232786 📠 01939 234097
e-mail: enquiries@soultonhall.co.uk
web: www.soultonhall.co.uk
dir: A49 between Shrewsbury & Whitchurch turn onto B5065 towards Wem. Soulton Hall 2m E of Wem on B5065

Located two miles from historic Wem, this 16th-century manor house incorporates part of an even older building. The house stands in 560 acres and provides high levels of comfort. Bedrooms are equipped with homely extras and the ground-floor areas include a spacious hall sitting room, lounge-bar and an attractive dining room, the setting for imaginative dinners.

Rooms 4 en suite 3 annexe en suite (2 fmly) (3 GF) S £44-£131; D £88-£142* **Facilities** FTV tea/coffee Dinner available Direct Dial Cen ht Licensed Wi-fi ch fac 🏊 Golf 18 Fishing Birdwatching in 50 acre private woodland **Conf** Max 100 Thtr 100 Class 60 Board 50 **Parking** 52 **Notes** LB Civ Wed 450

WESTBURY
Map 15 SJ30

Barley Mow House

★★★★ BED AND BREAKFAST

Aston Rogers SY5 9HQ
☎ 01743 891234 📠 01743 891234
e-mail: colinrigby@astonrogers.fsnet.co.uk
web: www.barleymowhouse.co.uk
dir: 2m S of Westbury. Off B4386 into Aston Rogers, house 400yds opp Aston Hall

Dating in part from the 17th century and extended in the 18th century, this charming property has been restored to provide comfortable accommodation with modern facilities. The house stands in a peaceful village and is surrounded by beautifully maintained gardens.

Rooms 3 en suite (1 fmly) (1 GF) **Facilities** FTV TVL tea/coffee Cen ht Wi-fi **Parking** 4 **Notes** ⊗

SOMERSET

BALTONSBOROUGH
Map 4 ST53

Lower Farm (ST572346)

★★★★ FARMHOUSE

Lottisham BA6 8PF
☎ 01458 850206
Diana Board
e-mail: dboard51@btinternet.com
dir: From Shepton Mallet take A37 over Wraxall Hill past Queens Arms. Follow road 3rd turning on right to Marsh Lottisham, 1st on right

Peacefully located and surrounded by pleasant countryside, this working farm offers a genuine welcome and traditional farmhouse hospitality. The one en suite bedroom is spacious and well equipped, and is located on the ground floor at one end of the main building. Breakfast is taken in the comfortable dining room where a wood-burning fire adds to the ambience during the winter.

Rooms 1 en suite (1 GF) **Facilities** FTV TVL tea/coffee Cen ht Golf **Parking** **Notes** ⊗ ⊛

BATCOMBE
Map 4 ST63

The Three Horseshoes

★★★★ INN

BA4 6HE
☎ 01749 850359 📠 01749 850615
e-mail: info@thethreehorseshoesinn.com
dir: 3m from Bruton signed on A359

This traditional village inn has a delightful rural setting and provides a peaceful and relaxing stay. Welcoming hospitality combines with a fine selection of good food and real ales. Bedrooms, while not large, are comfortably furnished and well equipped. Guests have the option of sitting beside a log fire in the bar or relaxing in the garden depending on the season.

Rooms 3 en suite D £70-£85* **Facilities** tea/coffee Dinner available Cen ht **Parking** 30 **Notes** No coaches

Home Farm

★★★ BED AND BREAKFAST

BA4 6HF
☎ 01749 850303
e-mail: camilla@wickedworm.co.uk

Peacefully located and surrounded by delightful countryside in the pleasant village of Batcombe. This relaxed family home offers two comfortable traditionally furnished en suite bedrooms located on the first floor. TVs are available on request but most guests prefer to enjoy the peace and tranquillity. Guests are welcome to use the comfortable lounge and outdoor seating. The village pub is just a few minutes' stroll for dinner.

Rooms 2 en suite **Facilities** STV FTV TVL tea/coffee Cen ht **Parking** 4 **Notes** LB ⊛

BATH
Map 4 ST76

For other locations surrounding Bath see also Box (Wiltshire), Bradford on Avon (Wiltshire), Farmborough, Frome & Trowbridge (Wiltshire)

PREMIER COLLECTION

Ayrlington

★★★★★ GUEST ACCOMMODATION

24/25 Pulteney Rd BA2 4EZ
☎ 01225 425495 📠 01225 469029
e-mail: mail@ayrlington.com
web: www.ayrlington.com
dir: A4 onto A36, pass Holburne Museum, premises 200yds on right

The charm of this impressive Victorian house is evident in the attractive exterior and throughout the rooms, many of which feature Oriental artefacts and pictures. The bedrooms, some with spa baths, four-poster beds and views over Bath cricket ground, are very comfortable. Breakfast is served in the elegant dining room, which shares the enjoyable view.

Rooms 16 en suite (3 fmly) (3 GF) D £105-£185 **Facilities** tea/coffee Cen ht Licensed Wi-fi Unlimited free golf at local golf club **Conf** Max 20 **Parking** 16 **Notes** LB ⊗ No Children 14yrs Closed 22 Dec-5 Jan

PREMIER COLLECTION

Bradford Old Windmill

★★★★★ BED AND BREAKFAST

4 Masons Ln BA15 1QN
☎ 01225 866842 📠 01225 866648
e-mail: aa@bradfordoldwindmill.co.uk

(For full entry see Bradford-on-Avon)

Save on B&Bs and Hotels. Book at **theAA.com/hotel**

SOMERSET 253 ENGLAND

PREMIER COLLECTION

One Three Nine

★★★★★ GUEST ACCOMMODATION

139 Wells Rd BA2 3AL
☎ 01225 314769 📠 01225 443079
e-mail: info@139bath.co.uk
dir: M4 junct 19 onto A46. A4 towards Bath, then A367 towards Wells and Shepton Mallet. On left 500mtrs up hill

Overlooking the historic city of Bath this quality establishment provides spacious accommodation paired with thoughtful design. Bedrooms are comfortably equipped providing a very good range of accessories to enhance guest comfort. A number of feature bathrooms add a dash of luxury. Breakfast is served in the bright and airy dining room, where an excellent choice of continental and hot items is served. Off-street parking is available.

Rooms 10 en suite (1 fmly) (2 GF) D £60-£170*
Facilities FTV tea/coffee Direct Dial Cen ht Wi-fi
Parking 10 **Notes** ⊗ Closed 24-25 Dec

PREMIER COLLECTION

Paradise House

★★★★★ GUEST ACCOMMODATION

Holloway BA2 4PX
☎ 01225 317723 📠 01225 482005
e-mail: info@paradise-house.co.uk
web: www.paradise-house.co.uk
dir: A36 onto A367 Wells Rd, 3rd left, down hill onto cul-de-sac, house 200yds on left

Set in half an acre of lovely walled gardens, this Georgian house, built of mellow Bath stone, is within walking distance of the city centre. Many bedrooms have fine views over the city, and all are decorated in opulent style. Furnishings are elegant and facilities modern. The lounge is comfortable and relaxing, and breakfast is served in the smart dining room. Hospitality and service are friendly and professional.

Rooms 11 en suite (2 fmly) (4 GF) S £65-£130; D £75-£175* **Facilities** FTV tea/coffee Direct Dial Cen ht Licensed Wi-fi **Parking** 11 **Notes** LB ⊗ Closed 24-25 Dec

PREMIER COLLECTION

Apsley House

★★★★★ 🛏 BED AND BREAKFAST

Newbridge Hill BA1 3PT
☎ 01225 336966 📠 01225 425462
e-mail: info@apsley-house.co.uk
dir: 1.3m W of city centre on A431

Built in 1830 for the Duke of Wellington, Apsley House is within walking distance (allow around half an hour) of the city centre. The house is extremely elegant, and the spacious bedrooms have pleasant views. There are family rooms and rooms with four-poster beds. A smart breakfast room and a delightful lounge are also available.

Rooms 11 en suite (2 fmly) (1 GF) S £65-£145; D £79-£190* **Facilities** STV FTV tea/coffee Dinner available Direct Dial Cen ht Licensed Wi-fi **Parking** 12 **Notes** LB ⊗ Closed 3 days Xmas

PREMIER COLLECTION

Cheriton House

★★★★★ GUEST ACCOMMODATION

9 Upper Oldfield Park BA2 3JX
☎ 01225 429862 📠 01225 428403
e-mail: info@cheritonhouse.co.uk
web: www.cheritonhouse.co.uk
dir: A36 onto A367 Wells Rd, 1st right

Expect a friendly welcome and a relaxed atmosphere at this well-presented Victorian house with panoramic views over Bath. The carefully decorated bedrooms are well equipped and include a two-bedroom suite in a converted coach house. A substantial breakfast is served in the conservatory-breakfast room overlooking the rear garden. There is also a comfortable lounge.

Rooms 11 en suite (2 fmly) (2 GF) S £55-£95; D £80-£145 **Facilities** tea/coffee Direct Dial Cen ht Wi-fi **Parking** 11 **Notes** LB ⊗ No Children 12yrs

PREMIER COLLECTION

Chestnuts House

★★★★★ 🛏 GUEST ACCOMMODATION

16 Henrietta Rd BA2 6LY
☎ 01225 334279 📠 01225 312236
e-mail: reservations@chestnutshouse.co.uk
web: www.chestnutshouse.co.uk

Located just a few minutes' walk from the city centre and totally renovated using light shades and oak, the accommodation is fresh and airy. Bedrooms are attractively co-ordinated, well equipped and comfortable. Added enhancements, such as Wi-fi make the rooms suitable for both business and leisure guests. Breakfast, which features quite an extensive buffet and daily specials, is served in the dining room that opens onto the pretty rear garden. There is a cosy lounge, and the small car park is a bonus.

Rooms 5 en suite (1 fmly) (2 GF) S £80-£99; D £85-£125* **Facilities** STV FTV TVL tea/coffee Cen ht Wi-fi Riding **Parking** 5 **Notes** ⊗

BATH *continued*

Dorian House

★★★★★ GUEST ACCOMMODATION

1 Upper Oldfield Park BA2 3JX
☎ 01225 426336 📠 01225 444699
e-mail: info@dorianhouse.co.uk
web: www.dorianhouse.co.uk
dir: *A36 onto A367 Wells Rd, right onto Upper Oldfield Park, 3rd building on left*

This elegant Victorian property has stunning views over the city. The atmosphere is welcoming and the accommodation of high quality. Several of the rooms have fine period four-poster beds and all offer a range of extra facilities. The attractive lounge has an honesty bar and views of the terraced gardens.

Rooms 13 en suite (4 fmly) (2 GF) S £65-£95; D £65-£165* **Facilities** FTV tea/coffee Direct Dial Cen ht Licensed Wi-fi **Parking** 9 **Notes** LB ⊗ Closed 25 & 26 Dec

Tasburgh House

★★★★★ GUEST ACCOMMODATION

Warminster Rd BA2 6SH
☎ 01225 425096 📠 01225 463842
e-mail: stay@tasburghhouse.co.uk
dir: *On N side of A36, next to Bathampton Ln junct*

Located on the main road just outside of Bath, this elegant, detached property has undergone a complete refurbishment and provides high levels of quality and comfort throughout. Relaxing public areas include a guest lounge and the delightful conservatory-style breakfast room. Bedrooms vary in size but each includes a host of extras and very comfortable beds. Guests also have use of outdoor seating on the terrace, the large garden and off-street parking.

Rooms 12 en suite (3 fmly) (2 GF) S £85-£100; D £120-£180 **Facilities** FTV tea/coffee Dinner available Direct Dial Cen ht Licensed Wi-fi 🏌 Golf 18 Fishing **Conf** Max 15 Thtr 10 Class 10 Board 15 **Parking** 16 **Notes** ⊗ Closed 21 Dec-14 Jan

The Bailbrook Lodge

★★★★ GUEST HOUSE

35-37 London Road West BA1 7HZ
☎ 01225 859090 📠 01225 852299
e-mail: hotel@bailbrooklodge.co.uk
web: www.bailbrooklodge.co.uk
dir: *M4 junct 18, A46 S to A4 junct, left signed Batheaston. Lodge 1st on left*

Set in extensive gardens on the east edge of the city, this imposing Georgian building provides smart accommodation. The well-equipped bedrooms include some with four-poster beds and period furniture, and service is professional and efficient. The inviting lounge has a small bar, and light snacks are available from noon until evening. Breakfast is served in the elegant dining room.

Rooms 15 rms (14 en suite) (1 pri facs) (5 fmly) (1 GF) **Facilities** FTV tea/coffee Cen ht Licensed Wi-fi **Conf** Max 20 Thtr 20 Class 10 Board 12 **Parking** 15 **Notes** ⊗

Cranleigh

★★★★ BED AND BREAKFAST

159 Newbridge Hill BA1 3PX
☎ 01225 310197 📠 01225 423143
e-mail: cranleigh@btinternet.com
dir: *1.2m W of city centre on A431*

This pleasant Victorian house is in a quiet location near the city centre. The well-equipped bedrooms, some on the ground floor, are decorated in the period style and two rooms have four-poster beds. Breakfast is served in the elegant dining room, and there is also an attractive garden which includes a popular hot tub.

Rooms 9 en suite (2 fmly) (2 GF) S £65-£75; D £67-£136* **Facilities** FTV tea/coffee Direct Dial Cen ht Licensed Wi-fi Garden hot tub **Parking** 5 **Notes** ⊗ No Children 5yrs Closed 25-26 Dec

The Hollies

★★★★ GUEST ACCOMMODATION

Hatfield Rd BA2 2BD
☎ 01225 313366
e-mail: davcartwright@lineone.net
dir: *A36 onto A367 Wells Rd & Wellsway, 0.7m right opp Devonshire Arms*

This delightful house stands in impressive gardens overlooking a magnificent church, and is within easy reach of the city centre. The individually decorated, themed bedrooms are appointed to provide excellent levels of comfort and good facilities. Breakfast in the elegant dining room is an enjoyable start to the day.

Rooms 3 rms (2 en suite) (1 pri facs) **Facilities** FTV tea/coffee Cen ht Wi-fi **Parking** 3 **Notes** ⊗ No Children 16yrs Closed 15 Dec-Jan

The Kennard

★★★★ GUEST ACCOMMODATION

11 Henrietta St BA2 6LL
☎ 01225 310472 📠 01225 460054
e-mail: reception@kennard.co.uk
web: www.kennard.co.uk
dir: *A4 onto A36 Bathwick St, 2nd right onto Henrietta Rd & Henrietta St*

This attractive Georgian house dates from 1794 and is situated just off famous Great Pulteney Street, making it convenient for the city centre. The house is decorated and furnished in keeping with the elegance of the architecture. Bedrooms, some located at ground floor level, vary in style and size. Breakfast is served in the lower garden dining room and includes an excellent cold buffet, as well as a selection of hot items.

Rooms 12 rms (10 en suite) (2 GF) S £65-£70; D £110-£150* **Facilities** FTV tea/coffee Direct Dial Cen ht Licensed Wi-fi **Notes** ⊗ No Children 8yrs Closed 1wk Xmas

Marlborough House

★★★★ GUEST ACCOMMODATION

1 Marlborough Ln BA1 2NQ
☎ 01225 318175 📠 01225 466127
e-mail: mars@manque.dircon.co.uk
web: www.marlborough-house.net
dir: *450yds W of city centre, at A4 junct with Marlborough Ln*

Marlborough House is situated opposite Royal Victoria Park and close to the Royal Crescent. Some original features remain and the rooms are decorated with period furniture and pictures. The atmosphere is relaxed, and service is attentive and friendly. The breakfast, served from an open-plan kitchen, is vegetarian and organic.

Rooms 6 en suite (2 fmly) (1 GF) S £75-£110; D £85-£135 **Facilities** FTV tea/coffee Direct Dial Cen ht Licensed Wi-fi **Parking** 3 **Notes** LB Closed 24-26 Dec

Oldfields

★ ★ ★ ★ GUEST HOUSE

102 Wells Rd BA2 3AL
☎ 01225 317984 📄 01225 444471
e-mail: info@oldfields.co.uk
dir: 0.5m S of city centre. A36 onto A367

This guest house has been sensitively developed both to maintain some period features and to offer luxurious comfort. The attractive, light and airy bedrooms, some of which have four-poster beds and jacuzzis, are well equipped. The lounge has a welcoming fire on colder days. The elegant dining room offers a choice of dishes at breakfast.

Rooms 16 en suite (4 fmly) (2 GF) S £65–£99; D £65–£165* **Facilities** FTV tea/coffee Direct Dial Cen ht Wi-fi **Parking** 16 **Notes** LB ⊗ Closed 24-26 Dec

17 Lansdown Crescent

★ ★ ★ ★ BED AND BREAKFAST

BA1 5EX
☎ 01225 471741
e-mail: derries@globalnet.co.uk
dir: From A4 onto Lansdown Rd, 5th turn on left onto Lansdown Pl East then Lansdown Crescent

An impressive Georgian building full of charm and elegance located in a crescent overlooking the delightful city of Bath. Grade I listed, the building has very spacious bedrooms and a huge, tastefully decorated breakfast room. Guests are welcome to use the full-size snooker table in its own room; and parking permits are available. While not en suite due to the nature of the building, each bedroom has its own well decorated bathroom.

Rooms 2 rms (2 pri facs) (2 fmly) **Facilities** FTV tea/coffee Cen ht Wi-fi Snooker **Notes** LB ⊗ Closed 20-28 Dec 📷

Villa Claudia

★ ★ ★ ★ BED AND BREAKFAST

19 Forester Rd, Bathwick BA2 6QE
☎ 01225 329670 📄 01225 329670
e-mail: claudiaamato77@aol.com
dir: From A4 onto Cleveland Place East (A36), at next rdbt take 1st exit onto Beckford Rd, then left onto Forester Rd

Villa Claudia is a beautiful Victorian property located on a quiet tree-lined residential street within easy walking distance of the city centre's attractions and restaurants. The Italian owners of this family-run bed and breakfast provide attentive and personal service. The bedrooms and bathrooms are beautifully decorated and very comfortable; a four-poster room is available. Delicious breakfasts are served in the charming dining room at a communal table.

Rooms 3 en suite (1 fmly) S £85–£99; D £98–£125* **Facilities** FTV tea/coffee Cen ht Wi-fi **Parking** 4 **Notes** ⊗

Aquae Sulis

★ ★ ★ ★ GUEST ACCOMMODATION

174-176 Newbridge Rd BA1 3LE
☎ 01225 420061 📄 01225 446077
e-mail: enquiries@aquaesulishotel.co.uk
web: www.aquaesulishotel.co.uk
dir: On A4 1.8m W of city centre, on A4 (Upper Bristol Rd)

Located within easy reach of the city centre, this attractive Edwardian house offers a genuine welcome. Bedrooms are of a good size and well equipped, with many modern facilities such as internet access. There are two inviting lounges, one with a small but well-stocked bar. Breakfast is served in the comfortable dining room.

Rooms 13 rms (11 en suite) (2 pri facs) 1 annexe en suite (5 fmly) (3 GF) **Facilities** STV FTV tea/coffee Direct Dial Cen ht Licensed Wi-fi **Parking** 12 **Notes** Closed 24-26 Dec RS 27-30 Dec accommodation only, no room service

The Bath House

★ ★ ★ ★ GUEST ACCOMMODATION

40 Crescent Gardens BA1 2NB
☎ 0117 937 4495 & 07711 119847 📄 0117 337 6791
e-mail: info@thebathhouse.org
dir: 100yds from Queen Sq on A431

Now refurbished to high quality specifications, this accommodation is stylish and just a few minutes level walk from the city. Bedrooms are attractive, spacious, light and airy, and equipped with modern accessories, including flat-screen televisions and Wi-fi. Breakfast is room service only and a full height dining table provided in the bedroom ensures guests enjoy their meal experience. Limited parking space is available.

Rooms 5 en suite (1 GF) S £69–£109; D £69–£129* **Facilities** FTV tea/coffee Cen ht Wi-fi **Parking** 5 **Notes** LB ⊗ No Children 8yrs

Bathwick Gardens

★ ★ ★ ★ BED AND BREAKFAST

95 Sydney Place BA2 6NE
☎ 01225 469435 & 07737 793772
e-mail: visitus@bathwickgardens.co.uk
web: www.bathwickgardens.co.uk
dir: From A46 onto A4 for 2m. At lights turn left, over bridge at next lights turn right, pass Holburne Museum then immediate left

Situated close to the city centre, this substantial Regency town house featured in the film of Jane Austen's *Persuasion*. Architecturally restored with many original features, the house provides an insight into the 18th century. The en suite bedrooms are very spacious and decorated with period wallpapers. Breakfast is a choice of traditional English or the house special, an Austrian continental breakfast. Parking is by arrangement.

Rooms 3 rms (2 en suite) **Facilities** TVL TV1B tea/coffee Cen ht Wi-fi **Parking** 2 **Notes** ⊗ 📷

Brocks Guest House

★ ★ ★ ★ GUEST ACCOMMODATION

32 Brock St BA1 2LN
☎ 01225 338374 📄 01225 338425
e-mail: brocks@brocksguesthouse.co.uk
web: www.brocksguesthouse.co.uk
dir: Just off A4 between Circus & Royal Crescent

A warm welcome is extended at this delightful Georgian property, located in the heart of the city just a few hundred yards from Royal Crescent. All rooms reflect the comfortable elegance of the Georgian era. A traditional breakfast is served in the charming dining room, which also offers a lounge area with comfortable seating.

Rooms 6 en suite (2 fmly) **Facilities** FTV tea/coffee Cen ht Wi-fi **Parking** **Notes** ⊗ Closed 24 Dec-1 Jan

Devonshire House

★ ★ ★ ★ GUEST ACCOMMODATION

143 Wellsway BA2 4RZ
☎ 01225 312495
e-mail: enquiries@devonshire-house.uk.com
web: www.devonshire-house.uk.com
dir: 1m S of city centre. A36 onto A367 Wells Rd & Wellsway

Located within walking distance of the city centre, this charming house maintains Victorian style. The friendly proprietors make every effort to ensure a stay here is pleasant and memorable. The attractive bedrooms, some appointed to a very high quality standard, have many thoughtful extras. There is a small lounge area, and freshly cooked breakfasts are served in the pleasant dining room. Secure parking is available.

Rooms 4 en suite (1 fmly) (2 GF) S £60–£80; D £68–£98* **Facilities** FTV tea/coffee Cen ht Wi-fi **Parking** 6 **Notes** LB ⊗

Dolphin House

★ ★ ★ ★ BED AND BREAKFAST

8 Northend, Batheaston BA1 7EN
☎ 01225 858915 & 07801 444521
e-mail: georgeandjane@hotmail.com
dir: 2m NE of Bath. Off Batheaston High St to Northend, 100yds on right

This detached Grade II listed Georgian house is convenient for Bath and has a delightful terraced walled garden. Bedrooms, including a suite with lounge, twin bedroom and large bathroom, feature attractive period decor. Continental breakfasts are served in the bedrooms or on the terrace.

Rooms 2 rms (1 en suite) (1 pri facs) (1 GF) D £70–£85* **Facilities** FTV tea/coffee Cen ht Wi-fi **Parking** 2 **Notes** ⊗ No Children 12yrs Closed Xmas RS 24-27 Dec 📷

BATH *continued*

Eagle House

★★★★ GUEST ACCOMMODATION

Church St, Bathford BA1 7RS
☎ 01225 859946 📠 01225 859430
e-mail: jonap@eagleho.demon.co.uk
web: www.eaglehouse.co.uk
dir: *Off A363 onto Church St*

Set in attractive gardens, this delightful Georgian house is pleasantly located on the outskirts of the city. Bedrooms are individually styled, and each has a thoughtful range of extra facilities. The impressive lounge is adorned with attractive pictures, and the dining room has views of the grounds and tennis court.

Rooms 6 en suite 2 annexe en suite (2 fmly) (2 GF) S £48-£88.50; D £64-£115* **Facilities** FTV tea/coffee Direct Dial Cen ht Wi-fi 🏊 🚣 Treehouse Tarzan swing **Conf** Max 18 Thtr 18 Class 18 Board 14 **Parking** 10 **Notes** LB Closed 12 Dec-15 Jan

Grove Lodge

★★★★ GUEST ACCOMMODATION

11 Lambridge BA1 6BJ
☎ 01225 310860 📠 01225 429630
e-mail: stay@grovelodgebath.co.uk
dir: *0.6m NE of city centre. Off A4, 400yds W from junct A46*

This fine Georgian house lies within easy reach of the city centre and is accessed via a stone path through a neat garden surrounded by trees. The spacious bedrooms have period character and all are well equipped. There is an attractive breakfast room, and parking is available in nearby side streets. Guests may venture into the city for evening meals or alternatively, a short stroll along the canal leads to an inn which serves food.

Rooms 4 rms (3 en suite) (1 pri facs) S £60-£89; D £75-£90* **Facilities** FTV tea/coffee Cen ht Wi-fi **Notes** LB ⊗ No Children 7yrs Closed Xmas & New Year

Highways House

★★★★ GUEST ACCOMMODATION

143 Wells Rd BA2 3AL
☎ 01225 421238 📠 01225 481169
e-mail: stay@highwayshouse.co.uk
dir: *A36 onto A367 Wells Rd, 300yds on left*

This elegant Victorian house is just a 10-minute walk from the city centre; alternatively, there is a frequent bus service. The bedrooms are individually styled, well equipped and homely. A spacious, attractive lounge is available, and breakfast is served in the dining room at separate tables. Parking is a bonus.

Rooms 5 en suite 2 annexe en suite (2 fmly) (3 GF) S £50-£70; D £72-£85* **Facilities** FTV tea/coffee Cen ht Wi-fi **Parking** 7 **Notes** ⊗ No Children 8yrs

Milsoms Bath

★★★★ 🍽 RESTAURANT WITH ROOMS

24 Milsom St BA1 1DG
☎ 01225 750128 📠 01225 750121
e-mail: bath@milsomshotel.co.uk

Located at the end of the main street in busy, central Bath, this stylish restaurant with rooms offers a range of comfortable, well equipped accommodation. The ground-floor Loch Fyne Restaurant serves an excellent selection of dishes at both lunch and dinner with an emphasis on freshest quality fish and shellfish. A good selection of hot and cold items is also available in the same restaurant at breakfast.

Rooms 9 en suite D £85-£115* **Facilities** FTV tea/coffee Dinner available Direct Dial Cen ht **Notes** LB ⊗ No coaches

Rivers Street Rooms

★★★★ BED AND BREAKFAST

39 Rivers St BA1 2QA
☎ 07787 500345
e-mail: sharonabrahams3@yahoo.co.uk
dir: *From Lansdown Rd, take Julian Rd & left onto Rivers St*

This centrally located, five-storey, 1770s townhouse offers modern contemporary styling that blends seamlessly with the wealth of original features. There's a family suite that comprises two rooms, and a double room with king-size bed and the exclusive use of a small courtyard garden; both rooms have flat-screen Freeview TVs and refreshment trays. Breakfast is continental style but very generous, offering a wide variety of delicious home-baked goodies such as mini-quiches, pastries, scones and fresh fruits.

Rooms 2 rms (1 en suite) (1 pri facs) (1 fmly) **Facilities** FTV tea/coffee Cen ht Wi-fi **Notes** 📧

Elgin Villa

★★★ BED AND BREAKFAST

6 Marlborough Ln BA1 2NQ
☎ 01225 424557
e-mail: elginvilla@hotmail.co.uk
web: www.elginvilla.co.uk
dir: *From one way system at Queen Sq, exit NW & follow signs for A4, Bristol. By pedestrian crossing, right into car park, parking in far left corner behind wooden gate*

Located near the park and just a ten-minute walk from the centre of Bath, Elgin Villa offers a range of variously sized bedrooms. Most rooms have en suite facilities, although two just have a shower and washbasin in the room, and share a WC. Continental breakfast, including scrambled eggs and croissants, is served at two large tables in the comfortable dining room. Private parking is available to the rear.

Rooms 6 rms (4 en suite) (2 fmly) D £85-£110* **Facilities** FTV tea/coffee Wi-fi **Parking** 6 **Notes** ⊗

The Parade Park and Lambrettas Bar

★★★ GUEST ACCOMMODATION

8-10 North Pde BA2 4AL
☎ 01225 463384 📠 01225 442322
e-mail: info@paradepark.co.uk
web: www.paradepark.co.uk
dir: *In city centre. Off A36 Pulteney Rd onto North Parade Rd & North Parade*

This attractive Georgian property was formerly the home of William Wordsworth. The restored rooms are brightly decorated, and well equipped with modern facilities. A varied continental style breakfast is served in the impressive, panelled first-floor dining room. The mod scooter-themed Lambretta bar is open to the public.

Rooms 38 rms (32 en suite) (8 fmly) (2 GF) S £55-£70; D £75-£99* **Facilities** FTV tea/coffee Cen ht Licensed **Notes** LB ⊗ Closed Xmas

Pulteney House

★★★ GUEST ACCOMMODATION

14 Pulteney Rd BA2 4HA
☎ 01225 460991   📠 01225 460991
e-mail: pulteney@tinyworld.co.uk
web: www.pulteneyhotel.co.uk
dir: *A4 onto A36, 200yds past lights on right*

This large detached property, situated in a colourful garden is within walking distance of the city centre. Bedrooms vary in size including some annexe rooms, and are well equipped with useful facilities. Full English breakfasts are served in the dining room at individual tables. A guest lounge and car park are both welcome features.

Rooms 12 rms (11 en suite) (1 pri facs) 5 annexe en suite (6 fmly) (2 GF) S £50-£60; D £70-£130 **Facilities** FTV TVL tea/coffee Cen ht Wi-fi **Parking** 18 **Notes** LB ⊗ Closed 24-26 Dec

Roman City Guest House

★★★ GUEST HOUSE

18 Raby Place, Bathwick Hill BA2 4EH
☎ 01225 463668
e-mail: enquire@romancityguesthouse.co.uk
dir: *A4 onto A36 Bathwick St, turn right at lights, straight on at rdbt. Turn left at St Mary's church onto Bathwick Hill, on left*

A warm welcome is assured at this 18th-century end-of-terrace house, located just a stroll from the heart of the historic city. The spacious bedrooms, some with four-poster beds, are comfortable and well equipped with many extra facilities. A pleasant lounge is also available.

Rooms 4 rms (3 en suite) (1 pri facs) (2 fmly) (2 smoking) **Facilities** FTV tea/coffee Cen ht Wi-fi **Conf** Board 12 **Notes** ⊗

Waltons

★★★ GUEST HOUSE

17-19 Crescent Gardens, Upper Bristol Rd BA1 2NA
☎ 01225 426528   📠 01225 420350
e-mail: rose@waltonsguesthouse.co.uk
web: www.bathguesthouse.com
dir: *On A4 350yds W of city centre*

There is a warm welcome at Waltons, situated within strolling distance of the centre of Bath. The cosy bedrooms come with useful extra facilities, and a traditional English breakfast is served at individual tables in the dining room.

Rooms 7 en suite **Facilities** FTV tea/coffee Direct Dial Cen ht **Notes** ⊗ 📵

Hermitage

★★ GUEST ACCOMMODATION

Bath Rd SN13 8DT
☎ 01225 744187
e-mail: hermitagebb@btconnect.com

(For full entry see Box (Wiltshire))

Corston Fields Farm

[U]

Corston BA2 9EZ
☎ 01225 873305 & 07900 056568
e-mail: corston.fields@btinternet.com
dir: *300mtrs off A39 between Corston & Marksbury on lane running adjacent to Wheatsheaf pub*

Currently the rating for this establishment is not confirmed. This may be due to a change of ownership or because it has only recently joined the AA rating scheme.

Rooms 3 rms (2 en suite) (1 pri facs) 1 annexe en suite (1 GF) S £60; D £98 **Facilities** FTV TV3B tea/coffee Cen ht Wi-fi **Parking** 4 **Notes** ⊗ No Children 13yrs Closed 23 Dec-2 Jan

---

BECKINGTON   Map 4 ST85

Pickford House

★★★ GUEST ACCOMMODATION

23 Bath Rd BA11 6SJ
☎ 01373 830329   📠 01373 830329
e-mail: AmPritchar@aol.com
web: www.pickfordhouse.com
dir: *Off A36 (Little Chef rdbt) signed Beckington, follow for 300yds to 30mph signs by village hall, turn right then sharp left*

This peacefully located Regency-style house is set in secluded walled gardens. The proprietors are welcoming and attentive, and many guests visit this pleasant house on a regular basis. Dinner is an enjoyable experience with a 'pot luck' menu (unless you require vegetarian or special dietary dishes) and, along with the impressive wine list, provides fine dining.

Rooms 2 rms 3 annexe en suite (2 fmly) (1 GF) **Facilities** tea/coffee Dinner available Cen ht Licensed ⊀ **Parking** 15 **Notes** Closed Xmas 📵

Woolpack Inn

★★★ INN

BA12 6SP
☎ 01373 831244   📠 01373 831223
web: www.oldenglish.co.uk

This charming coaching inn dates back to the 16th century and retains many original features including flagstone floors, open fireplaces and exposed beams. The bar is popular with visitors and locals alike. There is a garden room lounge and a choice of places to eat: the bar for light snacks, the Oak Room for more substantial meals or the Garden Room which leads onto a pleasant courtyard.

Rooms 11 en suite (3 fmly) **Facilities** tea/coffee Dinner available Direct Dial Cen ht Wi-fi Golf 18 ⅃ **Conf** Max 40 Thtr 40 Class 20 Board 20 **Parking** 16 **Notes** LB

BEERCROCOMBE
Map 4 ST32

Whittles Farm *(ST324194)*

★★★★ FARMHOUSE

TA3 6AH
☎ 01823 480301 ▦ 01823 480301
Mr & Mrs Mitchem
e-mail: djcm.mitchem@btinternet.com
web: www.whittlesfarm.co.uk
dir: *Off A358 through Hatch Beauchamp to Beercrocombe, keep left through village, Whittles Farm 1st lane on right, no through road*

This 16th-century farmhouse set between the Quantock and Blackdown Hills is ideal for a relaxing break. The friendly and attentive owners have been receiving guests here for over 20 years, and everyone is assured of a caring and genuine welcome. Bedrooms are spacious and comfortable with an engaging homeliness. There's a choice of lounges in which to relax and perhaps curl up beside the fire. Breakfasts are impressive and a great way to start the day.

Rooms 2 en suite S £45-£50; D £70-£76 **Facilities** FTV tea/coffee Cen ht **Parking** 4 **Notes** ⊗ No Children 12yrs Closed Dec & Jan ⊛ 250 acres beef

BRIDGWATER
Map 4 ST23

Ash-Wembdon Farm *(ST281382)*

★★★★ FARMHOUSE

Hollow Ln, Wembdon TA5 2BD
☎ 01278 453097 ▦ 01278 445856
Mr & Mrs Rowe
e-mail: mary.rowe@btinternet.com
web: www.farmaccommodation.co.uk
dir: *M5, A38, A39 to Minehead, at rdbt 3rd exit Homeburg Way, at lights B3339, right onto Hollow Ln*

Near the Quantock Hills, this is a 17th-century farmhouse on a working beef and arable farm offering homely and comfortable accommodation. All rooms have en suite showers or private bathrooms, and English or continental breakfasts are served in the guest dining room. Guests also have use of a lounge and landscaped garden.

Rooms 3 rms (2 en suite) (1 pri facs) S £35-£38; D £54-£60 **Facilities** FTV TVL tea/coffee Cen ht Wi-fi **Parking** 3 **Notes** LB ⊗ No Children 10yrs Closed 22 Dec-3 Jan 340 acres arable/beef

AA GUEST ACCOMMODATION FOR ENGLAND

Blackmore Farm *(ST247385)*

★★★★ FARMHOUSE

Blackmore Ln, Cannington TA5 2NE
☎ 01278 653442 ▦ 01278 653427
Mrs Ann Dyer
e-mail: dyerfarm@aol.com
dir: *3m W of Bridgwater, turn left at Bridgwater Mowers (Cannington) onto Blackmore Ln. Farm 1m on left*

Dating back to the 15th century, this Grade I listed manor house is truly unique; there is a wealth of original features such as oak beams, huge open fireplaces, stone archways and even a chapel. Bedrooms located in the main house are individual in style and one has a wonderful four-poster and a lofty oak-beamed ceiling. Additional, more conventional bedrooms are located in a separate courtyard area. Breakfast is taken in the grandeur of the dining room around one, incredibly long table - a truly memorable experience! Blackmore Farm is the AA's Guest Accommodation of the Year for England (2011-2012).

Rooms 3 en suite 2 annexe en suite (1 fmly) (2 GF) S £48-£55; D £90-£100* **Facilities** FTV TVL tea/coffee Cen ht Licensed Wi-fi ⛳ Golf 18 Fishing **Conf** Max 30 Board 30 **Parking** 10 **Notes** LB ⊗ 900 acres dairy/arable

The Boat & Anchor Inn

★★★ INN

Huntworth TA7 0AQ
☎ 01278 662473 ▦ 01278 662542
dir: *M5 junct 24, 500yds NE to Huntworth, 0.5m N of village across canal bridge*

This popular canal-side inn has easy access to the M5 and is a useful stopover en route to and from the West Country. Bedrooms vary in size and style, and some have lovely views across the canal and open fields. An impressive selection of food is offered from the blackboard menus, served either in the bar and lounge areas, or the new conservatory.

Rooms 11 en suite (3 fmly) **Facilities** tea/coffee Dinner available Cen ht **Conf** Thtr 80 Class 50 Board 45 **Parking** 100 **Notes** ⊗ RS Nov-Mar Mon-Thu 12-3 & 5-11 Fri-Sun all day

The Malt Shovel

★★★ INN

Blackmore Ln, Cannington TA5 2NE
☎ 01278 653432
e-mail: themaltshovescannington@hotmail.co.uk
dir: *A39 from Bridgwater, left onto Blackmore Ln, just before Bridgwater Mowers*

Located in a quiet rural area and just a couple of miles from Bridgwater, this popular hostelry has a broad appeal. There's plenty of character here with log fires, low beams and a warm and genuine welcome. The well-stocked bar has a range of Butcombe Ales as well as guest beers, while the menu offers plenty of choice in addition to the impressive carvery. The bedrooms are located in the converted skittle alley, and provide good levels of space and comfort. Spacious gardens and patios make the perfect venues for a refreshing drink in the summer.

Rooms 8 annexe en suite (1 fmly) (8 GF) S £40-£45; D £60-£70* **Facilities** FTV TVL tea/coffee Dinner available Cen ht Wi-fi **Parking** 50 **Notes** LB

BROMPTON REGIS
Map 3 SS93

Holworthy Farm *(SS978308)*

★★★★ 🛏 FARMHOUSE

TA22 9NY
☎ 01398 371244 ▦ 01398 371244
Mrs G Payne
e-mail: holworthyfarm@aol.com
web: www.holworthyfarm.co.uk
dir: *2m E of Brompton Regis. Off A396 on E side of Wimbleball Lake*

Set in the south-east corner of Exmoor, this working livestock farm has spectacular views over Wimbleball Lake. Bedrooms are traditionally furnished and well equipped. The dining room overlooking the garden is the attractive setting for breakfast. Dinner is available by arrangement.

Rooms 5 rms (3 en suite) (2 pri facs) (2 fmly) (1 GF) **Facilities** TVL tea/coffee Dinner available Cen ht **Conf** Max 20 **Parking** 8 **Notes** LB ⊗ 200 acres beef/sheep

BURNHAM-ON-SEA — Map 4 ST34

Magnolia House

★★★★ GUEST HOUSE

26 Manor Rd TA8 2AS
☎ **01278 792460**
e-mail: enquiries@magnoliahouse.gb.com
web: www.magnoliahouse.gb.com
dir: M5 junct 22, follow signs to Burnham-on-Sea, at 2nd rdbt, Magnolia House on right

Within walking distance of the town centre and beach, this elegant Edwardian house has been totally refurbished to an impressive standard. Contemporary bedrooms offer comfort and quality with many extras such as Wi-fi and a large DVD film library. Bathrooms are also modern and stylish with invigorating showers. A family suite is offered with separate, interconnecting bedrooms. Traditional full English breakfast is served in the attractive, air-conditioned breakfast room, with vegetarian and continental options available.

Rooms 4 en suite (2 fmly) **Facilities** FTV tea/coffee Cen ht Wi-fi Golf 18 **Parking** 7 **Notes** LB ⊗ No Children 5yrs

CASTLE CARY — Map 4 ST63

Clanville Manor *(ST618330)*

★★★★ FARMHOUSE

BA7 7PJ
☎ **01963 350124** & **07966 512732** 📠 **01963 350719**
Mrs S Snook
e-mail: info@clanvillemanor.co.uk
web: www.clanvillemanor.co.uk
dir: A371 onto B3153, 0.75m entrance to Clanville Manor via white gate & cattle grid under bridge

Built in 1743, Clanville Manor is situated on a beef farm, and has been owned by the Snook family since 1898. A polished oak staircase leads up to the individually decorated bedrooms, which retain a great deal of their original character. Hearty breakfasts are served in the elegant dining room, which looks over open meadows. There is also a spacious and comfortable sitting room.

Rooms 4 en suite S £45-£60; D £90-£120 **Facilities** FTV TVL tea/coffee Cen ht Wi-fi ↘ 🐎 **Parking** 6 **Notes** LB ⊗ No Children 12yrs Closed 21 Dec-2 Jan 165 acres beef

The Pilgrims

★★★★ ⊚ 🍴 INN

Lovington BA7 7PT
☎ **01963 240600**
e-mail: jools@thepilgrimsatlovington.co.uk
web: www.thepilgrimsatlovington.co.uk
dir: On B3153, 1.5m E of lights on A37 at Lydford

This popular establishment describes itself as 'the pub that thinks it's a restaurant', which is pretty accurate. With a real emphasis on fresh, local and carefully prepared produce, both dinner and breakfast are the focus of any stay here. In addition, the resident family proprietors provide a friendly and relaxed atmosphere. Comfortable and well-equipped bedrooms are available in the adjacent, converted cider barn.

Rooms 5 annexe en suite (5 GF) S £90-£120; D £105-£130* **Facilities** FTV tea/coffee Dinner available Cen ht Wi-fi **Parking** 5 **Notes** LB No Children 14yrs Closed 1st 2wks Oct RS Sun eve-Tue lunch Restaurant & bar closed to non-residents No coaches

CATCOTT — Map 4 ST33

Honeysuckle

★★★★ GUEST ACCOMMODATION

King William Rd TA7 9HU
☎ **01278 722890**
dir: Off A39 to Catcott, pass King William pub, house 200yds on right

Situated in the village centre, this delightful modern house is a good base for visiting the many attractions in the area, including the bird-watching haven of the Somerset Levels. Bedrooms are comfortable, and there is a spacious lounge and a charming garden. Breakfast is served around a communal table in the pleasant dining room.

Rooms 3 rms (1 en suite) (1 GF) S £26-£28; D £56-£65* **Facilities** tea/coffee Cen ht **Parking** 3 **Notes** ⊗ No Children 7yrs Closed 20 Dec-3 Jan 🐕

CHARD — Map 4 ST30

Hornsbury Mill

★★★★ 🅰 GUEST ACCOMMODATION

Eleighwater TA20 3AQ
☎ **01460 63317** 📠 **01460 67758**
e-mail: info@hornsburymill.co.uk
Rooms 10 en suite (2 fmly) (1 GF) S £72; D £97* **Facilities** STV FTV tea/coffee Dinner available Direct Dial Cen ht Licensed Wi-fi **Conf** Max 150 Thtr 150 Class 50 Board 50 **Parking** 80 **Notes** ⊗ Closed 30 Dec-10 Jan RS Sun eve closed Civ Wed 120

Watermead

★★★ GUEST HOUSE

83 High St TA20 1QT
☎ **01460 62834** 📠 **01460 67448**
e-mail: trudy@watermeadguesthouse.co.uk
dir: On A30 in town centre

Guests will feel at home at this family-run house, a smart establishment in a convenient location. Hearty breakfasts are served in the dining room overlooking the garden. Bedrooms are neat, and the spacious, self-contained suite is popular with families. Free Wi-fi access is available.

Rooms 9 rms (6 en suite) 1 annexe en suite (1 fmly) S £35-£40; D £65-£75* **Facilities** FTV TVL tea/coffee Cen ht Wi-fi **Parking** 10 **Notes** LB

CHEDDAR

See Draycott

CLUTTON — Map 4 ST65

The Hunters Rest

★★★★ INN

King Ln, Clutton Hill BS39 5QL
☎ **01761 452303** 📠 **01761 453308**
e-mail: paul@huntersrest.co.uk
web: www.huntersrest.co.uk
dir: Off A37 onto A368 towards Bath, 100yds right onto lane, left at T-junct, inn 0.25m on left

This establishment was originally built around 1750 as a hunting lodge for the Earl of Warwick. Set in delightful countryside, it is ideally located for Bath, Bristol and Wells. Bedrooms and bathrooms are furnished and equipped to excellent standards, and the ground floor combines the character of a real country inn with an excellent range of home-cooked meals.

Rooms 5 en suite (1 fmly) S £67.50-£77.50; D £95-£130* **Facilities** FTV tea/coffee Dinner available Direct Dial Cen ht Wi-fi Golf 18 **Conf** Max 40 Thtr 40 Class 25 Board 25 **Parking** 90 **Notes** LB

CONGRESBURY
Map 4 ST46

The Ship & Castle
★★★★ ⊛ INN

High St BS49 5JA
☎ **01934 833535**
dir: *M5 junct 21, take A370 towards Bristol for 4m. In village centre at lights*

Now extensively refurbished throughout, The Ship & Castle is a 500-year-old traditional country inn located just four miles from the M5 and three miles from Bristol Airport. Bedrooms and bathrooms offer plenty of welcoming extras and have been decorated and furnished to provide high levels of quality and comfort. A wide range of dishes, utilising good quality ingredients, is available at both dinner and breakfast.

Rooms 6 en suite (2 fmly) **Facilities** FTV TVL tea/coffee Dinner available Cen ht Wi-fi **Parking** 48

CREWKERNE
Map 4 ST40

Manor Farm
★★★ GUEST ACCOMMODATION

Wayford TA18 8QL
☎ **01460 78865 & 0776 7620031** 📠 **01460 78865**
e-mail: theresaemery@hotmail.com
web: www.manorfarm.biz
dir: *B3165 from Crewkerne to Lyme Regis, 3m in Clapton right onto Dunsham Ln, Manor Farm 0.5m up hill on right*

Located off the beaten track, this fine Victorian country house has extensive views over Clapton towards the Axe Valley. The comfortably furnished bedrooms are well equipped, and front-facing rooms enjoy splendid views. Breakfast is served at separate tables in the dining room, and a spacious lounge is also provided.

Rooms 4 en suite 1 annexe en suite (2 fmly) S £35-£40; D £70-£75 **Facilities** STV FTV TVL TV4B tea/coffee Cen ht Fishing Riding **Parking** 14 **Notes** ⊗ ⊜

The George
★★★ INN

Market Square TA18 7LP
☎ **01460 73650** 📠 **01460 72974**
e-mail: georgecrewkerne@btconnect.com
web: www.thegeorgehotelcrewkerne.co.uk
dir: *In town centre on A30*

Situated in the heart of town, this welcoming inn has been providing rest and sustenance for over 400 years. The atmosphere is warm and inviting, and the bar is the ideal place for a natter and a refreshing pint. Comfortable bedrooms are traditionally styled and include four-poster rooms. A choice of menus is available, served either in the bar or attractive restaurant.

Rooms 13 rms (8 en suite) (2 pri facs) (2 fmly) S £40-£100; D £70-£150* **Facilities** FTV TVL tea/coffee Dinner available Direct Dial Cen ht Wi-fi George Suite has

a hydro-therapy spa bath **Conf** Max 100 Thtr 100 Class 100 Board 50 **Notes** LB ⊗

CROSCOMBE
Map 4 ST54

Bull Terrier
★★★ INN

BA5 3QJ
☎ **01749 343658**
e-mail: barry.vidler@bullterrierpub.co.uk
dir: *On A371 by village cross*

Located in the centre of the village, this attractive country inn has a relaxed and friendly atmosphere. The character of the inn has been retained with the flagstone floors and inglenook fireplace, and the public areas are particularly welcoming. Bedrooms are brightly decorated and well equipped. Freshly prepared lunches and dinners are available.

Rooms 2 en suite S £30-£40; D £60-£70* **Facilities** FTV tea/coffee Dinner available Cen ht **Conf** Max 16 **Parking** 3 **Notes** No Children 10yrs RS Oct-Mar Closed Mon

DRAYCOTT
Map 4 ST45

Oakland House
★★★★ GUEST ACCOMMODATION

Wells Rd BS27 3SU
☎ **01934 744195** 📠 **01934 744195**
e-mail: enquiries@oakland-house.co.uk
web: www.oakland-house.co.uk
dir: *Off A371 at S end of village*

Situated a short distance from Cheddar, this friendly home provides comfortable and spacious accommodation. There are splendid views of the Somerset moors and Glastonbury Tor from the sun lounge and the well-appointed and attractive bedrooms. Dinner features fresh fruit and vegetables from the garden.

Rooms 3 en suite (1 fmly) **Facilities** STV TVL tea/coffee Dinner available Cen ht Pool table **Parking** 6 **Notes** ⊗

DULVERTON
Map 3 SS92

PREMIER COLLECTION

Tarr Farm Inn
★★★★★ ⊛ INN

Tarr Steps, Exmoor National Park TA22 9PY
☎ **01643 851507** 📠 **01643 851111**
e-mail: enquiries@tarrfarm.co.uk
web: www.tarrfarm.co.uk
dir: *4m NW of Dulverton. Off B3223 signed Tarr Steps, signs to Tarr Farm Inn*

Tarr Farm, dating from the 16th century, nestles on the lower slopes of Exmoor overlooking the famous old clapper bridge, Tarr Steps. The majority of rooms are in the bedroom block that provides very stylish and comfortable accommodation with an impressive selection of thoughtful touches. Tarr Farm Inn, with much character and traditional charm, draws the crowds for cream teas and delicious dinners which are prepared from good local produce.

Rooms 9 en suite (4 GF) S £95; D £150* **Facilities** STV tea/coffee Dinner available Direct Dial Cen ht Wi-fi Fishing Riding **Conf** Max 18 **Parking** 10 **Notes** LB No Children 14yrs No coaches

FARMBOROUGH   Map 4 ST66

School Cottages Bed & Breakfast

★★★★ BED AND BREAKFAST

The Street, Near Bath BA2 0AR
☎ 01761 471167 & 07989 349428
e-mail: tim@schoolcottages.co.uk
web: www.schoolcottages.co.uk
dir: Off A39 in Farmborough onto The Street, 1st left opp
village school

This lovingly restored country house is conveniently
located to the south-west of Bath in the pretty Somerset
village of Farmborough. The contemporary, stylish
bedrooms are equipped with Wi-fi, while the excellent
bathrooms may include a power shower or a spa bath.
Home-made jams and freshly-laid eggs contribute to the
delicious breakfasts served in a charming conservatory
overlooking the garden.

Rooms 3 en suite S £50-£60; D £70-£90 Facilities FTV
TVL tea/coffee Cen ht Wi-fi Golf 18 Parking 3 Notes LB No
Children 10yrs

Menga Lodge

★★★★ BED AND BREAKFAST

Bath Rd BA2 0BG
☎ 01761 471089 & 07966 688387

Two self-contained units on the ground floor with either
double or twin accommodation. The large double family
room has a sofa bed and the twin benefits from a private
terrace overlooking far reaching views. Generous
continental breakfasts with boiled eggs are discreetly
served at the dining table in the privacy of your room.

Rooms 2 annexe en suite (1 fmly) (2 GF) Facilities FTV
tea/coffee Cen ht Wi-fi Parking 3 Notes ⊗ ⊛

FROME   Map 4 ST74

PREMIER COLLECTION

Lullington House

★★★★★ BED AND BREAKFAST

Lullington BA11 2PG
☎ 01373 831406 & 07979 290146
🖨 01373 831406
e-mail: info@lullingtonhouse.co.uk
web: www.lullingtonhouse.co.uk
dir: 2.5m N of Frome. Off A36 into Lullington

Built in 1866 as a rectory, this quintessentially English
stone country house stands in extensive grounds and
gardens which convey an air of peace, quiet and
tranquillity. The luxurious large bedrooms, some with
four-poster beds, are decorated to high standards
using beautiful fabrics, fine antique furniture and
many extras such as Wi-fi, decanters of sherry, fresh
flowers and well-stocked beverage trays. Breakfast is
served in the impressive dining room with an excellent
selection of dishes available.

Rooms 3 en suite S £60-£70; D £80-£100* Facilities
FTV tea/coffee Cen ht Wi-fi Golf 18 Parking 4
Notes ⊗ Closed Xmas & New Year ⊛

Archangel

★★★★ ⊛ RESTAURANT WITH ROOMS

1 King St BA11 1BH
☎ 01373 456111 🖨 01373 456110
e-mail: hello@archangelfrome.com

Located in the centre of Frome, this welcoming property
has been completely refurbished to create a stylish,
contemporary ambience in a building that is full of
character. The bedrooms might be described as funky;
they come in a varied range of shapes and sizes but
plenty of welcome extras are included. There is a variety
of lounges and bars, an outdoor patio with seating, and a
comfortable restaurant where high quality ingredients are
utilised at both dinner and breakfast.

Rooms 6 en suite S £80-£85; D £120-£140* Facilities
tea/coffee Dinner available Direct Dial Cen ht Wi-fi
Conf Max 40 Thtr 40 Class 20 Board 24 Parking 2

GLASTONBURY   Map 4 ST53

See also Catcott & Somerton

Wearyall Hill House

★★★★ BED AND BREAKFAST

78 The Roman Way BA6 8AD
☎ 01458 835510
e-mail: enquiries@wearyallhillhouse.co.uk
dir: 0.5m SW of town centre. A39 rdbt towards Street,
pass B&Q on right, left onto Roman Way

Set on an elevated position on the edge of town, and
close to places of interest, this delightful late Victorian
residence affords sweeping views. Restored to its former
glory by the present owners, the property is appropriately
decorated and furnished with many extra facilities. The
sumptuous breakfasts served in the attractive dining
room are a highlight.

Rooms 3 en suite Facilities STV FTV TVL tea/coffee Cen ht
Wi-fi Parking 8 Notes ⊗ No Children 10yrs ⊛

Belle-Vue Bed & Breakfast

★★★ GUEST ACCOMMODATION

2 Bere Ln BA6 8BA
☎ 01458 830385
e-mail: info@bellevueglastonbury.co.uk
web: www.bellevueglastonbury.co.uk
dir: M5 junct 23 onto A39, then A361 signed Glastonbury.
On right, past Fisher Hill junct

This fully refurbished 1920s property close to the town
centre provides a relaxed and cosy atmosphere. All
bedrooms are en suite, and some have fabulous far-
reaching views; they are all decorated in a contemporary
style with many extras provided. A hearty breakfast, using
quality produce, is served in the charming dining room.

Rooms 6 en suite (1 fmly) (2 GF) S £30-£35; D £60-£70
Facilities FTV tea/coffee Cen ht Licensed Wi-fi Golf 18
Fishing Riding Parking 6 Notes LB ⊗

No 1 Park Terrace

★★★ GUEST HOUSE

Street Rd BA6 9EA
☎ 01458 835845 🖨 01458 833296
e-mail: info@no1parkterrace.co.uk
dir: From High St, onto Magdalene St. At mini rdbt turn
right, 100mtrs on right

A spacious and charming Victorian guest house located
within walking distance of the High Street and the Abbey
ruins. The proprietors are friendly and welcoming;
bedrooms are bright and airy with single rooms available.
The fully licensed restaurant offers a Spanish influenced
menu. Limited parking is available at the rear of the
property.

Rooms 5 rms (2 en suite) (1 pri facs) S £35; D £60-£70*
Facilities FTV tea/coffee Dinner available Cen ht Licensed
Wi-fi Conf Max 20 Parking 5 Notes LB ⊗

HIGHBRIDGE · Map 4 ST34

The Greenwood

★★★★ GUEST ACCOMMODATION

76 Main Rd, West Huntspill TA9 3QU
☎ 01278 795886 📠 01278 795886
e-mail: info@the-greenwood.co.uk
web: www.the-greenwood.co.uk
dir: *On A38 in West Huntspill, between Orchard Inn & Sundowner Hotel*

Set in two acres of land, this 18th-century former farmhouse and family home offers comfortable accommodation in a friendly environment. Breakfast, featuring home-made preserves, is served in the dining room and home-cooked dinners are available by arrangement. There is a lounge for relaxation.

Rooms 7 rms (6 en suite) (1 pri facs) (3 fmly) (1 GF) S £45-£49.50; D £65-£72* **Facilities** FTV TVL tea/coffee Dinner available Cen ht Licensed Wi-fi Treatment room **Conf** Max 30 Thtr 30 Class 20 Board 12 **Parking** 8 **Notes** LB

ILCHESTER · Map 4 ST52

Liongate House B&B

★★★★ BED AND BREAKFAST

Northover BA22 8NG
☎ 01935 841741
e-mail: info@liongatehouse.com
dir: *A303 onto A37 towards Yeovil, after 800mtrs left at rdbt signed Ilchester. Through village over river, on left opposite garage*

Located in the central area of the pleasant town of Ilchester, this purpose-built bed and breakfast provides guests with comfortable, well-furnished bedrooms and modern bathrooms; one bedroom is on the ground floor. The welcoming resident proprietors greet guests with tea on arrival which may be taken in the pleasant rear garden if the weather allows. A choice of pubs and restaurants is available just a short stroll away.

Rooms 3 en suite (1 fmly) (1 GF) S £60-£65; D £75 **Facilities** FTV tea/coffee Cen ht Wi-fi **Parking** 3 **Notes** LB ⊗ Closed 23 Dec-2 Jan

---

ILMINSTER · Map 4 ST31

Herne Lea Guest House

★★★★ GUEST ACCOMMODATION

15 Station Rd TA19 9BE
☎ 01460 53067
e-mail: enquiries@hernelea-ilminster.co.uk
web: www.hernelea-ilminster.co.uk
dir: *M5 junct 25 onto A358 follow signs for Ilminster, 100mtrs past Best Western hotel*

This welcoming Edwardian house has been extensively refurbished to provide impressive levels of quality and character. Bedrooms provide good levels of comfort with well appointed and stylish bathrooms. Breakfast utilises local produce and is served in the elegant dining room which opens into the conservatory lounge with lovely views towards Herne Hill.

Rooms 3 en suite (1 fmly) S £50-£55; D £60-£65* **Facilities** FTV tea/coffee Cen ht Wi-fi **Notes** LB ⊗

The New Inn

★★★★ 🍽 INN

Dowlish Wake TA19 0NZ
☎ 01460 52413
e-mail: newinn-ilminster@btconnect.com
dir: *A358 or A303, follow signs for Perry's Cider, well-signed in village*

Situated in the tranquil and unspoilt village of Dowlish Wake, the New Inn is a proper local pub with a warm welcome at the convivial bar. All the bedrooms are on the ground floor; they are contemporary in style and located to the rear overlooking the garden. The menu offers a range of enduring favourites and daily specials with good local produce used whenever possible. Breakfast is a substantial offering, just right for healthy appetites.

Rooms 4 annexe en suite (4 GF) **Facilities** FTV tea/coffee Dinner available Cen ht **Parking** 20

Square & Compass

★★★★ INN

Windmill Hill, Ashill TA19 9NX
☎ 01823 480467 📠 01823 480467
e-mail: squareandcompass@tiscali.co.uk
dir: *M5 junct 25 onto A358, 5m S*

This peacefully located inn provides a genuinely warm welcome and traditional hospitality. The bedrooms and modern bathrooms provide high standards of quality and comfort, and are situated in converted stables adjacent to the main building. In addition to a range of excellent home-cooked meals, a selection of real ales is also available. Outdoor seating is provided in the warmer months.

Rooms 8 en suite (8 fmly) (8 GF) S fr £65; D fr £85* **Facilities** FTV tea/coffee Dinner available Cen ht Wi-fi **Conf** Max 100 Class 100 Board 50 **Parking** 50 **Notes** Closed 24-26 Dec No coaches Civ Wed 120

KEYNSHAM · Map 4 ST66

Grasmere Court

★★★★ GUEST HOUSE

22-24 Bath Rd BS31 1SN
☎ 0117 986 2662 📠 0117 986 2762
e-mail: grasmerecourt@aol.com
web: www.grasmerecourthotel.co.uk
dir: *On B3116 just off A4 between Bath & Bristol*

This very friendly, family-run establishment is located between Bath and Bristol. Bedrooms vary in size and one has a four-poster bed. A comfortable lounge and a well-stocked bar are available, and good-value, freshly prepared food is served in the attractive dining room.

Rooms 16 en suite (2 fmly) (4 GF) **Facilities** STV FTV TVL tea/coffee Dinner available Direct Dial Cen ht Licensed Wi-fi Golf 18 **Conf** Max 30 Thtr 30 Class 20 Board 20 **Parking** 11 **Notes** ⊗

KILVE   Map 3 ST14

Hood Arms Inn
★★★★ INN

TA5 1EA
☎ 01278 741210 & 741969   📠 01278 741210
e-mail: info@thehoodarms.com
dir: W of Bridgwater on A39, halfway between Bridgwater
& Minehead

A traditional inn providing good food, comfortable
bedrooms and a range of local beers in the bar. Bedrooms
are well equipped, and both the bar and restaurant have
a cosy feel enhanced by the open fire. Food is available
daily and fresh local produce features on the extensive
menu.

Rooms 8 en suite 4 annexe en suite (2 GF) S £75; D £95*
Facilities FTV TVL tea/coffee Dinner available Direct Dial
Wi-fi Riding Boules Bar billiards **Parking** 11

LANGPORT   Map 4 ST42

The Old Pound Inn
★★★ INN

Aller TA10 0RA
☎ 01458 250469
e-mail: oldpoundinn@btconnect.com
web: www.oldpoundinn.co.uk
dir: On A372 in village centre

Situated in the heart of a charming village, just two miles
from Langport, this popular inn was once a cider house,
and dates back to 1571. Its long tradition of hospitality
continues with a convivial and welcoming atmosphere for
both locals and visitors alike. Bedrooms are soundly
appointed and include a four-poster room and connecting
family room. Public areas include the traditional bar,
together with a snug and a restaurant. There is also a
skittle alley for those who fancy competitive activity with
their pint.

Rooms 8 en suite (2 fmly) S fr £50; D fr £80*
Facilities FTV tea/coffee Dinner available Cen ht Wi-fi
Snooker Pool table **Conf** Max 90 Thtr 90 Class 90 Board
90 **Parking** 15 **Notes** LB

LOWER LANGFORD   Map 4 ST46

The Langford Inn
★★★★ INN

BS40 5BL
☎ 01934 863059   📠 01934 863539
e-mail: longfordinn@aol.com
web: www.langfordinn.com
dir: M5 junct 21 onto A370 towards Bristol. At T-lights
right onto B3133 to Langford, at mini-rdbt turn left
signed Lower Langford

Located in a peaceful village, on the edge of The Mendips,
this traditional country pub offers a varied selection of
real ales, well chosen wines and carefully prepared,
home-made dishes at dinner. Bedrooms and bathrooms,
refurbished to a high standard, are housed in two
converted 17th-century barns that are adjacent to the
inn. They feature exposed beams, original brickwork and
oak floors combined with modern luxuries.

Rooms 7 annexe en suite (3 fmly) (6 GF) S £79-£110; D
£79-£110 (room only)* **Facilities** FTV TVL Dinner
available Cen ht Wi-fi **Conf** Max 30 Thtr 30 Class 20
Board 20 **Parking** 20

LOWER VOBSTER   Map 4 ST74

The Vobster Inn
★★★★ ◉◉ INN

BA3 5RJ
☎ 01373 812920   📠 01373 812920
e-mail: rdavila@btinternet.com
dir: From A361 follow signs for Whatley & Mells, then
Vobster

Peacefully located in four acres of Somerset countryside,
this is the ideal village inn with a real sense of personal
attention and a genuine welcome from the resident
proprietors. Bedrooms and bathrooms provide high levels
of quality and comfort. Dinner places an emphasis on
high quality, simply prepared food with regular seasonal
changes, and includes several dishes demonstrating the
Spanish heritage of the chef proprietor.

Rooms 3 annexe en suite (2 fmly) (3 GF) **Facilities** FTV
tea/coffee Dinner available Cen ht Wi-fi Petanque
Conf Max 40 Thtr 25 Class 32 Board 32 **Parking** 60
Notes LB ⊗ RS Sun eve & Mon (ex BH lunch) No food or
drinks available

LYMPSHAM   Map 4 ST35

Batch
★★★★ GUEST ACCOMMODATION

Batch Ln BS24 0EX
☎ 01934 750371   📠 01934 750501
web: www.batchcountryhotel.co.uk
dir: M5 junct 22, take last exit on rdbt signed A370 to
Weston-Super-Mare. After 3.5m, left into Lympsham, 1m,
sign at end of road

In a rural location between Weston-Super-Mare and
Burnham-on-Sea, this former farmhouse offers a relaxed,
friendly and peaceful environment. The comfortable
bedrooms have views to the Mendip and Quantock hills.
Spacious lounges overlook the extensive, well-tended
gardens, and the comfortably furnished function room,
together with the restaurant, make this a popular venue
for wedding ceremonies.

Rooms 11 en suite (3 fmly) (1 GF) **Facilities** tea/coffee
Direct Dial Fishing **Parking** 140 **Notes** Closed 25-26 Dec
Civ Wed 260

MARTOCK   Map 4 ST41

Higher Farm
★★★★ BED AND BREAKFAST

Bladon Hill, Kingsbury Episcopi TA12 6BJ
☎ 01935 823099
e-mail: boltonali@aol.com
dir: 2m NW of Martock. Off B3165 to Kingsbury Episcopi,
left at Wyndham Arms, farm on right

Located in the scenic village of Kingsbury Episcopi,
Higher Farm provides comfortable accommodation with a
relaxed and friendly atmosphere. Breakfast is served in
the pleasant dining room which opens onto the patio and
rear garden. There are two pubs serving evening meals
that are just a five-minute walk in either direction.

Rooms 2 en suite (1 fmly) S £35; D £60-£70
Facilities FTV tea/coffee Cen ht **Parking** 6 **Notes** ⊗ ⊜

MIDSOMER NORTON — Map 4 ST65

The Moody Goose at The Old Priory

★★★★ ◉◉ RESTAURANT WITH ROOMS

Church Square BA3 2HX
☎ 01761 416784 📠 01761 417851
e-mail: info@theoldpriory.co.uk
dir: *A362 for 1m left to High Street to lights, turn right to small rdbt by St John's church, turn right*

Dating back to the 12th century, this relaxing establishment, with plenty of historic charm and character has been sensitively restored to maintain original features. The bedrooms, including one with a four-poster, are individually styled with plenty of welcome extras. The intimate, open-plan restaurant serves innovative, carefully prepared dishes utilising local produce whenever possible. There are two cosy lounges with log fires blazing in the colder months.

Rooms 6 en suite (1 fmly) S £75-£80; D £85-£140*
Facilities FTV tea/coffee Dinner available Cen ht Wi-fi Golf 9 Fishing **Parking** 15 **Notes** ⊗ Closed 25 Dec & 1 Jan No coaches

MILVERTON — Map 3 ST12

The Globe

★★★ ◉ INN

Fore St TA4 1JX
☎ 01823 400534
e-mail: adele@theglobemilverton.co.uk
web: www.theglobemilverton.co.uk
dir: *M5 junct 27 follow B3277 to Milverton. In village centre*

This popular village local was once a coaching inn, and although it has been given contemporary styling it still retains much traditional charm. The welcome is warm and genuine with a convivial atmosphere always guaranteed. Bedrooms are appointed in a similar modern style and have comfy beds. The hard-working kitchen is committed to quality, with excellent locally-sourced produce used in impressive dishes. Continental breakfast is served.

Rooms 3 en suite (1 fmly) **Facilities** tea/coffee Dinner available Cen ht Wi-fi **Parking** 4 **Notes** ⊗ Closed 20 Dec-2 Jan No coaches

MINEHEAD — Map 3 SS94

Kenella House

★★★★ GUEST ACCOMMODATION

7 Tregonwell Rd TA24 5DT
☎ 01643 703128 & 07710 889079 📠 01643 703128
e-mail: kenellahouse@fsmail.net
dir: *Off A39 onto Townsend Rd & right onto Ponsford Rd & Tregonwell Rd*

A warm welcome and relaxed atmosphere are found at Kenella House. Located close to the town centre, this guest accommodation is also convenient for visitors to the steam railway, and walkers (a heated boot cupboard is available). The well-maintained bedrooms are very comfortable and have many extras. Home-cooked dinners, (available by prior arrangement) and hearty breakfasts are served in the smart dining room.

Rooms 6 en suite (1 GF) D £60-£70* **Facilities** FTV tea/coffee Dinner available Cen ht Wi-fi **Parking** 8 **Notes** LB ⊗ No Children 14yrs Closed 23-26 Dec ⊛

NORTH WOOTTON — Map 4 ST54

Crossways

★★★★ INN

Stocks Ln BA4 4EU
☎ 01749 899000 📠 01749 890476
e-mail: enquiries@thecrossways.co.uk
dir: *Exit M5 junct 22 towards Shepton Mallet, 0.2m from Pilton*

This family-run establishment is tucked away down a quiet lane, yet is with easy reach of Wells, Glastonbury and other interesting areas of Wiltshire and Somerset. The bedrooms and bathrooms are spacious and have recently undergone a major refurbishment throughout to provide high levels of quality and comfort. There is a large bar-restaurant and a smaller dining room where breakfast is served. The extensive menu (served Wed-Sun) features many home-cooked dishes.

Rooms 21 en suite (4 fmly) S £45-£70; D £60-£100*
Facilities tea/coffee Dinner available Cen ht Pool table **Conf** Max 40 Thtr 40 Class 40 Board 25 **Notes** ⊗ Closed 25 Dec RS 26 Dec-2 Jan Civ Wed 100

OAKHILL — Map 4 ST64

The Oakhill Inn

★★★★ ⊜ INN

Fosse Rd BA3 5HU
☎ 01749 840442 📠 01749 840289
e-mail: info@theoakhillinn.com
dir: *On A367 between Stratton-on-the-Fosse & Shepton Mallet*

A welcoming country inn, offering warm hospitality, locally-sourced food and a wide selection of fine ales from local micro-breweries. The comfortable bedrooms include luxuries such as Egyptian cotton sheets and DVD players.

Rooms 5 en suite (1 fmly) S £77.50-£107.50; D £90-£120* **Facilities** FTV tea/coffee Dinner available Cen ht Wi-fi Golf **Parking** 12 **Notes** LB

PORLOCK — Map 3 SS84

Tudor Cottage

★★★★ GUEST ACCOMMODATION

TA24 8HQ
☎ 01643 862255 & 07855 531593
e-mail: bookings@tudorcottage.net
dir: *M5 junct 25 onto A358 then A39 to Minehead, after 5m turn for Allerford & Bossington. After 1m, 1st house on left*

Parts of this engaging cottage date back to the 15th century, and many period features have been retained. The welcome couldn't be warmer with tea and cake served in the lovely garden, weather permitting. The setting is a haven of peace and tranquillity with a wonderful wooded hillside as a backdrop. Bedrooms are reassuringly cosy and cosseting with all the expected modern comforts including TV/DVD and guest-controlled heating. Breakfast features a host of locally-sourced produce and light snacks are offered in the evenings.

Rooms 3 rms (1 en suite) (2 pri facs) S £50; D £70*
Facilities FTV TVL tea/coffee Licensed Wi-fi **Parking** 3 **Notes** LB ⊗ No Children 10yrs

The Cottage

★★★★ GUEST ACCOMMODATION

High St TA24 8PU
☎ **01643 862996** 🖨 **01643 862996**
e-mail: cottageporlock@aol.com
web: www.cottageporlock.co.uk
dir: *In village centre on A39*

One of the oldest houses in the area, The Cottage is located right in the heart of this ancient village, and so is ideally placed to enjoy village life, for exploring Exmoor and for walking along the South West coastal path. Bedrooms are well equipped and there is a comfortable lounge solely for guest use. Breakfast is served in the pleasant dining room at the front of the house.

Rooms 4 en suite (1 fmly) S £35-£40; D £60-£80 **Facilities** FTV tea/coffee Cen ht Golf 18 **Parking** 3 **Notes** LB ⊗ Closed Jan & Feb

---

RODHUISH Map 3 ST03

Croydon Hall

★★★ GUEST ACCOMMODATION

Felons Oak TA24 6QT
☎ **01984 642200** 🖨 **01984 640052**
e-mail: info@croydonhall.co.uk

This is the perfect place for rest and relaxation, located in beautiful countryside, just a short drive from the coast and Exmoor National Park. It is a grand house with an interesting history and has been offering holistic workshops for a number of years. Bedrooms provide good levels of comfort; the extensive public areas include a bar, lounge and dining room, where vegetarian dinners and breakfasts are served. In addition to the extensive gardens, facilities include a heated outdoor pool, sauna and hot tub.

Rooms 24 rms (18 en suite) (6 pri facs) (3 fmly) (1 GF) **Facilities** TVL tea/coffee Dinner available Direct Dial Cen ht Licensed Wi-fi ⚲ 🏊 Sauna Spa facilities - Steam room Hot tub **Conf** Max 140 Thtr 140 Class 60 Board 60 **Parking** 45 **Notes** LB ⊗ No Children 14yrs

---

RUDGE Map 4 ST85

The Full Moon Inn

★★★ INN

BA11 2QF
☎ **01373 830936**
e-mail: info@thefullmoon.co.uk
dir: *From A36 S from Bath, 10m, left at Standerwick by The Bell pub. 4m from Warminster*

Peacefully located in the quiet village of Rudge, this traditional inn offers a warm welcome and a proper country pub atmosphere. In the bar area, guests mix well with the locals to enjoy a selection of real ales and a log fire in the colder months. In addition to bar meals, a comfortable restaurant serving excellent home-cooked dishes is also available. Bedrooms include some at the main inn and more in an adjacent annexe - all are comfortable and well equipped.

Rooms 5 en suite 12 annexe en suite (2 fmly) (3 GF) **Facilities** tea/coffee Dinner available Cen ht ⚲ **Conf** Max 65 Thtr 30 Class 12 Board 18 **Parking** 25

SHEPTON MALLET Map 4 ST64

Cannards Grave Farmhouse

★★★★ GUEST ACCOMMODATION

Cannards Grave BA4 4LY
☎ **01749 347091** 🖨 **01749 347091**
e-mail: sue@cannardsgravefarmhouse.co.uk
web: www.cannardsgravefarmhouse.co.uk
dir: *On A37 between Shepton Mallet & The Bath and West Showground, 100yds from Highwayman pub towards showground on left*

Conveniently located for the Royal Bath & West Showground, Longleat, Glastonbury and Wells, this 17th-century house provides thoughtfully equipped en suite bedrooms. There is also a well-furnished lounge, and breakfast is served in the conservatory dining room. The proprietors provide warm hospitality.

Rooms 4 en suite 1 annexe en suite (2 fmly) (1 GF) S £40-£50; D £60-£70* **Facilities** FTV TVL tea/coffee Cen ht Wi-fi **Parking** 6 **Notes** ⊗

The Abbey Barn

★★★ BED AND BREAKFAST

Doulting BA4 4QD
☎ **01749 880321**
e-mail: abbeybarn@btconnect.com
dir: *2m E of Shepton Mallet on A361 in Doulting centre*

Situated on the edge of the Mendips in the pretty village of Doulting, this Grade II listed property is renowned for its superb friendly welcome and top quality breakfasts. A licensed cosy residents' lounge bar provides a relaxing area to enjoy a drink or two. Log fires burn in the winter, and guests can enjoy the attractive garden in the summer. Private parking is available.

Rooms 3 en suite (1 fmly) S £49-£73; D £69-£73 **Facilities** FTV tea/coffee Licensed Wi-fi **Parking** 10 **Notes** LB ⊗ No Children

---

The Thatched Cottage

Ⓤ

63-67 Charlton Rd BA4 5QF
☎ **01749 342058** 🖨 **01749 343265**
e-mail: enquiries@thatchedcottage.info
dir: *0.6m E of town centre on A361*

Currently the rating for this establishment is not confirmed. This may be due to a change of ownership or because it has only recently joined the AA rating scheme.

Rooms 8 en suite

SOMERTON Map 4 ST42

The Devonshire Arms

★★★★ ⊛ INN

Long Sutton TA10 9LP
☎ **01458 241271** 🖨 **01458 241037**
e-mail: mail@thedevonshirearms.com
web: www.thedevonshirearms.com
dir: *A303 onto A372 at Podimore rdbt. After 4m left onto B3165, signed Martock & Long Sutton*

This popular village inn offers an appealing blend of traditional and contemporary styling throughout the spacious public areas and accommodation. Bedrooms are individually designed and provide impressive levels of comfort and quality. Public areas include the convivial bar and elegant restaurant where excellent local produce is utilised in skilfully executed dishes.

Rooms 7 rms (6 en suite) (1 pri facs) 2 annexe en suite (1 fmly) (2 GF) **Facilities** FTV tea/coffee Dinner available Cen ht Wi-fi 🏊 Golf 18 **Parking** 6 **Notes** Closed 25-26 Dec & 1 Jan

SOMERTON *continued*

Somerton Court Country House

★★★★ GUEST ACCOMMODATION

TA11 7AH
☎ 01458 274694 📠 01458 274694
e-mail: enquiries@somertoncourt.com
web: www.somertoncourt.com
dir: *From A303 onto A372 at Podimore rdbt. In 3m right onto B3151 to Somerton & follow signs*

Dating back to the 17th century and set in extensive gardens and grounds, this house provides a tranquil haven away from the pressures of modern life. The comfortable bedrooms have lovely views, and breakfast is served in a delightful dining room that overlooks the gardens.

Rooms 4 en suite 2 annexe en suite (2 fmly) S fr £50; D fr £80* **Facilities** tea/coffee Cen ht Licensed Riding **Conf** Max 200 Thtr 200 Class 150 **Parking** 30 **Notes** ⊗ Closed Xmas & New Year Civ Wed 150

| STANTON DREW | Map 4 ST56 |

Greenlands *(ST597636)*

★★★★ FARMHOUSE

BS39 4ES
☎ 01275 333487 📠 01275 331211
Mrs J Cleverley
dir: *A37 onto B3130, on right before Stanton Drew Garage*

Situated near the ancient village of Stanton Drew in the heart of the Chew Valley, Greenlands is convenient for Bristol Airport and Bath, Bristol and Wells. There are comfortable, well-equipped bedrooms and a downstairs lounge, and breakfast is the highlight of any stay here.

Rooms 4 en suite S £30; D £60* **Facilities** STV FTV TVL tea/coffee Cen ht Wi-fi **Parking** 8 **Notes** No Children 12yrs 🐾 3 acres hobby farm/poultry

---

Valley Farm

★★★★ BED AND BREAKFAST

Sandy Ln BS39 4EL
☎ 01275 332723 & 07799 768161 📠 01275 332723
e-mail: valleyfarm2000@tiscali.co.uk
dir: *Off B3130 into Stanton Drew, right onto Sandy Ln*

Located on a quiet country lane, Valley Farm offers relaxing and friendly accommodation. All bedrooms are comfortable and well equipped, and each has pleasant views over the countryside. Breakfast is served around a communal table in the dining room, and although dinner is not available, the village pub is just a stroll away.

Rooms 3 en suite (1 fmly) (1 GF) **Facilities** TVL tea/coffee Cen ht **Parking** 6 **Notes** ⊗ No Children 8yrs Closed 24-26 Dec 🐾

| STAPLE FITZPAINE | Map 4 ST21 |

Greyhound

★★★★ 🛏 INN

TA3 5SP
☎ 01823 480227 📠 01823 481117
e-mail: thegreyhound-inn@btconnect.com
web: www.thegreyhoundinn.biz
dir: *M5 junct 25, A358 signed Yeovil. In 3m turn right, signed Staple Fitzpaine*

Set in the heart of Somerset in the Blackdown Hills, this picturesque village inn has great atmosphere and character, complete with flagstone floors and open fires. An imaginative choice of freshly-prepared seasonal dishes using locally sourced ingredients is featured on the ever-changing blackboard menu. The delightful bedrooms are spacious, comfortable, and well equipped with many extra facilities.

Greyhound

Rooms 4 en suite **Facilities** FTV tea/coffee Dinner available Direct Dial Cen ht Wi-fi Pool table **Conf** Max 60 Thtr 60 Class 30 Board 20 **Parking** 40 **Notes** No Children 10yrs

---

| STOGUMBER | Map 3 ST03 |

Wick House

★★★★ 🄰 GUEST HOUSE

Brook St TA4 3SZ
☎ 01984 656422
e-mail: sheila@wickhouse.co.uk
web: www.wickhouse.co.uk
dir: *Off A358 into village, left at the x-rds, Wick House 3rd on left*

Rooms 9 en suite (1 GF) S £30-£50; D £60-£80* **Facilities** FTV tea/coffee Dinner available Licensed Wi-fi Stairlift **Parking** 6 **Notes** LB ⊗

| STREET | Map 4 ST43 |

The Two Brewers

★★★★ INN

38 Leigh Rd BA16 0HB
☎ 01458 442421
e-mail: richard@thetwobrewers.co.uk
web: www.thetwobrewers.co.uk

This traditional inn is very popular with locals and tourists alike offering a genuine welcome, excellent home-cooked food and a selection of fine real ales. Bedrooms are located in an annexe to the rear of the inn and are well equipped and comfortable. The absence of music and machines in the bar adds to the relaxing atmosphere, and the menu includes regularly-changing blackboard specials and guest real ales.

Rooms 3 annexe en suite (1 GF) D £49 **Facilities** FTV tea/coffee Dinner available Cen ht Wi-fi Skittle alley boules **Parking** 3 **Notes** LB ⊗ Closed 25-26 Dec No coaches

Kasuli

★★★ BED AND BREAKFAST

71 Somerton Rd BA16 0DN
☎ 01458 442063
dir: *B3151 from Street rdbt for Somerton, house 400yds past Street Inn on left*

This family home is located close to Clarks Village Outlet Centre and with easy access to local places of historical interest. Friendliness and a homely atmosphere are offered, and bedrooms are neatly presented. An enjoyable traditional breakfast is served in the dining room around the family dining table.

Rooms 2 rms S £26-£28; D £50-£56* **Facilities** FTV tea/coffee Cen ht **Parking** 2 **Notes** ⊗ No Children 10yrs ⊛

| **TAUNTON** | **Map 4 ST22** |

See also Staple Fitzpaine

PREMIER COLLECTION

Elm Villa

★★★★★ BED AND BREAKFAST

1 Private Rd, Staplegrove Rd TA2 6AJ
☎ 01823 336165
e-mail: ferguson@elmvilla10.freeserve.co.uk
dir: *M5 junct 25, A358 (Minehead road) to Staplegrove Inn, left & left again onto Private Rd*

This spacious and comfortable Victorian villa enjoys distant views of the Blackdown Hills, yet is within walking distance of the town centre, theatre, station and county cricket ground. Both bedrooms are en suite and have plenty of facilities. Ample parking is available.

Rooms 2 en suite S £45; D £56 **Facilities** FTV tea/coffee Cen ht Wi-fi **Parking** 2 **Notes** ⊗ No Children 10yrs ⊛

Meryan House

★★★★ GUEST ACCOMMODATION

Bishop's Hull TA1 5EG
☎ 01823 337445   🖨 01823 322355
e-mail: meryanhousehotel@yahoo.co.uk
web: www.meryanhouse.co.uk
dir: *1.5m W of town centre. Off A38 into Bishop's Hull*

Located in its own grounds just over a mile from the town centre, this 17th-century property has delightful individually furnished rooms. The comfortable bedrooms feature antiques along with modern facilities. Interesting dishes are available at dinner, and there is also a cosy bar and a spacious lounge.

Rooms 12 en suite (2 fmly) (2 GF) S £65-£75; D £70-£90* **Facilities** STV FTV TVL tea/coffee Dinner available Direct Dial Cen ht Licensed Wi-fi **Conf** Max 25 Thtr 25 Class 25 Board 18 **Parking** 17 **Notes** LB RS Sun No evening meal

The Spinney

★★★★ 🏠 GUEST ACCOMMODATION

Curland TA3 5SE
☎ 01460 234362   & 07514 589739
e-mail: enquiries@spinneybedandbreakfast.co.uk
web: www.spinneybedandbreakfast.co.uk
dir: *2m W off A358 (Taunton-Ilminster road)*

A warm welcome awaits at this delightful family home, set in well-tended gardens and with magnificent views of the Blackdown, Quantock and Mendip hills. The attractive bedrooms are equipped with modern comforts and include a ground-floor room with level access.

Rooms 3 en suite (2 GF) D £68-£73 **Facilities** FTV TVL tea/coffee Cen ht Wi-fi **Parking** 6 **Notes** ⊗ No Children 10yrs Closed Xmas & New Year

Wick House B&B

★★★★ BED AND BREAKFAST

Norton Fitzwarren TA4 1BT
☎ 01823 289614   & 07772 052063
e-mail: info@wick-house.co.uk
dir: *From Taunton take B3227 through Norton Fitzwarren, after old railway bridge, 1st house on right*

This family-run establishment is handily placed just a few minutes from Taunton and within 15 minutes of the M5. Bedrooms are located away from the main house, allowing guests the flexibility to come and go as they please. All bedrooms provide impressive levels of comfort and quality, including spacious wet rooms and a kitchenette area for preparation of beverages. Breakfast is taken in the well-appointed dining room which has lovely views across the orchard.

Rooms 3 annexe en suite (3 GF) S £45-£50; D £65-£75* **Facilities** FTV tea/coffee Cen ht **Parking** 3 **Notes** ⊗ No Children

Blorenge House

★★★★ GUEST ACCOMMODATION

57 Staple Grove Rd TA1 1DG
☎ 01823 283005   🖨 01823 283005
e-mail: enquiries@blorengehouse.co.uk
dir: *M5 junct 25, towards cricket ground & Morrisons on left, left at lights, right at 2nd lights, house 150yds on left*

This fine Victorian property offers spacious accommodation and is within walking distance of the town centre. The bedrooms, some at ground-floor level and some with four-poster beds, are individually furnished and vary in size. A lounge is available, and the garden, with an outdoor swimming pool, is open to guests during daytime hours most days of the week. There is also ample parking.

Rooms 23 rms (19 en suite) (4 pri facs) (2 fmly) (2 GF) S £50-£85; D £80-£100* **Facilities** FTV TVL tea/coffee Cen ht Wi-fi ✎ **Conf** Max 20 **Parking** 23 **Notes** LB

Brookfield House

★★★★ GUEST HOUSE

16 Wellington Rd TA1 4EQ
☎ 01823 272786   🖨 01823 240003
e-mail: info@brookfieldguesthouse.uk.com
web: www.brookfieldguesthouse.uk.com
dir: *From town centre signs to Musgrove Hospital, onto A38 Wellington Rd, on right opp turning to hospital*

This charming Grade II listed Georgian house is just a five-minute, level walk from the town centre. The family take great pride in caring for guests, and the brightly decorated bedrooms are well equipped. Breakfast, featuring local produce, is served in the attractive dining room. The property is entirely non-smoking.

Rooms 7 en suite (1 fmly) S £65-£68; D £75-£98* **Facilities** tea/coffee Dinner available Cen ht Wi-fi **Parking** 8 **Notes** ⊗ No Children 7yrs

Creechbarn

★★★★ BED AND BREAKFAST

Vicarage Ln, Creech St Michael TA3 5PP
☎ 01823 443955
e-mail: mick@somersite.co.uk
dir: *M5 junct 25, A358 to Creech St Michael, follow canal boat signs to end Vicarage Ln. Through brick gateposts, turn right*

Located next to the canal and on a Sustrans cycle route, this traditional Somerset barn was lovingly converted by the current owners. Bedrooms are comfortable and there is a spacious sitting room with books and TV. Breakfast is carefully prepared with free-range eggs and home-made bread.

Rooms 3 rms (1 en suite) S £44-£46; D £50-£58 **Facilities** TVL TV1B tea/coffee Direct Dial Cen ht Wi-fi **Parking** 6 **Notes** LB Closed 20 Dec-6 Jan ⊛

TAUNTON *continued*

Lower Farm *(ST281241)*

★★★★ FARMHOUSE

Thornfalcon TA3 5NR
☎ 01823 443549
Mrs D Titman
e-mail: doreen@titman.eclipse.co.uk
web: www.thornfalcon.co.uk
dir: *M5 junct 25, 2m SE on A358, left opp Nags Head pub, farm signed 1m on left*

This charming, thatched, 15th-century farmhouse is set in lovely gardens and is surrounded by open countryside. Hearty breakfasts, served in the farmhouse kitchen, feature home-produced eggs. Some bedrooms are located in the converted granary, some on the ground floor. There is a comfortable sitting room with a log fire.

Rooms 2 rms (1 en suite) (1 pri facs) 9 annexe rms 7 annexe en suite (2 pri facs) (2 fmly) (7 GF) S £45-£50; D £70-£75 **Facilities** FTV TVL TV9B tea/coffee Cen ht Wi-fi **Parking** 10 **Notes** LB ⊗ No Children 5yrs 10 acres beef/cows/poultry

Lower Marsh Farm *(ST224279)*

★★★★ FARMHOUSE

Kingston St Mary TA2 8AB
☎ 01823 451331   📠 01823 451331
Mr & Mrs J Gothard
e-mail: b&b@lowermarshfarm.co.uk
web: www.lowermarshfarm.co.uk
dir: *M5 junct 25. Farm between Taunton & Kingston St Mary just past King's Hall School on right*

Located at the foot of the Quantock Hills, this delightful family-run farm provides a warm welcome with a pot of tea and cake ready and waiting. Bedrooms are individually styled and reflect the traditional charm of the house; they provide impressive levels of quality and are complemented by numerous thoughtful extras. The Aga-cooked breakfast is a real treat, served in the dining room around one grand table; evening meals are also available by prior arrangement. There is also a spacious lounge warmed by a crackling log fire in winter.

Rooms 3 en suite (1 fmly) S £38-£45; D £70-£80 **Facilities** TVL tea/coffee Dinner available Cen ht Wi-fi **Parking** 6 **Notes** ⊗ 300 acres arable

Higher Dipford *(ST216205)*

★★★ FARMHOUSE

Trull TA3 7NU
☎ 01823 275770   📠 01823 275770
Mrs M Fewings
e-mail: mafewings@tesco.net
dir: *A38 S from town centre on Honiton Rd to Trull, right onto Dipford Rd, farm on left*

This Grade II listed, 17th-century longhouse is part of a working beef farm. Steeped in character with elm beams and inglenook fireplaces, the house provides well-equipped and homely accommodation. Bedrooms are comfortable and individually decorated, and there is an honesty bar and lounge. Breakfasts and home-cooked dinners, featuring local produce, are served in the spacious dining room.

Rooms 3 en suite (1 fmly) S £45-£55; D £70-£85 **Facilities** STV FTV TVL tea/coffee Dinner available Cen ht Licensed 🍴 **Parking** 6 **Notes** LB ⊗ ⌖ 120 acres beef

Rumwell Park

★★★ GUEST ACCOMMODATION

Rumwell TA4 1EH
☎ 01823 461050
e-mail: affordableuk@gmail.com

Rumwell Park is a house of great charm and character, that offers comfortable accommodation in a grand setting within minutes of both Taunton and the M5. There is a pleasant guest lounge, and breakfast is a continental offering served in the morning room with views across open fields.

Rooms 3 rms (1 en suite) (1 pri facs) **Facilities** FTV Cen ht Wi-fi **Parking** Notes ⊗ Closed Aug

| **TINTINHULL** | **Map 4 ST41** |

Crown & Victoria

★★★★ ⊛ INN

Farm St BA22 8PZ
☎ 01935 823341   📠 01935 825786
e-mail: info@thecrownandvictoria.co.uk
web: www.thecrownandvictoria.co.uk
dir: *Off A303, signs for Tintinhull Gardens*

Appointed to a high standard, this light and airy accommodation has very well-equipped bedrooms. The staff ensure guests are well cared for, and the contemporary bar and restaurant provide a good selection of carefully prepared dishes.

Rooms 5 en suite **Facilities** tea/coffee Dinner available Cen ht Wi-fi **Parking** 60 **Notes** No coaches

WATCHET   Map 3 ST04

The Georgian House

★★★★ GUEST HOUSE

28 Swain St TA23 0AD
☎ 01984 639279
e-mail: georgianhouse_watchet@virgin.net
dir: A39 over railway bridge onto Watchet main street

This elegant Georgian property is situated in the heart of this increasingly popular coastal resort and is within a short walk of the impressive marina. Refurbished with considerable care, the comfortable bedrooms combine quality and individuality. Breakfast (and dinner by arrangement) is served in the well-appointed dining room. Additional facilities for guests include a lounge and the garden.

Rooms 3 en suite S £35; D £60-£90* **Facilities** Dinner available Cen ht **Parking** 2 **Notes** LB ⊗ 🐾

WATERROW   Map 3 ST02

The Rock

★★★★ 🍺 INN

TA4 2AX
☎ 01984 623293   ▤ 01984 623293
e-mail: enquiries@rockinn.co.uk
dir: On B3227

Set in the lush greenery of the Tone Valley, this 16th-century inn, as its name suggests, is built against a rock face. There is an abundance of character, and the friendly atmosphere draws both locals and visitors alike. A range of freshly prepared, imaginative meals is available in the bar and restaurant, including Aberdeen Angus steaks from the owner's farm. The bedrooms are comfortable, light and airy.

Rooms 8 en suite (1 fmly) S fr £50; D fr £75* **Facilities** FTV TVL tea/coffee Dinner available Direct Dial Cen ht Wi-fi **Parking** 25 **Notes** LB

WELLINGTON   Map 3 ST12

The Cleve Spa

★★★★ GUEST ACCOMMODATION

Mantle St TA21 8SN
☎ 01823 662033   ▤ 01823 660874
e-mail: reception@clevehotel.com
web: www.clevehotel.com
dir: M5 junct 26 follow signs to Wellington town centre. Continue for 600mtrs, entrance on left

This elegant Victorian country house is situated in an elevated position with commanding views. Bedrooms provide high levels of comfort and quality with well appointed and stylish bathrooms. Dinner and breakfast are served in the attractive restaurant, after which a stroll around the extensive grounds may be appropriate. An impressive array of leisure facilities is also offered, including indoor pool, spa bath, steam room and fully-equipped fitness studio.

Rooms 20 en suite (5 fmly) (3 GF) S £65-£95; D £80-£110* **Facilities** FTV Dinner available Direct Dial Cen ht Licensed Wi-fi ◆ Snooker Sauna Solarium Gym Spa beauty treatments **Conf** Max 250 Thtr 250 Class 100 Board 60 **Parking** 100 **Notes** LB Civ Wed 200

WELLS   Map 4 ST54

See also Croscombe

PREMIER COLLECTION

Beaconsfield Farm

★★★★★ 🏠 BED AND BREAKFAST

Easton BA5 1DU
☎ 01749 870308
e-mail: carol@beaconsfieldfarm.co.uk
web: www.beaconsfieldfarm.co.uk
dir: 2.5m from Wells on A371, on right just before Easton

Set in pleasant, well-tended gardens on the west side of the Mendip Hills, Beaconsfield Farm is a convenient base for exploring this attractive area. The welcoming hosts are most friendly and attentive, and many guests return on a regular basis. The comfortable bedrooms are delightfully decorated with co-ordinated fabrics and have many guest extras. A choice of well-cooked dishes featuring fresh local produce is offered at breakfast.

Rooms 3 en suite **Facilities** FTV TVL tea/coffee Cen ht Wi-fi **Parking** 10 **Notes** ⊗ No Children 8yrs Closed 22 Dec-3 Jan 🐾

Beryl

★★★★★ 🅰 BED AND BREAKFAST

Hawkers Ln BA5 3JP
☎ 01749 678738   ▤ 01749 670508
e-mail: stay@beryl-wells.co.uk
dir: Off B3139 Radstock Rd, signed The Horringtons, onto Hawkers Ln to end

Rooms 9 rms (8 en suite) (1 pri facs) (2 fmly) **Facilities** TVL tea/coffee Direct Dial Cen ht Lift Licensed 🦅 🐾 childrens play area **Parking** 20 **Notes** Closed 25-26 Dec

Double-Gate Farm *(ST484424)*

★★★★ FARMHOUSE

Godney BA5 1RZ
☎ 01458 832217   ▤ 01458 835612
Mr Millard
e-mail: doublegatefarm@aol.com
web: www.doublegatefarm.com
dir: A39 from Wells towards Glastonbury, at Polsham right signed Godney/Polsham. 2m to x-rds, continue to farmhouse on left after inn

Expect a warm welcome not only from the owner Mr Millard, but also his friendly Labradors. Set on the banks of the River Sheppey on the Somerset Levels, this comfortable farmhouse is well known for its attractive summer flower garden, as well as delicious breakfasts. Guests have use of a games room and free internet access in the lounge.

Rooms 3 en suite 4 annexe en suite (4 fmly) (4 GF) S £60-£85; D £70-£120* **Facilities** FTV TVL tea/coffee Cen ht Fishing Snooker Table tennis **Parking** 9 **Notes** ⊗ Closed 20 Dec-5 Jan 100 acres mixed

WELLS *continued*

Riverside Grange

★ ★ ★ ★ BED AND BREAKFAST

Tanyard Ln, North Wootton BA4 4AE
☎ 01749 890761
e-mail: riversidegrange@hotmail.com
dir: *2.5m SE of Wells in North Wootton*

A delightful restored tannery, built in 1853, the foundations of which actually sit in the River Redlake. A warm welcome and attentive service is guaranteed from the friendly proprietor, who makes every effort to see that guests feel at home. The house, furnished throughout with rosewood, is very comfortable; the bedrooms are stylishly co-ordinated. Guests may relax in the attractive garden in summer or, in winter, the cosy snug that overlooks the orchard.

Rooms 2 rms (1 en suite) (1 pri facs) S £55; D £65
Facilities tea/coffee Cen ht Wi-fi **Parking** 6 **Notes** ⊗ No Children 10yrs Closed Xmas & New Year ⊠

The Crown at Wells

★ ★ ★ ★ INN

Market Place BA5 2RP
☎ 01749 673457 ▤ 01749 679792
e-mail: stay@crownatwells.co.uk
web: www.crownatwells.co.uk
dir: *On entering Wells follow signs for Hotels & Deliveries, in Market Place, car park at rear*

Retaining its original features and period charm, this historic inn is situated in the heart of the city, just a short stroll from the cathedral. The building's frontage has been used in many film productions. Bedrooms, all with modern facilities, vary in size and style. Public areas focus around Anton's, the popular bistro, which offers a light and airy environment and relaxed atmosphere. The Penn Bar offers an alternative eating option and real ales.

Rooms 15 en suite (2 fmly) S £65-£95; D £95-£115*
Facilities FTV tea/coffee Dinner available Cen ht Wi-fi Golf 18 **Parking** 10 **Notes** LB

Glengarth House

★ ★ ★ ★ GUEST ACCOMMODATION

7 Glastonbury Rd BA5 1TW
☎ 01749 674792 ▤ 01749 674792
e-mail: glengarthhouse@tiscali.co.uk
dir: *On A39 S, on left past mini-rdbt*

This pleasant guest accommodation is located on the edge of Wells, just a short walk from the central attractions. A continental breakfast is provided in the light and airy dining room. The comfortable bedrooms are modern and brightly decorated, and guests will benefit from the limited off-road parking.

Rooms 5 en suite (1 fmly) S £35-£65; D £68-£75*
Facilities FTV tea/coffee Cen ht Wi-fi **Parking** 5 **Notes** LB ⊗ ⊠

Highfield

★ ★ ★ ★ BED AND BREAKFAST

93 Portway BA5 2BR
☎ 01749 675330
dir: *Enter Wells & signs for A371 Cheddar, Highfield on Portway after last lights at top of hill*

Within walking distance of the city and cathedral, this delightful home maintains its Edwardian style and provides comfortable accommodation. A warm welcome is assured, and bedrooms are well equipped. Breakfast is served at one large table in the smart dining room, which overlooks the pretty garden.

Rooms 3 en suite (1 fmly) **Facilities** tea/coffee Cen ht **Parking** 7 **Notes** ⊗ No Children 2yrs Closed 23 Dec-1 Jan ⊠

Hollow Tree Farm

★ ★ ★ ★ GUEST ACCOMMODATION

Launcherley BA5 1QJ
☎ 01749 673715 & 07704 506513 ▤ 01749 673715
e-mail: jennifercoombes1@hotmail.co.uk
dir: *A39 from Wells for Glastonbury, 1st left at Brownes Garden Centre, farm 0.5m on right*

Delightfully appointed rooms with bright, cheery colour schemes and comfortable furnishings are provided at this non-working farm. Spectacular views of Wells Cathedral and Glastonbury Tor and delightful flower-filled gardens add to the charm. The friendly hosts are most welcoming and attentive, and home-baked bread, jams and marmalade are only a part of the delicious breakfast.

Rooms 2 en suite (2 GF) S £35-£45; D £55-£60*
Facilities TVL tea/coffee Cen ht **Parking** 4 **Notes** ⊗ No Children 12yrs Closed mid Dec-mid Jan ⊠

Infield House

★ ★ ★ ★ BED AND BREAKFAST

36 Portway BA5 2BN
☎ 01749 670989 ▤ 01749 679093
e-mail: infield@talk21.com
web: www.infieldhouse.co.uk
dir: *500yds W of city centre on A371 Portway*

This charming Victorian house offers comfortable, spacious rooms of elegance and style. The friendly hosts are very welcoming and provide a relaxing home-from-home. Guests may bring their pets, by arrangement. Dinners, also by arrangement, are served in the pleasant dining room where good home cooking ensures an enjoyable and varied range of options.

Rooms 3 en suite D £68-£70* **Facilities** FTV tea/coffee Dinner available Cen ht Wi-fi **Parking** 3 **Notes** No Children 12yrs

Littlewell Farm

★ ★ ★ ★ GUEST ACCOMMODATION

Coxley BA5 1QP
☎ 01749 677914
e-mail: info@littlewellfarm.co.uk
web: www.littlewellfarm.co.uk
dir: *A39 from Wells towards Glastonbury, farm 1m on right opp sign for Coxley*

This charming house stands in spacious gardens at Coxley, on the outskirts of Wells. It provides well-equipped accommodation and has a smart, comfortable lounge. Breakfast, featuring local produce when possible, is served in the bright, modern dining room at separate tables.

Rooms 5 rms (4 en suite) (1 pri facs) (1 GF) S £40-£50; D £65-£75* **Facilities** FTV TVL tea/coffee Cen ht Wi-fi **Parking** 10 **Notes** ⊗ No Children Closed 25 Dec ⊠

Amber House

★★★ BED AND BREAKFAST

Coxley BA5 1QZ
☎ 01749 679612
e-mail: amberhouse@wellscity27.freeserve.co.uk
dir: *On A39 in village, 0.25m S past Pound Inn on right*

Located just 1.5 miles south of the centre of Wells and ideally placed for touring the area's historic sites and countryside, this friendly family home offers a relaxed atmosphere. Bedrooms are well equipped; some look out over open countryside and farmland to the rear. A traditional English breakfast is served, at separate tables, in the cosy dining room, which guests are welcome to use at other times.

Rooms 3 en suite S £32; D £50–£58* **Facilities** FTV tea/coffee Cen ht Wi-fi **Parking** 3 **Notes** ⊗ ⓔ

Birdwood House

★★★ GUEST ACCOMMODATION

Birdwood, Bath Rd BA5 3EW
☎ 01749 679250
e-mail: info@birdwood-bandb.co.uk
web: www.birdwood-bandb.co.uk
dir: *1.5m NE of city centre. On B3139 between South & West Horrington*

Set in extensive grounds and gardens just a short drive from the town centre, this imposing detached house dates from the 1850s. The bedrooms are comfortable and equipped with a number of extra facilities. Breakfast is served around a communal table in the pleasant dining room or conservatory, which is also available for guest use and enjoyment throughout the day.

Rooms 3 rms (2 en suite) (1 pri facs) (1 fmly)
Facilities TVL tea/coffee Cen ht ⬥ **Parking** 12 **Notes** LB ⓔ

19 St Cuthbert Street

★★ BED AND BREAKFAST

BA5 2AW
☎ 01749 673166
dir: *At bottom of High St opp St Cuthbert's Church*

Guests are assured of a friendly welcome at this charming terrace house, which is within walking distance of the cathedral and bus station. The accommodation is fresh, light and comfortable and the atmosphere homely. Bedrooms are well appointed and there is a comfortable lounge. Breakfast, featuring home-made marmalade, is served in the dining room around a family table.

Rooms 2 rms S £34–£37.50; D £55–£65* **Facilities** FTV TVL tea/coffee Cen ht **Notes** ⊗ No Children 5yrs ⓔ

| WESTON-SUPER-MARE | Map 4 ST36 |

PREMIER COLLECTION

Church House

★★★★★ BED AND BREAKFAST

27 Kewstoke Rd, Kewstoke BS22 9YD
☎ 01934 633185
e-mail: churchhouse@kewstoke.net
web: www.churchhousekewstoke.co.uk
dir: *From M5 junct 21 follow signs for Kewstoke 2.5m, next to Kewstoke Church*

In a peaceful location at the foot of Monk's Hill, this delightful property enjoys wonderful views over the Bristol Channel and across to Wales on clear days. Bedrooms are stylish and spacious, with lots of thoughtful extras and well-equipped en suites. Public areas include a pleasant conservatory and an elegant dining room where impressive breakfasts are served.

Rooms 5 en suite **Facilities** tea/coffee Cen ht Wi-fi **Parking** 10

PREMIER COLLECTION

9 The Park

★★★★★ GUEST ACCOMMODATION

9 Ellenborough Park Rd BS23 1XJ
☎ 01934 415244 & 07792 184230
e-mail: info@9theparkbandb.co.uk
dir: *A370 towards town centre, through 5 rdbts, at next 1st exit onto Station Approach. Pass station onto Neva Rd, left onto Ellenborough Park Rd, 40mtrs on left*

This elegant property is peacefully located in a residential area, yet just a short walk to the beach and the town centre. The bedrooms and bathrooms are all decorated and furnished to high standards and the beds are especially comfortable. The attentive proprietors ensure guests are very well looked after at all times. Breakfast is a highlight, with plenty of fresh local produce including a varied choice of hot items together with a wide range of fruits, cheeses and other items.

Rooms 3 en suite (2 fmly) S £60; D £85 **Facilities** FTV tea/coffee Cen ht Wi-fi **Parking** 4 **Notes** ⊗

Oakover

★★★★ GUEST HOUSE

25 Clevedon Rd BS23 1DA
☎ 01934 620125 ▤ 01934 620173
e-mail: info@oakover.co.uk
web: www.oakover.co.uk
dir: *Off A370 (Beach Rd) near Sea Life Aquarium onto Clevedon Rd*

Oakover is a substantial Victorian property situated a short level walk from the town centre and seafront. Bedrooms and bathrooms offer very good levels of quality and comfort. A varied breakfast menu is offered in the bright dining room. The friendly resident proprietor maintains an easy-going and welcoming establishment.

Rooms 6 en suite (2 GF) S £45–£80; D £60–£80* **Facilities** FTV tea/coffee Cen ht Wi-fi **Parking** 7 **Notes** ⊗ No Children 12yrs

WESTON-SUPER-MARE *continued*

Beverley Guest House

★★★ GUEST HOUSE

11 Whitecross Rd BS23 1EP
☎ 01934 622956 & 07824 512085 📠 01934 622956
e-mail: beverley11@hushmail.com
dir: *Off A370 Beach Rd onto Ellenborough Park Rd South & take 2nd right*

This charming guest house is located in a quieter residential area, yet is only a short stroll from both the beach and the town centre. The bedrooms and bathrooms come in a range of shapes and sizes but all are equipped with a number of welcome extras. A good selection of hot and cold items is offered at breakfast and served in the comfortable dining room.

Rooms 5 en suite (1 fmly) (1 GF) S £40-£52.50; D £60-£72* **Facilities** FTV tea/coffee Cen ht Wi-fi **Notes** LB ⊗ Closed 20 Dec-2 Jan

Camellia Lodge

★★★★ BED AND BREAKFAST

76 Walliscote Rd BS23 1ED
☎ 01934 613534 📠 01934 613534
e-mail: dachefs@aol.com
dir: *200yds from seafront*

Guests return regularly for the warm welcome at this immaculate Victorian family home, which is just off the seafront and within walking distance of the town centre. Bedrooms have a range of thoughtful touches, and carefully prepared breakfasts are served in the relaxing dining room. Home-cooked dinners are also available by prior arrangement.

Rooms 5 en suite (2 fmly) S £30-£40; D £60-£80* **Facilities** FTV tea/coffee Dinner available Cen ht Wi-fi

Jamesfield Guest House

★★★★ GUEST HOUSE

1A Ellenborough Park North BS23 1XH
☎ 01934 642898
e-mail: jamesfield1@aol.com

A well-maintained property in an ideal location, a short walk from the seafront and only a few minutes stroll from town. Bedrooms are all comfortably furnished and well decorated, and include rooms on the ground floor. Guests are welcome to use the relaxing lounge, and the property also benefits from its own car park.

Rooms 7 rms (6 en suite) (1 pri facs) (2 GF) **Facilities** TVL tea/coffee Cen ht **Parking** 9 **Notes** ⊗

Linden Lodge Guest House

★★★★ GUEST ACCOMMODATION

27 Clevedon Rd BS23 1DA
☎ 01934 645797
e-mail: info@lindenlodge.com
dir: *Follow signs to seafront. 0.5m S of grand pier turn onto Clevedon Rd*

Just a short walk from the town centre and the seafront, Linden Lodge offers a traditional style of welcoming hospitality and guest care. Bedrooms offer a range of shapes and sizes and all are well decorated and equipped. A good selection is offered at breakfast and served in the pleasant conservatory.

Rooms 5 en suite (1 fmly) **Facilities** tea/coffee Cen ht **Parking** 3 **Notes** ⊗

The Owls Crest House

★★★★ BED AND BREAKFAST

39 Kewstoke Rd, Kewstoke BS22 9YE
☎ 01934 417672 & 07929 350017
e-mail: theowlscrest1@btinternet.com
dir: *M5 junct 21, A370 to Weston, 1st left towards Kewstoke. Through 4 rdbts, to T-junct in Kewstoke. Turn left. Owls Crest House after New Inn pub*

Located in the pleasant village of Kewstoke, guests will find an especially friendly welcome from the resident Irish hosts at this relaxed establishment. The comfortable bedrooms provide plenty of useful extras. Traditional home-cooked breakfasts are served in the dining room. Guests are welcome to use the lounge.

Rooms 4 en suite (1 fmly) S £55-£57; D £67-£75* **Facilities** STV FTV TVL tea/coffee Cen ht Licensed Wi-fi **Parking** 5 **Notes** LB No Children 7yrs Closed 28 Dec-5 Jan & annual holidays

Rookery Manor

★★★★ GUEST ACCOMMODATION

Edingworth Rd, Edingworth BS24 0JB
☎ 0845 4090909 📠 0845 4090908
e-mail: enquiries@rookery-manor.co.uk
web: www.rookery-manor.co.uk
dir: *M5 junct 22, A370 towards Weston, 2m right to Rookery Manor*

Situated in its own delightful gardens and grounds within easy reach of the M5 and all the resort attractions of Weston-Super-Mare, this 16th-century manor house is best known for its extensive wedding and conference facilities. Bedrooms, each with its own access to the garden, are modern and bright. A carte menu is offered in Truffles Restaurant.

Rooms 22 en suite (2 fmly) (10 GF) **Facilities** TVL tea/coffee Dinner available Direct Dial Cen ht Licensed 🏌 🎣 Golf 9 ⚜ Riding Snooker Pool table **Conf** Max 800 Thtr 800 Class 120 Board 120 **Parking** 460 **Notes** LB ⊗ Civ Wed 400

Goodrington

★★★ GUEST HOUSE

23 Charlton Rd BS23 4HB
☎ 01934 623229
e-mail: vera.bishop@talk21.com
web: www.goodrington.info
dir: *A370 Beach Rd S onto Uphill Rd, left onto Charlton Rd*

The owners make every effort to ensure guests enjoy their stay at this charming Victorian house tucked away in a quiet residential area. The bedrooms are comfortably furnished, and there is an attractive lounge. Families are especially welcome and this makes a good holiday base.

Rooms 3 rms (2 en suite) (1 pri facs) (1 fmly) (1 GF) S £30-£35; D £56-£60* **Facilities** FTV TVL tea/coffee Dinner available Cen ht Wi-fi **Notes** LB ⊗ Closed Oct-Etr ⊛

Parasol Guest House

★★★ GUEST HOUSE

49 Walliscote Rd BS23 1EE
☎ 01934 636409 & 07592 357619
e-mail: parasol49@hotmail.com

Located in a residential area with the seafront and town centre just a short stroll away, Parasol Guest House has been upgraded to offer a range of well decorated bedrooms in various sizes. Breakfast is served at individual tables in the comfortable dining room. Wi-fi is among the welcome extras available in the bedrooms.

Rooms 8 en suite (2 fmly) (1 GF) S £20-£35; D £40-£66 **Facilities** FTV TVL tea/coffee Dinner available Cen ht Wi-fi Pass available to fitness club **Parking** 2 **Notes** LB ⊗

Bella Vista

★★★ GUEST HOUSE

19 Upper Church Rd BS23 2DX
☎ 01934 631931 📠 01934 620126
web: www.bellavistawsm.co.uk
dir: *A370 to town and seafront, right past Grand Pier. Right after 300yds onto Upper Church Rd & right at x-rds*

Situated close to the seafront and town centre, this delightful terrace property has an attractive patio with seating at the front. The well decorated bedrooms have TVs and hospitality trays. There is a cosy dining room where full English breakfasts are served, and a large comfortable lounge is also available.

Rooms 8 en suite (3 fmly) **Facilities** FTV TVL tea/coffee Cen ht **Notes** LB ⊗ Closed 12 Dec-2 Jan ⊛

Corbiere Guest House

★★★ GUEST HOUSE

24 Upper Church Rd BS23 2DX
☎ 01934 629607 & 07932 029732 ▤ 01934 629607
e-mail: corbierehotel@btinternet.com
dir: *M5 junct 21 take A370 to town/seafront. Turn right for pier along Knightstone Rd, approx 300yds turn right onto Upper Church Rd & right at x-rds*

Located within walking distance of the city centre, this charming house maintains Victorian style. The friendly proprietors make every effort to ensure a stay is pleasant and memorable, and the attractive bedrooms have many considerate extras. There is a lounge, and freshly cooked breakfasts are served in the pleasant dining room.

Rooms 10 en suite (4 fmly) (2 GF) S £20-£30; D £45-£50* **Facilities** FTV TVL tea/coffee Dinner available Cen ht **Notes** LB ⊗ ⊜

Edelweiss Guest House

★★★ GUEST HOUSE

24 Clevedon Rd BS23 1DG
☎ 01934 624705 ▤ 01934 624705
e-mail: edelweissguesthouse@tiscali.co.uk
dir: *Turn onto Clevedon Rd off Beach Rd (Seafront) opposite Tropicana. Edelweiss 75yds on right*

Located in a residential area approximately 100 yards from the seafront and beach, Edelweiss is a traditional and comfortable guest house run in a welcoming manner. Bedrooms vary in size but all are nicely decorated. Although dinner is not available, guests are welcome to select from a light snack and beverage menu up until 10pm.

Rooms 5 rms (4 en suite) (1 pri facs) (3 fmly) (2 GF) **Facilities** FTV tea/coffee Cen ht **Notes** LB ⊗ Closed Xmas wk

Weston Bay Guest House

★★★ GUEST HOUSE

2-4 Clevedon Rd BS23 1DG
☎ 01934 628903 ▤ 01934 417661
e-mail: westonbayhotel@btinternet.com
web: www.westonbayhotel.co.uk
dir: *Opp Sea Quarium on seafront*

Located on the seafront, this family-run property has generally spacious, well-equipped bedrooms with modern en suites. The comfortable lounge and attractive breakfast room have sea views, and packed lunches are available on request. There is a small private car park.

Rooms 9 en suite (5 fmly) (1 GF) S £50-£55; D £69-£77 **Facilities** FTV TVL tea/coffee Cen ht Wi-fi **Parking** 11 **Notes** LB ⊗ Closed mid Nov-mid Mar

WHEDDON CROSS   Map 3 SS93

North Wheddon Farm *(SS923385)*

★★★★ ⚑ ⌂ FARMHOUSE

TA24 7EX
☎ 01643 841791
Mrs R Abraham
e-mail: rachael@go-exmoor.co.uk
dir: *500yds S of village x-rds on A396. Pass Moorland Hall on left, driveway next right*

North Wheddon Farm is a delightfully friendly and comfortable environment with great views, a perfect base for exploring the delights of Exmoor. The tranquil grounds include a pleasant garden and guests are welcome to roam the fields and say hello to the pigs, sheep, goats and any other new arrivals. Memorable dinners and breakfasts feature excellent produce, much of it straight from the farm. The bedrooms are thoughtfully equipped and individual in style with lovely comfy beds.

Rooms 3 rms (2 en suite) (1 pri facs) S £33-£38.50; D £66-£77* **Facilities** FTV tea/coffee Dinner available Cen ht Licensed Wi-fi Riding **Parking** 5 **Notes** LB 20 acres mixed

The Rest and Be Thankful Inn

★★★★ INN

TA24 7DR
☎ 01643 841222 ▤ 01643 841813
e-mail: stay@restandbethankful.co.uk
dir: *M5 junct 25, A358 to Minehead, left onto B3224 at sign to Wheddon Cross*

The Rest and Be Thankful is situated in the highest village on Exmoor overlooking Dunkery Beacon. The comfortable, refurbished bedrooms are extremely well equipped with extras such as mini-bars and trouser presses. The convivial bar, complete with crackling log fires, is a popular meeting point for locals and visitors alike. A range of wholesome dishes is offered either in the bar, restaurant or outside on the patio, from where lovely countryside views can be enjoyed.

Rooms 8 en suite (1 fmly) **Facilities** FTV tea/coffee Dinner available Direct Dial Cen ht Wi-fi Pool table Skittle alley **Conf** Max 50 Class 50 Board 50 **Parking** 10 **Notes** ⊗ Closed 25 Dec

WILLITON   Map 3 ST04

The White House

★★★★ GUEST ACCOMMODATION

11 Long St TA4 4QW
☎ 01984 632306 ▤ 0118 900 7881
e-mail: whitehouselive@btconnect.com
dir: *A39 Bridgwater to Minehead, in Williton on right prior to Watchet turning*

This Grade II listed Georgian house is in a perfect location for guests wishing to explore this beautiful countryside and coast. Many original features have been retained which add to the character of this charming establishment. Bedrooms are located both in the main house and an adjacent courtyard; all are impressive and have Egyptian cotton linen and fluffy towels. Breakfast is served in the elegant dining room, and there is a guest lounge for relaxation.

Rooms 8 rms (7 en suite) (1 pri facs) 6 annexe en suite (2 fmly) (6 GF) S £39-£49; D £78-£98* **Facilities** FTV TVL tea/coffee Cen ht Licensed Wi-fi **Parking** 12 **Notes** LB

WINSFORD — Map 3 SS93

Karslake Country Guest House

★★★★ GUEST ACCOMMODATION

Halse Ln TA24 7JE
☎ 01643 851242 ▤ 01643 851242
e-mail: enquiries@karslakehouse.co.uk
web: www.karslakehouse.co.uk
dir: In village centre, past pub, up hill

A warm and welcoming house offering comfortable, well appointed rooms and friendly, professional service. Off-street parking, a guest lounge with log burner, and a separate bar are just some of the additional features of this popular property.

Rooms 6 rms (5 en suite) (1 pri facs) Facilities tea/coffee Parking

WITHYPOOL — Map 3 SS83

PREMIER COLLECTION

Kings Farm

★★★★★ BED AND BREAKFAST

TA24 7RE
☎ 01643 831381
e-mail: info@kingsfarmexmoor.co.uk
dir: Off B3223 to Withypool, over bridge & sharp left to farm

This delightful farmhouse is set in over two acres of landscaped gardens in an idyllic valley beside the River Barle. It combines the character and charm of its 19th-century origins with modern comforts. From the carefully planned bedrooms to the sumptuously furnished sitting room, delicious home-cooked breakfasts and the warmest of welcomes, top quality is most definitely the hallmark of Kings Farm. Both stabling and fishing are available.

Rooms 2 rms (1 en suite) (1 pri facs) S £60; D £95-£105* Facilities STV FTV tea/coffee Cen ht Wi-fi Fishing Parking 3 Notes No Children 14yrs

The Royal Oak Inn

★★★★ INN

TA24 7QP
☎ 01643 831506 ▤ 01643 831659
e-mail: enquiries@royaloakwithypool.co.uk
dir: 7m N of Dulverton, off B3223

Set at the heart of Exmoor, this long established and popular inn continues to provide rest and sustenance for weary travellers. The atmosphere is warm and engaging with the bar always frequented by cheery locals. Bedrooms and bathrooms are stylish and very well appointed with added touches of luxury such as Egyptian cotton linen, bath robes and cosseting towels. Menus feature local produce and can be enjoyed either in the bars or in the elegant restaurant.

Rooms 8 rms (7 en suite) (1 pri facs) D £120* Facilities tea/coffee Dinner available Direct Dial Cen ht Parking 10 Notes LB No Children 10yrs No coaches

WIVELISCOMBE — Map 3 ST02

White Hart

★★★★ INN

West St TA4 2JP
☎ 01984 623344 ▤ 01984 624748
e-mail: reservations@whitehartwiveliscombe.co.uk
dir: M5 junct 25 then A38 to Taunton. Follow signs for A358 to Minehead then B3227 to Wiveliscombe

The White Hart is the focal point of this delightful town situated near the foot of the Quantock Hills. Exmoor is on the doorstep and the coast is just a few miles away. Bedrooms offer contemporary, comfortable accommodation with a good range of facilities. Innovative dishes are offered in the restaurant, and the bar has a good range of locally brewed beers.

Rooms 16 en suite (2 fmly) Facilities FTV tea/coffee Dinner available Direct Dial Cen ht Wi-fi Skittle alley Conf Max 30 Thtr 30 Class 15 Board 15 Parking 12

WRINGTON — Map 4 ST46

Stablegrove Bed & Breakfast

★★★★ BED AND BREAKFAST

West Hay Rd BS40 5NR
☎ 01934 862032
e-mail: info@stablegrovebedandbreakfast.co.uk
web: www.stablegrovebedandbreakfast.co.uk
dir: M5 junct 20 follow signs for Yatton (B3133), through Yatton, at x-rds left onto A370. After 0.25m right onto Wrington Rd, B&B on left 1.7m

Peacefully located with delightful views towards the Mendip Hills, Stablegrove is only a short drive to the M5 and also Bristol Airport. Guests are welcome to use the very comfortable, stylish lounge/dining room where a welcoming fire and glass of port await. Bedrooms and bathrooms come in a range of shapes and sizes but all are well appointed and include some useful extras. Breakfast utilises fresh produce including eggs from the hens that live at the back of the property. Keep an eye out for the pet llamas too.

Rooms 5 rms (1 en suite) (2 pri facs) (1 fmly) S £50-£75; D £60-£85* Facilities FTV tea/coffee Cen ht Licensed Wi-fi Pool table games room Parking 7 Notes LB ⊗ No Children 5yrs Closed Xmas & New Year ⊛

YEOVIL — Map 4 ST51

See also Crewkerne

PREMIER COLLECTION

Little Barwick House

★★★★★ ⊛⊛⊛ RESTAURANT WITH ROOMS

Barwick Village BA22 9TD
☎ 01935 423902 ▤ 01935 420908
e-mail: littlebarwick@hotmail.com
dir: From Yeovil A37 towards Dorchester, left at 1st rdbt, 1st left, 0.25m on left

Situated in a quiet hamlet in three and half acres of gardens and grounds, this listed Georgian dower house is an ideal retreat for those seeking peaceful surroundings and good food. Just one of the highlights of a stay here is a meal in the restaurant, where excellent use is made of local ingredients. Each of the bedrooms has its own character, and a range of thoughtful extras such as fresh flowers, bottled water and magazines is provided.

Rooms 6 en suite Facilities FTV tea/coffee Dinner available Direct Dial Cen ht Parking 30 Notes No Children 5yrs RS Sun eve & Mon closed No coaches

The Masons Arms

★★★★ 🏠 🍽 INN

41 Lower Odcombe BA22 8TX
☎ 01935 862591 📠 01935 862591
e-mail: paula@masonsarmsodcombe.co.uk
web: www.masonsarmsodcombe.co.uk
dir: *From A303 take A3088 to Yeovil, follow signs to Montacute after village, 3rd turning on right*

Dating back to the 16th century, this charming inn claims to be the oldest building in this small country village on the outskirts of Yeovil. The spacious bedrooms are contemporary in style, with clean lines, a high level of comfort and a wide range of considerate extras. The friendly hosts run their own micro-brewery, and their ales are available at the bar along with others. Public areas include the bar/restaurant, which offers a full menu of freshly prepared dishes, along with a choice of lighter snacks. There is a small caravan/touring park at the rear of the inn.

Rooms 6 en suite (1 fmly) (6 GF) S £55-£70; D £75-£85* **Facilities** FTV tea/coffee Dinner available Direct Dial Cen ht Wi-fi **Conf** Max 15 Class 15 Board 15 **Parking** 35 **Notes** No coaches

The Helyar Arms

★★★★ ⊛ INN

Moor Ln, East Coker BA22 9JR
☎ 01935 862332 📠 01935 864129
e-mail: info@helyar-arms.co.uk
dir: *3m S of Yeovil. Off A30 or A37 into East Coker*

A charming 15th-century inn, serving real food in the heart of a pretty Somerset village. The traditional friendly bar with hand-drawn ales retains many original features while the bedrooms offer well equipped, attractive accommodation and modern facilities.

Rooms 6 en suite (3 fmly) **Facilities** tea/coffee Dinner available Direct Dial Cen ht Wi-fi Skittle alley **Conf** Max 40 Thtr 40 Class 20 Board 30 **Parking** 40

The Manor

★★★★ INN

Hendford BA20 1TG
☎ 01935 423116 📠 01935 706607
e-mail: manor.yeovil@oldenglishinns.co.uk
dir: *A303 onto A3088 to Yeovil. Over River Yeo, 2nd exit at rdbt immediately left into Hendford*

This manor house, dating from 1735, stands in the centre of Yeovil and has the benefit of its own spacious car park. There is a bar and an open-plan lounge area where afternoon tea may be enjoyed. Breakfast and dinner are served in the light and airy conservatory dining area.

Rooms 21 rms (20 en suite) (1 pri facs) 21 annexe en suite (10 GF) S £35-£75; D £55-£125 **Facilities** tea/coffee Dinner available Direct Dial Cen ht Wi-fi **Conf** Max 150 Thtr 120 Class 80 Board 60 **Parking** 60 **Notes** ⊗ Civ Wed 60

The Halfway House Inn Country Lodge

★★★ INN

Ilchester Rd BA22 8RE
☎ 01935 840350 & 849005 📠 01935 849006
e-mail: paul@halfwayhouseinn.com
web: www.halfwayhouseinn.com
dir: *A303 onto A37 Yeovil road at Ilchester, inn 2m on left*

This roadside inn offers comfortable accommodation, which consists of bedrooms in the main house and other contemporary style rooms, each having its own front door, in the annexe. All rooms are bright and well equipped. Meals are available in the cosy restaurant and bar where friendly staff ensure a warm welcome.

Rooms 11 en suite 9 annexe en suite (7 fmly) (9 GF) S £51.95-£64.95; D £62.95-£72.95* **Facilities** STV tea/coffee Dinner available Cen ht Wi-fi Fishing Pool table **Conf** Max 120 Thtr 120 Class 50 Board 40 **Parking** 49 **Notes** LB

At Your Service B&B

★★★ BED AND BREAKFAST

102 West Coker Rd BA20 2JG
☎ 01935 706932 & 07590 960339
e-mail: randall9ee@btinternet.com

Conveniently located on the main through road, this relaxed bed and breakfast makes an ideal base from which to explore the various nearby attractions. Bedrooms come in a range of shapes and sizes including some on the ground floor. Guests have use of the lounge and there is a car park to the rear of the property.

Rooms 4 en suite (4 GF) S £35-£50; D £55-£70* **Facilities** FTV Cen ht **Parking** 4 **Notes** LB Closed 24-27 Dec

The Half Moon Inn

★★★ INN

Main St, Mudford BA21 5TF
☎ 01935 850289 📠 01935 850842
e-mail: enquiries@thehalfmooninn.co.uk
dir: *A303 at Sparkford onto A359 to Yeovil, 3.5m on left*

Situated north of Yeovil, this delightful village inn dates from the 17th century. It has a wealth of character including exposed beams and flagstone floors. The inn proves very popular for its extensive range of wholesome food, and there is a choice of bar and dining areas. Most of the spacious, well-equipped bedrooms are on the ground floor and situated in an adjacent building.

Rooms 14 en suite (4 fmly) (9 GF) S £54.95; D £64.95 (room only)* **Facilities** STV FTV tea/coffee Dinner available Cen ht Wi-fi **Parking** 36 **Notes** ⊗ Closed 25-26 Dec

STAFFORDSHIRE

ABBOTS BROMLEY   Map 10 SK02

Marsh Farm *(SK069261)*

★★★★ FARMHOUSE

WS15 3EJ
☎ 01283 840323
Mrs M K Hollins
e-mail: marshfarm@meads1967.co.uk
dir: *1m N of Abbots Bromley on B5013*

Guests are welcome to walk around the fields at this working farm and watch the activities. The farmhouse has been modernised and bedrooms are carefully furnished and equipped; three rooms are located in a sympathetic barn conversion. Comprehensive breakfasts are served in the spacious cottage-style dining room, which operates as a popular tea room during the summer.

Rooms 5 rms (3 en suite) (1 fmly) (1 GF) S £32-£35; D £60-£65* **Facilities** TVL tea/coffee Cen ht **Parking** 6 **Notes** ⊗ Closed 25-27 Dec 20 acres mixed

ALTON   Map 10 SK04

Chained Oak Farm

★★★★ GUEST ACCOMMODATION

Farley Ln ST10 4BZ
☎ 01538 702104 & 07966 713151
e-mail: cross@barn.fslife.co.uk
dir: *Between Alton & Farley, opp Alton Towers*

Within walking distance of Alton Towers, families are especially well catered for at this attractive property. The house is set in 24 acres of its own woodland with stunning views of the countryside beyond. Bedrooms are spacious with most located in the converted stable block. Breakfast is served in a beautiful solid oak framed garden room.

Rooms 1 en suite 3 annexe en suite (2 fmly) (4 GF) **Facilities** TVL tea/coffee Cen ht **Parking** 10 **Notes** LB ⊗ 🐾

BURTON UPON TRENT   Map 10 SK22

The Delter

★★★★ GUEST ACCOMMODATION

5 Derby Rd DE14 1RU
☎ 01283 535115 📠 01283 845261
e-mail: info@delterhotel.co.uk
web: www.thedelter.co.uk
dir: *A511 rdbt onto A5121 (Derby Rd), 50yds on left*

This relaxing guest accommodation is on the outskirts of Burton upon Trent, close to the famous Bass Museum. Bedrooms are thoughtfully equipped and carefully decorated, and there is a pleasant breakfast room. Expect friendly and attentive service.

Rooms 7 en suite (2 fmly) (2 GF) S £39-£45; D £50-£60* **Facilities** FTV tea/coffee Cen ht Wi-fi **Parking** 8 **Notes** ⊗ Closed Xmas

BURTON UPON TRENT *continued*

Riverside

★★★ INN

Riverside Dr, Branston DE14 3EP
☎ 01283 511234 📠 01283 511441
e-mail: riverside.branston@oldenglishinns.co.uk
web: www.oldenglish.co.uk
dir: From A38 onto A5121 to Burton upon Trent, on right entering Branston

With its quiet residential location and well-kept terraced garden stretching down to the River Trent, this inn has all the ingredients for a relaxing stay. Many of the tables in the Garden Room restaurant have views over the garden. Bedrooms are tastefully furnished and provide a good range of extras.

Rooms 23 en suite (15 GF) **Facilities** TVL tea/coffee Dinner available Direct Dial Cen ht Wi-fi ch fac Golf 18 **Parking** 60 **Notes** Civ Wed 170

| CHEDDLETON | Map 16 SJ95 |

PREMIER COLLECTION

Choir Cottage and Choir House

★★★★★ BED AND BREAKFAST

Ostlers Ln ST13 7HS
☎ 01538 360561 & 07719 617078
e-mail: enquiries@choircottage.co.uk
dir: Off A520 opp Red Lion onto Hollow Ln, pass church & left onto Ostlers Ln, cottage on right at top of hill

Original features complement this carefully decorated 17th-century stone cottage. The bedrooms have lots of thoughtful extras and feature four-poster beds, modern bathrooms and private entrances. Spacious lounge areas are available in an adjacent house, and the attractive dining room is the setting for breakfast.

Rooms 1 en suite 2 annexe en suite (1 fmly) (2 GF) S £60-£75; D £79-£90* **Facilities** tea/coffee Cen ht Wi-fi **Parking** 5 **Notes** LB ⊗ Closed Xmas ⊜

Prospect House

★★★★ GUEST HOUSE

334 Cheadle Rd ST13 7BW
☎ 01782 550639
e-mail: prospect@talk21.com
web: www.prospecthouse.tv
dir: 4m S of Leek on A520

Prospect House was built from local stone in 1838, and is situated between Cheddleton and Wetley Rocks. Bedrooms are in a converted coach house behind the house, and facilities include a traditionally-furnished dining room together with a cosy lounge, and a pleasant garden with a conservatory.

Rooms 4 en suite (1 GF) S £25-£30; D £50-£60* **Facilities** FTV TVL tea/coffee Dinner available Cen ht Wi-fi **Parking** 4 **Notes** LB ⊗

| ECCLESHALL | Map 15 SJ82 |

Slindon House Farm (SJ826324)

★★★★ 🏠 FARMHOUSE

Slindon ST21 6LX
☎ 01782 791237
Mrs H Bonsall
e-mail: helenbonsall@btconnect.com
dir: 2m N of Eccleshall on A519

This large, charming, Victorian farmhouse is fronted by a lovely garden and situated on a dairy, arable and sheep farm in the village of Slindon some two miles from Eccleshall. It has one twin and one double-bedded room, both of which are thoughtfully equipped. Breakfast is served at individual tables in the traditionally-furnished combined breakfast room and lounge.

Rooms 2 rms (1 en suite) (1 pri facs) S £35-£40; D £60* **Facilities** TVL tea/coffee Cen ht Wi-fi **Parking** 4 **Notes** ⊗ Closed 23 Dec-3 Jan ⊜ 175 acres arable/dairy/sheep/beef

| FROGHALL | Map 10 SK04 |

Hermitage Working Farm (SK037497)

★★★ FARMHOUSE

ST10 2HQ
☎ 01538 266515 📠 01538 266155
Mrs W Barlow
e-mail: wilma@hermitagefarm.co.uk
web: www.hermitagefarm.co.uk
dir: A52 onto B5053 in Froghall, farm 0.5m on left at top of hill

Parts of this charming sandstone house date from the 16th century. It is quietly located on an elevated position with panoramic views. There is traditionally-furnished accommodation in the main house as well as a converted barn that offers rooms suitable for families. Handy for visiting Alton Towers.

Rooms 3 en suite 6 annexe en suite (3 fmly) (3 GF) **Facilities** tea/coffee Cen ht Wi-fi Shooting **Parking** 13 **Notes** ⊗ 100 acres beef/sheep/poultry

| HALMER END | Map 15 SJ74 |

The Lodge

★★★★ BED AND BREAKFAST

Red Hall Ln ST7 8AX
☎ 01782 729047 & 07973 776797 📠 01782 729047
e-mail: freelancedobies@aol.com
dir: M6 junct 16 onto A500 signed Stoke, take turn signed Audley Head. At mini-rdbt right onto Nantwich Rd (B5500). After 0.75m left onto Shraleybrook Rd (B5367) then right onto Red Hall Ln

Beside a quiet bridleway, situated next to Bateswood nature reserve bird sanctuary this friendly bed and breakfast is a good touring base for walkers, cyclists or sightseeing. The new double bedrooms are particularly spacious and both bedrooms are en suite. Lovely breakfasts, using free range hen and duck eggs are served in a dining room which overlooks the guest patio.

Rooms 2 en suite S £30-£33; D £60-£65* **Facilities** FTV TVL tea/coffee Cen ht Wi-fi Fishing **Parking** 5 **Notes** ⊗ ⊜

| KINGSLEY | Map 10 SK04 |

The Church Farm (SK013466)

★★★★ FARMHOUSE

Holt Ln ST10 2BA
☎ 01538 754759
Mrs J Clowes
e-mail: thechurchfarm@yahoo.co.uk
dir: Off A52 in Kingsley onto Holt Ln, 150mtrs on right opposite school drive

A warm welcome is assured at this charming farmhouse situated in the village of Kingsley. Thoughtfully equipped bedrooms with stylish furnishing are available in the main house. A hearty breakfast is served on individual tables overlooking the cottage gardens.

Rooms 3 en suite S £30-£35; D £50-£55* **Facilities** FTV TVL TV2B tea/coffee Cen ht Wi-fi garden **Parking** 6 **Notes** ⊗ ⊜ 100 acres dairy/beef

LICHFIELD
Map 10 SK10

PREMIER COLLECTION

St Johns House

★★★★★ GUEST ACCOMMODATION

Saint Johns St WS13 6PB
☎ 01543 252080 📠 01543 254623
e-mail: luxury@stjohnshouse.co.uk
web: www.stjohnshouse.co.uk
dir: In Lichfield City, Saint John St opposite Frog Ln, entrance through gateway on left hand side of building

St Johns House is a Grade II listed Regency house which was once a preparatory school. The present owner Johann Popp has lovingly restored the property and retained authentic features in the main building. The modern bedrooms are situated across the courtyard in a separate stable building; stylishly designed with comfort in mind, they each have bathrooms of the highest quality. The breakfasts use freshly cooked, home-made and locally sourced ingredients that make for a good start to the day.

Rooms 4 annexe en suite (2 GF) **Facilities** FTV tea/coffee Direct Dial Cen ht Wi-fi **Parking** 4 **Notes** ⊗ No Children 12yrs

Netherstowe House

★★★★ 🍽 GUEST HOUSE

Netherstowe Ln WS13 6AY
☎ 01543 254270 📠 01543 254270
e-mail: reservations@netherstowehouse.com
web: www.netherstowehouse.com
dir: A38 onto A5192, 0.3m on right, turn onto Netherstowe Ln. Take 1st left & 1st right down private drive

Located in a residential area a few minutes drive from the city centre, this elegant Georgian house provides a range of bedrooms, some of which are quite spacious. Comprehensive breakfasts are taken in a cosy dining room and a comfortable guest lounge is also available.

Rooms 12 en suite 8 annexe en suite (2 fmly) (5 GF) **Facilities** FTV TVL tea/coffee Dinner available Cen ht Wi-fi 🏊 Gym **Parking** 35 **Notes** ⊗

The Hawthorns

★★★ BED AND BREAKFAST

30 Norwich Close WS13 7SJ
☎ 01543 250151
e-mail: bambrushton@hotmail.com
dir: 1m N of city centre. Off A5192 Eastern Av nr Bristol Street Motors left onto Norwich Close

Located in a residential area on the outskirts of the city, this modern house provides two homely bedrooms with separate side entrance and a modern private shower room. Breakfast is taken in an attractive kitchen/dining room overlooking a pretty rear garden.

Rooms 2 en suite (2 GF) S £36; D £50 **Facilities** FTV tea/coffee Cen ht **Parking** 2 **Notes** ⊗ No Children ⊛

OAKAMOOR
Map 10 SK04

The Beehive Guest House

★★★★ GUEST HOUSE

Churnet View Rd ST10 3AE
☎ 01538 702420 📠 01538 703735
e-mail: thebeehiveoakamoor@btinternet.com
web: www.thebeehiveguesthouse.co.uk
dir: Off B5417 in village N onto Eaves Ln, sharp left onto Churnet View Rd

Standing in the centre of the village and overlooking the river, this spacious detached house offers thoughtfully equipped and comfortable bedrooms. There is also a comfortable lounge-dining room, where substantial breakfasts are served. This guest house is renowned for its hospitality.

Rooms 5 en suite (1 fmly) (1 GF) S £38-£56; D £56-£60* **Facilities** TVL tea/coffee Cen ht Wi-fi **Parking** 6 **Notes** LB ⊗ No Children 5yrs

Crowtrees Farm (SK049459)

★★★★ FARMHOUSE

Eaves Ln ST10 3DY
☎ 01538 702260
Mrs D Bickle
e-mail: dianne@crowtreesfarm.co.uk
web: www.crowtreesfarm.co.uk
dir: Off B5417 in village N onto Eaves Ln, 1m on left

This impeccably maintained 200-year-old farmhouse is convenient for the Potteries, the Peak District and Alton Towers. Bedrooms are comfortable and well equipped. It is still a working farm with splendid views, and has a variety of pets. The friendly owners create a relaxing atmosphere.

Rooms 2 en suite 5 annexe en suite (3 fmly) (4 GF) S £45-£55; D £60-£64 **Facilities** FTV tea/coffee Cen ht **Parking** 8 **Notes** LB ⊗ Closed 25-26 Dec 70 acres sheep

The Laurels Guest House

★★★★ GUEST HOUSE

Star Bank ST10 3BN
☎ 01538 702629 📠 01538 702796
e-mail: bbthelaurels@aol.com
web: www.thelaurels.co.uk
dir: On B5147 from Cheadle, 250yds on right past Cricketers Arms public house in Oakamoor

Situated on the edge of Oakamoor, offering comfortable bedrooms, a bar lounge and a spacious dining room, this friendly guest house is ideally located for families wishing to visit Alton Towers or touring rural Staffordshire and the Potteries.

Rooms 9 en suite (5 fmly) (1 GF) S £35-£60; D £60-£70* **Facilities** FTV TVL tea/coffee Dinner available Cen ht Licensed Wi-fi Pool table **Parking** 9 **Notes** ⊗

Tenement Farm Guest House

★★★★ GUEST ACCOMMODATION

Three Lows, Ribden ST10 3BW
☎ 01538 702333 📠 01538 703603
e-mail: stanleese@aol.com
web: www.tenementfarm.co.uk
dir: 2m NE of Oakamoor. Off A52 onto B5417, 1st drive on left, signed

Families are particularly welcome at this non-smoking former farmhouse which has been renovated to provide high standards of comfort throughout. Popular with visitors to Alton Towers, Tenement Farm offers bedrooms equipped with homely extras. Public areas include a comfortable lounge with an honesty bar, an attractive dining room and a children's play room.

Rooms 8 en suite (6 fmly) (2 GF) **Facilities** TVL tea/coffee Dinner available Cen ht Licensed **Parking** 12 **Notes** ⊗ Closed Nov-Feb

Admirals House

★★★ GUEST HOUSE

Mill Rd ST10 3AG
☎ 01538 702187
e-mail: admiralshouse@btinternet.com
dir: A52 onto B5417. In Oakamoor opposite picnic site

Within the heart of the village a few minutes drive from Alton Towers, this half-timbered house is a popular community meeting point that offers a range of tasty bar meals and real ales. Homely bedrooms are equipped with thoughtful extras and family rooms are also available.

Rooms 6 en suite (4 fmly) (1 GF) **Facilities** tea/coffee Dinner available Cen ht Licensed **Parking** 10 **Notes** ⊗ Closed 23 Dec-3 Jan RS Nov-Mar Restaurant closed Sun & Mon eve

ONNELEY — Map 15 SJ74

The Wheatsheaf Inn
★★★★ INN

Barhill Rd CW3 9QF
☎ 01782 751581 ▤ 01782 751499
e-mail: pub@wheatsheafpub.co.uk
web: www.wheatsheafpub.co.uk
dir: On A525 between Madeley & Woore

A beautifully refurbished 18th-century inn that retains many original features. A wide choice of home-cooked meals are served in the spacious dining areas where there are also cosy alcoves, comfortable lounge seating and real fires. Bedrooms are spacious and well equipped. There is also a function room available.

Rooms 6 en suite 4 annexe en suite (4 GF) **Facilities** FTV tea/coffee Dinner available Cen ht Wi-fi Golf 18 Pool table **Conf** Thtr 60 Class 30 Board 30 **Notes** ✖ Civ Wed 60

RUGELEY — Map 10 SK01

PREMIER COLLECTION

Colton House
★★★★★ ⬥ GUEST HOUSE

Colton WS15 3LL
☎ 01889 578580 ▤ 01889 578580
e-mail: mail@coltonhouse.com
web: www.coltonhouse.com
dir: 1.5m N of Rugeley. Off B5013 into Colton, 0.25m on right

Set in the pretty village of Colton, this elegant early 18th-century house has been restored to retain original character and provide high standards of comfort and facilities. Bedrooms have a wealth of thoughtful extras, there is a spacious and comfortable lounge and a 1.5 acre garden.

Rooms 9 en suite **Facilities** FTV TVL tea/coffee Dinner available Cen ht Licensed Wi-fi **Conf** Max 15 Thtr 15 Class 15 Board 15 **Parking** 15 **Notes** ✖ No Children 12yrs

STAFFORD — Map 10 SJ92

Haywood Park Farm *(SJ991207)*
★★★★ FARMHOUSE

Shugborough ST17 0XA
☎ 01889 882736 ▤ 01889 882736
Mr T Nichols
e-mail: haywood.parkfarm@btopenworld.com
web: www.haywoodparkfarm.co.uk
dir: 4m SE of Stafford off A513. Brown signs to Shugborough, on right 400yds past estate exit

Part of the Shugborough Estate, this historic house commands panoramic views over the fruit, flower and sheep farm. Delightfully furnished bedrooms have a wealth of thoughtful extras. Breakfast is served in the attractive lounge-dining room and features home-grown and local produce.

Rooms 2 en suite **Facilities** STV TVL tea/coffee Cen ht Fishing Riding **Parking** 4 **Notes** ✖ No Children 14yrs ⊛ 120 acres sheep/horse livery/fruit farm

Leonards Croft
★★★ GUEST HOUSE

80 Lichfield Rd ST17 4LP
☎ 01785 223676 ▤ 01785 223676
e-mail: leonardscroft@hotmail.com
dir: A34 from town centre signed Cannock, 0.5m on left

Located south of the town centre, this well-proportioned late Victorian house has been carefully renovated and is convenient for both business and leisure guests. Bedrooms are practically furnished, with two situated on the ground floor. A spacious lounge and complimentary Wi-fi are also provided. The gardens are extensive.

Rooms 9 en suite (3 fmly) (2 GF) S £35-£45; D £50-£65* **Facilities** FTV TVL tea/coffee Dinner available Cen ht Licensed Wi-fi **Parking** 12

Old School
★★★ BED AND BREAKFAST

Newport Rd, Haughton ST18 9JH
☎ 01785 780358 ▤ 01785 780358
e-mail: info@theoldsc.co.uk
dir: A518 W from Stafford, 3m to Haughton, Old School next to church

Located in the heart of Haughton, this Grade II listed former Victorian school has been renovated to provide a range of modern bedrooms equipped with thoughtful extras. The three rooms include a single, a double and a twin. All three have colour TV. Breakfast is served at a family table in a cosy lounge-dining room.

Rooms 3 rms (3 GF) S £25; D £50 **Facilities** FTV tea/coffee Cen ht Wi-fi **Parking** 3 **Notes** No Children 14yrs ⊛

STONE — Map 10 SJ93

Field House
★★★ BED AND BREAKFAST

59 Stafford Rd ST15 0HE
☎ 01785 605712 ▤ 01785 605712
e-mail: fieldhouse@ntlworld.com
dir: A34 NW into town centre, right onto Stafford Rd, opp Walton Grange

This family home stands in secluded, pretty gardens close to the town centre. The Georgian house has traditionally furnished bedrooms, some with family pieces. Guests breakfast together in the lounge-dining room, and hospitality is very welcoming.

Rooms 2 rms (1 en suite) (1 pri facs) **Facilities** STV FTV TVL tea/coffee Cen ht Art tuition on request **Parking** 4 **Notes** ✖ ⊛

TAMWORTH — Map 10 SK20

PREMIER COLLECTION

Oak Tree Farm
★★★★★ GUEST ACCOMMODATION

Hints Rd, Hopwas B78 3AA
☎ 01827 56807 ▤ 01827 67271
e-mail: oaktreefarm1@aol.com
web: www.oaktreefarmhotel.co.uk
dir: 2m NW of Tamworth. Off A51 in Hopwas

A warm welcome is assured at this sympathetically restored farmhouse, located in peaceful rural surroundings yet only a short drive from the NEC. Spacious bedrooms are filled with homely extras. The elegant dining room, adorned with Oriental artefacts, is the setting for memorable breakfasts. A small conference room is available.

Rooms 4 en suite 10 annexe en suite (4 fmly) (7 GF) S £35-£70; D £50-£85 **Facilities** FTV TVL tea/coffee Cen ht Wi-fi ch fac ⬧ Fishing Sauna **Conf** Max 15 Thtr 15 Class 9 Board 15 **Parking** 20

Globe Inn

★★★ INN

Lower Gungate B79 7AW
☎ 01827 60455 📠 01827 63575
e-mail: info@theglobetamworth.com

Located in the centre of Tamworth, this popular inn provides well-equipped and pleasantly decorated accommodation. The public areas include a spacious lounge bar and a relaxed dining area where a varied selection of dishes is available. There is also a function room and adjacent parking.

Rooms 18 en suite (2 fmly) (18 smoking) S £38; D £55*
Facilities STV tea/coffee Dinner available Cen ht Wi-fi
Conf Thtr 90 Class 90 Board 90 **Parking** 30 **Notes** ⊗
Closed 25 Dec

UTTOXETER — Map 10 SK03

High View Cottage

★★★★ GUEST ACCOMMODATION

Toothill Rd ST14 8JU
☎ 01889 568183 & 07980 041670
e-mail: info@highviewcottage.co.uk
dir: 1m S of town centre. Off B5017 Highwood Rd onto Toothill Rd

Located on the edge of Uttoxeter and close to the racecourse, High View Cottage offers comfortable, well-equipped accommodation and a friendly atmosphere. Bedrooms are equipped with lots of thoughtful extras, and hearty breakfasts are served in the attractive Garden Room which overlooks the courtyard.

Rooms 5 en suite (2 fmly) (5 GF) S £25-£60; D £50-£80*
Facilities FTV tea/coffee Cen ht Wi-fi **Conf** Max 8 Board 8
Parking 10 **Notes** ⊗

WOODSEAVES — Map 15 SJ72

Tunstall Hall Farm (SJ771273)

★★★★ FARMHOUSE

ST20 0NH
☎ 01785 280232 📠 01785 280232
Mrs Cooke
e-mail: isabel.cooke@btinternet.com
dir: 2m NW of Woodseaves. A41onto A519, 1st left to Shebdon, in 3m right towards Woodseaves. Bishops Offley 1m on right

Located in a quiet hamlet, this impressive renovated farmhouse dates from the early 18th century and retains original exposed beams and open fires. The thoughtfully furnished bedrooms have smart modern shower rooms en suite, and breakfast is served in the attractive conservatory.

Rooms 2 en suite (1 fmly) **Facilities** TVL tea/coffee Cen ht
Wi-fi **Parking** 6 **Notes** ⊗ 📶 280 acres mixed/dairy

SUFFOLK

ALDEBURGH — Map 13 TM45

The Toll House

★★★★ GUEST HOUSE

50 Victoria Rd IP15 5EJ
☎ 01728 453239
e-mail: mail@tollhousealdeburgh.com
web: www.tollhousealdeburgh.com
dir: B1094 into town until rdbt, on right

Expect a warm welcome at this delightful red brick property situated just a short walk from the seafront and town centre. Bedrooms are tastefully furnished, have co-ordinated fabrics and many thoughtful touches. Breakfast is served at individual tables in the smart dining room, which overlooks the garden.

Rooms 7 en suite (3 GF) S £60-£65; D £70-£75*
Facilities tea/coffee Cen ht **Parking** 6 **Notes** ⊗

The Mill Inn

★★★ INN

Market Cross Place IP15 5BJ
☎ 01728 452563 📠 01728 452563
e-mail: peeldennisp@aol.com

A traditional seafront inn in a bustling coastal town. Public areas include a lounge bar, a restaurant and a public bar frequented by local fishermen and the lifeboat crew. Bedrooms are simply decorated and well equipped; some rooms have lovely sea views.

Rooms 4 rms (4 pri facs) **Facilities** tea/coffee Dinner available Cen ht ⛳ Golf 18

ALDRINGHAM — Map 13 TM46

The Follies Cottage

★★★ BED AND BREAKFAST

IP16 4LU
☎ 01728 830856 & 07757 133412
e-mail: sueandfred@hotmail.com
dir: B1353 Thorpeness Rd, 0.6m from x-rds with B1122, turn left onto track signed B&B, 0.5m

A delightful detached cottage set amidst open countryside close to the RSPB Nature Reserve just a short drive from Aldeburgh. The property is located down a private track and is adjacent to Thorpeness Golf Course. The bedrooms are bright and airy, and have lovely views of the countryside. Breakfast is served at a large table in the dining room.

Rooms 2 en suite (1 fmly) **Facilities** tea/coffee Cen ht
Parking 3 **Notes** ⊛

BURY ST EDMUNDS — Map 13 TL86

PREMIER COLLECTION

Clarice House

★★★★★ GUEST ACCOMMODATION

Horringer Court, Horringer Rd IP29 5PH
☎ 01284 705550 📠 01284 716120
e-mail: bury@claricehouse.co.uk
web: www.claricehouse.co.uk
dir: 1m SW from town centre on A143 towards Horringer

A large country property set amidst pretty landscaped grounds a short drive from the historic town centre. The spacious, well-equipped bedrooms have co-ordinated fabrics and many thoughtful touches. Public rooms have a wealth of charm and include a smart lounge bar, an intimate restaurant, a further lounge and a conservatory. The property also has superb leisure facilities.

Rooms 13 en suite S £70-£90; D £100-£160
Facilities FTV tea/coffee Dinner available Direct Dial
Cen ht Lift Licensed ⓢ Sauna Solarium Gym Spa &
Beauty facilities **Conf** Max 50 Thtr 50 Class 50 Board
50 **Parking** 85 **Notes** LB ⊗ No Children 5yrs Closed
24-26 Dec & 31 Dec-1 Jan Civ Wed 70

BURY ST EDMUNDS *continued*

The Abbey

★★★★ GUEST ACCOMMODATION

35 Southgate St IP33 2AZ
☎ 01284 762020 📠 01284 330279
e-mail: reception@abbeyhotel.co.uk
dir: *A14 junct 44, A1302 to town centre, onto Southgate St, premises 400yds*

The Abbey is well placed for visiting the historic town centre. The property is split between several historic buildings, the main core dating from the 15th century. The public rooms in the Tudor inn section feature a comfortable lounge and an informal dining area. Bedrooms vary in size and style, but all are comfortably furnished and well equipped.

Rooms 12 en suite (1 fmly) (2 GF) **Facilities** FTV tea/coffee Cen ht Wi-fi **Parking** 12 **Notes** ⊗ No Children 3yrs

The Black Boy

★★★★ INN

69 Guildhall St IP33 1QD
☎ 01284 752723
dir: *Off A14 to town centre*

The Black Boy is a popular inn situated in the centre of this historic town. The spacious bedrooms have co-ordinated fabrics, pine furniture and many thoughtful touches. Public areas feature a large open-plan bar with a good selection of ales and a range of bar snacks are also available.

Rooms 5 en suite S £35-£40; D £60-£70* **Facilities** tea/coffee Dinner available Cen ht Wi-fi Pool table **Parking** 6 **Notes** ⊗ No coaches

The Chantry

★★★★ GUEST ACCOMMODATION

8 Sparhawk St IP33 1RY
☎ 01284 767427 📠 01284 760946
e-mail: chantryhotel1@aol.com
dir: *From cathedral S onto Crown St, left onto Sparhawk St*

Expect a warm welcome at this attractive Georgian property, just a short walk from the town centre. The individually decorated bedrooms are furnished with well-chosen pieces and have many thoughtful touches. Dinner and breakfast are served in the smart restaurant, and there is a cosy lounge-bar.

Rooms 11 en suite 3 annexe en suite (1 fmly) (1 GF) **Facilities** FTV tea/coffee Dinner available Direct Dial Cen ht Licensed Wi-fi **Parking** 16

83 Whiting Street

★★★★ BED AND BREAKFAST

83 Whiting St IP33 1NX
☎ 01284 704153
e-mail: gordon.wagstaff@btinternet.com
dir: *In town centre*

An attractive three-storey terrace property convenient for exploring this historic town. The spacious, individually decorated bedrooms are furnished with pine and equipped with modern facilities. Breakfast is served in the beamed dining room that features an open fireplace and a wall painting dating from 1530.

Rooms 4 en suite (1 fmly) S £45; D £70* **Facilities** tea/coffee Cen ht Wi-fi **Notes** ⊗ ⊚

The Six Bells at Bardwell

★★★★ INN

The Green, Bardwell IP31 1AW
☎ 01359 250820 📠 01359 250820
e-mail: sixbellsbardwell@aol.com
web: www.sixbellsbardwell.co.uk
dir: *8m NE, off A143 on edge of village. Follow brown signs from A143*

This 16th-century inn lies in the peaceful village of Bardwell. The bedrooms are in a converted stable block next to the main building, and are furnished in a country style and thoughtfully equipped. Public rooms have original character and provide a choice of areas in which to relax.

Rooms 10 annexe en suite (1 fmly) (10 GF) **Facilities** FTV tea/coffee Dinner available Cen ht **Parking** 50 **Notes** Closed 25 Dec-3 Jan

The Three Kings

★★★★ INN

Hengrave Rd, Fornham All Saints IP28 6LA
☎ 01284 766979
e-mail: thethreekings@keme.co.uk
web: www.the-three-kings.com
dir: *A14 junct 42, B1106 to Fornham, left onto B1101, establishment on left*

Attractive inn situated in the pleasant village of Fornham All Saints. The bedrooms are in a building adjacent to the main property; each one is smartly furnished and thoughtfully equipped. Public rooms feature a smart lounge bar, a conservatory and a comfortable restaurant.

Rooms 9 annexe en suite (2 fmly) (6 GF) **Facilities** FTV tea/coffee Dinner available Direct Dial Cen ht Wi-fi Golf **Conf** Max 45 Thtr 12 Class 24 Board 24 **Parking** 28 **Notes** ⊗

Dog & Partridge, The Old Brewers House

★★★ 🍺 INN

29 Crown St IP33 1QU
☎ 01284 764792
e-mail: 1065@greeneking.co.uk
web: www.oldenglish.co.uk
dir: *In town centre. Off A134 Parkway onto Westgate St & left onto Crown St*

Charming inn situated just a short walk from the town centre. Public rooms include a smart conservatory, a lounge bar, a small dining area and a smartly decked terrace to the rear of the property for alfresco dining. Bedrooms are pleasantly decorated, have co-ordinated fabrics, natural wood furniture and many thoughtful touches.

Rooms 9 en suite (2 fmly) (3 GF) **Facilities** STV tea/coffee Dinner available Direct Dial **Parking** 11 **Notes** ⊗

6 Orchard Street

★★★ BED AND BREAKFAST

IP33 1EH
☎ 01284 750191 & 07946 590265
e-mail: mariellascarlett@me.com
dir: *In town centre near St John's Church on one-way system; Northgate St turn right onto Looms Ln, 2nd right onto Well St, straight on onto Orchard St*

Expect a warm welcome from the caring hosts at this terrace property situated just a short walk from the town centre. The pleasant bedrooms are comfortably appointed and have a good range of useful extras. Breakfast is served at a large communal table in the cosy dining room.

Rooms 2 rms (1 en suite) (1 pri facs) S £30-£35; D £45-£55 **Facilities** FTV tea/coffee Cen ht Wi-fi **Notes** No Children 6yrs ⊚

Hamilton House

★★★ BED AND BREAKFAST

4 Nelson Rd IP33 3AG
☎ 01284 703022 & 07787 146553
e-mail: hamiltonhouse@hotmail.co.uk
dir: *A14 junct 42, follow A1302 across rdbt, then 1st right*

A warm welcome awaits at this relaxing Edwardian villa, which is situated in a quiet side road just a short walk from the town centre. The bedrooms are brightly decorated with co-ordinated fabrics and have a good range of facilities. Breakfast is served at a large communal table in the dining room.

Rooms 4 rms (2 en suite) (1 fmly) S £27-£35; D £50-£60* **Facilities** FTV tea/coffee Cen ht Wi-fi **Notes** ⊗ ⊚

Save on B&Bs and Hotels. Book at **theAA.com/hotel**

SUFFOLK 281 **ENGLAND**

St Andrews Lodge

★★★ BED AND BREAKFAST

30 Saint Andrews Street North IP33 1SZ
☎ 01284 756733
e-mail: standrewslodge@hotmail.com
dir: A14 junct 43, A134 towards town centre, left onto
Saint Andrews St North, Lodge on right

This delightful property is situated close to the A14 and
the town centre. The well-equipped modern bedrooms are
on the ground floor of a separate purpose-built building
to the rear of the house. Breakfast is served at individual
tables in the smart dining room, which overlooks the neat
courtyard.

Rooms 3 annexe en suite (3 GF) **Facilities** FTV tea/coffee
Cen ht **Parking** 3

Dunston Guest House

★★★ A GUEST HOUSE

8 Springfield Rd IP33 3AN
☎ 01284 767981   01284 764574
e-mail: anndakin@btconnect.com
web: www.dunstonguesthouse.co.uk
dir: A14 from Cambridge, 1st slip road onto A1302, in
1.5m after pedestrian crossing & Falcon pub left onto
Springfield Rd, further down on left

Rooms 11 rms (7 en suite) (4 pri facs) 6 annexe rms 2
annexe en suite (5 fmly) (4 GF) **Facilities** TVL tea/coffee
Cen ht Wi-fi **Parking** 10 **Notes** ⊗ ⊛

CAVENDISH   Map 13 TL84

The George

★★★★ ◉ RESTAURANT WITH ROOMS

The Green CO10 8BA
☎ 01787 280248
e-mail: thegeorgecavendish@gmail.com
web: www.thecavendishgeorge.co.uk
dir: A1092 into Cavendish, The George next to village
green

The George is situated in the heart of the pretty village of
Cavendish and has four very stylish bedrooms. The front-
facing rooms overlook the village; the comfortable,
spacious bedrooms retain many of their original features.
The award-winning restaurant is very well appointed and
dinner should not be missed. Guests are guaranteed to
receive a warm welcome, attentive friendly service and
great food.

Rooms 4 en suite (1 fmly) S £50; D £65-£85*
Facilities FTV tea/coffee Dinner available Cen ht Wi-fi
Notes ⊗ Closed 25 Dec & 1 Jan

CLARE   Map 13 TL74

Ship Stores

★★★★ GUEST ACCOMMODATION

22 Callis St CO10 8PX
☎ 01787 277834   01787 277183
e-mail: shipclare@aol.com
dir: A1092 to Clare, onto B1063, past church 100yds
on right

A charming property situated in the heart of an historic
market town. Bedrooms are split between the main house
and a converted stable block; each room is furnished in a
country style with bright, co-ordinated soft furnishings
and many thoughtful touches. Public areas include a
lounge with comfy sofas, and a contemporary breakfast
room with a stripped pine floor.

Rooms 4 en suite 2 annexe en suite (1 fmly) (3 GF) S
£45-£65; D £65-£70 **Facilities** tea/coffee Cen ht Wi-fi
Parking 3 **Notes** LB ⊗

ELMSWELL   Map 13 TL96

Kiln Farm Guest House

★★★★ GUEST HOUSE

Kiln Ln IP30 9QR
☎ 01359 240442
e-mail: davejankilnfarm@btinternet.com
dir: Exit A14 junct 47 for A1088. Entrance to Kiln Ln off
eastbound slip road

A delightful Victorian farmhouse situated in a peaceful
rural location amid three acres of landscaped grounds.
The bedrooms are housed in converted farm buildings;
each one is smartly decorated and furnished in country
style. Breakfast is served in the smart conservatory and
there is also a cosy lounge and bar area. David Copeman
was a finalist in this year's Friendliest Landlady of the
Year award (2011-12).

Rooms 2 en suite 6 annexe en suite (2 fmly) (6 GF) S
£35-£40; D £70-£80 **Facilities** FTV TVL tea/coffee Dinner
available Cen ht Licensed Wi-fi **Parking** 20

EYE   Map 13 TM17

The White Horse Inn

★★★★ INN

Stoke Ash IP23 7ET
☎ 01379 678222   01379 678800
e-mail: mail@whitehorse-suffolk.co.uk
web: www.whitehorse-suffolk.co.uk
dir: On A140 halfway between Ipswich & Norwich

A 17th-century coaching inn situated in the village of
Stoke Ash. Bedrooms are located in an annexe adjacent to
the main building; each one is smartly decorated in
pastel shades, tastefully furnished with co-ordinated
fabrics, and thoughtfully equipped. An interesting choice
of dishes is served in the restaurant, which features
exposed beams and inglenook fireplaces.

Rooms 11 annexe en suite (1 fmly) (9 GF) **Facilities** FTV
tea/coffee Dinner available Direct Dial Cen ht Wi-fi
Conf Max 50 Thtr 50 Class 50 **Parking** 60 **Notes** LB ⊗

FRAMLINGHAM   Map 13 TM26

Church Farm (TM605267)

★★★★ FARMHOUSE

Church Rd, Kettleburgh IP13 7LF
☎ 01728 723532
Mrs A Bater
e-mail: jbater@suffolkonline.net
dir: Off A12 to Wickham Market, signs to Easton Farm Park & Kettleburgh 1.25m, house behind church

A charming 300-year-old farmhouse situated close to the village church amid superb grounds with a duck pond, mature shrubs and sweeping lawns. The converted property retains exposed beams and open fireplaces. Bedrooms are pleasantly decorated and equipped with useful extras, and ground-floor rooms are available.

Rooms 2 rms (1 en suite) (1 pri facs) 2 annexe rms 1 annexe en suite (1 pri facs) (3 GF) **Facilities** TVL tea/coffee Dinner available Cen ht Wi-fi Fishing **Parking** 10 **Notes** 🐾 70 acres mixed

Woodlands Farm (TM269709)

★★★★ FARMHOUSE

Brundish IP13 8BP
☎ 01379 384444
Mrs J Graham
e-mail: jillatwoodlands@aol.com
dir: 6m N of Framlingham. Off A1120 onto B1116 N, 4th left, 0.5m left onto no-through road

Quietly located north of the town, this charming house has a wealth of character, including original exposed beams and inglenook fireplaces in the sitting room and the elegant dining room. The pleasant bedrooms are carefully decorated and thoughtfully equipped.

Rooms 3 en suite S £30-£35; D £55-£60* **Facilities** TVL tea/coffee Cen ht Wi-fi **Parking** 6 **Notes** 🚫 No Children 10yrs Closed 24 Dec-2 Jan 🐾 4 acres smallholding

HOLTON   Map 13 TM47

PREMIER COLLECTION

Valley Farm

★★★★★ BED AND BREAKFAST

Bungay Rd IP19 8LY
☎ 01986 874521 & 07971 669270
e-mail: mail@valleyfarmholton.co.uk
web: www.valleyfarmholton.co.uk
dir: A144 onto B1123 to Holton, left at fork in village, left at school, 500yds on left

Expect a warm welcome from the caring hosts at this charming red-brick farmhouse situated in a peaceful rural location a short drive from Halesworth. The individually decorated bedrooms are tastefully appointed with co-ordinated soft furnishings and many thoughtful touches. Breakfast, which features locally sourced and home-grown produce, is served at a large communal table in the smartly appointed dining room. The property has lovely landscaped grounds, a summer house, and an indoor heated swimming pool.

Rooms 2 en suite (1 fmly) S £70-£90; D £70-£90* **Facilities** FTV tea/coffee Cen ht Wi-fi 🕭 🏊 Boules piste **Parking** 15 **Notes** LB 🚫 🐾

INGHAM   Map 13 TL87

The Cadogan Arms

★★★★ ☻ INN

The Street IP31 1NG
☎ 01284 728443
e-mail: info@thecadogan.co.uk
dir: 4m from Bury St Edmunds, follow A134 towards Thetford

The Cadogan Arms is a popular inn situated four miles from the centre of town. The smartly appointed bedrooms have been thoughtfully designed and have many useful touches such as, flat-screen TVs, Freeview and CD/radios. The open-plan public rooms are contemporary in style; they include a range of seating areas with leather sofas and a smart restaurant.

Rooms 7 en suite S £70; D £90* **Facilities** FTV tea/coffee Dinner available Cen ht Wi-fi **Parking** 30 **Notes** LB

IPSWICH   Map 13 TM14

Evelyn B&B

★★★ BED AND BREAKFAST

London Rd IP2 0SS
☎ 01473 604769 & 07850 415544
e-mail: cliffb@btinternet.com
dir: A1214 into Ipswich, 0.5m pass Tesco, 500yds into bus lane, Evelyn on left

This comfortable establishment is located just outside Ipswich town centre and within easy reach of the main arterial roads. The husband and wife team extends a warm welcome. Bedrooms are well-appointed and offer a good range of amenities. A home-cooked breakfast is served in the cosy breakfast room.

Rooms 2 en suite (2 GF) S £40; D £60* **Facilities** FTV tea/coffee Cen ht **Parking** 6 **Notes** 🚫 No Children 12yrs 🐾

LAVENHAM　　　　　　Map 13 TL94

PREMIER COLLECTION

Lavenham Great House 'Restaurant With Rooms'

☆☆☆☆☆ @@ ▤ RESTAURANT WITH ROOMS

Market Place CO10 9QZ
☎ 01787 247431 ▤ 01787 248007
e-mail: info@greathouse.co.uk
web: www.greathouse.co.uk
dir: Off A1141 onto Market Ln, behind cross on Market Place

The 18th-century frontage on Market Place conceals a 15th-century timber-framed building that is now a restaurant with rooms. The Great House remains a pocket of France offering high-quality rural cuisine served by French staff. The spacious bedrooms are individually decorated and thoughtfully equipped with many useful extras; some rooms have a separate lounge area.

Rooms 5 en suite (1 fmly) S £95-£225; D £95-£225 (room only)* **Facilities** FTV tea/coffee Dinner available Direct Dial Cen ht Wi-fi Free bicycle use for guests **Notes** LB Closed Jan RS Sun eve & Mon Restaurant closed No coaches

PREMIER COLLECTION

Lavenham Old Rectory

☆☆☆☆☆ ▤ BED AND BREAKFAST

Church St CO10 9SA
☎ 01787 247572
e-mail: susie_dwright@hotmail.co.uk

After four years of restoration work, the Old Rectory has been reborn and now offers sumptuous en suite accommodation where classic style meets modern technology to suit a discerning clientele. The two suites are decorated in understated contemporary style, while the other room has a more traditional, elegant feel. Three acres of garden include a classical formal pond, herbaceous borders, a rose garden with an arched walk, and a thatched summer house. The Old Rectory was the winner of last year's AA Guest Accommodation of the Year for England award.

Rooms 3 en suite S £165-£335; D £165-£335* **Facilities** FTV Cen ht Wi-fi **Parking** 10 **Notes** LB ⊗ No Children Closed 24-26 Dec

PREMIER COLLECTION

Lavenham Priory

☆☆☆☆☆ ▤ BED AND BREAKFAST

Water St CO10 9RW
☎ 01787 247404 ▤ 01787 248472
e-mail: mail@lavenhampriory.co.uk
web: www.lavenhampriory.co.uk
dir: A1141 to Lavenham, turn by side of Swan onto Water St & right after 50yds onto private drive

This superb Grade I listed building, dating from the 15th century, once belonged to Benedictine monks and has been lovingly restored to maintain its original character. Individually decorated bedrooms are very spacious; each is beautifully furnished and thoughtfully equipped. Breakfast is served in the spectacular dining room or in the sheltered courtyard herb garden. Guests also have use of the Great Hall, with inglenook fireplace, and an adjoining lounge.

Rooms 6 en suite (1 fmly) S £82-£182; D £110-£182* **Facilities** FTV TVL tea/coffee Cen ht Licensed Wi-fi **Parking** 11 **Notes** No Children 10yrs Closed 21 Dec-2 Jan

The Angel

★★★★ @ RESTAURANT WITH ROOMS

Market Place CO10 9QZ
☎ 01787 247388 ▤ 01787 248344
e-mail: angel@maypolehotels.com
web: www.maypolehotels.com
dir: From A14 follow Bury E & Sudbury signs onto A143. In 4m take A1141 to Lavenham. Establishment off High Street

A delightful 15th-century property overlooking the market place in the heart of this historic medieval town. The Angel is well known for its cuisine and offers an imaginative menu based on fresh ingredients. Public rooms include a residents' lounge and open-plan bar/dining area. Bedrooms are tastefully furnished, attractively decorated and thoughtfully equipped.

Rooms 8 en suite (1 fmly) (1 GF) **Facilities** FTV TVL tea/coffee Dinner available Direct Dial Cen ht Wi-fi **Parking** 5 **Notes** No coaches

LEISTON　　　　　　Map 13 TM46

Field End

☆☆☆☆ GUEST HOUSE

1 Kings Rd IP16 4DA
☎ 01728 833527 ▤ 01728 833527
e-mail: herbert@herbertwood.wanadoo.co.uk
web: www.fieldendbedandbreakfast.co.uk
dir: In town centre off B1122

This Edwardian house has been appointed to a high standard and is impeccably maintained by the present owners. Bedrooms have co-ordinated soft furnishings and many thoughtful touches. Breakfast is served in an attractive dining room, which has a large sofa and a range of puzzles and games.

Rooms 5 rms (2 en suite) (1 pri facs) (1 fmly) (1 GF) S £35; D £65* **Facilities** TVL tea/coffee Cen ht **Parking** 5 **Notes** ⊗ No Children 6mths ☺

LOWESTOFT　　　　　Map 13 TM59

Abbe Guest House

★★★★ GUEST ACCOMMODATION

322 London Road South NR33 0BG
☎ 01502 581083
e-mail: abbehouse@btconnect.com
dir: On A12, 1.5m from the Pakefield Water Tower rdbt, 50yds past Rectory Rd

Expect a warm welcome from the caring hosts at this charming property situated just a short walk from the seafront and town centre. Bedrooms are pleasantly decorated, have co-ordinated soft furnishings and benefit from many thoughtful touches. Breakfast is served in the smart dining room, and guests have the use of a cosy lounge bar with plush leather sofas.

Rooms 4 rms (3 en suite) (1 pri facs) (1 fmly) **Facilities** FTV TVL tea/coffee Dinner available Cen ht Licensed Wi-fi **Notes** ⊗ No Children 5yrs Closed 21 Dec-6 Jan

Edingworth

★★★★ GUEST HOUSE

395 London Road South NR33 0BJ
☎ 01502 572051 ▤ 01502 572051
e-mail: enquiries@edingworth.co.uk
web: www.edingworth.co.uk
dir: 600yds on left after start of Pakefield/Kirkley one-way system, N towards town centre

A friendly, family-run guest house situated within easy walking distance of the town centre and seafront. The spacious bedrooms are pleasantly decorated and thoughtfully equipped. Breakfast is served in the smart dining room.

Rooms 6 rms (6 pri facs) (5 fmly) (1 GF) S £30-£32; D £56-£58 **Facilities** FTV tea/coffee Dinner available Cen ht Wi-fi **Parking** 3 **Notes** LB ⊗ Closed 24-26 Dec ☺

LOWESTOFT *continued*

Katherine Guest House

★★★★ 💭 GUEST ACCOMMODATION

49 Kirkley Cliff Rd NR33 0DF
☎ 01502 567858   📠 01502 581341
e-mail: beauthaicuisine@aol.com
web: www.beauthaikatherine.co.uk
dir: *On A12 seafront road next to Kensington Garden*

This large Victorian property lies opposite the beach in the quiet part of town. The spacious public rooms include a smart lounge bar with leather sofas and an intimate restaurant serving authentic Thai cuisine. The pleasant bedrooms have co-ordinated fabrics and many thoughtful touches.

Rooms 10 en suite (5 fmly) **Facilities** tea/coffee Dinner available Direct Dial Cen ht Licensed Wi-fi **Parking** 4

Somerton House

★★★★ GUEST ACCOMMODATION

7 Kirkley Cliff NR33 0BY
☎ 01502 565665
e-mail: pippin.somerton@btinternet.com
dir: *On old A12, 100yds from Claremont Pier*

Somerton House is a Grade II Victorian terrace situated in a peaceful area of town overlooking the sea. Bedrooms are smartly furnished in a period style and have many thoughtful touches; some rooms have four poster or half-tester beds. Breakfast is served in the smart dining room and guests have the use of a cosy lounge.

Rooms 7 rms (4 en suite) (2 pri facs) (1 fmly) (1 GF) S £36-£46; D £57-£62* **Facilities** FTV TVL tea/coffee Cen ht Licensed Wi-fi **Notes** LB Closed 25-26 Dec

Wavecrest Guest House

★★★★ GUEST HOUSE

31 Marine Pde NR33 0QN
☎ 01502 561268
e-mail: wavecrestguesthouse@googlemail.com
dir: *On seafront just S of Lowestoft Bridge*

This Victorian terrace house is situated on the seafront, overlooking the award-winning beach and within easy walking distance of the town centre. The bedrooms are smartly decorated with co-ordinated soft furnishings and equipped with modern facilities. Public areas include an elegant dining room where breakfast is served at individual tables.

Rooms 5 rms (4 en suite) (1 pri facs) (1 fmly) S £29-£45; D £45-£60* **Facilities** FTV tea/coffee Cen ht Wi-fi cycles available **Notes** ⊗ Closed 24-31 Dec

Coventry House

★★★ GUEST HOUSE

8 Kirkley Cliff NR33 0BY
☎ 01502 573865
dir: *On seafront*

A well presented Victorian property situated on the seafront overlooking the beach with superb views of the sea. Breakfast is served at individual tables in the spacious dining room, which is situated on the lower ground floor. The bedrooms have co-ordinated soft furnishings and modern facilities such as Wi-fi and flat screen TVs.

Rooms 7 rms (5 en suite) (2 pri facs) (3 fmly) (1 GF) **Facilities** FTV tea/coffee Cen ht Wi-fi **Parking** 4 **Notes** Closed 22-28 Dec ⊛

Highbury House

★★★ GUEST HOUSE

397 London Road South NR33 0BJ
☎ 01502 589064   & 07760 227245
e-mail: highbury.house@hotmail.co.uk
dir: *On A12 follow signs to Lowestoft then follow South Beach signs, then London Rd South. On left after St Peters Rd*

A friendly, family-run guest house situated just a short walk from the town centre and seafront. Bedrooms are generally quite spacious; each one is pleasantly decorated and equipped with a good range of useful facilities. Breakfast and dinner are served at individual tables in the dining room.

Rooms 4 en suite (2 fmly) S £29-£30; D £50-£54* **Facilities** FTV tea/coffee Dinner available Cen ht **Parking** 3 **Notes** ⊗ ⊛

Seavilla

★★★ GUEST ACCOMMODATION

43 Kirkley Cliff Rd NR33 0DF
☎ 01502 574657
dir: *A12 into town, right at South Beach, 300yds past Claremont Pier*

Expect a warm welcome at the Seavilla which is situated on the southern side of town overlooking the beach. The pleasant bedrooms are thoughtfully equipped and many have superb sea views. Breakfast is served at individual tables in the attractive dining room and guests have the use of a cosy lounge.

Rooms 9 rms (5 en suite) S £20-£40; D £50-£60 **Facilities** FTV TVL tea/coffee Cen ht **Parking** **Notes** LB ⊗

MELTON Map 13 TM25

Jarvis Cottage

★★★★ BED AND BREAKFAST

Foxburrow Farm Ln IP12 1NA
☎ 01394 380848   & 07899 843426
e-mail: jarviscottage@dsl.pipex.com
web: www.jarviscottage.co.uk
dir: *A12 signed Woodbridge, at rdbt left towards Lowestoft. Over next 2 rdbts, stay on A12. Turn right onto Saddlemakers Ln, opposite Bredfield turn. Next left, cottage 1st house on left*

A lovely detached property surrounded by Suffolk Wildlife Trust land, and situated down a private country lane on the outskirts of Woodbridge. The guest bedroom is situated in a converted building adjacent to the main house, and has light wood furniture, bright co-ordinated fabrics and many thoughtful touches. Breakfast is served at a large table in the smart conservatory dining room.

Rooms 1 annexe en suite (1 GF) D £75* **Facilities** STV FTV tea/coffee Cen ht **Parking** 2 **Notes** ⊗ No Children Closed Dec-14 Jan ⊛

MENDHAM Map 13 TM28

Weston House Farm *(TM292828)*

★★★★ FARMHOUSE

IP20 0PB
☎ 01986 782206
Mrs J E Holden
e-mail: holden@farmline.com
web: www.westonhousefarm.co.uk
dir: *Off A143 or B1123 signed Mendham, signs from village centre*

Well maintained Grade II listed, 17th-century farmhouse set in an acre of pleasant gardens in the heart of the Waveney Valley. The individually decorated bedrooms are thoughtfully furnished, well-equipped and generally quite spacious. Breakfast is served in the smart dining room which overlooks the garden.

Rooms 3 en suite (1 GF) S £38-£46; D £56-£70* **Facilities** TVL tea/coffee Cen ht Wi-fi **Parking** 6 **Notes** No Children 10yrs Closed Dec-Feb ⊛ 600 acres mixed

NEWMARKET Map 12 TL66

The Garden Lodge

★★★★ BED AND BREAKFAST

11 Vicarage Ln, Woodditton CB8 9SG
☎ 01638 731116
e-mail: swedishgardenlodge@hotmail.com
web: www.gardenlodge.net
dir: 3m S of Newmarket in Woodditton

A warm welcome is assured in this home-from-home, not far from the famous racecourse. The accommodation, in quality chalets, is very well equipped and features a wealth of thoughtful extras. Freshly prepared home-cooked breakfasts are served in an elegant dining room in the main house.

Rooms 3 en suite (3 GF) S £35-£40; D £60-£70* **Facilities** FTV tea/coffee Dinner available Cen ht Wi-fi **Parking** 6 **Notes** ◉

SAXMUNDHAM Map 13 TM36

Sandpit Farm

★★★★ BED AND BREAKFAST

Bruisyard IP17 2EB
☎ 01728 663445
e-mail: smarshall@aldevalleybreaks.co.uk
web: www.aldevalleybreaks.co.uk
dir: 4m W of Saxmundham. A1120 onto B1120, 1st left for Bruisyard, house 1.5m on left

Sandpit Farm is a delightful Grade II listed farmhouse set in 20 acres of grounds. Bedrooms have many thoughtful touches and lovely country views, and there are two cosy lounges to enjoy. Breakfast features quality local produce and freshly laid free-range eggs.

Rooms 2 en suite S £40-£60; D £65-£90 **Facilities** TVL tea/coffee Cen ht Wi-fi ☃ **Parking** 4 **Notes** LB Closed 24-26 Dec ◉

SIBTON Map 13 TM36

Sibton White Horse Inn

★★★★ ◉ INN

Halesworth Rd IP17 2JJ
☎ 01728 660337
e-mail: info@sibtonwhitehorseinn.co.uk
dir: A12 at Yoxford onto A1120 for 3m until Peasenhall. Turn right opposite butchers, White Horse 600mtrs

A delightful Grade II listed 16th-century Tudor inn set in a rural location surrounded by open countryside, a few miles from the Suffolk coast. Public rooms include a traditional beamed bar with exposed brick fireplaces and a choice of dining areas. The attractive bedrooms are situated in a converted building adjacent.

Rooms 6 annexe en suite (3 GF) S £60-£75; D £65-£90* **Facilities** FTV tea/coffee Dinner available Cen ht Wi-fi **Parking** 50 **Notes** LB No Children 12yrs Closed 26-27 Dec No coaches

SOUTHWOLD Map 13 TM57

PREMIER COLLECTION

Sutherland House

★★★★★ ◉◉ RESTAURANT WITH ROOMS

56 High St IP18 6DN
☎ 01502 724544
e-mail: enquiries@sutherlandhouse.co.uk
web: www.sutherlandhouse.co.uk
dir: A1095 into Southwold, on High St on left after Victoria St

A delightful 16th-century house situated in the heart of the bustling town centre with a wealth of character; there are oak beams, exposed brickwork, open fireplaces and two superb ornate plasterwork ceilings. The stylish bedrooms are tastefully decorated, have co-ordinated fabrics and many thoughtful touches. Public rooms feature a large open-plan contemporary restaurant with plush furniture.

Rooms 4 en suite (1 fmly) D £140-£250* **Facilities** FTV tea/coffee Dinner available Direct Dial Cen ht Wi-fi **Conf** Max 80 Thtr 80 Class 30 Board 30 **Parking** 1 **Notes** ✪ RS Mon Rest closed in winter No coaches

Home@ 21 North Parade

★★★★ BED AND BREAKFAST

21 North Pde IP18 6LT
☎ 01502 722573
e-mail: pauline.archer@btconnect.com
web: www.homeat21northparade.co.uk
dir: A12 onto B1095. At mini rdbt, left onto Pier Av, right onto North Parade. Premises 100yds on right

This delightful Victorian property is situated on the promenade overlooking the sea. The stylish bedrooms have co-ordinated soft furnishings and many thoughtful touches, also some rooms have superb sea views. Breakfast, which includes fresh local produce, is served in the smart lounge/dining room at a large polished table.

Rooms 3 rms (2 en suite) (1 pri facs) **Facilities** FTV tea/coffee Cen ht Wi-fi ☃ **Notes** LB ✪ No Children 10yrs Closed Xmas & New Year ◉

STOWMARKET Map 13 TM05

PREMIER COLLECTION

Bays Farm

★★★★★ GUEST ACCOMMODATION

Forward Green IP14 5HU
☎ 01449 711286
e-mail: info@baysfarmsuffolk.co.uk
web: www.baysfarmsuffolk.co.uk
dir: A14 junct 50, onto A1120. 1m after Stowupland, turn right at sharp left bend signed Broad Green. Bays Farm 1st house on right

Tea and home-made cake are offered on arrival at this delightful 17th-century former farmhouse, situated amid four acres of mature grounds. The property has a wealth of character. Bedrooms are carefully decorated and have co-ordinated soft furnishings as well as many thoughtful touches. Breakfast, which includes locally sourced produce, is served around a large polished table in the stylish dining room.

Rooms 3 en suite 1 annexe en suite S £65-£100; D £75-£110* **Facilities** FTV tea/coffee Cen ht Licensed Wi-fi **Parking** 6 **Notes** No Children 12yrs

SUDBURY — Map 13 TL84

The Case Restaurant with Rooms

★★★★ ⊛ RESTAURANT WITH ROOMS

Further St, Assington CO10 5LD
☎ 01787 210483 📄 01787 211725
e-mail: restaurant@thecaserestaurantwithrooms.co.uk
dir: Exit A12 at Colchester onto A134 to Sudbury. 7m from Colchester on left

The Case Restaurant with Rooms offers dining in comfortable surroundings, along with luxurious accommodation in bedrooms that all enjoy independent access. Some bathrooms come complete with corner jacuzzi, while internet access comes as standard. In the restaurant, local produce is used in all dishes, and fresh bread and desserts are made every day.

Rooms 7 en suite (2 fmly) (7 GF) **Facilities** FTV tea/coffee Dinner available Cen ht Wi-fi **Parking** 25 **Notes** LB ⊗

WOODBRIDGE — Map 13 TM24

Grove House

★★★ GUEST HOUSE

39 Grove Rd IP12 4LG
☎ 01394 382202
e-mail: reception@grovehousehotel.ltd.uk
dir: W of town centre on A12

A warm welcome is assured at this owner-managed establishment on the west side of town. The bedrooms are pleasantly decorated and thoughtfully equipped with a good range of useful facilities. The smart public rooms include a cosy bar, a comfortable lounge and a large dining room with individual tables.

Rooms 10 en suite (1 fmly) (6 GF) **Facilities** tea/coffee Dinner available Cen ht Licensed Wi-fi **Conf** Max 20 Thtr 20 Class 20 Board 20 **Parking** 12 **Notes** ⊗

WORLINGWORTH — Map 13 TM26

Pond Farm B&B (TM219697)

★★★ FARMHOUSE

Fingal St IP13 7PD
☎ 01728 628565 & 0798 0914768
Mrs S Bridges
e-mail: enquiries@featherdown.co.uk

A Grade II listed farmhouse set in twelve acres of grounds, close to the market towns of Framlingham and Woodbridge. The property is part of a working farm with Aberdeen Angus cattle, horse livery and free-range chickens. The well-equipped bedrooms are situated in an annexe adjacent to the main building. Breakfast is served at a large communal table in the cosy dining room.

Rooms 2 en suite (2 fmly) (2 GF) S fr £35; D fr £70*
Facilities STV FTV TVL tea/coffee Dinner available Direct Dial Cen ht ch fac Fishing **Parking** 10 **Notes** LB 100 acres beef/pigs

YAXLEY — Map 13 TM17

PREMIER COLLECTION

The Auberge

☆☆☆☆☆ ⊛⊛ RESTAURANT WITH ROOMS

Ipswich Rd IP23 8BZ
☎ 01379 783604 📄 01379 788486
e-mail: aubmail@the-auberge.co.uk
web: www.the-auberge.co.uk
dir: On A140 between Norwich & Ipswich at B1117 x-rds with Eye & Thornham Parva

A warm welcome awaits at this charming 15th-century property, which has been lovingly converted by the present owners from a rural pub into a smart restaurant with rooms, the restaurant side of which has gained two AA Rosettes for its good use of fresh quality produce. The public areas have a wealth of character, such as exposed brickwork and beams, and the grounds are particularly well-kept and attractive. The spacious bedrooms are tastefully appointed and have many thoughtful touches. One includes a four-poster.

Rooms 11 annexe en suite (2 fmly) (6 GF) S £75–£90; D £95–£140* **Facilities** FTV tea/coffee Dinner available Direct Dial Cen ht Wi-fi **Conf** Max 46 Thtr 30 Class 30 Board 20 **Parking** 40 **Notes** LB ⊗ No coaches

SURREY

ALBURY — Map 6 TQ04

The Drummond at Albury

★★★ ⊜ INN

High St GU5 9AG
☎ 01483 202039 📄 01483 205361

The Drummond Inn is centrally located in this picturesque village, with attractive gardens running down to a small river at the rear of the property. The bedrooms are individually appointed and offer all the modern comforts. Breakfast is served in the light and airy conservatory whilst the restaurant offers mouth-watering dishes.

Rooms 9 en suite **Facilities** Dinner available **Conf** Max 40 Thtr 40 Class 40

BETCHWORTH — Map 6 TQ25

The Red Lion

★★★ INN

Old Rd, Buckland RH3 7DS
☎ 01737 843336
e-mail: info@redlionbetchworth.co.uk
dir: Off A25 between Reigate & Dorking, turn left to Betchworth. At rdbt turn left at T-junct, 500mtrs pub on left

The Red Lion is conveniently located just 20 minutes from Gatwick in the quiet village of Betchworth. The garden and some bedrooms have views of the neighbouring village cricket green. Bedrooms have spacious, modern decor with LCD TVs and beverage-making facilities. The pub serves lunch and dinner daily, and a continental breakfast is available.

Rooms 6 annexe en suite (3 GF) **Facilities** FTV tea/coffee Dinner available Wi-fi Cricket pitch **Conf** Max 40 Thtr 40 Class 25 Board 25 **Parking** 40 **Notes** LB No coaches

CAMBERLEY — Map 6 SU86

Burwood House

★★★★ ⊜ GUEST ACCOMMODATION

15 London Rd GU15 3UQ
☎ 01276 685686 📄 01276 62220
e-mail: enquiries@burwoodhouse.co.uk
dir: On A30 between Camberley and Bagshot

Burwood House is a very stylish establishment with individually designed bedrooms that offer all modern conveniences including Wi-fi. Every Monday to Thursday evening the kitchen offers a varied menu full of traditional favourites, as well as seasonal house specialties. Breakfast can be taken either buffet-style or as a fresh-cooked meal prepared upon request. Public areas include a lounge, bar and garden.

Rooms 22 en suite (3 fmly) (7 GF) **Facilities** tea/coffee Dinner available Direct Dial Cen ht Licensed Wi-fi ⤳ Golf 18 **Conf** Max 60 Thtr 50 Class 16 Board 20 **Parking** 22 **Notes** Closed 22 Dec-4 Jan

Save on B&Bs and Hotels. Book at **theAA.com/hotel**

SURREY 287 ENGLAND

Hatsue Guest House

★★★★ GUEST ACCOMMODATION

17 Southwell Park Rd GU15 3PU
☎ 01276 22160 & 07791 267620 📠 01276 671415
e-mail: welcome@hatsueguesthouse.com
dir: M3 junct 4, A331 N, A30 E, at Arena sports centre
turn right. At T-junct, turn right, 2nd house on left before
church

Hatsue Guest House offers comfortable, well-appointed
accommodation within a period house, which has been
sympathetically modernised to meet the needs of the
modern guest. Flat screen TV and free Wi-fi are only two
of the amenities provided. The breakfast room overlooks
the quiet rear garden. Ample parking is provided.

Rooms 5 en suite S £60; D £70* **Facilities** FTV Direct Dial
Cen ht Wi-fi **Parking** 5 **Notes** ⊗

CHARLWOOD

For accommodation details see under Gatwick Airport
(London), (Sussex, West)

CHIDDINGFOLD   Map 6 SU93

PREMIER COLLECTION

The Crown Inn

★★★★★ INN

The Green, Petworth Rd GU8 4TX
☎ 01428 682255 📠 01428 683313
e-mail: enquiries@thecrownchiddingfold.com

Set in a tranquil location in a picturesque village, the
inn dates back to as early as 1216. This charming
property has been completely renovated and offers
stylish, modern accommodation which has been
tastefully renovated without losing any period features.
Breakfast and dinner can be enjoyed in the oak-
panelled dining room, and there is a spacious bar,
outside seating and small courtyard.

Rooms 8 en suite (4 fmly) S £100; D £125-£200
Facilities FTV tea/coffee Dinner available Direct Dial
Cen ht Wi-fi **Conf** Max 40 **Parking** 15 **Notes** ⊗

The Swan Inn

★★★★ ⊛ INN

Petworth Rd GU8 4TY
☎ 01428 684688 📠 01428 685991
e-mail: info@theswaninnchiddingfold.com
web: www.theswaninnchiddingfold.com
dir: M25 junct 10, A3 to Milford junct. At rdbt 1st exit
onto A283, at lights turn left. Next rdbt 2nd exit, 5m to
Swan Inn

This new addition to the West Sussex dining scene offers
well-sourced, seasonal food within an elegant
environment. The well-appointed bedrooms are air-
conditioned and equipped to meet the needs of both the
leisure and business traveller. The rear garden is a
peaceful option during the warm months.

Rooms 10 en suite (1 fmly) D £100-£170* **Facilities** STV
tea/coffee Dinner available Direct Dial Wi-fi **Conf** Max 20
Thtr 20 Class 20 Board 20 **Parking** 30 **Notes** No coaches

CHOBHAM   Map 6 SU96

Pembroke House

★★★★ GUEST ACCOMMODATION

Valley End Rd GU24 8TB
☎ 01276 857654 📠 01276 856080
e-mail: pembroke_house@btinternet.com
dir: A30 onto B383 signed Chobham, 3m right onto Valley
End Rd, 1m on left

Proprietor Julia Holland takes obvious pleasure in
welcoming guests to her beautifully appointed and
spacious home. The elegantly proportioned public areas
include an imposing entrance hall and dining room with
views over the surrounding countryside. Bedrooms are
restful and filled with thoughtful extras.

Rooms 4 rms (2 en suite) (2 pri facs) (1 fmly) S £40-£60;
D £80-£150* **Facilities** STV tea/coffee Cen ht Wi-fi 🐾
Parking 10 **Notes** ⊛

CRANLEIGH   Map 6 TQ03

The Cranley

★★★ INN

The Common GU6 8SQ
☎ 01483 272827 📠 01483 548576
e-mail: thecranleyhotel@gmail.com
dir: From Guildford on A281 left to Cranleigh

This traditional pub, located in the picturesque village of
Cranleigh, offers freshly prepared food, using local
produce, at lunch and dinner. Regular entertainment is
provided, and the rear garden is popular with families.
The comfortable bedrooms have TVs and tea- and coffee-
making facilities.

Rooms 7 en suite S £45-£55; D £50-£65* **Facilities** TVL
Dinner available Cen ht Wi-fi Pool table **Parking** 50
Notes ⊗

EAST HORSLEY   Map 6 TQ05

The Duke of Wellington

★★★ INN

Guildford Rd KT24 6AA
☎ 01483 282164
e-mail: info@dukeofwellington.uk.com

Built in the 16th century, this former coaching inn is
close to Guildford, Leatherhead and the M25. The
courtyard, previously a stable block, houses all the en
suite bedrooms; each is spacious and modern yet retains
original features. A hearty breakfast is served, and a
selection of home-cooked meals is available for both
lunch and dinner.

Rooms 9 en suite (2 fmly) (9 GF) S £45-£60; D £45-£60
(room only)* **Facilities** FTV tea/coffee Dinner available
Wi-fi Pool table **Parking** 30

EFFINGHAM   Map 6 TQ15

Sir Douglas Haig

★★★ INN

The Street KT24 5LU
☎ 01372 456886 📠 01372 450987
e-mail: sirdouglashaig@hotmail.com
dir: M25 junct 9 onto A243 then A24, at rdbt take 2nd exit
onto A246. Through Bookham, at lights with golf club on
left, turn right. Pub located on right

A traditional public house located in the village centre,
the Sir Douglas Haig has retained a country atmosphere
and offers comfortable accommodation for the modern
traveller. The bar is well stocked and provides regular
entertainment whilst the restaurant serves a choice of
traditional dishes. Ample parking is available.

Rooms 7 en suite (1 fmly) S £60-£75; D £70-£95 (room
only)* **Facilities** FTV tea/coffee Dinner available Cen ht
Wi-fi **Parking** 15 **Notes** LB

FARNHAM — Map 5 SU84

Sandiway

★★★ BED AND BREAKFAST

24 Shortheath Rd GU9 8SR
☎ 01252 710721
e-mail: john@shortheath.freeserve.co.uk
dir: *Onto A287 Hindhead, at lights at top of hill right onto Ridgway Rd, past green on left, Sandiway 300yds on right*

Guests are warmly welcomed at this delightful house, set in attractive gardens in a quiet residential area. Smart bedrooms have a thoughtful range of facilities and share a spacious, well-appointed bathroom. Guests have use of a comfortable lounge during the day and evening, which doubles as the dining room at breakfast.

Rooms 3 rms S £33; D £53* **Facilities** FTV TVL tea/coffee Cen ht Wi-fi **Parking** 3 **Notes** ⊗ No Children 10yrs Closed 21-31 Dec ⊛

GUILDFORD — Map 6 SU94

Asperion Hillside

★★★★ ⊜ GUEST ACCOMMODATION

Perry Hill, Worplesdon GU3 3RF
☎ 01483 232051 ☒ 01483 237015
e-mail: info@thehillsidehotel.com

Located just a short drive away from central Guildford this accommodation is popular with both business and leisure travellers. Bedrooms are comfortable and well equipped with good facilities. Public areas include a spacious lounge bar where dinner is served, and a bright well-styled breakfast room. Gardens are well maintained and are enhanced by a guest terrace. Intimate meetings and events can also be catered for here.

Rooms 15 en suite (6 GF) **Facilities** FTV tea/coffee Dinner available Cen ht Licensed Wi-fi **Conf** Max 20 Thtr 20 Class 10 Board 12 **Parking** 15 **Notes** ⊗ Closed 21 Dec-7 Jan

Asperion

★★★★ GUEST ACCOMMODATION

73 Farnham Rd GU2 7PF
☎ 01483 579299 ☒ 01483 457977
e-mail: enquiries@asperion.co.uk
dir: *Exit A3 at Surrey University only, 2nd exit from rdbt onto Chase Rd. Right onto Agraria Rd to Farnham Rd junct. Turn right onto Farnham Rd (A31), 3rd on right*

The stylish Asperion provides comfortable, modern, and contemporary styled bedrooms in a convenient location close to the city centre of Guildford. The owners are committed to a "more than for profit" business ethos, part of which involves a healthy organic breakfast.

Rooms 15 rms (14 en suite) (1 pri facs) (1 fmly) (9 GF) S £50-£65; D £75-£85* **Facilities** STV FTV TVL tea/coffee Direct Dial Cen ht Licensed **Notes** ⊗ No Children 12yrs Closed 21 Dec-5 Jan

HASLEMERE — Map 6 SU93

Ashleigh (SU949313)

★★★ FARMHOUSE

Fisherstreet Farm GU28 9EJ
☎ 01428 707229 ☒ 01428 707229
Mr & Mrs S Thomas
e-mail: gu284sx@yahoo.co.uk
dir: *3.5m E of Haslemere. B2131 onto A283 S*

Stephen and Madeleine Thomas make you feel like friends at their charming farmhouse. A homely ambience is evident throughout the spacious bedrooms, the cosy lounge and the elegant dining room. Breakfast, served family style, uses farm produce whenever possible.

Rooms 2 en suite (1 fmly) **Facilities** STV TVL tea/coffee Dinner available Cen ht Wi-fi **Parking** 6 **Notes** ⊗ ⊛ 450 acres beef/arable

Wheatsheaf

★★★ ⊜ INN

Grayswood Rd, Grayswood GU27 2DE
☎ 01428 644440 ☒ 01428 641285
e-mail: ken@thewheatsheafgrayswood.co.uk
web: www.thewheatsheafgrayswood.co.uk
dir: *1m N of Haslemere on A286 in Grayswood*

Situated in a small village just outside Haslemere, this well-presented inn has a friendly atmosphere. The smart conservatory restaurant is a new addition, which complements the attractive dining area and popular bar. Bedrooms are furnished to a good standard, all but one on the ground floor.

Rooms 7 en suite (6 GF) S £59; D £79* **Facilities** tea/coffee Dinner available Direct Dial Cen ht Wi-fi **Parking** 21 **Notes** No coaches

HORLEY

For accommodation details see under Gatwick Airport (London), (Sussex, West)

RIPLEY — Map 6 TQ05

The Talbot Inn

★★★★★ ⊚ ⊜ INN

High St GU23 6BB
☎ 01483 225188 ☒ 01483 211332
e-mail: info@thetalbotinn.com
web: www.thetalbotinn.com
dir: *Exit A3 signed Ripley, on left on High St*

The Talbot Inn simply oozes charm and character and has retained many of its historical features even having undergone a recent major transformation. Public areas are very comfortable, with real ales and delicious home-cooked food on offer. Alfresco dining is available in summer months. Traditional bedrooms are in the main house and more contemporary-styled rooms are featured in the 'stable block'.

Rooms 9 en suite 30 annexe en suite (17 GF) **Facilities** STV FTV tea/coffee Dinner available Cen ht Wi-fi **Conf** Max 120 Thtr 120 Class 58 Board 36 **Parking** 60 **Notes** Civ Wed 120

SUSSEX, EAST

BODIAM — Map 7 TQ72

Spring Farm

★★★★ BED AND BREAKFAST

Northlands TN32 5UX
☎ 01580 831222
e-mail: springfarmbandb@tiscali.co.uk
web: www.springfarmbodiam.co.uk
dir: *A21, 1m S of Hurst Green, turn left, follow signs for Bodiam Castle. After 2m across x-rds, 400mtrs on left*

Spring Farm is located just one mile from Bodiam Castle and is within close proximity to Hastings, Rye and Tenterden. Bedrooms and bathrooms are stylishly decorated, providing guests with comfortable accommodation that includes flat-screen LCD TVs; free Wi-fi is available throughout. The guest lounge on the ground floor provides additional space for relaxing during the day, and is the venue for a cooked or continental breakfast. There is an outdoor swimming pool in the beautiful gardens.

Rooms 3 en suite S £65-£80; D £80-£100 **Facilities** FTV TVL tea/coffee Dinner available Cen ht Wi-fi ⟍ **Parking** 3 **Notes** LB ⊗ No Children 12yrs ⊛

BRIGHTON & HOVE — Map 6 TQ30

Brighton Pavilions
★★★★ GUEST ACCOMMODATION

7 Charlotte St BN2 1AG
☎ 01273 621750 📠 01273 622477
e-mail: sanchez-crespo@lineone.net
web: www.brightonpavilions.com
dir: A23 to Brighton Pier, left onto A259 Marine Parade, Charlotte St 15th left

This well-run operation is in one of Brighton's Regency streets, a short walk from the seafront and town centre. Bedrooms have themes such as Mikado or Pompeii, and are very smartly presented with many thoughtful extras including room service breakfast in superior rooms and free Wi-fi. The bright breakfast room is styled after the Titanic garden restaurant.

Rooms 10 rms (7 en suite) (1 fmly) (1 GF) S £45-£47; D £86-£148* **Facilities** FTV tea/coffee Direct Dial Cen ht Wi-fi **Notes** LB

Five
★★★★ GUEST ACCOMMODATION

5 New Steine BN2 1PB
☎ 01273 686547 📠 0871 522 7472
e-mail: info@fivehotel.com
dir: On A259 towards E, 8th turn on left into square

An attractive townhouse in a traditional Georgian square just a stone's throw from the famous Brighton beaches, cafés and shops. Comfortable bedrooms and bathrooms are well equipped. A copious organic breakfast is served by cheerful hosts in the spacious, contemporary dining room.

Rooms 10 en suite **Facilities** FTV TVL tea/coffee Cen ht Wi-fi **Conf** Max 20 Board 20 **Notes** ⊗ No Children 5yrs

New Steine
★★★★ 🏠 🍴 GUEST ACCOMMODATION

10-11 New Steine BN2 1PB
☎ 01273 695415 & 681546 📠 01273 622663
e-mail: reservation@newsteinehotel.com
dir: A23 to Brighton Pier, left onto Marine Parade, New Steine on left after Wentworth St

Close to the seafront off the Esplanade, the New Steine provides spacious bedrooms. There is a cosy lounge, where a wide choice of English, vegetarian, vegan or continental breakfasts is served. There is street parking in front of the property.

Rooms 20 rms (16 en suite) (4 pri facs) (4 fmly) (2 GF) S £29.50-£59; D £57.50-£119 **Facilities** FTV tea/coffee Dinner available Direct Dial Cen ht Licensed Wi-fi **Conf** Max 50 Thtr 50 Class 20 Board 26 **Notes** LB No Children 4yrs

The Twenty One
★★★★ GUEST ACCOMMODATION

21 Charlotte St, Marine Pde BN2 1AG
☎ 01273 686450
e-mail: enquiries@thetwentyone.co.uk
web: www.thetwentyone.co.uk
dir: From Brighton Pier turn left onto Marine Parade, 16th turning on left

This stylishly refurbished townhouse property is situated in Kemp Town within easy reach of clubs, bars and restaurants and just a short walk from the beach. Rooms are elegantly furnished and comfortable, with an abundance of thoughtful extras provided. A smart dining room is the setting for a delicious, freshly-cooked breakfast.

Rooms 8 en suite (1 fmly) S £50-£60; D £90-£149* **Facilities** FTV tea/coffee Cen ht Wi-fi **Notes** LB ⊗ No Children 10yrs

See advert on this page

BRIGHTON & HOVE *continued*

The White House

★★★★ ⌂ GUEST ACCOMMODATION

6 Bedford St BN2 1AN
☎ 01273 626266
e-mail: info@whitehousebrighton.com
web: www.whitehousebrighton.com
dir: *A23 to Brighton, follow signs to town centre. At rdbt opposite pier take 1st exit, through 2 sets of lights, left onto Bedford St*

The White House is a small Regency residence only 100 metres from the seafront, and a short walk from Brighton's centre. There are sea views from the south-facing rooms and a courtyard garden where guests may sit and relax. All rooms are smartly and stylishly decorated and there is a relaxed atmosphere. Breakfast is served in the dining room, or alfresco. The extensive breakfast menu uses only best quality ingredients.

Rooms 10 rms (8 en suite) (2 GF) **Facilities** tea/coffee Cen ht Wi-fi **Notes** ⊗ Closed Jan

Alvia

★★★★ GUEST ACCOMMODATION

36 Upper Rock Gardens BN2 1QF
☎ 01273 682939 ⊟ 01273 626287
e-mail: enquiries@alviahotel.co.uk
web: www.alviahotel.co.uk
dir: *A23 to Brighton Pier, left onto Marine Parade, 500yds left at lights onto Lower Rock Gdns & Upper Rock Gdns*

Located in the popular Kemp Town area of Brighton, this townhouse establishment offers modern accommodation with a spacious dining room where guests can enjoy a cooked or continental breakfast. Fairly unique for this area, the property also benefits from an on-site private car park, which it is advisable to book in advance.

Rooms 10 rms (9 en suite) (1 fmly) **Facilities** tea/coffee Cen ht Wi-fi **Parking** 4 **Notes** ⊗

Ambassador Brighton

★★★★ GUEST ACCOMMODATION

22-23 New Steine, Marine Pde BN2 1PD
☎ 01273 676869 ⊟ 01273 689988
e-mail: info@ambassadorbrighton.co.uk
web: www.ambassadorbrighton.co.uk
dir: *A23 to Brighton Pier, left onto A259, 9th left, onto Garden Sq, 1st left*

At the heart of bustling Kemp Town, overlooking the attractive garden square next to the seaside, this well-established property has a friendly and relaxing atmosphere. Bedrooms are well equipped and vary in size, with the largest having the best views. A small lounge with a separate bar is available.

Rooms 24 en suite (9 fmly) (3 GF) (8 smoking) S £50-£77; D £75.50-£128* **Facilities** tea/coffee Direct Dial Cen ht Licensed **Conf** Max 20 Thtr 20 Board 14 **Notes** LB

Bannings@ Number 14

★★★★ GUEST ACCOMMODATION

14 Upper Rock Gardens BN2 1QE
☎ 01273 681403
e-mail: christopher.c.darnell@btinternet.com
dir: *Left onto A259 towards pier front, left at next lights, left to Tower Rock Garden, straight on to Upper Rock Gdns*

This attractive Victorian property is situated close to the seafront and just steps away from restaurants and shops. The comfortably furnished bedrooms are fresh and bright, and the cheerful dining room is the setting for a healthy breakfast. Parking tokens are available for a small charge.

Rooms 6 en suite D £85-£98* **Facilities** FTV tea/coffee Cen ht Wi-fi **Notes** ⊗ No Children

Brighton House

★★★★ ⌂ GUEST ACCOMMODATION

52 Regency Square BN1 2FF
☎ 01273 323282
e-mail: info@brighton-house.co.uk
web: www.brighton-house.co.uk
dir: *Opp West Pier*

Situated close to the seafront is the elegant, environmentally-friendly, Brighton House. Comfortably appointed bedrooms and bathrooms come in a variety of sizes and are located on four floors. An impressively abundant, organic continental breakfast is served in the spacious elegant dining room. Parking is in the nearby underground car park.

Rooms 16 en suite (2 fmly) **Facilities** tea/coffee Cen ht Licensed **Notes** ⊗ No Children 12yrs

Colson House

★★★★ GUEST ACCOMMODATION

17 Upper Rock Gardens BN2 1QE
☎ 01273 694922 ⊟ 01273 694922
e-mail: info@colsonhouse.co.uk
dir: *From Brighton Pier, east on A259 then left at lights*

Just a short walk from Kemp Town this listed Regency property offers a warm friendly welcome and some comfortable accommodation. Bedrooms are named after movie icons and include DVD players with films by the artiste. Breakfast is served in a light and airy dining room.

Rooms 8 en suite (1 GF) D £69-£119* **Facilities** FTV tea/coffee Cen ht Wi-fi **Notes** ⊗ No Children 12yrs

Four Seasons Guest House

★★★★ GUEST ACCOMMODATION

3 Upper Rock Gardens BN2 1QE
☎ 01273 673574
e-mail: info@fourseasonsbrighton.com
web: www.fourseasonsbrighton.com
dir: *At rdbt take first exit proceed along Marine Parade, at lights, turn left onto Lower Rock Gdns*

Caring hosts William and Thommy provide smart accommodation with a variety of stylish contemporary bedrooms, each with ample facilities including Wi-fi and hairdryers. A healthy breakfast is served in the sunny dining room. Beaches, restaurants and shops are within close walking distance.

Rooms 7 rms (6 pri facs) (1 GF) **Facilities** FTV tea/coffee Cen ht Wi-fi **Notes** LB ⊗ No Children 10yrs

George IV

★★★★ GUEST ACCOMMODATION

34 Regency Square BN1 2FJ
☎ 01273 321196
e-mail: info@georgeivbrighton.co.uk
web: www.georgeivbrighton.co.uk
dir: *Opp West Pier, at top of square*

Situated at the top of the prominent Regency Square overlooking the gardens and sea, this restored property provides elegantly furnished bedrooms with modern bathrooms and good facilities. There is a lift to all floors and a freshly prepared continental breakfast is served in your bedroom.

Rooms 8 en suite (1 fmly) S £50-£58; D £72-£155 (room only)* **Facilities** FTV tea/coffee Cen ht Lift Wi-fi **Notes** ⊗ Closed Jan

Gullivers

★★★★ GUEST ACCOMMODATION

12a New Steine BN2 1PB
☎ 01273 681546 & 695415 ⊟ 01273 622663
e-mail: reservation@gullivershotel.com
web: www.gullivershotel.com
dir: *A23 to Brighton Pier, left onto Marine Parade, premises 300yds on left*

Situated in an impressive Regency square close to the town and seafront, Gullivers has much to offer. Compact rooms use clever design and contemporary colours to ensure comfort, and some have quality shower rooms en suite. The lounge and brasserie, decorated with fine art, are super areas in which to relax and dine.

Rooms 12 rms (9 en suite) (3 pri facs) (2 GF) (4 smoking) S £27.50-£55; D £55-£115 **Facilities** FTV tea/coffee Dinner available Direct Dial Cen ht Licensed Wi-fi **Conf** Max 30 Thtr 30 Class 10 Board 20 **Notes** LB ⊗ No Children 4yrs

Marine View

★★★★ GUEST ACCOMMODATION

24 New Steine BN2 1PD
☎ 01273 603870   📠 01273 357257
e-mail: info@mvbrighton.co.uk
web: www.mvbrighton.co.uk
dir: *From A23, left onto Marine Pde, left onto New Steine, 300mtrs*

Overlooking the elegant Steine Square with the sea just a glance away, this 18th-century property offers comfortable, well-designed accommodation. Plenty of accessories are provided, including free Wi-fi. A hearty breakfast is available in the bright lounge/dining room.

Rooms 11 rms (8 en suite) (1 pri facs) (2 fmly) (2 GF) **Facilities** tea/coffee Cen ht Wi-fi **Notes** ⊗

Nineteen

★★★★ GUEST ACCOMMODATION

19 Broad St BN2 1TJ
☎ 01273 675529   📠 01273 675531
e-mail: info@hotelnineteen.co.uk
web: www.hotelnineteen.co.uk
dir: *A23 to Brighton Pier, left onto Marine Parade, 1st left onto Manchester St, right onto Saint James St. Broad St 2nd on right*

This contemporary establishment lies close to the town centre, only minutes from Brighton Pier. Bedrooms are decorated with white walls, wooden floors and stylish artworks. The continental breakfast (served with champagne at the weekend) is superb, providing a fine start to the day.

Rooms 8 en suite (2 GF) S £60-£90; D £80-£250* **Facilities** FTV Cen ht Wi-fi Outdoor Hot Tub in 1 bedroom **Notes** ⊗ No Children 10yrs Closed 24-26 Dec

The Oriental

★★★★ GUEST ACCOMMODATION

9 Oriental Place BN1 2LJ
☎ 01273 205050   📠 01273 205050
e-mail: info@orientalbrighton.co.uk
dir: *A23 right onto A259 at seafront, right into Oriental Place, on right*

The Oriental is situated close to the seafront and enjoys easy access to all areas. The accommodation is comfortable and modern, and there is a licensed bar. A tasty Sussex breakfast using locally sourced produce is offered in a friendly, relaxed atmosphere.

Rooms 9 en suite (4 fmly) (1 GF) S £45-£79; D £75-£150* **Facilities** FTV tea/coffee Cen ht Licensed Wi-fi Massage Aromatherapy Beauty treatments **Conf** Max 10 Thtr 10 Class 10 Board 10

Paskins Town House

★★★★ 🏠 GUEST ACCOMMODATION

18/19 Charlotte St BN2 1AG
☎ 01273 601203   📠 01273 621973
e-mail: welcome@paskins.co.uk
web: www.paskins.co.uk
dir: *A23 to pier, turn left, Charlotte St 11th left*

This environmentally-friendly, family-run Victorian house is in a quiet street within walking distance of the seafront and town centre. Bedrooms are a comfortable mix of Victorian and art nouveau styles. The Art Deco breakfast room offers a variety of vegetarian and vegan dishes and traditional English breakfasts, featuring home-made vegetarian sausages and much organic produce.

Rooms 19 rms (16 en suite) (2 fmly) (3 GF) **Facilities** FTV tea/coffee Cen ht Wi-fi **Notes** LB

Snooze

★★★★ GUEST ACCOMMODATION

25 St George Ter BN2 1JJ
☎ 01273 605797
e-mail: info@snoozebrighton.com

This splendid Victorian terraced property is close to the beach and the popular Kemptown bars and restaurants. Bedrooms have a distinctly 'retro' feel and all are comfortably presented. A choice of hearty breakfasts is served in the spacious dining room enhanced with large bay windows.

Rooms 8 en suite (2 GF) D £65-£130* **Facilities** FTV tea/coffee Cen ht Wi-fi **Notes** ⊗

Brighton Marina House

★★★ GUEST ACCOMMODATION

8 Charlotte St BN2 1AG
☎ 01273 605349   📠 01273 679484
e-mail: rooms@jungs.co.uk
web: www.brighton-mh-hotel.co.uk

Brighton Marina House occupies a period building in the heart of the town and the seafront is only a short walk away. The bedrooms are individually themed and nicely equipped and many rooms have four-poster beds. Breakfast is particularly interesting with special emphasis on vegan and vegetarian options.

Rooms 9 rms (6 en suite) (3 pri facs) (3 fmly) S £30-£49; D £99-£129* **Facilities** FTV tea/coffee Cen ht Wi-fi **Notes** LB ⊗ Closed Jan

Motel Schmotel

★★★ GUEST ACCOMMODATION

37 Russell Square BN1 2EF
☎ 01273 326129
e-mail: info@motelschmotel.co.uk

Charming family-run establishment situated on a quiet square just minutes away from beaches and shops. Bright en suite bedrooms include thoughtful amenities such as free Wi-fi and Freeview TV. A substantial breakfast menu uses fresh, local produce and is served in rooms.

Rooms 8 en suite (1 fmly) (2 GF) **Facilities** tea/coffee Cen ht Wi-fi **Parking** 2 **Notes** ⊗

Regency Landsdowne Guest House

★★★ GUEST ACCOMMODATION

45 Landsdowne Place BN3 1HF
☎ 01273 321830   📠 01273 777067
e-mail: regencylansdowne@aol.com
web: www.regencylansdowne.co.uk
dir: *A23 to Brighton Pier, right onto A259, 1m right onto Lansdowne Place, house on left before Western Rd*

A warm welcome is guaranteed at this Regency house, located only minutes from the seafront. Comfortable bedrooms are functionally equipped with a good range of facilities. An extensive continental breakfast is served at a communal table overlooking attractive gardens. On-road parking is a short walk away.

Rooms 7 rms (5 en suite) (2 pri facs) S £30-£55; D £46-£89* **Facilities** FTV tea/coffee Cen ht Lift Wi-fi **Notes** ⊗ Closed 20-27 Dec

Ainsley House

★★★ GUEST ACCOMMODATION

28 New Steine BN2 1PD
☎ 01273 605310   📠 01273 688604
e-mail: rooms@ainsleyhotel.com

Situated on the stylish Steine Square and with good views of the Pier, this popular property has a range of well equipped rooms; most are en suite and all are comfortably presented. Breakfast, served by the cheerful proprietor, is in the well positioned dining room with views over the square.

Rooms 12 rms (10 en suite) (3 fmly) **Facilities** TVL TV11B tea/coffee Cen ht **Notes** LB

BRIGHTON & HOVE *continued*

Avalon

★★★ GUEST ACCOMMODATION

7 Upper Rock Gardens BN2 1QE
☎ 01273 692344 📠 01273 692344
e-mail: info@avalonbrighton.co.uk
dir: *A23 to Brighton Pier, left onto Marine Parade, 300yds at lights left onto Lower Rock Gdns, over lights Avalon on left*

A warm welcome is assured at this guest accommodation just a short walk from the seafront and The Lanes. The en suite bedrooms vary in size and style but all are attractively presented with plenty of useful accessories including free Wi-fi. Parking vouchers are available for purchase from the proprietor.

Rooms 7 en suite (3 fmly) (1 GF) **Facilities** FTV tea/coffee Cen ht Wi-fi

The Market Inn

★★★ INN

1 Market St BN1 1HH
☎ 01273 329483 📠 01273 777227
e-mail: marketinn@reallondonpubs.com
web: www.reallondonpubs.com/market.html
dir: *In city centre, on pedestrian road 50yds from junct North St & East St*

This lively period inn is within walking distance of many local attractions. Bedrooms are attractively decorated and feature a range of extra facilities. Breakfast is served in the bedrooms, and popular bar food is served at lunchtimes in the bar, which retains its original character.

Rooms 2 en suite S £50-£60; D £65-£85* **Facilities** FTV tea/coffee Dinner available Cen ht Wi-fi **Notes** LB No Children 18yrs No coaches

Westbourne Guest House

★★★ GUEST ACCOMMODATION

46 Upper Rock Gardens BN2 1QF
☎ 01273 686920 📠 01273 686920
e-mail: welcome@westbournehotel.net
dir: *A23 to Brighton Pier, left onto Marine Parade, 100yds left at lights, premises on right*

Just a short walk from the seafront, this Victorian house is run by friendly owners. The attractive bedrooms are bright and well furnished, and some have flat screen TVs. Spacious dining area is complemented by a large bay window.

Rooms 11 rms (7 en suite) (1 fmly) (2 GF) (2 smoking) S £25-£55; D £38-£100* **Facilities** FTV tea/coffee Licensed Wi-fi **Parking** 1 **Notes** ⊗ Closed 23-30 Dec

Sandpiper Guest House

★★★ 🅰 GUEST HOUSE

11 Russell Square BN1 2EE
☎ 01273 328202 📠 01273 329974
e-mail: sandpiper@brighton.co.uk
dir: *After conference centre on King's Rd, right onto Cannon Place. Russell Sq at end of street*

Rooms 6 rms (1 fmly) **Facilities** tea/coffee Cen ht **Notes** LB ⊗

CROWBOROUGH   **Map 6 TQ53**

Plough & Horses

★★★ INN

Walshes Rd TN6 3RE
☎ 01892 652614 📠 01892 652614
dir: *A26 onto B2100, under railway bridge, right onto Western Rd, over railway to Walshes Rd*

This pleasant inn has been welcoming guests for many years, and over the last two decades the present owners have made this a very attractive and popular place. The spacious bedrooms feature well-chosen pine furniture, and public rooms include a traditional bar, a restaurant, and a further lounge bar.

Rooms 15 en suite (3 fmly) **Facilities** TVL tea/coffee Dinner available Cen ht **Parking** 40 **Notes** Closed 24-25 Dec

---

DITCHLING   **Map 6 TQ31**

PREMIER COLLECTION

Tovey Lodge

★★★★★ GUEST ACCOMMODATION

Underhill Ln BN6 8XE
☎ 08456 120544 📠 08456 120533
e-mail: info@sussexcountryholidays.co.uk
dir: *From Ditchling village, N on Beacon Rd. After 0.5m left onto Underhill Ln, 100yds 1st drive on left*

Tovey Lodge is set within three acres of garden and great views of the South Downs. There is an indoor swimming pool, sauna and hot tub. Bedrooms and bathrooms are spacious and stylishly decorated. Bedrooms also include Wi-fi and DVD plasma TVs. There is a guest lounge which backs on to a patio, offering additional space to relax. The lounge is spacious and features a 50-inch plasma TV. A cooked or continental breakfast can be enjoyed in the dining room.

Rooms 5 en suite (4 fmly) (2 GF) **Facilities** FTV TVL tea/coffee Dinner available Cen ht Licensed Wi-fi ⊗ Golf Riding Sauna Hot tub spa **Conf** Max 12 Thtr 12 Board 12 **Parking** 28

The Bull

★★★★ 🍴 INN

2 High St BN6 8TA
☎ 01273 843147 📠 01273 843147
e-mail: info@thebullditchling.com

Dating back to 1563, the Bull is one of the oldest buildings in this famously pretty Sussex village. First used as an overnight resting place for travelling monks, the inn has also served as a courthouse and staging post for the London-Brighton coach. Home-cooked meals and local ales are available in the restaurant. A huge garden commands stunning views over the South Downs. A selection of modern en suite bedrooms are stylishly decorated and comfortably furnished.

Rooms 4 en suite **Facilities** FTV Dinner available Cen ht Wi-fi **Parking** 30

EASTBOURNE   **Map 6 TV69**

PREMIER COLLECTION

The Manse B&B

BED AND BREAKFAST

7 Dittons Rd BN21 1DW
☎ 01323 737851
e-mail: anne@themansebb.com
web: www.themansebb.com
dir: *A22 to town centre railway station, onto Old Orchard Rd, right onto Arlington Rd*

This delightful home is in a quiet residential area only a five minute walk from the town centre. Built as a Presbyterian manse at the turn of the 19th century, much of the original character has been retained. The beautifully decorated bedrooms are very comfortable and have a wide range of accessories such as flat screen TV and DVD. Breakfast is served in the elegant dining room, with its stripped wooden floors and pretty courtyard view.

Rooms 3 en suite S £55-£60; D £80-£92* **Facilities** FTV tea/coffee Cen ht Wi-fi **Parking** 2

Save on B&Bs and Hotels. Book at **theAA.com/hotel**

SUSSEX, EAST 293 **ENGLAND**

PREMIER COLLECTION

Ocklynge Manor

★★★★★ BED AND BREAKFAST

Mill Rd BN21 2PG
☎ 01323 734121 & 07979 627172
e-mail: ocklyngemanor@hotmail.com
web: www.ocklyngemanor.co.uk
dir: *From Eastbourne Hospital follow town centre/
seafront sign, 1st right onto Kings Av, Ocklynge Manor
at top of road*

This charming home has seen a variety of uses through
the years, including as a commanderie for the Knights
of St John in the 12th century. An air of peace and
relaxation is evident in the delightful public rooms,
well-tended gardens and the spacious, comfortable
bedrooms filled with thoughtful extras, including free
Wi-fi. Hospitality is a plus and home-baked bread is
just one of the delights on offer.

Rooms 3 rms (2 en suite) (1 pri facs) S £50; D £90
Facilities FTV tea/coffee Cen ht Wi-fi Walks **Parking** 3
Notes ⊗ No Children 16yrs ⊛

PREMIER COLLECTION

The Berkeley

★★★★★ GUEST ACCOMMODATION

3 Lascelles Ter BN21 4BJ
☎ 01323 645055 📠 01323 400128
e-mail: info@theberkeley.net
dir: *Follow seafront from pier, take 7th turn on right*

The Berkeley's central location is convenient for the
seafront, theatres and town centre. Spacious bedrooms
are smartly furnished and decorated, and some offer
sea views and views over the South Downs and
Devonshire Park. A stylish lounge is provided for
guests' relaxation. Here they can enjoy a drink and a
snack while choosing a book from the library or playing
one of the many board games available. Continental
and full English breakfasts are served in the attractive
dining room.

Rooms 13 en suite (4 fmly) (1 GF) **Facilities** STV tea/
coffee Cen ht Wi-fi

PREMIER COLLECTION

The Gables

★★★★★ BED AND BREAKFAST

21 Southfields Rd BN21 1BU
☎ 01323 644600
e-mail: info@gablesbandb.co.uk
dir: *A2270 into town centre, 2nd exit at rdbt by station,
bear right onto Southfields Rd*

The Gables is a splendid Edwardian property with lots
of character, spacious accommodation and friendly
hosts. A freshly-cooked breakfast is served in the
elegant dining room. Free Wi-fi is available for guests.
A short walk will take you to the station, town centre
and pier. Some off-road parking is available.

Rooms 3 rms (2 en suite) (1 pri facs) **Facilities** TVL
tea/coffee Cen ht Lift Wi-fi **Parking** 2 **Notes** ⊗ ⊛

The Camelot Lodge

★★★★ GUEST ACCOMMODATION

35 Lewes Rd BN21 2BU
☎ 01323 725207 📠 01323 722799
e-mail: info@camelotlodgehotel.com
web: www.camelotlodgehotel.com
dir: *A22 onto A2021, premises 0.5m after hospital on left*

This delightful Edwardian property is within walking
distance of the seafront and local amenities. The
beautifully styled bedrooms feature a range of facilities
including free Wi-fi access, and there is a spacious
lounge-bar area. Meals are served in the conservatory
dining room, and dinner is available by arrangement.

Rooms 8 en suite (3 fmly) (1 GF) S £34.95-£50; D
£70-£90* **Facilities** FTV TVL tea/coffee Dinner available
Cen ht Licensed Wi-fi **Parking** 11 **Notes** LB ⊗

Arden House

★★★★ GUEST ACCOMMODATION

17 Burlington Place BN21 4AR
☎ 01323 639639 📠 01323 417840
e-mail: info@theardenhotel.co.uk
dir: *On seafront, towards W, 5th turn after pier*

This attractive Regency property sits just minutes away
from the seafront and town centre. Bedrooms are
comfortable and bright, many with new en suite
bathrooms. Guests can enjoy a hearty breakfast at the
beginning of the day then relax in the cosy lounge in the
evening.

Rooms 11 rms (10 en suite) (1 pri facs) (1 fmly) S
£38-£42; D £62-£68* **Facilities** STV FTV TVL tea/coffee
Cen ht Wi-fi **Parking** 3 **Notes** LB

The Bay Lodge

★★★★ GUEST ACCOMMODATION

61-62 Royal Pde BN22 7AQ
☎ 01323 732515 📠 01323 735009
e-mail: baylodgehotel@fsmail.net
dir: *From A22 follow signs to seafront. Bay Lodge on right
opposite Pavilion Tea Gardens*

This family-run guest accommodation offers a warm
welcome in comfortable surrounds opposite the Redoubt
and Pavilion gardens. Bedrooms are bright and spacious,
some with balconies. There is a sun lounge and a cosy
bar that enjoy superb sea views.

Rooms 10 en suite (2 fmly) (2 GF) S £30-£42; D
£56-£84* **Facilities** TVL tea/coffee Cen ht Licensed Wi-fi
Parking 6 **Notes** LB ⊗

Bella Vista

★★★★ GUEST ACCOMMODATION

30 Redoubt Rd BN22 7DH
☎ 01323 724222
e-mail: enquiries@hotelbellavista.co.uk
dir: *500yds NE of town centre. Off A259 (Seaside Rd)*

Situated on the east side of town, just off the seafront,
this is an attractive flint house with the bonus of a car
park. Bedrooms are generally spacious, comfortable and
neatly appointed with modern facilities including free Wi-
fi. There is a large lounge and dining room where dinner
and breakfast is served.

Rooms 9 en suite (1 fmly) (3 GF) **Facilities** TVL tea/coffee
Dinner available Cen ht Licensed **Parking** 10 **Notes** ⊗

Ivydene

★★★★ GUEST ACCOMMODATION

5-6 Hampden Ter, Latimer Rd BN22 7BL
☎ 01323 720547 📠 01323 411247
e-mail: ivydenehotel@hotmail.co.uk
web: www.ivydenehotel-eastbourne.co.uk
dir: *From town centre/pier NE along seafront, towards
Redoubt Fortress, onto St Aubyns Rd, 1st right onto
Hampden Terrace*

This friendly family-run property is situated a short walk
from the pier and seafront. Bedrooms are bright and
cheerful with comfortable, stylish furnishings. Public
areas include a spacious lounge/bar, sunny conservatory
and attractive dining room.

Rooms 14 en suite (2 fmly) (1 GF) S £32-£37; D
£63-£73* **Facilities** FTV TVL tea/coffee Dinner available
Cen ht Licensed Wi-fi **Notes** LB ⊗ RS Oct-Etr No evening
meal

EASTBOURNE *continued*

The Mowbray

★★★★ GUEST ACCOMMODATION

2 Lascelles Ter BN21 4BJ
☎ 01323 720012 📄 01323 733579
e-mail: info@themowbray.com
dir: *Opp Devonshire Park Theatre*

This elegant townhouse is located opposite the Devonshire Park Theatre and a few minutes walk from the seafront. Bedrooms are accessible by a lift to all floors and vary in size, but all are attractively furnished and comfortable. There are a spacious well presented lounge, small modern bar and a stylish dining room. Breakfast is home-cooked, as are evening meals, available by prior arrangement

Rooms 13 en suite (2 fmly) (1 GF) S £38-£43; D £75-£102* Facilities FTV TVL tea/coffee Dinner available Cen ht Lift Licensed Wi-fi Therapist available (massage) Conf Max 20 Thtr 20 Class 10 Board 10 Notes LB

The Royal

★★★★ GUEST ACCOMMODATION

8-9 Marine Pde BN21 3DX
☎ 01323 649222 📄 0560 1500 065
e-mail: info@royaleastbourne.org.uk
dir: *On seafront 100mtrs E of pier*

This property enjoys a central seafront location close to the pier and within easy walking distance of the town centre. Spectacular uninterrupted sea views are guaranteed. Now fully renovated and eco-friendly, the comfortable bedrooms are modern with flat-screen TVs and free Wi-fi. One of the ten rooms has private facilities, while the others are fully en suite. A substantial continental breakfast is served. The Royal offers a full pet-sitting service.

Rooms 10 rms (9 en suite) (1 pri facs) (1 fmly) (1 GF) S £35-£55; D £59-£90* Facilities STV FTV tea/coffee Cen ht Wi-fi Golf Free Wi-fi, Dogs stay free of charge Notes LB No Children 12yrs

The Sherwood

★★★★ GUEST ACCOMMODATION

7 Lascelles Ter BN21 4BJ
☎ 01323 724002 📄 01323 400133
e-mail: info@thesherwood.net
dir: *Follow signs to seafront (Grand Parade). Next to Eastbourne Centre*

Attractive Victorian property just a minute's walk from the seafront, offering well-appointed bedrooms with comfortable, co-ordinated furnishings. The cosy lounge is a nice environment to relax in, and the attractive dining room serves a robust breakfast.

Rooms 13 en suite (5 fmly) (1 GF) S £38-£43; D £76-£86* Facilities STV FTV TVL tea/coffee Dinner available Cen ht Licensed Wi-fi

Beach Haven

★★★ GUEST ACCOMMODATION

61 Pevensey Rd BN21 3HS
☎ 01323 726195
e-mail: enquiries@beach-haven.co.uk
web: www.beach-haven.co.uk
dir: *250yds E of town centre off A259*

This attractive terrace property is just a short walk from the seafront and attractions. Bedrooms are located on three floors, some offer en suite facilities and all have a thoughtful range of guest extras. There is also a comfortable dining room, a cosy lounge and a small private chapel.

Rooms 7 rms (3 en suite) (1 GF) S £28-£45; D £56-£90* Facilities tea/coffee Dinner available Cen ht Notes LB ⊗ No Children 1yr

Beachy Rise

★★★ GUEST HOUSE

5 Beachy Head Rd BN20 7QN
☎ 01323 639171 📄 01323 645006
e-mail: susanne234@hotmail.co.uk
dir: *1m SW of town centre. Off B2103 Upper Dukes Rd*

This friendly family-run guest house has a quiet residential location close to Meads Village. Bedrooms are individually styled with co-ordinated soft furnishings and feature some useful extras. Breakfast is served in the light and airy dining room overlooking the garden, which guests are welcome to use.

Rooms 4 en suite (2 fmly) S £35-£45; D £55-£70* Facilities tea/coffee Cen ht Wi-fi

The Sheldon

Ⓤ

9-11Burlington Place BN21 4AS
☎ 01323 724120 & 07803 147082 📄 01323 644327
e-mail: info@thesheldonhotel.co.uk
dir: *Just off The Grand Parade*

Currently the rating for this establishment is not confirmed. This may be due to a change of ownership or because it has only recently joined the AA rating scheme.

Rooms 20 en suite (6 fmly) (4 GF) S £40-£50; D £90-£120* Facilities STV FTV tea/coffee Lift Wi-fi Conf Thtr 20 Class 30 Board 15 Parking 20 Notes ⊗ No Children 1yr Closed 3 Jan-1 Mar

FOREST ROW — Map 6 TQ43

The Roebuck

★★★ INN

Wych Cross RH18 5JL
☎ 01342 823811 📄 01342 824790
e-mail: 6499@greeneking.co.uk

This 17th-century country house is located just minutes from Forest Row just off the A22. Public areas have many original features and log fires are lit during the winter months. Free Wi-fi is available throughout. Bedrooms are well equipped and offer comfortable facilities. Dinner and breakfast are served in Antlers Restaurant.

Rooms 28 en suite (8 GF) Facilities TVL tea/coffee Dinner available Direct Dial Cen ht Wi-fi Pool table Conf Max 100 Thtr 10 Class 20 Parking 100 Notes Civ Wed 100

HALLAND — Map 6 TQ41

PREMIER COLLECTION

Tamberry Hall

★★★★★ GUEST ACCOMMODATION

Eastbourne Rd BN8 6PS
☎ 01825 880090 📄 01825 880090
e-mail: rosi@tamberryhall.co.uk
web: www.tamberryhall.co.uk
dir: *In Halland on A22, 200yds N of junct with B2192 at Black Lion Inn*

A warm welcome is assured at this attractive house sitting in three acres of wonderful landscaped gardens. Individually decorated bedrooms vary in size and are all equipped with a variety of thoughtful extras. An inglenook fireplace and exposed beams are a character of this establishment. Hearty breakfasts are served in a delightful dining room or on the terrace, weather permitting.

Rooms 3 en suite (1 fmly) Facilities TVL tea/coffee Cen ht Parking 3 Notes ⊗ RS 24-27 Dec Continental breakfast only

Save on B&Bs and Hotels. Book at **theAA.com/hotel**

SUSSEX, EAST 295 ENGLAND

Beechwood B&B

★★★★★ 🅰 GUEST ACCOMMODATION

Eastbourne Rd BN8 6PS
☎ 01825 840936 📄 01825 840936
e-mail: chyland1956@aol.com
web: www.beechwoodbandb.co.uk
dir: *On A22 directly before speed camera in Halland*
Rooms 3 rms (2 en suite) (1 pri facs) (1 fmly)
Facilities TVL tea/coffee Cen ht Wi-fi ⚡ Hot Tub
Parking 5 **Notes** LB

HASTINGS & ST LEONARDS | Map 7 TQ80

PREMIER COLLECTION

Stream House

★★★★★ BED AND BREAKFAST

Pett Level Rd, Fairlight TN35 4ED
☎ 01424 814916 & 0794 191 1379
e-mail: info@stream-house.co.uk
web: www.stream-house.co.uk
dir: *4m NE of Hastings. Off A259 on unclassified road between Fairlight & Cliff End*

Lovingly converted from three cottages, Stream House stands in three acres of tranquil grounds, just one mile from Winchelsea beach. The well-appointed bedrooms are beautifully decorated. Delicious breakfasts are served in the lounge-dining room with an original inglenook fireplace, and during warmer months you can enjoy the extensive garden with its rippling stream and Koi pond.

Rooms 3 rms (2 en suite) (1 pri facs) D £75-£95*
Facilities FTV TVL tea/coffee Cen ht Wi-fi **Parking** 4
Notes LB ⊗ No Children 10yrs Closed Dec-Feb ⊛

PREMIER COLLECTION

Barn House Seaview B&B

★★★★★ BED AND BREAKFAST

Warren Rd, Fairlight TN35 4AN
☎ 01424 813821
e-mail: enquiries@seaviewbnb.co.uk
web: www.seaviewbnb.co.uk
dir: *From Hastings on A259, right onto Fairlight Rd to Battery Hill. Turn right at Warren Rd*

Barn House Seaview B&B is located in Fairlight, just a couple of miles from Hastings. In a quiet location down a country lane, this 16th-century converted barn has an elevated position with far reaching sea views, and is set in 14 acres of garden and woodland. During summer months guests can enjoy the tennis court or play boules. Rooms are stylishly decorated and equipped with a number of thoughtful extras including well stocked beverage trays and free Wi-fi. There are also two large guest lounges. Dinner is available on request and guests can enjoy authentic Chinese cooking. A cooked and continental breakfast can be enjoyed in the conservatory.

Rooms 3 en suite (1 fmly) S £60-£80; D £80-£100
Facilities STV FTV TVL tea/coffee Dinner available Direct Dial Cen ht Wi-fi 🏊 Boules **Conf** Max 12 Thtr 12 Class 12 Board 12 **Parking** 6 **Notes** LB ☎

PREMIER COLLECTION

The Cloudesley

★★★★★ GUEST ACCOMMODATION

7 Cloudesley Rd TN37 6JN
☎ 01424 442524 & 07507 000148
e-mail: info@thecloudesley.co.uk
dir: *A21 London Rd onto A2102, left turn onto Tower Rd. Right turn onto Cloudesley Rd, situated at top of road on left*

The Cloudesley is located just minutes from Hastings in the quiet residential area of St Leonard's, and offers high standards of quality and comfort. The bedrooms have been environmentally designed - the walls have been eco-limewashed, the beds are handmade and have Siberian goosedown pillows and the shampoos are free of parabens and sodiam lauryl sulphate. There is a treatment room for holistic therapies. The two guest lounges are stylish and decorated with photographs taken by the proprietor. An extensive selection of cooked and continental dishes is available for breakfast, which includes locally sourced, organic ingredients.

Rooms 4 en suite **Facilities** tea/coffee Dinner available Cen ht Licensed Wi-fi Holistic therapies & massage **Notes** ⊗ No Children

---

PREMIER COLLECTION

The Laindons

★★★★★ BED AND BREAKFAST

23 High St, Old Town TN34 3EY
☎ 01424 437710
e-mail: jacksonchris2007@yahoo.co.uk
dir: *A21 onto seafront, turn left towards the old town. Left at lights onto High St, situated next to pharmacy*

The Laindons is a Georgian townhouse, formerly a coaching house, set on this attractive high street in Hastings. Bedrooms have been stylishly decorated offering guests comfortable accommodation; rooms include Freeview TV and Wi-fi. Whilst bedrooms are spacious, there is a guest lounge providing additional space for guests to relax. A cooked or continental breakfast can be enjoyed in the upper-floor conservatory with views of the downs and Hastings church.

Rooms 3 en suite S £80-£100; D £110-£125*
Facilities STV TVL tea/coffee Cen ht Wi-fi **Notes** ⊗ No Children 5yrs Closed Dec-Jan

HASTINGS & ST LEONARDS *continued*

Parkside House

★★★★ GUEST ACCOMMODATION

59 Lower Park Rd TN34 2LD
☎ 01424 433096
e-mail: bkentparksidehse@aol.com
dir: *A2101 to town centre, right at rdbt, 1st right*

You can expect a friendly welcome at this attractive Victorian house overlooking Alexandra Park, just a 10-minute walk from the town centre and seafront. The bedrooms are carefully furnished and have an abundance of thoughtful touches including free Wi-fi and a 'tuck shop' for midnight snackers. Breakfast is served at individual tables in the elegant dining room.

Rooms 5 rms (4 en suite) (1 pri facs) (1 fmly) S £35-£50; D £55-£70* **Facilities** TVL tea/coffee Cen ht Wi-fi **Notes** LB ⊗

White Cottage

★★★★ GUEST ACCOMMODATION

Battery Hill, Fairlight TN35 4AP
☎ 01424 812528 ▧ 01424 812285
dir: *3m E off A259 (Hastings-Rye), signed Fairlight*

This modern house is set among mature gardens on the outskirts of the peaceful village of Fairlight, between Hastings and Rye. White Cottage offers pleasantly decorated, thoughtfully furnished and well-equipped bedrooms. Breakfast is served in the bright and airy lounge-dining area which overlooks the beautiful garden.

Rooms 3 en suite (1 GF) S fr £50; D £75-£80 **Facilities** tea/coffee Cen ht **Parking** 4 **Notes** LB ⊗ No Children 12yrs Closed Dec ⊛

Seaspray Bed & Breakfast

★★★★ ⚄ GUEST HOUSE

54 Eversfield Place TN37 6DB
☎ 01424 436583
e-mail: jo@seaspraybb.co.uk
web: www.seaspraybb.co.uk
dir: *A21 to town centre & seafront, Seaspray 100yds W of pier*
Rooms 10 rms (8 en suite) (2 pri facs) (1 fmly) (1 GF) S £30-£50; D £60-£85* **Facilities** FTV tea/coffee Cen ht Wi-fi **Notes** LB ⊗ Closed 10 Jan-10 Feb

Eagle House

★★★ GUEST ACCOMMODATION

Pevensey Rd TN38 0JZ
☎ 01424 430535 & 437771
e-mail: info@eaglehousehotel.co.uk
web: www.eaglehousehotel.co.uk
dir: *Off seafront onto London Rd, premises next to St Leonards Shopping Centre*

Victorian property situated in a peaceful residential area within easy walking distance of the shops, college and seafront. Public areas are sumptuously decorated in a traditional style and the spacious 'retro' bedrooms are simply furnished. A hearty breakfast can be enjoyed in the dining room, which overlooks the gardens.

Rooms 19 en suite (4 fmly) (3 GF) S £45-£50; D £65-£85* **Facilities** FTV TVL tea/coffee Direct Dial Cen ht Licensed Wi-fi **Parking** 13 **Notes** ⊗

HEATHFIELD Map 6 TQ52

Holly Grove

★★★★ BED AND BREAKFAST

Little London TN21 0NU
☎ 01435 863375 & 07811 963193
e-mail: joedance@btconnect.com
dir: *A267 to Horam, turn right at Little London garage, proceed to bottom of lane*

Holly Grove is set in a quiet rural location with heated outdoor swimming pool, satellite TV, Wi-fi and parking facilities. Bedrooms are appointed to a very high standard. There is a separate lounge available for guests, and breakfast is served in the dining room or on the terrace, weather permitting.

Rooms 3 rms (2 en suite) (1 pri facs) (1 fmly) (2 GF) **Facilities** STV TVL tea/coffee Dinner available Cen ht Wi-fi ⚄ Pool table Table tennis Table hockey **Parking** 7

Stone House

★★★★ ⚄ ⚄ GUEST ACCOMMODATION

Rushlake Green TN21 9QJ
☎ 01435 830553 ▧ 01435 830726
e-mail: stonehousehotel@aol.co.uk

The Dunn family built the house in 1495 and has lived here ever since; they personally take care of their guests and Mrs Dunn only uses products from the estate in her acclaimed cuisine. The accommodation is traditional in style yet offers all modern amenities.

Rooms 7 en suite S £102-£138; D £138-£293* **Facilities** tea/coffee Dinner available Direct Dial Licensed Wi-fi ⚄ Snooker **Conf** Max 12 Thtr 12 Board 12 **Parking** 10 **Notes** LB No Children 9yrs Closed 23 Dec-3 Jan & 20 Feb-20 Mar

HERSTMONCEUX Map 6 TQ61

PREMIER COLLECTION

Wartling Place

★★★★★ GUEST ACCOMMODATION

Wartling Place, Wartling BN27 1RY
☎ 01323 832590 ▧ 01323 831558
e-mail: accom@wartlingplace.prestel.co.uk
dir: *2.5m SE of Herstmonceux. Off A271 to Wartling. Wartling Place opp village church*

Located in a sleepy village, this beautiful Grade II listed country home is set in two acres of well-tended gardens. The individually decorated bedrooms, two featuring four-poster beds, are luxurious and have a host of thoughtful extras. Delicious breakfasts are served in the elegant dining room. For business travellers, there is free broadband access.

Rooms 4 en suite (1 fmly) **Facilities** tea/coffee Dinner available Cen ht **Conf** Max 12 **Parking** 10 **Notes** ⊗

Cleavers Lyng Country House

★★★★ GUEST ACCOMMODATION

Church Rd BN27 1QJ
☎ 01323 833644
e-mail: cleaverslyng@btinternet.com
web: www.cleaverslyng.co.uk
dir: *A271at Herstmonceux, turn onto Chapel Row leading onto Church Rd, 1.5m on right*

Expect a warm welcome at this Grade II listed country house, parts of which date back to 1577. A spacious downstairs lounge and breakfast room offers the perfect place to relax with its log burning fireplace. Alternatively guests can enjoy the peaceful, landscaped gardens with fantastic views of beautiful Sussex countryside. Rooms are well appointed with LCD TVs, free Wi-fi and many with amazing scenic views.

Rooms 4 en suite (1 fmly) **Facilities** tea/coffee Cen ht Wi-fi **Parking** 10

HOVE

See Brighton & Hove

Save on B&Bs and Hotels. Book at **theAA.com/hotel**

SUSSEX, EAST 297 ENGLAND

LEWES
Map 6 TQ41

The Blacksmiths Arms
★★★★ INN

London Rd, Offham BN7 3QD
☎ 01273 472971
e-mail: blacksmithsarms@shineadsl.co.uk
web: www.theblacksmithsarms-offham.co.uk
dir: 1m N of Lewes. On A275 in Offham

Situated just outside Lewes, this is a great location for touring the South coast, offering high quality accommodation in comfortable bedrooms. Enjoyable meals are available in the cosy bar downstairs, and this is where the hearty cooked breakfast is also served.

Rooms 4 en suite **Facilities** FTV tea/coffee Dinner available Cen ht Wi-fi **Parking** 22 **Notes** ⊗ No coaches

The Granary
★★★★ GUEST ACCOMMODATION

Southerham BN8 6JN
☎ 01273 480728
e-mail: alison@thegranarylewes.co.uk

Located at the foot of the South Downs in the hamlet of Southerham, with easy access to both Lewes, Alfriston and Brighton, this converted barn offers modern and comfortable bedrooms. Guests can enjoy a cooked or continental breakfast in the conservatory or outside patio with views of the garden. The South Downs are very close to the property and neighbouring Lewes is just a short walk away.

Rooms 4 en suite (1 fmly) (4 GF) D £100-£120*
Facilities FTV TVL tea/coffee Cen ht Wi-fi Golf 18 **Parking** 10 **Notes** ⊗ Closed Jan

Nightingales
★★★★ GUEST ACCOMMODATION

The Avenue, Kingston BN7 3LL
☎ 01273 475673
e-mail: nightingalesbandb@gmail.com
dir: 2m SW of Lewes. A23 onto A27 to Lewes, at Ashcombe rdbt 3rd exit for Kingston, under rail bridge, 2nd right into The Avenue, house 2nd from end on right

A warm welcome is assured at this delightful modern bungalow, set in beautifully kept gardens and grounds. The spacious bedrooms and bathrooms are well appointed and come with a wide range of thoughtful extras, including fresh fruit and sherry. Refreshment is served on arrival in the lounge or conservatory, both of which overlook the garden.

Rooms 2 en suite (2 GF) **Facilities** TVL tea/coffee Cen ht **Parking** 2 **Notes** ⊗ No Children

ROTTINGDEAN
Map 6 TQ30

White Horse
★★★ INN

Marine Dr BN2 7HR
☎ 01273 300301 ⊟ 01273 308716
e-mail: 5308@greeneking.co.uk
dir: A27 Lewes towards Rottingdean on B1223

The White Horse is conveniently located just a couple of miles from Brighton, and is right on the seafront with uninterrupted views. Bedrooms are comfortable with modern fixtures and fittings, and there is free Wi-fi throughout. Dinner is served daily and a cooked or continental breakfast can be enjoyed in the restaurant. There is plenty of outside seating available.

Rooms 18 en suite (1 fmly) S £54-£69; D £69-£109*
Facilities Dinner available Direct Dial Cen ht Wi-fi Golf **Conf** Max 60 Thtr 60 Class 30 Board 30 **Parking** 40 **Notes** No coaches

RYE
Map 7 TQ92

See also Hastings & St Leonards

PREMIER COLLECTION

Jeake's House
★★★★★ ⌂ GUEST ACCOMMODATION

Mermaid St TN31 7ET
☎ 01797 222828
e-mail: stay@jeakeshouse.com
web: www.jeakeshouse.com
dir: Approach from High St or The Strand

Previously a 17th-century wool store and then a 19th-century Baptist school, this delightful house stands on a cobbled street in one of the most beautiful parts of this small, bustling town. The individually decorated bedrooms combine elegance and comfort with modern facilities. Breakfast is served at separate tables in the galleried dining room, and there is an oak-beamed lounge as well as a stylish book-lined bar with old pews. Jenny Hadfield was a finalist in this year's Friendliest Landlady of the Year award (2011-12).

Rooms 11 rms (10 en suite) (1 pri facs) (2 fmly) S £70-£80; D £90-£140 **Facilities** FTV tea/coffee Direct Dial Cen ht Licensed Wi-fi **Parking** 20 **Notes** LB No Children 5yrs

RYE *continued*

Manor Farm Oast

★★★★★ 🛏 🍽 BED AND BREAKFAST

Windmill Ln TN36 4WL
☎ 01424 813787 & 07866 818952
📠 01424 813787
e-mail: manor.farm.oast@lineone.net
web: www.manorfarmoast.co.uk
dir: *4m SW of Rye. A259 W past Icklesham church, left at x-rds onto Windmill Ln, after sharp left bend left into orchards*

A charming 19th-century, environmentally-friendly oast house peacefully located amid orchards in open countryside. Spacious bedrooms are individually styled and include numerous thoughtful extras including free Wi-fi. A choice of lounges is available, one heated by a roaring log fire during the winter, and locally sourced, home-produced dinners are a feature of any stay.

Rooms 3 rms (2 en suite) (1 pri facs) (1 fmly) S £85-£105; D £105* **Facilities** FTV tea/coffee Dinner available Cen ht Licensed Wi-fi **Conf** Max 20 Thtr 20 Board 12 **Parking** 8 **Notes** LB ⊗ No Children 11yrs Closed 23 Dec-15 Jan Civ Wed 50

Olde Moat House

★★★★★ 🏛 GUEST ACCOMMODATION

TN29 0AZ
☎ 01797 344700 📠 01797 343919
e-mail: oldemoathouse@hotmail.com
web: www.oldemoathouse.co.uk

(For full entry see Ivychurch (Kent))

White Vine House

★★★★★ 🍽 RESTAURANT WITH ROOMS

24 High St TN31 7JF
☎ 01797 224748
e-mail: info@whitevinehouse.co.uk
dir: *In town centre*

Situated in the heart of the ancient Cinque Port town of Rye, this property's origins go back to the 13th century. The cellar is the oldest part, but the current building dates from 1560 and boasts an impressive Georgian frontage. The original timber framework is visible in many areas, and certainly adds to the house's sense of history. The bedrooms have period furniture along with luxury bath or shower rooms; one bedroom has an antique four-poster.

Rooms 7 en suite (1 fmly) **Facilities** tea/coffee Dinner available Cen ht Wi-fi **Conf** Max 30 Thtr 30 Class 30 Board 30 **Notes** ⊗ No coaches Civ Wed 30

The Rise

★★★★★ 🅰 BED AND BREAKFAST

82 Udimore Rd TN31 7DY
☎ 01797 222285
e-mail: theriserye@aol.com
dir: *A21 Johns Cross take B2089 towards Rye. On entering Rye on right on bottom of hill*

Rooms 3 en suite S £70-£90; D £90-£120 **Facilities** FTV tea/coffee Cen ht Wi-fi **Parking** 3 **Notes** ⊗ No Children 12yrs Closed 23 Dec-3 Jan

Strand House

★★★★ 🏛 🍽 GUEST ACCOMMODATION

Tanyards Ln, Winchelsea TN36 4JT
☎ 01797 226276 📠 01797 224806
e-mail: info@thestrandhouse.co.uk
dir: *M20 junct 10 onto A2070 to Lydd. Follow A259 through Rye to Winchelsea, 2m past Rye*

This charming 15th-century house is just a few miles drive from Rye. Traditional character is maintained in comfortably appointed rooms and public areas. Local produce is a feature of the home-cooked evening meals and breakfasts.

Rooms 10 rms (9 en suite) (1 pri facs) 3 annexe en suite (4 fmly) (3 GF) S £55-£120; D £65-£155* **Facilities** FTV TVL tea/coffee Dinner available Cen ht Licensed Wi-fi **Parking** 15 **Notes** LB No Children 10yrs RS wknds (high season) 2 night bookings only Civ Wed 30

Little Saltcote

★★★★ 🏛 GUEST ACCOMMODATION

22 Military Rd TN31 7NY
☎ 01797 223210 & 07940 742646 📠 01797 224474
e-mail: info@littlesaltcote.co.uk
web: www.littlesaltcote.co.uk
dir: *0.5m N of town centre. Off A268 onto Military Rd signed Appledore, house 300yds on left*

This delightful family-run guest accommodation stands in quiet surroundings within walking distance of Rye town centre. The bright and airy en suite bedrooms are equipped with modern facilities including Wi-fi, and you can enjoy afternoon tea in the garden conservatory. A hearty breakfast is served at individual tables in the dining room.

Rooms 4 en suite (2 fmly) (1 GF) S £40-£75; D £70-£80* **Facilities** FTV tea/coffee Cen ht Wi-fi **Parking** 5 **Notes** LB

he Windmill Guest House

★★★★ GUEST ACCOMMODATION

erry Rd TN31 7DW
☎ 01797 224027
-mail: info@ryewindmill.co.uk
eb: www.ryewindmill.co.uk

his white smock windmill has been a Rye landmark
ince 1820 and was more recently a bakery. Bedrooms
ocated in the purpose-built extension have good beds
nd en suite facilities are generously proportioned.
reakfast taken in the old granary is a freshly-cooked
ffair from well-sourced local ingredients including local
utchers' sausages and some good local fruit juices.

ooms 10 en suite (1 fmly) (4 GF) **Facilities** FTV TVL tea/
offee Cen ht Licensed Wi-fi **Conf** Thtr 25 Class 30 Board
2 **Parking** 12 **Notes** No Children 12yrs Closed 24-26 Dec

---

Cliff Farm (TQ933237)

★★★ FARMHOUSE

Military Rd, Iden Lock TN31 7QD
☎ 01797 280331   🖹 01797 280331
Mrs P Sullivin
-mail: info@cliff-farm.com
ir: 2m along Military Rd to Appledore, turn left at
anging milk churn

Beautiful views and wonderful hospitality are what you'll
nd at this farmhouse situated in a peaceful rural
ocation just a short drive from Rye and Hastings.
Bedrooms are pleasantly decorated and comfortably
urnished. Breakfast is served at individual tables in the
ining room, and there is also a cosy sitting room with a
wood-burning stove and TV.

Rooms 3 rms (1 fmly) **Facilities** TVL tea/coffee Cen ht
Parking 6 **Notes** Closed Nov-Feb 🍽 6 acres smallholding

Tower House

★★★ BED AND BREAKFAST

Hilders Cliff TN31 7LD
☎ 01797 226865 & 07940 817438   🖹 01797 226865

This expansive Georgian property is conveniently located
n the heart of historic Rye. Benefiting from off-road car
parking, the house is set back off the road within its own
well tended gated gardens. Bedrooms are traditionally
decorated, and there is a TV lounge, as well as a spacious
dining room where guests can enjoy a cooked or
continental breakfast. There is a large snooker room with
full size table, large inglenook fireplace and seating for
guests to relax.

Rooms 3 rms (2 en suite) (1 pri facs) (1 GF) S £55-£60; D
£85-£95* **Facilities** TVL tea/coffee Cen ht Licensed
Snooker **Parking** 3 **Notes** ⊗ No Children 12yrs Closed
Dec-Wed before Etr 🍽

ST LEONARDS

See Hastings & St Leonards

SEAFORD   Map 6 TV49

Ab Fab Rooms

★★★★ 🏠 BED AND BREAKFAST

11 Station Rd, Bishopstone BN25 2RB
☎ 01323 895001 & 07713 197915   🖹 0705 360 3204
e-mail: stay@abfabrooms.co.uk

Just a short walk from Bishopstone station and sandy
beaches, this is a perfect base for visiting local sights
and attractions. Contemporary-styled bedrooms offer
superior comfort and amenities. Breakfast, served in the
garden conservatory, includes home-made jams and local
Sussex produce.

Rooms 3 en suite S £55-£65; D £70-£80 **Facilities** STV
tea/coffee Cen ht Wi-fi **Parking** 2 **Notes** ⊗ 🍽

The Avondale

★★★ GUEST ACCOMMODATION

Avondale Rd BN25 1RJ
☎ 01323 890008   🖹 01323 490598
e-mail: avondalehotel@btconnect.com
dir: In town centre, off A259 behind war memorial

A warm welcome is offered by the caring owners at this
friendly, family-run guest accommodation which is ideally
placed for the Newhaven to Dieppe ferry service. The
bedrooms are pleasantly furnished and thoughtfully
equipped. Breakfast is served in the attractive dining
room and guests also have the use of a cosy lounge.

Rooms 14 rms (8 en suite) (4 fmly) S £35-£45; D
£65-£85 **Facilities** TVL tea/coffee Cen ht Lift Licensed
Wi-fi **Conf** Max 15 Class 15 Board 15 **Notes** LB ⊗

SEDLESCOMBE   Map 7 TQ71

Kester House B&B

★★★★ 🏠 BED AND BREAKFAST

The Street TN33 0QB
☎ 01424 870035
e-mail: derek@kesterhouse.co.uk
dir: Off A21 onto B2244 signed Sedlescombe, turn left
after 0.75m. On entering village, Kester House on right

This 16th-century Grade II listed house is located in the
tranquil village of Sedlescombe, close to Hastings, Battle
and Rye. Bedrooms have been tastefully refurbished
offering stylish, comfortable accommodation while still
boasting many of the building's original features. There
is a guest lounge next to the dining room area where
guests can enjoy home-made refreshments on arrival and
a hearty cooked or continental breakfast which features
high quality, locally sourced produce.

Rooms 3 rms (1 en suite) (2 pri facs) (1 fmly) D
£75-£105* **Facilities** tea/coffee Cen ht Wi-fi **Notes** ⊗
No Children 7yrs Closed 24 Dec-2 Jan

WADHURST   Map 6 TQ63

Little Tidebrook Farm (TQ621304)

★★★★ FARMHOUSE

Riseden TN5 6NY
☎ 01892 782688 & 07970 159988
Mrs Sally Marley-Ward
e-mail: info@littletidebrook.co.uk
web: www.littletidebrook.co.uk
dir: A267 from Tunbridge Wells to Mark Cross, left onto
B2100, 2m turn right at Best Beech Inn, left after 1m
onto Riseden Rd, farm on left

This traditional farmhouse has cosy log fires in winter
and wonderful garden dining in warm months. The
imaginative decor combines with modern amenities such
as Wi-fi to provide leisure and business travellers with
the ideal setting. Close to Bewl Water and Royal
Tunbridge Wells.

Rooms 3 rms (2 en suite) (1 pri facs) S £50-£75; D
£50-£75* **Facilities** TVL tea/coffee Cen ht Wi-fi **Parking** 8
Notes No Children 12yrs 🍽 50 acres horses

WADHURST *continued*

The Greyhound Inn

★★★ INN

High St TN5 6AP
☎ 01892 783224
e-mail: info@thegreyhoundwadhurst.co.uk

This 16th-century inn is located in the centre of Wadhurst. The pub and restaurant area are traditional in style and feature a large open fireplace. Breakfast, lunch and dinner are served daily. Bedrooms are all annexed and have been converted from the original stable blocks. Bedrooms are spacious and comfortable and combine traditional features such as exposed oak beams with modern decor and furnishings.

Rooms 5 en suite (1 fmly) (3 GF) S £65; D £79*
Facilities FTV tea/coffee Dinner available Cen ht Wi-fi
Parking 8

WILMINGTON Map 6 TQ50

Crossways

★★★★ ⓖⓖ RESTAURANT WITH ROOMS

Lewes Rd BN26 5SG
☎ 01323 482455 ▤ 01323 487811
e-mail: stay@crosswayshotel.co.uk
web: www.crosswayshotel.co.uk
dir: *On A27 between Lewes & Polegate, 2m E of Alfriston rdbt*

Amidst stunning gardens and attractively tended grounds sits this well-established, popular restaurant. The well-presented bedrooms are tastefully decorated and provide an abundance of thoughtful amenities including free Wi-fi. Guest comfort is paramount and the naturally warm hospitality ensures guests often return.

Rooms 7 en suite S £79-£85; D £130-£170 **Facilities** FTV tea/coffee Dinner available Direct Dial Cen ht Wi-fi
Parking 30 **Notes** LB ⊗ No Children 12yrs Closed 24 Dec-23 Jan No coaches

SUSSEX, WEST

AMBERLEY Map 6 TQ01

Woody Banks Cottage

★★★★ BED AND BREAKFAST

Crossgates BN18 9NR
☎ 01798 831295 & 07719 916703
e-mail: woodybanks@btinternet.com
web: www.woodybanks.co.uk
dir: *Off B2139 into village, right at Black Horse pub, Woody Banks 0.5m on left past Sportsman pub*

Located close to Arundel on an elevated position with stunning views over the Wildbrooks, this immaculately maintained house and gardens is very popular with walkers. It provides two comfortable, homely bedrooms filled with thoughtful extras. Imaginative breakfasts are served in the panoramic lounge-dining room.

Rooms 2 rms (1 pri facs) (1 fmly) S £35-£45; D £70-£75 **Facilities** TVL tea/coffee Cen ht **Parking** 3 **Notes** LB ⊗ No Children 6yrs Closed 24-27 Dec ⓔ

ANGMERING Map 6 TQ00

Angmering Manor

★★★★ ⌨ GUEST ACCOMMODATION

High St BN16 4AG
☎ 01903 859849 ▤ 01903 783268
e-mail: angmeringmanor@thechapmansgroup.co.uk
web: www.relaxinnz.co.uk
dir: *Follow A27 towards Portsmouth, exit A280, follow signs for Angmering*

This former manor house in the heart of the village has been stylishly appointed. It offers good food, a bar, an indoor pool, and good parking. Staff are friendly and helpful and rooms are very comfortable.

Rooms 17 en suite (3 fmly) (4 GF) **Facilities** FTV TVL tea/coffee Dinner available Direct Dial Cen ht Licensed Wi-fi ⓢ Sauna Gym Beauty salon **Parking** 25 **Notes** LB ⊗ Civ Wed

ARUNDEL Map 6 TQ00

See also Amberley

Hanger Down House B&B

★★★★ BED AND BREAKFAST

Priory Ln, Tortington BN18 0BG
☎ 01903 882904 & 07753 595191
e-mail: aayling@btinternet.com
web: www.hangerdownhouse.co.uk
dir: *A27 to Arundel, take road signed Ford/Climping at Arundel rdbt. Priory Ln 0.5m on right*

Set in picturesque Sussex countryside, Hanger Down House is conveniently and quietly located one mile from the historic town of Arundel. Both bedrooms are stylishly decorated and provide comfortable accommodation for guests. Bedrooms include king-sized beds, a leather sofa, refrigerators, digital LCD TVs and free Wi-fi. There are great views of the local countryside and a walled garden which guests are free to use. A cooked or continental breakfast can be enjoyed downstairs in the dining room.

Rooms 3 en suite (2 fmly) (1 GF) S £60-£80; D £80-£120 **Facilities** FTV TVL TV2B tea/coffee Cen ht Wi-fi ⛳ Pool table Trampoline Football pitch Outdoor table tennis **Parking** 5 **Notes** LB ⊗ ⊗ ⓔ

The Townhouse

★★★★ ⓖⓖ RESTAURANT WITH ROOMS

65 High St BN18 9AJ
☎ 01903 883847
e-mail: enquiries@thetownhouse.co.uk
web: www.thetownhouse.co.uk
dir: *A27 to Arundel, into High Street, establishment on left at top of hill*

This is an elegant, Grade II-listed Regency building overlooking Arundel Castle, just a short walk from the shops and centre of the town. Bedrooms and public areas retain the building's unspoilt character. The ceiling in the dining room is particularly spectacular and originated in Florence in the 16th century. The owners can be justifiably proud of the enterprise they undertook just a few years ago.

Rooms 4 en suite S £75; D £95-£130* **Facilities** FTV tea/coffee Dinner available Cen ht Wi-fi **Notes** ⊗ Closed 2wks Feb & 2wks Oct RS Sun-Mon Restaurant closed No coaches

Save on B&Bs and Hotels. Book at **theAA.com/hotel**

SUSSEX, WEST 301 ENGLAND

Arden

★★★ GUEST ACCOMMODATION

4 Queens Ln BN18 9JN
☎ **01903 882544**
e-mail: info@ardenguesthouse.net
dir: From station, at rdbt take turning for town centre. Take next left onto Queens Ln

This is a comfortable guest accommodation situated a few minutes from the town centre and station. The property has a selection of single, double and twin bedrooms, some of which are en suite. Traditional cooked breakfasts are served in the well-lit dining room. Off-street parking is available.

Rooms 8 rms (5 en suite) (2 GF) S £47-£55; D £60-£75 **Facilities** tea/coffee Cen ht **Parking** 5 **Notes** ⊗ No Children 14yrs Closed 31 Dec

BOGNOR REGIS   Map 6 SZ99

Arbor D'Oak

★★★★ BED AND BREAKFAST

221 Hawthorn Rd PO21 2UW
☎ **01243 861280**
e-mail: arbordoak@uwclub.net
dir: A29 to Bognor Regis, pass hospital, take last exit from rdbt Chichester Rd A259. Over lights next left onto Hawthorn Rd, past sports field, 50yds on left

A modern property offering guests stylish, comfortable accommodation. Bedrooms and bathrooms are spacious with excellent quality fixtures and fittings. Useful features include hairdryers and irons in the rooms. The guest lounge on the ground floor creates additional space in which to relax. Breakfast can be enjoyed around the family-style breakfast table in the conservatory that looks out over the garden.

Rooms 2 rms (1 en suite) (1 pri facs) S £55-£85; D £90-£130* **Facilities** FTV TVL tea/coffee Cen ht cycle storage available **Parking** 4 **Notes** LB ⊗ No Children Closed Oct-Mar

Old Priory

★★★★ GUEST HOUSE

80 North Bersted St PO22 9AQ
☎ **01243 863580**   📠 **01243 826597**
e-mail: old.priory@btinternet.com
web: www.old-priory.com
dir: 1.6m NW of Bognor. Off A259 (Chichester road) to North Bersted. Old Priory sign on left

Located in the mainly residential area of North Bersted, this 400-year-old property retains many original features. Bedrooms which are all individual in style are homely, and one has a four-poster waterbed and a double air bath. There is an outdoor pool and attractive grounds, perfect for the summer.

Rooms 3 rms (2 en suite) (1 pri facs) 3 annexe en suite (3 GF) S £40-£50; D £65-£100* **Facilities** STV tea/coffee Cen ht Wi-fi ⏲ Hot tub **Parking** 6

Jubilee Guest House

★★★ GUEST ACCOMMODATION

5 Gloucester Rd PO21 1NU
☎ **01243 863016**
dir: A259 to seafront, house opp Day Entrance to Butlins

This property is conveniently located opposite Butlins and in close proximity to the sea front and town centre. Comfortably appointed bedrooms come well equipped with free Wi-fi, flat screen digital TVs and heating/cooling systems. A cooked breakfast can be enjoyed in the attractive dining room.

Rooms 6 rms (2 en suite) (4 pri facs) (3 fmly) S £25-£40; D £50-£80* **Facilities** tea/coffee Cen ht **Parking** 4 **Notes** LB ⊗ Closed Xmas, Jan & Feb

BOLNEY   Map 6 TQ22

8 Bells Bed & Breakfast

★★★★ ⊜ INN

The Long House, The Street RH17 5QP
☎ **01444 881396**
e-mail: stay@8bellsbandb.com
dir: A23/A272 junct. Village situated between Ansty & Cowfold on A272

Situated in a peaceful village and in close proximity to both Heathfield and Crawley, this Tudor property has been restored following a complete refurbishment. Many original features, including exposed beams, remain, along with high quality, modern and comfortable accommodation. Guests check in at the establishment's pub located directly opposite and it is here that breakfast, lunch and dinner can be enjoyed.

Rooms 3 en suite (1 fmly) (1 GF) S £50-£105; D £60-£105* **Facilities** FTV tea/coffee Dinner available Cen ht Wi-fi Golf 18 Pool table Billiards **Parking** 15 **Notes** LB ⊗

BOSHAM   Map 5 SU80

Charters B&B

★★★★ BED AND BREAKFAST

Bosham Ln PO18 8HG
☎ **01243 572644 & 07967 010530**
e-mail: louise@chartersbandb.co.uk
dir: A27 onto A259, 3m left at rdbt, right at T-junct, 100yds on right

This establishment provides comfortable accommodation in a peaceful location close to Bosham Harbour and the Goodwood racing circuit. The stylish, modern bedrooms and bathrooms are spacious, and have their own separate entrances. A continental breakfast is served in the comfort of the bedrooms mid-week; a fully-cooked, freshly prepared, hot breakfast is offered on Saturday and Sunday mornings, and is served in the bright and airy conservatory.

Rooms 2 annexe en suite (1 GF) S £65-£80; D £75-£100* **Facilities** tea/coffee Cen ht Wi-fi **Parking** 3 **Notes** ⊗ No Children 10yrs Closed Xmas & New Year

BOSHAM *continued*

White Barn

☆☆☆☆ BED AND BREAKFAST

Crede Ln PO18 8NX
☎ 01243 573113   📠 01243 573113
e-mail: chrissie@whitebarn.biz
web: www.whitebarn.biz
dir: *A259 Bosham rdbt, turn S signed Bosham Quay, 0.5m to T-junct, left signed White Barn, 0.25m turn left signed White Barn, 50yds turn right*

This delightful single storey property is close to Bosham Harbour, Goodwood Race Circuit, Chichester and Portsmouth, and has cosy bedrooms with colour co-ordinated soft furnishings and many thoughtful extras. The open-plan dining room overlooks an attractive garden, where breakfast is served if the weather permits.

Rooms 2 en suite 1 annexe en suite (3 GF) S £65-£75; D £80-£99* Facilities FTV tea/coffee Cen ht Wi-fi Parking 3 Notes ⊗ No Children 12yrs Closed Xmas & New Year

---

BURGESS HILL Map 6 TQ31

Abbey House

☆☆☆☆ BED AND BREAKFAST

2 The Holt RH15 0RF
☎ 01444 233299
e-mail: info@abbey-house.biz
dir: *0.5m E of town centre. Off A2113 Folders Ln onto Kings Way, 3rd left onto The Holt*

This excellent accommodation is set in a comfortable family home, in a pleasant residential area, just a short walk from the town centre and railway station. The modern bedrooms are well equipped and include hairdryers, TVs, fridges and CD players. Welcoming touches include wine and fruit. A good breakfast is served around a large communal dining table.

Rooms 4 rms (3 en suite) (1 pri facs) (1 GF) Facilities FTV tea/coffee Direct Dial Cen ht Wi-fi Parking 5 Notes ⊗ No Children 11yrs Closed 24 Dec-2 Jan

---

CHARLTON Map 6 SU81

The Fox Goes Free

★★★★ INN

PO18 0HU
☎ 01243 811461   📠 01243 811712
e-mail: enquiries@thefoxgoesfree.com

This former hunting lodge has retained much original character and is located in lovely countryside at the foot of the South Downs National Park. It is well equipped to offer the modern traveller a comfortable bed for the night. The bedrooms are well appointed and the pub boasts low ceilings, brick floors and three inglenook fireplaces. The inn serves its own ale and has an inviting daily-changing menu. During the summer months, guests can take advantage of the rear garden.

Rooms 5 en suite S £65-£120; D £90-£120 (room only)* Facilities FTV tea/coffee Dinner available Cen ht Wi-fi Parking 50

CHICHESTER Map 5 SU80

See also Bosham & West Marden

PREMIER COLLECTION

Rooks Hill

☆☆☆☆☆ GUEST HOUSE

Lavant Rd, Lavant PO18 0BQ
☎ 01243 528400
e-mail: enquiries@rookshill.co.uk

Rooks Hill occupies a convenient and picturesque location near Goodwood and the city of Chichester. The warm and friendly proprietors create a wonderful home-from-home atmosphere. Rooms offer powerful thermostatic showers and additional thoughtful extras. A delicious breakfast served in the stylish dining room or on the patio overlooking the pretty gardens in warmer weather provides a substantial start to the day.

Rooms 3 en suite (1 GF) S £80-£135; D £90-£175* Facilities FTV TVL tea/coffee Cen ht Wi-fi Golf 19 Parking 6 Notes LB ⊗ No Children 12yrs

---

PREMIER COLLECTION

The Royal Oak Inn

★★★★★ ⊚ INN

Pook Ln PO18 0AX
☎ 01243 527434
e-mail: info@royaloakeastlavant.co.uk
dir: *2m N of Chichester. Off A286 into East Lavant centre*

Located close to the Goodwood estate and Rolls Royce HQ this delightful inn is full of character with beamed ceilings, timber floors and open fires in the public areas. Bedrooms are finished to a very high standard with comfortable beds and state-of-the-art electronic equipment. Award-winning meals are served in the popular restaurant.

Rooms 3 en suite 5 annexe en suite (1 fmly) (2 GF) S £95-£160; D £105-£295* Facilities STV FTV tea/coffee Dinner available Direct Dial Cen ht Wi-fi Riding Parking 25 Notes ⊗ No coaches

---

Richmond House Boutique B&B

☆☆☆☆ BED AND BREAKFAST

230 Oving Rd PO19 7EJ
☎ 01243 771464   & 07909 971736
e-mail: richmondhousechichester@hotmail.co.uk
web: www.richmondhousechichester.co.uk
dir: *From A27 bypass enter Chichester from lights E of city on Oving Rd. 1m on left*

Richmond House is conveniently located within a short walking distance of the town centre. Bedrooms and bathrooms are stylishly decorated and offer guests high quality comfort. All bedrooms come equipped with digital TVs, free Wi-fi and beverage making facilities. An extensive cooked or continental breakfast can be enjoyed in the private dining area

Rooms 3 en suite S £70-£115; D £80-£120* Facilities FTV tea/coffee Cen ht Wi-fi Parking 1 Notes LB ⊗

Abelands Barn B&B

★★★★ BED AND BREAKFAST

Bognor Rd, Merston PO20 1DY
☎ 01243 533826 📠 01243 783576
e-mail: snooze@abelandsbarn.co.uk
dir: 2.5m E of city centre on A259

Abelands Barn is located just two miles south of Chichester on the A259 with close proximity to Goodwood, Bognor Regis and Arundel. Bedrooms in the main house are traditionally decorated and comfortable, with far reaching countryside views and large open-plan lounge area. The annexed flint stone barn conversion offers stylish, modern and spacious rooms. Breakfast is served in the main house where guests can enjoy a cooked or continental breakfast.

Rooms 1 en suite 1 annexe en suite S £35-£70; D £60-£120 **Facilities** FTV TVL tea/coffee Cen ht Wi-fi **Parking** 5 **Notes** LB ⊗ 🐾

The Bull's Head

★★★★ INN

99 Fishbourne Road West PO19 3JP
☎ 01243 839895
e-mail: julie@bullsheadfishbourne.net
dir: A27 onto A259, 0.5m on left

The Bull's Head is a charming traditionally-styled inn which has a roaring open fire during winter months. By contrast, the accommodation is modern and contemporary and offers very good levels of comfort, spacious showers and generously sized fluffy towels. Evening meals and enjoyable breakfasts are provided daily. The establishment is perfectly located for Fishbourne Roman Palace, Goodwood, Portsmouth, Chichester Theatre and Bosham Harbour.

Rooms 4 en suite (1 fmly) (4 GF) **Facilities** FTV tea/coffee Dinner available Cen ht Wi-fi **Parking** 35 **Notes** LB

82 Fishbourne

★★★★ BED AND BREAKFAST

82 Fishbourne Road West PO19 3JL
☎ 07854 051013
e-mail: nik@nikwestacott.plus.com
dir: A27 Chichester rdbt, towards Fishbourne and Bosham on A259. 0.5m on right diagonally opp Woolpack pub

Warm and friendly hospitality abounds at 82 Fishbourne which is located only a short drive from the historic city of Chichester. Accommodation is spacious and well equipped. Breakfast provides a substantial start to the day and includes delicious fresh eggs from the free range hens which live in the back garden. Scheduled activities include 'Mushroom Hunts' and wine tastings held throughout the year.

Rooms 3 en suite (1 fmly) (1 GF) **Facilities** FTV tea/coffee Dinner available Cen ht Licensed Wi-fi **Parking** 3

Englewood B&B

★★★★ ⌂ BED AND BREAKFAST

East Ashling PO18 9AS
☎ 01243 575407
e-mail: sjenglewood@hotmail.co.uk
dir: Bosham rdbt A259, N exit. At T-junct turn right, next left to B2178, left again, Englewood on left

Set well back from the main road and in the South Downs National Park, Englewood has a very pretty garden, and is surrounded by pleasant lanes and footpaths. The two bedrooms have lots of thoughtful facilities and extras including bottled water, boiled sweets and fruit squash.

Rooms 2 rms (1 en suite) (1 pri facs) (2 GF) S £35-£45; D £50-£75* **Facilities** FTV tea/coffee Cen ht Wi-fi **Parking** 2 **Notes** LB ⊗ No Children 🐾

Gable End

★★★★ BED AND BREAKFAST

Main Rd, Nutbourne PO18 8RT
☎ 01243 573356
e-mail: jill@po188rt.freeserve.co.uk
dir: A259 W past Barleycorn pub on left, after 0.3m turn left & immediately right, 150yds 4th house on left, set back from road

You are guaranteed a genuinely warm welcome at Gable End which occupies a peaceful location close to Bosham and Emsworth Marina. Enjoy a delicious home-cooked breakfast in attractive surroundings with views from the rear of the property overlooking the sea and pretty garden.

Rooms 1 rms (1 pri facs) D £70-£80* **Facilities** tea/coffee Cen ht Wi-fi **Parking** 8 **Notes** ⊗ No Children 11yrs Closed 23 Dec-2 Jan 🐾

Horse and Groom

★★★★ INN

East Ashling PO18 9AX
☎ 01243 575339
e-mail: info@thehorseandgroomchichester.co.uk
web: www.thehorseandgroomchichester.co.uk
dir: 3m N of Chichester, on B2178 towards Rowland's Castle

The Horse and Groom is a unique 17th-century country pub and restaurant offering spacious and comfortable accommodation and warm, friendly hospitality. The substantial, freshly prepared breakfasts, lunches and dinners make good use of freshly caught fish and locally sourced ingredients.

Rooms 11 en suite (11 GF) S £45-£55; D £70-£80 **Facilities** tea/coffee Dinner available Cen ht Wi-fi **Parking** 40 **Notes** RS Sun eve Bar & Restaurant close 6pm

Old Chapel Forge

★★★★ ⌂ BED AND BREAKFAST

Lower Bognor Rd, Lagness PO20 1LR
☎ 01243 264380
e-mail: info@oldchapelforge.co.uk
dir: 4m SE of Chichester. Off A27 Chichester bypass at Bognor rdbt signed Pagham/Runcton, onto B2166 Pagham Rd & Lower Bognor Rd, Old Chapel Forge on right

Great local produce features in the hearty breakfasts at this comfortable, eco-friendly property, an idyllic 17th-century house and chapel set in mature gardens with panoramic views of the South Downs. Old Chapel Forge is a short drive from Chichester, Goodwood, Pagham Harbour Nature Reserve and the beach. Bedrooms, including suites in the chapel, are luxurious, and all have internet access.

Rooms 4 annexe en suite (2 fmly) (4 GF) S £45-£90; D £50-£120* **Facilities** tea/coffee Dinner available Cen ht Wi-fi Golf 18 **Parking** 6 **Notes** LB

CHICHESTER *continued*

The Vestry

★★★ INN

23 Southgate PO19 1ES
☎ 01243 773358 🖃 08720 220801
e-mail: info@the-vestry.com

The Vestry is conveniently located in the town centre. Bedrooms are spacious and well equipped including beverage making facilities and Wi-fi. The bar and restaurant are spacious with comfortable seating areas; during the winter months guests can keep cosy in front of the log fires. Lunch and dinner are served daily; both continental and range of wholesome cooked breakfasts are available.

Rooms 11 en suite (2 fmly) S £55-£65; D £65-£75*
Facilities FTV tea/coffee Dinner available Wi-fi
Notes Closed 24-26 Dec & 31 Dec-1 Jan

CLIMPING   Map 6 SU90

Derwent House

★★★★ BED AND BREAKFAST

Climping St BN17 5RQ
☎ 01903 726204
e-mail: jonshorrock@yahoo.co.uk
dir: Turn S off A259 at Yapton onto Climping St

Derwent House is situated in the Conservation Area of the Climping Gap, the last undeveloped stretch of coastline between Brighton and Bognor Regis. Guests will find a warm and friendly welcome at this attractive country house, which offers well-appointed rooms, a dining room and a cosy lounge overlooking the garden.

Rooms 2 en suite D £70* **Facilities** FTV TVL tea/coffee Cen ht Wi-fi Golf 18 Fishing Riding Snooker **Parking** 8
Notes LB No Children

CRAWLEY

For accommodation details see Gatwick Airport (London)

GATWICK AIRPORT (LONDON)   Map 6 TQ24

Acorn Lodge Gatwick

★★★★ GUEST ACCOMMODATION

79 Massetts Rd RH6 7EB
☎ 01293 774550
e-mail: info@acornlodgegatwick.co.uk
web: www.acornlodgegatwick.co.uk
dir: M23 junct 9, A23 into Horley, off A23 Brighton Rd

This property provides a 24-hour transfer service to the airport and has on-site parking. Bedrooms are comfortably furnished, come with a practical desk area and useful touches. The breakfasts served in the comfortable dining room make a good start to the day; dinner is also available.

Rooms 15 en suite (4 fmly) (7 GF) **Facilities** FTV TVL tea/coffee Dinner available Cen ht Licensed Wi-fi **Parking** 20
Notes ⊗

Corner House

★★★★ GUEST ACCOMMODATION

72 Massetts Rd RH6 7ED
☎ 01293 784574 🖃 01293 784620
e-mail: info@thecornerhouse.co.uk
web: www.thecornerhouse.co.uk
dir: M23 junct 9, to Gatwick, 1st rdbt 2nd exit (straight ahead) next rdbt 4th exit signed Redhill. Onto A23 towards Redhill, turn off 2nd right Massetts Rd, on left

Well located for Gatwick Airport with a 24-hour courtesy transfer service, the Corner House provides a range of thoughtfully furnished bedrooms, some in a separate house. Ground-floor areas include an attractive dining room and a comfortable lounge bar.

Rooms 19 rms (13 en suite) 12 annexe en suite (6 fmly) (9 GF) **Facilities** FTV TVL tea/coffee Dinner available Direct Dial Cen ht Licensed Golf 18 Membership to local sports centre **Conf** Max 15 Class 15 Board 15 **Parking** 12

The Lawn Guest House

★★★★ GUEST HOUSE

30 Massetts Rd RH6 7DF
☎ 01293 775751 🖃 01293 821803
e-mail: info@lawnguesthouse.co.uk
web: www.lawnguesthouse.com
dir: M25 junct 7, M23 S towards Brighton/Gatwick Airport. Exit at junct 9. At either South or North Terminal rdbts take A23 towards Redhill. At 3rd rdbt (Esso garage on left) take 3rd exit. (Texaco garage on right). In 200yds right at lights onto Massetts Rd. Guest house 400yds on left

Once a Victorian school, this friendly guest house is well-positioned on a quiet leafy street close to Gatwick. Bedrooms are spacious with thoughtful amenities such as free Wi-fi, and fans for use in warm weather. Airport parking is available.

Rooms 12 en suite (4 fmly) **Facilities** STV tea/coffee Direct Dial Cen ht Wi-fi **Parking** 4

Trumbles

★★★★ GUEST ACCOMMODATION

Stan Hill RH6 0EP
☎ 01293 863418 🖃 01293 862925
e-mail: stay@trumbles.co.uk
web: www.trumbles.co.uk
dir: 0.5m N of Charlwood. From village centre onto Norwoodhill Rd, 1st left onto Stan Hill

This attractive house, within easy reach of Gatwick, enjoys a quiet and secluded setting in this charming village. Bedrooms are spacious with a good range of facilities. The conservatory offers an ideal environment for guests to relax and enjoy either continental or full English breakfast. Parking is available, along with airport transfers.

Rooms 6 en suite (2 fmly) (1 GF) S £60; D £70-£75*
Facilities FTV TVL tea/coffee Cen ht Wi-fi **Parking** 20
Notes ⊗ Closed 24-25 Dec

Vulcan Lodge

★★★★ BED AND BREAKFAST

27 Massetts Rd RH6 7DQ
☎ 01293 771522 & 07980 576012 🖃 01737 720153
e-mail: reservations@vulcan-lodge.com
dir: M23 junct 9, A23 into Horley, off A23 Brighton Rd

A particularly warm and friendly welcome is offered by the hosts of this charming period house, which sits back from the main road and is convenient for Gatwick Airport. Bedrooms are well equipped and feature many thoughtful extras. A choice of breakfast is offered, including vegetarian, and is served in a delightful dining room.

Rooms 4 rms (3 en suite) (1 pri facs) (1 fmly) S £40-£45; D £55-£60* **Facilities** FTV TVL tea/coffee Cen ht Wi-fi **Parking** 13

Save on B&Bs and Hotels. Book at **theAA.com/hotel**

SUSSEX, WEST 305 **ENGLAND**

Gainsborough Lodge

★★★ GUEST ACCOMMODATION

39 Massetts Rd RH6 7DT
☎ 01293 783982 ▤ 01293 785365
e-mail: enquiries@gainsborough-lodge.co.uk
dir: 2m NE of airport off A23 Brighton Rd

Close to Gatwick, this fine Edwardian house offers a courtesy service to and from the airport. The bright bedrooms are comfortably appointed, and a varied breakfast, including a vegetarian option, is served in the cheerful conservatory-dining room. There is also an attractive lounge and bar.

Rooms 16 rms (14 en suite) 14 annexe en suite (5 fmly) (12 GF) **Facilities** TVL tea/coffee Direct Dial Cen ht Free membership of local Gym **Parking** 30 **Notes** ⊗

Gatwick White House

★★ GUEST ACCOMMODATION

50-52 Church Rd RH6 7EX
☎ 01293 402777 & 784322 ▤ 01293 424135
e-mail: hotel@gwhh.com
web: www.gwhh.com
dir: In Horley centre off A23 (Brighton Rd)

Convenient for the airport and major routes, this establishment offers efficient and functional accommodation. There is a bar, restaurant with good curries as well as traditional dishes, parking, and a 24-hour transfer service to Gatwick is available on request.

Rooms 27 en suite (2 fmly) (10 GF) **Facilities** TVL tea/coffee Dinner available Direct Dial Cen ht Licensed Wi-fi **Parking** 30 **Notes** ⊗

HENFIELD Map 6 TQ21

Frylands (TQ231197)

★★★★ FARMHOUSE

Wineham BN5 9BP
☎ 01403 710214
Mrs S Fowler
e-mail: frylandsfarm@gmail.com
dir: 2m NE of Henfield. Off B2116 towards Wineham, 1.5m left onto Fryland Ln, Frylands 0.3m on left

The friendly hosts offer comfortable accommodation at this delightful 16th-century timber-framed farmhouse, set in peaceful countryside. Day rooms and bedrooms are full of character and the well-appointed dining room is the setting for freshly cooked breakfasts. Ample off-road parking and free car storage for travellers using Gatwick Airport is available.

Rooms 3 rms (2 pri facs) (1 fmly) S £35-£37.50; D £55-£60* **Facilities** tea/coffee Cen ht Wi-fi ⚞ Fishing **Parking** 4 **Notes** ⊗ Closed 21 Dec-2 Jan ⊜ 250 acres mixed

---

HORSHAM Map 6 TQ13

Denham Cottage

★★★★ BED AND BREAKFAST

1 Friday St, Warnham RH12 3QY
☎ 01403 243362
e-mail: denhamcottage@btinternet.com
dir: From A24 into Warnham, past church on left, 2nd right, cottage 2nd on left

Denham Cottage is situated in the picturesque village of Warnham, near Horsham on the edge of the famous deer park. Very smart and spacious accommodation with a private lounge/study adjoining and lots of useful extras, whether staying on business or for pleasure.

Rooms 1 en suite **Facilities** TVL tea/coffee Cen ht Wi-fi **Parking** 2 **Notes** ⊗ Closed Xmas ⊜

Random Hall

★★★★ GUEST ACCOMMODATION

Stane St, Slinfold RH13 0QX
☎ 01403 790558 ▤ 01403 330475
e-mail: nigelrandomhall@btconnect.com
web: www.randomhall.co.uk
dir: 4m W of Horsham. On A29 W of Slinfold

This 16th-century farmhouse combines character with good quality accommodation and service from the resident proprietors. The comfortable bedrooms are equipped with useful extras. Beams, flagstone floors and quality fabrics add style to the bar and public areas, and an enjoyable dinner is served Monday to Saturday.

Rooms 13 en suite (5 GF) **Facilities** STV tea/coffee Dinner available Direct Dial Cen ht Licensed Wi-fi Golf 18 **Conf** Max 20 Thtr 20 Class 10 Board 10 **Parking** 40 **Notes** ⊗

LINDFIELD Map 6 TQ32

PREMIER COLLECTION

The Pilstyes

★★★★★ BED AND BREAKFAST

106-108 High St RH16 2HS
☎ 01444 484101
e-mail: carol@pontifexes.co.uk
web: www.sussex-bedandbreakfast.co.uk
dir: On High Street (B2028), 8 houses down from church

Pilstyes is a Grade II-listed village house that was built around 1575. The spacious bedrooms are beautifully furnished and provide all the comforts of home. A healthy breakfast is served in the charming country kitchen or, on sunny days, in the flower-filled cottage courtyard. Carol and Roy are caring hosts providing a warm welcome and ensuring a pleasant stay.

Rooms 2 en suite S £75-£100; D £85-£105* **Facilities** FTV TVL tea/coffee Cen ht Wi-fi **Parking** 4 **Notes** ⊗ No Children 5yrs

---

LITTLEHAMPTON Map 6 TQ00

Leeside

★★★★ GUEST ACCOMMODATION

Rope Walk BN17 5DE
☎ 01903 723666 & 07791 797131
e-mail: leeside1@tiscali.co.uk
dir: Off A259. Onto Ferry Road 1m, turn right, up on right

This bright bungalow is close to local sailing clubs, the River Arun and the beach. Visitors will enjoy a warm welcome in the comfortable modern bedrooms that have flat-screen TVs and free Wi-fi. The hearty breakfasts make a good start to the day.

Rooms 4 en suite (3 GF) **Facilities** FTV TVL tea/coffee Cen ht Wi-fi **Parking** 4 **Notes** ⊗ No Children 14yrs

East Beach Guest House

★★★★ GUEST HOUSE

71 South Ter BN17 5LQ
☎ 01903 714270 ▤ 01903 714270
e-mail: info@eastbeachguesthouse.co.uk
web: www.eastbeachguesthouse.co.uk
dir: On South Terrace, opposite beach, 200mtrs from junct with Pier Rd

A newly refurbished guest house which offers individually styled and comfortable accommodation; all rooms are equipped with a good range of amenities including flat-screen TVs and Wi-fi. Some bedrooms have sea views. A freshly cooked breakfast, using local produce, is served on the first-floor breakfast room that overlooks the sea.

Rooms 9 en suite (2 fmly) (2 GF) **Facilities** FTV TVL tea/coffee Cen ht Wi-fi **Notes** LB ⊗ No Children 3yrs

MIDHURST — Map 6 SU82

See also Rogate

Loves Farm *(SU912235)*

★★★★ FARMHOUSE

Easebourne St GU29 0BG
☎ 01730 813212 & 07789 228400
Mr J Renwick
e-mail: renwick@lovesl.fsnet.co.uk
dir: *2m NE of town centre. Off A272 at Easebourne church onto Easebourne St, signs for Loves Farm*

This 17th-century farmhouse is set on a 300-acre farm with wonderful views of the South Downs from the windows. The comfortable rooms have their own entrance and benefit from king-size beds and en suite or private shower rooms. This is a great location for access to Midhurst, Cowdray Park and Goodwood.

Rooms 3 rms (2 en suite) (1 pri facs) (2 fmly) (1 GF) S £50-£55; D £75-£85* **Facilities** FTV tea/coffee Cen ht Wi-fi **Parking** 3 **Notes** ⊗ ⊜ 300 acres arable/horses

ROGATE — Map 5 SU82

PREMIER COLLECTION

Mizzards

★★★★★ BED AND BREAKFAST

GU31 5HS
☎ 01730 821656 📠 01730 821655
e-mail: francis@mizzards.co.uk
dir: *0.6m S from Rogate x-rds, over river & signed 300yds on right*

This charming 16th-century house stands near the River Rother in two acres of beautiful landscaped gardens with a lake and the proprietor's own sculptures. Guests can relax in either the conservatory or the split-level drawing room, and the airy, well-appointed bedrooms look over the grounds. There is an entrance hall, dining room, and a swimming pool is available in summer.

Rooms 3 en suite S £55-£65; D £80-£92* **Facilities** tea/coffee Cen ht Wi-fi ⚹ ⛵ **Parking** 12 **Notes** ⊗ No Children 9yrs Closed Xmas ⊜

RUSTINGTON — Map 6 TQ00

Kenmore Guest House

★★★★ GUEST ACCOMMODATION

Claigmar Rd BN16 2NL
☎ 01903 784634
e-mail: enquiries@kenmoreguesthouse.co.uk
dir: *A259 follow signs for Rustington, turn for Claigmar Rd by war memorial. Kenmore on right as Claigmar Rd bends*

A warm welcome is assured at this Edwardian house, located close to the sea and convenient for touring West Sussex. Spacious bedrooms, all individually decorated, are provided with many useful extras. There is a comfortable lounge in which to relax and a bright dining room where a good choice of breakfast is served.

Rooms 8 rms (7 en suite) (1 pri facs) (1 fmly) (2 GF) S £30-£40; D £65-£85* **Facilities** FTV tea/coffee Cen ht Wi-fi **Parking** 7

SELSEY — Map 5 SZ89

Greenacre

★★★★ 🅰 BED AND BREAKFAST

5 Manor Farm Court PO20 0LY
☎ 01243 602912
e-mail: greenacre@zoom.co.uk
dir: *B2145 to Selsey, over a small rdbt, next left (Manor Farm Court), bear left & Greenacre on left*
Rooms 4 rms (3 en suite) (1 fmly) (1 GF) **Facilities** STV TVL tea/coffee Cen ht Wi-fi **Parking** 7

St Andrews Lodge

★★★★ 🅰 GUEST ACCOMMODATION

Chichester Rd PO20 0LX
☎ 01243 606899 📠 01243 607826
e-mail: info@standrewslodge.co.uk
web: www.standrewslodge.co.uk
dir: *B2145 into Selsey, on right just before church*
Rooms 5 en suite 5 annexe en suite (3 fmly) (5 GF) S £45-£60; D £70-£95 **Facilities** FTV TVL tea/coffee Direct Dial Cen ht Licensed Wi-fi **Conf** Max 15 **Parking** 14 **Notes** LB

SIDLESHAM — Map 5 SZ89

PREMIER COLLECTION

The Crab & Lobster

★★★★★ ⊛ RESTAURANT WITH ROOMS

Mill Ln PO20 7NB
☎ 01243 641233
e-mail: enquiries@crab-lobster.co.uk
dir: *A27 onto B2145 signed Selsey. 1st left after garage at Sidlesham onto Rookery Ln to Crab & Lobster*

Hidden away on the south coast near Pagham Harbour and only a short drive from Chichester is the stylish Crab & Lobster. Bedrooms are superbly appointed, and bathrooms are a feature with luxury toiletries and powerful 'raindrop' showers. Guests can enjoy lunch or dinner in the smart restaurant where the menu offers a range of locally caught fresh fish amongst other regionally-sourced, seasonal produce.

Rooms 4 en suite S £80-£90; D £140-£180 **Facilities** FTV tea/coffee Dinner available Cen ht Wi-fi **Parking** 12 **Notes** ⊗ No coaches

The Jolly Fisherman B&B

★★★★ BED AND BREAKFAST

Selsey Rd PO20 7LS
☎ 01243 641544
e-mail: pamela.brett@btinternet.com

The Jolly Fisherman B&B benefits from its location halfway between the historic city of Chichester and Selsey. It is perfect for exploring the South coast harbours and ideal for Goodwood. Accommodation is comfortable and a traditional substantial breakfast is available in the dining room or on the rear patio overlooking fields, weather permitting.

Rooms 3 en suite **Facilities** FTV Cen ht Wi-fi Golf **Parking** 3 **Notes** ⊗ ⊜

Lockgate Cottage B&B

Ⓤ

Sidlesham Common PO20 7QH
☎ 01243 641452
e-mail: buchanan.j@virgin.net
dir: *4.5m S of Chichester, access from A286 or B2145*

Currently the rating for this establishment is not confirmed. This may be due to a change of ownership or because it has only recently joined the AA rating scheme.

Rooms 2 annexe en suite (2 GF) D £75-£95* **Facilities** FTV tea/coffee Cen ht Wi-fi **Parking** 4 **Notes** LB ⊗ No Children 16yrs

Save on B&Bs and Hotels. Book at **theAA.com/hotel**

SUSSEX, WEST 307 ENGLAND

The Red Lyon

[U]

The Street RH13 0RR
☎ 01403 790339   📄 01403 330450
e-mail: simon@theredlyon.co.uk
dir: *A29 signed Slinfold, turn right into village, past the church, on right*

Currently the rating for this establishment is not confirmed. This may be due to a change of ownership or because it has only recently joined the AA rating scheme.

Rooms 4 rms (3 en suite) (1 pri facs) (1 fmly) S £50-£60; D fr £55 (room only)* **Facilities** FTV TVL tea/coffee Dinner available Cen ht Licensed Wi-fi Golf 18 **Parking** 30

The Horse Guards Inn

★★★★ ⊛ INN

GU28 9AF
☎ 01798 342332   📄 01798 345126
e-mail: info@thehorseguardsinn.co.uk
dir: *Off A272 to Tillington, up hill opposite All Hallows church*

The Horse Guards Inn is conveniently located close to Petworth and Midhurst in a quiet village setting opposite the quaint church, and is perfect for exploring the beautiful surrounding countryside. The comfortable bedrooms are simply decorated, and delicious breakfasts are prepared to order using the finest local ingredients. The same principles apply to the substantial and flavoursome meals served in the cosy restaurant/bar dining areas.

Rooms 2 en suite 1 annexe en suite (1 fmly) S £80-£145; D £80-£145* **Facilities** FTV tea/coffee Dinner available Cen ht Wi-fi

PREMIER COLLECTION

West Marden Farmhouse *(SU770135)*

★★★★★ FARMHOUSE

PO18 9ES
☎ 023 9263 1761
Mrs C M Edney
e-mail: carole.edney@btinternet.com

Located in the small rural village of West Marden is the delightful West Marden Farmhouse, (a working arable farm) which provides extremely comfortable and stylish accommodation comprising of one guest bedroom, an en suite bathroom plus shower room, and a fabulous private lounge with sofas, where the log fire is lit in cooler weather. The Farmhouse provides a sumptuous home-cooked, freshly prepared breakfast for all of its welcome visitors. Free Wi-fi is available throughout.

Rooms 1 en suite **Facilities** FTV tea/coffee Cen ht Wi-fi **Parking** 5 **Notes** ⊛ Closed 23-28 Dec ⊛ 1000 acres arable

Grandwood House

★★★★ GUEST ACCOMMODATION

Watergate PO18 9EG
☎ 07971 845153   & 023 9263 1436
e-mail: info@grandwoodhouse.co.uk
web: www.grandwoodhouse.co.uk

Set in the South Downs and built in 1907, Grandwood House was originally a lodge belonging to Watergate House, which was accidentally burnt down by troops during WWII. Only a short walk away is the local pub in nearby Walderton which serves lunches and evening meals. All rooms are en suite and enjoy views of the garden, open farmland or both. Large security gates leading onto the driveway ensure secure parking at all times.

Rooms 4 annexe en suite (4 GF) S £40-£60; D £50-£85* **Facilities** FTV tea/coffee Cen ht Wi-fi **Parking** 8 **Notes** LB

The Beacons

★★★★ GUEST ACCOMMODATION

18 Shelley Rd BN11 1TU
☎ 01903 230948
e-mail: thebeacons@btconnect.com
dir: *0.5m W of town centre. Off A259 Richmond Rd onto Crescent Rd & 3rd left*

This splendid Edwardian property is ideally situated close to the shopping centre, marine garden and pier. Bedrooms are bright, spacious and attractively furnished with many thoughtful amenities, including free Wi-fi. Guests can enjoy the comfortable lounge with honesty bar and breakfast is served in the sunny dining room.

Rooms 8 en suite (1 fmly) (3 GF) S £45-£50; D £72-£80* **Facilities** FTV tea/coffee Cen ht Licensed Wi-fi **Parking** 8

The Burlington

★★★★ GUEST ACCOMMODATION

Marine Pde BN11 3QL
☎ 01903 211222   📄 01903 209561
e-mail: info@theburlingtonworthing.co.uk
web: www.theburlingtonworthing.co.uk
dir: *On seafront 0.5m W of Worthing Pier, Wordsworth Rd junct*

This imposing seafront building offers a modern contemporary look that appeals to a mainly youthful clientele. The light spacious bar and terrace extends to a night club open at the weekends. Bedrooms are spacious and thoughtfully furnished with some modern touches. Friendly staff.

Rooms 26 en suite (6 fmly) S £70; D £75-£130* **Facilities** FTV tea/coffee Dinner available Direct Dial Cen ht Licensed Wi-fi **Conf** Max 100 Thtr 50 Class 35 Board 40 **Notes** ⊛

The Conifers

★★★★ 🏠 GUEST ACCOMMODATION

43 Parkfield Rd BN13 1EP
☎ 01903 265066   & 07947 321096
e-mail: conifers@hews.org.uk
dir: *A24 or A27 onto A2031 at Offington rdbt, over lights, Parkfield Rd 5th right*

This charming home with its award-winning garden is located in a quiet residential area within easy reach of the town centre. Bedrooms are bright and comfortable with plenty of thoughtful extras. A hearty English breakfast is served by friendly host Barbara in a traditionally furnished, oak-panelled dining room.

Rooms 2 rms (1 pri facs) (2 fmly) S £42.50-£45; D £70-£75* **Facilities** tea/coffee Cen ht Wi-fi **Notes** LB ⊛ No Children 12yrs Closed Xmas & New Year ⊛

WORTHING *continued*

Moorings

★★★★ GUEST ACCOMMODATION

4 Selden Rd BN11 2LL
☎ **01903 208882**
e-mail: themooringsworthing@hotmail.co.uk
dir: 0.5m E of pier off A259 towards Brighton

This well-presented Victorian house is located in a quiet residential street just a short walk from the seafront and town centre. Bedrooms are attractively co-ordinated with plenty of extras such as Wi-fi and Freeview TV. Breakfast is served in a smart dining room and there is a small lounge with books and games. Sarah Huckwell was a finalist in this year's Friendliest Landlady of the Year award (2011-12).

Rooms 7 en suite (1 fmly) (1 GF) S £35-£45; D £60-£85* **Facilities** FTV tea/coffee Direct Dial Cen ht Wi-fi **Notes** LB ⊗

Olinda Guest House

★★★★ GUEST ACCOMMODATION

199 Brighton Rd BN11 2EX
☎ **01903 206114**
e-mail: info@olindaguesthouse.co.uk
web: www.olindaguesthouse.co.uk
dir: 1m E of pier on Brighton Rd along Worthing seafront

Guests are assured a warm welcome at this establishment which is located on the seafront just a walk away from the town centre. The bedrooms are cosy and comfortable, and breakfast is taken in the attractively appointed dining room overlooking the seafront.

Rooms 6 rms (3 en suite) S £26-£35; D £52-£70* **Facilities** FTV tea/coffee Cen ht Wi-fi **Notes** ⊗ No Children 12yrs

Tudor Guest House

★★★★ GUEST ACCOMMODATION

5 Windsor Rd BN11 2LU
☎ **01903 210265**
e-mail: info@tudor-worthing.co.uk
dir: Off A259 (seafront road)

The Tudor Guest House is a friendly and attractive establishment situated just off the seafront on the east side of town. Bedrooms are generally spacious and neatly appointed with modern facilities. Fresh organic produce is served in the bright breakfast room.

Rooms 7 en suite (1 GF) **Facilities** tea/coffee Cen ht **Parking** 6 **Notes** ⊗ No Children 8yrs Closed 24 Dec-3 Jan

Merton House

★★★★ Ⓐ GUEST HOUSE

96 Broadwater Rd BN14 8AW
☎ **01903 238222**
e-mail: stay@mertonhouse.co.uk
dir: 0.5m from A27, S onto A24 towards pier. 0.25m after St Marys Church

Rooms 7 en suite (2 GF) S £50-£75; D £85-£100* **Facilities** FTV tea/coffee Dinner available Cen ht Wi-fi **Parking** 7 **Notes** LB ⊗ No Children 10yrs

Beechwood Hall

★★★ INN

Wykeham BN11 4JD
☎ **01903 232375** 📠 **01903 219778**
e-mail: admin@beechwoodhall.net
dir: A259 to town centre towards Littlehampton, 0.5m on right

Located on the outskirts of Worthing, this Swiss Cottage has been restored to its former glory under the careful management of Paul and Rose. The eight en suite bedrooms all offer good levels of comfort. Food is served daily, and where possible dishes feature good use of local produce.

Rooms 8 en suite (2 fmly) **Facilities** FTV tea/coffee Dinner available Cen ht Wi-fi **Conf** Max 25 Thtr 25 Class 25 Board 25 **Parking** 40 **Notes** ⊗ No coaches

High Beach Guest House

★★★ GUEST ACCOMMODATION

201 Brighton Rd BN11 2EX
☎ **01903 236389**
e-mail: info@highbeachworthing.com
web: www.highbeachworthing.com
dir: On A259, 200yds past Aqurena swimming pool

This property is situated within a short walking distance of Worthing town centre, and its seafront location offers uninterrupted sea views from front facing rooms and the breakfast room. Bedrooms are traditionally decorated and come well-equipped. A conservatory with comfortable seating leads onto the front garden which guests can enjoy during summer months.

Rooms 7 rms (3 en suite) (1 GF) S £27-£32.50; D £56-£65* **Facilities** FTV TVL tea/coffee Cen ht Wi-fi **Parking** 3 **Notes** ⊗

Marina Guest House

★★★ GUEST ACCOMMODATION

191 Brighton Rd BN11 2EX
☎ **01903 207844**
e-mail: marinaworthing@ntlworld.com
dir: M27 onto A259 to Worthing; or M23 onto A24 to Worthing

This Victorian establishment is in a great location with uninterrupted sea views, and just a short distance from

the town centre. The property is well maintained with comfortable accommodation. A cooked breakfast can be enjoyed in the family-style breakfast room that looks out over the sea.

Rooms 5 rms (2 en suite) (2 fmly) **Facilities** tea/coffee Direct Dial Cen ht Wi-fi **Notes** ⊗

GATESHEAD 🗺 Map 21 NZ26

PREMIER COLLECTION

The Stables Lodge

★★★★★ 🏠 GUEST HOUSE

South Farm, Lamesley NE11 0ET
☎ **0191 492 1756** 📠 **0191 410 6192**
e-mail: janet@thestableslodge.co.uk
dir: From A1, take Team Valley/Retail World slip road and turn off towards Lamesley/Kibblesworth

The Stables Lodge is in a semi-rural setting not far from Newcastle and Gateshead, with the Metro Centre and Angel of the North only minutes away. The Stables was thoughtfully converted presenting a 'Hunting Lodge' theme. Features include luxurious surroundings and excellent guest care. The Red room has a sauna and steam room, while the Garden room has an outside seating area.

Rooms 3 en suite (1 fmly) (1 GF) **Facilities** STV TVL tea/coffee Cen ht Sauna **Parking** 6 **Notes** ⊗

SOUTH SHIELDS Map 21 NZ36

Ocean Breeze

★★★★ GUEST HOUSE

11 Urfa Ter NE33 2ES
☎ **0191 456 7442**
e-mail: info@oceanbreezeguesthouse.co.uk
dir: A183 towards town centre, onto Lawe Rd, 3rd left

Situated just a short walk from the seafront and town centre, this smartly appointed terrace house offers modern, fully-equipped bedrooms, most with en suite shower rooms. Guests are given a genuine warm welcome and hearty breakfasts, made using fresh local ingredients are served in the pleasant dining room.

Rooms 6 rms (3 en suite) (1 fmly) **Facilities** FTV tea/coffee Cen ht Wi-fi **Notes** ⊗ No Children 5yrs Closed 16 Dec-6 Jan

SUNNISIDE   Map 19 NZ25

PREMIER COLLECTION

Hedley Hall Country House

★★★★★ GUEST ACCOMMODATION

Hedley Ln NE16 5EH
☎ **01207 231835**
e-mail: hedleyhall@aol.com
web: www.hedleyhall.com
dir: *From A1 follow signs for Lanseley, at mini rdbt turn right 2m, left at Birkheads Garden/Nursery sign. Straight over x-rds, turn left to Hedley Hall Country House*

Located within easy reach of Beamish, Hedley Hall Country House was once a working farm that was part of the Queen Mother's estate. A warm welcome and quality accommodation is guaranteed. The stylish modern bedrooms, one with a super-king-sized bed, are very thoughtfully equipped. Delightful day rooms include a spacious lounge with deep sofas. Breakfasts are served in the conservatory or the elegant dining room.

Rooms 4 en suite (1 fmly) **Facilities** TVL tea/coffee Dinner available Cen ht Wi-fi **Parking** 6 **Notes** LB ⊗ Closed 22 Dec-2 Jan

WHITLEY BAY   Map 21 NZ37

Park Lodge

★★★★ GUEST HOUSE

158-160 Park Av NE26 1AU
☎ **0191 253 0288**   📠 **0191 252 6879**
e-mail: parklodgehotel@hotmail.com
dir: *From S A19 through Tyne Tunnel, right onto A1058 to seafront. Turn left, after 2m left at lights onto A191. On left*

A friendly atmosphere prevails at this refurbished Victorian house, located on a leafy avenue, overlooking the park and just minutes from the town centre and coastline. Bedrooms are very comfortable, stylishly furnished and feature homely extras. A hearty breakfast is served and free Wi-fi is available.

Rooms 5 en suite (1 fmly) (2 GF) S £65-£85; D £85-£95 **Facilities** FTV TVL tea/coffee Cen ht Wi-fi **Parking** 2 **Notes** ⊗ Closed 24-30 Dec

Sandsides Guest House

★★★ GUEST ACCOMMODATION

122 Park Av NE26 1AY
☎ **0191 253 0399   & 07947 447695**
e-mail: sandsides@btinternet.com
dir: *A19 Tyne Tunnel exit A1058. At rdbt follow A192 Whitley Bay, next rdbt turn left. Located in one-way system*

Situated opposite the park and close to the beach and town centre, Sandsides offers a variety of room sizes, two with en suite shower rooms and the others with shared facilities. Freshly-cooked breakfasts are served in the dining room.

Rooms 5 rms (2 en suite) (2 fmly) **Facilities** FTV tea/coffee Cen ht **Parking** 1 **Notes** LB ⊗ ⊜

WARWICKSHIRE

ATHERSTONE   Map 10 SP39

PREMIER COLLECTION

Chapel House Restaurant With Rooms

★★★★★ ⊛ RESTAURANT WITH ROOMS

Friar's Gate CV9 1EY
☎ **01827 718949**   📠 **01827 717702**
e-mail: info@chapelhouse.eu
web: www.chapelhouse.eu
dir: *A5 to town centre, right onto Church St. Right onto Sheepy Rd & left onto Friar's Gate*

Sitting next to the church this 18th-century town house offers excellent hospitality and service while the cooking, using much local produce, is very notable. Bedrooms are well equipped and lounges are extensive; there is also a delightful walled garden for guests to use.

Rooms 11 en suite **Facilities** tea/coffee Dinner available Direct Dial Cen ht Wi-fi **Notes** LB ⊗ Closed Etr wk, Aug BH wk & Xmas wk No coaches

BAGINTON   Map 11 SP37

The Oak

★★★ INN

Coventry Rd CV8 3AU
☎ **024 7651 8855**   📠 **024 7651 8866**
e-mail: thebagintonoak@aol.com
web: http://theoak.greatpubs.net

Located close to major road links and Coventry Airport, this popular inn provides a wide range of food throughout the themed, open-plan public areas. Families are especially welcome. Modern, well-equipped bedrooms are situated in a separate accommodation building.

Rooms 13 annexe en suite (1 fmly) (6 GF) S £45-£60; D £45-£60 **Facilities** FTV tea/coffee Dinner available Cen ht Wi-fi Free use of local gym **Conf** Max 40 Thtr 40 Class 40 Board 25 **Parking** 110

COLESHILL — Map 10 SP28

Coleshill

★★★ INN

152 High St B46 3BG
☎ 01675 465527 ⊜ 01675 464013
e-mail: 9130@greeneking.co.uk
dir: M6 junct 4, after 2nd island turn right onto Coventry road. On left approx 100yds after mini rdbt

The Coleshill offers a convenient location for both the NEC and Birmingham International Airport. Bedrooms, some of which are in a separate house opposite, provide comfortable and well-equipped facilities. The bar and bistro are attractively appointed. Additional features include a car park and self-contained function suite.

Rooms 15 en suite 8 annexe en suite (3 fmly) (3 GF) **Facilities** tea/coffee Direct Dial **Parking** 30

ETTINGTON — Map 10 SP24

PREMIER COLLECTION

Fulready Manor

✭✭✭✭✭ ⌂ BED AND BREAKFAST

Fulready CV37 7PE
☎ 01789 740152
e-mail: stay@fulreadymanor.co.uk
web: www.fulreadymanor.co.uk
dir: 2.5m SE of Ettington. 0.5m S off A422 at Pillerton Priors

Located in 120 acres of arable farmland, this impressive, new Cotswold-stone house provides very high levels of comfort. The spacious ground-floor areas are furnished with quality and flair, and feature fine furniture and art. The individually themed bedrooms have a wealth of thoughtful extras, and memorable breakfasts are served in the elegant dining room overlooking immaculate gardens.

Rooms 3 en suite D £125-£140 **Facilities** Cen ht Wi-fi **Parking** 6 **Notes** ⊗ No Children 15yrs ⊜

FILLONGLEY — Map 10 SP28

Heart of England Conference & Events Centre

★★★★ GUEST ACCOMMODATION

Meriden Rd CV7 8DX
☎ 01676 540333 ⊜ 01676 540365
e-mail: pa@heartofengland.co.uk
web: www.heartofengland.co.uk

A charming stone-built house with attractively presented, well-equipped bedrooms and sleek modern bathrooms. This fine old house has bags of character and the spacious, comfortable lounge has a wood burning stove, which is a real feature on cooler evenings. Delicious hot breakfasts are served at individual tables in the well-appointed breakfast room. The nearby Quicken Tree restaurant serves an extensive choice of imaginative dishes and is an ideal dinner venue. First-rate conference and business facilities are available on site.

Rooms 7 en suite (1 GF) **Facilities** FTV TVL tea/coffee Dinner available Direct Dial Cen ht Licensed Wi-fi **Conf** Max 450 Thtr 450 Class 200 Board 50 **Parking** 36 **Notes** LB Civ Wed 200

KENILWORTH — Map 10 SP27

Milsoms Kenilworth

★★★★ ⊜ INN

Clarendon House Hotel, High St CV8 1LZ
☎ 01926 515450 ⊜ 01926 515451
e-mail: kenilworth@milsomshotel.co.uk
web: www.milsomshotel.co.uk
dir: A452 signs to town centre, at small rdbt with clock tower, 2nd exit Abbey Hill. At lights, Milsoms immediately on left

Milsoms enjoys a prominent position in the heart of Kenilworth and benefits from secure car parking for guests. Recently refurbished bedrooms are all of a very high standard, very well equipped and complimentary Wi-fi is available for residents. Dinner in the Loch Fyne restaurant is not to be missed and guests are assured of attentive friendly service along with great seafood. There is a charming bar and a comfortable lounge for guests. The NEC and Birmingham Airport are a short drive away

Rooms 28 en suite 3 annexe en suite (1 fmly) (5 GF) S £50-£75; D £55-£95* **Facilities** FTV tea/coffee Dinner available Wi-fi **Conf** Max 25 Thtr 16 Class 18 **Parking** 19 **Notes** ⊗

Stoneleigh Park Lodge

★★★★ GUEST HOUSE

Stoneleigh Park CV8 2LZ
☎ 024 7669 0123 ⊜ 024 7669 0789
e-mail: info@stoneleighparklodge.com
web: www.stoneleighparklodge.com
dir: 2m E of Kenilworth in National Agricultural Centre

This house lies within the grounds of the National Agricultural Centre and provides modern, well-equipped accommodation. Meals, using local produce, are served in the Park View Restaurant overlooking the showground. Various conference and meeting facilities are available.

Rooms 58 en suite (4 fmly) (26 GF) S £50-£100; D £50-£130* **Facilities** FTV TVL tea/coffee Dinner available Direct Dial Cen ht Licensed Wi-fi Fishing **Conf** Max 10 **Parking** 60 **Notes** Closed Xmas

Victoria Lodge

★★★★ GUEST ACCOMMODATION

180 Warwick Rd CV8 1HU
☎ 01926 512020 ⊜ 01926 858703
e-mail: info@victorialodgekenilworth.co.uk
dir: 250yds SE of town centre on A452 opp St John's Church

Situated within walking distance of Kenilworth Castle and the historic town's many acclaimed restaurants, Victoria Lodge is a family-run establishment. All of the well-appointed rooms are en suite and thoughtfully furnished with homely extras. There is a Victorian walled garden for guests' use, plus a car park.

Rooms 10 en suite (1 fmly) (2 GF) S £49-£65; D £72-£85* **Facilities** FTV tea/coffee Direct Dial Cen ht Licensed Wi-fi **Parking** 9 **Notes** ⊗ Closed 24 Dec-1 Jan

Hollyhurst

★★★ GUEST HOUSE

47 Priory Rd CV8 1LL
☎ 01926 853882 ⊜ 01926 853882
e-mail: admin@hollyhurstguesthouse.co.uk
dir: On A452 in town centre

Located on a mainly residential avenue within easy walking distance of the castle and town centre, this constantly improving establishment offers a range of bedrooms, some of which have the benefit of modern shower rooms. Ground-floor areas include a comfortable lounge in addition to an attractive dining room.

Rooms 4 rms (3 en suite) (1 pri facs) (1 fmly) S £35-£38; D £52-£58* **Facilities** FTV tea/coffee Cen ht Wi-fi **Parking** 7 **Notes** ⊗ Closed Xmas & New Year

Save on B&Bs and Hotels. Book at **theAA.com/hotel**

WARWICKSHIRE 311 **ENGLAND**

Howden House

★★★ BED AND BREAKFAST

70 Warwick Rd CV8 1HS
☎ **01926 850310**
e-mail: howdenhouse@hotmail.co.uk
dir: From A46 take Leamington exit onto A452, follow sign to Kenilworth, on left of Warwick Rd

Guests will find a warm welcome awaits them at Howden House which is situated at the end of the main street, convenient for the town centre, the National Exhibition Centre and motorway networks. The bedrooms are homely and comfortable.

Rooms 3 rms (1 en suite) (1 fmly) (1 GF) S £35-£45; D £55-£70* **Facilities** TVL tea/coffee Cen ht ⏚ Golf 36 **Parking** 1 **Notes** ⊗ Closed Xmas & New Year 🐾

LEAMINGTON SPA (ROYAL)   Map 10 SP36

The Adams

★★★★ GUEST ACCOMMODATION

22 Avenue Rd CV31 3PQ
☎ **01926 450742** 📠 **01926 313110**
e-mail: bookings@adams-hotel.co.uk
dir: 500yds W of town centre. Off A452 (Adelaide Rd) onto Avenue Rd

Just a short walk from the town centre, this elegant 1827 Regency house offers a relaxing setting and quality accommodation. Public areas include a lounge bar with leather armchairs, and a pretty garden. The attractive bedrooms are very well appointed, and have modem points and bathrobes.

Rooms 10 en suite (2 GF) **Facilities** tea/coffee Direct Dial Cen ht Licensed Wi-fi **Parking** 14 **Notes** ⊗ No Children 12yrs Closed 23 Dec-2 Jan

LIGHTHORNE   Map 10 SP35

Redlands Farm

★★★★ BED AND BREAKFAST

Banbury Rd CV35 0AH
☎ **01926 651241**
e-mail: redlandsfarm@btinternet.com
dir: Off B4100, 5m S of Warwick

Redlands Farm offers a tranquil location, just six miles from Warwick, Leamington Spa and Stratford-upon-Avon. Bedrooms promise a comfortable stay and breakfast features fresh eggs laid by the chickens in the garden.

Rooms 3 en suite (1 fmly) S £35-£45; D £60-£65* **Facilities** FTV TVL tea/coffee Cen ht Wi-fi 🎣 **Parking** 7 **Notes** ⊗ Closed Xmas & New Year

LONG COMPTON   Map 10 SP23

The Red Lion

★★★★ ◉ INN

Main St CV36 5JS
☎ **01608 684221** 📠 **01608 684968**
e-mail: info@redlion-longcompton.co.uk
dir: 5m S of Shipston on Stour on A3400

Located in the pretty rural village of Long Compton, this mid 18th-century posting house retains many original features which are complemented by rustic furniture in the public areas. A good range of ales is offered, and interesting menus make good use of quality local produce. Newly refurbished bedrooms are well appointed, and furnished with a good range of facilities.

Rooms 5 en suite (1 fmly) S £55-£75; D £85-£185* **Facilities** tea/coffee Dinner available Cen ht Wi-fi **Parking** 60 **Notes** No coaches

Tallet Barn B&B

★★★★ BED AND BREAKFAST

Yerdley Farm CV36 5LH
☎ **01608 684248** 📠 **01608 684248**
e-mail: talletbarn@googlemail.com
dir: Off A3400 in village onto Vicarage Ln opp village stores, 3rd entrance on right

This converted barn and grain store in the heart of an unspoiled Cotswold village provides comfortable bedrooms with thoughtful extras. Comprehensive breakfasts are served in the elegant beamed dining room in the main house, which also has a comfortable lounge.

Rooms 2 annexe en suite (1 fmly) (1 GF) S £40-£45; D £60-£65* **Facilities** tea/coffee Cen ht **Parking** 2 **Notes** ⊗ No Children 6yrs 🐾

RUGBY   Map 11 SP57

Number Seven Guest House

★★★ GUEST HOUSE

7 Eastfield Place CV21 3AT
☎ **01788 541010** 📠 **01788 544996**
dir: Follow signs to town centre & Rugby school, onto Hillmorton Rd then Littlechurch St. 1st right onto Eastfield Pl, before black & white pub

Located in a quiet side road, just minutes from Rugby town centre, this guest house, originally a private residence, offers good quality accommodation, some with en suite facilities. Ground-floor areas include a comfortable lounge in addition to an open plan kitchen/dining room where hearty breakfasts are served.

Rooms 7 rms (1 en suite) (6 pri facs) 3 annexe en suite (1 fmly) (4 GF) S £36-£70; D £55-£70* **Facilities** FTV TVL tea/coffee Cen ht Wi-fi **Notes** LB 🐾

SHIPSTON ON STOUR   Map 10 SP24

PREMIER COLLECTION

The Old Mill

★★★★★ ◉◉ RESTAURANT WITH ROOMS

Mill St CV36 4AW
☎ **01608 661421** 📠 **01608 610600**
e-mail: jl@theoldmillshipston.co.uk
web: www.theoldmillshipston.com

This former mill sits of the banks of the fast flowing River Stour and is close to the centre of the pretty village of Shipston. The individually styled bedrooms are beautifully presented and very well equipped. The cosy bar has many original features and the potbelly stove creates a warm welcoming atmosphere. No stay here is complete without a visit to the award-winning restaurant and guests are assured of a warm welcome and attentive service.

Rooms 5 en suite (2 fmly) S £75-£90; D £110-£175* **Facilities** FTV tea/coffee Dinner available Cen ht Wi-fi **Conf** Max 40 Thtr 40 Class 25 Board 25 **Parking** 10 **Notes** No coaches

SHIPSTON ON STOUR *continued*

Holly End Bed & Breakfast

★ ★ ★ ★ 🏠 BED AND BREAKFAST

London Rd CV36 4EP
☎ **01608 664064**
e-mail: hollyend.hunt@btinternet.com
web: www.holly-end.co.uk
dir: *0.5m S of Shipston on Stour on A3400*

Located between Oxford and Stratford-upon-Avon and a short walk from the town centre, this immaculate detached house offers bedrooms with lots of thoughtful extras. Comprehensive breakfasts use the best of local produce.

Rooms 3 rms (2 en suite) (1 pri facs) S £50-£60; D £75-£95* **Facilities** FTV tea/coffee Cen ht Wi-fi **Parking** 6 **Notes** LB ⊗ No Children 9yrs 🐾

Folly Farm Cottage

★ ★ ★ ★ 🄰 GUEST ACCOMMODATION

Ilmington CV36 4LJ
☎ **01608 682425** 📠 **0808 280 2264**
e-mail: bruceandpam@follyfarm.co.uk
dir: *A3400 S of Stratford-upon-Avon, turn right signed Wimpstone/Ilmington*

Rooms 3 en suite S £55-£65; D £72-£88* **Facilities** FTV tea/coffee Dinner available Cen ht Wi-fi 🐾 **Parking** 8 **Notes** LB ⊗ No Children 18yrs

---

STRATFORD-UPON-AVON Map 10 SP25

PREMIER COLLECTION

Cherry Trees

★ ★ ★ ★ ★ 🏠 GUEST HOUSE

Swans Nest Ln CV37 7LS
☎ **01789 292989**
e-mail: gotocherrytrees@aol.com
web: www.cherrytrees-stratford.co.uk
dir: *250yds SE of town centre over bridge. Off A422, next to Butterfly Farm*

Comfortably located close to the theatre and the centre of town, Cherry Trees offers three spacious, luxurious and well-equipped rooms. The Garden Room has a king-size four-poster, while the Terrace Room and the Tiffany Suite both include king-size beds. The Tiffany Suite is so named thanks to its round Tiffany stained-glass window. Guests have a separate entrance and hearty breakfasts are served in the attractive upstairs dining room. As well as Continental and full English choices, guests can enjoy Belgian waffles or eggs Benedict.

Rooms 3 en suite (3 GF) D £98-£120* **Facilities** FTV tea/coffee Cen ht Wi-fi **Parking** 11 **Notes** LB ⊗ No Children 10yrs

Ambleside

★ ★ ★ ★ GUEST HOUSE

41 Grove Rd CV37 6PB
☎ **01789 297239** 📠 **01789 295670**
e-mail: peter@amblesideguesthouse.com
dir: *250mtrs from town centre on A4390 opposite Firs Gdns*

Ambleside is a very comfortable house in the heart of Stratford where a refurbishment and meticulous on-going redecoration has left it in sparkling condition. Breakfast is served in the bright and airy dining room, which overlooks the park at the front. Free on-site parking and Wi-fi are provided.

Rooms 7 rms (5 en suite) (2 pri facs) (2 fmly) (2 GF) S £30-£45; D £55-£85 **Facilities** FTV tea/coffee Cen ht Wi-fi **Parking** 9 **Notes** ⊗ No Children 7yrs

Adelphi Guest House

★ ★ ★ ★ 🏠 GUEST ACCOMMODATION

39 Grove Rd CV37 6PB
☎ **01789 204469**
e-mail: info@adelphi-guesthouse.com

The Adelphi is a Victorian town house just minutes from the centre of Stratford-upon-Avon and within walking distance of all the town's theatres and historic attractions. The property is decorated in period style and a warm welcome awaits from the proprietors. The comfortable bedrooms are suitably decorated and provide a good range of extras. Breakfast offers an excellent choice and is served in the elegant dining room which has views out over the park. Parking is provided to the rear of the property.

Rooms 6 en suite S £35-£40; D £70-£85* **Facilities** FTV tea/coffee Cen ht Wi-fi **Parking** 5 **Notes** ⊗ No Children 10yrs

Clopton Orchard Farm *(SP165455)*

★ ★ ★ ★ FARMHOUSE

Lower Clopton, Upper Quinton CV37 8LH
☎ **01386 438669** & **07765 414636** 📠 **01386 438669**
Mrs A Coldicott
e-mail: mail@clopton-orchard.fsnet.co.uk
dir: *6m S of Stratford on B4632. S through Lower Clopton, on right opposite farm shop*

A warm welcome is assured at this attractive modern farmhouse located between Broadway and Stratford-upon-Avon. The spacious bedrooms come with practical and thoughtful extras, and comprehensive breakfasts are served around a family table in the cosy pine-furnished first-floor dining room.

Rooms 2 en suite (1 fmly) S £50-£65; D £70 **Facilities** FTV tea/coffee Cen ht Wi-fi **Parking** 5 **Notes** LB 🐾 300 acres arable/sheep/mixed

Monk's Barn *(SP206516)*

★ ★ ★ ★ FARMHOUSE

Shipston Rd CV37 8NA
☎ **01789 293714** & **205886**
Mrs R M Meadows
e-mail: ritameadows@btconnect.com
dir: *2m S of Stratford on A3400, on right after bungalows on left*

With stunning views of the surrounding countryside, a warm welcome is assured at this impressive renovated house. Bedrooms, some of which are located in former outbuildings, are filled with a wealth of thoughtful extras. Memorable breakfasts are served in the spacious and cosy lounge-dining room.

Rooms 2 en suite 3 annexe en suite (1 fmly) (3 GF) S £29-£35; D £58 **Facilities** FTV TVL tea/coffee Cen ht Wi-fi **Parking** 7 **Notes** ⊗ Closed 25-27 Dec 75 acres mixed

Save on B&Bs and Hotels. Book at theAA.com/hotel

WARWICKSHIRE 313 ENGLAND

Moonraker House

★★★★ GUEST ACCOMMODATION

40 Alcester Rd CV37 9DB
☎ 01789 268774 📠 01789 268774
e-mail: info@moonrakerhouse.com
dir: 200yds from rail station on A422 (Alcester Rd)

Just a short walk from the railway station and the central attractions, this establishment provides a range of stylish bedrooms. The sitting area during the day is the setting for the freshly cooked breakfasts. The attractive exterior is enhanced by a magnificent floral display during the warmer months.

Rooms 7 en suite (1 fmly) (2 GF) S £40-£47; D £65-£87*
Facilities FTV tea/coffee Cen ht Wi-fi **Parking** 7 **Notes** LB ⊗ No Children 6yrs

Victoria Spa Lodge

★★★★ GUEST HOUSE

Bishopton Ln, Bishopton CV37 9QY
☎ 01789 267985 📠 01789 204728
e-mail: ptozer@victoriaspalodge.demon.co.uk
web: www.victoriaspa.co.uk
dir: A3400 1.5m N to junct A46, 1st left onto Bishopton Ln, 1st house on right

Located within immaculate mature gardens beside the canal on the outskirts of town, this impressive Victorian house retains many original features enhanced by the lovely furnishings and decor. Bedrooms are filled with thoughtful extras and the spacious dining room, furnished with quality antiques and ornaments, also contains a cosy lounge area.

Rooms 7 en suite (3 fmly) S £50-£55; D £65-£70*
Facilities FTV tea/coffee Cen ht Wi-fi **Parking** 12
Notes ⊗

Caterham House

★★★★ Ⓐ GUEST HOUSE

58-59 Rother St CV37 6LT
☎ 01789 267309
e-mail: CaterhamSoA@btconnect.com
dir: 200yds on Rother St from Clocktower
Rooms 10 en suite S £70; D £80-£100 **Facilities** FTV TVL tea/coffee Cen ht Licensed Wi-fi **Conf** Max 25 Thtr 25 Class 25 Board 25 **Parking** 10 **Notes** ⊗ Closed 24-26 Dec

Arden Way Guest House

★★★ GUEST HOUSE

22 Shipston Rd CV37 7LP
☎ 01789 205646 📠 01789 205646
e-mail: info@ardenwayguesthouse.co.uk
web: www.ardenwayguesthouse.co.uk
dir: On A3400, S of River Avon, 100mtrs on left

A warm welcome is assured at this constantly improving non-smoking house, located within easy walking distance of the Butterfly Farm and cricket ground. The homely bedrooms are filled with lots of thoughtful extras and an attractive dining room, overlooking the pretty rear garden, is the setting for comprehensive breakfasts.

Rooms 6 en suite (1 fmly) (2 GF) S £35-£55; D £58-£74*
Facilities FTV tea/coffee Cen ht Wi-fi **Parking** 6 **Notes** LB ⊗

Travellers Rest

★★★ GUEST ACCOMMODATION

146 Alcester Rd CV37 9DR
☎ 01789 266589
e-mail: enquiries@travellersrest.biz
web: www.travellersrest.biz
dir: 0.5m W of town centre on A422, past railway station

Located with easy access to the town centre, this attractive semi-detached house provides cosy bedrooms, each with a modern shower room and filled with thoughtful extras. Breakfast is taken in an attractive front-facing dining room, and a warm welcome is assured.

Rooms 4 en suite (1 fmly) **Facilities** tea/coffee Cen ht Wi-fi **Parking** 5 **Notes** Closed 24-26 Dec

Cherry Blossom House

★★★ GUEST ACCOMMODATION

51 Grove Rd CV37 6PB
☎ 01789 293404
e-mail: enqs@cherryblossomhouse.com
web: www.cherryblossomhouse.com

Cherry Blossom House is situated on a main road within easy walking distance of the town centre, theatres and the many attractions of Shakespeare's birthplace. The accommodation is comfortable with a good range of extras provided including Wi-fi. The welcoming dining room provides well spaced tables with friendly service from host Christine, who serves a hearty breakfast using fresh local ingredients. Parking is available to the front of the property.

Rooms 6 rms (4 en suite) (1 GF) **Facilities** tea/coffee Cen ht **Parking** 4 **Notes** ⊗ No Children 12yrs

Clomendy

★★★ BED AND BREAKFAST

10 Broad Walk CV37 6HS
☎ 01789 266957
e-mail: clomendy@amserve.com
dir: In town centre, turn left off B439 at Evesham Place onto Broad Walk

Located on a peaceful avenue within easy walking distance of central attractions, this wonderfully maintained house offers homely, thoughtfully equipped bedrooms with modern bathrooms. Breakfast is served at a family table in the elegant dining room, which opens to the pretty rear patio garden.

Rooms 2 rms (1 en suite) (1 pri facs) S £45; D £50-£60*
Facilities FTV tea/coffee Cen ht **Parking** 1 **Notes** LB ⊗ No Children 5yrs 🐕

Forget-me-Not

★★★ GUEST ACCOMMODATION

18 Evesham Place CV37 6HT
☎ 01789 204907
e-mail: kate@forgetmenotguesthouse.co.uk
dir: W side of town centre on A4390 ring road, near Chestnut Walk junct

This guest accommodation benefits from lots of care and attention applied by its enthusiastic owners. Bedrooms of varying sizes offer comfortable beds and modern shower rooms. Breakfast is offered in a pretty, bright ground-floor dining room.

Rooms 5 en suite (1 fmly) **Facilities** tea/coffee Cen ht Wi-fi **Parking** 2 **Notes** ⊗

STRATFORD-UPON-AVON *continued*

Stretton House

★★★ GUEST ACCOMMODATION

38 Grove Rd CV37 6PB
☎ **01789 268647**
e-mail: shortpbshort@aol.com
web: www.strettonhouse.co.uk
dir: *On A439 in town centre road behind police station*

This attractive Edwardian terrace house is within easy walking distance of the railway station and Shakespeare's birthplace. Bedrooms are carefully decorated, well equipped, and many have modern shower rooms en suite. The pretty front garden is a very welcoming feature.

Rooms 6 rms (5 en suite) (1 pri facs) (3 fmly) (1 GF) S £30-£40; D £50-£70* **Facilities** tea/coffee Cen ht Wi-fi **Parking** 7

Salamander Guest House

★★★ Ⓐ GUEST HOUSE

40 Grove Rd CV37 6PB
☎ **01789 205728** ▤ **01789 205728**
e-mail: p.delin@btinternet.com
web: www.salamanderguesthouse.co.uk
dir: *250yds W of town centre on A439 ring road, opp Firs Garden*

Rooms 7 rms (6 en suite) (1 pri facs) (5 fmly) (1 GF) S £20-£40; D £40-£65 **Facilities** FTV tea/coffee Dinner available Cen ht Wi-fi **Parking** 12 **Notes** LB ⊗

Barbette Guest House

★★ BED AND BREAKFAST

165 Evesham Rd CV37 9BP
☎ **01789 297822**
e-mail: barbette@sitgetan.demon.co.uk
dir: *B439 S, 0.5m from town centre*

Expect a friendly welcome at this guest house, a compact but comfortable establishment close to the main road with ample parking and a landscaped rear garden. Bedrooms are comfortable and well-equipped, and guests have use of a TV lounge.

Rooms 4 rms (2 en suite) **Facilities** FTV TVL tea/coffee Cen ht Wi-fi **Parking** 5 **Notes** ⊗ ⊜

WEST MIDLANDS

BIRMINGHAM Map 10 SP08

PREMIER COLLECTION

Westbourne Lodge

★★★★★ ⬭ GUEST ACCOMMODATION

25-31 Fountain Rd, Edgbaston B17 8NJ
☎ **0121 429 1003** ▤ **0121 429 7436**
e-mail: info@westbournelodge.co.uk
web: www.westbournelodge.co.uk
dir: *100yds from A456*

Located on a quiet residential avenue close to Hagley Road, this well-maintained property provides a range of no-smoking, thoughtfully furnished bedrooms; some are on the ground floor. Breakfasts (and dinner by arrangement) are served in an attractive dining room overlooking a pretty patio garden. A comfortable sitting room and lounge bar are also available.

Rooms 18 en suite (4 fmly) (2 GF) S £49.50-£69.50; D £69.50-£89.50 **Facilities** FTV TVL tea/coffee Dinner available Cen ht Licensed Wi-fi **Parking** 12 **Notes** Closed 24 Dec-1 Jan

---

Black Firs

★★★★ GUEST HOUSE

113 Coleshill Rd, Marston Green B37 7HT
☎ **0121 779 2727** ▤ **0121 779 2727**
e-mail: julie@b-firs.co.uk
web: www.b-firs.co.uk
dir: *M42 junct 6, A45 W, onto B4438, signs for Marston Green*

This elegant house is set in immaculate gardens in a mainly residential area close to the NEC. Thoughtfully equipped bedrooms with Wi-fi access are complemented by smart shower rooms. Memorable breakfasts are served in an attractive dining room and a lounge is also available. Julie Matthews was a finalist in this year's Friendliest Landlady of the Year award (2011-12).

Rooms 6 en suite **Facilities** TVL tea/coffee Cen ht **Conf** Max 14 **Parking** 6 **Notes** ⊗ ⊜

Olton Cottage

★★★★ GUEST HOUSE

School Ln, Old Yardley Village, Yardley B33 8PD
☎ **0121 783 9249** ▤ **0121 789 6545**
e-mail: olton.cottage@virgin.net
dir: *3.5m E of city centre. Off A45 onto A4040 to Yardley onto Stoney Ln via Yew Tree rdbt then 1m right onto Vicarage Rd, right onto Church Rd, left onto School Ln*

A warm welcome is assured at this carefully renovated Victorian house, located in a peaceful residential area close to the city centre. The cosy bedrooms contain a wealth of thoughtful extras, and ground-floor areas include a cottage-style dining room and comfortable lounge overlooking the pretty enclosed garden.

Rooms 5 rms (2 en suite) S £30; D £60* **Facilities** FTV TVL tea/coffee Cen ht Wi-fi **Parking** 2 **Notes** Closed Xmas & New Year ⊜

Tri-Star

★★★ GUEST ACCOMMODATION

Coventry Rd, Elmdon B26 3QR
☎ **0121 782 1010** & 782 6131 ▤ **0121 782 6131**
e-mail: info@tristarhotel.co.uk
dir: *On A45*

Located a short drive from the airport, the international station and the NEC, this owner-managed property provides a range of thoughtfully furnished bedrooms with modern bathrooms. The open-plan ground-floor area includes a bright, attractive dining room, a comfortable lounge bar and a separate conference room.

Rooms 15 en suite (3 fmly) (6 GF) S £39-£79; D £49-£89* **Facilities** FTV TVL tea/coffee Dinner available Cen ht Licensed Wi-fi Pool table Games room **Conf** Max 20 Thtr 20 Class 10 Board 20 **Parking** 25 **Notes** ⊗

Save on B&Bs and Hotels. Book at **theAA.com/hotel**

WEST MIDLANDS 315 ENGLAND

Rollason Wood

★★ GUEST ACCOMMODATION

130 Wood End Rd, Erdington B24 8BJ
☎ 0121 373 1230 🖶 0121 382 2578
e-mail: rollwood@globalnet.co.uk
dir: M6 junct 6, A5127 to Erdington, right onto A4040,
0.25m on left

Well situated for many road networks and the city centre, this owner-managed establishment is popular with contractors. The choice of three different bedroom styles suits most budgets, and rates include full English breakfasts. Ground-floor areas include a popular bar, cosy TV lounge and a dining room.

Rooms 35 rms (11 en suite) (5 fmly) (9 smoking) **Facilities** TVL tea/coffee Dinner available Cen ht Licensed Wi-fi Pool table **Parking** 35

BIRMINGHAM (NATIONAL EXHIBITION CENTRE)

See Solihull

COVENTRY   Map 10 SP37

Ashdowns

★★★ 🄰 GUEST HOUSE

12 Regent St CV1 3EP
☎ 024 7622 9280
dir: A429 to city centre, over rdbt before ring road, 1st left onto Grosvenor Rd, right onto Westminster Rd, right onto Regent St

Rooms 8 rms (7 en suite) (3 fmly) (1 GF) (8 smoking) S £40-£45; D £50-£60* **Facilities** FTV TVL tea/coffee Cen ht **Parking** 8 **Notes** LB ⊗ No Children 13yrs Closed 22 Dec-1 Jan ⊛

DORRIDGE   Map 10 SP17

The Forest

★★★★ ◉◉ RESTAURANT WITH ROOMS

25 Station Rd B93 8JA
☎ 01564 772120 🖶 01564 732680
e-mail: info@forest-hotel.com
web: www.forest-hotel.com
dir: In town centre near station

This very individual and stylish restaurant with rooms is well placed for routes to Birmingham, Stratford-upon-Avon and Warwick. The 12 individually designed bedrooms are very well equipped with modern facilities, and imaginative food is served in the bars and intimate restaurant. A warm welcome is assured.

Rooms 12 en suite **Facilities** FTV tea/coffee Dinner available Direct Dial Cen ht Wi-fi **Conf** Max 100 Thtr 100 Class 60 Board 40 **Parking** 50 **Notes** ⊗ RS Sun eve Restaurant closed No coaches Civ Wed 120

MERIDEN   Map 10 SP28

Grove House Bed & Breakfast

★★★★ BED AND BREAKFAST

8 Whichcote Av CV7 7LR
☎ 01676 523295
e-mail: enquiries@grovehousebandb.co.uk
web: www.grovehousebandb.co.uk
dir: M42 junct 6 onto A45 then A452, at rdbt onto B4102 signed Meriden. Pass Bulls Head, 3rd turning on left (Leys Ln), house on left

Located in the quiet village of Meriden just 10 minutes from Birmingham International Airport and the NEC. A warm welcome is guaranteed at Grove House. Bedrooms are spacious and well equipped providing impressive quality and comfort. Ground-floor areas include a comfortable lounge in addition to the cosy breakfast room that overlooks the garden.

Rooms 2 rms (1 en suite) (1 pri facs) **Facilities** FTV TVL tea/coffee Dinner available Cen ht Wi-fi **Parking** 6 **Notes** LB ⊗ ⊛

Swallowfield Country House

★★★★ GUEST ACCOMMODATION

Hampton Ln CV7 7JR
☎ 01676 521262

Swallowfield Country House is a beautifully presented house located on a quiet side road in the busy town of Meriden. The house is a five-minute drive from the NEC and is ideally situated for Birmingham Airport and The Bullring shopping complex. Bedrooms are all very attractively presented; free Wi-fi is available along with ample secure car parking. Breakfast is not to be missed and is served in the light filled conservatory. Guests are assured of a warm welcome from the very friendly proprietors.

Rooms 8 en suite (5 GF) S fr £65; D fr £75* **Facilities** TVL Cen ht Wi-fi **Parking** 15 **Notes** ⊗ No Children Closed 22 Dec-6 Jan

SOLIHULL   Map 10 SP17

The Gate House

★★★ BED AND BREAKFAST

Barston Ln, Barston B92 0JN
☎ 01675 443274
e-mail: enquiries@gatehousesolihull.co.uk
web: www.gatehousesolihull.co.uk
dir: 4m E of Solihull. Off B4101 or B4102 to Barston, on W side of village

This elegant Victorian building stands in landscaped grounds with secure parking, and is within easy driving distance of the NEC in Birmingham. The resident proprietor is most welcoming and provides spacious comfortable accommodation. Breakfast is served in an elegant dining room overlooking the pretty gardens.

Rooms 4 rms (2 en suite) **Facilities** tea/coffee Cen ht Wi-fi **Parking** 20 **Notes** ⊗ No Children 5yrs ⊛

Windrush

★★★★ 🏠 BED AND BREAKFAST

337 Birmingham Rd, Wylde Green B72 1DL
☎ 0121 384 7534 & 07884 226552
e-mail: windrush59@hotmail.com
dir: *M6 junct 6, on A5127 to Sutton Coldfield, pass shopping centre on left. 75yds then house just before Hawthorn's Surgery on right immediately before traffic bollards*

A warm welcome is assured at this Victorian home from home. The recently refurbished accommocation offers considerable luxury. Memorable breakfasts are served in the elegant dining room.

Rooms 2 rms (1 en suite) (1 pri facs) S £40-£45; D £60-£65* **Facilities** FTV tea/coffee Cen ht Wi-fi **Parking** 5 **Notes** ⊗ No Children 16yrs Closed 19 Dec-3 Jan ⊜

WIGHT, ISLE OF

Blandings

★★★★ BED AND BREAKFAST

Horringford PO30 3AP
☎ 01983 865720 & 865331 📠 01983 862099
e-mail: robin.oulton@horringford.com
web: www.horringford.com/bedandbreakfast.htm
dir: *S through Arreton (B3056), pass Stickworth Hall on right, 300yds on left farm entrance signed Horringford Gdns. U-turn to left, at end of poplar trees turn right. Blandings on left*

This recently-built detached home stands in the grounds of Horringford Gardens. One bedroom has private access and a decking area for warm summer evenings. Breakfast is a highlight with local island produce gracing the table.

Blandings

Rooms 2 en suite (1 GF) **Facilities** FTV TV1B tea/coffee Cen ht **Parking** 3 **Notes** LB ⊜

The Crab & Lobster Inn

★★★★ INN

32 Forelands Field Rd PO35 5TR
☎ 01983 872244 📠 01983 873495
e-mail: info@crabandlobsterinn.co.uk
dir: *From Bembridge village, 1st left after Boots onto Forelands Rd to Windmill Hotel. Left onto Lane End Rd, 2nd right onto Egerton Rd, left onto Howgate Rd & immediately right onto Forelands Field Rd*

A traditional beamed inn enjoying a coastal location overlooking Bembridge Ledge with panoramic sea views. Bedrooms and bathrooms are traditionally fitted, comfortable and spacious, offering a good range of accessories. Locally-caught crab and lobster is the specialty during lunch and dinner at this popular dining destination.

Rooms 5 en suite (1 fmly) S £25-£70; D £60-£100* **Facilities** tea/coffee Dinner available Cen ht Wi-fi **Parking** 20 **Notes** Closed 24-26 Dec No coaches

Windmill Inn

★★★★ INN

1 Steyne Rd PO35 5UH
☎ 01983 872875 📠 01983 874760
e-mail: enquiries@windmill-inn.com

This popular Inn is located in the quiet village location of Bembridge. Bedrooms are modern throughout with good quality decoration and comfortable furnishings appealing to both business and leisure guests alike. Food is served throughout the day in the popular bar and restaurant. Guests can choose from snacks, meals including locally sourced Bembridge Lobster and on Sundays there is a Carvery.

Rooms 14 en suite (2 fmly) S £40-£50; D £80-£100* **Facilities** FTV TVL Dinner available Cen ht Wi-fi **Parking** 50

The Lake

★★★★ GUEST ACCOMMODATION

Shore Rd PO38 1RF
☎ 01983 852613
e-mail: enquiries@lakehotel.co.uk
dir: *0.5m E of Ventnor. Off A3055 to Bonchurch, opp village pond*

A warm welcome is assured at this friendly, family-run property set in two acres of well-tended gardens close to the sea. Bedrooms are equipped with modern facilities and the elegant public rooms offer a high standard of comfort. The breakfast menu offers a good choice of cold and hot options.

Rooms 11 en suite 9 annexe en suite (7 fmly) (4 GF) S £36-£47; D £72-£94* **Facilities** TVL tea/coffee Cen ht Licensed Wi-fi Golf 9 **Parking** 20 **Notes** LB No Children 3yrs Closed 20 Dec-2 Jan

The Old House

★★★★ 🏠 BED AND BREAKFAST

Gotten Manor, Gotten Ln PO38 2HQ
☎ 01983 551368 & 07746 453398
e-mail: aa@gottenmanor.co.uk
web: www.gottenmanor.co.uk
dir: *1m N of Chale. Turn right off B3399 onto Gotten Ln (opp chapel), house at end*

Located in countryside close to the coast, this 17th-century house has 18th- and 19th-century additions. Restoration has created comfortable, rustic bedrooms with antique bathtubs. Comprehensive breakfasts using the finest ingredients are served in the cosy dining room, and there is a spacious lounge with an open fire.

Rooms 2 en suite D £80-£100* **Facilities** STV FTV tea/coffee Cen ht Wi-fi 🎣 **Parking** 3 **Notes** LB ⊗ No Children 12yrs ⊜

Save on B&Bs and Hotels. Book at **theAA.com/hotel**

WIGHT, ISLE OF 317 ENGLAND

COWES — Map 5 SZ49

Duke of York

★★★ INN

Mill Hill Rd PO31 7BT
☎ 01983 295171 📠 01983 295047
e-mail: dukeofyorkcowes@btconnect.com

This family-run inn is situated very close to the town centre of Cowes. Comfortable bedrooms are divided between the main building and a separate building only seconds away. Home-cooked meals, with a number of fish and seafood dishes, feature on the menu every evening and are served in the newly redecorated bar and dining area. Parking is a bonus at this location, and outdoor, covered dining is also an option.

Rooms 8 en suite 5 annexe en suite (1 fmly) (1 GF)
Facilities FTV tea/coffee Dinner available Wi-fi
Parking 10

The Fountain Inn

★★★ INN

High St PO31 7AW
☎ 01983 292397 📠 01983 299554
e-mail: fountain.cowes@oldenglishinns.co.uk
dir: Adjacent to Red Jet passenger ferry in town centre

The Fountain Inn is located in the heart of the harbourside town of Cowes where a number of bedrooms have beautiful views across the water. Bedrooms and bathrooms are modern in their design, and provide comfortable accommodation. Substantial bar meals are served in the public areas, and breakfast offers a wide range of options. Public transport operates a regular service with a convenient drop-off point at the rear of this inn. Local pay-and-display car parking is a short walk away.

Rooms 20 en suite Facilities STV FTV tea/coffee Dinner available Direct Dial Cen ht Wi-fi Notes LB No coaches

EAST COWES — Map 5 SZ59

The Moorings

U

3 Cambridge Rd PO32 6AE
☎ 01983 292779
e-mail: themooringsbandb@hotmail.com
dir: By East Cowes Esplanade opposite harbour breakwater

Currently the rating for this establishment is not confirmed. This may be due to a change of ownership or because it has only recently joined the AA rating scheme. Please note that this establishment is open from mid-June to mid-September only.

Rooms 4 rms (1 GF) Facilities TVL Notes ⊗ No Children
Closed Oct-May 🖂

FRESHWATER — Map 5 SZ38

Seagulls Rest

★★★★ GUEST ACCOMMODATION

Colwell Chine Rd PO40 9NP
☎ 01983 754037 & 754929
e-mail: selena.flint@btinternet.com
dir: A3054 W from Yarmouth, 2.5m at Colwell Bay Inn right for beach, 300yds on left

Situated just a stroll from the beach, this smart modern detached house has bright and spacious bedrooms, and there is a comfortable lounge. Breakfast and evening meals (by arrangement) are served in the cheery dining room.

Rooms 4 en suite (2 fmly) (1 GF) S £37-£44; D £64-£68
Facilities FTV tea/coffee Dinner available Cen ht Wi-fi
Parking 9 Notes LB ⊗ 🖂

GATCOMBE — Map 5 SZ48

Little Gatcombe Farm

★★★ BED AND BREAKFAST

Newbarn Ln PO30 3EQ
☎ 01983 721580 & 07968 462513
e-mail: anita@littlegatcombefarm.co.uk
dir: From Newport head towards Chillerton, 1m past Wightcroft clocktower turn right onto Gatcombe Rd, 1m further on left

Nestled in beautiful countryside only a couple of miles away from Carisbrooke, and only a ten minute drive from Newport, is the delightful Little Gatcombe Farm. Accommodation is comfortable and guests can enjoy a delicious home-cooked breakfast in the bright conservatory overlooking rolling hills and grounds which are usually packed with grazing sheep. Cream teas are served here daily during the summer months.

Rooms 2 en suite D £70-£90 Facilities FTV tea/coffee
Cen ht Parking 20 Notes ⊗ No Children 🖂

GODSHILL — Map 5 SZ58

PREMIER COLLECTION

Godshill Park Farm House

★★★★★ 🏠 BED AND BREAKFAST

Shanklin Rd PO38 3JF
☎ 01983 840781
e-mail: info@godshillparkfarm.uk.com
web: www.godshillparkfarm.uk.com
dir: From ferry teminal towards Newport, onto A3020 & signs to Sandown, at Blackwater Corner right to Godshill, farm on right after Griffin pub

This delightful 200-year-old stone farmhouse is set in 270 acres of organic farmland with lakes and woodlands. Bedrooms, one with a four-poster bed and the other overlooking the millpond, are comfortably furnished with many extra facilities. Delicious full English breakfasts are served at one large table in the oak panelled Great Hall.

Rooms 2 en suite D £80-£110* Facilities tea/coffee
Cen ht Wi-fi Fishing Parking 4 Notes ⊗ No Children 8yrs

'Arndale'

★★★★ BED AND BREAKFAST

High St PO38 3HH
☎ 01983 842003
e-mail: arndalebandb@aol.com
dir: On A3020 High St

Arndale is situated in the pretty village of Godshill. Expect a warm welcome from the resident dogs, Bayley and Arrow. Breakfast is served in the private lounge-dining room. Guests have access to the patio and garden during the warmer months of the year

Rooms 2 rms (2 pri facs) (1 GF) S £35-£65; D £65*
Facilities TVL Cen ht Riding Parking 4 Notes ⊗ No Children 14yrs 🖂

NEWPORT — Map 5 SZ58

Castle Lodge

★ ★ ★ GUEST ACCOMMODATION

54 Castle Rd PO30 1DP
☎ 01983 527862 & 07789 228203 📄 01983 559030
e-mail: castlelodge@hotmail.co.uk
web: www.castlelodgeiow.co.uk
dir: 0.5m SW of town centre. On B3323 towards Carisbrooke Castle

This well-presented establishment is located in a quiet residential area within close walking distance of the famous Carisbrooke Castle. A comfortable stay is assured in attractive and restful bedrooms, together with a bright and airy dining room where a substantial breakfast can be enjoyed.

Rooms 2 en suite 5 annexe en suite (1 fmly) (5 GF) S £35-£45; D £55-£75* **Facilities** FTV tea/coffee Cen ht Wi-fi **Parking** 5 **Notes** ⊗

NITON — Map 5 SZ57

PREMIER COLLECTION

Enchanted Manor

★ ★ ★ ★ ★ GUEST ACCOMMODATION

Sandrock Rd PO38 2NG
☎ 01983 730215
e-mail: info@enchantedmanor.co.uk
web: www.enchantedmanor.co.uk

This delightful property, set in charming grounds, enjoys an enviable location within walking distance of the sea. An unusual theme of magic and enchantment prevails throughout the beautifully appointed suites and spacious public areas that are all furnished and decorated to a very high standard. A host of extra touches are provided such as DVD players, well-stocked mini-fridges and welcome baskets. Guests are ensured of friendly, attentive personalised service and an excellent breakfast.

Rooms 7 en suite (2 GF) **Facilities** STV FTV tea/coffee Cen ht Licensed Wi-fi Snooker Pool table Spa/hot tub Massage beauty treatment room **Conf** Max 30 Board 30 **Parking** 15 **Notes** LB No Children Civ Wed 50

RYDE — Map 5 SZ59

1 The Lawn

★ ★ ★ ★ BED AND BREAKFAST

Spencer Rd PO33 2NU
☎ 01983 568742
dir: A3054, left into West St. Left at T-junct, 100yds on left up drive signed Veterinary Surgery

Attractive Victorian house in quiet area, convenient for the town centre as well as the hovercraft and catamaran terminals. Off-road parking is available.

Rooms 2 rms (2 pri facs) D £50-£60* **Facilities** TV1B tea/coffee Cen ht **Parking** 2 **Notes** ⊗ No Children 5yrs 🐾

Ryde Castle

★ ★ ★ INN

The Esplanade PO33 1JA
☎ 01983 563755 📄 01983 566906
e-mail: 6505@greeneking.co.uk

Located overlooking Ryde esplanade with sea views out to the Solent and beyond, this historic building provides comfortable bedroom accommodation with en suite facilities. This majestic setting houses a popular brasserie and lounge/bar whilst the external decking areas are a welcome place to relax for a summer-time drink. Ample off-road parking is an additional bonus.

Rooms 18 en suite (1 fmly) D £59-£99* **Facilities** FTV tea/coffee Dinner available Cen ht Wi-fi **Conf** Max 100 Thtr 100 Class 75 Board 30 **Parking** 70 **Notes** ⊗ No coaches Civ Wed 120

SANDOWN — Map 5 SZ58

The Lawns

★ ★ ★ ★ GUEST ACCOMMODATION

72 Broadway PO36 9AA
☎ 01983 402549
e-mail: lawnshotel@aol.com
web: www.lawnshotelisleofwight.co.uk
dir: On A3055 N of town centre

The Lawns stands in grounds just a short walk from the beach, public transport and town centre. There is a comfortable lounge and bar, and evening meals (by arrangement) and breakfast are served in the bright dining room. Service is friendly and attentive, and the bedrooms are comfortably equipped.

Rooms 13 en suite (2 fmly) (2 GF) S £40-£50; D £76-£92* **Facilities** FTV TVL tea/coffee Dinner available Cen ht Licensed Wi-fi **Parking** 13 **Notes** LB ⊗ Closed Nov-Jan

Montague House

★ ★ ★ ★ GUEST HOUSE

109 Station Av PO36 8HD
☎ 01983 404295
e-mail: enquiries@montaguehousehotel.fsnet.co.uk
dir: A3055 from Ryde to Sandown, onto Station Av, follow signs for beach

This large, detached, late Victorian house is just a short walk from the town centre and seafront. The friendly hosts provide good quality, well-equipped modern accommodation. Separate tables are provided in the very attractive dining room and you can relax in the pleasant conservatory.

Rooms 10 rms (9 en suite) (1 pri facs) (2 fmly) (2 GF) S £35; D £70* **Facilities** TVL tea/coffee Cen ht **Notes** LB ⊗ No Children 5yrs 🐾

Carisbrooke House

★★★ GUEST HOUSE

1 Beachfield Rd PO36 8NA
☎ 01983 402257 ▧ 01983 402257
e-mail: wmch583@aol.com
dir: *Opposite Ferncliff Gardens*

Expect a friendly welcome at this family-run guest house situated opposite Ferncliff Gardens and within walking distance of the town centre and seafront. A full English breakfast is served in the dining room overlooking the sun terrace. Enjoy a drink in the bar/lounge. Dinner by arrangement.

Rooms 11 rms (9 en suite) (2 pri facs) (3 fmly) (3 GF) **Facilities** TVL tea/coffee Dinner available Cen ht Licensed Wi-fi **Parking** 3

Chester Lodge

★★★ GUEST HOUSE

8 Beachfield Rd PO36 8NA
☎ 01983 402773
dir: *On B3395 S from seafront/High St*

This family-run property is within walking distance of the seafront and shops. The neat bedrooms include some on the ground floor with easier access, and there is a comfortable bar and lounge. Breakfast is served in the bright dining room.

Rooms 13 en suite (3 fmly) (4 GF) S £28-£35; D £56-£70* **Facilities** TVL tea/coffee Dinner available Licensed Wi-fi **Parking** 14 **Notes** LB ⊗

The Sandhill

★★★ 🅰 GUEST ACCOMMODATION

6 Hill St PO36 9DB
☎ 01983 403635 ▧ 01983 403695
e-mail: sandhillsandown@aol.com
dir: *In Sandown proceed along main broadway, turn onto Leed St, The Sandhill at top of road*

Rooms 16 en suite (6 fmly) (4 GF) S £28-£38; D £56-£76* **Facilities** TVL tea/coffee Dinner available Direct Dial Cen ht Licensed Wi-fi **Parking** 10 **Notes** LB

SEAVIEW   Map 5 SZ69

The Boathouse

★★★★ 🍴 INN

Springvale Rd PO34 5AW
☎ 01983 810616
e-mail: info@theboathouseiow.co.uk

This very pleasant inn has a shore side location and is a relaxing, friendly and comfortable place to stay. Food is a focus here with fresh, local produce and speciality lobster and crab dishes. The inn provides a contemporary style throughout; bedrooms are pleasantly spacious and most have beach views. There is ample parking and a garden where in warmer times drinks and food are served.

Rooms 4 en suite (1 fmly) **Facilities** FTV tea/coffee Dinner available Cen ht Wi-fi **Parking** 20 **Notes** No coaches

---

SHANKLIN   Map 5 SZ58

Fernbank

★★★★ GUEST ACCOMMODATION

6 Highfield Rd PO37 6PP
☎ 01983 862790
e-mail: fernbank2010@btconnect.com
dir: *Approaching Shanklin on A3020, right onto Highfield Rd. 300yds on left*

Located in the Shanklin Old Village, this newly renovated establishment offers modern, comfortable and spacious accommodation. Home-made refreshments are available throughout the afternoon and guests can enjoy a wide range of both cooked and continental breakfasts in the airy dining room. There is an indoor swimming pool and plenty of outside space within the sup-tropical landscaped gardens in which to relax. Free Wi-fi is available throughout.

Rooms 17 en suite (2 fmly) (2 GF) S £35-£42; D £70-£84 **Facilities** FTV tea/coffee Cen ht Licensed Wi-fi 🔁 Petanque **Parking** 13 **Notes** LB ⊗ No Children 5yrs Closed Nov-Feb

---

The Finches

★★★★ BED AND BREAKFAST

9 Highfield Rd PO37 6PP
☎ 01983 863899
e-mail: sally@kmg.org.uk
dir: *A3020 towards Shanklin, turn right onto Highfield Rd*

Located a short walk from Shanklin Old Village and benefiting from off-road car parking, is the beautifully maintained The Finches. Accommodation is very smart with amazingly comfortable beds, a substantial, enjoyable breakfast, and a warm welcome from the friendly owners.

Rooms 2 en suite S £55-£65; D £70-£80* **Facilities** STV FTV tea/coffee Cen ht Wi-fi **Parking** 4 **Notes** ⊗ No Children 8yrs ⊗

The Avenue

★★★★ GUEST ACCOMMODATION

6 Avenue Rd PO37 7BG
☎ 01983 862746
e-mail: info@avenuehotelshanklin.co.uk
dir: *A3055 from Sandown, through Lake, right onto Avenue Rd before x-rds lights*

This friendly, family-run guest accommodation is in a quiet location just a 5-minute walk from the town centre and beaches. The well-equipped bedrooms are generally spacious, and there is a bar-lounge, a conservatory and a comfortable breakfast room. An attractive terraced courtyard lies to the rear.

Rooms 10 en suite (2 GF) S £35-£39; D £69-£79* **Facilities** FTV tea/coffee Cen ht Licensed Wi-fi **Parking** 6 **Notes** LB ⊗ Closed Nov-Feb

SHANKLIN *continued*

The Bedford Lodge

★★★★ GUEST ACCOMMODATION

4 Chine Av PO37 6AA
☎ 01983 862416 📄 01983 868704
e-mail: mail@bedfordlodge.co.uk
dir: *A3055 onto Chine Av, opp Tower Cottage Gardens*

A particularly warm welcome is guaranteed at this delightful property. The Bedford Lodge benefits from an unspoilt and quiet location with pretty gardens and is extremely close to Shanklin Old Village and Shanklin beach. Bedrooms are well equipped and comfortable. A delicious breakfast is served at individual dining tables in the attractive dining room; in addition a bar and lounge is available for guests' use.

Rooms 14 en suite (1 fmly) (2 GF) **Facilities** TVL tea/coffee Cen ht Wi-fi **Parking** 8 **Notes** No Children 5yrs

The Belmont

★★★★ GUEST ACCOMMODATION

8 Queens Rd PO37 6AN
☎ 01983 862864 & 867875
e-mail: enquiries@belmont-iow.co.uk
dir: *From Sandown (on A3055), half left at Fiveways lights signed Ventnor. Belmont 400mtrs on right, opp St Saviour's church*

Situated less than 10 minutes walk from Shanklin beach and only five minutes from Shanklin Old Village is The Belmont. This establishment offers comfortable accommodation and several rooms have stunning sea views. The Belmont is licensed, and beverages and sandwiches are available during the day time and evening. Off-road parking is a benefit, and during summer months guests can enjoy the outdoor swimming pool.

Rooms 13 en suite (2 fmly) (2 GF) **Facilities** FTV tea/coffee Direct Dial Licensed Wi-fi ⌇ **Parking** 9 **Notes** LB ⊗ No Children 5yrs

The Grange

★★★★ GUEST ACCOMMODATION

9 Eastcliff Rd PO37 6AA
☎ 01983 867644 📄 01983 865537
e-mail: jenni@thegrangebythesea.com
web: www.thegrangebythesea.com
dir: *Off A3055, High St*

This delightful house specialises in holistic breaks and enjoys a tranquil yet convenient setting in manicured grounds close to the seafront and village centre. Extensive refurbishment has resulted in beautifully presented bedrooms and spacious public areas. Breakfast is taken en famille (outside in fine weather).

Rooms 16 en suite (2 fmly) (6 GF) S £58; D £88-£116* **Facilities** TVL tea/coffee Cen ht Licensed Wi-fi Sauna Beauty treatments & massage **Parking** 8 **Notes** LB ⊗ Civ Wed 100

See advert on this page

Hayes Barton

★★★★ ⬤ GUEST ACCOMMODATION

7 Highfield Rd PO37 6PP
☎ **01983 867747**
e-mail: williams.2000@virgin.net
web: www.hayesbarton.co.uk
dir: *A3055 onto A3020 Victoria Av, 3rd left*

Hayes Barton has the relaxed atmosphere of a family home and provides well-equipped bedrooms and a range of comfortable public areas. Dinner is available from a short selection of home-cooked dishes, and there is a cosy bar lounge. The old village, beach and promenade are all within walking distance.

Rooms 9 en suite (4 fmly) (2 GF) **Facilities** TVL tea/coffee Dinner available Cen ht Licensed Wi-fi **Parking** 9 **Notes** LB Closed Nov-Mar

The Richmond

★★★★ GUEST HOUSE

23 Palmerston Rd PO37 6AS
☎ **01983 862874**
e-mail: info@richmondhotel-shanklin.co.uk
dir: *Off Shanklin High St at Conservative Club*

This friendly guest house is a stroll from the town centre and beach. The carefully furnished bedrooms have a good range of facilities, and the public rooms include a cosy lounge bar and an attractive dining room.

Rooms 9 en suite (3 fmly) S £28-£33; D £56-£74* **Facilities** TVL tea/coffee Dinner available Cen ht Licensed Wi-fi **Parking** 5 **Notes** LB ⊗ No Children 3yrs

Rowborough

★★★★ GUEST ACCOMMODATION

32 Arthurs Hill PO37 6EX
☎ **01983 866072 & 863070** 📠 **01983 867703**
e-mail: susanpatricia@btconnect.com
web: www.rowboroughhotel.com
dir: *Between Sandown & Shanklin*

Located on the main road into town, this charming, family-run establishment provides comfortable bedrooms with many extra facilities. The non-smoking conservatory overlooks the garden, along with a lounge and a bar. Dinner is available by arrangement.

Rooms 9 en suite (5 fmly) (1 GF) S £46-£52; D £92-£104* **Facilities** TVL tea/coffee Dinner available Cen ht Licensed Wi-fi DVD players in all rooms **Parking** 5 **Notes** LB

St Georges House

★★★★ GUEST ACCOMMODATION

2 St Georges Rd PO37 6BA
☎ **01983 863691** 📠 **01983 861597**
e-mail: info@stgeorgesiow.com
web: www.stgeorgesiow.com
dir: *S from Fiveways turn 2nd right off A3055, next right*

A warm welcome is assured at this family-run property located in a quiet area between the town centre and cliff top. Bedrooms vary in size but all are comfortable and well appointed. Guests have use of the lounge and bar.

Rooms 9 en suite (1 fmly) (1 GF) S £30-£42; D £60-£84* **Facilities** FTV TVL tea/coffee Cen ht Licensed Wi-fi **Parking** 7 **Notes** LB Closed mid Dec-mid Jan

The Braemar

★★★ GUEST HOUSE

1 Grange Rd PO37 6NN
☎ **01983 863172** 📠 **01983 863172**
e-mail: djsherfield@aol.com

Tucked away in Shanklin Old Village, expect a warm welcome at this family-run, licensed guest house. Bedrooms are comfortable and vary in size. Breakfast is served in the bright dining room overlooking the gardens.

Rooms 11 en suite (2 fmly) (3 GF) S fr £30; D fr £60* **Facilities** TVL tea/coffee Cen ht Licensed Wi-fi Pool table **Parking** 10 **Notes** LB

TOTLAND BAY   **Map 5 SZ38**

PREMIER COLLECTION

Sentry Mead

★★★★★ ⬤ GUEST ACCOMMODATION

Madeira Rd PO39 0BJ
☎ **01983 753212** 📠 **01983 754710**
e-mail: info@sentrymead.co.uk
dir: *From Yarmouth onto A3054 to Freshwater, after 2m straight over at rdbt, right at next rdbt, Madeira Rd, 300yds on right*

This country house is located in Totland Bay, the West Wight part of the Isle of Wight. Bedrooms have been tastefully decorated to offer guests traditional yet stylish accommodation, all well equipped with Wi-fi and digital TVs. Public areas are spacious; guests can relax in the main lounge or conservatory area both with views of the large well tended garden. Dinner is served daily in the dining room where guests can also enjoy a selection of cooked breakfasts and continental dishes.

Rooms 11 en suite (1 fmly) S £55; D £70-£125* **Facilities** FTV tea/coffee Dinner available Direct Dial Cen ht Licensed Wi-fi Golf 18 Day membership to West Bay Country Club **Parking** 9 **Notes** LB

The Golf House

★★★★ 🏠 BED AND BREAKFAST

Alum Bay New Rd PO39 0JA
☎ **01983 753293**
e-mail: sue@thegolfhouse.info
dir: *Totland B3322, at War Memorial rdbt take 2nd exit onto Church Hill 1m, entrance on left*

The Golf House is a detached house in its own grounds situated at the western tip of the Isle of Wight with all rooms enjoying amazing views. Two bedrooms, each with TVs, create a two-bedroom suite with one bathroom which can accommodate up to four guests, and the second bedroom has en suite facilities. Local produce is used where possible and evening snacks are available by prior arrangement. Transport to and from Yarmouth can be arranged.

Rooms 3 rms (1 en suite) (2 pri facs) S £40-£50; D £75-£90 **Facilities** STV FTV TVL tea/coffee Cen ht Wi-fi Snooker **Parking** 3 **Notes** LB ⊗

The Hoo

★★★★ BED AND BREAKFAST

Colwell Rd PO39 0AB
☎ **01983 753592** 📠 **01983 753592**
e-mail: the.hoo@btinternet.com
dir: *From Yarmouth ferry right onto A3054, 2.25m enter Colwell Common, The Hoo on corner of Colwell Rd & Warden Rd*

Located close to the port and beaches, this friendly family home provides a peaceful setting. The house has many Japanese features and guests are asked to wear slippers. The spacious bedrooms are well equipped and comfortably furnished. English breakfast is most enjoyable and is served overlooking the attractive gardens.

Rooms 3 rms (1 en suite) (2 fmly) **Facilities** FTV tea/coffee Cen ht Wi-fi **Parking** 1 **Notes** No Children 5yrs

The Hermitage

★★★ GUEST ACCOMMODATION

Cliff Rd PO39 0EW
☎ **01983 752518**
e-mail: blake_david@btconnect.com
web: www.thehermitagebnb.co.uk
dir: *Church Hill B3322, right onto Eden Rd, left onto Cliff Rd, 0.5m on right*

The Hermitage is an extremely pet and people friendly establishment which occupies a stunning and unspoilt location near to the cliff top in Totland Bay. Extensive gardens are well maintained and off-road parking is a bonus. Accommodation is comfortable and you are assured of a genuinely warm welcome at this traditionally styled establishment. A range of delicious items at breakfast provide a substantial start to the day.

Rooms 6 rms (5 en suite) (1 pri facs) (1 fmly) **Facilities** TVL tea/coffee Dinner available **Parking** 6 **Notes** LB

PREMIER COLLECTION

The Hambrough

★★★★★ @@@ RESTAURANT WITH ROOMS

Hambrough Rd PO38 1SQ
☎ 01983 856333 📄 01983 857260
e-mail: info@thehambrough.com
dir: *Telephone for directions*

A former Victorian villa set on the hillside above
Ventnor and with memorable views out to sea, The
Hambrough has a modern, stylish interior with well
equipped, boutique-style accommodation. The kitchen
team's passion for food is clearly evident in the superb
cuisine served in the minimalistic styled restaurant.
The Hambrough was a runner-up for the AA's Funkiest
B&B of the Year Award (2011-2012).

Rooms 7 en suite (3 fmly) D £170-£280* **Facilities** STV
tea/coffee Dinner available Direct Dial Cen ht Wi-fi
Notes LB ⊗ Closed 2wks Xmas-Jan, 1wk Apr & 2wks
Nov No coaches

PREMIER COLLECTION

The Leconfield

★★★★★ @ 🏠 GUEST ACCOMMODATION

85 Leeson Rd, Upper Bonchurch PO38 1PU
☎ 01983 852196
e-mail: enquiries@leconfieldhotel.com
web: www.leconfieldhotel.com
dir: *On A3055, 3m from Shanklin Old Village*

This country house is situated on an elevated position
with panoramic sea views above the historic village of
Bonchurch. Luxury bedrooms and suites are spacious
and individually styled. Public rooms include two
lounges and a conservatory, in addition to the Sea
Scape restaurant, named after the views, where freshly
prepared breakfast and imaginative dinner menus are
served. Additional facilities include the outdoor pool,
terrace area and ample off-road parking.

Rooms 6 en suite 5 annexe en suite (3 GF) S £40-£180;
D £80-£200* **Facilities** tea/coffee Dinner available
Cen ht Licensed Wi-fi ⊰ **Parking** 14 **Notes** LB ⊗ No
Children 16yrs Closed 24-26 Dec & 3-27 Jan

St. Augustine Villa

★★★★ GUEST ACCOMMODATION

Esplanade PO38 1TA
☎ 01983 852285 📄 01983 856630
e-mail: info@harbourviewhotel.co.uk
web: www.harbourviewhotel.co.uk
dir: *Opp harbour*

Located on an elevated position with spectacular sea
views, this delightful Victorian property next to the Winter
Gardens provides well-equipped and comfortable
bedrooms. Public areas include a conservatory dining
room, lounge, cosy bar, small garden and patio area, all
with sea views.

Rooms 9 en suite **Facilities** STV FTV TVL tea/coffee Direct
Dial Cen ht Licensed Wi-fi **Parking** 8 **Notes** ⊗ No
Children 21yrs Closed 5 Jan-1 Feb

St Maur

★★★★ GUEST ACCOMMODATION

Castle Rd PO38 1LG
☎ 01983 852570 & 853645 📄 01983 852306
e-mail: sales@stmaur.co.uk
dir: *Exit A3055 at end of Park Av onto Castle Rd, premises
150yds on left*

A warm welcome awaits guests at this Victorian villa,
which is pleasantly and quietly located in an elevated
position overlooking the bay. The well-equipped bedrooms
are traditionally decorated, while public areas include a
spacious lounge and cosy residents' bar. The gardens
here are a delight.

Rooms 9 en suite (2 fmly) **Facilities** STV tea/coffee
Dinner available Cen ht Licensed **Parking** 9 **Notes** ⊗ No
Children 5yrs Closed Dec

Cornerways

★★★ GUEST ACCOMMODATION

39 Madeira Rd PO38 1QS
☎ 01983 852323 📄 01983 852323
e-mail: cornerwayshotel@aol.com
web: www.cornerwaysventnor.co.uk
dir: *Off Trinity Rd (south coast road) near Trinity Church
onto Madeira Rd, house on left*

This property is quietly located between Bonchurch and
the town centre, yet is only a stroll from the beach, shops
and many places of interest. Bedrooms are comfortable
and well equipped and there is a lounge and cosy bar.
Full English breakfasts are served at individual tables.

Rooms 9 en suite (1 fmly) (1 GF) S £32-£36; D £64-£72*
Facilities TVL tea/coffee Cen ht Licensed Wi-fi Pool table
Parking 4 **Notes** LB ⊗ No Children 5yrs Closed 22 Dec-3
Jan

Gothic View B&B

★★★ 🏠 🍽 BED AND BREAKFAST

Town Ln, Chale Green PO38 2JS
☎ 01983 551120 & 07818 864967
e-mail: info@gothicview.co.uk
dir: *From Cowes A3021, A3054 to Newport (or from
Fishbourne B3339 to Newport). Then B3323 to Shorwell,
B3399 to Chale. From Yarmouth A3054 to Totland, A3055
to Chale*

This establishment provides comfortable accommodation
in a converted gothic chapel located in the picturesque
village of Chale Green. Delicious meals are prepared with
the personal tastes of the guest fully catered for, and
breakfast is also a treat with a number of home-made,
freshly created and healthy items available.

Rooms 3 rms (2 en suite) (1 pri facs) (2 fmly) (3 GF) S
£30-£35; D £60-£70* **Facilities** tea/coffee Dinner
available Cen ht Wi-fi **Parking** 1 **Notes** LB ⊗ 🍽

Little Span Farm *(SZ545792)*

★★★ FARMHOUSE

Rew Ln, Wroxall PO38 3AU
☎ 01983 852419
Mrs F J Corry
e-mail: info@spanfarm.co.uk
dir: *A3020 onto B3327 to Wroxall, in centre of village turn
onto West St. Up hill, 200yds from sharp bend on right*

Enjoy the peace and tranquillity on offer at Little Span
Farm which is a working farm located near Wroxall, and
only a short drive from the seaside town of Ventnor. All
rooms are comfortable with en suite facilities and some
occupy the most beautiful views across the countryside.
Breakfast is usually served in the 17th-century dining
area or in summer months in the more modern, bright
and airy conservatory.

Rooms 2 en suite 1 annexe en suite (1 fmly)
Facilities FTV TVL tea/coffee Cen ht Wi-fi **Parking** 3
Notes RS 3/4wks Etr lambing season 🍽 180 acres sheep

Save on B&Bs and Hotels. Book at **theAA.com/hotel**

WILTSHIRE 323 **ENGLAND**

WILTSHIRE

AMESBURY
Map 5 SU14

Mandalay

★★★★ GUEST ACCOMMODATION

15 Stonehenge Rd SP4 7BA
☎ **01980 623733**
e-mail: nick.ramplin@btinternet.com
dir: *500yds W of town centre, off High St onto Church St & Stonehenge Rd*

Quietly located on the edge of the town, yet within easy reach of Stonehenge and the cathedral, this delightful property provides individually decorated rooms. Freshly cooked breakfasts are served in the pleasant breakfast room, which overlooks the landscaped gardens. Please note that a 48 hour cancellation policy is in operation.

Rooms 5 en suite (2 fmly) S £50-£60; D £65-£75
Facilities FTV TVL tea/coffee Cen ht Wi-fi **Parking** 5
Notes ⊗

Park House Motel

★★★★ GUEST ACCOMMODATION

SP4 0EG
☎ **01980 629256** 🖷 **01980 629256**
e-mail: info@parkhousemotel.com
dir: *5m E of Amesbury. Junct A303 & A338*

This family-run establishment offers a warm welcome and is extremely convenient for the A303. Bedrooms are practically equipped with modern facilities and come in a variety of sizes. There is a large dining room where dinner is served during the week, and a cosy bar in which to relax.

Rooms 30 rms (27 en suite) (1 pri facs) (9 fmly) (25 GF)
S £56-£65; D £75* **Facilities** STV FTV TVL tea/coffee
Dinner available Cen ht Licensed Wi-fi **Parking** 40

Catkin Lodge

★★★ BED AND BREAKFAST

93 Countess Rd SP4 7AT
☎ **01980 624810 & 622139** 🖷 **01980 622139**
e-mail: info@catkinlodge.fsnet.co.uk
web: www.catkinlodge.fsnet.co.uk
dir: *From A303 at Amesbury onto A345 (Marlborough road), 400yds on left*

Popular for business and leisure, Catkin Lodge is close to Stonehenge and offers off-road parking. The three bedrooms, including two on the ground floor, offer good levels of comfort and can accommodate children if required. The artwork of the talented proprietor is displayed around the property, adding further interest.

Rooms 3 en suite (1 fmly) (2 GF) S £30-£45; D £65-£80*
Facilities FTV tea/coffee Cen ht **Parking** 7 **Notes** ⊗ No Children 7yrs ⊛

BOX
Map 4 ST86

Lorne House

★★★★ GUEST HOUSE

London Rd SN13 8NA
☎ **01225 742597**
e-mail: info@lornehousebox.co.uk
web: www.lornehousebox.co.uk
dir: *On A4 in village, E of High St next to doctors surgery*

Lorne House offers guests a high standard of quality and comfort throughout, and a genuinely warm welcome is extended by the resident proprietors. The bedrooms and bathrooms have undergone a complete refurbishment and now include air conditioning, DVD players and luxury showers. At breakfast there's a good selection of carefully prepared dishes using local and home-made produce. Parking is available adjacent to the house.

Rooms 5 en suite (2 fmly) (1 GF) S £55-£70; D £85-£95*
Facilities FTV TVL tea/coffee Cen ht Wi-fi ➷ **Conf** Max 12
Thtr 12 Class 12 Board 12 **Parking** 6 **Notes** ⊗ Closed Xmas

White Smocks

★★★★ BED AND BREAKFAST

Ashley SN13 8AJ
☎ **01225 742154** 🖷 **01225 742212**
e-mail: whitesmocksashley@hotmail.com
dir: *A4 1m W of Box turn opp The Northy, at T-junct White Smocks right of thatched cottage*

Quietly located in the pleasant village of Ashley, and just a short drive from Bath with its many attractions, White Smocks offers a relaxing escape where guests are encouraged to enjoy the pleasant garden in the summer, real fires in the winter and the jacuzzi all year round. The two bedrooms and bathrooms are immaculately presented and comfortably furnished. Guests are also welcome to use the lounge.

Rooms 2 en suite (1 fmly) **Facilities** FTV TVL tea/coffee
Dinner available Cen ht Wi-fi **Parking** 3 **Notes** ⊗

Hermitage

★★ GUEST ACCOMMODATION

Bath Rd SN13 8DT
☎ **01225 744187**
e-mail: hermitagebb@btconnect.com
dir: *On A4 at W end of village*

This 16th-century house is located in a pleasant village five miles from Bath. The spacious bedrooms are comfortably furnished, with two rooms in a small adjacent cottage. Breakfast is served in the dining room. There is also a lounge area, and delightful gardens with a heated swimming pool.

Rooms 3 en suite 2 annexe en suite (1 fmly) (1 GF) S
£37-£40; D £60-£65* **Facilities** FTV tea/coffee Cen ht ⬩
Parking 6 **Notes** ⊗ Closed 22 Dec-6 Jan ⊛

The Northey Arms

Ⓤ

Bath Rd SN13 8AE
☎ **01225 891166**

Currently the rating for this establishment is not confirmed. This may be due to a change of ownership or because it has only recently joined the AA rating scheme.

Rooms 3 en suite S £87.50-£160; D £87.50-£160*

BRADFORD-ON-AVON　　Map 4 ST86

PREMIER COLLECTION

Bradford Old Windmill

★★★★★ 🛌 BED AND BREAKFAST

4 Masons Ln BA15 1QN
☎ 01225 866842 📠 01225 866648
e-mail: aa@bradfordoldwindmill.co.uk
dir: *N of town centre off A363. Driveway on E side of Masons Ln, no sign or number, 100mtrs before Castle public house*

This unique property has been restored to retain many original features. Bedrooms are individually decorated, and include a number of interesting options such as a round room, a waterbed or a suite with minstrels' gallery. An extensive breakfast menu, featuring local and organic products whenever possible, offers a range of alternatives from devilled mushrooms or passion fruit pancakes to the more traditional choices. A comfortable lounge is also available.

Rooms 3 en suite (1 fmly) **Facilities** tea/coffee Dinner available Cen ht Wi-fi **Parking** 3 **Notes** ⊗ No Children 6yrs Closed Dec-Jan RS Tue, Fri & Sun (Mar-Oct) No dinner

Stillmeadow

★★★★★ 🅰 BED AND BREAKFAST

18 Bradford Rd, Winsley BA15 2HW
☎ 01225 722119
e-mail: sue.gilby@btinternet.com
dir: *From Bradford-on-Avon on B3108 to rdbt, take 1st exit, 0.25m on left*

Rooms 3 en suite (2 fmly) S £60-£95; D £80-£95* **Facilities** tea/coffee Cen ht Wi-fi Golf 18 Storage for bicycles **Parking** 6 **Notes** LB ⊗ Closed 24-26 Dec

Midway Place

★★★★ BED AND BREAKFAST

10 Farleigh Wick BA15 2PU
☎ 01225 863932
e-mail: info@midwayplace.co.uk
web: www.midwayplace.co.uk
dir: *On A363 between Bath & Bradford-on-Avon, next to Fox & Hounds pub*

This property has been extensively renovated throughout and now offers contemporary bedrooms and bathrooms and a breakfast area. The resident host offers a naturally relaxed, welcoming style of hospitality. Bedrooms vary in size but are well laid out for guests' comfort and include useful extras. Dinner and lunch are available at the pub next door where guests can usually park their cars while they stay at Midway Place.

Rooms 6 en suite S £55-£78; D £78-£85* **Facilities** FTV TVL tea/coffee Cen ht Wi-fi **Parking** 6 **Notes** ⊗ Closed 14 Dec-14 Jan

Serendipity

★★★★ BED AND BREAKFAST

19f Bradford Rd, Winsley BA15 2HW
☎ 01225 722380 & 07941 778397
e-mail: vanda.shepherd@tesco.net
dir: *A36 onto B3108, 1.5m right into Winsley, establishment on right on main road*

Set in a quiet residential area, Serendipity is convenient for visiting nearby Bath. The proprietors are friendly and welcoming, and bedrooms are brightly decorated and equipped with a range of extras. Two are on the ground floor. Guests can watch badgers and other wildlife in the gardens during the evening. Breakfast is served in the conservatory overlooking the garden.

Rooms 3 en suite (1 fmly) (2 GF) S £45-£63; D £55-£69* **Facilities** FTV tea/coffee Cen ht Wi-fi 🏌 Golf 36 **Parking** 5 **Notes** LB ⊗ ⊛

The Swan

★★★★ 🍽 INN

1 Church St BA15 1LN
☎ 01225 868686 📠 01225 868681
e-mail: theswanbradford@yahoo.co.uk
dir: *On A363 in town centre*

A delightful Grade II listed building located right in the heart of this pleasant town. Bedrooms come in a range of shapes and sizes and offer plenty of quality and comfort. Downstairs guests relax in the lounge areas and unwind with a drink, or choose the character bar with its selection of real ales. Dinner and breakfast are highlights of any stay, and utilise fresh, high quality produce in dishes to suit all tastes.

Rooms 12 en suite (1 fmly) S £70-£90; D £80-£140* **Facilities** FTV tea/coffee Dinner available Cen ht Wi-fi Golf 18 **Conf** Thtr 60 Class 30 Board 24 **Parking** 15

The Tollgate Inn

★★★★ ◎◎ INN

Ham Green, Holt BA14 6PX
☎ 01225 782326 📠 01225 782805
e-mail: alison@tollgateholt.co.uk
web: www.tollgateholt.co.uk
dir: *A363 Bradford-on-Avon turn left onto B3105, left onto B3107, 100yds on right at W end of Holt*

The Tollgate combines the comforts of a traditional inn with excellent food served in delightful surroundings. It stands near the village green in Holt, and is only a short drive from Bath. The bedrooms, varying in size, are well decorated and thoughtfully equipped with welcome extras.

Rooms 4 en suite S £60-£110; D £90-£110* **Facilities** FTV tea/coffee Dinner available Direct Dial Cen ht Wi-fi Farm shop & animals **Conf** Max 36 Thtr 36 Board 30 **Parking** 40 **Notes** ⊗ Closed 25-26 Dec & 1 Jan No coaches

BROMHAM　　Map 4 ST96

Wayside

★★★ BED AND BREAKFAST

Chittoe Heath SN15 2EH
☎ 01380 850695 & 07770 774460 📠 01380 850696
e-mail: mail@waysideofwiltshire.co.uk
web: www.waysideofwiltshire.co.uk
dir: *From A342 take road signed Spye Park & Chittoe, Wayside 1st on right*

Peacefully located yet only just off the main road, Wayside offers relaxed and comfortable accommodation and bedrooms with a range of shapes and sizes. Guests are welcome to use the lounge and there is even a wood to the rear of the property where guests can enjoy a private walk. Good quality ingredients are offered at breakfast and a wide choice of local inns and restaurants is available for dinner.

Rooms 2 en suite (1 fmly) (1 GF) (2 smoking) S £40; D £70* **Facilities** STV FTV TVL Cen ht Wi-fi Golf 18 Riding **Parking** 3 **Notes** LB ⊛

BURTON　　Map 4 ST87

PREMIER COLLECTION

The Old House at Home

★★★★★ 🍽 INN

SN14 7LT
☎ 01454 218227
e-mail: office@ohhcompany.co.uk
web: www.ohhcompany.co.uk
dir: M4 junct 18 to Acton Turvill, right onto B4039.
1.5m to Burton

In a pleasant setting and just a couple of miles from
the delightful village of Castle Combe, this well-
established country inn is run personally by the
resident proprietors and their family. Six purpose-built,
high quality bedrooms and bathrooms provide plenty of
welcome extras, and are located in a stylish block
adjacent to the main building. Dinner here should not
be missed, with a varied selection of high quality,
carefully prepared ingredients used in the dishes,
including daily specials.

Rooms 6 annexe en suite (1 fmly) (6 GF) **Facilities** FTV
tea/coffee Dinner available Direct Dial Cen ht Wi-fi
Parking 20 **Notes** LB ❌ Closed 25 Dec

CHAPMANSLADE　　Map 4 ST84

Huntenhull Farm

★★★★ BED AND BREAKFAST

Huntenhull Ln BA13 4AS
☎ 01373 832960 & 07585 969646
e-mail: info@huntenhull.com
dir: A36 between Warminster & Beckington, take exit
signed Chapmanslade. In village take 1st left signed
Corsley onto Huntenhull Ln, 500yds on right

This establishment is peacefully located in the grounds of
a Grade II listed Georgian farmhouse. The accommodation
itself is set in a newly converted and stylish barn which
provides plenty of quality and comfort. There is no dining
room but guests can enjoy breakfast (cooked or
continental) in the comfort of their own room. A luxurious
spa with swimming pool and sauna is also available, as
is a recording studio should the need arise!

Rooms 1 en suite (1 fmly) S £60-£65; D £65-£75*
Facilities STV FTV tea/coffee Cen ht Wi-fi 🍵 Sauna
Jacuzzi Steam room **Parking** 10 **Notes** LB ❌

CHICKLADE　　Map 4 ST93

The Old Rectory

Ⓤ

SP3 5SU
☎ 01747 820000 📠 01747 820000
e-mail: lynda@theoldrectory-bandb.co.uk
dir: On A303 in village behind lay-by

Currently the rating for this establishment is not
confirmed. This may be due to a change of ownership or
because it has only recently joined the AA rating scheme.

Rooms 3 en suite (1 fmly) S £60-£65; D £70-£80*
Facilities FTV Cen ht Wi-fi **Parking** 6 **Notes** LB Closed
Xmas 🐾

CHIPPENHAM　　Map 4 ST97

Diana Lodge Bed & Breakfast

★★★ BED AND BREAKFAST

Grathie Cottage, 72 Marshfield Rd SN15 1JR
☎ 01249 650306
e-mail: diana.lodge@talktalk.net
dir: 500yds NW of town centre on A420, into West End
Club car park

A cheerful welcome awaits guests at this late 19th-
century cottage that is within walking distance of the
town centre and the railway station. The comfortable
bedrooms are well appointed, and adjacent parking is
available.

Rooms 5 rms (3 en suite) (2 pri facs) (1 fmly) (2 GF)
Facilities FTV tea/coffee Cen ht Wi-fi **Parking** 1 **Notes** ❌

CORSHAM　　Map 4 ST87

PREMIER COLLECTION

The Methuen Arms

★★★★★ 🍴🍴 RESTAURANT WITH ROOMS

2 High St SN13 0HB
☎ 01249 717060
e-mail: info@themethuenarms.com
web: www.themethuenarms.com
dir: M4 junct 17, A350 towards Chippenham, at rdbt
take A4 towards Bath. 1m after lights, at next rdbt
sharp left onto Pickwick Rd, establishment 0.5m on left

This well-established restaurant with rooms in the
centre of the thriving town of Corsham has undergone
a complete refurb to provide high levels of quality and
comfort. The bedrooms are modern and stylish with
large comfortable beds and spacious, well-equipped
bathrooms. Guests can enjoy a drink in the relaxing
bar, a light snack in the day or evening, and should not
miss the award-winning, high quality, carefully
prepared dishes at dinner.

Rooms 12 en suite (3 fmly) S £75-£95; D £100-£160*
Facilities FTV tea/coffee Dinner available Direct Dial
Cen ht Wi-fi **Conf** Thtr 50 Board 14 **Parking** 50

Thurlestone Lodge

★★★★ BED AND BREAKFAST

13 Prospect SN13 9AD
☎ 01249 713397 & 07815 731131
e-mail: v_ogilvie_robb@hotmail.com
web: www.thurlestone.webeden.co.uk
dir: 0.25m from Corsham Centre on B3353. 150yds on
right after Great Western pub halfway between turnings
to Lypiatt Rd & Dicketts Rd

This charming Victorian house is delightfully located in
the attractive town of Corsham, convenient for the
attractions of the Cotswolds and of Bath. Bedrooms are
comfortable, spacious and well appointed. Breakfast is
served in the spacious dining room and provides a hearty
start to the day.

Rooms 2 en suite (1 fmly) S £52-£68; D £70-£78*
Facilities FTV tea/coffee Cen ht Wi-fi **Parking** 5 **Notes** ❌
No Children 7yrs Closed Xmas & New Year RS 22 Dec-2
Jan

Pickwick Lodge Farm (ST857708)

★★★★ 🏠 FARMHOUSE

Guyers Ln SN13 0PS
☎ 01249 712207 📠 01249 701904
Mrs G Stafford
e-mail: bandb@pickwickfarm.co.uk
web: www.pickwickfarm.co.uk
dir: Off A4, Bath side of Corsham, onto Guyers Ln,
farmhouse at end on right

This Grade II listed, 17th-century farmhouse is peacefully
located on a 300-acre beef and arable farm, within easy
reach of Bath. The spacious bedrooms are well equipped
with modern facilities and many thoughtful extras. A
hearty breakfast using the best local produce is served at
a communal table in the dining room.

Rooms 3 rms (2 en suite) (1 pri facs) D £70-£80*
Facilities FTV TVL tea/coffee Cen ht Wi-fi Fishing
Parking 6 **Notes** LB ❌ No Children 12yrs 🐾 300 acres
arable/beef

CRICKLADE
Map 5 SU09

Upper Chelworth Farm

★★★ BED AND BREAKFAST

Upper Chelworth SN6 6HD
☎ 01793 750440
dir: *1.5m W of Cricklade. Off B4040 x-rds for Chelworth Upper Green*

Close to the M4 and Swindon, Upper Chelworth Farm offers a genuinely friendly welcome in addition to comfortable bedrooms of varying sizes. There is a spacious lounge with a wood-burning stove, a games room with a pool table and a lovely garden. Breakfast is served in the dining room.

Rooms 7 rms (6 en suite) (1 fmly) **Facilities** TVL TV6B tea/coffee Cen ht Pool table **Parking** 10 **Notes** No Children 5yrs Closed mid Dec-mid Jan 🅿

DEVIZES
Map 4 SU06

PREMIER COLLECTION

Blounts Court Farm

★★★★★ 🏠 BED AND BREAKFAST

Coxhill Ln, Potterne SN10 5PH
☎ 01380 727180
e-mail: carys@blountscourtfarm.co.uk
dir: *A360 to Potterne, into Coxhill Ln opp George & Dragon, at fork turn left, follow drive uphill to farmhouse*

A warm welcome is assured at this peacefully located, delightful arable farm, overlooking the village cricket field. The character barn has been converted to provide three attractive bedrooms on the ground floor - one has a four-poster bed. The elegant decor is in keeping with the character of the house. Breakfast, which features home-made and local produce, is served in the farmhouse dining room.

Rooms 3 en suite (3 GF) S £38-£55; D £68-£75*
Facilities FTV TVL tea/coffee Cen ht Wi-fi **Parking** 5 **Notes** ✖ No Children 8yrs

Summerhayes B&B

★★★★★ 🅰 BED AND BREAKFAST

143 High St, Littleton Panell SN10 4EU
☎ 01380 813521
e-mail: summerhayesbandb@btinternet.com
web: www.summerhayesbandb.co.uk
dir: *5m S of Devizes on A360, near x-rds with B3098*

Rooms 2 rms (1 en suite) (1 pri facs) S £50-£60; D £70-£80 **Facilities** STV FTV TVL tea/coffee Cen ht Wi-fi Sauna Hot tub **Parking** 6 **Notes** LB ✖

FIRSDOWN
Map 5 SU23

Junipers

★★★★ BED AND BREAKFAST

3 Juniper Rd SP5 1SS
☎ 01980 862330
e-mail: junipersbedandbreakfast@btinternet.com
web: www.junipersbedandbreakfast.co.uk
dir: *5m from Salisbury on A30, A343 to London follow Junipers brown signs into Firsdown*

Located in a quiet residential area, just five miles from the city, this homely bed and breakfast offers ground floor bedrooms that are well equipped with thoughtful extras. The hosts, who have craft skills, are happy to show guests their interesting items constructed in medieval style. Breakfast, featuring local produce, is served in the cosy dining room/lounge.

Rooms 3 en suite (3 GF) S £50; D £70 **Facilities** FTV tea/coffee Cen ht Wi-fi **Parking** 6 **Notes** LB ✖ No Children

FONTHILL BISHOP
Map 4 ST93

The River Barn

★★★ 🍴 GUEST HOUSE

SP3 5SF
☎ 01747 820232
dir: *Off A303 to Tisbury/Fonthill Bishop. 1m to junct then right onto B3089, 100yds on left*

Surrounded by lawns stretching down to the river, The River Barn is the central hub of the village of Fonthill Bishop. Parts of the barn are 600 years old and it has operated as a business for the last 100 years. The annexe bedrooms are spacious and well appointed. The café-bar offers sumptuous cakes and cream teas, light lunches and evening meals.

Rooms 4 annexe en suite (1 fmly) (3 GF) **Facilities** tea/coffee Dinner available Cen ht Licensed **Parking** 20 **Notes** ✖

GRITTLETON
Map 4 ST88

Staddlestones

★★ BED AND BREAKFAST

SN14 6AW
☎ 01249 782458 📠 01249 782458
e-mail: staddlestonesbb@btinternet.com
dir: *500yds E of village x-rds*

The large modern bungalow lies at the east end of the small village, and is convenient for the M4. The local pub is just a stroll away and ample parking is available.

Rooms 3 rms (3 GF) S £40-£60; D £60-£80*
Facilities FTV TVL tea/coffee Cen ht **Parking** 5 **Notes** 🅿

HIGHWORTH
Map 5 SU29

Highlands of Highworth

★★★★ GUEST HOUSE

1 Swindon Rd SN6 7DE
☎ 01793 765131
e-mail: highlandsofhighworth@yahoo.co.uk
web: www.highlandsofhighworth.co.uk
dir: *A361 from Swindon, after Shell garage, last house on left before rdbt*

Conveniently located on the edge of Highworth, this detached accommodation offers a range of very well decorated and equipped bedrooms including one on the ground floor. Extras such as free Wi-fi in rooms are welcome features. Ample parking is provided, and a good selection of pubs and restaurants are within easy walking distance.

Rooms 4 en suite (1 fmly) (1 GF) S £45-£50; D £50-£60 **Facilities** FTV TVL tea/coffee Cen ht Wi-fi **Parking** 6 **Notes** LB ✖

HINDON
Map 4 ST93

The Lamb Inn

★★★★ 🍴 INN

SP3 6DP
☎ 01747 820573 🖨 01747 820605
e-mail: info@thelambathindon.co.uk
dir: *Off B3089 in village centre*

This 17th-century coaching inn is in a pretty village within easy reach of Salisbury and Bath. It has been refurbished in an eclectic style, and some of the well-equipped bedrooms have four-poster beds. Enjoyable, freshly prepared dishes are available at lunch and dinner in the restaurant or bar, where log fires provide a welcoming atmosphere on colder days.

Rooms 19 rms (13 en suite) 6 annexe en suite (1 fmly) (3 GF) **Facilities** FTV tea/coffee Dinner available Direct Dial Cen ht Wi-fi Boules court **Conf** Max 40 Thtr 40 Class 16 Board 24 **Parking** 16

Save on B&Bs and Hotels. Book at **theAA.com/hotel**

WILTSHIRE 327 ENGLAND

HORNINGSHAM
Map 4 ST84

The Bath Arms at Longleat

★★★★ ◉◉ INN

Longleat Estate BA12 7LY
☎ 01985 844308 📠 01985 845187
e-mail: enquiries@batharms.co.uk
dir: In village, on Longleat Estate

Peacefully located at the edges of The Longleat Estate, this delightful inn has perhaps best been described as 'quirky luxury'. Bedrooms come in a variety of shapes and sizes; each individually decorated in a range of styles and designs. High quality produce is used to prepare delicious dishes at dinner which is served in the relaxed main restaurant.

Rooms 9 en suite 6 annexe en suite (9 fmly) (1 GF)
Facilities FTV tea/coffee Dinner available Direct Dial Cen ht Wi-fi Golf 18 Treatment room **Parking** 6

LACOCK
Map 4 ST96

At the Sign of the Angel

★★★★ GUEST ACCOMMODATION

6 Church St SN15 2LB
☎ 01249 730230 📠 01249 730527
e-mail: angel@lacock.co.uk
dir: Off A350 into Lacock, follow 'Local Traffic' sign

Visitors will surely be impressed by the character of this 15th-century former wool merchant's house, set in the National Trust village of Lacock. Bedrooms come in a range of sizes and styles including the atmospheric rooms in the main house and others in an adjacent building. Excellent dinners and breakfasts are served in the beamed dining rooms, and there is also a first-floor lounge and a pleasant rear garden.

Rooms 6 en suite 5 annexe en suite (4 GF) S £85; D £129-£159* **Facilities** FTV tea/coffee Dinner available Direct Dial Cen ht Licensed Wi-fi **Conf** Max 14 Board 14 **Parking** 6 **Notes** Closed 23-27 Dec RS Mon (ex BHs) Closed for lunch Civ Wed 27

LOWER CHICKSGROVE
Map 4 ST92

Compasses Inn

★★★★ ◉ INN

SP3 6NB
☎ 01722 714318 📠 01722 714318
e-mail: thecompasses@aol.com
web: www.thecompassesinn.com
dir: Off A30 signed Lower Chicksgrove, 1st left onto Lagpond Ln, single-track lane to village

This charming 17th-century inn, within easy reach of Bath, Salisbury, Glastonbury and the Dorset coast, offers comfortable accommodation in a peaceful setting. Carefully prepared dinners are enjoyed in the warm atmosphere of the bar-restaurant, while breakfast is served in a separate dining room.

Rooms 5 en suite (2 fmly) S £50-£65; D £65-£85
Facilities FTV tea/coffee Dinner available Cen ht Wi-fi ch fac **Conf** Max 14 **Parking** 40 **Notes** LB Closed 25-26 Dec

LUDWELL
Map 4 ST92

The Grove Arms

★★★★ INN

SP7 9ND
☎ 01747 828811 📠 01747 828844
e-mail: bename@golf727.fsnet.co.uk
web: www.grovearms-ludwell.co.uk
dir: 2m E of Shaftesbury on A30

This 16th-century, Grade II listed building has recently been refurbished. Located between Salisbury and Shaftesbury, the inn provides a great base for exploring the Wiltshire and Dorset countryside. The six en suite bedrooms are comfortable and well equipped. Lunch and dinner menus offer a great choice enhanced with daily specials. Traditional ales are also available.

Rooms 6 en suite (2 fmly) S £75-£80; D £90-£100*
Facilities tea/coffee Dinner available Cen ht Wi-fi Golf 18 **Parking** 32 **Notes** ⊗ No coaches

MARLBOROUGH
Map 5 SU16

The Lamb Inn

★★★ ⬭ INN

The Parade SN8 1NE
☎ 01672 512668 & 07885 275568 📠 01672 512668
e-mail: thelambinnmarlboro@fsmail.net
dir: From High St, right onto Parade, 50yds on left

Located in a quieter area of Marlborough, yet just a couple of minutes from the bustle of the main street, this traditional inn provides a friendly welcome and relaxed ambience. Bedrooms vary in size and are located above the main inn, and in modernised stables adjacent to the pleasant rear garden. Dinner here is a highlight with a good selection of very well cooked and presented dishes using fresh ingredients.

Rooms 6 en suite (1 fmly) S fr £50; D fr £75* **Facilities** tea/coffee Dinner available Cen ht Wi-fi Golf 18 **Conf** Max 24 **Notes** No coaches

NETTLETON
Map 4 ST87

Fosse Farmhouse Chambre d'Hote

★★★★ ⬭ BED AND BREAKFAST

Nettleton Shrub SN14 7NJ
☎ 01249 782286 📠 01249 783066
e-mail: caroncooper@fossefarmhouse.com
web: www.fossefarmhouse.com
dir: 1.5m N from Castle Combe on B4039, left at Gib, 1m on right

Set in quiet countryside not far from Castle Combe, this bed and breakfast has well-equipped bedrooms decorated in keeping with its 18th-century origins. Excellent dinners are served in the farmhouse, and cream teas can be enjoyed in the old stables or the delightful garden.

Rooms 2 en suite (1 fmly) S £70-£80; D £95-£125*
Facilities tea/coffee Dinner available Cen ht Licensed Wi-fi Golf 18 **Conf** Max 15 Thtr 10 Class 10 Board 10 **Parking** 12 **Notes** LB

REDLYNCH — Map 5 SU22

Rookseat B&B

★★★ BED AND BREAKFAST

Grove Ln SP5 2NR
☎ 01725 512522 & 07748 550481
e-mail: deanransome@btinternet.com

Expect a friendly welcome at this family-run bed and breakfast situated in the quiet New Forest village of Redlynch, perfect for visiting Salisbury and Bournemouth. Comfortable bedrooms all have en suite shower rooms. A delicious breakfast with plenty of choice is served in the dining room.

Rooms 3 en suite S fr £40; D fr £60* **Facilities** FTV tea/coffee Cen ht Wi-fi **Parking** 3 **Notes** ⊗ No Children 12yrs ⊛

ROWDE — Map 4 ST96

The George & Dragon

★★★★ ◉◉ RESTAURANT WITH ROOMS

High St SN10 2PN
☎ 01380 723053
e-mail: thegandd@tiscali.co.uk
dir: 1.5m from Devizes on A350 towards Chippenham

The George & Dragon dates back to the 14th century when it was a meeting house. Exposed beams, wooden floors, antique rugs and open fires create a warm atmosphere in the bar and restaurant. Bedrooms and bathrooms are very well decorated and equipped with some welcome extras. Dining in the bar or restaurant should not be missed, as local produce and fresh fish deliveries from Cornwall are offered on the daily-changing blackboard menu.

Rooms 3 rms (2 en suite) (1 pri facs) (1 fmly) D £55-£105* **Facilities** FTV TVL tea/coffee Dinner available Cen ht Wi-fi **Parking** 15 **Notes** No coaches

SALISBURY — Map 5 SU12

See also Amesbury & Stoford

PREMIER COLLECTION

Quidhampton Mill

★★★★★ ⌂ BED AND BREAKFAST

Lower Rd, Quidhampton SP2 9BB
☎ 01722 741171
e-mail: quidhamptonmill@waitrose.com
dir: From Salisbury on A36 towards Wilton, at lights turn left onto B3094 signed Blandford. On left just after turning for Quidhampton

A warm welcome is assured here at Quidhampton Mill. Situated just two miles out of Salisbury, this makes for an ideal base from which to explore the many attractions that Wiltshire has to offer. There are three recently converted en suite bedrooms each with its own external access. Rooms are tastefully designed and offer excellent quality and comfort. Award-winning breakfasts are served in the main house and feature a range of excellent coffees and daily specials. Secure off-road parking is available.

Rooms 3 en suite (1 fmly) (2 GF) S £60-£80; D £65-£109* **Facilities** STV FTV tea/coffee Dinner available Cen ht Wi-fi Golf 18 **Parking** 7 **Notes** ⊗

St Anns House

★★★★ GUEST ACCOMMODATION

32-34 Saint Ann St SP1 2DP
☎ 01722 335657
e-mail: info@stannshouse.co.uk
web: www.stannshouse.co.uk
dir: From Brown St turn left onto Saint Ann St

St Anns House is a newly refurbished former public house close to the cathedral and city centre. Lovingly restored with many original features and modern creature comforts such as flat-screen TVs, this is a high quality operation with a friendly host.

Rooms 8 en suite S £50-£60; D £64-£89* **Facilities** FTV tea/coffee Cen ht Licensed Wi-fi **Conf** Max 16 Thtr 14 Class 14 Board 16 **Notes** ⊗ Closed 23 Dec-2 Jan

Salisbury Old Mill House

★★★★ BED AND BREAKFAST

Warminster Rd, South Newton SP2 0QD
☎ 01722 742458
e-mail: salisburymill@yahoo.com
dir: 4m NW of Salisbury on A36 in South Newton

This restored watermill exudes character, and the mill machinery is still on view. Friendly and welcoming, the property offers comfortable, well-appointed bedrooms, a lounge with wood-burning stove, and a dining area where dinners are available by arrangement. The garden features the original millpond.

Rooms 3 rms (2 en suite) (1 pri facs) 1 annexe en suite (2 fmly) (2 GF) S £40-£45; D £60-£80* **Facilities** FTV tea/coffee Dinner available Cen ht Licensed Wi-fi Golf 9 Riding Outdoor table tennis **Parking** 6 **Notes** ⊗ Closed 25 Dec & 1 Jan ⊛

Websters

★★★★ GUEST HOUSE

11 Hartington Rd SP2 7LG
☎ 01722 339779
e-mail: enquiries@websters-bed-breakfast.com
dir: From city centre onto A360 Devizes Rd, 1st turning on left

A warm welcome is assured at this delightful property, located in a quiet cul-de-sac close to the city centre. The charming, well-presented bedrooms are equipped with numerous extras including broadband. There is one ground-floor room with easier access.

Rooms 5 en suite (1 GF) S £48-£55; D £55-£80 **Facilities** FTV TVL tea/coffee Cen ht Wi-fi **Parking** 5 **Notes** LB ⊗ No Children 12yrs Closed 31 Dec & 1 Jan RS Xmas & New Year Continental breakfast only at Xmas

Save on B&Bs and Hotels. Book at **theAA.com/hotel**

WILTSHIRE 329 **ENGLAND**

Avonlea House

★★★★ BED AND BREAKFAST

231 Castle Rd SP1 3RY
☎ 01722 338351
e-mail: guests@avonleahouse.co.uk
web: www.avonleahouse.co.uk
dir: 1.5m N of city centre. On A345 near Old Sarum

Avonlea House has very comfortable and well equipped bedrooms. Breakfast is offered with a choice of fresh local items. The property is located close to Old Sarum and within walking distance of Salisbury city centre, the Cathedral and riverside walks. There are leisure facilities close by in the shape of a swimming pool and gym, and there is easy access to Stonehenge, the New Forest and the South coast.

Rooms 3 en suite S £40-£50; D £63-£70* **Facilities** FTV tea/coffee Cen ht Wi-fi **Parking** 3 **Notes** ⊗ No Children 2yrs

Cricket Field House

★★★★ GUEST ACCOMMODATION

Skew Bridge, Wilton Rd SP2 9NS
☎ 01722 322595 ᤜ 01722 444970
e-mail: cricketfieldcottage@btinternet.com
dir: A36, 1m W of Salisbury, towards Wilton & Warminster

The 19th-century gamekeeper's cottage stands in award-winning gardens overlooking the South Wiltshire Cricket Ground. Within walking distance of the city centre and railway station, Cricket Field House provides a high level of accommodation, hospitality and customer care.

Rooms 7 en suite 10 annexe en suite (10 GF) S £50-£65; D £55-£105 **Facilities** FTV tea/coffee Cen ht Wi-fi Licensed **Wi-fi Conf** Thtr 20 Class 14 Board 16 **Parking** 25 **Notes** ⊗ No Children 14yrs RS 24-26 Dec room only

Newton Farmhouse (SU230223)

★★★★ FARMHOUSE

Southampton Rd SP5 2QL
☎ 01794 884416
Mr & Mrs Guild
e-mail: lizzie@newtonfarmhouse.com
web: www.newtonfarmhouse.com

(For full entry see Whiteparish)

The Old House

★★★★ GUEST ACCOMMODATION

161 Wilton Rd SP2 7JQ
☎ 01722 333433 ᤜ 01722 335551
dir: 1m W of city centre on A36

Located close to the city centre, this non-smoking property dates from the 17th century. Bedrooms have modern facilities and one room has a four-poster bed. There is a spacious lounge and large gardens to enjoy - weather permitting.

Rooms 7 en suite (1 fmly) **Facilities** FTV TVL tea/coffee Cen ht Wi-fi **Parking** 10 **Notes** LB ⊗ No Children 7yrs

2 Park Lane

★★★★ GUEST ACCOMMODATION

2 Park Ln SP1 3NP
☎ 01722 321001
web: www.2parklane.co.uk

A stylish period property that has been completely renovated, within walking distance of the city centre and its attractions. Light, airy rooms, comfortable beds and good off-road parking are available.

Rooms 6 en suite S £50-£65; D £60-£80* **Facilities** FTV tea/coffee Cen ht Wi-fi **Parking** 6 **Notes** ⊗ No Children 6yrs

Melbury House

★★★ BED AND BREAKFAST

46 Stonehenge Rd, Durrington SP4 8BP
☎ 01980 653151
e-mail: jonandcarol@daytons.co.uk
dir: From A303 Countess Rd rdbt, take A345. At rdbt turn right signed Durrington 5yds, turn left onto Stonehenge Rd

Melbury House is a traditional small bed and breakfast with warm, friendly hosts. Rooms are fresh and comfortable and it has a great location, handy for Stonehenge and Salisbury. Breakfast is at a family table and is freshly cooked to order - a good start to the day.

Rooms 2 rms (1 en suite) (1 pri facs) (2 fmly) (2 GF) S £40; D £65* **Facilities** FTV tea/coffee Cen ht Wi-fi **Parking** 4 **Notes** ⊗ No Children 10yrs ⊛

Sarum Heights

★★★ BED AND BREAKFAST

289 Castle Rd SP1 3SB
☎ 01722 421596 & 07931 582357
e-mail: reservations@sarumheights.co.uk

Sarum Heights is a large family home on the outskirts of the city with good off-road parking. Rooms are smart, clean and well appointed with quality beds and linen. Freshly-cooked breakfasts are served at a family table in the kitchen.

Rooms 3 rms (2 en suite) (1 pri facs) S £43-£46; D £60-£70 **Facilities** tea/coffee Cen ht Wi-fi **Parking** 3 **Notes** ⊗ ⊛

Byways Guest House

★★★ GUEST ACCOMMODATION

31 Fowlers Rd SP1 2QP
☎ 01722 328364 ᤜ 01722 322146
e-mail: info@bywayshouse.co.uk
web: www.bywayshouse.co.uk
dir: 500yds E of city centre. A30 onto A36 signed Southampton, follow Youth Hostel signs to hostel, Fowlers Rd opp

Located in a quiet street with off-road parking, Byways is within walking distance of the town centre. Several bedrooms have been decorated in a Victorian style and another two have four-poster beds. All rooms offer good levels of comfort, with one adapted for easier access.

Rooms 23 rms (19 en suite) (6 fmly) (13 GF) S £39-£60; D £55-£90* **Facilities** tea/coffee Cen ht Licensed Wi-fi **Conf** Max 8 **Parking** 15 **Notes** Closed Xmas & New Year

Old Mill

★★★ INN

Town Path SP2 8EU
☎ 01722 327517 ᤜ 01722 333367
e-mail: theoldmill@simonandsteve.com
web: www.simonandsteve.com
dir: Turn right from A338 onto A3094, then third turning on right

Full of character, The Old Mill has an interesting history going back well over five hundred years. Located in tranquil water meadows, the medieval city of Salisbury is just a 10-minute walk along the footpath. Bedrooms come in a range of shapes and sizes and include two above the lively bar. Dinner here is a highlight; the carefully prepared dishes, utilising local produce, should suit all tastes.

Rooms 11 en suite S £55-£65; D £65-£110* **Facilities** FTV tea/coffee Dinner available Direct Dial Cen ht Wi-fi Fishing **Conf** Max 43 Class 43 Board 28 **Parking** 17

SEMINGTON   Map 4 ST86

The Somerset Arms

★★★★ INN

High St BA14 6JR
☎ 01380 870067
e-mail: contact@somersetarmssemington.co.uk
dir: *From Melksham take 3rd exit at Semington rdbt signed High St, 1st exit from Trowbridge Way*

Located in a quiet village, this refurbished, former coaching inn has been providing a warm welcome to visitors for centuries. Its tradition of hospitality is endorsed by the crackling log fires, comfy sofas and an engaging blend of old and new. The bedrooms offer high standards of comfort and quality that include those little extras which make all the difference. The exciting menu utilises local produce whenever possible, and can be enjoyed in the elegant informality of the restaurant.

Rooms 3 en suite S fr £70; D fr £80* **Facilities** FTV TVL tea/coffee Dinner available Wi-fi **Parking** 20 **Notes** LB No coaches

---

STAPLEFORD   Map 5 SU03

Oak Bluffs

★★★ BED AND BREAKFAST

4 Church Furlong SP3 4QE
☎ 01722 790663 & 07796 893502 ▤ 01722 790663
dir: *In village centre off B3083*

A warm and friendly welcome awaits at this immaculately presented bungalow situated in a delightful village, complete with an ancient church and many thatched properties. Well located for visiting Stonehenge, the well appointed bedroom has its own separate entrance, with lots of thoughtful extras provided. A couple of pubs are within walking distance.

Rooms 1 en suite (1 GF) S £35-£40; D £55-£60* **Facilities** tea/coffee Cen ht Golf 9 **Parking** 1 **Notes** ⊗ ✉

STOFORD   Map 5 SU03

The Swan Inn

★★★★ INN

Warminster Rd SP2 0PR
☎ 01722 790236 ▤ 01722 444972
e-mail: info@theswanatstoford.co.uk
web: www.theswanatstoford.co.uk
dir: *On A36 in village centre*

This centrally located, family-run inn is ideal for touring the area. Good-sized bedrooms are available, and the newly refurbished bar and restaurant serve an excellent choice of meals with an emphasis on locally sourced produce. Other facilities include Wi-fi, private fishing on the river and a skittle alley.

Rooms 8 en suite (1 fmly) S £53-£78; D £53-£78* **Facilities** FTV tea/coffee Dinner available Cen ht Wi-fi Fishing Skittle alley **Conf** Thtr 40 Class 30 Board 20 **Parking** 70

STOURTON   Map 4 ST73

Spread Eagle Inn

★★★★ 🍴 INN

Church Lawn BA12 6QE
☎ 01747 840587
e-mail: enquiries@spreadeagleinn.com
web: www.spreadeagleinn.com
dir: *0.5m W off B3092 at entrance to Stourhead Gardens*

Set in the beautiful grounds of Stourhead House with its Palladian temples, lakes and inspiring vistas, the Spread Eagle is an impressive red-brick building with a good reputation for simple, honest and locally-sourced food. In the bedrooms, National Trust antiques sit side by side with modern comforts. The large Georgian windows, low ceilings and uneven floors add to the authentic atmosphere of this delightful country house.

Rooms 5 en suite **Facilities** tea/coffee Dinner available Direct Dial Cen ht Wi-fi **Conf** Max 30 Thtr 30 Board 20 **Notes** ⊗

SWINDON   Map 5 SU18

Ardecca

★★★★ GUEST ACCOMMODATION

Fieldrise Farm, Kingsdown Ln, Blunsdon SN25 5DL
☎ 01793 721238 & 07791 120826
e-mail: chris-graham.ardecca@fsmail.net
web: www.ardecca-bedandbreakfast.co.uk
dir: *Off A419 onto B4019 to Blunsdon/Highworth then onto Turnpike Rd at Cold Harbour pub, then left down Kingsdown Ln*

Ardecca is quietly located in 16 acres of pastureland with easy access to Swindon and the Cotswolds. All bedrooms are on the ground floor and are well furnished and equipped. An especially friendly welcome is provided, and arts and crafts workshops are available on site.

Rooms 4 rms (4 pri facs) (1 fmly) (4 GF) (4 smoking) **Facilities** FTV tea/coffee Cen ht Wi-fi Art & Crafts workshops **Conf** Class 16 **Parking** 5 **Notes** ⊗ No Children 6yrs ✉

The Old Post Office Guest House

★★★★ GUEST HOUSE

Thornhill Rd, South Marston SN3 4RY
☎ 01793 823114 ▤ 01793 823441
e-mail: theoldpostofficeguesthouse@yahoo.co.uk
web: www.theoldpostofficeguesthouse.co.uk
dir: *A420 onto Thornhill Rd at Gablecross rdbt 0.75m on left before Old Vicarage Lane*

Sympathetically extended, this attractive property is about two miles from Swindon. Guests are welcomed by the enthusiastic owner, a professional opera singer with a wonderful sense of humour. The comfortable bedrooms vary in size, and all are equipped with numerous facilities. An extensive choice is offered at breakfast, freshly cooked using the best of local produce.

Rooms 5 en suite (1 fmly) **Facilities** FTV tea/coffee Cen ht Wi-fi **Parking** 6 **Notes** ⊗

Portquin Guest House

★★★★ GUEST ACCOMMODATION

Broadbush, Broad Blunsdon SN26 7DH
☎ 01793 721261
e-mail: portquin@msn.com
dir: A419 onto B4019 at Blunsdon signed Highworth, continue 0.5m

This friendly guest house, situated not far from Swindon, offers a warm welcome and views of the Lambourn Downs. The rooms vary in shape and size, with six in the main house and three in an adjacent annexe. Full English breakfasts are served at two large tables in the kitchen-dining area.

Rooms 6 en suite 3 annexe en suite (2 fmly) (4 GF) S £45-£50; D £55-£80* **Facilities** FTV tea/coffee Cen ht Wi-fi **Conf** Max 20 Thtr 20 Class 20 Board 20 **Parking** 12

Tawny Owl

★★★★ INN

Queen Elizabeth Dr, Taw Hill SN25 1WP
☎ 01793 706770   ▤ 01793 706785
e-mail: tawnyowl@arkells.com
dir: 2.5m NW of town centre, signed from A419

Expect a genuinely friendly welcome from the staff at this modern inn on the north-west outskirts of Swindon. It has comfortable, well-equipped bedrooms and bathrooms. A varied selection of enjoyable home-cooked meals is on offer at dinner, and a range of Arkells ales and wines. A private function room is available.

Rooms 5 en suite (1 fmly) **Facilities** TVL tea/coffee Dinner available Direct Dial Cen ht Stairlift **Conf** Max 55 Thtr 55 Class 55 Board 55 **Parking** 75 **Notes** ⊗ RS Xmas/New Year Civ Wed 50

Fairview Guest House

★★★ GUEST HOUSE

52 Swindon Rd, Wootton Bassett SN4 8EU
☎ 01793 852283
e-mail: fairview@woottonb.wanadoo.co.uk
web: http://fairviewguesthouse.website.orange.co.uk
dir: On A3102 to Wootton Bassett. 1.25m from M4 junct 16. 5m from Swindon centre

A welcoming, family-run property with easy access to the M4 and the town of Swindon. Bedrooms are split between the main house and the bungalow annexe, and breakfast is served in an open-plan dining/sitting room with an open fire on cooler mornings.

Rooms 8 rms (3 en suite) 4 annexe rms 3 annexe en suite (1 pri facs) (2 fmly) (4 GF) S £30-£38; D £50-£55* **Facilities** FTV TVL tea/coffee Cen ht Wi-fi **Parking** 14 **Notes** LB ⊗

Heart in Hand

★★★ INN

43 High St, Blunsdon SN26 7AG
☎ 01793 721314   ▤ 01793 727026
e-mail: leppardsteve@aol.com
dir: Off A419 at High St, 200yds on right

Located in the village centre, this family-run inn offers a friendly welcome together with a wide selection of home-cooked food. Bedrooms are spacious, well equipped and offer a number of useful extras. A pleasant patio and rear garden with seating is also available.

Rooms 4 en suite (1 fmly) **Facilities** tea/coffee Dinner available Cen ht **Parking** 17 **Notes** ⊗

Internos B&B

★★★ BED AND BREAKFAST

3 Turnpike Rd, Blunsdon SN26 7EA
☎ 01793 721496   ▤ 01793 721496
web: www.internos-bedandbreakfast.co.uk
dir: 4m N of Swindon. Alongside A419 access from Cold Harbour End

Situated just off the A419 towards Cirencester, this establishment offers comfortable accommodation and a relaxed and informal atmosphere. The gardens open onto a field, which is a haven for wildlife. Guests enjoy a freshly-cooked breakfast served in the dining room, and a cosy lounge is also available.

Rooms 3 rms (1 fmly) S £27-£32; D fr £42* **Facilities** FTV TVL tea/coffee Cen ht Wi-fi **Parking** 6 **Notes** ⊗ ⊠

Saracens Head

★★ INN

High St, Highworth SN6 7AG
☎ 01793 762284   ▤ 01793 767869
e-mail: arkells@arkells.com
dir: 5m NE of Swindon

This establishment stands on the main street of a pleasant market town, close to Swindon. It offers plenty of character, including a popular bar dating from 1828. A fine selection of real ales and home-cooked food are highlights. Bedrooms, which vary in size, are generally compact. A rear car park and a patio area are available.

Rooms 13 en suite (2 fmly) **Facilities** tea/coffee Dinner available Direct Dial Cen ht Wi-fi **Conf** Max 10 Thtr 10 Class 10 Board 10 **Parking** 30

TROWBRIDGE   Map 4 ST85

Eastbrook Cottage

★★★★ BED AND BREAKFAST

Hoopers Pool, Southwick BA14 9NG
☎ 01225 764403
e-mail: enquiries@eastbrookcottage.co.uk
web: www.eastbrookcottage.co.uk
dir: 2m SW of Trowbridge. Off A361 between Rode & Southwick

This cottage, situated just off the main Frome road, offers fresh, smart accommodation. Although the bedrooms are not the most spacious, they are finished to a high level of quality and equipped with many thoughtful extras. To add to this, the host offers genuine hospitality and friendliness. Guests may not want to move from the wood-burning stove in the snug lounge. Breakfast, featuring local produce wherever possible, is enjoyed around a large oak table.

Rooms 3 rms (2 en suite) (1 pri facs) S £45-£50; D £65-£75* **Facilities** tea/coffee Cen ht Wi-fi **Parking** 5 **Notes** ⊗ No Children 10yrs ⊠

The George Inn

★★★★ INN

Longbridge Deverill BA12 7DG
☎ 01985 840396 📠 01985 841333
e-mail: info@the-georgeinn.co.uk
web: www.the-georgeinn.co.uk
dir: 3m S on A350

The George Inn combines a friendly village pub atmosphere with modern well-equipped bedrooms; one with a four-poster bed. In addition to the pleasant bar/restaurant, there is a cosy first-floor lounge and a charming river garden in which to enjoy a cool summer drink. There is an extensive menu available featuring a selection of home-cooked dishes.

Rooms 12 en suite (5 fmly) S £45-£70; D £55-£90*
Facilities FTV tea/coffee Dinner available Direct Dial
Cen ht Wi-fi Conf Max 120 Thtr 50 Class 50 Board 30
Parking 100 Notes LB ⊗ RS Xmas closed pm

The Granary Bed & Breakfast

★★★★ BED AND BREAKFAST

Manor Farm, Upton Scudamore BA12 0AG
☎ 01985 214835 📠 01985 214835
dir: 2m NW of Warminster. Off A350 into Upton Scudamore

The Granary is located in the peaceful village of Upton Scudamore and has delightful country views. It offers ground-floor bedrooms, each with a private terrace, stylishly decorated with co-ordinated fabrics and comfortable furnishings. There are many thoughtful extras including a fridge, and breakfast is served in the guests' room.

Rooms 3 annexe en suite (3 GF) Facilities FTV tea/coffee
Cen ht Wi-fi Parking 4 Notes ⊗ No Children 8yrs Closed
20 Dec-3 Jan 🐾

White Lodge

★★★★ GUEST ACCOMMODATION

22 Westbury Rd BA12 0AW
☎ 01985 212378 📠 01985 212378
e-mail: carol@lioncountry.co.uk
dir: 0.5m N of town centre. Off High St onto Portway signed Westbury, White Lodge 0.75m on left

Situated on the outskirts of Warminster, this attractive house, with art deco features, is well placed for touring Wiltshire and Somerset. Individually styled bedrooms, which overlook well-tended grounds, are comfortable and well appointed.

Rooms 3 rms (1 en suite) (2 pri facs) (1 fmly) S £50-£60;
D £65-£72* Facilities FTV tea/coffee Cen ht Wi-fi
Parking 8 Notes ⊗ No Children 5yrs Closed Xmas RS
Jan-Feb 🐾

The Dove Inn

★★★ ⊛ INN

Corton BA12 0SZ
☎ 01985 850109 📠 01985 851041
e-mail: info@thedove.co.uk
dir: 5m SE of Warminster. Off A36 to Corton village

Quietly located in the village of Corton, this traditional style Inn has undergone many changes in recent months and now provides plenty of quality and comfort and a friendly welcome. In addition to lighter options, a range of well sourced, quality produce is used in the enjoyable dinners served in the main restaurant. Bedrooms offer a choice of standard rooms adjacent to the inn or two more luxurious rooms in a cottage recently completed to high standards.

Rooms 7 annexe en suite (1 fmly) (5 GF) S £60-£80; D £80-£120 Facilities FTV tea/coffee Dinner available Cen ht Wi-fi Parking 24 Notes LB

Brayford

★★★★ BED AND BREAKFAST

Newton Ln SP5 2QQ
☎ 01794 884216
e-mail: reservations@brayford.org.uk
dir: Off A36 at Newton x-rds onto Newton Ln towards Whiteparish, Brayford 150yds on right

A genuine welcome awaits guests at this comfortable family home. Peacefully located with views over neighbouring farmland, the house is just a short drive from the A36. Suitable for business and leisure travellers, bedrooms are well equipped with many thoughtful extras. Guests are invited to relax in the lounge dining room, where a tasty breakfast is served.

Rooms 3 rms (2 pri facs) (1 fmly) (2 GF) S £40-£50; D £65-£75 Facilities FTV TVL tea/coffee Cen ht Wi-fi Parking 2 Notes ⊗ Closed Xmas & New Year 🐾

Newton Farmhouse (SU230223)

★★★★ FARMHOUSE

Southampton Rd SP5 2QL
☎ 01794 884416
Mr & Mrs Guild
e-mail: lizzie@newtonfarmhouse.com
web: www.newtonfarmhouse.com
dir: 7m SE of Salisbury on A36, 1m S of A27 junct

Dating back to the 16th century, this delightful farmhouse was gifted to Lord Nelson's family as part of the Trafalgar estate. The house has been thoughtfully restored and bedrooms, most with four-poster beds, have been adorned with personal touches. Delicious breakfasts are available in the relaxing conservatory. The pleasant gardens include an outdoor swimming pool.

Rooms 6 en suite 2 annexe en suite (1 fmly) (4 GF) Facilities FTV TVL tea/coffee Cen ht Wi-fi 🏊 🐾 Parking 8 Notes ⊗ 2.5 acres non-working

---

Cornerways Cottage

★★★★ BED AND BREAKFAST

Longcross BA12 6LL
☎ 01747 840477
e-mail: cornerways.cottage@btinternet.com
dir: From A303 onto B3092 signed Stourhead. At bottom of slip road, turn right under bridge & follow signs for Zeals. On left by 40mph sign

A warm friendly welcome, comfortable rooms and hearty breakfasts await in this charming 250-year-old stone cottage. Situated right on the borders of Somerset, Dorset and Wiltshire it is ideal for visiting Longleat, Stourhead House and Gardens or for simply touring the local area. Horseriding, fishing, the Wiltshire Cycleway and plenty of great walks are all on the doorstep.

Rooms 3 rms (2 en suite) (1 pri facs) S £45-£50; D £60-£65* Facilities FTV TVL Cen ht Golf 9 Parking 10 Notes ⊗ No Children 8yrs Closed Xmas & New Year

---

WORCESTERSHIRE

Alcott Farm (SP056739)

★★★ ⬛ FARMHOUSE

Icknield St, Weatheroak B48 7EH
☎ 01564 824051 📠 01564 829799
Mrs J Poole
e-mail: alcottfarm@btinternet.com
web: www.alcottfarm.co.uk
dir: 2m NE of Alvechurch. M42 junct 3, A435 for Birmingham, left signed Weatheroak, left at x-rds down steep hill, left opp pub, farm 0.5m on right up long driveway

Rooms 4 en suite (1 GF) Facilities TVL tea/coffee Cen ht Wi-fi Fishing Parking 20 Notes ⊗ No Children 10yrs 66 acres horses

---

Corner Cottage

★★★ BED AND BREAKFAST

1194 Evesham Rd B96 6AA
☎ 01527 459122 & 07917 582884 📠 01527 459122
e-mail: marilyn_alan1194@hotmail.co.uk
dir: A441 through Astwood Bank, at T-lights

A warm welcome awaits you at Corner Cottage, a beautiful Victorian cottage set in a pristine village location within walking distance of pubs, shops and restaurants. Convenient for Statford-upon-Avon, Evesham, Warwick, Birmingham and Worcester.

Rooms 3 rms (2 en suite) (1 pri facs) (3 fmly) S £50-£55; D £50-£55* Facilities FTV TVL tea/coffee Cen ht Wi-fi Parking 3 Notes LB ⊗ ⊗ 🐾

BECKFORD   Map 10 S093

The Beckford Inn

★★★★ INN

Cheltenham Rd GL20 7AN
☎ 01386 881532
e-mail: enquiries@thebeckford.com
dir: Off A46 nr junct Station Rd to Beckford

Looking more like a country mansion than a typical inn, this is a superb Cotswold-stone building with 18th-century origins. Comfortable accommodation is provided and there's a good range of choices at dinner and breakfast; a snug is available with a widescreen TV. The Beckford is a good venue for parties, weddings or conferences. There is ample parking and disabled access.

Rooms 11 rms (8 en suite) (3 pri facs) 2 annexe en suite (2 fmly) S fr £80; D fr £100 **Facilities** FTV tea/coffee Dinner available Cen ht Wi-fi **Conf** Max 100 Thtr 100 Class 60 Board 100 **Parking** 70 **Notes** LB Civ Wed 60

BEWDLEY   Map 10 S077

PREMIER COLLECTION

Number Thirty

★★★★★ BED AND BREAKFAST

30 Gardners Meadow DY12 2DG
☎ 01299 402404   📠 01299 402404
e-mail: info@numberthirty.net
dir: Turn left off Load St after Bewdley bridge onto Severnside South, 2nd right onto Gardners Meadow

A warm welcome is assured at this smart modern house, a short stroll from the River Severn and the Georgian town centre. Bedrooms are luxuriously furnished and have lots of thoughtful extras. Comprehensive breakfasts are taken in an attractive dining room that overlooks the immaculate gardens and cricket ground; guests can enjoy watching a game from a raised sun deck. A sumptuous guest lounge is also available.

Rooms 3 en suite S fr £65; D fr £75 **Facilities** FTV TVL tea/coffee Cen ht Wi-fi Golf 18 **Parking** 6 **Notes** ⊗ No Children 10yrs 🐾

The Mug House Inn

★★★★ ⊚ INN

12 Severnside North DY12 2EE
☎ 01299 402543
e-mail: drew@mughousebewdley.co.uk
web: www.mughousebewdley.co.uk
dir: In town centre on riverfront

Located on the opposite side of the River Severn to Bewdley Rowing Club, this 18th-century inn has been renovated to combine high standards of comfort and facilities with many original features. Bedrooms are thoughtfully furnished, there is a separate breakfast room, and imaginative dinners are served in the restaurant.

Rooms 4 en suite 3 annexe en suite (2 fmly) (1 GF) S £67-£97; D £77-£97* **Facilities** tea/coffee Dinner available Cen ht Wi-fi **Notes** ⊗ No Children 10yrs No coaches

Royal Forester Country Inn

★★★★ ⊚ INN

Callow Hill DY14 9XW
☎ 01299 266286
e-mail: contact@royalforesterinn.co.uk

Located opposite The Wyre Forest on the town's outskirts, this inn dates back to 1411 and has been sympathetically restored to provide high standards of comfort. Stylish modern bedrooms are complemented by smart bathrooms, and equipped with many thoughtful extras. Decor styles throughout the public areas highlight the many period features, and the restaurant serves imaginative food featuring locally sourced produce.

Rooms 7 en suite (2 fmly) **Facilities** STV FTV tea/coffee Dinner available Cen ht Wi-fi **Parking** 40 **Notes** No coaches

Welchgate Guest House

★★★★ GUEST HOUSE

1 Welch Gate DY12 2AT
☎ 01299 402655
e-mail: info@welchgate-guesthouse.co.uk
web: www.welchgate-guesthouse.co.uk

A warm welcome is assured at this 400-year-old former inn, which has been sympathetically restored to provide modern comforts and good facilities. Bedrooms are equipped with fine furnishings and thoughtful extras, and have smart modern en suite shower rooms. Hearty breakfasts are taken in a rustically furnished café which is also open to the public during the day.

Rooms 4 en suite S £35-£50; D £70-£90* **Facilities** tea/coffee Cen ht Licensed Wi-fi **Parking** 4 **Notes** LB ⊗ No Children

Bank House

★★★ BED AND BREAKFAST

14 Lower Park DY12 2DP
☎ 01299 402652
e-mail: fleur.nightingale@virgin.net
web: www.bewdley-accommodation.co.uk
dir: In town centre. From junct High St & Lax Ln, Bank House after junct on left

Once a private bank, this Victorian house retains many original features and offers comfortable accommodation. The cosy dining room is the setting for tasty English breakfasts served at one family table. Owner Mrs Nightingale has a comprehensive knowledge of the town and its history.

Rooms 4 rms (1 fmly) S £33-£35; D £57-£60* **Facilities** FTV tea/coffee Cen ht **Parking** 2 **Notes** ⊗ Closed 24-26 Dec 🐾

Woodcolliers Arms

★★★ INN

76 Welch Gate DY12 2AU
☎ 01299 400589
e-mail: roger@woodcolliers.co.uk
web: www.woodcolliers.co.uk
dir: Exit A456, follow road behind church and turn left into Welch Gate (B4190)

Dating from before 1780, the Woodcolliers Arms is a family-run establishment located in the renowned Georgian town of Bewdley. This is a traditional inn offering an interesting menu with both traditional British pub food and a speciality Russian menu. Accommodation is comfortable and rooms are well equipped.

Rooms 5 rms (4 en suite) (1 pri facs) S £26-£36; D £51-£61 (room only)* **Facilities** FTV tea/coffee Dinner available Cen ht Wi-fi **Parking** 2 **Notes** LB

BROADWAY
Map 10 SP03

PREMIER COLLECTION

Abbots Grange

★★★★★ 🏠 GUEST HOUSE

Church St WR12 7AE
☎ 020 8133 8698
e-mail: rooms@abbotsgrange.com
web: www.abbotsgrange.com
dir: *M5 junct 9 follow signs to Evesham & Broadway*

A warm welcome waits at this 14th-century monastic manor house believed to be the oldest dwelling in Broadway; a Grade II listed building it stands proudly in eight acres of grounds. The bedrooms are luxurious and comprise twin and four-poster suites. The stunning medieval Great Hall is the guests' lounge and makes a romantic setting with its log fire and candles. The quality breakfasts are served at the large communal table in the wood panelled dining room. The Grange also offers a tennis court and croquet lawn along with a helicopter landing pad.

Rooms 4 rms (3 en suite) (1 pri facs) S £105-£185; D £125-£200* **Facilities** STV FTV TVL tea/coffee Cen ht Wi-fi 🏊 ⛳ **Conf** Board 10 **Parking** 8 **Notes** ⊗ No Children 6yrs

PREMIER COLLECTION

East House

★★★★★ 🏠 GUEST ACCOMMODATION

162 High St WR12 7AJ
☎ 01386 853789 & 07738 290855
e-mail: enquiries@vacationcotswolds.co.uk
dir: *M40 junct 8 then A44 to Broadway, left at mini-rdbt to Upper High Street. 600mtrs on left*

A very warm welcome is assured at this fine house, located in a quiet residential area of Broadway. For guests looking to relax in the Cotswolds, this home is certainly a special place to reside. Day rooms include an elegant reception room with open fire, drawing room with grand piano, and a cosy breakfast room where memorable breakfasts are served. Individually furnished bedrooms, equipped with many thoughtful extras are in keeping with the house. Off-road parking is a bonus.

Rooms 4 en suite D £165-£195 **Facilities** FTV TVL tea/coffee Cen ht Wi-fi Table tennis Treadmill **Parking** 7 **Notes** ⊗ No Children 18yrs

PREMIER COLLECTION

Mill Hay House

★★★★★ 🏠 GUEST ACCOMMODATION

Snowshill Rd WR12 7JS
☎ 01386 852498 📠 01386 858038
e-mail: info@millhay.co.uk
web: www.millhay.co.uk
dir: *0.7m S of Broadway towards Snowshill, house on right*

Set in three acres of immaculate grounds beside a medieval watermill, this impressive early 18th-century stone house has many original features complemented by quality decor, period furniture and works of art. The spacious bedrooms are filled with thoughtful extras and one has a balcony. Imaginative breakfasts are served in the elegant dining room, and there is a spacious drawing room.

Rooms 3 en suite S £120-£160; D £160-£190* **Facilities** FTV TVL tea/coffee Direct Dial Cen ht Wi-fi **Parking** 15 **Notes** LB ⊗ No Children 12yrs

PREMIER COLLECTION

Russell's

★★★★★ ◉◉ 🏠 RESTAURANT WITH ROOMS

20 High St WR12 7DT
☎ 01386 853555 📠 01386 853555
e-mail: info@russellsofbroadway.co.uk
dir: *Opposite village green*

Situated in the centre of a picturesque Cotswold village this restaurant with rooms makes a great base for exploring local attractions. The superbly appointed bedrooms, each with its own character, have air conditioning and a wide range of extras for guests. The cuisine is a real draw here with freshly-prepared, local produce skilfully utilised.

Rooms 4 en suite 3 annexe en suite (4 fmly) S £80; D £98-£300* **Facilities** STV FTV TV3B tea/coffee Dinner available Direct Dial Cen ht **Conf** Max 12 Board 12 **Parking** 16 **Notes** No coaches

Bowers Hill Farm *(SP086420)*

★★★★ FARMHOUSE

Bowers Hill, Willersey WR11 7HG
☎ 01386 834585 & 07966 171861 📠 01386 830234
Mr & Mrs M Bent
e-mail: sarah@bowershillfarm.com
web: www.bowershillfarm.com
dir: *3m NW of Broadway. A44 onto B4632 to Willersey, at mini rdbt signs to Badsey/industrial estate, farm 2m on right by postbox*

An impressive Victorian house set in immaculate gardens on a diverse farm, where point-to-point horses are bred. The house has been renovated to provide very comfortable bedrooms with modern bathrooms. Breakfast is served in the elegant dining room or the magnificent conservatory, and a lounge, with an open fire, is available to guests.

Rooms 3 en suite (1 fmly) S £50-£60; D £70-£80 **Facilities** FTV TVL tea/coffee Cen ht Wi-fi **Conf** Max 8 Class 8 Board 8 **Parking** 5 **Notes** LB ⊗ 98 acres horse breeding/grassland

Cowley House

★★★★ GUEST ACCOMMODATION

Church St WR12 7AE
☎ 01386 858148
e-mail: cowleyhouse.broadway@tiscali.co.uk
dir: *Follow signs for Broadway. Church St adjacent to village green, 3rd on left*

A warm welcome is assured at this 18th-century Cotswold-stone house, just a stroll from the village green. Fine period furniture enhances the interior, and the elegant hall has a polished flagstone floor. Tastefully equipped bedrooms include thoughtful extras and smart modern shower rooms. Comprehensive breakfasts feature local produce.

Rooms 7 rms (6 en suite) (1 pri facs) (2 fmly) (2 GF) S £50-£75; D £69-£110* **Facilities** FTV tea/coffee Cen ht Wi-fi **Parking** 7 **Notes** LB

Horse & Hound

★★★★ INN

54 High St WR12 7DT
☎ 01386 852287 📠 01386 853784
e-mail: djttruesdale@msn.com
dir: *Off A46 to Evesham*

The Horse & Hound is at the heart of the beautiful Cotswold village of Broadway. There are many areas of interest to visit within easy distance of this well established inn. A warm welcome is guaranteed from hosts David and Diane whether dining in the inviting pub or staying overnight in attractive and well-appointed bedrooms. Breakfast and dinner provide quality ingredients which are freshly prepared.

Rooms 5 en suite (1 fmly) S £60-£70; D £70-£80* **Facilities** tea/coffee Dinner available Cen ht Wi-fi **Parking** 15 **Notes** LB RS Winter

Save on B&Bs and Hotels. Book at theAA.com/hotel

WORCESTERSHIRE 335 ENGLAND

Mount Pleasant Farm (SP056392)

★★★★ FARMHOUSE

Childswickham WR12 7HZ
☎ 01386 853424 & 07515 651560 📄 01386 853424
Mrs H Perry
e-mail: helen@mountpleasantfarm.biz
dir: Onto B4632 for Cheltenham & Winchcombe, 50yds
right to Childswickham (3m). Farm 1.5m W on left

Located in immaculate, mature grounds in a pretty
hamlet, this impressive Victorian house provides
spacious, traditionally furnished bedrooms with smart
modern bathrooms. Comprehensive breakfasts are served
in an elegant dining room, and a comfortable lounge is
available.

Rooms 3 en suite (1 fmly) S £50; D £70* Facilities tea/
coffee Cen ht Golf Parking 10 Notes ⊗ No Children 5yrs
950 acres arable

Whiteacres Guest House

★★★★ 🏠 GUEST ACCOMMODATION

Station Rd WR12 7DE
☎ 01386 852320
e-mail: whiteacres@btinternet.com
web: www.broadwaybandb.com
dir: 500yds NW from E end of High St

Located a few minutes' walk from the historic village
centre, this elegant Edwardian house has been lovingly
renovated to provide high standards of comfort and good
facilities. The bedrooms are equipped with a wealth of
thoughtful extras, and memorable breakfasts can be
enjoyed in an attractive dining room. A comfortable guest
lounge is also available and a warm welcome is assured.

Rooms 5 en suite S £55-£70; D £70-£90* Facilities FTV
TVL tea/coffee Cen ht Wi-fi Golf 18 Parking 5 Notes LB No
Children 5yrs

Windrush House

★★★★ 🅰 GUEST ACCOMMODATION

Station Rd WR12 7DE
☎ 01386 853577 📄 01386 853790
e-mail: richard.pinder@virgin.net
dir: From A44 take turn for Broadway, Windrush House is
opp junct with B4632

Rooms 5 en suite Facilities tea/coffee Wi-fi

FLYFORD FLAVELL   Map 10 SO95

The Boot Inn

★★★★ 🍽 INN

Radford Rd WR7 4BS
☎ 01386 462658 📄 01386 462547
e-mail: enquiries@thebootinn.com
web: www.thebootinn.com
dir: In village centre, signed from A422

An inn has occupied this site since the 13th century,
though the Boot itself dates from the Georgian period.
Modernisation has retained historic charm, while the
bedrooms, furnished in antique pine, are equipped with
practical extras and have modern bathrooms. A range of
ales, wines and imaginative food is offered in the cosy
public areas, which include an attractive conservatory
and patio.

Rooms 5 annexe en suite (2 GF) S £50-£65; D £65-£95
Facilities FTV tea/coffee Dinner available Cen ht Wi-fi
Golf 27 Pool table Parking 30 Notes LB

The Flyford Arms Inn & Brasserie

★★★★ 🍽 INN

Flyford WR7 4DA
☎ 01905 381890
e-mail: info@flyfordarms.com
web: wwww.flyfordarms.com
dir: On A422 midway between Worcester & Stratford-
upon-Avon

This attractive country inn is full of charm, and enjoys a
pleasant location with adjacent gardens and terraces for
warmer months. Public areas include a contemporary
stylish brasserie and a pleasant bar with small lounge
area. En suite bedrooms are well appointed and benefit
from free Wi-fi. Management and staff are friendly and
attentive.

Rooms 3 en suite Facilities FTV tea/coffee Dinner
available Cen ht Wi-fi Golf 18 Parking 25 Notes ⊗ No
Children 10yrs No coaches

HANLEY SWAN   Map 10 SO84

The Swan Inn

★★★★ INN

Worcester Rd WR8 0EA
☎ 01684 311870
e-mail: info@theswanhanleyswan.co.uk
web: www.theswanhanleyswan.co.uk
dir: M5 junct 7, follow signs for Three Counties
Showground, 1m before

This 17th-century property, often described as a
quintessential country inn, is located right on the village
green, and has a warm, cosy, home-from-home
atmosphere. Ideally situated at the foot of the beautiful
Malvern Hills, it has five en suite bedrooms that are
pleasantly furnished, modern and comfortable. Dining,
particularly on warmer days in the garden and the patio,
is a delight. There is ample parking to the rear of the
property.

Rooms 5 en suite (2 fmly) S £62; D £84* Facilities tea/
coffee Dinner available Cen ht Wi-fi Parking 30

KEMPSEY   Map 10 SO84

Walter de Cantelupe Inn

★★★ INN

Main Rd WR5 3NA
☎ 01905 820572
e-mail: walter.depub@fsbdial.co.uk
web: www.walterdecantelupeinn.com
dir: On A38 in village centre

This inn provides cosy bedrooms with smart bathrooms,
and is convenient for the M5 and Worcester. The intimate,
open-plan public areas are the setting for a range of
real ales, and imaginative food featuring local produce and a
fine selection of British cheeses.

Rooms 3 rms (2 en suite) (1 pri facs) Facilities tea/
coffee Dinner available Cen ht Wi-fi Parking 24 Notes No
coaches

MALVERN — Map 10 SO74

The Dell House

★★★★ BED AND BREAKFAST

Green Ln, Malvern Wells WR14 4HU
☎ 01684 564448 📠 01684 893974
e-mail: burrage@dellhouse.co.uk
web: www.dellhouse.co.uk
dir: *2m S of Great Malvern on A449. Turn left off A449 onto Green Ln. House at top of road on right, just below old church*

This impressive, well-proportioned Victorian house retains many unique features, several of which were introduced by the resident scholar and vicar during the time it was a rectory. Spacious bedrooms are filled with thoughtful extras, and a comprehensive breakfast is served in an elegant dining room that has superb views over the mature gardens to the countryside beyond. Babies under one year are catered for.

Rooms 3 en suite **Facilities** TVL tea/coffee Cen ht Wi-fi **Parking** 3 **Notes** ⊗ No Children 10yrs

Bredon House

★★★★ GUEST ACCOMMODATION

34 Worcester Rd WR14 4AA
☎ 01684 566990
e-mail: enquiries@bredonhouse.co.uk
web: www.bredonhouse.co.uk
dir: *200yds N of Great Malvern centre on A449, large fir tree in front car park*

Superbly located on the east side of the Malvern Hills, with stunning views of the Vale of Evesham and the Severn Valley, this elegant Regency house retains many original features. Bedrooms, some with spectacular views, offer both thoughtful and practical extras, and a comfortable licensed lounge is also available.

Bredon House

Rooms 10 en suite (2 fmly) (1 GF) S £55-£65; D £75-£100 **Facilities** FTV TVL tea/coffee Direct Dial Cen ht Licensed Wi-fi **Parking** 7

Gilberts End Farm B&B

★★★★ BED AND BREAKFAST

Gilberts End, Harley Castle WR8 0AR
☎ 01684 311392 📠 01684 311392
e-mail: chrissy.bacon@btinternet.com
dir: *From Hanley Castle (B4211) onto B4209 signed to Malvern Wells. Take immediate left to Gilberts End, follow brick wall on right round sharp right hand bend (approx 1m), entrance on right on exit of bend*

A warm welcome awaits guests from hosts Chrissy and Roy Bacon at this Grade II listed farm building, with parts dating back some 600 years. Peacefully located in its own grounds, the house is close to Upton-upon-Severn and Hanley Swan, and just a short drive to the Malvern Hills and Worcester. Therapeutic massage treatments and other complementary therapies are available. The bedrooms are comfortable with a good range of extras. The farmhouse breakfasts are served at individual tables in the welcoming dining room.

Rooms 3 en suite **Facilities** tea/coffee Cen ht Wi-fi Complementary therapies available **Parking** 6 **Notes** ⊗ No Children 5yrs

Wyche Inn

★★★★ INN

74 Wyche Rd WR14 4EQ
☎ 01684 575396
e-mail: thewycheinn@googlemail.com
web: www.thewycheinn.co.uk
dir: *1.5m S of Malvern. On B4218 towards Malvern & Colwall. Off A449 (Worcester to Ross/Ledbury road)*

Located in an elevated position on the outskirts of Malvern, this inn is popular with locals and visiting walkers. The thoughtfully furnished bedrooms provide good levels of comfort with suitable guest extras; all bathrooms have a bath and shower. All bedrooms have stunning countryside views. A good range of real ales is available from the bar. The menus offer a good choice of home-cooked dishes, and most evenings there is a choice of good value, themed choices.

Rooms 4 en suite 1 annexe rms (1 pri facs) **Facilities** FTV tea/coffee Dinner available Cen ht Wi-fi Pool table **Parking** 6 **Notes** LB No coaches

The Pembridge

★★★ GUEST ACCOMMODATION

114 Graham Rd WR14 2HX
☎ 01684 574813 📠 01684 566885
e-mail: info@thepembridge.co.uk
dir: *A449 onto Church St, 1st left*

Located on a leafy residential road close to the town centre, this large Victorian house retains many original features, including a superb staircase. Bedrooms, which include a ground-floor room, are well equipped. Other areas include a comfortable sitting room with a small bar and an elegant dining room.

Rooms 8 en suite (1 fmly) (1 GF) S £45-£60; D £59-£69* **Facilities** FTV TVL tea/coffee Direct Dial Cen ht Licensed Wi-fi **Conf** Max 8 **Parking** 10 **Notes** LB ⊗ No Children 7yrs RS 25-26 Dec No cooked English breakfast

Portocks End House

★★★ BED AND BREAKFAST

Little Clevelode WR13 6PE
☎ 01684 310276
e-mail: email@portocksendbandb.co.uk
dir: *On B4424, 4m N of Upton upon Severn, opposite Riverside Caravan Park*

Peacefully located, yet convenient for the showground and major road links, this period house retains many original features; the traditional furnishings and decor highlight its intrinsic charm. The bedrooms are equipped with lots of thoughtful extras, and breakfasts are taken in a cosy dining room overlooking the pretty garden.

Rooms 2 rms (1 en suite) (1 pri facs) (1 fmly) S £30; D £50* **Facilities** tea/coffee **Parking** 4 **Notes** Closed Dec-Feb 🚭

Save on B&Bs and Hotels. Book at theAA.com/hotel

WORCESTERSHIRE 337 **ENGLAND**

Sidney House

★★★ GUEST ACCOMMODATION

40 Worcester Rd WR14 4AA
☎ 01684 574994 📠 01684 574994
e-mail: info@sidneyhouse.co.uk
web: www.sidneyhouse.co.uk
dir: On A449, 200yds N from town centre

This impressive Grade II listed Georgian house is close to the central attractions and has stunning views. Bedrooms are filled with thoughtful extras, and some have small, en suite shower rooms. The spacious dining room overlooks the Cotswold escarpment and a comfortable lounge is also available.

Rooms 8 rms (6 en suite) (2 pri facs) (1 fmly) S £25-£55; D £59-£75* **Facilities** FTV TVL tea/coffee Cen ht Licensed Wi-fi **Parking** 9 **Notes** Closed 24 Dec-3 Jan

Four Hedges

★★ GUEST ACCOMMODATION

The Rhydd, Hanley Castle WR8 0AD
☎ 01684 310405
e-mail: fredgies@aol.com
dir: 4m E of Malvern at junct of B4211 & B4424

Situated in a rural location, this detached house stands in mature grounds with wild birds in abundance. The bedrooms are equipped with thoughtful extras. Tasty English breakfasts, using free-range eggs, are served in a cosy dining room at a table made from a 300-year-old elm tree.

Rooms 4 rms (2 en suite) S £25; D £50 **Facilities** TVL TV2B tea/coffee Cen ht 🎣 Fishing **Parking** 5 **Notes** No Children 1yr Closed Xmas ⊗

MARTLEY Map 10 SO76

Admiral Rodney Inn

★★★★ INN

Berrow Green WR6 6PL
☎ 01886 821375
e-mail: rodney@admiral.fslife.co.uk
dir: A44 onto B4197 at Knightwick, 2m on left

Located in the pretty village of Berrow Green, this 16th-century inn has been renovated to provide high standards of comfort and facilities. Hosts Karen and Desmond offer a warm welcome to all their customers, and provide spacious, carefully furnished bedrooms, complemented by luxurious modern bathrooms. Ground-floor areas include quality bars with log fires and a unique tiered and beamed restaurant, where imaginative dishes are served. There are also outside seating areas to front and rear, and excellent parking facilities.

Rooms 3 en suite **Facilities** tea/coffee Cen ht Wi-fi Pool table **Parking** 40

WORCESTER Map 10 SO85

Bants

★★★★ INN

Worcester Rd WR7 4NN
☎ 01905 381282 📠 01905 381173
e-mail: info@bants.co.uk
web: www.bants.co.uk
dir: 5m E of Worcester. On A422 at Upton Snodsbury

A family-run, 16th-century pub with a modern atmosphere. Bedrooms are carefully decorated and well equipped, with some rooms separate from the inn. A wide range of freshly-cooked meals is available in the free house bar or served in the large conservatory.

Rooms 4 en suite 5 annexe en suite (3 GF) S £65-£75; D £75-£85* **Facilities** FTV tea/coffee Dinner available Cen ht Wi-fi **Conf** Max 50 **Parking** 40 **Notes** LB

The Dewdrop Inn

★★★★ INN

Bell Ln, Lower Broadheath WR2 6RR
☎ 01905 640012 📠 01905 640265
e-mail: enquiries@thedewdrop-inn.co.uk
dir: From A44 follow signs for Elgar Birthplace Museum, 0.5m past museum turn right at x-rds. 800yds on left

This country pub with rooms is set in the pretty village of Lower Broadheath on the outskirts of Worcester. The accommodation offers seven comfortable, en suite bedrooms that are well equipped with thoughtful extras. Dining in the open-plan contemporary bar and restaurant is especially popular at weekends for the carvery, however a full menu of enticing options is available at other times. Alfresco dining is available in the summer months.

Rooms 7 en suite (7 GF) S £69; D £90* **Facilities** FTV tea/coffee Dinner available Direct Dial Cen ht Wi-fi **Parking** 40 **Notes** LB

Oaklands B&B

★★★★ GUEST ACCOMMODATION

Claines WR3 7RS
☎ 01905 458871 📠 01905 759362
e-mail: barbara.gadd@zoom.co.uk
dir: M5 junct 6 onto A449. At rdbt take 1st exit signed Claines. 1st left onto School Bank. Oaklands 1st house on right

A warm welcome is guaranteed at this converted stable, which is well located in a peaceful setting just a short drive from major routes. The property stands in abundant mature gardens, and the well-appointed bedrooms are mostly spacious. There is also a snooker room. Parking is available.

Rooms 4 en suite (2 fmly) **Facilities** tea/coffee Cen ht Wi-fi Snooker **Parking** 7 **Notes** LB Closed Xmas & New Year ⊗

Wyatt

★★★★ GUEST HOUSE

40 Barbourne Rd WR1 1HU
☎ 01905 26311 📠 01905 26311
e-mail: wyatt.guest@virgin.net
dir: On A38 0.5m N from city centre

Located within easy walking distance of shops, restaurants and central attractions, this constantly improving Victorian house provides a range of thoughtfully furnished bedrooms. Breakfast is served in an attractive dining room, a warm welcome is assured, and the attractive frontage is a regular winner in the Worcester Britain in Bloom competition.

Rooms 8 rms (7 en suite) (1 fmly) (1 GF) S £40-£45; D £56-£60 **Facilities** STV tea/coffee Cen ht Wi-fi

Ye Olde Talbot

★★★ INN

Friar St WR1 2NA
☎ 01905 23573 📠 01905 612760
e-mail: 9250@greeneking.co.uk
web: www.oldenglish.co.uk

Located in the heart of the city, close to the cathedral, this period inn has been sympathetically renovated to provide attractive and cosy public areas where guests can enjoy a wide range of imaginative food, wine and real ales. Bedrooms are thoughtfully furnished. Parking is available at the adjacent NCP Cathedral car park.

Rooms 29 en suite (6 fmly) (6 GF) **Facilities** FTV tea/coffee Direct Dial Wi-fi **Notes** ⊗

Croft Guest House

★★ GUEST HOUSE

Bransford WR6 5JD
☎ 01886 832227
e-mail: accom@brianporter.orangehome.co.uk
web: www.croftguesthouse.com
dir: 4m SW of Worcester. On A4103 Leigh exit at Bransford rdbt, driveway on left after 30yds

This cottage-style property, dating in parts from the 16th century, is convenient for the city centre and the Malvern Hills, and offers homely bedrooms. Freshly-cooked breakfasts feature home-made sausages. Dogs are welcome provided they have a current vaccination certificate.

Rooms 3 en suite (1 fmly) **Facilities** TVL tea/coffee Cen ht Licensed **Parking** 5

YORKSHIRE, EAST RIDING OF

BEVERLEY — Map 17 TA03

PREMIER COLLECTION

Burton Mount Country House

★★★★★ ⌂ GUEST ACCOMMODATION

Malton Rd, Cherry Burton HU17 7RA
☎ 01964 550541
e-mail: pg@burtonmount.co.uk
web: www.burtonmount.co.uk
dir: *2m NW of Beverley. B1248 for Malton, 2m right at x-rds, house on left*

A charming country house three miles from Beverley, set in delightful gardens and offering luxurious accommodation. Bedrooms are well equipped and have thoughtful extra touches. The spacious drawing room has a blazing fire in the cooler months, and an excellent, Aga-cooked Yorkshire breakfast is served in the morning room. Pauline Greenwood is renowned locally for her customer care, culinary skills and warm hospitality.

Rooms 3 en suite **Facilities** STV TVL tea/coffee Dinner available Cen ht Licensed Wi-fi ⛳ ♨ **Conf** Max 30 Thtr 30 Class 20 Board 20 **Parking** 20 **Notes** LB ⊗ No Children 12yrs

The Ferguson Fawsitt Arms & Country Lodge

★★★★ Ⓐ INN

East End, Walkington HU17 8RX
☎ 01482 882665 📠 01482 882665
e-mail: admin@fergusonfawsitt.com
web: www.fergusonfawsitt.co.uk
dir: *M62 junct 38 onto B1230, left on A1034, right onto B1230, on left in centre of Walkington*

Rooms 10 en suite (2 fmly) (10 GF) S £60-£70; D £60-£70* **Facilities** FTV tea/coffee Dinner available Cen ht Wi-fi **Conf** Max 80 Thtr 60 Class 40 Board 20 **Parking** 120 **Notes** ⊗ RS 25-26 & 31 Dec No breakfast available

---

BRIDLINGTON — Map 17 TA16

PREMIER COLLECTION

Marton Grange

★★★★★ GUEST ACCOMMODATION

Flamborough Rd, Marton cum Sewerby YO15 1DU
☎ 01262 602034 & 07891 682687
📠 01262 602034
e-mail: info@marton-grange.co.uk
web: www.marton-grange.co.uk
dir: *2m NE of Bridlington. On B1255, 600yds W of Links golf club*

This Grade II listed former farmhouse is set in well maintained gardens offering high levels of comfort, service and hospitality. Bedrooms are well appointed with quality fixtures and fittings. Public areas offer wonderful views of the gardens. Thoughtful extras provided as standard make for a delightful guest experience.

Rooms 11 en suite (3 GF) **Facilities** FTV tea/coffee Cen ht Lift Licensed Wi-fi Golf 18 **Parking** 11 **Notes** LB RS Dec-Jan Restricted opening for refurbishments

Burlington Quays

★★★★ GUEST ACCOMMODATION

20 Meadowfield Rd YO15 3LD
☎ 01262 676052
e-mail: burlingtonquays@axis-connect.com
dir: *A165 into Bridlington, 1st right past golf course onto Kingston Rd. Bear left to seafront, take 3rd left*

In a peaceful street close to the seafront, this spacious house features modern, well appointed bedrooms, all with en suite bath or shower rooms. Guests also have use of a comfortable lounge and a cosy, fully licensed bar. Tasty breakfasts are served in the pleasant dining room at individual tables.

Rooms 5 en suite (4 fmly) S £40-£45; D £64-£85* **Facilities** TVL tea/coffee Cen ht Licensed Wi-fi **Parking** 2 **Notes** LB ⊗

Longcroft Lodge

★★★★ GUEST HOUSE

100 Trinity Rd YO15 2HF
☎ 01262 672180
e-mail: longcroft_hotel@hotmail.com
dir: *M62 junct 37, A614 to Bridlington*

Situated just two minutes from the north beach, and town centre, this well-maintained accommodation consists of bright, cheerful, and thoughtfully equipped bedrooms, with a friendly and relaxed atmosphere. Cooked breakfasts are served in the dining room, which has a lounge area with a bar and TV.

Rooms 7 rms (6 en suite) (1 pri facs) (1 fmly) (3 smoking) S £24-£30; D £50-£65 **Facilities** FTV tea/coffee Dinner available Cen ht Licensed **Parking** 2 **Notes** LB

Longleigh

★★★★ BED AND BREAKFAST

12 Swanland Av YO15 2HH
☎ 01262 676234 & 07980 310777
e-mail: geraldineross@hotmail.co.uk
dir: *Flamborough Rd, N past Holy Trinity Church*

In a quiet location ten minutes walk from the town centre or beach, Longleigh offers comfortable, tastefully appointed accommodation in a friendly atmosphere. Rooms are well equipped and breakfast is served in the attractive dining room. Free parking permits available for on-street parking.

Rooms 3 en suite S £32-£35 **Facilities** STV FTV TVL tea/coffee Cen ht **Notes** ⊗ No Children

The Royal Bridlington

★★★★ GUEST ACCOMMODATION

1 Shaftesbury Rd YO15 3NP
☎ 01262 672433 📠 01262 672118
e-mail: info@royalhotelbrid.co.uk
dir: *A615 N to Bridlington (Kingsgate), right onto Shaftesbury Rd*

Located just off the promenade, this immaculate property has a range of thoughtfully furnished bedrooms with smart modern bathrooms. Spacious public areas include a large dining room, conservatory-sitting room, and a cosy television lounge. Freshly-cooked dinners are a feature and a warm welcome is assured.

Rooms 14 rms (13 en suite) (1 pri facs) 4 annexe en suite (7 fmly) (4 GF) S £46-£50; D £72-£80* **Facilities** FTV TVL tea/coffee Dinner available Cen ht Licensed Wi-fi Golf 18 **Conf** Max 85 Thtr 85 Class 20 Board 40 **Parking** 7 **Notes** LB ⊗

The Marina

★★★★ Ⓐ GUEST HOUSE

8 Summerfield Rd YO15 3LF
☎ 01262 677138 & 0800 970 0591
e-mail: themarina8@hotmail.com
web: www.themarina-bridlington.com
dir: *From A165 take 1st right after Broadacres pub on left. Onto promenade, 5th turning on left*

Rooms 7 en suite (1 fmly) (1 GF) S £22.50-£26; D £50-£60* **Facilities** FTV tea/coffee Dinner available Cen ht Licensed Wi-fi **Notes** LB No Children 4yrs

The Tennyson

★★★ GUEST ACCOMMODATION

19 Tennyson Av YO15 2EU
☎ 01262 604382 & 07729 149729
e-mail: dianew2@live.co.uk
web: www.thetennyson-brid.co.uk
dir: *500yds NE of town centre. B1254 Promenade from town centre towards Flamborough, Tennyson Av on left*

Situated in a quiet side road close to the town centre and attractions, this friendly guest accommodation offers attentive service and comfortable bedrooms. Dinner is also available by prior arrangement.

Rooms 8 rms (7 en suite) (1 pri facs) (2 fmly) (1 GF) D £56-£65* Facilities FTV tea/coffee Dinner available Cen ht Wi-fi Notes LB

Aidansdale

★★★ GUEST HOUSE

92 Trinity Rd YO15 2HF
☎ 01262 676723

This friendly family-run house is located on a street next to North Beach and is only five minutes from the town centre. The attractive bedrooms are comfortable and well equipped, with good quality en suite shower rooms. Tasty breakfasts are served in the pleasant dining room and service is very attentive.

Rooms 7 rms (6 en suite) (4 fmly) Facilities TVL tea/coffee Cen ht Notes

Lansdowne House

★★★ GUEST ACCOMMODATION

33 Lansdowne Rd YO15 2QT
☎ 01262 604184 📠 01262 604184
e-mail: stephennunn@sky.com
dir: *N of town centre. Off B1254 Promenade near Leisure World onto Lansdowne Rd, last house on left*

A well maintained and friendly house located close to the seafront and only a short walk from the shops and attractions. Bedrooms are comfortable and appropriately equipped. Breakfasts are served in the dining room at individual tables. There is also a licensed bar with small lounge area.

Rooms 8 rms (6 en suite) (2 pri facs) (3 fmly) S £30-£35; D £58-£60* Facilities FTV TVL tea/coffee Direct Dial Cen ht Licensed Notes LB

The Ransdale

★★★ GUEST ACCOMMODATION

30 Flamborough Rd YO15 2JQ
☎ 01262 674334
e-mail: info@ransdalehotel.com

Close to all main attractions this establishment offers comfortable bedrooms and friendly service. Guests have use of a small, modern lounge. Evening meals and tasty breakfasts are served in the spacious dining room which also has a bar area. Limited off-street parking is also available.

Rooms 16 en suite (4 fmly) (4 GF) S fr £47; D fr £68* Facilities FTV TVL tea/coffee Dinner available Cen ht Licensed Wi-fi Golf 18 Parking 10 Notes LB

Sandra's Guest House

★★★ GUEST HOUSE

6 Summerfield Rd, South Marine Dr YO15 3LF
☎ 01262 677791
e-mail: sandrasguesthouse@yahoo.com
dir: *250yds SW of town centre. Off seafront South Marine Dr*

Close to the south beach and the Spa Theatre, this friendly guest house is in a quiet residential area. Bedrooms are furnished in a fresh, modern style and hearty full English breakfasts are prepared by the resident proprietors and served in the bright, airy dining room.

Rooms 9 rms (8 en suite) (1 pri facs) (1 GF) S £25-£30; D £50-£70* Facilities tea/coffee Dinner available Cen ht Licensed Wi-fi Notes LB No Children 12yrs Closed 24-27 Dec

The Brockton

Ⓤ

4 Shaftesbury Rd YO15 3NP
☎ 01262 673967 & 401771 📠 01262 673967
e-mail: brocktonhotel@yahoo.co.uk
dir: *Off A167 coast road, right at golf course, through lights, 2nd on left*

Currently the rating for this establishment is not confirmed. This may be due to a change of ownership or because it has only recently joined the AA rating scheme.

Rooms 10 en suite (1 fmly) (2 GF) S £28-£34; D £56-£60* Facilities FTV TVL tea/coffee Dinner available Cen ht Licensed Wi-fi Golf 18 Conf Max 20 Parking 10 Notes LB

The Wolds Inn

★★★ 🍽 INN

Driffield Rd YO42 1YH
☎ 01377 288217
e-mail: huggate@woldsinn.freeserve.co.uk
dir: *Huggate signed off A166 & brown signs to Wolds Inn*

At the end of the highest village in the Yorkshire Wolds, midway between York and the coast, this ancient inn is a rural haven beside the Wolds Way walk. Substantial meals are served in the dining room and a good range of well-kept beers is available in the bar. Bedrooms, varying in size, are well equipped and comfortable.

Rooms 3 en suite S £42; D £55-£57 (room only) Facilities FTV tea/coffee Dinner available Cen ht Pool table Parking 30 Notes

Robeanne House

★★★ GUEST ACCOMMODATION

Driffield Ln, Shiptonthorpe YO43 3PW
☎ 01430 873312 & 07720 468811 📠 01430 879142
e-mail: enquiries@robeannehouse.co.uk
web: www.robeannehouse.co.uk
dir: *1.5m NW on A614*

Set back off the A614 in a quiet location, this delightful modern family home was built as a farmhouse. York, the coast, and the Yorkshire Moors and Dales are within easy driving distance. All bedrooms have country views and include a large family room. A charming wooden chalet is available in the garden.

Rooms 2 en suite 6 annexe en suite (2 fmly) (3 GF) S £35-£45; D £60-£75* Facilities FTV TVL tea/coffee Dinner available Cen ht Wi-fi Conf Max 8 Parking 10 Notes LB

Lucy Cross Farm

★★★ GUEST ACCOMMODATION

DL11 7AD
☎ 01325 374319 & 07931 545985
e-mail: sally@lucycross.co.uk
web: www.lucycross.co.uk
dir: *A1 junct 56 onto B6275 at Barton, white house 3m from Barton rdbt on left towards Piercebridge*

Located close to major road links, a relaxed atmosphere and friendly welcome is assured. Traditionally furnished bedrooms are very comfortably equipped; one is on the ground floor. A lounge is available and hearty breakfasts are served in the pleasant dining room.

Rooms 5 rms (3 en suite) (2 pri facs) (1 fmly) (1 GF) Facilities FTV TVL tea/coffee Dinner available Cen ht Wi-fi Fishing Riding Conf Max 12 Board 12 Parking 10

ALLERSTON — Map 19 SE88

Rains Farm (SE888808)

★★★★ 🏠 FARMHOUSE

YO18 7PQ
☎ 01723 859333
Mr N Allanson
e-mail: rainsholidays@btconnect.com
web: www.rains-farm-holidays.co.uk

This 17th-century farmhouse located on the edge of the North Yorkshire Moors and central for Pickering Moors, the coast, and steam trains, is a quiet and peaceful destination. The accommodation is comfortable and the lounge and attractive garden provide a relaxing place to sit and view the wildlife. Exclusively for adults.

Rooms 5 en suite (1 GF) S £36-£50; D £72-£100*
Facilities FTV TVL tea/coffee Cen ht Wi-fi **Parking** 7
Notes LB ⊗ No Children Closed mid Oct-Etr 7 acres non-working

AMPLEFORTH — Map 19 SE57

PREMIER COLLECTION

Shallowdale House

★★★★★ 🍽 GUEST ACCOMMODATION

West End YO62 4DY
☎ 01439 788325 📄 01439 788885
e-mail: stay@shallowdalehouse.co.uk
web: www.shallowdalehouse.co.uk
dir: Off A170 at W end of village, on turn to Hambleton

An outstanding example of an architect-designed 1960s house, Shallowdale lies in two acres of hillside gardens. There are stunning views from every room, and the elegant public rooms include a choice of lounges. Spacious bedrooms blend traditional and 1960s style with many home comforts. Expect excellent service and genuine hospitality from Anton and Phillip. The very imaginative, freshly cooked dinners are not to be missed.

Rooms 3 rms (2 en suite) (1 pri facs) S £80-£95; D £99.50-£125 **Facilities** FTV tea/coffee Dinner available Cen ht Licensed Wi-fi **Parking** 3 **Notes** ⊗ No Children 12yrs Closed Xmas & New Year

APPLETREEWICK — Map 19 SE06

PREMIER COLLECTION

Knowles Lodge

★★★★★ 🏠 BED AND BREAKFAST

BD23 6DQ
☎ 01756 720228 📄 01756 720381
e-mail: pam@knowleslodge.com
web: www.knowleslodge.com
dir: From Bolton Abbey B6160 3.5m, turn right after Barden Tower 1.5m, entrance on left

Located in the heart of Wharfedale and surrounded by 17 acres of meadow and woodland, this delightful Canadian-style ranch has been lovingly restored. The house is attractively furnished, with well appointed bedrooms, and whether guests are there to walk, cycle, fish, or simply relax and enjoy the scenery, they are sure to be given a warm welcome. Delicious breakfasts featuring home-made dishes are served around a large gate-leg table.

Rooms 4 en suite (1 fmly) (3 GF) S £60-£65; D £100*
Facilities TVL tea/coffee Cen ht Wi-fi 🚣 Fishing
Parking 6 **Notes** No Children 8yrs Civ Wed 100

AUSTWICK — Map 18 SD76

The Traddock

★★★★ ⌘⌘ 🏠 RESTAURANT WITH ROOMS

LA2 8BY
☎ 015242 51224 📄 015242 51796
e-mail: info@austwicktraddock.co.uk
dir: From Skipton take A65 towards Kendal, 3m after Settle turn right signed Austwick, cross hump back bridge, 100yds on left

Situated within the Yorkshire Dales National Park and a peaceful village environment, this fine Georgian country house with well-tended gardens offers a haven of calm and good hospitality. There are two comfortable lounges with real fires and fine furnishings, as well as a cosy bar and an elegant dining room serving fine cuisine. Bedrooms are individually styled with many homely touches.

Rooms 12 en suite (2 fmly) (1 GF) S £85-£95; D £95-£185* **Facilities** FTV tea/coffee Dinner available Direct Dial Cen ht Wi-fi ch fac 🚣 Golf 18 **Conf** Max 24 Thtr 24 Class 16 Board 16 **Parking** 20 **Notes** LB No coaches

AYSGARTH — Map 19 SE08

Stow House

★★★★ 🅰 GUEST ACCOMMODATION

DL8 3SR
☎ 01969 663635
e-mail: info@stowhouse.co.uk
web: www.stowhouse.co.uk
dir: 0.6m E of Aysgarth on A684

Rooms 9 en suite (1 GF) S £42-£57; D £80-£104*
Facilities tea/coffee Dinner available Cen ht Licensed Wi-fi 🐾 🚣 **Parking** 10 **Notes** LB Closed 24-26 Dec

BAINBRIDGE — Map 18 SD99

PREMIER COLLECTION

Yorebridge House

★★★★★ ⌘⌘ 🏠 RESTAURANT WITH ROOMS

DL8 3EE
☎ 01969 652060 📄 01969 650258
e-mail: enquiries@yorebridgehouse.co.uk

Yorebridge House is situated by the river on the edge of Bainbridge, in the heart of the North Yorkshire Dales. Formerly a schoolmaster's house and school in the Victorian era, this building now offers luxury boutique-style accommodation. Each bedroom is individually designed with high quality furnishings and thoughtful extras. All rooms have stunning views of the Dales and some have their own terrace with hot tubs. There is a comfortable lounge bar where guests can relax before enjoying dinner in the attractive and elegant dining room.

Rooms 7 en suite 4 annexe en suite (11 fmly) (5 GF) S £155-£225; D £180-£250* **Facilities** STV FTV tea/coffee Dinner available Direct Dial Cen ht Wi-fi **Conf** Max 70 Thtr 70 Class 60 Board 30 **Parking** 30 **Notes** LB No coaches Civ Wed 100

BEDALE
Map 19 SE28

PREMIER COLLECTION

Mill Close Farm *(SE232922)*

★★★★★ FARMHOUSE

Patrick Brompton DL8 1JY
☎ 01677 450257 🖨 01748 813612
Mrs P Knox
e-mail: pat@millclose.co.uk
dir: *3m NW of Bedale. A684 to Patrick Brompton & brown tourist signs to farm*

A real home-from-home atmosphere prevails at this working farm. Bedrooms are furnished with quality and style; one has a four-poster and two have spa baths, but all rooms feature homely extras including fridges. Well-prepared breakfasts are one of the highlights of a stay and feature home-made produce cooked on the Aga of the farm kitchen.

Rooms 3 en suite D £80-£95* **Facilities** tea/coffee Cen ht Wi-fi Squash **Parking** 6 **Notes** LB ⊗ No Children 10yrs Closed Dec-Feb 240 acres mixed

Castle Arms

★★★★ 🍽 INN

Snape DL8 2TB
☎ 01677 470270 🖨 01677 470837
e-mail: castlearms@aol.com
dir: *2m S of Bedale. Off B6268 into Snape*

Nestled in the quiet village of Snape, this former coaching inn is full of character. Bedrooms are in a converted barn, and each room is very comfortable and carefully furnished. The restaurant and public bar offer a good selection of fine ales, along with an interesting selection of freshly-prepared dishes.

Rooms 9 annexe en suite (8 GF) S £60-£65; D £70-£80* **Facilities** FTV tea/coffee Dinner available Cen ht Wi-fi **Parking** 15 **Notes** LB No coaches

Elmfield House

★★★★ 🅰 GUEST HOUSE

Arrathorne DL8 1NE
☎ 01677 450558
e-mail: stay@elmfieldhouse.co.uk
dir: *4m NW of Bedale. A684 from Bedale for Leyburn, right after Patrick Brompton towards Richmond, 1.5m on right*
Rooms 4 en suite (1 fmly) **Facilities** FTV tea/coffee Dinner available Cen ht Licensed Wi-fi Fishing **Parking** 4 **Notes** LB ⊗

BISHOP MONKTON
Map 19 SE36

Lamb & Flag Inn

★★★★ INN

Boroughbridge Rd HG3 3QN
☎ 01765 677322
e-mail: carol@lambandflagbarn.co.uk
dir: *A61 turn E onto Moor Rd crossing Knaresbrough Rd*

A delightful country inn set in the countryside yet close to Harrogate, York and Leeds. The inn provides a warm welcome and freshly prepared local food. The three comfortably furnished and equipped bedrooms are a conversion from a barn and are annexed next to the pub. A continental-style breakfast is provided in your bedroom.

Rooms 3 annexe en suite (1 fmly) (3 GF) D £55-£65* **Facilities** FTV tea/coffee Dinner available Cen ht Wi-fi Pool table **Parking** 20 **Notes** ⊗ No coaches

BOLTON ABBEY
Map 19 SE05

Howgill Lodge

★★★★ GUEST ACCOMMODATION

Barden BD23 6DJ
☎ 01756 720655
e-mail: info@howgill-lodge.co.uk
dir: *B6160 from Bolton Abbey signed Burnsall, 3m right at Barden Tower signed Appletreewick, Howgill Lodge 1.25m on right at phone box*

Having an idyllic position high above the valley, this converted stone granary provides a quality get-away-from-it-all experience. The uniquely styled bedrooms provide a host of thoughtful touches and are designed to feature original stonewalls, flagstone floors and timber beams. All of the rooms boast spectacular, memorable views. Breakfasts make excellent use of fresh local ingredients.

Rooms 4 en suite (1 fmly) (4 GF) S £49; D £78* **Facilities** FTV tea/coffee Cen ht **Parking** 6 **Notes** LB ⊗ Closed 24-26 Dec

BOROUGHBRIDGE
Map 19 SE36

PREMIER COLLECTION

The Crown Inn

★★★★★ ⊛ INN

Roecliffe YO51 9LY
☎ 01423 322300 🖨 01423 322033
e-mail: info@crowninnroecliffe.com
web: www.crowninnroecliffe.com
dir: *A1(M) junct 48, follow signs for Boroughbridge. At rdbt exit towards Roecliffe & brown tourist signs*

The Crown is a 16th-century coaching inn that has undergone full refurbishment to provide an excellent combination of traditional charm and modern comforts. Service is friendly and professional and food is a highlight of any stay. Bedrooms are attractively furnished with stylish en suite bathrooms.

Rooms 4 en suite (1 fmly) S £82-£90; D £97-£120* **Facilities** FTV tea/coffee Dinner available Cen ht Wi-fi **Conf** Max 100 Thtr 100 Class 60 Board 30 **Parking** 40

BURNSALL
Map 19 SE06

The Devonshire Fell

★★★★ ⊛⊛ RESTAURANT WITH ROOMS

BD23 6BT
☎ 01756 729000 🖨 01756 729009
e-mail: manager@devonshirefell.co.uk
web: www.devonshirefell.co.uk
dir: *On B6160, 6m from Bolton Abbey rdbt, A59 junct*

Located on the edge of the attractive village of Burnsall, this establishment offers comfortable, well-equipped accommodation in a relaxing atmosphere. There is an extensive menu featuring local produce, and meals can be taken either in the bar area or the more formal restaurant. A function room with views over the valley is also available.

Rooms 12 en suite (2 fmly) S £134-£176; D £165-£206 (incl.dinner) **Facilities** STV FTV tea/coffee Dinner available Direct Dial Cen ht Wi-fi Fishing Free use of Spa facilities at sister hotel **Conf** Max 50 Thtr 50 Class 30 Board 24 **Parking** 30 **Notes** LB Civ Wed 90

CARPERBY
Map 19 SE08

The Wheatsheaf

★★★ 🅰 INN

DL8 4DF
☎ 01969 663216 🖨 01969 663019
e-mail: wheatsheaf@paulmit.globalnet.co.uk
dir: *Off A684 signed Aysgarth Falls to village centre*
Rooms 12 en suite 1 annexe en suite (2 fmly) (1 GF) S fr £35; D £70-£87* **Facilities** FTV tea/coffee Dinner available Cen ht Wi-fi Fishing **Conf** Max 20 Board 20 **Parking** 40 **Notes** LB No coaches

CATTERICK — Map 19 SE29

Rose Cottage

★★★ GUEST ACCOMMODATION

26 High St DL10 7LJ
☎ 01748 811164
dir: Off A1 in village centre, opp village pharmacy

Convenient for exploring the Dales and Moors, this well-maintained guest accommodation lies in the middle of Catterick. Bedrooms are nicely presented and comfortable. The cosy public rooms include a cottage-style dining room adorned with Mrs Archer's paintings, and a lounge. Dinner is available by arrangement during the summer.

Rooms 3 rms (2 en suite) (1 pri facs) (1 fmly) (3 smoking) S £30-£36; D £48-£54* Facilities tea/coffee Dinner available Cen ht Parking 3 Notes Closed 24-26 Dec ✿

CAWOOD — Map 16 SE53

Maypole Farm B&B

★★★ BED AND BREAKFAST

14 Wistowgate YO8 3SH
☎ 01757 268849
e-mail: bookings@maypole-farm.co.uk
web: www.maypole-farm.co.uk

Located in a quiet village, Maypole Farm B&B offers a peaceful and relaxing stay. Each of the three bedrooms are uniquely designed, with thoughtful accessories. The conservatory overlooking the garden offers a relaxing place to sit, or even a game of pool. Breakfast is served in the very pleasant and well-appointed dining room.

Rooms 3 en suite S £40; D £70* Facilities FTV tea/coffee Cen ht Wi-fi Golf 18 Pool table Parking 3 Notes ✿

CLAPHAM — Map 18 SD76

Brookhouse Guest House

★★★★ ⬤ GUEST HOUSE

Station Rd LA2 8ER
☎ 015242 51580
e-mail: admin@brookhouseclapham.co.uk
web: www.brookhouse-clapham.co.uk
dir: Off A65 into village

Located in the pretty conservation village of Clapham beside the river, this well-maintained and friendly guest house provides thoughtfully furnished bedrooms and a popular evening bistro, offering an interesting selection of home-made meals.

Rooms 3 rms (2 en suite) (1 pri facs) (1 fmly) Facilities FTV tea/coffee Dinner available Cen ht Licensed Wi-fi ⬤ Golf 18 Notes ✕ ✿

CLOUGHTON — Map 19 TA09

Blacksmiths Arms

★★★★ INN

High St YO13 0AE
☎ 01723 870244
e-mail: enquiries@blacksmithsarmsinn.co.uk
dir: On A171 in village centre. 6m N of Scarborough

Located six miles north of Scarborough, this inn features smartly furnished bedrooms. Four are in converted stone buildings that have private entrances. A good range of dishes is served in the bar and dining room, which have the ambience of a country inn, including open fires and traditional furniture.

Rooms 6 en suite 4 annexe en suite (1 fmly) (4 GF) Facilities FTV tea/coffee Dinner available Cen ht Wi-fi Parking 35 Notes LB ✕ RS 25-27 Dec No breakfast or room service No coaches

CRAYKE — Map 19 SE57

The Durham Ox

★★★★ 🅰 RESTAURANT WITH ROOMS

Westway YO61 4TE
☎ 01347 821506   ▤ 01347 823326
e-mail: enquiries@thedurhamox.com
dir: A19 to Easingwold. Through market place to Crayke, 1st left up hill

Rooms 1 en suite 4 annexe en suite (2 fmly) (2 GF) Facilities tea/coffee Dinner available Wi-fi Shooting, fishing, riding by arrangement Conf Max 18 Thtr 18 Board 18 Parking 35 Notes LB Closed 25 Dec No coaches

FLIXTON — Map 17 TA07

Orchard Lodge

★★★★ GUEST ACCOMMODATION

North St YO11 3UA
☎ 01723 890202   ▤ 01723 890202
e-mail: c.pummell@btinternet.com
web: www.orchard-lodge.com
dir: Off A1039 in village centre

Located six miles south of Scarborough, just off the main road, this establishment offers spacious and comfortable bedrooms. It is a good base for touring the coast, the North York Moors or the Wolds. Hearty breakfasts feature home-made preserves.

Rooms 6 en suite S fr £45; D fr £70* Facilities FTV tea/coffee Cen ht Parking 8 Notes LB ✕ No Children 3yrs Closed Jan-Feb

GIGGLESWICK — Map 18 SD86

Harts Head Inn

★★★★ 🅰 INN

Belle Hill BD24 0BA
☎ 01729 822086   & 07894 939495
e-mail: info@hartsheadinn.co.uk
web: www.hartsheadinn.co.uk
dir: On B6480, 1m from A65

Rooms 7 en suite 3 annexe en suite (1 fmly) S £45-£55; D £75-£95 Facilities STV FTV tea/coffee Dinner available Cen ht Wi-fi Golf 9 Snooker Pool table Conf Max 30 Class 30 Board 20 Parking 25 Notes LB

GOLDSBOROUGH — Map 19 SE35

PREMIER COLLECTION

Goldsborough Hall

★★★★★ ⬤ GUEST ACCOMMODATION

Church St HG5 8NR
☎ 01423 867321   ▤ 0845 638 3806
e-mail: accommodation@goldsboroughhall.com
dir: A1(M) junct 47, take A59 to Knaresborough. Take 2nd left onto Station Rd, at T-junct left onto Church St

It's not everyday that you get the chance to stay in the former residence of a Royal Princess, in this case HRH Princess Mary. Hospitality at Goldsborough Hall is second to none. Six luxury rooms have been refurbished to the highest standards, and the bathrooms offer a real "wow" factor. Bedrooms feature hand-made mahogany 8ft four-poster beds, Chesterfields and 50-inch televisions.

Rooms 6 en suite (3 fmly) S £125-£370; D £150-£395* Facilities FTV TVL tea/coffee Dinner available Direct Dial Cen ht Lift Licensed Wi-fi Outdoor Hot Tub Conf Max 150 Thtr 150 Class 50 Board 30 Parking 50 Notes LB ✕ Civ Wed 110

GRASSINGTON — Map 19 SE06

PREMIER COLLECTION

Ashfield House

★★★★★ 🏠 🍴 GUEST ACCOMMODATION

Summers Fold BD23 5AE
☎ 01756 752584 📠 07092 376562
e-mail: sales@ashfieldhouse.co.uk
web: www.ashfieldhouse.co.uk
dir: B6265 to village centre, main street, left onto Summers Fold

Guests are greeted like old friends at this beautifully maintained 17th-century house, peacefully tucked away a few yards from the village square. The smart lounges offer a high level of comfort and an honesty bar. The freshly prepared three-course dinner (by arrangement) is a highlight of any stay. The attractive bedrooms are well furnished and thoughtfully equipped.

Rooms 7 en suite 1 annexe en suite S £65-£110; D £95-£125* **Facilities** FTV tea/coffee Dinner available Cen ht Licensed Wi-fi **Conf** Max 8 Board 8 **Parking** 8 **Notes** LB ⊗ No Children 5yrs RS Nov-Mar No dinner on Sun & Wed eve

PREMIER COLLECTION

Grassington House

★★★★★ @@ 🍴 RESTAURANT WITH ROOMS

5 The Square BD23 5AQ
☎ 01756 752406 📠 01756 752050
e-mail: bookings@grassingtonhousehotel.co.uk
web: www.grassingtonhousehotel.co.uk
dir: A59 into Grassington, in town square opposite post office

Located in the square of the popular village of Grassington this beautiful converted Georgian house is personally run by owners John and Sue. Delicious food, individually designed bedrooms and warm hospitality ensure an enjoyable stay. There is a stylish lounge bar looking out to the square and the restaurant is split between two rooms; here guests will find the emphasis is on fresh, local ingredients and attentive, yet friendly service.

Rooms 9 en suite (2 fmly) S £70-£90; D £100-£145* **Facilities** STV FTV tea/coffee Dinner available Direct Dial Cen ht Wi-fi **Conf** Thtr 26 Class 20 Board 20 **Parking** 25 **Notes** LB ⊗

GREAT AYTON — Map 19 NZ51

Royal Oak

★★★ INN

123 High St TS9 6BW
☎ 01642 722361 & 723270 📠 01642 724047
e-mail: info@royaloak-hotel.co.uk
dir: Off the A173, on High Street

This 18th-century former coaching inn is very popular with locals and visitors to the village. Bedrooms are all comfortably equipped. The restaurant and public bar retain many original features and offer a good selection of fine ales; an extensive range of food is available all day and is served in the bar or the dining room.

Rooms 5 rms (4 en suite) S £30-£35; D £70* **Facilities** tea/coffee Dinner available Direct Dial Cen ht Wi-fi **Conf** Max 30 Thtr 30 Class 30 Board 30

GUISBOROUGH — Map 19 NZ61

The Kings Head at Newton

★★★★ GUEST ACCOMMODATION

The Green TS9 6QR
☎ 01642 722318 📠 01642 724750
e-mail: info@kingsheadhotel.co.uk
web: www.kingsheadhotel.co.uk
dir: A171 towards Guisborough, at rdbt onto A173 to Newton under Roseberry, under Roseberry Topping landmark

Converted from a row of traditional cottages, the friendly, family-owned Kings Head offers modern accommodation yet retains original features. The stylish bedrooms are thoughtfully equipped, and the adjacent restaurant offers a very good range of dishes.

Rooms 8 en suite (1 fmly) (2 GF) **Facilities** FTV TVL tea/coffee Direct Dial Cen ht Licensed Wi-fi Mountain biking **Parking** 100 **Notes** ⊗ Closed 25 Dec & 1 Jan

HACKNESS — Map 19 SE99

Troutsdale Lodge

★★★★ GUEST ACCOMMODATION

Troutsdale YO13 0BS
☎ 01723 882209
e-mail: captroutsdale@yahoo.co.uk
web: www.troutsdalelodge.com
dir: Off A170 at Snainton signed Troutsdale

Commanding magnificent views across a peaceful valley and the forest beyond, this Edwardian house showcases many original features combined with modern art. Bedrooms offer good all-round comforts and guests receive fine hospitality from the resident owners.

Rooms 4 en suite (1 fmly) (4 GF) **Facilities** TVL tea/coffee Dinner available Cen ht Licensed 🏌 **Parking** 8 **Notes** ⊗

See advert on page 344

HARROGATE — Map 19 SE35

Cold Cotes

★★★★★ 🅰 GUEST ACCOMMODATION

Cold Cotes Rd, Felliscliffe HG3 2LW
☎ 01423 770937
e-mail: info@coldcotes.com
web: www.coldcotes.com
dir: W of Harrogate. Off A59 after Black Bull, 3rd entrance on right

Rooms 3 en suite 3 annexe en suite (2 GF) S £60-£99; D £72-£99* **Facilities** FTV tea/coffee Dinner available Cen ht Licensed Wi-fi **Conf** Max 50 Thtr 30 Class 24 Board 14 **Parking** 20 **Notes** ⊗ No Children 12yrs

HARROGATE *continued*

Alexa House

★★★★ GUEST HOUSE

26 Ripon Rd HG1 2JJ
☎ 01423 501988
e-mail: enquiries@alexa-house.co.uk
web: www.alexa-house.co.uk
dir: *On A61, 0.25m from junct A59*

This popular establishment has stylish, well-equipped bedrooms split between the main house and cottage rooms. All rooms come with homely extras. The opulent day rooms include an elegant lounge with honesty bar, and a bright dining room. The hands-on proprietors ensure high levels of customer care.

Rooms 9 en suite 4 annexe en suite (2 fmly) (4 GF) S £47-£62; D £82-£94 **Facilities** tea/coffee Cen ht Licensed Wi-fi **Parking** 10 **Notes** Closed 23-26 Dec

The Grafton

★★★★ GUEST ACCOMMODATION

1-3 Franklin Mount HG1 5EJ
☎ 01423 508491   📠 01423 523168
e-mail: enquiries@graftonhotel.co.uk
web: www.graftonhotel.co.uk
dir: *Follow signs to International Centre, onto Kings Rd with Centre on left, Franklin Mount 450yds on right*

The delightful family-run Grafton is in a quiet location just a short walk from the conference centre and town. This smartly appointed period property provides stylish accommodation; bedrooms vary between modern and traditional. There is a beautifully appointed lounge looking out to the garden.

Rooms 14 en suite (1 fmly) (1 GF) S £55-£75; D £75-£130* **Facilities** FTV TVL tea/coffee Direct Dial Cen ht Licensed Wi-fi Golf 18 **Parking** 1 **Notes** LB ⊗ Closed 15 Dec-6 Jan

Shelbourne House

★★★★ GUEST ACCOMMODATION

78 Kings Rd HG1 5JX
☎ 01423 504390
e-mail: sue@shelbournehouse.co.uk
web: www.shelbournehouse.co.uk
dir: *Follow signs to International Centre, over lights by Holiday Inn, premises on right*

Situated opposite the conference centre and near to the town centre, this elegant Victorian house extends a warm welcome to all guests. Bedrooms are tastefully decorated and well equipped. There is a guests' lounge and an attractive breakfast room, where hearty breakfasts are served at the individual tables.

Rooms 8 en suite (2 fmly) S £40-£45; D £68-£90* **Facilities** TVL tea/coffee Cen ht Wi-fi **Conf** Board 16 **Parking** 1 **Notes** LB ⊗

Wynnstay House

★★★★ 🏠 GUEST ACCOMMODATION

60 Franklin Rd HG1 5EE
☎ 01423 560476
e-mail: wynnstayhouse@tiscali.co.uk
web: www.wynnstayhouse.com
dir: *Off A61 in town centre onto Kings Rd, right onto Strawberry Dale, left at top of road onto Franklin Rd*

Located in a residential area a short distance from the conference centre, shops and attractions, this friendly, family-run guest accommodation is ideal for business or leisure. There is a passion for ruined castles at Wynnstay House: the attractive, well-equipped bedrooms are each named after a spectacular fortress.

Rooms 5 en suite S £65-£90; D £80-£95* **Facilities** FTV tea/coffee Cen ht Wi-fi **Notes** LB ⊗ No Children 14yrs

April House

★★★★ GUEST ACCOMMODATION

3 Studley Rd HG1 5JU
☎ 01423 561879
e-mail: info@aprilhouse.com
dir: *Off A59/A61 onto Kings Rd signed Harrogate International Centre. Opposite Holiday Inn turn onto Alexandra Rd. Establishment at top of road on right*

Located in a quiet residential area just a short walk from the conference centre, this impeccable Victorian house retains many original features. The comfortable bedrooms come with an array of homely touches, and breakfast is served in an attractive dining room.

Rooms 5 rms (4 en suite) (1 pri facs) (1 fmly) S £40-£50; D £60-£80* **Facilities** FTV tea/coffee Wi-fi **Notes** LB ⊗

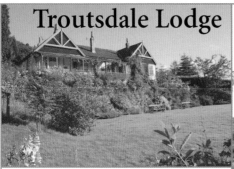

Troutsdale Lodge

This Edwardian Shooting Lodge provides luxurious ground floor accommodation with south facing veranda ensuring one of the best views in Yorkshire. Set within two acres of beautiful tiered English country gardens with its own private car park. Located overlooking a stunning hidden dale in the National Park. Easy access to Dalby Forest and heritage coastal towns of Scarborough and Whitby.

Hackness, Scarborough, North Yorkshire, YO13 0BS
Tel: 01723 882209
Email: clive@troutsdalelodge.fsnet.co.uk
Website: www.troutsdalelodge.com

The Arc - Boutique B&B

★★★★ GUEST ACCOMMODATION

68 Kings Rd HG1 5JR
☎ **01423 542571 & 07956 577303** 📠 **01423 740571**
e-mail: info@harrogatearc.co.uk
dir: *Opposite Holiday Inn on Kings Rd*

Situated directly opposite the Harrogate Conference Centre, the Arc offers contemporary accommodation and a friendly welcome. All bedrooms have been refurbished in a modern style. Wi-fi is available throughout. Bed and breakfast is available or a room-only rate if preferred.

Rooms 8 en suite (1 fmly) (1 GF) S £40-£65; D £55-£99 (room only)* **Facilities** FTV tea/coffee Cen ht Wi-fi **Parking** 4 **Notes** ⊗

Ashwood House

★★★★ GUEST ACCOMMODATION

7 Spring Grove HG1 2HS
☎ **01423 560081** 📠 **01423 527928**
e-mail: ashwoodhouse@aol.com
web: www.ashwoodhouse.co.uk
dir: *A61 Ripon Rd onto Springfield Av, 3rd left*

This delightfully decorated and furnished Edwardian house is situated in a quiet area of town. The spacious bedrooms are individually styled and thoughtfully equipped, and one has a four-poster bed. There is a cosy lounge and an elegant dining room where full English breakfasts are served.

Rooms 5 en suite (1 fmly) S £40-£50; D £70-£80* **Facilities** FTV TVL tea/coffee Cen ht Wi-fi **Parking** 3 **Notes** LB ⊗ No Children 7yrs Closed Xmas & New Year

Harrogate Brasserie with Rooms

★★★★ GUEST ACCOMMODATION

28-30 Cheltenham Pde HG1 1DB
☎ **01423 505041** 📠 **01423 722300**
e-mail: info@harrogatebrasserie.co.uk
web: www.harrogatebrasserie.co.uk
dir: *On A61 town centre behind theatre*

This town centre establishment is distinctly continental in style. The brasserie covers three cosy dining areas, richly decorated and adorned with artefacts. Live jazz is featured on Wednesday, Friday and Sunday nights. The individual bedrooms feature period collectibles; many rooms have DVD players and all have lots to read.

Rooms 15 en suite 1 annexe en suite (3 fmly) S £60-£75; D £80-£95* **Facilities** tea/coffee Dinner available Direct Dial Cen ht Licensed Wi-fi **Parking** 12 **Notes** LB

Ruskin

★★★★ GUEST ACCOMMODATION

1 Swan Rd HG1 2SS
☎ **01423 502045** 📠 **01423 506131**
e-mail: ruskin.hotel@virgin.net
dir: *Off A61 Ripon road, left opp The Majestic Hotel*

The mid 19th-century house stands in secluded tree-studded gardens, only a 5-minute walk from the town centre. It retains many original features and has a relaxing lounge. Breakfasts are served in the elegant dining room, and the thoughtfully equipped bedrooms range from compact to spacious, all furnished in stylish Victorian pine.

Rooms 7 en suite (2 fmly) (1 GF) **Facilities** tea/coffee Direct Dial Cen ht Licensed **Parking** 7

Shannon Court

★★★★ GUEST HOUSE

65 Dragon Av HG1 5DS
☎ **01423 509858** 📠 **01423 530606**
e-mail: info@shannoncourtguesthouse.co.uk
web: www.shannoncourtguesthouse.co.uk
dir: *Adjacent to A59, 1m S of junct with A61*

Shannon Court is situated within easy walking distance of the town and conference centre, and offers individually decorated, pleasantly furnished and thoughtfully equipped bedrooms. Friendly service complements an attractive breakfast room and memorable breakfasts.

Rooms 8 en suite (2 fmly) S £49-£60; D £59-£85* **Facilities** FTV tea/coffee Cen ht Wi-fi **Parking** 3 **Notes** LB ⊗

HAWNBY   Map 19 SE58

The Inn at Hawnby

★★★★★ ⓜ INN

YO62 5QS
☎ **01439 798202** 📠 **01439 798344**
e-mail: info@innathawnby.co.uk
web: www.innathawnby.co.uk
dir: *Off B1257 between Stokesley & Helmsley*

A charming 19th-century inn located in a peaceful village. Service is attentive and friendly, with guests able to relax and browse menus in the cosy bar where there is a good wine list and range of ales. Delicious, home-cooked meals are served in the restaurant, overlooking the gardens and surrounding countryside. Bedrooms are well equipped, with some in the converted stables.

Rooms 6 en suite 3 annexe en suite (1 fmly) (3 GF) S £75-£79; D £90-£99* **Facilities** FTV tea/coffee Dinner available Direct Dial Cen ht Wi-fi Fishing Riding **Conf** Max 20 Thtr 12 Class 20 **Parking** 9 **Notes** LB Closed 25 Dec RS Feb & Mar Restricted lunch service Mon & Tue

Laskill Grange

★★★★ GUEST ACCOMMODATION

YO62 5NB
☎ **01439 798268**
e-mail: laskillgrange@tiscali.co.uk
web: www.laskillgrange.co.uk
dir: *From York A19 to Thirsk, A170 to Helmsley then B1257 N, after 6m sign on left to Laskill Grange*

Lovers of the countryside will enjoy this charming 19th-century farmhouse. Guests can take a walk in the surrounds, fish the River Seph, which runs through the grounds, or visit nearby Rievaulx Abbey. The comfortable, well furnished bedrooms are in the main house and are supplied with many thoughtful extras.

Rooms 3 rms (2 en suite) (1 pri facs) (3 GF) S £40-£50; D £80-£90* **Facilities** FTV TVL tea/coffee Dinner available Cen ht Licensed Wi-fi Fishing Riding Outdoor activity area Hot tubs **Conf** Max 20 **Parking** 20 **Notes** LB Civ Wed 60

HELMSLEY   Map 19 SE68

See also Hawnby

PREMIER COLLECTION

Shallowdale House

★★★★★ 🍴 GUEST ACCOMMODATION

West End YO62 4DY
☎ **01439 788325** 📠 **01439 788885**
e-mail: stay@shallowdalehouse.co.uk
web: www.shallowdalehouse.co.uk

(For full entry see Ampleforth)

Plumpton Court

★★★★ GUEST ACCOMMODATION

High St, Nawton YO62 7TT
☎ **01439 771223**
e-mail: mail@plumptoncourt.com
web: www.plumptoncourt.com
dir: *2.5m E of Helmsley. Off A170 in Nawton, signed*

Located in the village of Nawton, in the foothills of the North Yorkshire Moors, this characteristic 17th-century, stone-built house offers a warm welcome. The cosy lounge bar has an open fire. Bedrooms are comfortable, modern and well equipped, one with a four-poster bed.

Rooms 6 en suite (1 GF) S £50-£70; D £68-£72* **Facilities** FTV tea/coffee Cen ht Licensed Wi-fi Golf 18 **Parking** 8 **Notes** ⊗ No Children 12yrs Closed 22-29 Dec

HELMSLEY *continued*

The Carlton Lodge

★★★★ 🅰 GUEST HOUSE

Bondgate YO62 5EY
☎ 01439 770557
e-mail: enquiries@carlton-lodge.com
dir: *400yds E of Market Sq on A170*
Rooms 8 rms (7 en suite) (1 pri facs) (1 fmly) (2 GF) S
£50-£60; D £85-£95* **Facilities** FTV tea/coffee Cen ht
Licensed Wi-fi **Parking** 10 **Notes** LB

HETTON   Map 18 SD95

PREMIER COLLECTION

The Angel Inn

★★★★★ ◉◉ RESTAURANT WITH ROOMS

BD23 6LT
☎ 01756 730263 🖨 01756 730363
e-mail: info@angelhetton.co.uk
dir: *B6265 from Skipton towards Grassington. At
Rylstone turn left by pond, follow signs to Hetton*

This roadside inn is steeped in history; parts of the
building go back over 500 years. The restaurant and
bar are in the main building which has ivy and green
canopies at the front. The large and stylish bedrooms
are across the road in a converted barn which has
great views of the Dales, its own wine cave and private
parking.

Rooms 9 en suite (3 GF) D £140-£190* **Facilities** FTV
tea/coffee Dinner available Direct Dial Cen ht Wi-fi
Wine tasting cave **Conf** Max 16 Board 14 **Parking** 40
Notes LB Closed 25 Dec & 1wk Jan No coaches Civ Wed
40

HUBY   Map 19 SE56

The New Inn Motel

★★★ GUEST ACCOMMODATION

Main St YO61 1HQ
☎ 01347 810219 🖨 01347 810219
e-mail: enquiries@newinnmotel.freeserve.co.uk
web: www.newinnmotel.co.uk
dir: *Off A19 E into village centre, motel on left*

Located behind the New Inn, this modern motel-style
accommodation has a quiet location in the village of
Huby, nine miles north of York. Comfortable bedrooms are
spacious and neatly furnished, and breakfast is served in
the cosy dining room. The reception area hosts an array of
tourist information and the resident owners provide a
friendly and helpful service.

Rooms 8 en suite (3 fmly) (8 GF) S £40-£50; D £70-£80*
Facilities FTV tea/coffee Cen ht **Parking** 8 **Notes** LB
Closed mid Nov-mid Dec & part Feb

HUNTON   Map 19 SE19

The Countryman's Inn

★★★ INN

Bedale DL8 1PY
☎ 01677 450554
e-mail: tony@countrymansinn.co.uk
dir: *Between Bedale & Leyburn, 2m N of A684*

Set in the heart of this quiet village, the inn is popular
with visitors and locals and serves good home-made
food. The resident owner and staff provide warm
hospitality, and the bedrooms are smartly furnished and
comfortably equipped.

Rooms 3 en suite **Facilities** FTV TVL tea/coffee Dinner
available Cen ht Wi-fi **Parking** 11 **Notes** RS Mon-Tue
Restaurant closed

INGLETON   Map 18 SD67

Gale Green Cottage

★★★★ BED AND BREAKFAST

Westhouse LA6 3NJ
☎ 015242 41245 & 077867 82088
e-mail: jill@galegreen.com
dir: *2m NW of Ingleton. S of A65 at Masongill x-rds*

Peacefully located in a rural hamlet, this 300-year-old
house has been lovingly renovated to provide modern
facilities without compromising original charm and
character. Thoughtfully furnished bedrooms feature
smart modern en suite shower rooms, and a guest lounge
is also available.

Rooms 3 en suite (1 fmly) S £35-£39; D £58-£64*
Facilities FTV TVL tea/coffee Cen ht **Parking** 6
Notes Closed Xmas & New Year 🐾

KIRKBY FLEETHAM   Map 19 SE29

PREMIER COLLECTION

The Black Horse

★★★★★ ◉◉ RESTAURANT WITH ROOMS

Lumley Ln DL7 0SH
☎ 01609 749010 & 749011 🖨 01423 507836
e-mail: gm@blackhorsekirkbyfleetham.com
web: www.blackhorsekirkbyfleetham.com
dir: *A1 onto A684 then Ham Hall Ln. On Lumley Ln, on
left past Post Office*

Set in a small village, the Black Horse provides
everything needed for a getaway break including
award-winning food. The spacious bedrooms, named
after famous racehorses, are beautifully designed in
New England/French style with pastel colours, co-
ordinating fabrics and excellent beds; many of the
superb bathrooms feature slipper or roll-top baths.
There is a large dining room and bar that attracts
locals as well as visitors from further afield.

Rooms 7 en suite (1 fmly) (2 GF) S £40-£70; D
£50-£120 **Facilities** FTV tea/coffee Dinner available
Cen ht Wi-fi ch fac Golf 18 Fishing quoits pitch
Conf Max 40 Thtr 40 Class 30 Board 24 **Parking** 90
Notes LB

KNARESBOROUGH   Map 19 SE35

PREMIER COLLECTION

General Tarleton Inn

★★★★★ ◉◉ RESTAURANT WITH ROOMS

Boroughbridge Rd, Ferrensby HG5 0PZ
☎ **01423 340284** 🖷 **01423 340288**
e-mail: gti@generaltarleton.co.uk
dir: A1(M) junct 48 at Boroughbridge, take A6055 to
Knaresborough. 4m on right

Food is a real feature here with skilfully prepared meals
served in the restaurant, traditional bar and modern
conservatory. Accommodation is provided in brightly
decorated and airy rooms, and the bathrooms are
thoughtfully equipped. Enjoying a country location, yet
close to the A1(M), the General Tarleton remains
popular with both business and leisure guests.

Rooms 14 en suite (7 GF) S £75–£107; D £129–£150*
Facilities tea/coffee Dinner available Direct Dial
Cen ht Wi-fi **Conf** Max 40 Thtr 40 Class 35 Board 20
Parking 40 **Notes** LB ⊗ Closed 24-26 Dec, 1 Jan No
coaches Civ Wed 50

LEEMING BAR   Map 19 SE57

Little Holtby

★★★★ 🅰 BED AND BREAKFAST

DL7 9LH
☎ **01609 748762**
e-mail: littleholtby@yahoo.co.uk
dir: 2m N of A684 (junct with A1)

Rooms 3 en suite £40-£45; D £75-£80 **Facilities** FTV
TVL tea/coffee Cen ht Wi-fi Golf 18 **Parking** 6 **Notes** LB ⊗
No Children 12yrs ⊛

LEVISHAM   Map 19 SE89

The Horseshoe Inn

★★★★ INN

Main St YO18 7NL
☎ **01751 460240** 🖷 **01751 460052**
e-mail: info@horseshoelevisham.co.uk
dir: From Pickering on A169, after 4m past Fox & Rabbit
Inn on right. 0.5m left to Lockton, then steep winding
road to village

A charming 19th-century inn with a peaceful location in
Levisham village. The spacious bar and dining area are
traditionally furnished and food is a highlight with a wide
choice and generous portions. The attractive bedrooms
include two garden rooms, and most rooms in the main
house have lovely views of the village.

Rooms 9 en suite (3 fmly) (3 GF) S £45; D £70-£90
Facilities tea/coffee Dinner available Cen ht Wi-fi
Parking 30 **Notes** LB No coaches

LEYBURN   Map 19 SE19

PREMIER COLLECTION

Capple Bank Farm

★★★★★ BED AND BREAKFAST

West Witton DL8 4ND
☎ **01969 625825** & **07836 645238**
e-mail: julian.smithers@btinternet.com
dir: A1 to Bedale. Turn off onto A684 to Leyburn.
Continue towards Hawes through Wensley, take 1st left
in West Witton. Up hill, round left bend, gates straight
ahead

Ideal for walking and touring in the Yorkshire Dales
National Park, this spacious house has been recently
converted and refurbished. Guests have use of a lovely
lounge with a real fire lit on cooler days, and breakfast
is served at a beautiful table in the open-plan kitchen
and dining room.

Rooms 2 en suite £60; D £90* **Facilities** STV FTV tea/
coffee Cen ht **Parking** 6 **Notes** ⊗ No Children 10yrs ⊛

PREMIER COLLECTION

Thorney Hall

★★★★★ BED AND BREAKFAST

Spennithorne DL8 5PW
☎ **01969 622120** & **07836 269453**
e-mail: nesbit1954@btinternet.com

This beautiful, lovingly restored country house offers
period features, open fireplaces and elegant
furnishings. Bedrooms are well appointed and each
has either a modern en suite or private bathroom.
Guests receive a warm welcome and have use of an
attractive lounge. Well-cooked evening meals and
hearty breakfasts are served at a traditional table in
the grand dining room.

Rooms 3 rms (2 en suite) (1 pri facs) S £76-£110; D
£76-£110 **Facilities** tea/coffee Dinner available Cen ht
⬚ ⬚ Golf **Parking** 10 **Notes** ⊗ No Children 12yrs ⊛

The Queens Head

★★★★ ⬚ INN

Westmoor Ln, Finghall DL8 5ND
☎ **01677 450259**
e-mail: enquiries@queensfinghall.co.uk
web: www.queensfinghall.co.uk
dir: From Bedale follow A684 W towards Leyburn, just
after pub & caravan park turn left signed to Finghall.
Follow road, on left

Located in the quiet village of Finghall this country inn
dates back to the 18th century, with original oak beams.
A wide choice of freshly prepared meals are served in
either the bar or more contemporary restaurant, which
has lovely views of the surrounding countryside.
Bedrooms are spacious and located in an adjacent
annexe.

Rooms 3 annexe en suite (1 fmly) (3 GF) D £60-£90*
Facilities FTV TVL tea/coffee Dinner available Cen ht Pool
table **Parking** 40 **Notes** LB

LOW ROW   Map 18 SD99

The Punch Bowl Inn

★★★★ ⬚ ⬚ INN

DL11 6PF
☎ **01748 886233** 🖷 **01748 886945**
e-mail: info@pbinn.co.uk
dir: From Scotch Corner take A6108 to Richmond then
B6270 to Low Row

This friendly inn has now been refurbished in a
contemporary style. Real ales and freshly-cooked meals
are served in either the spacious bar or dining room. The
modern bedrooms are stylish yet simply furnished, with
well-equipped bathrooms. Guests also have use of a
lounge which has stunning views of the Dales.

Rooms 9 en suite 2 annexe en suite (1 GF) D £92-£123*
Facilities FTV tea/coffee Dinner available Direct Dial
Cen ht Wi-fi Fishing Riding **Parking** 20 **Notes** LB ⊗
Closed 25 Dec

MALHAM — Map 18 SD96

The Lister Arms

★★★★ INN

BD23 4DB
☎ 01729 830330
e-mail: relax@listerarms.co.uk
dir: From A59 into Malham, right in centre of village

Located in Malham in the Yorkshire Dales National Park, the Lister Arms is a traditional country inn with wood beams and open fires, close to a village green and a babbling stream. The accommodation is comfortable and well equipped, and a wide selection of imaginative dishes together with real ales and fine wines are served in the busy bar and restaurant, where the atmosphere is relaxed and comfortable.

Rooms 9 en suite (1 fmly) S £65-£100; D £90-£120*
Facilities FTV tea/coffee Dinner available Cen ht Wi-fi
Parking 20 Notes LB No coaches

River House

★★★★ 🏠 🍴 GUEST HOUSE

BD23 4DA
☎ 01729 830315
e-mail: info@riverhousehotel.co.uk
web: www.riverhousehotel.co.uk
dir: Off A65, N to Malham

A warm welcome awaits you at this attractive house, which dates from 1664. The bedrooms are bright and comfortable, with one on the ground floor. Public areas include a cosy lounge and a large, well-appointed dining room. Breakfasts and evening meals offer choice and quality above expectation.

Rooms 8 en suite (1 GF) S £45-£75; D £70-£80*
Facilities FTV tea/coffee Dinner available Cen ht Licensed
Wi-fi Fishing Parking 5 Notes LB No Children 9yrs

Beck Hall

★★★ GUEST HOUSE

Cove Rd BD23 4DJ
☎ 01729 830332
e-mail: alice@beckhallmalham.com
web: www.beckhallmalham.com
dir: A65 to Gargrave, turn right to Malham. Beck Hall 100yds on right after mini rdbt

A small stone bridge over Malham Beck leads to this delightful property. Dating from 1710, the house has true character, with bedrooms carefully furnished with four-poster beds. Delicious afternoon teas are available in the colourful garden in warmer months, while roaring log fires welcome you in the winter.

Rooms 11 en suite 7 annexe en suite (4 fmly) (4 GF) S £25-£65; D £50-£90 Facilities STV tea/coffee Dinner available Cen ht Licensed Wi-fi Fishing Conf Max 35 Thtr 30 Class 30 Board 30 Parking 40 Notes LB

MASHAM — Map 19 SE28

Bank Villa

★★★★ 🏠 🍴 GUEST HOUSE

HG4 4DB
☎ 01765 689605
e-mail: stay@bankvilla.com
web: www.bankvilla.com
dir: Enter on A6108 from Ripon, property on right

An elegant Georgian house set in a pretty walled garden. Individually decorated bedrooms feature stripped pine, period furniture and crisp, white linen. Imaginative home-cooked meals are served in the attractive dining room. Character public rooms include a choice of lounges, or you can relax in the garden in summer.

Rooms 6 rms (4 en suite) (2 pri facs) (2 fmly)
Facilities FTV TVL TV2B tea/coffee Dinner available
Cen ht Licensed Wi-fi Conf Max 12 Thtr 12 Class 12 Board
12 Parking 6 Notes LB No Children 5yrs

MIDDLESBROUGH — Map 19 NZ41

The Grey House

★★★★ GUEST ACCOMMODATION

79 Cambridge Rd, Linthorpe TS5 5NL
☎ 01642 817485 📠 01642 817485
e-mail: denistaylor-100@btinternet.com
web: www.greyhousehotel.co.uk
dir: A19 N onto A1130 & A1032 Acklam Rd, right at lights

This Edwardian mansion stands in mature gardens in a quiet residential area, and is lovingly maintained to provide a relaxing retreat. The master bedrooms are well sized, and the upper rooms, though smaller, also offer good comfort. Downstairs there is an attractive lounge and the breakfast room.

Rooms 9 en suite (1 fmly) Facilities FTV TVL tea/coffee
Direct Dial Cen ht Wi-fi Parking 10

MOULTON — Map 19 NZ20

The Black Bull

[U]

DL10 6QJ
☎ 01325 377289
e-mail: info@blackbullmoulton.com
web: www.blackbullmoulton.com
dir: At Scotch Corner join A1 Sbound, after 1m take exit signed Moulton, in centre of village

Currently the rating for this establishment is not confirmed. This may be due to a change of ownership or because it has only recently joined the AA rating scheme.

Rooms 9 en suite (1 fmly) S £40-£70; D £50-£120*
Facilities FTV tea/coffee Dinner available Direct Dial
Cen ht Licensed Wi-fi Parking 65 Notes LB

MUKER — Map 18 SD99

Oxnop Hall (SD931973)

★★★★ FARMHOUSE

Low Oxnop, Gunnerside DL11 6JJ
☎ 01748 886253 📠 01748 886253
Mrs A Porter
dir: Off B6270 between Muker & Gunnerside

Set in beautiful Swaledale scenery, this smartly presented 17th-century farmhouse has been furnished with thought and care. The attractive bedrooms are well equipped and some boast original exposed beams and mullion windows. Hearty farmhouse breakfasts are served, using local and home-made produce where possible. A cosy lounge is also available.

Rooms 4 en suite 1 annexe en suite (1 GF) Facilities FTV tea/coffee Cen ht Parking 10 Notes ⊗ No Children 10yrs Closed Nov-Mar ☻ 1300 acres beef/sheep/hill farming

NORTHALLERTON — Map 19 SE39

Windsor Guest House

★★★★ GUEST HOUSE

56 South Pde DL7 8SL
☎ 01609 774100 📠 01609 774100
e-mail: windsorguesthouse@yahoo.co.uk
dir: On A684 at S end of High St

This Victorian terrace house is convenient for the town centre. The well maintained accommodation consists of bright, cheerful and thoughtfully equipped bedrooms. The attractive dining room looks out to the back garden and is a pleasant venue for tasty breakfasts served by the friendly proprietors.

Rooms 6 rms (5 en suite) (1 pri facs) (1 fmly) S £40; D £60-£75* Facilities FTV tea/coffee Cen ht Wi-fi Parking 1 Notes ⊗ No Children 1.5yrs

OLDSTEAD　　Map 19 SE57

PREMIER COLLECTION

The Black Swan at Oldstead

★★★★★ ◉◉◉ 🏠 RESTAURANT WITH ROOMS

YO61 4BL

☎ 01347 868387

e-mail: enquiries@blackswanoldstead.co.uk

dir: *Exit A19, 3m S Thirsk for Coxwold, left in Coxwold, left at Byland Abbey for Oldstead*

The Black Swan is set amidst the stunning scenery of the North Yorkshire National Park, and parts of the building date back to the 16th century. Well appointed, very comfortable bedrooms and bathrooms provide the perfect get-away-from-it-all. Open fires, a traditional bar and a restaurant, serving award-winning food, is the icing on the cake for this little gem of a property.

Rooms 4 en suite (4 GF) D £190-£310* (incl.dinner) **Facilities** FTV tea/coffee Dinner available Cen ht Wi-fi **Parking** 24 **Notes** LB ⊗ No Children 10yrs Closed 2wks Jan No coaches

PATELEY BRIDGE　　Map 19 SE16

Roslyn House

★★★★ GUEST ACCOMMODATION

9 King St HG3 5AT

☎ 01423 711374　🖨 01423 715995

e-mail: enquiries@roslynhouse.co.uk

web: www.roslynhouse.co.uk

dir: *B6165 into Pateley Bridge, end of High St turn right at newsagents onto King Street, house 200yds on left*

You are assured of a very warm welcome at this well-maintained guest accommodation in the village centre. Bedrooms are sensibly furnished and offer many homely touches. A very comfortable lounge is available, and hearty breakfasts set you up for the day. Roslyn House caters well for cyclists and walkers on the famous Nidderdale Way.

Rooms 6 en suite (1 fmly) S £49-£55; D £69-£74* **Facilities** STV TVL tea/coffee Cen ht Wi-fi **Conf** Max 8 Board 8 **Parking** 6 **Notes** LB ⊗ No Children 3yrs

PICKERING　　Map 19 SE78

PREMIER COLLECTION

17 Burgate

★★★★★ 🏠 GUEST ACCOMMODATION

17 Burgate YO18 7AU

☎ 01751 473463

e-mail: info@17burgate.co.uk

dir: *From A170 follow sign to Castle. 17 Burgate on right*

An elegant market town house close to the centre and the castle, offering comfortable individually designed bedrooms with all modern facilities, including free broadband. Public areas include a comfortable lounge bar, and breakfast includes a wide choice of local, healthy foods.

Rooms 5 en suite S £70-£110; D £83-£120* **Facilities** FTV tea/coffee Cen ht Licensed Wi-fi **Parking** 7 **Notes** LB No Children 10yrs Closed Xmas

PICKHILL　　Map 19 SE38

Nags Head Country Inn

★★★★ ◉◉ INN

YO7 4JG

☎ 01845 567391　🖨 01845 567212

e-mail: reservations@nagsheadpickhill.co.uk

dir: *2m E of A1*

This country inn, situated in the centre of the attractive village, is only a mile from the A1, and 9 miles northwest of Thirsk. It is renowned for the excellence of its food and traditional real ales, complemented by the atmosphere and character of its cosy bars. Some bedrooms are in a cottage next door, and they all have en suite bathrooms and are very well equipped with TV, clock radios, telephones and tea and coffee making facilities. The smartly appointed restaurant and cocktail bar is open to both residents and non-residents for dinner.

Rooms 7 en suite 7 annexe en suite (3 GF) S £60-£77.50; D £80-£97* **Facilities** FTV TVL tea/coffee Dinner available Direct Dial Cen ht Wi-fi ⛳ Golf 18 **Conf** Thtr 30 Class 18 Board 16 **Parking** 40 **Notes** LB ⊗ Closed 25 Dec

RAVENSCAR　　Map 19 NZ90

Smugglers Rock Country House

★★★★ 🅰 GUEST HOUSE

YO13 0ER

☎ 01723 870044

e-mail: info@smugglersrock.co.uk

dir: *0.5m S of Ravenscar. Off A171 towards Ravenscar, opp stone windmill*

Rooms 8 en suite (3 fmly) S £39-£47; D £68-£84* **Facilities** FTV TVL tea/coffee Cen ht Wi-fi **Parking** 12 **Notes** LB ⊗ Closed Nov-Mar RS end Mar-early Oct

REETH　　Map 19 SE09

Charles Bathurst Inn

★★★★ 🍽 INN

Arkengarthdale DL11 6EN

☎ 01748 884567　🖨 01748 884599

e-mail: info@cbinn.co.uk

dir: *B6270 to Reeth, at Buck Hotel turn N to Langthwaite, pass church on right, inn 0.5m on right*

The CB Inn, as it is known, is surrounded by magnificent scenery high in the Dales. Food is the focus of the pub, where a choice of rustic eating areas makes for atmospheric dining. The well-equipped bedrooms blend contemporary and traditional styles, and cosy lounge areas are available. A well-equipped function suite is also available.

Rooms 19 en suite (2 fmly) (5 GF) D £92-£123* **Facilities** FTV tea/coffee Dinner available Direct Dial Cen ht Wi-fi Fishing Riding Pool table **Conf** Max 70 Thtr 70 Class 30 Board 30 **Parking** 35 **Notes** LB ⊗ Closed 25 Dec

RICCALL　　Map 16 SE63

The Park View

★★★★ GUEST ACCOMMODATION

20 Main St YO19 6PX

☎ 01757 248458　🖨 01757 249211

e-mail: mail@parkviewriccall.co.uk

web: www.parkviewriccall.co.uk

dir: *A19 from Selby, left for Riccall by water tower, 100yds on right*

The well-furnished and comfortable Park View stands in grounds and offers well-equipped bedrooms. There is a cosy lounge plus a small bar, while breakfasts are served in the dining room. Dinner is available midweek.

Rooms 7 en suite (1 fmly) S fr £52; D fr £74* **Facilities** FTV TVL tea/coffee Dinner available Cen ht Licensed Wi-fi **Parking** 10

RICCALL *continued*

White Rose Villa

★★★★ 🄰 BED AND BREAKFAST

33 York Rd YO19 6QG
☎ 01757 248115
e-mail: whiterosevilla@btinternet.com
web: www.whiterosevilla.info
dir: *S of York, from A19, signed Riccall, 50mtrs on right*

Rooms 3 en suite (2 fmly) S £35-£40; D £65
Facilities FTV TVL tea/coffee Cen ht Wi-fi Parking 4
Notes LB ⊗ Closed 24-26 & 31 Dec 🍽

RICHMOND   Map 19 NZ10

See also Reeth

Rosedale Guest House

★★★★ 🏠 GUEST HOUSE

2 Pottergate DL10 4AB
☎ 01748 823926
e-mail: gary53uk@hotmail.com
dir: *A1(M), A6108 into Richmond onto Pottergate, 0.5m before town centre*

A short stroll away from the small town of Richmond, this attractive Grade II listed building has been tastefully decorated throughout. Warm hospitality features alongside stylishly furnished and comfortably equipped bedrooms. The public rooms include a dining area and a private lounge offering free Wi-fi.

Rooms 4 en suite (1 fmly) D £78-£88 Facilities FTV TVL tea/coffee Cen ht Wi-fi Notes LB ⊗ No Children 5yrs

---

Whashton Springs Farm (NZ149046)

★★★★ 🏠 FARMHOUSE

DL11 7JS
☎ 01748 822884   📠 01748 826285
Mrs J M Turnbull
e-mail: whashtonsprings@btconnect.com
dir: *In Richmond N at lights towards Ravensworth, 3m down steep hill, farm at bottom on left*

A friendly welcome awaits at this farmhouse accommodation, situated in the heart of the countryside yet convenient for major routes. Bedrooms are split between the courtyard rooms and the main farmhouse. Hearty breakfasts are served in the spacious dining room overlooking the gardens. A stylish lounge is also available.

Rooms 3 en suite 5 annexe en suite (2 fmly) (5 GF) Facilities FTV tea/coffee Cen ht Wi-fi Conf Max 16 Board 16 Parking 10 Notes ⊗ No Children 3yrs Closed late Dec-Jan ⊚ 600 acres arable/beef/mixed/sheep

---

RIPON   Map 19 SE37

PREMIER COLLECTION

Mallard Grange (SE270704)

★★★★★ 🏠 FARMHOUSE

Aldfield HG4 3BE
☎ 01765 620242   📠 01765 620242
Mrs M Johnson
e-mail: maggie@mallardgrange.co.uk
web: www.mallardgrange.co.uk
dir: *B6265 W fom Ripon, Mallard Grange 2.5m on right*

Located near Fountains Abbey a genuine welcome is always guaranteed at Mallard Grange. The original features of this early 16th-century, Grade II listed farmhouse are highlighted by quality furnishings and decor. Bedrooms, two of which are in a converted smithy, are filled with a wealth of thoughtful extras, and comprehensive breakfasts feature home-reared and local produce.

Rooms 2 en suite 2 annexe en suite (2 GF) S £65-£90; D £75-£99 Facilities FTV tea/coffee Cen ht Wi-fi Parking 6 Notes LB ⊗ No Children 12yrs Closed Xmas & New Year 500 acres mixed/beef/sheep/arable

---

The Old Coach House

★★★★★ 🄰 GUEST ACCOMMODATION

2 Stable Cottages, North Stanley HG4 3HT
☎ 01765 634900   📠 01765 635352
e-mail: enquiries@oldcoachhouse.info
web: www.oldcoachhouse.info
dir: *From Ripon take A6108 to Masham. Once in North Stainley, on left opposite Staveley Arms*

Rooms 8 en suite (4 GF) Facilities FTV tea/coffee Direct Dial Cen ht Wi-fi Parking 8 Notes ⊗ No Children 14yrs Closed Jan

---

Bay Tree Farm (SE263685)

★★★★ 🏠 FARMHOUSE

Aldfield HG4 3BE
☎ 01765 620394   📠 01765 620394
Mrs V Leeming
e-mail: val@btfarm.entadsl.com
web: www.baytreefarm.co.uk
dir: *4m W of Ripon. S off B6265 in village of Aldfield*

A warm welcome awaits at this farmhouse set in the countryside close to Fountains Abbey and Studley Park. Bedrooms are suitably equipped, there is a cosy lounge with a log-burning stove, and breakfast is traditional home-cooked fare. Dinner is available for groups of eight or more by arrangement.

Rooms 4 en suite 2 annexe en suite (1 fmly) (3 GF) S £50-£70; D £80-£100 Facilities FTV tea/coffee Dinner available Cen ht Wi-fi Parking 10 Notes LB 400 acres beef/arable

---

The George at Wath

★★★★ INN

Main St, Wath HG4 5EN
☎ 01765 641324
e-mail: richard@thegeorgeatwath.co.uk
web: www.thegeorgeatwath.co.uk
dir: *From A1 (dual carriageway) N'bound turn left signed Melmerby & Wath. From A 1 S'bound exit at slip road signed A61. At T-junct right (signed Ripon). Approx 0.5m turn right for Melmerby & Wath*

Located in the centre of the beautiful North Yorkshire village of Wath, this popular village inn provides well-equipped and pleasantly decorated accommodation. The public areas include a spacious lounge bar complete with log burning stove and a relaxed dining area where a varied selection of dishes are available. Wi-fi connection available throughout.

Rooms 5 en suite (1 fmly) S £60-£65; D £75-£120* Facilities FTV tea/coffee Dinner available Cen ht Wi-fi Pool table Conf Max 45 Thtr 45 Class 32 Board 16 Parking 25 Notes Civ Wed 70

The Royal Oak

★★★★ ⊛ INN

36 Kirkgate HG4 1PB

☎ 01765 602284

e-mail: info@royaloakripon.co.uk

dir: *In town centre*

Ideally located in the heart of the city centre close to the cathedral and museum. The Royal Oak offers modern, stylish, and comfortable en suite rooms with a genuine warm welcome on arrival. The inn has a restaurant and separate bar area which organises food and wine tasting events on a regular basis. The menu boasts a varied range of traditional dishes with a European influence in the attractively designed restaurant. A good selection of Timothy Taylor ales can be found along with a varied selection of wines.

Rooms 6 en suite (1 fmly) S £65-£90; D £80-£90*
Facilities FTV tea/coffee Dinner available Cen ht Wi-fi
Parking 4 **Notes** ⊗ No coaches

St George's Court (SE237697)

★★★★ 🏠 FARMHOUSE

Old Home Farm, Grantley HG4 3PJ

☎ 01765 620618

Mrs Hitchen

e-mail: info@stgeorgescourt.co.uk

web: www.stgeorges-court.co.uk

dir: *B6265 W from Ripon, up hill 1m past Risplith sign & next right, 1m on right*

This renovated farmhouse is a great location to get away from it all, in the delightful countryside close to Fountains Abbey. The attractive, well-equipped, upgraded ground-floor bedrooms are located around a central courtyard. Imaginative breakfasts are served in the new breakfast room, and a guest lounge is now available, both with views of the surrounding countryside.

Rooms 5 en suite (1 fmly) (5 GF) **Facilities** tea/coffee Cen ht Wi-fi Fishing **Conf** Max 12 **Parking** 12 **Notes** 20 acres beef /sheep/pigs

---

SCARBOROUGH　　Map 17 TA08

Columbus

★★★★ GUEST ACCOMMODATION

124 Columbus Ravine YO12 7QZ

☎ 01723 374634　& 07930 545964

e-mail: hotel.columbus@lineone.net

dir: *On A165 towards North Bay, near Peasholm Park*

Yorkshire hospitality at its best is offered here, and Bonnie Purchon is a welcoming hostess. The establishment is well located for the beach and attractions. Bedrooms are compact, well equipped and homely. A very comfortable lounge is provided. In the dining room a good breakfast is served, as are evening meals during the main season.

Rooms 10 en suite (2 fmly) S £39.50; D £79-£82*
Facilities tea/coffee Dinner available Cen ht Licensed Wi-fi **Parking** 8 **Notes** LB ⊗ No Children 3yrs

The Danielle

★★★★ GUEST ACCOMMODATION

9 Esplanade Rd, South Cliff YO11 2AS

☎ 01723 366206

e-mail: hoteldanielle@yahoo.co.uk

dir: *S of town centre. Off A165 Filey Rd onto Victoria Av, left onto Esplanade, left onto Esplanade Rd*

A warm welcome is assured at this elegant Victorian house situated a short walk from the Spa Cliff Lift. Bedrooms are equipped with thoughtful extras, and day rooms include an attractive dining room and a lounge.

Rooms 9 rms (7 en suite) (2 pri facs) (1 fmly) S £29-£30; D £62-£65* **Facilities** TVL tea/coffee Cen ht Licensed **Notes** LB ⊗ No Children 2yrs Closed Dec-mid Feb

---

The Hillcrest

★★★★ GUEST ACCOMMODATION

2 Peasholm Av YO12 7NE

☎ 01723 361981

e-mail: enquiries@hillcresthotel.co.uk

dir: *A165 to North Bay/leisure parks, onto Peasholm Dr & Peasholm Crescent*

Hillcrest is in a residential area close to Peasholm Park, within walking distance of the cricket ground and the North Bay attractions, and its individually furnished bedrooms contain many extras. There is a dining room where breakfast and dinner are served.

Rooms 7 en suite (1 fmly) S £28-£35; D £56-£70*
Facilities FTV tea/coffee Dinner available Cen ht Licensed Wi-fi **Parking** 2 **Notes** LB ⊗ No Children 3yrs Closed Dec-1 Feb

The Moorings

★★★★ GUEST ACCOMMODATION

3 Burniston Rd YO12 6PG

☎ 01723 373786

e-mail: post@scarboroughmoorings.co.uk

dir: *300mtrs from North Bay Beach, next to the Peasholm Park entrance*

Located in a quiet area close to the North Bay, this large detached house offers a friendly welcome, spacious dining room and private parking. There are a variety of bedroom styles including family rooms, a wheelchair accessible annexe room and several with separate lounges.

Rooms 11 en suite 1 annexe en suite (2 fmly) (1 GF) S £35-£38; D £66-£84* **Facilities** FTV TVL tea/coffee Dinner available Cen ht Wi-fi **Parking** 12 **Notes** LB ⊗ Closed 2wks Xmas RS Nov-Feb annexe closed

SCARBOROUGH *continued*

Olivers

★★★★ GUEST ACCOMMODATION

34 West St YO11 2QP
☎ 01723 368717
e-mail: info@olivershotelscarborough.co.uk
dir: *Take A64 to B1427 (Margarets Rd). Right onto A165 (Filey Rd). Take 2nd left onto Granville Rd*

Well-equipped, spacious bedrooms are a feature of this old Victorian gentleman's residence, and one bedroom was originally the nursery. Close to the cliff lift down to the spa, beaches and gardens, and centrally located on the South Cliff.

Rooms 6 en suite (2 fmly) (1 GF) D £56-£62
Facilities FTV tea/coffee Dinner available Cen ht
Notes LB ⊗ Closed 20-28 Dec

Paragon

★★★★ GUEST ACCOMMODATION

123 Queens Pde YO12 7HU
☎ 01723 372676 📠 01723 372676
web: www.paragonhotel.com
dir: *On A64, follow signs for North Bay. Establishment on clifftop*

This welcoming Victorian terrace house has been carefully renovated to provide stylish, thoughtfully equipped, non-smoking accommodation. Hearty English breakfasts are served in the attractive dining room and there is also a lounge bar with a fabulous sea view.

Rooms 14 en suite (1 fmly) S £35-£50; D £60-£68
Facilities tea/coffee Direct Dial Cen ht Licensed Wi-fi
Parking 6 **Notes** LB Closed 20 Nov-24 Jan

The Ramleh

★★★★ GUEST ACCOMMODATION

135 Queens Pde YO12 7HY
☎ 01723 365745
e-mail: info@theramleh.co.uk
dir: *A64/A165 to North Bay & Alexandra Bowling Centre. At Bowling Centre, follow Queens Parade*

Overlooking North Bay, this welcoming terrace house has a friendly atmosphere. The modern bedrooms are bright and comfortable, and tasty breakfasts are served in the spacious dining room, which also has a well-stocked bar and a stunning view.

Rooms 9 rms (8 en suite) (1 pri facs) (3 fmly) S £30-£40; D £50-£70* **Facilities** FTV TVL tea/coffee Dinner available Cen ht Licensed **Parking** 5 **Notes** LB ⊗ No Children 3yrs Closed Xmas

The Whiteley

★★★★ GUEST ACCOMMODATION

99-101 Queens Pde YO12 7HY
☎ 01723 373514 📠 01723 373007
e-mail: whiteleyhotel@bigfoot.com
dir: *A64/A165 to North Bay & Peasholm Park, right onto Peasholm Rd, 1st left*

The Whiteley is an immaculately run, sea-facing home-from-home. Bedrooms, though compact, are carefully decorated and have many thoughtful extras. There's a small garden at the rear, a choice of lounges and a bar. The establishment has superb views, and the owners provide personal attention and a substantial breakfast.

Rooms 10 en suite (3 fmly) (1 GF) S £34.50-£36; D £59-£68 **Facilities** TVL tea/coffee Cen ht Licensed **Parking** 8 **Notes** LB ⊗ No Children 3yrs Closed 30 Nov-Jan

The Windmill Bed & Breakfast

★★★★ GUEST ACCOMMODATION

Mill St YO11 1SZ
☎ 01723 372735 📠 01723 377190
e-mail: info@windmill-hotel.co.uk
dir: *A64 into Scarborough, pass Sainsbury's, left onto Victoria Rd, 3rd left onto Mill St*

Situated in the centre of town but having its own car park, this unique establishment has modern bedrooms situated around a courtyard next to a windmill dating from 1784. The base of the mill includes a spacious breakfast room and a toy museum which is only viewable by guests.

Rooms 11 en suite (2 fmly) (6 GF) D £85-£140*
Facilities FTV tea/coffee Cen ht **Parking** 7 **Notes** LB ⊗

Ainsley Court Guest House

★★★★ Ⓐ GUEST HOUSE

112 North Marine Rd YO12 7JA
☎ 01723 500352
e-mail: lynn@ainsleycourt.co.uk
dir: *Next to Scarborough cricket ground*

Rooms 6 rms (4 en suite) (2 pri facs) (2 fmly) S £17.50-£26; D £40-£52 **Facilities** TVL tea/coffee Cen ht **Notes** LB ⊗

Howdale

★★★★ Ⓐ GUEST HOUSE

121 Queen's Pde YO12 7HU
☎ 01723 372696
e-mail: mail@howdale.co.uk
web: www.howdale.co.uk
dir: *At lights opp railway station turn left, stay in left lane. Straight over at next lights onto Northway then Columbus Ravine. Right onto Victoria Park, continue onto Queen's Parade*

Rooms 15 rms (13 en suite) (1 fmly) S fr £25; D fr £56
Facilities FTV TVL tea/coffee Cen ht Wi-fi **Parking** 9
Notes LB Closed Nov-Feb

Marine View Guest House

★★★★ Ⓐ GUEST HOUSE

34 Blenheim Ter YO12 7HD
☎ 01723 361864
e-mail: info@marineview.co.uk
dir: *From A64 left onto B1364, turn left onto Rutland Ter. After 0.1m straight onto Blenheim Ter*

Rooms 6 en suite (2 fmly) S fr £32; D £56-£60*
Facilities FTV TVL tea/coffee Cen ht Wi-fi **Notes** LB ⊗ No Children 3yrs

The Wharncliffe

★★★★ Ⓐ GUEST ACCOMMODATION

26 Blenheim Ter YO12 7HD
☎ 01723 374635
e-mail: info@thewharncliffescarborough.co.uk
dir: *Follow signs to Castle, left onto Blenheim St, left onto Blenheim Ter*

Rooms 12 en suite D £58-£78 **Facilities** FTV TVL tea/coffee Cen ht Licensed Wi-fi **Notes** LB ⊗ No Children 18yrs

Chessington

★★★ GUEST ACCOMMODATION

The Crescent YO11 2PP
☎ 01723 365207   📠 01723 375206
e-mail: info@thechessington.co.uk
web: www.thechessington.co.uk
dir: A64 to town centre lights, right, left at next lights & right at next lights, Chessington on left

This Grade II listed building occupies a fine position overlooking The Crescent and is close to the town centre. The bedrooms are well equipped, and the spacious dining room is the setting for comprehensive breakfasts. A sitting room and lounge bar are available.

Rooms 10 en suite (2 fmly) S £27.50-£34; D £55-£68*
Facilities TVL tea/coffee Cen ht Licensed Wi-fi **Conf** Max 10 **Notes** LB ⊗ Closed Dec & Jan

The Croft

★★★ 🏠 GUEST ACCOMMODATION

87 Queens Pde YO12 7HT
☎ 01723 373904
e-mail: information@crofthotel.co.uk
web: www.crofthotel.co.uk
dir: Follow tourist signs for North Bay seafront, along front towards castle headland, right turn up cliff, right at top, premises on left

A flexible approach to your needs is a key feature of this friendly establishment. It overlooks the bay, so you can enjoy the spectacular view from the comfortable lounge or from the patio in fine weather. Breakfast is served in the very pleasant well-appointed dining room.

Rooms 6 rms (5 en suite) (1 pri facs) (4 fmly) S £30-£35; D £50-£60* **Facilities** FTV TVL tea/coffee Cen ht Licensed **Parking** 4 **Notes** LB ⊗ Closed Dec-Feb

Palace Hill

★★★ GUEST HOUSE

1 Palace Hill, Eastborough YO11 1NL
☎ 01723 374535
e-mail: info@palace-hill.co.uk
web: www.palace-hill.co.uk
dir: N on Foreshore road, left at lights onto Eastborough, 300yds on right

With its central location in the Old Town this smartly presented 18th-century building is only a minute's walk from the South Bay beach and seafront. The house has been fully refurbished to offer attractively decorated, modern bedrooms with good quality en suite shower rooms. Wi-fi access is also available.

Rooms 9 en suite (3 fmly) (1 GF) S £40-£60; D £55-£60*
Facilities Cen ht **Notes** LB ⊗ Closed Dec & Jan

Plane Tree Cottage Farm (SE999984)

★★★ FARMHOUSE

Staintondale YO13 0EY
☎ 01723 870796
Mrs M A Edmondson
dir: A171, N from Scarborough. At Cloughton onto Staintondale road, farm 2m N of Cloughton

The Edmondson family are welcoming hosts, and the animals on the farm include unusual breeds of sheep and hens. This is an interesting and pleasant venue, either for its tranquil, secluded setting, or as a base for walking. Expect good home cooking, comfortable bedrooms, and a cosy lounge and dining room.

Rooms 3 rms (2 en suite) (1 pri facs) (1 GF) D £60*
Facilities TVL tea/coffee Dinner available Cen ht **Parking** 3 **Notes** ⊗ No Children Closed Oct-Mar 🐾 60 acres sheep/hens/Highland cattle

Argo

★★★ GUEST HOUSE

134 North Marine Rd YO12 7HZ
☎ 01723 375745
dir: Close to entrance of Scarborough Cricket Ground

This friendly house is a haven for cricket fans, with some of the comfortable bedrooms overlooking the championship ground. Day rooms include a well appointed lounge and a dining room where tasty cooked breakfasts are served at individual tables.

Rooms 8 rms (5 en suite) (2 fmly) **Facilities** TVL tea/coffee Cen ht **Notes** ⊗ 🐾

The Barrington Guest House

★★★ GUEST HOUSE

3 Palace Hill, Eastborough YO11 1NL
☎ 01723 379494
e-mail: valeriehotchin@aol.com

This charming house has an elevated position just a short walk from the sandy beaches of South Bay and all the amenities of the town. Bedrooms are ranged over three floors and all are tastefully decorated in a contemporary style; they include family rooms and en suite rooms.

Rooms 6 en suite (2 fmly) S £37.50-£45; D £55*
Facilities FTV tea/coffee Cen ht Wi-fi **Notes** LB Closed 24 Dec-2 Jan

The Grosvenor

★★★ GUEST ACCOMMODATION

51 Grosvenor Rd YO11 2LZ
☎ 01723 363801   📠 01723 363801
e-mail: grosvenorhotelscarborough@msn.com
web: www.grosvenor-scarborough.co.uk
dir: Follow signs for South Bay along Valley Rd, Grosvenor Rd on right

Guests can expect a good level of hospitality at this large, family-run property which is a short walk from the town and the seafront. All bedrooms have a contemporary feel. Freshly cooked breakfasts are served on the ground floor, and guests can also relax in the spacious lounge.

Rooms 8 en suite S £30-£45; D £60-£75 **Facilities** FTV TVL tea/coffee Cen ht Wi-fi Holistic Therapist & Treatment room **Notes** LB ⊗ Closed Nov-Etr

North End Farm Country Guesthouse

★★★ GUEST ACCOMMODATION

88 Main St, Seamer YO12 4RF
☎ 01723 862965
e-mail: northendfarm@tiscali.co.uk
dir: A64 N onto B1261 through Seamer, farmhouse next to rdbt

Located in Seamer, a village inland from Scarborough, this 18th-century farmhouse contains comfortable, well-equipped en suite bedrooms. Breakfast is served at individual tables in the smart dining room, and the cosy lounge has a large-screen TV.

Rooms 3 en suite (1 fmly) S £30-£40; D £55-£65
Facilities FTV TVL tea/coffee Cen ht **Parking** 6 **Notes** 🐾

SCARBOROUGH *continued*

Peasholm Park

★★★ GUEST ACCOMMODATION

21-23 Victoria Park YO12 7TS
☎ 01723 500954
e-mail: peasholmparkhotel@btconnect.com
web: www.peasholmpark.co.uk
dir: *Opp entrance to Peasholm Park*

A warm welcome awaits you at this family-run guest accommodation, which is within easy walking distance of the beach or the town centre. Bedrooms are comfortable, and feature homely extras. Breakfast is served at individual tables in the dining room, which looks over Peasholm Park.

Rooms 12 en suite (3 fmly) **Facilities** TVL tea/coffee Cen ht Licensed **Parking** 2 **Notes** ⊗ No Children 4yrs RS 22 Dec-2 Jan bed & breakfast only

Dolphin Guest House

★★★ 🅰 GUEST HOUSE

151 Columbus Ravine YO12 7QZ
☎ 01723 341914 📠 08715 284118
e-mail: dolphinguesthouse@btinternet.com
web: www.thedolphin.info
dir: *At train station turn left onto Northway then onto Columbus Ravine, guest house on right*
Rooms 6 rms (5 en suite) (1 pri facs) (4 fmly) S £25-£30; D £50-£56 **Facilities** FTV TVL tea/coffee Cen ht Wi-fi **Notes** LB ⊗

Lyness Guest House

★★★ 🅰 GUEST HOUSE

145 Columbus Ravine YO12 7QZ
☎ 01723 375952 📠 01723 372550
e-mail: info@thelyness.co.uk
dir: *Follow signs for North Bay, leading onto Northway. Continue onto Columbus Ravine, over 2 rdbts, 200mtrs on right*
Rooms 8 rms (6 en suite) (2 pri facs) (2 fmly) S £26-£28; D £54-£58* **Facilities** TVL tea/coffee Dinner available Cen ht Wi-fi **Notes** LB ⊗ Closed 20 Dec-3 Jan

The Sheridan

★★★ 🅰 GUEST ACCOMMODATION

108 Columbus Ravine YO12 7QZ
☎ 01723 372094
e-mail: kim@thesheridan.co.uk
dir: *Turn left at railway station onto Northway, then over 2 mini-rdbts, 300yds on left*
Rooms 8 en suite (2 fmly) (1 GF) S £35-£45; D £52-£64* **Facilities** FTV tea/coffee Dinner available Cen ht **Parking** 6 **Notes** LB ⊗ No Children 5yrs

Warwick House

★★ GUEST ACCOMMODATION

70 Westborough YO11 1TS
☎ 01723 374343 📠 01723 374343
e-mail: warwick-house@talktalk.net
dir: *On outskirts of town centre, just before railway station on left*

Close to the Stephen Joseph Theatre, station and shops, this friendly guest accommodation has some en suite and some shared facility rooms. Hearty breakfasts are served in the pleasant basement dining room. Private parking is available.

Rooms 6 rms (2 en suite) (4 fmly) S £18.50-£24.50; D £37-£49 (room only)* **Facilities** FTV tea/coffee Cen ht Wi-fi **Parking** 5 **Notes** LB ⊜

SCOTCH CORNER Map 19 NZ20

The Vintage

★★★ 🅰 INN

DL10 6NP
☎ 01748 824424 & 822961 📠 01748 826272
e-mail: thevintagescotchcorner@btinternet.com
web: www.thevintagehotel.co.uk
dir: *Leave A1 at Scotch Corner onto A66 towards Penrith, premises 200yds on left*
Rooms 8 rms (5 en suite) S £23.50-£39.50; D £39.50-£49.50 (room only)* **Facilities** TVL tea/coffee Dinner available Direct Dial Cen ht Wi-fi **Conf** Max 48 Thtr 40 Class 24 Board 20 **Parking** 40 **Notes** LB ⊗ Closed Xmas & New Year

SETTLE Map 18 SD86

See also Clapham

The Lion at Settle

★★★★ INN

Duke St BD24 9DU
☎ 01729 822203
e-mail: relax@thelionsettle.co.uk
dir: *In town centre opp Barclays Bank*

Located in the heart of the market town of Settle, The Lion at Settle is a traditional coaching inn, with inglenook fire place and alfresco dining in the new courtyard. The accommodation is comfortable and well equipped. A wide selection of imaginative dishes together with real ales and fine wines are served in the busy bar and restaurant, where the atmosphere is relaxed and comfortable.

Rooms 14 en suite (2 fmly) S £65-£100; D £90-£120* **Facilities** FTV tea/coffee Dinner available Cen ht Wi-fi **Notes** LB

Whitefriars Country Guesthouse

★★★★ GUEST ACCOMMODATION

Church St BD24 9JD
☎ 01729 823753
e-mail: info@whitefriars-settle.co.uk
dir: *Off A65 through Settle market place, premises signed 50yds on left*

This friendly, family-run house stands in peaceful gardens just a stroll from the town centre and railway station. Bedrooms, some quite spacious, are attractively furnished in a traditional style and thoughtfully equipped. A hearty breakfast is served in the traditional, beamed dining room, and a cosy lounge is available.

Rooms 10 rms (6 en suite) (1 pri facs) (1 fmly) **Facilities** FTV TVL tea/coffee Cen ht **Parking** 10 **Notes** ⊗ Closed 25 Dec ⊜

SKIPTON Map 18 SD95

Clay Hall

★★★★ GUEST ACCOMMODATION

Broughton Rd BD23 3AA
☎ 01756 794391
dir: *On A6069, 1m from Skipton towards Broughton*

A warm welcome is assured here on the outskirts of the town next to the Leeds and Liverpool canal. The house has been restored to provide carefully furnished bedrooms with smart modern shower rooms en suite, and a wealth of thoughtful extras. Comprehensive breakfasts are served in an attractive dining room.

Rooms 2 en suite **Facilities** tea/coffee Cen ht **Parking** 4 **Notes** ⊗ No Children 12yrs ⊜

Westfield House

★★★★ ⌂ GUEST HOUSE

50 Keighley Rd BD23 2NB
☎ 01756 790849
dir: *500yds S of town centre on A6131, S of canal bridge*

Just a stroll from the town centre, this friendly, non-smoking guest house provides smart accommodation. Bedrooms are well presented and most have large beds and many accessories including bathrobes. A hearty breakfast is served in the cosy dining room, and permission to use nearby parking is a bonus. Hospitality here is warm and nothing is too much trouble for the owners.

Rooms 4 en suite D £55-£60* **Facilities** tea/coffee Cen ht **Notes** ⊗ No Children ⊗

The Woolly Sheep

★★★★ INN

38 Sheep St BD23 1HY
☎ 01756 700966
e-mail: woolly.sheep@btconnect.com
dir: *At bottom of High St*

Situated right in the centre of Skipton's vibrant market town, close to the medieval castle and railway station, this popular inn offers good quality and comfortable accommodation. All bedrooms are en suite and well equipped with traditional country pine furniture, colour TV and tea/coffee making facilities. Food is the focus, with good home-cooked food, and serving a range of award-winning Timothy Taylor real ales. Free secure car parking to the rear.

Rooms 9 en suite (3 fmly) S £50-£55; D £80-£95* **Facilities** FTV tea/coffee Dinner available Cen ht Wi-fi **Parking** 14 **Notes** LB ⊗ No coaches

Low Skibeden House (SD013526)

★★★ FARMHOUSE

Harrogate Rd BD23 6AB
☎ 01756 793849
Mrs H Simpson
web: www.lowskibeden.co.uk
dir: *1m E of Skipton on right before A59/A65 rdbt, set back from road*

A lovely stone, 16th-century farmhouse located one mile from Skipton and surrounded by open countryside. Bedrooms are traditionally furnished and there is a spacious, comfortable lounge where guests are offered tea or coffee and cake on arrival, and supper time drinks from hosts, Bill and Heather.

Rooms 4 rms (2 en suite) (2 fmly) S £40-£56; D £60-£68* **Facilities** TVL tea/coffee Cen ht **Parking** 4 **Notes** LB ⊗ No Children 14yrs 40 acres sheep/non-working

Rockwood House

★★★ GUEST ACCOMMODATION

14 Main St, Embsay BD23 6RE
☎ 01756 799755 & 07976 314980 📄 01756 799755
e-mail: rockwood@steadonline.com
web: www.stayinyorkshire.co.uk
dir: *2m NE of Skipton. Off A59 into Embsay village centre*

This Victorian terrace house has a peaceful location in the village of Embsay. Bedrooms are thoughtfully furnished, individually styled and reassuringly comfortable. The traditionally styled dining room sets the venue for hearty breakfasts. Hospitality is a feature here with a genuine and friendly welcome.

Rooms 3 en suite (1 fmly) (1 GF) S £35-£50; D £65-£75* **Facilities** TVL tea/coffee Cen ht Wi-fi Golf 18 **Parking** 3 **Notes** LB ⊗

SNAINTON   Map 17 SE98

The Coachman Inn

★★★★ ⊛ RESTAURANT WITH ROOMS

Pickering Road West YO13 9PL
☎ 01723 859231 📄 01723 850008
e-mail: info@coachmaninn.co.uk
web: www.coachmaninn.co.uk
dir: *From A170 in village onto B1258, establishment sign at side of road*

This Grade II listed property was built in 1776 as a coaching inn and stands just on the outskirts of Snainton. It now offers comfortable, double, en suite rooms, fine dining in a wonderful large dining room, a locals' bar, a quiet lounge for residents and ample parking.

Rooms 6 en suite **Facilities** FTV tea/coffee Dinner available Cen ht Wi-fi Golf 9 Riding **Conf** Max 60 **Parking** 28 **Notes** No coaches

STILLINGTON   Map 19 SE56

The Baytree

★★★★ ⊛ RESTAURANT WITH ROOMS

High St YO61 1JU
☎ 01347 811394
e-mail: info@baytreestillington.com
web: www.baytreestillington.com
dir: *A19 onto Tollerton Rd (signed Huby, Public Weighbridge, Sutton Park). In Huby left onto Main St, right onto Stillington Rd. 1m, right onto Roseberry Ln. 0.5m, left onto Carr Ln (B1363), right onto Main St*

Just a 20-minute drive from York, The Baytree enjoys a quiet country village location. It is spacious with comfortable seating, a large conservatory restaurant, and a small, private dining area - perfect for small parties. The bar has open fires, stone-flagged floors and a great ambiance. The accommodation includes rooms suitable for families. The award-winning food is the highlight of any stay; the outside eating areas are delightful, and even if it's chilly, there are patio heaters.

Rooms 4 en suite (2 fmly) (2 GF) S £40-£70; D £50-£120* **Facilities** FTV tea/coffee Dinner available Direct Dial Cen ht Wi-fi **Parking** 8 **Notes** LB No coaches

SUTTON-ON-THE-FOREST   Map 19 SE56

The Blackwell Ox Inn

★★★★ ⊛ ⌂ INN

Huby Rd YO61 1DT
☎ 01347 810328 📄 01347 812738
e-mail: enquiries@blackwelloxinn.co.uk
web: www.blackwelloxinn.co.uk
dir: *A1237 onto B1363 to Sutton-on-the-Forest. Left at T-junct, 50yds on right*

Standing in the lovely village, this refurbished inn and restaurant offers very good bedrooms and pleasing public rooms. Cooking is well worth seeking out and staff are very keen and friendly.

Rooms 7 en suite S £65; D £95-£110* **Facilities** FTV tea/coffee Dinner available Direct Dial Cen ht Lift Wi-fi **Parking** 18 **Notes** LB ⊗ No coaches

TADCASTER — Map 16 SE44

The Old Presbytery Guest House

★★★ BED AND BREAKFAST

London Rd, Saxton LS24 9PU
☎ 01937 557708
e-mail: guest@presbytery.plus.com
web: www.presbyteryguesthouse.co.uk
dir: 4m S of Tadcaster on A162. 100yds N of Barkston Ash
on E side of road

Dating from the 18th century, this former dower house
has been modernised to provide comfortable
accommodation with original features. The hall lounge
features a wood-burning stove, and extensive breakfasts
are served at an old oak dining table in a cosy breakfast
room.

Rooms 4 rms (3 en suite) (1 pri facs) (1 fmly) S £43-£51;
D £82 Facilities FTV TVL tea/coffee Cen ht Wi-fi Golf 18
Parking 6 Notes ⊗

THIRSK — Map 19 SE48

PREMIER COLLECTION

Spital Hill

★★★★★ ⊞ ➰ GUEST ACCOMMODATION

York Rd YO7 3AE
☎ 01845 522273 🖷 01845 524970
e-mail: spitalhill@spitalhill.entadsl.com
web: www.spitalhill.co.uk
dir: 1.5m SE of town, set back 200yds from A19,
driveway marked by 2 white posts

Set in gardens, this substantial Victorian country house
is delightfully furnished. The spacious bedrooms are
thoughtfully equipped with many extras, one even has
a piano, but no TVs or kettles; the proprietor prefers to
offer tea as a service. Delicious meals feature local and
home-grown produce and are served house-party style
around one table in the interesting dining room. Ann
and Robin Clough were finalists in this year's
Friendliest Landlady of the Year award (2011-12).

Rooms 3 rms (2 en suite) (1 pri facs) 2 annexe en suite
(1 GF) S £70-£75; D £110-£120 Facilities TVL Dinner
available Direct Dial Cen ht Licensed Wi-fi ➰ Golf
Parking 6 Notes LB ⊗ No Children 12yrs

THORNTON WATLASS — Map 19 SE28

PREMIER COLLECTION

Thornton Watlass Hall

★★★★★ GUEST ACCOMMODATION

HG4 4AS
☎ 01677 422803 🖷 01677 424160
e-mail: enquiries@thorntonwatlasshall.co.uk
dir: Off B6268, at N end of village

Thornton Watlass Hall dates from the 11th century and
has been occupied by the same family for just under
1000 years. The Hall has featured in TV dramas over
the years, such as All Creatures Great and Small and
Heartbeat. The Hall is finely furnished in period style
and is unspoilt but still offers all the modern
amenities. David and Liz Smith-Dodsworth offer a very
friendly welcome and breakfasts are served in the
grand dining room offering local produce. Relax in the
palatial drawing room with its large open fireplace and
honesty bar.

Rooms 6 en suite (1 fmly) S £80; D £125-£135*
Facilities FTV TVL tea/coffee Direct Dial Cen ht
Licensed Wi-fi ➰ Snooker Parking 50 Notes Closed 24
Dec-1 Jan RS Nov-Apr Full house parties only

Buck Inn

★★★ INN

HG4 4AH
☎ 01677 422461 🖷 01677 422447
e-mail: innwatlass1@btconnect.com
web: www.thebuckinn.net
dir: From A1 at Leeming Bar take A684 towards Bedale,
B6268 towards Masham 2m, turn right at x-rds to
Thornton Watlass

This traditional country inn is situated on the edge of the
village green overlooking the cricket pitch. Cricket prints
and old photographs are found throughout, and an open
fire in the bar adds to the warm and intimate
atmosphere. Wholesome lunches and dinners, from an
extensive menu, are served in the bar or dining room.
Bedrooms are brightly decorated and well equipped.

Rooms 7 rms (5 en suite) (1 fmly) (1 GF) Facilities TVL
tea/coffee Dinner available Cen ht Wi-fi Fishing Pool table
Quoits Conf Max 50 Thtr 50 Class 45 Board 30
Parking 10 Notes RS 24-25 Dec No accommodation, no
food 25 Dec

WESTOW — Map 19 SE76

Woodhouse Farm (SE749637)

★★★★ FARMHOUSE

YO60 7LL
☎ 01653 618378 & 07904 293422 🖷 01653 618378
Mrs S Wardle
e-mail: stay@wood-house-farm.co.uk
web: www.wood-house-farm.co.uk
dir: Off A64 to Kirkham Priory & Westow. Right at T-junct,
farm drive 0.5m out of village on right

The owners of this house are a young farming family who
open their home and offer caring hospitality. Home-made
bread, preserves and farm produce turn breakfast into a
feast, and the views from the house across open fields
are splendid.

Rooms 2 en suite (1 fmly) S £40-£50; D £65-£75*
Facilities FTV TVL tea/coffee Cen ht Wi-fi ch fac Fishing
Parking 12 Notes LB ⊗ Closed Xmas, New Year & mid
Mar-mid Apr ➰ 500 acres arable/sheep

WEST WITTON — Map 19 SE08

AA FUNKIEST B&B OF THE YEAR

The Wensleydale Heifer

★★★★ ◉◉ RESTAURANT WITH ROOMS

Main St DL8 4LS
☎ 01969 622322
web: www.wensleydaleheifer.co.uk
dir: A1 to Leeming Bar junct, A684 towards Bedale for
approx 10m to Leyburn, then towards Hawes 3.5m to
West Witton

Describing itself as 'boutique style', this 17th-century
coaching inn is very much in the 21st-century. The
bedrooms, with Egyptian cotton linen and Molton Brown
toiletries as standard, are each designed with a unique
and interesting theme - for example, Black Sheep, Night
at the Movies, True Romantics and Shooters, and for
chocolate lovers there's a bedroom where they can eat as
much chocolate as they like! The food is very much the
focus here in both the informal fish bar and the
contemporary style restaurant. The kitchen prides itself
on sourcing the freshest fish and locally reared meats.
The Wensleydale Heifer is the AA's Funkiest B&B of the
Year (2011-2012).

Rooms 9 en suite 4 annexe en suite (2 GF) S £100-£140;
D £120-£190* Facilities FTV tea/coffee Dinner available
Direct Dial Cen ht Wi-fi Parking 20 Notes LB

WHITBY   Map 19 NZ81

Estbek House

★★★★★ ⊛⊛ 🖹 RESTAURANT WITH ROOMS

East Row, Sandsend YO21 3SU
☎ 01947 893424 📠 01947 893625
e-mail: info@estbekhouse.co.uk
dir: From Whitby take A174. In Sandsend, left into East Row

A speciality seafood restaurant on the first floor is the focus of this listed building in a small coastal village north west of Whitby. There is also a small bar and breakfast room, and four individually appointed bedrooms offering luxury and comfort.

Rooms 4 rms (3 en suite) (1 pri facs) **Facilities** tea/coffee Dinner available Cen ht Wi-fi **Conf** Board 20 **Parking** 6 **Notes** ⊗ No Children 14yrs No coaches

Netherby House

★★★★ 🖹 ⇔ GUEST ACCOMMODATION

90 Coach Rd, Sleights YO22 5EQ
☎ 01947 810211 📠 01947 810211
e-mail: info@netherby-house.co.uk
web: www.netherby-house.co.uk
dir: In village of Sleights, off A169 (Whitby-Pickering road)

This fine Victorian house has been lovingly refurbished and now offers thoughtfully furnished, individually styled bedrooms together with delightful day rooms. There is a fine conservatory and the grounds are extensive, with exceptional views from the summerhouse at the bottom of the garden. Imaginative dinners feature produce from the extensive kitchen garden.

Rooms 6 en suite 5 annexe en suite (1 fmly) (5 GF) S £39-£49.50; D £78-£99* **Facilities** FTV TVL tea/coffee Dinner available Cen ht Licensed Wi-fi ⛲ **Parking** 17 **Notes** LB ⊗ No Children 2yrs Closed 25-26 Dec

Chiltern Guest House

★★★★ GUEST HOUSE

13 Normanby Ter, West Cliff YO21 3ES
☎ 01947 604981
e-mail: Jjchiltern@aol.com
dir: Whalebones next to Harbour, sea on right. Royal Hotel on left, 200yds. Royal Gardens turn left, 2nd road on left, 6th house on right

This Victorian terrace house offers a warm welcome and comfortable accommodation within walking distance of the town centre and seafront. Public areas include a smartly decorated lounge and a bright, attractive dining room. Bedrooms are thoughtfully equipped and many have modern en suites.

Rooms 9 en suite (2 fmly) **Facilities** TVL tea/coffee Cen ht Wi-fi Golf 18

Corra Lynn

★★★★ GUEST ACCOMMODATION

28 Crescent Av YO21 3EW
☎ 01947 602214 📠 01947 602214
dir: Corner A174 & Crescent Av

Occupying a prominent corner position, this property mixes traditional values with a trendy and artistic style. Bedrooms are thoughtfully equipped, individually furnished and have bright colour schemes, but it is the delightful dining room with corner bar, and a wall adorned with clocks that catch the eye.

Rooms 5 en suite (1 fmly) D fr £70* **Facilities** STV FTV tea/coffee Direct Dial Cen ht Licensed **Parking** 5 **Notes** ⊗ Closed 21 Dec-14 Feb ⊛

Lansbury Guesthouse

★★★★ GUEST ACCOMMODATION

29 Hudson St YO21 3EP
☎ 01947 604821
e-mail: jill@lansbury44.fsnet.co.uk
dir: In town centre. Off A174 Upgang Ln onto Crescent Av, 2nd right

A short walk from the historic harbour, a warm welcome is assured at this elegant Victorian terrace house which has been renovated to provide good standards of comfort and facilities. Bedrooms are equipped with thoughtful extras, and comprehensive breakfasts using local produce are served in an attractive dining room.

Rooms 7 en suite **Facilities** FTV tea/coffee Cen ht **Parking** 3 **Notes** ⊗

Rosslyn Guest House

★★★★ GUEST HOUSE

11 Abbey Ter YO21 3HQ
☎ 01947 604086
e-mail: rosslynhouse@googlemail.com

Guests are sure of a friendly atmosphere, high standards of cleanliness and comfortable bedrooms at this lovely house, close to the sea front. Breakfast is served in a beautifully appointed dining room. Additional facilities include a small guest kitchen, complimentary Wi-fi, Sky TV and secure outside storage for bikes.

Rooms 6 en suite (2 fmly) (1 GF) S £40-£60; D £55-£70* **Facilities** STV tea/coffee Cen ht Wi-fi **Parking** 1 **Notes** LB ⊗

WHITBY *continued*

Sandpiper Guest House

★★★★ GUEST HOUSE

4 Belle Vue Ter YO21 3EY
☎ 01947 600246
e-mail: enquiries@sandpiperhouse.wanadoo.co.uk
dir: *A169, 2nd left at rdbt signed Whitby, follow signs to West Cliffe on N Prom, 4th right, take Esplanade straight onto Belle Vue Terrace. Guest House on left*

This well presented Victorian house is just a few minutes walk from Whitby's golden sands and the quaint streets of its historic harbour area. The contemporary bedrooms vary in size with a choice of singles, twins, a four-poster room and family room available. Hearty breakfasts are served in the cheerful lower ground-floor dining room.

Rooms 7 en suite (1 fmly) (1 GF) **Facilities** tea/coffee Cen ht Wi-fi **Parking** 3 **Notes** ⊗ No Children 4yrs ⊜

The Waverley

★★★★ GUEST HOUSE

17 Crescent Av YO21 3ED
☎ 01947 604389 ⋕ 0870 0063 3129
e-mail: stephen@whitbywaverley.com
dir: *A174 towards Saltburn, turn right, 250mtrs on right at bend*

This terraced house was originally built as a guest house in 1898, and is located on the West Cliff. Bedrooms vary in size, but all are comfortable and well equipped. Day rooms include a smartly appointed dining room and first-floor lounge. All guests are assured a warm welcome and a hearty breakfast.

Rooms 6 rms (5 en suite) (1 pri facs) **Facilities** TVL tea/coffee Cen ht Wi-fi **Parking** 3 **Notes** ⊗ No Children Closed Nov-Jan

Whitehaven Guest House

★★★★ GUEST ACCOMMODATION

29 Crescent Av YO21 3EW
☎ 01947 601569
e-mail: simon@whitehavenguesthouse.co.uk
web: www.whitehavenguesthouse.co.uk
dir: *Signs to West Cliff, A174 onto Crescent Av*

Occupying a corner position close to the sports complex and indoor swimming pool, this house provides colourful bedrooms in contrasting styles. All rooms have mini-fridges and most have DVD players. Vegetarian options are available at breakfast, which is served in the attractive dining room.

Rooms 4 rms (3 en suite) (1 fmly) D £65-£70* **Facilities** FTV tea/coffee Cen ht Wi-fi **Notes** LB ⊗ Closed 23-26 Dec ⊜

Arundel House

★★★ GUEST ACCOMMODATION

Bagdale YO21 1QJ
☎ 01947 603645 ⋕ 08703 121974
e-mail: arundel_house@hotmail.com
dir: *A171 town centre, onto Arundel Pl at bottom of hill*

In a prime location within walking distance of all the attractions, Arundel House's bedrooms are simply furnished and offer good value for money. Expect a helping of true Yorkshire hospitality, and look out for the unique collection of walking canes on show in the house.

Rooms 12 en suite (2 fmly) (2 GF) S £40-£45; D £60-£90* **Facilities** tea/coffee Cen ht Wi-fi **Parking** 6 **Notes** LB

WOMBLETON   **Map 19 SE68**

New Buckland

★★★★ BED AND BREAKFAST

Flatts Ln YO62 7RU
☎ 01751 433369 & 07738 430519
e-mail: junedrake138@btinternet.com
dir: *From A170 turn right 3m from Helmsley, left at Plough Inn follow round, last property on right*

Two attractive bedrooms and excellent bathrooms in a well presented countryside property. Whether one or both rooms are booked, guests have exclusive use of the spacious, contemporary lounge and a very well equipped small kitchen. Complimentary Wi-fi access is available. Guests also have use of an area of the attractive garden with summer house and garden furniture.

Rooms 2 rms (2 pri facs) S £45; D £69 **Facilities** FTV TVL Cen ht Wi-fi **Parking** 2 **Notes** LB ⊗ No Children

---

YORK   **Map 16 SE65**

See also Sutton-on-the-Forest

Guy Fawkes Inn

★★★★ ⊚ INN

25 High Petergate YO1 7HP
☎ 01904 623716
e-mail: enquiry@gfyork.com
web: www.gfyork.com
dir: *A64 onto A1036 signed York & inner ring road. Over bridge onto Duncombe Pl then right onto High Petergate*

This inn is only feet away from The Minster and was the birthplace of the notorious plotter, Guy Fawkes. Steeped in history, it is full of character and has been restored to retain many original features including the timber staircase, gas lighting and open fires. The bar is a real gathering place for locals and visitors to the city. The bedrooms are wonderfully appointed with antique furniture, Italian fabrics and luxury beds; some of the modern bathrooms have roll-top baths. An outside courtyard at the back of the inn provides ample space for dining and enjoying a drink.

Rooms 13 en suite (1 fmly) (2 GF) S £50-£70; D £60-£150* **Facilities** FTV tea/coffee Dinner available Direct Dial Wi-fi **Notes** LB

The Hazelwood

★★★★ GUEST ACCOMMODATION

24-25 Portland St YO31 7EH
☎ 01904 626548 ⋕ 01904 628032
e-mail: reservations@thehazelwoodyork.com
web: www.thehazelwoodyork.com
dir: *400yds N of York Minster, off inner ring road Gillygate*

A renovation of two elegant Victorian houses in a residential side street near the Minster. Bedrooms are equipped with thoughtful extras, and comprehensive breakfasts are served in an attractive dining room. There is a cosy garden-level lounge and a private car park.

Rooms 13 en suite (2 fmly) (2 GF) S £65-£105; D £80-£125* **Facilities** FTV tea/coffee Cen ht Licensed Wi-fi **Parking** 8 **Notes** LB ⊗ No Children 8yrs

See advert on opposite page

The Lamb & Lion

★★★★ ⊚ INN

2-4 High Petergate YO1 7EH
☎ 01904 612078
e-mail: enquiry@lambandlionyork.com
web: www.lambandlionyork.com
dir: *A64 onto A1036, after 3.5m at rdbt take 3rd exit & continue on A1036. After 2m turn right onto High Petergate*

This inn, steeped in history and full of character, stands in the shadows of the medieval city gate on Bootham Bar. The stylish bedrooms are well appointed and have wonderfully comfortable beds; some benefit from views of the city wall and The Minster itself. The public areas have winding passages leading to a 'Parlour' dining room complete with church pews and open fire; cosy little rooms off the corridor afford much privacy.

Rooms 12 en suite S £50-£70; D £60-£150* **Facilities** FTV tea/coffee Dinner available Cen ht Wi-fi **Conf** Max 20 Thtr 20 Class 20 Board 20 **Notes** ⊗

Ascot House

★★★★ GUEST ACCOMMODATION

0 East Pde YO31 7YH
☎ 01904 426826 📠 01904 431077
e-mail: admin@ascothouseyork.com
web: www.ascothouseyork.com
dir: 0.5m NE of city centre. Off A1036 Heworth Green onto
Mill Ln, 2nd left

June and Keith Wood provide friendly service at the 1869
Ascot House, a 15-minute walk from the town centre.
Bedrooms are thoughtfully equipped, many with four-
poster or canopy beds and other period furniture.
Reception rooms include a cosy lounge that also retains
its original features.

Rooms 12 en suite (3 fmly) (2 GF) S £60-£80; D £70-£90
Facilities FTV TVL tea/coffee Cen ht Licensed Wi-fi
Parking 13 **Notes** LB Closed 21-28 Dec

Ashley Guest House

★★★★ GUEST HOUSE

76 Scott St YO23 1NS
☎ 01904 647520 & 07955 250271
e-mail: taylor.philip.j@googlemail.com
dir: Pass racecourse, turn right at 2nd lights onto
Scarcroft Rd. Scott St 2nd last on right

Ashley Guest House is a Victorian end-terrace that has
been given a very modern treatment with stylish interiors
and distinctive character. Attractively furnished
bedrooms and caring hospitality are hallmarks of this
well located city-centre establishment.

Rooms 6 rms (5 en suite) (1 pri facs) S £40-£53; D
£50-£86 **Facilities** FTV tea/coffee Cen ht Wi-fi **Notes** ⊗
No Children 12yrs

City Guest House

★★★★ GUEST ACCOMMODATION

68 Monkgate YO31 7PF
☎ 01904 622483
e-mail: info@cityguesthouse.co.uk
dir: NE of city centre on B1036

Just a stroll from the historic Monk Bar, this guest
accommodation is well located for business, shopping
and sightseeing. Carefully furnished bedrooms boast
stylish interior design and come equipped with a host of
thoughtful touches. The smart dining room is the venue
for a good breakfast.

Rooms 7 rms (6 en suite) (1 pri facs) (1 fmly) (1 GF) S
£39-£43; D £68-£76 **Facilities** FTV tea/coffee Cen ht Wi-fi
Golf 9 **Parking** 6 **Notes** ⊗ No Children 8yrs Closed Xmas
& 1st 2wks Jan

YORK *continued*

The Heathers

★★★★ GUEST ACCOMMODATION

54 Shipton Rd, Clifton-Without YO30 5RQ
☎ 01904 640989 📄 01904 640989
e-mail: aabbg@heathers-guest-house.co.uk
web: www.heathers-guest-house.co.uk
dir: *N of York on A19, halfway between A1237 ring road & York city centre*

Recent remodelling and refurbishment at The Heathers has resulted in a most comfortable and welcoming establishment. Heather and Graham Fisher have designed each room individually, using quality fabrics and decor to provide a feeling of luxury. The light and airy breakfast room looks out on to a well tended garden area.

Rooms 6 rms (4 en suite) (2 pri facs) (1 fmly) S £52-£126; D £56-£130 **Facilities** tea/coffee Cen ht Wi-fi **Parking** 9 **Notes** ⊗ No Children 10yrs Closed Xmas

Holly Lodge

★★★★ GUEST ACCOMMODATION

204-206 Fulford Rd YO10 4DD
☎ 01904 646005
e-mail: geoff@thehollylodge.co.uk
web: www.thehollylodge.co.uk
dir: *On A19 south side, 1.5m on left from A64/A19 junct, or follow A19 Selby signs from city centre to Fulford Rd*

Located just a short walk from the historic centre, this pleasant Georgian property has coordinated, well-equipped bedrooms. The spacious lounge houses a grand piano, and hearty breakfasts are served in the cosy dining room. You may also enjoy the delightful walled garden. Complimentary Wi-fi is also available.

Rooms 5 en suite (1 fmly) (1 GF) S £58-£88; D £78-£98 **Facilities** FTV tea/coffee Cen ht Wi-fi **Parking** 6 **Notes** ⊗ No Children 7yrs Closed 24-27 Dec

Midway House

★★★★ 🅰 GUEST ACCOMMODATION

145 Fulford Rd YO10 4HG
☎ 01904 659272 📄 01904 638496
e-mail: info@midwayhouseyork.co.uk
dir: *A64 to York, 3rd exit A19 to York city centre, over 2nd lights, house 50yds on right*

Rooms 12 rms (10 en suite) (3 fmly) (1 GF) S £48-£66; D £60-£84* **Facilities** FTV TVL tea/coffee Cen ht Wi-fi **Parking** 14 **Notes** LB ⊗ No Children 6yrs Closed 18 Dec-20 Jan

Adam's House

★★★ GUEST HOUSE

5 Main St, Fulford YO10 4HJ
☎ 01904 655413 📄 01904 643203
e-mail: adams.house2@virgin.net
dir: *A64 onto A19, 200yds on right after lights*

Adam's House offers comfortable accommodation not far from York centre in the suburb of Fulford, close to the university. It has many fine period features, pleasant, well-proportioned bedrooms, and an attractive dining room. The resident owners are friendly and attentive.

Rooms 8 rms (7 en suite) (4 fmly) (2 GF) **Facilities** tea/coffee Cen ht Wi-fi **Parking** 8 **Notes** ⊗

Cumbria House

★★★ GUEST ACCOMMODATION

2 Vyner St, Haxby Rd YO31 8HS
☎ 01904 636817
e-mail: candj@cumbriahouse.freeserve.co.uk
web: www.cumbriahouse.com
dir: *A1237 onto B1363 S towards city centre, pass hospital, left at lights, 400yds on left*

Expect a warm welcome at this family-run guest accommodation, which is ten minutes walk from the Minster. The attractive bedrooms are well furnished and equipped with many useful extras. Freshly-cooked breakfasts are served in the smart dining room at individual tables.

Rooms 6 rms (2 en suite) (2 fmly) S £25-£30; D £54-£60 **Facilities** tea/coffee Cen ht Wi-fi **Parking** 5 **Notes** LB ⊗

Dalescroft Guest House

★★★ GUEST HOUSE

10 Southlands Rd YO23 1NP
☎ 01904 626801 📄 01904 626801
e-mail: info@dalescroft-york.co.uk
web: www.dalescroft-york.co.uk
dir: *A64 until A1036 towards race course, right at Kwik-Fit onto Scarcroft Rd. Pass green on left, right on Russell St, at top turn left onto Southlands Rd*

Originally built in 1908, this smartly appointed Victorian terrace house is located in a quiet residential area just ten minutes walk from the city of York. Bedrooms and bathrooms are comfortably furnished. Freshly cooked breakfasts are served at individual tables in the cosy dining room. Permits are available for the on-street parking.

Rooms 5 en suite **Facilities** FTV tea/coffee Cen ht **Notes** ⊗ No Children 12yrs

Greenside

★★★ GUEST HOUSE

124 Clifton YO30 6BQ
☎ 01904 623631 📄 01904 623631
e-mail: greenside@onebillnet.co.uk
web: www.greensideguesthouse.co.uk
dir: *A19 N towards city centre, over lights for Greenside, on left opp Clifton Green*

Overlooking Clifton Green, this detached house is just within walking distance of the city centre. Accommodation consists of simply furnished bedrooms and there is a cosy lounge and a dining room, where traditional breakfasts are served. It is a family home, and other families are welcome.

Rooms 6 rms (3 en suite) (2 fmly) (3 GF) S fr £30; D fr £58* **Facilities** TVL tea/coffee Cen ht Wi-fi **Parking** 6 **Notes** LB Closed Xmas & New Year 🅰

St Georges

★★★ 🅰 GUEST ACCOMMODATION

6 St Georges Place, Tadcaster Rd YO24 1DR
☎ 01904 625056 📄 01904 625009
e-mail: sixstgeorg@aol.com
web: www.stgeorgesyork.com
dir: *A64 onto A1036 N to city centre, as racecourse ends, St Georges Place on left*

Rooms 10 en suite (5 fmly) (1 GF) S £40-£65; D £60-£70* **Facilities** tea/coffee Cen ht Wi-fi **Parking** 7 **Notes** LB No Children 12yrs Closed 20 Dec-2 Jan

Save on B&Bs and Hotels. Book at **theAA.com/hotel**

YORKSHIRE, SOUTH 361 | ENGLAND

YORKSHIRE, SOUTH

ROTHERHAM | Map 16 SK49

he Stonecroft

★★★★ GUEST ACCOMMODATION

38 Main St, Bramley S66 2SF
☎ 01709 540922 ▤ 01709 540922
-mail: stonecrofthotel@btconnect.com
ir: 3m E of Rotherham. Off A631 into Bramley village
entre

hese converted stone cottages in the centre of Bramley
rovide a good base for visiting Rotherham or Sheffield.
ome bedrooms are around a landscaped courtyard with
rivate parking, and there is a lounge with a bar.
maginative home-cooked meals are available.

ooms 3 en suite 4 annexe en suite (1 fmly) (4 GF)
acilities FTV TVL tea/coffee Dinner available Cen ht
icensed Wi-fi Golf 18 Parking 7 Notes LB ⊗ Closed 24
ec-2 Jan

SHEFFIELD | Map 16 SK38

ross Scythes

★★★★ INN

aslow Rd, Totley S17 4AE
☎ 0114 236 0204
-mail: enquiries@cross-scythes.com

ocated approximately five miles south of Sheffield city
entre and just 10 minutes drive from Chatsworth House,
his 18th-century building has been sympathetically
enovated. There are four tastefully decorated double
ooms and all are en suite. Food is available and is
erved all day throughout the spacious public areas.

ooms 4 en suite S fr £55; D fr £55 (room only)*
acilities FTV tea/coffee Dinner available Cen ht Wi-fi
olf 18 Parking 51 Notes ⊗

Padley Farm B&B

★★★★ GUEST ACCOMMODATION

Dungworth Green S6 6HE
☎ 0114 285 1427 ▤ 0114 285 1427
e-mail: aandlmbestall@btinternet.com
web: www.padleyfarm.co.uk
dir: M1 junct 33 follow ring road (A61 Barnsley), turn left
onto B6077 signed Bradfield

The barn conversion offers high quality en suite rooms
with spectacular views of open countryside. An allergy
free environment and warm hospitality ensure a pleasant
stay.

Rooms 7 en suite (3 fmly) (2 GF) S £30-£37; D £54-£60*
Facilities FTV tea/coffee Cen ht Fishing Snooker Conf Max
15 Class 15 Parking 8 Notes LB ⊗

Westbourne House Guest Accommodation

★★★★ GUEST ACCOMMODATION

25 Westbourne Rd, Broomhill S10 2QQ
☎ 0114 266 0109 ▤ 0114 266 7778
e-mail: guests@westbournehousehotel.com
web: www.westbournehousehotel.com
dir: A61 onto B6069 Glossop Rd, past university, after
Hallamshire Hospital over lights to next T-junct, straight
through next lights, left onto Westbourne Rd

Westbourne House is a Victorian residence situated in
beautiful gardens close to the university and
hospitals. The modern bedrooms are individually
furnished and decorated, and extremely well
equipped. Wi-fi is available throughout the property. A
comfortable lounge overlooks the terrace and garden.

Rooms 8 rms (7 en suite) (1 pri facs) (2 fmly) S £52-£65;
D £75-£85* Facilities FTV TVL tea/coffee Cen ht Licensed
Wi-fi Parking 6 Notes ⊗

THROAPHAM | Map 16 SK58

Throapham House

★★★★★ Ⓐ GUEST ACCOMMODATION

Oldcotes Rd S25 2QS
☎ 01909 562208 ▤ 01909 567825
e-mail: enquiries@throapham-house.co.uk
web: www.throapham-house.co.uk
dir: M1 junct 31 onto A57 E towards Worksop. After 1m
left at lights, at rdbt take 2nd exit onto Common Rd. In
Throapham, 200yds on left after sign

Rooms 3 en suite D £70-£90* Facilities FTV TVL tea/
coffee Cen ht Wi-fi Parking 3 Notes LB ⊗

TODWICK | Map 16 SK48

The Red Lion

★★★ INN

Worksop Rd S26 1DJ
☎ 01909 771654 ▤ 01909 773704
e-mail: 7933@greeneking.co.uk
dir: On A57, 1m from M1 junct 31 towards Worksop

Originally a roadside public house, the Red Lion is now a
popular bar and restaurant offering a wide range of
drinks and food. Bedrooms are well equipped, modern
and comfortable, and there are three meeting rooms and
ample parking facilities.

Rooms 27 en suite (1 fmly) (14 GF) Facilities tea/coffee
Direct Dial Parking 80

WORTLEY | Map 16 SK39

Wortley Hall

★★★★ GUEST ACCOMMODATION

Wortley Village S35 7DB
☎ 0114 288 2100 ▤ 0114 283 0695
e-mail: info@wortleyhall.org.uk
web: www.wortleyhall.org.uk
dir: Exit M1 junct 35a, straight over 2nd rdbt signed
A616/Manchester. In 3m turn left to Wortley

Standing in 26 acres of parkland, this listed country
house has been in the custody of the Trades Union
Movement for the last 50 years and displays much of
their history. Bedrooms are mixed in size and quality, but
all are comfortable and there are spacious day rooms
reminiscent of the hall's original grandeur.

Rooms 49 en suite (7 fmly) (4 GF) S £46-£99; D
£99-£142* Facilities TVL tea/coffee Dinner available
Direct Dial Cen ht Lift Licensed Wi-fi Conf Thtr 150 Class
70 Board 30 Parking 60 Notes ⊗ Civ Wed 100

YORKSHIRE, WEST

HALIFAX
Map 19 SE02

Shibden Mill
★★★★ ⊛⊛ INN

Shibden Mill Fold, Shibden HX3 7UL
☎ 01422 365840 📠 01422 362971
e-mail: enquiries@shibdenmillinn.com
web: www.shibdenmillinn.com
dir: *3m NE of Halifax off A58*

Nestling in a fold of Shibden Dale, this 17th-century inn features exposed beams and open fires. Guests can dine well in the two lounge-style bars, the restaurant, or outside in summer. The stylish bedrooms come in a variety of sizes, and all are thoughtfully equipped and have access to a free video library. Service is friendly and obliging.

Rooms 11 en suite (1 GF) S £81-£133; D £100-£158*
Facilities FTV tea/coffee Dinner available Direct Dial
Cen ht Wi-fi Golf 18 Free use of local fitness centre
Conf Max 50 Thtr 50 Class 21 Board 24 **Parking** 100

HAWORTH
Map 19 SE03

Weavers Restaurant with Rooms
★★★★ ⊛ RESTAURANT WITH ROOMS

15 West Ln BD22 8DU
☎ 01535 643822 📠 01535 644832
e-mail: weaversltd@btconnect.com
dir: *In village centre. Pass Brontë Weaving Shed on right, 100yds left to Parsonage car park*

Centrally located on the cobbled main street, this family-owned restaurant with rooms provides well-equipped, stylish and comfortable accommodation. Each of the three en suite bedrooms has many thoughtful extras. The kitchen serves both modern and traditional dishes with flair and creativity.

Rooms 3 en suite S £65-£75; D £90-£120* **Facilities** FTV
tea/coffee Dinner available Direct Dial Cen ht Wi-fi
Notes ⊗ Closed 24 Dec-10 Jan RS Sun & Mon No
arrivals/rest

HEBDEN BRIDGE
Map 19 SD92

Moyles
★★★★ ⊛ RESTAURANT WITH ROOMS

6-10 New Rd HX7 8AD
☎ 01422 845272 📠 01422 847663
e-mail: enquire@moyles.com
dir: *A646 to Hebden Bridge, opposite marina*

Centrally located in the charming town of Hebden Bridge, this Victorian building as been modernised to offer a high standard of contemporary accommodation. Fresh, local produce features on the imaginative menus served in the bar and in the restaurant. There's a relaxing ambience throughout.

Rooms 12 en suite (6 fmly) **Facilities** FTV tea/coffee
Dinner available Cen ht Wi-fi **Conf** Max 12 Thtr 12 Class
12 Board 12 **Notes** ⊗

HOLMFIRTH
Map 16 SE10

Uppergate Farm
★★★★ 🅰 GUEST ACCOMMODATION

Hepworth HD9 1TG
☎ 01484 681369 📠 01484 687343
e-mail: info@uppergatefarm.co.uk
dir: *0.5m off A616*

Rooms 2 en suite (1 fmly) S £55; D £80 **Facilities** TVL
tea/coffee Cen ht Wi-fi ch fac 🕙 Sauna Pool table Table
tennis **Parking** 6 **Notes** LB ⊗

HUDDERSFIELD
Map 16 SE11

The Huddersfield Central Lodge
★★★★ GUEST ACCOMMODATION

11/15 Beast Market HD1 1QF
☎ 01484 515551 📠 01484 432349
e-mail: angela@centrallodge.com
web: www.centrallodge.com
dir: *In town centre off Lord St, signs for Beast Market from ring road*

This friendly, family-run operation offers smart spacious bedrooms with modern en suites. Some rooms are in the main building, while new rooms, many with kitchenettes, are situated across a courtyard. Public rooms include a bar and a conservatory, and there are arrangements for local restaurants to charge meals to guests' accounts. Secure complimentary parking.

Rooms 9 en suite 13 annexe en suite (2 fmly) (6 smoking)
S £53-£59; D £70* **Facilities** FTV TVL tea/coffee Direct
Dial Cen ht Licensed Wi-fi **Parking** 50

The Woodman Inn
★★★★ ⊜ INN

Thunder Bridge Ln HD8 0PX
☎ 01484 605778 📠 01484 604110
e-mail: thewoodman@connectfree.co.uk
web: www.woodman-inn.co.uk

(For full entry see Kirkburton)

Griffin Lodge Guest House
★★★ GUEST HOUSE

273 Manchester Rd HD4 5AG
☎ 01484 431042 📠 01484 431043
e-mail: info@griffinlodge.co.uk
web: www.griffinlodge.co.uk

Located on the outskirts of Huddersfield and close to the villages of Holmfirth and Marsden, Griffin Lodge is famil run and offers comfortable well appointed accommodation. Either continental or a full cooked breakfast is served in the small dining room and there is parking to the rear.

Rooms 6 en suite (4 fmly) (6 GF) **Facilities** FTV tea/coffe
Cen ht Wi-fi **Parking** 10

KIRKBURTON
Map 16 SE11

The Woodman Inn
★★★★ ⊜ INN

Thunder Bridge Ln HD8 0PX
☎ 01484 605778 📠 01484 604110
e-mail: thewoodman@connectfree.co.uk
web: www.woodman-inn.co.uk
dir: *1m SW of Kirkburton. Off A629 in Thunder Bridge*

The Woodman offers traditional innkeeping and is extremely popular with locals. The air-conditioned restaurant holds an extensive range of wines, while the popular bar offers a wide selection of ales and lagers. Bedrooms are comfortable and comprehensively furnished, making this an ideal base for walking, visitin the National Mining Museum, or simply escaping to the country.

Rooms 12 en suite (3 GF) **Facilities** tea/coffee Dinner
available Direct Dial Cen ht Pool table **Conf** Max 60 Thtr
50 Class 60 Board 30 **Parking** 50 **Notes** ⊗

he Olive Branch Restaurant with ooms

★★★ ◉ RESTAURANT WITH ROOMS

anchester Rd HD7 6LU
☎ 01484 844487
mail: eat@olivebranch.uk.com
eb: www.olivebranch.uk.com
r: 1m NE of Marsden on A62

e Olive Branch, once a roadside inn, was developed
to a popular restaurant with three comfortable
drooms. The menu features the best of seasonal
oduce cooked with flair and enthusiasm. The
rrounding countryside has many historic attractions
d offers pleasant walking opportunities.

ooms 3 en suite S £60; D £80 (room only) **Facilities**
a/coffee Dinner available Cen ht Wi-fi **Parking** 25
tes ⊗ Closed 2-17 Jan No coaches

eath House

★★★ GUEST ACCOMMODATION

hancery Rd WF5 9RZ
☎ 01924 260654 & 07890 385622 📠 01924 263131
mail: bookings@heath-house.co.uk
eb: www.heath-house.co.uk
r: M1 junct 40, A638 towards Dewsbury, at end dual
arriageway exit rdbt 2nd left, house 20yds on right

e spacious Victorian family home stands in four acres
tranquil gardens a short distance from the M1. It has
egant en suite bedrooms, and the courteous and
endly owners provide healthy, freshly-cooked
eakfasts.

ooms 2 en suite (1 fmly) S £35-£39; D £49-£52
acilities tea/coffee Cen ht Wi-fi **Parking** 16

lidgley Lodge Motel and Golf Course

★★★ 🅰 GUEST ACCOMMODATION

arr Ln, Midgley WF4 4JJ
☎ 01924 830069 📠 01924 830087
mail: midgleylodgemotel@tiscali.co.uk
r: SW of Wakefield. M1 junct 38, A637 Huddersfield road
Midgley

ooms 25 en suite (10 fmly) (13 GF) S fr £54; D fr £64
oom only)* **Facilities** STV FTV TVL tea/coffee Direct Dial
en ht Licensed Wi-fi Golf 9 ⛳ **Parking** 90 Notes ⊗
losed 25 Dec-2 Jan

Stanley View Guest House

★★★ GUEST HOUSE

226-230 Stanley Rd WF1 4AE
☎ 01924 376803 📠 01924 369123
e-mail: enquiries@stanleyviewguesthouse.co.uk
dir: M62 junct 30, follow Aberford Rd 3m. Signed on left

Part of an attractive terrace, this well-established guest
house is just half a mile from the city centre and has
private parking at the rear. The well equipped bedrooms
are brightly decorated, and there is a licensed bar and
comfortable lounge. Hearty home-cooked meals are
served in the attractive dining room.

Rooms 17 rms (13 en suite) (6 fmly) (7 GF) **Facilities** STV
TVL tea/coffee Dinner available Direct Dial Cen ht
Licensed Wi-fi **Parking** 10

CHANNEL ISLANDS

JERSEY

PREMIER COLLECTION

The Panorama

★★★★★ 🏠 GUEST ACCOMMODATION

La Rue du Crocquet JE3 8BZ
☎ 01534 742429 📠 01534 745940
e-mail: info@panoramajersey.com
web: www.panoramajersey.com
dir: In village centre

With spectacular views across St Aubin's Bay, the
Panorama is a long-established favourite with visitors.
The welcome is genuine and many of the well-equipped
bedrooms have wonderful views. Public areas also look
seaward and have attractive antique fireplaces.
Breakfast is excellent and served in two dining areas.

Rooms 14 en suite (3 GF) S £40-£73; D £90-£146*
Facilities STV tea/coffee Cen ht Wi-fi **Notes** ⊗ No
Children 18yrs Closed mid Oct-mid Apr

Harbour View

★★★★ GUEST HOUSE

Le Boulevard JE3 8AB
☎ 01534 741585 📠 01534 499460
e-mail: harbourview@localdial.com

The Harbour View is situated in a beautiful location
overlooking St Aubin Harbour. The guest house has been
lovingly restored over recent years and it retains many
original features. Bedrooms are all smartly presented and
come with a host of facilities. Food can be taken at
'Danny's at the Harbour View' and car parking is an
added bonus.

Rooms 16 en suite (4 fmly) (2 GF) **Facilities** STV TVL tea/
coffee Cen ht Licensed Wi-fi Golf 18 **Parking** 8 **Notes** LB
Closed Dec-Feb

Peterborough House

★★★ GUEST ACCOMMODATION

La Rue du Croquet JE3 8BZ
☎ 01534 741568 📠 01534 746787
e-mail: fernando@localdial.com
dir: A13 to St Aubin, left at La Haule Slip, 1st left. Left
fork, half way down on left

Situated on the old St Aubin high street, this well-
presented house dates back to 1690. The bedrooms are
comfortably appointed and the sea-facing rooms are
always in high demand. One of the two lounge areas has
a bar, or guests can enjoy the view with a drink on the
outdoor terrace. Breakfast has a choice of traditional and
continental options.

Rooms 14 rms (12 en suite) (1 fmly) (2 GF) S
£30.50-£41.10; D £51-£72.20* **Facilities** TVL tea/coffee
Cen ht Licensed Wi-fi **Notes** LB ⊗ No Children 12yrs
Closed Nov-Feb

Bay View Guest House

★★★★ GUEST ACCOMMODATION

12 Havre des Pas JE2 4UQ
☎ 01534 720950 & 07700 720100 📠 01534 720950
e-mail: bayview.guesthouse@jerseymail.co.uk
dir: Through tunnel, right at rdbt, down Green St & left,
100yds on left

The Bay View is located across the road from the Havre
des Pas Lido and beach, and just a ten minute walk from
the centre of St Helier. Bedrooms are well equipped, and
extra facilities include a bar and a television lounge with
free Wi-fi internet access. There is a small garden terrace
to the front of the establishment.

Rooms 13 rms (12 pri facs) (3 fmly) S £28-£48; D
£60-£112* **Facilities** FTV TVL tea/coffee Cen ht Licensed
Wi-fi **Notes** LB ⊗

ISLE OF MAN

DOUGLAS
Map 24 SC37

Dreem Ard

★ ★ ★ ★ ⊖ BED AND BREAKFAST

Ballanard Rd IM2 5PR
☎ 01624 621491 📄 01624 621491
dir: *From St Ninian's Church along Ballanard Rd for 1m, over Johnny Watterson Ln x-rds, past farm on left, Dreem Ard on left*

Dreem Ard is a relaxing sanctuary, with superb views over the glens just to the north of Douglas. Bedrooms are spacious and well equipped, and the caring hosts are genuinely hospitable and attentive. Breakfast and dinner are served around a large table, where good food and good company go hand-in-hand.

Rooms 3 en suite (1 fmly) (2 GF) D £60-£80*
Facilities STV FTV tea/coffee Dinner available Cen ht
Parking 6 **Notes** LB ⊗ No Children 8yrs ⊕

All Seasons

★ ★ ★ 🅰 GUEST HOUSE

11 Clifton Ter, Broadway IM2 3HX
☎ 01624 676323 📄 08718 553 465
dir: *Off Central Promenade at Villa Marina, premises in 1st row of hotels on left*
Rooms 6 rms (4 en suite) (2 pri facs) (6 fmly) S £36-£45; D £59-£110* **Facilities** FTV TVL tea/coffee Dinner available Cen ht Licensed Wi-fi **Notes** LB ⊗ No Children 12yrs

PORT ST MARY
Map 24 SC26

PREMIER COLLECTION

Aaron House

★ ★ ★ ★ ★ 🏛 GUEST HOUSE

The Promenade IM9 5DE
☎ 01624 835702 📄 01624 837731
web: www.aaronhouse.co.uk
dir: *Follow signs for South & Port St Mary, left at Post Office. House in centre of Promenade*

Aaron House is truly individual. From the parlour down to the detail of the cast-iron baths, the house, overlooking the harbour, has been restored to its Victorian origins. The family work hard to offer the best quality, whether its providing luxury and comfort in the bedrooms, or offering home-made cakes on arrival.

Rooms 4 rms (3 en suite) (1 pri facs) **Facilities** TVL TV1B tea/coffee Cen ht **Notes** ⊗ No Children 12yrs Closed 21 Dec-3 Jan ⊕

ST JOHN'S
Map 24 SC28

Glen Helen Inn

★ ★ ★ ★ ⊖ INN

Glen Helen IM4 3NP
☎ 01624 801294 & 666186 📄 01624 803294
e-mail: info@glenheleninn.com
web: www.glenheleninn.com

This charming inn is in a glorious location in the heart of the island and close to some lovely country walks. Bedrooms are all very well planned and have a contemporary appearance. The stylish bar is ideal for pre dinner drinks and there is a popular restaurant, which serves a wide range of dishes.

Rooms 17 en suite (4 fmly) S £45-£55; D £65-£85
Facilities FTV tea/coffee Dinner available Cen ht Wi-fi
Conf Max 80 Thtr 80 Class 24 Board 40 **Parking** 70
Notes LB

Why not spend less and relax more on UK breaks?

cottages4you property ref GRL

Make AA Travel your first destination and you're on the way to a more relaxing short break or holiday.

AA Members and customers can get great deals on accommodation, from B&Bs to farmhouses, inns and hotels.

You can also save up to 10% at cottages4you, enjoy a 5% discount with Hoseasons, and up to 60% off the very best West End shows.

Thinking of going further afield?

Check out our attractive discounts on car hire, airport parking, ferry bookings, travel insurance and much more.

Then simply relax.

These are just some of our well-known partners:

cottages4you Hoseasons **Hertz** **P&O** Ferries

Visit theAA.com/travel

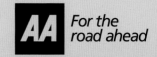

Scotland

Loch Morlich, Cairngorms National Park

CITY OF ABERDEEN

ABERDEEN
Map 23 NJ90

The Jays Guest House

★★★★ GUEST HOUSE

422 King St AB24 3BR
☎ 01224 638295 ▤ 01224 638360
e-mail: alice@jaysguesthouse.co.uk
web: www.jaysguesthouse.co.uk
dir: A90 from S onto Main St & Union St & A92 to King St N

Guests are warmly welcomed to this attractive granite house on the north side of the city. Maintained in first-class order throughout, it offers attractive bedrooms, smartly furnished to appeal to business guests and tourists. Freshly prepared breakfasts are enjoyed in the carefully appointed dining room.

Rooms 10 rms (8 en suite) (2 pri facs) (1 GF) S £55-£65; D £90-£110* Facilities STV FTV tea/coffee Cen ht Wi-fi Parking 9 Notes ⊗ No Children 12yrs Closed mid Dec-mid Jan

Arkaig

★★★ GUEST HOUSE

43 Powis Ter AB25 3PP
☎ 01224 638872 ▤ 01224 622189
e-mail: info@arkaig.co.uk
dir: On A96 at junct with Bedford Rd

A friendly welcome and relaxed atmosphere is assured at this well-presented guest house, situated on the north side of the city close to the university and city centre. Bedrooms vary in size, are attractively decorated, and are all thoughtfully equipped to appeal to business and leisure guests. There is a cosy sun lounge with magazines, and an attractive breakfast room where delicious, freshly cooked breakfasts are served. Parking is also available.

Rooms 9 rms (7 en suite) (1 fmly) (5 GF) Facilities FTV TVL tea/coffee Direct Dial Cen ht Parking 10

PETERCULTER
Map 23 NJ80

Furain

★★★ Ⓐ GUEST HOUSE

92 North Deeside Rd AB14 0QN
☎ 01224 732189 ▤ 01224 739070
e-mail: furain@btinternet.com
dir: 7m W of city centre on A93
Rooms 8 en suite (2 fmly) (3 GF) S £45-£53; D £60-£70 Facilities FTV tea/coffee Cen ht Wi-fi Parking 7 Notes Closed Xmas & New Year

ABERDEENSHIRE

BALLATER
Map 23 NO39

The Green Inn

★★★★★ ⑳⑳⑳ 🍴 RESTAURANT WITH ROOMS

9 Victoria Rd AB35 5QQ
☎ 013397 55701
e-mail: info@green-inn.com
web: www.green-inn.com
dir: In village centre

A former temperance hotel, the Green Inn enjoys a central location in the pretty village of Ballater. Bedrooms are of a high standard and attractively presented. The kitchen has a strong reputation for its fine cuisine, which can be enjoyed in the stylish conservatory restaurant. The head chef is Chris O'Halloran, son of owners Trevor and Evelyn. Breakfast is equally enjoyable and should not be missed. Genuine hospitality from the enthusiastic proprietors is a real feature of any stay.

Rooms 2 en suite S £59.50; D £79 Facilities FTV TVL tea/coffee Dinner available Cen ht Wi-fi Notes Closed 1st 2wks Nov, last 2wks Jan No coaches

The Auld Kirk

★★★★ ⑳⑳ RESTAURANT WITH ROOMS

Braemar Rd AB35 5RQ
☎ 01339 755762 & 07918 698000 ▤ 0700 6037 559
e-mail: info@theauldkirk.com
dir: From A93 Braemar, on right just before village centre

A Victorian Scottish Free Church building that is now a contemporary restaurant with rooms, boasting well-appointed bedrooms and bathrooms. Many original features of this kirk have been restored and incorporated in the design. The Spirit Restaurant with its high ceilings and tall windows provides a wonderful setting to enjoy the award-winning, seasonal food. There is a stylish bar with a good selection of malts and a terrace for alfresco eating when the weather permits.

Rooms 7 en suite (1 fmly) S £70-£75; D £110-£140* Facilities tea/coffee Dinner available Direct Dial Cen ht Wi-fi Conf Max 25 Thtr 25 Class 18 Board 16 Parking 7 Notes RS Sun closed No coaches Civ Wed 34

BRAEMAR
Map 23 NO19

Callater Lodge Guest House

★★★★ GUEST HOUSE

9 Glenshee Rd AB35 5YQ
☎ 013397 41275
e-mail: info@hotel-braemar.co.uk
web: www.callaterlodge.co.uk
dir: Next to A93, 300yds S of Braemar centre

Located in the picturesque village of Braemar, this grand Victorian villa is very well presented with stunning views and lots of period features. Bedrooms are attractively decorated with many thoughtful extras. The spacious lounge is inviting and homely. Breakfast is served at individual tables, and uses quality local ingredients. The gardens are a very pleasant feature.

Rooms 6 en suite (1 fmly) S fr £40; D fr £78* Facilities tea/coffee Cen ht Licensed Wi-fi Parking 6 Notes ⊗ Closed Xmas

INVERURIE
Map 23 NJ72

Kintore Arms

★★★★ INN

83 High St AB51 3QJ
☎ 01467 621367 ▤ 01467 625620
e-mail: manager.kintore@ohiml.com
web: www.oxfordhotelsandinns.com
dir: From A96 at rdbt turn signed Inverurie, onto main High St, on left

Well situated within easy walking distance of the town centre and benefiting from off-road parking, this traditional inn has recently undergone a programme of refurbishment. Good-sized bedrooms are thoughtfully equipped for the modern traveller. Regular evening entertainment is provided.

Rooms 28 en suite (1 fmly) Facilities FTV TVL tea/coffee Dinner available Cen ht Wi-fi Conf Max 150 Thtr 150 Class 75 Board 75 Parking 30 Notes Civ Wed 150

STRATHDON
Map 23 NJ31

The Glenkindie Arms

★★★ ⑳⑳ INN

Glenkindie AB33 8SX
☎ 01975 641288
e-mail: iansimpson.glenkindiearms@gmail.com

Good food is a real feature here with skilfully prepared meals served in the cosy traditional bar which has an open fire, and serves real ales and quality wines. Accommodation is provided in brightly decorated and airy rooms, and the bathrooms are thoughtfully equipped. The inn enjoys a peaceful rural location, and has built up a good reputation and a loyal following. Breakfast is not to be missed, and lunches feature traditional dishes made from the best local produce.

Rooms 3 en suite (1 fmly) S £35-£50; D £70-£100* Facilities STV FTV tea/coffee Dinner available Cen ht Wi-fi Golf 18 Fishing Conf Max 40 Thtr 20 Class 20 Board 30 Parking 25 Notes LB ⊗ Closed 3wks Nov RS Jan wknds only

ANGUS

INVERKEILOR
Map 23 NO64

Gordon's

★★★★★ ⑧⑧ 🏛 RESTAURANT WITH ROOMS

Main St DD11 5RN
☎ **01241 830364** 📄 **01241 830364**
e-mail: gordonsrest@aol.com
dir: Off A92, follow signs for Inverkeilor

It's worth a detour off the main road to this family-run restaurant with rooms set in the centre of the village. It has earned AA Rosettes for dinner, and the excellent breakfasts are equally memorable. A huge fire dominates the restaurant on cooler evenings, and there is a small lounge with limited seating. The attractive bedrooms are tastefully decorated and thoughtfully equipped; the larger two are furnished in pine.

Rooms 4 en suite 1 annexe en suite (1 GF) S £60-£75; D £100-£130 **Facilities** FTV Dinner available Cen ht **Parking** 6 **Notes** ⊗ No Children 12yrs Closed 2wks Jan No coaches

MONTROSE
Map 23 NO75

Oaklands

★★★ GUEST HOUSE

10 Rossie Island Rd DD10 9NN
☎ **01674 672018** 📄 **01674 672018**
e-mail: oaklands1@btopenworld.com
dir: On A92 at S end of town

A genuine welcome and attentive service are assured at this smart detached house situated on the south side of the town. Bedrooms come in a variety of sizes and are neatly presented. There is a lounge on the ground floor next to the attractive dining room, where hearty breakfasts are served. Motorcycle guided tours can be arranged for those travelling with their own motorbikes.

Rooms 7 en suite (1 fmly) (1 GF) S £35-£40; D £60-£70* **Facilities** FTV TVL tea/coffee Cen ht Wi-fi **Parking** 8 **Notes** ⊗

ARGYLL & BUTE

APPIN
Map 20 NM94

Pineapple House

★★★★ 🍴 GUEST HOUSE

Duror PA38 4BP
☎ **01631 740557** 📄 **01631 740557**
e-mail: info@pineapplehouse.co.uk
dir: In Duror, off A828. 5m S of A82

Ideally located just south of Glencoe and just north of Appin, this period farmhouse has been lovingly restored and is extremely well presented using a great mix of modern and traditional. Dinners are available on request and use the best local quality produce. Service is friendly and genuine, and makes this a wonderful base for touring this area of Scotland.

Rooms 6 en suite (1 fmly) S £45; D £75-£95 **Facilities** FTV tea/coffee Dinner available Cen ht Wi-fi **Parking** 10 **Notes** ⊗ No Children 7yrs Closed Oct-25 Mar

BARCALDINE
Map 20 NM94

Barcaldine House

★★★★★ ⑧⑧ GUEST ACCOMMODATION

PA37 1SG
☎ **01631 720219**
e-mail: enquiries@barcaldinehouse.co.uk
web: www.barcaldinehouse.co.uk

Originally built in 1709 by Patrick Campbell IV of Barcaldine, this fine country house enjoys a peaceful location on lands that were once part of the extensive estates of the Campbells of Breadalbane. The house has been sympathetically restored, and the attractive bedrooms are spacious and very well equipped. The award-winning restaurant serves the best in local produce and has a well deserved reputation. Guests have a choice of comfortable lounges with real fires and the billiard room is a popular feature. The house is an ideal base when exploring Argyll & Bute, the Highlands and the islands of Scotland.

Rooms 8 en suite (1 fmly) **Facilities** STV FTV tea/coffee Dinner available Direct Dial Cen ht Licensed Snooker **Conf** Max 24 Thtr 24 Board 24 **Parking** 16 **Notes** Civ Wed 40

CAIRNDOW
Map 20 NN11

Cairndow Stagecoach Inn

★★★ INN

PA26 8BN
☎ **01499 600286** & **600252** 📄 **01499 600252**
e-mail: enq@cairndowinn.com
dir: From N, take either A82 to Tarbet, A83 to Cairndow, or A85 to Palmally, A819 to Inveraray & A83 to Cairndow

A relaxed, friendly atmosphere prevails at this 18th-century inn, overlooking the beautiful Loch Fyne. Bedrooms offer individual decor and thoughtful extras.Traditional public areas include a comfortable beamed lounge, a well-stocked bar where food is served throughout the day, and a spacious restaurant with conservatory extension. Deluxe bedrooms offer more space and luxury.

Rooms 13 en suite 5 annexe en suite (2 fmly) (5 GF) **Facilities** STV FTV tea/coffee Dinner available Direct Dial Cen ht Wi-fi Sauna Solarium **Conf** Max 30 Thtr 30 Class 30 Board 30

CARRADALE
Map 20 NR83

Dunvalanree

★★★★ ⑧ GUEST ACCOMMODATION

Port Righ Bay PA28 6SE
☎ **01583 431226**
e-mail: stay@dunvalanree.com
web: www.dunvalanree.com
dir: From centre of Carradale, turn right at x-rds, continue to end of road

Set in stunning scenery on the Mull of Kintyre, Dunvalanree has been welcoming guests for over 70 years. The restaurant menu, which has earned an AA Rosette, uses local seafood and farm produce. Standing in delightful gardens on the edge of Port Righ Bay, the house enjoys splendid views over Kilbrannan Sound, to the Isle of Arran.

Rooms 5 en suite (1 GF) S £95; D £140-£175* (incl. dinner) **Facilities** tea/coffee Dinner available Cen ht Licensed Wi-fi Golf 9 Fishing **Parking** 8 **Notes** LB Civ Wed

CONNEL   Map 20 NM93

PREMIER COLLECTION

Ards House

★★★★★ 🏠 GUEST HOUSE

PA37 1PT
☎ **01631 710255 & 07703 438341**
📠 **01631 710857**
e-mail: info@ardshouse.com
web: www.ardshouse.com
dir: On A85, 4m N of Oban

This delightful Victorian villa on the approaches to Loch Etive has stunning views over the Firth of Lorne and the Morven Hills beyond. The stylish bedrooms come with added touches such as mineral water and home-made shortbread. There is an inviting drawing room complete with piano, games and books, plus a fire on cooler evenings. The attractive dining room is the setting for delicious breakfasts.

Rooms 4 en suite S £50-£65; D £80-£90*
Facilities FTV TVL tea/coffee Cen ht Wi-fi **Parking** 12
Notes LB ⊗ No Children 10yrs Closed mid Dec-mid Jan

HELENSBURGH   Map 20 NS28

PREMIER COLLECTION

Lethamhill

★★★★★ GUEST ACCOMMODATION

West Dhuhill Dr G84 9AW
☎ **01436 676016 & 07974 798593**
📠 **01436 676016**
e-mail: jane@lethamhill.co.uk
web: www.lethamhill.co.uk
dir: 1m N of pier/town centre. Off A818 onto West Dhuhill Dr. Cross Upper Colquhoun St, then 3rd entrance on right

From the red phone box in the garden to the old typewriters and slot machines inside, this fine house is an Aladdin's cave of unusual collectibles and memorabilia. The house itself offers spacious and comfortable bedrooms with superb bathrooms. The home-cooked breakfasts and delicious baking earn much praise.

Rooms 3 en suite S £65-£70; D £85-£90*
Facilities FTV tea/coffee Cen ht Wi-fi **Parking** 6
Notes LB ⊗

LUSS   Map 20 NS39

The Inn at Inverbeg

★★★★ 🏠 🛏 INN

Inverbeg G83 8PD
☎ **01436 860678** 📠 **01436 860203**
e-mail: inverbeg.reception@loch-lomond.co.uk
dir: A82 N of Balloch

Dating back to the 18th century this inn offers very stylish, comfortable bedrooms, bathrooms, and equally stylish public areas that boast open fires and cow-hide sofas. Food is as much as a feature as the property itself, serving unusual but quality dishes including deep-fried Mars bars and Irn Bru sorbet. The Beach House accommodation is a real treat for that special occasion.

Rooms 12 en suite 8 annexe en suite (1 fmly) (5 GF)
Facilities STV FTV TVL tea/coffee Dinner available Cen ht Wi-fi **Parking** 60 **Notes** ⊗ Civ Wed 60

OBAN   Map 20 NM82

PREMIER COLLECTION

Blarcreen House

★★★★★ GUEST HOUSE

Ardchattan, Connel PA37 1RG
☎ **01631 750272**
e-mail: info@blarcreenhouse.com
web: www.blarcreenhouse.com
dir: 9.5m NE of Oban. N over Connel Bridge, 1st right, 7m, pass church & Ardchattan Priory Gardens. Blarcreen House 2m

Built in 1886 this elegant Victorian farmhouse stands on the shores of Loch Etive and has lovely views of the surrounding mountains. Bedrooms are beautifully furnished and very well equipped. There is a comfortable drawing room with deep sofas, a plentiful supply of books and videos, and a log-burning fire. A delicious breakfast offers a great start to the day, and is served in the dining room. Hospitality is strong, and the atmosphere relaxed, in this charming house.

Rooms 3 en suite S £61-£77.50; D £82-£115*
Facilities STV TVL tea/coffee Cen ht Licensed Wi-fi **Parking** 5 **Notes** LB ⊗ No Children 16yrs

Glenburnie House

★★★★ GUEST HOUSE

The Esplanade PA34 5AQ
☎ **01631 562089** 📠 **01631 562089**
e-mail: graeme.strachan@btinternet.com
dir: On Oban seafront. Follow signs for Ganavan

This impressive seafront Victorian house has been lovingly restored to a high standard. Bedrooms (including a four-poster room and a mini-suite) are beautifully decorated and very well equipped. There is a cosy ground floor lounge and an elegant dining room, where hearty traditional breakfasts are served at individual tables.

Rooms 12 en suite (2 GF) S £55-£60; D £90-£110*
Facilities FTV tea/coffee Cen ht Wi-fi **Parking** 12
Notes LB ⊗ No Children 12yrs Closed Dec-Feb

Braeside

★★★★ GUEST HOUSE

Kilmore PA34 4QR
☎ **01631 770243** 📠 **01631 770343**
e-mail: braeside.guesthouse@virgin.net
web: www.braesideguesthouse.net
dir: On A816 5m from Oban

This family-run bungalow stands in gardens overlooking the spectacular Loch Feochan. Bedrooms, all en suite, are bright and airy, well equipped and have easy access. The lounge-dining room has a loch view, a bar with a range of single malts, wines and a wonderful array of local beers, and offers a varied choice of tasty home-cooked evening meals and breakfasts.

Rooms 5 en suite (1 fmly) (5 GF) **Facilities** tea/coffee Dinner available Cen ht Licensed Wi-fi **Parking** 6
Notes LB ⊗ No Children 8yrs

Corriemar House

★★★★ GUEST HOUSE

Corran Esplanade PA34 5AQ
☎ **01631 562476** 📠 **01631 564339**
e-mail: info@corriemarhouse.co.uk
web: www.corriemarhouse.co.uk
dir: A85 to Oban. Down hill in right lane & follow sign for Ganavan at mini rdbt onto Esplanade

Billy and Sandra Russell have created a stylish haven of tranquillity at this detached Victorian house close to the town centre. Bedrooms are furnished with panache, ranging from massive to cosy, and even include a suite. Those to the front of the house have stunning views across Oban Bay to the Isle of Mull. Expect a substantial breakfast and friendly attentive service.

Rooms 9 en suite 4 annexe en suite (3 fmly) (1 GF)
Facilities tea/coffee Cen ht **Parking** 9 **Notes** ⊗

ancaster

★★ GUEST ACCOMMODATION

Corran Esplanade PA34 5AD
☎ 01631 562587 ▤ 01631 562587
e-mail: lancasteroban@btconnect.com
dir: On seafront next to Columba's Cathedral

A family-run establishment on the esplanade that offers budget accommodation; many bedrooms boast lovely views out over the bay towards the Isle of Mull. Public areas include a choice of lounges and bars that also benefit from the panoramic views. A swimming pool, sauna and jacuzzi are added benefits.

Rooms 27 rms (24 en suite) (3 fmly) (10 smoking) Facilities FTV TVL tea/coffee Cen ht Licensed ⓒ Sauna Pool table Jacuzzi Steam room Conf Max 30 Thtr 30 Class 20 Board 12 Parking 20 Notes LB

DUMFRIES & GALLOWAY

CASTLE DOUGLAS — Map 21 NX76

Craigadam

★★★★ 🏠 🍽 GUEST HOUSE

Craigadam DG7 3HU
☎ 01556 650233 & 650100 ▤ 01556 650233
e-mail: inquiry@craigadam.com
web: www.craigadam.com
dir: From Castle Douglas E on A75 to Crocketford. In Crocketford turn left on A712 for 2m. House on hill

Set on a farm, this elegant country house offers gracious living in a relaxed environment. The large bedrooms, most set around a courtyard, are strikingly individual in style. Public areas include a billiard room with comprehensive honesty bar, and the panelled dining room which features a magnificent 15-seater table, the setting for Celia Pickup's delightful meals.

Rooms 10 en suite (2 fmly) (7 GF) S £60-£94; D £94-£110* Facilities FTV TVL tea/coffee Dinner available Cen ht Licensed Wi-fi 🎣 Fishing Snooker Private fishing & shooting Conf Max 22 Parking 12 Notes LB Closed Xmas & New Year Civ Wed 150

West Barmoffity Farmhouse (NX785705)

★★★★ FARMHOUSE

DG7 3HL
☎ 01556 650631
Ms J Wilson
e-mail: jeniffer.wilson@sky.com
dir: A75 to Springholm, follow signs for Kirkpatrick Durham. Straight ahead at x-rds, after 20yds turn right, follow farm track 0.5m, on left

Located on a working farm in rolling countryside, this is an ideal base for touring, and is within easy reach of Castle Douglas. The bedrooms are spacious and well presented, plus there is a comfortable lounge and dining room where home-cooked dinner and hearty breakfasts are served.

Rooms 2 en suite (1 fmly) S £30-£35; D £60-£70* Facilities FTV TVL tea/coffee Dinner available Cen ht Parking 4 Notes LB ❀ 170 acres beef/sheep

DUMFRIES — Map 21 NX97

Wallamhill House

★★★★ BED AND BREAKFAST

Kirkton DG1 1SL
☎ 01387 248249
e-mail: wallamhill@aol.com
dir: 3m N of Dumfries. Off A701 signed Kirkton, 1.5m on right

Wallamhill House is set in well-tended gardens, in a delightful rural area three miles from Dumfries. Bedrooms are spacious and extremely well equipped. There is a peaceful drawing room, and a mini health club with sauna, steam shower and gym equipment.

Rooms 3 en suite (1 fmly) Facilities FTV TVL tea/coffee Cen ht Wi-fi 🎣 Sauna Gym Steam room Parking 6 Notes ❀

Rivendell

★★★★ GUEST HOUSE

105 Edinburgh Rd DG1 1JX
☎ 01387 252251 ▤ 01387 263084
e-mail: info@rivendellbnb.co.uk
web: www.rivendellbnb.co.uk
dir: On A701 Edinburgh Rd, 400yds S of A75 junct

Situated just north of the town and close to the bypass, this lovely 1920s house, standing in extensive landscaped gardens, has been restored to reflect the period style of the property. Bedrooms are thoughtfully equipped, many are spacious and all offer modern facilities. Traditional breakfasts are served in the elegant dining room.

Rooms 6 en suite (2 fmly) (1 GF) S £35-£45; D £60* Facilities FTV tea/coffee Cen ht Wi-fi Parking 12 Notes LB ❀

Southpark House

★★★★ GUEST ACCOMMODATION

Quarry Rd, Locharbriggs DG1 1QR
☎ 01387 711188 & 0800 970 1588 ▤ 01387 711155
e-mail: info@southparkhouse.co.uk
web: www.southparkhouse.co.uk
dir: 3.5m NE of Dumfries. Off A701 in Locharbriggs onto Quarry Rd, last house on left

With a peaceful location commanding stunning views, this well-maintained property offers comfortable, attractive and well-equipped bedrooms. The peaceful lounge has a log fire on colder evenings, and fax and e-mail facilities are available. Friendly proprietor Ewan Maxwell personally oversees the hearty Scottish breakfasts served in the conservatory breakfast room.

Rooms 4 en suite (1 fmly) S £29.99-£49.99; D £49.99-£69.99* Facilities STV FTV TVL tea/coffee Cen ht Wi-fi ch fac 2 acres of garden Parking 13 Notes LB ❀

GRETNA (WITH GRETNA GREEN) — Map 21 NY36

Barrasgate

★★★★ GUEST ACCOMMODATION

Millhill DG16 5HU
☎ 01461 337577 & 07711 661938 ▤ 01461 337577
e-mail: info@barrasgate.co.uk
web: www.barrasgate.co.uk
dir: From N: A74 (M) junct 22 signed Gretna Green/ Longtown. At 2nd rdbt right, signed Longtown. Approx 1.5m, establishment on right. From S: M6 junct 45 (A74(M) junct 24) take A6071 signed Gretna/Longtown. Approx 1m turn 2nd left, signed Gretna Green/Springfield. Establishment 1st left

This detached house lies in attractive gardens in a rural setting near Gretna, the Blacksmith Centre, and motorway links. Bedrooms are well presented and equipped; some have recently been refurbished with good results. Hearty breakfasts featuring local produce are taken in an attractive dining room, overlooking the gardens.

Rooms 5 en suite (2 fmly) (1 GF) Facilities FTV tea/coffee Cen ht Wi-fi Parking 10 Notes Closed Jan-Feb

GRETNA (WITH GRETNA GREEN) *continued*

Surrone House

★ ★ ★ GUEST ACCOMMODATION

Annan Rd DG16 5DL
☎ 01461 338341 📄 01461 338341
e-mail: enquiries@surronehouse.co.uk
web: www.surronehouse.co.uk
dir: *In town centre on B721*

Guests are assured of a warm welcome at this well-maintained guest accommodation set in attractive gardens well back from the road. Bedrooms are sensibly furnished and include a delightful honeymoon suite. Dinner, drinks and light refreshments are available.

Rooms 7 en suite (3 fmly) (2 GF) S fr £40; D fr £70* **Facilities** FTV TVL tea/coffee Dinner available Cen ht Licensed Wi-fi **Parking** 10 **Notes** ⊗

LANGHOLM Map 21 NY38

Glengarth Guest Rooms

★ ★ ★ ★ GUEST ACCOMMODATION

Maxwell Rd DG13 0DX
☎ 01387 380777 & 07802 771137
e-mail: info@glengarthguestrooms.co.uk
web: www.glengarthguestrooms.co.uk
dir: *M6 junct 44 onto A7, in Langholm 500yds past co-op*

Glengarth Guest Rooms is located in a quiet residential area in the Borders town of Langholm. Strong hospitality and customer care is provided. Bedrooms and en suites are well appointed, comfortable and cater well for the needs of the guest. Quality breakfast is served in the lounge/dining room using locally sourced produce.

Rooms 2 en suite (2 GF) S £40; D £60* **Facilities** STV tea/coffee Cen ht Wi-fi Golf 9 Fishing **Parking** 1 **Notes** LB ⊗ No Children ⊗

LOCKERBIE Map 21 NY18

Blackyett Mains

★ ★ ★ ★ 📶 BED AND BREAKFAST

DG11 3ND
☎ 01461 500750
e-mail: mail@blackyettmains.co.uk
web: www.blackyettmains.co.uk
dir: *M74 junct 21 towards Kirkpatrick Fleming, B6357 to Annan. At Hollee turn right to Irvington after 0.5m, left to Blackyett Mains. 1st on left*

Set in the rolling Dumfriesshire countryside but just 5 minutes from the M74, Blackyett Mains is a converted farmhouse with many original features, and wonderful wooden floors. Bedrooms and en suites are generous in size and very well appointed. Award-winning breakfasts use locally sourced produce and a large garden is available for guests to enjoy.

Rooms 3 rms (2 en suite) (1 pri facs) (1 GF) S £45-£55; D £60-£75* **Facilities** FTV TVL tea/coffee Dinner available Cen ht Wi-fi **Parking** 3 **Notes** LB ⊗

MOFFAT Map 21 NT00

PREMIER COLLECTION

Well View

★ ★ ★ ★ ★ ❀ ❀ GUEST ACCOMMODATION

Ballplay Rd DG10 9JU
☎ 01683 220184
e-mail: johnwellview@aol.com
dir: *From Moffat on A708 towards Selkirk, 0.5m, left onto Ballplay Rd. Well View 300mtrs on right*

Well View is set on an elevated position with outstanding views. The house is tastefully and traditionally decorated and furnished with many personal touches. Service and attention to detail are key features, as is the fine food that is personally cooked by the proprietors.

Rooms 3 en suite S £55-£80; D £75-£115 **Facilities** tea/coffee Dinner available Cen ht **Conf** Max 8 Board 8 **Parking** 4 **Notes** LB

Bridge House

★ ★ ★ ★ 🍴 GUEST HOUSE

Well Rd DG10 9JT
☎ 01683 220558 📄 01683 220558
e-mail: info@bridgehousemoffat.co.uk
dir: *Off A708 The Holm onto Burnside & Well Rd, house 0.5m on left*

A fine Victorian property, Bridge House lies in attractive gardens in a quiet residential area on the outskirts of the town. The atmosphere is very friendly and relaxed. The chef-proprietor provides interesting dinners (by arrangement) featuring local produce. The cosy guest lounge is the ideal venue for pre-dinner drinks.

Rooms 7 en suite (1 fmly) S £55; D £70-£95* **Facilities** FTV tea/coffee Dinner available Cen ht Licensed **Parking** 7 **Notes** LB ⊗ No Children 2yrs Closed Xmas & New Year

---

Hartfell House & The Limetree Restaurant

★ ★ ★ ★ ❀ GUEST HOUSE

Hartfell Crescent DG10 9AL
☎ 01683 220153
e-mail: enquiries@hartfellhouse.co.uk
web: www.hartfellhouse.co.uk
dir: *Off High St at war memorial onto Well St & Old Well Rd. Hartfell Crescent on right*

Built in 1850, this impressive Victorian house is in a peaceful terrace high above the town and has lovely countryside views. Beautifully maintained, the bedrooms offer high quality and comfort. The attractive dining room is transformed in the evening into the Limetree Restaurant (previously situated in the town centre) offering chef Matt Seddon's culinary delights.

Rooms 7 en suite (2 fmly) (1 GF) S £35-£40; D £60-£70* **Facilities** FTV tea/coffee Dinner available Cen ht Licensed Wi-fi Golf 18 **Parking** 6 **Notes** LB ⊗ Closed Xmas

---

Limetree House

★ ★ ★ ★ GUEST ACCOMMODATION

Eastgate DG10 9AE
☎ 01683 220001
e-mail: info@limetreehouse.co.uk
web: www.limetreehouse.co.uk
dir: *Off High St onto Well St, left onto Eastgate, house 100yds on left*

A warm welcome is assured at this well-maintained guest accommodation, quietly situated behind the main high street. Recognisable by its colourful flower baskets in season, it provides an inviting lounge and a bright cheerful breakfast room. Bedrooms are smartly furnished and include a large family room.

Rooms 6 en suite (1 fmly) (1 GF) S £40-£45; D £60-£80* **Facilities** FTV TVL tea/coffee Cen ht Wi-fi Golf 18 **Parking** 3 **Notes** LB No Children 5yrs RS Xmas & New Year

No 29 Well Street

★★★★ BED AND BREAKFAST

9 Well St DG10 9DP
☎ 01683 221905
e-mail: mcleancamm1956@btinternet.com
dir: M74 junct 15 follow signs to High St, Well St on right

Located in the heart of Moffat just minutes drive from the rolling countryside of the Scottish Borders, this is a very comfortable and well presented property offering high standards of hospitality and service. Bedrooms are well appointed with many useful extras provided as standard. Breakfast is hearty with local produce used to good effect.

Rooms 3 en suite (2 GF) S £30-£40; D £50-£60 Facilities FTV tea/coffee Cen ht Wi-fi Parking 1 Notes ⊗ No Children 10yrs Closed 24-26 & 31 Dec, 1 Jan

The Balmoral

★★★ INN

High St DG10 9DL
☎ 01683 220288 ᦵ 01683 220451
web: www.thebalmoralhotel-moffat.co.uk
dir: 0.5m from A/M74 junct 15, halfway up High St on right

The Balmoral is situated in the centre of the town with free parking in the town square, and a friendly welcome is guaranteed. Bar meals are available all day until 9.30pm. Bedrooms are very comfortably equipped with thoughtful extras. Moffat is a former spa town and is within easy reach of many major tourist attractions.

Rooms 16 en suite (2 fmly) Facilities tea/coffee Dinner available Cen ht Notes ⊗

Barnhill Springs Country Guest House

★★ GUEST ACCOMMODATION

DG10 9QS
☎ 01683 220580
e-mail: barnhillsprings@yahoo.co.uk
dir: A74(M) junct 15, A701 towards Moffat, Barnhill Rd 250yds on right

This former farmhouse is in a quiet, rural location south of the town and within easy reach of the M74. Bedrooms are well proportioned; and have private bathrooms. There is a comfortable lounge and separate dining room. Barnhill Spring continues to welcome pets.

Rooms 5 rms (5 pri facs) (1 fmly) (1 GF) S £35-£36; D £70-£72 Facilities TVL tea/coffee Dinner available Cen ht Parking 10 Notes LB ⊗

THORNHILL   Map 21 NX89

PREMIER COLLECTION

Gillbank House

★★★★★ GUEST ACCOMMODATION

8 East Morton St DG3 5LZ
☎ 01848 330597 ᦵ 01848 331713
e-mail: hanne@gillbank.co.uk
web: www.gillbank.co.uk
dir: In town centre off A76

Gillbank House was originally built for a wealthy Edinburgh merchant. Convenient for the many outdoor pursuits in this area, such as fishing and golfing, this delightful house offers comfortable and spacious bedrooms and smart shower rooms en suite. Breakfast is served at individual tables in the bright, airy dining room, which is next to the comfortable lounge.

Rooms 6 en suite (2 GF) S £50; D £75* Facilities tea/coffee Cen ht Wi-fi Golf 18 Parking 8 Notes ⊗ No Children 8yrs

---

EAST AYRSHIRE

SORN   Map 20 NS52

The Sorn Inn

★★★★ ◉◉ ᦵ RESTAURANT WITH ROOMS

35 Main St KA5 6HU
☎ 01290 551305 ᦵ 01290 553470
e-mail: craig@sorninn.com
dir: A70 from S or A76 from N onto B743 to Sorn

Centrally situated in a rural village, which is convenient for many of Ayrshire's attractions, this inn has a fine dining restaurant with a cosy lounge area. There is also a popular chop house with a pub-like environment. The freshly decorated bedrooms have comfortable beds and good facilities.

Rooms 4 en suite (1 fmly) S £35-£50; D £50-£90 Facilities tea/coffee Dinner available Direct Dial Cen ht Wi-fi Fishing Parking 9 Notes Closed 2wks Jan RS Mon Closed

---

EAST LOTHIAN

GIFFORD   Map 21 NT56

The Old Farmhouse (NT521651)

★★★★ FARMHOUSE

Redshill Farm EH41 4JN
☎ 01620 810406 & 07971 115848
Mr G Tait
e-mail: redshill@btinternet.com
web: www.haddingtonaccomodation.com
dir: Exit A1 at Haddington onto B6369 signed to Gifford. Leaving Gifford straight across staggered xrds with golf course on right. Turn left at next xrds then 2nd right

Dating back to the early 19th century but fully refurbished The Old Farmhouse is part of a working arable farm. Bedrooms are well presented and very comfortable, with a welcoming lounge and many extras provided as standard. East Lothian, the Borders and Edinburgh are all within easy striking distance of this peaceful rural setting. A drying room is available.

Rooms 3 en suite (2 GF) S £45-£55; D £70-£80* Facilities FTV TVL tea/coffee Cen ht Wi-fi Parking 6 Notes LB ⊗ 300 acres arable

CITY OF EDINBURGH

EDINBURGH Map 21 NT27

See also East Calder (West Lothian)

PREMIER COLLECTION

Elmview

★★★★★ 🏠 GUEST ACCOMMODATION

15 Glengyle Ter EH3 9LN
☎ 0131 228 1973
e-mail: nici@elmview.co.uk
web: www.elmview.co.uk
dir: *0.5m S of city centre. Off A702 Leven St onto Valleyfield St, one-way to Glengyle Ter*

Elmview offers stylish accommodation on the lower ground level of a fine Victorian terrace house. The bedrooms and smart bathrooms are comfortable and extremely well equipped, with thoughtful extras such as safes, and fridges with fresh milk and water. Breakfasts are excellent and are served at a large, elegantly appointed table in the charming dining room.

Rooms 3 en suite (3 GF) S £70-£105; D £90-£130*
Facilities FTV tea/coffee Direct Dial Cen ht Wi-fi
Notes ⊗ No Children 15yrs Closed Dec-Feb

PREMIER COLLECTION

Kew House

★★★★★ 🏠 GUEST ACCOMMODATION

1 Kew Ter, Murrayfield EH12 5JE
☎ 0131 313 0700 📠 0131 313 0747
e-mail: info@kewhouse.com
web: www.kewhouse.com
dir: *1m W of city centre A8*

Forming part of a listed Victorian terrace, Kew House lies within walking distance of the city centre, and is convenient for Murrayfield Stadium and tourist attractions. Meticulously maintained throughout, it offers attractive bedrooms in a variety of sizes, all thoughtfully equipped to suit business and leisure guests. There is a comfortable lounge offering a supper and snack menu. Internet access is also available.

Rooms 6 en suite (1 fmly) (2 GF) S £79-£96; D £94-£194* **Facilities** FTV tea/coffee Direct Dial Cen ht Wi-fi **Parking** 6 **Notes** LB ⊗ Closed approx 5-23 Jan

PREMIER COLLECTION

21212

★★★★★ 🎖🎖🎖 RESTAURANT WITH ROOMS

3 Royal Ter EH7 5AB
☎ 0131 523 1030 & 0845 222 1212
📠 0131 553 1038
e-mail: reservations@21212restaurant.co.uk

A real gem in Edinburgh's crown, this establishment takes its name from the numbers of choices at each course on the five-course dinner menu. Located on the prestigious Royal Terrace this is a light and airy, renovated Georgian townhouse stretching over four floors. The four individually designed bedrooms epitomise luxury living and the bathrooms certainly have the 'wow' factor. At the heart of this restaurant with rooms is the creative, award-winning cooking of Paul Kitching. Service throughout is friendly and very attentive.

Rooms 4 en suite D £175-£325* **Facilities** STV FTV Dinner available Cen ht Wi-fi **Notes** ⊗ No Children 5yrs Closed 1wk Jan RS Sun & Mon closed No coaches

PREMIER COLLECTION

The Witchery by the Castle

★★★★★ 🎖 🏠 RESTAURANT WITH ROOMS

352 Castlehill, The Royal Mile EH1 2NF
☎ 0131 225 5613 📠 0131 220 4392
e-mail: mail@thewitchery.com
web: www.thewitchery.com
dir: *Top of Royal Mile at gates of Edinburgh Castle*

Originally built in 1595, The Witchery by the Castle is situated in a historic building at the gates of Edinburgh Castle. The two luxurious and theatrically decorated suites, known as the Inner Sanctum and the Old Rectory are located above the restaurant and are reached via a winding stone staircase. Filled with antiques, opulently draped beds, large roll-top baths and a plethora of memorabilia, this ancient and exciting establishment is often described as one of the country's most romantic destinations.

Rooms 3 en suite 5 annexe en suite (1 GF)
Facilities STV FTV tea/coffee Dinner available Direct Dial Cen ht **Notes** ⊗ No Children 12yrs Closed 25-26 Dec No coaches

PREMIER COLLECTION

23 Mayfield

★★★★★ 🏠 GUEST ACCOMMODATION

23 Mayfield Gardens EH9 2BX
☎ 0131 667 5806 📠 0131 667 6833
e-mail: info@23mayfield.co.uk
web: www.23mayfield.co.uk
dir: *A720 bypass S, follow city centre signs. Left at Craigmillar Park, 0.5m on right*

23 Mayfield is well located en route into Edinburgh with the added benefit of off-road parking. The spacious accommodation has retained many of its original period features. Breakfast is a real delight, with the very best local produce used to give guests a great start to their day. 23 Mayfield is the AA's Guest Accommodation of the Year for Scotland (2011-2012).

Rooms 9 en suite (2 fmly) (2 GF) S £75-£110; D £90-£170 **Facilities** FTV tea/coffee Cen ht Wi-fi Bike hire **Parking** 10 **Notes** LB ⊗

Bonnington Guest House

★★★★ GUEST HOUSE

202 Ferry Rd EH6 4NW
☎ 0131 554 7610
e-mail: booking@thebonningtonguesthouse.com
web: www.thebonningtonguesthouse.com
dir: *On A902, near corner of Ferry Rd & Newhaven Rd*

This delightful Georgian house offers individually furnished bedrooms on two floors, that retain many of their original features. Family rooms are also available. A substantial freshly prepared breakfast is served in the refurbished dining room. Off-street parking is an added bonus.

Rooms 7 rms (5 en suite) (2 pri facs) (4 fmly) (1 GF) **Facilities** FTV tea/coffee Cen ht Wi-fi **Parking** 9 **Notes** ⊗

Fraoch House

★★★★ 🛏 GUEST ACCOMMODATION

66 Pilrig St EH6 5AS
☎ 0131 554 1353
e-mail: info@fraochhouse.com
dir: *1m from Princes St*

Situated within walking distance of the city centre and convenient for many attractions, Fraoch House, which dates from the 1900s, has been appointed to offer well-equipped and thoughtfully furnished bedrooms. Delicious, freshly cooked breakfasts are served in the charming dining room on the ground floor.

Rooms 9 rms (7 en suite) (2 pri facs) (1 fmly) (1 GF) **Facilities** FTV tea/coffee Cen ht Wi-fi Free use of DVDs and CDs & internet access **Notes** ⊗

Southside

★★★★ 🛏 GUEST HOUSE

8 Newington Rd EH9 1QS
☎ 0131 668 4422   📄 0131 667 7771
e-mail: info@southsideguesthouse.co.uk
web: www.southsideguesthouse.co.uk
dir: *E end of Princes St onto North Bridge to Royal Mile, continue S, 0.5m, house on right*

Situated within easy reach of the city centre and convenient for the major attractions, Southside is an elegant sandstone house. Bedrooms are individually styled, comfortable and thoughtfully equipped. Traditional, freshly cooked Scottish breakfasts are served at individual tables in the smart ground-floor dining room.

Rooms 8 en suite (2 fmly) (1 GF) S £68-£85; D £90-£180 **Facilities** FTV tea/coffee Direct Dial Cen ht Licensed Wi-fi **Notes** LB ⊗ No Children 10yrs

Allison House

★★★★ GUEST ACCOMMODATION

17 Mayfield Gardens EH9 2AX
☎ 0131 667 8049   📄 0131 667 5001
e-mail: info@allisonhousehotel.com
web: www.allisonhousehotel.com

Part of a Victorian terrace, Allison House offers modern comforts in a splendid building. It's convenient for the city centre, theatres and tourist attractions, and is on the main bus route. The attractive bedrooms are generally spacious and very well equipped. Breakfast is served at individual tables in the ground-floor dining room. Off-road parking is available.

Rooms 11 rms (10 en suite) (1 pri facs) (1 fmly) (2 GF) (2 smoking) **Facilities** tea/coffee Direct Dial Cen ht Wi-fi **Parking** 6 **Notes** ⊗

Ashlyn Guest House

★★★★ GUEST HOUSE

42 Inverleith Row EH3 5PY
☎ 0131 552 2954
e-mail: info@ashlynguesthouse.com
web: www.ashlynguesthouse.com
dir: *Adjacent to Edinburgh Botanic Gardens, then follow signs for North Edinburgh & Botanics*

The Ashlyn Guest House is a warm and friendly Georgian home, ideally located to take advantage of Edinburgh's attractions. The city centre is within walking distance and the Royal Botanical Gardens are minutes away. Bedrooms are all individually decorated and furnished to a high standard. A generous and hearty breakfast gives a great start to the day.

Rooms 8 rms (4 en suite) (2 pri facs) (1 fmly) (1 GF) S £35-£40; D £70-£90* **Facilities** FTV TVL tea/coffee Cen ht Wi-fi **Notes** ⊗ No Children 7yrs Closed 23-28 Dec

The Edinburgh Lodge

★★★★ GUEST HOUSE

6 Hampton Ter, West Coates EH12 5JD
☎ 0131 337 3682   📄 0131 313 1700
e-mail: info@thelodgehotel.co.uk
dir: *On A8, 0.75m W of Princes St*

Situated at the west end of Edinburgh, benefiting from off-road parking this well presented property offers comfortable bedrooms with many thoughtful extras, including complimentary Wi-fi. A well-cooked breakfast is served on individual tables which overlook the well maintained gardens.

Rooms 12 en suite (2 fmly) (4 GF) **Facilities** STV TVL tea/coffee Direct Dial Cen ht Licensed Wi-fi **Conf** Max 16 **Parking** 8 **Notes** ⊗

EDINBURGH *continued*

Heriott Park

★★★★ GUEST HOUSE

256 Ferry Rd, Goldenacre EH5 3AN
☎ **0131 552 3456**
e-mail: reservations@heriottpark.co.uk
web: www.heriottpark.co.uk
dir: *1.5m N of city centre on A902*

A conversion of two adjoining properties, which retain many original features. Heriott Park is on the north side of the city and has lovely panoramic views of the Edinburgh skyline, including the castle and Arthur's Seat. The attractive bedrooms are well equipped and have excellent en suite bathrooms.

Rooms 15 en suite (7 fmly) (1 GF) S £40-£80; D £60-£110* **Facilities** FTV tea/coffee Cen ht Wi-fi
Notes ⊗

International Guest House

★★★★ GUEST HOUSE

37 Mayfield Gardens EH9 2BX
☎ **0131 667 2511 & 0845 241 7551** 📠 **0131 667 1112**
e-mail: intergh1@yahoo.co.uk
web: www.accommodation-edinburgh.com
dir: *On A701 1.5m S of Princes St*

Guests are assured of a warm and friendly welcome at this attractive Victorian terraced house, situated to the south of the city centre. The smartly presented bedrooms are thoughtfully decorated, comfortably furnished and well equipped. Hearty Scottish breakfasts are served at individual tables in the traditionally styled dining room, which boasts a beautiful ornate ceiling.

Rooms 9 en suite (3 fmly) (1 GF) S £40-£80; D £70-£140
Facilities FTV tea/coffee Direct Dial Cen ht Wi-fi
Parking 3 **Notes** LB ⊗

See advert on this page

Kingsway Guest House

★★★★ GUEST HOUSE

5 East Mayfield EH9 1SD
☎ **0131 667 5029**
e-mail: room@edinburgh-guesthouse.com
web: www.edinburgh-guesthouse.com
dir: *A701 to city centre, after 4m road name changes to Mayfield Gdns. Turn right at lights onto East Mayfield*

Well situated for the city centre and with off-road parking, this well presented Victorian building maintains a number of original features, and genuine and warm hospitality is assured. All the bedrooms are comfortable, and the quality Scottish breakfasts make an excellent start to the day

Rooms 7 rms (6 en suite) (1 pri facs) (2 fmly) S £40-£60; D £60-£100 **Facilities** FTV tea/coffee Cen ht Wi-fi Golf 18
Parking 4 **Notes** ⊗

Save on B&Bs and Hotels. Book at **theAA.com/hotel**

CITY OF EDINBURGH 377 SCOTLAND

Sherwood

★★★★ GUEST HOUSE

42 Minto St EH9 2BR
☎ 0131 667 1200 📠 0131 667 2344
e-mail: enquiries@sherwood-edinburgh.com
web: www.sherwood-edinburgh.com
dir: On A701, S of city centre

Lying on the south side of the city, this guest house is immaculately maintained and attractively presented throughout. Bedrooms vary in size, the smaller ones being thoughtfully appointed to make the best use of space. All include iron and ironing board, and several come with a fridge and microwave. Continental breakfast is served in the elegant dining room.

Rooms 6 rms (5 en suite) (1 pri facs) (2 fmly) (1 GF) S £40-£75; D £55-£90* **Facilities** FTV tea/coffee Cen ht Wi-fi **Parking** 3 **Notes** LB ⊗ Closed 20-29 Dec & 5 Jan-2 Mar

Gildun

★★★★ 🅐 GUEST HOUSE

9 Spence St EH16 5AG
☎ 0131 667 1368 📠 0131 668 4989
e-mail: gildun.edin@btinternet.com
dir: A720 city bypass to Sheriffhall rdbt onto A7 for 4m to Cameron Toll rdbt. Under rail bridge follow A7 sign onto Dalkeith Rd. Spence St 4th left opp church

Rooms 8 rms (7 en suite) (1 pri facs) (5 fmly) (2 GF) S £30-£68; D £60-£134* **Facilities** FTV tea/coffee Cen ht Wi-fi **Parking** 4 **Notes** LB

Arden Guest House

★★★ GUEST HOUSE

126 Old Dalkeith Rd EH16 4SD
☎ 0131 664 3985 📠 0131 621 0866
e-mail: ardenguesthouse@btinternet.com
dir: 2m SE of city centre nr Craigmillar Castle. On A7 200yds W of hospital

Arden Guest House is well situated on the south side of the city, close to the hospital, benefiting from off-road parking. Many thoughtful extras are provided as standard, including Wi-fi. Attentive and friendly service enhances the guest experience.

Rooms 8 en suite (2 fmly) (3 GF) S £30-£45; D £50-£90* **Facilities** STV tea/coffee Cen ht Wi-fi **Parking** 8 **Notes** Closed 22-27 Dec

Averon City Centre Guest House

★★★ GUEST HOUSE

44 Gilmore Place EH3 9NQ
☎ 0131 229 9932
e-mail: info@averon.co.uk
web: www.averon.co.uk
dir: From W end of Princes St onto A702, right at Kings Theatre

Situated within walking distance of the west end of the city and close to the Kings Theatre, Mrs Iliazova's guest house offers comfortable good value accommodation, with a secure car park to the rear.

Rooms 10 rms (6 en suite) (1 pri facs) (3 fmly) (5 GF) S £28-£44; D £48-£90 **Facilities** tea/coffee Cen ht **Parking** 19 **Notes** ⊗

See advert on this page

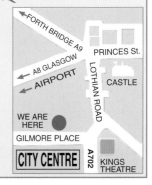

EDINBURGH *continued*

Elder York Guest House

★★★ GUEST HOUSE

38 Elder St EH1 3DX
☎ 0131 556 1926 📠 0131 624 7140
e-mail: reception@elderyork.co.uk
web: www.elderyork.co.uk
dir: *Close to Princes St, next to bus station*

Centrally located just minutes from the bus station, Harvey Nichols and the St James Shopping Centre. Accommodation is situated up flights of stairs but all bedrooms are well appointed with many thoughtful extras including Wi-fi. Quality breakfast is served on individual tables overlooking Queen Street.

Rooms 13 rms (10 en suite) (1 fmly) **Facilities** FTV tea/coffee Cen ht Wi-fi **Notes** ⊗

Ardbrae House B&B

★★★ 🅰 BED AND BREAKFAST

85 Drum Brae South, Corstorphine EH12 8TD
☎ 0131 467 5787
e-mail: info@ardbrae.com
dir: *From W enter Edinburgh on A8. At PC World/Drum Brae rdbt turn left, up hill, on left, adjacent to speed camera*

Rooms 3 en suite (3 GF) S £35-£60; D £50-£80 **Facilities** FTV tea/coffee Cen ht Wi-fi ch fac **Parking** 5 **Notes** LB ⊗ Closed 24-28 Dec

Classic House

★★★ 🅰 GUEST HOUSE

50 Mayfield Rd EH9 2NH
☎ 0131 667 5847 📠 0131 662 1016
e-mail: info@classicguesthouse.co.uk
web: www.classichouse.demon.co.uk
dir: *From bypass follow signs for A701 city centre. At Liberton Brae, keep left, 0.5m on left*

Rooms 7 rms (6 en suite) (1 pri facs) (2 fmly) S £35-£60; D £50-£90* **Facilities** TVL Cen ht **Notes** LB ⊗

Ravensdown Guest House

★★★ 🅰 GUEST HOUSE

248 Ferry Rd EH5 3AN
☎ 0131 552 5438
e-mail: david@ravensdownhouse.com
web: www.ravensdownhouse.com
dir: *N of city centre, close to Royal Botanic Gardens, A902 Goldenacre*

Rooms 7 en suite (5 fmly) (1 GF) S £50-£115; D £80-£125 **Facilities** FTV tea/coffee Cen ht Wi-fi **Parking** 2 **Notes** LB ⊗

ANSTRUTHER	Map 21 NO50

The Spindrift

★★★★ 🏠 ⌨ GUEST HOUSE

Pittenweem Rd KY10 3DT
☎ 01333 310573 📠 01333 310573
e-mail: info@thespindrift.co.uk
web: www.thespindrift.co.uk
dir: *Enter town from W on A917, 1st building on left*

This immaculate Victorian villa stands on the western edge of the village. The attractive bedrooms offer a wide range of extra touches; the Captain's Room, a replica of a wood-panelled cabin, is a particular feature. The inviting lounge has an honesty bar, while imaginative breakfasts, and enjoyable home-cooked meals by arrangement, are served in the cheerful dining room.

The Spindrift

Rooms 8 rms (7 en suite) (1 pri facs) (2 fmly) S £40-£80; D £66-£80 **Facilities** FTV TVL tea/coffee Dinner available Direct Dial Cen ht Licensed Wi-fi Golf 18 **Parking** 12 **Notes** LB No Children 10yrs Closed Xmas-late Jan

The Waterfront

★★★★ 🏠 ⌨ RESTAURANT WITH ROOMS

18-20 Shore St KY10 3EA
☎ 01333 312200 📠 01333 312288
e-mail: chris@anstruther-waterfront.co.uk
dir: *Off A917 opposite marina*

Situated overlooking the harbour, The Waterfront offers spacious, stylish, contemporary accommodation, with bedrooms located in lovingly restored buildings in a courtyard behind the restaurant. There is a comfortable lounge with a smartly fitted kitchen and dining room, and laundry facilities are available in the granary. Dinner and breakfast are served in the attractive restaurant that offers a comprehensive menu featuring the best of local produce.

Rooms 8 annexe en suite (3 fmly) (1 GF) **Facilities** STV TVL tea/coffee Dinner available Cen ht **Notes** ⊗

Save on B&Bs and Hotels. Book at **theAA.com/hotel**

FIFE 379 SCOTLAND

INVERKEITHING   Map 21 NT18

The Roods

★★★★ BED AND BREAKFAST

16 Bannerman Av KY11 1NG
☎ 01383 415049   📄 01383 415049
e-mail: isobelmarley@hotmail.com
web: www.the-roods.co.uk
dir: *N of town centre off B981(Church St/Chapel Place)*

This charming house stands in secluded, well-tended gardens close to the station. Bedrooms are individually styled and have state-of-the-art bathrooms. There is an inviting lounge, and breakfast is served at individual tables in an attractive conservatory.

Rooms 2 en suite (2 GF) S fr £35; D £70-£80*
Facilities FTV TVL tea/coffee Direct Dial Cen ht Wi-fi
Parking 4 **Notes** LB ⊗

LEUCHARS   Map 21 NO42

Hillpark House

★★★★ GUEST HOUSE

96 Main St KY16 0HF
☎ 01334 839280   📄 01334 839051
e-mail: enquiries@hillparkhouse.com
web: www.hillparkhouse.com
dir: *Leaving Leuchars for St Michaels, house last on right*

Lying peacefully on the edge of the village, Hillpark House is an impressive Edwardian home offering comfortable, well-appointed and equipped bedrooms. There is an inviting lounge, a conservatory and a peaceful dining room.

Rooms 5 rms (3 en suite) (1 pri facs) (1 fmly) S £38-£45; D £76-£90 **Facilities** TVL tea/coffee Cen ht Wi-fi Golf
Parking 6 **Notes** ⊗

LEVEN   Map 21 NO30

Dunclutha Guest House

★★★★ GUEST HOUSE

16 Victoria Rd KY8 4EX
☎ 01333 425515   📄 01333 422311
e-mail: pam.leven@blueyonder.co.uk
web: www.dunclutha.myby.co.uk
dir: *A915, B933 Glenlyon Rd into Leven, rdbt left onto Commercial Rd & Victoria Rd, Dunclutha opp church on right*

Set in a quiet street close to the town centre, Dunclutha is an inviting Victorian property that was formerly the rectory for the nearby Episcopalian church. Lovingly restored and refurbished to its original splendour it offers comfortable, well-equipped accommodation. A splendid lounge adjoins the dining room where hearty breakfasts are served at individual tables.

Rooms 4 rms (3 en suite) (1 pri facs) (2 fmly) S £35-£40; D £64-£80* **Facilities** FTV TVL tea/coffee Cen ht Wi-fi Piano **Parking** 3 **Notes** ⊗ Closed 2wks Jan

MARKINCH   Map 21 NO20

Town House

★★★★ RESTAURANT WITH ROOMS

1 High St KY7 6DQ
☎ 01592 758459   📄 01592 755039
e-mail: townhousehotel@aol.com
web: www.townhousehotel-fife.co.uk
dir: *In town centre opposite railway station*

Well situated on the edge of town and close to the railway station, this friendly establishment offers well presented bedrooms with pleasant colour schemes, modern furnishings, and a good range of facilities and extras. The attractive bar-restaurant is popular with locals and serves a choice of good-value dishes.

Rooms 3 en suite (1 fmly) S £50-£65; D £80-£90*
Facilities FTV tea/coffee Dinner available Cen ht Wi-fi
Notes ⊗ Closed 25-26 Dec & 1-2 Jan No coaches

PEAT INN   Map 21 NO40

PREMIER COLLECTION

The Peat Inn

★★★★★ ◉◉◉ RESTAURANT WITH ROOMS

KY15 5LH
☎ 01334 840206   📄 01334 840530
e-mail: stay@thepeatinn.co.uk
dir: *At junct of B940 & B941, 5m SW of St Andrews*

This 300-year-old former coaching inn enjoys a rural location, yet is close to St Andrews. The spacious restaurant with rooms is very well appointed and all rooms have lounge areas. The inn is steeped in history and is a real haven for food lovers. The three dining areas create a romantic setting, and chef/owner Geoffrey Smeddle turns out excellent 3 AA Rosette-worthy dishes. Expect open fires and a relaxed ambiance.

Rooms 8 annexe en suite (3 fmly) (8 GF) S £150; D £195* **Facilities** FTV tea/coffee Dinner available Direct Dial Cen ht Wi-fi **Parking** 24 **Notes** LB ⊗ Closed 25-26 Dec, 2wks Jan RS Sun-Mon Closed No coaches

ST ANDREWS   Map 21 NO51

PREMIER COLLECTION

The Paddock

★★★★★ 🏠 GUEST ACCOMMODATION

Sunnyside, Strathkinness KY16 9XP
☎ 01334 850888   📄 01334 850870
e-mail: thepaddock@btinternet.com
web: www.thepadd.co.uk
dir: *3m W from St Andrews off B939. The Paddock signed from village centre*

Situated in a peaceful village overlooking rolling countryside, this friendly, family-run guest accommodation offers stylish and very well-equipped bedrooms. Superb fish tanks, one freshwater, the other salt, line the entrance hall and contain beautiful and unusual fish. The lounge-dining room in the conservatory is a lovely setting for the delicious breakfasts.

Rooms 4 en suite (1 fmly) (2 GF) **Facilities** FTV tea/coffee Cen ht Wi-fi **Parking** 8 **Notes** ⊗ No Children 12yrs Closed Nov-Mar

ST ANDREWS continued

Nethan House

★ ★ ★ ★ GUEST HOUSE

17 Murray Park KY16 9AW
☎ 01334 472104 📠 01334 850870
e-mail: enquiries@nethan-standrews.com
dir: *A91 towards St Andrews, over 2nd rdbt onto North St, Murray Park on left before cinema*

This large Victorian terrace house is set in the heart of St Andrews; a short walk from the main tourist attractions and the famous golf course. The bright bedrooms are stylish and well appointed. The freshly cooked breakfast is a highlight and is served in the attractive dining room.

Rooms 7 en suite (1 fmly) (1 GF) **Facilities** FTV TVL tea/coffee Cen ht Wi-fi **Notes** ⊗ Closed 24-26 Dec

The Inn at Lathones

★ ★ ★ ★ ◉ ◉ INN

Largoward KY9 1JE
☎ 01334 840494 📠 01334 840694
e-mail: lathones@theinn.co.uk
web: www.theinn.co.uk
dir: *5m S of St Andrews on A915, 0.5m before village of Largoward on left just after hidden dip*

This lovely country inn, parts of which are 400 years old, is full of character and individuality. The friendly staff help to create a relaxed atmosphere. Smart contemporary bedrooms are in two separate wings. The colourful, cosy restaurant is the main focus, where the menu offers modern interpretations of Scottish and European dishes.

Rooms 21 annexe en suite (1 fmly) (18 GF) **Facilities** STV TVL tea/coffee Dinner available Direct Dial Cen ht Wi-fi **Conf** Max 40 Thtr 40 Class 10 Board 20 **Parking** 35 **Notes** Closed 26 Dec & 3-16 Jan RS 24 Dec Civ Wed 45

Lorimer House

★ ★ ★ ★ GUEST HOUSE

19 Murray Park KY16 9AW
☎ 01334 476599 📠 01334 476599
e-mail: info@lorimerhouse.com
dir: *A91 to St Andrews, left onto Golf Place, right onto The Scores, right onto Murray Park*

Rooms 5 en suite (1 GF) D £80-£110* **Facilities** STV FTV TVL tea/coffee Cen ht Wi-fi **Notes** ⊗ No Children 12yrs

Millhouse B&B

★ ★ ★ ★ ▲ BED AND BREAKFAST

2 Cauldside Farm Steading, Strathkinness High Rd KY16 9TY
☎ 01334 850557
e-mail: millhousebandb@yahoo.co.uk
web: www.bandbinstandrews.co.uk
dir: *B939 W of St Andrews, right onto Strathkinness High Rd. After 1m, right onto farm track*

Rooms 2 en suite D £65-£75* **Facilities** FTV TVL tea/coffee Cen ht Wi-fi **Parking** 3 **Notes** ⊗ No Children 12yrs

CITY OF GLASGOW

GLASGOW	Map 20 NS56

Argyll Guest House

★ ★ ★ GUEST ACCOMMODATION

960 Sauchiehall St G3 7TH
☎ 0141 357 5155 📠 0141 337 3283
e-mail: info@argyllguesthouseglasgow.co.uk
web: www.argyllguesthouseglasgow.co.uk
dir: *M8 junct 18 right hand lane, at 2nd set of lights turn right onto Berkley St. Right onto Elderslie St, 1st left onto Sauchiehall St*

This very popular guest accommodation is close to the city centre, the Scottish Conference and Exhibition centre and the University. The bedrooms have all been refurbished and each room is attractively presented, well equipped and includes features like free Wi-fi. A full hot and cold buffet breakfast is served at the adjacent Argyll Hotel.

Rooms 20 en suite (5 fmly) (5 GF) **Facilities** FTV tea/coffee Direct Dial Cen ht Wi-fi **Notes** LB ⊗

Clifton Guest House

★ ★ ★ GUEST HOUSE

26-27 Buckingham Ter, Great Western Rd G12 8ED
☎ 0141 334 8080 📠 0141 337 3468
e-mail: kalam@cliftonhotelglasgow.co.uk
web: www.cliftonhotelglasgow.com
dir: *1.25m NW of city centre off A82 (Inverquhomery Rd)*

Located north-west of the city centre, the Clifton forms part of an elegant terrace and is ideal for business and leisure. The attractive bedrooms are spacious, and there is an elegant lounge. Hearty breakfasts are served at individual tables in the dining room.

Rooms 23 rms (17 en suite) (6 fmly) (3 GF) **Facilities** STV TVL tea/coffee Direct Dial Cen ht **Parking** 8 **Notes** ⊗

Georgian House

★ ★ ★ GUEST HOUSE

29 Buckingham Ter, Great Western Rd G12 8ED
☎ 0141 339 0008 & 07973 971563
e-mail: thegeorgianhouse@yahoo.com
web: www.thegeorgianhousehotel.com
dir: *M8 junct 17 towards Dumbarton, through 4 sets of lights & right onto Queen Margaret Dr, then right onto Buckingham Ter*

Georgian House offers good value accommodation at the west end of the city in a peaceful tree-lined Victorian terrace near the Botanic Gardens. Bedrooms vary in size and are furnished in modern style. A continental style breakfast is served in the first-floor lounge-dining room.

Rooms 11 rms (10 en suite) (1 pri facs) (4 fmly) (3 GF) S £40-£60; D £70-£110* **Facilities** FTV tea/coffee Cen ht Wi-fi **Parking** 6 **Notes** LB

The Kelvin

★ ★ ★ GUEST HOUSE

15 Buckingham Ter, Great Western Rd, Hillhead G12 8EB
☎ 0141 339 7143 📠 0141 339 5215
e-mail: enquiries@kelvinhotel.com
web: www.kelvinhotel.com
dir: *M8 junct 17, A82 Kelvinside/Dumbarton, 1m on right before Botanic Gardens*

Two substantial Victorian terrace houses on the west side of the city have been combined to create this friendly establishment close to the Botanic Gardens. The attractive bedrooms are comfortably proportioned and well equipped with flat screen TVs offering an array of channels and Wi-fi available also. The dining room on the first floor is the setting for breakfasts served at individual tables.

Rooms 21 rms (9 en suite) (4 fmly) (2 GF) (14 smoking) S £30-£48; D £60-£68 **Facilities** FTV tea/coffee Cen ht Wi-fi **Parking** 5

Lomond

★ ★ ★ GUEST ACCOMMODATION

6 Buckingham Ter, Great Western Rd, Hillhead G12 8EB
☎ 0141 339 2339 📠 0141 339 0477
e-mail: info@lomondhotel.co.uk
web: www.lomondhotel.co.uk
dir: *M8 junct 17, A82 Dumbarton, 1m on right before Botanic Gardens*

Situated in the west end of the city in a tree-lined Victorian terrace, the Lomond offers well maintained, good value accommodation in a friendly environment. Bedrooms are brightly appointed and suitably equipped for leisure guests. Hearty breakfasts are served at individual tables in the bright ground-floor dining room.

Rooms 17 rms (6 en suite) (5 fmly) (3 GF) **Facilities** tea/coffee Direct Dial Cen ht

Craigielea House B&B

★★ Ⓐ BED AND BREAKFAST

35 Westercraigs G31 2HY
☎ 0141 554 3446 & 07890 991063
e-mail: craigieleahouse@yahoo.co.uk
dir: *1m E of city centre. M8 junct 15, onto A8, left onto Duke St, pass Tennents Brewery & left onto road after lights onto Craigpark. 3rd on left, then right onto Westercraigs*

Rooms 3 rms (1 GF) S £28-£33; D £40-£50*
Facilities FTV tea/coffee Cen ht Wi-fi **Parking** 3 **Notes** ⊗ No Children 3yrs ⊜

HIGHLAND

ARDELVE   Map 22 NG82

Caberfeidh House

★★★ GUEST HOUSE

IV40 8DY
☎ 01599 555293
e-mail: info@caberfeidh.plus.com
web: www.caberfeidh.plus.com
dir: *A87 over Dornie Bridge into Ardelve, 1st left, 100yds on right*

Set in a peaceful location overlooking Lochs Alsh and Duich, Caberfeidh House offers good value, comfortable accommodation in relaxed and friendly surroundings. Bedrooms are traditionally furnished and thoughtfully equipped, and there is a cosy lounge with a wide selection of books, games and magazines. Hearty breakfasts are served at individual tables in the dining room. Discount available for stays of two or more nights.

Rooms 5 rms (4 en suite) (1 pri facs) (3 fmly) S £32; D £64 **Facilities** FTV tea/coffee Cen ht **Parking** 4 **Notes** ⊗ Closed 25-26 Dec

ARISAIG   Map 22 NM68

Cnoc-na-Faire

★★★★★ ⓖ ⌂ INN

Back of Keppoch PH39 4NS
☎ 01687 450249   ▤ 01687 450249
e-mail: cnocnafaire@googlemail.com
dir: *A830 1m past Arisaig, turn left onto B0080, 0.5m on left into driveway*

Gaelic for Hill of Vigil the property boasts picture postcard views down to the white sandy beach and further afield to the Inner Hebridean Isles. Modern bedrooms and bathrooms cater well for the needs of the guest. AA Rosette-winning food is served in the cosy bar and restaurant. Warm and genuine service and hospitality complete this wonderful guest experience.

Rooms 6 en suite **Facilities** STV tea/coffee Dinner available Cen ht Wi-fi Golf 9 **Conf** Max 20 Thtr 20 Class 16 Board 16 **Parking** 15 **Notes** Closed 23-27 Dec No coaches Civ Wed 25

AVIEMORE   Map 23 NH81

PREMIER COLLECTION

The Old Minister's House

★★★★★ GUEST HOUSE

Rothiemurchus PH22 1QH
☎ 01479 812181   ▤ 01479 811925
e-mail: kate@theoldministershouse.co.uk
web: www.theoldministershouse.co.uk
dir: *B970 from Aviemore signed Glenmore & Coylumbridge, establishment 0.75m at Inverdruie*

Built originally as a manse in 1906, the Old Minister's House stands in well-tended grounds close to Aviemore. The house is beautifully furnished and immaculately maintained. Bedrooms are spacious, attractively decorated and thoughtfully equipped. There is an inviting lounge and a dining room where hearty breakfasts are served.

Rooms 4 en suite (1 fmly) **Facilities** FTV tea/coffee Cen ht Wi-fi **Parking** 4 **Notes** ⊗ No Children 10yrs

Ravenscraig

★★★★ GUEST HOUSE

Grampian Rd PH22 1RP
☎ 01479 810278   ▤ 01479 810210
e-mail: info@aviemoreonline.com
web: www.aviemoreonline.com
dir: *N end of main street, 250yds N of police station*

This friendly, family-run guest house is on the north side of the village, a short walk from local amenities. Bedrooms vary between the traditionally styled rooms in the main house and modern spacious rooms in a chalet-style annexe. There is a relaxing lounge and separate dining room, where freshly prepared breakfasts are served at individual tables.

Rooms 6 en suite 6 annexe en suite (6 fmly) (6 GF) S £35-£42; D £70-£84* **Facilities** FTV TVL tea/coffee Cen ht Wi-fi **Parking** 15 **Notes** ⊗

BALLACHULISH   Map 22 NN05

Lyn-Leven

★★★★ GUEST HOUSE

West Laroch PH49 4JP
☎ 01855 811392   ▤ 01855 811600
e-mail: macleodcilla@aol.com
web: www.lynleven.co.uk
dir: *Off A82 signed on left West Laroch*

Genuine Highland hospitality and high standards are part of the appeal of this comfortable guest house. The attractive bedrooms vary in size, are well equipped, and offer many thoughtful extra touches. There is a spacious lounge, and a smart dining room where delicious home-cooked breakfasts are served at individual tables.

Rooms 8 en suite 4 annexe en suite (3 fmly) (12 GF) S £45-£55; D £56-£70* **Facilities** TVL tea/coffee Cen ht Licensed **Parking** 12 **Notes** LB Closed Xmas

BONAR BRIDGE — Map 23 NH69

Kyle House

★★★ GUEST ACCOMMODATION

Dornoch Rd IV24 3EB
☎ 01863 766360
e-mail: kylehouse360@msn.com
dir: On A949 N from village centre

A spacious house with splendid views of the Kyle of Sutherland and the hills beyond. Bedrooms are comfortably furnished in traditional style and equipped with all the expected facilities. There is a lounge, and hearty breakfasts are enjoyed in the dining room.

Rooms 5 rms (3 en suite) (2 fmly) S £30-£50; D £60*
Facilities FTV TVL tea/coffee Cen ht **Parking** 5 **Notes** ⊗
No Children 5yrs Closed Dec-Jan RS Oct & Apr Occasional closure (phone in advance) ⊜

BRACHLA — Map 23 NH53

PREMIER COLLECTION

Loch Ness Lodge

★★★★★ ⊛⊛ 🍴 RESTAURANT WITH ROOMS

Loch Ness-Side IV3 8LA
☎ 01456 459469 🖷 01456 459439
e-mail: escape@loch-ness-lodge
dir: From A9 Inverness onto A82 signed Fort William, after 9m & 30mph speed sign, Lodge on right immediately after Clansman Hotel

This house enjoys a prominent position overlooking Loch Ness, and each of the individually designed bedrooms enjoys views of the loch. The bedrooms are of the highest standard, and are beautifully presented with a mix of traditional luxury and up-to-date technology, including Wi-fi. There is a spa with a hot tub, sauna and a therapy room offering a variety of treatments. Award-winning evening meals are served in the restaurant, and guests have a choice of attractive lounges which feature real fires in the colder months.

Rooms 7 en suite (1 GF) S £204-£369; D £254-£419*
(incl.dinner) **Facilities** Dinner available Direct Dial
Cen ht Wi-fi Golf 18 Fishing Sauna Hot tub Therapy
room **Conf** Max 14 Thtr 14 Class 10 Board 14
Parking 10 **Notes** LB ⊗ No Children 16yrs Closed 2-31
Jan No coaches Civ Wed 24

CARRBRIDGE — Map 23 NH92

The Pines Country House

★★★ BED AND BREAKFAST

Duthil PH23 3ND
☎ 01479 841520 🖷 01479 841520
e-mail: lynn@thepines-duthil.co.uk
dir: 2m E of Carrbridge in Duthil on A938

A warm welcome is assured at this comfortable home in the Cairngorms National Park. The bright bedrooms are traditionally furnished and offer good amenities. Enjoyable home-cooked fare is served around a communal table. Guests can relax in the conservatory-lounge and watch squirrels feed in the nearby wood.

Rooms 3 en suite (1 fmly) S £41.50-£45; D £60-£63.50*
Facilities STV tea/coffee Dinner available Cen ht Wi-fi
ch fac **Parking** 5 **Notes** LB

DORNOCH — Map 23 NH78

PREMIER COLLECTION

2 Quail

★★★★★ GUEST ACCOMMODATION

Castle St IV25 3SN
☎ 01862 811811
e-mail: theaa@2quail.com
dir: On main street, 200yds from cathedral

The saying 'small is beautiful' aptly applies to this guest accommodation. Set in the main street the careful renovation of its Victorian origins transports guests back in time. Cosy public rooms are ideal for conversation, but there are masses of books for those just wishing to relax. The stylish, individual bedrooms match the character of the house but are thoughtfully equipped to include DVD players.

Rooms 3 en suite (1 fmly) S £70-£110; D £80-£120*
Facilities FTV tea/coffee Direct Dial Cen ht Licensed
Wi-fi **Notes** LB ⊗ No Children 8yrs Closed Xmas & 2
wks Feb/Mar RS Nov-Mar winter hours - check when
booking

DRUMNADROCHIT — Map 23 NH53

Ferness Cottage

★★★★ BED AND BREAKFAST

Lewiston IV63 6UW
☎ 01456 450564
e-mail: info@lochnessaccommodation.co.uk
web: www.lochnessaccommodation.co.uk
dir: A82, from Inverness turn right after Esso service station; from Fort William left before Esso service station, 100mtrs phone box on left. 100mtrs on right

This rose-covered cottage dating from the 1840s has a peaceful location and is within easy walking distance of the village centre. The two charming bedrooms are well equipped, with many thoughtful extra touches. Traditional breakfasts in the cosy lounge-dining room feature the best of local produce. Guests can use the grass area, with seating, beside the River Coiltie, where fishing is available.

Rooms 2 rms (1 en suite) (1 pri facs) S £50-£70; D
£50-£70 **Facilities** STV tea/coffee Cen ht Wi-fi Fishing
Parking 2 **Notes** LB ⊗ No Children 10yrs

EVANTON — Map 23 NH66

Kiltearn House

★★★★ 🅰 GUEST HOUSE

Kiltearn, Dingwall IV16 9UY
☎ 01349 830617 🖷 01349 830617
e-mail: info@kiltearn.co.uk
dir: Off A9 towards Evanton, follow signs for burial
ground

Rooms 5 en suite S £72-£84; D £120-£150*
Facilities FTV TVL tea/coffee Dinner available Cen ht
Licensed Wi-fi **Parking** 6 **Notes** LB ⊗ No Children 12yrs

Save on B&Bs and Hotels. Book at **theAA.com/hotel**

HIGHLAND 383 SCOTLAND

FORT WILLIAM — Map 22 NN17

See also Spean Bridge

Distillery Guest House

★★★★ GUEST HOUSE

Nevis Bridge, North Rd PH33 6LR
☎ 01397 700103
e-mail: disthouse@aol.com
dir: *A82 from Fort William towards Inverness, on left after Glen Nevis rdbt*

Situated in the grounds of the former Glenlochy Distillery, this friendly guest house was once the distillery manager's home. Bedrooms are attractively decorated, comfortably furnished and very well equipped. There is a relaxing lounge, which features a superb range of games, and a bright airy dining room where traditional Scottish breakfasts are served at individual tables.

Rooms 10 en suite (1 fmly) (1 GF) **Facilities** tea/coffee Cen ht Licensed **Parking** 21 **Notes** ⊗

See advert on this page

Mansfield Guest House

★★★★ GUEST HOUSE

Corpach PH33 7LT
☎ 01397 772262 & 0845 6449432
e-mail: mansfield@btinternet.com
web: www.fortwilliamaccommodation.com
dir: *2m N of Fort William A82 onto A830, house 2m on A830 in Corpach*

Peacefully set in its own well-tended garden this friendly, family-run guest house provides comfortable, attractively decorated and well-equipped accommodation. There is a cosy lounge, where a roaring coal fire burns on cold evenings, and an attractive dining room where delicious, home-cooked evening meals and breakfasts are served at individual tables.

Rooms 6 en suite (1 GF) S £35-£40; D £60-£65
Facilities FTV TVL tea/coffee Dinner available Cen ht Wi-fi Golf 18 **Parking** 7 **Notes** LB ⊗ No Children 12yrs

Stobhan B&B

★★★ BED AND BREAKFAST

Fassifern Rd PH33 6BD
☎ 01397 702790 📠 01397 702790
e-mail: boggi@supanet.com
dir: *In town centre. A82 onto Victoria Rd beside St Mary's Church, right onto Fassifern Rd*

Stobhan B&B occupies an elevated location overlooking Loch Linnhe and offers comfortable, good-value accommodation. Bedrooms, one of which is on the ground floor, are traditionally furnished and have en suite facilities. Breakfast is served in the ground-floor dining room, which is adjacent to the lounge.

Rooms 4 en suite (1 GF) S £28-£35; D £56-£70
Facilities FTV tea/coffee Cen ht

FOYERS — Map 23 NH42

Craigdarroch House

★★★★ 🍴 RESTAURANT WITH ROOMS

IV2 6XU
☎ 01456 486400 📠 01456 486444
e-mail: info@hotel-loch-ness.co.uk
dir: *Take B862 from either end of loch, then B852 signed Foyers*

Craigdarroch is located in an elevated position high above Loch Ness on the south side. Bedrooms vary in style and size but all are comfortable and well equipped; those that are front-facing have wonderful views. Dinner is well worth staying in for, and breakfast is also memorable.

Rooms 8 en suite (1 fmly) S £65-£95; D £99-£160
Facilities FTV TVL tea/coffee Dinner available Direct Dial Cen ht Wi-fi **Conf** Max 30 Thtr 30 Class 30 Board 30 **Parking** 24 **Notes** No coaches Civ Wed 30

FOYERS continued

Foyers Bay Country House

★★★ GUEST HOUSE

Lochness IV2 6YB
☎ 01456 486624
e-mail: enquiries@foyersbay.co.uk
dir: Off B852 into Lower Foyers

Situated in sloping grounds with pines and abundant colourful rhododendrons, this delightful Victorian villa has stunning views of Loch Ness. The attractive bedrooms vary in size and are well equipped. There is a comfortable lounge next to the plant-filled conservatory-café, where delicious evening meals and traditional breakfasts are served.

Rooms 6 en suite (1 GF) S £55-£65; D £70-£95*
Facilities FTV TVL tea/coffee Dinner available Cen ht Licensed Wi-fi **Conf** Max 20 Thtr 20 Class 20 Board 20 **Parking** 6 **Notes** LB ⊗ No Children 16yrs Civ Wed 20

GLENCOE   Map 22 NN15

Lyn-Leven

★★★★ GUEST HOUSE

West Laroch PH49 4JP
☎ 01855 811392   01855 811600
e-mail: macleodcilla@aol.com
web: www.lynleven.co.uk

(For full entry see Ballachulish)

Scorrybreac

★★★★ GUEST ACCOMMODATION

PH49 4HT
☎ 01855 811354
e-mail: info@scorrybreac.co.uk
web: www.scorrybreacglencoe.com
dir: Off A82 just outside village, 500yds from River Coe bridge

With a stunning location above the village and overlooking the loch, this charming family-run guest accommodation offers guests a warm welcome. Bedrooms are attractive, well equipped and comfortably furnished. There is a cosy lounge with plenty of books, board games and maps, and a bright airy dining room where delicious breakfasts are served at individual tables.

Rooms 6 en suite (6 GF) **Facilities** tea/coffee Cen ht **Parking** 7 **Notes** ⊗ Closed 25-26 Dec

---

GOLSPIE   Map 23 NC80

Granite Villa Guest House

★★★★ GUEST ACCOMMODATION

Fountain Rd KW10 6TH
☎ 01408 633146
e-mail: info@granite-villa.co.uk
dir: Left from A9 (N'bound) onto Fountain Rd, immediately before pedestrian crossing lights

Originally built in 1892 for a wealthy local merchant, this traditional Victorian house has been sympathetically restored in recent years. Bedrooms are comfortable and all come with a range of thoughtful extras. Guests can relax in the large lounge, with its views over the landscaped garden where complimentary tea and coffee is often served. A warm welcome is assured in this charming period house.

Rooms 5 en suite (1 fmly) (1 GF) (2 smoking) S £45-£50; D £70* **Facilities** FTV tea/coffee Cen ht Wi-fi Golf 18 **Parking** 6 **Notes** ⊛

GRANTOWN-ON-SPEY   Map 23 NJ02

An Cala

★★★★★ A GUEST HOUSE

Woodlands Ter PH26 3JU
☎ 01479 873293   01479 873610
e-mail: ancala@globalnet.co.uk
web: www.ancalaguesthouse.co.uk
dir: From Aviemore on A95 left onto B9102 at rdbt outside Grantown. After 400yds, 1st left, An Cala opposite

Rooms 4 en suite (1 fmly) D £80-£86* **Facilities** FTV TVL tea/coffee Dinner available Cen ht Wi-fi **Parking** 7 **Notes** LB ⊗ No Children 3yrs Closed Xmas RS Nov-Mar Phone/e-mail bookings only

---

Holmhill House

★★★★ GUEST ACCOMMODATION

Woodside Av PH26 3JR
☎ 01479 873977
e-mail: enquiries@holmhillhouse.co.uk
web: www.holmhillhouse.co.uk
dir: S of town centre off A939 Spey Av

Built in 1895, and situated in a large well-tended garden within walking distance of the town centre, Holmhill House combines Victorian character with modern comforts. The attractive bedrooms are well equipped, and en suite. There are a ramp and lift available for easier access plus a specially equipped bathroom.

Rooms 3 en suite D £80-£90* **Facilities** FTV tea/coffee Cen ht Lift Wi-fi **Parking** 9 **Notes** ⊗ No Children 12yrs Closed Nov-Mar

---

INVERGARRY   Map 22 NH30

Forest Lodge Guest House

★★★ A GUEST HOUSE

South Laggan PH34 4EA
☎ 01809 501219   & 07790 907477
e-mail: info@flgh.co.uk
web: www.flgh.co.uk
dir: 2.5m S of Invergarry. Off A82 in South Laggan

Rooms 8 rms (7 en suite) (1 pri facs) (3 fmly) (4 GF) S £38-£40; D £60-£64* **Facilities** TVL TV1B tea/coffee Dinner available Cen ht Wi-fi **Parking** 10 **Notes** LB Closed 20 Dec-7 Jan

---

INVERNESS   Map 23 NH64

PREMIER COLLECTION

Daviot Lodge

★★★★★ GUEST ACCOMMODATION

Daviot Mains IV2 5ER
☎ 01463 772215   01463 772099
e-mail: margaret.hutcheson@btopenworld.com
dir: Off A9 5m S of Inverness onto B851 signed Croy. 1m on left

Standing in 80 acres of peaceful pasture land, this impressive establishment offers attractive, well-appointed and equipped bedrooms. The master bedroom is furnished with a four-poster bed. There is a tranquil lounge with deep sofas and a real fire, and a peaceful dining room where hearty breakfasts featuring the best of local produce are served. Full disabled access for wheelchairs.

Rooms 4 en suite (1 GF) S £40-£50; D £80-£100* **Facilities** FTV TVL tea/coffee Direct Dial Cen ht Licensed Wi-fi **Parking** 10 **Notes** LB No Children 5yrs Closed 23 Dec-2 Jan

PREMIER COLLECTION

Trafford Bank

★★★★★ 🏛 GUEST HOUSE

96 Fairfield Rd IV3 5LL
☎ **01463 241414**
e-mail: enquiries@invernesshotelaccommodation.co.uk
dir: *Off A82 at Kenneth St, Fairfield Rd 2nd left, 600yds on right*

This impressive Victorian house lies in a residential area close to the canal. Lorraine Freel has utilised her interior design skills to blend the best in contemporary styles with the house's period character and the results are simply stunning. Delightful public areas offer a choice of lounges, while breakfast is taken in a beautiful conservatory featuring eye-catching wrought-iron chairs. Each bedroom is unique in design and has TV, DVDs and CDs, sherry, silent mini-fridges and much more.

Rooms 5 en suite (2 fmly) **Facilities** STV FTV TVL tea/coffee Cen ht Wi-fi **Parking** 10 **Notes** ⊗

See advert on this page

Avalon Guest House

★★★★ GUEST HOUSE

79 Glenurquhart Rd IV3 5PB
☎ **01463 239075** 📠 **01463 709827**
e-mail: avalon@inverness-loch-ness.co.uk
web: www.inverness-loch-ness.co.uk
dir: *Exit A9 at Longman rdbt, 1st exit onto A82, at Telford St rdbt, 2nd exit. Right at lights onto Tomnahurich St/ Glenurquhart Rd*

Avalon Guest House is just a short walk from the city centre, and five minutes drive from Loch Ness. Each bedroom has a flatscreen LCD TV with Freeview (some with DVD), Wi-fi, fluffy white towels and complimentary toiletries; bathrobes and slippers are available on request as well as various other useful items. A delicious breakfast, freshly cooked from a varied menu, is served in the dining room; most dietary requirements can be catered for. Public areas include a guest lounge; and the owners have a range of maps, guidebooks and brochures that guests can refer to.

Rooms 6 rms (5 en suite) (1 pri facs) (4 GF) S £45-£75; D £60-£85 **Facilities** FTV TVL tea/coffee Cen ht Wi-fi **Parking** 12 **Notes** LB ⊗ No Children 12yrs

---

Ballifeary Guest House

★★★★ 🏛 GUEST HOUSE

10 Ballifeary Rd IV3 5PJ
☎ **01463 235572** 📠 **01463 717583**
e-mail: william.gilbert@btconnect.com
web: www.ballifearyguesthouse.co.uk
dir: *Off A82, 0.5m from town centre, turn left onto Bishops Rd & sharp right onto Ballifeary Rd*

This charming detached house has a peaceful residential location within easy walking distance of the town centre and Eden Court Theatre. The attractive bedrooms are carefully appointed and well equipped. There is an elegant ground-floor drawing room and a comfortable dining room, where delicious breakfasts, featuring the best of local produce, are served at individual tables.

Rooms 7 en suite (1 GF) S £40-£70; D £70-£85 **Facilities** FTV TV6B tea/coffee Cen ht Wi-fi **Parking** 6 **Notes** LB ⊗ No Children 15yrs Closed 24-28 Dec

---

INVERNESS continued

The Ghillies Lodge

★★★★ 🛏 BED AND BREAKFAST

16 Island Bank Rd IV2 4QS
☎ 01463 232137 & 07817 956533
e-mail: info@ghillieslodge.com
dir: *1m SW from town centre on B862, pink house facing river*

Situated on the banks of the River Ness not far from the city centre, Ghillies Lodge offers comfortable accommodation in a relaxed, peaceful environment. The attractive bedrooms, one of which is on the ground floor, are all en suite, and are individually styled and well equipped. There is a comfortable lounge-dining room, and a conservatory that overlooks the river.

Rooms 3 en suite (1 GF) S £40-£55; D £62-£72
Facilities STV tea/coffee Cen ht Wi-fi **Parking** 4 **Notes** ⊗

Moyness House

★★★★ 🛏 GUEST ACCOMMODATION

6 Bruce Gardens IV3 5EN
☎ 01463 233836 🖨 01463 233836
e-mail: stay@moyness.co.uk
web: www.moyness.co.uk
dir: *Off A82 (Fort William road), almost opp Highland Regional Council headquarters*

Situated in a quiet residential area just a short distance from the city centre, this elegant Victorian villa dates from 1880 and offers beautifully decorated, comfortable bedrooms and well-appointed bathrooms. There is an attractive sitting room and an inviting dining room, where traditional Scottish breakfasts are served. Guests are welcome to use the secluded and well-maintained back garden.

Moyness House

Rooms 6 en suite (1 fmly) (2 GF) S £60-£85; D £68-£100* **Facilities** FTV tea/coffee Cen ht Wi-fi **Parking** 10 **Notes** LB ⊗ No Children 5yrs

The Alexander

★★★★ 🛏 GUEST HOUSE

16 Ness Bank IV2 4SF
☎ 01463 231151 🖨 01463 232220
e-mail: info@thealexander.net
web: www.thealexander.net
dir: *On E bank of river, opposite cathedral*

Built in 1830 this impressive house has been extensively renovated by the current owners and many of the original Georgian features have been retained. Bedrooms are simply furnished and beds have luxurious mattresses dressed in fine Egyptian cotton. All rooms have flatscreen TVs with DVD players, there is a payphone in the hall, and ironing facilities are available. Light sleepers will welcome the silent running fridges in each room. Public rooms include a charming lounge with views over the River Ness and the house is a short walk from the city centre.

Rooms 7 en suite 3 annexe en suite (1 GF) S £45-£60; D £75-£95* **Facilities** FTV tea/coffee Cen ht Wi-fi **Parking** 8 **Notes** ⊗

Lyndon Guest House

★★★★ GUEST HOUSE

50 Telford St IV3 5LE
☎ 01463 232551 🖨 01463 225827
e-mail: lyndon@invernessbedandbreakfast.com
web: www.invernessbedandbreakfast.com
dir: *From A9 onto A82 over Friars Bridge, right at rdbt onto Telford St. House on right*

A warm Highland welcome awaits at this family-run accommodation close to the centre of Inverness. All rooms are en suite and are equipped with plenty of useful facilities including full internet access. Gaelic Spoken.

Rooms 6 en suite (4 fmly) (2 GF) S £28-£40; D £56-£80* **Facilities** STV FTV TVL tea/coffee Cen ht Wi-fi **Parking** 6 **Notes** ⊗ Closed 20 Dec-5 Jan

Westbourne

★★★★ 🛏 GUEST ACCOMMODATION

50 Huntly St IV3 5HS
☎ 01463 220700 🖨 01463 220700
e-mail: richard@westbourne.org.uk
dir: *A9 onto A82 at football stadium over 3 rdbts, at 4th rdbt 1st left onto Wells St & Huntly St*

The immaculately maintained Westbourne looks across the River Ness to the city centre. This friendly, family-run house has bright modern bedrooms of varying size, all attractively furnished in pine and very well equipped. A relaxing lounge with internet access, books, games and puzzles is available.

Rooms 9 en suite (2 fmly) S £45-£55; D £80-£90* **Facilities** FTV tea/coffee Cen ht Wi-fi **Parking** 6 **Notes** LB Closed Xmas & New Year

Sunnyholm

★★★ GUEST ACCOMMODATION

12 Mayfield Rd IV2 4AE
☎ 01463 231336
e-mail: sunnyholm@aol.com
web: www.invernessguesthouse.com
dir: *500yds SE of town centre. Off B861 Culduthel Rd onto Mayfield Rd*

Situated in a peaceful residential area within easy walking distance of the city centre, Sunnyholm offers comfortably proportioned and well-equipped bedrooms. A spacious conservatory-lounge overlooks the rear garden, and there is a another lounge next to the bright, airy dining room.

Rooms 4 en suite (4 GF) S £38-£42; D £60-£64* **Facilities** FTV tea/coffee Cen ht Wi-fi **Parking** 6 **Notes** ⊗ No Children 3yrs 🐾

Save on B&Bs and Hotels. Book at **theAA.com/hotel**

HIGHLAND 387 SCOTLAND

Acorn House

★★★ GUEST HOUSE

2A Bruce Gardens IV3 5EN
☎ 01463 717021 & 240000 📠 01463 714236
e-mail: enquiries@acorn-house.freeserve.co.uk
web: www.acorn-house.freeserve.co.uk
dir: *From town centre onto A82, on W side of river, right onto Bruce Gardens*

This attractive detached house is just a five-minute walk from the town centre. Bedrooms are smartly presented and well equipped. Breakfast is served at individual tables in the spacious dining room.

Rooms 6 en suite (2 fmly) **Facilities** STV TVL tea/coffee Cen ht Wi-fi Sauna Hot tub **Parking** 7 **Notes** Closed 25-26 Dec

Fraser House

★★★ GUEST ACCOMMODATION

9 Huntly St IV3 5HS
☎ 01463 716488 & 07900 676799 📠 01463 716488
e-mail: fraserlea@btopenworld.com
dir: *A82 W over bridge, left onto Huntly St, house 100yds*

Situated on the west bank of the River Ness, Fraser House has a commanding position overlooking the city, and is within easy walking distance of the central amenities. Bedrooms, all en suite, vary in size and are comfortably furnished and well equipped. The ground-floor dining room is the setting for freshly cooked Scottish breakfasts.

Rooms 5 en suite (2 fmly) S £30-£35; D £50-£60* **Facilities** FTV tea/coffee Cen ht Wi-fi **Notes** Closed Feb-Mar ⊛

KINGUSSIE Map 23 NH70

PREMIER COLLECTION

The Cross at Kingussie

★★★★★ ⊛⊛⊛ 🍴 RESTAURANT WITH ROOMS

Tweed Mill Brae, Ardbroilach Rd PH21 1LB
☎ 01540 661166 📠 01540 661080
e-mail: relax@thecross.co.uk
dir: *From lights in Kingussie centre along Ardbroilach Rd, 300yds left onto Tweed Mill Brae*

Situated in the valley near Kingussie, this former tweed mill sits next to a river, with wild flower gardens and a sunny terrace. Hospitality and food are clearly highlights of any stay at this special restaurant with rooms. Locally sourced produce is carefully prepared with passion and skill. Bedrooms are spacious and airy, with little touches such as fluffy towels and hand-made toiletries providing extra luxury.

Rooms 8 en suite (1 fmly) S £140-£165; D £180-£280* (incl.dinner) **Facilities** FTV tea/coffee Dinner available Direct Dial Cen ht Wi-fi Golf 18 Petanque **Conf** Max 20 Thtr 20 Class 20 Board 20 **Parking** 12 **Notes** LB ⊗ No Children 8yrs Closed Xmas & Jan (ex New Year) RS Sun & Mon Accommodation/dinner not available No coaches

Allt Gynack Guest House

★★★ Ⓐ GUEST HOUSE

Gynack Villa, 1 High St PH21 1HS
☎ 01540 661081
e-mail: alltgynack@tiscali.co.uk
web: www.alltgynack.com
dir: *A9 onto A86 through Newtonmore, 2m to Kingussie, on left after bridge*

Rooms 5 rms (3 en suite) (2 pri facs) (1 fmly) S £30-£32; D £56-£64* **Facilities** FTV tea/coffee Cen ht Wi-fi Golf 18 **Parking** 5 **Notes** LB No Children 14yrs

---

LYBSTER Map 23 ND23

Portland Arms

★★★★ ⊜ INN

Main St KW3 6BS
☎ 01593 721721 📠 01593 721722
e-mail: manager@portland-arms.co.uk
web: www.portlandarms.co.uk
dir: *On A99, 4m N of Thurso junct*

Originally built in the 1850s as a coaching inn, the Portland Arms has a range of stylish comfortable bedrooms with front facing rooms having a wonderful sea view. Fine dining can be enjoyed in the refurbished Library restaurant while more informal meals are served in the Farmhouse Kitchen. The resident's lounge has a range of comfortable seating and an open log fire burns brightly in the colder months.

Rooms 23 en suite (4 fmly) (4 GF) **Facilities** FTV tea/coffee Dinner available Direct Dial Cen ht Wi-fi ch fac Golf 9 **Conf** Max 150 Thtr 150 Class 150 Board 50 **Parking** 72 **Notes** ⊗ Civ Wed 280

MUIR OF ORD Map 23 NH55

Carndaisy House

★★★★ BED AND BREAKFAST

Easter Urray IV6 7UL
☎ 01463 870244 & 07780 923316 📠 0808 280 1771
e-mail: info@carndaisyhouse.co.uk
dir: *A9, at Tore rdbt 1st left onto A832 to Muir of Ord. At junct with A862 turn right over bridge, then 1st left onto A832. 2m W, turn right, 0.5m on left*

Carndaisy House offers very comfortable bed and breakfast in Easter Urray a short drive from Muir of Ord just outside Inverness. Accommodation includes three en suite rooms including a large family room with its own entrance and patio. All bedrooms are contemporarily decorated, and finished to a high standard. A well-cooked traditional Scottish breakfast provides a good start to the day.

Rooms 3 en suite (2 fmly) (1 GF) S £29-£49; D £49-£75* **Facilities** FTV tea/coffee Cen ht Wi-fi Riding **Parking** 5 **Notes** LB ⊗ ⊛

NAIRN · Map 23 NH85

North End

★★★★ BED AND BREAKFAST

18 Waverley Rd IV12 4RQ
☎ 01667 456338
e-mail: reservations@northendnairn.co.uk
dir: On corner of A96 (Academy St) & Waverley Rd

Built in 1895, North End is a delightful Victorian villa that has been sympathetically restored in recent years. The spacious bedrooms are comfortable and well equipped. The cosy lounge has a wood-burning stove and the original features of the house are complemented by contemporary furnishings. The house is within easy walking distance of Nairn and is a 20-minute drive from Inverness.

Rooms 3 rms (2 en suite) (1 pri facs) **Facilities** TVL tea/coffee Cen ht **Parking** 4 **Notes** ⊗ Closed Sep-Apr ⊛

NEWTONMORE · Map 23 NN79

Crubenbeg House

★★★★ GUEST HOUSE

Falls of Truim PH20 1BE
☎ 01540 673300
e-mail: enquiries@crubenbeghouse.com
web: www.crubenbeghouse.com
dir: 4m S of Newtonmore. Off A9 for Crubenmore, over railway bridge & right, signed

Set in a peaceful rural location, Crubenbeg House has stunning country views and is well located for touring the Highlands. The attractive bedrooms are individually styled and well equipped, while the ground-floor bedroom provides easier access. Guests can enjoy a dram in front of the fire in the inviting lounge, while breakfast features the best of local produce in the adjacent dining room.

Rooms 4 rms (3 en suite) (1 pri facs) (1 GF) S £33-£40; D £55-£87* **Facilities** STV tea/coffee Dinner available Cen ht Licensed Wi-fi **Parking** 10 **Notes** LB No Children 12yrs

POOLEWE · Map 22 NG88

PREMIER COLLECTION

Pool House

★★★★★ GUEST ACCOMMODATION

IV22 2LD
☎ 01445 781272 ▤ 01445 781403
e-mail: stay@pool-house.co.uk
dir: 6m N of Gairloch on A832 in the centre of village by bridge

Set on the shores of Loch Ewe where the river meets the bay, the understated roadside façade gives little hint of its splendid interior, nor of the views facing the bay. Memorable features are its delightful public rooms, and stunningly romantic suites, each individually designed with feature bathrooms. Pool House is run very much as a country house - the hospitality and guest care by the Harrison Family are second to none.

Rooms 5 en suite 1 annexe en suite (2 GF) S £125-£150; D £250-£300* **Facilities** FTV tea/coffee Dinner available Direct Dial Cen ht Licensed Wi-fi Fishing Snooker **Parking** 12 **Notes** LB ⊗ No Children 16yrs Closed 6 Jan-12 Feb RS Mon closed

SHIEL BRIDGE · Map 22 NG91

Grants at Craigellachie

★★★★ ⊛ RESTAURANT WITH ROOMS

Craigellachie, Ratagan IV40 8HP
☎ 01599 511331
e-mail: info@housebytheloch.co.uk
dir: From A87 exit for Glenelg, 1st right to Ratagan, opposite Youth Hostel sign

Sitting on the tranquil shores of Loch Duin and overlooked by the Five Sisters Mountains, Grants really does occupy a stunning location. The restaurant has a well deserved reputation for its cuisine, and the bedrooms are stylish and have all the creature comforts. Guests are guaranteed a warm welcome at this charming house.

Rooms 2 en suite 2 annexe en suite (3 GF) S £92.50-£112.50; D £155-£240* (incl.dinner) **Facilities** STV tea/coffee Dinner available Cen ht Wi-fi Riding **Parking** 8 **Notes** LB No Children 12yrs Closed Dec-mid Feb RS Oct-Apr reservation only No coaches

SOUTH BALLACHULISH · Map 22 NN05

Craiglinnhe House

★★★★ GUEST HOUSE

Lettermore PH49 4JD
☎ 01855 811270
e-mail: info@craiglinnhe.co.uk
web: www.craiglinnhe.co.uk
dir: From village A82 onto A828, Craiglinnhe 1.5m on left

Built during the reign of Queen Victoria, Craiglinnhe House enjoys an elevated position with stunning views across Loch Linnhe to the village of Onich, and up to the Ballachulish Bridge and the Pap of Glencoe. The attractive bedrooms vary in size, are stylishly furnished, and are well equipped. There is a ground-floor lounge and a charming dining room where delicious breakfasts, and evening meals by arrangement, are served at individual tables.

Rooms 5 en suite S £48-£55.50; D £60-£85 **Facilities** FTV tea/coffee Dinner available Cen ht Licensed Wi-fi **Parking** 5 **Notes** LB ⊗ No Children 13yrs Closed 24-26 Dec

SPEAN BRIDGE · Map 22 NN28

Corriechoille Lodge

★★★★ ⊜ GUEST HOUSE

PH34 4EY
☎ 01397 712002
web: www.corriechoille.com
dir: Off A82 signed Corriechoille, 2.5m, left at fork (10mph sign). At end of tarmac, turn right up hill & left

This fine country house stands above the River Spean. There are magnificent views of the Nevis range and surrounding mountains from the comfortable first-floor lounge and some of the spacious, well-appointed bedrooms. Friendly and attentive service is provided, as are traditional breakfasts and delicious evening meals by arrangement.

Rooms 4 en suite (2 fmly) (1 GF) S £42-£48; D £64-£76* **Facilities** STV FTV tea/coffee Dinner available Cen ht Licensed Wi-fi **Parking** 7 **Notes** ⊗ No Children 7yrs Closed Nov-Mar RS Sun-Mon closed

Smiddy House

★ ★ ★ ★ ⊛⊛ ≙ RESTAURANT WITH ROOMS

Roy Bridge Rd PH34 4EU
☎ 01397 712335 📠 01397 712043
e-mail: enquiry@smiddyhouse.co.uk
web: www.smiddyhouse.co.uk
dir: In village centre, A82 onto A86

Set in the Great Glen which stretches from Fort William to Inverness, this was once the village smithy, and is now a very friendly establishment. The attractive bedrooms, named after places in Scotland, are comfortably furnished and well equipped. A relaxing garden room is available for guest use. Delicious evening meals are served in Russell's restaurant.

Rooms 4 en suite (1 fmly) **Facilities** tea/coffee Dinner available Wi-fi **Parking** 15 **Notes** No coaches

Achnabobane (NN195811)

★ ★ ★ FARMHOUSE

PH34 4EX
☎ 01397 712919
Mr and Mrs N Ockenden
e-mail: enquiries@achnabobane.co.uk
web: www.achnabobane.co.uk
dir: 2m S of Spean Bridge on A82

With breathtaking views of Ben Nevis, Aonach Mhor and the Grey Corries, the farmhouse offers comfortable, good-value accommodation in a friendly family environment. Bedrooms are traditional in style and well equipped. Breakfast and evening meals are served in the conservatory-dining room. Pets are welcome.

Rooms 4 rms (1 en suite) (1 fmly) (1 GF) S £30-£34; D £60-£68* **Facilities** TVL tea/coffee Dinner available Cen ht Wi-fi **Parking** 5 **Notes** Closed Xmas red deer/woodland

STRATHPEFFER   Map 23 NH45

Inver Lodge

★ ★ ★ GUEST HOUSE

IV14 9DL
☎ 01997 421392
e-mail: derbyshire@inverlg.fsnet.co.uk
dir: A834 through Strathpeffer centre, turn beside Spa Pavilion signed Bowling Green, Inver Lodge on right

You are assured of a warm welcome at this Victorian lodge, secluded in its own tree-studded gardens yet within easy walking distance of the town centre. Bedrooms are comfortable and well equipped, and the cosy lounge is ideal for relaxation. Breakfasts, and evening meals (by arrangement), are served at a communal table.

Rooms 2 rms (1 fmly) S £32.50; D £50* **Facilities** FTV tea/coffee Dinner available Cen ht Wi-fi **Parking** 2 **Notes** LB ⊗ Closed Xmas & New Year ⊛

TOMATIN   Map 23 NH82

Glenan Lodge

★ ★ ★ ★ GUEST HOUSE

IV13 7YT
☎ 01808 511217 📠 08082 801125
e-mail: enquiries@glenanlodge.co.uk
web: www.glenanlodge.co.uk
dir: Off A9 to Tomatin, turn left to distillery, then right into distillery drive. Proceed to top of hill, take right fork & follow road to Glenan Lodge

Peacefully located on the edge of the village, this relaxed and homely guest house offers a warm welcome. The comfortable bedrooms are traditionally furnished and suitably equipped. An inviting lounge is available, and delicious home-cooked evening meals and breakfasts are served in the dining room. A two mile stretch of the River Findhorn is available for fly-fishing, and golfers, walkers and bird watchers are also well provided for locally.

Rooms 7 en suite (2 fmly) S £31-£41; D £62-£72* **Facilities** FTV TVL tea/coffee Dinner available Cen ht Licensed Wi-fi Fishing **Parking** 7 **Notes** LB ⊗ No Children 5yrs

TORRIDON — Map 22 NG95

The Torridon Inn

★★★ 🍴 INN

IV22 2EY
☎ 01445 791242 📠 01445 712253
e-mail: inn@thetorridon.com

The Torridon Inn enjoys an idyllic location and is set in 58 acres of parkland overlooking Loch Torridon and surrounded by steep mountains on all sides. The inn is very popular with walkers, and guests can also avail themselves of the many outdoor pursuits that are provided at the Torridon Hotel. Each of the spacious bedrooms are well equipped and comfortable. Evening meals and lunches are available at the inn where over 80 whiskies, and several real ales including a local Torridon Ale are firm favourites.

Rooms 12 en suite (3 fmly) (5 GF) S £99; D £99*
Facilities STV tea/coffee Dinner available Cen ht Wi-fi 🏊 Fishing Pool table Outdoor adventure activities available **Parking** 12 **Notes** LB Closed Jan

See advert on page 389

ULLAPOOL — Map 22 NH19

The Archinn

★★★ 🍴🍴 INN

10-11 West Shore St IV26 2UR
☎ 01854 612454
e-mail: info@thearchinn.co.uk

The Archinn is situated on Ullapool waterfront on the shores of Loch Broom, only a two-minute walk from the Outer Hebrides ferry terminal. The accommodation provided is comfortable and most rooms have stunning views over the loch to the mountains in the distance. Two dining options are available - the relaxed bar and grill on the ground floor, and a more formal Seafood Restaurant on the first floor.

Rooms 10 en suite (1 fmly) (2 GF) S fr £40; D fr £80*
Facilities FTV tea/coffee Dinner available Cen ht Wi-fi Pool table **Conf** Max 60 Thtr 40 Class 30 Board 35 **Parking** 5 **Notes** ⊗

WICK — Map 23 ND35

The Clachan

★★★★ BED AND BREAKFAST

13 Randolph Place, South Rd KW1 5NJ
☎ 01955 605384 & 600467
e-mail: enquiry@theclachan.co.uk
dir: *Off A99 0.5m S of town centre*

A warm welcome is assured at this immaculate detached home, by the main road on the south edge of the town. The bright, airy bedrooms (all on the ground floor) though compact, are attractively furnished to make good use of available space. Breakfast offers an extensive choice and is served at individual tables in the cosy dining room.

Rooms 3 en suite (3 GF) S £35-£55; D £64-£70*
Facilities FTV tea/coffee Cen ht Wi-fi **Parking** 3 **Notes** ⊗ No Children 12yrs Closed Xmas & New Year 🍴

MIDLOTHIAN

DALKEITH — Map 21 NT36

The Sun Inn

★★★★ 🍴 INN

Lothian Bridge EH22 4TR
☎ 0131 663 2456 & 07967 585850
e-mail: thesuninn@live.co.uk
dir: *On A7 towards Galashiels, opposite Newbattle Viaduct*

The Sun Inn dates back to 1697 and is situated within easy striking distance of Edinburgh. Major refurbishment has totally transformed this property and it now has boutique-style bedrooms (one featuring a copper bath) and modern bathrooms. High quality, award-winning food is served in stylish surroundings; drinks can be enjoyed in the terraced garden area.

Rooms 5 en suite S £70-£100; D £85-£150*
Facilities STV FTV tea/coffee Dinner available Cen ht Wi-fi Golf 18 Fishing **Parking** 50 **Notes** LB ⊗ No coaches

ROSLIN — Map 21 NT26

The Original Rosslyn Inn

★★★★ INN

4 Main St EH25 9LE
☎ 0131 440 2384 📠 0131 440 2514
e-mail: enquiries@theoriginalhotel.co.uk
dir: *Off city bypass at Straiton for A703 (inn near Rosslyn Chapel)*

Whether you find yourself on the Da Vinci Code trail or in the area on business, this property a very short walk from the famous Rosslyn Chapel which is well worth visiting. A delightful village inn offers well-equipped bedrooms with upgraded en suites. Four of the rooms have four-poster beds. The Grail Restaurant, the lounge and conservatory offer a comprehensive selection of dining options.

Rooms 6 en suite (2 fmly) (1 smoking) **Facilities** STV tea/coffee Dinner available Cen ht Wi-fi **Conf** Max 130 Thtr 130 Class 80 Board 60 **Parking** 8 **Notes** Civ Wed 180

NORTH AYRSHIRE

LARGS — Map 20 NS25

South Whittlieburn Farm

★★★★ 🏠 BED AND BREAKFAST

Brisbane Glen KA30 8SN
☎ 01475 675881 📠 01475 675080
e-mail: largsbandb@southwhittlieburnfarm.freeserve.co.uk
dir: *2m NE of Largs off A78 signed Brisbane Glen, after Vikingar centre*

This comfortable and welcoming farmhouse is on a working sheep farm surrounded by gently rolling countryside. The attractive bedrooms are well equipped with all having DVD and video players. There is a spacious ground-floor lounge, and a bright airy dining room where delicious breakfasts are served.

Rooms 3 en suite (1 fmly) S £37.50-£40; D £60-£65*
Facilities STV FTV TVL tea/coffee Cen ht Golf 18 **Parking** 10 **Notes** LB ⊗ RS Xmas 🍴

NORTH LANARKSHIRE

AIRDRIE
Map 21 NS76

Shawlee Cottage

★★★ 🅰 BED AND BREAKFAST

108 Lauchope St, Chapelhall ML6 8SW
☎ 01236 753774 📠 01236 749300
e-mail: shawleecottage@blueyonder.co.uk
web: www.airdriebedbreakfast.co.uk
dir: M8 junct 6, A73 to Chapelhall, left onto B799,
Shawlee 600yds on right

Rooms 5 en suite (5 GF) S £36-£46; D £55-£75*
Facilities tea/coffee Direct Dial Cen ht Wi-fi Golf 18
Parking 6 Notes ⊗

COATBRIDGE
Map 20 NS76

Auchenlea

★★★ GUEST HOUSE

153 Langmuir Rd, Bargeddie G69 7RT
☎ 0141 771 6870 & 07775 791381 📠 0141 771 6870
e-mail: helenbarr06@btinternet.com
dir: N off A8 onto A752 for 0.4m

Backing onto farmland, yet only a short distance from the
motorway, this detached house is well placed for Glasgow
and Edinburgh. Satisfying, well-cooked breakfasts are
served at a communal table in the bright dining room,
and there is an attractive conservatory and adjoining
lounge. The bedrooms, all on the ground floor, are modern
in style with one designed for easier access.

Rooms 6 en suite (1 fmly) (6 GF) Facilities FTV TVL tea/
coffee Cen ht Parking 10 Notes ⊗

PERTH & KINROSS

ALYTH
Map 23 NO24

PREMIER COLLECTION

Tigh Na Leigh Guesthouse

★★★★★ 🍴 🚗 GUEST ACCOMMODATION

22-24 Airlie St PH11 8AJ
☎ 01828 632372 📠 01828 632279
e-mail: bandcblack@yahoo.co.uk
web: www.tighnaleigh.co.uk
dir: In town centre on B952

Situated in the heart of this country town, Tigh Na
Leigh is Gaelic for 'The House of the Doctor'. Its
location and somewhat sombre façade are in stunning
contrast to what lies inside. The house has been
completely restored to blend its Victorian architecture
with contemporary interior design. Bedrooms, including
a superb suite, have state-of-the-art bathrooms. There
are three entirely different lounges, while delicious
meals are served in the conservatory/dining room
overlooking a spectacular landscaped garden.

Rooms 5 en suite (1 GF) S £42-£48; D £84-£122.50*
Facilities FTV TVL tea/coffee Dinner available Cen ht
Licensed Wi-fi Golf 18 Parking 5 Notes No Children
12yrs Closed Dec-Feb

BLAIRGOWRIE
Map 21 NO14

Gilmore House

★★★★ 🍴 BED AND BREAKFAST

Perth Rd PH10 6EJ
☎ 01250 872791 📠 01250 872791
e-mail: jill@gilmorehouse.co.uk
dir: On A93 S

This Victorian villa stands in a well-tended garden on the
south side of town. Sympathetically restored to enhance
its period features it offers individual bedrooms tastefully
furnished in antique pine, and thoughtfully equipped to
include modern amenities such as Freeview TV. There are
two inviting lounges, one of which has lovely views over
the gardens. Hearty traditional breakfasts are served in
the attractive dining room.

Rooms 3 en suite D £60-£80* Facilities FTV TVL tea/
coffee Cen ht Wi-fi Parking 3 Notes Closed Xmas

CRIEFF
Map 21 NN82

Merlindale

★★★★ BED AND BREAKFAST

Perth Rd PH7 3EQ
☎ 01764 655205 📠 01764 655205
e-mail: merlin.dale@virgin.net
web: www.merlindale.co.uk
dir: On A85, 350yds from E end of High St

Situated in a quiet residential area within walking
distance of the town centre, this delightful detached
house stands in well-tended grounds and offers a warm
welcome. The pretty bedrooms are comfortably furnished
and well equipped. There is a spacious lounge, an
impressive library, and an elegant dining room where
delicious evening meals and traditional breakfasts are
served.

Rooms 3 en suite (1 fmly) S £50-£65; D £75-£90*
Facilities STV FTV TVL tea/coffee Dinner available Cen ht
Wi-fi Parking 3 Notes LB ⊗ Closed 9 Dec-10 Feb

GLENFARG
Map 21 NO11

The Famous Bein Inn

★★★ 🕸 INN

PH2 9PY
☎ 01577 830216 📠 01577 830211
e-mail: enquiries@beininn.com
web: www.beininn.com
dir: From S: M90 junct 8, A91 towards Cupar, Left onto
B996 to Bein Inn. From N: M90 junct 9, A912 towards
Gateside

This inn, in a peaceful rural setting, was originally built
to accommodate travellers on a journey between
Edinburgh and the Highlands. A friendly welcome is
guaranteed and there is a relaxed informal atmosphere
with blazing log fires a feature on colder evenings. Short
breaks for golf, fishing and shooting are offered. The
restaurant has a well deserved reputation for the careful
preparation of the finest local produce.

Rooms 7 en suite 4 annexe en suite (4 fmly) (4 GF)
Facilities tea/coffee Dinner available Direct Dial Cen ht
Wi-fi Conf Max 32 Thtr 32 Class 25 Board 25 Parking 26
Notes Closed 25 Dec

Barley Bree Restaurant with Rooms

★★★★ ◉◉ RESTAURANT WITH ROOMS

6 Willoughby St PH5 2AB
☎ 01764 681451 📄 01764 910055
e-mail: info@barleybree.com
dir: *A9 onto A822 in centre of Muthill*

Situated in the heart of the small village of Muthill, and is just a short drive from Crieff, genuine hospitality and quality food are obvious attractions at this charming restaurant with rooms. The property has been transformed by the current owners, and the stylish bedrooms are appointed to a very high standard. The restaurant has a rustic feel and and boasts a log burning fire.

Rooms 6 en suite (1 fmly) S £60-£70; D £100-£150*
Facilities FTV tea/coffee Dinner available Cen ht Wi-fi
Parking 10 **Notes** LB ⊗ Closed 2wks Autumn/Jan RS
Mon & Tue Restaurant closed to public No coaches

Cherrybank Guesthouse

★★★★ 🏠 GUEST ACCOMMODATION

217-219 Glasgow Rd PH2 0NB
☎ 01738 451982 📄 01738 561336
e-mail: m.r.cherrybank@blueyonder.co.uk
dir: *1m SW of town centre on A93*

Convenient for the town and major roads, Cherrybank has been extended and carefully refurbished to offer well equipped and beautifully presented bedrooms, one of which is on the ground floor. The delightful lounge is ideal for relaxation, while delicious breakfasts are served at individual tables in the bright airy dining room. Margaret and Robert Miller were finalists in this year's Friendliest Landlady of the Year award (2011-12).

Rooms 5 rms (4 en suite) (1 pri facs) (2 fmly) (1 GF)
Facilities tea/coffee Cen ht Wi-fi **Parking** 4 **Notes** ⊗

Clunie

★★★★ GUEST HOUSE

12 Pitcullen Crescent PH2 7HT
☎ 01738 623625 📄 01738 623238
e-mail: ann@clunieguesthouse.co.uk
dir: *On A94 on E side of river*

Lying on the north east side of town, this family-run guest house offers a friendly welcome. The comfortable bedrooms, which vary in size, are attractively decorated and well equipped. Breakfast is served at individual tables in the elegant ground-floor dining room.

Rooms 7 en suite (1 fmly) S £30-£40; D £60-£70*
Facilities tea/coffee Cen ht Wi-fi **Parking** 8 **Notes** LB ⊗

The Anglers Inn

★★★ INN

Main Rd, Guildtown PH2 6BS
☎ 01821 640329
e-mail: info@theanglersinn.co.uk
dir: *6m N of Perth on A93*

This charming country inn enjoys a peaceful rural setting, and yet is only a short drive from Perth city centre. It is popular with fishing and shooting parties along with race goers. The inn has been tastefully refurbished and the accommodation consists of en suite bedrooms that vary in size, each equipped with flat-screen television. The restaurant offers local produce and a daily changing blackboard. Ample car parking.

Rooms 6 en suite (1 fmly) S £40-£75; D £100-£150
Facilities FTV TVL tea/coffee Dinner available Cen ht Wi-fi
🎱 Pool table **Parking** 40 **Notes** LB No Children

Ballabeg Guest House

★★★ BED AND BREAKFAST

14 Keir St PH2 7HJ
☎ 01738 620434
e-mail: ballabeg@btopenworld.com
dir: *NE of city centre, off A94*

Well situated for the town centre and benefiting from off-road parking, this property offers modern, comfortable bedrooms of a good overall size with a number of extras provided as standard. Well-cooked breakfasts with warm and genuine hospitality ensure a pleasant stay.

Rooms 4 rms (3 en suite) (1 pri facs) D £57-£60*
Facilities FTV tea/coffee Cen ht **Parking** 4 **Notes** ⊗ No
Children 16yrs Closed 5 Dec-Jan

Craigroyston House

★★★★ GUEST HOUSE

2 Lower Oakfield PH16 5HQ
☎ 01796 472053 📄 01796 472053
e-mail: reservations@craigroyston.co.uk
web: www.craigroyston.co.uk
dir: *In town centre near information centre car park*

The Maxwell family delight in welcoming guests to their home, an impressive detached Victorian villa set in a colourful garden. The bedrooms have pretty colour schemes and are comfortably furnished in period style. There is an inviting sitting room, complete with deep sofas for those wishing to relax and enjoy the peaceful atmosphere. Scottish breakfasts are served at individual tables in the attractive dining room.

Rooms 8 en suite (1 fmly) (1 GF) D £70-£95
Facilities FTV tea/coffee Cen ht Wi-fi **Parking** 9 **Notes** LB
⊗ 🚭

Wellwood House

★★★★ GUEST HOUSE

13 West Moulin Rd PH16 5EA
☎ 01796 474288 📄 01796 474299
e-mail: wellwoodhouse@aol.com
web: www.wellwoodhouse.com
dir: *In town centre opp town hall*

Set in lovely grounds on an elevated position overlooking the town, Wellwood House has stunning views of the Vale of Atholl and the surrounding countryside. The comfortably proportioned bedrooms are attractively decorated and well equipped. The elegant lounge has an honesty bar and a fire on cooler evenings, and the spacious dining room is the setting for hearty breakfasts served at individual tables.

Rooms 10 rms (8 en suite) (2 pri facs) (1 fmly) (1 GF) S
£45-£55; D £66-£80* **Facilities** FTV TVL tea/coffee Cen ht
Licensed Wi-fi **Parking** 20 **Notes** ⊗ Closed 10 Nov-14
Feb

The Glenholm Centre

★★★ 🏠 GUEST ACCOMMODATION

ML12 6JF
☎ 01899 830408
e-mail: info@glenholm.co.uk
dir: *1m S of Broughton. Off A701 to Glenholm*

Surrounded by peaceful farmland, this former schoolhouse has a distinct African theme. The home-cooked meals and baking have received much praise and are served in the spacious lounge-dining room. The bright airy bedrooms are thoughtfully equipped, and the service is friendly and attentive. Computer courses are available.

Rooms 3 en suite 1 annexe en suite (1 fmly) (2 GF) S
£39-£42; D £64 **Facilities** TVL tea/coffee Dinner available
Cen ht Licensed Wi-fi ♿ **Conf** Max 24 Thtr 24 Class 24
Board 24 **Parking** 14 **Notes** LB Closed 20 Dec-1 Feb

Save on B&Bs and Hotels. Book at **theAA.com/hotel**

SCOTTISH BORDERS 393 SCOTLAND

| **EDDLESTON** | Map 21 NT24 |

The Horseshoe Inn

★★★★★ ❀❀❀ RESTAURANT WITH ROOMS

EH45 8QP
☎ 01721 730225　📠 01721 730268
e-mail: reservations@horseshoeinn.co.uk
web: www.horseshoeinn.co.uk
dir: A703, 5m N of Peebles

This inn is five miles north of Peebles and only 18 miles south of Edinburgh. Originally a blacksmith's shop, it now has a very good reputation for delightful atmosphere and excellent cuisine. There are eight luxuriously appointed and individually designed bedrooms.

Rooms 8 en suite (1 fmly) (6 GF) **Facilities** FTV tea/coffee Dinner available Direct Dial Cen ht Wi-fi Fishing **Parking** 20 **Notes** LB Closed 25 Dec & Mon & 2wks Jan RS Sun eve Rest closed, bistro open

| **GALASHIELS** | Map 21 NT43 |

Over Langshaw *(NT524400)*

★★★ FARMHOUSE

Langshaw TD1 2PE
☎ 01896 860244　📠 01896 860668
Mrs S Bergius
e-mail: overlangshaw@btconnect.com
dir: 3m N of Galashiels. A7 N from Galashiels, 1m right signed Langshaw, right at T-junct into Langshaw, left signed Earlston, Over Langshaw 1m, signed

There are fine panoramic views from this organic hillside farm which offers two comfortable and spacious bedrooms. Hearty breakfasts are provided at individual tables in the lounge and a friendly welcome is guaranteed.

Rooms 2 en suite (1 fmly) (1 GF) D £65-£75*
Facilities TVL tea/coffee Cen ht Wi-fi **Parking** 4 **Notes** ❀ 500 acres dairy/sheep/organic

| **JEDBURGH** | Map 21 NT62 |

Ferniehirst Mill Lodge

★★ GUEST HOUSE

TD8 6PQ
☎ 01835 863279
e-mail: ferniehirstmill@aol.com
web: www.ferniehirstmill.co.uk
dir: 2.5m S of Jedburgh on A68, onto private track to end

Reached by a narrow farm track and a rustic wooden bridge, this chalet-style house has a secluded setting by the River Jed. Bedrooms are small and functional but there is a comfortable lounge in which to relax. Home-cooked dinners are available by arrangement, and hearty breakfasts are served in the cosy dining room.

Rooms 7 en suite (1 GF) S £30; D £60 **Facilities** TVL tea/coffee Dinner available Cen ht Fishing Riding **Parking** 10

| **LAUDER** | Map 21 NT54 |

The Black Bull

★★★★ INN

Market Place TD2 6SR
☎ 01578 722208　📠 01578 722419
e-mail: enquiries@blackbull-lauder.com
dir: On A68 in village centre

This 18th-century coaching inn has been completely transformed. The lovely bedrooms are furnished in the period character and thoughtfully equipped with modern amenities. The wooden floored cosy bar and four dining areas are charming, the main dining room being a former chapel. A very good range of food makes this a popular gastro-pub.

Rooms 8 en suite (2 fmly) **Facilities** FTV tea/coffee Dinner available Direct Dial Cen ht Wi-fi **Parking** 8

16 Market Place

★★★ 🅰 BED AND BREAKFAST

16 Market Place TD2 6SR
☎ 01578 718776　& 07725 472543
e-mail: wendymcv@talktalk.net
dir: In centre of Lauder, opp Black Bull

Rooms 2 en suite S £25-£30; D £60-£70* **Facilities** FTV tea/coffee Cen ht Wi-fi Golf 9 **Parking** 1 **Notes** Closed Xmas ❀

| **MELROSE** | Map 21 NT53 |

PREMIER COLLECTION

Fauhope House

★★★★★ 🏡 GUEST HOUSE

Gattonside TD6 9LU
☎ 01896 823184　📠 01896 823184
e-mail: info@fauhopehouse.com
dir: 0.7m N of Melrose over River Tweed. N off B6360 at Gattonside 30mph sign (E) up long driveway

It's hard to imagine a more complete experience than a stay at Fauhope, set high on a hillside on the north-east edge of the village. Hospitality is first class, breakfasts are excellent, and the delightful country house has a splendid interior. Bedrooms are luxurious, each individual and superbly equipped. Public areas are elegantly decorated and furnished, and enhanced by beautiful floral arrangements; the dining room is particularly stunning.

Rooms 3 en suite **Facilities** tea/coffee Dinner available Cen ht 🐴 Riding **Parking** 10 **Notes** LB ❌

NEWCASTLETON — Map 21 NY48

Liddesdale

★★★★ INN

Douglas Sq TD9 0QD
☎ 01387 375255 ≣ 01387 752577
e-mail: reception@theliddesdalehotel.co.uk

Liddesdale is located in the peaceful 17th-century village of Newcastleton overlooking the village square. There are well-appointed bedrooms and bathrooms, and the public areas offer various locations in which to dine. The welcoming public bar is well used by locals and residents alike. Relaxed and informal menus use the best local produce available. The new welcome addition of the beer garden this year shows very good results.

Rooms 6 en suite (2 fmly) S £45; D £80* **Facilities** STV FTV TVL tea/coffee Dinner available Direct Dial Cen ht Wi-fi ⌣ Golf 9 Fishing **Conf** Max 60 Thtr 40 Class 40 Board 40 **Notes** LB ⊗

SOUTH AYRSHIRE

AYR — Map 20 NS32

PREMIER COLLECTION

26 The Crescent

★★★★★ GUEST HOUSE

26 Bellevue Crescent KA7 2DR
☎ 01292 287329 ≣ 01292 201003
e-mail: enquiries@26crescent.co.uk
web: www.26crescent.co.uk
dir: Leave A79 onto rdbt, 3rd exit onto King St. Left onto Bellevue Crescent

Located in a quiet residential area of Ayr, close to the seafront, town centre and race course, this guest house offers a traditional warm welcome with well appointed and comfortable bedrooms. Bathrooms are of a high standard, as is the hearty breakfast served on individual tables in the charming dining room. Joyce and Michael Brennan were finalists in this year's Friendliest Landlady of the Year award (2011-12).

Rooms 5 en suite S £45-£50; D £55-£80*
Facilities FTV tea/coffee Cen ht Wi-fi **Notes** LB ⊗

Daviot House

★★★★ GUEST HOUSE

12 Queens Ter KA7 1DU
☎ 01292 269678
e-mail: daviothouse@hotmail.com
web: www.daviothouse.com
dir: Off A719 onto Wellington Sq & Bath Place, turn right

This well-maintained Victorian house stands in a peaceful location close to the beach and town centre. Bedrooms are modern in style and well equipped. Hearty breakfasts are served in the dining room. Daviot House is a member of Golf South Ayrshire - a golf booking service for local municipal courses, so let your hosts know if you'd like a round booked.

Rooms 6 rms (5 en suite) (1 pri facs) (1 fmly) (1 GF) S £25-£40; D £46-£65* **Facilities** FTV tea/coffee Cen ht Wi-fi **Notes** LB ⊗

BALLANTRAE — Map 20 NX08

Balkissock Lodge

★★★★ ☎ ☎ GUEST ACCOMMODATION

Balkissock KA26 0LP
☎ 01465 831537
e-mail: howard.balkissock@btinternet.com
dir: S through Ballantrae (A77) over river, 1st left at campsite sign. Right at T-junct, 1.5m

A warm and genuine welcome awaits after a scenic drive. Set in the rolling South Ayrshire countryside, surrounded by wonderful gardens, Balkissock Lodge is a perfect getaway. The owners show great hospitality and customer care in a very comfortable and well-appointed property.

Rooms 3 en suite (1 fmly) (2 GF) **Facilities** STV TVL tea/coffee Dinner available Cen ht **Parking** 3 **Notes** ⊗ No Children

SOUTH LANARKSHIRE

STRATHAVEN — Map 20 NS74

Rissons at Springvale

★★★ ⊛ RESTAURANT WITH ROOMS

18 Lethame Rd ML10 6AD
☎ 01357 521131 & 520234 ≣ 01357 521131
e-mail: rissons@msn.com
dir: A71 into Strathaven, W of town centre off Townhead St

Guests are assured of a warm welcome at this charming establishment close to the town centre. The bedrooms and bathrooms are stylish and well equipped. The main attraction here is the food - a range of interesting, well-prepared dishes served in Rissons Restaurant.

Rooms 9 en suite (1 fmly) (1 GF) S £42.50-£45; D £75-£80* **Facilities** tea/coffee Dinner available Cen ht Wi-fi **Parking** 10 **Notes** ⊗ Closed 1st wk Jan No coaches

STIRLING

CALLANDER — Map 20 NN60

Annfield Guest House

★★★★ ≣ GUEST HOUSE

18 North Church St FK17 8EG
☎ 01877 330204
e-mail: reservations@annfieldguesthouse.co.uk
dir: Off A84 Main St onto North Church St, at top on right

Situated within easy reach of the town centre, this welcoming guest house offers comfortable, good-value accommodation. The spacious bedrooms are attractively decorated and well equipped. An elegant first-floor lounge is ideal for relaxation, and hearty breakfasts are served at individual tables in the pretty dining room.

Rooms 7 rms (4 en suite) (2 pri facs) (1 fmly) S £40-£65; D £60-£70 **Facilities** FTV TVL tea/coffee Cen ht Wi-fi Golf 18 **Parking** 7 **Notes** LB ⊗ No Children 6yrs Closed Xmas RS Dec-Feb Maybe closed for 2 months over winter ⊛

Arden House

★★★★ ≣ GUEST ACCOMMODATION

Bracklinn Rd FK17 8EQ
☎ 01877 330235
e-mail: ardenhouse@onetel.com
dir: Off A84 Main St onto Bracklinn Rd, house 200yds on left

This impressive Victorian villa lies in beautiful mature grounds in a peaceful area of the town. It featured in the 1960s hit television series Dr Finlay's Casebook and is a friendly, welcoming house. The comfortable bedrooms are thoughtfully furnished and equipped. There is a stylish lounge in addition to the attractive breakfast room where delicious breakfasts are served at individual tables.

Rooms 6 en suite (2 GF) **Facilities** tea/coffee Cen ht Wi-fi ⌣ **Parking** 10 **Notes** ⊗ No Children 14yrs Closed Nov-Mar

Callander Meadows

★★★★ @ RESTAURANT WITH ROOMS

24 Main St FK17 8BB
☎ 01877 330181
e-mail: mail@callandermeadows.co.uk
web: www.callandermeadows.co.uk
dir: M9 junct 10 onto A84 to Callander, on main street just past A81 junct

Located on the high street in Callander, this family-run business offers comfortable accommodation and a restaurant that has quickly become very popular with the locals. The bedrooms have been appointed to a high standard. Private parking is available to the rear.

Rooms 3 en suite **Facilities** STV tea/coffee Dinner available Cen ht Wi-fi **Parking** 4 **Notes** ⊗ RS Winter Restaurant open Thu-Sun only No coaches

Lubnaig House

★★★★ 🅰 GUEST HOUSE

Leny Feus FK17 8AS
☎ 01877 330376
e-mail: info@lubnaighouse.co.uk
web: www.lubnaighouse.co.uk
dir: From town centre A84 W, right onto Leny Feus. Lubnaig House after Poppies Hotel

Rooms 6 en suite 2 annexe en suite (4 GF) S £45-£55; D £70-£80* **Facilities** FTV tea/coffee Cen ht Wi-fi **Parking** 10 **Notes** LB ⊗ No Children 7yrs Closed Nov-Apr

Mansewood Country House

★★★★ GUEST HOUSE

FK19 8NS
☎ 01567 830213
e-mail: stay@mansewoodcountryhouse.co.uk
dir: A84 N to Lochearnhead, 1st building on left; A84 S to Lochearnhead

Mansewood Country House is a spacious former manse that dates back to the 18th century and lies in a well-tended garden to the south of the village. Bedrooms are well appointed and equipped and offer high standards of comfort. Refreshments can be enjoyed in the cosy bar or the elegant lounge, and meals prepared with flair are served in the attractive restaurant. There is also a log cabin where pets are allowed.

Rooms 6 en suite (1 GF) **Facilities** FTV TVL tea/coffee Dinner available Cen ht Licensed Wi-fi **Parking** 6 **Notes** LB ⊗ RS Nov-Mar Phone for advance bookings

Tigh Na Crich

★★★★ BED AND BREAKFAST

FK19 8PR
☎ 01567 830235
e-mail: johntippett2@aol.com
web: www.tighnacrich.co.uk
dir: On junct of A84 & A85, next to village shop

Tich Na Crich is located in the heart of the small village of Lochearnhead, surrounded by mountains on three sides and Loch Earn on the fourth. Inside is very well presented accommodation with many thoughtful extras provided. The generous breakfast is served in the comfortable dining room on individual tables looking out to the front of the property.

Rooms 3 en suite (1 fmly) S £40-£45; D £60-£65 **Facilities** FTV tea/coffee Cen ht **Parking** 3 **Notes** ⊜

Linden Guest House

★★★★ GUEST HOUSE

22 Linden Av FK7 7PQ
☎ 01786 448850 & 07974 116573 🖷 01786 448850
e-mail: fay@lindenguesthouse.co.uk
web: www.lindenguesthouse.co.uk
dir: 0.5m SE of city centre off A9

Situated within walking distance of the town centre, this friendly guest house offers attractive and very well-equipped bedrooms, including a large family room that sleeps five comfortably. There is a bright dining room where delicious breakfasts are served at individual tables with quality Wedgwood crockery.

Rooms 4 en suite (2 fmly) (1 GF) S £40-£70; D £50-£80* **Facilities** STV FTV tea/coffee Cen ht Wi-fi **Parking** 2 **Notes** LB

PREMIER COLLECTION

Creagan House

★★★★★ @@ ≡ RESTAURANT WITH ROOMS

FK18 8ND
☎ 01877 384638 🖷 01877 384319
e-mail: eatandstay@creaganhouse.co.uk
web: www.creaganhouse.co.uk
dir: 0.25m N of Strathyre on A84

Originally a farmhouse dating from the 17th century, Creagan House has operated as a restaurant with rooms for many years. The baronial-style dining room provides a wonderful setting for the cuisine which is classic French with some Scottish influences. Warm hospitality and attentive service are the highlights of any stay.

Rooms 5 en suite (1 fmly) (1 GF) S £75-£95; D £130-£150 **Facilities** FTV tea/coffee Dinner available Cen ht Wi-fi **Conf** Max 35 Thtr 35 Class 12 Board 35 **Parking** 16 **Notes** LB Closed 7-22 Nov, Xmas & 18 Jan-8 Mar RS Wed & Thu Closed

The Waterhouse Inn

★★★★ INN

34 Balloch Rd G83 8LE
☎ 01389 752120 🖷 01389 752125
e-mail: info@waterhouseinn.co.uk
web: www.waterhouseinn.co.uk

This welcoming modern Inn is located on the high street of Balloch close to the park and the mouth of Loch Lomond. Bedrooms are well equipped and spacious, with modern bright bathrooms. The café serves home-cooked food throughout the day. A perfect base for touring Loch Lomond and the Trossachs National Park.

Rooms 7 en suite (2 fmly) **Facilities** STV FTV TVL tea/coffee Dinner available Cen ht Wi-fi **Notes** ⊗

BALLOCH *continued*

Sunnyside

★★★ BED AND BREAKFAST

35 Main St G83 9JX
☎ 01389 750282 & 07717 397548
e-mail: enquiries@sunnysidebb.co.uk
dir: *From A82 take A811 then A813 for 1m, over mini-rdbt 150mtrs on left*

Set in its own grounds well back from the road by Loch Lomond, Sunnyside is an attractive, traditional detached house, parts of which date back to the 1830s. Bedrooms are attractively decorated and provide comfortable modern accommodation. Free Wi-fi is also available. The dining room is located on the ground floor, and is an appropriate setting for hearty Scottish breakfasts.

Rooms 6 en suite (2 fmly) (1 GF) S £32-£38; D £54-£65*
Facilities FTV tea/coffee Dinner available Cen ht Wi-fi
Parking 8

WEST LOTHIAN

BLACKBURN	Map 21 NS96

Cruachan B&B

★★★★ GUEST ACCOMMODATION

78 East Main St EH47 7QS
☎ 01506 655221   📠 01506 652395
e-mail: enquiries@cruachan.co.uk
web: www.cruachan.co.uk
dir: *On A705 in Blackburn, 1m from M8 junct 4*

Ideally located for both the leisure and business traveller to central Scotland, with Edinburgh only 30 minutes away by train and Glasgow only 35 minutes away by car. Cruachan is the comfortable, friendly home of the Harkins family. Bedrooms are bright, attractive and very well equipped. Breakfast, featuring the best of local produce is served at individual tables in the ground-floor dining room.

Rooms 4 rms (3 en suite) (1 pri facs) (1 fmly) S £40-£45; D £60-£65* **Facilities** FTV tea/coffee Cen ht Wi-fi **Parking** 5 **Notes** ⊗

EAST CALDER	Map 21 NT06

PREMIER COLLECTION

Ashcroft Farmhouse

★★★★★ 🍴 GUEST HOUSE

East Calder EH53 0ET
☎ 01506 881810   📠 01506 884327
e-mail: scottashcroft7@aol.com
web: www.ashcroftfarmhouse.com

See advert on opposite page

(For full entry see Livingston)

Whitecroft

★★★★ BED AND BREAKFAST

7 Raw Holdings, East Calder EH53 0ET
☎ 01506 882494   📠 01506 882598
e-mail: lornascot@aol.com

(For full entry see Livingston)

FAULDHOUSE	Map 21 NS96

East Badallan Farm *(NS919598)*

★★★★ FARMHOUSE

EH47 9AG
☎ 01501 770251
Ms Struthers
e-mail: mary@eastbadallan.co.uk
web: www.eastbadallan.co.uk
dir: *M8 junct 3 or 4 onto B7010*

Equidistant from Edinburgh and Glasgow with great transportation links, this working beef farm has been in the same family since the 18th century. Inside are well appointed bedrooms with modern facilities provided as standard. Hospitality is a strength, as is the breakfast, made with award-winning local produce.

Rooms 3 en suite (1 fmly) (1 GF) S £35-£45; D £60-£80* **Facilities** FTV tea/coffee Cen ht Wi-fi **Parking Notes** LB ⊗ 🐾 300 acres beef

LINLITHGOW	Map 21 NS97

PREMIER COLLECTION

Arden Country House

★★★★★ 🍴 GUEST ACCOMMODATION

Belsyde EH49 6QE
☎ 01506 670172   📠 01506 670172
e-mail: info@ardencountryhouse.com
dir: *1.3m SW of Linlithgow. A706 over Union Canal, entrance 200yds on left at Lodge Cottage*

Situated in the picturesque grounds of the Belsyde Country Estate and close to the Royal Burgh of Linlithgow, Arden Country House offers immaculate, stylishly furnished and spacious bedrooms. There is a cosy ground-floor lounge and a charming dining room where delicious breakfasts feature the best of local produce.

Rooms 3 en suite (1 GF) S £54-£100; D £79-£108
Facilities FTV tea/coffee Cen ht Wi-fi **Parking** 4
Notes LB ⊗ No Children 12yrs Closed 25-26 Dec

Belsyde House

★★★★ 🍴 GUEST ACCOMMODATION

Lanark Rd EH49 6QE
☎ 01506 842098   📠 01506 842098
e-mail: info@belsydehouse.com
web: www.belsyde.com
dir: *1.5m SW on A706, 1st left over Union Canal*

Reached by a tree-lined driveway, this welcoming farmhouse is peacefully situated in attractive grounds close to the Union Canal. There are well-proportioned double, twin and family rooms, and a cosy single. All are nicely furnished and well equipped. Breakfast, including a vegetarian menu, is served at good-sized tables in the dining room, next to the lounge.

Rooms 3 en suite (1 fmly) **Facilities** FTV TVL tea/coffee Cen ht Wi-fi **Parking** 10 **Notes** ⊗ No Children 12yrs Closed Xmas

Save on B&Bs and Hotels. Book at **theAA.com/hotel**

WEST LOTHIAN 397 SCOTLAND

Bomains Farm

★★★★ GUEST HOUSE

Bo'ness EH49 7RQ
☎ 01506 822188 & 822861 📠 01506 824433
e-mail: bunty.kirk@onetel.net
web: www.bomains.co.uk
dir: A706, 1.5m N towards Bo'ness, left at golf course
x-rds, 1st farm on right

From its elevated location this friendly farmhouse has
stunning views of the Firth of Forth. The bedrooms which
vary in size are beautifully decorated, well equipped and
enhanced by quality fabrics, with many thoughtful extra
touches. Delicious home-cooked fare featuring the best of
local produce is served in a stylish lounge-dining room.

Rooms 6 rms (4 en suite) (1 pri facs) (1 fmly)
Facilities STV FTV TVL tea/coffee Cen ht Wi-fi Golf 18
Fishing **Parking** 12

| LIVINGSTON | Map 21 NT06 |

PREMIER COLLECTION

Ashcroft Farmhouse

★★★★★ 🏠 GUEST HOUSE

East Calder EH53 0ET
☎ 01506 881810 📠 01506 884327
e-mail: scottashcroft7@aol.com
web: www.ashcroftfarmhouse.com
dir: On B7015, off A71, 0.5m E of East Calder, near
Almondell Country Park

With over 40 years' experience in caring for guests,
Derek and Elizabeth Scott ensure a stay at Ashcroft will
be memorable. Their modern home sits in lovely award-
winning landscaped gardens and provides attractive
and well-equipped ground-floor bedrooms. The
comfortable lounge includes a video and DVD library.
Breakfast, featuring home-made sausages and the
best of local produce, is served at individual tables in
the stylish dining room. Free Wi-fi is now available, and
a Park and Ride facility is nearby.

Rooms 6 en suite (2 fmly) (6 GF) **Facilities** FTV TVL tea/
coffee Cen ht Wi-fi **Parking** 8 **Notes** ⊗ No Children
12yrs

See advert on this page

Whitecroft

★★★★ BED AND BREAKFAST

7 Raw Holdings, East Calder EH53 0ET
☎ 01506 882494 📠 01506 882598
e-mail: lornascot@aol.com
dir: A71 onto B7015, establishment on right

A relaxed and friendly atmosphere prevails at this
charming modern bed and breakfast. The bedrooms, all
of which are on the ground floor, are attractively colour
co-ordinated, well-equipped and contain many thoughtful
extra touches. Breakfast is served at individual tables in
the smart dining room.

Rooms 3 en suite (3 GF) S £45-£55; D £64-£76*
Facilities FTV tea/coffee Cen ht Wi-fi **Parking** 5 **Notes** ⊗
No Children 12yrs

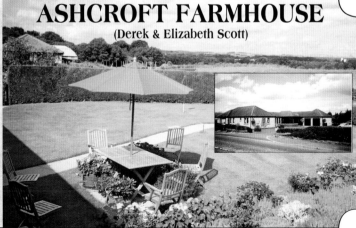

SCOTTISH ISLANDS

ARRAN, ISLE OF

BRODICK   Map 20 NS03

Allandale

★★★★ GUEST HOUSE

KA27 8BJ
☎ 01770 302278
e-mail: info@allandalehouse.co.uk
dir: *500yds S of Brodick Pier, off A841 towards Lamlash, up hill 2nd left at Corriegills sign*

Under enthusiastic ownership, this comfortable guest house is set in delightful gardens in beautiful countryside. Guests can relax in the lounge with its attractive garden views. Bedrooms vary in size and have pleasing colour schemes and mixed modern furnishings, along with thoughtful amenities. In a peaceful location, Allandale is convenient for the CalMac ferry and Brodick centre.

Rooms 4 rms (3 en suite) (1 pri facs) 2 annexe en suite (3 fmly) (2 GF) **Facilities** FTV tea/coffee Cen ht **Parking** 6 **Notes** ⊗ Closed Nov-Feb

HARRIS, ISLE OF

SCARISTA (SGARASTA BHEAG)   Map 22 NG09

Scarista House

★★★★ ◉◉ ▥ RESTAURANT WITH ROOMS

HS3 3HX
☎ 01859 550238   🖹 01859 550277
e-mail: timandpatricia@scaristahouse.com
dir: *On A859, 15m S of Tarbert*

A former manse, Scarista House is a haven for food lovers who seek to explore this magnificent island. It enjoys breathtaking views of the Atlantic and is just a short stroll from miles of golden sandy beaches. The house is run in a relaxed country-house manner by the friendly hosts. Expect wellies in the hall and masses of books and CDs in one of two lounges. Bedrooms are cosy, and delicious set dinners and memorable breakfasts are provided.

Rooms 3 en suite 2 annexe en suite (2 GF) **Facilities** tea/coffee Dinner available Direct Dial Cen ht **Parking** 12 **Notes** Closed Xmas, Jan & Feb No coaches Civ Wed 40

ORKNEY

ST MARGARET'S HOPE   Map 24 ND49

The Creel Restaurant with Rooms

★★★★ ◉◉ ▥ RESTAURANT WITH ROOMS

Front Rd KW17 2SL
☎ 01856 831311
e-mail: alan@thecreel.freeserve.co.uk
web: www.thecreel.co.uk
dir: *A961 into village, establishment on seafront*

With wonderful sea views, The Creel enjoys a prominent position in the pretty fishing village of St Margaret's Hope. The award-winning restaurant has a well deserved reputation for the quality of its seafood and a window seat is a must in the charming restaurant. The stylish bedrooms are appointed to a high standard and most enjoy views over the bay. Breakfasts should not be missed, with local Orkney produce and freshly baked breads on the menu.

Rooms 3 en suite S £70-£80; D £110-£120* **Facilities** Dinner available Cen ht **Parking** 6 **Notes** ⊗ Closed mid Oct-Apr No coaches

SHETLAND

LERWICK   Map 24 HU44

Glen Orchy House

★★★★ GUEST HOUSE

20 Knab Rd ZE1 0AX
☎ 01595 692031   🖹 01595 692031
e-mail: glenorchy.house@virgin.net
dir: *Next to coastguard station*

This welcoming and well-presented house lies above the town with views over the Knab, and is within easy walking distance of the town centre. Bedrooms are modern in design and there is a choice of lounges with books and board games, one with an honesty bar. Substantial breakfasts are served, and the restaurant offers a delicious Thai menu.

Rooms 24 en suite (4 fmly) (4 GF) S £65; D £90* **Facilities** STV FTV TVL tea/coffee Dinner available Cen ht Licensed Wi-fi **Parking** 10 **Notes** Closed 25-26 Dec & 1-2 Jan

SKYE, ISLE OF

EDINBANE   Map 22 NG35

Shorefield House

★★★★ ▥ GUEST HOUSE

IV51 9PW
☎ 01470 582444
e-mail: stay@shorefield-house.com
dir: *12m from Portree & 8m from Dunvegan, off A850 into Edinbane, 1st on right*

Shorefield stands in the village of Edinbane and looks out to Loch Greshornish. Bedrooms range from single to family, while one ground-floor room has easier access. All rooms are thoughtfully equipped and have CD players. Breakfast is an impressive choice and there is also a child-friendly garden.

Rooms 3 en suite (1 fmly) (2 GF) D £80-£97 **Facilities** STV FTV TVL tea/coffee Cen ht Wi-fi **Parking** 10 **Notes** LB ⊗ Closed Xmas

Save on B&Bs and Hotels. Book at **theAA.com/hotel**

SCOTTISH ISLANDS (SKYE) 399 SCOTLAND

STAFFIN
Map 22 NG46

The Glenview

★ ★ ★ ◉ RESTAURANT WITH ROOMS

Culnacnoc IV51 9JH
☎ **01470 562248**
e-mail: enquiries@glenviewskye.co.uk
dir: *12m N of Portree on A855*

The Glenview is located in one of the most beautiful parts of Skye with stunning sea views; it is close to the famous rock formation, the Old Man of Storr. The individually styled bedrooms are very comfortable and front-facing rooms enjoy the dramatic views. Evening meals should not to be missed as the restaurant has a well deserved reputation for its locally sourced produce.

Rooms 5 en suite (1 GF) **Facilities** tea/coffee Dinner available Wi-fi **Parking** 12 **Notes** ⊗ RS Sun & Mon closed

STRUAN
Map 22 NG33

PREMIER COLLECTION

Ullinish Country Lodge

★ ★ ★ ★ ★ ◉◉◉ 🍴 RESTAURANT WITH ROOMS

IV56 8FD
☎ **01470 572214** 📠 **01470 572341**
e-mail: ullinish@theisleofskye.co.uk
dir: *N on A863*

Set in some of Scotland's most dramatic landscape, with views of the Black Cuillin and MacLeod's Tables, this lodge has lochs on three sides. Samuel Johnson and James Boswell stayed here in 1773 and were impressed with the hospitality even then. Hosts Brian and Pam hope to extend the same welcome to their guests today. As you would expect, all bedrooms have amazing views, and come with half-tester beds. The cuisine in the restaurant is impressive and uses the best of Skye's produce including locally sourced seafood and game.

Rooms 6 en suite S £90-£120; D £125-£165* **Facilities** tea/coffee Dinner available Cen ht **Parking** 8 **Notes** LB ⊗ No Children 16yrs Closed Jan & 1wk Nov No coaches

UIG
Map 22 NG36

Woodbine House

★ ★ ★ GUEST ACCOMMODATION

IV51 9XP
☎ **01470 542243** & **07904 267561**
e-mail: contact@skyeactivities.co.uk
dir: *From Portree into Uig Bay, pass Ferry Inn & right onto A855 Staffin Rd, house 300yds on right*

Built in the late 19th century, Woodbine House occupies an elevated position overlooking Uig Bay and the surrounding countryside, and is well suited for walking and bird-watching enthusiasts. The ground-floor dining room has lovely sea views, as do the front-facing bedrooms.

Rooms 5 en suite (1 fmly) (1 GF) S £50-£64; D £64-£69* **Facilities** FTV TVL tea/coffee Dinner available Cen ht Wi-fi Archery Mountain bike/sea kayak hire & boat trips **Parking** 4 **Notes** LB ⊗ RS Nov-Feb long stays or group bookings only

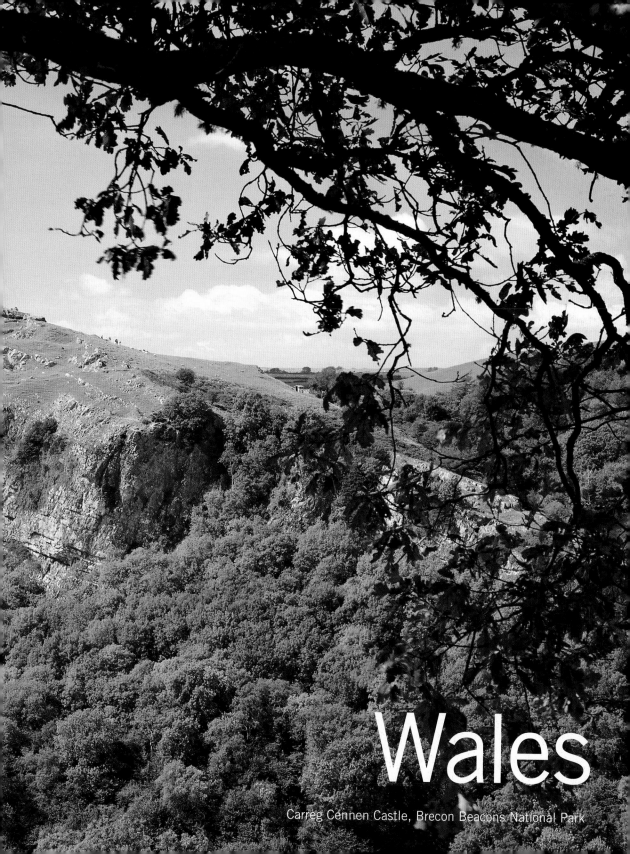

Wales

Carreg Cennen Castle, Brecon Beacons National Park

ANGLESEY, ISLE OF

BEAUMARIS   Map 14 SH67

PREMIER COLLECTION

Ye Olde Bulls Head Inn

★★★★★ ◎◎ INN

Castle St LL58 8AP
☎ 01248 810329   📄 01248 811294
e-mail: info@bullsheadinn.co.uk
dir: *Located on Main St in town centre*

Charles Dickens and Samuel Johnson were regular visitors to this Inn that features exposed beams and antique weaponry. Richly decorated traditional bedrooms are situated in the Inn with vibrant boutique bedrooms across in the Townhouse. Meetings and small functions are catered for, and food continues to attract praise in both The Loft restaurant and the less formal brasserie. Cask-conditioned ales are served in the traditional bar.

Rooms 25 en suite 1 annexe en suite (2 fmly) (5 GF) S £80-£100; D £100-£165* **Facilities** FTV tea/coffee Dinner available Direct Dial Cen ht Lift Wi-fi Golf 18 **Parking** 10 **Notes** LB ⊗ Closed 25 & 26 Dec No coaches

CEMAES BAY   Map 14 SH39

Hafod Country House

★★★★ BED AND BREAKFAST

LL67 0DS
☎ 01407 711645
e-mail: hbr@osmol.co.uk
dir: *0.5m S of Cemaes. Off A5025 Cemaes rdbt signed Llanfechell, Hafod 500yds on left*

Guests are assured of a warm welcome at this large and spacious Edwardian house, which stands in extensive gardens and is quietly located on the outskirts of the village. It provides well equipped accommodation, as well as a comfortable lounge and an elegant dining room, the setting for comprehensive Welsh breakfasts.

Rooms 3 en suite S £42.50; D £65-£75* **Facilities** FTV tea/coffee Cen ht ⤳ Golf 18 **Parking** 3 **Notes** ⊗ No Children 7yrs Closed Oct-Mar

HOLYHEAD   Map 14 SH28

Blackthorn Farm

★★★★ 🅰 GUEST ACCOMMODATION

Penrhosfeilw, Trearddur Bay LL65 2LT
☎ 01407 765262   📄 01407 765336
e-mail: enquiries@blackthornfarm.co.uk
web: www.blackthornleisure.co.uk
dir: *A55 to Holyhead, take 1st exit at rdbt, turn immediately right between two pubs. At end of road, turn right, 0.5m on left*

Rooms 7 rms (5 en suite) (2 fmly) S £52-£70; D £65-£85* **Facilities** FTV tea/coffee Cen ht Wi-fi **Parking** 10 **Notes** LB Closed 22-31 Dec

LLANERCHYMEDD   Map 14 SH48

Tre-Wyn (SH454851)

★★★★ FARMHOUSE

Maenaddwyn LL71 8AE
☎ 01248 470875
Mrs N Bown
e-mail: nia@trewyn.fsnet.co.uk
dir: *A5025 to Benllech Bay, B5108 to Brynteg x-rds, take Llannerchymedd road 3m to Maenaddwyn. Right after 6 houses, 0.5m to farm*

An extremely friendly welcome is extended at this spacious farmhouse. Rooms are well equipped and attractively furnished. The dining room and the relaxing lounge with its log fire have wonderful views across the gardens and countryside to Bodafon Mountain.

Rooms 3 en suite (1 fmly) **Facilities** TVL tea/coffee Cen ht **Parking** 5 **Notes** ⊗ 240 acres arable/beef/sheep

CARMARTHENSHIRE

CARMARTHEN   Map 8 SN42

Capel Dewi Uchaf Country House

★★★★ 🏠 BED AND BREAKFAST

Capel Dewi SA32 8AY
☎ 01267 290799   📄 01267 290003
e-mail: uchaffarm@aol.com
dir: *On B4300 between Capel Dewi & junct B4310*

Located in 35 acres of grounds with stunning views and private fishing in the River Towy, this Grade II listed, 16th-century house retains many magnificent features and has a wealth of character. Generous Welsh breakfasts are a feature here.

Rooms 3 en suite **Facilities** TVL tea/coffee Dinner available Cen ht Fishing Riding **Conf** Max 8 Board 8 **Parking** 10 **Notes** ⊗ Closed Xmas

Sarnau Mansion

★★★★ GUEST ACCOMMODATION

Llysonnen Rd SA33 5DZ
☎ 01267 211404   📄 01267 211404
e-mail: d.fernihough@btinternet.com
web: www.sarnaumansion.co.uk
dir: *5m W of Carmarthen. Off A40 onto B4298 & Bancyfelin road, Sarnau on right*

Located west of Carmarthen in 16 acres of grounds and gardens, including a tennis court, this large Grade II listed, late Georgian house retains much original character and is stylishly decorated. There is a lounge with a log fire, an elegant dining room, and spacious bedrooms with stunning rural views.

Rooms 4 rms (3 en suite) (1 pri facs) S £45-£50; D £75-£80 **Facilities** TVL tea/coffee Dinner available Cen ht ⤳ **Parking** 10 **Notes** ⊗ No Children 5yrs

FELINGWM UCHAF   Map 8 SN52

Allt Y Golau Farmhouse (SN510261)

★★★★ 🏠 FARMHOUSE

Allt Y Golau Uchaf SA32 7BB
☎ 01267 290455
Dr C Rouse
e-mail: alltygolau@btinternet.com
web: www.alltygolau.com
dir: *A40 onto B4310, N for 2m. 1st on left after Felingwm Uchaf*

This delightful Georgian farmhouse has been furnished and decorated to a high standard by the present owners, and enjoys panoramic views over the Tywi Valley to the Black Mountains beyond. Guests are welcome to take a relaxing walk through two acres of mature garden. Many thoughtful extras are provided in the comfortable bedrooms, and there is as a separate lounge. Breakfast is provided in the cosy dining room around a communal table.

Rooms 3 rms (2 en suite) (1 pri facs) (2 GF) S £45; D £68 **Facilities** TVL tea/coffee Cen ht **Parking** 3 **Notes** ⊗ Closed 20 Dec-2 Jan ⊜ 2 acres smallholding

LLANDOVERY
Map 9 SN73

Dan Y Parc (SN795378)

★★★★ 🅰 FARMHOUSE

Cynghordy SA20 0LD
☎ 01550 720401
Mrs G Kilmartin
e-mail: info@danyparc.com
dir: *3m from Llandovery on A483 heading to Builth Wells*

Rooms 3 rms (2 en suite) (1 pri facs) S £32-£35; D
£64-£70 **Facilities** FTV TVL tea/coffee Dinner available
Cen ht Wi-fi **Parking** 6 **Notes** LB Closed 20-31 Dec 🐾 14
acres non-working/horses/sheep

LLANDYBIE
Map 8 SN61

Glynhir Mansion

★★★ BED AND BREAKFAST

Glynhir Rd SA18 2TD
☎ 01269 850438   📠 01269 851275
e-mail: enquiries@theglynhirestate.com
web: www.theglynhirestate.com
dir: *1m N of Ammanford on A483*

Nestling at the foot of the Black Mountains, an
outstandingly beautiful area, Glynhir Mansion dates from
the end of the 17th century. The dining room and lounge
have open fires and attractive period furnishings. The
200-acre grounds include lovely walks alongside the
River Loughor, where the 30-foot waterfall is a spectacle
not to be missed.

Rooms 4 en suite (1 fmly) **Facilities** TVL Dinner available
Cen ht Licensed Golf 18 Pool table Table tennis **Conf** Max
40 Thtr 40 Class 40 Board 30 **Parking** 12 **Notes** ✪
Closed mid Dec-mid Jan Civ Wed 45

ST CLEARS
Map 8 SN21

PREMIER COLLECTION

Coedllys Country House

★★★★★ BED AND BREAKFAST

Coedllys Uchaf, Llangynin SA33 4JY
☎ 01994 231455   📠 01994 231441
e-mail: coedllys@btinternet.com
web: www.coedllyscountryhouse.co.uk
dir: *A40 St Clears rdbt, take 3rd exit, at lights turn left.
After 100yds turn right, 3m to Llangynin, pass village
sign. 30mph sign on left, turn immediately down track
(private drive)*

Set in a peaceful valley, Coedllys is the home of Mr and
Mrs Harber, who make visitors feel like honoured
guests. Bedrooms are lavishly furnished, and the
thoughtful and useful extras make a stay most
memorable. There is a cosy, well-furnished lounge and
an extensive menu choice at breakfast is served in the
pleasant dining room. A further annexe, cottage-style
room with two bedrooms is now available which is also
suitable as a self-catering let. For the energetic there
is a fitness suite, but guests can also relax in the
sauna or small indoor pool.

Rooms 3 en suite 1 annexe en suite (1 fmly) (1 GF) D
£90-£150* **Facilities** FTV tea/coffee Cen ht Wi-fi 📶
Sauna Gym **Parking** 6 **Notes** LB No Children 12yrs
Closed Xmas

CEREDIGION

ABERAERON
Map 8 SN46

PREMIER COLLECTION

The Harbourmaster

★★★★★ ◉ 🍴 INN

Pen Cei SA46 0BA
☎ 01545 570755
e-mail: info@harbour-master.com
web: www.harbour-master.com
dir: *In town centre beside tourist office & harbour*

Located right on the harbour in a picturesque seaside
town, this Grade II listed building was once the
harbourmaster's house. The bedrooms are delightfully
furnished and comfortable, and some rooms have sea
views; four are particularly modern in design and one
first-floor room is accessible by lift. The ever-popular
lunches and dinners offer a varied range of carefully
prepared dishes using locally sourced, fresh produce.
Breakfasts are a real treat too. The proprietors and
staff are very friendly and professional.

Rooms 13 rms (10 en suite) (3 pri facs) S £65; D
£110-£250* **Facilities** FTV tea/coffee Dinner available
Direct Dial Cen ht Lift Wi-fi **Parking** 7 **Notes** LB ✪ No
Children 5yrs Closed 25 Dec No coaches

PREMIER COLLECTION

Ty Mawr Mansion

★★★★★ ◉◉ 🍴 RESTAURANT WITH ROOMS

Cilcennin SA48 8DB
☎ 01570 470033
e-mail: info@tymawrmansion.co.uk
web: www.tymawrmansion.co.uk
dir: *On A482 (Lampeter to Aberaeron road), 4m from
Aberaeron*

Surrounded by rolling countryside in its own naturally
beautiful gardens, this fine country mansion house is a
haven of perfect peace and tranquillity. Careful
renovation has restored it to its former glory and,
combined with lush fabrics, top quality beds and
sumptuous furnishings, the accommodation is
spacious, superbly equipped and very comfortable.
Award-winning chefs create mouth-watering dishes
from local and seasonal produce. There is also a 27-
seat cinema with all the authenticity of the real thing.
Martin and Cath McAlpine offer the sort of welcome
which makes every visit to Ty Mawr a memorable one.

Rooms 8 en suite 1 annexe en suite (1 fmly) (2 GF)
Facilities FTV tea/coffee Dinner available Direct Dial
Cen ht Wi-fi Fishing Cinema **Conf** Max 25 Thtr 25 Class
25 Board 16 **Parking** 20 **Notes** ✪ No Children 12yrs
Closed 28 Dec-10 Jan No coaches Civ Wed 30

PREMIER COLLECTION

Feathers Royal

★★★★★ INN

Alban Square SA46 0AQ
☎ 01545 571750   📠 01545 571760
e-mail: enquiries@feathersroyal.co.uk
dir: *A482, Lampeter Road, Feathers Royal opposite
recreation grounds*

This is a family-run inn, ideally located in the
picturesque Georgian town of Aberaeron. It is a
charming, Grade II listed property, built in 1815 as a
traditional coaching house that underwent a
transformation to coincide with the town's bicentenary
celebrations. Accommodation is very comfortable with
modern fittings and accessories provided, and the
public areas are well appointed. There is a large suite
available for private or business functions. A friendly
welcome can be expected.

Rooms 13 en suite (2 fmly) S £75; D £115*
Facilities STV tea/coffee Direct Dial Wi-fi **Parking** 20
Notes ✪ Civ Wed 200

ABERAERON *continued*

Arosfa Harbourside Guesthouse

★★★★ 🏠 GUEST HOUSE

SA46 0BU
☎ 01545 570120

e-mail: info@arosfaguesthouse.co.uk
dir: *A487 in town centre onto Market St towards sea, 150yds to Arosfa, harbourside car park*

A warm welcome is assured at this renovated Georgian house, located by the historic harbour. Bedrooms are filled with thoughtful extras and have modern bathrooms. Other areas include a cosy lounge, stairways enhanced by quality art and memorabilia, and a bright, attractive dining room, the setting for imaginative Welsh breakfasts.

Rooms 3 en suite 1 annexe en suite (1 fmly) (1 GF) S £40-£65; D £64-£100 **Facilities** FTV tea/coffee Cen ht Wi-fi **Notes** LB ⊗ 🐾

Gwennaul

★★★★ 🅰 BED AND BREAKFAST

Drefach SA46 0JR
☎ 01545 571756

e-mail: gwennaul@hotmail.co.uk
dir: *From Aberaeron on A487 towards Aberystwyth, after petrol station take 2nd lane on left, 1st bungalow on left*

Rooms 2 en suite (2 GF) D £70-£80* **Facilities** FTV tea/coffee Cen ht **Parking** 2 **Notes** ⊗ No Children 16yrs Closed Dec 🐾

Aromatherapy Reflexology Centre

★★★ BED AND BREAKFAST

The Barn House, Pennant Rd SY23 5LZ
☎ 01974 202581

e-mail: aromareflex@googlemail.com
web: www.aromatherapy-breaks-wales.co.uk
dir: *S of Aberystwyth to Llanon, leaving village turn left at 40mph sign. 2nd left to Barn House*

Expect a warm welcome from this family-run bed and breakfast where Welsh is spoken. Set in its own grounds in a tranquil position with lovely views of Cardigan Bay. Bedrooms are comfortable and smartly presented. There is a choice of traditional, vegetarian or vegan breakfast available. Aromatherapy and Reflexology are available at the centre.

Rooms 3 rms (2 en suite) (1 pri facs) S £33-£45; D £60-£90 **Facilities** FTV tea/coffee Wi-fi Massage/Reflexology by appointment **Parking** 7 **Notes** LB 🐾

ABERYSTWYTH
Map 8 SN58

PREMIER COLLECTION

Awel-Deg

★★★★★ BED AND BREAKFAST

Capel Bangor SY23 3LR
☎ 01970 880681

e-mail: awel-deg@tiscali.co.uk
web: www.awel-deg.co.uk
dir: *5m E of Aberystwyth. On A44 in Capel Bangor*

Located five miles from the historic university town, this attractive bungalow, set in pretty gardens, provides high standards of hospitality, comfort and facilities. Immaculately maintained throughout, spacious bedrooms are equipped with a wealth of thoughtful extras and smart, modern en suite shower rooms. Comprehensive breakfasts are served at one table in the elegant dining room and a choice of lounges is available.

Rooms 2 en suite (2 GF) D £59* **Facilities** FTV TVL tea/coffee Cen ht **Parking** 8 **Notes** LB ⊗ No Children 11yrs Closed 20-30 Dec 🐾

Bodalwyn

★★★★ GUEST HOUSE

Queen's Av SY23 2EG
☎ 01970 612578 📠 01970 639261

e-mail: enquiries@bodalwyn.co.uk
web: www.bodalwyn.co.uk
dir: *500yds N of town centre. Off A487 Northgate St onto North Rd to end*

Located a short walk from the promenade, this imposing Edwardian house, built for a college professor, has been totally refurbished to provide high standards of comfort and good facilities. Smart modern bathrooms complement the spacious bedrooms, which are equipped with a wealth of thoughtful extras. Family rooms are available. Comprehensive Welsh breakfasts are served in the elegant conservatory-dining room.

Rooms 8 en suite (2 fmly) **Facilities** FTV tea/coffee Cen ht Wi-fi **Notes** ⊗ Closed 24 Dec-1 Jan 🐾

Glyn-Garth

★★★★ GUEST HOUSE

South Rd SY23 1JS
☎ **01970 615050**
e-mail: glyngarth@aol.com
web: www.glyngarth.cjb.net
dir: *In town centre. Off A487 onto South Rd off South Promenade*

Privately owned and personally run by the same family for over 50 years, this immaculately maintained guest house provides a range of thoughtfully furnished bedrooms with smart modern bathrooms. Breakfast is served in the attractive dining room and a lounge is also available.

Rooms 10 rms (6 en suite) (2 fmly) (1 GF) S £30–£60; D £60–£80* **Facilities** STV FTV TVL tea/coffee Cen ht Wi-fi **Parking** 2 **Notes** ⊗ Closed 2wks Xmas & New Year ⊛

Llety Ceiro Country House

★★★★ GUEST HOUSE

Peggy Ln, Bow St, Llandre SY24 5AB
☎ **01970 821900** ▤ **01970 820966**
e-mail: marinehotel1@btconnect.com
dir: *4m NE of Aberystwyth. Off A487 onto B4353 for 300yds*

Located north of Aberystwyth, this house is well maintained throughout. Bedrooms are equipped with a range of thoughtful extras in addition to smart modern bathrooms. Morning coffees, afternoon teas and dinner are available in an attractive dining room, with a conservatory extension, and bicycle hire is also available.

Rooms 11 en suite (2 fmly) (3 GF) (1 smoking) **Facilities** FTV TVL tea/coffee Dinner available Direct Dial Cen ht Licensed Wi-fi Free use of facilities at sister hotel **Conf** Max 60 Thtr 60 Class 40 Board 40 **Parking** 21 **Notes** Civ Wed 65

Yr Hafod

★★★★ GUEST HOUSE

1 South Marine Ter SY23 1JX
☎ **01970 617579** ▤ **01970 636835**
e-mail: johnyrhafod@aol.com
dir: *On south promenade between harbour & castle*

An immaculately maintained, end of terrace Victorian house in a commanding location overlooking the South Bay. The spacious bedrooms are comfortable and some have smart modern shower rooms. Breakfast is served in the attractive front-facing dining room.

Rooms 6 rms (3 en suite) (1 pri facs) S £30–£31; D £60–£82* **Facilities** STV FTV TVL tea/coffee Cen ht Wi-fi **Parking** 1 **Notes** ⊗ Closed Xmas & New Year ⊛

Y Gelli

★★★ GUEST HOUSE

Dolau, Lovesgrove SY23 3HP
☎ **01970 617834**
e-mail: pat.twigg@virgin.net
dir: *Off A44 2.75m E of town centre*

Located in spacious grounds on the town's outskirts, this modern detached house contains a range of practical furnished bedrooms and three further rooms are available in an adjacent Victorian property. Comprehensive breakfasts are served in the attractive dining room with evening meals available on request. A comfortable lounge is also available for guest use.

Rooms 5 rms (2 en suite) 3 annexe rms 1 annexe en suite (3 fmly) (1 GF) **Facilities** TVL tea/coffee Dinner available Cen ht Snooker Pool table Table tennis Stabling can be provided **Conf** Thtr 30 Class 30 Board 20 **Parking** 20 **Notes** ⊗ ⊛

PONTERWYD   Map 9 SN78

Ffynnon Cadno Guest House

★★★★ ▲ BED AND BREAKFAST

SY23 3AD
☎ **01970 890224**
e-mail: ffynnoncadno@btinternet.com
dir: *Adjacent to A44 (Aberystwyth to Llangurig road), on Aberystwyth side of village*

Rooms 3 rms (2 en suite) (1 pri facs) (1 fmly) S £20–£35; D £40–£70* **Facilities** STV FTV TVL tea/coffee Cen ht Wi-fi Pool table **Parking** 6 **Notes** ⊗ No Children 3yrs

CONWY

ABERGELE   Map 14 SH97

PREMIER COLLECTION

The Kinmel Arms

★★★★★ ⊛⊛ RESTAURANT WITH ROOMS

The Village, St George LL22 9BP
☎ **01745 832207** ▤ **01745 822044**
e-mail: info@thekinmelarms.co.uk
dir: *From A55 junct 24a to St George. E on A55, junct 25. 1st left to Rhuddlan, then 1st right into St George. Take 2nd right*

This converted 17th-century coaching inn stands close to the church in the village of St George in the beautiful Elwy Valley. The popular restaurant specialises in produce from Wales and north west England, and the friendly and helpful staff ensure an enjoyable stay. The four attractive suites are luxuriously furnished and feature stunning bathrooms. Substantial continental breakfasts are served in the rooms.

Rooms 4 en suite (2 GF) **Facilities** STV tea/coffee Dinner available Cen ht **Parking** 8 **Notes** ⊗ No Children 16yrs Closed 25 Dec & 1 Jan RS Sun & Mon Closed Sun pm & all day Mon (ex BHs) No coaches

BETWS-Y-COED — Map 14 SH75

PREMIER COLLECTION

Penmachno Hall

★★★★★ 🍽 GUEST ACCOMMODATION

Penmachno LL24 0PU
☎ 01690 760410 🖷 01690 760410
e-mail: stay@penmachnohall.co.uk
web: www.penmachnohall.co.uk
dir: 4m S of Betws-y-Coed. A5 onto B4406 to
Penmachno, over bridge, right at Eagles pub signed Ty
Mawr. 500yds at stone bridge

Set in more than two acres of mature grounds
including a mountain stream and woodland, this
impressive Victorian rectory has been lovingly restored
to provide high standards of comfort and facilities.
Stylish decor and quality furnishings highlight the
many original features throughout the ground-floor
areas, and the bedrooms have a wealth of thoughtful
extras. Alongside the main building is a superb two-
bedroom, self-catering unit created from a sympathetic
renovation of a former coach house. Pre-booked set
dinner party-style evening meals are served on
Saturday night, while a buffet-style meal is served
Tuesday through Friday.

Rooms 3 en suite D £85-£100 **Facilities** STV tea/coffee
Dinner available Cen ht Licensed Wi-fi **Parking** 5
Notes LB ⊗ Closed Xmas & New Year RS Sun-Mon No
evening meals

PREMIER COLLECTION

Tan-y-Foel Country House

★★★★★ ◉◉◉ 🍽 GUEST HOUSE

Capel Garmon LL26 0RE
☎ 01690 710507 🖷 01690 710681
e-mail: enquiries@tyfhotel.co.uk
web: www.tyfhotel.co.uk
dir: 1.5m E of Betws-y-Coed. Off A5 onto A470 N, 2m
right for Capel Garmon, establishment signed 1.5m
on left

Situated high above the Conwy valley and set in six
acres of woodland with attractive gardens and country
walks leading from the grounds, this delightful 17th-
century country house has superb views in all
directions. The bedrooms are individually decorated
and include four-poster king, canopied and king-size
beds along with modern facilities. There is a stylish
sitting room and restaurant where fires burn in winter,
and fresh local produce features on the small but
interesting menu.

Rooms 4 en suite 2 annexe en suite (1 GF) S £90-£145;
D £115-£245* **Facilities** tea/coffee Dinner available
Direct Dial Cen ht Licensed Wi-fi **Parking** 14 **Notes** LB
⊗ No Children 12yrs Closed Dec RS Jan Limited
availability

Afon View Guest House

★★★★ GUEST HOUSE

Holyhead Rd LL24 0AN
☎ 01690 710726 🖷 01690 710726
e-mail: welcome@afon-view.co.uk
web: www.afon-view.co.uk
dir: On A5, 150yds E of HSBC bank

A warm welcome is assured at this elegant Victorian
house, located between Waterloo Bridge and the village
centre. Bedrooms are equipped with lots of thoughtful
extras and day rooms include an attractive dining room
and comfortable guest lounge.

Rooms 7 en suite (1 fmly) S £45; D £75-£95*
Facilities FTV tea/coffee Cen ht Wi-fi **Parking** 7 **Notes** LB
⊗ No Children 4yrs Closed 23-26 Dec

Bryn Bella Guest House

★★★★ GUEST HOUSE

Lon Muriau, Llanrwst Rd LL24 0HD
☎ 01690 710627
e-mail: welcome@bryn-bella.co.uk
web: www.bryn-bella.co.uk
dir: A5 onto A470, 0.5m right onto driveway signed Bryn
Bella

Located on an elevated position on the town's outskirts
and having stunning views of the surrounding
countryside, this elegant Victorian house provides a range
of thoughtfully equipped bedrooms with smart modern
bathrooms. A fine collection of memorabilia adorns the
public areas, which include an attractive dining room
and a comfortable lounge. A warm welcome is assured
and guest services include a daily weather forecast.

Rooms 5 en suite (1 GF) D £75-£90 **Facilities** FTV TVL
tea/coffee Cen ht Wi-fi **Parking** 7 **Notes** LB ⊗

Cwmanog Isaf Farm (SH799546)

★★★★ FARMHOUSE

Fairy Glen LL24 0SL
☎ 01690 710225 & 07808 421634
Mrs H M Hughes
e-mail: h.hughes165@btinternet.com
dir: 1m S of Betws-y-Coed off A470 by Fairy Glen Hotel,
500yds on farm lane

Peacefully located on 30 acres of undulating land, which
also contains the renowned Fairy Glen, this 200-year-old
house on a working livestock farm has been restored to
provide comfortable, thoughtfully furnished bedrooms.
Breakfast includes home-reared or organic produce, and
the raised position of the property provides stunning
views of the surrounding countryside.

Rooms 3 rms (2 en suite) (1 pri facs) (1 GF) S £45-£60; D
£62-£75* **Facilities** STV tea/coffee Cen ht **Parking** 4
Notes ⊗ No Children 15yrs Closed 15 Nov-1 Mar ☺ 30
acres mixed

Park Hill

★★★★ GUEST HOUSE

Llanrwst Rd LL24 0HD
☎ 01690 710540 🖷 01690 710540
e-mail: welcome@park-hill.co.uk
web: www.park-hill.co.uk
dir: 0.5m N of Betws-y-Coed on A470 (Llanrwst road)

This friendly guest house benefits from a peaceful
location overlooking the village. Comfortable bedrooms
come in a wide range of sizes and are well equipped, one
with a four-poster bed. There is a choice of lounges, a
heated swimming pool, sauna and whirlpool bath for
guests' use.

Rooms 8 en suite S £50-£92; D £66-£97.50*
Facilities FTV tea/coffee Cen ht Wi-fi ☜ Sauna
Parking 11 **Notes** LB ⊗ No Children 8yrs

Save on B&Bs and Hotels. Book at **theAA.com/hotel**

CONWY 407 WALES

Ty Gwyn Inn

★★★ INN

LL24 0SG
☎ 01690 710383 📠 01690 710383
e-mail: mratcl1050@aol.com
dir: *Junct of A5 & A470, by Waterloo Bridge*

Situated on the edge of the village, close to the Waterloo Bridge, this historic coaching inn retains many original features. Quality furnishing styles and memorabilia throughout enhance its intrinsic charm. Bedrooms, some of which feature antique beds, are equipped with thoughtful extras, and imaginative food is provided in the cosy bars or restaurant.

Rooms 13 rms (10 en suite) (3 fmly) (1 GF) **Facilities** TVL tea/coffee Dinner available Cen ht Wi-fi **Parking** 14 **Notes** Closed Mon-Wed in Jan

COLWYN BAY   Map 14 SH87

Whitehall

★★★★ GUEST HOUSE

51 Cayley Promenade, Rhos-on-Sea LL28 4EP
☎ 01492 547296
e-mail: mossd.cymru@virgin.net
dir: *A55 onto B5115 (Brompton Av), right at rdbt onto Whitehall Rd to seafront*

Overlooking Rhos-on-Sea promenade, this popular, family-run establishment is convenient for the shops and local amenities. Attractively appointed bedrooms include family rooms and a room on the ground floor; all benefit from an excellent range of facilities such as video and CD players as well as air-conditioning. Facilities include a bar and a foyer lounge. Home-cooked dinners are available.

Rooms 12 en suite (4 fmly) (1 GF) S £28-£45; D £56-£76* **Facilities** FTV TVL tea/coffee Dinner available Direct Dial Cen ht Licensed Wi-fi **Parking** 5 **Notes** LB

The Northwood

★★★ GUEST HOUSE

47 Rhos Rd, Rhos-on-Sea LL28 4RS
☎ 01492 549931
e-mail: welcome@thenorthwood.co.uk
web: www.thenorthwood.co.uk
dir: *Leave A55 junct 22 (Old Colwyn), at T-junct turn right to next T-junct (facing sea). Turn left, go past pier, opposite harbour turn left onto Rhos Rd. On left next to church*

A short walk from the seafront and shops, this constantly improving guest house has a warm and friendly atmosphere and welcomes back many regular guests. Bedrooms are furnished in modern style, and freshly prepared meals utilising fresh produce (some home grown), can be enjoyed in the spacious dining room that overlooks the pretty patio.

Rooms 11 rms (10 en suite) (1 pri facs) (3 fmly) (2 GF) **Facilities** TVL tea/coffee Dinner available Cen ht Licensed Wi-fi **Conf** Max 20 Class 20 Board 20 **Parking** 12

See advert on this page

CONWY   Map 14 SH77

The Groes Inn

★★★★★ ⚜ INN

Tyn-y-Groes LL32 8TN
☎ 01492 650545 📠 01492 650855
e-mail: enquiries@thegroes.com
web: www.groesinn.com
dir: *A55, over Old Conwy Bridge, 1st left through Castle Walls on B5106 (Trefriw Road), 2m on right*

Located in the picturesque Conwy Valley, this historic inn dates from 1573 and was the first licensed house in Wales. The exterior and gardens have an abundance of shrubs and seasonal flowers and create an immediate welcome, which is matched by a friendly and professional staff. Public areas are decorated and furnished with flair to highlight the many period features, and a formal dining room is also available. Spacious bedrooms, in sympathetically renovated former outbuildings are equipped with a wealth of thoughtful extras, and many have balconies overlooking the surrounding countryside.

Rooms 14 en suite (1 fmly) (6 GF) S £91-£190; D £115-£220* **Facilities** FTV tea/coffee Dinner available Direct Dial Cen ht Wi-fi Golf 18 Squash **Conf** Max 20 Thtr 20 Class 20 Board 20 **Parking** 100 **Notes** LB Closed 25 Dec

---

CONWY *continued*

PREMIER COLLECTION

The Old Rectory Country House

★★★★★ 🏠 GUEST ACCOMMODATION

Llanrwst Rd, Llansanffraid Glan Conwy LL28 5LF
☎ 01492 580611
e-mail: info@oldrectorycountryhouse.co.uk
web: www.oldrectorycountryhouse.co.uk
dir: *0.5m S from A470/A55 junct on left, by 30mph sign*

This very welcoming accommodation has fine views over the Conwy estuary and towards Snowdonia. The elegant day rooms are luxurious and afternoon tea is available in the lounge. Bedrooms share the delightful views and are thoughtfully furnished, while the genuine hospitality creates a real home from home.

Rooms 3 en suite 2 annexe en suite (1 fmly) (2 GF) S £79-£119; D £99-£159* **Facilities** STV FTV tea/coffee Direct Dial Cen ht Wi-fi **Parking** 10 **Notes** LB No Children 3yrs Closed 14 Dec-15 Jan

Gwern Borter Country Manor

★★★★ GUEST ACCOMMODATION

Barkers Ln LL32 8YL
☎ 01492 650360 🖩 01492 650360
e-mail: mail@snowdoniaholidays.co.uk
dir: *From Conwy B5106 for 2.25m, right towards Rowen for 0.5m then right, left as road forks, Gwern Borter 0.5m on left*

This delightful mansion has walls covered in climbing plants and is set in several acres of lawns and gardens. Children are very welcome and there is a rustic play area, games room and many farmyard pets. Bedrooms are furnished with antiques and modern facilities, and one room has an Edwardian four-poster bed. There is an elegant lounge and Victorian-style dining room, where freshly cooked breakfasts are served. Self-catering cottages are also available.

Rooms 4 rms (3 en suite) (1 pri facs) (1 fmly) **Facilities** STV FTV TVL tea/coffee Cen ht Wi-fi Riding Sauna Gym Pool table **Parking** 4 **Notes** LB ⊗ No Children 4yrs

---

DWYGYFYLCHI   Map 14 SH77

The Gladstone

★★★★ INN

Ygborwen Rd LL34 6PS
☎ 01492 623231
e-mail: thegladstonepub@hotmail.co.uk
dir: *A55 junct 16 turn left, then left again towards Dwygyfylchi, 0.25m on right*

The Gladstone offers modern seaside accommodation; the comfortable, stylish bedrooms are individually designed, equipped with plenty of thoughtful extras and have luxurious bathrooms. The bar and front bedrooms have views of Puffin Island and Anglesey. There is seating outside for alfresco dining and for enjoying the sunsets. Off-road parking is available.

Rooms 6 en suite S £50-£90; D £70-£120* **Facilities** FTV TVL tea/coffee Dinner available Cen ht Wi-fi **Parking** 25 **Notes** LB ⊗ No coaches

---

LLANDUDNO   Map 14 SH78

PREMIER COLLECTION

Bryn Derwen

★★★★★ GUEST HOUSE

34 Abbey Rd LL30 2EE
☎ 01492 876804 🖩 01492 876804
e-mail: brynderwen34@btinternet.com
dir: *A470 into Llandudno, left at The Parade promenade to cenotaph, left, over rdbt, 4th right onto York Rd, Bryn Derwen at top*

A warm welcome is assured at this impressive Victorian house, which retains original tiled floors and some fine stained-glass windows. Quality decor and furnishings highlight the historic charm of the property, which is apparent in the sumptuous lounges and attractive dining room, the setting for imaginative breakfasts. Bedrooms are equipped with a wealth of thoughtful extras, and the establishment also has a fully-equipped beauty salon.

Rooms 9 en suite (1 fmly) S £50-£55; D £80-£100* **Facilities** FTV tea/coffee Dinner available Cen ht Licensed Wi-fi Golf 18 Solarium Beauty Salon **Parking** 9 **Notes** LB ⊗ No Children 12yrs Closed Dec-Jan

---

Abbey Lodge

★★★★ GUEST HOUSE

14 Abbey Rd LL30 2EA
☎ 01492 878042
e-mail: enquiries@abbeylodgeuk.com
dir: *A546 to N end of town, onto Clement Av, right onto Abbey Rd*

This impressive Victorian villa is on a leafy avenue within easy walking distance of the promenade. It has been lovingly restored, and stylish decor and furniture add to its charm. Bedrooms come with a wealth of thoughtful extras, and there is a choice of sumptuous lounges and an elegant dining room.

Rooms 4 en suite S £37.50-£40; D £75 **Facilities** FTV tea/coffee Cen ht Wi-fi **Parking** 4 **Notes** ⊗ Closed Dec-1 Mar ⊛

Brigstock House

★★★★ GUEST HOUSE

1 St David's Place LL30 2UG
☎ 01492 876416 🖩 01492 879292
e-mail: simon.hanson4@virgin.net
dir: *A470 into Llandudno, left onto The Parade promenade, left onto Lloyd St, left onto St David's Rd & left onto St David's Place*

This impressive Edwardian property is on a quiet residential cul-de-sac within easy walking distance of the seafront and central shopping area. The attractive bedrooms are well equipped, and a comfortable lounge is available. Substantial breakfasts and dinners, by arrangement, are served in the elegant dining room.

Rooms 8 en suite S £36-£42; D £72-£84* **Facilities** FTV TVL tea/coffee Dinner available Cen ht Licensed Wi-fi **Parking** 6 **Notes** LB ⊗ No Children 12yrs Closed Dec-Jan

Save on B&Bs and Hotels. Book at **theAA.com/hotel**

CONWY 409 WALES

St Hilary Guest House

★★★★ GUEST ACCOMMODATION

16 Craig-y-Don Pde, The Promenade LL30 1BG
☎ 01492 875551 📄 01492 877538
e-mail: info@sthilaryguesthouse.co.uk
web: www.sthilaryguesthouse.co.uk
dir: 0.5m E of town centre. On B5115 seafront road near
Venue Cymru

A warm welcome is assured at this constantly improving
guest accommodation, located at the Craig-y-Don end of
the Promenade, and many of the thoughtfully furnished
bedrooms have superb sea views. Day rooms include a
spacious attractive front-facing dining room. A cosy
guest lounge is also available.

Rooms 9 en suite (2 fmly) (1 GF) S £45-£47; D £68-£82
Facilities FTV tea/coffee Cen ht Wi-fi **Notes** LB ⊗ No
Children 8yrs Closed end Nov-early Feb

Stratford House

★★★★ GUEST ACCOMMODATION

8 Craig-y-Don Pde, The Promenade LL30 1BG
☎ 01492 877962
e-mail: stratfordhtl@aol.com
dir: A470 rdbt 4th exit on Queens Rd to promenade, on
right

This immaculately presented spacious house is located
on the sea front with spectacular views. Bedrooms are
attractively decorated, some with four-poster beds and
all have an excellent range of accessories, such as flat
screen televisions. The traditionally decorated dining
room is also beautifully presented. The friendly owners
are very welcoming.

Rooms 9 en suite (2 fmly) (1 GF) S £45-£55; D £55-£70*
Facilities FTV tea/coffee Cen ht Wi-fi **Notes** LB ⊗ No
Children 8yrs Closed Jan

Britannia Guest House

★★★★ GUEST HOUSE

Promenade, 15 Craig-y-Don Pde LL30 1BG
☎ 01492 877185 📄 01492 233300
e-mail: info@thebritanniaguesthouse.co.uk
web: www.thebritanniaguesthouse.co.uk
dir: A55 onto A470 to Llandudno, at rdbt take 4th exit
signed Craig-y-Don, right at promenade

This family-run Victorian guest house offers a warm
welcome and friendly service. The bedrooms are very
comfortable and well equipped, and many have fantastic
views of Llandudno Bay. Ground floor rooms are available.
Hearty breakfasts are served in the sea view dining room.

Rooms 10 rms (9 en suite) (1 pri facs) (3 fmly) (2 GF) D
£60-£78* **Facilities** FTV tea/coffee Cen ht Wi-fi **Notes** LB
⊗ No Children 10yrs Closed 28 Nov-13 Feb

Bryn-y-Mor

★★★★ GUEST ACCOMMODATION

25 North Pde LL30 2LP
☎ 01492 876790 📄 01492 874990
e-mail: info@bryn-y-mor.net
web: www.bryn-y-mor.net
dir: A55 take Llandudno junct, head for Promenade turn
left, by pier on left

Located at the foot of the Great Orme and close to the
town centre and its main attractions, the family-run
Bryn-y-Mor offers comfortable well-equipped rooms,
many with sea views. There is an attractive lounge
looking over the bay to the Little Orme. There is also a
small bar and an outside patio which also overlooks the
bay.

Rooms 12 en suite **Facilities** FTV tea/coffee Cen ht
Licensed **Notes** ⊗ No Children 16yrs Closed 15 Nov-9
Feb

Can-Y-Bae

★★★★ GUEST ACCOMMODATION

10 Mostyn Crescent, Central Promenade LL30 1AR
☎ 01492 874188 📄 01492 868376
e-mail: canybae@btconnect.com
web: www.can-y-baehotel.com
dir: A55 junct 10 onto A470, signed Llandudno/
Promenade. Can-Y-Bae on seafront promenade between
Venue Cymru Theatre & Band Stand

A warm welcome is assured at this tastefully renovated
house, centrally located on the Promenade. Bedrooms are
equipped with both practical and homely extras and
upper floors are serviced by a modern lift. Day rooms
include a panoramic lounge, cosy bar and attractive
basement dining room.

Rooms 16 en suite (2 GF) S £35-£45; D £80-£100*
Facilities FTV tea/coffee Dinner available Direct Dial
Cen ht Lift Licensed Wi-fi **Notes** LB No Children 12yrs

The Cliffbury

★★★★ GUEST ACCOMMODATION

34 St David's Rd LL30 2UH
☎ 01492 877224
e-mail: info@thecliffbury.co.uk

Located on a leafy avenue within easy walking distance
of the town centre, this elegant Edwardian house has
been sympathetically refurbished to provide high
standards of comfort. Bedrooms, furnished in minimalist
style, provide a range of practical and thoughtful extras
and smart modern bath/shower rooms are an additional
benefit. Breakfast is taken in an attractive dining room
and a warm welcome is assured.

Rooms 6 en suite D £62-£80* **Facilities** FTV tea/coffee
Cen ht Wi-fi **Parking** 6 **Notes** LB ⊗ No Children 11yrs

Epperstone

★★★★ GUEST ACCOMMODATION

15 Abbey Rd LL30 2EE
☎ 01492 878746 📄 01492 871223
e-mail: epperstonehotel@btconnect.com
dir: A550/A470 to Mostyn St. Left at rdbt, 4th right onto
York Rd, Epperstone on junct of York Rd & Abbey Rd

This delightful property is located in wonderful gardens in
a residential part of town, within easy walking distance
of the seafront and shopping area. Bedrooms are
attractively decorated and thoughtfully equipped. Two
lounges and a Victorian-style conservatory are available.
A daily-changing menu is offered in the bright dining
room.

Rooms 8 en suite (5 fmly) **Facilities** FTV tea/coffee Direct
Dial Wi-fi **Parking** 8

Glenavon Guest House

★★★★ GUEST HOUSE

27 St Mary's Rd LL30 2UB
☎ 01492 877687 📄 0870 706 2247
e-mail: postmaster@glenavon.plus.com
dir: From A470 signed Llandudno, turn left at lights
onto Trinity Av. 3rd on right into St Mary's Rd. Glenavon
on right

Supporters of Liverpool Football Club are especially
welcome here and they can admire the extensive range of
memorabilia throughout the comfortable day rooms.
Bedrooms are equipped with thoughtful extras and Welsh
breakfasts provide a good start to the day.

Rooms 7 en suite (1 fmly) S £40-£45; D £60-£75
Facilities FTV TVL tea/coffee Cen ht Wi-fi **Parking** 4
Notes LB ⊗

LLANDUDNO *continued*

The Lilly Restaurant with Rooms

★★★ 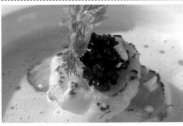 RESTAURANT WITH ROOMS

West Pde, West Shore LL30 2BD
☎ 01492 876513
e-mail: thelilly@live.co.uk

Located on the seafront on the West Shore with views over the Great Orme, this establishment has bedrooms that offer high standards of comfort and good facilities. Children are very welcome here, and a relaxed atmosphere can be found in Madhatters Brasserie, which takes its name from Lewis Caroll's *Alice's Adventures in Wonderland* which was written on the West Shore. A fine dining restaurant is also available.

Rooms 12 en suite (2 fmly) (2 GF) Facilities FTV tea/coffee Dinner available Direct Dial Cen ht Wi-fi Conf Max 35 Thtr 25 Board 20 Notes ⊗ No coaches

Minion

★★★ GUEST ACCOMMODATION

21-23 Carmen Sylva Rd, Craig-y-Don LL30 1EQ
☎ 01492 877740
dir: *A55 junct 19 onto A470 to Llandudno. At 4th rdbt take Craig-y-Don turn-off. 2nd right after park*

Situated in a quiet residential area a few minutes walk from the eastern promenade, the Minion has been owned by the same family for over 60 years and continues to extend a warm welcome. Bedrooms are smart and comfortable, and two are on the ground floor. There is a cosy bar and a colourful garden.

Rooms 10 en suite (1 fmly) (2 GF) S £26-£28.50; D £52-£57* Facilities FTV TVL tea/coffee Dinner available Licensed Parking 8 Notes No Children 2yrs Closed Nov-Mar ⊜

LLANRWST	Map 14 SH86

PREMIER COLLECTION

Plas Maenan Country House

★★★★★ ◉◉ GUEST ACCOMMODATION

Maenan LL26 0YR
☎ 01492 660232 📠 01492 660363
e-mail: james.burt@btconnect.com
dir: *On A470 between Glan Conwy & Llanrwst*

A beautifully refurbished Edwardian mansion house with stunning views over the Conwy Valley. The friendly owners and their staff provide attentive service. The bedrooms are tastefully furnished and well equipped. There is an elegant sitting room with open fire, mountain-view conservatory and a Steinway piano in the Music Room which leads through to a cosy bar. Dinner is a highlight, and features skilfully prepared dishes made with high quality ingredients. Plas Maenan is the AA's Guest Accommodation of the Year for Wales (2011-2012).

Rooms 10 en suite (2 fmly) S fr £65; D £120-£160* Facilities FTV TVL tea/coffee Dinner available Direct Dial Cen ht Licensed Wi-fi Conf Max 80 Thtr 80 Class 60 Board 40 Parking 60 Notes LB No Children 6yrs Closed 1-10 Jan RS Sun eve & Mon closed Civ Wed 85

RHOS-ON-SEA	Map 14 SH88

See also Colwyn Bay

PREMIER COLLECTION

Plas Rhos

★★★★★ ⌂ GUEST ACCOMMODATION

Cayley Promenade LL28 4EP
☎ 01492 543698 📠 01492 540088
e-mail: info@plasrhos.co.uk
dir: *A55 junct 20 onto B5115 for Rhos-on-Sea, right at rdbt onto Whitehall Rd to promenade*

Stunning sea views are a feature of this renovated Victorian house, which provides high standards of comfort and hospitality. Cosy bedrooms are filled with a wealth of thoughtful extras, and public areas include a

---

choice of sumptuous lounges featuring smart decor, quality soft furnishings and memorabilia. Breakfast is served in the attractive dining room, overlooking the pretty patio garden.

Plas Rhos

Rooms 7 en suite S £50; D £70-£100* Facilities FTV TVL tea/coffee Cen ht Licensed Wi-fi Parking 4 Notes LB ⊗ No Children 12yrs Closed 21 Dec-Jan

DENBIGHSHIRE

CORWEN	Map 15 SJ04

Bron-y-Graig

★★★★ ⌂ GUEST HOUSE

LL21 0DR
☎ 01490 413007 📠 01490 413007
e-mail: info@north-wales-hotel.co.uk
web: www.north-wales-hotel.co.uk
dir: *On A5 on E edge of Corwen*

A short walk from the town centre, this impressive Victorian house retains many original features including fireplaces, stained glass and a tiled floor in the entrance hall. Bedrooms, complemented by luxurious bathrooms, are thoughtfully furnished, and two are in a renovated coach house. Ground-floor areas include a traditionally furnished dining room and a comfortable lounge. A warm welcome, attentive service and imaginative food is assured.

Rooms 8 en suite 2 annexe en suite (3 fmly) Facilities STV tea/coffee Dinner available Direct Dial Cen ht Licensed Conf Max 20 Class 20 Board 15 Parking 15

Save on B&Bs and Hotels. Book at **theAA.com/hotel**

DENBIGHSHIRE 411 | WALES

Plas Derwen Country House

★★★★ GUEST ACCOMMODATION

London Rd LL21 0DR
☎ **01490 412742**
e-mail: bandb@plasderwen.supanet.com
dir: On A5 0.5m E of Corwen

Set in four acres of fields and mature gardens in an elevated position with superb views of the River Dee, this elegant late 18th-century house has been restored to provide high levels of comfort and facilities. Quality furnishings and decor highlight the many original features, and a warm welcome is assured.

Rooms 3 rms (2 en suite) (1 pri facs) (2 fmly)
Facilities FTV TVL tea/coffee Cen ht Wi-fi **Parking** 6
Notes ✦ Closed Dec-Jan

DENBIGH	Map 15 SJ06

PREMIER COLLECTION

Castle House

★★★★★ BED AND BREAKFAST

Bull Lane (Love Lane) LL16 3LY
☎ **01745 816860** 🖶 **01745 817214**
e-mail: stay@castlehousebandb.co.uk
web: www.castlehousebandb.co.uk
dir: A55 junct 27 onto A525 to Denbigh. From Vale St take 1st exit at rdbt, pass supermarket, 1st left to T-junct then right. 20yds on left onto unmarked drive

Located within the medieval town walls and overlooking the Vale of Clwyd, this elegant Georgian house has been lovingly restored to provide high standards of comfort and facilities. Spacious, individually themed bedrooms are equipped with quality furnishings, a wealth of thoughtful extras and smart efficient bathrooms. The furnishing and decor styles throughout the day rooms highlight the many period features, and the notable unfinished Leister's Church and town walls are within the nine-acre grounds.

Rooms 3 en suite S £65-£110; D £120-£160*
Facilities FTV tea/coffee Dinner available Cen ht Licensed Wi-fi ⛳ **Parking** 6 **Notes** ✦ Closed 20-30 Dec Civ Wed 40

Cayo

★★★ GUEST HOUSE

74 Vale St LL16 3BW
☎ **01745 812686**
e-mail: stay@cayo.co.uk
dir: Off A525 into town, at lights turn up hill, supermarket on right. Guest house up hill on left

A warm welcome is assured at this Victorian house, which is situated on the main street, just a short walk from the town centre. Bedrooms are comfortably and thoughtfully furnished with lots of homely extras. Good home cooking is provided in a Victorian-themed dining room, and a cosy basement lounge is also available.

Rooms 4 en suite S £28-£30; D £56-£60 **Facilities** FTV TVL tea/coffee Cen ht Wi-fi **Notes** Closed Xmas-New Year

LLANDRILLO	Map 15 SJ03

PREMIER COLLECTION

Tyddyn Llan Restaurant

★★★★★ ◉◉ 🍴 RESTAURANT WITH ROOMS

LL21 0ST
☎ **01490 440264** 🖶 **01490 440414**
e-mail: info@tyddynllan.co.uk
web: www.tyddynllan.co.uk

Tyddyn Llan is a very well appointed property set in the Edeyrnion Valley at the gateway to Snowdonia. Whilst not all the individually styled bedrooms are spacious, they do offer many home comforts. The public areas are beautifully furnished and have open fires in the colder months. Susan runs the front of the house with friendly informed staff; service is formal and in keeping with the style of the establishment. Husband and chef Bryan sources ingredients as locally as possible and his cooking is sympathetic to the produce. An extensive breakfast menu is available.

Rooms 13 en suite S £150; D £100-£320 (incl.dinner)
Facilities FTV Dinner available Direct Dial Cen ht
Conf Max 30 Thtr 30 Class 10 Board 20 **Parking** 20
Notes LB Closed 2wks Jan No coaches Civ Wed

LLANDYRNOG	Map 15 SJ16

PREMIER COLLECTION

Pentre Mawr Country House

★★★★★ 🛏 GUEST ACCOMMODATION

LL16 4LA
☎ **01824 790732** 🖶 **01824 790441**
e-mail: info@pentremawrcountryhouse.co.uk
dir: From Denbigh follow signs to Bodfari/Llandyrnog. Left at rdbt to Bodfari, after 50yds turn left onto country lane, follow road and Pentre Mawr on left

Expect a warm welcome from Graham and Bre at this superb family country house set in nearly 200 acres of meadows, park and woodland. The property has been in Graham's family for over 400 years. Bedrooms are individually decorated, very spacious and each is thoughtfully equipped. Breakfast is served in either the morning room or, on warmer mornings, on the Georgian terrace. Dinner is served in the formal dining room. There is a salt water swimming pool in the walled garden.

Rooms 3 en suite 8 annexe en suite (7 GF) D £130-£190* **Facilities** FTV TV5B tea/coffee Dinner available Cen ht Licensed Wi-fi ✦ ⛳ Fishing
Conf Max 16 **Parking** 14 **Notes** LB No Children 13yrs

LLANGOLLEN	Map 15 SJ24

See also Corwen

Tyn Celyn Farmhouse

★★★★ BED AND BREAKFAST

Tyndwr LL20 8AR
☎ **01978 861117**
e-mail: j.m.bather-tyncelyn@talk21.com
dir: A5 to Llangollen, pass golf club on right, next left signed Tyndwr outdoor centre, 0.5m sharp left onto Tyndwr Rd, past outdoor centre on left. Tyn Celyn 0.5m on left

This 300-year-old timber-framed farmhouse has stunning views over the Vale of Llangollen. Bedrooms, one of which is located on the ground floor, provide a range of thoughtful extras in addition to fine period furniture. Breakfast is served at a magnificent carved table in a spacious sitting-dining room.

Rooms 3 en suite (1 fmly) (1 GF) D £60-£64
Facilities TVL tea/coffee Cen ht **Parking** 5 **Notes** LB ✦ 🚗

RHYL   Map 14 SJ08

Barratt's of Ty'n Rhyl

★★★★ ◉◉ ≘ RESTAURANT WITH ROOMS

Ty'n Rhyl, 167 Vale Rd LL18 2PH
☎ **01745 344138 & 0773 095 4994** 🖷 **01745 344138**
e-mail: ebarratt5@aol.com
dir: *A55 onto A525 to Rhyl, pass Sainsburys & B&Q, pass Roger Jones on left, 50yds on right*

This delightful 16th-century house lies in a secluded location surrounded by attractive gardens. The quality of the food reflects the skill of the owner-chef. Public areas are smartly furnished and include a panelled lounge, cosy library and an attractive conservatory. Bedrooms are comfortable and equipped with lots of thoughtful extras.

Rooms 3 en suite **Facilities** FTV TVL tea/coffee Dinner available Cen ht Wi-fi ⤳ **Parking** 20 **Notes** ⊗

RUTHIN   Map 15 SJ15

PREMIER COLLECTION

Firgrove Country House B&B

★★★★★ ≘ ⇒ BED AND BREAKFAST

Firgrove, Llanfwrog LL15 2LL
☎ **01824 702677** 🖷 **01824 702677**
e-mail: meadway@firgrovecountryhouse.co.uk
web: www.firgrovecountryhouse.co.uk
dir: *0.5m SW of Ruthin. A494 onto B5105, 0.25m past Llanfwrog church on right*

Standing in immaculate mature gardens in a peaceful rural retreat, this well-proportioned house retains many original features, highlighted by the quality decor and furnishings throughout the interior. Bedrooms, complemented by smart modern bathrooms, are equipped with a wealth of thoughtful extras and memorable breakfasts, using home-made or local produce, are served in an elegant dining room. Imaginative dinners are also available by prior arrangement and a warm welcome is assured.

Rooms 2 en suite 1 annexe en suite (1 GF) S £50-£80; D £70-£100* **Facilities** FTV tea/coffee Dinner available Cen ht Wi-fi **Parking** 4 **Notes** ⊗ No Children Closed Dec-Jan

Tyddyn Chambers *(SJ102543)*

★★★★ FARMHOUSE

Pwllglas LL15 2LS
☎ **01824 750683 & 07745 589946**
Mrs E Williams
e-mail: ella.williams@btconnect.com
web: www.tyddynchambers.co.uk
dir: *3m S of Ruthin. W off A494 after Fox & Hounds pub in Pwllglas, signed*

This charming little farmhouse has been extended to provide carefully appointed, modern accommodation, which includes a family room. The pleasant, traditionally furnished breakfast room has separate tables and a lounge is also available. The house stands in an elevated position with panoramic views.

Rooms 3 en suite (1 fmly) S £35-£38; D £56-£64* **Facilities** TVL tea/coffee Cen ht **Parking** 3 **Notes** ⊗ No Children 4yrs Closed Xmas & New Year ⊕ 180 acres beef/sheep

The Wynnstay Arms

★★★★ INN

Well St LL15 1AN
☎ **01824 703147** 🖷 **01824 705428**
e-mail: resevations@wynnstayarms.com
web: www.wynnstayarms.com
dir: *In town centre*

Established in 1549, this former coaching inn in the town centre has been sympathetically renovated to provide good quality accommodation and a smart café-bar. Imaginative food is served in Fusions Brasserie, where the contemporary decor highlights the many retained period features.

Rooms 7 en suite (1 fmly) S £45-£65; D £65-£105* **Facilities** FTV tea/coffee Dinner available Cen ht Wi-fi **Conf** Max 30 Thtr 30 Class 20 Board 16 **Parking** 14 **Notes** LB

ST ASAPH   Map 15 SJ07

PREMIER COLLECTION

Tan-Yr-Onnen Guest House

★★★★★ GUEST HOUSE

Waen LL17 0DU
☎ **01745 583821** 🖷 **01745 583821**
e-mail: tanyronnenvisit@aol.com
web: www.northwalesbreaks.co.uk
dir: *W on A55 junct 28, turn left in 300yds*

A warm welcome is assured at Tan-Yr-Onnen, which is quietly located in six acres of gardens, yet conveniently close to the A55. The very well equipped accommodation includes four ground floor rooms with French windows opening onto the terrace with tables and chairs. Upstairs there are two luxury suites, with lounge areas. Hearty breakfasts are served in the dining room overlooking the gardens. A conservatory lounge and Wi-fi is also available.

Rooms 6 en suite (1 fmly) (4 GF) S £69-£90; D £89-£125* **Facilities** FTV tea/coffee Dinner available Cen ht Licensed Wi-fi **Parking** 8

Bach-Y-Graig *(SJ075713)*

★★★★ FARMHOUSE

Tremeirchion LL17 0UH
☎ **01745 730627** 🖷 **01745 730627**
Mrs A Roberts
e-mail: anwen@bachygraig.co.uk
dir: *3m SE of St Asaph. Off A525 at Trefnant onto A541 to x-rds with white railings, left down hill, over bridge & then right*

Dating from the 16th century, this listed building was the first brick-built house in Wales and retains many original features including a wealth of exposed beams and inglenook fireplaces. Bedrooms are furnished with fine period pieces and quality soft fabrics. Ground-floor areas include a quiet lounge and a combined sitting and dining room, featuring a superb Jacobean oak table.

Rooms 3 rms (2 en suite) (1 pri facs) (1 fmly) S £38-£50; D £73-£80* **Facilities** FTV TVL tea/coffee Cen ht Wi-fi Fishing Woodland trail **Parking** 3 **Notes** LB ⊗ Closed Xmas & New Year 200 acres dairy/mixed

FLINTSHIRE

NANNERCH   Map 15 SJ16

The Old Mill Guest Accommodation

★★★★ GUEST ACCOMMODATION

Melin-Y-Wern, Denbigh Rd CH7 5RH
☎ 01352 741542
e-mail: mail@old-mill.co.uk
web: www.old-mill.co.uk
dir: A541, NW from Mold, 7m into Melin-Y-Wern, Old Mill
on right

This converted stone stable block was once part of a
Victorian watermill complex. Immediately adjacent is The
Cherry Pie Inn where evening meals can be taken. The
non-smoking guest accommodation offers modern, well-
equipped bedrooms with en suite bathrooms.

Rooms 6 en suite (1 fmly) (2 GF) S £45-£59; D £60-£82*
Facilities FTV tea/coffee Direct Dial Cen ht Wi-fi
Parking 12 Notes LB ⊗ Closed Feb

GWYNEDD

ABERSOCH   Map 14 SH32

Llysfor Guest House

★★★★ GUEST HOUSE

LL53 7AL
☎ 01758 712248   📠 01758 712248
e-mail: emma@llysforguesthouse.co.uk
web: www.llysforguesthouse.com
dir: Take A499, at bottom of hill on right

This large Victorian house stands opposite the harbour
and is within a short walk of the beach and the town
centre. It provides good quality, modern accommodation,
which is complemented by a pleasant lounge and an
attractive breakfast room.

Rooms 6 rms (4 en suite) (2 pri facs) S £45-£50; D
£70-£80* Facilities FTV tea/coffee Cen ht Wi-fi Parking 8
Notes ⊗ Closed Dec-Jan ⊚

BALA   Map 14 SH93

Erw Feurig

★★★★ GUEST HOUSE

Cefnddwysarn LL23 7LL
☎ 01678 530262   & 07786 168399   📠 01678 530262
e-mail: erwfeurig@yahoo.com
web: www.erwfeurig.com
dir: 3m NE of Bala off A494. 2nd left after x-rds at
Cefnddwysarn, turn at B&B sign

A warm welcome is assured at this delightful and
peaceful farm cottage situated on a hillside with
panoramic views of the Berwyn Mountains. The
individually styled bedrooms have a range of additional
extras, and a cosy lounge and a cheerful ground-floor
breakfast room are available.

Rooms 4 rms (2 en suite) (2 pri facs) (1 GF) S £30-£35; D
£55-£60* Facilities FTV TVL tea/coffee Cen ht Fishing
Parking 6 Notes LB ⊗ No Children Closed Nov-Feb ⊚

BARMOUTH   Map 14 SH61

See also Dyffryn Ardudwy

Richmond House

★ ★ ★ ★ GUEST HOUSE

High St LL42 1DW
☎ 01341 281366   & 07976 833069
e-mail: info@barmouthbedandbreakfast.co.uk
web: www.barmouthbedandbreakfast.co.uk
dir: In town centre. Car park at rear on Jubilee Rd

A warm welcome awaits you at this lovely Victorian
house, which has been modernised to provide good
quality and thoughtfully equipped accommodation. Two
of the bedrooms have sea views, as do the lounge and
dining room, where there are separate tables. There is
also a pleasant garden.

Rooms 3 en suite (1 fmly) S £60; D £75* Facilities FTV
tea/coffee Cen ht Wi-fi Parking 5 Notes LB ⊗

Llwyndu Farmhouse

★★★★ ⌂ GUEST ACCOMMODATION

Llanaber LL42 1RR
☎ 01341 280144
e-mail: intouch@llwyndu-farmhouse.co.uk
web: www.llwyndu-farmhouse.co.uk
dir: A496 towards Harlech where street lights end, on
outskirts of Barmouth, take next right

This converted 16th-century farmhouse retains many
original features including inglenook fireplaces, exposed
beams and timbers. There is a cosy lounge and meals
can be enjoyed in the licensed restaurant; two and three
course dinners are offered. Bedrooms are modern and
well equipped, and some have four-poster beds. Four
rooms are in nearby buildings.

Rooms 3 en suite 4 annexe en suite (2 fmly) S fr £60; D
£100-£120* Facilities FTV TVL tea/coffee Dinner
available Cen ht Licensed Wi-fi Conf Max 10 Parking 10
Notes LB Closed 25-26 Dec RS Sun no dinner

Morwendon House

★★★★ ⌂ ⌂ GUEST ACCOMMODATION

Llanaber LL42 1RR
☎ 01341 280566   📠 07092 197785
e-mail: info@morwendon-house.co.uk
dir: A496 at Llanaber N of Barmouth. On Seaward side
250yds past Llanaber Church

With its impressive position overlooking Cardigan Bay,
Morwendon House is an ideal base for exploring the
surrounding area and its many attractions. The bedrooms
offer well-equipped accommodation, with many rooms
having sea views. Dinner is available by arrangement
and meals are taken in the attractive dining room
overlooking the bay. There is also a comfortable lounge,
again with views over the bay.

Rooms 5 en suite 1 annexe en suite (1 fmly) (1 GF) S
£51-£71.40; D £73-£102* Facilities FTV TVL tea/coffee
Dinner available Cen ht Licensed Wi-fi Parking 6
Notes LB ⊗ No Children 12yrs Closed 24-27 Dec

BEDDGELERT   Map 14 SH54

Tanronnen Inn

★★★★ INN

LL55 4YB
☎ 01766 890347   📠 01766 890606
dir: In village centre opposite river bridge

This delightful inn offers comfortable, well equipped and
attractively appointed accommodation, including a family
room. There is also a selection of pleasant and relaxing
public areas. The wide range of bar food is popular with
tourists, and more formal meals are served in the
restaurant.

Rooms 7 en suite (3 fmly) Facilities FTV tea/coffee Dinner
available Direct Dial Cen ht Parking 15 Notes LB ⊗

BETHESDA
Map 14 SH66

Snowdonia Mountain Lodge

★★ GUEST ACCOMMODATION

Nant Ffrancon LL57 3LX
☎ 01248 600500
e-mail: info@snowdoniamountainlodge.com

Located on the A5, south of Bethesda and surrounded by mountains in a stunningly beautiful area, this establishment is very popular with walkers and climbers. A World Peace Flame Monument is a feature on the attractive frontage. Bedrooms are located in chalet-style buildings and a comprehensive continental breakfast is served in an adjacent café. Specialist yoga and meditation classes are offered.

Rooms 19 en suite **Facilities** tea/coffee **Parking**
Notes Closed 22 Dec-4 Jan

BETWS GARMON
Map 14 SH55

Betws Inn

★★★★ BED AND BREAKFAST

LL54 7YY
☎ 01286 650324
e-mail: stay@betws-inn.co.uk
dir: On A4085 Caernarfon to Beddgelert, opp Bryn Gloch Caravan Park

Set in the western foothills of the Snowdonia, this 17th-century inn has been restored to create an establishment of immense charm. A warm welcome and caring service are assured. Bedrooms have a wealth of homely extras, and imaginative dinners feature local produce. Breakfast includes home-made bread and preserves.

Rooms 3 en suite D £65-£90* **Facilities** FTV TVL tea/coffee Dinner available Cen ht Wi-fi **Parking** 3 **Notes** LB ⊗

CAERNARFON
Map 14 SH46

See also Penygroes

PREMIER COLLECTION

Plas Dinas Country House

★★★★★ GUEST ACCOMMODATION

Bontnewydd LL54 7YF
☎ 01286 830214
e-mail: info@plasdinas.co.uk
dir: 3m S of Caernarfon, off A487, 0.5m down private drive

Situated in 15 acres of beautiful grounds in Snowdonia, this delightful Grade II listed building dates back to the mid-17th century, but with many Victorian additions. Once the home of the Armstrong-Jones family; there are many family portraits, memorabilia and original pieces of furniture for guests to view. The bedrooms are individually decorated and include four-poster beds along with modern facilities. There is a stylish drawing room where the fire burns in the winter, and fresh local produce features on the dinner menu.

Rooms 10 en suite (1 GF) S £95-£110; D £140-£250* **Facilities** FTV tea/coffee Dinner available Direct Dial Cen ht Licensed Wi-fi Golf 18 **Conf** Max 20 Thtr 20 Class 20 Board 20 **Parking** 10 **Notes** LB No Children 13yrs Closed Xmas & New Year Civ Wed 60

Rhiwafallen Restaurant with Rooms

★★★★★ ⓖⓖ RESTAURANT WITH ROOMS

Rhiwafallen, LLandwrog LL54 5SW
☎ 01286 830172
e-mail: ktandrobjohn@aol.com
dir: Off A499

Located south of Caernarfon on the Llyn Peninsula link, this former farmhouse has been tastefully renovated to provide high levels of comfort and facilities. Quality bedrooms are furnished in minimalist style with a wealth of thoughtful extras. The original modern art in public areas adds vibrancy to the interior. Warm hospitality and imaginative cooking ensure a memorable stay at this owner-managed establishment.

Rooms 5 en suite (1 GF) **Facilities** FTV tea/coffee Dinner available Cen ht Golf **Parking** 10 **Notes** ⊗ No Children 12yrs Closed 25-26 Dec No coaches

Black Boy Inn

★★★★ INN

LL55 1RW
☎ 01286 673604 📠 01286 674955
e-mail: office@black-boy-inn.com
dir: A55 junct 9 onto A487, follow signs for Caernarfon. Within town walls between castle & Victoria Dock

Located within Caernarfon's historic town wall, this fine 16th-century inn has low ceilings, narrow staircases and thick wooden beams from old ships. The Black Boy Inn is one of the oldest inns in North Wales, and has a wealth of charm and character. Bedrooms have been fully renovated and provide modern accommodation. Hearty meals are available in both the restaurant and bar area. On-site parking available.

Rooms 15 en suite **Facilities** FTV tea/coffee Dinner available Direct Dial Cen ht Wi-fi Golf 18 **Conf** Max 40 Thtr 40 Class 20 Board 30 **Parking** 20 **Notes** LB ⊗

The Stables

★★★★ GUEST ACCOMMODATION

Llanwnda LL54 5SD
☎ 01286 830711 📠 01286 830711
dir: 3m S of Caernarfon on A499 towards Pwllheli

This privately-owned and personally-run establishment is set in 15 acres of its own land, south of Caernarfon. Very well equipped bedrooms are located within two motel style buildings and breakfast is taken in a spacious dining room decorated with a wealth of unusual memorabilia.

Rooms 22 annexe en suite (8 fmly) (22 GF) (5 smoking) **Facilities** TVL tea/coffee Direct Dial Cen ht Licensed **Conf** Max 50 Thtr 50 Class 30 Board 30 **Parking** 40

Save on B&Bs and Hotels. Book at **theAA.com/hotel**

GWYNEDD 415 WALES

CRICCIETH — Map 14 SH43

The Abereistedd

★★★★ GUEST ACCOMMODATION

West Pde LL52 0EN
☎ 01766 522710 📠 01766 523526
e-mail: info@abereistedd.co.uk
web: www.abereistedd.co.uk
dir: *A487 through Criccieth towards Pwllheli, left 400yds after fuel station following signs for beach, on left at seafront*

An extremely warm welcome is assured at this Victorian property with uninterrupted mountain and coastal views. The attractive bedrooms are very well equipped with thoughtful extras, the ground-floor lounge has a bar extension, and the bright dining room overlooks the seafront.

Rooms 12 en suite (2 fmly) S £38; D £68-£76*
Facilities FTV tea/coffee Dinner available Direct Dial Cen ht Licensed Wi-fi **Parking** 9 **Notes** LB ⊗ Closed Nov-Mar

Bron Rhiw

★★★★ GUEST ACCOMMODATION

Caernarfon Rd LL52 0AP
☎ 01766 522257
e-mail: clairecriccieth@yahoo.co.uk
web: www.bronrhiwhotel.co.uk
dir: *Off High St onto B4411*

A warm welcome and high standards of comfort and facilities are assured at this constantly improving Victorian property, just a short walk from the seafront. Bedrooms are equipped with lots of thoughtful extras and ground-floor areas include a sumptuous lounge, a cosy bar, and an elegant dining room, the setting for imaginative breakfasts.

Rooms 9 en suite (2 fmly) S £46-£60; D £70-£74*
Facilities FTV tea/coffee Cen ht Licensed Wi-fi **Parking** 3
Notes LB ⊗ No Children 10yrs Closed Nov-Feb

Min y Gaer

★★★★ GUEST HOUSE

Porthmadog Rd LL52 0HP
☎ 01766 522151
e-mail: info@minygaer.co.uk
dir: *On A497 200yds E of junct with B4411*

The friendly, family-run Min y Gaer has superb views from many of the rooms. The smart, modern bedrooms are furnished in pine, and the welcoming proprietors also provide a bar and a traditionally furnished lounge.

Rooms 10 en suite (1 fmly) S £35-£40; D £66-£75
Facilities FTV tea/coffee Cen ht Licensed Wi-fi **Parking** 12
Notes Closed Nov-14 Mar

DOLGELLAU — Map 14 SH71

PREMIER COLLECTION

Tyddynmawr Farmhouse (SH704159)

★★★★★ FARMHOUSE

Cader Rd, Islawrdref LL40 1TL
☎ 01341 422331
Mrs Evans
dir: *From town centre left at top of square, left at garage onto Cader Rd for 3m, 1st farm on left after Gwernan Lake*

A warm welcome is assured at this 18th-century farmhouse which lies at the foot of Cader Idris amidst breathtaking scenery. The bedrooms are spacious and have Welsh oak furniture; the upper room has a balcony and the ground-floor room has a patio area. The bathrooms are large and luxurious. The superb breakfasts offer an excellent choice of home-made items including bread, preserves, muesli or smoked fish. Self-catering cottages are also available.

Rooms 2 en suite (1 GF) D £78 **Facilities** TVL tea/coffee Cen ht Wi-fi Fishing **Parking** 8 **Notes** ⊗ No Children Closed Jan 🐾 800 acres beef/sheep

Dolgun Uchaf Guesthouse

★★★★ GUEST HOUSE

Dolgun Uchaf LL40 2AB
☎ 01341 422269
e-mail: dolgunuchaf@aol.com
web: www.guesthousessnowdonia.com
dir: *Off A470 at Little Chef just S of Dolgellau, Dolgun Uchaf 1st property on right*

Located in a peaceful area with stunning views of the surrounding countryside, this 500-year-old late medieval hall house retains many original features, including exposed beams and open fireplaces. Bedrooms are equipped with thoughtful extras and a lounge is also available.

Rooms 3 en suite 1 annexe en suite (1 GF) **Facilities** TVL tea/coffee Dinner available Cen ht Wi-fi **Parking** 6 **Notes** No Children 5yrs

Ivy House

★★★ GUEST HOUSE

Finsbury Square LL40 1RF
☎ 01341 422535 📠 01341 422689
e-mail: marg.bamford@btconnect.com
dir: *In town centre. Straight across top of main square, house on left after bend*

Friendly hospitality is offered at this house, situated in the centre of Dolgellau at the foot of Cader Idris. Bedrooms are brightly decorated and thoughtfully equipped. Ground floor rooms include a comfortable lounge and a spacious dining room.

Rooms 6 rms (4 en suite) (1 fmly) S £45-£53; D £65-£75* **Facilities** FTV TVL tea/coffee Cen ht Wi-fi **Notes** ⊗

DOLGELLAU *continued*

Royal Ship

★★★ INN

Queens Square LL40 1AR
☎ 01341 422209 🖹 01341 424693
e-mail: royalship.hotel@btconnect.com
dir: *In town centre*

The Royal Ship is very much at the centre of local activities and dates from 1813 when it was a coaching inn. There are three bars and several lounges, all comfortably furnished and attractively appointed. A wide range of food is offered, and the well-equipped bedrooms include family rooms. The property has a secure car park.

Rooms 24 en suite (4 fmly) S £50-£60; D £90-£100*
Facilities FTV Wi-fi **Parking** 12

DYFFRYN ARDUDWY	Map 14 SH52

Cadwgan Inn

★★★★ INN

LL44 2HA
☎ 01341 247240
e-mail: cadwgan.hotel@virgin.net
dir: *In Dyffryn Ardudwy onto Station Rd, over railway crossing*

This very pleasant, privately-owned pub stands in grounds close to Dyffryn Ardudwy station, between Barmouth and Harlech. The beach is a short walk away. The good quality, well-equipped modern accommodation includes family rooms and a room with a four-poster bed. Public areas include an attractive dining room, popular bar and a beer garden.

Rooms 6 en suite (3 fmly) **Facilities** TVL tea/coffee Dinner available Cen ht Sauna Gym Pool table **Notes** ⊗ No coaches Civ Wed 60

HARLECH	Map 14 SH53

Gwrach Ynys Country

★★★★ GUEST HOUSE

Talsarnau LL47 6TS
☎ 01766 780742
e-mail: deborah@gwrachynys.co.uk
web: www.gwrachynys.co.uk
dir: *2m N of Harlech on A496*

This delightful Edwardian house nestles in idyllic lawns and gardens with dramatic views of the surrounding mountains. Bedrooms are thoughtfully equipped with modern facilities. Two comfortably furnished lounges promote a home-from-home feel and hospitality is welcoming. Hearty breakfast can be enjoyed at separate tables in the dining room. Deborah and Gwynfor Williams were finalists in this year's Friendliest Landlady of the Year award (2011-12).

Rooms 7 rms (6 en suite) (1 pri facs) (3 fmly) S £30-£35; D £60-£80 **Facilities** FTV TVL tea/coffee Cen ht Wi-fi **Parking** 10 **Notes** LB ⊗ Closed mid Nov-mid Jan ⊛

LLANBEDR	Map 14 SH52

Victoria Inn

★★★★ INN

LL45 2LD
☎ 01341 241213 🖹 01341 241644
e-mail: junevicinn@aol.com
dir: *In village centre*

This former coaching inn lies beside the River Artro in a very pretty village. Many original features remain, including the Settle bar with its flagstone floor, black polished fireplace and unusual circular wooden settle. The menu is extensive and is supplemented by blackboard specials. Bedrooms are spacious and thoughtfully furnished.

Rooms 5 en suite **Facilities** tea/coffee Dinner available Cen ht **Conf** Max 30 **Parking** 75

LLANDDEINIOLEN	Map 14 SH56

Ty'n-Rhos Country House & Restaurant

★★★★★ 🅐 GUEST ACCOMMODATION

Seion LL55 3AE
☎ 01248 670489 🖹 01248 671772
e-mail: enquiries@tynrhos.co.uk
web: www.tynrhos.co.uk
dir: *A55 junct 11 onto A5 for 50yds, right at mini-rdbt onto A4244. After 4m, take 2nd exit at rdbt, signed in 0.5m*

Rooms 12 en suite 4 annexe en suite (3 fmly) (8 GF) **Facilities** FTV tea/coffee Dinner available Cen ht Licensed Wi-fi ⬆ Golf 18 Fishing **Conf** Max 60 Thtr 60 Class 40 Board 40 **Parking** 50 **Notes** LB Civ Wed 60

PENYGROES	Map 14 SH45

Llwyndu Mawr *(SH475536)*

★★ FARMHOUSE

Carmel Rd LL54 6PU
☎ 01286 880419 🖹 01286 880845
Mrs N R Williams
e-mail: queri@live.co.uk
dir: *From village onto B4418, 500yds left for Carmel, 500yds up hill after cemetery, 1st left*

This hillside farmhouse dates from the 19th century and is quietly located on the outskirts of the village. Home-from-home hospitality is provided, with simply appointed accommodation, and guests are welcome to take part in the life of this working sheep farm, where there are also boarding kennels.

Rooms 4 rms (2 en suite) (2 pri facs) (1 fmly) (1 GF) S £28-£30; D £56-£60 **Facilities** FTV TVL tea/coffee Dinner available Cen ht **Parking** 7 **Notes** Closed 20 Dec-6 Jan ⊛ 98 acres sheep/ducks/geese/chickens

---

PORTHMADOG	Map 14 SH53

Tudor Lodge

★★★★ GUEST ACCOMMODATION

Tan-Yr-Onnen, Penamser Rd LL49 9NY
☎ 01766 515530
e-mail: info@tudor-lodge.co.uk
dir: *At main Porthmadog rdbt turn onto Criccieth Rd, 40mtrs on left*

This large guest accommodation is conveniently located within a short walk of the town centre. It has been considerably renovated to provide good quality modern accommodation, including family rooms. Separate tables are provided in the breakfast room, where a substantial self-service continental breakfast buffet is provided. There is also a pleasant garden for guests to use.

Rooms 13 en suite (3 fmly) (6 GF) S £48-£65; D £74-£84 **Facilities** STV tea/coffee Cen ht Wi-fi Golf **Parking** 25 **Notes** LB ⊗

TYWYN	Map 14 SH50

Eisteddfa *(SH651055)*

★★★★ FARMHOUSE

Eisteddfa, Abergynolwyn LL36 9UP
☎ 01654 782385 🖹 01654 782385
Mrs G Pugh
e-mail: hugh.pugh01@btinternet.com
dir: *5m NE of Tywyn on B4405 nr Dolgoch Falls*

Eisteddfa is a modern stone bungalow situated less than a mile from Abergynolwyn, in a spot ideal for walking or for visiting the local historic railway. Rooms are well equipped and stunning views are a feature from the attractive dining room.

Rooms 3 rms (2 en suite) (3 GF) **Facilities** STV FTV TVL tea/coffee Cen ht **Parking** 6 **Notes** LB Closed Dec-Feb ⊛ 1200 acres mixed

Y FELINHELI — Map 14 SH56

Plas Dinorwic Country House

★★★★ GUEST HOUSE

Ffordd Siabod LL56 4XA
☎ 01248 670559 & 0800 328 3910 📠 01248 670300
e-mail: plasdinorwic@btconnect.com
dir: *A55 junct 10 signed to Caernarfon. At mini rdbt take 1st exit, at next rdbt take 2nd exit. Follow road to village, turn left at Halfway House pub, over bridge and up hill*

Plas Dinorwic has an idyllic location alongside the Menai Strait and is an integral part of a marina and village development. Most of the spacious modern bedrooms have spectacular views; many are located in separate cottages and are also available as self-catering accommodation. Facilities include a lounge bar, function room and an indoor swimming pool.

Rooms 12 en suite 18 annexe en suite (6 fmly) (10 GF) S £60-£69; D £70-£79 (room only) **Facilities** FTV tea/coffee Dinner available Cen ht Licensed Wi-fi 🐾 Sauna **Conf** Max 50 Thtr 50 Class 50 Board 35 **Notes** LB ⊛

MERTHYR TYDFIL

MERTHYR TYDFIL — Map 9 SO00

Llwyn Onn

★★★★ GUEST HOUSE

Cwmtaf CF48 2HT
☎ 01685 384384 📠 01685 359310
e-mail: reception@llwynonn.co.uk
dir: *Off A470 2m N of Cefn Coed, overlooking Llwyn-Onn Reservoir*

Fronted by a large pleasant garden, this delightful house overlooks Llwyn Onn Reservoir. This property offers traditional bedrooms that are spacious and comfortable, with all modern facilities. The cosy lounge opens onto the terrace and garden, as does the bright breakfast room.

Rooms 11 en suite (3 GF) **Facilities** STV TVL tea/coffee Cen ht **Conf** Max 10 Class 10 Board 10 **Parking** 9 **Notes** LB ⊛ RS 2wks Xmas

Penrhadw Farm

★★★★ GUEST HOUSE

Pontsticill CF48 2TU
☎ 01685 723481 & 722461 📠 01685 722461
e-mail: treghotel@aol.com
web: www.penrhadwfarm.co.uk
dir: *5m N of Merthyr Tydfil. (Please see map on website)*

Expect a warm welcome at this former farmhouse, dating from Victorian times, in the glorious Brecon Beacons National Park. The house is appointed to provide quality modern accommodation. The well-equipped, spacious bedrooms include two large suites in cottages adjacent to the main building. There is also a comfortable lounge. Separate tables are provided in the cosy breakfast room.

Rooms 5 en suite 5 annexe en suite (5 fmly) (1 GF) S £45-£60; D £70-£90 **Facilities** FTV TVL tea/coffee Dinner available Cen ht Wi-fi Golf 18 **Conf** Max 10 Thtr 10 Class 10 **Parking** 22 **Notes** LB ⊛

MONMOUTHSHIRE

ABERGAVENNY — Map 9 SO21

Hardwick Farm (SO306115)

★★★★ FARMHOUSE

NP7 9BT
☎ 01873 853513 & 07773 775179 📠 01873 854238
Mrs A Price
e-mail: carol@hardwickfarm.co.uk
dir: *1m from Abergavenny, off A4042, farm sign on right*

Quietly located in the Usk Valley with wonderful views, this large family-run farmhouse provides warm hospitality. The spacious bedrooms are comfortably furnished, well equipped, and include one suitable for families. Farmhouse breakfasts are served at the communal table in the traditionally furnished dining room. Carol Jones was a finalist in this year's Friendliest Landlady of the Year award (2011-12).

Rooms 3 rms (2 en suite) (1 pri facs) (1 fmly) **Facilities** FTV tea/coffee Cen ht **Parking** 3 **Notes** Closed Dec-Jan ⊛ 230 acres dairy/mixed

Black Lion Guest House

★★★★ 🅰 GUEST HOUSE

43 Hereford Rd NP7 5PY
☎ 01873 851920 📠 01873 857885
e-mail: blacklionaber@aol.com
Rooms 5 rms (2 en suite) (3 pri facs) (1 fmly) **Facilities** STV FTV tea/coffee Dinner available Cen ht **Parking** 3 **Notes** ⊛

LLANDOGO — Map 4 SO50

The Sloop Inn

★★★★ INN

NP25 4TW
☎ 01594 530291
e-mail: thesloopinn@btconnect.com
dir: *On A466 in village centre*

This welcoming inn is centrally located in the village of Llandogo, close to the River Wye in an outstandingly beautiful valley. It offers a selection of traditional food, as well as friendly hospitality. The dining room has delightful views over the valley, and the spacious bedrooms and bathrooms are equipped for both business and leisure guests.

Rooms 4 en suite (1 fmly) **Facilities** tea/coffee Dinner available Cen ht Pool table **Parking** 50 **Notes** RS Mon-Fri closed between 3-6

LLANTRISANT — Map 9 ST39

Greyhound Inn

★★★ 🅰 INN

NP15 1LE
☎ 01291 673447 & 672505 📠 01291 673255
e-mail: enquiry@greyhound-inn.com
web: www.greyhound-inn.com
dir: *M4 junct 24, A449, 1st exit for Usk, 2.5m from town square, follow Llantrisant signs*

Rooms 10 en suite (2 fmly) (5 GF) S £60-£66; D £78-£88* **Facilities** tea/coffee Direct Dial Cen ht Wi-fi **Parking** 75 **Notes** LB Closed 25-26 Dec RS Sun eve no food No coaches

MONMOUTH — Map 10 SO51

Penylan Farm

★★★★ Ⓐ BED AND BREAKFAST

The Hendre NP25 5NL
☎ 01600 716435 📠 01600 719391
e-mail: penylanfarm@gmail.com
dir: *5m NW of Monmouth. B4233 through Rockfield towards Hendre. 0.5m before Hendre turn right towards Newcastle. After 1.5m turn left, farm 0.5 m on right*

Rooms 3 en suite 3 annexe en suite (1 fmly) (2 GF) S £40-£50; D £65-£80 **Facilities** tea/coffee Dinner available Cen ht Wi-fi 🕳 **Parking** 10 **Notes** LB ⊗ Closed Xmas & New Year

Church Farm

★★★ GUEST HOUSE

Mitchel Troy NP25 4HZ
☎ 01600 712176
e-mail: info@churchfarmguesthouse.eclipse.co.uk
dir: *From A40 S, left onto B4293 for Trelleck before tunnel, 150yds turn left and follow signs to Mitchel Troy. Guest House on main road, on left 200yds beyond campsite*

Located in the village of Mitchel Troy, this 16th-century former farmhouse retains many original features including exposed beams and open fireplaces. There is a range of bedrooms and a spacious lounge, and breakfast is served in the traditionally furnished dining room. Dinner is available by prior arrangement.

Rooms 9 rms (7 en suite) (2 pri facs) (3 fmly) S £33-£36; D £66-£72 **Facilities** TVL TV2B tea/coffee Dinner available Cen ht ch fac **Parking** 12 **Notes** LB Closed Xmas 🐾

ROCKFIELD — Map 9 SO41

The Stonemill & Steppes Farm Cottages

★★★★ ◉◉ RESTAURANT WITH ROOMS

NP25 5SW
☎ 01600 775424
e-mail: bookings@thestonemill.co.uk
dir: *A48 to Monmouth, B4233 to Rockfield. 2.6m from Monmouth town centre*

Located in a small hamlet just west of Monmouth, close to the Forest of Dean and the Wye Valley, this operation offers accommodation comprising six very well-appointed cottages. The comfortable rooms (for self-catering or on a B&B basis) are architect designed and have been lovingly restored to retain many original features. In a separate, converted 16th-century barn is Stonemill Restaurant with oak beams, vaulted ceilings and an old cider press. Breakfast is served in the cottages on request. This establishment's location proves handy for golfers with a choice of many courses in the area.

Rooms 6 en suite (6 fmly) (6 GF) **Facilities** FTV TVL tea/coffee Dinner available Cen ht Golf 18 Free golf **Conf** Max 60 Thtr 60 Class 56 Board 40 **Parking** 53 **Notes** LB ⊗ RS Sun eve & Mon closed No coaches Civ Wed 120

SKENFRITH — Map 9 SO42

The Bell at Skenfrith

★★★★★ ◉◉ RESTAURANT WITH ROOMS

NP7 8UH
☎ 01600 750235 📠 01600 750525
e-mail: enquiries@skenfrith.co.uk
web: www.skenfrith.co.uk
dir: *On B4521 in Skenfrith, opposite castle*

The Bell is a beautifully restored, 17th-century former coaching inn which still retains much original charm and character. It is peacefully situated on the banks of the Monnow, a tributary of the River Wye, and is ideally placed for exploring the numerous delights of the area. Natural materials have been used to create a relaxing atmosphere, while the bedrooms, which include full suites and rooms with four-poster beds, are stylish, luxurious and equipped with DVD players. The garden produces many of the fresh ingredients used in the kitchen where award-winning quality food is produced for relaxed dining in the welcoming restaurant.

Rooms 11 en suite (2 fmly) S £75-£120; D £110-£220* **Facilities** tea/coffee Dinner available Direct Dial Cen ht Wi-fi **Conf** Max 20 Thtr 20 Board 16 **Parking** 36 **Notes** No Children 8yrs Closed last wk Jan-1st wk Feb RS Nov-Mar Closed Tue No coaches

TINTERN PARVA — Map 4 SO50

Parva Farmhouse Riverside Guest House & Restaurant

★★★★ ⛱ GUEST HOUSE

Monmouth Rd NP16 6SQ
☎ 01291 689411 📠 01291 689941
e-mail: parvahoteltintern@fsmail.net
dir: *On A466 at N edge of Tintern. Next to St Michael's Church on the riverside*

This relaxed and friendly, family-run guest house is situated on a sweep of the River Wye with far-reaching views of the valley. Originally a farmhouse dating from the 17th century, many features have been retained, providing character and comfort in an informal atmosphere. The cosy Inglenook Restaurant is the place where quality ingredients are offered at breakfast and dinner. The individually designed bedrooms are tastefully decorated and enjoy pleasant views; one has a four-poster.

Rooms 8 en suite (2 fmly) S £45-£69; D £66-£99* **Facilities** FTV tea/coffee Dinner available Cen ht Licensed **Parking** 8 **Notes** No Children 12yrs

USK — Map 9 SO30

Newbridge on Usk

★★★★ ◉ ⛱ RESTAURANT WITH ROOMS

Tredunnock NP15 1LY
☎ 01633 451000 & 410262
e-mail: newbridgeonusk@celtic-manor.com
dir: *M4 junct 24 signed Newport, onto B4236. At Ship Inn turn right, over mini-rdbt onto Llangybi/Usk road. Turn right opposite Cwrt Bleddyn Hotel, signed Tredunnock, through village & down hill*

This cosy, gastro-pub is tucked away in a beautiful village setting with the River Usk nearby. The well-equipped bedrooms, in a separate building, provide comfort and a good range of extras. Guests can eat at rustic tables around the bar or in the upstairs dining room where award-winning, seasonal food is served; there is also a small private dining room. Breakfast is one of the highlights of a stay with quality local ingredients offered in abundance.

Rooms 6 en suite (2 fmly) (4 GF) D £59-£108* **Facilities** FTV Dinner available Direct Dial Cen ht Wi-fi Facilities available at Celtic Manor Resort **Conf** Max 14 Thtr 14 Class 14 Board 14 **Parking** 60 **Notes** LB Civ Wed 80

WHITEBROOK Map 4 SO50

PREMIER COLLECTION

The Crown at Whitebrook

★★★★★ ◉◉◉ 🖺 RESTAURANT WITH ROOMS

NP25 4TX
☎ 01600 860254 🖷 01600 860607
e-mail: info@crownatwhitebrook.co.uk
dir: *4m from Monmouth on B4293, left at sign to Whitebrook, 2m on unmarked road, Crown on right*

In a secluded spot in the wooded valley of the River Wye, this former drover's cottage dates back to the 17th century. Individually decorated bedrooms boast a contemporary feel with smart modern facilities. The restaurant and lounge combine many original features with a bright fresh look. Memorable cuisine features locally sourced ingredients, skilfully prepared.

Rooms 8 en suite S £90–£120; D £135–£170*
Facilities FTV tea/coffee Dinner available Direct Dial Cen ht Wi-fi Fishing Shooting **Conf** Max 12 Board 12
Parking 20 **Notes** LB ⊗ No Children 12yrs Closed 22 Dec-4 Jan No coaches

See advert on this page

NEATH PORT TALBOT

NEATH Map 9 SS79

Cwmbach Cottages Guest House

★★★★ GUEST HOUSE

Cwmbach Rd, Cadoxton SA10 8AH
☎ 01639 639825
e-mail: l.morgan5@btinternet.com
web: www.cwmbachcottages.co.uk
dir: *1.5m NE of Neath. A465 onto A474 & A4230 towards Aberdulais, left opp Cadoxton church, guest house signed*

A terrace of former miners' cottages has been restored to provide a range of thoughtfully furnished bedrooms, with one on the ground floor for easier access. Spacious public areas include a comfortable lounge and a pleasant breakfast room with separate tables. A superb decked patio overlooks a wooded hillside rich with wildlife.

Rooms 5 en suite (1 fmly) (1 GF) S £44–£54; D £60–£70*
Facilities FTV TVL tea/coffee Cen ht Wi-fi Golf 18
Parking 9 **Notes** LB ⊗

NEWPORT

NEWPORT Map 9 ST38

Labuan Guest House

★★★★ GUEST HOUSE

464 Chepstow Rd NP19 8JF
☎ 01633 664533 🖷 01633 664533
e-mail: patricia.bees@ntlworld.com
dir: *M4 junct 24, 1.5m on B4237*

Expect a warm welcome from owners Pat and John at this delightful guest house which is set on the main road into Newport. The accommodation is comfortable and includes a ground-floor twin room; all bedrooms are of a good size and bathrooms feature a wide range of extras. The hearty breakfasts, with a good choice on the menu, are taken in the welcoming dining room at separate tables. Off-street parking is available.

Rooms 5 rms (3 en suite) (2 pri facs) (1 GF)
Facilities FTV TVL tea/coffee Dinner available Cen ht Wi-fi
Parking 6 **Notes** LB ⊜

Kepe Lodge

★★★ GUEST HOUSE

46A Caerau Rd NP20 4HH
☎ 01633 262351 🖷 01633 262351
e-mail: kepelodge@hotmail.com
dir: *500yds W of town centre. M4 junct 27, town centre signs, 2nd lights left, premises on right*

This attractive guest house in a quiet residential area is set back from the road in pleasant gardens. Guests can expect attentive service and comfortable homely bedrooms. Breakfast is served at individual tables in the well-appointed dining room. A comfortable lounge is also available.

Rooms 8 rms (3 en suite) **Facilities** FTV tea/coffee Cen ht
Parking 12 **Notes** ⊗ No Children 10yrs ⊜

REDWICK
Map 9 ST48

Brickhouse Country Guest House

★★★★ GUEST HOUSE

North Row NP26 3DX
☎ 01633 880230 📠 01633 882441
e-mail: brickhouse@compuserve.com
dir: *M4 junct 23A, follow steelworks road for 1.5m. Left after sign for Redwick, Brickhouse 1.5m on left*

This impressive country house is in a peaceful location with attractive, well-tended gardens. The friendly hosts are most attentive and provide a relaxing atmosphere. Bedrooms are spacious and traditionally furnished, while the public areas include a choice of lounges. Dinners featuring home-grown produce are sometimes available by prior arrangement.

Rooms 7 rms (5 en suite) (2 pri facs) (1 fmly) S £40-£50; D £65* **Facilities** FTV TVL tea/coffee Dinner available Cen ht Licensed Wi-fi **Parking** 7 Notes ⊗

PEMBROKESHIRE

FISHGUARD
Map 8 SM93

PREMIER COLLECTION

Erw-Lon (SN028325)

★★★★★ FARMHOUSE

Pontfaen SA65 9TS
☎ 01348 881297
Mrs L McAllister
e-mail: lilwenmcallister@btinternet.com
dir: *5.5m SE of Fishguard on B4313*

Located in the Pembrokeshire Coast National Park, with stunning views of the Gwaun Valley, this attractive farmhouse has been converted to provide modern well-equipped bedrooms with a wealth of homely extras. The McAllisters give the warmest of welcomes, and their memorable dinners feature the finest local produce.

Rooms 3 en suite (3 smoking) S £45; D £66-£70* **Facilities** FTV TVL tea/coffee Dinner available Cen ht Wi-fi **Parking** 5 **Notes** LB ⊗ No Children 10yrs Closed Dec-Mar ⊛ 128 acres beef/sheep

HAVERFORDWEST
Map 8 SM91

See also Narberth

College Guest House

★★★★ GUEST HOUSE

93 Hill St, St Thomas Green SA61 1QL
☎ 01437 763710 📠 01437 763710
e-mail: colinlarby@aol.com
dir: *In town centre, along High St, pass church, keep in left lane. 1st exit by Stonemason Arms pub, follow signs for St Thomas Green. 300mtrs on left by No Entry sign*

Located in a mainly residential area within easy walking distance of the attractions, this impressive Georgian house has been upgraded to offer good levels of comfort and facilities. There is range of practically equipped bedrooms, along with public areas that include a spacious lounge (with internet access) and an attractive pine-furnished dining room, the setting for comprehensive breakfasts.

Rooms 8 en suite (4 fmly) S £51-£57; D £70-£75 **Facilities** FTV TVL tea/coffee Cen ht Wi-fi

MANORBIER
Map 8 SS09

Castlemead

★★★★ RESTAURANT WITH ROOMS

SA70 7TA
☎ 01834 871358 📠 01834 871358
e-mail: castlemeadhotel@aol.com
web: www.castlemeadhotel.com
dir: *A4139 towards Pembroke, B4585 into village, follow signs to beach & castle, establishment on left*

Benefiting from a superb location with spectacular views of the bay, the Norman church and Manorbier Castle, this family-run property is friendly and welcoming. Bedrooms, which include some in a converted former coach house at ground floor level, are generally quite spacious and have modern facilities. The public areas include a cosy bar, a sea-view residents' lounge and a restaurant which is also open to non-residents. There are extensive gardens to the rear.

Rooms 5 en suite 3 annexe en suite (2 fmly) (3 GF) S £43-£50; D fr £85* **Facilities** FTV tea/coffee Dinner available Direct Dial Cen ht Wi-fi **Parking** 20 **Notes** Closed Jan-Feb RS Nov maybe B&B only No coaches

NARBERTH
Map 8 SN11

PREMIER COLLECTION

The Grove

★★★★★ ◉◉ RESTAURANT WITH ROOMS

Molleston SA67 8BX
☎ 01834 860915
e-mail: info@thegrove-narberth.co.uk
web: www.thegrove-narberth.co.uk
dir: *A48 to Carmarthen, then A40 to Haverfordwest. At A478 rdbt 1st exit to Narberth, through town towards Tenby. At bottom of hill right, 1m, The Grove on right*

The Grove is an elegant 18th-century country house set on a hillside in 24 acres of rolling countryside. The enthusiastic owners have lovingly restored this building with care, combining period features with excellent modern decor. There are six bedrooms in the main house and six additional rooms in separate buildings; all are appointed with quality and comfort. Some bedrooms are on the ground floor, and most have fantastic views out over the Preseli Hills. There are two sumptuous lounge areas, one with an open fire and a small bar, and two separate dining rooms that offer award-winning cuisine. Self catering cottages are available.

Rooms 6 en suite 6 annexe en suite (4 fmly) (3 GF) £130-£300; D £130-£320* **Facilities** FTV tea/coffee Dinner available Direct Dial Cen ht Wi-fi ch fac **Conf** Max 25 Thtr 25 Class 25 Board 18 **Parking** 45 **Notes** LB ⊗ Civ Wed 35

Save on B&Bs and Hotels. Book at **theAA.com/hotel**

PEMBROKESHIRE 421 WALES

Highland Grange Farm (SN077154)

★★★ FARMHOUSE

Robeston Wathen SA67 8EP
☎ 01834 860952 & 07855 359919 ▤ 01834 860952
Mrs N Jones
e-mail: highlandgrange@hotmail.co.uk
web: www.highlandgrange.co.uk
dir: 2m NW of Narberth at Robeston Wathen, 400mtrs off
A40 at rdbt

Awake to birdsong in comfortable accommodation at this
peaceful farmhouse property, with spacious bedrooms
that are all on the ground floor. The property is set in the
small hilltop village of Robeston Wathen, 400 metres
from the A40, between Whitland and Haverfordwest, and
enjoys wonderful panoramic views. The dining room has
separate tables where a good hearty breakfast is
provided. There is also a spacious and comfortable
lounge.

Rooms 3 rms (2 en suite) (1 pri facs) (1 fmly) (3 GF) S
£35-£52; D £57-£68* **Facilities** FTV TVL tea/coffee Dinner
available Cen ht Wi-fi ch fac Golf **Parking** 6 **Notes** LB ☺
.50 acres mixed/sheep

NEVERN   Map 8 SN04

Trewern Arms

★★★★ INN

SA42 0NB
☎ 01239 820395 ▤ 01239 820173
e-mail: trewernarms@btconnect.com
dir: Off A48. Midway between Cardigan & Fishguard

Set in a peaceful and picturesque village, this charming
16th-century inn is well positioned to offer a relaxing
stay. There are many original features to be seen in the
two character bars and attractive restaurant, and the
spacious bedrooms are appointed to a high standard and
include some family rooms.

Rooms 10 en suite (4 fmly) **Facilities** TVL Cen ht Fishing
Riding **Parking** 100

NEWPORT   Map 8 SN03

Llysmeddyg

★★★★ ◉◉ RESTAURANT WITH ROOMS

East St SA42 0SY
☎ 01239 820008
e-mail: contact@llysmeddyg.com
dir: On A487 in centre of town on Main St

Llysmeddyg is a Georgian townhouse offering a blend of
old and new, with elegant furnishings, deep sofas and a
welcoming fire. The owners of this property employed
local craftsmen to create a lovely interior that has an
eclectic style. The focus of the quality restaurant menu is
the use of fresh, seasonal, locally sourced ingredients.
The spacious bedrooms are comfortable and
contemporary in design; bathrooms vary in style.

Rooms 5 en suite 3 annexe en suite (3 fmly) (1 GF) S
£85-£165; D £100-£180* **Facilities** FTV tea/coffee Dinner
available Cen ht Wi-fi ch fac ⌣ Golf 18 Riding **Conf** Max
20 Class 20 Board 20 **Parking** 8 **Notes** LB No coaches Civ
Wed 90

Salutation Inn

★★★ Ⓐ INN

Filindre Farchog SA41 3UY
☎ 01239 820564 ▤ 01239 820355
e-mail: johndenley@aol.com
web: www.salutationcountryhotel.co.uk
dir: On A487 between Cardigan & Fishguard. 3m N of
Newport

Rooms 8 en suite (2 fmly) (8 GF) S £60; D £75*
Facilities FTV tea/coffee Dinner available Direct Dial
Cen ht Wi-fi Golf 18 Pool table **Conf** Max 25 Thtr 25 Class
12 Board 12 **Parking** 60 **Notes** LB

ST DAVID'S   Map 8 SM72

See also Solva

PREMIER COLLECTION

Ramsey House

★★★★★ ▩ ☕ GUEST HOUSE

Lower Moor SA62 6RP
☎ 01437 720321 & 07795 575005
e-mail: info@ramseyhouse.co.uk
web: www.ramseyhouse.co.uk
dir: From Cross Sq in St David's towards Porthclais,
house 0.25m on left

This pleasant guest house, under the ownership of
Suzanne and Shaun Ellison, offers the ideal
combination of professional management and the
warmth of a family-run guest house. The property is
quietly located on the outskirts of St David's and
surrounded by unspoilt countryside. It provides modern,
well-equipped bedrooms and refurbished en suite
bathrooms along with a good range of welcome extras.
Carefully prepared dinners by chef Shaun feature
quality local Welsh produce, and breakfast provides a
choice of home-made items including breads and
preserves. Suzanne and Shaun were finalists in this
year's Friendliest Landlady of the Year award
(2011-12).

Rooms 6 rms (5 en suite) (1 pri facs) (3 GF) S
£60-£110; D £100-£110* **Facilities** FTV tea/coffee
Dinner available Cen ht Licensed Wi-fi **Parking** 10
Notes LB ⊗ No Children 16yrs Closed Nov-13 Feb

ST DAVID'S *continued*

Lochmeyler Farm Guest House *(SM855275)*

★★★★★ 🐾 FARMHOUSE

Llandeloy, Pen-y-Cwm SA62 6LL
☎ 01348 837724 📠 01348 837622
Mrs Margo Evans
e-mail: stay@lochmeyler.co.uk
web: www.lochmeyler.co.uk

(For full entry see SOLVA)

The Waterings

★★★★ BED AND BREAKFAST

Anchor Dr, High St SA62 6QH
☎ 01437 720876 📠 01437 720876
e-mail: enquiries@waterings.co.uk
web: www.waterings.co.uk
dir: *On A487 on E edge of St David's*

Situated a short walk from the centre of St David's, the Waterings offers spacious bedrooms that are accessed from a courtyard garden. Most rooms have their own separate seating area. Breakfast, from a good selection of local produce, is served in a smart dining room in the main house.

Rooms 5 annexe en suite (4 fmly) (5 GF) S £50-£85; D £75-£85* **Facilities** FTV tea/coffee Cen ht Licensed Wi-fi 🏌 Golf 9 **Conf** Max 15 Board 15 **Parking** 20 **Notes** No Children 5yrs

Y-Gorlan

★★★★ GUEST HOUSE

77 Nun St SA62 6NU
☎ 01437 720837 & 07974 108029
e-mail: mikebohlen@aol.com
dir: *In centre of St David's*

This personally-run guest house is just a stroll from the city's attractions. The well-maintained accommodation includes a family room and a room with a four-poster bed. The comfortable first-floor lounge has excellent views towards the coast across the surrounding countryside. A hearty breakfast is offered with a good choice of items available.

Rooms 5 en suite (1 fmly) S £40-£45; D £70-£85* **Facilities** STV FTV TVL tea/coffee Cen ht **Parking** 3 **Notes** ⊗ No Children 5yrs

Vine Cottage

★★★★ GUEST HOUSE

The Ridgeway SA69 9LA
☎ 01834 814422
e-mail: enquiries@vinecottageguesthouse.co.uk
web: www.vinecottageguesthouse.co.uk
dir: *A477 S onto A478, left onto B4316, after railway bridge right signed Saundersfoot, cottage 100yds beyond 30mph sign*

A warm welcome awaits guests at this pleasant former farmhouse located on the outskirts of Saundersfoot, yet within easy walking distance of the village. Set in extensive, mature gardens which include some rare and exotic plants and a summer house where guests can sit and relax on warmer evenings. Bedrooms, including a ground-floor room, are modern and well equipped, and some are suitable for families. There is a comfortable, airy lounge. Breakfast is served in the cosy dining room.

Rooms 5 en suite (2 fmly) (1 GF) S £42-£48; D £70-£76* **Facilities** FTV tea/coffee Dinner available Cen ht **Parking** 10 **Notes** LB No Children 6yrs 🐾

Crug-Glas Country House

★★★★★ 🍴 🐾 RESTAURANT WITH ROOMS

SA62 6XX
☎ 01348 831302
e-mail: janet@crugglas.plus.com

This house is on a mixed dairy, beef and cereal farm of approximately 600 acres, and is situated about a mile inland from the coast at the end of the St David's Peninsula. A delightful property provides comfort and relaxation, along with flawless attention to detail provided by the charming host, Janet Evans. Each spacious bedroom has the hallmarks of assured design, with warm, well-chosen fabrics, grand furnishings and luxury bathrooms, each with a bath and shower; one suite on the top floor affords great views. There are an additional two suites now in separate buildings with private frontage. Award-winning breakfasts and dinners, using the finest local produce, are served. The sunsets are stunning.

Rooms 7 en suite (1 fmly) (2 GF) S £80-£100; D £100-£150* **Facilities** FTV tea/coffee Dinner available Cen ht Wi-fi **Conf** Max 20 Thtr 20 Class 20 Board 20 **Parking** 10 **Notes** ⊗ No Children 12yrs Closed 24-27 Dec

PREMIER COLLECTION

Lochmeyler Farm Guest House (SM855275)

★★★★★ FARMHOUSE

Llandeloy, Pen-y-Cwm SA62 6LL
☎ 01348 837724 ▤ 01348 837622
Mrs Margo Evans
e-mail: stay@lochmeyler.co.uk
web: www.lochmeyler.co.uk
dir: From Haverfordwest A487 (St David's road) to Pen-y-Cwm, right to Llandeloy

Located on a 220-acre dairy farm in a beautiful area, with easy access to the Pembrokeshire coast line, Lochmeyler provides high levels of comfort and excellent facilities. The spacious bedrooms, of which four are cottage style converted outbuildings, are equipped with a wealth of thoughtful extras and have private sitting rooms. Three are in the main house which has its own separate entrance. Comprehensive breakfasts are served in the dining room as well as dinner on request; a pleasant lounge is also available.

Rooms 7 en suite (5 GF) S £40-£50; D £70-£80*
Facilities FTV tea/coffee Dinner available Direct Dial Cen ht Licensed Wi-fi **Parking** 7 **Notes** LB 220 acres dairy

---

TENBY   Map 8 SN10

Panorama

★★★★ GUEST ACCOMMODATION

The Esplanade SA70 7DU
☎ 01834 844976 ▤ 01834 844976
e-mail: mail@tenby-hotel.co.uk
web: www.tenby-hotel.co.uk
dir: A478 follow South Beach & Town Centre signs. Sharp left under railway arches, up Greenhill Rd, onto South Pde then Esplanade

This charming property is part of a Victorian terrace, overlooking the South Beach and Caldy Island in Tenby. All the bedrooms are well equipped and comfortable. Facilities include a cosy seating area and a large elegant dining room with sea views. There's a good selection at breakfast with dishes prepared from fresh and local ingredients.

Rooms 8 en suite (1 fmly) S £45-£50; D £75-£110
Facilities FTV tea/coffee Cen ht Licensed Wi-fi **Notes** ⊗ No Children 5yrs Closed 22-28 Dec

---

Rosendale Guesthouse

★★★★ GUEST HOUSE

Lydstep SA70 7SQ
☎ 01834 870040
e-mail: rosendalewales@yahoo.com
web: www.rosendalepembrokeshire.co.uk
dir: 3m SW of Tenby. A4139 W towards Pembroke. Rosendale on right after Lydstep

A warm welcome awaits all guests at this family-run establishment that is ideally located on the outskirts of the pretty village of Lydstep, not far from the seaside town of Tenby. Rosendale provides modern, well-equipped bedrooms; some with coast or country views, and three rooms that are on the ground floor of a separate building to the rear of the main house. The attractive welcoming dining room is the setting for breakfast served at well appointed tables.

Rooms 3 en suite 3 annexe en suite (3 GF) **Facilities** FTV tea/coffee Cen ht Wi-fi **Parking** 6 **Notes** LB No Children 16yrs

---

Elm Grove Country House

★★★★ GUEST ACCOMMODATION

Elm Grove, St Florence SA70 8LS
☎ 01834 871255 ▤ 01834 871673
e-mail: enquiries@elmgrovecountryhouse.co.uk
web: www.elmgrovecountryhouse.co.uk
dir: From A40 onto A477, signed Tenby & Pembroke Dock. At Sageston rdbt turn left onto B4318, after 1.25m turn right to St Florence

This elegant Georgian country house has been run by the Rees Family since 1958. It is set in 20 acres of lawned gardens and fields, just three miles from Tenby and a short drive from Pembroke's coastline and beaches. The property has marble fireplaces, chandeliers, panelled doorways, high ceilings and large picture windows. The bedrooms are spacious and all have flat-screen TVs and a good range of extras including Wi-fi. Breakfast is served in the light and airy dining room at separate tables; dinner, using fresh local produce, is available on request. There is a games room, grass tennis court, and a bar. Self-catering units are also available.

Rooms 10 en suite (2 fmly) (2 GF) S £46-£75; D £84-£96* **Facilities** FTV TVL tea/coffee Dinner available Direct Dial Cen ht Licensed Wi-fi ♨ ⚓ Pool table Table tennis **Parking** 10 **Notes** ⊗ Closed Nov-Mar

---

Esplanade

★★★★ GUEST ACCOMMODATION

The Esplanade SA70 7DU
☎ 01834 842760 & 843333 ▤ 01834 845633
e-mail: esplanadetenby@googlemail.com
web: www.esplanadetenby.co.uk
dir: Follow signs to South Beach, turn off South Parade onto St Florence Parade. Premises on seafront next to town walls

Located beside the historic town walls of Tenby and with stunning views over the sea to Caldey Island, the Esplanade provides a range of standard and luxury bedrooms, some ideal for families. Breakfast is offered in the elegant front-facing dining room, which contains a comfortable lounge-bar area.

Rooms 14 en suite (4 fmly) (1 GF) S £55-£120; D £70-£130 **Facilities** tea/coffee Direct Dial Cen ht Licensed Wi-fi **Notes** LB Closed 15-27 Dec

---

Giltar Grove Country House

★★★ GUEST ACCOMMODATION

Penally SA70 7RY
☎ 01834 871568
e-mail: giltarbnb@aol.com
dir: 2m SW of Tenby. Off A4139, 2nd right after railway bridge

Just a short walk from the spectacular Pembrokeshire Coastal Path, this impressive Victorian farmhouse retains many original features. Some bedrooms have four-poster beds and some are on the ground floor; all are filled with homely extras. There is a cosy sitting room, an elegant dining room, and a spacious conservatory where breakfast is served.

Rooms 6 rms (5 en suite) (1 pri facs) (2 GF) S £30-£35; D £60-£70 **Facilities** FTV tea/coffee Cen ht **Parking** 10 **Notes** ⊗ No Children 8yrs Closed Dec-Feb ◉

BRECON   Map 9 SO02

See also Sennybridge

PREMIER COLLECTION

The Coach House

★★★★★ 🏛 GUEST ACCOMMODATION

Orchard St LD3 8AN
☎ **01874 620043 & 07974 328437**
e-mail: coachhousebrecon@gmail.com
dir: *From town centre W over bridge onto B4601, Coach House 200yds on right*

A warm welcome awaits at this former coach house that now provides contemporary accommodation; the friendly and enthusiastic proprietors ensure a memorable stay. The bedrooms are well equipped and extremely comfortable. A selection of imaginative Welsh home-cooked breakfast items is served in the spacious dining room. The property has a lovely garden and is within easy walking distance of Brecon.

Rooms 6 en suite S £50–£65; D £65–£95 **Facilities** FTV tea/coffee Direct Dial Cen ht Licensed Wi-fi Resident holistic therapist, massage & reflexology **Parking** 6 **Notes** LB ⊗ No Children 16yrs

PREMIER COLLECTION

Canal Bank

★★★★★ BED AND BREAKFAST

Ty Gardd, Canal Bank LD3 7HG
☎ **01874 623464 & 07929 369149**
e-mail:
enquiries@accommodation-breconbeacons.co.uk
dir: *B4601 signed Brecon, left over bridge before petrol station, turn right, continue to end of lane*

Expect a warm welcome at this delightful property, which was developed from a row of five 18th-century cottages. It provides very high quality, comfortable and well-equipped accommodation, and stands alongside the canal in a semi-rural area on the outskirts of Brecon, yet within walking distance of the town centre. Facilities here include a comfortable lounge, a very attractive breakfast room and a lovely garden.

Rooms 3 en suite D £75–£98* **Facilities** FTV tea/coffee Cen ht Wi-fi **Parking** 5 **Notes** No Children 16yrs 🐾

PREMIER COLLECTION

Peterstone Court

★★★★★ ◉◉ 🏛 RESTAURANT WITH ROOMS

Llanhamlach LD3 7YB
☎ **01874 665387**
e-mail: info@peterstone-court.com
dir: *3m from Brecon on A40 towards Abergavenny*

Situated on the edge of the Brecons Beacons this establishment affords stunning views and overlooks the River Usk. The style is friendly and informal. No two bedrooms are alike, but all share comparable levels of comfort, quality and elegance. Public areas reflect similar standards, eclectically styled with a blend of the contemporary and the traditional. Quality produce is cooked with care in a range of enjoyable dishes.

Rooms 8 en suite 4 annexe en suite (2 fmly) **Facilities** tea/coffee Dinner available Direct Dial Cen ht Wi-fi 🌡 Fishing Riding Sauna Gym Pool open mid Apr-1 Oct, Spa facilities **Conf** Max 100 Thtr 100 Class 100 Board 60 **Parking** 60 **Notes** Civ Wed

The Felin Fach Griffin

★★★★ ◉◉ INN

Felin Fach LD3 0UB
☎ **01874 620111**
e-mail: enquiries@eatdrinksleep.ltd.uk
dir: *4m NE of Brecon on A470*

This delightful inn stands in an extensive garden at the northern end of the village of Felin Fach. The public areas have a wealth of rustic charm and provide the setting for the excellent food that is served. The bedrooms are carefully appointed and have modern equipment and facilities. The service and hospitality are commendable.

Rooms 7 en suite (1 fmly) **Facilities** tea/coffee Dinner available Direct Dial Cen ht ch fac 🌡 **Conf** Max 15 Board 15 **Parking** 61 **Notes** Closed 24-25 Dec No coaches

Llanddetty Hall Farm *(SO124205)*

★★★★ FARMHOUSE

Talybont-on-Usk LD3 7YR
☎ **01874 676415** 🖷 **01874 676415**
Mrs H E Atkins
dir: *SE of Brecon. Off B4558*

This impressive Grade II listed, 17th-century farmhouse in the beautiful Usk Valley is full of character, and the friendly proprietors ensure a comfortable stay. Bedrooms are very pleasant and feature traditional furnishings, exposed timbers and polished floorboards. Welcoming log fires are lit during cold weather in the comfortable lounge, and guests dine around one table in the dining room.

Rooms 3 rms (2 en suite) (1 pri facs) 1 annexe en suite (1 GF) S £40; D £65–£70 **Facilities** TVL TV1B tea/coffee Cen ht **Parking** 6 **Notes** ⊗ No Children 12yrs Closed 16 Dec-14 Jan RS Feb-Apr restricted service at lambing season 🐾 48 acres sheep

The Usk Inn

★★★★ 🍽 INN

Station Rd, Talybont-on-Usk LD3 7JE
☎ **01874 676251** 🖷 **01874 676392**
e-mail: stay@uskinn.co.uk
dir: *Off A40, 6m E of Brecon*

This delightful inn is personally run in a friendly manner by the owners Jill and Andrew Felix, who have renovated the property to a high standard during their tenure. The thoughtfully equipped and well-appointed bedrooms include a family room, and one room has a four-poster bed. Public areas have a wealth of charm including a welcoming log fire on colder days. The inn has a well-deserved reputation for good food.

Rooms 10 en suite (1 fmly) **Facilities** TVL tea/coffee Dinner available Direct Dial Cen ht **Conf** Max 60 Thtr 60 Class 40 Board 20 **Parking** 30 **Notes** ⊗ Closed 25-27 Dec

...e Beacons Guest House

★★ GUEST HOUSE

Bridge St LD3 8AH
☎ 01874 623339   📄 01874 623339
...mail: guesthouse@thebreconbeacons.co.uk
...r: On B4601 opp Christ College

...cated west of the historic town centre over the bridge,
...s 17th-century former farmhouse by the river has been
...novated to provide a range of homely bedrooms, some
...converted barns and outbuildings. There is a guests'
...unge and a cosy bar. This is a non-smoking
...tablishment.

...ooms 11 rms (9 en suite) (2 pri facs) 3 annexe en suite
...fmly) (3 GF) S £37-£84; D £58-£84* **Facilities** FTV TVL
...a/coffee Cen ht Licensed Wi-fi **Conf** Max 30 Thtr 30
...ass 25 Board 20 **Parking** 20 **Notes** LB ⊗

...orderers

★★ GUEST ACCOMMODATION

The Watton LD3 7EG
☎ 01874 623559
...mail: info@borderers.com
...eb: www.borderers.com
...r: 200yds SE of town centre on B4601, opp church

...is guest accommodation was originally a 17th-century
...rovers' inn. The courtyard, now a car park, is surrounded
...y many of the bedrooms, and pretty hanging baskets
...an be seen everywhere. The bedrooms are attractively
...ecorated with rich floral fabrics, and there is one room
...at has easier access.

...ooms 4 rms (3 en suite) (1 pri facs) 5 annexe en suite
...fmly) (4 GF) S £40-£50; D £56-£65* **Facilities** FTV tea/
...offee Cen ht Wi-fi **Parking** 6

The Lansdowne

★★★ GUEST ACCOMMODATION

The Watton LD3 7EG
☎ 01874 623321   📄 01874 610438
e-mail: reception@lansdownehotel.co.uk
dir: A40/A470 onto B4601

Privately-owned and personally-run, this Georgian house
is conveniently located close to the town centre. The
accommodation is well equipped and includes family
rooms and a bedroom on ground-floor level. There is a
comfortable lounge, a small bar and an attractive split-
level dining room where dinner is available to residents.

Rooms 9 en suite (2 fmly) (1 GF) S £40-£45; D £60-£65*
Facilities FTV tea/coffee Dinner available Direct Dial
Cen ht Licensed **Notes** LB No Children 5yrs

PREMIER COLLECTION

The Talkhouse

★★★★★ ⑧⑩ RESTAURANT WITH ROOMS

Pontdolgoch SY17 5JE
☎ 01686 688919   & 07876 086183
e-mail: info@talkhouse.co.uk
dir: 1.5m NW of Caersws on A470

Unsurprisingly, a highlight of this delightful 19th-
century restaurant with rooms is the food - home-made
dishes make good use of local produce. The bedrooms
offer luxury in every area and the cosy lounge, filled
with sofas, is the place to while away some time with a
glass of wine or a pot of tea. The bar features a large
fireplace.

Rooms 3 en suite S £70; D £125 **Facilities** FTV Dinner
available Cen ht **Conf** Max 20 **Parking** 50 **Notes** LB ⊗
No Children 12yrs Closed 1st 2wks Jan RS Mon & Tue
open for group bookings only No coaches

PREMIER COLLECTION

Glangrwyney Court

★★★★★ BED AND BREAKFAST

NP8 1ES
☎ 01873 811288   📄 01873 810317
e-mail: info@glancourt.co.uk
web: www.glancourt.co.uk
dir: 2m SE of Crickhowell on A40 (near county
boundary)

Located in extensive mature grounds, this impressive
Georgian house has been renovated to provide high
standards of comfort and facilities. The spacious
bedrooms are equipped with a range of homely extras,
and bathrooms include a jacuzzi or steam shower.
There are also comfortable bedrooms in an annexe; two
have their own lounge and kitchen area.
Comprehensive breakfasts are taken in the elegant
dining room and a luxurious lounge is also provided.

Rooms 6 en suite 4 annexe en suite (1 fmly) (1 GF)
Facilities STV TVL tea/coffee Cen ht Licensed Wi-fi 🍴
Boules **Parking** 12 **Notes** Civ Wed 23

See advert on this page

Brimford House *(SJ310150)*

★ ★ ★ ★ FARMHOUSE

Criggion SY5 9AU
☎ **01938 570235**
Mrs Dawson
e-mail: info@brimford.co.uk
dir: *Off B4393 after Crew Green turn left for Criggion, Brimford 1st on left after pub*

This elegant Georgian house stands in lovely open countryside and is a good base for touring central Wales and the Marches. Bedrooms are spacious, and thoughtful extras enhance guest comfort. A cheery log fire burns in the lounge during colder weather and the hospitality is equally warm, providing a relaxing atmosphere throughout.

Rooms 3 en suite S £45-£60; D £60-£75* **Facilities** FTV TVL tea/coffee Cen ht Wi-fi Fishing **Parking** 4 **Notes** LB 🐾 250 acres arable/beef/sheep

Lane Farm *(SJ305161)*

★ ★ ★ ★ FARMHOUSE

SY5 9BG
☎ **01743 884288**
Mrs L Burrowes
e-mail: lesley@lanefarmbedandbreakfast.co.uk
dir: *On B4393 between Crew Green & Llandrinio*

A warm welcome awaits at Lane Farm, a traditional 380-acre, organic, working beef and sheep farm, set beneath the tranquil Breidden Hills. Bedrooms are comfortably furnished with pine furniture and provide a good range of guest extras. There are two bedrooms at ground floor level. A substantial farmhouse breakfast is on offer and served in the beamed dining room around a communal table. Plenty of parking is available, free fishing on the Severn, and attractive gardens.

Rooms 4 en suite (2 GF) S £30-£35; D £50-£54* **Facilities** FTV tea/coffee Cen ht Fishing **Parking** 8 **Notes** LB Closed 23-27 Dec 380 acres organic beef/sheep

See advert on this page

Hafod-y-Garreg

★ ★ ★ ★ 🍴 BED AND BREAKFAST

LD2 3TQ
☎ **01982 560400**
e-mail: john-annie@hafod-y.wanadoo.co.uk
web: www.hafodygarreg.co.uk
dir: *1m S of Erwood. Off A470 at Trericket Mill, sharp right, up track past cream farmhouse towards pine forest, through gate*

This remote Grade II listed farmhouse dates in part from 1401 and has been confirmed, by dendrochronology, as the 'oldest dwelling in Wales'. As you would expect the house has tremendous character, and is decorated and furnished to befit its age; the bedrooms have all the modern facilities. There is an impressive dining room and a lounge with an open fireplace. Warm hospitality from John Marchant and Annie McKay is a major strength here and they were both finalists in this year's Friendliest Landlady of the Year award (2011-12).

Rooms 2 en suite D £82 **Facilities** STV tea/coffee Dinner available Cen ht Wi-fi **Parking** 6 **Notes** No Children Closed Xmas 🐾

Save on B&Bs and Hotels. Book at **theAA.com/hotel**

POWYS 427 WALES

HAY-ON-WYE
Map 9 SO24

ee also Erwood

ld Black Lion Inn
★★★ ◉ INN

6 Lion St HR3 5AD
☎ 01497 820841 📠 01497 822960
-mail: info@oldblacklion.co.uk

his fine old coaching inn, with a history stretching back
everal centuries, has a wealth of charm and character.
was occupied by Oliver Cromwell during the siege of
ay Castle. Privately-owned and personally-run, it
rovides cosy and well-equipped bedrooms, some located
an adjacent building. A wide range of well-prepared
ood is provided, and the service is relaxed and friendly.

ooms 6 rms (5 en suite) (1 pri facs) 4 annexe en suite
2 GF) S £45-£95; D fr £115* **Facilities** FTV tea/coffee
inner available Direct Dial Cen ht Wi-fi **Parking** 12
otes ⊗ No Children 8yrs Closed 24-26 Dec

LLANDRINDOD WELLS
Map 9 SO06

Guidfa House
★★★★★ 🏠 GUEST ACCOMMODATION

Crossgates LD1 6RF
☎ 01597 851241 📠 01597 737269
e-mail: guidfa@globalnet.co.uk
web: www.guidfa-house.co.uk
dir: *3m N of Llandrindod Wells, at junct of A483 & A44*

Expect a relaxed and pampered stay at this elegant
Georgian house just outside the town. Comfort is the
keynote here, whether in the attractive and well-
equipped bedrooms or in the homely lounge, where a
real fire burns in cold weather. Breakfast is also a
strength, due to the proprietor's skilful touch in the
kitchen; a wide choice of expertly cooked options are
offered.

Rooms 5 en suite 1 annexe en suite (1 GF) S £65-£90;
D £85-£110* **Facilities** FTV tea/coffee Cen ht Licensed
Wi-fi **Parking** 10 **Notes** LB ⊗ No Children 10yrs

Holly Farm *(SO045593)*
★★★★ FARMHOUSE

Holly Ln, Howey LD1 5PP
☎ 01597 822402 📠 01597 822402
Mrs R Jones
dir: *2m S on A483 of Llandrindod Wells near Howey*

This working farm dates from Tudor times. Bedrooms are
homely and full of character, and the comfortable lounge
has a log fire in cooler months. Traditional home cooking,
using local produce, can be enjoyed in the dining room.

Rooms 3 en suite (1 fmly) S £35-£40; D £58-£64*
Facilities FTV TVL tea/coffee Dinner available Cen ht
Parking 4 **Notes** LB ⊗ 70 acres beef/sheep

LLANGAMMARCH WELLS
Map 9 SN94

The Cammarch
★★★★ GUEST ACCOMMODATION

LD4 4BY
☎ 01591 610802
e-mail: mail@cammarch.com
web: www.cammarch.com
dir: *Off A483 at Garth signed Llangammarch Wells, opp
T-junct*

This property dates from the 1850s and was built as a
hotel by the railway company. Owner Kathryn Dangerfield
offers a warm welcome to all guests and the
establishment provides modern, well-equipped bedrooms
that are tastefully decorated. There is a comfortable
spacious bar and lounge, with a log-burning fire, ideal for
colder evenings. The conservatory dining room,
overlooking the attractive gardens and pond, offers fresh
local produce on the dinner menu and the hearty Welsh
breakfast makes a good start to the day. Parking is
provided at the side of the property.

Rooms 11 en suite (3 fmly) S £59-£69; D £79-£89
Facilities FTV tea/coffee Dinner available Cen ht Licensed
Wi-fi 🎣 Fishing **Conf** Max 20 Thtr 20 Class 15 Board 13
Parking 16 **Notes** LB RS Xmas-New Year Self catering
only

LLANGEDWYN
Map 15 SJ12

Plas Uchaf Country Guest House
★★★★ 🦢 GUEST HOUSE

SY10 9LD
☎ 01691 780588 & 07817 419747
e-mail: info@plasuchaf.com
dir: *Mile End services Oswestry A483/Welshpool, 2m
White Lion right, 4.5m Llangedwyn, 150yds after school
on right*

Located in a superb elevated position amongst extensive
mature parkland, this elegant Queen Anne house has
been sympathetically renovated to provide high standards
of comfort and facilities. The interior flooring was created
from recycled ship timbers from The Armada fleet of
1588, and furnishing styles highlight the many period
features. Imaginative dinners are available, and a warm
welcome is assured.

Rooms 6 en suite (1 fmly) (1 GF) S £52.50-£90; D
£70-£90* **Facilities** FTV tea/coffee Dinner available
Cen ht Licensed Wi-fi 🍷 🦢 **Conf** Max 15 Thtr 15 Class 15
Board 15 **Parking** 30 **Notes** LB Civ Wed 50

LLANGURIG — Map 9 SN97

The Old Vicarage

★★★★ GUEST HOUSE

SY18 6RN
☎ 01686 440280   📠 01686 440280
e-mail: info@theoldvicaragellangurig.co.uk
dir: *A470 onto A44, signed*

Located on pretty mature grounds, which feature a magnificent holly tree, this elegant Victorian house provides a range of thoughtfully furnished bedrooms, some with fine period items. Breakfast is served in a spacious dining room, and a comfortable guest lounge is also available. Afternoon teas are served in the garden during the warmer months.

Rooms 4 en suite (1 fmly) S £34-£40; D £56-£64*
Facilities TVL tea/coffee Dinner available Cen ht Licensed Wi-fi **Parking** 6 **Notes** LB ⊛

LLANIDLOES — Map 9 SN98

Mount Inn

★★★ INN

China St SY18 6AB
☎ 01686 412247   📠 01686 412247
e-mail: mountllani@aol.com
dir: *In town centre*

This establishment is believed to occupy part of the site of an old motte and bailey castle, and started life as a coaching inn. The traditional bars are full of character, with exposed beams and timbers as well as cobbled flooring and log fires. Bedrooms, which include some in a separate building, are carefully furnished and equipped with practical and thoughtful extras.

Rooms 3 en suite 6 annexe en suite (3 fmly) (3 GF) S £45; D £68 **Facilities** FTV TVL tea/coffee Dinner available Cen ht Golf 9 Pool table **Conf** Max 20 Thtr 12 Class 20 Board 12 **Parking** 12

LLANWRTYD WELLS — Map 9 SN84

Carlton Riverside

★★★★ ◉◉ RESTAURANT WITH ROOMS

Irfon Crescent LD5 4SP
☎ 01591 610248
e-mail: info@carltonriverside.com
dir: *In town centre beside bridge*

Guests become part of the family at this character property, set beside the river in Wales's smallest town. Carlton Riverside offers award-winning cuisine for which Mary Ann Gilchrist relies on the very best of local ingredients. The set menu is complemented by a well-chosen wine list and dinner is served in the delightfully stylish restaurant which offers a memorable blend of traditional comfort, modern design and river views. Four comfortable bedrooms have tasteful combinations of antique and contemporary furniture, along with welcome personal touches.

Rooms 4 en suite S £50; D £75-£100* **Facilities** tea/coffee Dinner available Cen ht Wi-fi **Notes** LB Closed 20-30 Dec No coaches

Lasswade Country House

★★★★ ◉◉ RESTAURANT WITH ROOMS

Station Rd LD5 4RW
☎ 01591 610515   📠 01591 610611
e-mail: info@lasswadehotel.co.uk
dir: *Exit A483 onto Irfon Terrace, right onto Station Rd, 350yds on right*

This friendly establishment on the edge of the town has impressive views over the countryside. Bedrooms are comfortably furnished and well equipped, while the public areas consist of a tastefully decorated lounge, an elegant restaurant with a bar, and an airy conservatory which looks towards the neighbouring hills. The kitchen utilises fresh, local produce to provide an enjoyable dining experience.

Rooms 8 en suite S £55-£70; D £70-£100* **Facilities** TVL Dinner available Cen ht Riding **Conf** Max 18 Thtr 18 Class 14 Board 14 **Parking** 6 **Notes** LB No coaches

LLANYMYNECH — Map 15 SJ22

The Bradford Arms

★★★★ INN

Llanymynech SY22 6EJ
☎ 01691 830582   📠 01691 839009
e-mail: catelou@tesco.net

(For full entry see Oswestry (Shropshire))

SENNYBRIDGE — Map 9 SN92

Maeswalter

★★★★ GUEST ACCOMMODATION

Heol Senni LD3 8SU
☎ 01874 636629
e-mail: bb@maeswalter.co.uk
web: www.maeswalter.co.uk
dir: *A470 onto A4215, 2.5m left for Heol Senni, 1.5m on right over cattle grid*

Set in a peaceful country location with splendid views of the Senni Valley, this 17th-century farmhouse offers a friendly and relaxing place to stay. The accommodation well maintained and includes a suite on the ground floor of an adjacent building. A lounge-dining room is provided, and freshly cooked farmhouse breakfasts are a pleasure.

Rooms 4 en suite (1 fmly) (2 GF) **Facilities** STV FTV TVL tea/coffee Dinner available Cen ht **Parking** 12 **Notes** ⊗ No Children 5yrs

WELSHPOOL — Map 15 SJ20

See also Criggion

PREMIER COLLECTION

Moors Farm B&B

★★★★★ BED AND BREAKFAST

Oswestry Rd SY21 9JR
☎ 01938 553395   & 07957 882967
e-mail: moorsfarm@tiscali.co.uk
web: www.moors-farm.com
dir: *1.5m NE of Welshpool off A483*

A very warm welcome awaits at this impressive house, parts of which date from the early 18th century. The property has a wealth of character, including exposed beams and log-burning fires, and the day rooms are spacious and tastefully furnished. The bedrooms feature smart modern bathrooms and are equipped with a wealth of thoughtful extras.

Rooms 5 en suite (2 fmly) **Facilities** TVL tea/coffee Cen ht **Notes** ⊗

Heath Cottage *(SJ239023)*

★★ 🏠 FARMHOUSE

ngswood, Forden SY21 8LX
☎ 01938 580453 📠 01938 580453
r & Mrs M C Payne
e-mail: heathcottagewales@tiscali.co.uk
r: 4m S of Welshpool. Off A490 behind Forden Old Post
ffice, opp Parrys Garage

ne furnishings and decor highlight the original features
f this early 18th-century farmhouse. Bedrooms have
unning country views, and a choice of lounges, one with
log fire, is available. Memorable breakfasts feature
ee-range eggs and home-made preserves.

Rooms 3 en suite (1 fmly) S fr £30; D fr £60*
Facilities TVL tea/coffee Cen ht **Parking** 4 **Notes** ⊗
Closed Oct-Etr 🐾 6 acres poultry/sheep

SWANSEA

LLANGENNITH Map 8 SS49

Kings Head

★★★ INN

own House SA3 1HX
☎ 01792 386212 📠 01792 386477
e-mail: info@kingsheadgower.co.uk

anding opposite the church in this coastal village, The
ings Head is made up from three 17th-century buildings
et behind a splendid rough stone wall. The comfortable,
ell-equipped bedrooms, including some on the ground
por, can be found in two of the buildings. This
stablishment makes an ideal base for exploring the
ower Peninsula, whether for walking, cycling or surfing.
vening meals and breakfasts can be taken in the inn.

Rooms 27 en suite (3 fmly) (14 GF) **Facilities** FTV tea/
offee Dinner available Direct Dial Cen ht Pool table
Parking 35 **Notes** LB Closed 25 Dec RS 24 Dec closed for
heck-in

MUMBLES Map 8 SS68

PREMIER COLLECTION

Little Langland

★★★★★ GUEST ACCOMMODATION

2 Rotherslade Rd, Langland SA3 4QN
☎ 01792 369696
e-mail: enquiries@littlelangland.co.uk
dir: Off A4067 in Mumbles onto Newton Rd, 4th left
onto Langland Rd, 2nd left onto Rotherslade Rd

Little Langland is only five miles from Swansea's city
centre and within easy access of the stunning Gower
Peninsula with its many coves and bays. The bedrooms
are stylish, comfortable and include free broadband.
There is a new café bar, ideal for a relaxing drink, and
also a bar menu of freshly prepared snacks. Breakfast
is served in the comfortable dining area.

Rooms 6 en suite S £70; D £90* **Facilities** FTV tea/
coffee Direct Dial Cen ht Licensed Wi-fi **Parking** 6
Notes ⊗ No Children 8yrs

PARKMILL (NEAR SWANSEA) Map 8 SS58

PREMIER COLLECTION

Maes-Yr-Haf Restaurant with Rooms

★★★★★ 🍴 RESTAURANT WITH ROOMS

SA3 2EH
☎ 01792 371000 📠 01792 234922
e-mail: enquiries@maes-yr-haf.com
dir: Take A4118 W from Swansea

Set in the peaceful location on The Gower in the small
village of Parkmill, this property is well situated for
easy access to Swansea and the coast. It offers
contemporary, individually styled bedrooms with a very
good range of guest extras, where comfort is the key.
Bathrooms have both bath and shower. The food is
created from high quality, locally sourced ingredients;
dinner is a highlight, served in the modern restaurant,
and breakfast provides a very good start to the day.

Rooms 5 en suite **Facilities** FTV tea/coffee Dinner
available Direct Dial Cen ht Wi-fi **Parking** 20 **Notes** ⊗
No Children 6yrs Closed 11-31 Jan

Parc-le-Breos House *(SS529896)*

★★★★ FARMHOUSE

SA3 2HA
☎ 01792 371636 📠 01792 371287
Mrs O Edwards
e-mail: info@parclebreos.co.uk
dir: On A4118, right 300yds after Shepherds shop, next
left, signed

This imposing early 19th-century house is at the end of a
forest drive and set in 70 acres of delightful grounds.
Many charming original features have been retained in
the public rooms, which include a lounge and a games
room. The bedrooms have comfortable furnishings, and
many are suitable for families.

Rooms 10 en suite (7 fmly) (1 GF) **Facilities** FTV TVL tea/
coffee Dinner available Cen ht Licensed Wi-fi Fishing
Riding Pool table **Conf** Max 30 Thtr 30 **Parking** 12
Notes ⊗ Closed 25-26 Dec 65 acres arable/horses/pigs/
chickens

REYNOLDSTON Map 8 SS48

PREMIER COLLECTION

Fairyhill

★★★★★ 🍴🍴 🏠 RESTAURANT WITH ROOMS

SA3 1BS
☎ 01792 390139 📠 01792 391358
e-mail: postbox@fairyhill.net
web: www.fairyhill.net
dir: M4 junct 47 onto A483, at next rdbt turn right onto
A484. At Gowerton take B4295 10m

Peace and tranquillity are never far away at this
charming Georgian mansion set in the heart of the
beautiful Gower peninsula. Bedrooms are furnished
with care and are filled with many thoughtful extras.
There is also a range of comfortable seating areas,
with crackling log fires, to choose from, and the smart
restaurant offers menus based on local produce and
complemented by an excellent wine list.

Rooms 8 en suite S £160-£260; D £180-£280*
Facilities FTV TVL Dinner available Direct Dial Cen ht
Wi-fi ♨ Holistic treatments **Conf** Max 32 Thtr 32 Board
16 **Parking** 50 **Notes** LB No Children 8yrs Closed 26
Dec & 1-27 Jan No coaches Civ Wed 40

SWANSEA — Map 9 SS69

The Alexander

★★★★ GUEST ACCOMMODATION

3 Sketty Rd, Uplands SA2 0EU
☎ 01792 470045 ≣ 01792 476012
e-mail: reception@alexander-hotel.co.uk

Located in fashionable Uplands between The Gower and
the city centre, this Victorian house has been modernised
to provide good levels of comfort and facilities. Bedrooms
are comfortable with family rooms, doubles and twins
available; all are filled with a very good range of practical
extras. Other areas include a cosy dining room where a
hearty breakfast is served and a comfortably furnished
lounge with a guest bar. The lower-ground floor provides
an office with broadband connection for guests' use.

Rooms 9 rms (8 en suite) (1 pri facs) (4 fmly) S £35-£52;
D £65-£77* Facilities FTV tea/coffee Direct Dial Cen ht
Licensed Wi-fi Notes ✇

The White House

★★★★ GUEST ACCOMMODATION

4 Nyanza Ter SA1 4QQ
☎ 01792 473856 ≣ 01792 455300
e-mail: reception@thewhitehousehotel.co.uk
dir: On A4118, 1m W of city centre at junct with Eaton
Crescent

Part of a short early-Victorian terrace in fashionable
Uplands, this house retains many original features. It has
been restored to provide thoughtfully furnished and
equipped quality accommodation. Bedrooms are filled
with many extras, and the memorable Welsh breakfasts
include cockles and laverbread.

Rooms 9 en suite (4 fmly) S £59-£69; D £89
Facilities FTV TVL tea/coffee Dinner available Direct Dial
Cen ht Licensed Wi-fi Conf Max 16 Thtr 16 Class 16 Board
10 Parking 8 Notes LB

Hurst Dene

★★★ GUEST HOUSE

10 Sketty Rd, Uplands SA2 0LJ
☎ 01792 280920 ≣ 01792 280920
e-mail: hurstdenehotel@yahoo.co.uk
dir: 1m W of city centre. A4118 through Uplands shopping
area onto Sketty Rd, Hurst Dene on right

This friendly guest house has a private car park and
provides soundly maintained bedrooms with modern
furnishings and equipment. Facilities include an
attractive breakfast room with separate tables and there
is a small comfortable lounge.

Rooms 10 rms (8 en suite) (3 fmly) (1 GF) S £40-£45; D
£65* Facilities FTV TVL tea/coffee Cen ht Wi-fi Parking 7
Notes ✇ Closed 22 Dec-1 Jan

See advert on this page

GLYN CEIRIOG — Map 15 SJ23

The Golden Pheasant

★★★★ INN

Llwynmawr LL20 7BB
☎ 01691 718281 ≣ 01691 718479
e-mail: info@goldenpheasanthotel.co.uk
web: www.goldenpheasanthotel.co.uk
dir: B4500, 5m to Dolywern, after bridge into Llynmawr.
200mtrs at top of road

This 18th-century inn is located in the heart of the Cerio₀
Valley with a peaceful setting and lovely views. Public
areas include a traditional bar with slate floor and open
fire, and there is a spacious lounge. A wide choice of
meals is offered in the bar or smartly presented
restaurant.

Rooms 19 en suite (1 fmly) Facilities FTV TVL tea/coffee
Dinner available Direct Dial Cen ht Wi-fi Conf Max 30 Th▮
30 Board 15 Parking 50 Notes Civ Wed 40

Save on B&Bs and Hotels. Book at **theAA.com/hotel**

WREXHAM 431 WALES

HANMER	Map 15 SJ43

The Hanmer Arms

★★★★ INN

SY13 3DE
☎ 01948 830532   📠 01948 830740
e-mail: info@hanmerarms.co.uk
web: www.hanmerarms.co.uk
dir: On A539, just off A525 Whitchurch/Wrexham road

Located in the centre of the village and also home to the local crown-green bowling club, this former farm has been sympathetically renovated to provide a good range of facilities. Well-equipped bedrooms are situated in the former stables or barns, and rustic furniture styles highlight the many period features in the public areas, which also feature an attractive first-floor function room.

Rooms 12 annexe en suite (2 fmly) (8 GF) S fr £68; D fr £99* **Facilities** FTV TVL tea/coffee Dinner available Cen ht Wi-fi **Conf** Max 140 Thtr 140 Class 100 Board 60 **Parking** 50 **Notes** LB Civ Wed 60

HORSEMAN'S GREEN	Map 15 SJ44

Murefield Bed & Breakfast

★★★★ BED AND BREAKFAST

Murefield SY13 3EA
☎ 01948 830790   📠 01948 830790
e-mail: enquiries@murefield.com
dir: Turn off A525 to Horseman's Green, in centre of village turn left for Little Arowry. 350mtrs on right

Located in a peaceful rural setting between Whitchurch and Wrexham this modern house provides very high standards of comfort and facilities throughout, along with well presented gardens and parking. The thoughtfully furnished bedrooms are comfortable, well equipped with many extras, and have modern efficient bathrooms. One bedroom is on the ground floor for easy access. Comprehensive breakfasts offer home-made and locally sourced produce.

Rooms 2 en suite (1 GF) S £40-£60; D £60-£70 **Facilities** FTV tea/coffee Cen ht Wi-fi **Parking** 2 **Notes** LB ⊗ No Children 8yrs Closed 22 Dec-3 Jan ⊗

LLANARMON DYFFRYN CEIRIOG	Map 15 SJ13

The Hand at Llanarmon

★★★★ ⊚ INN

LL20 7LD
☎ 01691 600666   📠 01691 600262
e-mail: reception@thehandhotel.co.uk
dir: Exit A5 at Chirk onto B4500 signed Ceiriog Valley, continue for 11m

This owner managed inn provides a range of thoughtfully furnished bedrooms, with smart modern bathrooms. Public areas retain many original features including exposed beams and open fires. Imaginative food utilises the finest of local produce. A warm welcome and attentive service ensure a memorable guest experience.

Rooms 13 en suite (4 GF) **Facilities** tea/coffee Dinner available Direct Dial Cen ht Wi-fi Pool table **Conf** Max 15 Thtr 10 Class 10 Board 15 **Parking** 19 **Notes** Civ Wed 60

West Arms

★★★★ ⊚ INN

LL20 7LD
☎ 01691 600665 & 600612   📠 01691 600622
e-mail: gowestarms@aol.com
dir: Off A483/A5 at Chirk, take B4500 to Ceiriog Valley

Set in the beautiful Ceiriog Valley, this delightful 17th-century inn has a wealth of charm and character. There is a comfortable lounge, a room for private dining and two bars, as well as an elegant, award-winning restaurant offering a set-price menu of imaginative dishes, utilising quality local produce. The attractive bedrooms have a mixture of modern and period furnishings.

Rooms 15 en suite (2 fmly) (3 GF) **Facilities** FTV tea/coffee Dinner available Direct Dial Cen ht Wi-fi Fishing **Conf** Max 35 Thtr 35 Class 25 Board 20 **Parking** 22 **Notes** Civ Wed 50

Ireland

Kinsale harbour, Co Cork

NORTHERN IRELAND

CO ANTRIM

BUSHMILLS   Map 1 C6

PREMIER COLLECTION

Whitepark House

★★★★★ GUEST ACCOMMODATION

150 Whitepark Rd, Ballintoy BT54 6NH
☎ 028 2073 1482
e-mail: bob@whiteparkhouse.com
dir: On A2 at Whitepark Bay, 6m E of Bushmills

Whitepark House nestles above a sandy beach and has super views of the ocean and Scotland's Western Isles. The house features bijouterie gathered from Far Eastern travels, while the traditional bedrooms are homely. Breakfasts are served around a central table in the open-plan hallway, and hospitality is warm and memorable.

Rooms 3 en suite S £75; D £100* Facilities tea/coffee Cen ht Wi-fi Parking 6 Notes ⊗ No Children 10yrs

PREMIER COLLECTION

Causeway Lodge

★★★★★ GUEST HOUSE

52 Moycraig Rd, Dunseverick BT57 8TB
☎ 028 2073 0333   📄 0800 7565433
e-mail: stay@causewaylodge.com

Causeway Lodge offers high quality contemporary accommodation in an idyllic peaceful setting on the North Antrim Coast. Each of the individually designed bedrooms are thoughtfully presented and the Causeway Suite is very stylish. The house is close to the Giants Causeway, Carrick-A-Rede rope bridge and the famous Bushmill's Distillery. Wi-fi is available and a warm welcome is assured from the friendly owners.

Rooms 4 rms (3 en suite) (1 pri facs) (1 fmly) (1 GF) S £70; D £100-£120* Facilities STV FTV TVL tea/coffee Cen ht Wi-fi Parking 6 Notes ⊗

LARNE   Map 1 D5

Derrin House

★★★★ GUEST ACCOMMODATION

2 Princes Gardens BT40 1RQ
☎ 028 2827 3269   📄 028 2827 3269
e-mail: info@derrinhouse.co.uk
dir: Off A8 Harbour Highway onto A2 (coast route), 1st left after lights at Main St

Just a short walk from the town centre, and a short drive from the harbour, this comfortable Victorian house offers a very friendly welcome. The bedrooms are gradually being refurbished to offer smartly presented modern facilities. Public areas are light and inviting, hearty breakfasts are offered in the stylish dining room.

Rooms 7 en suite (2 fmly) (2 GF) S £35-£40; D £55-£57* Facilities TVL tea/coffee Cen ht Wi-fi Parking 3 Notes LB

Manor Guest House

★★★★ GUEST HOUSE

23 Older Fleet Rd, Harbour Highway BT40 1AS
☎ 028 2827 3305   📄 028 2826 0505
e-mail: welcome@themanorguesthouse.com
dir: Near Larne ferry terminal & harbour train station

This grand Victorian house continues to prove popular with travellers thanks to its convenient location next to the ferry terminal. There is an elegant sitting room and a separate cosy breakfast room. The well-equipped bedrooms vary in size and are furnished in modern or period style. Hospitality is especially good and ensures a real home-from-home experience.

Rooms 8 en suite (2 fmly) S £30-£35; D £55-£60 Facilities FTV tea/coffee Cen ht Wi-fi Parking 6 Notes LB ⊗ Closed 25-26 Dec

PORTRUSH   Map 1 C6

Beulah Guest House

★★★ GUEST ACCOMMODATION

16 Causeway St BT56 8AB
☎ 028 7082 2413
e-mail: stay@beulahguesthouse.com
dir: Approach Portrush, signs for Bushmills/East Strand car park, onto Causeway St, house 300yds on left

Situated just a stroll from the East Strand and the town's attractions, this guest accommodation offers a friendly welcome. Bright and attractive throughout, the comfortable bedrooms are well equipped. There is also a first-floor lounge and secure parking behind the house.

Rooms 9 en suite (3 fmly) S £35-£55; D £55-£80 Facilities TVL tea/coffee Cen ht Wi-fi Parking 10 Notes LB ⊗ Closed 25-26 Dec

BELFAST

BELFAST   Map 1 D5

Tara Lodge

★★★★ GUEST ACCOMMODATION

36 Cromwell Rd BT7 1JW
☎ 028 9059 0900   📄 028 9059 0901
e-mail: info@taralodge.com
web: www.taralodge.com
dir: M1 onto A55, left onto A1, right onto Fitzwilliam St, left onto University Rd, proceed to Botanic Av

Friendly staff and comfortable bedrooms make this new establishment popular for tourism and business. The stylish dining room is the scene for memorable breakfasts, while secure off-road parking is a bonus so close to the city centre.

Rooms 19 en suite 9 annexe en suite (3 GF) S £60-£70; D £70-£90* Facilities STV FTV TVL tea/coffee Direct Dial Cen ht Lift Wi-fi Parking 19 Notes LB ⊗ Closed 24-28 Dec

CO DOWN

BANGOR   Map 1 D5

PREMIER COLLECTION

Hebron House

★★★★★ 🏠 BED AND BREAKFAST

68 Princetown Rd BT20 3TD
☎ 028 9146 3126   📄 028 9146 3126
e-mail: reception@hebron-house.com
web: www.hebron-house.com
dir: A20 onto B20 for 3m, 1st rdbt onto Princetown Rd

Hebron House stands in a peaceful elevated location within easy walking distance of the town amenities. Bedrooms are luxuriously furnished and have many thoughtful extras. The elegant lounge is richly styled and very comfortable. Breakfast offers home-made and local produce around a communal table in the smart dining room.

Rooms 3 en suite (1 GF) S £35-£80; D £55-£80 Facilities TVL tea/coffee Cen ht Wi-fi Parking 2 Notes ⊗ Closed 22 Dec-1 Jan

Shelleven House

★★★★ GUEST HOUSE

61 Princetown Rd BT20 3TA
☎ 028 9127 1777 📠 028 9127 1777
e-mail: shellevenhouse@aol.com
web: www.shellevenhouse.com
dir: A2 from Belfast, left at rail station rdbt. Onto Dufferin Av, proceed to rdbt, over to Princetown Rd

Shelleven is a large Victorian townhouse situated in a quiet conservation area and close to the marina, the promenade and a short walk from the town centre. Bedrooms are all spacious and very comfortable, with rooms at the front of the house having wonderful sea views. There is an extensive choice available at breakfast, which is served in the elegant dining room.

Rooms 10 en suite (2 fmly) (1 GF) S £37-£38; D £70-£80 **Facilities** STV TVL tea/coffee Direct Dial Cen ht Licensed Wi-fi **Parking** 10 **Notes** LB ⊗

DONAGHADEE　　　　　　Map 1 D5

Pier 36

★★★★ A GUEST HOUSE

36 The Parade BT21 0HE
☎ 028 9188 4466 📠 028 9188 4636
e-mail: info@pier36.co.uk
dir: A2 left onto flyover before Bangor, follow signs for Donaghadee (right across bridge). After 3m take 3rd exit at rdbt towards harbour, Pier 36 on right

Rooms 6 en suite (2 fmly) **Facilities** STV TVL tea/coffee Dinner available Cen ht Licensed Wi-fi **Notes** ⊗

GREYABBEY　　　　　　　Map 1 D5

Ballynester House

★★★★ GUEST HOUSE

1a Cardy Rd BT22 2LS
☎ 028 4278 8386 📠 028 4278 8986
e-mail: rc.davison@virgin.net
dir: A20 S from Newtownards to Greyabbey, or A20 N from Portaferry to Greyabbey, signed at Greyabbey rdbt

Located in the rolling hills above Strangford Lough, this stylish, modern house provides a tranquil haven and a warm welcome. Smart day rooms make the most of the super views; hearty breakfasts are served in the bright dining room. Richly furnished bedrooms include a host of thoughtful extras.

Rooms 3 en suite (3 GF) S £30; D £60-£70* **Facilities** FTV tea/coffee Cen ht Wi-fi Professional Genealogy consultation for guests **Parking** 10 **Notes** ⊗ No Children 11yrs

---

HOLYWOOD　　　　　　　Map 1 D5

PREMIER COLLECTION

Rayanne House

★★★★★ 🛎 GUEST HOUSE

60 Desmesne Rd BT18 9EX
☎ 028 9042 5859 📠 028 9042 5859
e-mail: info@rayannehouse.com
web: www.rayannehouse.com
dir: Exit A2 at Holywood, left onto Jacksons Rd, pass golf club, 200yds on right

This elegant period house, set in its own grounds, is full of charm and enjoys a commanding position overlooking Belfast Lough and the Antrim Hills beyond. Bedrooms are all of a high standard and a host of thoughtful extras is provided. The house is a short drive from Belfast City centre and the City Airport. Breakfasts are not to be missed and evening meals are served in the spacious dining room.

Rooms 10 en suite (2 fmly) (1 GF) S £67.50-£75; D £110-£130* **Facilities** FTV tea/coffee Dinner available Direct Dial Cen ht Licensed Wi-fi ch fac Golf 18 **Conf** Max 17 Thtr 17 Class 17 Board 17 **Parking** 15 **Notes** LB ⊗ RS 25-26 Dec no breakfast service

---

STRANGFORD　　　　　　Map 1 D5

The Cuan Licensed Guest Inn

★★★★ 🎖 INN

6-12 The Square BT30 7ND
☎ 028 4488 1222
e-mail: info@thecuan.com
web: www.thecuan.com
dir: A7 to Downpatrick, follow A25 for Strangford ferry. Located in centre of village

This popular family-run inn is located in the heart of the pretty village of Strangford. The bedrooms are equipped with a range of thoughtful extras including digital TV, free internet access and direct dial telephone. A number of bedrooms overlook the square offering 'a fly on the wall' opportunity to watch village life go by. Strangford offers an ideal base for exploring the extensive range of activities on offer in the area, including the burial site of St Patrick, Ireland's patron saint in nearby Downpatrick.

Rooms 9 en suite (3 fmly) **Facilities** FTV TVL tea/coffee Dinner available Direct Dial Cen ht Wi-fi Golf 18 **Conf** Max 80 Thtr 60 Class 30 Board 24 **Parking** 5 **Notes** LB

CO FERMANAGH

ENNISKILLEN　　　　　　Map 1 C5

Belmore Court & Motel

★★★★ GUEST ACCOMMODATION

Tempo Rd BT74 6HX
☎ 028 6632 6633 📠 028 6632 6362
e-mail: info@motel.co.uk
web: www.motel.co.uk
dir: On A4 Belfast-Enniskillen Rd, opp Tesco

Situated in the centre of Enniskillen, the Belmore Court offers an ideal location for visiting the North West and Fermanagh lakes. The accommodation offered has a range of styles from rooms with small kitchen areas to executive suites. They are stylish and have all the modern attractions of flat-screen TVs and free Wi-fi. Some also come with espresso coffee makers. The public areas are also modern, and the breakfast room catches all the morning sun. Excellent free parking.

Rooms 30 en suite 30 annexe en suite (17 fmly) (12 GF) S £50-£130; D £60-£145 **Facilities** FTV TVL tea/coffee Direct Dial Cen ht Lift Wi-fi **Conf** Max 45 Thtr 45 Class 25 Board 16 **Parking Notes** LB ⊗ Closed 24-27 Dec

---

Aghnacarra Guest House

★★★ GUEST ACCOMMODATION

Carrybridge, Lisbellaw BT94 5HX
☎ 028 6638 7077
e-mail: normaensor@talk21.com
web: www.guesthouseireland.com
dir: From Belfast A4 left to Lisbellaw-Carrybridge

Surrounded by spacious grounds, gardens and countryside on the shores of Lough Erne, this delightful modern extended house is a haven of peace and quiet. It is understandably very popular with anglers, who may fish from the grounds. Bedrooms are well maintained, and day rooms include an elegant lounge, bright dining room and a spacious bar and games room.

Rooms 7 en suite (4 fmly) (5 GF) **Facilities** TVL tea/coffee Dinner available Cen ht Licensed Pool table **Parking** 8 **Notes** ⊗

CO LONDONDERRY

CASTLEDAWSON   Map 1 C5

The Inn Castledawson

★★★★ ◉◉ INN

47 Main St BT45 8AA
☎ 028 7946 9777   📄 028 7946 9751
e-mail: info@theinncastledawson.com
web: www.theinncastledawson.com
dir: A6 at Magherafelt rdbt exit onto A54 into Castledawson. Next to post office on Main Street

Located in the heart of the pretty village of Castledawson, the Inn has been totally refurbished and now offers a range of spacious comfortable bedrooms. Rear facing rooms overlook both the garden and the tranquil River Moyola. The award-winning restaurant is very stylish and the cosy bar area is ideal for pre-dinner drinks. Business facilities are available and private parties are also catered for.

Rooms 10 en suite (3 fmly) (5 GF) S £60-£67.50; D £100-£115* **Facilities** FTV tea/coffee Dinner available Direct Dial Cen ht Wi-fi **Conf** Max 60 Thtr 60 Class 40 Board 40 **Parking** 6 **Notes** LB ⊗

COLERAINE   Map 1 C6

PREMIER COLLECTION

Greenhill House (C849210)

★★★★★ 📄 FARMHOUSE

24 Greenhill Rd, Aghadowey BT51 4EU
☎ 028 7086 8241   📄 028 7086 8365
Mrs E Hegarty
e-mail: greenhill.house@btinternet.com
web: www.greenhill-house.co.uk
dir: A29 from Coleraine S for 7m, left onto B66 Greenhill Rd for 300yds. House on right, AA sign at front gate

Located in the tranquil Bann Valley, overlooking the Antrim Hills, this delightful Georgian house nestles in well-tended gardens with views to open rolling countryside. Public rooms are traditionally styled and include a comfortable lounge and an elegant dining room. The pleasant bedrooms vary in size and style and have a host of thoughtful extras.

Rooms 6 en suite (2 fmly) S £45; D £70 **Facilities** FTV TVL tea/coffee Direct Dial Cen ht Wi-fi **Parking** 10 **Notes** ⊗ Closed Nov-Feb RS Mar-Oct 150 acres beef

Bellevue Country House

★★★★ GUEST HOUSE

43 Greenhill Rd, Aghadowey BT51 4EU
☎ 028 7086 8797
e-mail: info@bellevuecountryhouse.co.uk
dir: On B66 just off A29, 7m S of Coleraine

This fine country house, dating from 1840, stands in peaceful grounds. A variety of bedrooms are offered, including a family room and ground-floor accommodation, and there is also a comfortable drawing room. Generous breakfasts are freshly prepared and served around one large table.

Rooms 3 en suite (1 fmly) (1 GF) S £38-£40; D £60* **Facilities** TVL tea/coffee Cen ht Wi-fi Fishing **Parking** 9 **Notes** ⊗ Closed Nov-3 Mar ⊜

Heathfield (NW012782)

★★★★ FARMHOUSE

31 Drumcroone Rd, Killykergan BT51 4EB
☎ 028 2955 8245   & 07745 209296
Ms H Torrens
e-mail: relax@heathfieldfarm.com
dir: 8m S of Coleraine. On A29 nr Killykergan, 2m N of Garvagh

Heathfield is a delightful traditional farmhouse that is an integral part of a working cattle farm. The house enjoys a rural setting and is a short drive from the towns of Garvagh and Coleraine making it an ideal base from which to explore the North Antrim Coast. Bedrooms are comfortable and all enjoy views of the surrounding countryside. Guests enjoy a hearty breakfast in the dining room or relax in the lounge after a day's sightseeing.

Rooms 3 en suite S £40-£45; D £65* **Facilities** FTV TVL tea/coffee Cen ht Wi-fi **Parking** 10 **Notes** ⊗ No Children 10yrs Closed Xmas & New Year

LONDONDERRY   Map 1 C5

Killennan House

★★★★ 📄 BED AND BREAKFAST

40 Killennan Rd, Drumahoe BT47 3NG
☎ 028 7130 1710   📄 028 7130 1710
e-mail: averil@killennan.co.uk
dir: From A6 onto B118 Eglinton Rd, turn left onto Killennan Rd, 1st house on right

A warm welcome from hosts Averil and Jim Campbell awaits all guests at their 19th-century restored farmhouse which stands in its own grounds at the end of a winding drive. It is set in the countryside outside Londonderry yet within easy reach of Belfast, the coast and many tourist attractions. Bedrooms are comfortable and a very good range of extras is provided. There's a cosy lounge and substantial quality breakfasts are served at the communal table in the dining room. Averil Campbell was a finalist in this year's Friendliest Landlady of the Year award (2011-12).

Rooms 3 en suite (2 fmly) S £38-£40; D £56-£60* **Facilities** TVL tea/coffee Cen ht **Parking** 4 **Notes** ⊗ No Children 3yrs Closed Nov-1 Mar

CO TYRONE

DUNGANNON   Map 1 C5

PREMIER COLLECTION

Grange Lodge

★★★★★ 🏆 ⊜ GUEST HOUSE

7 Grange Rd BT71 7EJ
☎ 028 8778 4212   & 07970 429965
📄 028 8778 4313
e-mail: stay@grangelodgecountryhouse.com
web: www.grangelodgecountryhouse.com
dir: M1 junct 15, A29 towards Armagh, 1m Grange Lodge signed, 1st right & 1st white-walled entrance on right

Grange Lodge dates from 1698 and nestles in 20 acres of well-tended grounds. It continues to set high standards in hospitality and food, and excellent meals are served in the bright and airy extension. Home-baked afternoon teas can be enjoyed in the sumptuous drawing room.

Rooms 5 en suite S £60-£69; D £80-£89 **Facilities** STV FTV TVL tea/coffee Dinner available Direct Dial Cen ht Licensed Wi-fi ⤵ Golf 18 Snooker **Conf** Max 25 **Parking** 12 **Notes** ⊗ No Children 12yrs Closed 21 Dec-1 Feb

Millbrook Bed & Breakfast

★★★★ BED AND BREAKFAST

46 Moy Rd BT71 7DT
☎ 028 8772 3715
e-mail: info@millbrookonline.co.uk
dir: On A29 1m S of Dungannon, 0.25m N of M1 junct 15

This well-presented bungalow is situated just outside the town of Dungannon and close to main routes. Comfortable ground-floor bedrooms and a stylish lounge are complemented by a substantial, freshly prepared breakfast. The owners' natural hospitality is memorable.

Rooms 2 en suite (2 GF) S fr £45; D fr £65* **Facilities** TVL tea/coffee Cen ht Wi-fi **Parking** 4 **Notes** ⊗ ⊜

REPUBLIC OF IRELAND

CO CARLOW

CARLOW Map 1 C3

Avlon House Bed & Breakfast

★★★★ BED AND BREAKFAST

Green Ln, Dublin Rd
☎ 059 9174222   📄 059 9173829
e-mail: avlonhouse@eircom.net
web: www.carlowbedandbreakfast.com
dir: N of town centre

Avlon House was built with visiting guests in mind. Located on the main approach from Dublin, there is secure car-parking and an attractively landscaped garden terrace. All of the bedrooms are comfortably appointed, and guests have the choice of two comfortable lounge areas. While it is a non-smoking house, there is a dedicated smoking lodge in the garden.

Rooms 5 en suite (1 fmly) Facilities STV FTV TVL tea/coffee Dinner available Direct Dial Cen ht Wi-fi Parking 7 Notes ⊗

Barrowville Town House

★★★★ GUEST HOUSE

Kilkenny Rd
☎ 059 914 3324 & 086 2520013
e-mail: barrowvilletownhouse@eircom.net
dir: Carlow Town, N9 Kilkenny Rd near Institute of Technology

The Smyths are the friendly owners of this carefully maintained 18th-century town house. Many of the very comfortable bedrooms are spacious, and the public rooms are elegant and relaxing. The conservatory, with its fruiting vine, is where Barrowvilles's legendary breakfasts are served, overlooking well tended gardens. Ample car parking.

Rooms 7 en suite (3 fmly) Facilities STV TVL tea/coffee Direct Dial Cen ht Wi-fi Parking 11 Notes ⊗ No Children 10yrs Closed 24-26 Dec

CO CAVAN

BALLYCONNELL Map 1 C4

Prospect Bay Lakeside Accommodation

★★★★ BED AND BREAKFAST

Brackley Lake
☎ 049 9523930
e-mail: info@prospectbay.ie
dir: N87 through Ballyconnell & Bawnboy to Brackley Lake. 1st left after Lakeside car park

Prospect Bay promises you eco-friendly comfort, hospitality and home baking. The accommodation is on a 30-acre site overlooking Brackley Lake, where boats are available for fishing. Bedrooms and guest sitting/dining room are all smartly appointed and lead on to the lovely garden patio. Convenient for Slieve Russell Hotel and Golf Course.

Rooms 4 en suite (2 fmly) (2 GF) S €60; D €80*
Facilities TVL tea/coffee Cen ht Wi-fi ch fac Fishing Clay pigeon shooting Hovercrafting Mud buggies Parking 5 Notes LB Closed 20 Dec-6 Jan

CO CLARE

DOOLIN Map 1 B3

Sea View House

★★★★ BED AND BREAKFAST

☎ 087 2679617
e-mail: darra@seaviewhouse.eu
dir: From R478 down hill to Doolin. At x-rds left for 0.5km, beside Doolin hostel

Perched on the hillside overlooking the Atlantic Ocean and Doolin village which is renowned for traditional live music sessions and great pubs, the Hughes family home has beautifully decorated bedrooms. Guests can relax and enjoy a cup of tea on arrival in the guest sitting room or the deck outside, while taking in the breathtaking views. Breakfast is served at one large family table and the menu includes locally smoked fish and Darra's home baking. The Cliffs of Moher and Aran Islands are close by.

Rooms 4 en suite (1 fmly) Facilities STV FTV tea/coffee Cen ht Wi-fi Parking 4 Notes ⊗ Closed 15 Dec-15 Jan 🌐

Cullinan's Seafood Restaurant & Guest House

★★★ ⊚ 🏠 GUEST HOUSE

☎ 065 7074183   📄 065 7074239
e-mail: cullinans@eircom.net
dir: In town centre at x-rds between McGanns Pub & O'Connors Pub

This charming guest house and restaurant is situated in the village of Doolin. Bedrooms are attractively decorated and comfortably decorated in a traditional style. Chef patron James Cullinan features locally caught fresh fish on his dinner menu which also includes steaks, lamb and vegetarian dishes, and there is a popular Early Bird menu. Dinner is served in the conservatory dining room overlooking the River Aille (closed Wed and Sun) in season. There is cosy guest lounge and ample off-street parking.

Rooms 8 en suite (3 fmly) (3 GF) Facilities STV FTV TVL TV6B tea/coffee Dinner available Direct Dial Cen ht Wi-fi Parking 15 Notes ⊗ Closed Jan-Feb

LAHINCH Map 1 B3

PREMIER COLLECTION

Moy House

★★★★★ ⊚⊚ 🏠 GUEST HOUSE

☎ 065 7082800   📄 065 7082500
e-mail: moyhouse@eircom.net
web: www.moyhouse.com
dir: 1km from Lahinch on Miltown Malbay Rd, signed from Lahinch N67

This 18th-century hunting lodge overlooks Lahinch Bay the world-famous surfing beach and championship golf links. Individually designed bedrooms are decorated with luxurious fabrics and fine antique furniture. The elegant drawing room has an open turf fire where guests can enjoy the breathtaking views of the ever-changing ocean. The skilful and carefully prepared dinner menu has an emphasis on local seafood and must be pre-booked. A gourmet tasting menu is served on selected nights. Breakfast is also a treat. This is a charming house where hospitality is memorable.

Rooms 9 en suite (2 fmly) (4 GF) S €145-€175; D €185-€360* Facilities STV FTV Dinner available Direct Dial Cen ht Licensed Wi-fi Private access to beach Conf Max 16 Board 16 Parking 30 Notes LB ⊗ Closed Jan-13 Feb RS Nov-Dec & Feb-Mar wknds only - open New Year

LISCANNOR
Map 1 B3

Moher Lodge (R043917)

★★★★ FARMHOUSE

Cliffs of Moher
☎ 065 7081269   065 7081589
Mr & Mrs Considine
e-mail: moherlodge@gmail.com
dir: *1m from Cliffs of Moher on R478*

This very comfortable farmhouse is situated within
walking distance of the world famous Cliffs of Moher.
Three of the well appointed bedrooms are on the ground
floor. There is a cosy sitting room with a turf fire and
guests are greeted with tea and Mary's Guinness cake on
arrival and there is a selection of dishes and freshly
baked scones for breakfast. The locality offers
restaurants, pubs with Irish Music, ferries to the Aran
Islands and the Links Golf course at Lahinch.

Rooms 4 en suite (1 fmly) (3 GF) **Facilities** FTV TVL tea/
coffee Cen ht Wi-fi **Parking** 4 **Notes** ⊗ Closed Nov-Mar
⊛ 300 acres dairy/beef

TUAMGRANEY
Map 1 B3

Clareville House

★★★★ BED AND BREAKFAST

☎ 061 922925 & 087 6867548   061 922925
e-mail: clarevillehouse@ireland.com
web: www.clarevillehouse.net
dir: *On R352 in village adjacent to Scarriff*

Clareville House is attractively decorated and is situated
in the pretty lakeside village of Tuamgraney. Bedrooms
are furnished to a high standard and there is a cosy
guest sitting room. Teresa's breakfast is a special treat.
Walking tours are organised by Derek who has all the
knowledge about fishing and golf in the area, and offers
a taxi service and airport collection.

Rooms 4 en suite (4 fmly) **Facilities** TVL tea/coffee Cen ht
Wi-fi Golf 18 Riding **Parking** 8 **Notes** ⊗ Closed 20-27
Dec

CO CORK

BANDON
Map 1 B2

Glebe Country House

★★★★ BED AND BREAKFAST

Ballinadee
☎ 021 4778294   021 4778456
e-mail: glebehse@indigo.ie
dir: *Off N71 at Innishannon Bridge signed Ballinadee,
8km along river bank, left after village sign*

Situated in the charming village of Ballinadee this lovely
bed and breakfast stands in well-kept gardens, and is
run with great attention to detail. Antique furnishings
predominate throughout this comfortable house, which
has an elegant, lounge and dining room. Bedrooms are
spacious and well appointed; the ground-floor room has
access to the lovely garden. There is an interesting
breakfast menu featuring local and garden produce. A
country-house style dinner is available by arrangement.

Rooms 4 en suite (2 fmly) **Facilities** TVL tea/coffee Dinner
available Direct Dial Cen ht Wi-fi **Parking** 10
Notes Closed 21 Dec-3 Jan

BLARNEY
Map 1 B2

PREMIER COLLECTION

Ashlee Lodge

★★★★★ GUEST HOUSE

Tower
☎ 021 4385346   021 4385726
e-mail: info@ashleelodge.com
dir: *4km from Blarney on R617*

Ashlee Lodge is a purpose-built guest house, situated
in the village of Tower, close to Blarney and local pubs
and restaurants. Bedrooms are decorated with comfort
and elegance in mind, some with whirlpool baths.
Bedrooms are on two floors and one room has its own
entrance. The extensive breakfast menu is memorable
which includes home baking and quality local produce.
Guests can unwind in the sauna or the outdoor hot tub.
Transfers to the nearest airport and railway station can
be arranged, and tee times can be booked at many of
the nearby golf courses

Rooms 10 en suite (2 fmly) (6 GF) S €65-€95; D
€80-€140 **Facilities** STV FTV TVL tea/coffee Dinner
available Direct Dial Cen ht Licensed Wi-fi Sauna Hot
tub **Parking** 12 **Notes** LB

Blarney Vale House

★★★★ BED AND BREAKFAST

Cork Rd, Sheanlower
☎ 021 4381511
e-mail: info@blarneyvale.com
dir: *On R617*

Anne and Ray Hennessy welcome you to this, their family
home, a dormer bungalow, located on an elevated
position above the Cork Road, just minutes walk from the
village green. Set in attractively landscaped gardens the
house offers good comfort in all rooms and the lounge.

Rooms 4 en suite (2 fmly) (1 GF) **Facilities** FTV TVL tea/
coffee Cen ht **Notes** ⊗ No Children 7yrs Closed Nov-Mar
⊛

Killarney House

★★★★ BED AND BREAKFAST

Station Rd
☎ 021 4381841   021 4381841
e-mail: info@killarneyhouseblarney.com
dir: *From Cork N20 towards Limerick, after 8km onto
R617 signed Blarney. In village turn right beyond petrol
station onto Station Rd, 1km on right*

This attractive house has four ground-floor bedrooms and
two spacious family rooms on the first floor. Caroline
Morgan is a charming, attentive hostess whose
comfortable house is very well appointed. There is a cosy
television lounge, drying facilities for wet gear, off-road
parking and a lovely garden. This non-smoking house is
within walking distance of the village of Blarney and
close to golf, horse riding and Blarney Woollen Mills.

Rooms 6 en suite (2 fmly) (4 GF) S €43-€55; D €60-€80
Facilities FTV TVL tea/coffee Cen ht Wi-fi Golf 18 Riding
Gym **Parking** 8 **Notes** LB ⊗ ⊛

White House

★★★★ BED AND BREAKFAST

Shean Lower
☎ 021 4385338
e-mail: info@thewhitehouseblarney.com
web: www.thewhitehouseblarney.com
dir: *On R617 (Cork-Blarney road)*

Situated on an elevated position near to the town, with
views of Blarney Castle, this carefully maintained
bungalow has prize-winning gardens. Bedrooms are all
on the ground floor and they are well appointed and
comfortably furnished. Breakfast is a real treat and there
is a choice of hot dishes that are all cooked to order.
Ample off-street car parking is available.

Rooms 6 en suite (1 fmly) (6 GF) S €40-€50; D €60-€76*
Facilities STV tea/coffee Cen ht Wi-fi Golf 18 **Parking** 7
Notes ⊗

CLONAKILTY　　　　　　　　Map 1 B2

PREMIER COLLECTION

An Garran Coir (W332358)

★★★★★ 　FARMHOUSE

Rathbarry, Rosscarbery Coast Route
☎ 023 8848236 　📠 023 8848236
Mr & Mrs M Calnan
e-mail: angarrancoir@eircom.net
web: www.angarrancoir.com
dir: *Signed at Maxol station in Clonakilty. 6.5km W of town off N71, 1.5km on right*

Situated on the coast road to Rosscarbery from Clonakilty, close to sandy beaches and the village, this comfortable farmhouse has lovely views. Bedrooms are attractively decorated to a high standard with well fitted bathrooms. Jo Calnan's cooking is a special treat, evening meals are available on request with produce from the garden and fresh eggs from the farm. Also available, a tennis court and lovely garden.

Rooms 5 en suite (2 fmly) **Facilities** tea/coffee Dinner available Cen ht ♨ Local leisure club available - rates negotiated **Parking** 5 **Notes** ⊗

Duvane House (W349405)

★★★★ FARMHOUSE

Ballyduvane
☎ 023 8833129
Mrs N McCarthy
e-mail: duvanefarm@eircom.net
dir: *1km SW from Clonakilty on N71*

This Georgian farmhouse is on the N71 Skibbereen road. Bedrooms are comfortable and include four-poster and brass beds. There is a lovely sitting room and dining room, and a wide choice is available at breakfast (dinner is available by arrangement). Local amenities include Blue Flag beaches, riding and golf.

Rooms 4 en suite (1 fmly) **Facilities** TVL tea/coffee Dinner available Cen ht Wi-fi Golf 9 ⌕ Fishing Pool table **Parking** 20 **Notes** LB ⊗ Closed Nov-Mar 😊 100 acres beef/dairy/mixed/sheep/horses

Springfield House (W330342)

★★★★ FARMHOUSE

Kilkern, Rathbarry, Castlefreke
☎ 023 8840622 　📠 023 8840622
Mr & Mrs J Callanan
e-mail: jandmcallanan@eircom.net
dir: *N71 from Clonakilty for Skibbereen, 0.5km left after Pike Bar & signed for 5km*

A Georgian-style farmhouse in a picturesque rural setting. Maureen and John Callanan are genuine and welcoming hosts, and their comfortable home has well-appointed bedrooms and lovely gardens. You are welcome to watch the cows being milked. Home cooking is a speciality.

Rooms 4 rms (3 en suite) (2 fmly) **Facilities** TVL TV3B Cen ht **Parking** 8 **Notes** ⊗ Closed 20-27 Dec 😊 130 acres dairy/beef

CORK　　　　　　　　　Map 1 B2

Crawford House

★★★★ GUEST HOUSE

Western Rd
☎ 021 4279000 　📠 021 4279927
e-mail: info@crawfordguesthouse.com
dir: *0.8km from city on N22 Cork-Killarney road, opp University College*

Two adjoining Victorian houses form this friendly guest house, close to the university and city centre. Refurbished in a contemporary style, the bedrooms have refreshing natural colour schemes. The attractive dining room and conservatory overlook a colourful patio. An interesting breakfast menu is available and there is ample secure parking.

Rooms 12 en suite (2 fmly) (2 GF) S €50-€70; D €60-€80 **Facilities** STV tea/coffee Direct Dial Cen ht Wi-fi **Parking** 12 **Notes** ⊗ Closed 22 Dec-15 Jan

Garnish House

★★★★ GUEST HOUSE

1 Aldergrove, Western Rd
☎ 021 4275111 　📠 021 4273872
e-mail: garnish@iol.ie
web: www.garnish.ie
dir: *Opp Cork University College*

A stay in Garnish House is memorable for its carefully appointed rooms, with an optional jacuzzi en suite, and the extensive breakfast menu. Only a five-minute walk to the city centre, and convenient for the ferry and airport, the guest house has 24-hour reception for reservations, departures and late arrivals.

Rooms 21 en suite (4 fmly) (1 GF) (10 smoking) S €50-€85; D €75-€130 **Facilities** STV FTV TVL tea/coffee Direct Dial Cen ht Wi-fi **Parking** 20 **Notes** LB ⊗

Killarney

★★★★ GUEST HOUSE

Western Rd
☎ 021 4270290 　📠 021 4271010
e-mail: killarneyhouse@iol.ie
dir: *On N22 Cork-Killarney opp University College*

Mrs O'Leary is the welcoming owner of this well-equipped guest house, which stands near Cork University and within walking distance of the city centre. The bedrooms are all comfortably furnished and brightly decorated. There is a comfortable lounge, a spacious dining room, and ample parking to the rear of the house. Breakfast is a special treat cooked to order including delicious freshly baked scones and breads.

Rooms 19 en suite (3 fmly) **Facilities** STV TVL tea/coffee Direct Dial Cen ht Wi-fi **Parking** 15 **Notes** ⊗ Closed 24-26 Dec

DURRUS	Map 1 B2

Blairscove House & Restaurant

★ ★ ★ ★ ⑳⑳ RESTAURANT WITH ROOMS

☎ **027 61127** 🖨 **027 61487**

e-mail: mail@blairscove.ie

dir: *From Durrus on R591 towards Crookhaven, 2.4km, house (blue gate) on right*

Blairscove comprises four elegant suites located in the courtyard of a Georgian country house outside the pretty village of Durrus near Bantry; they are individually decorated in a contemporary style and have stunning views over Dunmanus Bay and the mountains. The restaurant is renowned for its wide range of hors d'oeuvres and its open wood-fire grill. The piano playing and candle light add to a unique dining experience.

Rooms 4 annexe en suite (1 fmly) (4 smoking) **Facilities** STV tea/coffee Dinner available Direct Dial Cen ht **Parking** 30 **Notes** ⊗ Closed Nov, Jan & Feb RS Dec wknds only No coaches Civ Wed 20

FERMOY	Map 1 B2

Abbeyville House

★ ★ ★ ★ BED AND BREAKFAST

Abercomby Place

☎ **025 32767** 🖨 **025 32767**

e-mail: info@abbeyvillehouse.com

dir: *N8 (Cork to Dublin road). In town centre across road from town park*

This delightful 19th-century town house is situated on the crossroads of Munster, on the Rosslare to Killarney and Cork to Dublin routes. The smart bedrooms, drawing room and dining room are furnished to a high standard. Guests have complimentary use of the facilities in the Health and Fitness Club in the town park near by.

Rooms 6 en suite (2 fmly) (1 GF) **Facilities** FTV TVL tea/coffee Cen ht Wi-fi ch fac **Parking** 12 **Notes** ⊗ Closed 30 Oct-1 Apr

GOLEEN	Map 1 A1

Heron's Cove

★★★★ ⑳ BED AND BREAKFAST

The Harbour

☎ **028 35225** 🖨 **028 35422**

e-mail: suehill@eircom.net

web: www.heronscove.com

dir: *By harbour in Goleen*

There are charming views of the harbour, fast-flowing stream and inland hills from Heron's Cove, at Ireland's most south-westerly point, near Mizen Head. The restaurant and wine bar is run by chef-patron Sue Hill, where the freshest fish and local produce feature. Bedrooms are comfortable, some with balconies overlooking the harbour.

Rooms 5 en suite (2 fmly) **Facilities** STV tea/coffee Dinner available Direct Dial Cen ht Licensed Wi-fi **Parking** 10 **Notes** ⊗ Closed Xmas & New Year

See advert on this page

Save on B&Bs and Hotels. Book at **theAA.com/hotel**

CO CORK 441 | IRELAND

KINSALE · Map 1 B2

PREMIER COLLECTION

Friar's Lodge

★★★★★ GUEST HOUSE

5 Friars St
☎ 086 2895075 & 021 4777384 📄 021 4774363
e-mail: mtierney@indigo.ie
dir: *In town centre next to parish church*

This new, purpose-built property near the Friary, has been developed with every comfort in mind. Bedrooms are particularly spacious. Located on a quiet street just a short walk from the town centre, with secure parking to the rear. A very good choice is offered from the breakfast menu.

Rooms 18 en suite (2 fmly) (4 GF) **Facilities** STV tea/coffee Direct Dial Cen ht Lift Wi-fi **Parking** 20 **Notes** Closed Xmas ⊛

PREMIER COLLECTION

Old Bank House

★★★★★ GUEST HOUSE

11 Pearse St
☎ 021 4774075 📄 021 4774296
e-mail: info@oldbankhousekinsale.com
dir: *On main road into Kinsale from Cork Airport (R600). House on right at start of Kinsale, next to Post Office*

The Fitzgerald family has restored this delightful Georgian house to its former elegance. The en suite bedrooms, with period furniture and attractive decor, combine charm with modern comforts. Sailing, deep-sea fishing and horse riding can be arranged. Dinner is available at the sister Blue Haven Hotel.

Rooms 17 en suite (3 fmly) **Facilities** STV TVL Direct Dial Cen ht Lift Licensed Wi-fi **Notes** LB ⊛ Closed 23-28 Dec

PREMIER COLLECTION

Rivermount House

★★★★★ BED AND BREAKFAST

Knocknabinny, Barrells Cross
☎ 021 4778033 📄 021 4778225
e-mail: info@rivermount.com
dir: *3km from Kinsale. R600 W towards Old Head of Kinsale, right at Barrells Cross*

There are spectacular views over the Bandon River from this charming modern family home which is close to the Old Head Golf links and Kinsale. The smartly decorated bedrooms are furnished to a high standard with many thoughtful extras. Guests can relax in the contemporary conservatory lounge where an interesting snack menu is available, Claire's breakfast and packed lunches are a speciality.

Rooms 6 en suite (3 fmly) (2 GF) **Facilities** TVL tea/coffee Direct Dial Cen ht Wi-fi **Parking** 10 **Notes** ⊛ Closed Dec-Jan

The White House

★★★★ ⊛ RESTAURANT WITH ROOMS

Pearse St, The Glen
☎ 021 4772125 📄 021 4772045
e-mail: whitehse@indigo.ie
dir: *In town centre*

Centrally located among the narrow, twisting streets of the charming town of Kinsale, this restaurant with rooms dates from 1850, and is a welcoming hostelry with modern, smart, comfortable bedrooms. The bar and bistro are open for lunch and dinner, and the varied menu features local fish and beef. The courtyard makes a perfect setting in summer and there is traditional music in the bar most nights.

Rooms 10 en suite (2 fmly) S €55-€100; D €100-€160* **Facilities** STV tea/coffee Dinner available Direct Dial Cen ht Wi-fi **Notes** LB ⊛ Closed 24-25 Dec

Woodlands House B&B

★★★★ BED AND BREAKFAST

Cappagh
☎ 021 4772633 📄 021 4772649
e-mail: info@woodlandskinsale.com
dir: *R605 NW from Kinsale, pass St Multose's Church, 0.5km on left*

Situated on a height overlooking the town, about a 10-minute walk away on the Bandon road, this new house offers great comfort and the personal attention of Brian and Valerie Hosford. Rooms are individually decorated, some with views towards the harbour. Breakfast is a particular pleasure, featuring home-made breads and preserves. Free Wi-fi is also available.

Rooms 6 en suite (1 fmly) (2 GF) S €50-€80; D €70-€100 **Facilities** FTV TVL tea/coffee Direct Dial Cen ht Wi-fi Golf 18 **Parking** 8 **Notes** ⊛ Closed 16 Nov-Feb

MALLOW · Map 1 B2

Greenfield House B&B

★★★★ BED AND BREAKFAST

Navigation Rd
☎ 022 50231 & 08723 63535
e-mail: greenfieldhouse@hotmail.com
dir: *N20 at Mallow rdbt onto N72 (Killarney road), last house 300mtrs on left*

This purpose built bed and breakfast is situated within walking distance of the centre of Mallow, the railway station and Cork Racecourse. The bedrooms offer good space and are well appointed. There is a cosy guest sitting room and the breakfast menu includes gluten-free and vegetarian dishes as well as the full Irish breakfast. There is ample off-street car parking available.

Rooms 6 en suite (1 GF) S €40-€45; D €60-€70* **Facilities** STV TVL tea/coffee Cen ht Wi-fi **Parking** 10 **Notes** ⊛

SHANAGARRY · Map 1 C2

PREMIER COLLECTION

Ballymaloe House

★★★★★ ⊛⊛ GUEST HOUSE

☎ 021 4652531 📄 021 4652021
e-mail: res@ballymaloe.ie
dir: *From N25 take R630 at Midleton rdbt. After 0.5m, left onto R631 to Cloyne. 2m beyond Cloyne on Ballycotton Rd*

This charming country house is on a 400 acre farm, part of the Geraldine estate in East Cork. Bedrooms upstairs in the main house retain many original features. The ground floor and court yard room feature garden patios. The relaxing drawing room and dining rooms have enchanting old-world charm. Ballymaloe is renowned for excellent meals, many of which are created using ingredients produced on the farm. There are a craft shop, café, tennis and small golf course on the estate.

Rooms 21 en suite 9 annexe en suite (2 fmly) (3 GF) S €85-€110; D €170-€250* **Facilities** TVL Dinner available Direct Dial Cen ht Licensed Wi-fi ↝ ⌣ ⚒ Golf 9 ⚓ Fishing Children's sand pit/slide **Conf** Max 200 Thtr 200 Class 50 Board 50 **Parking** 50 **Notes** LB Closed 23-26 Dec, 8-28 Jan Civ Wed 170

SKIBBEREEN — Map 1 B2

Ilenroy House

★★★ BED AND BREAKFAST

10 North St
☎ 028 22751 & 22193 ▤ 028 23228
e-mail: ilenroyhouse@gmail.com
dir: *90mtrs from main street on N71 (Clonakilty road)*

Conveniently situated in the centre of Skibbereen this well maintained house has comfortable bedrooms that are equipped to a high standard. This is an excellent base from which to tour South West Cork and the Islands.

Rooms 5 en suite (2 smoking) S €35-€45; D €70-€75*
Facilities STV tea/coffee Direct Dial Cen ht **Notes** ⊗

YOUGHAL — Map 1 C2

PREMIER COLLECTION

Ahernes

★★★★★ ⊛ GUEST HOUSE

163 North Main St
☎ 024 92424 ▤ 024 93633
e-mail: ahernes@eircom.net

In the same family since 1923, Ahernes offers a warm welcome, with turf fires and a traditional atmosphere. Spacious bedrooms are furnished to the highest standard and include antiques and modern facilities. There is a restaurant, well known for its daily-changing menu of the freshest seafood specialities, in addition to a cosy drawing room.

Rooms 12 en suite (2 fmly) (3 GF) **Facilities** FTV tea/coffee Dinner available Direct Dial Cen ht Licensed Wi-fi **Conf** Max 20 Thtr 20 Class 20 Board 12 **Parking** 20 **Notes** LB Closed 23-26 Dec

CO DONEGAL

BALLYSHANNON — Map 1 B5

Dún Na Sí

★★★★ GUEST HOUSE

Bundoran Rd
☎ 071 985 2322 & 085 122 2813
e-mail: dun-na-si@oceanfree.net
dir: *0.4km from Ballyshannon on R267*

A smart purpose-built guest house set back from the road and within walking distance of the town. The spacious bedrooms are comfortable and well equipped, and one of the two ground-floor rooms is suitable for the less mobile.

Rooms 7 en suite (2 fmly) (2 GF) S €40-€50; D €60-€80*
Facilities STV tea/coffee Direct Dial Cen ht Wi-fi
Parking 15 **Notes** ⊗

CARRIGANS — Map 1 C5

Mount Royd Country Home

★★★★ ⊜ BED AND BREAKFAST

☎ 074 914 0163 ▤ 074 914 0400
e-mail: jmartin@mountroyd.com
dir: *Off N13/N14 onto R236. A40 from Northern Ireland (Derry City)*

Mount Royd is a creeper-clad house with lovely gardens in the pretty village of Carrigans a short distance from Derry. The friendly Martins have brought hospitality to new heights - nothing is too much trouble for them. Breakfast is a feast of choices including home baking and eggs from their own hens. Bedrooms are very comfortable, with lots of personal touches.

Rooms 4 en suite (1 fmly) (1 GF) S €45; D €65-€70
Facilities FTV TVL tea/coffee Cen ht Wi-fi **Parking** 7
Notes LB ⊗ No Children 12yrs RS Nov-Feb ⊜

DONEGAL — Map 1 B5

The Arches Country House

★★★★ BED AND BREAKFAST

Lough Eske
☎ 074 972 2029
e-mail: archescountryhse@eircom.net
dir: *5km from Donegal. Signed off N15, 300mtrs past garage turn left*

Located on an elevated site overlooking Lough Eske, this fine house is set amid beautifully manicured lawns. Each of the bedrooms shares the spectacular view, as do the breakfast room and comfortable lounge. A warm welcome is assured from the McGinty family.

Rooms 6 en suite (3 fmly) (2 GF) S €50; D €70
Facilities STV FTV TVL tea/coffee Cen ht Wi-fi **Parking** 10
Notes ⊗

Ardeevin

★★★★ BED AND BREAKFAST

Lough Eske, Barnesmore
☎ 074 972 1790 & 0868 229753 ▤ 074 972 1790
e-mail: seanmcginty@eircom.net
dir: *N15 Derry road from Donegal for 5km, left at junct after garage for Ardeevin & Lough Eske & signs for Ardeevin*

Enjoying commanding views over Lough Eske, this is a very comfortable home with individually designed and decorated bedrooms that have many thoughtful additional touches. The varied breakfast is tempting and features Mary McGinty's home baking.

Rooms 6 en suite (2 fmly) (2 GF) S €45-€50; D €65-€70
Facilities STV FTV TVL tea/coffee Cen ht Wi-fi **Parking** 10
Notes ⊗ Closed Dec-mid Mar

Ard Na Breatha

★★★★ ⌂ GUEST HOUSE

Drumrooske Middle
☎ 074 972 2288 & 086 842 1330 ▤ 074 974 0720
e-mail: info@ardnabreatha.com
web: www.ardnabreatha.com
dir: *From town centre onto Killybegs road, 2nd right continue to mini rdbt, sharp right at XL shop*

This family-run guest house is just a short drive from Donegal town centre. Bedrooms are all well-appointed and very comfortable, with a relaxing lounge for residents. Evening meals are served in the popular restaurant at weekends and during high season, but can be arranged for residents at other times. The menu features much of the produce of the family farm which surrounds the house.

Rooms 6 en suite (1 fmly) (3 GF) S €50-€69; D €70-€110
Facilities TVL tea/coffee Dinner available Direct Dial Cen ht Licensed Golf swimming pool & gym available at local hotel **Conf** Thtr 20 Class 30 Board 20 **Parking** 16
Notes LB Closed Nov-Jan

DUNKINEELY — Map 1 B5

Castle Murray House and Restaurant

★★★★ ⊛ RESTAURANT WITH ROOMS

St Johns Point
☎ 074 973 7022 ▤ 074 973 7330
e-mail: info@castlemurray.com
dir: *From Donegal take N56 towards Killybegs. Left to Dunkineely*

Situated on the coast road of St Johns Point, this charming family-run restaurant with rooms overlooks McSwynes Bay and the castle. The bedrooms are individually decorated with guest comfort very much in mind, as is the cosy bar and sun lounge. There is a strong French influence in the cooking; locally landed fish, and prime lamb and beef are featured on the menus. Closed dates are subject to change, please telephone for details.

Rooms 10 en suite (2 fmly) S €50-€65; D €80-€110*
Facilities FTV tea/coffee Dinner available Direct Dial Cen ht Wi-fi ch fac **Parking** 40 **Notes** LB RS Wknds Oct-Mar, 5 days May, Jun & Sep Civ Wed 30

Save on B&Bs and Hotels. Book at **theAA.com/hotel**

DUBLIN 443 IRELAND

DUBLIN

DUBLIN	Map 1 D4

PREMIER COLLECTION

Butlers Town House

★★★★★ GUEST HOUSE

44 Lansdowne Rd, Ballsbridge
☎ 01 6674022 📠 01 6673960
e-mail: reservations@butlers-hotel.com

This fine Victorian house, in the heart of Dublin's Embassy belt, has been restored and retains the charm of a gracious family home. Bedrooms are air-conditioned and individually furnished and decorated. The public areas are particularly relaxing and there is a charming and comfortable drawing room and conservatory style breakfast room. Limited off-street parking is available.

Rooms 20 en suite **Facilities** STV FTV Direct Dial Licensed Wi-fi **Parking** 14 **Notes** ⊗ Closed 22-28 Dec

PREMIER COLLECTION

Glenogra Town House

★★★★★ GUEST HOUSE

64 Merrion Rd, Ballsbridge
☎ 01 6683661 📠 01 6683698
e-mail: info@glenogra.com
web: www.glenogra.com
dir: *Opp Royal Dublin Showgrounds & Four Seasons Hotel*

This fine 19th-century red brick house is situated across from the RDS and close to the Aviva Stadium. The bedrooms are comfortably appointed and include many thoughtful extras; three bedrooms are on the ground floor. There is an elegant drawing room and dining room, and the interesting breakfast menu offers a range of dishes. Secure parking is available, and The Aircoach and city-centre buses stop in Merrion Road; the DART rail is around the corner.

Rooms 13 en suite (1 fmly) (3 GF) S €59-€99; D €89-€199* **Facilities** STV TVL tea/coffee Direct Dial Cen ht Wi-fi **Parking** 10 **Notes** LB ⊗ Closed 23-28 Dec

PREMIER COLLECTION

Harrington Hall

★★★★★ GUEST HOUSE

69-70 Harcourt St
☎ 01 4753497 📠 01 4754544
e-mail: harringtonhall@eircom.net
web: www.harringtonhall.com
dir: *St Stephens Green via O'Connell St, in Earlsfort Ter pass National Concert Hall & right onto Hatch St, right onto Harcourt St*

This restored Georgian house is on a one-way street system, just off the south west corner of St Stephen's Green in the centre of the city. The spacious bedrooms are well appointed and include comfortable suites. A lovely plasterwork ceiling adorns the relaxing drawing room. An extensive breakfast menu is served in the basement dining room. A lift, porter service and limited off-street parking is available.

Rooms 28 en suite (3 fmly) (3 GF) **Facilities** STV tea/coffee Direct Dial Cen ht Lift **Conf** Max 20 Thtr 20 Class 6 Board 12 **Parking** 8 **Notes** ⊗

Charleville Lodge

★★★★ GUEST HOUSE

268/272 North Circular Rd, Phibsborough
☎ 01 8386633 📠 01 8385854
e-mail: info@charlevillelodge.ie
web: www.charlevillelodge.ie
dir: *N from O'Connell St to Phibsborough, left fork at St Peter's Church, house 250mtrs on left*

Situated close to the city centre near Phoenix Park, this elegant terrace of Victorian houses has been restored to a high standard. The two interconnecting lounges are welcoming, and the smart dining room offers a choice of breakfasts. Bedrooms are very comfortable with pleasant decor, and there is a secure car park.

Rooms 30 en suite (2 fmly) (4 GF) S €30-€90; D €35-€95 (room only) **Facilities** STV FTV TVL Direct Dial Cen ht Licensed Wi-fi Golf 18 **Conf** Max 10 Thtr 10 Class 10 Board 10 **Parking** 18 **Notes** LB ⊗ Closed 21-26 Dec

Glenshandan Lodge

★★★★ GUEST ACCOMMODATION

Dublin Rd, Swords
☎ 01 8408838 & 08765 92114 📠 01 8408838
e-mail: glenshandan@eircom.net
dir: *Beside Topaz on airport side of Swords Main St*

Glenshandan Lodge is a family and dog-friendly house with hospitable owners and good facilities including e-mail access. Bedrooms are comfortable and one room has easier access. Secure parking available. Close to pubs, restaurants, golf, airport and the Kennel Club.

Rooms 9 en suite (5 fmly) (5 GF) S €25-€40; D €45-€60 (room only)* **Facilities** FTV TVL tea/coffee Cen ht Wi-fi ch fac Golf 36 **Conf** Max 20 **Parking** 10 **Notes** LB Closed Xmas & New Year

Airport Tirconaill B&B

★★★ BED AND BREAKFAST

2 Longlands, Malahide Rd
☎ 01 8407962 & 087 2384705
e-mail: patriciamariaduffy@eircom.net
dir: *From M1 exit onto R125 to Swords (from N), at Malahide Rd rdbt take exit towards Pavilion shopping centre. At rdbt take 2nd exit, establishment in 100yds*

Located in Swords town centre, a short drive from Dublin Airport, this house is perfect for visitors enjoying their last night of a holiday. The town has many restaurants and atmospheric pubs. The recently refurbished cosy bedrooms all have en suite shower rooms and complimentary Wi-fi. Guests are welcome to use the relaxing lounge, and ample car parking is provided to the rear.

Rooms 4 en suite (3 fmly) (1 GF) S €40-€45; D €60-€70* **Facilities** FTV tea/coffee Cen ht Wi-fi ch fac Golf 18 **Parking** 10 **Notes** ⊗ Closed 23 Dec-7 Jan

DUBLIN *continued*

Ardagh House

★★★ GUEST HOUSE

1 Highfield Rd, Rathgar
☎ 01 4977068 📄 01 4973991
e-mail: enquiries@ardahouse.com
dir: *S of city centre through Rathmines*

Ardagh House is an early 19th-century house with modern additions, and stands in a premier residential area on the outskirts of the city close to local restaurants and pubs. It retains many original features and has a relaxing lounge that overlooks a delightful garden. There is an attractive dining room where hearty breakfasts are served at the individual tables. The comfortable bedrooms vary in size. Ample off-street parking is available.

Rooms 19 en suite (4 fmly) (1 GF) S €60-€95; D €70-€150 **Facilities** FTV TVL tea/coffee Direct Dial Cen ht Wi-fi **Parking** 20 **Notes** ⊗ Closed 22 Dec-3 Jan

Leeson Bridge Guest House

★★★ GUEST HOUSE

1 Upper Leeson St
☎ 01 6681000 & 6682255 📄 01 6681444
e-mail: info@leesonbridgehouse.ie
dir: *At junct of N11 & N7, Leeson St*

This guest house is located right by Leeson Street Bridge, close to the city centre and easily accessible from the ferry ports. Centred around a Georgian house, many of its original architectural features are retained. It offers a range of en suite bedroom styles, some with spa baths, sauna or galley kitchenette. Residents have access to ample car parking at the rear. A take-away breakfast is offered to early morning departing guests.

Rooms 20 en suite (1 fmly) (2 GF) (10 smoking) **Facilities** STV FTV TVL tea/coffee Direct Dial Cen ht Lift Wi-fi Fishing **Parking** 18 **Notes** ⊗

RUSH   Map 1 D4

Sandyhills Bed & Breakfast

★★★★ 🛏 BED AND BREAKFAST

Sandyhills
☎ 01 8437148 & 086 242 3660 📄 01 8437148
e-mail: mary@sandyhills.ie
dir: *Exit M1 onto N1, right to Lusk on R127. 3rd exit at rdbt in Lusk to Rush. Right towards church car park, right to Corrs Ln, then 2nd right*

Set just a stroll from the sea and the village of Rush, within easy reach of Dublin Airport, Sandyhills has spacious bedrooms, well equipped with thoughtful extra facilities. Breakfast is a special treat featuring local produce along with Mary Buckley's preserves, freshly baked cakes and breads. There is a cosy sitting room and a lovely garden with secure car parking.

Rooms 5 en suite (2 fmly) **Facilities** Direct Dial Cen ht Wi-fi **Parking** 20 **Notes** ⊗ No Children 12yrs

CLIFDEN   Map 1 A4

Ardmore House (*L589523*)

★★★★ FARMHOUSE

Sky Rd
☎ 095 21221 & 076 6030227
Mr & Mrs J Mullen
e-mail: info@ardmore-house.com
web: www.ardmore-house.com
dir: *5km W of Clifden. From Clifden signs for Sky Rd, pass bank onto the Abbey Glen Castle, house signed*

Ardmore is set among the wild scenery of Connemara between hills and the sea on the Sky Road. Bedrooms are attractively decorated and the house is very comfortable throughout. A pathway leads from the house to the coast. A good hearty breakfast is provided featuring Kathy's home baking.

Rooms 6 en suite (3 fmly) (6 GF) S €40-€60; D €70-€80* **Facilities** STV FTV TVL tea/coffee Cen ht Wi-fi **Parking** 8 **Notes** LB ⊗ Closed Oct-Mar 🔌 25 acres non-working

Faul House (*L650475*)

★★★★ FARMHOUSE

Ballyconneely Rd
☎ 095 21239 📄 095 21998
Mrs K Conneely
e-mail: info@ireland.com
dir: *1.5km from town right at rugby pitch signed Rockglen Hotel*

A fine modern farmhouse stands on a quiet and secluded road overlooking Clifden Bay. It is smart and comfortable with large bedrooms, all well furnished and with good views. Kathleen offers a hearty breakfast with home baking. There are Connemara ponies available for trekking.

Rooms 6 en suite (3 fmly) (3 GF) S €40-€50; D €70-€80* **Facilities** FTV TVL tea/coffee Cen ht Wi-fi **Parking** 10 **Notes** Closed Nov-26 Mar 🔌 35 acres sheep/ponies/hens/ducks

Mallmore House

★★★★ BED AND BREAKFAST

Ballyconneely Rd
☎ 095 21460
e-mail: info@mallmore.com
dir: *1.5km from Clifden towards Ballyconneely take 1st right*

A charming Georgian-style house built in the 17th century set in fourteen hectares of woodland overlooking Clifden Bay, close to the Rock Glen Hotel. Alan and Kathy Hardman have restored the house with parquet flooring and some favourite antiques, while turf fires provide warmth and atmosphere.

Rooms 6 en suite (2 fmly) (6 GF) D €60-€80 **Facilities** FTV tea/coffee Cen ht Wi-fi **Parking** 15 **Notes** ⊗ Closed Nov-1 Mar 🔌

Ben View House

★★★ GUEST HOUSE

Bridge St
☎ 095 21256 📄 095 21226
e-mail: benviewhouse@ireland.com
dir: *Enter town on N59, opp Esso fuel station*

This house is well located in the centre of the town with ample on-street parking. Dating from 1824, it offers good quality accommodation at a moderate cost. The breakfast room and lounge feature an old world atmosphere, with antique furniture and sparkling silverware in everyday use.

Rooms 10 rms (9 en suite) (3 fmly) **Facilities** TVL TV9B tea/coffee Cen ht **Notes** ⊗

Save on B&Bs and Hotels. Book at **theAA.com/hotel**

CO GALWAY – CO KERRY 445 IRELAND

GALWAY
Map 1 B3

Marian Lodge
★★★ GUEST HOUSE

Knocknacarra Rd, Salthill Upper
☎ 091 521678 ▤ 091 528103
e-mail: celine@iol.ie
dir: From Galway to Salthill on R336, through Salthill, 1st
right after Spinnaker Hotel onto Knocknacarra Rd

This large modern house is only 50 metres from the
seafront. The fully equipped bedrooms have orthopaedic
beds and en suite facilities. There is also a lounge and
separate breakfast room available.

Rooms 6 en suite (4 fmly) Facilities STV TVL tea/coffee
Direct Dial Cen ht Parking 10 Notes ⊗ No Children 3yrs
Closed 23-28 Dec

Clochard Bed & Breakfast
★★★ BED AND BREAKFAST

Spires Gardens, Shantalla Rd
☎ 091 521533 & 086 0523132 ▤ 091 522536
e-mail: clochard@eircom.net
dir: N59 Galway ring road, after Quincentennial Bridge,
left at 4th set of lights & right onto Shantalla Rd. Spires
Gdns opp school

Clochard is part of a small development in the Galway
City Council award-winning Spires Gardens which is
located within walking distance from the Galway
University College and Hospital and close to the city
centre and Salthill. Bedrooms, guest sitting and dining
room are attractively decorated and comfortably
furnished. Freshly baked scones and barm brack loaf are
included with a substantial breakfast. Guests can be
dropped off at the shuttle bus for the Aran Island Ferry
and routes for day trips are organised with maps supplied
by the Hanlon family.

Rooms 4 en suite (2 fmly) (1 GF) D €60-€86
Facilities FTV TVL tea/coffee Cen ht Wi-fi Parking 4
Notes LB ⊗ No Children Closed Dec-Feb

SPIDDAL (AN SPIDÉAL)
Map 1 B3

Ardmor Country House
★★★★ BED AND BREAKFAST

Greenhill
☎ 091 553145
e-mail: ardmorcountryhouse@yahoo.com
dir: On R336 (coast road) from Galway, 1km W of Spiddal

There are superb views of Galway Bay and the Aran
Islands from this beautifully appointed luxury home.
Bedrooms are spacious and there are relaxing lounges, a
well-stocked library and delightful gardens.

Rooms 5 en suite (2 fmly) (5 GF) S €40-€50; D €70-€76*
Facilities TVL tea/coffee Cen ht Wi-fi ch fac Parking 20
Notes ⊗ Closed Dec-Feb RS Mar-Nov 🐾

Ard Aoibhinn
★★★ BED AND BREAKFAST

☎ 091 553179
e-mail: aoibhinn@gofree.indigo.ie
dir: 500mtrs W of Spiddal village on right hand side of
R336 Coast road

This long established bed and breakfast is a modern
bungalow set back from the road in a lovely garden. It is
just a five minute walk from the Gaeltacht village (Irish
language speaking area) of An Spidéal. It has benefited
from a recent renovation and refurbishment programme.
The lounge features a picture window with panoramic
views of Galway Bay towards the Aran Islands. Bedrooms
are well appointed and comfortable, with beverage
making facilities. This is an ideal base for touring
Connemara or a day trip to the islands.

Rooms 5 en suite (1 fmly) (5 GF) D €60-€70*
Facilities FTV TVL tea/coffee Cen ht Wi-fi Parking 5
Notes LB ⊗ Closed Xmas wk

CO KERRY

CASTLEGREGORY
Map 1 A2

Sea-Mount House
★★★★ BED AND BREAKFAST

Cappatigue, Conor Pass Rd
☎ 066 7139229 ▤ 066 7139229
e-mail: seamount@unison.ie
web: www.seamounthouse.com
dir: N86 from Tralee for 15km, at Camp take R560 for
15km, establishment 1.5km past Stradbally village

Located on the Conor Pass road between Tralee and
Dingle, this friendly house has great views of Brandon
Bay. It is a good base for exploring the Dingle Peninsula.
The cosy sitting areas and bedrooms make the most of
the views, a great way to enjoy home baking and welcome
tea on arrival.

Rooms 2 en suite (1 GF) Facilities TVL tea/coffee Cen ht
Wi-fi Parking 5 Notes LB ⊗ No Children 6yrs Closed Nov-
Feb

Griffin's Palm Beach Country House (Q525085)
★★★ FARMHOUSE

Goulane, Conor Pass Rd
☎ 066 7139147 & 0872 111901
Mrs C Griffin
e-mail: griffinspalmbeach@eircom.net
dir: 1.5km from Stradbally

This farmhouse is a good base for exploring the Dingle
Peninsula and unspoiled beaches. The comfortable
bedrooms have fine views over Brandon Bay, and the
delightful garden can be enjoyed from the dining room
and sitting room. Mrs Griffin offers a warm welcome and
her home baking is a feature on the breakfast menu.

Rooms 6 en suite (3 fmly) (1 GF) S €40-€45; D €70-€80*
Facilities FTV TVL TV5B tea/coffee Cen ht ch fac Golf 9
Parking 10 Notes LB Closed Nov-Feb 150 acres mixed/
arable/sheep

DINGLE (AN DAINGEAN)
Map 1 A2

PREMIER COLLECTION

Emlagh House
★★★★★ GUEST ACCOMMODATION

☎ 066 9152345 ▤ 066 9152369
e-mail: info@emlaghhouse.com
web: www.emlaghhouse.com
dir: Pass rdbt at entrance to town, turn left. House
ahead

An impressive Georgian-style house, on the outskirts of
Dingle, where attention to detail and luxury combine to
make a stay memorable. The stylish drawing room,
conservatory and dining room overlook the harbour.
Bedrooms and bathrooms are individually decorated to
a high standard with antique furniture, with ground
floor rooms having private patios. Breakfasts are very
special here and make good use of fresh local produce.

Rooms 10 en suite (1 fmly) (4 GF) S €95-€125; D
€130-€210 Facilities STV Direct Dial Cen ht Lift
Licensed Wi-fi Golf 18 Parking 20 Notes LB ⊗ No
Children 8yrs Closed 5 Nov-10 Mar Civ Wed 35

DINGLE (AN DAINGEAN) *continued*

PREMIER COLLECTION

Gormans Clifftop House & Restaurant

★★★★★ ⊛ GUEST HOUSE

Glaise Bheag, Ballydavid
☎ 066 9155162 & 083 0033133 📄 066 9155003
e-mail: info@gormans-clifftophouse.com
dir: *R559 to An Mhuirioch, turn right at T-junct, N for 3km*

Sile and Vincent Gorman's guest house and restaurant is perched over the cliffs on the western tip of the Slea Head Peninsula near Ballydavid village. The beauty of the rugged coastline, rhythm of the sea and the sun going down on Smerwick Harbour can be enjoyed over a delicious dinner in the smart dining room. The menu includes produce from the garden, local seafood and lamb. Bedrooms are comfortably proportioned and thoughtfully equipped and have breathtaking views of the ocean or mountains, the ground floor rooms are adapted for the less mobile. Bracing cliff walks can be accessed across from the house. Gormans is the AA's Guest Accommodation of the Year for Ireland (2011-2012).

Rooms 8 en suite (2 fmly) (4 GF) S €75-€95; D €100-€150* **Facilities** tea/coffee Dinner available Direct Dial Cen ht Licensed Wi-fi Bicycles for hire **Parking** 15 **Notes** LB ⊗ Closed 24-26 Dec RS Oct-Mar reservation only Civ Wed 25

An Bothar Pub

★★★ GUEST HOUSE

Cuas, Ballydavid
☎ 066 9155342
e-mail: botharpub@eircom.net

This traditional guest house and pub is located close to the town of Dingle on the Slea Head Drive at the foot of Mount Brandon. The Walsh family has been welcoming guests for three generations and the pub is famous for music and dancing. Fresh fish, their own farm produce and home baking are included on the daily menu. Walking, cycling, horse riding, golf, swimming, and windsurfing are all locally available activities. The comfortable bedrooms are attractively decorated and furnished, some suitable for families.

Rooms 7 en suite (2 fmly) S €40-€50; D €70-€80* **Facilities** STV FTV TVL Dinner available Direct Dial Cen ht Licensed Pool table **Parking** 30 **Notes** ⊗ Closed 24-25 Dec RS Oct-Mar No evening meals available

Barr Na Sraide Inn

★★★ GUEST HOUSE

Upper Main St
☎ 066 9151331 & 9151446 📄 066 9151446
e-mail: barrnasraide@eircom.net

Barr na Sraide Inn is a family-run guest house, which has its very own traditional pub on site and free car parking at the rear. It is situated in the heart of Dingle town and just a stroll from many restaurants, traditional music venues and shops. The en suite bedrooms are attractively decorated and comfortably furnished. There is a cosy guest sitting room and a hearty breakfast can be chosen from the breakfast menu which includes Patricia's home-baked breads.

Rooms 26 en suite (7 fmly) (4 GF) S €40-€55; D €70-€100* **Facilities** STV FTV TVL Direct Dial Cen ht Licensed Wi-fi Golf 18 **Parking** 18 **Notes** ⊗ Closed 19-25 Dec

Hurleys *(Q392080)*

★★★ FARMHOUSE

An Dooneen, Kilcooley
☎ 066 9155112 & 0862 142580
Ms Hurley
e-mail: andooneen@eircom.net
dir: *11km W of Dingle town on Ballydavid-Muirioch road*

Hurleys Farm is tucked away behind the church in Kilcooley, 1.5 kilometres from the beach and sheltered by Mount Brandon, a popular place for hill walkers. Accommodation includes a cosy TV room, dining room and comfortable en suite bedrooms, graced by some special pieces of high quality furniture. The whole area is rich in early historic and prehistoric relics: ogham stones, ring forts and the famous dry-stone masonry 'beehive' huts.

Rooms 4 en suite (2 GF) S €45-€55; D €70-€85* **Facilities** TVL Cen ht **Parking** 6 **Notes** LB ⊗ Closed Nov-Mar ⊕ 38 acres non-working

GLENBEIGH

Map 1 A2

Mountain View

★★★ BED AND BREAKFAST

Droum West
☎ 066 9768541 & 087 6241658 📄 066 9768541
e-mail: mountainstage@eircom.net
dir: *4km W of Glenbeigh, 200mtrs off N70*

The O'Riordan's bed and breakfast is an ideal place to stay when touring the Ring of Kerry; it is located just off the N70 road between Glenbeigh and Kells. There is a lovely large garden and ample car parking. The bedrooms are well appointed, three of them are on the ground floor and there are spacious rooms to accommodate families. There are lovely views of the mountains from the comfortable guest sitting room and Anne serves a substantial breakfast.

Rooms 4 en suite (4 fmly) (3 GF) S €40-€45; D €60-€70 **Facilities** STV FTV TVL Dinner available Cen ht Wi-fi ch fac **Parking** 8 **Notes** LB ⊗ Closed Nov-Feb RS Mar

KENMARE

Map 1 B2

Shelburne Lodge

★★★★ ⌂ GUEST HOUSE

Cork Rd
☎ 064 6641013 📄 064 6642135
e-mail: shelburnekenmare@eircom.net
dir: *On Cork road (R569), 500mtrs from Kenmare centre*

Dating from the mid 18th century, this long established guest house is well deserving of its reputation. Located within easy walking distance of the town, it offers a range of individually decorated bedrooms, together with reception rooms that ooze comfort and relaxation. Breakfast is a highlight of a stay, with a wide selection of fruits, preserves and home bakery, complementing a menu of cooked items that feature carefully selected local and artisan foods.

Rooms 8 en suite 2 annexe en suite (1 fmly) S €75-€100; D €100-€160 **Facilities** STV Direct Dial Cen ht Wi-fi ⌂ **Parking** 20 **Notes** ⊗ Closed 16 Nov-15 Mar

Davitts

★★★ GUEST HOUSE

Henry St
☎ 064 6642741   📠 064 6642757
e-mail: info@davitts-kenmare.com
dir: *On N22 (Cork-Killarney rd) at Kenmare junct (R569). In town centre*

This family-run guest house is situated in the centre of the heritage town of Kenmare. With the popular Davitts Bar Bistro at street level serving excellent food, it is the perfect location for an enjoyable holiday all under the one roof. The spacious, well-appointed bedrooms are decorated in a contemporary style, and there is a cosy sitting room on the first floor.

Rooms 11 en suite (1 fmly) **Facilities** STV TVL Dinner available Direct Dial Cen ht Licensed Wi-fi **Parking** 4 **Notes** ⊗ Closed 1-14 Nov & 24-26 Dec

Harbour View

★★★★ BED AND BREAKFAST

Castletownbere Rd, Dauros
☎ 064 6641755   & 087 7684564
e-mail: maureenmccarthy@eircom.net
dir: *From Kenmare towards Glengarriffe, onto Castletownbere Haven road (571), 1st right after bridge. Harbour View 6.5km on left on seashore*

This charming house is situated on the seashore, with lovely views of Kenmare Bay and the mountains beyond. Maureen McCarthy is a cheerful, caring hostess with infectious enthusiasm, and her attention to detail is evident throughout the comfortable bedrooms. The breakfast menu includes fresh and smoked seafood and the home baking is excellent.

Rooms 4 en suite (1 fmly) (4 GF) S €60-€65; D €90 **Facilities** STV TVL tea/coffee Cen ht Wi-fi **Parking** 6 **Notes** ⊗ Closed Oct-Apr 🍴

Kenmare House B&B

★★★★ BED AND BREAKFAST

Sneem Rd
☎ 064 6641283   📠 064 6642765
e-mail: info@kenmarehousebandb.com
dir: *500mtrs from town centre, turn left onto N70 towards Sneem on the Ring of Kerry. 400mtrs on right*

Annagry House is owned and run by the O'Sullivan family; it is situated on the Ring of Kerry road (N70) only minutes from Kenmare town. Bedrooms are spacious and comfortably furnished to accommodate families and there are two ground floor rooms. The relaxing guest sitting room has books, maps and information on the area. The extensive breakfast menu includes Fionnuala's home baking, and Danny will advise on tours and activities available

Rooms 6 en suite (3 fmly) (2 GF) **Facilities** FTV TVL tea/coffee Cen ht Wi-fi **Parking** 11 **Notes** ⊗ Closed 26 Oct-Apr 🍴

Sea Shore Farm Guest House

★★★★ GUEST HOUSE

Tubrid
☎ 064 6641270   & 6641675   📠 064 6641270
e-mail: seashore@eircom.net
dir: *1.6km from Kenmare off N70 Ring of Kerry road. Signed at junct N70 & N71*

Overlooking Kenmare Bay on the Ring of Kerry road, this modern farm guest house is close to town and has spacious bedrooms. Ground-floor rooms open onto the patio and have easier access. Guests are welcome to enjoy the farm walks through the fields to the shore, and salmon and trout fishing on the Roughty River. There is a comfortable sitting room and dining room and a delightful garden.

Rooms 6 en suite (2 fmly) (2 GF) S €60-€90; D €90-€120* **Facilities** FTV tea/coffee Direct Dial Cen ht Wi-fi **Parking** 10 **Notes** ⊗ Closed Nov-19 Mar

The Caha's

★★★ BED AND BREAKFAST

Hospital Rd
☎ 064 6641271   & 086 0723590   📠 064 6641271
e-mail: osheacahas@eircom.net
dir: *Pass church & shopping centre, take left at next junct, 200mtrs on left*

This charming family home is situated in a peaceful residential area and within walking distance of the town centre. Home baking and local produce feature on Eilish O'Shea's delicious breakfast menu. The bedrooms are comfortably furnished and there are two ground floor rooms. The combined dining/sitting room overlooks the lovely colourful garden and there is ample off-street car or bicycle parking. An ideal location for touring the Ring of Kerry, Ring of Beara and The Kerry Way.

Rooms 4 en suite (2 fmly) (2 GF) S €40-€50; D €60-€80* **Facilities** STV TVL tea/coffee Cen ht Wi-fi **Parking** 4 **Notes** ⊗ Closed Nov-1 Apr 🍴

Muxnaw Lodge

[U]

Casletownbere Rd
☎ 064 6641252
e-mail: muxnaw@eircom.net

Currently the rating for this establishment is not confirmed. This may be due to a change of ownership or because it has only recently joined the AA rating scheme.

Rooms 5 en suite (1 fmly) **Facilities** STV TVL tea/coffee Cen ht Wi-fi 🛶 **Parking** 5 **Notes** ⊗ Closed 24-25 Dec 🍴

KILGARVAN   Map 1 B2

Birchwood

★★★★ BED AND BREAKFAST

Church Ground
☎ 064 6685473   📠 064 6685570
e-mail: birchwood1@eircom.net
dir: *500mtrs E of Kilgarvan on R569*

Birchwood stands in extensive gardens facing a natural forest and backed by the Mangerton Mountains, an area ideal for hill-walking and touring. The MacDonnells are caring hosts in this tranquil location, and offer comfortable and attractively decorated bedrooms. The nearby Rivers Roughty and Slaheny provide good salmon and trout fishing.

Rooms 5 en suite (3 fmly) **Facilities** FTV TVL tea/coffee Cen ht **Parking** 6 **Notes** ⊗ 🍴

KILLARNEY   Map 1 B2

PREMIER COLLECTION

Fairview

★★★★★ 🏠 GUEST HOUSE

College St
☎ 064 6634164   📄 064 6671777
e-mail: info@fairviewkillarney.com
dir: *In town centre off College St*

This smart guest house is situated in the town centre and close to the bus/railway station. Great attention to detail has been taken in the furnishing and design of bedrooms to ensure guest comfort including some with air conditioning and jacuzzi baths. There is a lift to all floors and the impressive penthouse suite enjoys views of the mountains. There is a relaxing guest sitting room and the breakfast menu offers a selection of dishes cooked to order. Local activities include lake cruises, Killarney National Park and championship golf courses.

Rooms 29 en suite (1 GF) (2 smoking) **Facilities** STV TVL tea/coffee Dinner available Direct Dial Cen ht Lift Licensed Wi-fi Jacuzzi suites available **Parking** 11

PREMIER COLLECTION

Foleys Town House

★★★★★ 🍽 GUEST HOUSE

22/23 High St
☎ 064 6631217   📄 064 6634683
e-mail: info@foleystownhouse.com
dir: *In town centre*

Charming, individually-designed bedrooms are a feature of this well-established house, which has good parking facilities and a comfortable lounge. Family owned and run by Carol Hartnett who is also the chef in the adjoining restaurant that specialises in seafood.

Rooms 28 en suite **Facilities** STV TVL tea/coffee Dinner available Direct Dial Cen ht Lift Licensed Wi-fi **Parking** 60 **Notes** LB ⊗ Closed 6 Nov-16 Mar

PREMIER COLLECTION

Old Weir Lodge

★★★★★ GUEST HOUSE

Muckross Rd
☎ 064 6635593   📄 064 6635583
e-mail: oldweirlodge@eircom.net
web: www.oldweirlodge.com
dir: *On N71 (Muckross Rd), 500mtrs from Killarney*

This purpose-built Tudor-style guest house is situated within walking distance of the town. There are comfortable lounges and the dining room is a lovely bright room with a conservatory that overlooks the garden. The comfortable bedrooms are equipped to a high standard. A varied range of tasty options is available at breakfast including Maureen's freshly baked breads. Dermot will help with boat trips on the Killarney Lakes, golf, fishing and walking tours. There is also a drying room and ample off-road parking.

Rooms 30 en suite (2 fmly) (6 GF) S €50-€70; D €70-€120 **Facilities** STV TVL tea/coffee Dinner available Direct Dial Cen ht Lift Licensed Wi-fi Golf 18 **Parking** 30 **Notes** ⊗ Closed 23-26 Dec

Ashville House

★★★★ GUEST HOUSE

Rock Rd
☎ 064 6636405   📄 064 6636778
e-mail: info@ashvillekillarney.com
dir: *In town centre. Off N end of High St onto Rock Rd*

This inviting house is just a stroll from the town centre and near the N22 (Tralee road). Bedrooms are comfortably furnished, and there is a pleasant sitting room and dining room. There is a private car park, and tours can be arranged.

Rooms 12 en suite (4 fmly) (4 GF) S €50-€100; D €70-€110 **Facilities** STV FTV TVL tea/coffee Direct Dial Cen ht Wi-fi **Parking** 13 **Notes** LB ⊗ Closed Nov-1 Mar

Killarney Villa Country House & Gardens

★★★★ BED AND BREAKFAST

Mallow Rd
☎ 064 6631878   📄 064 6631878
e-mail: killarneyvilla@ie-post.com
web: www.killarneyvilla.com
dir: *N22 E from Killarney, over 1st rdbt, continue after 2nd rdbt on N22 & N72 for 2km, left at rdbt onto Mallow Rd, Villa 300mtrs on right*

This luxurious country home has a rooftop conservatory where complimentary beverages are available. It is situated on the outskirts of the town within easy reach of the beautiful Killarney lakes and mountains. Bedrooms are very comfortable and well equipped, and there is a lovely dining room where a variety of dishes are available at breakfast.

Rooms 6 en suite (3 fmly) (1 GF) S €35-€40; D €60-€70 **Facilities** STV TVL tea/coffee Cen ht Wi-fi **Parking** 20 **Notes** LB ⊗ No Children 6yrs Closed Nov-Apr

Kingfisher Lodge

★★★★ GUEST HOUSE

Lewis Rd
☎ 064 6637131   📄 064 6639871
e-mail: info@kingfisherlodgekillarney.com
dir: *Dublin link straight through 1st rdbt. Right at next rdbt towards town centre, Lodge on left*

This welcoming, family-run modern guest house, situated within walking distance of the town centre, has comfortable well-appointed bedrooms. A delicious breakfast is served in the attractively decorated dining room and there is also a relaxing lounge. A drying room is available for fishing and wet gear. Golf, walking and fishing trips can be arranged.

Rooms 10 en suite (1 fmly) (2 GF) D €60-€110* **Facilities** STV FTV TVL tea/coffee Direct Dial Cen ht Wi-fi Golf 18 Walking, fishing, horseriding, golf can be booked **Parking** 11 **Notes** LB Closed 15 Dec-13 Feb

Shraheen House

★★★★ BED AND BREAKFAST

Ballycasheen, Off Cork Rd (N22)
☎ 064 6631286
e-mail: info@shraheenhouse.com
dir: *On Ballycasheen-Woodlawn road, 1.6km off N71 at lights by Dromhall Hotel. Off N22 at Whitebridge Caravan Park Sign*

The large modern house stands in extensive grounds on a quiet road. The bedrooms are all well equipped and have attractive soft furnishings. The quiet gardens and the pleasant sun lounge are very relaxing. Within easy reach of three golf courses or local fishing.

Rooms 6 en suite (2 fmly) (3 GF) **Facilities** STV TVL tea/coffee Cen ht Wi-fi **Parking** 8 **Notes** ⊗ No Children 4yrs Closed Dec-Jan 🍴

KILLORGLIN
Map 1 A2

PREMIER COLLECTION

Carrig House Country House & Restaurant

★★★★★ ◉ ⌂ GUEST HOUSE

Caragh Lake
☎ 066 9769100 ▤ 066 9769166
e-mail: info@carrighouse.com

The hospitality shown by hosts Mary and Frank Slattery and their team make a visit to Carrig House a memorable event. The house has a range of relaxing lounges and individually decorated, spacious bedrooms; those on the ground floor benefit from garden patios. Country-house cooking can be enjoyed in the dining room which has splendid views of the delightful garden and beyond to Caragh Lake and the mountains.

Rooms 16 en suite **Facilities** TVL Dinner available Direct Dial Cen ht Licensed ⌕ Fishing **Parking** 20 **Notes** No Children 8yrs Closed Oct-Feb

Grove Lodge

★★★ GUEST HOUSE

Killarney Rd
☎ 066 9761157 & 08720 73238 ▤ 066 9762726
-mail: info@grovelodge.com
dir: 800mtrs from Killorglin Bridge on N72 (Killarney road)

lovely riverside house extended and developed to a high standard, with all the rooms en suite and fully equipped. Mrs Foley is an enthusiastic host who likes to please her guests and for those who just want to relax there is a patio seating area in the garden by the river.

Rooms 10 en suite (4 fmly) (4 GF) **Facilities** STV FTV tea/coffee Direct Dial Cen ht Wi-fi Fishing **Parking** 15 **Notes** ⊗ Closed 22-30 Dec

O'Regan's Country Home & Gardens

★★★★ BED AND BREAKFAST

Gansha
☎ 066 9761200 & 087 8651333 ▤ 066 9761200
-mail: jeromeoregan@eircom.net
dir: 1.6km from Killorglin on N70, turn right at sign for An Bainseach

The O'Regan family have been welcoming guests to their family home for many years, with some returning regularly. Set in beautifully kept gardens overlooking the Kerry Mountains, the house is particularly comfortable and welcoming. The lounge and breakfast room overlook the gardens. The bedrooms have benefited from refurbishment and are well appointed. Breakfast features a wide selection, including Christina's delicious home baking.

Rooms 4 en suite (1 fmly) (4 GF) **Facilities** TVL tea/coffee Cen ht Wi-fi Golf 18 **Parking** 8 **Notes** ⊗ Closed Nov-Feb

Torine House

Ⓤ

Sunhill Rd
☎ 066 9761352 & 087 9297329 ▤ 066 9761352
e-mail: torinehouse@eircom.net
dir: Entering town from Tralee at rdbt take Sunhill Rd to top of hill. 1st right, 3rd house on left

Currently the rating for this establishment is not confirmed. This may be due to a change of ownership or because it has only recently joined the AA rating scheme.

Rooms 6 rms (5 en suite) (1 pri facs) (3 fmly) (4 GF) S €30; D €54* **Facilities** FTV TVL tea/coffee Dinner available Cen ht Wi-fi Golf 18 **Parking** 20 **Notes** LB ⊗ No Children 5yrs Closed Dec-Feb

TRALEE
Map 1 A2

Brianville Guest House

★★★★ BED AND BREAKFAST

Clogherbrien, Fenit Rd
☎ 066 7126645 ▤ 066 7126645
e-mail: michsmit@gofree.indigo.ie
web: www.brianville-tralee.com
dir: R558 (Tralee-Fenit road), 2km from Tralee

This welcoming large yellow bungalow, situated on the road to Fenit on the outskirts of Tralee, is within easy reach of beaches, golf and the Aqua Dome. Bedrooms vary in size and are attractively furnished with hand-crafted pine. Breakfast is served in the bright sitting/dining room overlooking the well-tended garden.

Rooms 5 en suite (1 fmly) **Facilities** STV TVL tea/coffee Cen ht Wi-fi Golf 18 **Parking** 10 **Notes** ⊗ ☻

Tralee Townhouse

★★★ GUEST HOUSE

1-2 High St
☎ 066 7181111 ▤ 066 7181112
e-mail: traleetownhouse@eircom.net
dir: In town

Located in the town centre, close to pubs, restaurants and Aqua Dome, this friendly guest house offers well-equipped bedrooms with a lift to all floors. Guests can relax in the comfortable lounge and Eleanor Collins serves a variety of breakfast dishes and home-baked breads.

Rooms 19 en suite (2 fmly) (9 smoking) **Facilities** STV FTV TVL tea/coffee Direct Dial Cen ht Lift Wi-fi **Notes** ⊗ Closed 24-28 Dec

CO KILDARE

ATHY
Map 1 C3

PREMIER COLLECTION

Coursetown Country House

★★★★★ BED AND BREAKFAST

Stradbally Rd
☎ 059 8631101 ▤ 059 8632740
dir: M7 exit to M9, then exit at Ballitore onto N78 to Athy, take R428

This charming Victorian country house stands on a 100-hectare tillage farm and bird sanctuary. It has been extensively refurbished, and all bedrooms are furnished to the highest standards. Convalescent and disabled guests are especially welcome, and Iris and Jim Fox are happy to share their knowledge of the Irish countryside and its wildlife.

Rooms 5 en suite (1 GF) S €65-€85; D €90-€130 **Facilities** TVL tea/coffee Direct Dial Cen ht **Parking** 22 **Notes** No Children 12yrs Closed 15 Nov-15 Mar

CO KILKENNY

KILKENNY
Map 1 C3

Rosquil House

★★★★ GUEST HOUSE

Castlecomer Rd
☎ 056 7721419 ▤ 056 7750398
e-mail: info@rosquilhouse.com
dir: From N77, 1km from rail & bus staions, near Newpark Hotel

Just a few minutes from the Kilkenny town centre, Rosquil House is newly built and furnished with great attention to design and detail. Bedrooms are stylishly furnished, as are the guest sitting and breakfast rooms. There is a real treat in store at breakfast where stewed fruits and a choice of hot dishes are complemented by Rhoda Nolan's home baking. There is ample off-street parking available.

Rooms 7 en suite (1 fmly) (3 GF) **Facilities** STV tea/coffee Direct Dial Cen ht Wi-fi **Parking** 10 **Notes** ⊗

KILKENNY *continued*

Butler House

★★★★ GUEST HOUSE

Patrick St
☎ 056 7765707 & 7722828 📠 056 7765626
e-mail: res@butler.ie
web: www.butler.ie
dir: *In centre near Kilkenny Castle*

Once the dower house of Kilkenny Castle, this fine Georgian building fronts onto the main street with secluded gardens at the rear, through which you stroll to have full breakfast in Kilkenny Design Centre. A continental breakfast is served in bedrooms, which feature contemporary decor. There is a comfortable foyer lounge and conference-banqueting suites.

Rooms 13 en suite (4 fmly) Facilities STV FTV tea/coffee Direct Dial Cen ht Wi-fi Conf Max 120 Thtr 120 Class 40 Board 40 Parking 24 Notes ⊗ Closed 24-29 Dec Civ Wed 70

CO LAOIS

PORTLAOISE   Map 1 C3

O'Sullivan

★★★ BED AND BREAKFAST

8 Kelly Ville Park
☎ 0502 22774
dir: *In town centre opp County Hall car park*

This family-run semi-detached house on the edge of the town offers a homely atmosphere. The en suite bedrooms are comfortable and secure parking is available.

Rooms 4 en suite (1 fmly) (2 GF) Facilities STV TVL Cen ht Parking 8 Notes LB ⊗ 🐾

CO LIMERICK

ADARE   Map 1 B3

Berkeley Lodge

★★★★ BED AND BREAKFAST

Station Rd
☎ 061 396857 📠 061 396857
e-mail: berlodge@iol.ie
dir: *In village centre*

Situated in the pretty village of Adare this homely bed and breakfast has very comfortably furnished and attractively decorated bedrooms. The lounge leads on to an attractive conservatory-style breakfast room, which offers Bridie's home baking and a choice of hot dishes. Adare Manor and many other golf courses and horse riding stables are close by.

Rooms 6 en suite (2 fmly) (1 GF) S €45-€50; D €70-€75 Facilities TVL tea/coffee Cen ht Wi-fi Parking 6 Notes ⊗

BRUFF   Map 1 B3

The Old Bank Bed & Breakfast

★★★★ BED AND BREAKFAST

Main St
☎ 061 389969 📠 061 389969
e-mail: info@theoldbank.ie
dir: *From Limerick on R512, on right on main street*

The Old Bank is an inviting and imposing building in the town of Bruff. It has been lovingly refurbished and decorated by Miriam and Pat Sadlier-Barry. There are interconnecting bedrooms. All are spacious and furnished with guest comfort in mind; some have four-poster beds. There is a cosy library lounge with open fire, and breakfast is served where the original bank transactions took place.

Rooms 8 en suite Facilities TVL tea/coffee Cen ht Wi-fi Golf Gym Conf Max 20 Thtr 20 Class 20 Board 12 Parking 9 Notes ⊗ Closed 24-25 Dec

CO LOUTH

CARLINGFORD   Map 1 D4

Ghan House

★★★★ ⊛ 🏡 GUEST ACCOMMODATION

☎ 042 9373682 & 086 6000399 📠 042 9373772
e-mail: info@ghanhouse.com
dir: *M1 junct 18 signed Carlingford, 50mtrs on left after speed sign*

Dating from 1727, Ghan House has been restored to a high standard. Set in two acres of walled gardens, it is within 50 metres of the centre of this medieval village, making it an ideal base for walking and touring the Cooley peninsula. Bedrooms are warm and well appointed, either in the house itself or in a converted barn in the grounds. Public rooms are comfortable, featuring log fires and relaxing armchairs. Food is an important element of the business, and a successful cookery school has operated here for many years. Dinner is a highlight, with an emphasis on artisan produce and Cooley Lamb. Breakfast is a real treat with a great choice of fruit compôtes and preserves.

Rooms 4 en suite 8 annexe en suite (3 fmly) (4 GF) S €65-€95; D €130-€220 Facilities tea/coffee Dinner available Cen ht Licensed Wi-fi Riding Conf Max 50 Thtr 50 Board 32 Parking 35 Notes LB ⊗ Civ Wed 45

DROGHEDA   Map 1 D4

Windsor Lodge

★★★★ BED AND BREAKFAST

1 The Court
☎ 041 9841966 📠 041 9841966
e-mail: unagarvey@eircom.net
dir: *From M1 take exit 10 (Drogheda N). Through 3 rdbts & lights, driveway 60mtrs*

The home of Olive Murphy is delightfully furnished and decorated with guest comfort in mind. Two of the bedrooms are on the ground floor and the guest lounge is very relaxing and comfortable. A hearty breakfast is served in the conservatory style dining room. Windsor Lodge is situated just off the M1 on the north road and within walking distance of the hospital and Drogheda town centre. Close to Newgrange and many historical sites and golf courses.

Rooms 7 en suite (2 fmly) (2 GF) Facilities STV FTV TVL tea/coffee Cen ht Wi-fi Golf 18 Parking 12 Notes ⊗

CO MAYO

ACHILL ISLAND   Map 1 A4

Lavelle's Seaside House

★★★ GUEST ACCOMMODATION

Dooega
☎ 098 45116 & 01 2828142
e-mail: info@lavellesseasidehouse.com
web: www.lavellesseasidehouse.com
dir: *R319, NW from Achill Sound, Gob an Choire. Continue for 5km turn left onto L1405 Dooega/Dumma Eige junct & continue for 5km*

Friendliness and good food are offered at this comfortable house close to the beach. Facilities include a lounge, breakfast room, and a traditional pub where seafood is available during the high season. The more-spacious bedrooms are in the new wing.

Rooms 14 en suite (5 fmly) (14 GF) Facilities TVL tea/coffee Dinner available Cen ht Licensed Pool table Parking 20 Notes ⊗ Closed 2 Nov-mid Mar RS Dinner served Jul/Aug only

BALLINA
Map 1 B4

Red River Lodge B&B

★★★ BED AND BREAKFAST

Ceford, The Quay Rd
☎ 096 22841
e-mail: redriverlodge@eircom.net
dir: 3km from quay

Located on the N59 just 5 miles from Ballina Town, Red River Lodge is a very comfortable family home set in half an acre of beautifully landscaped gardens. Bedrooms are very well appointed in a contemporary style, with many of them having spectacular views of the estuary of the River Moy. Dolores and Mark are perfect hosts, and are renowned for the quality of their breakfasts, served in the bright and airy conservatory. This house is an ideal location for visitors touring the counties of Mayo and Sligo.

Rooms 4 en suite (2 fmly) (1 GF) D €60-€65*
Facilities STV FTV Cen ht Wi-fi Golf 18 **Parking** 6
Notes ⊗ Closed 30 Sep-1 May

Abbey B&B

★★★ BED AND BREAKFAST

Foxford Rd
☎ 096 78499
e-mail: knockglasslodge@ireland.com

This welcoming house is set in landscaped gardens near the train station close to the town. The first floor's individually styled bedrooms all feature comfortable beds and furniture made from reclaimed pine. The hosts are always on hand to recommend one of the many restaurants in the town.

Rooms 4 en suite **Facilities** FTV tea/coffee Cen ht **Parking** 9 **Notes** ⊗ Closed 22 Dec-1 Jan

BELMULLET
Map 1 A5

Drom Caoin Bed & Breakfast

★★★ BED AND BREAKFAST

Sraid na hEaglaise
☎ 097 81195   📄 097 81195
e-mail: stay@dromcaoin.ie
dir: N59 to Bangor Erris, then R313 to Belmullet. 1st left off rdbt, 0.5km on left

Set in sloping gardens overlooking Blacksod Bay, Drom Caoin is the welcoming family home of Máirín and Gerry Murphy. Bedrooms are comfortable and include two spacious apartments for extended stays. The breakfast room and lounge are relaxing with good reading materials and lovely views. Drying rooms and cycle storage facilities make this an ideal base for those who enjoy outdoor pursuits.

Rooms 5 en suite 1 annexe en suite (1 fmly) (2 GF)
Facilities TVL tea/coffee Dinner available Cen ht Wi-fi
Parking 7 **Notes** Closed 15 Dec-15 Jan

CASTLEBAR
Map 1 B4

Kennys Guest House

★★★ GUEST HOUSE

Lucan St
☎ 094 9023091
e-mail: info@kennysguesthouse.com
dir: N5 follow signs to town centre

The Kenny family have been running this charming guest house for ten years. It is situated in the heart of Castlebar town close to singing bars, restaurants, Mayo Movie Centre, Royal Theatre and Museum of Country Life. Bedrooms are attractively decorated and well appointed with two ground floor rooms suitable for the less able. There is a cosy sitting room, and breakfast, served in the dining room includes eggs from their own farm and delicious home baking.

Rooms 8 en suite (2 fmly) (2 GF) S €35-€40; D €70-€80*
Facilities STV FTV TVL tea/coffee Direct Dial Cen ht Wi-fi ch fac Golf 18 **Parking** 6 **Notes** LB ⊗

Lough Lannagh Lodge

★★★ GUEST ACCOMMODATION

Old Westport Rd
☎ 094 9027111   📄 094 9027295
e-mail: info@loughlannagh.ie
web: www.loughlannagh.ie
dir: N5 around Castlebar. 3rd rdbt, 2nd exit. Next left, past playground, 1st building on right

Lough Lannagh is in a delightful wooded area within walking distance of Castlebar. There is a conference centre, fitness centre, tennis, table tennis, laundry and drying facilities, a private kitchen, and many activities for children. Bedrooms are well appointed and breakfast is served in the café. Dinner is available by appointment for groups.

Rooms 24 en suite (24 fmly) (12 GF) **Facilities** FTV TVL Dinner available Direct Dial Cen ht Wi-fi ch fac ♨ Sauna Gym Steam room Table tennis **Conf** Max 100 Thtr 100 Class 54 Board 34 **Parking** 24 **Notes** ⊗ Closed 8 Dec-11 Jan

Carrabaun House

★★★★ BED AND BREAKFAST

Carrabaun, Leenane Rd
☎ 098 26196 📠 098 28466
e-mail: carrabaun@anu.ie
dir: *On N59 S. Leave Westport town, 1.6km pass Maxol station on left, house 200mtrs*

This elevated house has stunning views of Croagh Patrick and Clew Bay, situated on the outskirts of Westport town. The Gavin family are friendly hosts and serve a hearty breakfast. Bedrooms are attractively furnished and there is a comfortable guest sitting room and dining room. There is private parking, and lovely gardens surround the house.

Rooms 6 en suite (6 fmly) (1 GF) **Facilities** TVL tea/coffee Cen ht **Parking** 12 **Notes** ⊗ Closed 16-31 Dec

Bertra House (L903823)

★★★ FARMHOUSE

Thornhill, Murrisk
☎ 098 64833 📠 098 64833
Mrs M Gill
e-mail: bertrahse@eircom.net
dir: *W of Westport off R335, near Croagh Patrick on L1833*

This attractive bungalow overlooks the Blue Flag Bertra beach. Four bedrooms are en suite and the fifth has its own bathroom. Breakfast is generous and Mrs Gill offers tea and home-baked cakes on arrival in the cosy lounge.

Rooms 5 rms (4 en suite) (1 pri facs) (3 fmly) (5 GF) **Facilities** FTV TVL tea/coffee Cen ht **Parking** 7 **Notes** ⊗ No Children 6yrs Closed 15 Nov-15 Mar 🐄 40 acres beef

Killyon

★★★★ GUEST ACCOMMODATION

Dublin Rd
☎ 046 9071224 & 08681 71061 📠 046 9072766
e-mail: info@killyonguesthouse.ie
dir: *On N3, River Boyne side, opp Ardboyne Hotel*

This luxurious house has fine views over the River Boyne from the balcony and cosy guest lounge. The comfortable bedrooms are individually decorated with antique beds and quality soft furnishings. Sheila Fogarty's breakfast is a special treat which includes home baking, jams and local products, and is served in the sun lounge or on the balcony. There is off-street parking at the front of the house in the colourfully planted garden.

Rooms 6 en suite (1 fmly) (1 GF) S €40-€50; D €60-€70* **Facilities** STV TVL Direct Dial Cen ht Wi-fi ch fac Fishing **Parking** 10 **Notes** ⊗ Closed 23-25 Dec

The Yellow House

★★★★ BED AND BREAKFAST

Springfield Glen, Dublin Rd
☎ 046 9073338 & 086 3280458
e-mail: info@theyellowhouse.ie
dir: *N3 from Dublin, left at 2nd lights on approach to Navan*

Located on the southern approach to the town, this friendly house is popular with return guests. It offers well-appointed rooms and a comfortable lounge reserved for residents. A number of choices are available at breakfast, and off-road parking is provided in mature gardens.

Rooms 4 rms (3 en suite) (1 pri facs) (2 fmly) **Facilities** FTV TVL tea/coffee Cen ht Wi-fi **Parking** 12 **Notes** ⊗

Dalys B&B

★★★ BED AND BREAKFAST

R153, Mooretown
☎ 046 9023219 & 085 7089813
e-mail: info@dalysbandb.com
web: www.dalysbandb.com
dir: *Take R153 from Navan, B&B is 2km on the right*

The Daly family provide a home-from-home atmosphere in this lovely house which is on a sheep farm 2 kms from Navan town. Brian gives advice on the many historical sights, and the Hill of Tara can been seen from the comfortable bedrooms. There is a combined sitting/dining room and breakfast is served at a communal table set with lovely china and includes Pauline's bread and

preserves. There is ample car parking and a lovely garden to relax in.

Rooms 3 en suite (1 fmly) S €45-€50; D €70-€74 **Facilities** STV FTV TVL tea/coffee Cen ht Golf 27 **Parking** 8 **Notes** ⊗

Brogans

★★★ GUEST HOUSE

High St
☎ 046 9431237 📠 046 9437648
e-mail: info@brogans.ie
web: www.brogans.ie
dir: *Exit M50 junct 6 at rdbt, 1st exit to Blanchardstown, N3 rdbt 2nd exit, turn 1st left, left again onto R154. Continue to High St*

Brogans is situated in the designated heritage town of Trim, and was built nearly two centuries ago using much of the original stone from Trim Castle. Bedrooms in the main house have been refurbished and there are new rooms in the courtyard. There is a cosy traditional bar where food is served throughout the day and at weekends in the Beacon Restaurant. This guest house is convenient for New Grange, the Hill of Tara and many championship golf courses.

Rooms 18 en suite (3 fmly) (4 GF) S €35-€70; D €45-€110* **Facilities** TVL tea/coffee Dinner available Direct Dial Cen ht Licensed **Notes** LB Closed 24-25 Dec

An Teach Bán

★★★★ BED AND BREAKFAST

Main St
☎ 047 87198 & 086 6072996 📠 047 87198
e-mail: anteachban@eircom.net
dir: *On N2, 11km N of Monaghan town*

An Teach Bán bed and breakfast is situated in the picturesque village of Emyvale where there is a selection of traditional pubs and restaurants as well as fishing, golf and equestrian centre. The area is ideal for walking and cycling enthusiasts. The house is attractively decorated throughout and bedrooms are comfortably furnished and well appointed. Two ground floor rooms have the added benefit of access to the garden and car park and one is fitted to accommodate the less able. The garden is available for guests to relax in and listen to the birds in. A hearty breakfast is cooked to order and includes the local mushrooms and freshly baked breads.

Rooms 5 en suite (3 fmly) (3 GF) S €50; D €70* **Facilities** FTV TVL tea/coffee Cen ht Wi-fi ch fac Fishing Riding **Parking** 7 **Notes** ⊗ Closed Dec-Jan

GLASLOUGH — Map 1 C5

PREMIER COLLECTION

The Castle at Castle Leslie Estate

★★★★★ @ GUEST HOUSE

☎ 047 88100 🖹 047 88256

e-mail: info@castleleslie.com

dir: M1 junct 14 onto N2 to Monaghan then N12 to N185 Glaslough

Set in 1000 acres of rolling countryside, the Castle is the centre of the Leslie estate which has been in the family since the 1660s. Bedrooms are all decorated in keeping with the age and style of the period, and are ideal for relaxing breaks where guests enjoy the peace and tranquillity of the property without any interference from televisions or other distractions. The restaurant is renowned for the quality of its food and ornate setting. With a successful equestrian centre and a private fishing lake, this is an ideal location for those who enjoy country pursuits.

Rooms 20 rms (19 en suite) (1 pri facs) S €150-€250; D €240-€300 **Facilities** Dinner available Direct Dial Cen ht Lift Licensed Wi-fi 🏊 Golf 18 Fishing Riding Snooker Spa treatment rooms Private cinema **Conf** Max 150 Thtr 150 Class 100 Board 44 **Parking** 100 **Notes** LB ⊗ Closed 22-27 Dec Civ Wed 70

CO SLIGO

BALLYSADARE — Map 1 B5

Seashore House

★★★ BED AND BREAKFAST

Lisduff

☎ 071 9167827 🖹 071 9167827

e-mail: seashore@oceanfree.net

dir: N4 onto N59 W at Ballisadore, 4km Seashore signed, 0.6km right to house

Seashore House is an attractive dormer bungalow in a quiet seashore location. A comfortable lounge with open turf fire and sunny conservatory dining room look out over attractive landscaped gardens to sea and mountain scenery. Bedrooms are attractively appointed and comfortable, and there is also a tennis court and bicycle storage.

Rooms 5 rms (4 en suite) (2 fmly) (3 GF) S €45; D €70* **Facilities** STV FTV TVL Cen ht Wi-fi 🏊 Fishing Solarium **Parking** 6 **Notes** LB ⊗ No Children

BELTRA — Map 1 B5

Rafter's Woodfield Inn

★★★★ GUEST ACCOMMODATION

Larkhill

☎ 071 9166610 🖹 071 9166610

dir: On N59

This delightful property is attached to a cosy traditional pub, established in 1775, that serves bar food in the evening. Guests can relax in the conservatory lounge while enjoying the views of the Ox Mountains. Three of the bedrooms are on the ground floor and are fitted to accommodate less able guests; all bedrooms are well furnished, individually decorated and identified by names from the local area. Breakfast menu includes Carol's brown bread, spotted dog scones and preserves.

Rooms 5 en suite (3 fmly) (3 GF) **Facilities** FTV TVL Cen ht Licensed Wi-fi **Parking** 25 **Notes** ⊗ 🐾

GRANGE — Map 1 B5

Rowanville Lodge

★★★★ BED AND BREAKFAST

Moneygold

☎ 071 9163958 🖹 353 71 9163958

e-mail: rowanville@hotmail.com

dir: On N15, 1km N of Grange village

This smart bed and breakfast is just five minutes from the town centre, and is part of Manor West retail park which has many shopping opportunities. Spacious well-appointed bedrooms are matched by comfortable public areas including the Bar and Bistro where food is served throughout the day, with fine dining available in the Walnut Room. There is a high spec Leisure Club, and a variety of treatments are offered in the Harmony Wellness suites. A range of meeting and banqueting rooms are also available.

Rooms 4 en suite (4 fmly) (2 GF) S €40; D €60-€75* **Facilities** STV FTV TVL tea/coffee Dinner available Cen ht Wi-fi Golf 18 **Parking** 9 **Notes** LB Closed 20-27 Dec

CO TIPPERARY

CASHEL — Map 1 C3

Ard Ri House

★★★★ BED AND BREAKFAST

Dualla Rd

☎ 062 63143 🖹 062 63037

e-mail: ardrihouse@gmail.com

dir: Turn 1st right after Information Office onto R688, turn left after church onto R691, 1km on right

A warm welcome awaits you at this non-smoking house, only a short distance from the town on the Kilkenny Road. All of the bedrooms are comfortably furnished with thoughtful extras, and are on the ground floor. The breakfast served by Eileen features locally sourced ingredients from a varied menu. Facilities are available for children.

Rooms 4 en suite (1 fmly) (4 GF) D €70-€90 **Facilities** TVL tea/coffee Cen ht Wi-fi **Parking** 8 **Notes** ⊗ Closed Nov-Feb

Ashmore House

★★★ BED AND BREAKFAST

John St

☎ 062 61286 & 0861 037010 🖹 062 62789

e-mail: info@ashmorehouse.ie

dir: Off N8 in town centre onto John St, house 100mtrs on right

Ashmore House is set in a pretty walled garden in the town centre with an enclosed car park. Guests have use of a large sitting and dining room, and bedrooms come in a variety of sizes from big family rooms to a more compact double.

Rooms 5 en suite (2 fmly) D €70-€80 **Facilities** STV FTV TVL tea/coffee Dinner available Cen ht Wi-fi **Parking** 10 **Notes** ⊗

NENAGH   Map 1 B3

Ashley Park House

★★★★ BED AND BREAKFAST

☎ 067 38223 & 38013   📄 067 38013
e-mail: margaret@ashleypark.com
web: www.ashleypark.com
dir: 6.5km N of Nenagh. Off N52 across lake, signed on
left & left under arch

This attractive, colonial style farmhouse was built in
1770. Set in gardens that run down to Lake Ourna, it has
spacious bedrooms with quality antique furnishings.
Breakfast is served in the dining room overlooking the
lake, and dinner is available by arrangement. There is a
delightful walled garden, and a boat for fishing on the
lake is available.

Rooms 5 en suite (3 fmly) **Facilities** TVL tea/coffee Dinner
available Cen ht Licensed Wi-fi ch fac Golf 18 Fishing
Rowing boat on lake **Conf** Max 30 Board 30 **Parking** 30
Notes LB 🐾

THURLES   Map 1 C3

PREMIER COLLECTION

Inch House Country House &
Restaurant

★★★★★ 🍴 GUEST HOUSE

☎ 0504 51348 & 51261   📄 0504 51754
e-mail: mairin@inchhouse.ie
dir: 6.5km NE of Thurles on R498

This lovely Georgian house, at the heart of a working
farm, was built in 1720 and has been carefully restored
by the Egan family. The elegant drawing room ceiling is
particularly outstanding among the grand public
rooms, and the five spacious bedrooms are delightfully
appointed. Reservations are essential in the fine
restaurant, where an imaginative choice of freshly
prepared dishes is on offer, with an emphasis on local
produce. Some of the produce from the kitchen is
available in a number of specialist outlets throughout
the country.

Rooms 5 en suite (1 fmly) S €50-€60; D €90-€110
Facilities TVL tea/coffee Dinner available Direct Dial
Cen ht Licensed Wi-fi **Parking** 40 **Notes** LB 🐾 Closed 2
wks Xmas RS Sun & Mon Restaurant closed evening
Civ Wed 30

PREMIER COLLECTION

The Castle

★★★★★ BED AND BREAKFAST

Twomileborris
☎ 0504 44324   📄 0504 44352
e-mail: bandb@thecastletmb.com
dir: 7km E of Thurles. On N75 200mtrs W of
Twomileborris at Castle

Pierce and Joan are very welcoming hosts. Their
fascinating house, sheltered by a 16th-century tower
house, has been in the Duggan family for 200 years.
Bedrooms are comfortable and spacious, there is a
relaxing lounge, and the dining room overlooks the
delightful garden. Golf, fishing, hill walking, and
traditional pubs and restaurants are all nearby. Dinner
is available by arrangement.

Rooms 4 en suite (3 fmly) S €45-€60; D €70-€100
Facilities STV FTV TVL tea/coffee Dinner available
Cen ht Wi-fi 🐾 🦆 Fishing Pool table **Conf** Max 40
Board 20 **Parking** 30 **Notes** LB 🐾

TIPPERARY   Map 1 C3

Ach-na-Sheen House

★★★ GUEST HOUSE

Clonmel Rd
☎ 062 51298   📄 062 80467
e-mail: gernoonan@eircom.net
dir: In town centre

This large, modern bungalow is set in a lovely garden and
is only five minutes walk from the main street of Tipperary
town on the N24 road. Public areas include a guest
sitting room and dining room and bedrooms are well
appointed. There is good off-street parking.

Rooms 8 en suite (5 fmly) (6 GF) S €45-€55; D €75-€85*
Facilities STV tea/coffee Cen ht **Parking** 13 **Notes** 🐾
Closed 11 Dec-8 Jan

Aisling

★★★ BED AND BREAKFAST

Glen of Aherlow
☎ 062 33307 & 087 2278230   📄 062 82955
e-mail: ladygreg@oceanfree.net
web: www.aislingbedandbreakfast.com
dir: From town centre R664 for 2.4km

Aisling is close to Tipperary on the R664, Glen of Aherlow
road. The bedrooms are well furnished and attractively
decorated. There is a comfortable guest sitting room and
a delightful garden with patio seating. Marian and Bob
will arrange day trips and have maps and good
information on the locality.

Rooms 5 rms (4 en suite) (1 pri facs) (2 fmly) (5 GF) (2
smoking) **Facilities** FTV TVL tea/coffee Dinner available
Cen ht Wi-fi **Conf** Max 6 Class 6 **Parking** 4

CO WATERFORD

BALLYMACARBRY   Map 1 C2

PREMIER COLLECTION

Hanoras Cottage

★★★★★ GUEST HOUSE

Nire Valley
☎ 052 6136134 & 6136442   📄 052 6136540
e-mail: hanorascottage@eircom.net
dir: From Clonmel or Dungarvan R672 to
Ballymacarbry, at Melodys Bar turn into Nire Valley,
establishment by bridge beside church

Nestling in the beautiful Nire Valley, Hanoras Cottage
is very popular with hill and forest walkers, bird
watchers and nature lovers. The spacious bedrooms are
comfortably and beautifully furnished. There are cosy
lounge areas and the award-winning restaurant serves
fresh local produce. Mary Wall's breakfasts are a real
feast and deserve to be savoured at leisure.

Rooms 10 en suite **Facilities** STV FTV TVL tea/coffee
Dinner available Direct Dial Cen ht Licensed Golf 18
Fishing Jacuzzi in all rooms **Conf** Class 40 **Parking** 15
Notes LB 🐾 No Children Closed Xmas wk RS Sun
Restaurant closed Civ Wed 40

TRAMORE — Map 1 C2

Cliff House

★★★★ BED AND BREAKFAST

Cliff Rd
☎ 051 381497 & 391296 📠 051 381497
e-mail: hilary@cliffhouse.ie
dir: Off R675, left at Ritz thatched pub

This comfortable and spacious home of the O'Sullivan family is situated overlooking Tramore Bay and has beautiful gardens and a conservatory lounge where guests can relax while enjoying the breathtaking views. All bedrooms are decorated to a high standard, there are rooms with balconies and some rooms are suitable for families. The extensive breakfast menu offers many delicious choices.

Rooms 6 en suite (3 fmly) (3 GF) **Facilities** STV TVL tea/coffee Cen ht Wi-fi **Parking** 10 **Notes** ⊗ No Children 4yrs Closed Nov-Mar

Cloneen

★★★★ BED AND BREAKFAST

Love Ln
☎ 051 381264 📠 051 381264
e-mail: cloneen@iol.ie
dir: N25 onto R675 to Tramore, Majestic Hotel on right, continue up hill until road bears left, take 1st left

This pleasant family home is situated on a quiet residential area off the coast road and within walking distance of the seaside town of Tramore. Bedrooms are stylishly furnished with guest comfort in mind; some of the ground floor rooms have their own patio overlooking the lovely garden. Guests can relax in the conservatory-style sitting room and enjoy a hearty breakfast in the bright dining room.

Rooms 6 en suite (2 fmly) (4 GF) S €45-€50; D €70-€80 **Facilities** STV TVL tea/coffee Cen ht Wi-fi **Parking** 8

WATERFORD — Map 1 C2

PREMIER COLLECTION

Sion Hill House & Gardens

★★★★★ GUEST ACCOMMODATION

Sion Hill, Ferrybank
☎ 051 851558 📠 051 851678
e-mail: sionhill@eircom.net
dir: Near city centre on R711, 300mtrs from Rice Bridge & railway station

Situated close to the city, this 18th-century residence has extensive peaceful gardens, which include a walled garden, a meadow and woodlands. Flanked by two pavilions, the house has been refurbished to provide two fine reception rooms and comfortable en suite bedrooms. The friendly owners like to mix with their guests, as the visitors' book shows.

Rooms 4 en suite (2 fmly) **Facilities** STV FTV TVL tea/coffee Cen ht **Parking** 16 **Notes** ⊗ Closed 23-28 Dec

Belmont House

★★★ BED AND BREAKFAST

Belmont Rd, Rosslare Rd, Ferrybank
☎ 051 832174 📠 051 832174
e-mail: belmonthouse@eircom.net
dir: Exit N25 at Luffany rdbt, follow R711 (Waterford N). Belmont House 4km from junct, 2nd B&B on left after service station

This comfortable bed and breakfast is within walking distance of the city centre. A hospitality tray is available in the relaxing guest sitting room and a hearty breakfast is served in the dining room at separate tables. Bedrooms are well appointed and offer good quality and space.

Rooms 6 rms (4 en suite) (2 pri facs) (3 fmly) S €45-€55; D €64-€76* **Facilities** TVL Cen ht Wi-fi **Parking** 6 **Notes** ⊗ No Children 7yrs Closed Nov-Apr ☺

CO WESTMEATH

HORSELEAP — Map 1 C4

Woodlands Farm House (N286426)

★★★★ FARMHOUSE

Streamstown
☎ 044 9226414
Mrs M Maxwell
e-mail: maxwells.woodlandsfarm@gmail.com
dir: N6 N onto R391 at Horseleap, farm signed 4km

This very comfortable and charming house has a delightful setting on a farm. The spacious sitting and dining rooms are very relaxing, and there is a hospitality kitchen where tea and coffee are available at all times.

Rooms 5 rms (4 en suite) (1 pri facs) (2 fmly) (2 GF) **Facilities** TVL Cen ht **Parking Notes** Closed Nov-Feb ☺ 120 acres mixed

CO WEXFORD

CAMPILE — Map 1 C2

PREMIER COLLECTION

Kilmokea Country Manor & Gardens

★★★★★ GUEST ACCOMMODATION

Great Island
☎ 051 388109 📠 051 388776
e-mail: stay@kilmokea.com
dir: R733 from New Ross to Campile, right before village for Great Island & Kilmokea Gardens

This fine property is an 18th-century former rectory, lovingly restored to its original glory by the hospitable Emma Hewlett and her husband Mark. It is located in wooded and beautifully landscaped gardens that are in themselves a popular visitor attraction. The bedrooms are richly furnished in a mix of styles, but all have particularly comfortable beds. The drawing and reading rooms all retain the style and proportions of the era, with an honesty bar for those tempted to have a night-cap. Dinner is available by prior arrangement, served in what was the original dining room of the house, or in summer, in the conservatory. This is where a hearty and delicious breakfast is also served. Recent additions in the grounds include a swimming pool and an aromatherapy treatment service.

Rooms 4 en suite 2 annexe en suite (1 fmly) (2 GF) S fr €75; D €160-€300* **Facilities** STV TVL TV2B tea/coffee Dinner available Direct Dial Cen ht Licensed Wi-fi ch fac 🏊 ♨ 🌳 Fishing Riding Sauna Gym Aromatherapy treatments Meditation room Jacuzzi **Conf** Max 75 Thtr 40 Class 30 Board 25 **Parking** 23 **Notes** LB RS Nov-end Jan

NEW ROSS
Map 1 C3

Woodlands House

★★★ BED AND BREAKFAST

Carrigbyrne
☎ 051 428287 📄 051 428287
e-mail: woodwex@eircom.net
dir: *On N25 (New Ross-Wexford route), 0.4km from Cedar Lodge Hotel towards New Ross*

Commanding panoramic views, this is a recently refurbished bungalow with pretty gardens. It is only a 30-minute drive to Rosslare Harbour. Snacks are available, and dinner by arrangement. Bedrooms vary in size, though all are very comfortable. There is a guest sitting room.

Rooms 4 en suite (4 GF) **Facilities** tea/coffee Dinner available Cen ht Licensed **Parking** 6 **Notes** LB ⊗ No Children 5yrs

ROSSLARE HARBOUR
Map 1 D2

Archways

★★★★ BED AND BREAKFAST

Rosslare Road (N25), Tagoat
☎ 053 9158111 & 0870 929597
e-mail: thearchways@eircom.net
dir: *6km from Rosslare Harbour*

Located 6km from Rosslare Ferry port, which is served by sailings from Fishguard and Pembroke, Archways is a comfortable family home recently refurbished by the new owners Eileen and Chris Hadlington. Each bedroom is decorated and furnished in a contemporary style. The lounge and dining room are bright and airy, and form the backdrop for relaxing evenings where guests enjoy the fruits of Chris's labours in the kitchen. An experienced chef, his dinner menu features the best of seasonal and local ingredients. Breakfast offers a choice of interesting options. There is secure storage for bicycles and ample car parking. This welcoming house is popular with bird watchers visiting nearby Kilmore Quay.

Rooms 6 en suite (2 fmly) (6 GF) S €48-€64; D €68-€84* **Facilities** FTV TVL tea/coffee Dinner available Cen ht Wi-fi Golf 18 **Parking** 14 **Notes** LB Closed 15 Dec-1 Mar

WEXFORD
Map 1 D3

Killiane Castle *(T058168)*

★★★★ 🏠 FARMHOUSE

Drinagh
☎ 053 9158885 📄 053 9158885
Mr & Mrs J Mernagh
e-mail: killianecastle@yahoo.com
dir: *Off N25 between Wexford and Rosslare*

This 17th-century house is part of a 13th-century Norman castle where the Mernagh family run a charming house on a dairy farm close to Wexford town. The comfortable reception rooms and bedrooms are beautifully furnished. Breakfast is a real treat and includes farm produce and Kathleen's baking and preserves. There is a hard tennis court, croquet lawn, a golf driving range and walks to wander through the farm.

Rooms 8 en suite (2 fmly) S €65-€70; D €90-€100* **Facilities** TVL Cen ht Wi-fi 🐾 🦆 Driving range 18 hole pitch & putt **Parking** 8 **Notes** ⊗ Closed Dec-Feb 230 acres dairy

Maple Lodge

★★★★ BED AND BREAKFAST

Castlebridge
☎ 053 9159195 📄 053 9159195
e-mail: sreenan@eircom.net
dir: *5km N of Wexford. On R741, N on outskirts of Castlebridge, pink house on left*

This imposing house, set in extensive mature gardens, is in a peaceful location close to Curracloe Beach. Eamonn and Margaret Sreenan offer warm hospitality in their comfortable home. There is a varied breakfast menu offered and secure parking in the grounds.

Rooms 4 en suite (2 fmly) **Facilities** STV TVL Cen ht Wi-fi **Parking** 5 **Notes** ⊗ No Children 10yrs Closed mid Nov-mid Mar

Slaney Manor

★★★★ GUEST ACCOMMODATION

☎ 053 9120051 📄 053 9120510
e-mail: info@slaneymanor.ie
dir: *On N25, 0.8km W of N11 junct*

This attractive manor house stands in 24 hectares of woodland overlooking the River Slaney. Restored by the owners, the house retains many fine features. The elegant, high-ceilinged drawing room and dining room have views of the river, and four-poster beds feature in all bedrooms. The rooms in the converted coach house can be reserved on a room only basis for those travelling on the Rosslare ferry.

Rooms 9 en suite (2 fmly) (4 GF) S €65-€105; D €80-€190* **Facilities** TVL tea/coffee Dinner available Direct Dial Cen ht Lift Licensed **Conf** Max 250 Thtr 250 Class 100 Board 100 **Parking** 30 **Notes** LB ⊗ Closed 24-26 Dec Civ Wed 250

CO WICKLOW

ASHFORD
Map 1 D3

Ballyknocken House & Cookery School

★★★★ 🏠 🍴 GUEST HOUSE

☎ 0404 44627 📄 0404 44696
e-mail: cfulvio@ballyknocken.com
web: www.ballyknocken.com
dir: *N11, S into Ashford, right after petrol station, house 5km on right*

This charming Victorian farmhouse stands in the foothills of the Wicklow Mountains. Catherine Fulvio is an enthusiastic hostess and reservations are necessary for dinner, which includes imaginative, freshly prepared dishes using produce from the garden and farm. The smart bedrooms are comfortable, and the farm buildings have been converted into a cookery school.

Rooms 7 en suite (1 fmly) **Facilities** tea/coffee Dinner available Direct Dial Cen ht Licensed 🍴 Cookery school **Conf** Max 80 Thtr 80 Class 50 Board 30 **Parking** 8 **Notes** ⊗ Closed 14 Dec-8 Jan

Save on B&Bs and Hotels. Book at **theAA.com/hotel**

CO WICKLOW 457 | IRELAND

AUGHRIM	Map 1 D3

Clone House

★★★★ BED AND BREAKFAST

☎ 0402 36121 & 087 2517587
e-mail: stay@clonehouse.com
dir: *From Dublin take N11 to Ashford, turn right at Texaco station signed Gleneally, turn right again signed Rathdrum, continue to Aughrim and continue 2m S*

Clone House dates from the 16th and 17th centuries and is located between Arklow and Aughrim. Liam has refurbished the house with care and attention to both age and style to create a truly comfortable retreat. There is a drawing room, library, parlour and dining room for guest use each with open log fire places and a wonderful selection of Irish art and literature to enjoy. The bedrooms have been beautifully decorated and furnished with guest comfort in mind; Aine is responsible for the home baking and delicious dinners which are available on reservation.

Rooms 4 en suite **Facilities** TVL Dinner available Cen ht Wi-fi Golf 18 Fishing Riding **Parking** 10 **Notes** ⊛

DUNLAVIN	Map 1 C3

Tynte House (N870015)

★★★★ FARMHOUSE

☎ 045 401561 📄 045 401586
Mr & Mrs J Lawler
e-mail: info@tyntehouse.com
web: www.tyntehouse.com
dir: *N81 at Hollywood Cross, right at Dunlavin, follow finger signs for Tynte House, past market house in town centre*

This 19th-century farmhouse stands in the square of the quiet country village of Dunlavin in the west of County Wicklow. The friendly hosts have carried out a lot of restoration resulting in cosy bedrooms and a relaxing guest sitting room. Breakfast, featuring Caroline's home baking, is a highlight of a visit to this house. An all-weather tennis court is located in the grounds, together with an indoor games room. This house is an ideal base for touring the Wicklow and Kildare areas with their many sporting attractions

Rooms 7 en suite (2 fmly) **Facilities** TVL tea/coffee Direct Dial Cen ht Wi-fi ⌇ Golf 18 Pool table Playground Games room **Parking** 16 **Notes** Closed 16 Dec-9 Jan 200 acres beef/tillage

WICKLOW	Map 1 D3

Kilpatrick House (T257808)

★★★★ FARMHOUSE

Redcross
☎ 0404 47137 & 087 6358325 📄 0404 47866
Mr H Kingston
e-mail: info@kilpatrickhouse.com
dir: *13km S, 3.2km off N11, signed from Jack Whites pub*

This elegant 18th-century Georgian residence is set on a beef farm just off the N11 north of Arklow. Bedrooms are carefully furnished and thoughtfully equipped. The interesting breakfast menu includes home baking and country produce. There is a delightful garden and relaxing guest sitting room. Close to Brittas Bay, there is a choice of golf courses and horse riding available locally

Rooms 4 rms (3 en suite) (1 pri facs) (2 fmly)
Facilities TVL tea/coffee Cen ht ⌇ Fishing **Parking** 20
Notes ⊛ Closed Oct-Apr 150 acres beef

County Maps

England

1 Bedfordshire
2 Berkshire
3 Bristol
4 Buckinghamshire
5 Cambridgeshire
6 Greater Manchester
7 Herefordshire
8 Hertfordshire
9 Leicestershire
10 Northamptonshire
11 Nottinghamshire
12 Rutland
13 Staffordshire
14 Warwickshire
15 West Midlands
16 Worcestershire

Scotland

17 City of Glasgow
18 Clackmannanshire
19 East Ayrshire
20 East Dunbartonshire
21 East Renfrewshire
22 Perth & Kinross
23 Renfrewshire
24 South Lanarkshire
25 West Dunbartonshire

Wales

26 Blaenau Gwent
27 Bridgend
28 Caerphilly
29 Denbighshire
30 Flintshire
31 Merthyr Tydfil
32 Monmouthshire
33 Neath Port Talbot
34 Newport
35 Rhondda Cynon Taff
36 Torfaen
37 Vale of Glamorgan
38 Wrexham

Na h-Eileanan
an Iar

Highland

Moray

City of
Aberdeen

Aberdeenshire

SCOTLAND

Angus

Perth &
Kinross

City of
Dundee

Argyll
& Bute

Stirling

Fife

East
Lothian

North
Ayrshire

19   24

South
Ayrshire

Dumfries &
Galloway

Scottish
Borders

Northumberland

Tyne & Wear

Durham

Cumbria

North
Yorkshire

East Riding
of Yorkshire

Lancashire

West
Yorkshire

Isle
of Man

Isle of
Anglesey

Merseyside

6

South
Yorkshire

Lincolnshire

Conwy

30

Cheshire

Derbyshire

29

38

11

Gwynedd

ENGLAND

13

Norfolk

Shropshire

9   12

Ceredigion

Powys

15

Suffolk

WALES

16   14   10   5

Carmarthenshire

7   1

Pembrokeshire

Essex

Swansea

Gloucestershire

4   8

Oxfordshire

Greater
London

Kent

3

Wiltshire

2

Surrey

Somerset

Hampshire

East
Sussex

West
Sussex

Devon

Dorset

Isle of
Wight

Cornwall

Isles of
Scilly

Guernsey

Jersey

Orkney Islands   Shetland Islands

Argyll
& Bute

Stirling

18   22

Fife

Inverclyde

25   20

Falkirk

23   17

North
Lanarkshire

West
Lothian

City of
Edinburgh

North
Ayrshire

21

Midlothian

19

South Lanarkshire

Scottish
Borders

31   26   32

33   35   28   36   34

27

Cardiff

37

| 0 | 20 | 40 | 60 | 80 | 100 miles |

| 0 | 20 40 60 80 100 120 140 | 160 kilometres |

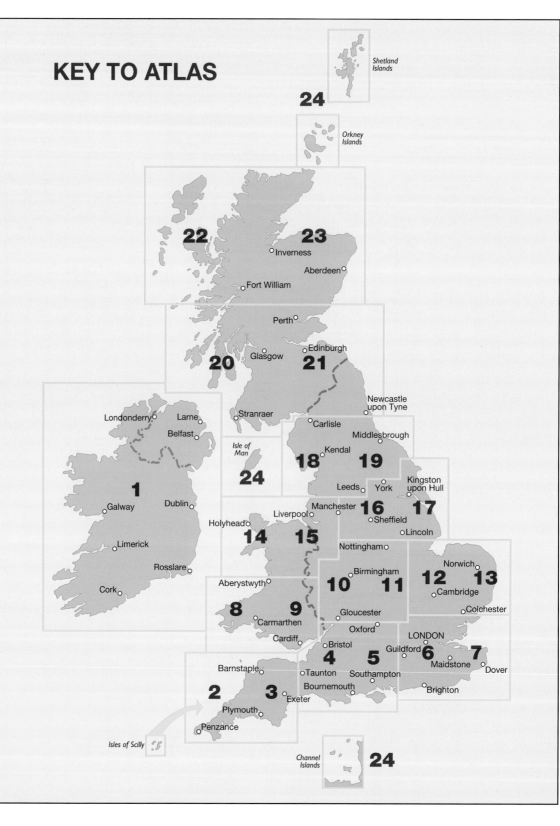

KEY TO ATLAS

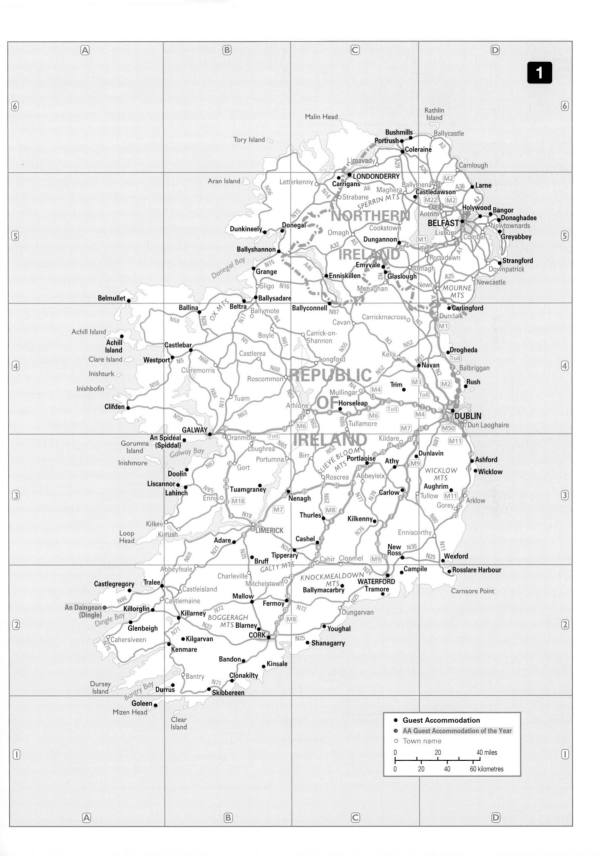

2

For continuation pages refer to numbered arrows

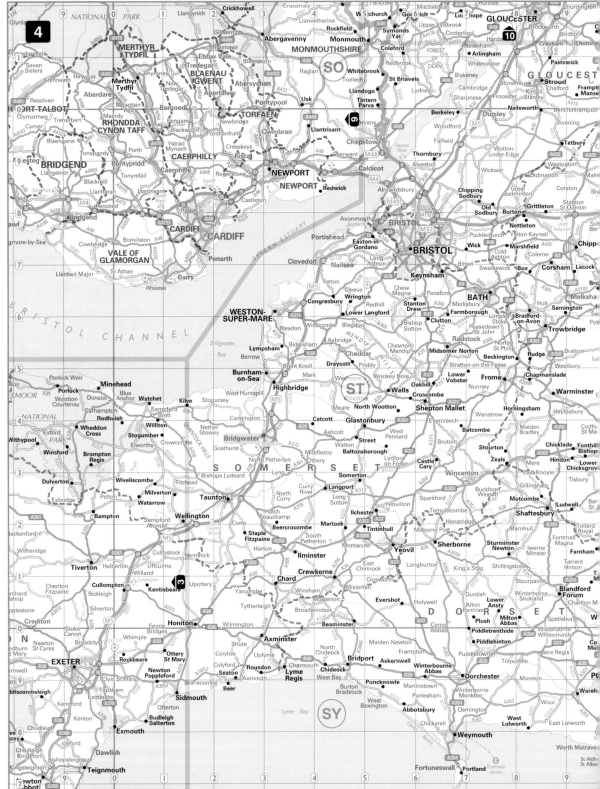

For continuation pages refer to numbered arrows

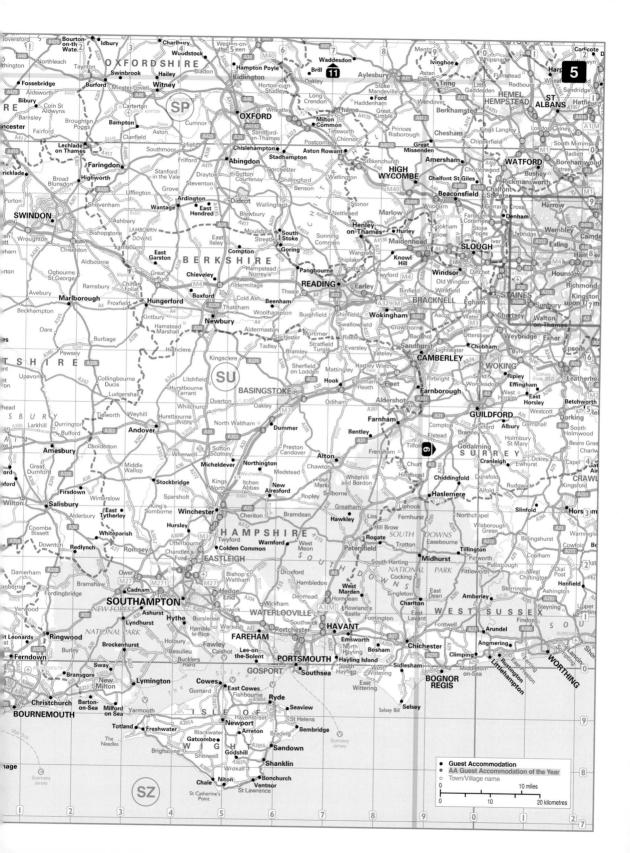

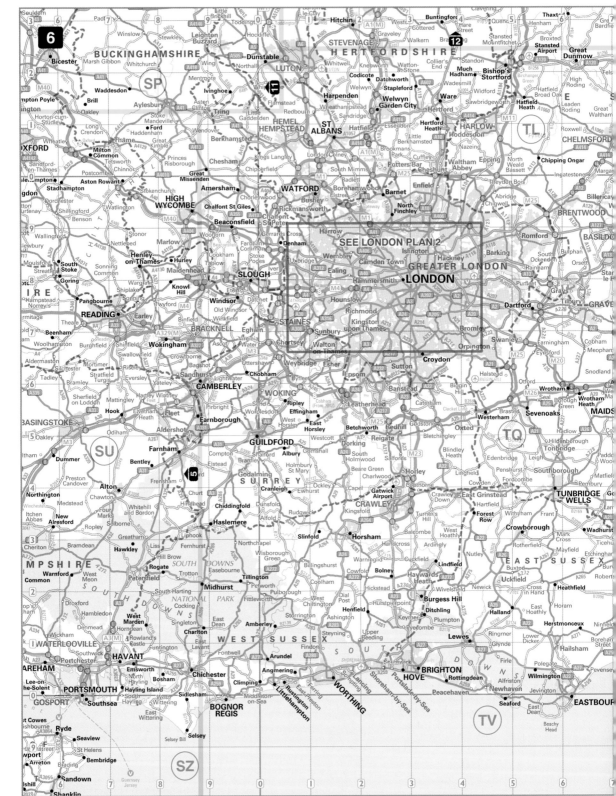

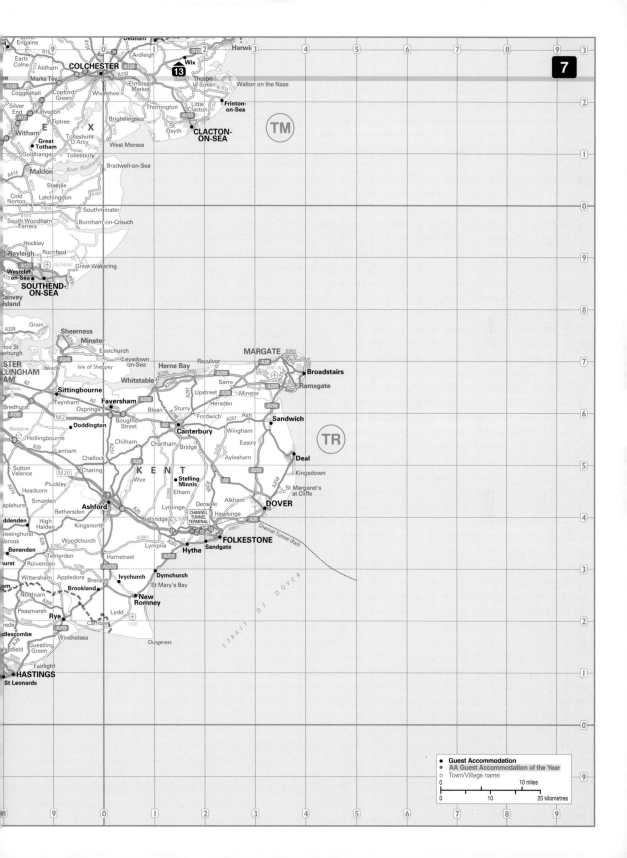

CARDIGAN BAY

Aberystwyth

Llanfarian

Llanrhystud

Llansantffraid

Aberarth

New Quay · Aberaeron

C E

Llangranog

Aberporth

Temple Bar

Tan-y-groes

Blaenporth

Talgarreg

Rhydowen

Cardigan

Llechryd

Llanybydder

St Dogmaels

Llandysul

Newcastle Emlyn

Llangeler

SN

SM

Strumble Head

Nevern

Newport

Eglwyswrw

Brechfa

Fishguard

PEMBROKESHIRE COAST NATIONAL PARK

MYNYDD PRESELI

Cynwyl Elfed

CARMARTHENSHIRE

Felingwm Ucha

St David's Head

Letterston

Nantgaredig

Wolf's Castle

St David's

Solva

PEMBROKESHIRE

Brawdy

Carmarthen

Llanarthne

Llanddarog

Llandy

Newgale

Roch

Llandissilio

Cross Hands

Amma

Robeston Wathen

Whitland

St Clears

St Brides Bay

PEMBROKESHIRE COAST NATIONAL PARK

Broad Haven

Haverfordwest

Narberth

Laugharne

Red Roses

Pontyberem

Pontyates

Llansteffan

Johnston

Kilgetty

Amroth

Pendine

Kidwelly

Pont Ab

Marloes

Dale

Broad Sound

Milford Haven

Neyland

Carew

Pembroke Dock

St Florence

Saundersfoot

Carmarthen Bay

Pembrey

Pwll

Llanell

Burry Port

Gorsei

Angle

Pembroke

Tenby

Penally

Castlemartin

PEMBROKESHIRE COAST NATIONAL PARK

Bosherston

Manorbier

Gowerton

Dunvant

Llanrhidian

SWANSEA

Llangennith

Reynoldston

Bishe

Rhossili

Parkmill

The Mur

Worms Head

Oxwich

Port Einon

SR

SS

Guest Accommodation
AA Guest Accommodation of the Year
○ Town/Village name

0   10 miles

0   10   20 kilometres

Lundy

Ilfracombe

Mortehoe Lee Berrynarbor

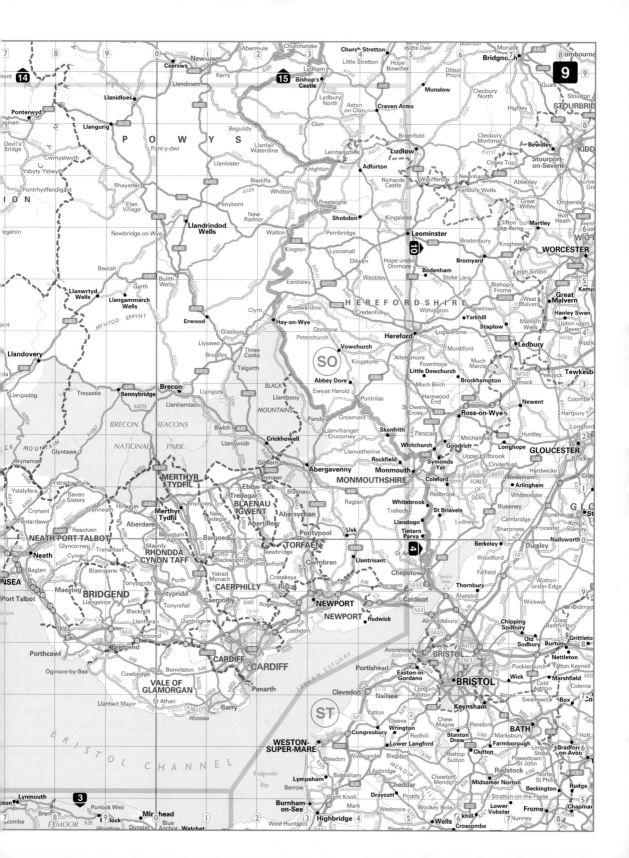

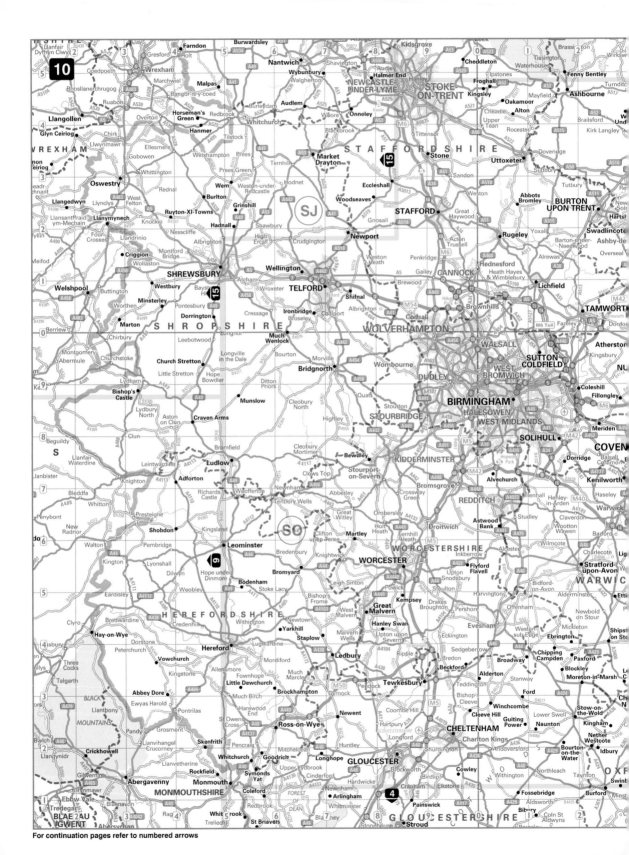

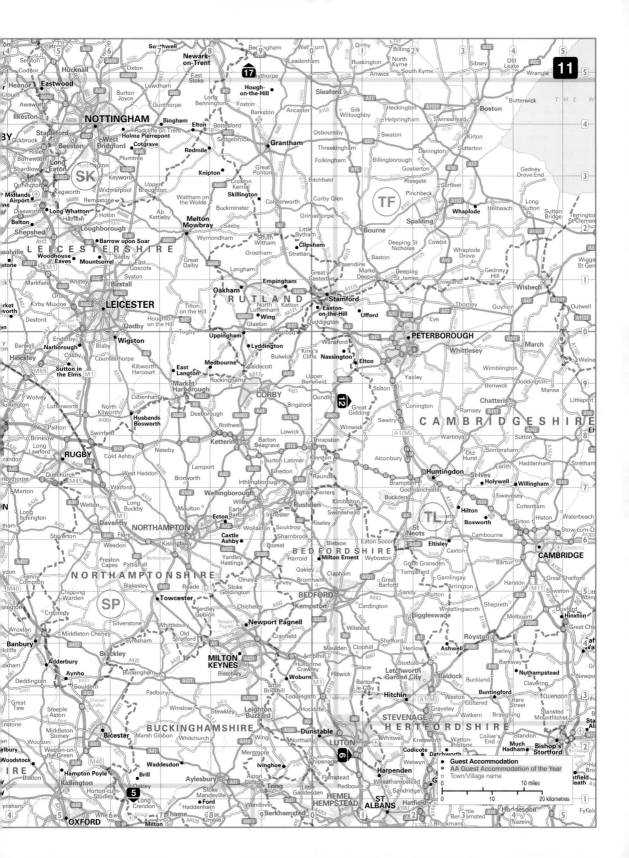

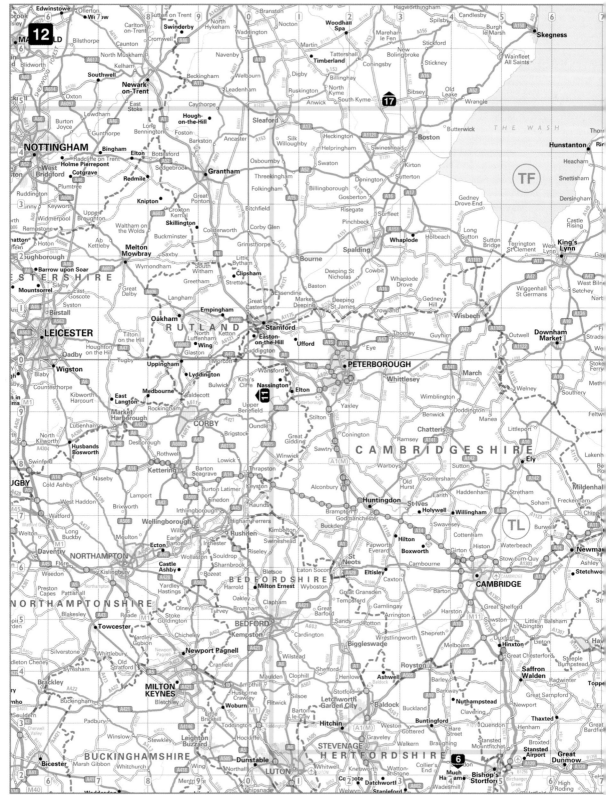

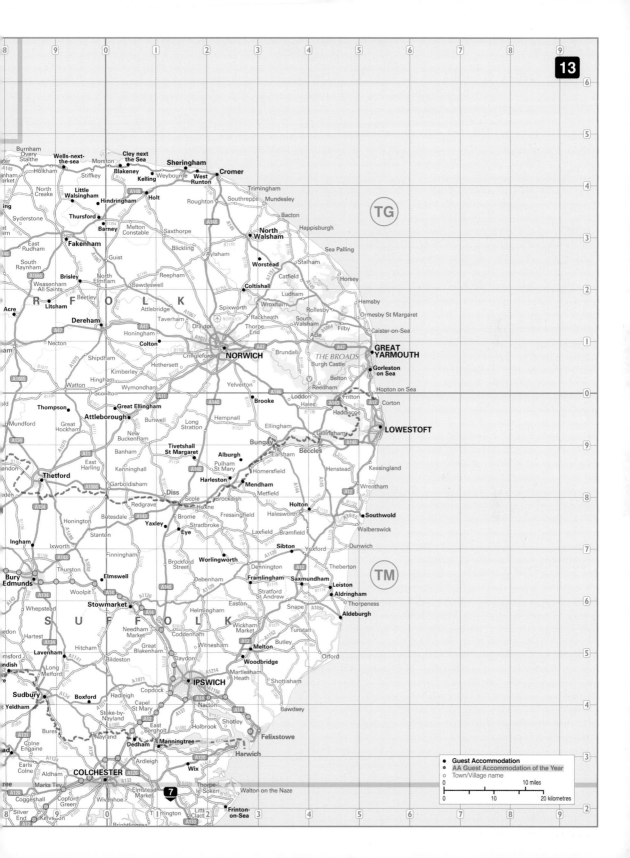

14

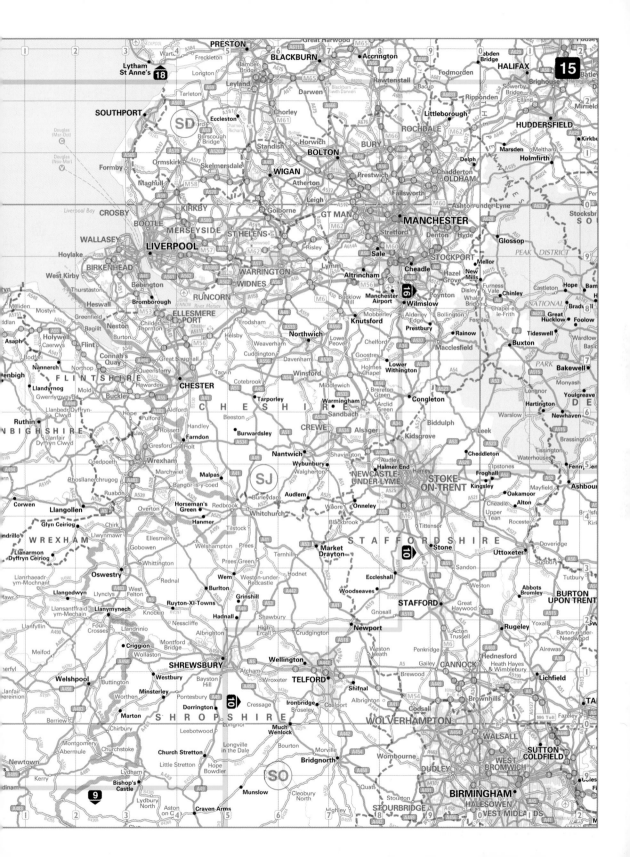

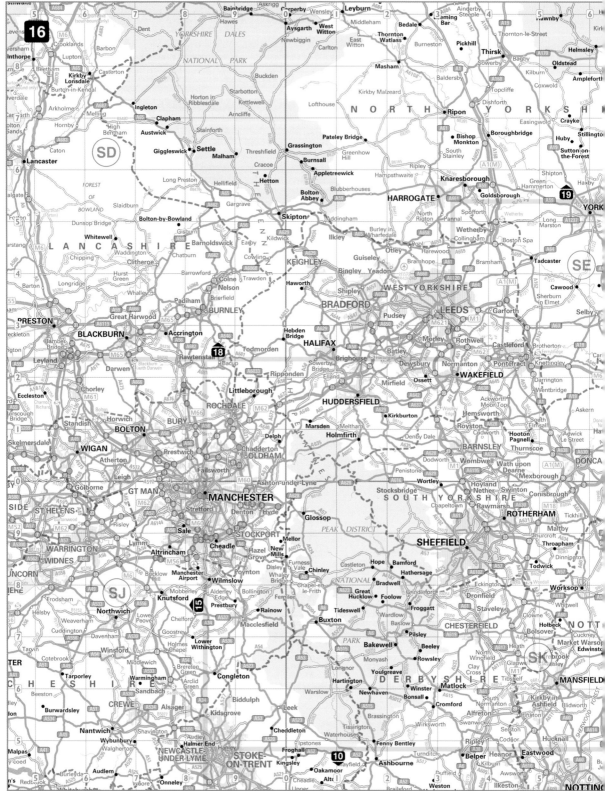

C EDIN	City of Edinburgh
C GLAS	City of Glasgow
CLACKS	Clackmannanshire
C DUND	City of Dundee
E DUNS	East Dunbartonshire
E RENS	East Renfrewshire
INVER	Inverclyde
MDLOTH	Midlothian
N LANS	North Lanarkshire
RENS	Renfrewshire
W DUNS	West Dunbartonshire
W LOTH	West Lothian

NA

NB

NA H–EILEANAN
AN IAR

NF

NG

NL

NM

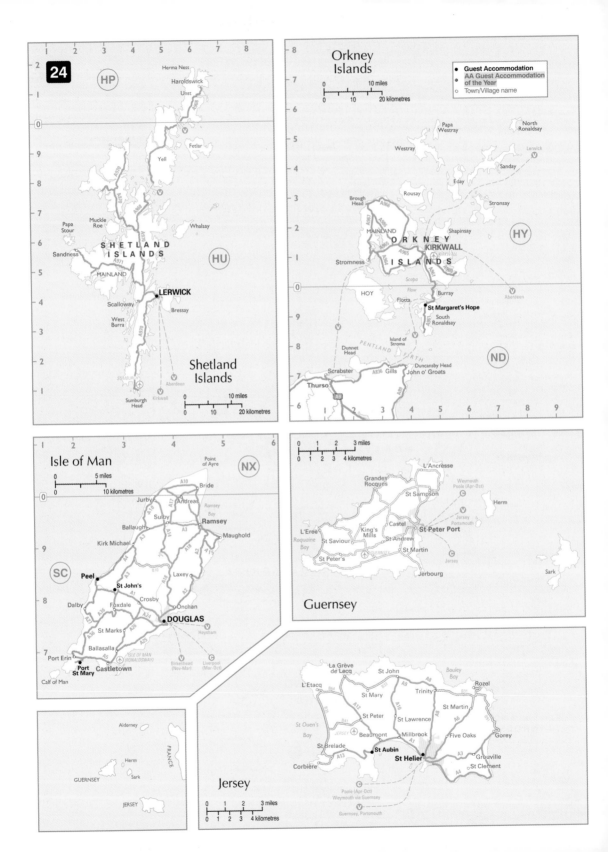

Central London

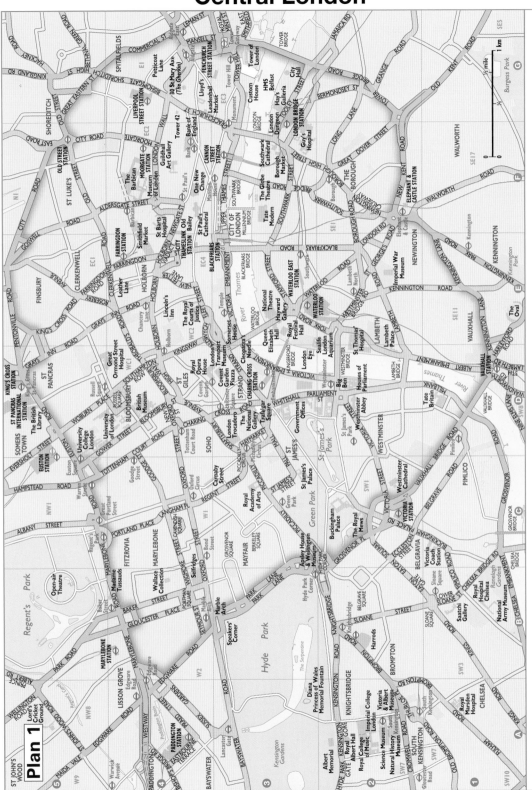

KEY TO B & B LOCATIONS

Each B & B in London has a map reference, eg C2. The letter 'C' refers to the grid square located at the left hand edge of the map. The figure '2' refers to the grid square located at the bottom of the map. For example, where these two intersect, Buckingham Palace can be found. Due to the scale of the map, only a rough guide to the location of a B & B can be given. A more detailed map will be necessary to be precise.

Congestion Charging Zone boundary

London Plan 2

0   2 miles
0   2   3 kilometres

Central London Congestion Charging Zone

Guest Accommodation

Index of Bed & Breakfasts

Acknowledgements

The Automobile Association wishes to thank the following photographers and organisations for their assistance in the preparation of this book.

Abbreviations for the picture credits are as follows – (t) top; (b) bottom; (l) left; (r) right; (c) centre; (AA) AA World Travel Library

1 Hazel Bank Country House, Rosthwaite; 2 Berkeley Photographs; 3 The Red Lion, Shipston on Stour; 4 The Swan Inn, Hungerford; 5 Elerkey Guest House, Veryan; 6 AA/K Fanner; 7 David Dalgety; 9 The Round House, Horns Cross; 10 ©nicksmithphotography.com; 11 AA/T Mackie; 12 AA/K Fanner; 13t The Wensleydale Heifer, West Witton; 13b Park Grand, Paddington; 14t Blackmore Farm, Bridgwater; 14b 23 Mayfield, Edinburgh; 15t Plas Maenan Country House, Llanrwst; 15b Gorman's Clifftop House & Restaurant, Dingle; 16 AA; 17 Compton House, Newark; 18l Compton House, Newark; 18r Compton House, Newark; 19 Compton House, Newark; 26/27 AA/M Kipling; 366/367 AA/M Hamblin; 400/401 AA/D Santillo; 432/433 AA/D Forss

Every effort has been made to trace the copyright holders, and we apologise in advance for any unintentional omissions or errors. We would be pleased to apply any corrections in a following edition of this publication.

Readers' Report Form

Please send this form to:–
Editor, The B&B Guide,
Lifestyle Guides,
AA Publishing,
Fanum House, FH13
Basingstoke RG21 4EA

or e-mail: lifestyleguides@theAA.com

Use this form to recommend any guest house, farmhouse or inn where you have stayed that is not already in the guide.

If you have any comments about your stay at an establishment listed in the Guide, please let us know, as feedback from readers helps to keep our Guide accurate and up to date. If you have a complaint during your stay, we recommend that you discuss the matter with the establishment.

Please note that the AA does not undertake to arbitrate between you and the establishment, to obtain compensation, or to engage in protracted correspondence.

Date

Your name (BLOCK CAPITALS)

Your address (BLOCK CAPITALS)

Post code

E-mail address

Name of hotel

Comments (Please include the name and address of the establishment)

(please attach a separate sheet if necessary)

Please tick here ☐ if you DO NOT wish to receive details of AA offers or products

PTO

Readers' Report Form *continued*

Have you bought this guide before? ☐ YES ☐ NO

What other accommodation, restaurant, pub or food guides have you bought recently?

Why did you buy this guide? (tick all that apply)
Holiday ☐   Short break ☐   Business travel ☐   Special occasion ☐   Overnight stop ☐   Conference ☐
Other (please state)

How often do you stay in B&Bs? (tick one choice)
More than once a month ☐   Once a month ☐   Once in two to three months ☐   Once in six months ☐
Once a year ☐   Less than once a year ☐

Please answer these questions to help us make improvements to the guide.
Which of these factors is most important when choosing a B&B?
Price ☐   Location ☐   Awards/ratings ☐   Service ☐   Décor/surroundings ☐
Previous experience ☐   Recommendation ☐
Other (please state)

Do you read the editorial features in the guide? ☐ YES ☐ NO

Do you use the location atlas?   ☐ YES ☐ NO

What elements of the guide do you find most useful when choosing somewhere to stay?
Description ☐   Photo ☐   Advertisement ☐   Star rating ☐

Can you suggest any improvements to the guide?

Thank you for completing and returning this form

Readers' Report Form

Please send this form to:–
Editor, The B&B Guide,
Lifestyle Guides,
AA Publishing,
Fanum House, FH13
Basingstoke RG21 4EA

or e-mail: lifestyleguides@theAA.com

Use this form to recommend any guest house, farmhouse or inn where you have stayed that is not already in the guide.

If you have any comments about your stay at an establishment listed in the Guide, please let us know, as feedback from readers helps to keep our Guide accurate and up to date. If you have a complaint during your stay, we recommend that you discuss the matter with the establishment.

Please note that the AA does not undertake to arbitrate between you and the establishment, to obtain compensation, or to engage in protracted correspondence.

Date

Your name (BLOCK CAPITALS)

Your address (BLOCK CAPITALS)

Post code

E-mail address

Name of hotel

Comments (Please include the name and address of the establishment)

(please attach a separate sheet if necessary)

Please tick here ☐ if you DO NOT wish to receive details of AA offers or products

PTO

Readers' Report Form *continued*

Have you bought this guide before? ☐ YES ☐ NO

What other accommodation, restaurant, pub or food guides have you bought recently?

....

....

....

Why did you buy this guide? (tick all that apply)
Holiday ☐   Short break ☐   Business travel ☐   Special occasion ☐   Overnight stop ☐   Conference ☐
Other (please state)

How often do you stay in B&Bs? (tick one choice)
More than once a month ☐   Once a month ☐   Once in two to three months ☐   Once in six months ☐
Once a year ☐   Less than once a year ☐

Please answer these questions to help us make improvements to the guide.
Which of these factors is most important when choosing a B&B?
Price ☐   Location ☐   Awards/ratings ☐   Service ☐   Décor/surroundings ☐
Previous experience ☐   Recommendation ☐
Other (please state)

Do you read the editorial features in the guide?   ☐ YES   ☐ NO

Do you use the location atlas?   ☐ YES   ☐ NO

What elements of the guide do you find most useful when choosing somewhere to stay?
Description ☐   Photo ☐   Advertisement ☐   Star rating ☐

Can you suggest any improvements to the guide?

....

....

....

....

Thank you for completing and returning this form

Readers' Report Form

Please send this form to:–
Editor, The B&B Guide,
Lifestyle Guides,
AA Publishing,
Fanum House, FH13
Basingstoke RG21 4EA

or e-mail: lifestyleguides@theAA.com

Use this form to recommend any guest house, farmhouse or inn where you have stayed that is not already in the guide.

If you have any comments about your stay at an establishment listed in the Guide, please let us know, as feedback from readers helps to keep our Guide accurate and up to date. If you have a complaint during your stay, we recommend that you discuss the matter with the establishment.

Please note that the AA does not undertake to arbitrate between you and the establishment, to obtain compensation, or to engage in protracted correspondence.

Date

Your name (BLOCK CAPITALS)

Your address (BLOCK CAPITALS)

Post code

E-mail address

Name of hotel

Comments (Please include the name and address of the establishment)

(please attach a separate sheet if necessary)

Please tick here ☐ if you DO NOT wish to receive details of AA offers or products

PTO

Readers' Report Form *continued*

Have you bought this guide before? ☐ YES ☐ NO

What other accommodation, restaurant, pub or food guides have you bought recently?

Why did you buy this guide? (tick all that apply)
Holiday ☐   Short break ☐   Business travel ☐   Special occasion ☐   Overnight stop ☐   Conference ☐
Other (please state)

How often do you stay in B&Bs? (tick one choice)
More than once a month ☐   Once a month ☐   Once in two to three months ☐   Once in six months ☐
Once a year ☐   Less than once a year ☐

Please answer these questions to help us make improvements to the guide.
Which of these factors is most important when choosing a B&B?
Price ☐   Location ☐   Awards/ratings ☐   Service ☐   Décor/surroundings ☐
Previous experience ☐   Recommendation ☐
Other (please state)

Do you read the editorial features in the guide?   ☐ YES   ☐ NO

Do you use the location atlas?   ☐ YES   ☐ NO

What elements of the guide do you find most useful when choosing somewhere to stay?
Description ☐   Photo ☐   Advertisement ☐   Star rating ☐

Can you suggest any improvements to the guide?

Thank you for completing and returning this form

Readers' Report Form

Please send this form to:–
Editor, The B&B Guide,
Lifestyle Guides,
AA Publishing,
Fanum House, FH13
Basingstoke RG21 4EA

or e-mail: lifestyleguides@theAA.com

Use this form to recommend any guest house, farmhouse or inn where you have stayed that is not already in the guide.

If you have any comments about your stay at an establishment listed in the Guide, please let us know, as feedback from readers helps to keep our Guide accurate and up to date. If you have a complaint during your stay, we recommend that you discuss the matter with the establishment.

Please note that the AA does not undertake to arbitrate between you and the establishment, to obtain compensation, or to engage in protracted correspondence.

Date

Your name (BLOCK CAPITALS)

Your address (BLOCK CAPITALS)

Post code

E-mail address

Name of hotel

Comments (Please include the name and address of the establishment)

(please attach a separate sheet if necessary)

Please tick here ☐ if you DO NOT wish to receive details of AA offers or products

PTO

Readers' Report Form *continued*

Have you bought this guide before? ☐ YES ☐ NO

What other accommodation, restaurant, pub or food guides have you bought recently?

Why did you buy this guide? (tick all that apply)
Holiday ☐   Short break ☐   Business travel ☐   Special occasion ☐   Overnight stop ☐   Conference ☐
Other (please state)

How often do you stay in B&Bs? (tick one choice)
More than once a month ☐   Once a month ☐   Once in two to three months ☐   Once in six months ☐
Once a year ☐   Less than once a year ☐

Please answer these questions to help us make improvements to the guide.
Which of these factors is most important when choosing a B&B?
Price ☐   Location ☐   Awards/ratings ☐   Service ☐   Décor/surroundings ☐
Previous experience ☐   Recommendation ☐
Other (please state)

Do you read the editorial features in the guide? ☐ YES ☐ NO

Do you use the location atlas?   ☐ YES ☐ NO

What elements of the guide do you find most useful when choosing somewhere to stay?
Description ☐   Photo ☐   Advertisement ☐   Star rating ☐

Can you suggest any improvements to the guide?

Thank you for completing and returning this form